# THE THEORY
# OF BUSINESS FINANCE
## A BOOK OF READINGS

# THE THEORY

# OF BUSINESS FINANCE

## A Book of Readings

SECOND EDITION

### STEPHEN H. ARCHER
*Dean, Graduate School of Administration*
*Willamette University*

### CHARLES A. D'AMBROSIO
*Graduate School of Business Administration*
*University of Washington*

Macmillan Publishing Co., Inc.
NEW YORK
Collier Macmillan Publishers
LONDON

Macmillan Publishing Co., Inc.
866 Third Avenue, New York, New York 10022

Collier Macmillan Canada, Ltd.

Library of Congress Cataloging in Publication Data

Archer, Stephen Hunt, comp.
  The theory of business finance.

  Includes bibliographies.
  1. Corporations—Finance—Addresses, essays,
lectures. 2. Business enterprises—Finance—
Addresses, essays, lectures. 3. Capital—
Addresses, essays, lectures. I. D'Ambrosio, Charles A.,
joint comp. II. Title.
HG4011.A82   1976          658.1'5          75–15618
ISBN 0–02–303820–9


Printing: 1 2 3 4 5 6 7 8      Year: 6 7 8 9 0 1 2

# PREFACE

Nine years ago, in the preface to the first edition, we felt that the "explosion" that had taken place in the literature of finance warranted a collection of a set of readings basic to the understanding of the field. Apparently, the marketplace felt the same way, as evidenced by the initial and sustained reception of the book. Since the first edition of *The Theory of Business Finance: A Book of Readings*, the literature has expanded considerably. Thus the selection of articles for this second edition was even more difficult because of a greater quantity of excellent choices.

Our goal in this edition is the same as that of the first edition, namely, to collate those readings that clearly stand out as landmarks in the study of finance and that constitute the minimal set of literature for every serious student.

The present set of readings represents our efforts, together with the advice of others, then, to present a reasonable body of substantive, analytical work for microfinance. We have tended to exclude readings in such other important areas as international finance, money markets, financial institutions, and investments, although many of the works included here serve as a foundation for all fields of finance.

Hence, the present version of *The Theory of Business Finance: A Book of Readings* accomplishes two things. First, it sets forth a "core" set of necessary readings. Second, each article sets forth the "core" parameters for financial decision making. We hope that this two-stage distillation will make progress through the literature maze more meaningful, more efficient, and more elegant.

It should also be noted that this revision excludes many areas of microfinance, for example, short-term capital management. Although we gave some attention to this subject in the first edition, space limitations forced us to include only those articles that addressed themselves to noncurrent financial deliberations.

Perforce, not everyone will agree with our selections. It is doubtful that an "optimal" set is attainable, given the taste functions of each possible user.

Nevertheless, in many areas of finance there seems to be a reasonable consensus regarding what constitutes the important articles to be studied. We have tried to restrict our collection to that set. In other areas, however, there seems to be little consensus. In those cases we had to exercise our judgment regarding the "reasonably acceptable" set. For reasons readily explicable by imperfect knowledge and other human frailties, the emergent set is necessarily preferred, *in toto*, perhaps only by us. Our hope is that it will be a preferred one to others also, at least within the theory of second best.

The foregoing implies, among other things, that many, many fine articles have been excluded. As in the first edition, such exclusion is not intended to slight these significant contributions. The budget constraint of a collection of readings also had to be acknowledged.

As anyone who has followed the recent development of the literature knows, the overlap in content and coverage among published works can be considerable. Of necessity then, much of each selection, when incorporated into a collection such as this, is duplicative. Paradoxically, to have shorn the various selections of paragraphs or sections redundant of materials in other selections would have been to detract from their overall flavor and intent. As a result, each reading is presented intact.

Along these lines, segmentation of these readings according to various section headings has been a somewhat hazardous task inasmuch as some of the selections could have been included in more than one section. The current topical arrangement is the preferred choice of the editors. Obviously, as the articles are unedited, each user can freely create his own variation. In general, the papers within each section are put in chronological order. Some articles are comments, criticisms, or replies of other works and therefore some care should be exercised in jumping around.

The nature of the readings, it will quickly be observed, is challenging. However, many can be handled by the beginning student, requiring in most cases acquaintance with simple mathematical expressions. The first edition found use in many types of classes. It has been used as a supplementary text for a beginning class in finance, as the main body of material for advanced classes, and in graduate seminars. The choice depended on the selection of the articles and the preparation of the students.

The second edition includes the following six sections:

    I. Profits
   II. Risk, Return, and Utility
  III. Capital Markets
  IV. Capital Budgeting
   V. Cost of Capital
  VI. Dividend Policy

We have added four important contributions to Part II—articles by Latané, Hadar and Russel, Pratt, and Roy. We have added the Mossin article to the

"Capital Markets" section, and three articles were added to "Capital Budgeting," those by Lorie and Savage, Tuttle and Litzenberger, and Myers. The "Cost of Capital" section is enhanced by the inclusion of articles by Heins and Sprenkle, Modigliani and Miller's "Reply," and articles by Stiglitz and Hamada. To "Dividend Policy," we added the Fama and Babiak article. We wish we could have included more. Those pages we had to delete to make room for the new caused considerable anguish.

We acknowledge the generosity of each of the authors for his permission to reproduce his paper. Our gratitude is also extended to the various editors and copyright holders who are acknowledged herein. Also, we give special thanks to the reviewers of the first edition and to Macmillan for bringing the new edition to fruition.

STEPHEN H. ARCHER
CHARLES A. D'AMBROSIO

# CONTENTS

# THE THEORY
# OF BUSINESS FINANCE
## A BOOK OF READINGS

PART I

PROFITS

\* \* \* \* \* \* \* \* \* \* \* \* \* \* \* \* \* \* \* \* \* \* \*

# 1. A CASH-FLOW CONCEPT OF PROFIT*

DIRAN BODENHORN†

Reprinted from *The Journal of Finance*, Vol. *XIX*, No. 1
(March, 1964), pp. 16–31, by permission of the author and
the publisher.

## I. INTRODUCTION AND SUMMARY

The traditional theory of the firm is based on the assumption that the firm
acts in the stockholders' interests and that the stockholders are interested in
profit, so that the objective of the firm is to maximize profit. There have been
many theoretical discussions of the concept of profit but there is no consensus
of opinion as to the precise definition of this theoretical construct.[1] Nevertheless the theory of the firm has been based on the assumption of profit
maximization and profit has been thought of (loosely) as the difference between the revenue received from the product sold and the payments made to
the productive factors which together produced that product.

This concept of profit has been difficult to apply to investment decisions,
and wealth maximization and cash-flow concepts have been developed in
connection with this problem. This paper presents a cash-flow concept of
profit which is associated with the cash-flow theory of stock value. This
concept of profit has three desirable properties which make it more useful
than the traditional concept. (1) It can be used in decision making within the
firm since profit maximization is in the stockholders' interest. (2) The profit
of the firm coincides with the stockholders' income in each time period. (3)
Past profit can be measured from market values so that it is an objective
measure of performance.

* The author is indebted to many friends for innumerable discussions of the concept of
profit over many years. Professors Alan Batchelder and Robert Gallman have been particularly helpful in discussing the organization and content of this paper.

† Professor of Economics, Ohio State University.

[1] See, for example, Weston (10), and the references cited therein.

New cash flows are defined in Section II as the cash flows between the firm and its stockholders. The value of the stock is then the present value of the future net cash flows. In Section III cash-flow profit is defined as the increase in the stock value plus the net cash flow of the period. If the expectations for the period are observed and those for the future are unchanged, a normal profit is made on the initial stock value (investment). If expectations change, pure profits arise.

The cash-flow concept is then compared to the traditional concept. Section IV is concerned with the handling of depreciation, a concept which is not required in cash-flow analysis. It is shown that depreciation expenses understate capital costs unless implicit interest is charged on the book value of net worth. It follows in Section V that the traditional profit concept cannot be used in decision making unless this implicit interest is charged as an expense. It develops, however, that the decision is independent of the pattern of depreciation, which confirms the cash-flow analysis.

In Section VI it is shown that cash-flow profit and stockholders' income coincide in every time period, since it is based on the return which the stockholder would get if the firm liquidated as a going concern. Traditional profit is based on the return which the stockholders would get if the firm liquidated its assets piecemeal instead of as a going concern, and is therefore of less economic interest. The last section points out briefly the advantages of having a profit concept which can be measured from market values.

## II. CASH FLOWS AND STOCK VALUATION

In this section we present a definition of cash flows and a theory of stock pricing based on cash-flow analysis.[2] A careful definition of cash flows is required because previous discussions have been concerned with investment decisions rather than stock pricing. They have therefore been concerned with the cash flows associated with a particular investment project, rather than with the flows to the firm as a whole, and we must recognize the possibility that cash flows generated by one project will be used to finance another project. Furthermore, other discussions tend to separate the investment decision from the financing decision, and we want to include financing considerations.

In defining cash flows, we need to distinguish transactions involving goods or services, financial obligations, and cash balances. The purchase of any good or service, whether for current use (expense) or future use (asset), results in an immediate cash payment, by our definitions. If in fact the goods are purchased on account, then a second transaction, the borrowing of money from the seller, is recorded. The sale of goods or services results in an immediate cash receipt. If credit is extended, then a second transaction, the lending of money to the buyer, is also recorded.

With respect to financial transactions, we distinguish between transactions

---

[2] For further discussion and justification of cash-flow analysis, see Bodenhorn (2) and (3), Dean (4), and Lorie and Savage (6).

involving the financial obligations of the firm itself, i.e., obligations which call for a payment by the firm to someone outside the firm, and transactions involving the financial obligations of outsiders. Cash receipts and cash payments are defined to include all transactions with the financial obligations of outsiders.

In considering the firm's own obligations, it is useful to distinguish debt and equity obligations. This distinction would not be important in a world of certainty. If everyone knew precisely what payments would be made on all financial obligations, all future payments would be discounted by the lender at the same interest rate, and the terms of the contract between the borrower and the lender would be irrelevant. With uncertainty, however, the discount rate applied to equity obligations is higher than that applied to debt. We can handle this problem more readily if we define cash receipts and payments to include transactions involving debt obligations but to exclude equity transactions.

The problem of cash balances is somewhat peculiar. In a world of certainty it would be unprofitable for a firm to hold cash. Any cash not needed immediately to make payments would be lent at interest, as liquidity is worthless if all future cash needs can be perfectly foreseen, and there are no flotation costs associated with lending, borrowing, or repaying money.

In the presence of uncertainty, cash balances are held because they provide liquidity. In principle, the decision to purchase liquidity by increasing cash balances or to sell liquidity by reducing cash balances should be analyzed in the same way any other (investment) decision is analyzed. Management should project the future cash receipts and cash payments of the firm with various cash balances, subtract the payments from the receipts to determine *net* cash flows, and then select that cash balance (i.e., purchase that amount of liquidity) which maximizes the present value of the net cash flows.

An increase in cash balances is therefore considered as a purchase of liquidity and is defined as a cash payment. A reduction in cash balances is a sale of liquidity and defined as a cash receipt. If a firm receives cash from the sale of a product and increases its bank balance, this involves both a cash receipt and a cash payment, so that the net cash flow is zero. Subsequently, when the firm reduces its bank balance to pay wages, this is again both a cash receipt and a cash payment, with a net cash flow of zero.

The net cash flow in any period therefore is the difference between cash received by the firm from purchasers, debtors, or banks, and the cash used by the firm to increase cash balances, to pay for goods and services, to pay interest or repay debt, or to lend. Such flows must be associated with equity obligations, i.e., the net cash flow is the cash flow between the firm and its stockholders. A positive net cash flow represents a cash payment by the firm to the stockholders, i.e., a dividend payment or a stock repurchase, while a negative net cash flow represents a cash payment by the stockholders to the firm, i.e., a new stock subscription.

The associated theory of stock valuation is based on the assumption that the cash receipts and the cash payments of the firm have been projected for each time period forever.[3] Second, we assume that there are no transaction or flotation costs, or any costs other than interest (or dividends) involved in borrowing or repaying money, or in buying or selling financial obligations. Third, we assume that stockholders are indifferent between capital gains and dividend income, so that we ignore problems which arise because of the different taxes on income and capital gains.

Cash-flow theory then says that the value of the stock is the present value of the future net cash flows.[4] This provides the justification for our treatment of cash balances. The definition of cash flows can be determined to suit the purpose of the user, and the cash-flow concept will be most useful if we define the flows so that the present value of the net cash flows is the value of the stock. Since the stock value is logically the discounted value of the dividends, not the dividends plus the increase in cash balances, our somewhat peculiar treatment of cash balances is required.

Within the more usual context of investment decisions, the decision has a favorable influence on stock price if the present value of the net cash flows associated with the investment project is positive, i.e., if the firm could pay enough dividends to justify raising the necessary funds by a new stock issue. If the net cash flows generated by the project are not used to pay dividends, but are reinvested in the firm (perhaps to purchase liquidity) this is a second investment project, and the two projects should be evaluated independently. The net cash flows associated with the second (reinvestment) project are negative and offset the positive net cash flow of the first project so that the net cash flow to the firm is zero. Since the peculiar treatment of cash balances does not arise in evaluating any decision except the decision about the level of cash balances themselves, our treatment of cash balances does not impair the usefulness of the cash-flow concept in investment decisions, and adds to its usefulness in stock valuation.

This theory implies that stockholders do not care whether the firm repurchases stock or pays dividends, since either one is a cash flow from the firm to the stockholder. This can be seen with a simple example. Suppose that a firm has 100 shares outstanding and is going to return $2500 to stockholders. The value of the firm after the money has been distributed, which we can assume to be $10,000, is the discounted value of the net cash flows after that

---

[3] In principle, the time period should be of zero duration, and discounting should be continuous, but it is easier to think in terms of discrete time periods and to discount all the receipts and payments of a period for the same amount of time in calculating the present value. The duration of the time period makes no difference to any of the principles or conclusions in this paper.

[4] We could exclude all dealings in the firm's financial obligations from the cash receipts and payments. The net cash flow would then include transactions with debtholders as well as stockholders. The present value of the net cash flows would be the total value of all the firm's financial obligations, and the value of the stock would be the total value of the obligations less the value of the debt. This would be more in keeping with the stock valuation theory suggested by Modigliani and Miller (8).

date and is not influenced by the way the funds are returned to the stockholders. If the stockholders expect a $25 dividend per share, each shareholder,
subsequent to the dividend distribution, will have a share worth $100 and a
$25 dividend. Before the dividend is paid, therefore, the shares must be valued
at $125.

The shares must also be valued at $125 if the firm is expected to use the
$2500 to repurchase stock rather than to pay dividends, since the price of
each share must be the same before and after the stock repurchase. If the shares
are worth $125 before the purchase, the company can purchase 20 shares for
$2500. The stockholders who sell will receive $125 per share, and each share
still outstanding will represent 1/80th of the total stock (which still has a
total value of $10,000) and therefore will be valued at $125.[5] In short, if the
firm returns $2500 to the stockholders, they do not care whether it is called
a cash dividend or whether this firm buys a given proportion of each stockholder's shares. Each stockholder owns the same proportion of the shares
outstanding and receives the same amount of cash.[6]

This theory has some interesting implications with respect to future investment projects, future financing decisions, and future dividend payments. The
emphasis on dividend payments might be misinterpreted to mean that
dividend policy is important in determining stock value. This is not the case.
If a firm has decided to undertake an investment project which involves the
outlay of, say, one million dollars, it makes no difference whether the million
dollars is obtained by reducing dividends or is paid out in dividends and then
borrowed by issuing new stock.

The net cash flows which determine the stock value have been defined as the
flows between the firm and its stockholders, and these flows are not changed
by the decision to finance internally or to issue new stock. If the stockholders
receive a dividend of $1 million, this is a net cash flow of plus $1 million. If
$1 million of new stock is sold, this is a net cash flow of minus $1 million. If
both transactions take place in the same period, the net cash flow is the sum
of the two, or zero. This, however, is exactly what the net cash flow would be
if no dividends were paid, no new stock were issued, and the project were
financed internally.[7]

The theory also implies that a decision to undertake investment projects in
the future influences the value of the stock today. The stock value is based
entirely upon future cash flows, and it makes no difference whether the flows
are expected in connection with a project that has already been undertaken or
a project that is going to be undertaken in the future.[8] It makes no difference,

[5] This proof follows the pattern used by Miller and Modigliani (7).

[6] This, of course, relies on the assumptions that there are no transaction costs and that
stockholders are indifferent between capital gains and dividend income.

[7] For a more complete discussion of the influence of dividend policy on stock valuation,
see Miller and Modigliani (7).

[8] For further discussion of this point, see Alchian (1), Bodenhorn (3), and Miller and
Modigliani (7).

that is, unless the cash flows associated with future projects are considered to be more risky than those associated with current projects and therefore are discounted at a higher rate. The determination of the appropriate rate at which to discount future cash flows, which is sometimes called the normal rate of return on investment, is unfortunately beyond the scope of this paper.

## III. THE CASH-FLOW CONCEPT OF PROFIT

Profit is defined in connection with a particular time period, and reflects some of the activities of the firm during the period. We consider first three concepts relating to the status of the firm at the beginning and end of the period.

*Stockholders' initial investment.*   This is the market value of the stock at the beginning of the period. It is the stockholders' initial investment in the sense that it represents what the stockholders could get by selling their shares at the beginning of the period, and is the amount of their wealth which they have entrusted to the firm for the period. Symbolically, the theory says:

$$S_o = \frac{N_1}{(1+r)} + \frac{N_2}{(1+r)^2} + \frac{N_3}{(1+r)^3} + \cdots = \sum_{i=1}^{\infty} \frac{N_i}{(1+r)^i}$$

where   $S_0$ = Stock value at the start of the period = Stockholders' initial investment

$N_1, N_2, \ldots$ = Net cash flows expected in future periods

$r$ = Discount rate[9]

*Stockholders' expected end-of-period wealth.*   At the start of the period, the stockholders expect that their initial investment will yield a return during the period. Their expected end-of-period wealth, $E(W_1)$, consists of the expected net cash flow of the period, $N_1$, plus the expected end-of-period stock value:

$$E(W_1) = N_1 + \frac{N_2}{(1+r)} + \frac{N_3}{(1+r)^2} + \cdots = \sum_{i=1}^{\infty} \frac{N_i}{(1+r)^{i-1}} = S_o(1+r)$$

This means that the expected return during the period is the normal rate of return on the initial investment as given by the discount rate.

*Stockholders' actual end-of-period wealth.*   This is the cash flow that actually takes place during the period, $C_1$, plus the actual stock value at the end of the period, i.e., the investment that the stockholders carry over into the next period, $S_1$.

$$W_1 = C_1 + S_1 = C_1 + \frac{M_2}{(1+r)} + \frac{M_3}{(1+r)^2} + \cdots = C_1 + \sum_{i=2}^{\infty} \frac{M_i}{(1+r)^{i-1}}$$

[9] We shall assume throughout that this rate is determined in the market, but shall not seek to explain how it is determined.

where $W_1$ = End of period wealth

$\quad C_1$ = Actual cash flow of period

$\quad S_1$ = Stock value at end of period = Investment carried forward to next period

$M_2, M_3$ = Net cash flows expected in future periods

Actual wealth can differ from expected wealth for any of three reasons: the cash flow of the period is different from what had been expected, $C_1 \neq N_1$; the cash flows expected in future periods have changed since the start of the period, $M_1 \neq N_1$; or the discount rate has changed. In a world of certainty where expectations always come true and are never changed, actual wealth would be the same as expected wealth and would increase from period to period by the discount rate multiplied by the initial investment.

*Pure profit.*   The economist usually defines pure profit as a return in excess of the normal on invested capital, which in this case is the discount rate, since the normal return is regarded as a cost. The corresponding cash-flow definition is the difference between actual end-of-period wealth and expected end-of-period wealth.

$$\text{Pure profit} = W_1 - E(W_1) = W_1 - S_o(1 + r)$$

*Business profit or income.*   Businessmen and accountants usually look upon the entire return to stockholders as profit or income, and do not regard any return on stockholder investment as a cost. Thus business profit is pure profit plus the normal return on investment, which is also the difference between end-of-period wealth and initial investment.

$$\text{Business profit} = W_1 - S_o = \text{Pure Profit} + rS_o$$

If expectations for the period are fulfilled ($N_1 = C_1$), future expectations unchanged ($M_1 = N_1$), and the discount rate unchanged, then pure profit is zero and business profit is the normal return on initial investment, $rS_o$.

Management's decisions during the period will be in the best interests of its stockholders if it maximizes end-of-period wealth, business profit or pure profit. These three criteria are logically equivalent because wealth, business profit and pure profit differ by values which depend upon the initial expectations but cannot change during the period. End-of-period wealth and business profit differ by the initial stock value or investment and business profit and pure profit differ by the normal return on the initial investment.

This concept of profit is significantly different from the conventional concept which we shall call "earnings" so that the word "profit" can be reserved for the cash-flow concept. Earnings of a period are associated with the difference between the sales value and the cost of production of the goods sold[10] during the period. Earnings are therefore concerned primarily with activity during the period. Earlier and later periods are involved only to the

[10] Sometimes the goods produced are considered but this would not affect the argument in this paper.

extent that expenses associated with current sales are paid in other periods or revenues associated with current sales are received in other periods. Earnings are not influenced by changed expectations about the future as profits are.

The differences between the cash-flow profit approach and the traditional earnings approach can be illustrated by considering the analysis of a simple investment project. The project requires a capital outlay of $1000 at the beginning of the first year. At the end of the first year the firm will receive $1120 in sales revenue and will pay $400 in wages and $60 in corporate income taxes. At the end of the second year the firm will receive $1310 in sales revenue and pay $500 in wages and $205 in corporate income taxes. The income taxes are calculated by charging $600 of depreciation expenses the first year and $400 the second, which we assume the tax laws to permit. A 50 per cent tax rate is then applied to taxable income (revenue minus wages minus depreciation) of $120 the first year and $410 the second year. No other receipts or payments are associated with the project.

The project therefore has a net cash flow of $-\$1000$ at the start of the first year, $+\$660$ at the end of the first year and $+\$605$ at the end of the second year. If we assume a discount rate of 10 per cent, the present (start of first year) value of the net cash flow is $+\$100$ for the project.

It is easier to see the implications of the cash-flow analysis of this project with its associated profit and stock values if we assume that an entrepreneur incorporates solely for the purpose of engaging in this project, and that the project is equity financed. Indeed, we have already assumed equity financing by assuming a net cash flow of $-\$1000$ when the asset is purchased. By definition, a net cash flow is a transaction with stockholders, and the negative sign implies a flow of cash from the stockholders to the firm.[11] The analysis would not be changed in any important way if we assumed this project to be an addition to a going concern. It would become more complicated, however, since it might be financed internally, i.e., the funds to buy the asset might be obtained from cash receipts generated by other projects, and the receipts associated with this project might be used to finance other projects instead of being returned to stockholders. The principles are clearer, but not different, if we assume that the firm and the project coincide, so that cash flows generated by the project are also net cash flows from the point of view of the firm.

The simplest case to consider is one in which the investment project was not anticipated by the market, but the market adopts the firm's forecast of the future net cash flows immediately when the asset is purchased.[12] The sequence of events is as follows:

1. An entrepreneur takes $1,000 of his own money and buys an asset with the expectation that he can get a net cash flow of $660 at the end of the first year, and $605 at the end of the second.

[11] We will discuss below some of the problems which arise if the project is partially debt financed.

[12] Complications arise if the market delays in adopting the firm's forecasts, or has anticipated the project in the case of a going concern, but again there is no difference in

2. He incorporates and issues stock to himself at the same time that he buys the asset.
3. The market values this stock at $1100 when it is issued, because this is the present value of the expected future cash flows, discounted at 10 per cent.
4. The entrepreneur therefore makes a capital gain of $100 at the time that he issues the stock since he has paid $1,000 for the asset and has stock which he could liquidate for $1100. This increase in his wealth takes place whether or not he actually sells the stock, and is his "initial investment" in the firm according to our definitions. It is also a business profit, and a pure profit, received at the start of the first year, since his actual wealth is $1100, and his expected (by the market) wealth had been $1000.
5. If all goes as expected, the firm returns $660 to its stockholders (who may or may not include the original entrepreneur) at the end of the first year. If the expectations for the second year are unchanged, the stockholders also have stock valued at $550, which is the present (start of the second year) value of the cash flow of $605 expected at the end of the year. The stockholders' actual end-of-period wealth is $660 + $550 = $1210, and *business profit* is $110 in the first year. *Pure profit* is zero since the stockholders' normal 10 per cent rate of return on their initial investment of $1100 is also $110.
6. If expectations continue to be realized, the firm returns $605 to its stockholders at the end of the second year, and the stock becomes worthless. End-of-period wealth is therefore $605. The initial investment for the second year is $550 since this is the stock value at the start of the year. *Business profit* is therefore $55 and *pure profit* is still zero.

Cash-flow theory says that all *pure* profit is earned when the stock value makes a change that had not been anticipated by the market. The market value of the stock is always determined in such a way that the *expected* return, net cash flow (dividends) plus capital gains, is the *normal* return on the market value at the start of the period. If all goes as expected, the actual return, *business* profit, will be the expected normal return, and *pure* profit will be zero. If expectations change, a *pure* profit (or loss) is made immediately as the stock price makes an unexpected adjustment so that the newly expected future returns will equal a normal return on the new stock value (investment).

Analysis of the project within the context of tr\ditional earnings theory requires information about *economic* depreciation vhich cash-flow analysis does not require. Cash-flow analysis requires only information about corporate income taxes, which requires knowledge abo\ t legal depreciation but not about economic depreciation.[13] While there is s me debate, particularly

---

[13] Another way of looking at this is to observe that no depreciation calculation would be required for cash-flow analysis if there were no income tax, while depreciation would still be required for earnings analysis.

among accountants, about the precise meaning of economic depreciation, we shall assume that it is the change in the market value of the asset.[14] We can also assume, for the time being, that legal depreciation and economic depreciation are the same, i.e., that the asset has a value of $400 at the end of the first year. Traditional earnings analysis then says that the firm raises $1000 in capital at the start of the first year. It earns (net of taxes) $60 the first year. Since it returns $660 at the end of the year, $600 of this represents a return of capital, and the stockholders still have $400 invested. The second year earnings are $205. Since $605 is paid to stockholders at the end of the year, this represents a disbursement of the earnings and a full return of the $400 investment.

We can summarize the cash-flow and the earnings analyses:

| Time | CASH-FLOW ANALYSIS | | | EARNINGS ANALYSIS | | |
|---|---|---|---|---|---|---|
| | Business Profit | Pure Profit | Stock-holders' Investment | Earnings | Pure Earnings* | Stock-holders' Investment |
| Start of First Year | $100 | $100 | $1100 | 0 | 0 | $1000 |
| End of First Year | $110 | 0 | $ 550 | $ 60 | $ −40 | $ 400 |
| End of Second Year | $ 55 | 0 | 0 | $205 | $ 165 | 0 |

* This concept is discussed in Section IV.

Cash-flow analysis therefore shows an immediate capital gain of $100, with subsequent business profits of a normal 10% on investment and no pure profit. Earnings analysis shows no immediate capital gain, earnings of 6% on investment the first year and $51\frac{1}{4}$% the second year.

We now turn to a discussion of the reasons for preferring the cash-flow approach.

## IV. THE DEPRECIATION PROBLEM

The fundamental criticism of the treatment of depreciation in earnings analysis is that the economic depreciation expense understates the capital costs involved. The actual cost is $1000 at the start of year one, while the depreciation expenses over the two years add (undiscounted) to $1,000. The present (start of year one) value of the depreciation expenses is therefore less than the actual cost of $1,000.[15]

[14] This definition has the advantage of being tied to market values, and so is unambiguously measurable after the fact. There is no other definition, except one tied to cash-flows in such a way that earnings and business profit become identical, which is not subject to the same criticisms we are about to make of this concept of depreciation.

[15] This criticism applies to long-run static equilibrium where depreciation just covers replacement in each period so that the initial investment never gets charged as an expense.

The solution to this problem, within the framework of earnings analysis, is to charge an implicit interest expense on the book value of the stockholders' investment (net worth) at the normal rate of return, 10%. In the case of equity financing which we have been considering, this is equivalent to charging implicit interest on the undepreciated asset balance.[16] However, if the asset is financed in whole or in part by debt,[17] on which interest is included explicitly, costs would be overstated by including an implicit interest expense on the entire undepreciated asset balance.

The inclusion of implicit interest on net worth makes the present (start of first year) value of the costs charged to equity capital in each year—depreciation minus debt repayment plus implicit interest—equal to the initial equity investment.[18] Since the present value of the debt repayment and associated interest expenses must equal the initial debt investment, all capital charges are accounted for.

---

Let the initial investment be $I$, with annual replacement of $R$. The present value of the investment plus replacement is therefore $I + R/r$. If the annual depreciation charge is $D$, the present value of the depreciation charges is $D/r$. In long-run static equilibrium $D = R$, and the true cost of the investment, $I + R/r$, exceeds the present value of the depreciation expenses by the initial investment, $I$.

[16] This suggestion was made by Edwards and Bell (5), page 68.

[17] This, of course, would change the net cash flows. In our example, if $500 is raised by debt borrowing the net cash flow at the start of the first year is only $-$500. There is a cash payment of $1000 for the asset and a cash receipt of $500 from debtholders. Only $500 is raised from stockholders, and this is the net cash flow. The net cash flows would be reduced in subsequent periods also, because debt repayment and interest are cash payments which must be subtracted from the cash receipts to get the cash flows (to stockholders). The debt financing might also raise the discount rate on the equity return (net cash flow), but we continue to assume that the appropriate discount rate, as influenced by the debt issue, is known.

[18] Consider a case in which the net cash flows are $N_0$ at the start of the first year, $N_1$ at the end of the year and $N_2$ at the end of the second year. Bonds ($B$) are issued at the start of the first year, of which $B_1$ are due at the end of the first year and $B - B_1$ at the end of the second year. The initial asset value is $A = B - N_0$, since we raise $N_0$ from stockholders. Depreciation is $D_1$ the first year and $A - D_1$ the second year. The book value of the net worth is $-N_0$ at the start of the first year, so the implicit interest charge is $-rN_0$. The firm returns $N_1$ to its stockholders at the end of the first year, of which $N_1 - D_1 + B_1$ represent earnings and $D_1 - B_1$ represent a return of capital. Book value of net worth is therefore $-N_0 - D_1 + B_1$ at the end of the first year, and implicit interest of $r(-N_0 - D_1 + B_1)$ must be charged in the second year. Charges ($C$) against equity capital are depreciation minus debt retirement plus implicit interest. So we have

$$C_1 = D_1 - B_1 - rN_0$$

$$C_2 = A - D_1 - (B - B_1) + r(-N_0 - D_1 + B_1)$$

$$= A - B - rN_0 + (1 + r)(B_1 - D_1)$$

$$= -N_0 - rN_0 + (1 + r)(B_1 - D_1)$$

$$= (1 + r)(B_1 - D_1 - N_0)$$

The present (start of year one) value of these charges is

We can now define *pure earnings* as earnings minus implicit interest, and pure earnings then account for all capital costs. In our example, the book value of the stockholders' investment is $1000 at the start of the first year and $400 at the start of the second, so implicit interest would be $100 the first year and $40 the second, and pure earnings would be $-$40$ the first year and $165 the second. The fact that the pure earnings account for capital costs means that the present (start of first year) value of the pure earnings is the same as the present value of the net cash flows, which also account for all capital costs.[19] Cash-flow analysis accounts for these costs much more simply, however, by charging the cost as a cash payment when the asset is bought. Depreciation and implicit interest need not be considered since they do not give rise to cash flows.

## V. THE MAXIMIZATION PROBLEM

The correct calculation of capital costs is necessary for decision making. This means that the maximization of earnings is not in the stockholders' interest, while the maximization of pure earnings is.

The maximization of earnings can be misleading even in the determination of the output rate by setting marginal cost equal to marginal revenue in the framework of comparative statics. In this case the marginal revenue is the same as the marginal cash receipts and marginal cost is the marginal cash

$$\frac{C_1}{1+r} + \frac{C_2}{(1+r)^2} = \frac{D_1 - B_1 - rN_0}{1+r} + \frac{(B_1 - D_1 - N_0)(1+r)}{(1+r)^2}$$

$$= \frac{D_1 - B_1 - rN_0 + B_1 - D_1 - N_0}{(1+r)}$$

$$= -N_0$$

[19] Since the discount rate is 10%, we have

$$\frac{-40}{1.1} + \frac{165}{1.2} = \frac{-44}{1.21} + \frac{165}{1.21} = \frac{121}{1.21} = 100$$

More generally, using the notation of the last footnote, and denoting the pure earnings by $P_1$ and $P_2$, we have

$$P_1 = N_1 - D_1 + B_1 + rN_0$$

$$P_2 = N_2 - (A - D_1) + (B - B_1) - r(-N_0 - D_1 + B_1)$$

$$= N_2 - A + B + rN_0 - (1+r)(B_1 - D_1)$$

$$= N_2 + N_0 + rN_0 - (1+r)(B_1 - D_1)$$

$$= N_2 - (1+r)(B_1 - D_1 - N_0)$$

The present (start of first year) value is

$$\frac{P_1}{1+r} + \frac{P_2}{(1+r)^2} = \frac{N_1 - D_1 + B_1 + rN_0}{1+r} + \frac{N_2}{(1+r)^2} - \frac{B_1 - D_1 - N_0}{(1+r)}$$

$$= N_0 + \frac{N_1}{1+r} + \frac{N_2}{(1+r)^2}$$

payment so that the difference between marginal revenue and marginal cost is the marginal net cash flow. Since a positive marginal net cash flow necessarily increases the present value of the future net cash flows and so increases profits, cash-flow theory confirms the traditional result that output should be increased if marginal revenue exceeds marginal cost.

This is true, however, only if both revenues and costs increase at the same time. If the cost increases first and some time elapses before the product is sold and revenue increases, then the cash outlay during this time interval must be regarded as an investment in the context of earnings analysis or as a net cash payment in the context of cash-flow analysis. Earnings will rise if marginal revenue exceeds marginal cost, but the output should be increased only if the difference is large enough to provide a normal rate of return on the additional (equity) investment, so that earnings maximization is an inadequate decision criterion. Cash-flow analysis gives the correct result by requiring that the present value of the future net cash receipts generated when the marginal revenue exceeds marginal cost be at least as large as the present value of the net cash payments generated after the marginal cost has risen but before the marginal revenue has risen.

An example related to the investment project discussed in the last two sections will also illuminate some of the problems. Suppose that a firm must select either that project or an alternative project which has identical cash flows,[20] but which has economic depreciation of $500 in each of the two years. Such a project would be indistinguishable from the first using cash-flow analysis. Earnings analysis, however, would show earnings of $160 the first year (instead of $60 as the original project) and of $105 the second year (instead of $205). Pure earnings would be $60 the first year (instead of $-40$) and $55 the second year (instead of $165). Earnings maximization would lead to the selection of the alternative project, since it earns $100 more the first year and $100 less the second year. Maximization of pure earnings, however, again leads to the conclusion that the projects are equally profitable since the present value of the pure earnings is $100 for either project.

This is not a coincidence and illustrates a very important point. The present value of the pure earnings of a project does not depend in any way on the economic depreciation pattern, even though the economic depreciation is charged as an expense in the various periods. We have already seen[21] that the present value of the pure earnings equals the present value of the net cash flows, and neither the net cash flows nor their present value is influenced by the pattern of economic depreciation.

The conclusion is that earnings maximization is not an appropriate decision criterion unless the earnings are corrected for implicit interest on the

---

[20] This implies that the tax payments are the same for the two projects and that they have the same tax depreciation. This is necessary if we are to distinguish the impact of economic depreciation from the impact of tax depreciation. For further discussion of this point see my paper (2).

[21] See footnote 19.

book value of the net worth to obtain pure earnings. The present value of the pure earnings, however, is independent of the depreciation pattern so that it hardly seems worthwhile to go to the trouble of determining depreciation and the implicit interest charge. It is simple (but logically the same) to maximize the present value of the net cash flows.

## VI. THE TIMING PROBLEM

The only possible advantages of pure earnings over cash-flow profit would be either that they give a more accurate picture of the timing of the benefits from the investment project, or that they are more easily measurable at the end of the period.

With respect to timing, cash-flow theory says that the original project creates a pure profit of $100 at the start of the first year, and then earns only a normal 10 per cent profit on investment in the next two years. Earnings theory says that there are no pure earnings at the start of the first year, that the return on investment during the first year falls short of a normal 10 per cent return by $40 (pure earnings of − $40) and exceeds a normal 10 per cent return by $165 during the second year. Since the present (start of first year) value of the pure earnings is the same as the present value of the pure profit, the dispute is really about the timing of the realization of the pure profit or earnings, not about the total amount involved.

The approaches agree in defining pure profit as the ordinary profit (which we have called business profit) or earnings less a normal return on invested capital. They differ both in their measurements of the ordinary profit or earnings and in their measurement of the amount of invested capital.[22] If we adopt the strongest version of traditional theory and value assets at market, so that depreciation is the change in market value, then both cash-flow and traditional theory base their measurements of profit (or earnings) and invested capital on market values. Earnings are associated with the potential (but usually hypothetical) sale of the firm's assets at market value. Cash-flow profit is associated with the potential (but usually hypothetical) sale of the firm's equities at market value.

Traditional earnings is the difference between the book value of the net worth at the end of the year and book value at the beginning of the year, plus the net cash flow. It is associated with asset values because the net worth is the residual when debt is subtracted from the market value of the assets. It therefore shows the gains accruing to the stockholder because the firm refrained from selling its assets at market for an additional year.[23] Cash-flow business profit is the difference between the market value of the stock at the end of the year and its market value at the beginning of the year also plus the net cash flow. It therefore shows the income accruing to stockholders because

---

[22] We are assuming that they agree in their measurement of the normal rate of return, although this is not necessarily the case.

[23] This concept of earnings, based on valuing assets at market, has been called "realizable profit" by Edwards and Bell (5, page 44ff).

they held their stock for an additional year, if we define income in the usual way as the maximum possible consumption without reducing wealth.

The traditional approach is to measure the stockholders' investment as the book value of the net worth, and we have already seen that this is the appropriate base in the determination of implicit interest. Cash-flow theory measures the stockholders' investment as the market value of the firm's stock.

This difference in the measurement of stockholders' investment extends to the analysis of static equilibrium, where there is no difference between earnings and business profit. In static equilibrium the liquidation value of the assets, the book value of net worth, and the market value of the stock must be the same at the start and the end of the year. Both earnings and business profit therefore equal the net cash flow. Nevertheless, traditional theory says that a monopoly earns a pure profit because its revenues exceed its costs, including implicit interest on net worth as a cost. Cash-flow theory says that no pure profit can exist in static equilibrium because nothing unexpected ever happens. The pure profit of traditional theory gets capitalized in the form of a higher stock price when the market realizes that the monopoly has been obtained. At that time the stockholders' investment increases by just enough to eliminate any pure profit in addition to the normal return on investment.

The advantage of cash-flow theory does not lie in the fact that it considers the potential sale of equities rather than the sale of assets. Indeed, cash-flow theory says that it makes no difference whether we sell assets or equities, provided that we sell the assets as a going concern rather than sell them piecemeal at market value. That is, cash-flow theory says that the going-concern value of the assets is the present value of the net cash flows, and that this is also the value which the market should place on the stock. Thus sale of the firm as a going concern will yield the same return to stockholders that they could get by selling their stock. The mistake of the traditional analysis is to consider the sale of the assets piecemeal at a price which is less than the maximum that could be obtained. Earnings calculations should not be based on the assumption that management would make such a blunder.

The effect of considering sale in the wrong market at too low a price is that earnings bear no relationship to stockholders' returns, and stockholders can be making money on their stock when the firm is losing money and vice-versa. The separation of the firm's earnings from the stockholders' earnings serves no useful purpose. Business profit is always the same as stockholders' income and its maximization is always in the stockholders' interest. Cash-flow theory also says that the allocation of the pure profit of $100 to subsequent years as pure earnings is unnecessary since the stockholders get an income in the form of a capital gain when the pure profit is recorded.

## VII. THE MEASUREMENT PROBLEM

If the objective of the firm is to earn a profit for its stockholders, the amount of profit earned during a period can be used as a criterion in measuring the performance of the firm. It is therefore desirable to have a profit concept which can be measured on the basis of market values, so that the measurement will be objective in the accounting sense.

Of the four profit concepts we have considered, two, business profit and earnings,[24] are measurable from market data. Neither pure earnings nor pure profit is so measurable since they both require the use of the normal rate of return and this is not directly observable in the market. As earnings maximization is not in the stockholders' interest, it is not a satisfactory measure of performance. This leaves business profit as the only satisfactory measure of performance.

## REFERENCES

1. Alchian, Armen. "Costs and Outputs" in Moses Abromovitz (*et al.*) *The Allocation of Economic Resources, Essays in Honor of Bernard Francis Haley*, 1959.
2. Bodenhorn, Diran. "Depreciation, Price Level Changes, and Investment Decision," *Journal of Business*, October, 1963, 448–457.
3. ——"On the Problem of Capital Budgeting," *Journal of Finance*, December, 1959, 473–492.
4. Dean, Joel. "Measuring the Productivity of Capital," *Harvard Business Review*, January–February, 1954. Also printed in (9).
5. Edwards, E. O. and Bell, P. W. *The Theory and Measurement of Business Income*, Berkeley, Calif., 1961.
6. Lorie, J. and Savage, L. J. "Three Problems in Capital Rationing," *Journal of Business*, October, 1955. Also reprinted in (9).
7. Miller, M. H. and Modigliani, F. "Dividend Policy, Growth, and the Valuation of Shares," *Journal of Business*, October, 1961, 411–433.
8. Modigliani, F. and Miller, M. H. "The Cost of Capital, Corporation Finance and the Theory of Investment," *American Economic Review*, June, 1958, 261–297. Also reprinted in (9).
9. Solomon, Ezra, Editor. *The Management of Corporate Capital*, Glencoe, Ill., 1959.
10. Weston, J. Fred. "The Profit Concept and Theory: A Restatement," *Journal of Political Economy*, April, 1954, 152–170.

---

[24] Earnings are measurable if, as we have been assuming, assets are carried on the books at market value. Otherwise there is likely to be a dispute about the objectivity of the depreciation calculation.

PART **II**

# RISK, RETURN, AND UTILITY

\* \* \* \* \* \* \* \* \* \* \* \* \* \* \* \* \* \* \* \* \* \* \* \* \*

# 2. THE UTILITY ANALYSIS OF CHOICES INVOLVING RISK[1]

MILTON FRIEDMAN*
and
LEONARD J. SAVAGE†

Reprinted from *The Journal of Political Economy*, Vol. *LVI*, No. 4 (August, 1948), pp. 279–304, by permission of the authors.

## I. THE PROBLEM AND ITS BACKGROUND

The purpose of this paper is to suggest that an important class of reactions of individuals to risk can be rationalized by a rather simple extension of orthodox utility analysis.

Individuals frequently must, or can, choose among alternatives that differ, among other things, in the degree of risk to which the individual will be subject. The clearest examples are provided by insurance and gambling. An individual who buys fire insurance on a house he owns is accepting the certain loss of a small sum (the insurance premium) in preference to the combination of a small chance of a much larger loss (the value of the house) and a large chance of no loss. That is, he is choosing certainty in preference to uncertainty. An individual who buys a lottery ticket is subjecting himself to a large chance of losing a small amount (the price of the lottery ticket) plus a small chance of winning a large amount (a prize) in preference to avoiding both risks. He is choosing uncertainty in preference to certainty.

This choice among different degrees of risk, so prominent in insurance and gambling, is clearly present and important in a much broader range of economic choices. Occupations differ greatly in the variability of the income they promise: in some, for example, civil service employment, the prospective income is rather clearly defined and is almost certain to be within rather narrow limits; in others, for example, salaried employment as an accountant, there is somewhat more variability yet almost no chance of either an extremely high or an extremely low income; in still others, for example, motion-picture acting, there is extreme variability, with a small chance of an extremely high income and a larger chance of an extremely low income. Securities vary similarly, from government bonds and industrial "blue chips" to "blue-sky" common stocks; and so do business enterprises or lines of business activity. Whether or not they realize it and whether or not they take explicit

* Professor of Economics, University of Chicago.

† Professor of Statistics, Yale University.

[1] The fundamental ideas of this paper were worked out jointly by the two authors. The paper was written primarily by the senior author.

account of the varying degree of risk involved, individuals choosing among occupations, securities, or lines of business activity are making choices analogous to those that they make when they decide whether to buy insurance or to gamble. Is there any consistency among the choices of this kind that individuals make? Do they neglect the element of risk? Or does it play a central role? If so, what is that role?

These problems have, of course, been considered by economic theorists, particularly in their discussions of earnings in different occupations and of profits in different lines of business.[2] Their treatment of these problems has, however, never been integrated with their explanation of choices among riskless alternatives. Choices among riskless alternatives are explained in terms of maximization of utility: individuals are supposed to choose as they would if they attributed some common quantitative characteristic—designated utility—to various goods and then selected the combination of goods that yielded the largest total amount of this common characteristic. Choices among alternatives involving different degrees of risk, for example, among different occupations, are explained in utterly different terms—by ignorance of the odds or by the fact that "young men of an adventurous disposition are more attracted by the prospects of a great success than they are deterred by the fear of failure," by "the overweening conceit which the greater part of men have of their own abilities," by "their absurd presumption in their own good fortune," or by some similar *deus ex machina*.[3]

The rejection of utility maximization as an explanation of choices among different degrees of risk was a direct consequence of the belief in diminishing marginal utility. If the marginal utility of money diminishes, an individual seeking to maximize utility will never participate in a "fair" game of chance, for example, a game in which he has an equal chance of winning or losing a dollar. The gain in utility from winning a dollar will be less than the loss in utility from losing a dollar, so that the expected utility from participation in the game is negative. Diminishing marginal utility plus maximization of expected utility would thus imply that individuals would always have to be paid to induce them to bear risk.[4] But this implication is clearly contradicted

[2] E.g., see Adam Smith, *The Wealth of Nations*, Book I, Ch. x (Modern Library reprint of Cannan ed.), pp. 106–11; Alfred Marshall, *Principles of Economics* (8th ed.; London: Macmillan & Co., Ltd., 1920), pp. 398–400, 554–55, 613.

[3] Marshall, *op. cit.*, p. 554 (first quotation); Smith, *op. cit.*, p. 107 (last two quotations).

[4] See Marshall, *op. cit.*, p. 135 n.; Mathematical Appendix, n. ix (p. 843). "Gambling involves an economic loss, even when conducted on perfectly fair and even terms. . . . A theoretically fair insurance against risks is always an economic gain" (p. 135). "The argument that fair gambling is an economic blunder . . . requires no further assumption than that, firstly the pleasures of gambling may be neglected; and, secondly $\phi''(x)$ is negative for all values of $x$, where $\phi(x)$ is the pleasure derived from wealth equal to $x$. . . . It is true that this loss of probable happiness need not be greater than the pleasure derived from the excitement of gambling, and we are then thrown back upon the induction that pleasures of gambling are in Bentham's phrase 'impure'; since experience shows that they are likely to engender a restless, feverish character, unsuited for steady work as well as for the higher and more solid pleasures of life" (p. 843).

by actual behavior. People not only engage in fair games of chance, they engage freely and often eagerly in such unfair games as lotteries. Not only do risky occupations and risky investments not always yield a higher average return than relatively safe occupations or investments, they frequently yield a much lower average return.

Marshall resolved this contradiction by rejecting utility maximization as an explanation of choices involving risk. He need not have done so, since he did not need diminishing marginal utility—or, indeed, any quantitative concept of utility—for the analysis of riskless choices. The shift from the kind of utility analysis employed by Marshall to the indifference-curve analysis of F. Y. Edgeworth, Irving Fisher, and Vilfredo Pareto revealed that to rationalize riskless choices, it is sufficient to suppose that individuals can rank baskets of goods by total utility. It is unnecessary to suppose that they can compare differences between utilities. But diminishing, or increasing, marginal utility implies a comparison of differences between utilities and hence is an entirely gratuitous assumption in interpreting riskless choices.

The idea that choices among alternatives involving risk can be explained by the maximization of expected utility is ancient, dating back at least to D. Bernoulli's celebrated analysis of the St. Petersburg paradox.[5] It has been repeatedly referred to since then but almost invariably rejected as the correct explanation—commonly because the prevailing belief in diminishing marginal utility made it appear that the existence of gambling could not be so explained. Even since the widespread recognition that the assumption of diminishing marginal utility is unnecessary to explain riskless choices, writers have continued to reject maximization of expected utility as "unrealistic."[6] This rejection of maximization of expected utility has been challenged by John von

---

[5] See Daniel Bernoulli, *Versuch einer neuen Theorie der Wertbestimmung von Glücksfällen* (Leipzig, 1896), translated by A. Pringsheim from "Specimen theoriae novae de mensura sortis," *Commentarii academiae scientiarum imperialis Petropolitanae*, Vol. V, for the years 1730 and 1731, published in 1738.

In an interesting note appended to his paper Bernoulli points out that Cramer [presumably Gabriel Cramer (1704–52)], a famous mathematician of the time, had anticipated some of his own views by a few years. The passages that he quotes from a letter in French by Cramer contain what, to us, is the truly essential point in Bernoulli's paper, namely, the idea of using the mathematical expectation of utility (the "moral expectation") instead of the mathematical expectation of income to compare alternatives involving risk. Cramer has not in general been attributed this much credit, apparently because the essential point in Bernoulli's paper has been taken to be the suggestion that the logarithm of income is an appropriate utility function.

[6] "It has been the assumption in the classical literature on this subject that the individual in question will always try to maximize the mathematical expectation of his gain or utility. . . . This may appear plausible, but it is certainly not an assumption which must hold true in all cases. It has been pointed out that the individual may also be interested in, and influenced by, the range or the standard deviation of the different possible utilities derived or some other measure of dispersion. It appears pretty evident from the behavior of people in lotteries or football pools that they are not a little influenced by the skewness of the probability distribution" [Gerhard Tintner, "A Contribution to the Non-Static Theory of Choice," *Quarterly Journal of Economics*, Vol. LVI (February, 1942), p. 278].

Neumann and Oskar Morgenstern in their recent book, *Theory of Games and Economic Behavior*.[7] They argue that "under the conditions on which the indifference curve analysis is based very little extra effort is needed to reach a numerical utility," the expected value of which is maximized in choosing among alternatives involving risk.[8] The present paper is based on their treatment but has been made self-contained by the paraphrasing of esssential parts of their argument.

If an individual shows by his market behavior that he prefers *A* to *B* and *B* to *C*, it is traditional to rationalize this behavior by supposing that he attaches more utility to *A* than to *B* and more utility to *B* than to *C*. All utility functions that give the same ranking to possible alternatives will provide equally good rationalizations of such choices, and it will make no difference which particular one is used. If, in addition, the individual should show by his market behavior that he prefers a 50-50 chance of *A* or *C* to the certainty of *B*, it seems natural to rationalize this behavior by supposing that the *difference* between the utilities he attaches to *A* and *B* is greater than the *difference* between the utilities he attaches to *B* and *C*, so that the *expected* utility of the preferred combination is greater than the utility of *B*. The class of utility functions, if there be any, that can provide the same ranking of alternatives that involve risk is much more restricted than the class that can provide the same ranking of alternatives that are certain. It consists of utility functions that differ only in origin and unit of measure (i.e., the utility functions in the class are linear functions of one another).[9] Thus, in effect, the ordinal properties of utility functions can be used to rationalize riskless choices, the numerical properties to rationalize choices involving risk.

It does not, of course, follow that there will exist a utility function that will rationalize in this way the reactions of individuals to risk. It may be that individuals behave inconsistently—sometimes choosing a 50-50 chance of *A* or *C* instead of *B* and sometimes the reverse; or sometimes choosing *A* instead of *B*, *B* instead of *C*, and *C* instead of *A*—or that in some other way their behavior is different from what it would be if they were seeking rationally to maximize expected utility in accordance with a given utility function. Or it may be that some types of reactions to risk can be rationalized in this way

---

"It would be definitely unrealistic . . . to confine ourselves to the mathematical expectation only, which is the usual but not justifiable practice of the traditional calculus of 'moral probabilities'" [J. Marschak, "Money and the Theory of Assets," *Econometrica*, Vol. VI (1938), p. 320].

Tintner's inference, apparently also shared by Marschak, that the facts he cites are necessarily inconsistent with maximization of expected utility is erroneous (see Secs. III and IV below). He is led to consider a formerly more general solution because of his failure to appreciate the real generality of the kinds of behavior explicable by the maximization of expected utility.

[7] Princeton University Press, 1st ed., 1944; 2d ed., 1947; pp. 15–31 (both eds.), pp. 617–32 (2d ed. only); succeeding references are to 2d ed.

[8] *Ibid.*, p. 17.

[9] *Ibid.*, pp. 15–31, esp. p. 25.

while others cannot. Whether a numerical utility function will in fact serve to rationalize any particular class of reactions to risk is an empirical question to be tested; there is no obvious contradiction such as was once thought to exist.

This paper attempts to provide a crude empirical test by bringing together a few broad observations about the behavior of individuals in choosing among alternatives involving risk (Sec. II) and investigating whether these observations are consistent with the hypothesis revived by von Neumann and Morgenstern (Secs. III and IV). It turns out that these empirical observations are entirely consistent with the hypothesis if a rather special shape is given to the total utility curve of money (Sec. IV). This special shape, which can be given a tolerably satisfactory interpretation (Sec. V), not only brings under the aegis of rational utility maximization much behavior that is ordinarily explained in other terms but also has implications about observable behavior not used in deriving it (Sec. VI). Further empirical work should make it possible to determine whether or not these implications conform to reality.

It is a testimony to the strength of the belief in diminishing marginal utility that it has taken so long for the possibility of interpreting gambling and similar phenomena as a contradiction of universal diminishing marginal utility, rather than of utility maximization, to be recognized. The initial mistake must have been at least partly a product of a strong introspective belief in diminishing marginal utility: a dollar must mean less to a rich man than to a poor man; see how much more a man will spend when he is rich than when he is poor to avoid any given amount of pain or discomfort.[10] Some of the comments that have been published by competent economists on the utility analysis of von Neumann and Morgenstern are even more remarkable testimony to the hold that diminishing marginal utility has on economists. Vickrey remarks: "There is abundant evidence that individual decisions in situations involving risk are not always made in ways that are compatible with the assumption that the decisions are made rationally with a view to maximizing the mathematical expectation of a utility function. The purchase of tickets in lotteries, sweepstakes, and 'numbers' pools would imply, on such a basis, that the marginal utility of money is an increasing rather than a decreasing function of income. Such a conclusion is obviously unacceptable as a guide to social policy."[11] Kaysen remarks, "Unfortunately, these postulates (underlying

---

[10] This elemental argument seems so clearly to justify diminishing marginal utility that it may be desirable even now to state explicitly how this phenomenon can be rationalized equally well on the assumption of increasing marginal utility of money. It is only necessary to suppose that the avoidance of pain and the other goods that can be bought with money are related goods and that, while the marginal utility of money increases as the amount of money increases, the marginal utility of avoiding pain increases even faster.

[11] William Vickrey, "Measuring Marginal Utility by Reactions to Risk," *Econometrica*, Vol. XIII (1945), pp. 319–33. The quotation is from pp. 327 and 328. "The purchase of tickets in lotteries, sweepstakes, and 'numbers' pools does not imply that marginal utility of money increases with income everywhere (see Sec. IV below). Moreover, it is entirely unnecessary to identify the quantity that individuals are to be interpreted as maximizing with a quantity that should be given special importance in public policy."

the von Neumann and Morgenstern discussion of utility measurement) involve an assumption about economic behavior which is contrary to experience.... That this assumption is contradicted by experience can easily be shown by hundreds of examples (including) the participation of individuals in lotteries in which their mathematical expectation of gain (utility) is negative."[12]

## II. OBSERVABLE BEHAVIOR TO BE RATIONALIZED

The economic phenomena to which the hypothesis revived by von Neumann and Morgenstern is relevant can be divided into, first, the phenomena ordinarily regarded as gambling and insurance; second, other economic phenomena involving risk. The latter are clearly the more important, and the ultimate significance of the hypothesis will depend primarily on the contribution it makes to an understanding of them. At the same time, the influence of risk is revealed most markedly in gambling and insurance, so that these phenomena have a significance for testing and elaborating the hypothesis out of proportion to their importance in actual economic behavior.

At the outset it should be confessed that we have conducted no extensive empirical investigation of either class of phenomena. For the present, we are content to use what is already available in the literature, or obvious from casual observation, to provide a first test of the hypothesis and to impose significant substantive restrictions on it.

The major economic decisions of an individual in which risk plays an important role concern the employment of the resources he controls: what occupation to follow, what entrepreneurial activity to engage in, how to invest (nonhuman) capital. Alternative possible uses of resources can be classified into three broad groups according to the degree of risk involved: (a) those involving little or no risk about the money return to be received— occupations like schoolteaching, other civil service employment, clerical work; business undertakings of a standard predictable type like many public utilities; securities like government bonds, high-grade industrial bonds; some real property, particularly owner-occupied housing; (b) those involving a moderate degree of risk but unlikely to lead to either extreme gains or extreme losses—occupations like dentistry, accountancy, some kinds of managerial work; business undertakings of fairly standard kinds in which, however, there is sufficient competition to make the outcome fairly uncertain; securities like lower-grade bonds, preferred stocks, higher-grade common stocks; (c) those involving much risk, with some possibility of extremely large gains and some of extremely large losses—occupations involving physical risks, like piloting aircraft, automobile racing, or professions like medicine and law; business undertakings in untried fields; securities like highly speculative stocks; some types of real property.

[12] C. Kaysen, "A Revolution in Economic Theory?" *Review of Economic Studies*, Vol. XIV, No. 35 (1946–47), pp. 1–15; quotation is from p. 13.

The most significant generalization in the literature about choices among these three uses of resources is that, other things the same, uses *a* or *c* tend in general to be preferred to use *b*; that is, people must in general be paid a premium to induce them to undertake moderate risks instead of subjecting themselves to either small or large risks. Thus Marshall says:

There are many people of a sober steady-going temper, who like to know what is before them, and who would far rather have an appointment which offered a certain income of say £400 a year than one which was not unlikely to yield £600, but had an equal chance of affording only £200. Uncertainty, therefore, which does not appeal to great ambitions and lofty aspirations, has special attractions for very few; while it acts as a deterrent to many of those who are making their choice of a career. And as a rule the certainty of moderate success attracts more than an expectation of an uncertain success that has an equal actuarial value.

But on the other hand, if an occupation offers a few extremely high prizes, its attractiveness is increased out of all proportion to their aggregate value.[13]

Adam Smith comments similarly about occupational choices and, in addition, says of entrepreneurial undertakings:

The ordinary rate of profits always rises more or less with the risk. It does not, however, seem to rise in proportion to it, or so as to compensate it completely. . . . The presumptuous hope of success seems to act here as upon all other occasions, and to entice so many adventurers into those hazardous trades, that their competition reduces the profit below what is sufficient to compensate the risk.[14]

Edwin Cannan, in discussing the rate of return on investments, concludes that "the probability is that the classes of investments which on the average return most to the investor are neither the very safest of all nor the very riskiest, but the intermediate classes which do not appeal either to timidity or to the gambling instinct."[15]

This asserted preference for extremely safe or extremely risky investments over investments with an intermediate degree of risk has its direct counterpart in the willingness of persons to buy insurance and also to buy lottery tickets or engage in other forms of gambling involving a small chance of a large gain. The extensive market for highly speculative stocks—the kind of stocks that "blue-sky" laws are intended to control—is a border-line case that could equally well be designated as investment or gambling.

The empirical evidence for the willingness of persons of all income classes to buy insurance is extensive.[16] Since insurance companies have costs of

---

[13] *Op. cit.*, pp. 554–55.

[14] *Op. cit.*, p. 111.

[15] Article on "Profit," in *Dictionary of Political Economy*, ed. R. H. Inglis Palgrave (new edition, ed. Henry Higgs; London, 1926); see also the summary of the views of different writers on risk-taking in F. H. Knight, *Risk, Uncertainty, and Profit* (New York, 1921; reprint London School of Economics and Political Science, 1933), pp. 362–67.

[16] E.g., see U.S. Bureau of Labor Statistics, *Bulletin 648: Family Expenditures in Selected Cities, 1935–36*; Vol. I: *Family Expenditures for Housing, 1935–36*; Vol. VI: *Family Expenditures for Transportation, 1935–36*; and Vol. VIII: *Changes in Assets and Liabilities, 1935–36.*

operation that are covered by their premium receipts, the purchaser is obviously paying a larger premium than the average compensation he can expect to receive for the losses against which he carries insurance. That is, he is paying something to escape risk.

The empirical evidence for the willingness of individuals to purchase lottery tickets, or engage in similar forms of gambling, is also extensive. Many governments find, and more governments have found, lotteries an effective

---

Table 6 of the Tabular Summary of Vol. I gives the percentage of home-owning families reporting the payment of premiums for insurance on the house. These percentages are given separately for each income class in each of a number of cities or groups of cities. Since premiums are often paid less frequently than once a year, the percentages given definitely understate the percentage of families carrying insurance. Yet the bulk of the percentages are well over 40.

Table 5 of the Tabular Summary of Vol. VI gives the percentage of families (again by income classes and cities or groups of cities) reporting expenditures for automobile insurance. These figures show a very rapid increase in the percentage of automobile operators that had insurance (this figure is derived by dividing the percentage of families reporting automobile insurance by the percentage of families operating cars) as income increases. In the bottom income classes, where operation of a car is infrequent, only a minority of those who operate cars carry insurance. In the upper income classes, where most families operate cars, the majority of operators carry insurance. A convenient summary of these percentages for selected income classes in six large cities, given in text Table 10 (p. 26), has 42 entries. These vary from 4% to 98%, and 23 are over 50%.

Table 3 of the Tabular Summary of Vol. VIII gives the percentage of families in each income class in various cities or groups of cities reporting the payment of life, endowment, or annuity insurance premiums. The percentages are uniformly high. For example, for New York City the percentage of white families reporting the payment of insurance premiums is 75% or higher for every income class listed and varies from 75% in the income class $500–$749 to over 95% in the upper-income classes; the percentage of Negro families purchasing insurance was 38% for the $1,000–$1,249 class but 60% or higher for every other class. This story is repeated for city after city, the bulk of the entries in the table for the percentage of families purchasing insurance being above 80%.

These figures cannot be regarded as direct estimates of the percentage of families willing to pay something—that is, to accept a smaller actuarial value—in order to escape risk, the technical meaning of the purchase of insurance that is relevant for our purpose. (1) The purchase of automobile and housing insurance may not be a matter of choice. Most owned homes have mortgages (see Vol. I, p. 361, Table L) and the mortgage may require that insurance be carried. The relevant figure for mortgaged homes would be the fraction of owners carrying a larger amount of insurance than is required by the mortgage. Similarly, finance companies generally require that insurance be carried on automobiles purchased on the instalment plan and not fully paid for, and the purchase of automobile insurance is compulsory in some states. (2) For automobile property damage and liability insurance (but not collision insurance) the risks to the operator and to the insurance company may not be the same, particularly to persons in the lower-income classes. The loss to the uninsured operator is limited by his wealth and borrowing power, and the maximum amount that he can lose may be well below the face value of the policy that he would purchase. The excess of the premium over the expected loss is thus greater for him than for a person with more wealth or borrowing power. The rise in the percentage of persons carrying automobile insurance as income rises may therefore reflect not an increased willingness to carry insurance but a reduction in the effective price that must be paid for insurance. (3) This tendency may be reversed for the relatively high-income classes for both automobile and housing insurance

means of raising revenue.[17] Though illegal, the "numbers" game and similar forms of gambling are reported to flourish in the United States,[18] particularly among the lower-income classes.

It seems highly unlikely that there is a sharp dichotomy between the individuals who purchase insurance and those who gamble. It seems much more likely that many do both or, at any rate, would be willing to. We can cite no direct evidence for this asserted fact, though indirect evidence and casual observation give us considerable confidence that it is correct. Its validity is suggested by the extensiveness of both gambling and the purchase of insurance. It is also suggested by some of the available evidence on how people invest their funds. The widespread legislation against "bucket shops" suggests that relatively poor people must have been willing to buy extremely speculative stocks of a "blue-sky" variety. Yet the bulk of the property income of the lower-income classes consists of interest and rents and relatively little of dividends, whereas the reverse is true for the upper-income classes.[19] Rents

---

by the operation of the income tax. Uninsured losses are in many instances deductible from income before computation of income tax under the United States federal income tax, while insurance premiums are not. This tends to make the net expected loss less for the individual than for the insurance company. This effect is almost certainly negligible for the figures cited above, both because they do not effectively cover very high incomes and because the federal income tax was relatively low in 1935–36. (4) Life insurance at times comes closer to gambling (the choice of an uncertain alternative in preference to a certain alternative with a higher expected value) than to the payment of a premium to escape risk. For example, special life insurance policies purchased to cover a single railroad or airplane trip are probably more nearly comparable to a lottery ticket than a means of achieving certainty. (5) Even aside from these qualifications, actual purchase of insurance would give at best a lower limit to the number willing to buy insurance, since there will always be some who will regard the price asked as too high.

These qualifications offset one another to some extent. It seems highly unlikely that their net effect could be sufficient to reverse the conclusion suggested by the evidence cited that a large fraction of people in all income classes are willing to buy insurance.

[17] France, Spain, and Mexico, to name but three examples, currently conduct lotteries for revenue. Russia attaches a lottery feature to bonds sold to the public. Great Britain conducted lotteries from 1694 to 1826. In the United States lotteries were used extensively before the Revolution and for some time thereafter, both directly by state governments and under state charters granted to further specific projects deemed to have a state interest. For the history of lotteries in Great Britain see C. L'Estrange Ewen, *Lotteries and Sweepstakes* (London, 1932); in New York State, A. F. Ross, "History of Lotteries in New York," *Magazine of History*, Vol. V (New York, 1907). There seem to be no direct estimates of the fraction of the people who purchase tickets in state or other legal lotteries, and it is clear that such figures would be difficult to get from data obtained in connection with running the lotteries. The receipts from legal lotteries, and casual impressions of observers, suggest that a substantial fraction of the relevant units (families or, alternatively, individual income recipients) purchase tickets.

[18] Evidence from wagering on horse races, where this has been legalized, is too ambiguous to be of much value. Since most legal wagering is at the track, gambling is available only to those who go to watch the races and is combined with participation in the mechanics of the game of chance.

[19] *Delaware Income Statistics*, Vol. I (Bureau of Economic and Business Research,

and interest are types of receipts that tend to be derived from investments with relatively little risk, and so correspond to the purchase of insurance, whereas investment in speculative stocks corresponds to the purchase of lottery tickets.

Offhand it appears inconsistent for the same person both to buy insurance and to gamble: he is willing to pay a premium, in the one case, to avoid risk, in the other, to bear risk. And indeed it would be inconsistent for a person to be willing to pay something (no matter how little) in excess of actuarial value to avoid every possible risk and also something in excess of actuarial value to assume every possible risk. One must distinguish among different kinds of insurance and different kinds of gambling, since a willingness to pay something for only some kinds of insurance would not necessarily be inconsistent with a willingness to engage in only some kinds of gambling. Unfortunately, very little empirical evidence is readily available on the kinds of insurance that people are willing to buy and the kinds of gambling that they are willing to engage in. About the only clear indication is that people are willing to enter into gambles that offer a small chance of a large gain—as in lotteries and "blue-sky" securities.

Lotteries seem to be an extremely fruitful, and much neglected, source of information about reactions of individuals to risk. They present risk in relatively pure form, with little admixture of other factors; they have been conducted in many countries and for many centuries, so that a great deal of evidence is available about them; there has been extensive experimentation with the terms and conditions that would make them attractive, and much competition in conducting them, so that any regularities they may show would have to be interpreted as reflecting corresponding regularities in human behavior.[20] It is, of course, not certain that inferences from lotteries would carry over to other choices involving risk. There would, however, seem to be some presumption that they would do so, though of course the validity of this presumption would have to be tested.[21]

The one general feature of lotteries that is worth noting in this preliminary survey, in addition to the general willingness of people to participate in them, is the structure of prizes that seems to have developed. Lotteries rarely have just a single prize equal to the total sum to be paid out as prizes. Instead, they tend to have several or many prizes. The largest prize is ordinarily not very

---

University of Delaware, 1941), Table 1; *Minnesota Incomes*, 1938–39, Vol. II (Minnesota Resources Commission, 1942), Table 27; F. A. Hanna, J. A. Pechman, S. M. Lerner, *Analysis of Wisconsin Income* ["Studies in Income and Wealth," Vol. IX (National Bureau of Economic Research, 1948)], Part II, Table 1.

[20] Aside from their value in providing information about reactions to risk, data from lotteries may be of broader interest in providing evidence about the stability of tastes and preferences over time and their similarity in different parts of the world. Here is a "commodity" which has remained unchanged over centuries, which is the same all over the globe, and which has been dealt in widely for the entire period and over much of the globe. It is hard to conceive of any other commodity for which this is true.

[21] See Smith, *op. cit.*, p. 108, for a precedent.

much larger than the next largest, and often there is not one largest prize but several of the same size.[22] This tendency is so general that one would expect it to reflect some consistent feature of individual reactions, and any hypothesis designed to explain reactions to uncertainty should explain it.

## III. THE FORMAL HYPOTHESIS

The hypothesis that is proposed for rationalizing the behavior just summarized can be stated compactly as follows: In choosing among alternatives open to it, whether or not these alternatives involve risk, a consumer unit (generally a family, sometimes an individual) behaves as if (a) it had a consistent set of preferences; (b) these preferences could be completely described by a function attaching a numerical value—to be designated "utility"—to alternatives each of which is regarded as certain; (c) its objective were to make its expected utility as large as possible. It is the contribution of von Neumann and Morgenstern to have shown that an alternative statement of the same hypothesis is: An individual chooses in accordance with a system of preferences which has the following properties:

1. The system is complete and consistent; that is, an individual can tell which of two objects he prefers or whether he is indifferent between them, and if he does not prefer C to B and does not prefer B to A, then he does not prefer C to A.[23] (In this context, the word "object" includes combinations of objects with stated probabilities; for example, if A and B are objects, a 40-60 chance of A or B is also an object.)

2. Any object which is a combination of other objects with stated probabilities is never preferred to every one of these other objects, nor is every one of them ever preferred to the combination.

3. If the object A is preferred to the object B and B to the object C, there will be some probability combination of A and C such that the individual is indifferent between it and B.[24]

---

[22] See Ewen, *op. cit.*, *passim*, but esp. descriptions of state lotteries in Ch. VII, pp. 199–244; see also the large numbers of bills advertising lotteries in John Ashton, *A History of English Lotteries* (London: Leadenhall Press, 1893).

[23] The transitivity of the relation of indifference assumed in this postulate is, of course, an idealization. It is clearly possible that the difference between successive pairs of alternatives in a series might be imperceptible to an individual, yet the first of the series definitely preferable to the last. This idealization, which is but a special case of the idealization involved in the geometric concept of a dimensionless point, seems to us unobjectionable. However, the use of this idealization in indifference-curve analysis is the major criticism offered by W. E. Armstrong in an attack on indifference-curve analysis in his article "The Determinateness of the Utility Function," *Economic Journal*, Vol. XLIX (September, 1939), pp. 453–67. In a more recent article ["Uncertainty and the Utility Function," *Economic Journal*, Vol. LVIII (March, 1948), pp. 1–10] Armstrong repeats this criticism and adds to it the criticism that choices involving risk cannot be rationalized by the ordinal properties of utility functions.

[24] For a rigorous presentation of the second statement and a rigorous proof that the statements are equivalent see von Neumann and Morgenstern, *op. cit.*, pp. 26–27, 617–32.

This form of statement is designed to show that there is little difference be-- tween the plausibility of this hypothesis and the usual indifference-curve explanation of riskless choices.

These statements of the hypothesis conceal by their very compactness most of its implications. It will pay us, therefore, to elaborate them. It simplifies matters, and involves no loss in generality, to regard the alternatives open to the consumer unit as capable of being expressed entirely in terms of money or money income. Actual alternatives are not, of course, capable of being so expressed: the same money income may be valued very differently according to the terms under which it is to be received, the nonpecuniary advantages or disadvantages associated with it, and so on. We can abstract from these factors, which play no role in the present problem, by supposing either that they are the same for different incomes compared or that they can be converted into equivalent sums of money income.[25] This permits us to consider total utility a function of money income alone.

Let $I$ represent the income of a consumer unit per unit time, and $U(I)$ the utility attached to that income if it is regarded as certain. Measure $I$ along the horizontal axis of a graph and $U$ along the vertical. In general, $U(I)$ will not be defined for all values of $I$, since there will be a lower limit to the income a consumer unit can receive, namely, a negative income equal (in absolute value to) the maximum amount that the consumer unit can lose per unit time for the period to which the utility curve refers.

Alternatives open to the consumer unit that involve no risk consist of possible incomes, say $I'$, $I''$, .... The hypothesis then implies simply that the consumer unit will choose the income to which it attaches the most utility. Other things the same, we know from even casual observation that the consumer unit will in general choose the largest income: put differently, we consider it pathological for an individual literally to throw money away, yet this means of choosing a smaller income is always available. It follows that the hypothesis can rationalize riskless choices of the limited kind considered here if, and only if, the utility of money income is larger, the higher the income. Consideration of riskless choices imposes no further requirements on the utility function.

Alternatives involving risk consist of probability distributions of possible incomes. Fortunately, it will suffice for our purpose to consider only a particularly simple kind of alternative involving risk, namely $(A)$ a chance $a(0 < a < 1)$ of an income $I_1$, and a chance $(1 - a)$ of an income $I_2$, where for

---

[25] The other factors abstracted from must not, of course, include any that cannot in fact be held constant while money income varies. For example, a higher income is desired because it enables a consumer unit to purchase a wider variety of commodities. The consumption pattern of the consumer unit must not therefore be supposed to be the same at different incomes. As another example, a higher income may mean that a consumer unit must pay a higher price for a particular commodity (e.g., medical service). Such variation in price should not be impounded in *ceteris paribus*, though price changes not necessarily associated with changes in the consumer unit's income should be.

simplicity $I_2$ is supposed always greater than $I_1$. This simplification is possible because, as we shall see later, the original hypothesis implies that choices of consumer units among more complicated alternatives can be predicted from complete knowledge of their preferences among alternatives like $A$ and a riskless alternative ($B$) consisting of a certain income $I_0$.

Since "other things" are supposed the same for alternatives $A$ and $B$, the utility of the two alternatives may be taken to be functions solely of the incomes and probabilities involved and not also of attendant circumstances. The utility of alternative $B$ is $U(I_0)$. The expected utility of $A$ is given by

$$\overline{U}(A) = aU(I_1) + (1 - a)U(I_2)$$

According to the hypothesis, a consumer unit will choose $A$ if $\overline{U} > U(I_0)$, will choose $B$ if $\overline{U} < U(I_0)$, and will be indifferent between $A$ and $B$ if $\overline{U} = U(I_0)$.

Let $\overline{I}(A)$ be the actuarial value of $A$, i.e., $\overline{I}(A) = aI_1 + (1 - a)I_2$. If $I_0$ is equal to $\overline{I}$, the "gamble" or "insurance" is said to be "fair" since the consumer unit gets the same actuarial value whichever alternative it chooses. If, under these circumstances, the consumer unit chooses $A$, it shows a preference for this risk. This is to be interpreted as meaning that $\overline{U} > U(\overline{I})$ and indeed $\overline{U} - U(\overline{I})$ may be taken to measure the utility it attaches to this particular risk.[26] If the consumer unit chooses $B$, it shows a preference for certainty. This is to be interpreted as meaning that $\overline{U} < U(\overline{I})$. Indifference between $A$ and $B$ is to be interpreted as meaning that $\overline{U} = U(\overline{I})$.

Let $I^*$ be the certain income that has the same utility as $A$, that is, $U(I^*) = \overline{U}$.[27] Call $I^*$ the income equivalent to $A$. The requirement, derived from consideration of riskless choices, that utility increase with income means that

$$\overline{U} \gtreqless U(\overline{I})$$

implies

$$I^* \gtreqless \overline{I}$$

If $I^*$ is greater than $\overline{I}$, the consumer unit prefers this particular risk to a certain income of the same actuarial value and would be willing to pay a

[26] This interpretation of $\overline{U} - U(I)$ as the utility attached to a particular risk is directly relevant to a point to which von Neumann and Morgenstern and commentators on their work have given a good deal of attention, namely, whether there may "not exist in an individual a (positive or negative) utility of the mere act of 'taking a chance,' of gambling, which the use of the mathematical expectation obliterates" (von Neumann and Morgenstern, *op. cit.*, p. 28). In our view the hypothesis is better interpreted as a rather special explanation why gambling has utility or disutility to a consumer unit, and as providing a particular measure of the utility or disutility, than as a denial that gambling has utility (see *ibid.*, pp. 28, 629–32).

[27] Since $U$ has been assumed strictly monotonic to rationalize riskless choices, there will be only one income, if any, that has the same utility as $A$. There will be one if $U$ is continuous which, for simplicity, we assume to be the case throughout this paper.

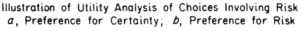

Illustration of Utility Analysis of Choices Involving Risk
*a*, Preference for Certainty; *b*, Preference for Risk

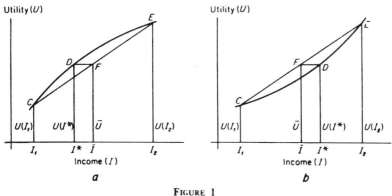

FIGURE 1

maximum of $I^* - \bar{I}$ for the privilege of "gambling." If $I^*$ is less than $\bar{I}$, the consumer unit prefers certainty and is willing to pay a maximum of $\bar{I} - I^*$ for "insurance" against this risk.

These concepts are illustrated for a consumer unit who is willing to pay for insurance ($\bar{I} > I^*$) in Figure 1a, and for a consumer unit who is willing to pay for the privilege of gambling ($\bar{I} < I^*$) in Figure 1b. In both figures, money income is measured along the horizontal axis, and utility along the vertical. On the horizontal axis, designate $I_1$ and $I_2$. $\bar{I}$, the actuarial value of $I_1$ and $I_2$, is then represented by a point that divides the interval $I_1$ to $I_2$ in the proportion

$$\frac{1-a}{a} \left( \text{i.e.,} \ \frac{\bar{I} - I_1}{I_2 - \bar{I}} = \frac{1-a}{a} \right)$$

Draw the utility curve ($CDE$ in both figures). Connect the points $[I_1, U(I_1)]$, $[I_2, U(I_2)]$ by a straight line ($CFE$). The vertical distance of this line from the horizontal axis at $\bar{I}$ is then equal to $\bar{U}$. [Since $\bar{I}$ divides the distance between $I_1$ and $I_2$ in the proportion $(1 - a)/a$, $F$ divides the vertical distance between $C$ and $E$ in the same proportion, so the vertical distance from $F$ to the horizontal axis is the expected value of $U(I_1)$ and $U(I_2)$.] Draw a horizontal line through $F$ and find the income corresponding to its intersection with the utility curve (point $D$). This is the income the utility of which is the same as the expected utility of $A$, hence by definition is $I^*$.

In Figure 1a, the utility curve is so drawn as to make $I^*$ less than $\bar{I}$. If the consumer unit is offered a choice between $A$ and a certain income $I_0$ greater than $I^*$, it will choose the certain income. If this certain income $I_0$ were less than $\bar{I}$, the consumer unit would be paying $\bar{I} - I_0$ for certainty—in ordinary parlance it would be "buying insurance"; if the certain income were greater than $\bar{I}$, it would be being paid $I_0 - \bar{I}$ for accepting certainty, even though it is willing to pay for certainty—we might say that it is "selling a gamble" rather than "buying insurance." If the consumer unit were offered a choice between $A$ and a certain income $I_0$ less than $I^*$, it would choose $A$ because, while it is willing to pay a price for certainty, it is being asked to pay more than the maximum amount $(\bar{I} - I^*)$ that it is willing to pay. The price of insurance has become so high that it has, as it were, been converted into a seller rather than a buyer of insurance.

In Figure 1b, the utility curve is so drawn as to make $I^*$ greater than $\bar{I}$. If the consumer unit is offered a choice between $A$ and a certain income $I_0$ less than $I^*$, it will choose $A$. If this certain income $I_0$ were greater than $\bar{I}$, the consumer unit would be paying $I_0 - \bar{I}$ for this risk—in ordinary parlance, it would be choosing to gamble or, one might say, "to buy a gamble"; if the certain income were less than $\bar{I}$, it would be being paid $\bar{I} - I_0$ for accepting this risk even though it is willing to pay for the risk—we might say that it is "selling insurance" rather than "buying a gamble." If the consumer unit is offered a choice between $A$ and a certain income $I_0$ greater than $I^*$, it will choose the certain income because, while it is willing to pay something for a gamble, it is not willing to pay more than $I^* - \bar{I}$. The price of the gamble has become so high that it is converted into a seller, rather than a buyer, of gambles.

It is clear that the graphical condition for a consumer unit to be willing to pay something for certainty is that the utility function be above its chord at $\bar{I}$. This is simply a direct translation of the condition that $U(\bar{I}) > \bar{U}$. Similarly, a consumer unit will be willing to pay something for a risk if the utility function is below its chord at $\bar{I}$. The relationship between these formalized "insurance" and "gambling" situations and what are ordinarily called insurance and gambling is fairly straight-forward. A consumer unit contemplating buying insurance is to be regarded as having a current income of $I_2$ and as being subject to a chance of losing a sum equal to $I_2 - I_1$, so that if this loss should occur its income would be reduced to $I_1$. It can insure against this loss by paying a premium equal to $I_2 - I_0$. The premium, in general, will be larger than $I_2 - \bar{I}$, the "loading" being equal to $\bar{I} - I_0$. Purchase of insurance therefore means accepting the certainty of an income equal to $I_0$ instead of a pair of alternative incomes having a higher expected value. Similarly, a consumer unit deciding whether to gamble (e.g., to purchase a lottery ticket) can be interpreted as having a current income equal to $I_0$. It can have a chance $(1 - a)$ of a gain equal to $I_2 - I_0$ by subjecting itself to a chance $a$ of losing a sum equal to $I_0 - I_1$. If it gambles, the actuarial value of its income is $\bar{I}$, which in general is less than $I_0$. $I_0 - \bar{I}$ is the premium it is paying for the chance to gamble (the "take" of the house, or the "banker's cut").

It should be emphasized that this analysis is all an elaboration of a particular hypothesis about the way consumer units choose among alternatives involving risk. This hypothesis describes the reactions of consumer units in terms of a utility function, unique except for origin and unit of measure, which gives the utility assigned to certain incomes and which has so far been taken for granted. Yet for choices among certain incomes only a trivial characteristic of this function is relevant, namely, that it rises with income. The remaining characteristics of the function are relevant only to choices among alternatives involving risk and can therefore be inferred only from observation of such choices. The precise manner in which these characteristics are implicit in the consumer unit's preferences among alternatives involving risk can be indicated most easily by describing a conceptual experiment for determining the utility function.

Select any two incomes, say $500 and $1,000. Assign any arbitrary utilities to these incomes, say 0 utiles and 1 utile, respectively. This corresponds to an arbitrary choice of origin and unit of measure. Select any intermediate income, say $600. Offer the consumer unit the choice between ($A$) a chance $a$ of $500 and $(1 - a)$ of $1,000$ or ($B$) a certainty of $600, varying $a$ until the consumer unit is indifferent between the two (i.e., until $I^* = \$600$). Suppose this indifference value of $a$ is 2/5. If the hypothesis is correct, it follows that

$$U(600) = 2/5\,U(500) + 3/5\,U(1000) = 2/5\cdot 0 + 3/5\cdot 1 = 3/5 = .60$$

In this way the utility attached to every income between $500 and $1,000 can be determined. To get the utility attached to any income outside the interval $500 to $1,000, say $10,000, offer the consumer unit a choice between ($A$) a chance $a$ of $500 and $(1 - a)$ of $10,000$ or ($B$) a certainty of $1,000, varying $a$ until the consumer unit is indifferent between the two (i.e., until $I^* = \$1,000$). Suppose this indifference value of $a$ is 4/5. If the hypothesis is correct, it follows that

$$4/5\,U(500) + 1/5\,U(10,000) = U(1000)$$

or

$$4/5\cdot 0 + 1/5\,U(10,000) = 1$$

or

$$U(10,000) = 5$$

In principle, the possibility of carrying out this experiment, and the reproducibility of the results, would provide a test of the hypothesis. For example, the consistency of behavior assumed by the hypothesis would be contradicted if a repetition of the experiment using two initial incomes other than $500 and $1,000 yielded a utility function differing in more than origin and unit of measure from the one initially obtained.

Given a utility function obtained in this way, it is possible, if the hypothesis is correct, to compute the utility attached to (that is, the expected utility of) any set or sets of possible incomes and associated probabilities and thereby to predict which of a number of such sets will be chosen. This is the precise meaning of the statement made toward the beginning of this section that, if the hypothesis were correct, complete knowledge of the preferences of consumer units among alternatives like $A$ and $B$ would make it possible to predict their reactions to any other choices involving risk.

The choices a consumer unit makes that involve risk are typically far more complicated than the simple choice between $A$ and $B$ that we have used to elaborate the hypothesis. There are two chief sources of complication: Any particular alternative typically offers an indefinitely large number of possible incomes, and "other things" are generally not the same.

The multiplicity of possible incomes is very general: losses insured against ordinarily have more than one possible value; lotteries ordinarily have more than one prize; the possible income from a particular occupation, investment, or business enterprise may be equal to any of an indefinitely large number of values. A hypothesis that the essence of choices among the degrees of risk involved in such complex alternatives is contained in such simple choices as the choice between $A$ and $B$ is by no means tautological.

The hypothesis does not, of course, pretend to say anything about how consumer choices will be affected by differences in things other than degree of risk. The significance for our purposes of such differences is rather that they greatly increase the difficulty of getting evidence about reactions to differences in risk alone. Much casual experience, particularly experience bearing on what is ordinarily regarded as gambling, is likely to be misinterpreted, and erroneously regarded as contradictory to the hypothesis, if this difficulty is not explicitly recognized. In much so-called gambling the individual chooses not only to bear risk but also to participate in the mechanics of a game of chance; he buys, that is, a gamble, in our technical sense, and entertainment. We can conceive of separating these two commodities: he could buy entertainment alone by paying admission to participate in a game using valueless chips; he could buy the gamble alone by having an agent play the game of chance for him according to detailed instructions.[28] Further, insurance and gambles are often purchased in almost pure form. This is notably true of insurance. It is true also of gambling by the purchase of lottery tickets when the purchaser is not a spectator to the drawing of the winners (e.g., Irish sweepstakes tickets bought in this country or the "numbers" game), and of much stockmarket speculation.

An example of behavior that would definitely contradict the assertion, contained in the hypothesis, that the same utility function can be used to explain choices that do and do not involve risk would be willingness by an individual to pay more for a gamble than the maximum amount he could win. In order to explain riskless choices it is necessary to suppose that utility increases with income. It follows that the average utility of two incomes can never exceed the utility of the larger income and hence that an individual will never be willing to pay, for example, a dollar for a chance of winning, at most, 99 cents.

More subtle observation would be required to contradict the assertion that

---

[28] It does not, of course, follow that the price an individual is willing to pay for the joint commodity is simply the sum of the prices he is willing to pay for them separately. Indeed, it may well be the possible existence of such a difference that people have in mind when they speak of a "specific utility of gambling."

the reactions of persons to complicated gambles can be inferred from their reactions to simple gambles. For example, suppose an individual refuses an opportunity to toss a coin for a dollar and also to toss a coin for two dollars but then accepts an opportunity to toss two coins in succession, the first to determine whether the second toss is to be for one dollar or for two dollars. This behavior would definitely contradict the hypothesis. On the hypothesis, the utility of the third gamble is an average of the utility of the first two. His refusal of the first two indicates that each of them has a lower utility than the alternative of not gambling; hence, if the hypothesis were correct, the third should have a lower utility than the same alternative, and he should refuse it.

## IV. RESTRICTIONS ON UTILITY FUNCTION REQUIRED TO RATIONALIZE OBSERVABLE BEHAVIOR

The one restriction imposed on the utility function in the preceding section is that total utility increase with the size of money income. This restriction was imposed to rationalize the first of the facts listed below. We are now ready to see whether the behavior described in Section II can be rationalized by the hypothesis, and, if so, what additional restrictions this behavior imposes on the utility function. To simplify the task, we shall take as a summary of the essential features of the behavior described in Section II the following five statements, alleged to be facts: (1) consumer units prefer larger to smaller certain incomes; (2) low-income consumer units buy, or are willing to buy, insurance; (3) low-income consumer units buy, or are willing to buy, lottery tickets; (4) many low-income consumer units buy, or are willing to buy, both insurance and lottery tickets; (5) lotteries typically have more than one prize.

These particular statements are selected not because they are the most important in and of themselves but because they are convenient to handle and the restrictions imposed to rationalize them turn out to be sufficient to rationalize all the behavior described in Section II.

It is obvious from Figure 1 and our discussion of it that if the utility function were everywhere convex from above (for utility functions with a continuous derivative, if the marginal utility of money does not increase for any income), the consumer unit, on our hypothesis, would be willing to enter into any fair insurance plan but would be unwilling to pay anything in excess of the actuarial value for any gamble. If the utility function were everywhere concave from above (for functions with a continuous derivative, if the marginal utility of money does not diminish for any income), the consumer unit would be willing to enter into any fair gamble but would be unwilling to pay anything in excess of the actuarial value for insurance against any risk.

It follows that our hypothesis can rationalize statement 2, the purchase of insurance by low-income consumer units, only if the utility functions of the corresponding units are not everywhere concave from above; that it can rationalize statement 3, the purchase of lottery tickets by low-income consumer units, only if the utility functions of the corresponding units are not everywhere convex from above; and that it can rationalize statement 4, the

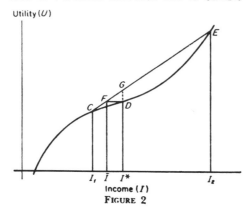

Illustration of Utility Function Consistent with
Willingness of a Low-Income Consumer Unit
Both to Purchase Insurance and to Gamble

FIGURE 2

purchase of both insurance and lottery tickets by low-income consumer units, only if the utility functions of the corresponding units are neither everywhere concave from above nor everywhere convex from above.

The simplest utility function (with a continuous derivative) that can rationalize all three statements simultaneously is one that has a segment convex from above followed by a segment concave from above and no other segments.[29] The convex segment must precede the concave segment because of the kind of insurance and of gambling the low-income consumer units are said to engage in: a chord from the existing income to a lower income must be below the utility function to rationalize the purchase of insurance against the risk of loss; a chord from the immediate neighborhood of the existing income to a higher income must be above the utility function at the existing income to rationalize the purchase for a small sum of a small chance of a large gain.[30]

Figure 2 illustrates a utility function satisfying these requirements. Let this utility function be for a low-income consumer unit whose current income is in the initial convex segment, say at the point designated $I^*$. If some risk should arise of incurring a loss, the consumer unit would clearly (on our hypothesis) be willing to insure against the loss (if it did not have to pay too much "loading") since a chord from the utility curve at $I^*$ to the utility curve at the lower income that would be the consequence of the actual occurrence of the loss would everywhere ʻ·e below the utility function. The consumer unit would not be willing to engage in small gambling. But suppose it is offered a fair gamble of the kind represented by a lottery involving a small chance of

[29] A kink or a jump in the utility function could rationalize either the gambling or the insurance. For example, the utility function could be composed of two convex or two concave segments joined in a kink. There is no essential loss in generality in neglecting such cases, as we shall do from here on, since one can always think of rounding the kink ever so slightly.

[30] If there are more than two segments and a continuous derivative, a convex segment necessarily precedes a concave segment.

winning a relatively large sum equal to $I_2 - I^*$ and a large chance of losing a relatively small sum equal to $I^* - I_1$. The consumer unit would clearly prefer the gamble, since the expected utility ($I^*G$) is greater than the utility of $I^*$. Indeed it would be willing to pay any premium up to $I^* - \bar{I}$ for the privilege of gambling; that is, even if the expected value of the gamble were almost as low as $\bar{I}$, it would accept the gamble in preference to a certainty of receiving $I^*$. The utility curve in Figure 2 is therefore clearly consistent with statements 2, 3, and 4.

These statements refer solely to the behavior of relatively low-income consumer units. It is tempting to seek to restrict further the shape of the utility function, and to test the restrictions so far imposed, by appealing to casual observation of the behavior of relatively high-income consumer units.[31] It does not seem desirable to do so, however, for two major reasons: (1) it is far more difficult to accumulate reliable information about the behavior of relatively high-income consumer units than about the behavior of the more numerous low-income units: (2) perhaps even more important, the progressive income tax so affects the terms under which the relatively high-income consumer units purchase insurance or gamble as to make evidence on their behavior hard to interpret for our purposes.[32] Therefore, instead of using

[31] For example, a high-income consumer unit that had a utility function like that in Fig. 2 and a current income of $I_2$ would be willing to participate in a wide variety of gambling, including the purchase of lottery tickets; it would be unwilling to insure against losses that had a small expected value (i.e., involved payment of a small premium) though it might be willing to insure against losses that had a large expected value. Consequently, unwillingness of relatively high-income consumer units to purchase lottery tickets, or willingness to purchase low-premium insurance, would contradict the utility function of Fig. 2 and require the imposition of further restrictions.

[32] The effect of the income tax, already referred to in footnote 16 above, depends greatly on the specific provisions of the tax law and of the insurance or gambling plan. For example, if an uninsured loss is deductible in computing taxable income (as is loss of an owned home by fire under the federal income tax) while the premium for insuring against the loss is not (as a fire insurance premium on an owned home is not), the expected value of the loss is less to the consumer unit than to the firm selling insurance. A premium equal to the actuarial value of the loss to the insurance company then exceeds the actuarial value of the loss to the consumer unit. That is, the government in effect pays part of the loss but none of the premium. On the other hand, if the premium is deductible (as a health insurance premium may be), while an uninsured loss is not (as the excess of medical bills over $2,500 for a family is not), the net premium to the consumer unit is less than the premium received by the insurance company. Similarly, gambling gains in excess of gambling losses are taxable under the federal income tax, while gambling losses in excess of gambling gains are not deductible. The special treatment of capital gains and losses under the existing United States federal income tax adds still further complications.

Even if both the premium and the uninsured loss are deductible, or a gain taxable and the corresponding loss deductible, the income tax may change the terms because of the progressive rates. The tax saving from a large loss may be a smaller fraction of the loss than the tax payable on the gain is of the gain.

These comments clearly apply not only to insurance and gambling proper but also to other economic decisions involving risk—the purchase of securities, choice of occupation or business, etc. The neglect of these considerations has frequently led to the erroneous belief

observations about the behavior of relatively high-income consumer units, we shall seek to learn more about the upper end of the curve by using statement 5, the tendency for lotteries to have more than one prize.

In order to determine the implications of this statement for the utility function, we must investigate briefly the economics of lotteries. Consider an entrepreneur conducting a lottery and seeking to maximize his income from it. For simplicity, suppose that he conducts the lottery by deciding in advance the number of tickets to offer and then auctioning them off at the highest price he can get.[33] Aside from advertising and the like, the variables at his disposal are the terms of the lottery: the number of tickets to sell, the total amount to offer as prizes (which together, of course, determine the actuarial value of a ticket), and the structure of prizes to offer. For any given values of the first two, the optimum structure of prizes is clearly that which maximizes the price he can get per ticket or, what is the same thing, the excess of the price of a ticket over its actuarial value—the "loading" per ticket.

In the discussion of Figure 2, it was noted that $I^* - \bar{I}$ was the maximum amount in excess of the actuarial value that the corresponding consumer unit would pay for a gamble involving a chance $(1 - a)$ of winning $I_2 - I^*$ and a chance $a$ of losing $I^* - I_1$. This gamble is equivalent to a lottery offering a chance $(1 - a)$ of a prize $I_2 - I_1$ in return for the purchase of a ticket at a price of $I^* - I_1$, the chance of winning the prize being such that $\bar{I} - I_1$ is the actuarial worth of a ticket [i.e., is equal to $(1 - a) \times (I_2 - I_1)$]. If the consumer unit won the prize, its net winnings would be $I_2 - I^*$, since it would have to subtract the cost of the ticket from the gross prize. The problem of the entrepreneur, then, is to choose the structure of prizes that will maximize $I^* - \bar{I}$ for a given actuarial value of a ticket, that is, for a given value of $\bar{I} - I_1$. Changes in the structure of prizes involve changes in $I_2 - I_1$. If there is a single prize, $I_2 - I_1$ is equal to the total amount to be distributed [$(1 - a)$ is equal to the reciprocal of the number of tickets]. If there are two equal prizes, $I_2 - I_1$ is cut in half [$(1 - a)$ is then equal to twice the reciprocal of the number of tickets]. Suppose Figure 2 referred to this latter situation in which there were two equal prizes, $I^*$ on the diagram designating both the current income of the consumer unit and the income equivalent to the lottery. If the price and actuarial worth of the ticket were kept unchanged, but a single prize was substituted for the two prizes [and $(1 - a)$ correspondingly reduced], the gamble would clearly become more attractive to the consumer unit. $I_2$ would move to the right, the chord connecting $U(I_1)$ and $U(I_2)$ would rotate upward, $\bar{U}$ would increase, and the consumer unit would be paying less

that a progressive income tax does not affect the allocation of resources and is in this way fundamentally different from excise taxes.

[33] This was, in fact, the way in which the British government conducted many of its official lotteries. It frequently auctioned off the tickets to lottery dealers, who served as the means of distributing the tickets to the public (see Ewen, *op. cit.*, pp. 234–40).

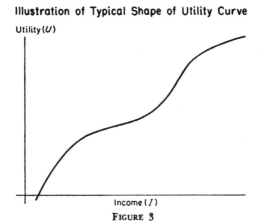

Illustration of Typical Shape of Utility Curve

Utility ($U$)

Income ($I$)

FIGURE 3

than the maximum amount it was willing to pay. The price of the ticket could accordingly be increased; that is, $I_2$, $\bar{I}$, and $I_1$ could be moved to the left until the $I^*$ for the new gamble were equal to the consumer unit's current income (the $I^*$ for the old gamble). The optimum structure of prizes clearly consists therefore of a single prize, since this makes $I_2 - I_1$ as large as possible.

Statement 5, that lotteries typically have more than one prize, is therefore inconsistent with the utility function of Figure 2. This additional fact can be rationalized by terminating the utility curve with a suitable convex segment. This yields a utility curve like that drawn in Figure 3. With such a utility curve, $I^* - \bar{I}$ would be a maximum at the point at which a chord from $U(I_1)$ was tangent to the utility curve, and a larger prize would yield a smaller value of $I^* - \bar{I}$.[34]

A utility curve like that drawn in Figure 3 is the simplest one consistent with the five statements listed at the outset of this section.

## V. A DIGRESSION

It seems well to digress at this point to consider two questions that, while not strictly relevant to our main theme, are likely to occur to many readers:

---

[34] An additional convex segment guarantees that there will always exist current incomes of the consumer unit for which (*a*) attractive gambles exist and (*b*) the optimum prize for attractive gambles has a maximum. It does not guarantee that *b* will be true for every income for which attractive gambles exist. The condition on the current income that attractive gambles exist is that the tangent to the utility curve at the current income be below the utility curve for some income (this argument, like many in later technical footnotes, holds not only for the utility function of Fig. 3 but for any differentiable utility function). A single prize will be the optimum, no matter what the amount distributed in prizes or the fixed actuarial worth of the prize if, and only if, every chord from the utility curve at the current income to the utility of a higher income is everywhere above the utility curve. A particular, and somewhat interesting, class of utility functions for which *b* will be true for every income for which *a* is true is the class for which utility approaches a finite limit as income increases.

first, is not the hypothesis patently unrealistic; second, can any plausible interpretation be given to the rather peculiar utility function of Figure 3?

## THE DESCRIPTIVE "REALISM" OF THE HYPOTHESIS

An objection to the hypothesis just presented that is likely to be raised by many, if not most, readers is that it conflicts with the way human beings actually behave and choose. Is it not patently unrealistic to suppose that individuals consult a wiggly utility curve before gambling or buying insurance, that they know the odds involved in the gambles or insurance plans open to them, that they can compute the expected utility of a gamble or insurance plan, and that they base their decision on the size of the expected utility?

While entirely natural and understandable, this objection is not strictly relevant. The hypothesis does not assert that individuals explicitly or consciously calculate and compare expected utilities. Indeed, it is not at all clear what such an assertion would mean or how it could be tested. The hypothesis asserts rather that, in making a particular class of decisions, individuals behave *as if* they calculated and compared expected utility and *as if* they knew the odds. The validity of this assertion does not depend on whether individuals know the precise odds, much less on whether they say that they calculate and compare expected utilities or think that they do, or whether it appears to others that they do, or whether psychologists can uncover any evidence that they do, but solely on whether it yields sufficiently accurate predictions about the class of decisions with which the hypothesis deals. Stated differently, the test by results is the only possible method of determining whether the *as if* statement is or is not a sufficiently good approximation to reality for the purpose at hand.

A simple example may help to clarify the point at issue. Consider the problem of predicting, before each shot, the direction of travel of a billiard ball hit by an expert billiard player. It would be possible to construct one or more mathematical formulas that would give the directions of travel that would score points and, among these, would indicate the one (or more) that would leave the balls in the best positions. The formulas might, of course, be extremely complicated, since they would necessarily take account of the location of the balls in relation to one another and to the cushions and of the complicated phenomena introduced by "english." Nonetheless, it seems not at all unreasonable that excellent predictions would be yielded by the hypothesis that the billiard player made his shots *as if* he knew the formulas, could estimate accurately by eye the angles, etc., describing the location of the balls, could make lightning calculations from the formulas, and could then make the ball travel in the direction indicated by the formulas. It would in no way disprove or contradict the hypothesis, or weaken our confidence in it, if it should turn out that the billiard player had never studied any branch of mathematics and was utterly incapable of making the necessary calculations: unless he was capable in some way of reaching approximately the same result as that obtained from the formulas, he would not in fact be likely to be an expert billiard player.

The same considerations are relevant to our utility hypothesis. Whatever the psychological mechanism whereby individuals make choices, these choices appear to display some consistency, which can apparently be described by our utility hypothesis. This hypothesis enables predictions to be made about phenomena on which there is not yet reliable evidence. The hypothesis cannot be declared invalid for a particular class of behavior until a prediction about that class proves false. No other test of its validity is decisive.

A POSSIBLE INTERPRETATION OF THE UTILITY FUNCTION

A possible interpretation of the utility function of Figure 3 is to regard the two convex segments as corresponding to qualitatively different socioeconomic levels, and the concave segment to the transition between the two levels. On this interpretation, increases in income that raise the relative position of the consumer unit in its own class but do not shift the unit out of its class yield diminishing marginal utility, while increases that shift it into a new class, that give it a new social and economic status, yield increasing marginal utility. An unskilled worker may prefer the certainty of an income about the same as that of the majority of unskilled workers to an actuarially fair gamble that at best would make him one of the most prosperous unskilled workers and at worst one of the least prosperous. Yet he may jump at an actuarially fair gamble that offers a small chance of lifting him out of the class of unskilled workers and into the " middle " or " upper " class, even though it is far more likely than the preceding gamble to make him one of the least prosperous unskilled workers. Men will and do take great risks to distinguish themselves, even when they know what the risks are. May not the concave segment of the utility curve of Figure 3 translate the economic counterpart of this phenomenon appropriately?

A number of additions to the hypothesis are suggested by this interpretation. In the first place, may there not be more than two qualitatively distinguishable socioeconomic classes? If so, might not each be reflected by a convex segment in the utility function? At the moment, there seems to be no observed behavior that requires the introduction of additional convex segments, so it seems undesirable and unnecessary to complicate the hypothesis further. It may well be, however, that it will be necessary to add such segments to account for behavior revealed by further empirical evidence. In the second place, if different segments of the curve correspond to different socioeconomic classes, should not the dividing points between the segments occur at roughly the same income for different consumer units in the same community? If they did, the fruitfulness of the hypothesis would be greatly extended. Not only could the general shape of the utility function be supposed typical; so also could the actual income separating the various segments. The initial convex segment could be described as applicable to "relatively low-income consumer units " and the terminal convex segment as applicable to

" relatively high-income consumer units "; and the groups so designated could be identified by the actual income or wealth of different consumer units.

Interpreting the different segments of the curve as corresponding to different socioeconomic classes would, of course, still permit wide variation among consumer units in the exact shape and height of the curve. In addition, it would not be necessary to suppose anything more than rough similarity in the location of the incomes separating the various segments. Different socioeconomic classes are not sharply demarcated from one another; each merges into the next by imperceptible gradations (which, of course, accounts for the income range encompassed by the concave segment); and the generally accepted dividing line between classes will vary from time to time, place to place, and consumer unit to consumer unit. Finally, it is not necessary that every consumer unit have a utility curve like that in Figure 3. Some may be inveterate gamblers; others, inveterately cautious. It is enough that many consumer units have such a utility curve.

## VI. FURTHER IMPLICATIONS OF THE HYPOTHESIS

To return to our main theme, we have two tasks yet to perform: first, to show that the utility function of Figure 3 is consistent with those features of the behavior described in Section II not used in deriving it; second, to suggest additional implications of the hypothesis capable of providing a test of it.

The chief generalization of Section II not so far used is that people must in general be paid a premium to induce them to bear moderate risks instead of either small or large risks. Is this generalization consistent with the utility function of Figure 3?

It clearly is for a consumer unit whose income places it in the initial convex segment. Such a relatively low-income consumer unit will be willing to pay something more than the actuarial value for insurance against any kind of risk that may arise; it will be averse to small fair gambles; it may be averse to all fair gambles; if not, it will be attracted by fair gambles that offer a small chance of a large gain; the attractiveness of such gambles, with a given possible loss and actuarial value, will initially increase as the size of the possible gain increases and will eventually decrease.[35] Such consumer units therefore

---

[35] The willingness of a consumer unit in the initial convex segment to pay something more than the actuarial value for insurance against any kind of risk follows from the fact that a chord connecting the utility of its current income with the utility of any lower income to which it might be reduced by the risk in question will everywhere be below the utility curve. The expected utility is therefore less than the utility of the expected income.

To analyze the reaction of such a consumer unit to different gambles, consider the limiting case in which the gamble is fair, i.e., $I = I_0$. $I$ then is both the expected income of the consumer unit if it takes the gamble and its actual income if it does not (i.e., its current income). The possible gains (and associated probabilities) that will be attractive to the unit for a given value of $I_1$ (i.e., a given possible loss) can be determined by drawing a straight line through $U(I_1)$ and $U(I)$. All values of $I_2 > I$ for which $U(I_2)$ is greater than the ordinate of the extended straight line will be attractive; no others will be.

Since $I$ is assumed to be in the first convex segment, there will always exist some values of

prefer either certainty or a risk that offers a small chance of a large gain to a risk that offers the possibility of moderate gains or losses. They will therefore have to be paid a premium to induce them to undertake such moderate risks.

The generalization is clearly false for a consumer unit whose income places it in the concave segment. Such an "intermediate-income" consumer unit will be attracted by every small fair gamble; it may be attracted by every fair gamble; it may be averse to all fair insurance; if not, it will be attracted by insurance against relatively large losses.[36] Such consumer units will therefore be willing to pay a premium in order to assume moderate risks.

The generalization is partly true, partly false, for a consumer unit whose income places it in the terminal convex segment. Such a relatively high-income consumer unit will be willing to insure against any small possible loss and may be attracted to every fair insurance plan; the only insurance plans it may be averse to are plans involving rather large losses; it may be averse to all fair gambles; if not, it will be attracted by gambles that involve a reasonably sure, though fairly small, gain, with a small possibility of a sizable loss; it will be averse to gambles of the lottery variety.[37] These consumer units therefore prefer certainty to moderate risks; in this respect they conform to the generalization. However, they may prefer moderate risks to extreme risks, though these adjectives hardly suffice to characterize the rather complex pattern of risk preferences implied for high-income consumer units by a utility curve like

---

$I_2 > I$ for which $U(I_2)$ is less than the ordinate of the extended straight line. This is the basis for the statement that the consumer unit will be averse to small gambles.

Consider the line that touches the curve at only two points and is nowhere below the utility curve. Call the income at the first of the points at which it touches the curve, which may be the lowest possible income, $I'$, and the income at the second point, $I''$. The consumer unit will be averse to all gambles if its income ($I_0 = I$) is equal to or less than $I'$. This follows from the fact that a tangent to the curve at $I$ will then be steeper than the "double tangent" and will intersect the latter prior to $I'$; a chord from $I$ to a lower income will be even steeper. This is the basis for the statement that the consumer unit may be averse to all gambles.

If the income is above $I'$, there will always be some attractive gambles. These will offer a small chance of a large gain. The statement about the changing attractiveness of the gamble as the size of the possible gain changes follows from the analysis in Sec. IV of the conditions under which it would be advantageous to have a single prize in a lottery.

[36] Consider the tangent to the utility curve at the income the consumer unit would have if it did not take the gamble ($I - I_0$). If this income is in the concave section, the tangent will be below the utility curve at least for an interval of incomes surrounding $I$. A chord connecting any two points of the utility curve on opposite sides of $I$ and within this interval will always be above the utility curve at $I$ (i.e., the expected utility will be above the utility of the expected income), so these gambles will be attractive. The tangent may lie below the utility curve for all incomes. In this case, every fair gamble will be attractive. The unit will be averse to insuring against a loss, whatever the chance of its occurring, if a chord from the current income to the lower income to which it would be reduced by the loss is everywhere above the utility curve. This will surely be true for small losses and may be true for all possible losses.

[37] These statements follow directly from considerations like those in the two preceding footnotes.

that of Figure 3. Nonetheless, in this respect the implied behavior of the high-income consumer units is either neutral or contrary to the generalization.

Our hypothesis does not therefore lead inevitably to a rate of return higher to uses of resources involving moderate risk than to uses involving little or much risk. It leads to a rate of return higher for uses involving moderate risk than for uses involving little risk only if consumer units in the two convex segments outweigh in importance, for the resource use in question, consumer units in the concave segment.[38] Similarly, it leads to a rate of return higher for uses involving moderate risk than for uses involving much risk only if consumer units in the initial convex segment outweigh in importance consumer units in both the concave and the terminal convex segments—though this may be a more stringent condition than is necessary in view of the uncertainty about the exact role of consumer units in the terminal convex segment.

This relative distribution of consumer units among the various segments could be considered an additional restriction that would have to be imposed to rationalize the alleged higher rate of return to moderately risky uses of resources. It is not clear, however, that it need be so considered, since there are two independent lines of reasoning that, taken together, establish something of a presumption that relatively few consumer units are in the concave segment.

One line of reasoning is based on the interpretation of the utility function suggested in Section V above. If the concave segment is a border line between two qualitatively different social classes, one would expect relatively few consumer units to be between the two classes.

The other line of reasoning is based on the implications of the hypothesis for the relative stability of the economic status of consumer units in the different segments. Units in the intermediate segment are tempted by every small gamble and at least some large ones. If opportunities are available, they will be continually subjecting themselves to risk. In consequence, they are likely to move out of the segment; upwards, if they are lucky; downwards, if they are not. Consumer units in the two convex segments, on the other hand, are less likely to move into the intermediate segment. The gambles that units in the initial segment accept will rarely pay off and, when they do, are likely to shift them all the way into the terminal convex segment. The gambles that units in the terminal segment accept will rarely involve losses and, when they do, may shift them all the way into the lower segment. Under these conditions, maintenance of a stable distribution of the population among the three segments would require that the two convex segments contain many more individuals than the concave segment. These considerations, while persuasive, are not, of course, conclusive. Opportunities to assume risks may

---

[38] This statement is deliberately vague. The actual relative rates of return will depend not only on the conditions of demand for risks of different kinds but also on the conditions of supply, and both would have to be taken into account in a comprehensive statement.

not exist. More important, the status of consumer units is determined not alone by the outcome of risks deliberately assumed but also by random events over which they cannot choose and have no control; and it is conceivable that these random events might be distributed in such a way that their main effect was to multiply the number in the concave segment.

The absolute number of persons in the various segments will count most for choices among the uses of human resources; wealth will count most for choices among uses of nonhuman resources.[39] In consequence, one might expect that the premium for bearing moderate risks instead of large risks would be greater for occupations than for investments. Indeed, for investments, the differential might in some cases be reversed, since the relatively high-income consumer units (those in the terminal segment) count for more in wealth than in numbers and they may prefer moderate to extreme risks.

In judging the implications of our hypothesis for the market as a whole, we have found it necessary to consider separately its implications for different income groups. These offer additional possibilities of empirical test. Perhaps the most fruitful source of data would be the investment policies of different income groups.

It was noted in Section II that, although many persons with low incomes are apparently willing to buy extremely speculative stocks, the low-income group receives the bulk of its property income in the form of interest and rents. These observations are clearly consistent with our hypothesis. Relatively high-income groups might be expected, on our hypothesis, to prefer bonds and relatively safe stocks. They might be expected to avoid the more speculative common stocks but to be attracted to higher-grade preferred stocks, which pay a higher nominal rate of return than high-grade bonds to compensate for a small risk of capital loss. Intermediate income groups might be expected to hold relatively large shares of their assets in moderately speculative common stocks and to furnish a disproportionate fraction of entrepreneurs.

Of course, any empirical study along these lines will have to take into account, as noted above, the effect of the progressive income tax in modifying the terms of investment. The current United States federal income tax has conflicting effects: the progressive rates discourage risky investments; the favored treatment of capital gains encourages them. In addition, such a study will have to consider the risk of investments as a group, rather than of individual investments, since the rich may be in a position to "average" risks.

Another implication referred to above that may be susceptible of empirical test, and the last one we shall cite, is the implied difference in the stability of the relative income status of various economic groups. The unattractiveness of small risks to both high- and low-income consumer units would tend to

[39] This distinction requires qualification because of the need for capital to enter some types of occupations and the consequent existence of "noncompeting groups"; see Milton Friedman and Simon Kuznets, *Income from Independent Professional Practice* (New York: National Bureau of Economic Research, 1945), Ch. III, Sec. 3; Ch. IV, Sec. 2.

give them a relatively stable status. By contrast, suppose the utility curve had no terminal convex segment but was like the curve of Figure 2. Low-income consumer units would still have a relatively stable status: their willingness to take gambles at long odds would pay off too seldom to shift many from one class to another. High-income consumer units would not. They would then take almost any gamble, and those who had high incomes today almost certainly would not have high incomes tomorrow. The average period from "shirt sleeves to shirt sleeves" would be far shorter than "three generations."[40] Unlike the other two groups, the middle-income class might be expected to display considerable instability of relative income status.[41]

## VII. CONCLUSION

A plausible generalization of the available empirical evidence on the behavior of consumer units in choosing among alternatives open to them is provided by the hypothesis that a consumer unit (generally a family, sometimes an individual) behaves as if

1. It had a consistent set of preferences;
2. These preferences could be completely described by attaching a numerical value—to be designated "utility"—to alternatives each of which is regarded as certain;
3. The consumer unit chose among alternatives not involving risk that one which has the largest utility;
4. It chose among alternatives involving risk that one for which the expected utility (as contrasted with the utility of the expected income) is largest;
5. The function describing the utility of money income had in general the following properties:
   a. Utility rises with income, i.e., marginal utility of money income everywhere positive;
   b. It is convex from above below some income, concave between that income and some larger income, and convex for all higher incomes, i.e., diminishing marginal utility of money income for incomes below some income, increasing marginal utility of money income for incomes between that income and some larger income, and diminishing marginal utility of money income for all higher incomes;

[40] We did not use the absence of such instability to derive the upper convex segment because of the difficulty of allowing for the effect of the income tax.

[41] The existing data on stability of relative income status are too meager to contradict or to confirm this implication. In their study of professional incomes Friedman and Kuznets found that relative income status was about equally stable at all income levels. However, this study is hardly relevant, since it was for homogeneous occupational groups that would tend to fall in a single one of the classes considered here. Mendershausen's analysis along similar lines for family incomes in 1929 and 1933 is inconclusive. See Friedman and Kuznets, *op. cit.*, chap. VII; Horst Mendershausen, *Changes in Income Distribution during the Great Depression* (New York: National Bureau of Economic Research, 1946), chap. III.

6. Most consumer units tend to have incomes that place them in the segments of the utility function for which marginal utility of money income diminishes.

Points 1, 2, 3, and 5a of this hypothesis are implicit in the orthodox theory of choice; point 4 is an ancient idea recently revived and given new content by von Neumann and Morgenstern; and points 5b and 6 are the consequence of the attempt in this paper to use this idea to rationalize existing knowledge about the choices people make among alternatives involving risk.

Point 5b is inferred from the following phenomena: (a) low-income consumer units buy, or are willing to buy, insurance; (b) low-income consumer units buy, or are willing to buy, lottery tickets; (c) many consumer units buy, or are willing to buy, both insurance and lottery tickets; (d) lotteries typically have more than one prize. These statements are taken as a summary of the essential features of observed behavior not because they are the most important features in and of themselves but because they are convenient to handle and the restrictions imposed to rationalize them turn out to be sufficient to rationalize all the behavior described in Section II of this paper.

A possible interpretation of the various segments of the utility curve specified in 5b is that the segments of diminishing marginal utility correspond to socioeconomic classes, the segment of increasing marginal utility to a transitional stage between a lower and a higher socioeconomic class. On this interpretation the boundaries of the segments should be roughly similar for different people in the same community; and this is one of several independent lines of reasoning leading to point 6.

This hypothesis has implications for behavior, in addition to those used in deriving it, that are capable of being contradicted by observable data. In particular, the fundamental supposition that a single utility curve can generalize both riskless choices and choices involving risk would be contradicted if (a) individuals were observed to choose the larger of two certain incomes offered to them but (b) individuals were willing to pay more than the largest possible gain for the privilege of bearing risk. The supposition that individuals seek to maximize expected utility would be contradicted if individuals' reactions to complicated gambles could not be inferred from their reactions to simple ones. The particular shape of the utility curve specified in 5b would be contradicted by any of a large number of observations, for example, (a) general willingness of individuals, whatever their income, who buy insurance against small risks to enter into small fair gambles under circumstances under which they are not also buying "entertainment," (b) the converse of (a), namely an unwillingness to engage in small fair gambles by individuals who are not willing to buy fair insurance against small risks, (c) a higher average rate of return to uses of resources involving little risk than to uses involving a moderate amount of risk when other things are the same, (d) a concentration of investment portfolios of relatively low-income groups on speculative (but not highly speculative) investments or of relatively high-income groups on either moderately or highly speculative investments, (e) great instability in the relative income status of high-income groups or of low-income groups as a consequence of a propensity to engage in speculative activities.

## 3. EXPOSITION OF A NEW THEORY ON THE MEASUREMENT OF RISK[1]

DANIEL BERNOULLI

Reprinted from *Econometrica*, Vol. 22, No. 1 (January, 1954), pp. 23–36, by permission of the publisher.

§1. Ever since mathematicians first began to study the measurement of risk there has been general agreement on the following proposition: *Expected values are computed by multiplying each possible gain by the number of ways in which it can occur, and then dividing the sum of these products by the total*

[1] Translated from Latin into English by Dr. Louise Sommer, The American University, Washington, D.C., from " Specimen Theoriae Novae de Mensura Sortis," *Commentarii Academiae Scientiarum Imperialis Petropolitanae*, Tomus V [*Papers of the Imperial Academy of Sciences in Petersburg*, Vol. V], 1738, pp. 175–192. Professor Karl Menger, Illinois Institute of Technology has written footnotes 4, 9, 10, and 15.

Editor's Note: In view of the frequency with which Bernoulli's famous paper has been referred to in recent economic discussion, it has been thought appropriate to make it more generally available by publishing this English version. In her translation Professor Sommer has sought, in so far as possible, to retain the eighteenth century spirit of the original. The mathematical notation and much of the punctuation are reproduced without change. References to some of the recent literature concerned with Bernoulli's theory are given at the end of the article.

Translator's Note: I highly appreciate the help of Karl Menger, Professor of Mathematics, Illinois Institute of Technology, a distinguished authority on the Bernoulli problem, who has read this translation and given me expert advice. I am also grateful to Mr. William J. Baumol, Professor of Economics, Princeton University, for his valuable assistance in interpreting Bernoulli's paper in the light of modern econometrics. I wish to thank also Mr. John H. Lingenfeld, Economist, U.S. Department of Labor, for his cooperation in the English rendition of this paper. The translation is based solely upon the original Latin text.

Biographical Note: Daniel Bernoulli, a member of the famous Swiss family of distinguished mathematicians, was born in Groningen, January 29, 1700, and died in Basle, March 17, 1782. He studied mathematics and medical sciences at the University of Basle. In 1725 he accepted an invitation to the newly established academy in Petersburg, but returned to Basle in 1733 where he was appointed professor of physics and philosophy. Bernoulli was a member of the academies of Paris, Berlin, and Petersburg and the Royal Academy in London. He was the first to apply mathematical analysis to the problem of the movement of liquid bodies.

*number of possible cases where, in this theory, the consideration of cases which are all of the same probability is insisted upon.* If this rule be accepted, what remains to be done within the framework of this theory amounts to the enumeration of all alternatives, their breakdown into equi-probable cases and, finally, their insertion into corresponding classifications.

§2. Proper examination of the numerous demonstrations of this proposition that have come forth indicates that they all rest upon one hypothesis: *since there is no reason to assume that of two persons encountering identical risks,[2] either should expect to have his desires more closely fulfilled, the risks anticipated by each must be deemed equal in value.* No characteristic of the persons themselves ought to be taken into consideration; only those matters should be weighed carefully that pertain to the terms of the risk. The relevant finding might then be made by the highest judges established by public authority. But really there is here no need for judgment but of deliberation, i.e., rules would be set up whereby anyone could estimate his prospects from any risky undertaking in light of one's specific financial circumstances.

§3. To make this clear it is perhaps advisable to consider the following example: Somehow a very poor fellow obtains a lottery ticket that will yield with equal probability either nothing or twenty thousand ducats. Will this man evaluate his chance of winning at ten thousand ducats? Would he not be ill-advised to sell this lottery ticket for nine thousand ducats? To me it seems that the answer is in the negative. On the other hand I am inclined to believe that a rich man would be ill-advised to refuse to buy the lottery ticket for nine thousand ducats. If I am not wrong then it seems clear that all men cannot use the same rule to evaluate the gamble. The rule established in §1 must, therefore, be discarded. But anyone who considers the problem with perspicacity and interest will ascertain that the concept of *value* which we have used in this rule may be defined in a way which renders the entire procedure universally acceptable without reservation. To do this the determination of the *value* of an item must not be based on its *price*, but rather on the *utility* it yields. The price of the item is dependent only on the thing itself and is equal for everyone; the utility, however, is dependent on the particular circumstances of the person making the estimate. Thus there is no doubt that a gain of one thousand ducats is more significant to a pauper than to a rich man though both gain the same amount.

§4. The discussion has now been developed to a point where anyone may proceed with the investigation by the mere paraphrasing of one and the same principle. However, since the hypothesis is entirely new, it may nevertheless

---

(On Bernoulli see: *Handwörterbuch der Naturwissenschaften*, second edition, 1931, pp. 800–801; "Die Basler Mathematiker Daniel Bernoulli und Leonhard Euler. Hundert Jahre nach ihrem Tode gefeiert von der Naturforschenden Gesellschaft," Basle, 1884. (Annex to part VII of the proceedings of this Society); and *Correspondance mathematique* ... , edited by Paul Heinrich Fuss, 1843 containing letters written by Daniel Bernoulli to Leonhard Euler, Nicolaus Fuss, and C. Goldbach.)

[2] i.e., risky propositions (gambles). [Translator].

require some elucidation. I have, therefore, decided to explain by example what I have explored. Meanwhile, let us use this as a fundamental rule: *If the utility of each possible profit expectation is multiplied by the number of ways in which it can occur, and we then divide the sum of these products by the total number of possible cases, a mean utility*[3] *[moral expectation] will be obtained, and the profit which corresponds to this utility will equal the value of the risk in question.*

§5. Thus it becomes evident that no valid measurement of the value of a risk can be obtained without consideration being given to its *utility*, that is to say, the utility of whatever gain accrues to the individual or, conversely, how much profit is required to yield a given utility. However it hardly seems plausible to make any precise generalizations since the utility of an item may change with circumstances. Thus, though a poor man generally obtains more utility than does a rich man from an equal gain, it is nevertheless conceivable, for example, that a rich prisoner who possesses two thousand ducats but needs two thousand ducats more to repurchase his freedom, will place a higher value on a gain of two thousand ducats than does another man who has less money than he. Though innumerable examples of this kind may be constructed, they represent exceedingly rare exceptions. We shall, therefore, do better to consider what usually happens, and in order to perceive the problem more correctly we shall assume that there is an imperceptibly small growth in the individual's wealth which proceeds continuously by infinitesimal increments. Now it is highly probable that *any increase in wealth, no matter how insignificant, will always result in an increase in utility which is inversely proportionate to the quantity of goods already possessed.* To explain this hypothesis it is necessary to define what is meant by the *quantity of goods.* By this expression I mean to connote food, clothing, all things which add to the conveniences of life, and even to luxury—anything that can contribute to the adequate satisfaction of any sort of want. There is then nobody who can be said to possess nothing at all in this sense unless he starves to death. For the great majority the most valuable portion of their possessions so defined will consist in their productive capacity, this term being taken to include even the beggar's talent: a man who is able to acquire ten ducats yearly by begging will scarcely be willing to accept a sum of fifty ducats on condition that he henceforth refrain from begging or otherwise trying to earn money. For he would have to live on this amount, and after he had spent it his existence must also come to an end. I doubt whether even those who do not possess a farthing and are burdened with financial obligations would be willing to free themselves of their debts or even to accept a still greater gift on such a condition. But if the beggar were to refuse such a contract unless immediately paid no less than one hundred ducats and the man pressed by creditors similarly demanded one thousand ducats, we might say that the former is possessed of wealth

---

[3] Free translation of Bernoulli's "emolumentum medium," literally: "mean utility." [Translator].

worth one hundred, and the latter of one thousand ducats, though in common parlance the former owns nothing and the latter less than nothing.

§6. Having stated this definition, I return to the statement made in the previous paragraph which maintained that, in the absence of the unusual, the *utility resulting from any small increase in wealth will be inversely proportionate to the quantity of goods previously possessed.* Considering the nature of man, it seems to me that the foregoing hypothesis is apt to be valid for many people to whom this sort of comparison can be applied. Only a few do not spend their entire yearly incomes. But, if among these, one has a fortune worth a hundred thousand ducats and another a fortune worth the same number of semi-ducats and if the former receives from it a yearly income of five thousand ducats while the latter obtains the same number of semi-ducats it is quite clear that to the former a ducat has exactly the same significance as a semi-ducat to the latter, and that, therefore, the gain of one ducat will have to the former no higher value than the gain of a semi-ducat to the latter. Accordingly, if each makes a gain of one ducat the latter receives twice as much utility from it, having been enriched by two semi-ducats. This argument applies to many other cases which, therefore, need not be discussed separately. The proposition is all the more valid for the majority of men who possess no fortune apart from their working capacity which is their only source of livelihood. True, there are men to whom one ducat means more than many ducats do to others who are less rich but more generous than they. But since we shall now concern ourselves only with one individual (in different states of affluence) distinctions of this sort do not concern us. The man who is emotionally less affected by a gain will support a loss with greater patience. Since, however, in special cases things can conceivably occur otherwise, I shall first deal with the most general case and then develop our special hypothesis in order thereby to satisfy everyone.

§7. Therefore, let *AB* represent the quantity of goods initially possessed. Then after extending *AB*, a curve *BGLS* must be constructed, whose ordinates *CG*, *DH*, *EL*, *FM*, etc., designate *utilities* corresponding to the abscissas *BC*, *BD*, *BE*, *BF*, etc., designating gains in wealth. Further, let *m*, *n*, *p*, *q*, etc., be the numbers which indicate the number of ways in which gains in wealth *BC*, *BD*, *BE*, *BF* [misprinted in the original as *CF*], etc., can occur. Then (in accord with §4) the *moral* expectation of the risky proposition referred to is given by:

$$PO = \frac{m \cdot CG + n \cdot DH + p \cdot EL + q \cdot FM + \cdots}{m + n + p + q + \cdots}$$

Now, if we erect *AQ* perpendicular to *AR*, and on it measure off $AN = PO$, the straight line $NO - AB$ represents the gain which may properly be expected, or the value of the risky proposition in question. If we wish, further, to know how large a stake the individual should be willing to venture on this risky proposition, our curve must be extended in the opposite direction in such a way that the abscissa *Bp* now represents a loss and the ordinate *po* represents

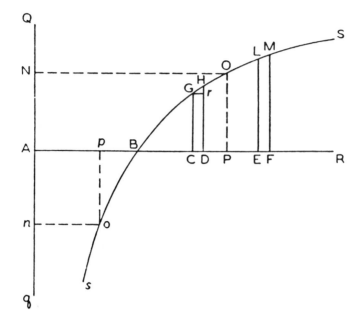

the corresponding decline in utility. Since in a fair game the disutility to be suffered by losing must be equal to the utility to be derived by winning, we must assume that $An = AN$, or $po = PO$. Thus $Bp$ will indicate the stake more than which persons who consider their own pecuniary status should not venture.

## COROLLARY I

§8. Until now scientists have usually rested their hypothesis on the assumption that all gains must be evaluated exclusively in terms of themselves, i.e., on the basis of their intrinsic qualities, and that these gains will always produce a *utility* directly proportionate to the gain. On this hypothesis the curve $BS$ becomes a straight line. Now if we again have:

$$PO = \frac{m \cdot CG + n \cdot DH + p \cdot EL + q \cdot FM + \cdots}{m + n + p + q + \cdots},$$

and if, on both sides, the respective factors are introduced it follows that:

$$BP = \frac{m \cdot BC + n \cdot BD + p \cdot BE + q \cdot BF + \cdots}{m + n + p + q + \cdots},$$

which is in conformity with the usually accepted rule.

## COROLLARY II

§9. If $AB$ were infinitely great, even in proportion to $BF$, the greatest possible gain, the arc $BM$ may be considered very like an infinitesimally small straight line. Again in this case the usual rule [for the evaluation of risky propositions] is applicable, and may continue to be considered approximately valid in games of insignificant moment.

§10. Having dealt with the problem in the most general way we turn now to the aforementioned particular hypothesis, which, indeed, deserves prior attention to all others. First of all the nature of curve $sBS$ must be investigated under the conditions postulated in §7. Since on our hypothesis we must consider infinitesimally small gains, we shall take gains $BC$ and $BD$ to be nearly equal, so that their difference $CD$ becomes infinitesimally small. If we draw $Gr$ parallel to $BR$, then $rH$ will represent the infinitesimally small gain in *utility* to a man whose fortune is $AC$ and who obtains the small gain, $CD$. This *utility*, however, should be related not only to the tiny gain $CD$, to which it is, other things being equal, proportionate, but also to $AC$, the fortune previously owned to which it is inversely proportionate. We therefore set: $AC = x$, $CD = dx$, $CG = y$, $rH = dy$ and $AB = \alpha$; and if $b$ designates some constant we obtain $dy = \dfrac{bdx}{x}$ or $y = b \log \dfrac{x}{\alpha}$. The curve $sBS$ is therefore a logarithmic curve, the subtangent[4] of which is everywhere $b$ and whose asymptote is $Qq$.

§11. If we now compare this result with what has been said in paragraph 7, it will appear that: $PO = b \log AP/AB$, $CG = b \log AC/AB$, $DH = b \log AD/AB$ and so on; but since we have

$$PO = \frac{m \cdot CG + n \cdot DH + p \cdot EL + q \cdot FM + \cdots}{m + n + p + q + \cdots}$$

it follows that

$$b \log \frac{AP}{AB} = \left( mb \log \frac{AC}{AB} + nb \log \frac{AD}{AB} + pb \log \frac{AE}{AB} + qb \log \frac{AF}{AB} + \cdots \right):$$

$$(m + n + p + q + \cdots)$$

and therefore

---

[4] The tangent to the curve $y = b \log \dfrac{x}{\alpha}$ at the point $\left( x_o, \log \dfrac{x_o}{\alpha} \right)$ is the line $y - b \log \dfrac{x_o}{\alpha} = \dfrac{b}{x_o}(x - x_o)$. This tangent intersects the $Y$-axis ($x = 0$) at the point with the ordinate $b \log \dfrac{x_o}{\alpha} - b$. The point of contact of the tangent with the curve has the ordinate $b \log \dfrac{x_o}{\alpha}$. So also does the projection of this point on the $Y$-axis. The segment between the two points on the $Y$-axis that have been mentioned has the length $b$. That segment is the projection of the segment on the tangent between its intersection with the $Y$-axis and the point of contact. The length of this projection (which is $b$) is what Bernoulli here calls the "sub-tangent." Today, by the subtangent of the curve $y = f(x)$ at the point $(x_o, f(x_o))$ is meant the length of the segment on the $X$-axis (and not the $Y$-axis) between its intersection with the tangent and the projection of the point of contact. This length is $f(x_o)/f'(x_o)$. In the case of the logarithmic curve it equals $x_o \log \dfrac{x_o}{\alpha}$. —Karl Menger.

$$AP = (AC^m \cdot AD^n \cdot AE^p \cdot AF^q \dots)^{1/m+n+p+q+ \cdots}$$

and if we subtract $AB$ from this, the remaining magnitude, $BP$, will represent the value of the risky proposition in question.

§12. Thus the preceding paragraph suggests the following rule: *Any gain must be added to the fortune previously possessed, then this sum must be raised to the power given by the number of possible ways in which the gain may be obtained; these terms should then be multiplied together. Then of this product a root must be extracted the degree of which is given by the number of all possible cases, and finally the value of the initial possessions must be subtracted therefrom; what then remains indicates the value of the risky proposition in question.* This principle is essential for the mesurement of the value of risky propositions in various cases. I would elaborate it into a complete theory as has been done with the traditional analysis, were it not that, despite its usefulness and originality, previous obligations do not permit me to undertake this task. I shall therefore, at this time, mention only the more significant points among those which have at first glance occurred to me.

§13. First, it appears that in many games, even those that are absolutely fair, both of the players may expect to suffer a loss; indeed this is Nature's admonition to avoid the dice altogether. . . . This follows from the concavity of curve $sBS$ to $BR$. For in making the stake, $Bp$, equal to the expected gain, $BP$, it is clear that the disutility $po$ which results from a loss will always exceed the expected gain in utility, $PO$. Although this result will be quite clear to the mathematician, I shall nevertheless explain it by example, so that it will be clear to everyone. Let us assume that of two players, both possessing one hundred ducats, each puts up half this sum as a stake in a game that offers the same probabilities to both players. Under this assumption each will then have fifty ducats plus the expectation of winning yet one hundred ducats more. However, the sum of the values of these two items amounts, by the rule of §12, to only $(50^1 \cdot 150^1)^{1/2}$ or $\sqrt{50 \cdot 150}$, i.e., less than eighty-seven ducats, so that, though the game be played under perfectly equal conditions for both, either will suffer an expected loss of more than thirteen ducats. We must strongly emphasize this truth, although it be self evident: the imprudence of a gambler will be the greater the larger the part of his fortune which he exposes to a game of chance. For this purpose we shall modify the previous example by assuming that one of the gamblers, before putting up his fifty ducat stake possessed two hundred ducats. This gambler suffers an expected loss of $200 - \sqrt{150 \cdot 250}$, which is not much greater than six ducats.

§14. Since, therefore, everyone who bets any part of his fortune, however small, on a mathematically fair game of chance acts irrationally, it may be of interest to inquire how great an advantage the gambler must enjoy over his opponent in order to avoid any expected loss. Let us again consider a game which is as simple as possible, defined by two equiprobable outcomes one of which is favorable and the other unfavorable. Let us take $a$ to be the gain to be won in case of a favorable outcome, and $x$ to be the stake which is lost in the unfavorable case. If the initial quantity of goods possessed is $\alpha$ we have $AB = \alpha$; $BP = a$; $PO = b \log \dfrac{\alpha + a}{\alpha}$ (see §10), and since (by §7) $po = PO$ it follows by the nature of a logarithmic curve that $Bp = \dfrac{\alpha a}{\alpha + a}$. Since however $Bp$ represents the stake $x$, we have $x = \dfrac{\alpha a}{\alpha + a}$ a magnitude which is always smaller than $a$, the expected gain. It also follows from this that a man who risks his entire fortune acts like a simpleton, however great may be the possible gain. No one will have difficulty in being persuaded of this if he has carefully examined our definitions given above. Moreover, this result sheds light on a statement which is universally accepted in practice: it may be reasonable for some individuals to invest in a doubtful enterprise and yet be unreasonable for others to do so.

§15. The procedure customarily employed by merchants in the insurance of commodities transported by sea seems to merit special attention. This may again be explained by an example. Suppose Caius,[5] a Petersburg merchant, has purchased commodities in Amsterdam which he could sell for ten thousand rubles if he had them in Petersburg. He therefore orders them to be shipped there by sea, but is in doubt whether or not to insure them. He is well aware of the fact that at this time of year of one hundred ships which sail from Amsterdam to Petersburg, five are usually lost. However, there is no insurance available below the price of eight hundred rubles a cargo, an amount which he considers outrageously high. The question is, therefore, how much wealth must Caius possess apart from the goods under consideration in order that it be sensible for him to abstain from insuring them? If $x$ represents his fortune, then this together with the value of the expectation of the safe arrival of his goods is given by

$$\sqrt[100]{(x + 10000)^{95} x^5} = \sqrt[20]{(x + 10000)^{19} x}$$

in case he abstains. With insurance he will have a certain fortune of $x + 9200$. Equating these two magnitudes we get: $(x + 10000)^{19} x = (x + 9200)^{20}$ or, approximately, $x = 5043$. If, therefore, Caius, apart from the expectation of receiving his commodities, possesses an amount greater than 5043 rubles he will be right in not buying insurance. If, on the contrary, his wealth is less than this amount he should insure his cargo. And if the question be asked "What minimum fortune should be possessed by the man who offers to provide this insurance in order for him to be rational in doing so?" We must answer thus: let $y$ be his fortune, then

$$\sqrt[20]{(y + 800)^{19} \cdot (y - 9200)} = y$$

or approximately, $y = 14243$, a figure which is obtained from the foregoing without additional calculation. A man less wealthy than this would be foolish to provide the surety, but it makes sense for a wealthier man to do so.

---

[5] Caius is a Roman name, used here in the sense of our "Mr. Jones." Caius is the older form; in the later Roman period it was spelled "Gaius." [Translator].

Fom this it is clear that the introduction of this sort of insurance has been so useful since it offers advantages to all persons concerned. Similarly, had Caius been able to obtain the insurance for six hundred rubles he would have been unwise to refuse it if he possessed less than 20478 rubles, but he would have acted much too cautiously had he insured his commodities at this rate when his fortune was greater than this amount. On the other hand a man would act unadvisedly if he were to offer to sponsor this insurance for six hundred rubles when he himself possesses less than 29878 rubles. However, he would be well advised to do so if he possessed more than that amount. But no one, however rich, would be managing his affairs properly if he individually undertook the insurance for less than five hundred rubles.

§16. Another rule which may prove useful can be derived from our theory. This is the rule that it is advisable to divide goods which are exposed to some danger into several portions rather than to risk them all together. Again I shall explain this more precisely by an example. Sempronius owns goods at home worth a total of 4000 ducats and in addition possesses 8000 ducats worth of commodities in foreign countries from where they can only be transported by sea. However, our daily experience teaches us that of ten ships one perishes. Under these conditions I maintain that if Sempronius trusted all his 8000 ducats of goods to one ship his expectation of the commodities is worth 6751 ducats. That is

$$\sqrt[10]{12000^9 \cdot 4000^1} - 4000.$$

If, however, he were to trust equal portions of these commodities to two ships the value of his expectation would be

$$\sqrt[100]{12000^{81} \cdot 8000^{18} \cdot 4000} - 4000, \quad \text{i.e., 7033 ducats.}$$

In this way the value of Sempronius' prospects of success will grow more favorable the smaller the proportion committed to each ship. However, his expectation will never rise in value above 7200 ducats. This counsel will be equally serviceable for those who invest their fortunes in foreign bills of exchange and other hazardous enterprises.

§17. I am forced to omit many novel remarks though these would clearly not be unserviceable. And, though a person who is fairly judicious by natural instinct might have realized and spontaneously applied much of what I have here explained, hardly anyone believed it possible to define these problems with the precision we have employed in our examples. Since all our propositions harmonize perfectly with experience it would be wrong to neglect them as abstractions resting upon precarious hypotheses. This is further confirmed by the following example which inspired these thoughts, and whose history is as follows: My most honorable cousin the celebrated *Nicolas Bernoulli*, Professor utriusque iuris[6] at the University of Basle, once submitted five

---

[6] Faculties of law of continental European universities bestow up to the present time the title of a Doctor utriusque juris, which means Doctor of both systems of laws, the Roman and the canon law. [Translator].

problems to the highly distinguished[7] mathematician *Montmort*.[8] These problems are reproduced in the work *L'analyse sur les jeux de hazard de M. de Montmort*, p. 402. The last of these problems runs as follows: *Peter tosses a coin and continues to do so until it should land "heads" when it comes to the ground. He agrees to give Paul one ducat if he gets "heads" on the very first throw, two ducats if he gets it on the second, four if on the third, eight if on the fourth, and so on, so that with each additional throw the number of ducats he must pay is doubled. Suppose we seek to determine the value of Paul's expectation.* My aforementioned cousin discussed this problem in a letter to me asking for my opinion. Although the standard calculation shows[9] that the value of Paul's expectation is infinitely great, it has, he said, to be admitted that any fairly reasonable man would sell his chance, with great pleasure, for twenty ducats. The accepted method of calculation does, indeed, value Paul's prospects at infinity though no one would be willing to purchase it at a moderately high price. If, however, we apply our new rule to this problem we may see the solution and thus unravel the knot. The solution of the problem by our principles is as follows:

§18. The number of cases to be considered here is infinite: in one half of the cases the game will end at the first throw, in one quarter of the cases it will conclude at the second, in an eighth part of the cases with the third, in a sixteenth part with the fourth, and so on.[10] If we designate the number of

---

[7] Cl., i.e., Vir Clarissimus, a title of respect. [Translator].

[8] Montmort, Pierre Remond, de (1678–1719). The work referred to here is the then famous "Essai d'analyse sur les jeux de hazard," Paris, 1708. Appended to the second edition, published in 1713, is Montmort's correspondence with Jean and Nicolas Bernoulli referring to the problems of chance and probabilities. [Translator].

[9] The probability of heads turning up on the 1st throw is $1/2$. Since in this case Paul receives one ducat, this probability contributes $1/2 . 1 = 1/2$ ducats to his expectation. The probability of heads turning up on the 2nd throw is $1/4$. Since in this case Paul receives 2 ducats, this possibility contributes $1/4 . 2 = 1/2$ to his expectation. Similarly, for every integer $n$, the possibility of heads turning up on the $n$-th throw contributes $1/2^n . 2^{n-1} = 1/2$ ducats to his expectation. Paul's total expectation is therefore $1/2 + 1/2 + \cdots + 1/2 + \cdots$, and that is infinite.—Karl Menger.

[10] Since the number of cases is infinite, it is impossible to speak about one half of the cases, one quarter of the cases, etc., and the letter $N$ in Bernoulli's argument is meaningless. However, Paul's expectation on the basis of Bernoulli's hypothesis concerning evaluation can be found by the same method by which, in footnote 9, Paul's classical expectation was determined. If Paul's fortune is ducats, then, according to Bernoulli, he attributes to a gain of $2^{n-1}$ ducats the value $b \log \dfrac{\alpha + 2^{n-1}}{\alpha}$. If the probability of this gain is $1/2^n$, his expectation is $b/2^n \log \dfrac{\alpha + 2^{n-1}}{\alpha}$. Paul's expectation resulting from the game is therefore $\dfrac{b}{2} \log \dfrac{\alpha + 1}{\alpha} + \dfrac{b}{4} \log \dfrac{\alpha + 2}{\alpha} + \cdots + \dfrac{b}{2^n} \log \dfrac{\alpha + 2^{n-1}}{\alpha} + \cdots = b \log [(\alpha + 1)^{1/2}(\alpha + 2)^{1/4} . \cdots . (\alpha + 2^{n-1})^{1/2^n}.$ $\cdots] - b \log \alpha$. What addition $D$ to Paul's fortune has the same value for him? Clearly, $b \log \dfrac{\alpha + D}{\alpha}$ must equal the above sum. Therefore $D = (\alpha + 1)^{1/2}(\alpha + 2)^{1/4} . \cdots .$ $(\alpha + 2^{n-1})^{1/2^n} . \cdots - \alpha$.—Karl Menger.

cases through infinity by $N$ it is clear that there are $\frac{1}{2}N$ cases in which Paul gains one ducat, $\frac{1}{4}N$ cases in which he gains two ducats, $\frac{1}{8}N$ in which he gains four, $\frac{1}{16}N$ in which he gains eight, and so on, ad infinitum. Let us represent Paul's fortune by $\alpha$; the proposition in question will then be worth

$$\sqrt[N]{(\alpha+1)^{N/2}.(\alpha+2)^{N/4}.(\alpha+4)^{N/8}.(\alpha+8)^{N/16}\cdots} - \alpha$$
$$= \sqrt{(\alpha+1)}.\sqrt[4]{(\alpha+2)}.\sqrt[8]{(\alpha+4)}.\sqrt[16]{(\alpha+8)}\cdots - \alpha.$$

§19. From this formula which evaluates Paul's prospective gain it follows that this value will increase with the size of Paul's fortune and will never attain an infinite value unless Paul's wealth simultaneously becomes infinite. In addition we obtain the following corollaries. If Paul owned nothing at all the value of his expectation would be

$$\sqrt[2]{1}.\sqrt[4]{2}.\sqrt[8]{4}.\sqrt[16]{8}\cdots$$

which amounts to two ducats, precisely. If he owned ten ducats his opportunity would be worth approximately three ducats; it would be worth approximately four if his wealth were one hundred, and six if he possessed one thousand. From this we can easily see what a tremendous fortune a man must own for it to make sense for him to purchase Paul's opportunity for twenty ducats. The amount which the buyer ought to pay for this proposition differs somewhat from the amount it would be worth to him were it already in his possession. Since, however, this difference is exceedingly small if $\alpha$ (Paul's fortune) is great, we can take them to be equal. If we designate the purchase price by $x$ its value can be determined by means of the equation

$$\sqrt[2]{(\alpha+1-x)}.\sqrt[4]{(\alpha+2-x)}.\sqrt[8]{(\alpha+4-x)}.\sqrt[16]{(\alpha+8-x)}\cdots = \alpha$$

and if $\alpha$ is a large number this equation will be approximately satisfied by

$$x = \sqrt[2]{\alpha+1}.\sqrt[4]{\alpha+2}.\sqrt[8]{\alpha+4}.\sqrt[16]{\alpha+8}\cdots - \alpha.$$

*After having read this paper to the Society[11] I sent a copy to the aforementioned Mr. Nicolas Bernoulli, to obtain his opinion of my proposed solution to the difficulty he had indicated. In a letter to me written in 1732 he declared that he was in no way dissatisfied with my proposition on the evaluation of risky propositions when applied to the case of a man who is to evaluate his own prospects. However, he thinks that the case is different if a third person, somewhat in the position of a judge, is to evaluate the prospects of any participant in a game in accord with equity and justice. I myself have discussed this problem in §2. Then this distinguished scholar informed me that the celebrated mathematician, Cramer,[12] had developed a theory on the same subject several years*

---

[11] Bernoulli's paper had been submitted to the Imperial Academy of Sciences in Petersburg. [Translator].

[12] Cramer, Gabriel, famous mathematician, born in Geneva, Switzerland (1704–1752). [Translator].

*before I produced my paper. Indeed I have found his theory so similar to mine that it seems miraculous that we independently reached such close agreement on this sort of subject. Therefore it seems worth quoting the words with which the celebrated Cramer himself first described his theory in his letter of 1728 to my cousin. His words are as follows:*[13]

" Perhaps I am mistaken, but I believe that I have solved the extraordinary problem which you submitted to M. *de Montmort*, in your letter of September 9, 1713 (problem 5, page 402). For the sake of simplicity I shall assume that A tosses a coin into the air and B commits himself to give A 1 ducat if, at the first throw, the coin falls with its cross upward; 2 if it falls thus only at the second throw, 4 if at the third throw, 8 if at the fourth throw, etc. The paradox consists in the infinite sum which calculation yields as the equivalent which A must pay to B. This seems absurd since no reasonable man would be willing to pay 20 ducats as equivalent. You ask for an explanation of the discrepancy between the mathematical calculation and the vulgar evaluation. I believe that it results from the fact that, *in their theory*, mathematicians evaluate money in proportion to its quantity while, *in practice*, people with common sense evaluate money in proportion to the utility they can obtain from it. The mathematical expectation is rendered infinite by the enormous amount which I can win if the coin does not fall with its cross upward until rather late, perhaps at the hundredth or thousandth throw. Now, as a matter of fact, if I reason as a sensible man, this sum is worth no more to me, causes me no more pleasure and influences me no more to accept the game than does a sum amounting only to ten or twenty million ducats. Let us suppose, therefore, that any amount above 10 millions, or (for the sake of simplicity) above $2^{24} = 166777216$ ducats be deemed by him equal in value to $2^{24}$ ducats or, better yet, that I can never win more than that amount, no matter how long it takes before the coin falls with its cross upward. In this case, my expectation is $\frac{1}{2}.1 + \frac{1}{4}.2 + \frac{1}{8}.4 \cdots + \frac{1}{2}25.2^{24} + \frac{1}{2}26.2^{24} + \frac{1}{2}27.2^{24} + \cdots = \frac{1}{2} + \frac{1}{2} + \frac{1}{2} + \cdots$ (24 times) $\cdots + \frac{1}{2} + \frac{1}{4} + \frac{1}{8} + \cdots = 12 + 1 = 13$. Thus, my moral expectation is reduced in value to 13 ducats and the equivalent to be paid for it is similarly reduced—a result which seems much more reasonable than does rendering it infinite."

*Thus far*[14] *the exposition is somewhat vague and subject to counter argument. If it, indeed, be true that the amount $2^{25}$ appears to us to be no greater than $2^{24}$, no attention whatsoever should be paid to the amount that may be won after the twenty-fourth throw, since just before making the twenty-fifth throw I am certain to end up with no less than $2^{24} - 1$,*[15] *an amount that, according to this theory, may be considered equivalent to $2^{24}$. Therefore it may be said correctly that my expectation is only worth twelve ducats, not thirteen. However, in*

---

[13] The following passage of the original text is in French. [Translator].

[14] From here on the text is again translated from Latin. [Translator].

[15] This remark of Bernoulli's is obscure. Under the conditions of the game a gain of $2^{24} - 1$ ducats is impossible.—Karl Menger.

*view of the coincidence between the basic principle developed by the afore-mentioned author and my own, the foregoing is clearly not intended to be taken to invalidate that principle. I refer to the proposition that reasonable men should evaluate money in accord with the utility they derive therefrom. I state this to avoid leading anyone to judge that entire theory adversely. And this is exactly what Cl. C.[16] Cramer states, expressing in the following manner precisely what we would ourselves conclude. He continues thus.[17]*

" The equivalent can turn out to be smaller yet if we adopt some alternative hypothesis on the moral value of wealth. For that which I have just assumed is not entirely valid since, while it is true that 100 millions yield more satis-faction than do 10 millions, they do not give ten times as much. If, for example, we suppose the moral value of goods to be directly proportionate to the square root of their mathematical quantities, e.g., that the satisfaction provided by 40000000 is double that provided by 10000000, my psychic expectation becomes

$$\tfrac{1}{2}\sqrt{1} + \tfrac{1}{4}\sqrt{2} + \tfrac{1}{8}\sqrt{4} + \tfrac{1}{16}\sqrt{8} + \cdots = \frac{1}{2 - \sqrt{2}}.$$

However this magnitude is not the equivalent we seek, for this equivalent need not be equal to my moral expectation but should rather be of such a magnitude that the pain caused by its loss is equal to the moral expectation of the pleasure I hope to derive from my gain. Therefore, the equivalent must, on our hypothesis, amount to $\left(\dfrac{1}{2-\sqrt{2}}\right)^2 = \left(\dfrac{1}{6-4\sqrt{2}}\right) = 2.9\ldots$, which is consequently less than 3, truly a trifling amount, but nevertheless, I believe, closer than is 13 to the vulgar evaluation."

## REFERENCES

There exists only one other translation of Bernoulli's paper:

Pringsheim, Alfred, *Die Grundlage der modernen Wertlehre: Daniel Bernoulli, Versucheiner neuen Theorie der Wertbestimmung von Glücksfällen* (Specimen Theoriae novae de Mensura Sortis). Aus dem Lateinischen übersetzt und mit Eläuterungen versehen von Alfred Pringsheim, Leipzig, Duncker und Humblot, 1896, Sammlung älterer und neuerer staats-wissenschaftlicher Schriften des Inund Auslandes hrsg. von L. Brentano und E. Leser, No. 9.

For an early discussion of the Bernoulli problem, reference is made to

Malfatti, Gianfrancesco, "Esame critico di un problema di probabilita del Signor Daniele Bernoulli, e soluzione d'un altro problema analogo al Bernoulliano" in "*Memorie di Matematica e Fisica della Societa italiana,*" Vol. I, Verona, 1782, pp. 768–824.

For more on the "St. Petersburg Paradox," including material on later discus-sions, see

Menger, Karl, "Das Unsicherheitsmoment in der Wertlehre. Betrachtungen im

---

[16] To be translated as "the distinguished Gabriel." [Translator].
[17] Text continues in French. [Translator].

Anschluss an das sogenannte Petersburger Spiel," *Zeitschrift für Nationalökonomie*, Vol. 5, 1934.

This paper by Professor Menger is the most extensive study on the literature of the problem, and the problem itself.

Recent interest in the Bernoulli hypothesis was aroused by its appearance in

von Neumann, John, and Oskar Morgenstern, *The Theory of Games and Economic Behavior*, second edition, Princeton: Princeton University Press, 1947, Ch. III and Appendix: "The Axiomatic Treatment of Utility."

Many contemporary references and a discussion of the utility maximization hypothesis are to be found in

Arrow, Kenneth J., "Alternative Approaches to the Theory of Choice in Risk-Taking Situations," *Econometrica*, Vol. 19, October, 1951.

More recent writings in the field include

Alchian, A. A., "The Meaning of Utility Measurement," *American Economic Review*, Vol. XLIII, March, 1953.

Friedman, M., and Savage, L. J., "The Expected Utility-Hypothesis and the Measurability of Utility," *Journal of Political Economy*, Vol. LX, December, 1952.

Herstein, I. N., and John Milnor, "An Axiomatic Approach to Measurable Utility," *Econometrica*, Vol. 21, April, 1953.

Marschak, J., "Why 'Should' Statisticians and Businessmen Maximize 'Moral Expectation'?," *Second Berkeley Symposium on Mathematical Statistics and Probability*, 1953.

Mosteller, Frederick, and Philip Nogee, "An Experimental Measurement of Utility," *Journal of Political Economy*, lix, 5, Oct., 1951.

Samuelson, Paul A., "Probability, Utility, and the Independence Axiom," *Econometrica*, Vol. 20, Oct., 1952.

Strotz, Robert H., "Cardinal Utility," *Papers and Proceedings of the Sixty-Fifth Annual Meeting of the American Economic Association, American Economic Review*, Vol. 43, May, 1953, and the comment by W. J. Baumol.

For dissenting views, see:

Allais, M., "Les Theories de la Psychologie du Risque de l'Ecole Americaine," *Revue d'Economie Politique*, Vol. 63, 1953.

——. "Le Comportement de l'Homme Rationnel devant le Risque: Critique des postulats et Axiomes de l'Ecole Americaine," *Econometrica*, Oct., 1953, and

Edwards, Ward, "Probability-Preferences in Gambling," *The American Journal of Psychology*, Vol. 66, July, 1953.

Textbooks dealing with Bernoulli:

Anderson, Oskar, *Einführung in die mathematische Statistik*, Wien: J. Springer, 1935.

Davis, Harold, *The Theory of Econometrics*, Bloomington, Ind.: Principia Press, 1941.

Loria, Gino, *Storia delle Matematiche, dall'albadella civiltá al secolo XIX*, Second revised ed., Milan: U. Hopli, 1950.

## 4. CRITERIA FOR CHOICE AMONG RISKY VENTURES

Reprinted by permission of the author and publishers from *The Journal of Political Economy*, Vol. LXVII, No. 2 (April 1959), pp. 144–55 (Chicago: Ill.: University of Chicago, Copyright, 1959 by the University of Chicago).

## THE SUBGOAL

This paper is concerned with the problem of how to make rational choices among strategies in situations involving uncertainty. Such choices can be expressed through payout matrices stated in terms of some measure of value to be maximized. These matrices show the probabilities of all relevant future occurrences and the payouts resulting from the combined effects of each possible strategy, on the one hand, and each relevant future occurrence, on the other.[1] All this information is needed to choose the proper strategy rationally. It would be impossible for a decision-maker to choose rationally among strategies if he disregarded either the probability of the relevant future occurrences or any of the possible payouts.

The problem of rational decision-making can be broken down into three steps: (1) deciding upon an objective and criteria for choosing among

---

* University of North Carolina, Chapel Hill.

[1] Payout matrices are shown in Tables 1, 2, and 3. The payouts represent the possible final outcomes of choices among strategies. The matrices have single-valued payouts and probabilities. Many, if not all, decision problems can be reduced to such form. Consider first the probabilities. A subjective probability distribution of an imperfectly known underlying probability can be reduced to a subjective probability of the event itself. For example, suppose a gambler believes that there is a 0.5 probability that a coin is biased so that it always comes up tails and a 0.5 probability that it is unbiased. He has a subjective probability of 0.25 for heads and 0.75 for tails, and these probabilities would be used in his payout matrix as long as his probability beliefs remain unchanged. Consider next the payouts. In much discussion of decision theory the payouts are taken as given, with only the probabilities subject to uncertainty. However, in real life the sizes of the payouts often are as subject to uncertainty as are the probabilities. But, even when the payouts are uncertain a matrix filled in with single values can be constructed. If we have probability distributions of payouts for all specified occurrences (such as heads and tails in the toss of a coin), a payout matrix can be constructed listing each possible payout and the subjective probability of its occurrence. These large matrices often can be reduced to simple two-valued distributions of payouts without much loss of information.

strategies; (2) filling out a payout matrix; and (3) choosing among available strategies on the basis of this matrix and the criteria. In real life, the second step—deciding upon the size of the payout matrix, measured by the number of columns representing relevant future occurrences and rows representing available strategies, and filling in the matrix with reasonable estimates of payouts and probabilities—is by far the most difficult part of the decision-maker's job. This paper has little to say about these problems. It deals largely with the first step: the problem of setting up criteria for choosing among strategies on the basis of a filled-in payout matrix.

A hierarchy of goals and guides for reaching these goals is involved in rational choices among strategies. This hierarchy consists of (1) a goal; (2) a subgoal; and (3) a criterion for choosing among strategies to reach the subgoal, that is, a measure that must be maximized to attain the subgoal. The goal in rational decision-making is the maximization of some measure of value. Each decision is made for the sake of the difference it will make in terms of this objective. The decision-maker is confronted with a payout matrix expressed in terms of either a subjective utility measure such as utiles or an objective measure such as money or bushels of wheat. He wishes to choose the strategy that will give him the maximum payout. This is his goal. When some one strategy gives a higher payout than any other strategy in all relevant future occurrences, the goal itself enables the decision-maker to choose among strategies. He merely chooses the dominant strategy.

When there is no strategy superior to all the rest in all possible future occurrences, the decision-maker needs some other guide for making decisions, since the goal itself does not enable him to make his choice. This guide is here called the "subgoal." The need for a subgoal exists because the outcome of specific strategies is subject to probabilistic uncertainty. In utility theory the payout matrix is expressed in terms of some measure of subjective utility, say, utiles. Choice of the strategy that will give the maximum payout in utiles is the goal, and choice of the strategy with the maximum expected utility[2] is taken as the subgoal. Given a completely filled-in matrix, this subgoal can surely be reached. Whether or not the goal is reached depends on future occurrences, but, in any event, the subgoal of maximization of the expected value of the payouts expressed in utiles is logically related to the goal of maximization of the forthcoming payout also expressed in utiles.

In this paper a second subgoal is proposed for use when the choice is repetitious and has cumulative effects and when the goal is maximization of wealth at the end of a large number of choices. Under these conditions the choice of the strategy that has a greater probability ($P'$) of leading to as much or more wealth than any other significantly different strategy at the end of a large number of choices also is a logical subgoal. The $P'$ subgoal is not as general as the maximum expected utility subgoal. For example, it would not

---

[2] The expected utility of a strategy is computed by multiplying all possible payouts expressed in utiles by their respective probabilities and then summing the products.

apply to unique choices. When a man is faced with a once-in-a-lifetime choice of risking his whole fortune and his life on a venture that will produce great rewards if successful, it does not help him to know that he is almost certain to be ruined if he takes such a risk often enough. The $P'$ subgoal is not logically related to the goal in this case.[3] Such a man, however, could set up a payout matrix expressed in utiles and decide which course of action maximized his expected utility. Here the maximum expected utility subgoal is logically related to the goal even though the $P'$ subgoal is not. The $P'$ subgoal is less general but would seem to be more operational than the expected utility subgoal because of the difficulty of constructing a payout matrix expressed in terms of utiles, especially if the decision involves a firm or group of people.

The $P'$ subgoal would seem to be particularly applicable to many business decisions such as those involved in portfolio management. Wealth-holders have the option of holding their wealth in many different combinations of stocks, bonds, and cash. The allocation of wealth among these types of assets involves a series of choices extending over time. The fact that these choices are repetitive in nature with cumulative effects may be used as the key factor in defining a goal, a subgoal, and a criterion for choosing among portfolios.

The problem of choice among portfolios may be stated in terms of the payout matrix in Table 1. In this table $p_j$ represents the probability of the $j$th occurrence, with $\sum p_j = 1$, and $a_{ij}$ represents the return from the $i$th portfolio with $i = 1, \ldots, t$, if the $j$th occurrence takes place, with $j = 1, \ldots, k$.

TABLE 1

PAYOUT MATRIX FOR VARYING PORTFOLIOS

| PORTFOLIO | RELEVANT FUTURE OCCURRENCES |
|---|---|
| | $1, \ldots, j, \ldots, k$ |
| 1 | $a_{ik}, \ldots, a_{1j}, \ldots, a_{1k}$ |
| $\vdots$ | |
| $i$ | $a_{j1}, \ldots, a_{ij}, \ldots, a_{ik}$ |
| $\vdots$ | |
| $l$ | $a_{t1}, \ldots, a_{tj}, \ldots, a_{tk}$ |
| Probability of occurrence | $p_1, \ldots, p_j, \ldots, p_k$ |

[3] For certain utility functions and for certain repeated gambles, no amount of repetition justifies the rule that the gamble which is almost sure to bring the greatest wealth is the preferable one. For example, the $P'$ subgoal is not appropriate for a decision-maker for whom the possibility of great gain, however small and diminishing, is more important than maximization of the probability of as much or more wealth than can be obtained by any other strategy in the long run. Such a decision-maker may adopt a course of action that is almost certain to result in less wealth in the long run. Whether or not his utility function is compatible with the specified goal of maximum long-run wealth is not at issue here.

A return is the payout, including return of principal, per dollar of portfolio value per investment period (here called "year"). Returns cannot be negative, so that $a_i \geq 0$. The portfolio manager is faced with such a payout matrix for $n$ years and wants to choose in a rational manner one portfolio from all available portfolios in each of the $n$ years.[4]

The goal of portfolio management is taken to be to select a portfolio so as to maximize wealth at the end of a period of years, assuming reinvestment of all returns.[5] Let $W_i^n$ be the final value of $1.00 placed in portfolio $i$ if returns are reinvested $n$ times. Then the goal of portfolio management is taken to be to select the optimum portfolio so that $W_{opt}^n \geq W_i^n$, with $i = 1, \ldots, t$. This goal cannot be used as a basis for choice among portfolios, since which portfolio will have the maximum $W^n$ depends on future occurrences.

The subgoal proposed here is the choice of the portfolio that has a greater probability ($P'$) of being as valuable or more valuable than any other significantly different portfolio at the end of $n$ years, $n$ being large. It is shown below that the portfolio having a probability distribution of returns with the highest geometric mean, $G$, also has the greatest $P'$.

The central fact of this paper is a simple one: If the value of an asset, say, portfolio $i$, priced initially at $1.00 is believed to change after a year to, alternatively, $a_{i1}$ or $a_{i2}, \ldots,$ or $a_{ik}$, with respective probabilities $p_1, p_2, \ldots, p_k$, and if the proceeds are reinvested $n$ times, then the compound average return $W_i$, "converges in probability" to $G_i = a_{i1}^{p1} \cdot a_{i2}^{p2} \cdots a_{ik}^{pk}$. The probability that the absolute difference between $W_i$ and $G_i$ is smaller than any preassigned

---

[4] The idea of maximizing wealth at the end of a large number of separate decisions based on the same payout matrix may appear unrealistic, but portfolio managers are continually being faced with choices having cumulative effects and involving approximately the same payouts and probabilities time after time. For example, year after year a portfolio manager may have probability beliefs such as: "I look for conditions in the next ten years to be very similar to those prevailing in 1926 through 1935. Bonds will yield about 4 per cent per annum during the whole period. Some day we are going to have a boom and a bust in the stock market, but I do not know which is going to come first." Choosing one portfolio to hold in each of the $n$ years is not the same as choosing one portfolio at the beginning of the period to hold throughout the $n$ years. For example, if the probability beliefs at the beginning of one year are such that the maximum $P'$ allocation of the portfolio is 40 per cent in bonds and 60 per cent in stock and if these beliefs remain the same at the beginning of the next year, then the maximum $P'$ allocation again will be 40 per cent in bonds and 60 per cent in stock at the beginning of the second year. If the relative prices of stocks and bonds have changed between the two dates, it will be necessary for the portfolio manager to make some sales and purchases in his portfolio to bring it into line with the desired proportions even if these proportions themselves have not changed.

[5] Few wealth-holders reinvest all returns, so the problem of maximizing wealth assuming no withdrawals is somewhat unrealistic. However, this restriction can be modified. If withdrawals per unit of time are a fixed proportion of wealth (considered as interest, for example), they will not affect proper maximizing action. Whatever would maximize wealth, assuming no withdrawals, would maximize wealth, assuming proportionate withdrawals.

positive number will approach 1 as $n$ increases indefinitely. In other words, the final return from \$1.00 invested in portfolio $i$, assuming reinvestment of all annual returns for $n$ years will converge in probability on $G_i$, the geometric mean of the probability distribution of annual returns from that portfolio. This relationship is intuitively obvious since the $a_{i1}$ return will "tend" to occur $np_1$ times, the $a_{ii}$ return will tend to occur $np_i$ times, and so forth, if $n$ is large. It can be proved rigorously by use of the law of large numbers applied to the logarithms of the annual returns.

Let $n_j$ be the number of occurrences of the $j$th relevant future occurrence, with $\sum n_j = n$, with $j = 1, \ldots, k$, then $n_j/n \xrightarrow[\text{lim}]{} p_j$ and $n_j/n \log a_{ij} \xrightarrow[\text{lim}]{} p_j \log a_{ij}$ as $n \to \infty$. But $\log W_i = \sum n_j/n \log a_{ij}$, with $j = 1, \ldots, k$ and $\log G_i = \sum_{ij} \log a_{ij}$, so $\log W_i \xrightarrow[\text{lim}]{} \log G_i$ and $W_i \xrightarrow[\text{lim}]{} G_i$ as $n \to \infty$.[6] It follows from this that, if $G_i > G_j$, then the probability, $P'$, that $W_i^n > W_j^n$ at the end of $n$ years approaches 1 as $n$ increases indefinitely. The portfolio with the highest $G$ is almost certain to be more valuable than any other significantly different portfolio in the long run. For this reason $G$ is accepted here as a rational criterion for choice among portfolios.

## SUBGOALS AND SUBJECTIVE UTILITY

Rational choice among strategies is the ancient problem of the gambler who has the option to choose among bets. Classical writers on probability theory recommended that problems of this kind be solved by first computing the expected winnings (possibly negative) for each available bet and then choosing the bet with the highest mathematical expectation of winning. Since there was no reason to assume that, of two persons encountering identical risks, either should expect to have his desires more closely fulfilled, the classical writers thought that no characteristic of the risk-takers themselves ought to be taken into consideration; only those matters should be weighed carefully that pertain to the terms of the risk.[7] In 1738 Daniel Bernoulli in four short paragraphs demonstrated that the use of the mathematical expectation of winnings did not always apply and proposed instead that gamblers should evaluate bets on the basis of the mathematical expectation of the utilities of winnings.[8]

In terms of subgoals as defined in this study, Bernoulli showed that use of the expected-value subgoal did not always lead to choices that seemed rational

---

[6] The asymptotic quality $G$ is used in information theory as developed by Dr. Claude Shannon and was applied to a gambling situation by John Kelly in "A New Interpretation of Information Rate," *Bell System Technical Journal*, August, 1956, pp. 917–26. See also R. Bellman and R. Kalaba, "Dynamic Programming and Statistical Communication Theory," *Proceedings of the National Academy of Science*, XLIII (1957), 749–51. I had no knowledge of this work when I first proposed the $P'$ subgoal at a Cowles Foundation Seminar in February, 1956.

[7] See Daniel Bernouilli, "Exposition of a New Theory on the Measurement of Risk," trans. Louise Sommer, *Econometrica*, XXII (January, 1954), 23.

[8] *Ibid.*, p. 24.

to him and proposed instead the use of the expected-utility subgoal. He used the following example:

Somehow a very poor fellow obtains a lottery ticket that will yield with equal probability either nothing or twenty thousand ducats. Will this man evaluate his chances of winning at ten thousand ducats? Would he not be ill-advised to sell this lottery ticket for nine thousand ducats? To me it seems that the answer is in the negative. On the other hand I am inclined to believe that a rich man would be ill-advised to refuse to buy the lottery ticket for nine thousand ducats. If I am not wrong then it seems clear that all men cannot use the same rule to evaluate the gamble.[9]

Bernoulli's example is somewhat aside from the daily business of living, but, when stripped of its gambling wrappings and expressed in terms of payouts and returns, it is seen to represent a major segment of economic decision-making. The hypothetical market price of the ticket, which has an equal probability of paying 20,000 ducats or nothing, is 9,000 ducats. Both the poor man and the rich man have the option either to hold the lottery ticket or to hold 9,000 ducats. Possible payouts range from 2.22 per ducat risked to 0. Payouts with ranges such as this—indeed, much greater ranges— are ordinary economic occurrences. The magnitude of the choice faced by the rich man is well within the range of ordinary business decisions, and the "poor man" today is continually faced with implicit or explicit decisions as serious as that faced by Bernoulli's lottery-ticket owner. He must decide whether to move to a new job, buy a new home, sign a second mortgage. He is continually offered the opportunity to undertake such risky ventures as purchasing his own truck, opening a restaurant, buying some uranium stock, some oil stock, or some investment shares. Some of these options may be highly advantageous, and he must choose some one course of action in each case. The effects of these choices are cumulative; that is, the decision-maker never comes back to exactly the same position he occupied before making his choice. The major difference between Bernoulli's problem and other choices is that the ticket-holder's choice is clearly defined, while the other opportunities are usually ignored, or the choices are muddled.

Thus Bernoulli's example is representative of a wide class of choices. The decision-maker is being faced continually with such choices, and the outcome of each decision affects his entire future. In the following discussion this example is stated in payout matrices constructed to illustrate choices based on (a) classical mathematical expectation (the expected value subgoal); (b) Bernoulli's subjective utility (the expected-utility subgoal); and (c) the minimum chance ($P'$) subgoal.

Table 2 shows the classical approach to choosing among risky ventures. The payout matrix, expressed in terms of thousands of ducats, shows the probability of the lottery ticket paying off or not and the net payout to the poor man and to the rich man for each of two courses of action. The classical

9 *Ibid.*

writers would calculate the mathematical expectation, $A$, of the net payouts and choose that strategy which maximizes $A$. In this case, they would recommend that the rich man buy the ticket for 9,000 ducats and that the poor man refuse to sell it at this price.

TABLE 2

PAYOUT MATRIX OF GAINS AND LOSSES

| | FUTURE OCCURRENCE | | |
| | Ticket | Ticket | |
| STRATEGY | Wins | Loses | CRITERION $A$ |
| --- | --- | --- | --- |
| a) Poor man: | | | |
|    Hold ticket | 20 | 0 | 10 |
|    Sell ticket | 9 | 9 | 9 |
| b) Rich man | | | |
|    Buy ticket | 11 | −9 | 1 |
|    Not buy ticket | 0 | 0 | 0 |
| Probability of occurrence | 0.5 | 0.5 | |

The mathematical expectation (that is, the arithmetic mean) of the probability distribution of payouts is, indeed, a good criterion when there are large numbers of independent trials. Even decision-makers who make repeated choices with cumulative effects (for example, the operators of roulette wheels and insurance companies) are rightly interested in this average when each risk is small in relation to total wealth. There is little or no conflict under these conditions between the use of the arithmetic mean as a criterion and the use of the geometric mean of the probability distribution of payouts per dollar of wealth as a criterion.[10] When a decision-maker can surely bet the same small amount on a large number of independent trials, he can maximize the expected value of his gain, and also the likelihood of having more gain than can be obtained by any other plan, by choosing that set of bets which gives him the greatest mathematically expected payout. For example, if Bernoulli's poor man had found 10,000 tickets involving 10,000 independent drawings, each with a payout equally likely to be 2 ducats or nothing, he clearly would be unwise to sell his block of tickets for 9,000 ducats. His winnings on 10,000 different trials would be almost certainly very close to 10,000 ducats, the mathematical expectation of the value of the set of tickets, and the advice of the classical writers would be sound.

[10] When a gambler who has the choice of betting or not betting bets all his wealth on the toss of a fair coin with a payout of $3.00 per $1.00 bet if heads occur and nothing per $1.00 bet if tails occur, he is maximizing the expected value of the payout but not $G$. When he can bet only 1 per cent of his wealth, however, he will maximize both $A$ and $G$ by betting.

Bernoulli used the lottery-ticket example to show that the expected values of the payouts are not good guides in making choices involving large risks. He proposed instead that the expected value of the utilities of the payouts be used as a criterion. He would fill in the payout matrix in Table 2 not with the money value of the gains and losses but with their utilities and then would use the mathematical expectation of these utilities as his criterion.

Whether or not particular payout matrices expressed in terms of subjective utility are realistic is not a problem here. But Bernoulli's procedure is very much at issue. He defines the "mean utility" of a course of action as the mathematical expectation of the probability distribution of the possible utilities from that course of action. He then states, with no discussion, that this mean utility can be used as a basis for valuing risks, that is, as a basis for choosing among courses of action. In other words, he explains why he expresses his profits (or losses) in terms of subjective utility, but he does not give any justification for maximizing the mathematical expectation of these utilities. Bernoulli's use of subjective utility has had wide recognition, and his use of mathematical expectation also has been widely adopted with little or no discussion.[11]

Bernoulli's problem can also be solved by the use of the maximum-chance $(P')$ subgoal. Table 3 shows the payout matrix of returns (that is, payouts, including return of principal, per dollar of wealth) for the poor man, who is assumed to have a wealth of 1,000 ducats aside from his lottery ticket, and for the rich man, who is assumed to have wealth of 100,000 ducats. The arithmetic mean, $A$, of the probability distribution of returns is higher for the poor man

TABLE 3
PAYOUT MATRIX OF RETURNS

| | FUTURE OCCURRENCE | | | |
| | Ticket | Ticket | CRITERION | |
| STRATEGY | Wins | Loses | A | G |
|---|---|---|---|---|
| a) Poor man: | | | | |
| Hold ticket | 2.1 | 0.1 | 1.1 | 0.46 |
| Sell ticket | 1.0 | 1.0 | 1.0 | 1.0 |
| b) Rich man: | | | | |
| Buy ticket | 1.11 | 0.91 | 1.01 | 1.005 |
| Not buy ticket | 1.00 | 1.00 | 1.00 | 1.00 |
| Probability of occurrence | 0.5 | 0.5 | | |

[11] Mathematical expectation now is used as a basis for defining utility. The present emphasis on the axiomatic approach to utility is largely derived from John von Neumann and Oskar Morgenstern, *Theory of Games and Economic Behavior* (rev. ed.; Princeton, N.J.: Princeton University Press, 1935). They say: "We have practically defined numerical utility as being that thing for which the calculus of mathematical expectations is legitimate" (p. 28).

when he holds the ticket and for the rich man when he buys the ticket. The geometric mean, $G$, of returns for the poor man is higher when the ticket is sold, however, and $G$ for the rich man is higher when he buys the ticket.

Over a long enough period of time many economic choices involving returns of the same order of magnitude repeat themselves. Bernoulli's poor man may never find another lottery ticket, but he probably will have many options among courses of action with as wide, or wider, a range of returns. It is assumed here that both the rich man and the poor man will have many opportunities to risk the same proportions of their respective fortunes on approximately the same terms and that both men prefer more wealth to less wealth, everything else being equal. If these assumptions are valid, the maximization of $P'$, the probability of having more wealth at the end of a long series of such choices than can be obtained by any other specified course of action, is a rational subgoal, and $G$ is a rational criterion. The use of the maximum-chance subgoal results in courses of action for both the rich man and the poor man which seemed rational to Bernoulli.

The decision-maker who is interested in maximizing his wealth at the end of a long series of choices should ask himself how he would come out in the long run if he made the same choice on the same terms over and over again. It is not necessary for him to ask himself what his individual subjective utility of winning is. This is not to say that other goals, rather than the goal of maximum wealth at the end of a long series of choices, are irrational. Indeed, the use of subgoals based on the goal of maximum wealth often may be irrational. For example, the man who desperately needs $10.00 to escape a jail sentence and who has only $1.00 may well be justified in taking a gamble to get his money, even though this gamble would not stand the maximum-chance subgoal test. Even under these conditions, however, it would be useful for the man to know that he should not often act in such a manner, if he wants to build up his fortune so as to avoid similar predicaments in the future.

In his paper Bernoulli uses the expected utilities of the payouts as his criterion. He then reaches the conclusion that the utility resulting from any small increase in wealth usually is inversely proportional to the quantity of goods previously possessed.[12] Under these conditions the utilities of the returns vary as their logarithms, and the geometric mean, $G$, of the probability distributions of returns can be used as a criterion instead of expected utility. The arithmetic mean of the logarithms (utilities) of returns is maximized when $G$ is maximized.[13]

Bernoulli gives a number of applications of his formula to gambling and to insurance. In each instance he is able to give a specific answer. He says that everyone who bets any part of his fortune on a mathematically fair game of

---

[12] This is generally credited with being the first use of a utility function.

[13] As pointed out to me by Professor L. J. Savage (in correspondence), not only is the maximization of $G$ the rule for maximum expected utility in connection with Bernoulli's function but (insofar as certain approximations are permissible) this same rule is approximately valid for all utility functions.

chance is acting irrationally, and he then determines what odds a gambler with a specified fortune must obtain to break even in the long run. Most of his problems still are interesting in their own right, and many have a bearing on proper portfolio management. For instance, he demonstrates with numerical examples the advantages of diversification among equally risky ventures and between risky and safe assets.

Bernoulli's approach to the valuation of risky ventures is not contradictory to the maximum-chance ($P'$) approach. Not only do the two approaches lead to the same conclusion when they both can be applied but they tend to support each other. Wealth-holders may be divided into two groups. The first group contains those to whom each risk is a unique event either because they do not expect it to recur or because they keep its effects entirely separate from the results of other risks. For example, the man who each year sets aside a small sum to bet on the races during his vacation, with the intention of "living it up" if he wins and writing it off to experience if he loses, presumably is not actuated by long-run profit-maximizing motives. The effects of each risk are kept separate. Analysis based on maximum chance has nothing to offer this first class of wealth-holders. The choice between profit and safety or expected return and variance is a matter of subjective utility. Bernoulli's assumption that the satisfaction derived from a small gain tends to vary in inverse proportion to the initial wealth may or may not be a shrewd guess.

The second class of wealth-holders includes those who expect to be faced repeatedly with risks of the same general type and magnitude. This group includes those making most business and portfolio decisions and hence is of great importance. It includes, specifically, all those who want to maximize the value of their portfolio at the end of $n$ years, assuming reinvestment of all returns. Here there is a definite rule for choosing between risk and return, the $P'$ subgoal, based on maximum-chance principles. This class may be subdivided further into ($a$) those who undertake only one risky venture at a time and ($b$) those who are able to diversify their risky ventures. Because so many economic phenomena, including yields on stocks, tend to fluctuate together over time, diversification among risky ventures cannot go as far toward eliminating risk as otherwise would be the case. Final choice among efficient portfolios for both groups, ($a$) and ($b$), is based on maximization of $G$, not because this maximizes subjective utility, but because it maximizes $P'$.

Bernoulli states that the wealth-holder should ask himself whether the added satisfaction associated with the expected gain justifies undertaking the risky venture. He bases an exact rule of behavior on his assumption as to how the added satisfaction varies with the size of the potential gain or loss in relation to the size of the portfolio. The rule may or may not be empirically useful, but it is grounded on rather shaky evidence about the exact shape of the utility function. According to maximum-chance analysis, the wealth-holder or portfolio manager should ask himself how he can maximize his chances of getting as good or better return than can be obtained with any other specific plan, assuming that he risks the same proportion of his portfolio on the same terms over and over again. It turns out that the formula which enables the portfolio manager to answer the maximum-chance question is the same as that developed by Bernoulli on grounds of subjective utility.

In conclusion Bernoulli says:

Though a person who is fairly judicious by natural instinct might have realized and spontaneously applied much of what I have here explained, hardly anyone believed it possible to define these problems with the precision we have employed in our examples. Since all of our propositions harmonize perfectly with experience it would be wrong to neglect them as abstractions resting upon precarious hypotheses.[14]

Professor Stigler, in a review article,[15] gives considerable space to Bernoulli's hypothesis about the slope of the wealth-holder's utility function, even though the major emphasis of the article is on utility not affected by probability. He mentions that Laplace and Marshall, among others, have accepted the law as a realistic guide. He also points out the similarity of Bernoulli's law to the Weber-Fechner psychological hypothesis that the just noticeable increment to any stimulus is proportional to the stimulus. Stigler says: "Bernoulli was right in seeking the explanation[16] in utility and he was wrong only in making a special assumption with respect to the slope of the utility curve for which there was no evidence and which he submitted to no tests."[17]

More recently Savage in a section on "Historical and Critical Comments on Utility" had this to say:

Bernoulli went further than the law of diminishing marginal utility and suggested that the slope of utility as a function of wealth might, at least as a rule of thumb, be supposed, not only to decrease with, but to be inversely proportional to, the cash value of wealth. To this day, no other function has been suggested as a better prototype for Everyman's utility function.... Though it might be a reasonable approximation to a person's utility in a moderate range of wealth, it cannot be taken seriously over extreme ranges.[18]

## INDIVIDUAL RISK PREFERENCE

As indicated in the previous section, Bernoulli took the following steps to develop his utility function and to justify diversification among risky ventures and between risk assets and safe assets. (1) He showed—subject to the implicit assumption about subgoals previously discussed—that the value of a

---

[14] *Op. cit.*, p. 31.

[15] George J. Stigler, "The Development of Utility Theory," *Journal of Political Economy*, LVIII (1950), 373–77.

[16] Bernoulli is explaining the reason for the limited value of the game involved in the St. Petersburg paradox. This game is a type of risky venture with an infinitely large mathematically expected value but with an extremely small probability of winning.

[17] Stigler, *op. cit.*, p. 375.

[18] Leonard J. Savage, *The Foundations of Statistics* (New York: John Wiley & Sons, 1954), p. 94.

risky venture to the individual wealth-holder is not the arithmetic mean of the probability distribution of returns (the mathematical expectation of returns) but may be taken to be the arithmetic mean of the probability distribution of the utilities of the returns. (2) He stated that, in the absence of the unusual, the gain in utility resulting from any small increase in wealth may be assumed to be inversely proportional to the quantity of goods previously possessed. (3) He developed a formula for calculating the utility of a risk asset to the individual wealth-holder using as a criterion the utility function developed in step 2. According to Bernoulli, the subjective utility of the wealth-holder's assets, including the risky venture, is measured by the geometric mean, $G$, of the probability distribution of payouts from such assets. (4) Using this formula, he was able to calculate exactly the utility of the wealth-holder's assets, including the risky venture, and to show that diversification among risky ventures increases the utility.[19]

Bernoulli's step 2 may be a reasonable assumption about utility,[20] but it is subject to so many qualifications and exceptions (it does not explain gambling, for example) that it has not been accepted as a suitable basis for erecting the superstructure of steps 3 and 4. The valuation of risky ventures has been left to individual risk preference without any criterion for deciding what this preference is likely to be. For example, Makower and Marschak present a hypothetical table in which an asset's marginal contribution is determined by adding together its contribution to "lucrativity" and safety measured in "lucrativity units" determined by the safety preference rate for a single individual.[21] These individual safety preference rates, in turn, are a matter of taste and must be accepted as given. Friedman and Savage build on Bernoulli's step 1 but modify step 2 by developing a doubly inflected curve comparing utility with income.[22]

Markowitz begins his analysis of portfolio selection by pointing out that "the portfolio with the maximum expected return is not necessarily the one with the minimum variance. There is a rate at which the investor can gain expected return by taking on variance, or reduce variance by giving up expected return."[23] He assumes that the investor considers, or should consider, expected return a desirable thing and variance of return an un-

[19] Bernoulli, op. cit., pp. 24, 25, 28, 30.

[20] Cf. Alfred Marshall, Principles of Economics (8th ed.; New York: Macmillan Co., 1950), p. 135. Marshall says: "In accordance with a suggestion made by Daniel Bernoulli, we may regard the satisfaction which a person derives from his income as commencing when he has enough to support life and afterwards as increasing by equal amounts with every equal successive percentage that is added to his income; and vice versa for loss of income."
See also Savage's comment quoted previously.

[21] Helen Makower and Jacob Marschak, "Assets, Prices and Marketing Theory," Economica, V (1938), 261–88. Reprinted in American Economic Association, Readings in Price Theory (Chicago: Richard D. Irwin, Inc., 1952), pp. 301–2.

[22] Milton Friedman and L. J. Savage, "The Utility Analysis of Choices Involving Risk," Journal of Political Economy, LVI (1948), 279–304.

[23] Harry Markowitz, "Portfolio Selection," Journal of Finance, VII (March, 1952), 79.

desirable thing, and he defines an efficient portfolio as a portfolio with minimum variance for a given expected return or more and a maximum expected return for a given variance or less. He develops a method for selecting efficient portfolios from the set of all possible portfolios but does not give any basis for choice among the efficient portfolios except the individual's safety preference rate.

## THE NEED FOR AN OBJECTIVE CRITERION

The difficulty of evaluating subjective risk preference and the need of an objective criterion are well indicated in the following quotation from a recent journal article dealing with selection of an optimum combination of crops for a farmer:

> The introduction of risk into an economic model of a firm and consequently into a linear programming model of a firm has been accomplished by describing risky outcomes as probability distributions and choosing from among alternate possible distributions by the expected utility hypothesis.
>
> Two basic weaknesses have appeared in applying this method of incorporating risk. One difficulty arises in choosing a value for the constant $a$, which in this case is some sort of risk aversion indicator, and is, to some degree, governed by the personal characteristics of the entrepreneur. A large value for $a$ indicates that the entrepreneur places a great weight on the variance as a deciding factor and is consequently highly averse to risk, and vice versa. The estimation of such a constant to be used in a model is thus quite important; the wrong choice will invalidate any results obtained. The derivation of this constant is a delicate task beyond the scope of this paper.[24]

A major advantage of the criterion for choice among risky ventures developed in this paper is that it avoids the necessity for direct subjective determination of such factors as Marschak's "lucrativity units" or Freund's "risk aversion indicator." As Roy remarks, "A man who seeks advice about his actions will not be grateful for the suggestion that he maximize expected utility."[25]

The criteria for choice between risk and safety in portfolio management can be illustrated by assuming that a gambler has the choice of holding his money in cash or of betting on a gambling device which, with equal probability, will return $R - s$ on loss occasions and $R + s$ on gain occasions with an expected return of $R$ per dollar played. The gambler's portfolio at any time consists of the proportion of his wealth held in cash plus the proportion bet on the gambling device. When the gambler bets none of his wealth, the expected return from his portfolio is 1, and the standard deviation of returns is 0. As the proportion bet increases, both the expected portfolio return and the standard deviation of returns increase. When he bets all his wealth, the expected portfolio return is $R$, and the expected standard deviation of returns

---

[24] Rudolph J. Freund, "The Introduction of Risk into a Programming Model," *Econometrica*, XXIV (July, 1956), 253–63.

[25] A. D. Roy, "Safety First and the Holding of Assets," *Econometrica*, XX (1952), 433.

is $s$. As long as $R$ is greater than 1, and $R - s$ is less than 1, all possible combinations of the two assets in this range are efficient portfolios in that any one of the combinations gives the maximum possible expected return for some standard deviation or variance and the minimum standard deviation or variance for some expected return. Neither Marschak nor Friedman and Savage nor Markowitz would be able to help the gambler in choosing among these efficient portfolios beyond telling him that he should gamble heavily if he has a high preference for risk and should be very conservative in his betting if he has a high risk-aversion factor. In this paper an attempt is made to give the gambler (and wealth-holders, in general) an objective criterion for making this choice.

The wealth-holder who adopts the maximum-chance ($P'$) subgoal can reach this subgoal by using the geometric mean, $G$, of the probability distribution of returns as his criterion and choose the strategy that has the probability distribution of returns with the highest $G$. Bernoulli has also shown that choice of that risky venture with the highest $G$ is a rational choice (1) if maximization of the mathematical expectation of the utilities of the payouts is a rational subgoal and (2) if the utility of a small gain or loss varies inversely with the amount of wealth already possessed.

Most economists recognize that the mathematical expectation and the variance of the probability distribution of returns and the chance of ruin are important to the wealth-holder—but they leave it to individual risk preference to balance one factor against the others. Since $G$ depends on both the mathematical expectation and the variance of the probability distribution of returns, when $G$ is maximized, there is no chance of ruin if the wealth-holder's probability beliefs are correct. Consequently, maximization of $G$ falls within the generally accepted range of rational behavior. This is not to say that $G$ is the only rational criterion for choice among strategies; it is to say, however, that it is a useful criterion in dealing with a broad range of problems.

## 5. INVESTMENT DECISION UNDER UNCERTAINTY: CHOICE—THEORETIC APPROACHES*

### J. HIRSHLEIFER

Reprinted by permission of the author and publishers from *The Quarterly Journal of Economics*, Vol. *LXXIX*, No. 4 (November, 1965), pp. 509–536 (Cambridge, Mass.: Harvard University Press, Copyright, 1965, by the President and Fellows of Harvard College).

Investment is, in essence, *present* sacrifice for *future* benefit. But the present is relatively well known, whereas the future is always an enigma. Investment is also, therefore, *certain* sacrifice for *uncertain* benefit. The theory of investment decision has been satisfactorily developed, in the great work of Irving Fisher,[1] only under the artificial assumption of certainty.[2] Despite the restrictiveness of this assumption, Fisher's theory does succeed in explaining substantial portions of observed investment behavior.[3] But other portions cannot apparently be explained without bringing in attitudes toward risk and differences of opinion, sources of behavior that only come into existence under uncertainty. Among the phenomena left unexplained under the certainty assumption are: the value attached to "liquidity," the willingness to buy insurance, the existence of debt and equity financing, and the bewildering variety of returns or yields on various forms of investment simultaneously ruling in the market.

---

* The editors have numbered all footnotes of this article consecutively although they are not presented that way in the original article. To aid in identification with the original article, at the end of each footnote, beginning with number 10, the editors have indicated in parenthesis the original footnote designation and the page on which it appears in the original article.

[1] Irving Fisher, *The Theory of Interest* (New York: Macmillan, 1930; reprinted, Augustus M. Kelley, 1961). Fisher's earlier work, *The Rate of Interest* (New York: Macmillan, 1907), is also important.

[2] Fisher takes account of uncertainty in his "third approximation" to the theory of interest. Significantly, Chap. 14 of *The Theory of Interest* is entitled: "The Third Approximation Unadapted to Mathematical Formulation."

[3] *Theory of Interest, op. cit.*, Chaps. 18–19.

The object of this paper is to develop, and show some of the implications of, a treatment of risky or uncertain choice that is a generalization of Fischer's theory of riskless choice over time (itself a generalization of the standard theory of timeless choice). In the section immediately following I provide an interpretation of Fisher's theory designed (a) to examine its character as a model of *choice-theoretic structure*, and (b) to introduce the *firm* as a decision-making unit, where Fisher treated only of atomic individuals. The next sections review alternative lines of approach to the theory of risky choice, showing how they diverge in specification of the *choice-objects* of individuals. The major analytical sections then follow, developing a theory of uncertain choice over time in terms of comparisons between consumption possibilities in different possible dated contingencies or "states of the world." A successor article[4] will apply this "time-state-preference" approach to several normative and positive issues: (1) risk aversion and the coexistence of gambling and insurance; (2) the Modigliani-Miller problem concerning the existence or nonexistence of an optimum corporate financial structure (debt-equity mix); and (3) the discount rate to be employed in evaluating public investment projects not subject to the market test.

## I. FISHER'S THEORY OF INVESTMENT DECISION: INTERPRETATION AND REFORMULATION

Only a brief exposition of Fisher's theory will be provided here, as a prelude to the introduction of the firm as an economic agent into Fisher's system. The concepts and terms of Fisher's presentation will be somewhat modified to suit my purposes. To avoid needless complications, the explicit presentation will be limited to two-period comparisons between the present (time "0") and the future (time "1").

In Fisher's system the primitive concept, in terms of which all others are defined, is *consumption*. The objects of choice are present consumption ($c_0$) and future consumption ($c_1$). The *time-preference* function for the $j$-th individual may be denoted $U^j = g^j(c_0^j, c_1^j), = 1, 2, \ldots, J$. Each individual attempts to maximize utility within his *opportunity set*. It is useful to distinguish three different categories within the opportunity set: endowment, financial opportunities, and productive opportunities. The endowment $Y^j = (y_0^j, y_1^j)$ is the individual's initial position (see Figure I); it provides a base point for the analysis of investment as a redistribution of consumption opportunities over time. The endowment element $y_0$ may be interpreted as *current income* and $y_1$ correspondingly as *future income*. The justification for this interpretation (which departs from Fisher's terminology, but is consistent with the spirit of his analysis) is that $y_0$ is the amount that can be consumed

---

[4] "Investment Decision Under Uncertainty: Applications of the State-Preference Approach," forthcoming in this *Journal*.

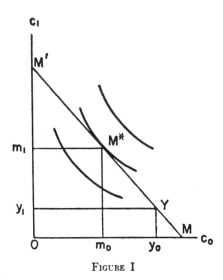

FIGURE I

without trenching on future consumptive possibilities.[5] We then define investment $i_0 = y_0 - c_0$, negative values of investment being possible.[6]

*Financial opportunities* for investment permit transormation of the endowment into alternative $(c_0, c_1)$ combinations, but only by trading with other individuals. In such trading, motivated by disparities between endowed or attained income-sequences and desired time-patterns of consumption, a rate of exchange between units of present consumption (present dollars) and of future consumption (future dollars) would be established in the market. This rate of exchange can be expressed as $(dc_1)/(dc_0) = -(1 + r)$, where $r$ is the *rate of interest*, or premium on current dollars. In Figure I the financial opportunities facing the investor are shown by the "market line" $MM'$

---

[5] "Income" is a troublesome concept. Fisher attempted to dispose of it by defining income as identical with consumption; this is unsatisfactory, since one cannot avoid distinguishing *actual* and *potential* consumption. Income is a potential-consumption concept: in principle, it is what can be consumed in the current period without impairing future income or consumption. But this statement of principle leaves open a number of possible interpretations. For accounting or tax purposes, a *net* concept of income is ordinarily adopted: the gross yield of any income source in the current period is reduced by allowance for "depreciation of capital." Depreciation represents the amount which, if reinvested, would replenish the income source so as to permit maintenance of the net income to the time-horizon envisaged—under the ordinary assumption of an infinite horizon, this is equivalent to maintaining capital value intact. The analytical inconvenience of this concept, for our purposes, is that depreciation (and therefore net income) cannot in general be calculated independently of the rate of interest—which is what we seek to explain. For this reason the income concept used here is *gross* income: for any time-period, this is the corresponding element of the gross yield sequence (the endowment) itself, without any accounting adjustments. This interpretation qualifies as a potential-consumption concept; it is what can be consumed without borrowing, or (equivalently) without trenching on the future-consumption elements of the endowment itself.

[6] This is a *gross* rather than a *net* investment concept (see footnote above).

through $Y$. Along this market line *wealth* $W = c_0 + c_1/(1 = r)$ equals $y_0 + y_1/(1 + r)$, a constant, so that the market line is a budget or wealth constraint. The time-preference optimum for the individual under pure exchange (financial opportunities only) is $M^*$, and at the interest rate $r$ he seeks to invest (lend) the amount $(y_0 - m_0)$. Under pure exchange the social totals of present and of future consumption, $\sum_j y_0^j$ and $\sum_j y_1^j$ are conserved, while the social total of investment is zero (for each borrower there is a lender). This condition determines the market interest rate $r$.

The basic equations under pure exchange may be represented as follows:

(1) $\quad U^j = g^j(c_0^j, c_1^j)$ 

Time-preference function wealth constraint, or

(2) $\quad c_0^j + c_1^j/(1 + r) = y_0^j + y_1^j/(1 + r)$ 

financial opportunities.

These equations also indicate that all loans are repaid.

(3) $\quad \dfrac{dc_1^j}{dc_0^j}\bigg|_{U^j} = -(1 + r)$ 

Time-preference optimum

The symbol on the left represents the marginal rate of substitution of $c_1$ for $c_0$ that leaves utility constant—the marginal rate of time preference. Note that this is equated for all individuals (if we rule out corner solutions).

(4) $\quad \left.\begin{aligned} \sum_{j=1}^{J} c_0^j &= \sum_{j=1}^{J} y_0^j \\ \sum_{j=1}^{J} c_1^j &= \sum_{j=1}^{J} y_1^j \end{aligned}\right\}$ 

Conservation equations[7]

These market-clearing equations also indicate that the social total of investment, $\sum(y_0 - c_0)$ is zero, as required for the case of pure exchange.

If the opportunity set also contains *productive opportunities*, then it is possible to engage in transactions with nature (e.g., planting a seed), as well as with other individuals. Under such circumstances, in Fisher's system the individual investor attains his utility optimum at $X^*$ (in Figure II) by a two-step procedure. First, he moves from his endowment $Y$ along his productive opportunity locus $PP'$ (note that his opportunities are ordered according to diminishing marginal productivity of investment) to his productive optimum $P^*$. The productive optimum is characterized by attainment of the highest possible market line—that is, highest wealth level. The productive investor can then "finance" by borrowing, if need be, to attain his utility optimum $X^*$. In Figure II, his productive investment is $(y_0 - p_0)$, and he borrows $(x_0 - p_0)$ to replenish current consumption. It is the transaction with nature that creates wealth; the associated financial transfers leave wealth unchanged.

---

[7] One of the conservation equations can be shown to follow from the remainder of the system.

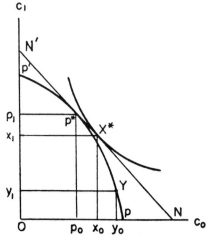

FIGURE II

In the equations allowing productive opportunities, the elements $(p_0, p_1)$ of the "productive solution" $P^*$ appear as variables:

(1')     $U^j = g^j(c_0^j, c_1^j)$                          Time-preference function
                                                                        wealth constraint, or

(2')     $c_0^j + c_1^j/(1 + r) = p_0^j + p_1^j/(1 + r)$   financial opportunities.

The wealth level attained by productive transformations, rather than the endowment wealth level, becomes the financial constraint.

(3')     $\dfrac{dc_1^j}{dc_0^j}\bigg|_{U^j} = -(1 + r)$     Time-preference optimum

(4')     $p^j(p_0^j, p_1^j; y_0^j, y_1^j) = 0$                Productive opportunity set

(5')     $\dfrac{dp_1^j}{dp_0^j} = -(1 + r)$                    Productive optimum

This condition also represents attainment of maximum wealth or "present value."[8]

(6')     $\left. \begin{array}{l} \sum\limits_{j=1}^{J} c_0^j = \sum\limits_{j=1}^{J} p_0^j \\[2ex] \sum\limits_{j=1}^{J} c_1^j = \sum\limits_{j=1}^{J} p_1^j \end{array} \right\}$          Conservation equations

[8] In more general cases, where the productive opportunity locus need not have the simple concavity properties of Figure II (because of lumpiness or interdependence among investments), the tangency condition of equation (5') is insufficient to determine the optimum. The more general maximum-wealth condition permits selection among multiple local maxima, whether tangencies or corner solutions. See J. Hirshleifer, "On the Theory of Optimal Investment Decision," *Journal of Political Economy, LXVI* (Aug. 1958), reprinted in E. Solomon (ed.), *The Management of Corporate Capital* (Glencoe, Ill.: Free Press, 1959).

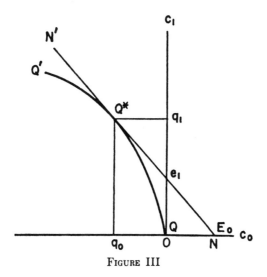

FIGURE III

These market-clearing equations make the interest rate depend upon the productive as well as the consumptive supply and demand for funds. The social total of current investment

$$\sum_{j=1}^{J} i_0^j = \sum_{j=1}^{J} (y_0^j - p_0^j).$$

We may now introduce firms as the specialized agencies of individuals in their time-productive capacities. We specify: (a) firms do not consume; (b) firms have null endowments; and (c) all productive opportunities appertain to firms. Let there be $F$ firms, and let $o_f^j$ be the fraction of the $f$-th firm owned by the $j$-th individual. The $o_f^j$ here are constants, such that $\sum_{j=1}^{J} o_f^j = 1$; for $f = 1; 2; \ldots, F$. The equilibrium of the firm (see Figure III) is the productive solution $Q^*$ where the highest market line $NN'$ is attained; this represents maximum wealth for the firm, and so for the owners. The firm, having null endowment, must borrow $q_0$, an amount equal to the productive investment. It repays lenders $-q_0(1 + r) = q_1 - e_1$ (see Figure III). The firm income $e_1^f$ is distributed to the owners as an increment to their endowments $y_1^j$.[9]

With the introduction of firms, the equation system may be represented:

(1″)        $U^j = g^j(c_0^j, c_1^j)$                          Time-preference function

(2″)        $c_0^j + c_1^j/(1 + r) =$

$y_0^j + \left(y_1^j + \sum_{f=1}^{F} o_f^j e_1^f\right)/(1 + r)$        Wealth constraint.

[9] Alternatively, in a world of certainty the firm's payout could be in current funds $c_0$. That is, the firm could immediately distribute to owners the amount $E_0$, the present value of the future net income $e_1$.

On this interpretation, the firms use no "equity" funds. In a world of certainty, full-debt financing is possible. However, the effect of profitable investment is an increment $e_1^f$ to equity (wealth of owners) in time "1".

(3") $$\left.\frac{dc_1^j}{dc_0^j}\right|_{U^j} = -(1 + r)$$ Time-preference optimum

(4") $$q^f(q_0^f, q_1^f) = 0$$ Productive opportunity set

(5") $$\frac{dq_1^f}{dq_0^f} = -(1 + r)$$ Productive optimum

The productive decisions are all made by the firms.

(6") $$q_1^f = -q_0^f(1 + r) + e_1^f$$ Firm's Financial Distributions

Since the firm does not consume, it must distribute its productive gross earnings, $q_1$. This amount is divided between repayment of debt and equity income to owners.

(7")
$$
\left.
\begin{aligned}
\sum_{j=1}^{J} y_0^j + \sum_{f=1}^{F} q_0^f = \sum_{j=1}^{J} c_0^j \\
\sum_{j=1}^{J} y_1^j + \sum_{f=1}^{F} q_1^f = \sum_{j=1}^{J} c_1^j
\end{aligned}
\right\}
$$
Conservation equations

Note that $\sum_{j=1}^{J} p_0^j$ in (6') of the previous formulation becomes $\sum_{j=1}^{J} y_0^j + \sum_{f=1}^{F} q_0^f$ here, and similarly $\sum p_1^j$ becomes $\sum y_1^j + \sum q_1^f$.

An alternative form of the wealth or financial constraints is also useful. Let $P_0$ be the price of $c_0$, and $P_1$ the price of $c_1$. If $c_0$ is taken as numeraire we have $P_0 = 1$ and $P_1 = 1/(1 + r)$. Then:

Equation (2) becomes: $P_0 c_0 + P_1 c_1 = P_0 y_0 + P_1 y_1$.

Equation (2') becomes: $P_0 c_0 + P_1 c_1 = P_0 p_0 + P_1 p_1$.

Equation (2") becomes: $P_0 c_0 + P_1 c_1 = P_0 y_0 + P_1 y_1 + P_1 \left[ \sum_{f=1}^{F} (_0{}_f e_1^f) \right]$.

And, after dividing through by $(1 + r)$, equation (6") becomes:

(6''') $$P_1 q_1 = -P_0 q_0 + P_1 e_1.$$

This can be given the interpretation: the "wealth of the firm" (i.e., the present worth of the firm's gross or productive income $q_1$) is the sum of the values of the debt and equity—the sum of the borrowings and the increment to wealth of the owners.[10]

[10] This looks very much like the famous "Proposition I" in F. Modigliani and M. H. Miller, "The Cost of Capital, Corporation Finance and the Theory of Investment," *American Economic Review*, XLVIII (June, 1958), 268. Of course, that the Modigliani-Miller theorem holds under conditions of certainty is not surprising; in the successor to this article it will be proved that the theorem continues to hold even under some forms of uncertainty. (1, p. 516).

## II. CHOICE-THEORETIC APPROACHES TO INVESTMENT DECISION UNDER UNCERTAINTY

While Fisher's model is a special application to the problem of investment decision under certainty, it can also be regarded as an archetype of choice-theoretic system for any decision problem. By "choice-theoretic system" I will mean a model containing the following features: (1) objects of choice (commodities), and decision-making units (economic agents); (2) a preference function ordering such objects, for each economic agent; (3) an opportunity set, again for each agent, which is equivalent to specifying the constraints upon the agent's range of choice; and (4) balancing or conservation equations, which specify the social interactions among the individual decisions. The competing approaches to investment decision considered in this section diverge in their specification of the basic objects of choice.

Investment decision under uncertainty involves purchase of *assets*—more or less complex claims or titles to present and future incomes. The most direct theoretical formulation of this decision is the *Asset-preference Approach*; this postulates that assets themselves are the desired objects of choice. On the theoretical level, comparisons usually run in terms of exchanges between a riskless asset and one or more risky assets (or lotteries) with arbitrary but specified probability distributions.[11] The main appeal of this approach is the attractiveness of the direct analogy between assets in investment theory and the commodities of ordinary price theory. The central disadvantage of the approach is that assets are clearly not the elemental desired objects; what we would like to do analytically would be to show how the prices of assets are determined by the valuations placed by individuals upon the underlying income opportunities to which the assets represent claims. In other words, what we really are seeking is a means of resolving assets into more fundamental choice-objects. A second difficulty, which will reappear below in connection with each of the alternative formulations for the objects of choice, is that the total of the various types of assets cannot be assumed fixed, even under pure exchange. Thus, an individual owning a real asset can issue claims against the security of his original asset—i.e., he can "finance" his holdings of assets, and in doing so has a wide variety of options ("debt-equity mix"). But each such action generates a more or less complex pattern of new "financial" assets which can substitute for productive assets in the portfolios of investors. It is clear, therefore, that conservation relations do not hold in any simple way when the objects of choice are taken to be assets.

The approach currently most popular in the analysis of investment decision under uncertainty postulates that the fundamental objects of choice, standing behind the particularities of individual assets, are the *mean* and the *variability* of future return—where variability refers to probabilistic rather

[11] An asset-preference approach is adopted in my paper, "Risk, the Discount Rate, and Investment Decisions," *American Economic Review*, LI (May 1961). A much more complete working out of this approach was independently developed by Gordon B. Pye in his 1963 M.I.T. Ph.D. thesis, "Investment Rules for Corporations." (2, p. 517)

than chronological fluctuation. This *Mean, Variability Approach*, to be critically analyzed in the next section, reduces assets (or portfolios of assets) to underlying mean and variability measures which, it is postulated, enter into investors' preference functions. An alternative reduction will be developed next, under the heading of *State-preference Approach*. Here the underlying objects of choice are postulated to be contingent consumption opportunities or claims defined over a complete listing of all possible " states of the world." It will be shown that this latter approach can easily be developed into a choice-theoretic system that represents a natural extension of Fisher's into the domain of uncertainty.

## III. THE MEAN, VARIABILITY APPROACH

The mean, variability approach to investment decision under uncertainty selects as the objects of choice *expected returns* and *variability of returns* from investments.[12] In accordance with the common beliefs of observers of

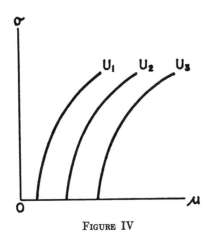

FIGURE IV

financial markets, the assumption is made that investors desire high values of the former and low values of the latter—as usually measured by the mean ($\mu$) and standard deviation ($\sigma$), respectively, of the probability distri-

---

[12] The most complete development of this viewpoint is in H. M. Markowitz, *Portfolio Selection* (New York: Wiley, 1959). The earliest conception is apparently that of Fisher in *The Nature of Capital and Income* (New York: Macmillan, 1912). Other important contributions are J. R. Hicks, "A Suggestion for Simplifying the Theory of Money," *Economica*, N.S., II (Feb. 1935); J. Marschak, " Money and the Theory of Assets," *Econometrica*, VI (Oct. 1938); and James Tobin, " Liquidity Preference as Behavior Towards Risk," *Review of Economic Studies*, XXV (Feb. 1958). A convenient condensed formulation will be found in D. E. Farrar, *The Investment Decision Under Uncertainty* (Englewood Cliffs, N.J.: Prentice-Hall, 1962). An important recent contribution, breaking into entirely new ground, is William F. Sharpe, "Capital Asset Prices: A Theory of Market Equilibrium under Conditions of Risk," *Journal of Finance*, XIX (Sept. 1964). (3, p. 518)

bution of returns—and show increasing aversion to σ as risk increases. Under these assumptions a preference function can be shown as in Figure IV ordering all possible (μ, σ) combinations.

Theorists following the mean, variability approach have concentrated upon the problem of portfolios, i.e., holdings of financial assets (securities). Little or no attention has been paid to productive assets or investments. Also, the usual portfolio analysis keeps constant the amount of current investment and concerns itself only with the distribution of that amount over the available securities. Neither restriction is, however, essential. The same approach could be extended, on the level of the individual investor, to include real productive investments in addition to a financial portfolio,[13] and a simultaneous solution could be provided for the amount of investment together with the choice of securities to be held.

For our purposes, it will suffice to present only the broad outlines of the mean, variability formulation. Turning first to the opportunity set, and letting X be the random variable of prospective gross portfolio value[14] consequent

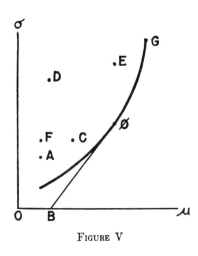

FIGURE V

upon given current investment, the possible combinations of $\mu(X)$ and $\sigma(X)$ attainable by holding individual securities (i.e., combinations attainable in one-security portfolios) are suggested by the typical points B, C, D, etc., in Figure V. The point B is on the horizontal axis; it is intended to represent investment in riskless bonds. The solid curve shows the efficient frontier (minimum σ attainable for each possible value of μ) when the investor does

[13] Although, as indicated above, such an extension would involve some difficulties in specifying conservation relations when both productive and financial assets are considered. (4, p. 519)

[14] Since a portfolio is a collection of assets, the gross value X cannot be negative. (5, p. 519)

*not* have the riskless opportunity $B$ available. In general, one-security port-folios are not on the efficient frontier, because of the advantage of diversi-fication: the over-all $\mu$ for any mixed portfolio will be the weighted average of the component $\mu_i$ values for the individual securities, but the over-all $\sigma$ will in general be lower than the corresponding average of the $\sigma_i$.[15] However, the security $G$, whose expected future value is greater than any other security's, is an efficient one-security portfolio. This suggests why the efficient frontier is convex to the right: as we move to higher and higher portfolio $\mu$, we are forced to concentrate increasingly on the small number of high-$\mu_i$ securities, thus progressively reducing the power of diversification. The introduction of the riskless security $B$, with mean future value $\mu_B$, changes the opportunity set to incorporate the area bounded by the line through $B$ and tangent at $\phi$ to the efficient frontier constructed from the risky securities.[16]

The preference function has been the focus of attention in controversial discussion of the mean, variability approach. There have been attempts to derive indifference maps like that portrayed in Figure IV from the Neumann-Morgenstern axioms of rational choice—together with a specification of a concave-downward utility-of-income $v(X)$ function like that shown in Figure VI. The latter shape is necessary in order to obtain risk aversion (positive-sloping U-curves in Figure IV).[17] (Whether observed behavior can be re-garded as reflecting risk aversion rather than risk preference, or some mixture of the two, is a subject of disagreement that will be considered in the succes-sor article alluded to earlier.) Here $v$ is the Neumann-Morgenstern utility indicator that permits use of the expected-utility theorem in rationalizing

---

[15] Let $X$ be the future value of the over-all portfolio, $x_i$ the future value of the $i$-th security, $a_i$ the fraction of the fixed original investment held in the $i$-th security, and $n$ the number of securities. Then:

(a)   $$X = \sum_{i=1}^{n} a_i x_i$$

(b)   $$\mu = E(X) = \sum_{i=1}^{n} a_i \mu_i$$

(c)   $$\sigma = \left[ \sum_{i=1}^{n} a_i^2 \sigma_i^2 + 2 \sum_{i=1}^{n} \sum_{j=1}^{i=1} a_i \sigma_i \sigma_j \right]^{1/2}$$

Here $\sigma_{ij}$ is the covariance of the $i$-th and the $j$-th security.

There are two important exceptions to the statement that $\sigma$ will be lower than the average of the $\sigma_i$: (1) if all the securities are perfectly correlated (each $\sigma_{ij} = \sigma_i \sigma_j$), or (2) if one secu-rity of a two-security portfolio has zero $\sigma_i$, from which it follows that covariance also equals zero. In either of these cases, $\sigma = \sum_{i=1}^{n} a_i \sigma_i$. (6, p. 520)

[16] The portfolio $\mu$ and $\sigma$ represented by combinations of $B$ and the "security" $\phi$ (itself generally a combination of securities) plot along a straight line because $\sigma_B$ and therefore $\sigma_{B\phi}$ equal zero (see footnote above). (7, p. 520)

[17] See M. Friedman and L. J. Savage, "The Utility Analysis of Choices Involving Risk," *Journal of Political Economy*, LVI (Aug. 1948). Reprinted in American Economic Associa-tion, *Readings in Price Theory* (Homewood, Ill.: Irwin, 1952). Page references to the latter volume. (8, p. 520)

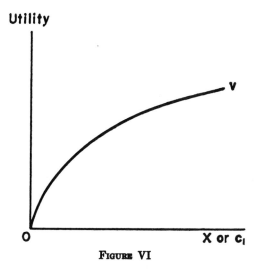

**Utility**

**v**

**X or $c_i$**

O

FIGURE VI

choice under uncertainty, and the argument $X$ is really consumption income in the future period. It has been shown that a $\mu$, $\sigma$ indifference map can be derived (i.e., that each indifference curve represents a locus of constant expected utility-of-income) only if one of the following conditions obtains: (a) the utility-of-income function $v$ is quadratic, or (b) in considering alternative portfolios, the investor's probability distributions for $X$ under the various portfolios considered are all members of a two-parameter family.[18]

It is clear that a quadratic utility-of-income function is unacceptable. To make $v(X)$ concave downward with such a function, the coefficient of the squared term must be negative—but in this case a point must be reached where additional income decreases utility! Furthermore, we cannot accept the quadratic even as an approximation, however well it may fit in the neighborhood of the mean return $\mu(X)$, because we are dealing with risky portfolios that require us to evaluate the utility of values for the random variable $X$ diverging considerably from the mean.

One's first impression is that the second condition should be much more widely applicable. In particular, if (on the efficient frontier, at least) all portfolios consist of relatively large numbers of securities, the Central Limit Theorem indicates that the probability distributions for the returns $X$ under any such "well-diversified" portfolio will approach normality—and, of course, the normal distribution is two-parameter. Nevertheless, this does not really help us, though to explain why will require an illustration anticipating the main ideas of the next section. Let us suppose that an investor contemplates the uncertain future as the set of three equally probable "states of the world" $A$, $B$, and $C$—one and only one of which will actually obtain. A

[18] Tobin, *loc. cit.*, pp. 74–77. (9, p. 521)

"state" here is a complete world-environment for the individual. For two different portfolios, the distribution of future values over these states ($X_A$, $X_B$, $X_C$), might be (3, 2, 1) and (1, 2, 3) respectively. Since these two distributions or "prospects" have the same $\mu$ and $\sigma$, they would have to .be identical in preference ordering in order for it to be possible to construct a preference map on $\mu$, $\sigma$ axes. But we have no right to assume that an investor would be indifferent between the two prospects. The nature of the world-environments $A$, $B$, and $C$ might be such that he prefers the distribution biased toward wealth in state $A$ over that biased toward wealth in state $C$. Here the *ordering* on $A$, $B$, and $C$ of the elements of the distribution cannot be neglected; a distribution that is two-parameter disregarding ordering turns out to be insufficiently specified, for preference ranking purposes, by the mean and standard deviation.

One element of the choice-theoretic structure under the mean, variability approach has not received the attention it deserves: the role of conservation relations. Waiving the difficulties turning upon the existence and shape of $\mu$, $\sigma$ preference functions, and accepting the efficient frontier as defining the useful limits of the opportunity set, the individual will presumably attain a tangency solution. Note in Figure V that there are two main classes of solutions: mixtures of riskless bonds and risky assets in the range $B\phi$, and portfolios excluding riskless bonds in the range $\phi G$.[19] But this is only an individual solution, not a market solution. The analytical system requires a specification of the social interactions that determine a set of asset prices $P_i$, which in turn modify the $\mu_i$, $\sigma_i$, and $\sigma_{ij}$ of the various securities until finally an equilibrium is reached.

In equations (4) describing Fisher's system, the social interaction takes the form of conservation equations fixing the social totals of the various objects of choice. Sharpe, apparently the first to realize the need for completion of the mean, variability theoretic structure, employed a formulation fixing the social totals of the various *securities* available. He has succeeded in deriving a number of theorems, based essentially upon the consideration that in equilibrium security prices $P_i$ must be such as to permit the existing totals of securities to be exactly held in terms of the summation of the individuals' tangency solutions. These results are important, but they cannot be regarded as a final completion of the choice-theoretic system.[20] The reason is that securities are artificial commodities or objects of choice. Without changing the underlying real investment yields, alternative patterns of securities can be

---

[19] Sharpe (*loc. cit.*) extends the line $B\phi$ beyond the point $\phi$, arguing that the extension represents negative amounts of the asset $B$, or "selling $B$ short" to hold more of the $\mu$, $\sigma$ combination represented by $\phi$. But this amounts to the investor issuing a new bond to "finance" his asset-holdings—which is inconsistent with the spirit of Sharpe's analysis that postulates fixed social totals of each class of risky and riskless assets. (If the analysis were to permit the investor to issue new bonds, it should also permit him to issue new risky securities as well.) (1, p. 522)

[20] They are analogous to the results derived in ordinary price theory in the so-called "very short run" where, with fixed supplies, demand alone governs price. (2, p. 523)

generated as claims to these real yields. On the individual or firm level, the question of the optimal pattern of securities to issue against one's assets— which latter may be real assets, or may themselves be securities one step or more removed from the ultimate real assets—is known in capital-budgeting literature as the "financing" problem, or in the simplest case as the problem of the "debt-equity mix." To complete the system fully under pure exchange, analysis must go beyond the principles on which individuals decide both to hold assets and to finance asset-holdings, to the social interactions that determine the equilibrium set of financial securities issued by all individuals together as the set of claims to the underlying real assets of the community. Presumably, these interactions will be governed by the $\mu$ and $\sigma$ represented by the given real assets. And, when production is introduced, the real assets themselves can no longer be held constant, and analysis must go back to the forces determining the balance between $\mu$ and $\sigma$ in the real investments undertaken. We are thus still a considerable distance from a market theory of the risk premium under the mean, variability approach.

## IV. THE STATE-PREFERENCE APPROACH

The approach to investment decision under uncertainty that begins by postulating the objects of choice to be contingent consumption opportunities, in alternative possible states of the world, is comparatively unfamiliar.[21] But it has great advantages. There is a close formal analogy with Fisher's model for riskless choice over time; in fact, the state-and-time-preference choice-theoretic model is a natural generalization of Fisher's system. The approach leads, we shall see, to important theorems concerning investment and financing decisions.

In the interest of minimizing complications, it will be assumed that there is only one present state; i.e., there is certainty as to the present (time "0"). The future is represented by a point in time (time "1"), in which there are two alternative "states of the world" (state $a$ or state $b$ must obtain). The two states might be thought of as war versus peace, or prosperity versus depression. Two-state uncertainty is, of course, a very radical oversimplification, adopted here for purposes of presentation only. In the two-period *certainty* case we needed to consider only the single type of exchange between present and future consumption, $c_0$ and $c_1$. But now there are three objects of choice: $c_0$, $c_{1a}$, and $c_{1b}$. We may think of two dimensions of choice: the contemporaneous balance of risky claims between $c_{1a}$ and $c_{1b}$ (Figure VII), and the time-plus-risk exchange between a present certain $c_0$ and a future uncertain $c_{1b}$ or

[21] The pioneering work here is Kenneth J. Arrow, "Le Rôle des Valeurs Boursières pour la Répartition la Meilleure des Risques," *International Colloquium on Econometrics*, 1952, Centre National de la Recherche Scientifique (Paris, 1953). An English version appeared under the title "The Role of Securities in the Optimal Allocation of Risk-bearing," *Review of Economic Studies*, XXXI (April 1964). See also G. Debreu, *Theory of Value* (New York: Wiley, 1959), Chap. 7, and J. Hirshleifer, "Efficient Allocation of Capital in an Uncertain World," *American Economic Review*, LIV (May 1964), 77–85. (3, p. 523)

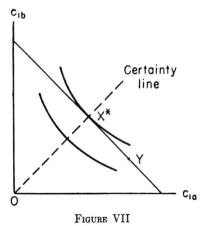

FIGURE VII

$c_{1a}$ (Figure VIII portrays the choice between $c_0$ and $c_{1b}$). We will consider here situations of pure exchange, deferring the problems introduced by the existence of productive opportunities.

Under the conditions of Figure VII, the amount of $c_0$ is implicitly fixed so that we can deal with simple exchange between contemporaneous risky claims. The 45° line through the origin represents points along which $c_{1a} = c_{1b}$, so that the amount $c_1$ is sure to be received—this is the "certainty line." The figure portrays the preference function for an individual attaching subjective probabilities $\pi_a = \pi_b = 1/2$ to the two possible states.

The convex indifference curves shown in Figure VII can be justified on several levels. General observation of behavior probably suffices to convince us that almost no one is so reckless to prefer, if $\pi_a = \pi_b = 1/2$, the prospect $(c_{1a}, c_{1b}) = (1000, 0)$ to a prospect like $(500, 500)$. (It must be understood that the statement $c_{1b} = 0$ does not mean merely a possibly tolerable loss of a

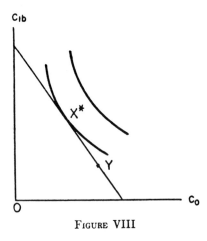

FIGURE VIII

gamble, but an actual zero consumption level—starvation—if state $b$ should occur.) Thus, even the very mild degree of conservatism, implicit in observed "nonspecialization" among claims to consumption in alternative states of the world, requires convex utility isoquants.[22]

Interesting questions arise concerning the interpretation of the convex preference function in Figure VII in terms of subjective probabilities and Neumann-Morgenstern utilities. Let a Neumann-Morgenstern function $v(c_1)$ be postulated, concave downward as in Figure VI, and assume that this function can be applied to the risky choice between $c_{1a}$ and $c_{1b}$. This special assumption says that the function $v(c_1)$ is independent of the state— the world-environment—that obtains; it will be called the "uniqueness" assumption. Then concavity of $v(c_1)$, or "diminishing marginal utility of (consumption) income," implies convexity of the utility isoquants in Figure VII. The converse also holds, so Neumann-Morgenstern risk aversion is implied by nonspecialization of risky choice. (Convexity is more general than diminishing marginal utility, in that convexity at a particular $(c_{1a}, c_{1b})$ point does not necessarily imply diminishing marginal utility at $c_{1a}$ and $c_{1b}$— but convexity *everywhere* requires diminishing marginal utility.)[23] In the

---

[22] The statement above is correct provided that the choice is between simple convex and simple concave curvature. Other, more complex, shapes would also be consistent with the observation. (4, p. 525)

[23] Convexity requires $(d^2c_{1b})/(dc_{1a}^2) > 0$. Under the Neumann-Morgenstern postulates, it is possible to attribute a utility function $v(c_1)$ to "income" (here, to consumption) such that the utility of a risky prospect equals the expectation of the $v$'s attached to the elements of the prospect. Then $U(c_{1a}, c_{1b}; \pi_a, \pi_b) = \pi_a v(c_{1a}) + \pi_b v(c_{1b})$, or, simplifying notation:

$$= \pi_a v_{1a} + \pi_b v_{1b}$$

$$\frac{dc_{1b}}{dc_{1a}}\bigg|_U = -\frac{\partial U/\partial c_{1a}}{\partial U/\partial c_{1b}} = -\frac{\pi_a v'_{1a}}{\pi_b v'_{1b}}$$

$$\frac{d^2c_{1b}}{dc^2_{1a}} = \frac{d}{dc_{1a}}\left(\frac{dc_{1b}}{dc_{1a}}\right) = \frac{\partial}{\partial c_{1a}}\left(\frac{dc_{1b}}{dc_{1a}}\right) + \frac{\partial}{\partial c_{1b}}\left(\frac{dc_{1b}}{dc_{1a}}\right) \cdot \frac{dc_{1b}}{dc_{1a}}$$

$$= -\frac{\pi_a v''_{1a}}{\pi_b v'_{1b}} + \frac{\pi_a v'_{1a} v''_{1b}}{\pi_b (v'_{1b})^2}\left(-\frac{\pi_a v'_{1a}}{\pi_b v'_{1b}}\right)$$

$$= -\frac{\pi_a v''_{1a}}{\pi_b v'_{1b}} - \frac{\pi_a^2 (v'_{1a})^2 v''_{1b}}{\pi_b^2 (v'_{1b})^2}$$

It should be noted that $\dfrac{\partial v'_{1b}}{\partial c_{1a}} = \dfrac{\partial v'_{1a}}{\partial c_{1b}} = 0$.

That is, the slope of the "utility-of-income" curve for state $b$ is independent of the amount scheduled for consumption in state $a$, and vice versa. This follows from the Neumann-Morgenstern "independence" or "substitutability" postulate (R. D. Luce and H. Raiffa, *Games and Decisions* (New York: Wiley, 1957), p. 27). Since $\pi_a, \pi_b, v'_{1a}, v'_{1b} > 0$, diminishing marginal utility ($v''_{1a} < 0$ and $v''_{1b} < 0$) is sufficient for convexity but is not a necessary condition for convexity at $(c_{1a}, c_{1b})$; a sufficiently negative $v''_{1a}$ may outweigh a positive $v''_{1b}$, or vice versa. But in this latter case it will be possible to find risky prospects for which $v''_{1a}$ and $v''_{1b}$ are both positive, so that convexity would not hold everywhere. (5, p. 526)

special case where $\pi_a = \pi_b = 1/2$, and holding to the uniqueness assumption so that the single function $v(c_1)$ is applicable to consumption in state $a$ or state $b$, concavity of $v(c_1)$ implies not merely convex indifference curves in Figure VII but indifference curves symmetrical about the 45° certainty line. For, with a single $v(c_1)$ function, utility of any prospect $(y, x; 1/2, 1/2)$ would then be the same as that of the prospect $(x, y; 1/2, 1/2)$.

Under the simplified model investigated here, any commodity basket consists of time-state consumption elements $c_0$, $c_{1a}$, and $c_{1b}$. In particular, the endowment $Y$ may be denoted $(y_0, y_{1a}, y_{1b})$. Since we are considering a pure-exchange situation, there are no productive opportunities. But financial opportunities exist for individuals to trade elements of their endowed combinations. In such trading each is constrained by his endowed wealth: $W = P_0 c_0 + P_{1a} c_{1a} + P_{1b} c_{1b}$. Here $P_0$, $P_{1a}$, and $P_{1b}$ are the prices of the correspondingly subscribed time-state claims—the commodities of this model. The constant $W$ is determined by $P_0 y_0 + P_{1a} y_{1a} + P_{1b} y_{1b}$, the present value of the endowment. Let $c_0$ be the numeraire, so that $P_0 = 1$. At this point we may generalize the concept of discount rate by defining the *time-and-state discount rates* $r_{1a}$ and $r_{1b}$ in terms of the prices of the corresponding time-state claims: $P_{1a} = 1/(1 + r_{1a})$ and $P_{1b} = 1/(1 + r_{1b})$. Note that these rates discount for both futurity and probability (or, rather, improbability). In the degenerate case of only one future state, the riskless rate, discounting for time only, is defined in $P_1 = 1/(1 + r_1)$.

In the special case where $\pi_a = \pi_b = 1/2$, and if the price of claims to $c_{1a}$ happens to equal that of claims to $c_{1b}$, under the uniqueness assumption the wealth constraint and preference function for contemporaneous exchanges (i.e., given the amount of $c_0$) are as portrayed in Figure VII—the former is a 135° line, and the latter is symmetrical about the 45° certainty line. Then, the state-preference tangency optimum must be along the certainty line. More generally, given uniqueness of $v(c_1)$, if the price ratio $P_{1b}/P_{1a}$ is equal to the probability ratio $\pi_b/\pi_a$, the optimum is along the certainty line.[24] This result corresponds to the well-known theorem that, if $v(c_1)$ is concave, a fair gamble will not be accepted.[25] (N.B., assuming the individual is already on the certainty line!)[26]

---

[24] The utility function is: $U = \pi_a v(c_{1a}) + \pi_b v(c_{1b})$. It is to be maximized subject to the constraint: $P_{1a} c_{1a} + P_{1b} c_{1b} = K$, a parameter equal to $W - c_0$. The condition resulting is:

$$\frac{P_{1b}}{P_{1a}} = \frac{\pi_b v'(c_{1b})}{\pi_a v'(c_{1a})}$$

The equality of price and probability ratios must hold along the certainty line, since there $c_{1b} = c_{1a}$. Convexity of the indifference curves assures that the condition cannot be met elsewhere. (6, p. 527)

[25] Friedman and Savage, *loc. cit.*, pp. 73 *ff.* (7, p. 527)

[26] If the individual is not on the certainty line, there may exist "gambles" that can move him toward that line. We call such gambles "insurance." Under the present assumptions fair insurance will be purchased. It is important to note that, depending on the endowed or attained position, the same contractual arrangement could be a risk-increasing gamble for

The final elements in the choice system are the conservation equations. These take on almost trivially simple forms: in each separate time-state, the total social endowment must be conserved (under pure exchange).

The entire time-and-state choice-theoretic system, for the special case of pure exchange with a single present state and two future states, and excluding generation of "financial" assets, may be summarized in the equations below:

(8) $\qquad U^j = g(c_0^j, c_{1a}^j, c_{1b}^j; \pi_a^j, \pi_b^j)$ $\qquad$ Time-and-state Preference Function

This formulation emphasizes that utility depends upon the subjective probability estimates, $\pi_a^j$ and $\pi_b^j$.[27]

(9) $\qquad c_0^j + \dfrac{c_{1a}^j}{1 + r_{1a}} + \dfrac{c_{1b}^j}{1 + r_{1b}} = y_0^j + \dfrac{y_{1a}^j}{1 + r_{1a}} + \dfrac{y_{1b}^j}{1 + r_{1b}}$ $\qquad$ Wealth constraint

(10) $\qquad \left. \begin{array}{l} \dfrac{\partial c_{1a}^j}{\partial c_0^j}\bigg|_{U^j} = -(1 + r_{1a}) \\[2mm] \dfrac{\partial c_{1b}^j}{\partial c_0^j}\bigg|_{U^j} = -(1 + r_{1b}) \\[2mm] \dfrac{\partial c_{1b}^j}{\partial c_{1a}^j}\bigg|_{U^j} = -\dfrac{1 + r_{1b}}{1 + r_{1a}} \end{array} \right\}$ $\qquad$ Optimum conditions

(11) $\qquad \left. \begin{array}{l} \sum c_0^j = \sum y_0^j \\[2mm] \sum c_{1a}^j = \sum y_{1a}^j \\[2mm] \sum c_{1b}^j = \sum y_{1b}^j \end{array} \right\}$ $\qquad$ Conservation equations

A numerical illustration may help provide an intuitive grasp of the above relationships. Imagine a simple economy consisting of 100 identically situated individuals with one consumption commodity ("corn"). Each individual has an endowment distributed as follows: 100 bushels of present corn ($y_0$),

---

one person and a risk-decreasing insurance for another. A very clear case exists in the futures market, where the same contract can be either a hedge or a speculation, depending upon the risk status of the purchaser. (8, p. 527)

[27] But note that the subjective probability estimates nowhere appear in the equations directly, so that up to this point the formulation does not require the existence of subjective probabilities. Actually, it is not necessary to go behind the preference function in this way. After specifying the time-state consumption claims as the basic objects of choice, we could assert convexity of indifference curves as a generalization of ordinary consumption theory. This is indeed the line pursued by Arrow and Debreu, and has the advantage of parsimony of assumptions. On the other hand, explicit introduction of probabilities does enable us to derive results (e.g., about fair gambles) not otherwise attainable. For discussions of the conditions permitting the simultaneous identification of subjective probabilities and numerical utilities, see L. J. Savage, *The Foundations of Statistics* (New York: Wiley, 1954) and Jacques Drèze, "Fondements Logiques de la Probabilité Subjective et de L'Utilité," *La Décision* (Centre National de la Recherche Scientifique, Paris, 1961). (9, p. 528)

and contingent claims to the future crop $y_{1a} = 150$ and $y_{1b} = 50$. Thus, the individual is entitled to 150 bushels if state $a$ obtains, but only 50 bushels if state $b$ obtains—only these two states, regarded as equally probable, being considered possible for the future crop. In a pure-exchange situation, it is impossible to change these endowments by planting seed, carry-over of crop, or "consumption of capital"; individuals can only modify their positions by trading. If, however, all individuals have identical preferences in addition to identical endowments and identical (null) productive opportunities, the markets must establish a set of prices such that each individual is satisfied to hold his original endowment. Let the numeraire $P_0 = 1$, and assume that with this time-state distribution there is on the margin for each individual zero time preference with respect to certainties. Thus, denoting the price of a certainty as $P_1$, where necessarily $P_1 = P_{1a} + P_{1b}$, we have $P_1 = 1$. To deal with the contemporaneous choices in time "1", it will be convenient to define a cardinal utility $U_1$ which assigns a numerical value to probabilistic combinations by the use of the expected-utility theorem and an underlying Neumann-Morgenstern utility-of-income function $v(c_1)$. Then $U_1 = 1/2v(c_{1a}) + 1/2v(c_{1b})$. For concreteness, we may use a logarithmic formulation: $v(c_1) = \ln c_1$. It may then be verified that the indifference curves are rectangular hyperbolas on axes as in Figure VII with slope $-c_{1b}/c_{1a}$, or at the endowment point $-1/3$. It follows that $P_{1a} = 1/4$, and $P_{1b} = 3/4$, at which prices everyone prefers to hold his endowment rather than exchange it for any alternative combination. Our numerical assumptions have implied discount rates $r_{1a} = 300$ per cent and $r_{1b} = 33\frac{1}{3}$ per cent.

It is often illuminating to introduce the concept of the riskless ("pure") interest rate, which we have denoted $r_1$. This would represent the marginal *time* preference alone. The relation defining the riskless discount rate in terms of the more basic time-and-risk exchanges is:

$$\frac{1}{1 + r_1} = \frac{1}{1 + r_{1a}} + \frac{1}{1 + r_{1b}}.$$

This follows immediately from $P_1 = P_{1a} + P_{1b}$—that is, the price of a riskless holding is simply the sum of the prices of a corresponding holding for each possible contingency. It would then be possible to reformulate the choice situation in terms of future risky and future riskless assets. The set of objects of choice, instead of $(c_0, c_{1a}, c_{1b})$ would be $(c_0, c_1, c_{1x})$, where $c_1$ is the lesser of $c_{1a}$ and $c_{1b}$, and $c_{1x}$ is the excess of the greater over the lesser of these two. This route leads toward the asset-preference approach alluded to earlier; its disadvantage lies in obscuring the state in which the risky asset pays off (that is, it will in general make a difference to an individual if a unit of $c_{1x}$ represents a claim to time-state $1a$ or $1b$).

Waiving explicit introduction of productive opportunities, and generalizations to $T$ times and $S$ states, it is possible in a few sentences to sum up the main nature of the results yielded by the time-and-state-preference approach. The discount rates are determined by the interaction of individual attempts to move to preferred time-and-state consumption combinations by productive and financial transformations. The equilibrium rates will depend upon the composition of endowments among individuals, states, and times; the natures of the productive and financial opportunities; and the time-and-state preferences of individuals, these in turn being connected with their subjective probability estimates for the states. In the case of certainty the interest rate was determined by the interaction of endowments, time preferences, and time productivity. The additional elements entering under certainty are state endowments, state productivity, and state preferences. Probability opinions will enter into state preferences.

Corresponding to the theorem under certainty that all investors (barring corner solutions) adapt their subjective marginal rates of time preference to the market rate of interest is the following: each investor will adapt his marginal rate of time-and-state preference to the market discount rate for claims of the corresponding state and time. This conclusion indicates that it is not necessary to allow an additional degree of freedom in the form of the interposition of a "personal discount rate" to reach an optimum under certainty.[28] The error here is analogous to that sometimes committed of imposing a personal *time-preference* discount rate on future certain returns— whereas attainment of an optimum requires adjusting the marginal personal rate of time preference to the objective market rate.

## V. RISK AVERSION AND THE UNIQUENESS ASSUMPTION

In the section preceding, the observation of "nonspecialization" among time-state contingencies was employed to justify convex indifference curves between state incomes. The further assumption of uniqueness of the underlying Neumann-Morgenstern utility-of-income $v(c_1)$ function, for uncertain future consumption, led to a kind of symmetry of state preferences such that if the price ratio for state incomes $P_{1b}/P_{1a}$ is equal to the probability ratio $\pi_b/\pi_a$, the preferred combination will be along the certainty line. This last condition is the ordinary definition of risk aversion: given an initial combination along the certainty line, a fair gamble would not be accepted.[29]

But, it may be asked, if reasonable assumptions under the state-preference approach lead to risk aversion in the ordinary sense, what is the advantage of the approach over the mean, variability formulation that directly postulates aversion to variability risk? The crucial advantage, developed at length in the previous sections, is that time-state claims are commodities capable of being exchanged in markets—so that a complete choice-theoretic structure, including

---

[28] Lacking a formal solution to investment decision under uncertainty, Fisher recommended discounting anticipated future receipts by a personal "caution coefficient" (*Rate of Interest, op. cit.*, p. 215). The analysis here indicates that the interaction of personal time-and-risk preferences will establish a *market* time-and-risk discount rate, to which individuals will adjust on the margin. (1, p. 530)

[29] As mentioned above, the proviso about the initial situation being one of certainty should not be omitted. (2, p. 531)

conservation equations, can be constructed as in equations (8) through (11) above. Mean return and variability of return are not commodities in this sense, or at least there are as yet unresolved difficulties in regarding them as such. Furthermore, even in terms of the preference function alone, there is a gain in depth of understanding in deriving risk aversion from more fundamental considerations as compared with merely postulating it.[30] But the consideration to be examined further in this section is whether some types of behavior that seem to violate risk aversion can be rationalized in terms of the state-preference approach.

If one asked a responsible family man why he carries life insurance, presumably he would give a reply consistent with our risk-avoiding picture in Figure VII. Letting the state *a* represent the contingency "Breadwinner dies" and *b* the contingency "Breadwinner lives," our family man purchases life insurance to move his heirs in the direction of the certainty line. But a similarly thoughtful man, who happened to be a bachelor without family, would be unlikely to purchase insurance. Are we to say that he prefers risk? In a sense, perhaps, but it is more natural to explain his behavior by saying that a consumption opportunity contingent upon his death does not have the same appeal to the bachelor as it does to the family man.

This extreme case suggests the more general consideration that the utility-of-income function for any individual may not be invariant with respect to the state that obtains. It will be useful here to distinguish between true *gambles* (artificially generated risks, as at roulette) and natural *hazards*. There seems no reason to believe that anyone would rationally value consumption opportunities differently depending upon which end of a winning gamble he held. Money won on Black at roulette means exactly the same as an equivalent sum won on Red.[31] Therefore, within our model and ruling out pleasure-oriented gambling,[32] it continues to follow that fair *gambles* would never be accepted. A natural *hazard*, in contrast, will in general affect the external or internal context for choice by modifying the significance of the "same" consumption opportunity or sum of money.[33] We might say, somewhat

[30] In suppressing the information about the state-distributed composition of a particular combination being analyzed, essential information may be lost. One example would be the comparison of two-state prospects like (3, 1) and (6, 2)—where, for each combination, the first number gives the income for state *a* and the second for state *b*, the two states being equally probable. Evidently, the combination (6, 2) is dominant. But in terms of mean and variability measures this would not be evident, since (6, 2) has both a larger mean and a larger standard deviation. A somewhat related point is discussed in W. J. Baumol, "An Expected Gain-Confidence Limit Criterion for Portfolio Selection," *Management Science*, X (Oct. 1963). (3, p. 531)

[31] Though one of the appeals of long-shot betting may be that it provides more thrill and conversation value than an equivalent sum won on favorites. (4, p. 532)

[32] The successor to this article will consider the question of how observed gambling can be rationalized. (5, p. 532)

[33] A rather similar conception has been put forward and analyzed by Jacques Drèze, *loc. cit.* (6, p. 532)

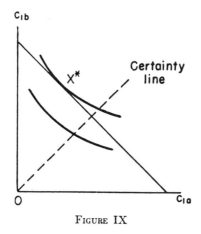

FIGURE IX

loosely, that states may vary in respect to "nonpecuniary income." As a result, state preferences for income become asymmetrical. For the bachelor in the above example, occurrence of the state " Death " eliminates practically any significance he might otherwise place upon titles to consumption. Again, a particular individual might weight his present choices in such a way as to have *more* income in depression· or famine than in prosperity, because he would then be able to assist his neighbors in their day of need. More typically, per- haps, we do not mind being poor so much if our neighbors (the Joneses) are also poor, since keeping up with them would then require less effort. The example cited in Section III, that an investor would not in general find the state-distributed portfolios (3, 2, 1) and (1, 2, 3) indifferent even if all three states were equally probable, would also be an instance of asymmetrical state preferences.

In all these cases we would observe risk-taking at fair odds in the sense that the preferred state distributions would not be along the certainty line (see Figure IX). But the reason is not nonconcavity of the $v(c_1)$ function—Neu- mann-Morgenstern risk preference—but rather nonuniqueness. That is, we would have to admit that, in general, we would have differing *conditional* utility-of-income functions $v_{1a}(c_{1a})$ and $v_{1b}(c_{1b})$. These separate functions can, however, be given a common scaling[34] so that we can find the utility of any prospect $(c_{1a}, c_{1b}; \pi_a, \pi_b)$ via the expected-utility theorem:

$$U(c_{1a}, c_{1b}; \pi_a, \pi_b) = \pi_a v_{1a}(c_{1a}) + \pi_b v_{1b}(c_{1b}).$$

Convexity of the state-distributed indifference curve follows, by the same reasoning employed in Section IV, making use again of the "independence" postulate which asserts that the marginal utilities of income in state *a* are unaffected by the level of consumption available for state *b*, and vice versa.

[34] See Appendix. (7, p. 533)

The equilibrium condition is

$$\frac{P_{1b}}{P_{1a}} = \frac{\pi_b v'_{1b}(c_{1b})}{\pi_a v'_{1a}(c_{1b})}.$$

However, since in general $v'_{1a}(c_{1a}) \neq v'_{1b}(c_{1b})$ when $c_{1a} = c_{1b}$, the tangencies will not occur on the certainty line, as was the case with a single utility-of-income function and consequent symmetrical state preferences.

The situation portrayed in Figure IX can be interpreted as indicating that in hazard situations people will be inclined to take risks. This is true in an actuarial sense (the decision-maker prefers at fair odds to move away from the certainty line), and yet the behavior remains essentially conservative. The "risk" is undertaken because quantitative equality of incomes in the two states does not properly balance the marginal utilities. We have shown, therefore, that the state-preference approach leads to a generalized concept which might be called "conservative behavior"—of which ordinary risk aversion in the sense of minimizing variability of outcome is only a special case.

## VI. CONCLUDING REMARK

One surprising aspect of the time-and-state preference model is that it leads to a theory of decision under uncertainty while entirely excluding the "vagueness" we usually associate with uncertainty.[35] Uncertainty in this model takes the form not of vagueness but rather of completely precise beliefs as to endowments, productive opportunities, etc., just as in the case of certainty—the only difference being that the beliefs span alternative possible states of the world as well as successive time periods. Again, precise beliefs as to the probabilities of these alternative states are assumed. The assumption that uncertainty takes the form of precise beliefs about alternative possible states of the world certainly lacks psychological verisimilitude to the mental state of confusion and doubt commonly experienced in this connection. It is generally recognized, however, that descriptive reality of assumptions is no essential criterion for a useful theory. So far as vagueness is concerned, we have already in our simplest timeless and riskless models assumed a precision in preference (as when we draw maps of indifference between shoes and apples) that can scarcely be regarded as closely descriptive of mental states. A similarly "unrealistic" or "depsychologized" portraying of uncertainty may really be what is required for comparably fruitful results in our analysis of risky choice.

## APPENDIX: SCALING OF UTILITY-OF-INCOME FUNCTIONS CONDITIONAL UPON STATE

We seek to show informally here that conditional utility-of-income functions, each defined for a particular state of the world, can nevertheless be

---

[35] Compare Fisher's declaration: "The third approximation cannot avoid some degree of vagueness" (*Theory of Interest, op. cit.*, p. 227). (8, p. 534)

given a common utility scaling consistent with the Neumann-Morgenstern postulates. In the case of a single (independent of state) utility-of-income function $v(c)$,[36] unique up to a linear transformation, a convenient scaling sets $v(0) = 0$, and $v(\overline{M}) = 1$, where $\overline{M}$ is the maximum income (consumption) level contemplated. The scaling used here will preserve analogues of these properties, for a hazard situation consisting of two alternative states of the world $a$ and $b$ $(\pi_a + \pi_b = 1)$, and where $v_a(c_a)$ is not identical with $v_b(c_b)$. As before, the elemental object of choice is a *conditional* claim to consumption in a specified state of the world. The "independence axiom" continues to apply: that is, $v_a(c_a)$ is independent of $c_b$, and *vice versa*.

To fix our desired scaling, it will suffice to assign utility values to two incomes on each conditional function: specifically to fix $v_a(0)$, $v_b(0)$, $v_a(\overline{M})$, and $v_b(\overline{M})$. We wish to continue assigning the utility value 1 to the certain receipt of $\overline{M}$, and the value 0 to the certain receipt of 0. Writing this in prospect notation, and using the expected-utility theorem:

$$U(\overline{M}, \overline{M}; \pi_a, \pi_b) = 1 = \pi_a v_a(\overline{M}) + \pi_b v_b(\overline{M})$$

$$U(0, 0; \pi_a, \pi_b) = 0 = \pi_a v_a(0) + \pi_b v_b(0).$$

We may now denote by the symbols $X_a$ and $X_b$ the prospects $(X, 0; \pi_a, \pi_b)$ and $(0, X; \pi_a, \pi_b)$, respectively. We can then adopt the scaling rule $v_a(X) = U(X_a)/\pi_a$, and similarly for $v_b(X)$. It follows immediately that $v_a(0) = v_b(0) = 0$, since $0_a$ and $0_b$ are identical and both have utility value zero; we may call this principle the Equivalence of Nulls. The interpretation is that, since we cannot do worse than zero in either state, a title or claim to zero in a particular state is worthless. Note that this does not deny that we might be happier with zero in state $a$ (should state $a$ obtain) than with zero in state $b$ (should state $b$ obtain) —but we cannot in fact ever be offered a choice among states, but only among claims to income conditional upon states occurring.

By the ordering postulate,[37] the individual can compare $\overline{M}_a$ with $\overline{M}_b$, and they need not be indifferent. Suppose he prefers the former. Then, by the continuity postulate[38] there is some probability $\pi$ (in a pure gamble) such that $\overline{M}_b$ is indifferent to a lottery ticket offering $\overline{M}_a$ or zero.[39] Thus:

$$U(0, \overline{M}; \pi_a, \pi_b) = U[(\overline{M}, 0; \pi_a, \pi_b), 0; \pi, 1 - \pi]$$

$$\pi_b v_b(\overline{M}) = \pi \pi_a v_a(\overline{M}).$$

Using the property that the certain receipt of $\overline{M}$ has utility 1, we get the results $v_a(\overline{M}) = 1/(\pi_a + \pi_a \pi)$ and $v_b(\overline{M}) = \pi/(\pi_b + \pi_b \pi)$. The import of this

---

[36] The time subscript will be dropped in this Appendix, which deals only with utility functions for synchronous decisions. (9, p. 534)

[37] Luce and Raiffa, *op. cit.*, p. 25. (1, p. 535)

[38] *Ibid.*, p. 27. (1, p. 535)

[39] This $\pi$ is a variable in an artificial gamble constructed to test preferences, whereas $\pi_a$ and $\pi_b$ are to be regarded as constants by nature (or at least by belief) in a real hazard situation. (1, p. 535)

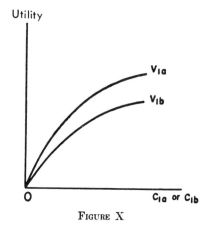

FIGURE X

is that we are now able, in principle, to use the two points thus provided for each state so as to construct in Figure X two separate curves, $v_{1a}(c_{1a})$ and $v_{1b}(c_{1b})$, to serve as *conditional* utility-of-income scales. The expected-utility theorem can then be used with these scales to calculate the over-all preference ordering of any income distribution over these states.

## 6. RULES FOR ORDERING UNCERTAIN PROSPECTS

JOSEF HADAR and WILLIAM R. RUSSELL*

Reprinted by permission of the authors and publisher from *The American Economic Review*, Vol. LIX, No. 1 (March 1969) pp. 25–34.

In many theoretical as well as practical situations one is frequently confronted with the necessity (or at least desirability) of making a prediction about a decision maker's preference (choice) between given pairs of uncertain alternatives without having any knowledge of the decision maker's utility function. Various approaches to this and related problems have appeared in the literature, the most popular of which involve comparisons of means and variances

* The authors are associate professors of economics at Case Western Reserve University and the University of Kentucky, respectively. They have benefitted from discussions with Richard Evans, Jan Kmenta, William Pierskalla, James Ramsey, and Thomas Saving. They are especially grateful to the referee for his helpful suggestions.

of the probability of distributions in question. Examples of these approaches are the works of Harry Markowitz [3] and James Tobin [6] [7]. It turns out, however, that since expected utility is, in general, a function of *all* the moments of the probability distribution, rules of comparison involving only two moments are valid only for limited classes of utility functions, or for special distributions. It is well known, for instance, that, if the utility function is quadratic, then only the mean and the variance enter into the calculation of expected utility. In that case the decision maker will always prefer the prospect with the lower variance (if he is a risk averter), given that the prospects under consideration have identical means; or prefer the prospect with the higher mean so long as the variances are the same. More generally, H. M. Markowitz [3] and Marcel Richter [5] have shown that, if the utility function is an $n$th-degree polynomial, then the first $n$ moments have to be considered. But it is clear that, if two distributions differ in all of their first $n$ moments, then in order to determine preference for these distributions, one needs to know the magnitudes as well as the signs of the $n$ derivatives of the utility function. In general, economists are reluctant to impose this many restrictions on the utility function because of the severe loss of generality incurred by such restrictions.

Thus, except for such special cases as the quadratic utility function, the specification of distributions in terms of their moments is not likely to yield strong results, essentially because information about the moments cannot be utilized efficiently for the purpose of ordering uncertain prospects under conditions in which the utility function is unknown. In this paper we propose two rules which are more powerful than the "moment method." Under the stronger of these rules, distributions may be ordered according to preference, given *any* utility function, while under the weaker rule orderability obtains for any utility function which exhibits nonincreasing marginal utility everywhere.

## I. PRELIMINARY DISCUSSION

Since in this paper we are concerned only with individuals who maximize expected utility, we may briefly go back to the axioms of expected utility maximization in order to show how these axioms are related to the proposed rules. Let $u_a$ and $u_b$ denote the utilities, respectively, of prospects $a$ and $b$, and assume $u_a < u_b$. (The prospects $a$ and $b$ may be either payoffs offered with certainty, or uncertain prospects; in the latter case the notation $u_a$ and $u_b$ should be interpreted as expected utilities.) If $\alpha$ and $\beta$ are probabilities, and $\alpha < \beta$, then it follows from the so-called independence axiom that

(1) $$(1 - \beta)u_a + \beta u_b > (1 - \alpha)u_a + \alpha u_b.^1$$

This preference between two prospects with identical payoffs has an intuitively appealing explanation: between any two uncertain prospects such as the

---

[1] For the proof see John von Neumann and Oskar Morgenstern [8, p. 618].

above, an individual will always prefer that prospect in which the probability of receiving the preferred payoff is higher. In fact, it may be helpful to suggest here that the preferred prospect in the above example may be thought of as having been constructed from the inferior prospect by a redistribution of probabilities from the lower payoff to the higher payoff.

Consider now a similar situation for $n$-payoff prospects. The utilities are denoted by $u_i$, and they are labeled in the order of their magnitudes; i.e., $u_i > u_j$ if and only if $i > j$. The respective probabilities are denoted by $\alpha_i$ and $\beta_i$. The following question may then be posed: Given an uncertain prospect with utilities $u_i$, $i = 1, 2, \ldots, n$, and respective probabilities $\alpha_i$, $i = 1, 2, \ldots, n$, is it possible to construct another uncertain prospect with the same utilities, and with probabilities $\beta_i$, $i = 1, 2, \ldots, n$, such that it will be preferred to the former prospect by any expected-utility-maximizing individual? The clue to how this can be done is, of course, to be found in the above two-payoff example; namely, by a redistribution of probabilities towards the higher payoffs. Thus, if we assume

$$(2) \qquad \begin{cases} \alpha_i > \beta_i, \alpha_k < \beta_k & \text{where } j < k, \\ \alpha_i = \beta_i & \text{for all } i,\ i \neq j,\ k, \end{cases}$$

then the new prospect is preferred to the initial one; i.e.,

$$(3) \qquad \sum_{i=1}^{n} \beta_i u_i > \sum_{i=1}^{n} \alpha_i u_i.$$

This result follows directly from (1); if we subtract

$$\sum_{\substack{i=1 \\ i \neq j \\ i \neq k}}^{n} a_i u_i$$

from both sides of the inequality in (3), then we obtain an inequality between two two-payoff prospects similar to that given in (1).

The concentration of probabilities at the higher payoffs which distinguishes the preferred prospects from the inferior ones in both (1) and (3) can be given a more formal characterization. We note that $\beta_i \leqq \alpha_i$, $i = 1, 2, \ldots j, \ldots, k - 1$, by assumption (2), hence

$$\sum_{i=1}^{k-1} \beta_i < \sum_{i=1}^{k-1} \alpha_i.$$

But since we also have $\beta_i = \alpha_i$, $i = k + 1, k + 2, \ldots, n$, it follows that

$$\sum_{i=1}^{r} \beta_i = \sum_{i=1}^{r} \alpha_i, \qquad r = k, k + 1, \ldots, n.$$

Therefore the following condition holds:

$$\sum_{i=1}^{r} \beta_i \leqq \sum_{i=1}^{r} \alpha_i \qquad r = 1, 2, \dots, n.$$

In words, the value of the cumulative distribution of the preferred prospect never exceeds that of the inferior prospect. This condition is known as *stochastic dominance*, and so we say that the preferred distributions (prospects) in examples (1) and (3) are *stochastically larger* than the inferior distributions (prospects).

It is clear that, in the absence of any specification of the utility function, the construction of a prospect that is preferred to any given prospect can be accomplished only by making use of condition (1), i.e., by a redistribution of probabilities toward the higher payoffs. While we demonstrated only one such construction in example (3), it should be obvious that by following this procedure iteratively, one can construct as many preferred prospects as one may desire; and it will, of course, be true, because of the transitivity of preferences, that all such prospects will be preferred to the original prospect. The above illustrations clearly show that there exists a close relationship between stochastic dominance, on the one hand, and preference between uncertain prospects on the other. In fact, this relationship can be stated more precisely in the form of two propositions, each of which is the converse of the other:

*Proposition 1.* Given any two prospects $P$ and $P'$, if $P$ is stochastically larger than $P'$, then $P$ is preferred to $P'$, regardless of the specifications of the utility function.

*Proposition 2.* Given any two prospects $P$ and $P'$, if $P$ is preferred to $P'$ for all utility functions, then $P$ is stochastically larger than $P'$.

The above propositions have been proved by James Quirk and Rubin Saposnik [4] for prospects with a finite number of payoffs. We provide proofs for discrete as well as continuous distributions. But more important, we show that the set of orderable distributions can be enlarged by placing a (frequently invoked) restriction on the utility function. The second set of results of this paper shows that, if the utility function has nonincreasing marginal utility everywhere, then propositions such as the above can be proved for pairs of distributions which satisfy a condition that is weaker than stochastic dominance.

## II. FORMAL RESULTS

First, we introduce the concept of stochastic dominance in a formal manner. Strictly speaking, since we are using two different types of dominance in this paper, we shall modify the accepted terminology slightly. Let $f$ and $g$ denote the probability functions of a (discrete or continuous) random variable taking the values $x_i$, or $x$, and let $F(x_i)$ and $G(x_i)$ be the respective cumulative distributions. Throughout the paper we shall adopt the convention of labeling the values of the random variable in accordance with their magnitudes; i.e., $x_i > x_j$ if and only if $i > j$. The set of the $x_i$ is denoted by $X$.

The first definition is that of *first-degree stochastic dominance* (FSD) which is the same concept as that which in the literature is known simply as stochastic dominance.[2] This condition holds between any two distributions whenever one cumulative distribution lies entirely, or partly, above the other.

*Definition 1.*   The probability function $g$ is said to be at least as large as $f$ in the sense of FSD if and only if

$$G(x_i) \leq F(x_i) \quad \text{for all } x_i \in X.$$

The second dominance condition is weaker than FSD, and we refer to it as *second-degree stochastic dominance* (SSD). It holds whenever the area under one cumulative distribution is equal to, or larger than, that under the other cumulative distribution.

*Definition 2.*   The probability function $g$ is said to be at least as large as $f$ in the sense of SSD if and only if

$$\sum_{i=1}^{r} G(x_i)\Delta x_i \leq \sum_{i=1}^{r} F(x_i)\Delta x_i \quad \text{for all } r < n,$$

where $\Delta x_i = x_{i+1} - x_i$, and $x_n$ is the largest value taken by the random variable. If the random variable is continuous, taking its value in the closed interval $I = x_1 - x_n$, then the above inequality takes the form

$$\int_{x_1}^{x} G(y)\, dy \leqq \int_{x_1}^{x} F(y)\, dy \quad \text{for all } x \in I.$$

It is easy to verify that FSD implies SSD.

Throughout the paper it is assumed that the random variable is one-dimensional.

## 1. ORDERABILITY UNDER FSD

In this section we are concerned with preference among uncertain prospects under conditions in which the utility function is not restricted in any essential fashion. More precisely, we shall consider utility functions $u = \phi(x)$ that are members of the set $U_1$, where $U_1 = \{\phi(x): \sigma \in D_1(x_1, x_n), \phi' > 0\}$, $D_1(x_1, x_n)$ represents the set of all functions that are continuous and have a continuous first derivative in the closed interval $I = x_1 - x_n$, and $\phi' = d\phi/dx$. At first we confine ourselves to probability distributions in which the random variable assumes only a finite number of distinct values, the latter being denoted by $x_i, i = 1, 2, \ldots, n$. We consider any two discrete probability functions defined on $X$, and write these as $f(x_i) = \alpha_i$, and $g(x_i) = \beta_i$. The respective cumulative distributions are given by

---

[2] For the definition and certain applications of this concept see e.g. [1] and [2].

$$F(x_i) = \sum_{i=1}^{r} f(x_r), \quad \text{and} \quad G(x_t) = \sum_{i=1}^{r} g(x_r).$$

*Theorem 1.* If $g$ is at least as large as $f$ in the sense of FSD, then $g$ is at least as preferred as $f$; i.e., if $G(x_i) \leq F(x_i)$ for all $x_i \in X$, then $\bar{u}_g - \bar{u}_f \geq 0$ for all $\phi \in U_1$, where

$$\bar{u}_j = \sum_{i=1}^{n} \alpha_i \phi(x_i), \quad \text{and} \quad \bar{u}_g = \sum_{i=1}^{n} \beta_i \phi(x_i).$$

*Proof.* Using the Theorem of the Mean it can be shown that

(4) $$\phi(x_i) = \phi(x_n) - \sum_{r=i}^{n-1} \phi'(\xi_r)\Delta x_r \quad i = 1, 2, \ldots, n - 1,$$

where $\xi_r$ is a properly chosen point between $x_r$ and $x_{r+1}$, and $\Delta x_r$ as defined in Definition 2. Since

$$\bar{u}_g - \bar{u}_f = \sum_{i=1}^{n} (\beta_i - \alpha_i)\phi(x_i),$$

we have

(5) $$\bar{u}_g - \bar{u}_f = \sum_{i=1}^{n} [\phi(x_n) - \sum_{r=i}^{n-1} \phi'(\xi_r)\Delta x_r](\beta_i - \alpha_i)$$

$$= -\sum_{r=1}^{n-1} \phi'(\xi_r) [G(x_r) - F(x_r)]\Delta x_r \geq 0.$$

The above inequality follows directly from the fact that $\phi' > 0$ and $\Delta x_r > 0$ by definition, while $[G(x_r) - F(x_r)] \leq 0$ by the hypothesis of FSD. It is also clear that, given the dominance condition, $g$ will be *strictly* preferred to $f$ if and only if $f$ and $g$ are different functions, in which case we have $[G(x_r) - F(x_r)] < 0$ for at least one $r$.

It should be pointed out here that a result such as (5), or (10) below, may be obtained not only for differences between expected utilities, but also for differences between the expectations of any monotonically increasing function (since monotonicity was the only property of $\phi(x)$ used in the above proof). In particular, since the functions $x^k$, $k = 1, 3, 5, \ldots$, are monotonic functions for all $x \in I$, it follows immediately that, if $g$ is at least as large as $f$ in the sense of FSD, then all the odd moments around zero of $g$ are at least as large as the respective moments of $f$. In the special case in which the domain of definition $I$ is a subset of the nonnegative half-line, then *all* the moments around zero of the dominant distribution are at least as large as the respective moments of the inferior distribution.

We now prove the converse of Theorem 1.

*Theorem 2.* If $g$ is preferred to $f$ for all utility functions, then $g$ is larger than $f$ in the sense of FSD; i.e., if $\bar{u}_g - \bar{u}_f > 0$ for all $\phi \in U_1$, then $G(x)_i \leq$

$F(x_i)$ for all $x_i \in X$, the strict inequality holding for at least one $x_i \in X$.

*Proof.* The proof is by contradiction. It is shown that, if the conclusion of the theorem fails to hold, then there exists a utility function in $U_1$ for which the hypothesis of the theorem is contradicted. For this purpose it is sufficient to assume that there exists $x_k \in X$, $x_k > x_1$ such that

$$G(x_i) \geq F(x_i) \quad \text{for } x_1 \leq x_i \leq x_k,$$

and

$$G(x_i) \leq F(x_i) \quad \text{for } x_k \leq x_i \leq x_n.$$

Consider the utility function (6) shown below. The parameters $a$ and $b$ may be chosen freely, subject only to the condition $a > b > 0$. Differentiating (6) with respect to $x$ gives equation (7). It is easily verified that $\phi \in U_1$. But by virtue of (5) we now have equation (8). Clearly, the first sum on the right-hand side of (8) is nonnegative, while the second sum is nonpositive. Furthermore, each of the terms $(A + B\xi_r)$ is an increasing function of the parameter $a$, hence the magnitude of the first sum can be made arbitrarily large by making $a$ sufficiently large. Therefore there exists a utility function in $U_1$, for which $\bar{u}_g - \bar{u}_f \leq 0$.[3]

$$(6) \quad \phi(x) = \begin{cases} \dfrac{x_k^2(b - a)}{2(x_k - x_1)} + \dfrac{(ax_k - bx_1)x}{(x_k - x_1)} + \dfrac{(b - a)x^2}{2(x_k - x_1)} & \text{for } x_1 \leq x \leq x_k, \\ bx & \text{for } x_k \leq x \leq x_n, \end{cases}$$

$$(7) \quad \phi'(x) = \begin{cases} \dfrac{(ax_k - bx_1)}{(x_k - x_1)} + \dfrac{(b - a)x}{(x_k - x_1)} & \text{for } x_1 \leq x \leq x_k, \\ b & \text{for } x_k \leq x \leq x_n. \end{cases}$$

$$(8) \quad \bar{u}_g - \bar{u}_f = - \sum_{r=1}^{k-1} (A + B\xi_r)[G(x_r) - F(x_r)]\Delta x_r - \sum_{r=k}^{n-1} b[G(x_r) - F(x_r)]\Delta x_r,$$

where

$$A = \frac{(ax_k - bx_1)}{(x_k - x_1)}, \quad \text{and} \quad B = \frac{(b - a)}{(x_k - x_1)}.$$

Since many economic variables (such as profit, income, rate of return, wealth, etc.) are continuous in nature, we feel that it is useful to provide also the continuous versions of the above theorems. For this purpose we need not redefine the concept of FSD, except that we now think of $f$ and $g$ as probability density functions. The latter, as well as the utility function $\phi(x)$, are

---

[3] For alternative proofs of Theorems 1 and 2 see Quirk and Saposnik [4].

defined on the interval $I = x_1 - x_n$.[4]

*Theorem 1'.*   If $G(x) \le F(x)$ for all $x \in I$, then $\bar{u}_g - \bar{u}_f \ge 0$ for all $\phi \in u_1$.

*Proof.*   By definition

(9) $$\bar{u}_g - \bar{u}_f = \int_{x_1}^{x_n} \phi(x) \, [g(x) - f(x)] \, dx.$$

Integrating by parts gives

(10) $$\bar{u}_g - \bar{u}_f = \phi(x) \, [G(x) - F(x)] \, \Big|_{x_1}^{x_n} - \int_{x_1}^{x_n} \phi'(x) \, [G(x) - F(x)] \, dx$$

$$= - \int_x^{x_n} \phi'(x) \, [G(x) - F(x)] \, dx \ge 0.$$

Here we see again that $g$ will be strictly preferred to $f$ if and only if the two density functions are not identical.

*Theorem 2'.*   If $\bar{u}_g - \bar{u}_f > 0$ for all $\phi \in U_1$, then $G(x) \le F(x)$ for all $x \in I$, the strict inequality holding for at least one $x \in I$.

*Proof.*   The proof is similar to that of Theroem 2. Suppose that there exists $x_k \in I$, $x_k > x_1$, such that $G(x) \ge F(x)$ for $x_1 \le x \le x_k$, and $G(x) \le F(x)$ for $x_k \le x \le x_n$. Then for the utility function given in (6) we have by virtue of (10)

(11) $$\bar{u}_g - \bar{u}_f = - \int_{x_1}^{x_k} (A + Bx) \, [G(x) - F(x)] \, dx - \int_{x_k}^{x_n} b[G(x) - F(x)] \, dx,$$

$A$ and $B$ as defined in the proof of Theorem 2. It is obvious again that, by choosing $a$ sufficiently large, the expression in (11) can be made nonpositive.

The most important implication of Theorems 1 and 2 (or 1' and 2') is the fact that, when no restrictions are placed on the utility function, then FSD is necessary and sufficient for preference among pairs of uncertain prospects. In other words, FSD is the weakest condition that will guarantee preference for one prospect over another for all utility functions in the set $U_1$. The significance of this result is discussed further in Section III below. At this point we turn to the problem of ordering uncertain prospects under the weaker of the two dominance conditions.

---

[4] The assumption that the range of the random variable is finite is not really a serious assumption, since the range can always be made as large as one may desire. After all, the maximum amount of income or wealth that an individual may either gain or lose is always finite. As a matter of fact, however, the results can also be proved for conditions under which the domain of definition is allowed to go to infinity. But since the proof then requires the introduction of fairly technical arguments that are likely to becloud the conceptual substance of the proposed rules, we felt that it was desirable not to do so in the present paper.

## 2. ORDERABILITY UNDER SSD

In this section we consider utility functions with nonincreasing marginal utility. More precisely, we are concerned with preference among uncertain prospects for all utility functions $u = \phi(x)$ in the set $U_2$, where $U_2 = \{\phi(x): \phi \in D_2(x_1, x_n), \phi' > 0, \phi'' \leq 0\}$, $D_2(x_1, x_n)$ is the set of all continuous functions with continuous derivatives of order one and two in the closed interval $I = x_1 - x_n$, and $\phi'' = d^2\phi/dx^2$. Utility functions that are members of $U_2$ exhibit what is known as weak global risk aversion.[5] We prove theorems similar to those in Section 1 above, starting with the discrete case.

*Theorem 3.* If $g$ is at least as large as $f$ in the sense of SSD, and marginal utility is everywhere nonincreasing, then $g$ is at least as preferred as $f$, i.e., if

$$\sum_{i=1}^{r} G(x_i)\Delta x_i \leq \sum_{i=1}^{r} F(x_i)\Delta x_i$$

for all $r < n$, then $\bar{u}_g - \bar{u}_f \geq 0$ for all $\phi \in U_2$.

*Proof.* Applying the Theorem of the Mean in a fashion similar to that which led to equation (4), we have

$$(12) \qquad \phi'(\xi_r) = \phi'(\xi_{n-1}) - \sum_{s=r}^{n-2} \phi''(\eta_s)\Delta\xi_s \qquad r = 1, 2, \ldots, n - 2,$$

where $\eta_s$ is a properly chosen point between $\xi_s$ and $\xi_{s+1}$, and $\Delta\xi_s = \xi_{s+1} - \xi_s$. Substituting for the $\phi'(\xi_r)$ in (5) from (12) yields

$$(13) \quad \bar{u}_g - \bar{u}_f = -\sum_{r=1}^{n-1} [\phi'(\xi_{n-1}) - \sum_{s=r}^{n-2} \phi''(\eta_s)\Delta\xi_s] [G(x_r) - F(x_r)]\Delta x_r$$

$$= -\phi'(\xi_{n-1}) \sum_{r=1}^{n-1} [G(x_r) - F(x_r)]\Delta x_r$$

$$+ \sum_{s=r}^{n-2} \phi''(\eta_s)\Delta\xi_s \sum_{r=1}^{n-1} [G(x_r) - F(x_r)]\Delta x_r \geq 0.$$

We may point out one implication of the result in (13): if SSD holds between any two distributions, then, just as in the case of FSD, the mean of the dominant distribution is at least as large as that of the other distribution, but the SSD condition imposes no general restrictions on the relative magnitudes of the higher moments of the distributions in question. It follows, therefore, that the set of distributions that can be ordered by means of SSD is, in general, larger than that which may be ordered by means of FSD. Moreover, SSD is

---

[5] That is, a decision maker whose preferences are represented by a utility function in $U_2$ will never prefer an uncertain prospect $P$ over a certain payoff which is equal to the expected value of $P$.

also necessary for preference among uncertain prospects for all utility functions in $U_2$. Hence we can prove the converse of Theorem 3.

*Theorem 4.* If $g$ is preferred to $f$ for all utility functions with nonincreasing marginal utility, then $g$ is larger than $f$ in the sense of SSD; i.e., if $\bar{u}_g - \bar{u}_f > 0$ for all $\phi \in U_2$, then

$$\sum_{i=1}^{r} G(x_i)\Delta x_i \leq \sum_{i=1}^{r} F(x_i)\Delta x_i$$

for all $r < n$, the strict inequality holding for at least one value of $r$.

$$(14) \quad \phi(x) = \begin{cases} -\dfrac{ax_k^3}{6(x_k - x_1)} + \left[\dfrac{ax_k^2}{2(x_k - x_1)} + b\right] x - \dfrac{ax_k x^2}{2(x_k - x_1)} \\ \qquad\qquad\qquad\qquad\qquad\qquad + \dfrac{ax^3}{6(x_k - x_1)} \\ \qquad\qquad\qquad\qquad\quad \text{for } x_1 \leq x \leq x_k, \\ bx \qquad\qquad\qquad\qquad\quad \text{for } x_k \leq x \leq x_n, \end{cases}$$

$$(15) \quad \phi'(x) = \begin{cases} \dfrac{ax_k^2}{2(x_k - x_1)} + b - \dfrac{ax_k x}{(x_k - x_1)} + \dfrac{ax^2}{2(x_k - x_1)} & \text{for } x_1 \leq x \leq x_k, \\ b & \text{for } x_k \leq x \leq x_n, \end{cases}$$

$$(16) \quad \phi''(x) = \begin{cases} -\dfrac{ax_k}{(x_k - x_1)} + \dfrac{ax}{(x_k - x_1)} & \text{for } x_1 \leq x \leq x_k, \\ 0 & \text{for } x_k \leq x \leq x_n. \end{cases}$$

*Proof.* We once more use a proof by contradiction. To simplify notation let

$$H(x_i) = \sum_{r=1}^{i} [G(x_r) - F(x_r)]\Delta x_r.$$

Suppose that there exists $x_k \in X$, $x_k > x_1$ such that $H(x)_i \geq 0$ for $x_1 \leq x_i \leq x_k$, and $H(x_i) \leq 0$ for $x_k \leq x_i \leq x_n$. Consider the utility function shown in (14) above, where $a$ and $b$ are freely chosen positive parameters. Differentiating (14) gives (15) and differentiating (15) yields (16) above. It is obvious that $\phi(x) \in U_2$. Now, however, we have

$$(17) \quad \bar{u}_g - \bar{u}_f = -\phi'(\xi_{n-1}) H(x_{n-1}) + \sum_{s=r}^{k-2} (A + B\eta_s)\Delta\xi_s H(x_{n-1}),$$

where

$$A = \frac{-ax_k}{(x_k - x_1)} \quad \text{and} \quad B = \frac{a}{(x_k - x_1)}.$$

The first term on the right-hand side of (17) is nonnegative, while the sum in

(17) is nonpositive. But each of the terms $[A + B\eta_s]$ is an increasing function of the parameter $a$, hence the magnitude of the sum can be made as large as desired by choosing $a$ sufficiently large. Therefore there exists a utility function in $U_2$ for which the hypothesis of the theorem is contradicted.

The last two theorems are the continuous versions of Theorems 3 and 4.

*Theorem 3'.*   If

$$\int_{x_1}^{x} G(y)\, dy \le \int_{x_1}^{x} F(y)\, dy$$

for all $x \in I$, then $\bar{u}_g - \bar{u}_f \ge 0$ for all $\phi \in U_2$.

*Proof.*   Integration by parts yields

$$(18) \quad \int_{x_1}^{x_n} \phi'(x)\, [G(x) - F(x)]\, dx = \phi'(x) \int_{x_1}^{x} [G(y) - F(y)]\, dy \, \Big|_{x_1}^{x_n}$$

$$- \int_{x_1}^{x_n} \phi''(x) \int_{x_1}^{x} [G(y) - F(y)]\, dy\, dx.$$

Substituting for the integral in (10) from (18) gives

$$(19) \quad \bar{u}_g - \bar{u}_f = -\phi'(x) \int_{x_1}^{x} [G(y) - F(y)]\, dy \, \Big|_{x_1}^{x_n}$$

$$+ \int_{x_1}^{x_n} \phi''(x) \int_{x_1}^{x} [G(y) - F(y)]\, dy\, dx \ge 0.$$

*Theorem 4'.*   If $\bar{u}_g - \bar{u}_f > 0$ for all $\phi \in U_2$, then

$$\int_{x_1}^{x} G(y)\, dy \le \int_{x_1}^{x} F(y)\, dy$$

for all $x \in I$, the strict inequality holding for at least one $x \in I$.

*Proof.*   The proof is similar to that of Theorem 4. To simplify notation let

$$H(x) = \int_{x_1}^{x} [G(y) - F(y)]\, dy.$$

Suppose that there exists $x_k \in I$, $x_k > x_1$ such that $H(x) \ge 0$ for $x_1 \le x \le x_k$, and $H(x) \le 0$ for $x_k \le x \le x_n$. Then for the utility function given in (14) we have by virtue of (19)

$$(20) \quad \bar{u}_g - \bar{u}_f = -bH(x_n) + \int_{x_1}^{x_k} (A + Bx)H(x)\, dx,$$

$A$ and $B$ as defined in the proof of Theorem 4. It is clear that, by choosing $a$ sufficiently large, the expression in (20) can be made nonpositive.

## III. SUMMARY AND CONCLUSION

One of the objectives of this paper was to suggest a set of rules for ordering uncertain prospects; that is, to specify conditions which will permit us to make predictions about preference. The single most important property of these rules is that they are not only sufficient, but also necessary for the respective class of utility functions. For example, in the absence of any restriction on the utility function (except monotonicity), we find that FSD implies preference. But at the same time, if an uncertain prospect is known to be preferred over another prospect for all monotonic utility functions, then FSD must hold. This means essentially that a state of preference implies something about the characteristics of the prospects in question. Thus by means of the FSD condition we can not only predict preference, but we can also make a statement about the characteristics of the uncertain prospects. For instance, we have indicated in the paper that FSD implies a certain relationship between the odd moments (and sometimes also between the even moments) of the prospects under consideration. Consequently, given that $P$ is preferred to $P'$ for all monotonic utility functions, we can immediately say that all the odd moments around zero of $P$ are larger than the respective moments of $P'$.

Similar relationships hold with respect to the SSD condition if the utility function is assumed to be concave. In fact, since SSD is a weaker condition than FSD, it is capable of ordering a larger set of distributions than that which is orderable under FSD. Indeed, the theorems that make use of SSD may be more important than those involving FSD because of the central position occupied by the concavity assumption. Not only is this assumption widely used in the literature, it is in fact a necessary condition for the existence of a maximum in a large class of problems involving the maximization of expected utility. Certainly, it is obvious that any result within the framework of the theory of risk aversion can be established directly by means of SSD. Conversely, any case of preference under risk aversion must imply SSD; if the latter condition fails to hold, then the result must necessarily be due to a special assumption about the functional form of the utility function.

Since FSD and SSD are both necessary and sufficient, rules involving the latter conditions must be superior to those involving comparisons of moments. The latter rules, as is well known, yield conclusive results only for a special class of utility functions (e.g., quadratic), or for special distributions (e.g., those depending only on mean and variance). The generality of the latter rules is, therefore, severely restricted. In fact, in those cases in which the application of the moment method is made possible by confining consideration to a special class of distributions, the utility function being either unrestricted or assumed concave, any determinate results must imply SSD, or even FSD, depending on the assumption about the utility function. If so, the same results can be established by using one of the dominance conditions directly, thereby, obviating the necessity of imposing a restriction on the class of admissible distributions. Since no such restriction is required in the application of the dominance conditions, it is clear that the moment method is, on the whole, less powerful as a means of ordering uncertain prospects.

The weakness inherent in methods involving comparisons of means and variances also manifests itself in Markowitz's efficiency frontier. For example, suppose we consider the case of global risk aversion. Then the true efficiency frontier consists of a set of prospects with no two prospects in that set satisfying the SSD condition (since otherwise there is preference, in which case both prospects cannot be on the frontier). But the Markowitz frontier may not satisfy this requirement. All we know about the latter frontier is that, between any two prospects on the frontier, one has a higher mean as well as a higher variance than the other prospect. However, it is not difficult to think of (or construct) examples of distributions where the one with the higher mean and variance is larger than the other in the sense of SSD (or FSD). It may, therefore, very well be the case that some pairs of distributions on the Markowitz frontier are in fact orderable by means of either SSD or FSD, in which case at least one prospect of each such pair does not belong on the frontier. Conversely, prospects that are off the Markowitz frontier could possibly be members of the true frontier set inasmuch as they may be neither larger nor smaller in the sense of either SSD or FSD than any other prospect on the frontier.[6]

On the practical level, the use of either FSD or SSD should prove to be the the most direct and efficient approach to a large number of specific problems. As was pointed out in Section I, the imposition of FSD is equivalent to a redistribution of probabilities from lower payoffs to higher payoffs; in terms of the cumulative distributions, it amounts to lowering the values of the cumulative distribution (relative to some other distribution) for some values of the random variable without raising them at any other points. Consequently, in order to test for the existence of FSD one needs only examine and compare the cumulative distributions of the prospects under consideration. The SSD condition, on the other hand, places a restriction on the areas under the respective cumulative distributions, and hence it may be applied with equal facility. We thus see that both FSD and SSD are specifications of the type that may be easily applied to actual problems since they are defined in terms of the very same concepts which are customarily used for the description of uncertain prospects.

In concluding, we may emphasize again that the superiority of the FSD and SSD conditions derives directly from the fact that these conditions are both necessary and sufficient, given the class of admissible utility functions. Thus, in the absence of any specification of the utility function, to say that prospect $P$ is larger than $P'$ in the sense of FSD is *equivalent* to saying that $P$ is preferred to $P'$ for all monotonic utility functions; and given risk aversion, to say that $P$ is larger than $P'$ in the sense of SSD is *equivalent* to saying that $P$

---

[6] For an example see Quirk and Saposnik [4].

is preferred to $P'$ for all concave utility functions. It is because of this equivalence relationship that the dominance conditions convey information which is more essential to the orderability of uncertain prospects than the information obtained from a comparison of moments. In fact, it is clear that any other rule that may yet be proposed cannot yield results that are stronger than those obtained from the use of either FSD or SSD. Thus any result about preference between uncertain prospects which is inconsistent with the theorems presented in this paper must be due to a more restrictive assumption about the utility function.

## REFERENCES

1. S. Karlin, "Dynamic Inventory Policy with Varying Stochastic Demands," *Manag. Sci.*, April 1960, *6*, 231–58.
2. E. L. Lehmann, "Ordered Families of Distributions," *Annals Math. Stat.*, Sept. 1955, *26*, 399–419.
3. H. M. Markowitz, *Portfolio Selection*. New York 1959.
4. J. P. Quirk and R. Saposnik, "Admissibility and Measurable Utility Functions," *Rev. Econ. Stud.*, 1962, *29*, 140–46.
5. M. K. Richter, "Cardinal Utility, Portfolio Selection and Taxation," *Rev. Econ. Stud.*, June 1960, *27*, 152–66.
6. J. Tobin, "Liquidity Preference as Behavior Toward Risk," *Rev. Econ. Stud.*, Feb. 1958, *25*, 65–86.
7. ———, "The Theory of Portfolio Selection," in F. H. Hahn and F. P. R. Brechling, eds., *The Theory of Interest Rates*. London 1965.
8. J. von Neumann and O. Morgenstern, *Theory of Games and Economic Behavior*. New York 1964.

# 7. RISK AVERSION IN THE SMALL AND IN THE LARGE[1]

JOHN W. PRATT*

Reprinted by permission of the author and publisher from *Econometrica*, Vol. 32, 1–2 (January–April 1964), pp. 122–136.

This paper concerns utility functions for money. A measure of risk aversion in the small, the risk premium or insurance premium for an arbitrary risk, and a natural concept of decreasing risk aversion are discussed and related to one another. Risks are also considered as a proportion of total assets.

## 1. SUMMARY AND INTRODUCTION

Let $u(x)$ be a utility function for money. The function $r(x) = -u''(x)/u'(x)$ will be interpreted in various ways as a measure of local risk aversion (risk aversion in the small); neither $u''(x)$ nor the curvature of the graph of $u$ is an appropriate measure. No simple measure of risk aversion in the large will be introduced. Global risks will, however, be considered, and it will be shown that one decision maker has greater local risk aversion $r(x)$ than another at all $x$ if and only if he is globally more risk-averse in the sense that, for every risk, his cash equivalent (the amount for which he would exchange the risk) is smaller than for the other decision maker. Equivalently, his risk premium (expected monetary value minus cash equivalent) is always larger, and he would be willing to pay more for insurance in any situation. From this it will be shown that a decision maker's local risk aversion $r(x)$ is a decreasing function of $x$ if and only if, for every risk, his cash equivalent is larger the larger his assets, and his risk premium and what he would be willing to pay for insurance are smaller. This condition, which many decision makers would subscribe to, involves the third derivative of $u$, as $r' \leq 0$ is equivalent to $u'''u' \geq u''^2$. It is not satisfied by quadratic utilities in any region. All this means that some natural ways of thinking casually about utility functions may be misleading. Except for one family, convenient utility functions for which $r(x)$ is decreasing are not so very easy to find. Help in this regard is given by some theorems showing that certain combinations of utility functions, in particular linear combinations with positive weights, have decreasing $r(x)$ if all the functions in the combination have decreasing $r(x)$.

[1] This research was supported by the National Science Foundation (grant NSF-G24035). Reproduction in whole or in part is permitted for any purpose of the United States Government.

* Harvard University.

The related function $r^*(x) = xr(x)$ will be interpreted as a local measure of aversion to risks measured as a proportion of assets, and monotonicity of $r^*(x)$ will be proved to be equivalent to monotonicity of every risk's cash equivalent measured as a proportion of assets, and similarly for the risk premium and insurance.

These results have both descriptive and normative implications. Utility functions for which $r(x)$ is decreasing are logical candidates to use when trying to describe the behavior of people who, one feels, might generally pay less for insurance against a given risk the greater their assets. And consideration of the yield and riskiness per investment dollar of investors' portfolios may suggest, at least in some contexts, description by utility functions for which $r^*(x)$ is first decreasing and then increasing.

Normatively, it seems likely that many decision makers would feel they ought to pay less for insurance against a given risk the greater their assets. Such a decision maker will want to choose a utility function for which $r(x)$ is decreasing, adding this condition to the others he must already consider (consistency and probably concavity) in forging a satisfactory utility from more or less malleable preliminary preferences. He may wish to add a further condition on $r^*(x)$.

We do not assume or assert that utility may not change with time. Strictly speaking, we are concerned with utility at a specified time (when a decision must be made) for money at a (possibly later) specified time. Of course, our results pertain also to behavior at different times if utility does not change with time. For instance, a decision maker whose utility for total assets is unchanging and whose assets are increasing would be willing to pay less and less for insurance against a given risk as time progresses if his $r(x)$ is a decreasing function of $x$. Notice that his actual expenditure for insurance might nevertheless increase if his risks are increasing along with his assets.

The risk premium, cash equivalent, and insurance premium are defined and related to one another in Section 2. The local risk aversion function $r(x)$ is introduced and interpreted in Sections 3 and 4. In Section 5, inequalities concerning global risks are obtained from inequalities between local risk aversion functions. Section 6 deals with constant risk aversion, and Section 7 demonstrates the equivalence of local and global definitions of decreasing (and increasing) risk aversion. Section 8 shows that certain operations preserve the property of decreasing risk aversion. Some examples are given in Section 9. Aversion to proportional risk is discussed in Sections 10 to 12. Section 13 concerns some related work of Kenneth J. Arrow.[2]

Throughout this paper, the utility $u(x)$ is regarded as a function of total

[2] The importance of the function $r(x)$ was discovered independently by Kenneth J. Arrow and by Robert Schlaifer, in different contexts. The work presented here was, unfortunately, essentially completed before I learned of Arrow's related work. It is, however, a pleasure to acknowledge Schlaifer's stimulation and participation throughout, as well as that of John Bishop at certain points.

assets rather than of changes which may result from a certain decision, so that $x = 0$ is equivalent to ruin, or perhaps to loss of all readily disposable assets. (This is essential only in connection with proportional risk aversion.) The symbol $\sim$ indicates that two functions are equivalent as utilities, that is, $u_1(x) \sim u_2(x)$ means there exist constants $a$ and $b$ (with $b > 0$) such that $u_1(x) = a + bu_2(x)$ for all $x$. The utility functions discussed may, but need not, be bounded. It is assumed, however, that they are sufficiently regular to justify the proofs; generally it is enough that they be twice continuously differentiable with positive first derivative, which is already required for $r(x)$ to be defined and continuous. A variable with a tilde over it, such as $\tilde{z}$, is a random variable. The risks $\tilde{z}$ considered may, but need not, have "objective" probability distributions. In formal statements, $\tilde{z}$ refers only to risks which are not degenerate, that is, not constant with probability one, and interval refers only to an interval with more than one point. Also, increasing and decreasing mean nondecreasing and nonincreasing respectively; if we mean strictly increasing or decreasing we will say so.

## 2. THE RISK PREMIUM

Consider a decision maker with assets $x$ and utility function $u$. We shall be interested in the *risk premium* $\pi$ such that he would be indifferent between receiving a risk $\tilde{z}$ and receiving the non-random amount $E(\tilde{z}) - \pi$, that is, $\pi$ less than the actuarial value $E(\tilde{z})$. If $u$ is concave, then $\pi \geq 0$, but we don't require this. The risk premium depends on $x$ and on the distribution of $\tilde{z}$, and will be denoted $\pi(x, \tilde{z})$. (It is not, as this notation might suggest, a function $\pi(x, z)$ evaluated at a randomly selected value of $z$, which would be random.) By the properties of utility,

$$(1) \qquad u(x + E(\tilde{z}) - \pi(x, \tilde{z})) = E\{u(x + \tilde{z})\}.$$

We shall consider only situations where $E\{u(x + \tilde{z})\}$ exists and is finite. Then $\pi(x, \tilde{z})$ exists and is uniquely defined by (1), since $u(x + E(\tilde{z}) - \pi)$ is a strictly decreasing, continuous function of $\pi$ ranging over all possible values of $u$. It follows immediately from (1) that, for any constant $\mu$,

$$(2) \qquad \pi(x, \tilde{z}) = \pi(x + \mu, \tilde{z} - \mu).$$

By choosing $\mu = E(\tilde{z})$ (assuming it exists and is finite), we may thus reduce consideration to a risk $\tilde{z} - \mu$ which is actuarially neutral, that is, $E(\tilde{z} - \mu) = 0$.

Since the decision maker is indifferent between receiving the risk $\tilde{z}$ and receiving for sure the amount $\pi_a(x, \tilde{z}) = E(\tilde{z}) - \pi(x, \tilde{z})$, this amount is sometimes called the cash equivalent or value of $\tilde{z}$. It is also the asking price for $\tilde{z}$, the smallest amount for which the decision maker would willingly sell $\tilde{z}$ if he had it. It is given by

$$(3a) \qquad u(x + \pi_a(x, \tilde{z})) = E\{u(x + \tilde{z})\}.$$

It is to be distinguished from the bid price $\pi_b(x, \tilde{z})$, the largest amount the decision maker would willingly pay to obtain $\tilde{z}$, which is given by

(3b) $$u(x) = E\{u(x + \tilde{z} - \pi_b(x, \tilde{z}))\}.$$

For an unfavorable risk $\tilde{z}$, it is natural to consider the insurance premium $\pi_I(x, \tilde{z})$ such that the decision maker is indifferent between facing the risk $\tilde{z}$ and paying the non-random amount $\pi_I(x, \tilde{z})$. Since paying $\pi_I$ is equivalent to receiving $-\pi_I$, we have

(3c) $$\pi_I(x, \tilde{z}) = -\pi_a(x, \tilde{z}) = \pi(x, \tilde{z}) - E(\tilde{z}).$$

If $\tilde{z}$ is actuarially neutral, the risk premium and insurance premium coincide.

The results of this paper will be stated in terms of the risk premium $\pi$, but could equally easily and meaningfully be stated in terms of the cash equivalent or insurance premium.

## 3. LOCAL RISK AVERSION

To measure a decision maker's local aversion to risk, it is natural to consider his risk premium for a small, actuarially neutral risk $\tilde{z}$. We therefore consider $\pi(x, \tilde{z})$ for a risk $\tilde{z}$ with $E(\tilde{z}) = 0$ and small variance $\sigma_z^2$; that is, we consider the behavior of $\pi(x, \tilde{z})$ as $\sigma_z^2 \to 0$. We assume the third absolute central moment of $\tilde{z}$ is of smaller order than $\sigma_z^2$. (Ordinarily it is of order $\sigma_z^3$.) Expanding $u$ around $x$ on both sides of (1), we obtain under suitable regularity conditions[3]

(4a) $$u(x - \pi) = u(x) - \pi u'(x) + O(\pi^2),$$

(4b) $$E\{u(x + \tilde{z})\} = E\{u(x) + \tilde{z}u'(x) + \tfrac{1}{2}\tilde{z}^2 u''(x) + O(\tilde{z}^3)\}$$
$$= u(x) + \tfrac{1}{2}\sigma_z^2 u''(x) + o(\sigma_z^2).$$

Setting these expressions equal, as required by (1), then gives

(5) $$\pi(x, \tilde{z}) = \tfrac{1}{2}\sigma_z^2 r(x) + o(\sigma_z^2),$$

where

(6) $$r(x) = -\frac{u''(x)}{u'(x)} = -\frac{d}{dx} \log u'(x).$$

Thus the decision maker's risk premium for a small, actuarially neutral risk $\tilde{z}$ is approximately $r(x)$ times half the variance of $\tilde{z}$; that is, $r(x)$ is twice the risk premium per unit of variance for infinitesimal risks. A sufficient regularity condition for (5) is that $u$ have a third derivative which is continuous and bounded over the range of all $\tilde{z}$ under discussion. The theorems to follow will not actually depend on (5), however.

If $\tilde{z}$ is not actuarially neutral, we have by (2), with $\mu = E(\tilde{z})$, and (5):

(7) $$\pi(x, \tilde{z}) = \tfrac{1}{2}\sigma_z^2 r(x + E(\tilde{z})) + o(\sigma_z^2).$$

---

[3] In expansions, $O(\ )$ means "terms of order at most" and $o(\ )$ means "terms of smaller order than."

Thus the risk premium for a risk $\tilde{z}$ with arbitrary mean $E(\tilde{z})$ but small variance is approximately $r(x + E(\tilde{z}))$ times half the variance of $\tilde{z}$. It follows also that the risk premium will just equal and hence offset the actuarial value $E(\tilde{z})$ of a small risk $(\tilde{z})$; that is, the decision maker will be indifferent between having $\tilde{z}$ and not having it when the actuarial value is approximately $r(x)$ times half the variance of $\tilde{z}$. Thus $r(x)$ may also be interpreted as twice the actuarial value the decision maker requires per unit of variance for infinitesimal risks.

Notice that it is the variance, not the standard deviation, that enters these formulas. To first order any (differentiable) utility is linear in small gambles. In this sense, these are second order formulas.

Still another interpretation of $r(x)$ arises in the special case $\tilde{z} = \pm h$, that is, where the risk is to gain or lose a fixed amount $h > 0$. Such a risk is actuarially neutral if $+h$ and $-h$ are equally probable, so $P(\tilde{z} = h) - P(\tilde{z} = -h)$ measures the *probability premium* of $\tilde{z}$. Let $p(x, h)$ be the probability premium such that the decision maker is indifferent between the status quo and a risk $\tilde{z} = \pm h$ with

$$(8) \qquad\qquad P(\tilde{z} = h) - P(\tilde{z} = -h) = p(x, h).$$

Then $P(\tilde{z} = h) = \frac{1}{2}[1 + p(x, h)]$, $P(\tilde{z} = -h) = \frac{1}{2}[1 - p(x, h)]$, and $p(x, h)$ is defined by

$$(9) \quad u(x) = E\{u(x + \tilde{z})\} = \frac{1}{2}[1 + p(x, h)]\, u(x + h) + \frac{1}{2}[1 - p(x, h)]u(x - h).$$

When $u$ is expanded around $x$ as before, (9) becomes

$$(10) \qquad\qquad u(x) = u(x) + hp(x, h)\, u'(x) + \frac{1}{2}h^2 u''(x) + O(h^3).$$

Solving for $p(x, h)$, we find

$$(11) \qquad\qquad p(x, h) = \frac{1}{2}hr(x) + O(h^2).$$

Thus for small $h$ the decision maker is indifferent between the status quo and a risk of $\pm h$ with a probability premium of $r(x)$ times $\frac{1}{2}h$; that is, $r(x)$ is twice the probability premium he requires for unit risked for small risks.

In these ways we may interpret $r(x)$ as a measure of the *local risk aversion* or *local propensity to insure* at the point $x$ under the utility function $u$; $-r(x)$ would measure locally liking for risk or propensity to gamble. Notice that we have not introduced any measure of risk aversion in the large. Aversion to ordinary (as opposed to infinitesimal) risks might be considered measured by $\pi(x, \tilde{z})$, but $\pi$ is a much more complicated function than $r$. Despite the absence of any simple measure of risk aversion in the large, we shall see that comparisons of aversion to risk can be made simply in the large as well as in the small.

By (6), integrating $-r(x)$ gives $\log u'(x) + c$; exponentiating and integrating again then gives $e^c u(x) + d$. The constants of integration are immaterial because $e^c u(x) + d \sim u(x)$. (Note $e^c > 0$). Thus we may write

(12)
$$u \sim \int e^{-\int r},$$

and we observe that the local risk aversion function $r$ associated with any utility function $u$ contains all essential information about $u$ while eliminating everything arbitrary about $u$. However, decisions about ordinary (as opposed to "small") risks are determined by $r$ only through $u$ as given by (12), so it is not convenient entirely to eliminate $u$ from consideration in favor of $r$.

## 4. CONCAVITY

The aversion to risk implied by a utility function $u$ seems to be a form of concavity, and one might set out to measure concavity as representing aversion to risk. It is clear from the foregoing that for this purpose $r(x) = -u''(x)/u'(x)$ can be considered a measure of the concavity of $u$ at the point $x$. A case might perhaps be made for using instead some one-to-one function of $r(x)$, but it should be noted that $u''(x)$ or $-u''(x)$ is not in itself a meaningful measure of concavity in utility theory, nor is the curvature (reciprocal of the signed radius of the tangent circle) $u''(x) (1 + [u'(x)]^2)^{-3/2}$. Multiplying $u$ by a positive constant, for example, does not alter behavior but does alter $u''$ and the curvature.

A more striking and instructive example is provided by the function $u(x) = -e^{-x}$. As $x$ increases, this function approaches the asymptote $u = 0$ and looks graphically less and less concave and more and more like a horizontal straight line, in accordance with the fact that $u'(x) = e^{-x}$ and $u''(x) = -e^{-x}$ both approach 0. As a utility function, however, it does not change at all with the level of assets $x$, that is, the behavior implied by $u(x)$ is the same for all $x$, since $u(k + x) = -e^{-k-x} \sim u(x)$. In particular, the risk premium $\pi(x, \tilde{z})$ for any risk $\tilde{z}$ and the probability premium $p(x, h)$ for any $h$ remain absolutely constant as $x$ varies, Thus, regardless of the appearance of its graph, $u(x) = -e^{-x}$ is just as far from implying linear behavior at $x = \infty$ as at $x = 0$ or $x = -\infty$. All this is duly reflected in $r(x)$, which is constant: $r(x) = -u''(x)/u'(x) = 1$ for all $x$.

One feature of $u''(x)$ does have a meaning, namely its sign, which equals that of $-r(x)$. A negative (positive) sign at $x$ implies unwillingness (willingness) to accept small, actuarially neutral risks with assets $x$. Furthermore, a negative (positive) sign for all $x$ implies strict concavity (convexity) and hence unwillingness (willingness) to accept any actuarially neutral risk with any assets. The absolute magnitude of $u''(x)$ does not in itself have any meaning in utility theory, however.

## 5. COMPARATIVE RISK AVERSION

Let $u_1$ and $u_2$ be utility functions with local risk aversion functions $r_1$ and $r_2$, respectively. If, at a point $x$, $r_1(x) > r_2(x)$, then $u_1$ is locally more risk-averse than $u_2$ at the point $x$; that is, the corresponding risk premiums satisfy

$\pi_1(x, \tilde{z}) > \pi_2(x, \tilde{z})$ for sufficiently small risks $\tilde{z}$, and the corresponding probability premiums satisfy $p_1(x, h) > p_2(x, h)$ for sufficiently small $h > 0$. The main point of the theorem we are about to prove is that the corresponding global properties also hold. For instance, if $r_1(x) > r_2(x)$ for all $x$, that is, $u_1$, has greater local risk aversion than $u_2$ everywhere, then $\pi_1(x, \tilde{z}) > \pi_2(x, \tilde{z})$ for every risk $\tilde{z}$, so that $u_1$ is also globally more risk-averse in a natural sense.

It is to be understood in this section that the probability distribution of $\tilde{z}$, which determines $\pi_1(x, \tilde{z})$ and $\pi_2(x, \tilde{z})$, is the same in each. We are comparing the risk premiums for the same probability distribution of risk but for two different utilities. This does not mean that when Theorem 1 is applied to two decision makers, they must have the same personal probability distributions, but only that the notation is imprecise. The theorem could be stated in terms of $\pi_1(x, \tilde{z}_1)$ and $\pi_2(x, \tilde{z}_2)$ where the distribution assigned to $\tilde{z}_1$ by the first decision maker is the same as that assigned to $\tilde{z}_2$ by the second decision maker. This would be less misleading, but also less convenient and less suggestive, especially for later use. More precise notation would be, for instance, $\pi_1(x, F)$ and $\pi_2(x, F)$, where $F$ is a cumulative distribution function.

*Theorem 1. Let $r_i(x)$, $\pi_i(x, \tilde{z})$, and $p_i(x)$ be the local risk aversion, risk premium, and probability premium corresponding to the utility function $u_i$, $i = 1, 2$. Then the following conditions are equivalent, in either the strong form (indicated in brackets), or the weak form (with the bracketed material omitted).*

(a) $r_1(x) \geqq r_2(x)$ *for all $x$ [and $>$ for at least one $x$ in every interval].*
(b) $\pi_1(x, \tilde{z}) \geqq [>] \pi_2(x, \tilde{z})$ *for all $x$ and $\tilde{z}$.*
(c) $p_1(x, h) \geqq [>] p_2(x, h)$ *for all $x$ and all $h > 0$.*
(d) $u_1(u_2^{-1}(t))$ *is a [strictly] concave function of $t$.*
(e) $\dfrac{u_1(y) - u_1(x)}{u_1(w) - u_1(v)} \leqq [<] \dfrac{u_2(y) - u_2(x)}{u_2(w) - u_2(v)}$ *for all $v$, $w$, $x$, $y$ with $v < w \leqq x < y$.*

*The same equivalences hold if attention is restricted throughout to an interval, that is, if the requirement is added that $x$, $x + \tilde{z}$, $x + h$, $x - h$, $u_2^{-1}(t)$, $v$, $w$, and $y$, all lie in a specified interval.*

*Proof.* We shall prove things in an order indicating somewhat how one might discover that (a) implies (b) and (c).

To show that (b) follows from (d), solve (1) to obtain

(13)     $\pi_i(x, \tilde{z}) = x + E(\tilde{z}) - u_i^{-1}(E\{u_i(x + \tilde{z})\}).$

Then

(14)   $\pi_1(x, \tilde{z}) - \pi_2(x, \tilde{z}) = u_2^{-1}(E\{u_2(x + \tilde{z})\}) - u_1^{-1}(E\{u_1(x + \tilde{z})\})$
$= u_2^{-1}(E\{\tilde{t}\}) - u_1^{-1}(E\{u_1(u_2^{-1}(\tilde{t}))\}),$

where $\tilde{t} = u_2(x + \tilde{z})$. If $u_1(u_2^{-1}(t))$ is [strictly] concave, then (by Jensen's inequality)

(15)     $E\{u_1(u_2^{-1}(\tilde{t}))\} \leqq [<] u_1(u_2^{-1}(E\{\tilde{t}\})).$

Substituting (15) in (14), we obtain (b).

To show that (a) implies (d), note that

$$(16) \qquad \frac{d}{dt} u_1(u_2^{-1}(t)) = \frac{u_1'(u_2^{-1}(t))}{u_2'(u_2^{-1}(t))},$$

which is [strictly] decreasing if (and only if) $\log u_1'(x)/u_2'(x)$ is. The latter follows from (a) and

$$(17) \qquad \frac{d}{dx} \log \frac{u_1'(x)}{u_2'(x)} = r_2(x) - r_1(x).$$

That (c) is implied by (e) follows immediately upon writing (9) in the form

$$(18) \qquad \frac{1 - p_i(x, h)}{1 + p_i(x, h)} = \frac{u_i(x + h) - u_i(x)}{u_i(x) - u_i(x - h)}.$$

To show that (a) implies (e), integrate (a) from $w$ to $x$, obtaining

$$(19) \qquad - \log \frac{u_1'(x)}{u_1'(w)} \geq [>] - \log \frac{u_2'(x)}{u_2'(w)} \quad \text{for } w < x,$$

which is equivalent to

$$(20) \qquad \frac{u_1'(x)}{u_1'(w)} \leq [<] \frac{u_2'(w)}{u_2'(w)} \quad \text{for } w < x.$$

This implies

$$(21) \qquad \frac{u_1(y) - u_1(x)}{u_1'(w)} \leq [<] \frac{u_2(y) - u_2(x)}{u_2'(w)} \quad \text{for } w \leq x < y,$$

as may be seen by applying the Mean Value Theorem of differential calculus to the difference of the two sides of (21) regarded as a function of $y$. Condition (e) follows from (21) upon application of the Mean Value Theorem to the difference of the reciprocals of the two sides of (e) regarded as a function of $w$.

We have now proved that (a) implies (d) implies (b), and (a) implies (e) implies (c). The equivalence of (a)–(e) will follow if we can prove that (b) implies (a), and (c) implies (a), or equivalently that not (a) implies not (b) and not (c). But this follows from what has already been proved, for if the weak [strong] form of (a) does not hold, then the strong [weak] form of (a) holds on some interval with $u_1$ and $u_2$ interchanged. Then the strong [weak] forms of (b) and (c) also hold on this interval with $u_1$ and $u_2$ interchanged, so the weak [strong] forms of (b) and (c) do not hold. This completes the proof.

We observe that (e) is equivalent to (20), (21), and

$$(22) \qquad \frac{u_1(w) - u_1(v)}{u_1'(x)} \geq [>] \frac{u_2(w) - u_2(v)}{u_2'(x)} \quad \text{for } v < w \leq x.$$

## 6. CONSTANT RISK AVERSION

If the local risk aversion function is constant, say $r(x) = c$, then by (12):

(23) $$u(x) \sim x \qquad \text{if } r(x) = 0;$$

(24) $$u(x) \sim -e^{-cx} \quad \text{if } r(x) = c > 0;$$

(25) $$u(x) \sim e^{-cx} \qquad \text{if } r(x) = c < 0.$$

These utilities are, respectively, linear, strictly concave and strictly convex.

If the risk aversion is constant locally, then it is also constant globally, that is, a change in assets makes no change in preference among risks. In fact, for any $k$, $u(k + x) \sim u(x)$ in each of the cases above, as is easily verified. Therefore it makes sense to speak of "constant risk aversion" without the qualification "local" or "global."

Similar remarks apply to constant risk aversion on an interval, except that global consideration must be restricted to assets $x$ and risks $\tilde{z}$ such that $x + \tilde{z}$ is certain to stay within the interval.

## 7. INCREASING AND DECREASING RISK AVERSION

Consider a decision maker who (i) attaches a positive risk premium to any risk, but (ii) attaches a smaller risk premium to any given risk the greater his assets $x$. Formally this means

(i) $\pi(x, \tilde{z}) > 0$ for all $x$ and $\tilde{z}$;
(ii) $\pi(x, \tilde{z})$ is a strictly decreasing function of $x$ for all $\tilde{z}$.

Restricting $\tilde{z}$ to be actuarially neutral would not affect (i) or (ii), by (2) with $\mu = E(\tilde{z})$.

We shall call a utility function (or a decision maker possessing it) *risk-averse* if the weak form of (i) holds, that is, if $\pi(x, \tilde{z}) \geq 0$ for all $x$ and $\tilde{z}$; it is well known that this is equivalent to concavity of $u$, and hence to $u'' \leq 0$ and to $r \geq 0$. A utility function is *strictly risk-averse* if (i) holds as stated; this is equivalent to strict concavity of $u$ and hence to the existence in every interval of at least one point where $u'' < 0, r > 0$.

We turn now to (ii). Notice that it amounts to a definition of strictly decreasing risk aversion in a global (as opposed to local) sense. One would hope that decreasing global risk aversion would be equivalent to decreasing local risk aversion $r(x)$. The following theorem asserts that this is indeed so. Therefore it makes sense to speak of "decreasing risk aversion" without the qualification "local" or "global." What is nontrivial is that $r(x)$ decreasing implies $\pi(x, \tilde{z})$ decreasing, inasmuch as $r(x)$ pertains directly only to infinitesimal gambles. Similar considerations apply to the probability premium $p(x, h)$.

*Theorem 2.   The following conditions are equivalent.*
(a)   *The local risk aversion function $r(x)$ is [strictly] decreasing.*
(b')   *The risk premium $\pi(x, \tilde{z})$ is a [strictly] decreasing function of $x$ for all $\tilde{z}$.*

(c') *The probability premium $p(x, h)$ is a [strictly] decreasing function of $x$ for all $h > 0$.*

*The same equivalences hold if "increasing" is substituted for "decreasing" throughout and/or attention is restricted throughout to an interval, that is, the requirement is added that $x$, $x + \tilde{z}$, $x + h$, and $x - h$ all lie in a specified interval.*

*Proof.* This theorem follows upon application of Theorem 1 to $u_1(x) = u(x)$ and $u_2(x) = u(x + k)$ for arbitrary $x$ and $k$.

It is easily verified that (a') and hence also (b') and (c') are equivalent to

(d')   $u'(u^{-1}(t))$ is a [strictly] convex function of $t$.

This corresponds to (d) of Theorem 1. Corresponding to (e) of Theorem 1 and (20)–(22) is

(e')   $u'(x)u'''(x) \geqq (u''(x))^2$ [and $>$ for at least one $x$ in every interval].

The equivalence of this to (a')–(c') follows from the fact that the sign of $r'(x)$ is the same as that of $(u''(x))^2 - u'(x)u'''(x)$. Theorem 2 can be and originally was proved by way of (d') and (e'), essentially as Theorem 1 is proved in the present paper.

## 8. OPERATIONS WHICH PRESERVE DECREASING RISK AVERSION

We have just seen that a utility function evinces decreasing risk aversion in a global sense if and only if its local risk aversion function $r(x)$ is decreasing. Such a utility function seems of interest mainly if it is also risk-averse (concave, $r \geqq 0$). Accordingly, we shall now formally define a utility function to be [strictly] *decreasingly risk-averse* if its local risk aversion function $r$ is [strictly] decreasing and nonnegative. Then by Theorem 2, conditions (i) and (ii) of Section 7 are equivalent to the utility's being strictly decreasingly risk-averse.

In this section we shall show that certain operations yield decreasingly risk-averse utility functions if applied to such functions. This facilitates proving that functions are decreasingly risk-averse and finding functions which have this property and also have reasonably simple formulas. In the proofs, $r(x)$, $r_1(x)$, etc., are the local risk aversion functions belonging to $u(x)$, $u_1(x)$, etc.

*Theorem 3.* *Suppose $a > 0$: $u_1(x) = u(ax + b)$ is [strictly] decreasingly risk-averse for $x_0 \leqq x \leqq x_1$ if and only if $u(x)$ is [strictly] decreasingly risk-averse for $ax_0 + b \leqq x \leqq ax_1 + b$.*

*Proof.* This follows directly from the easily verified formula:

(26) $$r_1(x) = ar(ax + b).$$

*Theorem 4.* *If $u_1(x)$ is decreasingly risk-averse for $x_0 \leqq x \leqq x_1$, and $u_2(x)$ is decreasingly risk-averse for $u_1(x_0) \leqq x \leqq u_1(x_1)$, then $u(x) = u_2(u_1(x))$ is decreasingly risk-averse for $x_0 \leqq x \leqq x_1$, and strictly so unless one of $u_1$ and*

$u_2$ is linear from some $x$ on and the other has constant risk aversion in some interval.

*Proof.*  We have $\log u'(x) = \log u_2'(u_1'(x)) + \log u_1'(x)$, and therefore

$$(27) \qquad\qquad r(x) = r_2(u_1(x))u_1'(x) + r_1(x).$$

The functions $r_2(u_1(x))$, $u_1'(x)$, and $r_1(x)$ are $\geq 0$ and decreasing, and therefore so is $r(x)$. Furthermore, $u_1'(x)$ is strictly decreasing as long as $r_1(x) > 0$, so $r(x)$ is strictly decreasing as long as $r_1(x)$ and $r_2(u_1(x))$ are both $> 0$. If one of them is 0 for some $x$, then it is 0 for all larger $x$, but if the other is strictly decreasing, then so is $r$.

*Theorem 5.*  If $u, \ldots, u_n$ are decreasingly risk-averse on an interval $[x_0, x_1]$, and $c, \ldots, c_n$ are positive constants, then $u = \sum_1^n c_i u_i$ is decreasingly risk-averse on $[x_0, x_1]$, and strictly so except on subintervals (if any) where all $u_i$ have equal and constant risk aversion.

*Proof.*  The general statement follows from the case $u = u_1 + u_2$.  For this case

$$(28) \qquad r = -\frac{u_1'' + u_2''}{u_1' + u_2'} = \frac{u_1'}{u_1' + u_2'} r_1 + \frac{u_2'}{u_1' + u_2'} r_2;$$

$$(29) \qquad r' = \frac{u_1'}{u_1' + u_2'} r_1' + \frac{u_2'}{u_1' + u_2'} r_2' + \frac{u_1'' u_2' - u_1' u_2''}{(u_1' + u_2')^2} (r_1 - r_2)$$

$$= \frac{u_1' r_1' + u_2' r_2'}{u_1' + u_2'} - \frac{u_1' u_2'}{(u_1' + u_2')^2} (r_1 - r_2)^2.$$

We have $u_1' > 0$, $u_2' > 0$, $r_1' \leq 0$, and $r_2' \leq 0$. Therefore $r \leq 0$, and $r' < 0$ unless $r_1 = r_2$ and $r_1' = r_2' = 0$. The conclusion follows.

## 9. EXAMPLES

9.1 *Example 1.*  The utility $u(x) = -(b - x)^c$ for $x \leq b$ and $c > 1$ is strictly increasing and strictly concave, but it also has strictly *increasing* risk aversion: $r(x) = (c - 1)/(b - x)$. Notice that the most general concave quadratic utility $u(x) = \alpha + \beta x - \gamma x^2$, $\beta > 0$, $\gamma > 0$, is equivalent as a utility to $-(b - x)^c$ with $c = 2$ and $b = \frac{1}{2}\beta/\gamma$. Therefore a quadratic utility cannot be decreasingly risk-averse on any interval whatever. This severely limits the usefulness of quadratic utility, however nice it would be to have expected utility depend only on the mean and variance of the probability distribution. Arguing "in the small" is no help: decreasing risk aversion is a local property as well as a global one.

9.2 *Example 2.*  If

$$(30) \qquad\qquad u'(x) = (x^a + b)^{-c} \quad \text{with} \quad a > 0, c > 0,$$

then $u(x)$ is strictly decreasingly risk-averse in the region

$$(31) \qquad\qquad x > [\max\{0, -b, b(a - 1)\}]^{1/a}.$$

To prove this, note

(32)
$$r(x) = -\frac{d}{dx} \log u'(x) = \frac{ac}{x + bx^{1-a}},$$

which is $\geq 0$ and strictly decreasing in the region where the denominator $x + bx^{1-a}$ is $\geq 0$ and strictly increasing, which is the region (30). (The condition $x \geq 0$ is included to insure that $x^a$ is defined; for $a \geq 1$ it follows from the other conditions.)

By Theorem 3, one can obtain a utility function that is strictly decreasingly risk-averse for $x > 0$ by substituting $x + d$ for $x$ above, where $d$ is at least the right-hand side of (31). Multiplying $x$ by a positive factor, as in Theorem 3, is equivalent to multuplying $b$ by a positive factor.

Given below are all the strictly decreasingly risk-averse utility functions $u(x)$ on $x > 0$ which can be obtained by applying Theorem 3 to (30) with the indicated choices of the parameters $a$ and $c$:

(33)  $a = 1, 0 < c < 1$: $u(x) \sim (x + d)^q$ with $d \geq 0, 0 < q < 1$;

(34)  $a = 1, c = 1$: $u(x) \sim \log(x + d)$ with $d \geq 0$;

(35)  $a = 1, c > 1$: $u(x) \sim -(x + d)^{-q}$ with $d \geq 0, q > 0$;

(36)  $a = 2, c = 5$: $u(x) \sim \log (x + d + [(x + d)^2 + b])$ with $d \geq |b|^{\frac{1}{2}}$;

(37)  $a = 2, c = 1$: $u(x) \sim \arctan(\alpha x + \beta)$ or $\log (1 - (\alpha x + \beta)^{-1})$ with $a > 0, \beta \geq 1$;

(38)  $a = 2, c = 1.5$: $u(x) \sim [1 + (\alpha x + \beta)^{-2}]^{-\frac{1}{2}}$ or $-[1 - (\alpha x + \beta)^{-2}]^{-\frac{1}{2}}$ with $\alpha > 0, \beta \geq 1$.

9.3 *Example 3.* Applying Theorems 4 and 5 to the utilities of Example 2 and Section 6 gives a very wide class of utilities which are strictly decreasingly risk-averse for $x > 0$, such as

(39)  $u(x) \sim -c_1 e^{-cx} - c_2 e^{-dx}$ with $c_1 > 0, c_2 > 0, c > 0, d > 0$.

(40)  $u(x) \sim \log (d_1 + \log (x + d_2))$ with $d_1 \geq 0, d_2 \geq 0, d_1 + \log d_2 \geq 0$.

## 10. PROPORTIONAL RISK AVERSION

So far we have been concerned with risks that remained fixed while assets varied. Let us now view everything as a proportion of assets. Specifically, let $\pi^*(x, \tilde{z})$ be the *proportional risk premium* corresponding to a proportional risk $\tilde{z}$; that is, a decision maker with assets $x$ and utility function $u$ would be indifferent between receiving a risk $x\tilde{z}$ and receiving the non-random amount $E(x\tilde{z}) - x\pi^*(x, \tilde{z})$. Then $x\pi^*(x, \tilde{z})$ equals the risk premium $\pi(x, x\tilde{z})$, so

$$(41) \qquad \pi^*(x, \tilde{z}) = \frac{1}{x} \, \pi(x, x\tilde{z}).$$

For a small, actuarially neutral, proportional risk $\tilde{z}$ we have, by (5),

$$(42) \qquad \pi^*(x, \tilde{z}) = \tfrac{1}{2}\sigma_z^2 \, r^*(x) + o(\sigma_z^2),$$

where

$$(43) \qquad r^*(x) = xr(x).$$

If $\tilde{z}$ is not actuarially neutral, we have, by (7),

$$(44) \qquad \pi^*(x, \tilde{z}) = \tfrac{1}{2}\sigma_z^2 r^*(x + E(\tilde{z})) + o(\sigma_z^2).$$

We will call $r^*$ the *local proportional risk aversion* at the point $x$ under the utility function $u$. Its interpretation by (42) and (44) is like that of $r$ by (5) and (7).

Similarly, we may define the *proportional probability premium* $p^*(x, h)$, corresponding to a risk of gaining or losing a proportional amount $h$, namely

$$(45) \qquad p^*(x, h) = p(x, xh).$$

Then another interpretation of $r^*(x)$ is provided by

$$(46) \qquad p^*(x, h) = \tfrac{1}{2}hr^*(x) + O(h^2),$$

which follows from (45) and (11).

## 11. CONSTANT PROPORTIONAL RISK AVERSION

If the local proportional risk aversion function is constant, say $r^*(x) = c$, then $r(x) = c/x$, so the utility is strictly decreasingly risk-averse for $c > 0$ and has negative, strictly increasing risk aversion for $c < 0$. By (12), the possibilities are:

$$(47) \qquad u(x) \sim x^{1-c} \qquad \text{if} \quad r^*(x) = c < 1,$$

$$(48) \qquad u(x) \sim \log x \qquad \text{if} \quad r^*(x) = 1,$$

$$(49) \qquad u(x) \sim -x^{-(c-1)} \quad \text{if} \quad r^*(x) = c > 1.$$

If the proportional risk aversion is constant locally, then it is constant globally, that is, a change in assets makes no change in preferences among proportional risks. This follows immediately from the fact that $u(kx) \sim u(x)$ in each of the cases above. Therefore it makes sense to speak of "constant proportional risk aversion" without the qualification "local" or "global." Similar remarks apply to constant proportional risk aversion on an interval.

## 12. INCREASING AND DECREASING PROPORTIONAL RISK AVERSION

We will call a utility function [strictly] increasingly or decreasingly proportionally risk-averse if it has a [strictly] increasing or decreasing local proportional risk aversion function. Again the corresponding local and global properties are equivalent, as the next theorem states.

*Theorem 6. The following conditions are equivalent.*

(a″) *The local proportional risk aversion function* $r^*(x)$ *is [strictly] decreasing.*

(b″) *The proportional risk premium* $\pi^*(x, \tilde{z})$ *is a [strictly] decreasing function of x for all* $\tilde{z}$.

(c″) *The proportional probability premium* $p^*(x, h)$ *is a [strictly] decreasing function of x for all* $h > 0$.

*The same equivalences hold if "increasing" is substituted for "decreasing" throughout and/or attention is restricted throughout to an interval, that is, if the requirement is added that* $x$, $x + x\tilde{z}$, $x + xh$, *and* $x - xh$ *all lie in a specified interval.*

*Proof.* This theorem follows upon application of Theorem 1 to $u_1(x) = u(x)$ and $u_2(x) = u(kx)$ for arbitrary $x$ and $k$.

A decreasingly risk-averse utility function may be increasingly or decreasingly proportionally risk-averse or neither. For instance, $u(x) \sim -\exp[-q^{-1}(x + b)^q]$, with $b \geq 0$, $q < 1, q \neq 0$, is strictly decreasingly risk-averse for $x > 0$ while its local proportional risk aversion function $r^*(x) = x(x + b)^{-1}[(x + b)^q + 1 - q]$ is strictly increasing if $0 < q < 1$, strictly decreasing if $q < 0$ and $b = 0$, and neither if $q < 0$ and $b > 0$.

## 13. RELATED WORK OF ARROW

Arrow[4] has discussed the optimum amount to invest when part of the assets $x$ are to be held as cash and the rest invested in a specified, actuarially favorable risk. If $\tilde{\imath}$ is the return per unit invested, then investing the amount $a$ will result in assets $x + a\tilde{\imath}$. Suppose $a(x, \tilde{\imath})$ is the optimum amount to invest, that is, $a(x, \tilde{\imath})$ maximizes $E\{u(x + a\tilde{\imath})\}$. Arrow proves that if $r(x)$ is [strictly] decreasing, increasing, or constant for all $x$, then $a(x, \tilde{\imath})$ is [strictly] increasing, decreasing, or constant, respectively, except that $a(x, \tilde{\imath}) = x$ for all $x$ below a certain value (depending on $\tilde{\imath}$). He also proves a theorem about the asset elasticity of the demand for cash which is equivalent to the statement that if $r^*(x)$ is [strictly] decreasing, increasing, or constant for all $x$, then the optimum proportional investment $a^*(x, \tilde{\imath}) = a(x, \tilde{\imath})/x$ is [strictly] increasing, decreasing, or constant, respectively, except that $a^*(x, \tilde{\imath}) = 1$ for all $x$ below a certain value. In the present framework it is natural to deduce these results from the following theorem, whose proof bears essentially the same relation to Arrow's proofs as the proof of Theorem 1 to direct proofs of Theorems 2 and 6. For convenience we assume that $a_1(x, \tilde{\imath})$ and $a_2(x, \tilde{\imath})$ are unique.

*Theorem 7. Condition* (a) *of Theorem 1 is equivalent to*

[4] Kenneth J. Arrow, "Liquidity Preference," Lecture VI in "Lecture Notes for Economics 285, The Economics of Uncertainty," pp. 33–53, undated, Stanford University.

(f)   $a_1(x, \bar{\imath}) \leq a_2(x, \bar{\imath})$ for all $x$ and $\bar{\imath}$ [and $<$ if $0 < a_1(x, \bar{\imath}) < x$].
The same equivalence holds if attention is restricted throughout to an interval, that is, if the requirement is added that $x$ and $x + \bar{\imath}x$ lie in a specified interval.

*Proof.*   To show that (a) implies (f), note that $a_j(x, \bar{\imath})$ maximizes

$$(50) \qquad v_j(a) = \frac{1}{u'_j(x)} E\{u_j(x + a\bar{\imath})\}, \qquad j = 1, 2.$$

Therefore (f) follows from

$$(51) \qquad \frac{d}{da}\{v_1(a) - v_2(a)\} = E\left\{\bar{\imath}\left(\frac{u'_1(x + a\bar{\imath})}{u'_1(x)} - \frac{u'_2(x + a\bar{\imath})}{u'_2(x)}\right)\right\} \leq [<] 0,$$

which follows from (a) by (20).

If, conversely, the weak [strong] form of (a) does not hold, then its strong [weak] form holds on some interval with $u_1$ and $u_2$ interchanged, in which case the weak [strong] form of (f) cannot hold, so (f) implies (a). (The fact must be used that the strong form of (f) is actually stronger than the weak form, even when $x$ and $x + \bar{\imath}x$ are restricted to a specified interval. This is easily shown.)

Assuming $u$ is bounded, Arrow proves that (i) it is impossible that $r^*(x) \leq 1$ for all $x > x_0$, and he implies that (ii) $r^*(0) \leq 1$. It follows, as he points out, that if $u$ is bounded and $r^*$ is monotonic, then $r^*$ is increasing. (i) and (ii) can be deduced naturally from the following theorem, which is an immediate consequence of Theorem 1 (a) and (e).

*Theorem 8.*   *If $r_1(x) \geq r_2(x)$ for all $x > x_0$ and $u_1(\infty) = \infty$, then $u_2(\infty) = \infty$. If $r_1(x) \geq r_2(x)$ for all $x < \varepsilon$, $\varepsilon > 0$, and $u_2(0) = -\infty$, then $u_1(0) = -\infty$.*
This gives (i) when $r_1(x) = 1/x$, $r_2(x) = r(x)$, $u_1(x) = \log x$, $u_2(x) = u(x)$. It gives (ii) when $r_1(x) = r(x)$, $r_2(x) = c/x$, $c > 1$, $u_1(x) = u(x)$, $u_2(x) = -x^{1-c}$.

This section is not intended to summarize Arrow's work,[4] but only to indicate its relation to the present paper. The main points of overlap are that Arrow introduces essentially the functions $r$ and $r^*$ (actually their negatives) and uses them in significant ways, in particular those mentioned already, and that he introduces essentially $p^*(x, h)$, proves an equation like (46) in order to interpret decreasing $r^*$, and mentions the possibility of a similar analysis for $r$.

# 8. SAFETY FIRST AND THE HOLDING OF ASSETS[1]

A. D. ROY*

Reprinted by permission of the author and the publisher
from *Econometrica*, Vol. 20 (July 1952), pp. 431–499.

This paper considers the implications of minimising the upper bound of the chance of a dread event, when the information available about the joint probability distribution of future occurrences is confined to the first- and second-order moments. The analysis is then applied to the particular problem of holding $n$ assets, either for speculative gain or for the income yielded. Some comments are made about the peculiar role of money, and finally the simple case of two assets is considered in more detail.

## INTRODUCTION

Early attempts to deal with the problem of behaviour under uncertainty were based upon the assumption that it is reasonable for an individual to maximise gain or profit in either real or money terms. There are two major objections to such an approach. First, the ordinary man has to consider the possible outcomes of a given course of action on one occasion only and the average (or expected) outcome, if this conduct were repeated a large number of times under similar conditions, is irrelevant. Second, the principle of maximising expected return does not explain the well-known phenomenon of the diversification of resources among a wide range of assets.

Recent writers have succeeded in overcoming each of the two difficulties singly, but so far as the author is aware both problems have not been solved simultaneously. Thus, Shackle in his recent contribution [5] to the theory of expectation in economies has tackled the first objection at the cost of a break away from orthodox probability theory, but even so he has not succeeded in explaining satisfactorily why people hold more than two assets.

Another school, of which the writings of von Neumann and Morgenstern [6], Friedman and Savage [3], and Marschak [4] are representative, has extended the theory of choice under certainty to problems involving expectation, by the assumption that individuals maximise expected utility. If the utility function is suitably chosen, this approach succeeds in explaining the diversifi-

[1] I am indebted to Professor C. F. Carter, Dr. H. E. Daniels, Mr. H. G. Johnson, and Dr. A. R. Prest for their helpful comments and to Mr. R. A. Arnould for the diagrams.

* Sydney-Sussex College, Cambridge.

cation of resources among different assets. But such a theory is still open to the criticism that the behaviour advocated is only *rational* if individuals are free to expose themselves to independent risks on a large number of occasions.

A third criticism can be leveled against both sets of theory. This objection is not, however, logical but practical. Is it reasonable that real people, have, or consider themselves to have, a precise knowledge of all possible outcomes of a given line of action, together with their respective probabilities or *potential surprise*? Both introspection and observation suggest that expectations are generally framed in a much more vague manner. Nor is it likely that the ordinary individual has much opportunity for extending his knowledge about what the future holds in store for him. What, therefore, appears to be required is some *simple* theory which meets in some measure all three of these major difficulties. An attempt to provide such an analysis will be given in the following discussion.

## THE PRINCIPLE OF SAFETY FIRST AND LIMITED KNOWLEDGE

A valid objection to much economic theory is that it is set against a background of case and safety. To dispel this artificial sense of security, theory should take account of the often close resemblance between economic life and navigation in poorly charted waters or manoeuvres in a hostile jungle. Decisions taken in practice are less concerned with whether a little more of this or of that will yield the largest net increase in satisfaction than with avoiding known rocks of uncertain position or with deploying forces so that, if there is an ambush round the next corner, total disaster is avoided. If economic survival is always taken for granted, the rules of behaviour applicable in an uncertain and ruthless world cannot be discovered.

In the economic world, disasters may occur if an individual makes a net loss as the result of some activity, if his resources are eroded by the process of inflation to, say, 70 per cent of their former worth, or if his income is less than what he would almost certainly obtain in some other occupation. For large numbers of people some such idea of a *disaster* exists, and the principle of Safety First asserts that it is reasonable, and probable in practice, that an individual will seek to reduce as far as is possible the chance of such a catastrophe occurring.[2] At every moment an individual's whole property is necessarily vulnerable to chance events, and the result of the current exposure to risk will determine his stake at fate's next throw.

From a formal standpoint, the minimisation of the chance of disaster can be interpreted as maximising expected utility if the utility function assumes only two values, e.g., one if disaster does not occur, and zero if it does. It would appear, however, that this formal analogy is scarcely helpful, since in the one case an individual is trying to make the expected *proportion* of occurrences of disaster as small as possible, while in maximising expected utility

---

[2] Such a principle has been applied to the theory of risk in insurance companies. See Cramér [1].

he is operating on a level of *satisfaction*. Readers, however, are open to interpret the principle in this way if they so desire, but the purpose of this discussion is not to suggest that individuals may possess a utility function of peculiar form but rather to find out the implication of a certain mode of behaviour, which appears both plausible and simple. In calling in a utility function to our aid, an appearance of generality is achieved at the cost of a loss of practical significance and applicability in our results. A man who seeks advice about his actions will not be grateful for the suggestion that he maximise expected utility.

There would appear to be no valid objection to the discontinuity in the preference scale that the existence of a single disaster value implies. In practice, death, bankruptcy, and a prison sentence are likely to be associated with sharp breaks in both our pattern of behaviour and in our scale of preferences.

It may be possible that the outcome of economic activity which is regarded as disaster is not independent of the expected value of the outcome. Thus, a person may be prepared to revise the level of disaster downwards if the expected return is at the same time raised. For example, he may at one and the same time regard a speculative loss of 10 per cent as a disaster if the expected gain is only 5 per cent, while, if the expected gain is 15 per cent, he will only get excited if his loss exceeds 25 per cent. Once again such individual psychology can no doubt be interpreted in terms of a utility function, but such a development will not be pursued here. In what follows, the disaster level of the outcome is taken to be a constant.

Let us suppose, then, that the principle of Safety First is adopted and that, when confronted with range of possible actions, we are concerned that our gross return should not be less than some quantity $d$. With every possible action is associated $m$, which is the expected value of the gross return. Since this outcome is not certain, there is coupled with $m$ a quantity $\sigma$ (the standard error of $m$) which is, very roughly, the average amount by which the prediction $m$ is expected to be wrong. In what follows, we assume that we know $m$ and $\sigma$ precisely, whereas in fact they must be estimated from information about the past. This raises all kinds of problems, which are beyond the scope of this discussion, since estimates of $m$ and $\sigma$, say $\hat{m}$ and $\hat{\sigma}$, will themselves have sampling distributions. Thus, a full analysis of the problem should discuss simultaneously not only behaviour under uncertainty but also action under uncertain uncertainty.[3]

In the particular application of the principle of Safety First that is examined here, it is postulated that $m$ and $\sigma$ are the only quantities that can be distilled out of our knowledge of the past. The slightest acquaintance with problems of analysing economic time series will suggest that this assumption is optimistic rather than unnecessarily restrictive.

Given the values of $m$ and $\sigma$ for all feasible choices of action, there will exist a functional relationship between these quantities, which will be denoted

[3] This brings us to the problem of statistical decision functions. See Wald [7].

by $f(\sigma, m) = 0$.[4] Since it is not possible to determine with this information, the precise probability of the final return being $d$ or less for a given pair of values of $m$ and $\sigma$, the only alternative open is a calculation of the upper bound of this probability. This can be done by an appeal to the Bienaymé-Tchebycheff inequality (see, for instance, H. Cramér [2]). Thus, if the final return is a random variable $\xi$, then[5]

$$P(|\xi - m| \geq m - d) \leq \frac{\sigma^2}{(m-d)^2}.$$

Then *a fortiori*

$$P(m - \xi \geq m - d) = P(\xi \leq d) \leq \frac{\sigma^2}{(m-d)^2}.$$

If then in default of minimising $P(\xi \leq d)$, we operate on $\sigma^2/(m-d)^2$, this is equivalent to maximising $(m-d)/\sigma$. In the subsequent analysis, we shall maximise this quantity and thus approach as near as is possible, under the circumstances, the true principle of Safety First. If $\xi$ was distributed normally with mean $m$ and standard deviation $\sigma$, then this line of conduct would minimise the probability of disaster itself; this fact is both interesting and reassuring.

If we find that $\sigma$ is constant for all values of $m$, then the maximising of $(m-d)/\sigma$ is equivalent to maximising expected gain or profit, though not, of course, to maximising expected utility. Thus, the procedure suggested here may be regarded as a generalisation of profit maximisation in an uncertain world.

The implication of the above argument can be represented graphically with great simplicity. The function $f(\sigma, m) = 0$ can be represented by a curve as in Figure 1. If we desire to avoid an outcome of $d$ or worse, we plot the point $D(0, d)$ on the $m$-axis. A tangent of positive slope is then drawn from the point $D$ to touch the $f(\sigma, m) = 0$ curve at $P$. Then if we adopt that course of action which produces an estimated outcome $m_0$, we shall have made the upper bound of the probability of $d$ or worse happening as small as possible. This upper bound is equal to the reciprocal of the square of the gradient of $DP$ and so the steeper the slope of $DP$, the smaller is the probability of disaster.[6] In Figure 1 the upper bound of the probability of $d'$ or worse is clearly less than that of $d$. If, however, the slope of $DP$ was less than 45 degrees (or 1 in 1), we should only be able to say that the chance of disaster was less than or equal to unity,[7] which is not very helpful.

This then is a particular application of the principle of Safety First; its

[4] There may be a whole family of such relationships: in this case $f(\sigma, m) = 0$ is their envelope.

[5] If $\xi$ has a unimodal and symmetrical distribution, the right-hand side of the inequality will be multiplied by the factor 4/9. See, once again, Cramér [2].

[6] One of the negative gradient would maximise the probability.

[7] Unless we could say that the outcomes had a unimodal probability distribution.

relevance to the problems of expectation is dependent on giving an everyday interpretation to the concept of an expected value and of a standard error. We shall show later that the principle can be used with advantage even if the standard errors are unknown.

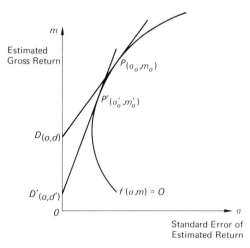

Figure 1.—The graphical determination of the best $\sigma$, $m$ combination.

## THE OPTIMUM DISTRIBUTION OF RESOURCES AMONG $n$ ASSETS

Now let us attack the problem of how we should distribute our resources between different assets, given certain expectations about the future. Let us suppose that we possess an amount $k$ of resources measured in real terms. For the moment we shall not discuss what we mean by *real* in this context. It is sufficient that our resources should not be reckoned in terms of any one asset. We wish to ensure that at the end of a given period our resources do not fall to or below an amount $d$ also in real terms.

On the basis of past experience we have estimated what the prices of the various assets are likely to be at the end of a certain period, and we have also investigated how the movements of the price of any one asset have been associated with those of the other assets.

Taking the present prices of all assets to be 1.00, the best estimates we can make of their level at the end of the period are $p_1, p_2, \ldots, p_n$[8] with which are coupled the standard errors $\alpha_1, \alpha_2, \ldots, \alpha_n$. Further, we have estimated that the correlation between the prices of the first two assets is $r_{12}$ and similarly for all other pairs of assets. If $x_1, x_2, \ldots, x_n$ are the amounts of our resources which we hold in the form of each asset, we can now calculate $m$ and $\sigma$.

(1)
$$m = \sum_{i=1}^{n} x_i p_i,$$

[8] These are not money prices but prices measured in terms of the composite numeraire which we use for reckoning our *real* resources.

(2)
$$\sigma^2 = \sum_{i=1}^{n} \sum_{j=1}^{n} x_i x_j r_{ij} a_i a_j,$$

for all values of $x_i$ such that

(3)
$$k = \sum_{i=1}^{n} x_i.$$

In general these three equations determine not one curve relating $m$ and $\sigma$ but a whole family of such curves. We can, however, determine the curve which forms the outer boundary or envelope of this family and this is the only curve that we need to know. In order to give it in a reasonably simple form we shall employ matrix notation.

Let us write $a$ for the column vector $(p_1/\alpha_1, p_2/\alpha_2, \ldots, p_n/\alpha_n)$ and $b$ for the column vector $(1/\alpha_1, 1/\alpha_2, \ldots, 1/\alpha_n)$. The correlation matrix of which the elements are $r_{ij}$, will be denoted by $W$ and its inverse by $W^{-1}$. The boundary curve which we require (derived in the Appendix) is then the hyperbola with the equation,

(4)
$$\left[ \frac{(a'W^{-1}a)(b'W^{-1}) - (a'W^{-1}b)^2}{b'W^{-1}b} \right] \left( \sigma^2 - \frac{k^2}{b'W^{-1}b} \right) = \left( m - k\frac{a'W^{-1}b}{b'W^{-1}b} \right)^2.$$

This rather formidable relationship can be shown graphically as in Figure 2. The shape of the curve shown in the figure holds quite generally and does not depend on any special assumptions.

We wish to know what values of $x_1, x_2, \ldots, x_n$ should be chosen if the outcome associated with $P$ (the point at which the tangent from $D$ touches the hyperbola) is the most safe from our point of view. We should also like to know how secure this most safe position actually is.

It is convenient to give the answer to the second query first. It can be shown (see the Appendix) that the reciprocal of the square of the gradient of $DP$, i.e., the upper bound of the probability of disaster, is equal to

$$\frac{1}{\left[ a - \left( \frac{d}{k} \right) b \right]' W^{-1} \left[ a - \left( \frac{d}{k} \right) b \right]}$$

or

(5)
$$\frac{|W|}{\sum_{i=1}^{n} \sum_{j=1}^{n} \frac{[p_i - (d/k)]}{\alpha_i} W_{ij} \frac{[p_j - (d/k)]}{\alpha_j}},$$

where $W_{ij}$ is the cofactor of $r_{ij}$ in the matrix $W$ and $|W|$ is the determinant of $W$. This result shows, as might be expected, that if $|W| = 0$ we can find a position of complete and blissful security.

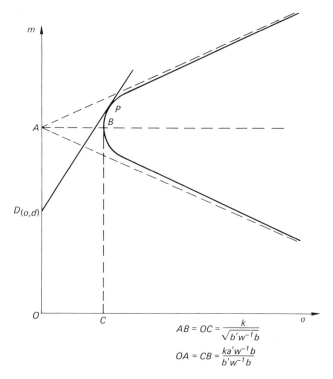

Figure 2—The graphical determination of the best $\sigma$, $m$ combination in the case of $n$ assets.

The required values of the $x$'s are given by the equations (derived in the Appendix),

$$(6) \qquad x_i = \frac{\lambda}{\alpha_i} \sum_{j=1}^{n} \frac{\left(p_j - \dfrac{d}{k}\right)}{\alpha_i} \frac{W_{ij}}{|W|} \qquad (i = 1, 2, \ldots, n)$$

where $\lambda$ is chosen so that $\sum_{i=1}^{n} x_i = k$. Despite the faintly discouraging appearance of the $n$ equations given by (6), they can be given a comparatively simple interpretation.

A cursory inspection of the results given at (5) and (6) above shows that a particular significance attaches to the ratio $d/k$ and this we shall call henceforward the *critical price*. For if we were to commit all our resources to one kind of asset and its price at the end of the period fell to or below (or rose no further than) $d/k$, then the disaster that we dread would have come about.

To decide which assets to hold and how much of them, we consider each asset in turn. We ask ourselves this question: "If the prices of all the other assets fell to the critical price, what is the best (linear) estimate of price of the asset under examination?" If the estimated price under these conditions exceeds the critical price, then we should hold some of our resources in this form. If the estimated price is less than the critical price, then either we should reject this asset altogether or, better still, we should contract liabilities in this form, if this is possible. Thus in the critical price we have a criterion which enables us to decide what things are eligible as assets and what as liabilities.

We must now find out how much a particular asset we should hold or how big a liability we should contract. To do this we allocate points to each asset or liability. First, we determine the difference between the estimated price of the asset when all other prices fall to the critical value, and the critical price. Then we calculate the standard error of this estimated price, which will be smaller than the standard error of our original estimate of the price of this asset. The points assigned to a particular asset are then equal to the difference already mentioned over the square of this standard error. The proportion of resources held in this form is obtained by calculating the points allotted to this asset as a proportion of the total points allotted to all assets. In other words we can rewrite (6), as,

$$(7) \qquad x_i = \lambda \frac{\left[\left(\begin{array}{c}\text{best estimate of price of } i\text{th asset}\\ \text{when all other prices are equal to } \dfrac{d}{k}\end{array}\right) - \dfrac{d}{k}\right]}{\left(\begin{array}{c}\text{Standard error of best estimate of } i\text{th asset's}\\ \text{price when all other prices are equal to } \dfrac{d}{k}\end{array}\right)^2}$$

where $\lambda$ is determined as before and $i = 1, 2, \ldots, n$.

We are thus enabled to discover the best structure of our assets and of our liabilities so that the chance[9] of a particular eventuality, at the end of a given period of time, shall be kept as small as possible. In general it will be desirable to hold our resources in a large number of different forms,[10] because although we may diminish the chance of a large gain somewhat by so doing we also reduce the probability of a really catastrophic outcome. We can also calculate the upper bound of the least chance of disaster and so we can tell how complacent or otherwise we should be in the existing situation.

In the simple case when all the correlations between the prices of assets are thought to be zero, the equations given at (6) and (7) become

$$(8) \qquad x_i = \lambda \frac{\left(p_i - \dfrac{d}{k}\right)}{a_i^2} \qquad (i = 1, 2, \ldots, n).$$

In this instance, we hold those assets the price of which we expect to exceed the critical price $d/k$. We contract liabilities in the form of those items of which the price is expected to be below $d/k$. If, further, our expectations about all assets are the same, we are not indifferent as to which assets we hold. For although we cannot affect the expected outcome by varying our

---

[9] Strictly the upper bound of the chance.

[10] This is an important difference between this theory and the theories which depend on the maximisation of expected gain.

holdings, we can affect our uncertainty about the outcome. This will be least when we spread our resources equally among all the assets.

If we hold only one of the exactly similar assets the upper bound of the chance of disaster would be $\alpha^2/(p - d/k)^2$, while if we held all $n$ of them in equal amounts this upper bound would become $\alpha^2/n(p - d/k)^i$. This is a demonstration of the folly of putting all one's eggs in one basket.

Even if we had no means of estimating the necessary standard errors of our estimates of future prices, we should still have a reasonable guide for action. If we decide to assume that all our estimates of prices were equally reliable, (8) would become

$$(9) \qquad x_i = \lambda \left( p_i - \frac{d}{k} \right) \qquad (i = 1, 2, \ldots, n).$$

If we thought that the estimates had equal proportionate reliability, which is perhaps a more plausible assumption in the economic world, we could determine our $x$'s from

$$(10) \qquad x_i = \lambda \frac{\left( p_i - \dfrac{d}{k} \right)}{p_i^2} \qquad (i = 1, 2, \ldots, n).$$

When we did not know the absolute values of the standard errors but we had some estimate of their relative magnitude, we could use (8) without modification. We should not know whether we were succeeding in reducing the upper bound of the probability below unity, but it would still be worth seeing that the upper bound was as small as possible.

## DISCUSSION OF ASSETS WITH YIELDS AND OF THE SPECIAL POSITION OF MONEY

Our discussion so far has considered only the best procedure to adopt when holding assets to ensure a given speculative gain (i.e., $d > k$) or to prevent an excesssive loss ($d < k$). We have implicitly assumed that none of the assets have any appreciable yield in the period of time under consideration.

If for the moment we consider the opposite extreme, we shall have a situation in which we are interested in yields alone and where the prices of the assets are of no immediate concern. In this case, the $p$'s become our best estimates of the yields of the various assets during the period which we are considering, and the $\alpha$'s are their standard errors. The quantity $100d/k$ is the percentage yield to or below which we have no desire to sink. We endeavour to minimise the chance that our real income over the period will be less than or equal to $d$.

When the period is sufficiently long for both yields over the period and prices at the end of the period to be of importance, then the $p$'s become our best estimates of the yields *and* the prices of the various assets and the $\alpha$'s are again the appropriate standard errors. We shall presumably be anxious to maintain our resources intact and to obtain a yield of more than 100 $(d - k)/k$ per cent over the period. If the period were $t$ years this would be equivalent to a return of 100 $(d - k)/kt$ per cent per annum at simple interest. So we see that the results we have obtained can be adapted to deal with problems other than those of pure speculative gain or loss.

Next we must discuss in more detail the implications of measuring our original resources in real terms. Money has certain limitations as a store of value, and it is therefore better to consider what goods our resources at any given moment will buy rather than what sum of money we can obtain by realising our assets. We should be well advised to measure our resources in terms of their purchasing power over consumer goods[11] if we are private individuals, or over capital goods and labour if we are entrepreneurs. Whatever standard we decide to use, money will be just another asset like the rest, about the future value of which we are uncertain. In times of rising prices we shall be encouraged to contract debts in terms of money and to use the proceeds to hold varying quantities of all other assets that appear eligible on the basis of the criterion that we have established. Likewise in times of falling prices we shall be happy to hold a substantial proportion of our resources in the form of money and we shall be anxious to incur liabilities in terms of things, the prices of which are expected to fall in real terms. In either situation there will be some stability in the sense that the amount of money we desire to borrow or hold will be limited by our uncertainty about what the value of money will actually be.

If, however, we reckon our resources in money terms, the whole position is radically altered and becomes most unstable. We might use a money standard of measurement either because we believed it to be an effective store of value or because we were bound by convention to attempt to maintain the money value of our resources intact. In either event the price of money in terms of itself is clearly unity and the standard error of this estimate is zero. Hence in times of rising prices our rules set no limits to the amount of money which should be borrowed in order to increase our holdings of assets with prices that are expected to rise in money terms. In practice the limit of our borrowing powers would be set by out credit worthiness alone and would be unaffected by our desire to minimise the chance that we made no more than a given speculative gain. When prices were expected to fall, there would be an indefinite encouragement to hold as much money as possible and to contract debts in the things of which the prices were falling.

Some sort of stability is restored when we are concerned not with prices alone but with yields as well. Uncertainty about the negative yield, i.e., the rate of interest, associated with borrowing money will set definite limits to the amount of money that we shall wish to borrow in a period of rising prices. This, however, is only true provided that the intervals, at which it is necessary to repay the loans and reborrow, are shorter than the period over which we

[11] Perhaps durable consumer goods.

are planning our distribution of resources. To give an example, if we are planning a scheme which will yield its fruit in ten years time, there are definite limits to the amounts we should like to borrow for periods of less than ten years; limits which are set, *inter alia*, by our uncertainty as to the rates of interest ruling when we have to reborrow. We should, however, be prepared to borrow an indefinitely large amount of money for more than ten years, provided always that the rate of interest charged is not greater than the least return we hoped to get.

We thus see that if we used money as our standard of value, we should be much more enterprising in periods of rising prices but that expectations of a general fall in prices would have a much more severe effect than when we used some kind of composite standard.

When deciding on the best distribution of assets, we have not as yet taken into account the fact that our current asset-holdings have been inherited from the past. Whatever the best distribution determined by our present expectation may be, there are costs, e.g., stamp duties, commissions and the like, involved in shifting our resources from one form of asset to another in order to achieve this distribution. Taking account of these costs causes no serious difficulty and our equations at 6 above can be suitably modified to allow for the pre-existing distribution of our assets. When making actual calculations a good procedure is first to find the desired distribution neglecting all such costs, in order to find the direction in which we should move from our present position. Having done this, the costs can be taken into account and the best distribution of assets calculated. The existence of these costs will merely damp down our desire to change the distribution whenever a change in our expectation takes place.

## A DETAILED EXAMINATION OF THE PARTICULAR CASE OF TWO ASSETS

When we examine the artificial but simple case of a world in which there are but two kinds of assets, the results that we have obtained for the case of $m$ assets assume less forbidding forms. Using the same symbols as before, the relation between $\sigma$ and $m$ given at (4) above now becomes

$$(p_1 - p_2)^2 \left[ \sigma^2 - \frac{k^2(1 - r^2)a_1^2 \alpha_2^2}{\alpha_1^2 - 2r\alpha_1\alpha_2 + \alpha_2^2} \right] = (\alpha_1^2 - 2r\alpha_1\alpha_2 + \alpha_2^2)$$

(11)
$$\left[ m - \frac{k\{\alpha_1^2 p_2 - r\alpha_1\alpha_2(p_1 + p_2) + \alpha_2^2 p_1\}}{(a_1^2 - 2r\alpha_1\alpha_2 + \alpha_2^2)} \right]^2$$

Figure 2 can be redrawn as in Figure 3. We also have useful relationships between $x_1$, $x_2$, and $m$:

(12)
$$x_1 = \frac{kp_2 - m}{p_2 - p_1}, \qquad x_2 = \frac{kp_1 - m}{p_1 - p_2}.$$

The points $X$, $Y$ in Figure 3 are of some interest. If the point $P$ lies between $X$

and $Y$ on the curve $f(\sigma, m) = 0$, then we shall find it advisable to hold some of both assets. If however $P$ lies above $X$ on the curve and $p_1$ is greater than $p_2$, then in order to be as secure as possible we must borrow in terms of the second asset in order to increase our holdings of the first.

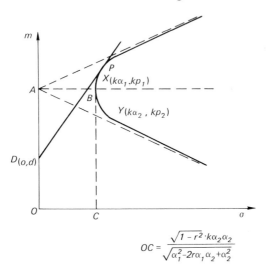

$$OC = \frac{\sqrt{1-r^2} \cdot k\alpha_2\alpha_2}{\sqrt{\alpha_1^2 - 2r\alpha_1\alpha_2 + \alpha_2^2}}$$

Figure 3—The graphical determination of the best $\sigma, m$ combination in the case of two assets only.

It can also be seen that the higher the correlation, either positive or negative, between the prices of the assets, the nearer will the curve move to the $m$-axis. Thus it might appear that, as the tangent from $D$ to the curve would necessarily become steeper the higher the correlation we assumed, so we should always be happier in a situation involving correlated prices. This, however, is not necessarily so because the existence of a correlation also has the effect of shifting the curve nearer or further from the $\sigma$ axis. *A priori* we cannot say what will happen since it depends on the relative sizes of $p_1$ and $p_2$, and of $\alpha_1$, and $\alpha_2$.

Equations (6) can now be written down again in a more simple form:

(13)
$$x_1 = \frac{\lambda}{\alpha_1(1-r^2)} \left[ \frac{\left(p_1 - \frac{d}{k}\right)}{\alpha_1} - \frac{r\left(p_2 - \frac{d}{k}\right)}{\alpha_2} \right]$$

$$x_2 = \frac{\lambda}{\alpha_2(1-r^2)} \left[ \frac{\left(p_2 - \frac{d}{k}\right)}{\alpha_2} - \frac{r\left(p_1 - \frac{d}{k}\right)}{\alpha_1} \right]$$

where $\lambda$ is such that $x_1 + x_2 = k$.

An increase in the estimated future price of an asset will, other things being equal, always increase our holdings of this asset. Similarly an increase in the reliability of the estimated price will have the same effect, if the correlation is zero or negative. If this is not so, then it may happen that the correlation exceeds a certain limiting positive value and in this case the holdings of the asset will be diminished.

If our total amount of resources, $k$, is increased, then the proportion of resources held in the form of the asset with the lower estimated future price will increase. In other words an increase in $k$ means that we can more than compensate the fall in $m$ by a fall in $\sigma$ as well. The wealthier man can rely more for his safety on the diversification of his holdings than the poorer man. Because of the symmetry existing between $d$ and $k$ in the formulae, the downward revision of the outcome, which we want most to avoid, has a precisely similar effect to an increase in total resources, other things being equal.

Some of these results can be illustrated by numerical examples. Suppose that we expected the prices of the assets at the end of a given period to be 1.00 and 1.10, the current prices being both 1.00. Suppose further that the standard error of the estimated price of the second asset is 0.05. Then we can tabulate the proportionate distribution of assets according to the variation in our desires and expectation as in the Table.

The Table calls for little comment. Perhaps the most interesting fact that it reveals is that small changes in the reliability of an estimated price may cause very heavy borrowing in an attempt to stave off disaster.

The demand for an asset in terms of variations in its own estimated price and the estimated price of the other asset can be shown diagrammatically as in Figure 4. For reasons of convenience the price is plotted along the horizon-

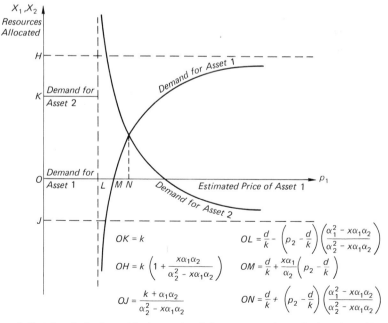

Figure 4—Variations in the demand for two assets only in response to changes in the estimated future price of one of them.

TABLE 1

PROPORTIONATE DISTRIBUTION OF ASSETS ACCORDING TO VARIATION IN DESIRES AND RELATIVE FIRMNESS OF EXPECTATIONS[a]

$[P_1 = 1.00; P_2 = 1.10; \alpha_2 = 0.05]$

| WE DESIRE TO AVOID: | A SPECULATIVE LOSS OF 10% OR MORE $d/k = 0.90$ | | | A SPECULATIVE LOSS OF 5% OR MORE $d/k = 0.95$ | | | NO SPECULATIVE GAIN OR WORSE $d/k = 1.00$ | | | A SPECULATIVE GAIN OF 5% OR LESS $d/k = 1.05$ | | |
|---|---|---|---|---|---|---|---|---|---|---|---|---|
| | PERCENTAGE HOLDING | | | PERCENTAGE HOLDING | | | PERCENTAGE HOLDING | | | PERCENTAGE HOLDING | | |
| RATIO OF STANDARD ERRORS $\alpha_1/\alpha_2$ | ASSET 1 | ASSET 2 | $(P)$ | ASSET 1 | ASSET 2 | $(P)$ | ASSET 1 | ASSET 2 | $(P)$ | ASSET 1 | ASSET 2 | $(P)$ |
| *Zero correlation* | | | | | | | | | | | | |
| 0.6 | 58 | 42 | (0.036) | 48 | 52 | (0.085) | 0 | 100 | (0.250) | 0 | 100 | (1.00) |
| 0.8 | 44 | 56 | (0.045) | 34 | 66 | (0.095) | 0 | 100 | (0.250) | 0 | 100 | (1.00) |
| 1.0 | 33 | 67 | (0.050) | 25 | 75 | (0.100) | 0 | 100 | (0.250) | 0 | 100 | (1.00) |
| 1.2 | 26 | 74 | (0.053) | 19 | 81 | (0.103) | 0 | 100 | (0.250) | -227 | 327 | (0.59) |
| 1.4 | 20 | 80 | (0.055) | 15 | 85 | (0.105) | 0 | 100 | (0.250) | -104 | 204 | (0.66) |
| *Correlation $= +\frac{1}{2}$* | | | | | | | | | | | | |
| 0.6 | 49 | 51 | (0.054) | 11 | 89 | (0.111) | -500 | 600 | (0.188) | 0 | 100 | (1.00) |
| 0.8 | 19 | 81 | (0.061) | -15 | 115 | (0.110) | -167 | 267 | (0.188) | 0 | 100 | (1.00) |
| 1.0 | 0 | 100 | (0.063) | -25 | 125 | (0.107) | -100 | 200 | (0.188) | 0 | 100 | (1.00) |
| 1.2 | -10 | 110 | (0.062) | -27 | 127 | (0.104) | -71 | 171 | (0.188) | -363 | 463 | (0.30) |
| 1.4 | -14 | 114 | (0.061) | -27 | 127 | (0.102) | -56 | 156 | (0.188) | -177 | 277 | (0.34) |
| *Correlation $= -\frac{1}{2}$* | | | | | | | | | | | | |
| 0.6 | 61 | 39 | (0.019) | 58 | 42 | (0.045) | 46 | 54 | (0.188) | 0 | 100 | (1.00) |
| 0.8 | 52 | 48 | (0.023) | 49 | 51 | (0.052) | 38 | 62 | (0.188) | 0 | 100 | (1.00) |
| 1.0 | 45 | 55 | (0.027) | 42 | 58 | (0.058) | 33 | 67 | (0.188) | 0 | 100 | (1.00) |
| 1.2 | 39 | 61 | (0.029) | 36 | 64 | (0.062) | 29 | 71 | (0.188) | -91 | 191 | (0.87) |
| 1.4 | 37 | 63 | (0.032) | 32 | 68 | (0.064) | 26 | 74 | (0.188) | -31 | 131 | (0.94) |

[a] $P$ is the upper bound of the probability that disaster occurs. If we assume distributions are unimodal and symmetrical all the $P$'s can be multiplied by the factor 4/9.

tal axis and not in the usual way. The variations in the upper bound of the probability of disaster can also be shown for variation in $p_1$ as in Figure 5. The main point of interest here is that although the estimated price of one asset is falling as we proceed from $M$ towards $L$ and no other variables are changing, yet nevertheless we are gradually getting into a safer position. The possibility of doing this depends on the relationship between the standard errors of the two estimated prices.

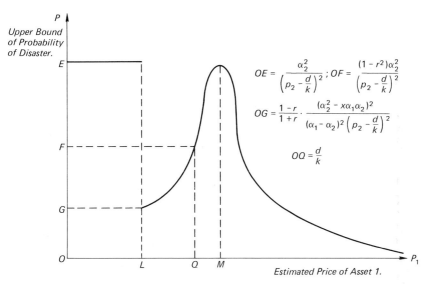

$$OE = \frac{\alpha_2^2}{\left(p_2 - \frac{d}{k}\right)^2} \; ; OF = \frac{(1 - r^2)\alpha_2^2}{\left(p_2 - \frac{d}{k}\right)^2}$$

$$OG = \frac{1-r}{1+r} \cdot \frac{(\alpha_2^2 - x\alpha_1\alpha_2)^2}{(\alpha_1 - \alpha_2)^2 \left(p_2 - \frac{d}{k}\right)^2}$$

$$OQ = \frac{d}{k}$$

Figure 5—Variations in the upper bound of the chance of disaster, in the case of two assets only, in response to changes in the estimated future price of one of them.

These diagrammatic and numerical illustrations should serve to clear up some at least of the obscurities that persist in the earlier exposition of the theory.

CONCLUSION

In conclusion we must consider how far the scheme of rational behaviour that has been sketched out here can be considered to be equivalent to the rules of thumb that guide the ordinary man in every day life. We cannot expect our laws to be obeyed in even a rudimentary way by the reckless gamblers who never consider the possibility of disaster. Our principles are, however, applicable to all those people in whose make-up caution plays some role however slight. They can be used by those whose main interest is speculative gain and by those who are content with modest yields over a long period. Different kinds of persons will use different ways of estimating future prices and the reliability of such estimates. Sometimes people may contemplate without undue dread the possibility of their wealth falling by ten per cent in real terms because in the existing circumstances such an outcome appears to be a minor evil. At other times the same people may try to make sure that they make a speculative gain of not less than five per cent. In all these various situations our rules remain relevant and useful.

Can we, however, expect people to arrive intuitively at rules of behaviour based on the theory of probability? Such a question cannot be answered directly by an economist. It is pertinent, however, to remark that the assumption that entrepreneurs maximise their profits and consumers their utility is not usually taken to imply that the rational man must be well-grounded in the differential calculus. It is not, therefore, an extravagance to suggest that our theory may well be a rationalisation of an already well-worn procedure. We have shown why it is a good thing for the property owner to disperse widely both his assets and liabilities, a principle that is always accepted in practice but rarely explained satisfactorily on relatively simple theoretical assumptions. We have also demonstrated that small changes in expectations about prices, whether they concern their future level or the reliability of existing predictions, may under certain circumstances produce very big changes in an individual's demand for some assets and liabilities. We have indicated too, how changes in expectations may affect the confidence of an individual or of a group of individuals with similar hopes and fears.

However plausible the explanations of individual behaviour given here may seem, in the last resort their validity must turn on their ability to stand up to statistical tests. Such tests cannot be used until the principles have been applied to large groups of people. To do this, the theory of the individual must be subjected to an extensive simplification. Although it is not at present obvious what kind of modification ought to be made, it seems that the basic theory developed here provides a secure base from which to launch attacks on the problems of aggregate market behaviour.

## APPENDIX

I. The envelope curve of $f(m, \sigma) = 0$ with $m$, $\sigma$ as in (1)–(3) of the text is obtained by minimising $\sigma^2$ for given $m$ and $k$. Using $W, a, b$ as in the text and $y$ for the column vector $(x_1\alpha_1, \ldots, x_n\alpha_n)$ we may write (1)–(3) as

$$(14) \qquad m = y'a, \qquad \sigma^2 = y'Wy, \qquad k = y'b.$$

We minimise then

$$y'Wy + 2\mu_1 (m - y'a) + 2\mu_2(k - y'b),$$

where $\mu_1$ and $\mu_2$ are undetermined multipliers. Substituting in (14) the $n$ solutions, $y = W^{-1}(\mu_1 a + \mu_2 b)$, of the simultaneous equations $Wy = \mu_1 a + \mu_2 b$, and eliminating $\mu_1$ and $\mu_2$ from the resulting three equations, we find the equation of the envelope to be

$$\begin{vmatrix} \sigma^2 & m & k \\ m & a'W^{-1}a & a'W^{-1}b \\ k & a'W^{-1}b & b'W^{-1}b \end{vmatrix} = 0,$$

which is (4) in the text.

II. We next find the least upper bound of the probability that $d$ or worse will occur.

Consider the line of slope $h$ through the point $\sigma = 0$, $m = d$, i.e., $D$. This line, $h\sigma = m - d$, is tangent to the envelope if

$$\begin{vmatrix} \sigma^2 & h\sigma + d & k \\ h\sigma + d & a'W^{-1}a & a'W^{-1}b \\ k & a'W^{-1}b & b'W^{-1}b \end{vmatrix}$$

is a perfect square. It is necessary then that

$$h^2 = \left[a - \frac{d}{k}b\right]' W^{-1} \left[a - \left(\frac{d}{k}\right)b\right].$$

Since on the line we have $\sigma^2/(m - d)^2 = 1/h^2$, the upper bound of the probability that $d$ or worse will occur is $1/h^2$. Thus as the upper bound of the probability of disaster we obtain (5) of the text.

III. The point at which the tangent line touches the envelope is given by

$$c = k \frac{\sqrt{\left[a - \left(\frac{d}{k}\right)b\right]' W^{-1} \left[a - \left(\frac{d}{k}\right)b\right]}}{\left[a - \left(\frac{d}{k}\right)b\right]' W^{-1}b}$$

$$m = k \frac{\left[a - \left(\frac{d}{k}\right)b\right]' W^{-1}a}{\left[a - \left(\frac{d}{k}\right)b\right]' W^{-1}b}$$

Using these values of $\sigma$ and $m$, we may evaluate $\mu_1$ and $\mu_2$ from the simultaneous equations obtained from the expressions for $m$ and $k$ of (14) by the substitution of the solutions of the equations $Wy = \mu_1 a + \mu_2 b$. We have then

$$\mu_1 = \frac{k}{\left[a - \left(\frac{d}{k}\right)b\right]' W^{-1}b}, \qquad \mu_2 = \frac{-d}{\left[a - \left(\frac{d}{k}\right)b\right]' W^{-1}b}.$$

Substituting in $y = W^{-1}(\mu_1 a + \mu_2 b)$,

(15)
$$y = \frac{kW^{-1}\left[a - \left(\frac{d}{k}\right)b\right]}{\left[a - \left(\frac{d}{k}\right)b\right]' W^{-1}b}.$$

which is equivalent to (6) of the text with

$$\lambda = \frac{k}{\left[a - \left(\dfrac{d}{k}\right)b\right]' W^{-1}b} = \frac{k}{\displaystyle\sum_{j=1}^{n}\sum_{l=1}^{n} \frac{[p_i - d/k)]}{\alpha_j\,\alpha_l} \dfrac{W_{ji}}{|W|}}.$$

Equation (15) gives us then the distribution of resources which minimises the upper bound of the probability of $d$ or worse occurring.

## REFERENCES

1. Cramér, H., "On the Mathematical Theory of Risk," *Försäkringsaktiebolaget Skandias Festkfrift*, Stockholm: Centraltryckeriet, 1930, pp. 7–84.
2. Cramér, H., *Mathematical Methods of Statistics*, Princeton: Princeton University Press, 1946, pp. 182–83.
3. Friedman, M., and L. J. Savage, "The Utility Analysis of Choices Involving Risk," *Journal of Political Economy*, Vol. 56, August, 1948, pp. 279–304.
4. Marschak, J., "Rational Behavior, Uncertain Prospects and Measurable Utility," *Econometrica*, Vol. 18, April, 1950, pp. 111–41.
5. Shackle, G. L. S., *Expectation in Economics*, Cambridge, England: Cambridge University Press, 1949, 146 pp.
6. von Neumann, J., and O. Morgenstern, *Theory of Games and Economic Behavior*, Princeton: Princeton University Press, 1947, 641 pp.
7. Wald, A., *Statistical Decision Functions*, New York: John Wiley and Sons, 1950, 179 pp.

PART **III**

CAPITAL MARKETS

\* \* \* \* \* \* \* \* \* \* \* \* \* \* \* \* \* \* \* \* \*

## 9. PORTFOLIO SELECTION*

HARRY MARKOWITZ†

Reprinted from *The Journal of Finance*, Vol. *VII*, No. 1, (March, 1952), pp. 77–91, by permission of the author and the publisher.

The process of selecting a portfolio may be divided into two stages. The first stage starts with observation and experience and ends with beliefs about the future performances of available securities. The second stage starts with the relevant beliefs about future performances and ends with the choice of portfolios. This paper is concerned with the second stage. We first consider the rule that the investor does (or should) maximize discounted expected, or anticipated, returns. This rule is rejected both as a hypothesis to explain, and as a maximum to guide investment behavior. We next consider the rule that the investor does (or should) consider expected return a desirable thing *and* variance of return an undesirable thing. This rule has many sound points, both as a maxim for, and hypothesis about, investment behavior. We illustrate geometrically relations between beliefs and choice of portfolio according to the "expected returns—variance of returns" rule.

One type of rule concerning choice of portfolio is that the investor does (or should) maximize the discounted (or capitalized) value of future returns.[1] Since the future is not known with certainty, it must be "expected" or "anticipated" returns which we discount. Variations of this type of rule can be suggested. Following Hicks, we could let "anticipated" returns include an

* This paper is based on work done by the author while at the Cowles Commission for Research in Economics and with the financial assistance of the Social Science Research Council. It will be reprinted as Cowles Commission Paper, New Series, No. 60.

† The Rand Corporation.

[1] See, for example, J. B. Williams, *The Theory of Investment Value* (Cambridge, Mass.: Harvard University Press, 1938), pp. 55–75.

allowance for risk.[2] Or, we could let the rate at which we capitalize the returns from particular securities vary with risk.

The hypothesis (or maxim) that the investor does (or should) maximize discounted return must be rejected. If we ignore market imperfections the foregoing rule never implies that there is a diversified portfolio which is preferable to all nondiversified portfolios. Diversification is both observed and sensible; a rule of behavior which does not imply the superiority of diversification must be rejected both as a hypothesis and as a maxim.

The foregoing rule fails to imply diversification no matter how the anticipated returns are formed; whether the same or different discount rates are used for different securities; no matter how these discount rates are decided upon or how they vary over time.[3] The hypothesis implies that the investor places all his funds in the security with the greatest discounted value. If two or more securities have the same value, then any of these or any combination of these is as good as any other.

We can see this analytically: suppose there are $N$ securities; let $r_{it}$ be the anticipated return (however decided upon) at time $t$ per dollar invested in security $i$; let $d_{it}$ be the rate at which the return on the $i^{th}$ security at time $t$ is discounted back to the present; let $X_i$ be the relative amount invested in security $i$. We exclude short sales, thus $X_i \geq 0$ for all $i$. Then the discounted anticipated return of the portfolio is

$$R = \sum_{t=1}^{\infty} \sum_{i=1}^{N} d_{it} r_{it} X$$

$$= \sum_{i=1}^{N} X_i \left( \sum_{t=1}^{\infty} d_{it} r_{it} \right)$$

$R_i = \sum_{t=1}^{\infty} d_{it} r_{it}$ is the discounted return of the $i^{th}$ security, therefore $R = \Sigma X_i R_i$ where $R_i$ is independent of $X_i$. Since $X_i \geq 0$ for all $i$ and $\Sigma X_i = 1$, $R$ is a weighted average of $R_i$ with the $X_i$ as non-negative weights. To maximize $R$, we let $X_i = 1$ for $i$ with maximum $R_i$. If several $Ra_a$, $a = 1, \ldots, K$ are maximum then any allocation with

$$\sum_{a=1}^{K} Xa_a = 1$$

maximizes $R$. In no case is a diversified portfolio preferred to all non-diversified portfolios.[4]

It will be convenient at this point to consider a static model. Instead of

[2] J. R. Hicks, *Value and Capital* (New York: Oxford University Press, 1939), p. 126. Hicks applies the rule to a firm rather than a portfolio.

[3] The results depend on the assumption that the anticipated returns and discount rates are independent of the particular investor's portfolio.

[4] If short sales were allowed, an infinite amount of money would be placed in the security with highest $r$.

speaking of the time series of returns from the $i^{th}$ security $(r_{i1}, r_{i2}, \ldots, r_{it}, \ldots)$ we will speak of "the flow of returns" $(r_i)$ from the $i^{th}$ security. The flow of returns from the portfolio as a whole is $R = \Sigma X_i r_i$. As in the dynamic case if the investor wished to maximize "anticipated" return from the portfolio he would place all his funds in that security with maximum anticipated returns.

There is a rule which implies both that the investor should diversify and that he should maximize expected return. The rule states that the investor does (or should) diversify his funds among all those securities which give maximum expected return. The law of large numbers will insure that the actual yield of the portfolio will be almost the same as the expected yield.[5] This rule is a special case of the expected returns—variance of returns rule (to be presented below). It assumes that there is a portfolio which gives both maximum expected return and minimum variance, and it commends this portfolio to the investor.

This presumption, that the law of large numbers applies to a portfolio of securities, cannot be accepted. The returns from securities are too intercorrelated. Diversification cannot eliminate all variance.

The portfolio with maximum expected return is not necessarily the one with minimum variance. There is a rate at which the investor can gain expected return by taking on variance, or reduce variance by giving up expected return.

We saw that the expected returns or anticipated returns rule is inadequate. Let us now consider the expected returns-variance of returns $(E\text{-}V)$ rule. It will be necessary to first present a few elementary concepts and results of mathematical statistics. We will then show some implications of the $E\text{-}V$ rule. After this we will discuss its plausibility.

In our presentation we try to avoid complicated mathematical statements and proofs. As a consequence a price is paid in terms of rigor and generality. The chief limitations from this source are 1) we do not derive our results analytically for the $n$-security case; instead, we present them geometrically for the 3 and 4 security cases; 2) we assume static probability beliefs. In a general presentation we must recognize that the probability distribution of yields of the various securities is a function of time. The writer intends to present, in the future, the general, mathematical treatment which removes this limitation.

We will need the following elementary concepts and results of mathematical statistics:

Let $Y$ be a random variable, i.e., a variable whose value is decided by chance. Suppose, for simplicity of exposition, that $Y$ can take on a finite number of values $y_1, y_2, \ldots, y_N$. Let the probability that $Y = y_1$, be $p_1$; that $Y = y_2$ be $p_2$; etc. The expected value (or mean) of $Y$ is defined to be

$$E = p_1 y_1 + p_2 y_2 + \cdots + p_N y_N$$

The variance of $Y$ is defined to be

[5] Williams, *op. cit.*, pp. 68, 69.

$$V = p_1(y_1 - E)^2 + p_2(y_2 - E)^2 + \cdots + p_N(y_N - E)^2$$

$V$ is the average squared deviation of $Y$ from its expected value. $V$ is a commonly used measure of dispersion. Other measures of dispersion, closely related to $V$ are the standard deviation, $\sigma = \sqrt{V}$, and the coefficient of variation, $\sigma/E$.

Suppose we have a number of random variables: $R_1, \ldots, R_n$. If $R$ is a weighted sum (linear combination) of the $R_i$

$$R = a_1 R_1 + a_2 R_2 + \cdots + a_n R_n$$

then $R$ is also a random variable. (For example, $R_1$ may be the number which turns up on one die; $R_2$, that of another die; and $R$ the sum of these numbers. In this case $n = 2$, $a_1 = a_2 = 1$.)

It will be important for us to know how the expected value and variance of the weighted sum ($R$) are related to the probability distribution of the $R_1$, $\ldots, R_n$. We state these relations below; we refer the reader to any standard text for proof.[6]

The expected value of a weighted sum is the weighted sum of the expected values. I.e. $E(R) = a_1 E(R_1) + a_2 E(R_2) + \ldots + a_n E(R_n)$. The variance of a weighted sum is not as simple. To express it we must define "covariance." The covariance of $R_1$ and $R_2$ is

$$\sigma_{12} = E\{[R_1 = E(R_1)][R_2 - E(R_2)]\}$$

i.e., the expected value of [(the deviation of $R_1$ from its mean) times (the deviation of $R_2$ from its mean)]. In general we define the covariance between $R_i$ and $R_j$ as

$$\sigma_{ij} = E\{[R_i - E(R_i)][R_j - E(R_j)]\}.$$

$\sigma_{ij}$ may be expressed in terms of the familiar correlation coefficient ($\rho_{ij}$). The covariance between $R_i$ and $R_j$ is equal to [(their correlation) times (the standard deviation of $R_i$) times (the standard deviation of $R_j$)]:

$$\sigma_{ij} = \rho_{ij}\sigma_i\sigma_j.$$

The variance of a weighted sum is

$$V(R) = \sum_{i=1}^{N} a_i^2 V(X_i) + 2\sum_{i=1}^{N} \sum_{i>1}^{N} a_i a_j \sigma_{ij}.$$

If we use the fact that the variance of $R_i$ is $\sigma_{ii}$ then

$$V(R) = \sum_{i=1}^{N} \sum_{j=1}^{N} a_i a_j \sigma_{ij}.$$

Let $R_i$ be the return on the $i^{th}$ security. Let $\mu_i$ be the expected value of $R_i$; $\sigma_{ij}$, be the covariance between $R_i$ and $R_j$ (thus $\sigma_{ii}$ is the variance of $R_i$). Let

---

[6] For example, J. V. Uspensky, *Introduction to Mathematical Probability* (New York: McGraw-Hill, 1937), Ch. 9, pp. 161–81.

$X_i$ be the percentage of the investor's assets which are allocated to the $i^{th}$ security. The yield ($R$) on the portfolio as a whole is

$$R = \sum R_i X_i .$$

The $R_i$ (and consequently $R$) are considered to be random variables.[7] The $X_i$ are not random variables, but are fixed by the investor. Since the $X_i$ are percentages we have $\Sigma X_i = 1$. In our analysis we will exclude negative values of the $X_i$ (i.e., short sales); therefore $X_i \geq 0$ for all $i$.

The return ($R$) on the portfolio as a whole is a weighted sum of random variables (where the investor can choose the weights). From our discussion of such weighted sums we see that the expected return $E$ from the portfolio as as a whole is

$$E = \sum_{i=1}^{N} X_i \mu_i$$

and the variance is

$$V = \sum_{i=1}^{N} \sum_{j=1}^{N} \sigma_{ij} X_i X .$$

For fixed probability beliefs ($\mu_i$, $\sigma_{ij}$) the investor has a choice of various combinations of $E$ and $V$ depending on his choice of portfolio $X_1, \ldots, X_N$. Suppose that the set of all obtainable ($E$, $V$) combinations were as in Figure 1. The $E$-$V$ rule states that the investor would (or should) want to select one of those portfolios which give rise to the ($E$, $V$) combinations indicated as efficient in the figure; i.e., those with minimum $V$ for given $E$ or more and maximum $E$ for given $V$ or less.

There are techniques by which we can compute the set of efficient portfolios and efficient ($E$, $V$) combinations associated with given $\mu_i$ and $\sigma_{ij}$. We will not present these techniques here. We will, however, illustrate geometrically the nature of the efficient surfaces for cases in which $N$ (the number of available securities) is small.

The calculation of efficient surfaces might possibly be of practical use. Perhaps there are ways, by combining statistical techniques and the judgment of experts, to form reasonable probability beliefs ($\mu_i$, $\sigma_{ij}$). We could use these beliefs to compute the attainable efficient combinations of ($E$, $V$).

---

[7] That is, we assume that the investor does (and should) act as if he had probability beliefs concerning these variables. In general we would expect that the investor could tell us, for any two events (A and B), whether he personally considered A more likely than B, B more likely than A, or both equally likely. If the investor were consistent in his opinions on such matters, he would possess a system of probability beliefs. We cannot expect the investor to be consistent in every detail. We can, however, expect his probability beliefs to be roughly consistent on important matters that have been carefully considered. We should also expect that he will base his actions upon these probability beliefs—even though they be in part subjective.

This paper does not consider the difficult question of how investors do (or should) form their probability beliefs.

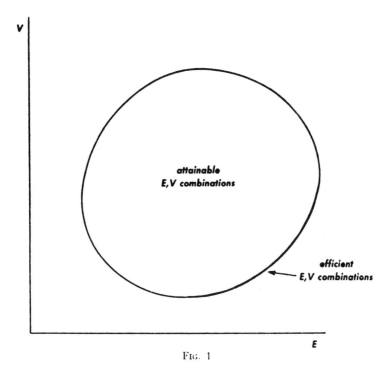

Fig. 1

The investor, being informed of what $(E, V)$ combinations were attainable, could state which he desired. We could then find the portfolio which gave this desired combination.

Two conditions—at least—must be satisfied before it would be practical to use efficient surfaces in the manner described above. First, the investor must desire to act according to the $E$-$V$ maxim. Second, we must be able to arrive at reasonable $\mu_i$ and $\sigma_{ij}$. We will return to these matters later.

Let us consider the case of three securities. In the three security case our model reduces to

(1)
$$E = \sum_{i=1}^{3} X_i \mu_i$$

(2)
$$V = \sum_{i=1}^{3} \sum_{j=1}^{3} X_i X_j \sigma_{ij}$$

(3)
$$\sum_{i=1}^{3} X_i = 1$$

(4)
$$X_i \geq 0 \quad \text{for } i = 1, 2, 3.$$

From (3) we get

(3')
$$X_3 = 1 - X_1 - X_2.$$

If we substitute (3′) in (1) and (2), we get $E$ and $V$ as functions of $X_1$ and $X_2$. For example we find

(1′)
$$E = \mu_3 + X_1(\mu_1 - \mu_3) + X_2(\mu_2 - \mu_3).$$

The exact formulas are not too important here (that of $V$ is given below).[8] We can simply write

(a)
$$E = E(X_1, X_2)$$

(b)
$$V = V(X_1, X_2)$$

(c)
$$X_1 \geq 0, X_2 \geq 0, 1 - X_1 - X_2 \geq 0.$$

By using relations (a), (b), (c), we can work with two dimensional geometry.

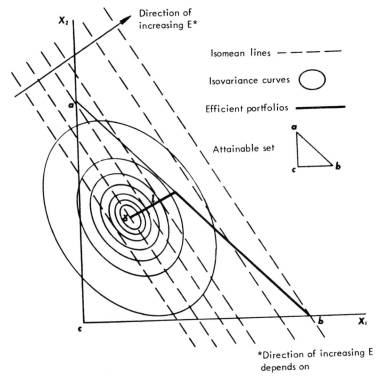

FIGURE 2.

The attainable set of portfolios consists of all portfolios which satisfy constraints (c) and (3′) (or equivalently (3) and (4)). The attainable combinations of $X_1$, $X_2$ are represented by the triangle $abc$ in Figure 2. Any point to the left of the $X_2$ axis is not attainable because it violates the condition that

[8]$V = X_1^2(\sigma_{11} - 2\sigma_{13} + \sigma_{33}) + X_2^2(\sigma_{22} - 2\sigma_{23} + \sigma_{33}) + 2 X_1 X_2(\sigma_{12} - \sigma_{13} - \sigma_{23} + \sigma_{33})$
$+ 2X_1(\sigma_{13} - \sigma_{33}) + 2X_2(\sigma_{23} - \sigma_{33}) + \sigma_{33}.$

$X_1 \geq 0$. Any point below the $X_1$ axis is not attainable because it violates the condition that $X_2 \geq 0$. Any point above the line $(1 - X_1 - X_2 = 0)$ is not attainable because it violates the condition that $X_3 = 1 - X_1 - X_2 \geq 0$.

We define an *isomean* curve to be the set of all points (portfolios) with a given expected return. Similarly an *isovariance* line is defined to be the set of all points (portfolios) with a given variance of return.

An examination of the formulae for $E$ and $V$ tells us the shapes of the iso-mean and isovariance curves. Specificallly, they tell us that typically[9] the isomean curves are a system of parallel straight lines; the isovariance curves are a system of concentric ellipses (see Fig 2). For example, if $\mu_2 \neq \mu_3$ equation (1') can be written in the familiar form $X_2 = a + bX_1$; specifically

$$X_2 = \frac{E - \mu_3}{\mu_2 - \mu_3} - \frac{\mu_1 - \mu_3}{\mu_2 - \mu_3} X_1.$$

Thus the slope of the isomean line associated with $E = E_o$ is $-(\mu_1 - \mu_3)/(\mu_2 - \mu_3)$; its intercept is $(E_o - \mu_3)/(\mu_2 - \mu_3)$. If we change $E$ we change the intercept but not the slope of the isomean line. This confirms the contention that the isomean lines form a system of parallel lines.

Similarly, by a somewhat less simple application of analytic geometry, we can confirm the contention that the isovariance lines form a family of concentric ellipses. The "center" of the system is the point which minimizes $V$. We will label this point $X$. Its expected return and variance we will label $E$ and $V$. Variance increases as you move away from $X$. More precisely, if one iso-variance curve, $C_1$, lies closer to $X$ than another, $C_2$, then $C_1$ is associated with a smaller variance than $C_2$.

With the aid of the foregoing geometric apparatus let us seek the efficient sets.

$X$, the center of the system of isovariance ellipses, may fall either inside or outside the attainable set. Figure 4 illustrates a case in which $X$ falls inside the attainable set. In this case: $X$ is efficient. For no other portfolio has a $V$ as low as $X$; therefore no portfolio can have either smaller $V$ (with the same or greater $E$) or greater $E$ with the same or smaller $V$. No point (portfolio) with expected return $E$ less than $E$ is efficient. For we have $E > E$ and $V < V$.

Consider all points with a given expected return $E$; i.e., all points on the isomean line associated with $E$. The point of the isomean line at which $V$ takes on its least value is the point at which the isomean line is tangent to an isovari-ance curve. We call this point $\hat{X}(E)$. If we let $E$ vary, $\hat{X}(E)$ traces out a curve.

Algebraic considerations (which we omit here) show us that this curve is a straight line. We will call it the critical line $l$. The critical line passes through $X$ for this point minimizes $V$ for all points with $E(X_1, X_2) = E$. As we go along

---

[9] The isomean "curves" are as described above except when $\mu_1 = \mu_2 = \mu_3$. In the latter case all portfolios have the same expected return and the investor chooses the one with minimum variance.

As to the assumptions implicit in our description of the isovariance curves, see foot-note 12.

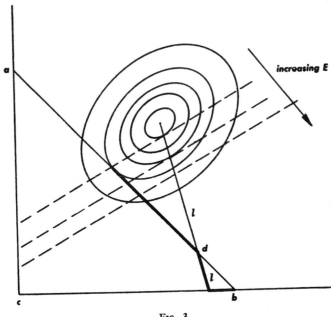

FIG. 3

$l$ in either direction from $X$, $V$ increases. The segment of the critical line from $X$ to the point where the critical line crosses the boundary of the attainable set is part of the efficient set. The rest of the efficient set is (in the case illustrated) the segment of the $\overline{ab}$ line from $d$ to $b$. $b$ is the point of maximum attainable $E$. In Figure 3, $X$ lies outside the admissible area but the critical line cuts the

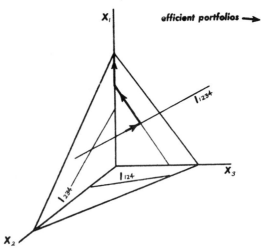

FIG. 4

admissible area. The efficient line begins at the attainable point with minimum variance (in this case on the $\overline{ab}$ line). It moves toward $b$ until it intersects the critical line, moves along the critical line until it intersects a boundary and finally moves along the boundary to $b$. The reader may wish to construct and examine the following other cases: (1) $X$ lies outside the attainable set and the critical line does not cut the attainable set. In this case there is a security which does not enter into any efficient portfolio. (2) Two securities have the same $\mu_i$. In this case the isomean lines are parallel to a boundary line. It may happen that the efficient portfolio with maximum $E$ is a diversified portfolio. (3) A case wherein only one portfolio is efficient.

The efficient set in the 4 security case is, as in the 3 security and also the $N$ security case, a series of connected line segments. At one end of the efficient set is the point of minimum variance; at the other end is a point of maximum expected return[10] (see Fig. 4).

Now that we have seen the nature of the set of efficient portfolios, it is not difficult to see the nature of the set of efficient $(E, V)$ combinations. In the three security case $E = a_o + a_1 X_1 + a_2 X_2$ is a plane; $V = b_o + b_1 X_1 + b_2 X_2 + b_{12} X_1 X_2 + b_{11} X_1^2 + b_{22} X_2^2$ is a paraboloid.[11] As shown in Figure 5, the section of the $E$-plane over the efficient portfolio set is a series of connected line segments. The section of the $V$-paraboloid over the efficient portfolio set is a series of connected parabola segments. If we plotted $V$ against $E$ for efficient portfolios we would again get a series of connected parabola segments (see Fig. 6). This result obtains for any number of securities.

Various reasons recommend the use of the expected return-variance of return rule, both as a hypothesis to explain well-established investment behavior and as a maxim to guide one's own action. The rule serves better, we

---

[10] Just as we used the equation $\sum_{i=1}^{4} X_i = 1$ to reduce the dimensionality in the three security case, we can use it to represent the four security case in 3 dimensional space. Eliminating $X_4$ we get $E = E(X_1, X_2, X_3)$, $V = V(X_1, X_2, X_3)$. The attainable set is represented, in three space, by the tetrahedron with vertices $(0, 0, 0)$, $(0, 0, 1)$, $(0, 1, 0)$, $(1, 0, 0)$, representing portfolios with, respectively, $X_4 = 1$, $X_3 = 1$, $X_2 = 1$, $X_1 = 1$.

Let $s_{123}$ be the subspace consisting of all points with $X_4 = 0$. Similarly we can define $s_{a1}, \ldots, a_a$ to be the subspace consisting of all points with $X_i = 0$, $i \neq a_1, \ldots, a_a$. For each subspace $s_{a1}, \ldots, a_a$ we can define a *critical line* $1a_1, \ldots a_a$. This line is the locus of points $P$ where $P$ minimizes $V$ for all points in $s_{a1}, \ldots, a_a$ with the same $E$ as $P$. If a point is in $s_{a1}, \ldots, a_a$ and is efficient it must be on $la_1, \ldots, a_a$. The efficient set may be traced out by starting at the point of minimum available variance, moving continuously along various $la_1, \ldots, a_a$ according to definite rules, ending in a point which gives maximum $E$. As in the two dimensional case the point with minimum available variance may be in the interior of the available set or on one of its boundaries. Typically we proceed along a given critical line until either this line intersects one of a larger subspace or meets a boundary (and simultaneously the critical line of a lower dimensional subspace). In either of these cases the efficient line turns and continues along the new line. The efficient line terminates when a point with maximum $E$ is reached.

[11] See footnote 8.

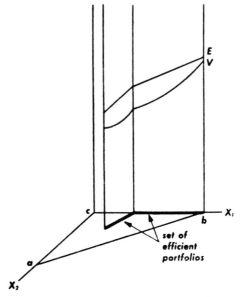

F<small>IG</small>. 5

will see, as an explanation of, and guide to, "investment" as distinguished from "speculative" behavior.

Earlier we rejected the expected returns rule on the grounds that it never implied the superiority of diversification. The expected return-variance of return rule, on the other hand, implies diversification for a wide range of $\mu_i$, $\sigma_{ij}$. This does not mean that the $E\text{-}V$ rule never implies the superiority of an undiversified portfolio. It is conceivable that one security might have an

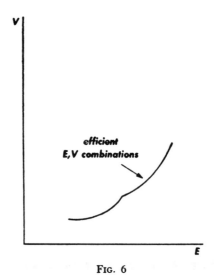

F<small>IG</small>. 6

extremely higher yield and lower variance than all other securities; so much so that one particular undiversified portfolio would give maximum $E$ and minimum $V$. But for a large, presumably representative range of $\mu_i$, $\sigma_{ij}$ the $E$-$V$ rule leads to efficient portfolios almost all of which are diversified.

Not only does the $E$-$V$ hypothesis imply diversification, it implies the " right kind " of diversification for the " right reason." The adequacy of diversification is not thought by investors to depend on the number of different securities held. A portfolio with sixty different railway securities for example, would not be as well diversified as the same size portfolio with some railroad, some public utility, mining, various sort of manufacturing, etc. The reason is that it is generally more likely for firms within the same industry to do poorly at the same time than for firms in dissimilar industries.

Similarly in trying to make variance small it is not enough to invest in many securities. It is necessary to avoid investing in securities with high covariances among themselves. We should diversify across industries because firms in different industries, especially industries with different economic characteristics, have lower covariances than firms within an industry.

The concepts " yield " and " risk " appear frequently in financial writings. Usually if the term " yield " were replaced by " expected yield " or " expected return," and " risk " by " variance of return," little change of apparent meaning would result.

Variance is a well-known measure of dispersion about the expected. If instead of variance the investor was concerned with standard error, $\sigma = \sqrt{V}$, or with the coefficient of dispersion, $\sigma/E$, his choice would still lie in the set of efficient portfolios.

Suppose an investor diversifies between two portfolios (i.e., if he puts some of his money in one portfolio, the rest of his money in the other. An example of diversifying among portfolios is the buying of the shares of two different investment companies). If the two original portfolios have *equal* variance then typically [12] the variance of the resulting (compound) portfolio will be less than the variance of either original portfolio. This is illustrated by Figure 7. To interpret Figure 7 we note that a portfolio $P$ which is built out of two portfolios $P' = (X'_1, X'_2)$ and $P'' = (X''_1, X''_2)$ is of the form $P = \lambda P' + (1 - \lambda)P''$ $= [\lambda X'_1 + (1 - \lambda)X''_1, \lambda X'_2 + (1 - \lambda)X''_2]$. $P$ is on the straight line connecting $P'$ and $P''$.

The $E$-$V$ principle is more plausible as a rule for investment behavior as distinguished from speculative behavior. The third moment [13] $M_3$ of the probability distribution of returns from the portfolio may be connected with a

[12] In no case will variance be increased. The only case in which variance will not be decreased is if the return from both portfolios are perfectly correlated. To draw the isovariance curves as ellipses it is both necessary and sufficient to assume that no two distinct portfolios have perfectly correlated returns.

[13] If $R$ is a random variable that takes on a finite number of values $r_1, \ldots, r_n$ with probabilities $p_1, \ldots, p_n$ respectively, and expected value $E$, then $M_3 = \sum_{i=1}^{n} p_i(r_i - E)^3$.

propensity to gamble. For example if the investor maximizes utility $U$ which depends on $E$ and $V$ $[U = U(E, V), \partial U/\partial E > 0, \partial U/\partial E < 0]$, he will never accept an actuarially fair[14] bet. But if $U = U(E, V, M_3)$ and if $\partial U/\partial M_3 \neq 0$ then there are some fair bets which would be accepted.

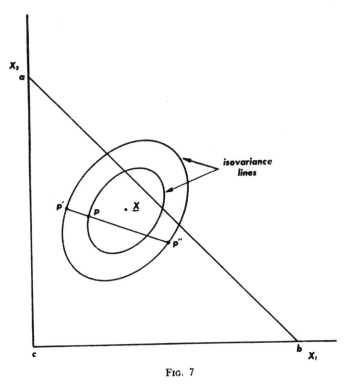

FIG. 7

Perhaps—for a great variety of investing institutions which consider yield to be a good thing; risk, a bad thing; gambling, to be avoided—$E$, $V$ efficiency is reasonable as a working hypothesis and a working maxim.

Two uses of the $E$-$V$ principle suggest themselves. We might use it in theoretical analyses, or we might use it in the actual selection of portfolios.

In theoretical analyses we might inquire, for example, about the various effects of a change in the beliefs generally held about a firm, or a general change in preference as to expected return versus variance of return, or a change in the supply of a security. In our analyses the $X_i$ might represent individual securities or they might represent aggregates such as, say, bonds, stocks, and real estate.[15]

To use the $E$-$V$ rule in the selection of securities we must have procedures

[14] One in which the amount gained by winning the bet times the probability of winning is equal to the amount lost by losing the bet, times the probability of losing.

[15] Care must be used in using and interpreting relations among aggregates. We cannot deal here with the problems and pitfalls of aggregation.

for finding reasonable $\mu_i$ and $\sigma_{ij}$. These procedures, I believe, should combine statistical techniques and the judgment of practical men. My feeling is that the statistical computations should be used to arrive at a tentative set of $\mu_i$ and $\sigma_{ij}$. Judgment should then be used in increasing or decreasing some of these $\mu_i$ and $\sigma_{ij}$ on the basis of factors or nuances not taken into account by the formal computations. Using this revised set of $\mu_i$ and $\sigma_{ij}$, the set of efficient $E$, $V$ combinations could be computed, the investor could select the combination he preferred, and the portfolio which gave rise to this $E$, $V$ combination could be found.

One suggestion as to tentative $\mu_i$, $\sigma_{ij}$ is to use the observed $\mu_i$, $\sigma_{ij}$ for some period of the past. I believe that better methods, which take into account more information, can be found. I believe that what is needed is essentially a "probabilistic" reformulation of security analysis. I will not pursue this subject here, for this is "another story." It is a story of which I have read only the first page of the first chapter.

In this paper we have considered the second stage in the process of selecting a portfolio. This stage starts with the relevant beliefs about the securities involved and ends with the selection of a portfolio. We have not considered the first stage: the information of the relevant beliefs on the basis of observation.

## 10. LIQUIDITY PREFERENCE AS BEHAVIOUR TOWARDS RISK*

J. TOBIN†

Reprinted from *The Review of Economic Studies*, Vol. *XXVI*, No. 1, (February, 1958), pp. 65–86, by permission of the author and the publisher.[1]

One of the basic functional relationships in the Keynesian model of the economy is the liquidity preference schedule, an inverse relationship between the demand for cash balances and the rate of interest. This aggregative function must be derived from some assumptions regarding the behavior of the decision-making units of the economy, and those assumptions are the concern

* I am grateful to Challis Hall, Arthur Okun, Walter Salant, and Leroy Wehrle for helpful comments on earlier drafts of this paper.

† New Haven, Conn., U.S.A.

[1] The footnotes below are numbered consecutively throughout, although in the original article they are numbered consecutively only on each page. To ease the reader's transference between this reprint and the original, at the end of each footnote, in parentheses, is the footnote citation and the page number of the original article.

of this paper. Nearly two decades of drawing downward-sloping liquidity preference curves in textbooks and on classroom blackboards should not blind us to the basic implausibility of the behavior they describe. Why should anyone hold the non-interest bearing obligations of the government instead of its interest bearing obligations? The apparent irrationality of holding cash is the same, moreover, whether the interest rate is 6%, 3% or $\frac{1}{2}$ of 1%. What needs to be explained is not only the existence of a demand for each when its yield is less than the yield on alternative assets but an inverse relationship between the aggregate demand for cash and the size of this differential in yields.[2]

## 1. TRANSACTIONS BALANCES AND INVESTMENT BALANCES.

Two kinds of reasons for holding cash are usually distinguished: transactions reasons and investment reasons.

1.1 *Transactions balances: size and composition.* No economic unit—firm or household or government—enjoys perfect synchronization between the seasonal patterns of its flow of receipts and its flow of expenditures. The discrepancies give rise to balances which accumulate temporarily, and are used up later in the year when expenditures catch up. Or, to put the same phenomenon the other way, the discrepancies give rise to the need for balances to meet seasonal excesses of expenditures over receipts. These balances are *transactions balances.* The aggregate requirement of the economy for such balances depends on the institutional arrangements that determine the degree of synchronization between individual receipts and expenditures. Given these institutions, the need for transactions balances is roughly proportionate to the aggregate volume of transactions.

The obvious importance of these institutional determinants of the demand for transactions balances has led to the general opinion that other possible determinants, including interest rates, are negligible.[3] This may be true of the

---

[2] " . . . in a world involving no transaction friction and no uncertainty, there would be no reason for a spread between the yield on any two assets, and hence there would be no difference in the yield on money and on securities . . . in such a world securities themselves would circulate as money and be acceptable in transactions; demand bank deposits would bear interest, just as they often did in this country in the period of the twenties." Paul A. Samuelson, *Foundations of Economic Analysis* (Cambridge: Harvard University Press, 1947), p. 123. The section pp. 122–124, from which the passage is quoted makes it clear that liquidity preference must be regarded as an explanation of the existence and level not of the interest rate but of the differential between the yield on money and the yields on other assets.

[3] The traditional theory of the velocity of money has, however, probably exaggerated the invariance of the institutions determining the extent of lack of synchronization between individual receipts and expenditures. It is no doubt true that such institutions as the degree of vertical integration of production and the periodicity of wage, salary, dividend, and tax payments are slow to change. But other relevant arrangements can be adjusted in response to money rates. For example, there is a good deal of flexibility in the promptness and regularity with which bills are rendered and settled. (1, p. 66)

size of transactions balances, but the composition of transactions balances is another matter. Cash is by no means the only asset in which transactions balances may be held. Many transactors have large enough balances so that holding part of them in earning assets, rather than in cash, is a relevant possibility. Even though these holdings are always for short periods, the interest earnings may be worth the cost and inconvenience of the financial transactions involved. Elsewhere[4] I have shown that, for such transactors, the proportion of cash in transactions balances varies inversely with the rate of interest; consequently this source of interest-elasticity in the demand for cash will not be further discussed here.

1.2 *Investment balances and portfolio decisions.*   In contrast to transactions balances, the investment balances of an economic unit are those that will survive all the expected seasonal excesses of cumulative expenditures over cumulative receipts during the year ahead. They are balances which will not have to be turned into cash within the year. Consequently the cost of financial transactions—converting other assets into cash and vice versa—does not operate to encourage the holding of investment balances in cash.[5] If cash is to have any part in the composition of investment balances, it must be because of expectations or fears of loss on other assets. It is here, in what Keynes called the speculative motives of investors, that the explanation of liquidity preference and of the interest-elasticity of the demand for cash has been sought.

The alternatives to cash considered, both in this paper and in prior discussions of the subject, in examining the speculative motive for holding cash are assets that differ from cash only in having a variable market yield. They are obligations to pay stated cash amounts at future dates, with no risk of default. They are, like cash, subject to changes in real value due to fluctuations in the price level. In a broader perspective, all these assets, including cash, are merely minor variants of the same species, a species we may call monetary assets—marketable, fixed in money value, free of default risk. The differences of members of this species from each other are negligible compared to their differences from the vast variety of other assets in which wealth may be invested: corporate stocks, real estate, unincorporated business and professional practice, etc. The theory of liquidity preference does not concern the choices investors make between the whole species of monetary assets, on the one hand, and other broad classes of assets, on the other.[6] Those choices are

---

[4] "The Interest Elasticity of the Transactions Demand for Cash," *Review of Economics and Statistics*, Volume 38 (August, 1956), pp. 241–247. (2, p. 66)

[5] Costs of financial transactions have the effect of deterring changes from the existing portfolio, whatever its composition; they may thus operate against the holding of cash as easily as for it. Because of these costs, the *status quo* may be optimal even when a different composition of assets would be preferred if the investor were starting over again. (3, p. 66)

[6] For an attempt by the author to apply to this wider choice some of the same theoretical tools that are here used to analyze choices among the narrow class of monetary assets, see "A Dynamic Aggregative Model," *Journal of Political Economy*, Vol. 63 (April, 1955), pp. 103–115. (4, p. 66)

the concern of other branches of economic theory, in particular theories of investment and of consumption. Liquidity preference theory takes as given the choices determining how much wealth is to be invested in monetary assets and concerns itself with the allocation of these amounts among cash and alternative monetary assets.

Why should any investment balances be held in cash, in preference to other monetary assets? We shall distinguish two possible sources of liquidity preference, while recognizing that they are not mutually exclusive. The first is inelasticity of expectations of future interest rates. The second is uncertainty about the future of interest rates. These two sources of liquidity preference will be examined in turn.

## 2. INELASTICITY OF INTEREST RATE EXPECTATIONS.

2.1 *Some simplifying assumptions.* To simplify the problem, assume that there is only one monetary asset other than cash, namely, consols. The current yield of consols is $r$ per "year." $1 invested in consols today will purchase an income of $r$ per "year" in perpetuity. The yield of cash is assumed to be zero; however, this is not essential, as it is the current and expected differentials of consols over cash that matter. An investor with a given total balance must decide what proportion of this balance to hold in cash, $A_1$, and what proportion in consols, $A_2$. This decision is assumed to fix the portfolio for a full "year."[7]

2.2 *Fixed expectations of future rate.* At the end of the year, the investor expects the rate on consols to be $r_e$. This expectation is assumed, for the present, to be held with certainty and to be independent of the current rate $r$. The investor may therefore expect with certainty that every dollar invested in consols today will earn over the year ahead not only the interest $r$, but also a capital gain or loss $g$:

$$g = \frac{r}{r_e} - 1. \qquad (2.1)$$

[7] As noted above, it is the costs of financial transactions that impart inertia to portfolio composition. Every reconsideration of the portfolio involves the investor in expenditure of time and effort as well as of money. The frequency with which it is worth while to review the portfolio will obviously vary with the investor and will depend on the size of his portfolio and on his situation with respect to costs of obtaining information and engaging in financial transactions. Thus the relevant "year" ahead for which portfolio decisions are made is not the same for all investors. Moreover, even if a decision is made with a view to fixing a portfolio for a given period of time, a portfolio is never so irrevocably frozen that there are no conceivable events during the period which would induce the investor to reconsider. The fact that this possibility is always open must influence the investor's decision. The fiction of a fixed investment period used in this paper is, therefore, not a wholly satisfactory way of taking account of the inertia in portfolio composition due to the costs of transactions and of decision making. (1, p. 67)

For this, investor, the division of his balance into proportions $A_1$ of cash and $A_2$ of consols is a simple all-or-nothing choice. If the current rate is such that $r + g$ is greater than zero, then he will put everything in consols. But if $r + g$ is less than zero, he will put everything in cash. These conditions can be expressed in terms of a critical level of the current rate $r_c$, where:

$$r_c = \frac{r_e}{1 + r_e}. \qquad (2.2)$$

At current rates above $r_c$, everything goes into consols; but for $r$ less than $r_c$, everything goes into cash.

2.3 *Sticky and certain interest rate expectations.* So far the investor's expected interest rate $r_e$ has been assumed to be completely independent of the current rate $r$. This assumption can be modified so long as some independence of the expected rate from the current rate is maintained. In Figure2.1,

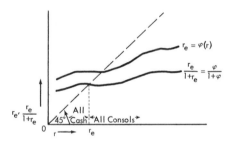

Fig. 2.1 — Stickiness in the relation between expected and current interest rate.

for example, $r_e$ is shown as a function of $r$, namely $\phi(r)$. Correspondingly $\frac{r_e}{1 + r_e}$ is a function of $r$. As shown in the figure, this function $\frac{\phi}{1 + \phi}$ has only one intersection with the 45° line, and at this intersection its slope $\frac{\phi'}{(1 + \phi)^2}$ is less than one. If these conditions are met, the intersection determines a critical rate $r_c$ such that if $r$ exceeds $r_c$ the investor holds no cash, while if $r$ is less than $r_c$ he holds no consols.

2.4 *Differences of opinion and the aggregate demand for cash.* According to this model, the relationship of the individual's investment demand for cash to the current rate of interest would be the discontinuous step function shown by the heavy vertical lines $LMNW$ in Figure 2.2. How then do we get the familiar Keynesian liquidity preference function, a smooth, continuous inverse relationship between the demand for cash and the rate of interest? For the economy as a whole, such a relationship can be derived from individual behavior of the sort depicted in Figure 2.2 by assuming that individual investors differ in their critical rates $r_c$. Such an aggregate relationship is shown in Figure 2.3.

At actual rates above the maximum of individual critical rates the aggregate demand for cash is zero, while at rates below the minimum critical rate it is

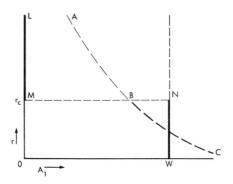

Fig. 2.2 — Individual demand for cash assuming certain but inelastic interest rate expectations.

equal to the total investment balances for the whole economy. Between these two extremes the demand for cash varies inversely with the rate of interest $r$. Such a relationship is shown as $LMN\Sigma W$ in Figure 2.3. The demand for cash at $r$ is the total of investment balances controlled by investors whose critical rates $r_c$ exceed $r$. Strictly speaking, the curve is a step function; but, if the number of investors is large, it can be approximated by a smooth curve. Its

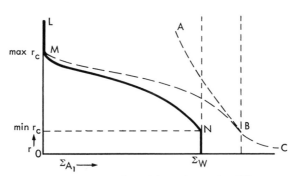

Fig. 2.3 — Aggregate demand for cash assuming differences among individuals in interest rate expectations.

shape depends on the distribution of dollars of investment balances by the critical rate of the investor controlling them; the shape of the curve in Figure 2.3 follows from a unimodal distribution.

2.5 *Capital gains or losses and open market operations.*   In the foregoing analysis the size of investment balances has been taken as independent of the current rate on consols $r$. This is not the case if there are already consols outstanding. Their value will depend inversely on the current rate of interest. Depending on the relation of the current rate to the previously fixed coupon on consols, owners of consols will receive capital gains or losses. Thus the investment balances of an individual owner of consols would not be constant at $W$ but would depend on $r$ in a manner illustrated by the curve $ABC$ in Figure 2.2.[8] Similarly, the investment balances for the whole economy would follow a curve like $ABC$ in Figure 2.3, instead of being constant at $\Sigma W$. The demand for cash would then be described by $LMBC$ in both figures. Correspondingly the demand for consols at any interest rate would be described by the horizontal distance between $LMBC$ and $ABC$. The value of consols goes to infinity as the rate of interest approaches zero; for this reason, the curve $BC$ may never reach the horizontal axis. The size of investment balances would be bounded if the monetary assets other than cash consisted of bonds with definite maturities rather than consols.

According to this theory, a curve like $LMBC$ depicts the terms on which a central bank can engage in open-market operations, given the claims for future payments outstanding in the form of bonds or consols. The curve tells what the quantity of cash must be in order for the central bank to establish a particular interest rate. However, the curve will be shifted by open market operations themselves, since they will change the volume of outstanding bonds or consols. For example, to establish the rate at or below min $r_c$, the central bank would have to buy all outstanding bonds or consols. The size of the community's investment balances would then be independent of the rate of interest; it would be represented by a vertical line through, or to the right of, $B$, rather than the curve $ABC$. Thus the new relation between cash and interest would be a curve lying above $LMB$, of the same general contour as $LMN\Sigma W$.

2.6 *Keynesian theory and its critics.*   I believe the theory of liquidity preference I have just presented is essentially the original Keynesian explanation. The *General Theory* suggests a number of possible theoretical explanations, supported and enriched by the experience and insight of the author. But the explanation to which Keynes gave the greatest emphasis is the notion of a "normal" long-term rate, to which investors expect the rate of interest to return. When he refers to uncertainty in the market, he appears to mean disagreement among investors concerning the future of the rate rather than subjective doubt in the mind of an individual investor.[9] Thus Kaldor's correction of Keynes is more verbal than substantive when he says, "It is . . . not

---

[8] The size of their investment balances, held in cash and consols may not vary by the full amount of these changes in wealth; some part of the changes may be reflected in holdings of assets other than monetary assets. But presumably the size of investment balances will reflect at least in part these capital gains and losses. (1, p. 69)

[9] J. M. Keynes, *The General Theory of Employment, Interest, and Money* (New York: Harcourt Brace, 1936), Chapters 13 and 15, especially pp. 168–172 and 201–203. One quotation from p. 172 will illustrate the point: "It is interesting that the stability of the system and its sensitiveness to changes in the quantity of money should be so dependent on the existence

so much the *uncertainty* concerning future interest rates as the *inelasticity* of interest expectations which is responsible for Mr. Keynes' 'liquidity preference function,' ... "[10]

Keynes' use of this explanation of liquidity preference as a part of his theory of underemployment equilibrium was the target of important criticism by Leontief and Fellner. Leontief argued that liquidity preference must necessarily be zero *in equilibrium*, regardless of the rate of interest. Divergence between the current and expected interest rate is bound to vanish as investors learn from experience; no matter how low an interest rate may be, it can be accepted as "normal" if it persists long enough. This criticism was a part of Leontief's general methodological criticism of Keynes, that unemployment was not a feature of equilibrium, subject to analysis by tools of static theory, but a phenomenon of disequilibrium requiring analysis by dynamic theory.[11] Fellner makes a similar criticism of the logical appropriateness of Keynes' explanation of liquidity preference for the purposes of his theory of underemployment equilibrium. Why, he asks, are interest rates the only variables to which inelastic expectations attach? Why don't wealth owners and others regard pre-depression price levels as "normal" levels to which prices will return? If they did, consumption and investment demand would respond to reductions in money wages and prices, no matter how strong and how elastic the liquidity preference of investors.[12]

These criticisms raise the question whether it is possible to dispense with the assumption of stickiness in interest rate expectations without losing the implication that Keynesian theory drew from it. Can the inverse relationship of demand for cash to the rate of interest be based on a different set of assumptions about the behavior of individual investors? This question is the subject of the next part of the paper.

### 3. UNCERTAINTY, RISK AVERSION, AND LIQUIDITY PREFERENCE.

3.1 *The locus of opportunity for risk and expected return.*   Suppose that an investor is not certain of the future rate of interest on consols; investment in consols then involves a risk of capital gain or loss. The higher the proportion of his investment balance that he holds in consols, the more risk the investor assumes. At the same time, increasing the proportion in consols also increases

---

of a variety of opinion about what is uncertain. Best of all that we should know the future. But if not, then, if we are to control the activity of the economic system by changing the quantity of money, it is important that opinions should differ." (1, p. 70)

[10] N. Kaldor, "Speculation and Economic Stability," *Review of Economic Studies*, Vol. 7 (1939), p. 15. (2, p. 70)

[11] W. Leontief, "Postulates: Keynes' General Theory and the Classicists," Chapter XIX in S. Harris, editor, *The New Economics* (New York: Knopf, 1947), pp. 232–242. Section 6, pp. 238–239, contains the specific criticism of Keynes' liquidity preference theory. (3, p. 70)

[12] W. Fellner, *Monetary Policies and Full Employment* (Berkeley: University of California Press, 1946), p. 149. (4, p. 70)

his expected return. In the upper half of Figure 3.1, the vertical axis represents expected return and the horizontal axis risk. A line such as $OC_1$ pictures the fact that the investor can expect more return if he assumes more risk. In the lower half of Figure 3.1, the left-hand vertical axis measures the proportion

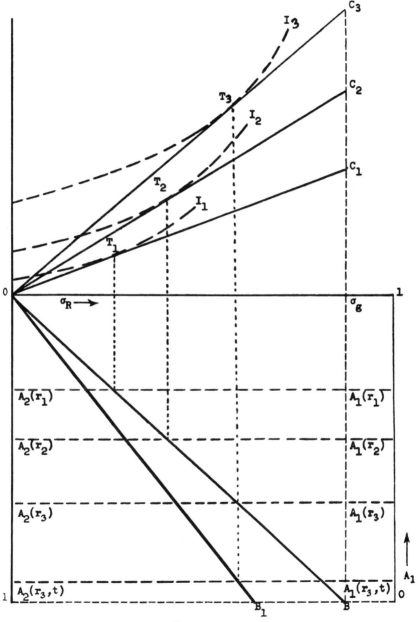

FIGURE 3.1
Portfolio Selection at Various Interest Rates and Before and After Taxation.

invested in consols. A line like $OB$ shows risk as proportional to the share of the total balance held in consols.

The concepts of expected return and risk must be given more precision.

The individual investor of the previous section was assumed to have, for any current rate of interest, a definite expectation of the capital gain or loss $g$ (defined in expression (2.1) above) he would obtain by investing one dollar in consols. Now he will be assumed instead to be uncertain about $g$ but to base his actions on his estimate of its probability distribution. This probability distribution, it will be assumed, has an expected value of zero and is independent of the level of $r$, the current rate on consols. Thus the investor considers a doubling of the rate just as likely when rate is 5% as when it is 2%, and a halving of the rate just as likely when it is 1% as when it is 6%.

A portfolio consists of a proportion $A_1$ of cash and $A_2$ of consols, where $A_1$ and $A_2$ add up to 1. We shall assume that $A_1$ and $A_2$ do not depend on the absolute size of the initial investment balance in dollars. Negative values of $A_1$ and $A_2$ are excluded by definition; only the government and the banking system can issue cash and government consols. The return on a portfolio $R$ is:

$$R = A_2(r + g) \qquad 0 \le A_2 \le 1. \tag{3.1}$$

Since $g$ is a random variable with expected value zero, the expected return on the portfolio is:

$$E(R) = \mu_R = A_2 r. \tag{3.2}$$

The risk attached to a portfolio is to be measured by the standard deviation of $R$, $\sigma_R$. The standard deviation is a measure of the dispersion of possible returns around the mean value $\mu_R$. A high standard deviation means, speaking roughly, high probability of large deviations from $\mu_R$, both positive and negative. A low standard deviation means low probability of large deviations from $\mu_R$; in the extreme case, a zero standard deviation would indicate certainty of receiving the return $\mu_R$. Thus a high-$\sigma_R$ portfolio offers the investor the chance of large capital gains at the price of equivalent chances of large capital losses. A low-$\sigma_R$ portfolio protects the investor from capital loss, and likewise gives him little prospect of unusual gains. Although it is intuitively clear that the risk of a portfolio is to be identified with the dispersion of possible returns, the standard deviation is neither the sole measure of dispersion nor the obviously most relevant measure. The case for the standard deviation will be further discussed in section 3.3 below.

The standard deviation of $R$ depends on the standard deviation of $g$, $\sigma_g$, and on the amount invested in consols:

$$\sigma_R = A_2 \sigma_g \qquad 0 \le A_2 \le 1. \tag{3.3}$$

Thus the proportion the investor holds in consols $A_2$ determines both his expected return $\mu_R$ and his risk $\sigma_R$. The terms on which the investor can obtain greater expected return at the expense of assuming more risk can be derived from (3.2) and (3.3):

$$\mu_R = \frac{r}{\sigma_g} \sigma_R \qquad 0 \le \sigma_R \le \sigma_g. \tag{3.4}$$

Such an *opportunity locus* is shown as line $OC_1$ (for $r = r_1$) in Figure 3.1. The slope of the line is $\dfrac{r_1}{\sigma_g}$. For a higher interest rate $r_2$, the opportunity locus would be $OC_2$; and for $r_3$, a still higher rate, it would be $OC_3$. The relationship (3.3) between risk and investment in consols is shown as line $OB$ in the lower half of the Figure. Cash holding $A_1 (= 1 - A_2)$ can also be read off the diagram on the right-hand vertical axis.

3.2 *Loci of indifference between combinations of risk and expected return.* The investor is assumed to have preferences between expected return $\mu_R$ and risk $\sigma_R$ that can be represented by a field of indifference curves. The investor is indifferent between all pairs $(\mu_R, \sigma_R)$ that lie on a curve such as $I_1$ in Figure 3.1. Points on $I_2$ are preferred to those on $I_1$; for given risk, an investor always prefers a greater to a smaller expectation of return. Conceivably, for some investors, *risk-lovers*, these indifference curves have negative slopes. Such individuals are willing to accept lower expected return in order to have the chance of unusually high capital gains afforded by high values of $\sigma_R$. *Risk-averters*, on the other hand, will not be satisfied to accept more risk unless they can also expect greater expected return. Their indifference curves will be positively sloped. Two kinds of risk-averters need to be distinguished. The first type, who may be called *diversifiers* for reasons that will become clear below, have indifference curves that are concave upward, like those in Figure 3.1. The second type, who may be called *plungers*, have indifference curves that are upward sloping, but either linear or convex upward.

3.3 *Indifference curves as loci of constant expected utility of wealth.* The reader who is willing to accept the indifference fields that have just been introduced into the analysis may skip to section 3.4 without losing the main thread of the argument. But these indifference curves need some explanation and defence. Indifference curves between $\mu_R$ and $\sigma_R$ do not necessarily exist. It is a simplification to assume that the investor chooses among the alternative probability distributions of $R$ available to him on the basis of only two parameters of those distributions. Even if this simplification is accepted, the mean and standard deviation may not be the pair of parameters that concern the investor.

3.3.1 One justification for the use of indifference curves between $\mu_R$ and $\sigma_R$ would be that the investor evaluates the future of consols only in terms of some two-parameter family of probability distributions of $g$. For example, the investor might think in terms of a range of equally likely gains or losses, centered on zero. Or he might think in terms that can be approximated by a normal distribution. Whatever two-parameter family is assumed—uniform, normal, or some other—the whole probability distribution is determined as soon as the mean and standard deviation are specified. Hence the investor's choice among probability distributions can be analyzed by $\mu_R$-$\sigma_R$ indifference curves; any other pair of independent parameters could serve equally well.

If the investor's probability distributions are assumed to belong to some two-parameter family, the shape of his indifference curves can be inferred from the general characteristics of his utility-of-return function. This function will be assumed to relate utility to $R$, the percentage growth in the investment balance by the end of the period. This way of formulating the utility function makes the investor's indifference map, and therefore his choices of proportions of cash and consols, independent of the absolute amount of his initial balance.

On certain postulates, it can be shown that an individual's choice among probability distributions can be described as the maximization of the expected value of a utility function.[13] The ranking of probability distributions with respect to the expected value of utility will not be changed if the scale on which utility is measured is altered either by the addition of a constant or by multiplication by a positive constant. Consequently we are free to choose arbitrarily the zero and unit of measurement of the utility function $U(R)$ as follows: $U(0) = 0$; $U(-1) = -1$.

Suppose that the probability distribution of $R$ can be described by a two-parameter density function $f(R; \mu_R, \sigma_R)$. Then the expected value of utility is:

$$E[U(R)] = \int_{-\infty}^{\infty} U(R)f(R; \mu_R, \sigma_R)dR. \qquad (3.5)$$

$$\text{Let } z = \frac{R - \mu_R}{\sigma_R}.$$

$$E[U(R)] = E(\mu_R, \sigma_R) = \int_{-\infty}^{\infty} U(\mu_R + \sigma_R z)f(z; 0, 1)dz. \qquad (3.6)$$

An indifference curve is a locus of points $(\mu_R, \sigma_R)$ along which expected utility is constant. We may find the slope of such a locus by differentiating (3.6) with

[13] See Von Neumann, J. and Morgenstern, O., *Theory of Games and Economic Behavior*, 3rd Edition (Princeton: Princeton University Press, 1953), pp. 15-30, pp. 617-632; Herstein, I. N. and Milnor, J., "An Axiomatic Approach to Measurable Utility," *Econometrica*, Vol. 23 (April, 1953), pp. 291-297; Marschak, J., "Rational Behavior, Uncertain Prospects, and Measurable Utility," *Econometrica*, Vol. 18 (April, 1950), pp. 111-141; Friedman, M. and Savage, L. J., "The Utility Analysis of Choices Involving Risk," *Journal of Political Economy*, Vol. 56 (August, 1948), pp. 279-304, and "The Expected Utility Hypothesis and the Measurability of Utility," *Journal of Political Economy*, Vol. 60 (December, 1952), pp. 463-474. For a treatment which also provides an axiomatic basis for the subjective probability estimates here assumed, see Savage, L. J., *The Foundations of Statistics* (New York: Wiley, 1954). (1, p. 74)

respect to $\sigma_R$:

$$0 = \int_{-\infty}^{\infty} U'(\mu_R + \sigma_R z)\left[\frac{d\mu_R}{d\sigma_R} + z\right]f(z; 0, 1)dz.$$

$$\frac{d\mu_R}{d\sigma_R} = -\frac{\displaystyle\int_{-\infty}^{\infty} zU'(R)f(z; 0, 1)dz}{\displaystyle\int_{-\infty}^{\infty} U'(R)f(z; 0, 1)dz}. \tag{3.7}$$

$U'(R)$, the marginal utility of return, is assumed to be everywhere non-negative. If it is also a decreasing function of $R$, then the slope of the indifference locus must be positive; an investor with such a utility function is a risk-averter. If it is an increasing function of $R$, the slope will be negative; this kind of utility function characterizes a risk-lover.

Similarly, the curvature of the indifference loci is related to the shape of the utility function. Suppose, that $(\mu_R, \sigma_R)$ and $(\mu'_R, \sigma'_R)$ are on the same indifference locus, so that $E(\mu_R, \sigma_R) = E(\mu'_R, \sigma'_R)$. Is $\left(\dfrac{\mu_R + \mu'_R}{2}, \dfrac{\sigma_R + \sigma'_R}{2}\right)$ on the same locus, or on a higher or a lower one? In the case of declining marginal utility we know that for every $z$:

$$\tfrac{1}{2}U(\mu_R + \sigma_R z) + \tfrac{1}{2}U(\mu'_R + \sigma'_R z) < U\left(\frac{\mu_R + \mu'_R}{2} + \frac{\sigma_R + \sigma'_R}{2}z\right)$$

Consequently $E\left(\dfrac{\mu_R + \mu'_R}{2}, \dfrac{\sigma_R + \sigma'_R}{2}\right)$ is greater than $E(\mu_R, \sigma_R)$ or $E(\mu'_R, \sigma'_R)$, and

$$\left(\frac{\mu_R + \mu'_R}{2}, \frac{\sigma_R + \sigma'_R}{2}\right),$$

which lies on a line between $(\mu_R, \sigma_R)$ and $(\mu'_R, \sigma'_R)$, is on a higher locus than those points. Thus it is shown that a risk-averter's indifference curve is necessarily concave upwards, provided it is derived in this manner from a two parameter family of probability distributions and declining marginal utility of return. All risk-averters are diversifiers; plungers do not exist. The same kind of argument shows that a risk-lover's indifference curve is concave downwards.

3.3.2 In the absence of restrictions on the subjective probability distribution of the investor, the parameters of the distribution relevant to his choice can be sought in parametric restrictions on his utility-of-return function. Two parameters of the utility function are determined by the choice of the utility scale. If specification of the utility function requires no additional parameters, one parameter of the probability distribution summarizes all the information relevant for the investor's choice. For example, if the utility function is linear

$[U(R) = R]$, then the expected value of utility is simply the expected value of $R$, and maximizing expected utility leads to the same behavior as maximizing return in a world of certainty. If, however, one additional parameter is needed to specify the utility function, then two parameters of the probability distribution will be relevant to the choice; and so on. Which parameters of the distribution are relevant depends on the form of the utility function.

Focus on the mean and standard deviation of return can be justified on the assumption that the utility function is quadratic. Following our conventions as to utility scale, the quadratic function would be:

$$U(R) = (1 + b)R + bR^2. \tag{3.8}$$

Here $0 < b < 1$ for a risk-lover, and $-1 < b < 0$ for a risk-averter. However (3.8) cannot describe the utility function for the whole range of $R$, because marginal utility cannot be negative. The function given in (3.8) can apply only for:

$$(1 + b) + 2bR \geq 0;$$

that is, for:

$$R \geq -\left(\frac{1 + b}{2b}\right)(b > 0) \quad \text{(Risk lover)} \tag{3.9}$$

$$R \leq -\left(\frac{1 + b}{2b}\right)(b < 0) \quad \text{(Risk averter)}.$$

In order to use (3.8), therefore, we must exclude from the range of possibility values of $R$ outside the limits (3.9). At the maximum investment in consols $(A_2 = 1)$, $R = r + g$. A risk-averter must be assumed therefore, to restrict the range of capital gains $g$ to which he attaches non-zero probability so that, for the highest rate of interest $r$ to be considered:

$$r + g \leq -\left(\frac{1 + b}{2b}\right). \tag{3.10}$$

The corresponding limitation for a risk-lover is that, for the lowest interest rate $r$ to be considered:

$$r + g \geq -\left(\frac{1 + b}{2b}\right). \tag{3.11}$$

Given the utility function (3.8), we can investigate the slope and curvature of the indifference curves it implies. The probability density function for $R$, $f(R)$, is restricted by the limit (3.10) or (3.11); but otherwise no restriction on its shape is assumed.

$$E[U(R)] = \int_{-\infty}^{\infty} U(R)f(R)dR = (1 + b)\mu_R + b(\sigma_R^2 + \mu_R^2). \tag{3.12}$$

Holding $E[U(R)]$ constant and differentiating with respect to $\sigma_R$ to obtain the slope of an indifference curve, we have:

$$\frac{d\mu_R}{d\sigma_R} = \frac{\sigma_R}{-\dfrac{1+b}{2b} - \mu_R}.$$ 

(3.13)

For a risk-averter, $-\dfrac{1+b}{2b}$ is positive and is the upper limit for $R$, according to (3.9); $-\dfrac{1+b}{2b}$ is necessarily larger than $\mu_R$. Therefore the slope of an indifference locus is positive. For a risk-lover, on the other hand, the corresponding argument shows that the slope is negative.

Differentiating (3.13) leads to the same conclusions regarding curvature as the alternative approach of section 3.3.1, namely that a risk-averter is necessarily a diversifier.

$$\frac{d^2\mu_R}{d\sigma_R} = \frac{1 + \left(\dfrac{d\mu_R^2}{d\sigma_R}\right)}{\left(-\dfrac{1+b}{2b} - \mu_R\right)^2}.$$ 

(3.14)

For a risk-averter, the second derivative is positive and the indifference locus is concave upwards; for a risk-lover, it is concave downwards.

3.4 *Effects of changes in the rate of interest.* In section 3.3 two alternative rationalizations of the indifference curves introduced in section 3.2 have been presented. Both rationalizations assume that the investor (1) estimates subjective probability distributions of capital gain or loss in holding consols, (2) evaluates his prospective increase in wealth in terms of a cardinal utility function, (3) ranks alternative prospects according to the expected value of utility. The rationalization of section 3.3.1 derives the indifference curves by restricting the subjective probability distributions to a two-parameter family. The rationalization of section 3.3.2 derives the indifference curves by assuming the utility function to be quadratic within the relevant range. On either rationalization, a risk-averter's indifference curves must be concave upwards, characteristic of the diversifiers of section 3.2, and those of a risk-lover concave downwards. If the category defined as *plungers* in 3.2 exists at all, their indifference curves must be determined by some process other than those described in 3.3.

The opportunity locus for the investor is described in 3.1 and summarized in equation (3.4). The investor decides the amount to invest in consols so as to reach the highest indifference curve permitted by his opportunity-locus. This maximization may be one of three kinds:

I. Tangency between an indifference curve and the opportunity locus, as

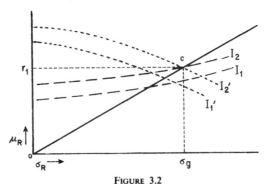

FIGURE 3.2
" Risk-lovers " and " Diversifiers " : Optimum Portfolio at Maximum Risk and Expected Return.

illustrated by points $T_1$, $T_2$, and $T_3$ in Figure 3.1. A regular maximum of this kind can occur only for a risk-averter, and will lead to diversification. Both $A_1$, cash holding, and $A_2$, consol holding, will be positive. They too are shown in Figure 3.1, in the bottom half of the diagram, where, for example, $A_1$ $(r_1)$ and $A_2$ $(r_1)$ depict the cash and consol holdings corresponding to point $T_1$.

II. A corner maximum at the point $\mu_R = r$, $\sigma_R = \sigma_g$, as illustrated in Figure 3.2. In Figure 3.2 the opportunity locus is the ray $OC$, and point $C$ represents the highest expected return and risk obtainable by the investor i.e. the expected return and risk from holding his entire balance in consols. A utility maximum at $C$ can occur either for a risk-averter or for a risk-lover. $I_1$ and $I_2$ represent indifference curves of a diversifier; $I_2$ passes through $C$ and has a lower slope, both at $C$ and everywhere to the left of $C$, than the opportunity locus. $I_1'$ and $I_2'$ represent the indifference curves of a risk-lover, for whom it is clear that $C$ is always the optimum position. Similarly, a plunger may, if his indifference curves stand with respect to his opportunity locus as in Figure 3.3 $(OC_2)$ plunge his entire balance in consols.

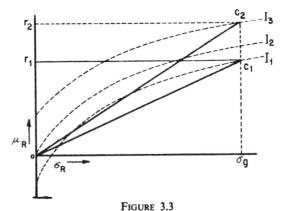

FIGURE 3.3
" Plungers "—Optimum Portfolio at Minimum or Maximum Risk and Expected Return.

III. A corner maximum at the origin, where the entire balance is held in cash. For a plunger, this case is illustrated in Figure 3.3, $(OC_1)$. Conceivably it could also occur for a diversifier, if the slope of his indifference curve at the origin exceeded the slope of the opportunity locus. However, case III is entirely excluded for investors whose indifference curves represent the constant-expected-utility loci of section 3.3. Such investors, we have already noted, cannot be plungers. Furthermore, the slope of all constant-expected-utility loci at $\sigma_R = 0$ must be zero, as can be seen from (3.7) and (3.13).

We can now examine the consequences of a change in the interest rate $r$, holding constant the investor's estimate of the risk of capital gain or loss. An increase in the interest rate will rotate the opportunity locus $OC$ to the left. How will this affect the investor's holdings of cash and consols? We must consider separately the three cases.

I. In Figure 3.1, $OC_1$, $OC_2$, and $OC_3$ represent opportunity loci for successively higher rates of interest. The indifference curves $I_1$, $I_2$, and $I_3$ are drawn so that the points of tangency $T_1$, $T_2$, and $T_3$, correspond to successively higher holdings of consols $A_2$. In this diagram, the investor's demand for cash depends inversely on the interest rate.

This relationship is, of course, in the direction liquidity preference theory has taught us to expect, but it is not the only possible direction of relationship. It is quite possible to draw indifference curves so that the point of tangency moves left as the opportunity locus is rotated counter-clockwise. The ambiguity is a familiar one in the theory of choice, and reflects the ubiquitous conflict between income and substitution effects. An increase in the rate of interest is an incentive to take more risk; so far as the substitution effect is concerned, it means a shift from security to yield. But an increase in the rate of interest also has an income effect, for it gives the opportunity to enjoy more security along with more yield. The ambiguity is analogous to the doubt concerning the effect of a change in the interest rate on saving; the substitution effect argues for a positive relationship, the income effect for an inverse relationship.

However, if the indifference curves are regarded as loci of constant expected utility, as derived in section 3.3, part of this ambiguity can be resolved. We have already observed that these loci all have zero slopes at $\sigma_R = 0$. As the interest rate $r$ rises from zero, so also will consul holding $A_2$. At higher interest rates, however, the inverse relationship may occur.

This reversal of direction can, however, virtually be excluded in the case of the quadratic utility function (section 3.3.2). The condition for a maximum is that the slope of an indifference locus as given by (3.13) equal the slope of the opportunity locus (3.4).

$$\frac{r}{\sigma_g} = \frac{A_2 \sigma_g}{-\dfrac{1+b}{2b} - A_2 r} \; ; \; A_2 = \frac{r}{r^2 + \sigma_g^2}\left(-\frac{1+b}{2b}\right). \tag{3.15}$$

Equation (3.15) expresses $A_2$ as a function of $r$, and differentiating gives:

$$\frac{dA_2}{dr} = \frac{\sigma_g^2 - r^2}{(\sigma_g^2 + r^2)^2}\left(-\frac{1+b}{2b}\right); \frac{r}{A_2}\frac{dA_2}{dr} = \frac{\sigma_g^2 - r^2}{\sigma_g^2 + r^2}. \tag{3.16}$$

Thus the share of consols in the portfolio increases with the interest rate for $r$ less than $\sigma_g$. Moreover, if $r$ exceeds $\sigma_g$, a tangency maximum cannot occur unless $r$ also exceeds $g_{max}$, the largest capital gain the investor conceives possible (see 3.10).[14] The demand for consols is less elastic at high interest rates than at low, but the elasticity is not likely to become negative.

II and III. A change in the interest rate cannot cause a risk-lover to alter his position, which is already the point of maximum risk and expected yield. Conceivably a "diversifier" might move from a corner maximum to a regular interior maximum in response either to a rise in the interest rate or to a fall. A "plunger" might find his position altered by an increase in the interest rate, as from $r_1$ to $r_2$ in Figure 3.3; this would lead him to shift his entire balance from cash to consols.

3.5 *Effects of changes in risk.*   Investor's estimates $\sigma_g$ of the risk of holding monetary assets other than cash, "consols," are subjective. But they are undoubtedly affected by market experience, and they are also subject to influence by measures of monetary and fiscal policy. By actions and words, the central bank can influence investors' estimates of the variability of interest rates; its influence on these estimates of risk may be as important in accomplishing or preventing changes in the rate as open-market operations and other direct interventions in the market. Tax rates, and differences in tax treatment of capital gains, losses, and interest earnings, affect in calculable ways the investor's risks and expected returns. For these reasons it is worth while to examine the effects of a change in an investor's estimate of risk on his allocation between cash and consols.

In Figure 3.4, $T_1$ and $A_2$ $(r_1, \sigma_g)$ represent the initial position of an investor, at interest rate $r_1$ and risk $\sigma_g$. $OC_1$ is the opportunity locus (3.4), and $OB_1$ is the risk-consols relationship (3.3). If the investor now cuts his estimate of risk in half, to $\frac{\sigma_g}{2}$, the opportunity locus will double in slope, from $OC_1$ to $OC_2$,

---

[14] For this statement and its proof, I am greatly indebted to my colleague Arthur Okun. The proof is as follows:

If $r^2 \geq \sigma_g^2$, then by (3.15) and (3.10):

$$1 \geq A_2 \geq \frac{r}{2r^2}\left(-\frac{1+b}{2b}\right) \geq \frac{1}{2r}(r + g_{max}).$$

From the two extremes of this series of inequalities it follows that $2r \geq r + g_{max}$ or $r \geq g_{max}$. Professor Okun also points out that this condition is incompatible with a tangency maximum if the distribution of g is symmetrical. For then $r \geq g_{max}$ would imply $r + g_{min} \geq 0$. There would be no possibility of net loss on consols and thus no reason to hold any cash. (1, p. 79)

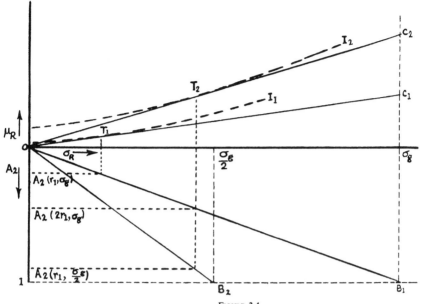

FIGURE 3.4

Comparison of effects of changes in interest rate $(r)$ and in " risk " $(\sigma_g)$ on holding of consols.

and the investor will shift to point $T_2$. The risk-consols relationship will have also doubled in slope, from $OB_1$ to $OB_2$. Consequently points $T_2$ corresponds to an investment in consols of $A_2 \left( r_1, \dfrac{\sigma_g}{2} \right)$. This same point $T_2$ would have been reached if the interest rate had doubled while the investor's risk estimate $\sigma_g$ remained unchanged. But in that case, since the risk-consols relationship would remain at $OB_1$, the corresponding investment in consols would have been only half as large, i.e., $A_2 (2r_1, \sigma_g)$. In general, the following relationship exists between the elasticity of the demand for consols with respect to risk and its elasticity with respect to the interest rate:

$$\frac{\sigma_g}{A_2} \frac{dA_2}{d\sigma_g} = -\frac{r}{A_2} \frac{dA_2}{dr} - 1. \tag{3.17}$$

The implications of this relationship for analysis of effects of taxation may be noted in passing, with the help of Figure 3.4. Suppose that the initial position of the investor is $T_2$ and $A_2 (2r_1, \sigma_g)$. A tax of 50% is now levied on interest income and capital gains alike, with complete loss offset provisions. The result of the tax is to reduce the expected net return per dollar of consols from $2r_1$ to $r_1$ and to reduce the risk to the investor per dollar of consols from $\sigma_g$ to $\sigma_g/2$. The opportunity locus will remain at $OC_2$, and the investor will still wish to obtain the combination of risk and expected return depicted by $T_2$. To obtain this combination, however, he must now double his holding of consols, to $A_2 (r_1, \sigma_g/2)$; the tax shifts the risk-consols line from $OB_1$ to $OB_2$.

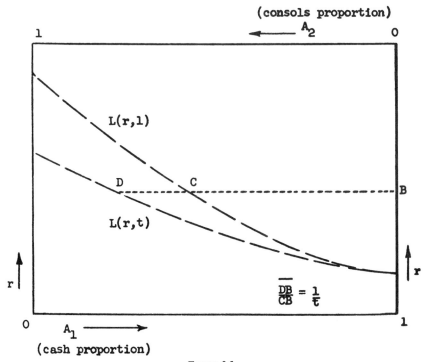

FIGURE 3.5
Effect of Tax (at Rate 1—*t*) on Liquidity Preference Function.

A tax of this kind, therefore, would reduce the demand for cash at any market rate of interest, shifting the investor's liquidity preference schedule in the manner shown in Figure 3.5. A tax on interest income only, with no tax on capital gains and no offset privileges for capital losses, would have quite different effects. If the Treasury began to split the interest income of the investor in Figure 3.4 but not to share the risk, the investor would move from his initial position, $T_2$ and $A_2 (2r_1, \sigma_g)$; to $T_1$ and $A_2 (r_1, \sigma_g)$. His demand for cash at a given market rate of interest would be increased and his liquidity preference curve shifted to the right.

3.6 *Multiple alternatives to cash.* So far it has been assumed that there is only one alternative to cash, and $A_2$ has represented the share of the investor's balance held in that asset, "consols." The argument is not essentially changed, however, if $A_2$ is taken to be the aggregate share invested in a variety of noncash assets, e.g. bonds and other debt instruments differing in maturity, debtor, and other features. The return $R$ and the risk $\sigma_g$ on "consols" will then represent the average return and risk on a composite of these assets.

Suppose that there are $m$ assets other than cash, and let $x_i(i = 1, 2, \dots m)$ be the amount invested in the $i$-th of these assets. All $x_i$ are non-negative, and $\sum_{i=1}^{m} x_i = A_2 \leq 1$. Let $r_i$ be the expected yield, and let $g_i$ be the capital gain or loss, per dollar invested in the $i$-th asset. We assume $E(g_i) = 0$ for all $i$. Let $v_{ij}$ be the variance or covariance of $g_i$ and $g_j$ as estimated by the investor.

$$v_{ij} = E(g_i g_j) \quad (i, j, = 1, 2, \dots m). \tag{3.18}$$

The over-all expected return is:

$$\mu_R = A_2 r = \sum_{i=1}^{m} x_i r_i. \tag{3.19}$$

The over-all variance of return is:

$$\sigma_R^2 = A_2^2 \sigma_g^2 = \sum_{i=1}^{m} \sum_{j=1}^{m} x_i x_j v_{ij}. \tag{3.20}$$

A set of points $x_i$ for which $\sum_{i=1}^{m} x_i r_i$ is constant may be defined as a *constant-return locus*. A constant-return locus is linear in the $x_i$. For two assets $x_1$ and $x_2$, two loci are illustrated in Figure 3.6. One locus of combinations of $x_1$ and $x_2$ that give the same expected return $\mu_R$ is the line from $\dfrac{\mu_R}{r_2}$ to $\dfrac{\mu_R}{r_1}$, through

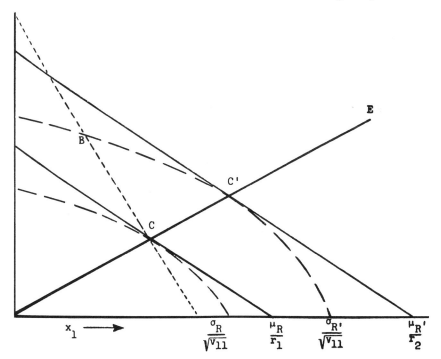

FIGURE 3.6
Dominant Combinations of Two Assets.

$C$; another locus, for a higher constant, $\mu'_R$, is the parallel line from $\dfrac{\mu'_R}{r_2}$ to $\dfrac{\mu'_R}{r_1}$, through $C'$.

A set of points $x_i$ for which $\sigma_R^2$ is constant may be defined as a *constant-risk locus*. These loci are ellipsoidal. For two assets $x_1$ and $x_2$, such a locus is illustrated by the quarter-ellipse from $\dfrac{\sigma_R}{\sqrt{v_{22}}}$ to $\dfrac{\sigma_R}{\sqrt{v_{11}}}$, through point $C$. The equation of such an ellipse is:

$$x_1^2 v_{11} + 2 x_1 x_2 v_{12} + x_2^2 v_{22} = \sigma_R^2 = \text{constant.}$$

Another such locus, for a higher risk level, $\sigma'_R$, is the quarter-ellipse from

$\dfrac{\sigma'_R}{\sqrt{v_{22}}}$ to $\dfrac{\sigma'_R}{\sqrt{v_{11}}}$ through point $C'$.

From Figure 3.6, it is clear that $C$ and $C'$ exemplify *dominant* combinations of $x_1$ and $x_2$. If the investor is incurring a risk of $\sigma a$, somewhere on the ellipse through $C$, he will to have the highest possible expectation of return available to him at that level of risk. The highest available expected return is represented by the constant-expected-return line tangent to the ellipse at $C$. Similarly $C'$ is a dominant point: it would not be possible to obtain a higher expected return than at $C'$ without incurring additional risk, or to diminish risk without sacrificing expected return.

In general, a dominant combination of assets is defined as a set $x_i$ which minimizes $\sigma_R^2$ for $\mu_R$ constant:

$$\sum_i \left( \sum_j v_{ij} x_j \right) x_i - \lambda \left( \sum_i r_i x_i - \mu_R \right) = \min \qquad (3.21)$$

where $\lambda$ is a Lagrange multiplier. The conditions for the minimum are that the $x_i$ satisfy the constraint (3.19) and the following set of $m$ simultaneous linear equations, written in matrix notation:

$$[v_{ij}][x_i] = [\lambda r_i]. \qquad (3.22)$$

All dominant sets lie on a ray from the origin. That is, if $[x_i^{(0)}]$ and $[x_i^{(1)}]$ are dominant sets, then there is some non-negative scalar $\kappa$ such that $[x_i^{(1)}] = [\kappa x_i^{(0)}]$. By definition of a dominant set, there is some $\lambda^{(0)}$ such that:

$$[v_{ij}][x_i^{(0)}] = [\lambda^{(0)} r_i],$$

and some $\lambda^{(1)}$ such that:

$$[v_{ij}][x_i^{(1)}] = [\lambda^{(1)} r_i].$$

Take $\kappa = \dfrac{\lambda(1)}{\lambda(0)}$. Then:

$$[v_{ij}][\kappa x_i^{(0)}] = [\kappa \lambda^{(0)} r_i] = [\lambda^{(1)} r_i] = [v_{ij}][x_i^{(1)}].$$

At the same time, $\Sigma r_i x_i^{(0)} = \mu_R^{(0)}$ and $\Sigma r_i x_i^{(1)} = \mu_R^{(1)}$.

Hence, $\mu_R^{(1)} = [\kappa \mu_R^{(0)}]$. Conversely, every set on this ray is a dominant set. If $[x_i^{(0)}]$ is a dominant set, then so is $[\kappa x_i^{(0)}]$ for any non-negative constant $\kappa$. This is easily proved. If $[x_i^{(0)}]$ satisfies (3.19) and (3.22) for $\mu_R^{(0)}$ and $\lambda^{(0)}$, then $[\kappa x_i^{(0)}]$ satisfies (3.19) and (3.22) for $\lambda^{(K)} = \kappa \lambda^{(0)}$ and $\mu_R^{(K)} = \kappa \mu_R^{(0)}$. In the two dimensional case pictured in Figure 3.6, the dominant pairs lie along the ray $OCC'E$.

There will be some point on the ray (say $E$ in Figure 3.6) at which the investor's holdings of non-cash assets will exhaust his investment balance $(\sum_i x_i = 1)$ and leave nothing for cash holding. Short of that point the balance will be divided among cash and non-cash assets in proportion to the distances along the ray; in Figure 3.6 at point $C$ for example, $\dfrac{OC}{OE}$ of the balance would be non-cash, and $\dfrac{CE}{OE}$ cash. But the convenient fact that has just been proved is that the proportionate composition of the non-cash assets is independent of their aggregate share of the investment balance. This fact makes it possible to describe the investor's decisions as if there were a single non-cash asset, a composite formed by combining the multitude of actual non-cash assets in fixed proportions.

Corresponding to every point on the ray of dominant sets is an expected return $\mu_R$ and risk $\sigma_R$; these pairs $(\mu_R, \sigma_R)$ are the opportunity locus of sections 3.1 and 3.4. By means of (3.22), the opportunity locus can be expressed in terms of the expected return and variances and covariances of the non-cash assets: Let:

$$[V_{ij}] = [V_{ij}]^{-1}.$$

Then:

$$\mu_R = \lambda \sum_i \sum_j r_i r_j V_{ij} \tag{3.23}$$

$$\sigma_R^2 = \lambda^2 \sum_i \sum_j r_i r_j V_{ij}. \tag{3.24}$$

Thus the opportunity locus is the line:

$$\mu_R = \sigma_R \sqrt{\sum_i \sum_j r_i r_j V_{ij}} = \sigma_R \frac{r}{\sigma_g} \tag{3.25}$$

This analysis is applicable only so long as cash is assumed to be a riskless asset. In the absence of a residual riskless asset, the investor has no reason to confine his choices to the ray of dominant sets. This may be easily verified in the two-asset case. Using Figure 3.6 for a different purpose now, suppose that the entire investment balance must be divided between $x_1$ and $x_2$. The point $(x_1, x_2)$ must fall on the line $x_1 + x_2 = 1$, represented by the line through $BC$ in the diagram. The investor will not necessarily choose point $C$. At point $B$, for example, he would obtain a higher expected yield as well as a higher risk;

he may prefer $B$ to $C$. His opportunity locus represents the pairs $(\mu_R, \sigma_R)$ along the line through $BC(x_1 + x_2 = 1)$ rather than along the ray $OC$, and is a hyperbola rather than a line. It is still possible to analyze portfolio choices by the apparatus of $(\mu_R, \sigma_R)$ indifference and opportunity loci, but such analysis is beyond the scope of the present paper.[15]

It is for this reason that the present analysis has been deliberately limited, as stated in section 1.2, to choices among monetary assets. Among these assets cash is relatively riskless, even though in the wider context of portfolio selection, the risk of changes in purchasing power, which all monetary assets share, may be relevant to many investors. Breaking down the portfolio selection problem into stages at different levels of aggregation—allocation first among, and then within, asset categories—seems to be a permissible and perhaps even indispensable simplification both for the theorist and for the investor himself.

### 4. IMPLICATIONS OF THE ANALYSIS FOR LIQUIDITY PREFERENCE THEORY

The theory of risk-avoiding behavior has been shown to provide a basis for liquidity preference and for an inverse relationship between the demand for cash and the rate of interest. This theory does not depend on inelasticity of expectations of future interest rates, but can proceed from the assumption that the expected value of capital gain or loss from holding interest-bearing assets is always zero. In this respect, it is a logically more satisfactory foundation for liquidity preference than the Keynesian theory described in section 2. Moreover, it has the empirical advantage of explaining diversification—the same individual holds both cash and "consols"—while Keynesian theory implies that each investor will hold only one asset.

The risk aversion theory of liquidity preference mitigates the major logical objection to which, according to the argument of section 2.6, the Keynesian theory is vulnerable. But it cannot completely meet Leontief's position that in a strict stationary equilibrium liquidity preference must be zero unless cash and consols bear equal rates. By their very nature consols and, to a lesser degree, all time obligations contain a potential for capital gain or loss that cash and other demand obligations lack. Presumably, however, there is some length of experience of constancy in the interest rate that would teach the most stubbornly timid investor to ignore that potential. In a pure stationary state, it could be argued, the interest rate on consols would have been the same for so long that investors would unanimously estimate $\sigma_g$ to be zero. So stationary a state is of very little interest. Fortunately the usefulness of comparative

---

[15] A forthcoming book by Harry Markowitz, *Techniques of Portfolio Selection*, will treat the general problem of finding dominant sets and computing the corresponding opportunity locus, for sets of securities all of which involve risk. Markowitz's main interest is prescription of rules of rational behavior for investors; the main concern of this paper is the implications for economic theory, mainly comparative statics, that can be derived from assuming that investors do in fact follow such rules. For the general nature of Markowitz's approach, see his article, "Portfolio Selection," *Journal of Finance*, Volume VII, No. 1 (March, 1952), pp. 77–91. (1, p. 85)

statics does not appear to be confined to comparisons of states each of which would take a generation or more to achieve. As compared to the Keynesian theory of liquidity preference, the risk aversion theory widens the applicability of comparative statics in aggregate analysis; this is all that need be claimed for it.

The theory, however, is somewhat ambiguous concerning the direction of relationship between the rate of interest and the demand for cash. For low interest rates, the theory implies a negative elasticity of demand for cash with respect to the interest rate, an elasticity that becomes larger and larger in absolute value as the rate approaches zero. This implication, of course, is in accord with the usual assumptions about liquidity preference. But for high interest rates, and especially for individuals whose estimates $\sigma_g$ of the risk of capital gain or loss on "consols" are low, the demand for cash may be an increasing, rather than a decreasing, function of the interest rate. However, the force of this reversal of direction is diluted by recognition, as in section 2.5, that the size of investment balances is not independent of the current rate of interest $r$. In section 3.4 we have considered the proportionate allocation between cash and "consols" on the assumption that it is independent of the size of the balance. An increase in the rate of interest may lead an investor to desire to shift towards cash. But to the extent that the increase in interest also reduces the value of the investor's consol holdings, it automatically gratifies this desire, at least in part.

The assumption that investors expect on balance no change in the rate of interest has been adopted for the theoretical reasons explained in section 2.6 rather than for reasons of realism. Clearly investors do form expectations of changes in interest rates and differ from each other in their expectations. For the purposes of dynamic theory and of analysis of specific market situations, the theories of sections 2 and 3 are complementary rather than competitive. The formal apparatus of section 3 will serve just as well for a non-zero expected capital gain or loss as for a zero expected value of $g$. Stickiness of interest rate expectations would mean that the expected value of $g$ is a function of the rate of interest $r$, going down when $r$ goes down and rising when $r$ goes up. In addition to the rotation of the opportunity locus due to a change in $r$ itself, there would be a further rotation in the same direction due to the accompanying change in the expected capital gain or loss. At low interest rates expectation of capital loss may push the opportunity locus into the negative quadrant, so that the optimal position is clearly no consols, all cash. At the other extreme, expectation of capital gain at high interest rates would increase sharply the slope of the opportunity locus and the frequency of no cash, all consols positions, like that of Figure 3.3. The stickier the investor's expectations, the more sensitive his demand for cash will be to changes in the rate of interest.

## 11. EFFICIENT ALLOCATION OF CAPITAL IN AN UNCERTAIN WORLD

### JACK HIRSHLEIFER*

Reprinted from *The American Economic Review*, Vol. *LIV*, No. 3 (May, 1964), pp. 77–85, by permission of the author and the publisher.

In a world of certainty, efficient allocation of capital would be evidenced by equality of the yield (value of marginal product per dollar of capital value) for all forms of investment, waiving certain complications in comparing differing time-shapes of yield streams [13] [2]. And, since in such a world expectations would always be borne out, the equality of yields would be true both prospectively and retrospectively.

When we turn to our actual world of uncertainty, we find that the yields realized on alternative forms of investment differ drastically. In general, there have been two main types of response to this evidence on the part of theorists. According to one school, the evidence indicates " the capital market to be imperfect, to be rife with rationing, ignorance, differential tax treatments, reluctance to finance investment from external funds, slow adjustment processes, etc., which destroy the normative significance of actual rates found in the market " [5, p. 503]. As indicated by the quotation, the positive conclusion about the malfunctioning of capital markets leads directly to a normative inference about the nonrelevance of market interest rates—most immediately, with reference to the controversial question of the appropriate rate of discount for use in evaluating government investment projects not subject to the market test. The other school of thought maintains that the divergences of observed yields conceal an underlying harmony of the capital markets (see, for example, [24]). This view is basically a programmatic hypothesis: those who hold it feel that the search for a consistent structure amidst the seeming confusion of observed yields will ultimately be rewarded. I shall pursue this line of thought here, developing and commenting on two proposed theoretical formulations explaining yield divergences—both turning upon investor attitudes toward risk and uncertainty.

We must note first, however, that in a world of uncertainty, the equilibrating market forces can only work on the prospective returns to investment. There are two possible sources of difficulty here: First, prospects or anticipations are not ordinarily observable and, second, in a world of uncertainty the returns

* University of California, Los Angeles.

anticipated are multivalued (usually expressed as a probability distribution). In what follows, I shall develop and compare alternative formulations of the investor's attitude toward multivalued returns; the question of how anticipations about such returns may be made operational for the purpose of direct empirical testing will not be considered here.

One general analytical consideration warrants emphasizing for its bearing upon the examination of alternative theoretical formulations below. Any economic theory of choice should contain, for formal completeness, certain elements: (1) Economic agents (individuals' consumption); (2) for each agent, preference functions among the objects of choice; (3) again for each agent, endowments of choice-objects and opportunity sets showing the possible transformations of endowments into alternative combinations of desired objects; and (4) conservation relations which constrain the net sum of individual decisions so as to be consistent with social totals of choice-objects available.

## I. MULTIVALUED RETURNS—$\mu$, $\sigma$ PREFERENCES

The most familiar formulation of investor attitudes toward the multivalued returns of an uncertain world takes for objects of choice the mathematical expectation $\mu$ and the standard deviation $\sigma$ of the (subjective) probability distribution of returns—$\sigma$ being interpreted as the measure of the "riskiness" of the investment in question [7] [11] [19] [23] [18] [6].[1] In accordance with the common beliefs of observers of financial markets, and in order to explain the observed phenomenon of diversification of assets, it is usually postulated that investors desire low values for $\sigma$—i.e., they are risk-avoiders—and that they show decreasing willingness to accept high $\mu$ to counterbalance high $\sigma$ (as $\mu$ and $\sigma$ both increase). These assumptions dictate a preference function like that illustrated in Figure 1.

In constructing the opportunity set, $\mu$, $\sigma$-theorists have concentrated upon the problem of portfolios; i.e., holdings of financial instruments. Little or no attention has been paid to productive investments. Also, the usual portfolio analysis keeps constant the amount of current investment and concerns itself only with the distribution of that amount over the available securities. Neither restriction is really essential: the same approach could be extended to include productive investments in addition to a financial portfolio, and a simultaneous solution could be provided for the scale of investment, together with the choice of securities held, by incorporating some kind of time-preference model.

In the usual portfolio analysis, the opportunity set is the area bordered by an efficient frontier showing (as in Figure 1) minimum $\sigma$ attainable for each possible value of $\mu$. Since holding a combination of securities whose returns are less than perfectly correlated tends to lower $\sigma$ relative to $\mu$ for the overall portfolio, one-security portfolios do not in general appear on the efficient

---

[1] Markowitz goes beyond the other works cited in examining alternative possible statistical measures of "riskiness."

frontier.[2] The curvature shown for the efficient frontier—opposite to that of the ($\mu$, $\sigma$) indifference curves—follows also from the covariance effect, since moving to higher values of portfolio $\mu$ progressively reduces the number of securities that can be held in combination so as to lower $\sigma$.[3]

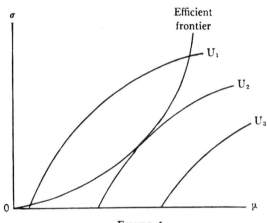

FIGURE 1<br>$\mu$, $\sigma$-PREFERENCES AND EFFICIENT FRONTIER

The approach in terms of $\mu$, $\sigma$-preferences has the advantages of plausibility, and a fairly direct connection between theoretical and measurable magnitudes (means, variances, covariances and so forth are all observable, though only retrospectively). A number of objections can be raised, however, of which only two will be mentioned here—leaving aside for the moment the complex question of the consistency of observed market behavior with the risk-aversion assumption.

1. It has been pointed out that it is not possible to derive $\mu$, $\sigma$ preference functions from the Neumann-Morgenstern postulates of rational choice except with the aid of arbitrary restrictions upon the subjective probability distributions or utility-of-wealth functions [23] [3].[4]

2. Another objection, less widely appreciated, is that current formulations in portfolio analysis do not meet the requirements for a complete choice-theoretic system. Granted that individuals have $\mu$, $\sigma$-preferences, it

---

[2] However, the security with highest $\mu$ (whatever its $\sigma$) is on the efficient frontier. Also, if there are riskless securities, the riskless security of highest $\mu$ must also constitute an efficient one-security portfolio.

[3] If, however, the available portfolios are all combinations of a single riskless security ($\mu = \mu_0$, $\sigma = 0$) and a risky one ($\mu = \mu_1$, $\sigma = \sigma_1$, where $\mu_1 > \mu_0$, $\sigma_1 > 0$), the efficient frontier reduces to a line (see [23]).

[4] The special assumptions are that the probability distribution must be two-parameter, or alternatively that the utility-of-wealth function be quadratic. The latter is especially objectionable, as it requires the marginal utility of wealth to become negative beyond a certain point.

remains to be shown how the resulting decisions of individuals in the market interact to determine security prices that permit the existing stocks of securities to be exactly held in market equilibrium.[5] Furthermore, securities are artificial commodities; still further steps are necessary to show how and why they are generated. Such an analysis must go back to the forces determining the balance between $\mu$ and $\sigma$ in real investments undertaken,[6] the principles on which owners of risky income streams partition $\mu$ and $\sigma$ to make up the various classes of securities that represent claims to such streams, and the conservation relations that apply to the social totals of $\mu$ and $\sigma$ in the economy. In short, what is lacking is a theory of the market risk-premium.

## II. MULTIVALUED RETURNS—TIME-STATE PREFERENCES

A less familiar, but (I feel) ultimately more satisfactory approach to decision under uncertainty has been pioneered by Arrow and Debreu [1]. In this formulation the objects of choice are not derivative statistical measures of the probability distribution of consumption opportunities but rather the contingent consumption claims themselves set out in extensive form. Combining Fisher's treatment of time-preference decisions under certainty with Arrow's conception of choice objects under uncertainty permits the formulation of a generalized theory in which the objects of choice are consumption opportunities as of alternative time-state claims. If the present and future are strictly determined, the objects of choice reduce simply to consumption opportunities of differing dates, as in Fisher's riskless time preference system [8].[7] It is evident that Fisher's time-claims to consumption generalize immediately to time-state claims, that under pure exchange the social total of each class of choice-objects must be conserved, and that analogous formulations for productive opportunities can be set down. The chief novel element is that, for state-preference at a given time, the Neumann-Morgenstern theorems permit a special formulation of the preference function.

In the interests of simplicity, in what follows it will be assumed that there is only one present state; i.e., there is certainty as to the present (time 0). The future is represented by a point in time (time 1) in which there are two alternative states (state $a$ or state $b$). The two states may be thought of as war versus peace, or prosperity versus depression. The fundamental objects of choice, contingent consumption opportunities, may be denoted $c_0$, $c_{1a}$, and $c_{1b}$. Whereas in the deterministic time-preference case there is only one independent dimension of choice (between $c_0$ and $c_1$), here there are two: a synchronous balance between the contingent claims $C_{1a}$ and $C_{1b}$, and a present—future balance (for the latter, it suffices to show the exchange between the contingent

---

[5] Some recent work by William Sharpe makes important progress in this direction [22].

[6] An important element in such decision must be the physical "productivity of risk" [14].

[7] Fisher, who may have been the first to suggest a $\mu$, $\sigma$ approach to risk-choices, apparently never employed a time-state formulation for uncertainty.

claims $c_0$ and $c_{1b}$, since the proportions of $c_{1a}$ and $c_{1b}$ are determined in the synchronous exchange).[8]

In Figure 2a the 45° "certainty line" through the origin represents points along which $c_{1a} = c_{1b}$. Convexity follows from the empirical observation of "nonspecialization" of risky choice. Almost no one is so reckless as to prefer —if, say, $p_a = p_b = \frac{1}{2}$—the prospect $(c_{1a}, c_{1b}) = (1000, 0)$ to a prospect like

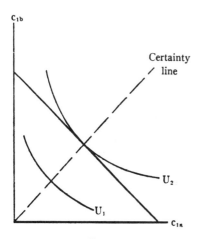

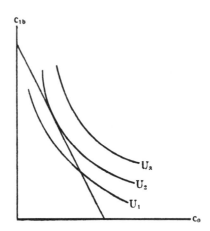

FIGURE 2a
CONTEMPORANEOUS STATE-PREFERENCES AND
FINANCIAL OPPORTUNITIES
$(t = 1, p_a = p_b = \frac{1}{2})$

FIGURE 2b
TIME-AND-STATE PREFERENCES AND
FINANCIAL OPPORTUNITIES

(500, 500). (It must be understood that $c_{1b} = 0$ does not mean merely the unfavorable outcome of a lottery, representing a possibly minor decrease in overall wealth but rather a zero-consumption situation—absolute impoverishment should state $b$ occur.) Thus, even a very mild degree of conservatism requires convex utility isoquants.

If we now introduce, for consumption at time 1, a Neumann-Morgenstern utility-of-income function $v(c_1)$ (see [9]), interesting results follow. It can be shown that, if the function $v(c_1)$ does not itself change whether state $a$ or $b$ obtains, everywhere-convex indifference curves require a "concave" utility-of-income function—that is, one characterized by diminishing marginal utility [15]. Thus, Neumann-Morgenstern risk-aversion follows from observed nonspecialization among contingencies.

In a pure-exchange situation, the individual's opportunities are limited to converting his endowment time-state distribution, $Y$, into a consumption time-state distribution, $C$, subject to a wealth-constraint $W$.

$$W = y_0 + y_{1a}/(1 + r_{1a}) + y_{1b}/(1 + r_{1b}) = c_0 + c_{1a}/(1 + r_{1a}) + c_{1b}/(1 + r_{1b}).$$

[8] For some purposes, it is more convenient to distinguish the synchronous (risky) exchange between $c_{1a}$ and $c_{1b}$ from the riskless time-exchange between $c_0$ and a certain claim to $c_1$ (see paragraph below).

Here $r_{1a}$ is the time-and-probability discount rate for contingent claims of date 1 and state $a$. We may also write the wealth constraint as $W = P_0 c_0 + P_{1a} c_{1a} + P_{1b} c_{1b}$ and, with $c_0$ as numeraire, $P_0 = 1$, $P_{1a} = 1/(1 + r_{1a})$, and $P_{1b} = 1/(1 + r_{1b})$.

For the contemporaneous exchange between $c_{1a}$ and $c_{1b}$, it can be shown that if the price ratio $P_{1b}/P_{1a}$ is equal to the probability ratio $p_b/p_a$, the optimum (for a consumer whose Neumann-Morgenstern $v(c)$ function is independent of state) must be along the certainty line. This corresponds to the well-known theorem that, if $v(c)$ is concave, a fair gamble—and, a fortiori, an adverse gamble—will not be accepted. Thus, an alternative explanation would have to be sought for the phenomenon of Las Vegas. (It may be noted here that the customary betting pattern at Las Vegas—repeated commitment of small stakes—makes the overall outcome close to a certainty; thus suggesting that participants in this game are not seriously attempting to change their wealth levels. If they were so attempting, they would hazard large fractions of their wealth on a single turn of a card or roll of a wheel. What they are really doing, one is forced to conclude, is paying a modest fee for a certain thrill or excitement under highly controlled conditions involving minimal real risk.)

A somewhat novel idea to which the time-state approach leads, however, is that the Neumann-Morgenstern function itself may not be independent of state—since different states are not mere gamble outcomes like Black or Red at roulette, but rather may represent objective differences in one's external or internal context for choice. If, for example, the states are personal health versus illness, even an unfair " gamble " might be accepted, provided it pays off disproportionately in the state in which income is more urgently needed; thus, purchase of health insurance, while an adverse gamble, remains essentially conservative.[9] Convexity of the indifference curves would ordinarily dictate an interior solution, so that only moderate gambles will be accepted.[10] This generalization of risk-aversion might be termed " conservative behavior."

To complete the choice-theoretic system under pure exchange, conservation equations must be incorporated which require that the entire social endowment, in each time-state, be exactly distributed among economic agents. If productive opportunities are introduced, the goal of production for each agent is wealth-maximization—where wealth is the sum of contingent income claims discounted, for time and state, by factors like $(1 + r_{1a})$. One problem is to explain why the capital markets ordinarily deal not in the " natural " units of time-state claims like $c_{1a}$ or $c_{1b}$, but in securities representing complex packages of such claims. The reason seems to be the huge number of conceivable contingencies; some aggregation of claims is required. The main aggregation procedure observed in the market is the separation of the claims resulting

[9] The variation of the $v(c)$ function might be attributed to the presence of positive or negative, "nonpecuniary income" in one of the states envisaged.

[10] Friedman and Savage [9], however, maintain that observed behavior shows aversion to moderate gambles as compared with either highly risky investments. Their illustrations can, I would maintain, be explained more satisfactorily on other grounds.

from investments into one package that is relatively certain or "senior" (bonds), and another covering the residuals (stocks). Treating each class of securities as a bundle of time-state claims, it is possible to show (under certain idealizing assumptions, most importantly zero taxation and absence of liquidity premiums) that the sum of values of alternative security combinations must be a constant—equal to the sum of values of the underlying physical time-state claims [15]. This is, of course, the Modigliani-Miller theorem [21, p. 268].

## III. HARMONY OF MARKET YIELDS

Does the foregoing formulation of investment theory for an uncertain world square with observed patterns of market yields? In particular, does it go some distance toward showing that observed divergences represent, when properly interpreted, a harmonious structure of yields? Only a few remarks on the evidence can be put forward here.

1. The great diversity of experienced yields, both cross-section and over time. This, of course, is exactly what one would expect as the economy threads its way among multiple possibilities over time [4]; different securities, although equally valued by the market *ex ante*, will be differentially affected *ex post* as some one of the set of mutually exclusive contingencies eventuates at each date.

2. Bond yields are less than stock yields (averaged over time) [17]. This is consistent with risk-aversion (postulated on the different ground of non-specialization among states). It may be worth noting that returns from holding high-grade bonds are better, from a risk-avoiding point of view, than a merely stable yield. A constant-dollar bond return will fluctuate upward in real terms during deep depression—just when income is most urgently needed.

3. Normally rising term-structure pattern.[11] This is usually interpreted as evidencing liquidity-preference, and in the Hicksion formulation is explained in terms of risk-avoiding behavior [12, pp. 145–47]. The pattern is thus consistent with convex time-and-state preferences. However, a time-state analysis employing a complete choice-theoretic system (too long to reproduce here) indicates that persistence of the long-short differential involves, in addition to risk-aversion, certain technological phenomena: positive net productivity of lengthening the "period of production," and limited reversibility of physical investments in the event of an adverse contingency (with consequent need for current income).

4. High yields on human investment. An implication of the foregoing is that investment in oneself—being exceptionally irreversible—should on the

[11] Meiselman [20] has shown that the term structure can, consistently with the data, be interpreted as reflecting changing expectations over time. But Kessel, in a still-unpublished N.B.E.R. study [16], has demonstrated that there remains a bias in the form of a normal excess of long rates over short. See also [25].

margin show high returns, which appears to be borne out by the evidence.[12]

## IV. CONCLUDING COMMENT

As indicated earlier, the harmonistic hypothesis is essentially a programmatic one. However, the formulation of investment choice under uncertainty in terms of time-state preferences, with the assumption of risk-aversion (or rather, the slightly generalized assumption of conservative behavior) does seem to promise progress toward harmonizing the bewildering diversity of market yields. I will conclude with the remark that validation of the harmonistic hypothesis would suggest, for the policy question alluded to earlier concerning the appropriate discount rate for government investment projects, the use of market yield rates comparably placed in the rate structure—taking account of risk, term, illiquidity, etc., or ultimately of the alternative time-states in which the investment income accrues. This would indicate considerably tougher standards than the current practice of employing the government's risk-free borrowing rate.

## REFERENCES

1. K. J. Arrow, "Le Role des Valeurs Boursieres pour la Repartition la Meilleure des Risques," *International Colloquium on Econometrics* (1952).
2. Martin J. Bailey, "Formal Criteria for Investment Decisions," *J.P.E.*, Oct., 1959.
3. Karl Borch, "A Note on Utility and Attitudes to Risk," *Management Science*, July, 1963.
4. Gerard Debreu, "Une Economique de L'Incertain," *Economie Appliquee*, 1960.
5. Otto Eckstein, in National Bureau of Economic Research, *Public Finances: Needs, Sources and Utilization* (Princeton Univ. Press, 1961).
6. D. E. Farrar, *The Investment Decision Under Uncertainty* (Prentice-Hall, 1962).
7. Irving Fisher, *The Nature of Capital and Income* (Macmillan, 1912), Chap. 16.
8. ——, *The Theory of Interest* (Macmillan, 1930; reprinted Augustus M. Kelley, 1955).
9. M. Friedman and L. J. Savage, "The Utility Analysis of Choices Involving Risk," *J.P.E.*, 1948. Reprinted, *Readings in Price Theory* (Irwin, 1952).
10. W. L. Hansen, "Total and Private Rates of Return to Investment in Schooling," *J.P.E.*, April, 1963.
11. J. R. Hicks, "A Suggestion for Simplifying the Theory of Money," *Economica*, Feb., 1935.
12. ——, *Value and Capital* (2nd ed., Oxford Univ. Press, 1946).
13. J. Hirshleifer, "On the Theory of Optimal Investment Decision," *J.P.E.*, Aug., 1958. Reprinted in E. Solomon, ed., *The Management of Corporate Capital* (Free. Press, 1959).
14. ——, "Risk, the Discount Rate, and Investment Decisions," *A.E.R.*, May, 1961.
15. ——, "Investment Decision Under Uncertainty" (1963).

[12] W. L. Hansen shows marginal private rates of return in schooling clustering mainly between 10 percent and 20 percent [10]. There are, it must be admitted, many difficulties in the data and interpretation.

16. Reuben A. Kessel, "The Cyclical Behavior of the Term Structure of Interest Rates" (1962).
17. Henry A. Latané, "Portfolio Balance—The Demand for Money, Bonds, and Stock," *Southern Econ. J.*, Oct., 1962.
18. Harry Markowitz, *Portfolio Selection* (Wiley, 1959).
19. J. Marschak, "Money and the Theory of Assets," *Econometrica*, Oct., 1938.
20. David Meiselman, *The Term Structure of Interest Rates* (Prentice-Hall, 1962).
21. F. Modigliani and M. H. Miller, "The Cost of Capital, Corporation Finance and the Theory of Investment," *A.E.R.*, June, 1958.
22. W. F. Sharpe, "Capital Asset Prices: A Theory of Market Equilibrium Under Conditions of Risk" (1963).
23. James Tobin, "Liquidity Preference as Behavior Towards Risk," *Rev. of Econ. Studies*, Feb., 1958.
24. ——, "Money, Capital, and Other Stores of Value," *A.E.R.*, May, 1961.
25. John H. Wood, "Expectations, Errors, and the Term Structure of Interest Rates," *J.P.E.*, April, 1963.

## 12. THE INTEGRATION OF CAPITAL BUDGETING AND STOCK VALUATION

EUGENE M. LERNER
and
WILLARD T. CARLETON*

Reprinted from *The American Economic Review*, Vol. *LIV*, No. 4 (September, 1964), pp. 683–702, by permission of the authors and the publisher.

It is widely recognized that a corporation's cost of capital cannot be determined until an analysis is made of how the market values the firm's common stock [5, p. 423] [6, p. 143]. There is, however, no widely accepted theoretical apparatus linking the market valuation of common stock to a corporation's investment-opportunities schedule, dividend payout function, and capital structure.

It is the position of this paper that a fundamental reason for the current stalemate over the theoretical apparatus is the single-equation nature of recent capital-budgeting and security-valuation models [3] [7] [11]. Since one

* The authors are, respectively, associate and assistant professor of finance at New York University, Graduate School of Business Administration. They wish to express their appreciation to Arnold Sametz and the members of the Investments Workshop for many helpful comments and criticisms, and to Howard Hendrikson who assisted in the design and execution of the figures.

equation can determine at most one unknown, manipulation of these models has, for the generation of results, necessitated a variety of *ad hoc* restrictions to reduce each equation to a relationship between *two* variables only—as, for example, between share price and capital structure.[1] Two consequences emerge: (a) Since there is no consensus, such restrictions tend to be different. (b) More importantly, such variables as share price, capital budget, dividend payout, and capital structure are in the real world jointly determined, and the suppression of this dependency unnecessarily limits the relevance of any theoretical results. That is, whether the problem is simply simultaneous determination of all the variables or maximization of one (e.g., share price) subject to one or more constraints, enumeration of the relevant relationships contained in the budgeting-valuation nexus must be explicit.

In this paper we depart from the single-equation convention and explicitly introduce two equations: an investment-opportunities (or capital-budgeting) schedule and a stock-valuation equation. Under reasonable assumptions these two equations are shown to determine simultaneously a corporation's internal rate of return, the percentage of earnings that it retains and the percentage that it distributes in dividends, and the price of its common stock. Furthermore, if the stock-valuation equation is treated as the corporation's objective function and the capital-budgeting equation as an internal constraint, we show that a unique maximum price can be found as a tangency solution.

The article falls into three major parts. Section I analyzes and modifies in two respects the stock-valuation model made popular by Myron Gordon in his *The Investment, Financing and Valuation of the Corporation* [3]. The Gordon model treats the price of a corporation's common stock as the present value of the expected future dividends, discounted at some given rate, $k$. Under the condition that the firm engages in no outside financing, retained earnings are reinvested by definition, so that a fixed relationship between dividend payout and capital budget emerges. A major difficulty of this model is that it generates unacceptable results when it is used as the sole determinant of the retention (hence, payout) rate which maximizes the value of the common stock. For example, the conclusion is reached that the corporation should retain and reinvest until the point at which the market value of stock equals book, or asset, value. The reason for anomalies of this sort is shown to be the implicit suppression of the mutual interaction within the firm of rate of return and size of capital budget. When a price map is drawn illustrating the substitutability of rate of return and dividend payout for shareholders at a given discount rate, the need for further specification of shareholder and corporation behavior becomes manifest. However, it is shown that even when $k$ is treated as an increasing linear function of expected growth (in recognition of the growth-stock paradox) and the corporation's capital structure is formally

---

[1] For example, see Lintner [7, pp. 250–51]. In order to generate the conclusion that investors will be indifferent to substitutions between elements in a corporation's time vector of dividends, it is necessary for Lintner to assume (among other things) given time vectors of earnings, capital budgets, and market discount rates.

introduced into the price model, the problem of what capital budget maximizes share price remains indeterminate.

Section II introduces an investment-opportunities schedule, positing the traditional inverse relationship between capital-budget size and internal rate of return. It then becomes obvious that there are two sets of rate of return and retention-rate expectations, one for the corporation and one for the shareholders. Under the necessary equilibrium condition that these two sets of expectations be equal, share price, dividend payout rate (and by construction, retention rate and capital budget), and internal rate of return are simultaneously determined. Finally, we demonstrate that there is a unique maximum share price attainable at some point along the corporation's investment-opportunities schedule. The more important implications of this tangency solution are: (1) a firm should not in general invest until internal rate of return equals the market discount rate; (2) most capital-budgeting "rules of thumb" are likely to be suboptimal; and (3) the consequences of changing the dividend payout rate depend upon whether the firm is operating above or below the point of tangency.

Finally, in Section III the obtained results are evaluated in an equilibrium economics context, subject to amendment in a dynamic framework. In particular, the implied prescription that the corporation adopt shareholders' risk preferences is not unreasonable when the problem of disappointed expectations is suppressed (as is necessary in comparative statics). Such a decision rule might need to be modified for a dynamic world. Also, the introduction of capital structure as a variable to be determined is shown to require another equation, perhaps linking capital financing to dividend payout. The most reasonable context in which to do this may turn out to be an adjustment model in which expectations are generated over time.

## I. THE STOCK-VALUATION EQUATION

### THE GORDON MODEL

The basic ingredients of any stock-valuation formula include: the particular stream of returns which is to be capitalized plus any time-dependent characteristics, such as a growth rate, that the stream possesses; the capitalization period (or investor time horizon); and the discount rate, or function. Academic debate over the proper definition of these ingredients has been exhaustive in recent years without being conclusive. The unfortunate fact is that normative results for corporate management depend rather strongly upon what definitions are adopted—whether the investor horizon is short-run or essentially infinite, for example. Rather than entering this terminological debate, we simply choose as a point of departure Myron Gordon's stock-valuation model [3, Ch. 4], which is a particularly well-developed and internally consistent approach to the valuation problem. Gordon defines investors' returns to be a growing stream of dividends, the market horizon as infinite, and the discount rate as a function, variously specified. He assumes no outside financing in his basic model, so that the establishment of a dividend payout automatically determines the capital budget as retained earnings.

Proceeding formally, assume that the corporation's dividends are expected to grow at a rate proportional to their present level,

(1.1)
$$\frac{dD}{dt} = gD,$$

and that, at time 0, the dividend payment is $D_o$. (Because new equity financing is excluded, $D$ in the subsequent development can be thought of in terms of either a per-share or a firm basis.)

Assume further that the value of a dividend stream decays at a rate proportional to its existing value,

(1.2)
$$\frac{dV}{dt} = -kV,$$

and that at time 0 the value of the stream is $V_o = 1$; $k$ can be taken as the market rate of discount.

The solutions of these two differential equations are

(1.1′)
$$D_t = D_o e^{gt},$$

(1.2′)
$$V_t = V_o e^{-kt}.$$

Since the price of a share is equal to the present value of the stream of all future dividends, equations (1.1′) and (1.2′) can be combined as follows:

(1.3)
$$P_o = \int_0^\infty D_o e^{gt} e^{-kt}\, dt$$

where $t = 0$ is now the date of valuation. A necessary condition for performing the integration is that $k > g$, for if $k \le g$, the value of the expression equals infinity, the well-known problem of growth-stock valuation [2].

Solving equation (1.3) yields

(1.4)
$$P_o = \frac{D_o}{k - g}.$$

The assumption that dividends grow at a constant rate is itself based on two assumed expectations; first, that the corporation is expected to earn a constant rate of return, $r$, on assets; and second, that the corporation is expected to retain a constant percentage, $b$, of its income. With the assumption that there is no debt in the capital structure of the corporation and that all growth of future dividends must come via retained earnings, equation (1.4) can then be rewritten in the form that Gordon gave it:

$$(1.4') \qquad P_o = \frac{(1-b)Y_o}{k-rb}$$

where $Y$ stands for income and $g = rb$, or as[2]

$$(1.4'') \qquad P_o = \frac{(1-b)rA_o}{k-rb}$$

where $A_o$ stands for total assets.

## THE "OPTIMUM" RETENTION RATE

The model described in equations (1.4) and (1.4') suggested ways in which the question of the optimum dividend rate (or optimum retention rate) could be approached. Assume $r$ is fixed, for clearly it is not independent of $b$. If the partial derivative of $P$ with respect to $b$ is set at zero, the price of the stock will be at a maximum if the second derivative is negative at this value. Taking the first partial derivative, it can be seen that $\partial P/\partial b = 0$ when $r$, the internal rate of return on assets, equals $k$, the market rate of discount. Upon taking the second derivative, however, it is seen that $\partial P/\partial b > 0$ only where $r > k$, and $\partial B/\partial b < 0$ only where $r < k$. Stated differently, where the first-order condition, $\partial P/\partial b = 0$, is satisfied, the second-order condition cannot be because the second and higher derivatives disappear. Therefore, the conclusion is reached that if $r$ is greater (less) than $k$, the price of the stock rises (falls) with a rise in retained earnings.[3]

Further implications can be derived from this unsuccessful attempt to find the optimum retention rate. Substituting $k$ for $r$,[4] its value when $\partial P/\partial b = 0$, in the denominator of equation (1.4') yields

$$(1.5) \qquad P = \frac{(1-b)Y}{k-kb} = \frac{Y}{k}.$$

---

[2] There is an implicit assumption that $g \geq 0$ and, hence $rb \geq 0$. Negative values of $g$, the expected rate of growth of dividends, are possible, but they contradict the assumption either of a constant rate of growth or of no outside financing. For example, consider a $g < 0$. This means that $r < 0$, since $0 \leq b < 1$. However, $r < 0$ implies a constant rate of deficit. $(1 - b)$ times a deficit is a negative expected dividend, or forced capital subscription, which contradicts the outside financing assumption. To allow outside financing only of this sort does not enhance the realism of the model. A heuristic resolution of the problem might be that the infinite-horizon model is an approximation, that the expectation of constant $r$ and $b$ is approximate, and that temporary negative $r$ (and therefore $g$) for a going concern is possible.

[3] Gordon proceeded in this manner and went on to state, "A moment's reflection on the conclusion just reached with respect to the variation in share price with $b$ reveals that a corporation should retain all of its income or liquidate depending on whether $r \lessgtr k$" [3, p. 48]. He then speculated that this curious result probably stemmed from the assumption of independence of $r$ and $b$, but with only one equation he was unable to follow the implications of this insight.

[4] Having developed present value valuation, subscripts from this point on refer to different values rather than different time periods.

Thus, in a single-equation valuation model such as (1.4″), the capitalized value of a corporation's dividend stream equals the capitalized value of its earnings stream if the corporation continues to invest until the rate of return on assets equals the market rate of discount.

This should not be considered a surprising result, considering the fixed definitional relationship between earnings and dividends. That an earnings model and a dividend model may lead to identical valuation of share prices has been demonstrated by Gordon [3, Ch. 5], Lintner [7, p. 256], and Miller and Modigliani [5][5] under various conditions and with different purposes in mind. What is significant is that $P$ in equation (1.5) does not depend upon $b$, nor in fact does it depend upon $r$ or $k$. If $r$ is substituted for $k$ in equation (1.4″), then at the point where $\partial P/\partial b = 0$,

$$(1.5') \qquad P = \frac{(1 - b)rA_o}{r - rb} = A_o,$$

or the price of the stock equals the book value of the corporation (since the assumption of no debt was made). With $r$ held constant and greater than $k$, the price of the stock commands a premium over book value and rises as $b$ increases. If $k$ is greater than a constant $r$, the price of the stock is less than book value and falls with a rise in $b$. While intuitively reasonable, the applicability of these results is limited because the manner in which they could be reached is unspecified. That is, if the retention rate is viewed as the firm's decision variable, it is reasonable to suppose that the value of the firm's stock would rise with an increase in its retention rate if internal opportunities remain greater than the shareholders' capitalization rate. On the other hand, the attempt of corporate management to proceed in its retention policy to the point where $r = k$ yields the unacceptable conclusion of equation (1.5′). The difficulty lies in not spelling out how $r$ and $k$ might, in fact, change with changes in $b$. Plainly, shareholders' discount rate and the rate of return on assets are not invariant with respect to changes in dividends and reinvestment of earnings. Instead of holding $r$ and $k$ fixed, and then tracing the effects of varying $b$ on $P$, a more useful way of working with equation (1.4″) may be to allow all four variables to change. As a first step, we continue to hold $k$ constant and map the $r$, $b$, and $P$ relationship.

If (1.4″) is written as

$$(1.4''') \qquad r = \frac{Pk}{b(P - A) + A}$$

iso-price lines can be traced on a graph whose axes are $r$ and $b$.

$P_2$ is higher than $P_1$ and both are greater than the corporation's book value. $P_{-1}$ is higher than $P_{-2}$ and both are less than book value. Figure 1 illustrates

---

[5] This study goes on to show that the valuation of shares will be identical not only under a dividend model and an earnings model, but also under a discounted cash-flow approach and the current earnings plus future investment-opportunities approach.

that for a given $r$, say $r_0 > k$, the price of the stock rises as $b$ increases from $b_1$ to $b_2$. If $r_0$ were less than $k$, the price would fall with increases in $b$. Moreover, for a given $b$, the price of the stock rises as $r$ increases.

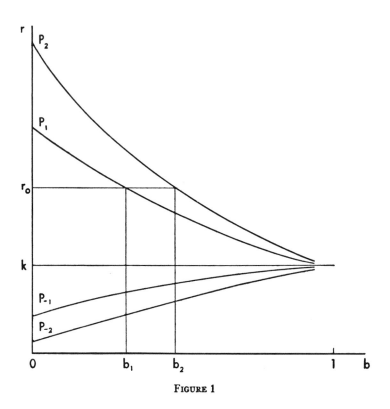

FIGURE 1

Figure 1 highlights the fact that all the iso-price lines approach $k$ as $b$ approaches 1.[6] It therefore follows that a given absolute change in $r$ will lead to a larger price change, the higher the level of $b$. This can be seen analytically by considering $\partial P/\partial r = (1 - b)kA/(k - rb)^2$ in the limiting cases where $b = 0$ and $b$ is close to 1. Phrased differently, stocks that have a right retention rate (low dividend payout rate) will fluctuate more in price for given changes in $r$ than securities with a low retention rate. A similar conclusion was reached by Malkiel [8].

A shift in $k$, the market rate of discount, will change the location of the iso-price lines. For example, if $k$ should fall as a result of a general decline in interest rates, and if $r$ and $b$ remain constant, some iso-price lines that formerly had positive slopes will now acquire negative slopes. Thus, if $k$ changes, the shares of a corporation may sell at a premium over book value (or any other

[6] Since $k > rb$ in general, but for $P > A$, $k < r$, it is clear that $b$ can only approach 1 for $k < r$. The integrability constraint would be violated if this were not the case.

specified price) at one time and at a discount from this price at another, even though the corporation continues to earn the same internal rate of return and follows the same dividend policy. More importantly, a corporation whose present price line shifted from negative to positive slope, say, would find that the consequence of an increase in the retention rate was a fall in share price, whereas formerly a rise would have resulted.

The difficulty with Figure 1 and its supporting equation as they now stand is that no provision is made for $k$ to vary and no bounds are placed on the interaction of $r$ and $b$ within the firm; hence, $P$ is indeterminate. Such also is the type of problem faced in the capital-budgeting decision. In that context, $P$ is usually assumed to be given and the question is asked: "What rate of return must be earned by the corporation if $P$ is to remain at its assumed level?" The more relevant question centers on the behavior of $P$ under various combinations of $r$ and $b$[7] and, more specifically, on the capital budget that will make $P$ a maximum. Without internal constraints on the firm or specification of how $k$ depends on $r$ and $b$, the problem cannot be resolved. Our next step is to specify $k$.

SPECIFYING $k$

Except for the constraint that $k$, the rate of discount, be greater than $rb$, the rate of growth of dividends, $k$ has not been specified. If for no other reason than to avoid the growth-stock paradox, $k$ should be related to the firm's expected growth. More importantly from a practical point of view, as indicated above, the suggestion that $k$ is a constant rather than a function leads to unacceptable capital-budgeting-decision results.

As a manageable form for such a function we propose:

(1.6)
$$k = \alpha + \psi rb$$

where $\alpha$ is the market interest rate on growthless shares[8] and $\psi$ is a risk class specification.[9] $\psi$ is a constant which can assume values between 0 and 1.[10]

At this stage of the analysis there is some parallel between Modigliani and Miller's risk-class concept and our own. That is, a $\psi$ class would be made up of corporations whose growth rates ($rb$'s) would be discounted in like fashion because in other respects they were similar. Since $\psi$ has not yet been specified

[7] One method of handling this problem was suggested by Cheng and Shelton [1].

[8] Under the assumption of an infinite stream of returns, yield to maturity equals current yield, a characteristic, for example, of consols. Because the dividend stream in this valuation model is discounted over an infinite horizon, $\alpha$, the market interest rate, is equivalent to a consol yield and might be approximated by the current yield on a growthless long-term security.

[9] Other forms for a risk-discount function are of course possible.

[10] This condition gives the limits of $\psi$ when $\alpha = 0$. Since in the real world $\alpha > 0$, equation (1.3) could still be integrated for some $\psi < 0$. Of course, if $\psi < 0$, this would imply that future dividends are worth more than current dividends. Furthermore, although $rb < 0$ gives rise to the logical problems of negative growth, as discussed in footnote 2, it is clear that with $0 \leq \psi \leq 1$, integrability conditions are not violated: $k - rb > 0$.

(except by its range of possible values) and since debt has not yet been introduced into the capital structure of the firm, principal sources of expected instability in the firm may include previous instability of growth due to industry competition, demand elasticity, vulnerability to technological change, and the like. The greater the degree to which these forces were operative in the past, the more likely, *ceteris paribus*, they are to be operative in the future. Put slightly differently, when such forces have been significant, there is a greater presumption that they will continue to be so. For example, a high expected growth rate for a firm is more likely to attract competition if barriers to entry have been low, and this possibility creates uncertainty with respect to the mean-value expectation of growth. Since Modigliani and Miller were interested primarily in the effect of leverage on the discount rate, they removed dividend payout from center stage by assuming it already decided in the stockholders' best interests [11, p. 266]. They then defined the discount rate as a linear function of leverage alone, suppressing the growth rate-discount relationship. We prefer to start at a more fundamental level and define $k$ as a linear function of growth even before introducing the leverage problem. At one extreme a $\psi$ value of 0 implies the uniform rate of discount we have already discussed. If $\psi = 1$, the rate of discount rises one-for-one with the expected rate of growth, and stockholders will pay no more for the high growth company than for the zero growth firm. As an example of the latter possibility, if the only source of growth was expected inflation of dividend dollars and shareholders insisted on evaluating their prospects in real terms, $\psi$ would equal 1.

Substituting equation (1.6) into (1.4″) yields

(1.7)
$$P = \frac{(1 - b)rA}{\alpha + \psi rb - rb}.$$

The first partial derivative of $P$ with respect to $b$ equals 0 when $r = \alpha/(1 - \psi)$, and once again the second derivative will be positive or negative depending upon whether $r(1 - \psi) \gtrless \alpha$.[11] A graph of this expression would be similar to that of Figure 1 above with the difference that $k$ would be replaced by $\alpha/(1 - \psi)$. Similarly, substituting the value for $r(1 - \psi)$ in equation (1.7) yields

(1.8)
$$P = \frac{rA}{\alpha}.$$

Once again, with $r$ a fixed number, there is a point $(\partial P/\partial b = 0)$ at which $P$ is independent of $b$, or the dividend model produces the same price as an earnings model. More importantly, at this point the risk class falls out. This result makes intuitive good sense and justifies the form given the discount function for, if $r$ is fixed and $b$ has been set by differentiation at the point at which it does not influence share price, then growth ($rb$) does not affect capitalization.

---

[11] Again, under the assumption that $dr/db = 0$ or that $r$ is fixed.

Equation (1.8) can also be rewritten as

$$(1.8') \qquad\qquad r = \frac{\alpha P}{A}.$$

In this form the equation focuses attention on the rate of return that a corporation must earn on its assets if its shares are to maintain their existing price. Equation (1.8') also serves to put to rest the alleged " IBM paradox ": Should not a corporation that sells at 50 times earnings invest in any asset yielding over 2 per cent? If $\alpha$, the market rate of interest on securities with no growth, equals 4 per cent, if the security sells at five times its book value, and if the retention rate is that which makes $\partial P/\partial b = 0$, then the required rate of return necessary to keep the price of the stock at its present level is 20 per cent, not any value greater than 2 per cent. As indicated earlier, however, equation (1.8') does not provide an answer to what rate must be earned to maximize $P$, let alone to what happens to $r$ when $b$ is determined.

A further interesting result can be obtained from equation (1.8'). When the firm's capital budget is set at $\partial P/\partial b = 0$, then $\alpha = r(1 - \psi)$, or

$$(1.9) \qquad\qquad \psi = 1 - \frac{\alpha}{r} = 1 - \frac{\alpha A}{Y}.$$

Since, under the assumption of an infinite shareholder time horizon, $\alpha$ can be replaced by the current earnings yield, the $\psi$ class of a security when $\partial P/\partial b = 0$ will be given by:

$$(1.10) \qquad\qquad \psi = \frac{P - A}{P}.$$

Note that $\psi = 0$ when the price of the stock equals its book value.[12] As the price rises from book value, $\psi$ increases. Equation (1.10), or some variant, has a long history of use among practitioners of security analysis and portfolio management. In the language of "The Street," risk rises when the security commands a substantial premium over book value. Indeed, one portfolio manager has gone so far as to state that when securities sell for more than six times book value (a $\psi$ class of .83 under our assumptions), they no longer belong in a prudent man's portfolio [4].

INTRODUCTION OF DEBT INTO THE CAPITAL STRUCTURE

Debt can be formally introduced into the single-equation valuation model as follows:

Let the change in assets in a continuous model be represented by the change

---

[12] Since $0 \leq \psi \leq 1, P \geq A$, which might seem to be an unnecessarily strong result. On the other hand, if $P < A$ and the firm is doing the best it can, then it probably should liquidate. This conclusion is equivalent to Gordon's and follows from essentially the same situation as his case of $r < k$.

in equity plus the change in liabilities:

(1.11)                     $dA = dE + dL.$

The change in equity equals retained earnings:

(1.12)                     $dE = Ar_L b,$

where $r_L$ is now the levered internal rate of return, or rate of return on assets less interest expenses imposed by the existence of debt. Let the change in debt be represented by $dL = L\mu$ where $\mu$ is some constant. If the ratio of debt to equity is assumed to remain constant,[13] then

$$\frac{dE}{dL} = \frac{E}{L} = \frac{Ar_L b}{L\mu}.$$

Therefore,

$$\mu = \frac{Ar_L b}{E}.$$

If $z = L/A$,

(1.13)                     $\mu = \dfrac{Ar_L b}{A - L} = \dfrac{Ar_L b}{A - A_z} = \dfrac{r_L b}{1 - z}.$

Substituting (1.12) and (1.13) into (1.11):

$$dA = Ar_L b + \frac{L(r_L b)}{(1 - z)}$$

$$= r_L b \left[ A + \frac{Az}{1 - z} \right] = \frac{Ar_L b}{1 - z},$$

or

(1.14)                     $\dfrac{dA}{A} = \dfrac{r_L b}{1 - z}.$

The percentage change in assets is precisely the term we have called $g$ in equation (1.4), by virtue of equation (1.1') and the assumption that $D = (1 - b)rA$. Substitution of equation (1.14) into (1.4) yields a valuation model for a corporation with a fixed percentage of debt in its capital structure ($k$, however, is unspecified at this point):

(1.15)                     $P = \dfrac{(1 - b)r_L A}{k - \dfrac{(r_L b)}{(1 - z)}}.$

Equation (1.15) suggests the following question: What is the optimum ratio

---

[13] For an empirical justification of this assumption, see Lindsay and Sametz [6, Chs. 18 and 19], and Miller [9].

of debt to assets for a corporation, abstracting from taxes? The first derivative of $P$ with respect to $z$ shows that so long as $k(1 - z) > r_L b$, the price of the security will rise with a rise in the ratio of debt to total assets, and as $k(1 - z)$ approaches $r_L b$, the change in price associated with a change in debt approaches infinity. The assumption that $k$ is independent of $z$, however, is not very useful. Indeed, one of the classic controversies in finance centers on the behavior of $k$ over various ranges of $z$. Modigliani and Miller's famous proposition—in terms of equation (1.15)—is, of course, that $k$ rises linearly with $z$ so that the average yield of the sum of debt plus equity remains constant. The more conventional position is that $k$ does not change for low levels of $z$; however, as $z$ continues to rise, $k$ rises faster than $r_L b/(1 - z)$. Under this conventional view, the price of a stock, therefore, first rises and then falls as progressively larger amounts of debt are introduced into the capital structure.

An alternative behavior assumption allows $k$ to change with changes in the debt-asset ratio. Such a specification may be given by

(1.16) $$k = \alpha + \psi r_L b + \phi z$$

where $\phi$ is same constant greater than zero. Substituting equation (1.16) into (1.15) gives a stock-valuation model that incorporates debt:

(1.17) $$P = \frac{(1 - b)r_L A}{\alpha + \psi r_L b + \phi z - \dfrac{(r_L b)}{(1 - z)}}.$$

For corporations that have no debt, it will be recalled that $\partial P/\partial b = 0$ when $r = \alpha/(1 - \psi)$, where the absence of a subscript means that $r$ is unlevered. The change in $P$ with respect to a change in $b$ for corporations with debt equals zero when

(1.18) $$r_L = \frac{(1 - z)(\alpha + \phi z)}{1 - \psi + \psi z}.$$

If $z = 0$, equation (1.18) is identical to the case of a corporation with no debt; $r_L$ is the rate of return after interest that a corporation must earn on assets if the price of the stock is to remain constant with respect to a change in retention rates.

The treatment of debt, however, suffers from being essentially arbitrary. Moreover, the implication of debt in the capital structure has not been carried through to the stream of dividends. Even if these difficulties are accounted for, the retention rate which maximizes $P$ is indeterminate.

## II. A GENERAL MODEL

In Section I we developed a stock-valuation model that specified $k$ and incorporated debt as part of the capital structure. While useful insights are obtained from this model, its usefulness is limited. The principal kinds of questions that can be answered within the model's framework are of the sort: given a $P$ and a $z$, what is the $b$ which will just maintain the present $P$? Of greater interest is a model which allows more logical "degrees of freedom." In this section we develop a set of two equations in $r$ and $P$, one the stock-valuation equation, the other an investment-opportunities schedule. Simultaneous solution of these for some $b$ yields $r$ and $P$.

### THE $LC$ SCHEDULE

The investment-opportunities schedule facing a corporation at a point in time can, with reliance upon traditional economic thinking on the subject, be taken as a function linking inversely the expected rate of return on total assets and size of capital budget.[14]

The development of a stock-valuation model invoked shareholders' expectations of $r$ and $b$; the present section deals with management's (expected) constraints on $r$ and $b$. Apart from equilibrium requirements, and undoubtedly in the everyday world, the possibility exists that shareholder and management point estimates of $r$ and $b$ will diverge. It, therefore, becomes useful to introduce new notation: $r_I$ and $b_I$ to stand for investor (shareholder) expectations of rate of return and retention rate, and $r_C$ and $b_C$ to be expectations of the same variables held by the corporation (management).

With this convention, and recalling that the capital budget is defined identically by the corporation's earnings-retention rate,[15] a reasonable form for the investment opportunity schedule would be:

$$(2.1) \qquad LC(r_C, b_C) = \gamma_0 \geq \frac{r_C}{1 + \gamma_1 b_C},$$

where $\gamma_0 (\geq 0)$ is the average rate of return expected when retained earnings are zero, and $\gamma_1 (<0)$ reflects the declining return associated with movement down an opportunities schedule as $b$ increases. To show the nature of the functional relationship of $r_C$ and $b_C$, inequality (2.1) may be written as

$$(2.2) \qquad r_C \leq \gamma_0 + \gamma_0 \gamma_1 b_C.$$

The shaded area in Figure 2 is feasible; for the efficient firm, (2.2) may be written as an equality:

$$(2.3) \qquad r_C = \gamma_0 + \gamma_0 \gamma_1 b_C.$$

It should be emphasized that this function is a set of equilibrium points, not a demand curve. For the corporation with no debt, no external financing, and

---

[14] The more common statement links the return on the marginal investment to the marginal investment. It is clear that our formulation is consistent, for if $r$, which is the average return on total assets, declines, then so does $r'$, the marginal return. The reason for our formulation rests on the fact that (from the stock-valuation equation) $r$ rather than $r'$ is the focus of capital-budget decisions designed to maximize share price.

[15] Depreciation is not considered a source of funds because we are interested only in net investment.

no liquidating dividends, the domain of $LC$ is from $b = 0$ to $b = 1$. The choice of $b_C$ (and, hence, of $r_C$) remains indeterminate for the corporation until it is known which retention rate will, in fact, maximize share price.

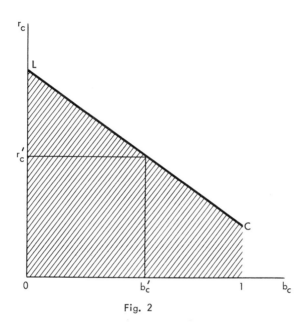

Fig. 2

## THE COMPLETE MODEL

Recall Figure 1 in which, from equation (1.4″), $r$ was expressed as a unique function of $b$, given $P$ and $k$. In terms of this section:

$$(1.4'') \qquad P = \frac{(1 - b_I)r_I A}{k - r_I b_I},$$

or

$$(1.4''') \qquad r_I = \frac{Pk}{b_I(P - A) + A} = \frac{P\alpha}{b_I[P(1 - \psi) - A] + A}.$$

As with equation (2.3), it is clear that the valuation model is incomplete. To state the matter differently, we can fix $P$ and $b_I$ and find $r_I$, but how do we arrive at a $P$, much less at a maximum $P$?

The answer lies in the simultaneous solution of equations (2.3) and (1.7). This can most easily be seen by tracing the steps from choice of $b$ (the corporation's decision variable) to final determination of $P$. As a first step, it is necessary to impose the equilibrium conditions that

$$(2.4) \qquad r_C = r_I$$

$$(2.5) \qquad b_C = b_I$$

in order that there be no divergence in expectations. That is, shareholders accept the firm's retention-rate decision and agree with its assessment of the consequences on rate of return (whether or not they like it).

Then it can be seen that, with exogenous $A$, $\alpha$, and $\psi$, equation (1.7) expresses share price as a function of $r$ and $b$ and that equation (2.3) is also a function in the same two variables. Once the firm chooses its retention rate, $b$, then $r$ is determined from the latter function. However, substitution of the values for these variables in the stock-valuation equation (1.7) produces a unique share price.

The problem of suboptimum price arises in an equilibrium context because, although shareholders may agree with the corporation's assessment of its retention policy, they would be better off with some other policy that produced some other return, which might be either higher or lower. Solution of maximum price is somewhat more easily described with equations (1.4''') and (2.3). The maximum price then is given by the familiar tangency condition:

(2.6)
$$\left(\frac{\partial r}{\partial b}\right)_{eq.(1.4''')} = \left(\frac{\partial r}{\partial b}\right)_{eq.(2.3)}$$

Under the conditions assumed, only one $P$, a unique maximum, satisfies the condition that these two slopes be equal.

$$\left(\frac{\partial r}{\partial b}\right)_{eq.(2.3)} = \gamma_0\gamma_1 < 0$$

and

$$\left(\frac{\partial r}{\partial b}\right)_{eq.(1.4''')} < 0 \quad \text{for } P(1-\psi) > A.$$

Furthermore, because the second partial derivative of $r$ with respect to $b$ is zero for the right-hand side and positive for the left-hand side of (2.6), for $P(1-\psi) > A$,[16] the appropriate convexity of the iso-price lines within the allowable range of the $rb$ plane is satisfied.[17] Figure 3 describes the solution of

[16] It may be asked why this statement of a general model was not handled by the more familiar technique of Lagrange multipliers: maximize equation (1.4) subject to equation (2.1). While such a method yields the same results plus valid economic insights into the nature of the valuation *cum* capital budget problem, a comment is in order. In general $b_c \neq b_i$ and $r_c \neq r_i$. Satisfaction of conditions (2.4) and (2.5) is necessary to secure simultaneous firm and market equilibrium *at any price*. Although the consequences of not meeting these conditions are best dealt with in dynamic models (and will be so handled in a forthcoming paper), we prefer not to suppress them this early in the game.

[17] We have drawn the $LC$ function *above* $\alpha/(1-\psi)$, indicating the firm has opportunity for an average internal return at least equal to the absolute required yield in the market adjusted for risk. For the firm whose $LC$ function is below $\alpha/(1-\psi)$, the iso-price lines are concave downward, indicating that the best the firm can do is distribute all earnings; retaining and reinvesting serves to lower $P$. As in Gordon's model, however, $b$ can only approach 1. For $r > \alpha/(1-\psi)$, if $b = 1$ the integrability constraint, $r < \alpha/b(1-\psi)$, is violated. The economic sense of this case—where the tangency is at or beyond the point

the stock-maximization problem, where $b'$ is the solution value of the corporation's decision variable.

The firm faces only one investment-opportunities schedule, downward-sloping, at a point in time, but an entire family of share prices. Without

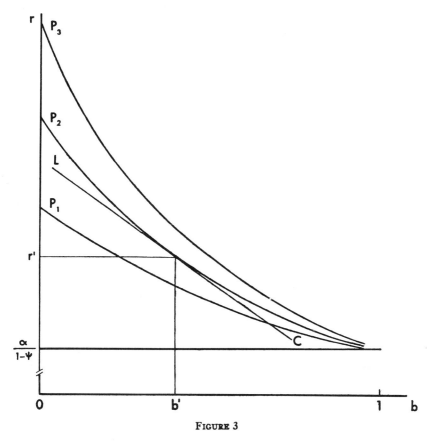

FIGURE 3

condition (2.6) an infinite number of prices are possible since the $LC$ function intersects infinitely many iso-price lines. Condition (2.6) allows us to find a

---

where $b = 1$—is that a switch to external financing is called for. For $r < \alpha/(1 - \psi)$, any $b > 0$ lowers $P$. Hence the case of $b = 1$ is not meaningful. Satisfaction of the second-order condition is guaranteed by the choice of a downward-sloping linear $LC$ function. It therefore may be argued that our specification of the investment-opportunities schedule is fortuitous. On the other hand, other specifications would produce the same results, and the one chosen is consistent with economic tradition. It is interesting to note that the condition $P(1 - \psi) > A$ which is necessary for negative first derivative and positive second derivative is at variance with the results of equation (1.9) and (1.10) above, in which $P(1 - \psi) = A$ for $\partial P/\partial b = 0$. The reason for this difference is, of course, that the earlier result ignored the $r, b$ relationship by considering $r$ to be fixed.

maximum price, i.e., where the slope of the $LC$ function equals the slope of an iso-price line.

Maximizing profits, that is, carrying on investment projects until $r = \alpha/(1 - \psi)$, is an inadequate criterion for either capital budgeting or dividend payout policy. In the case of Figure 3, investment to the point where $r = \alpha/(1 - \psi)$ (or equivalently until $r = k$) would clearly not be optimal, for once the point of tangency with an iso-price line is passed, movement down the $LC$ function toward $b = 1$ produces lower and lower share prices as (implicitly) less-profitable projects are undertaken. Such a course would only be another example of the alleged IBM paradox: Investment to the point where $r = \alpha/(1 - \psi)$ (or $r = k$) represents the undertaking of projects whose returns are not regarded by the market as valuable as using the funds to pay greater dividends.

This conclusion that firms should not in general invest until $r = \alpha/(1 - \psi)$ is admittedly at variance with traditional statements on the subject. Such statements have assumed either a single equation which took $P$ as given or an infinitely elastic investment-opportunities schedule. Positing a downward-sloping investment-opportunities schedule and a separate valuation equation leads to the results described above.

Figure 3 and the supporting equations also illustrate the fallacy of the proposition that a firm should retain all earnings or distribute all earnings depending upon whether $r \gtrless \alpha/(1 - \psi)$. The idea that such a policy could be relevant arises only because the requirements of internal (rate of return) and external (share price) equilibrium are not dealt with simultaneously. For the growing firm $(P > A)$, equilibrium at a maximum $P$ is obtained only with an $r > \alpha/(1 - \psi)$ (i.e., $r > k$), which could require a $b$ anywhere between 0 and 1. As discussed in footnote 17, for $r < \alpha/(1 - \psi)$, the maximum obtainable $P$ is at $b = 0$.

This analysis also indicates the limitations of two other "rules of thumb" that allegedly characterize some corporate actions: adopting only those projects that yield more than a given rate of return and paying out a fixed percentage of earnings in dividends. If a corporation rejects all projects that yield less than an arbitrary set $r_o$, a dividend payment is dictated which is likely to be suboptimal with respect to share prices. Similarly, if a corporation adopts a fixed payout (retention) policy, the rate of return that will be earned may not maximize share prices.

A variety of possible situations are manageable within the comparative statics framework of this model. Consider first the effect of an upward shift in $LC$, the investment-opportunities schedule. The result is an increase in $b$ and $P$, and possibly in $r$.

Consider now the selection of a retention rate higher than $b'$. Equilibrium for shareholders is possible now only at a lower $P$ because the exploitation of too many internal opportunities lowers the average rate of return. Similarly, too low a retention rate will not maximize $P$ because dividends are not valued as highly as some margin of the remaining internal opportunities. Securing equilibrium $r$ and $b$ together with a maximum $P$ requires the firm to find a unique retention rate and its associated unique rate of return.

Consider finally the effect of a change in $k$. If, for example, $k$ should rise because of a change in the demand for and supply of loanable funds (equivalently, if $\alpha$ should rise), the iso-price lines will shift so that any given $r$ and $b$ will be associated with lower iso-price lines. With an unchanged $LC$ schedule, the equilibrium $P$ will fall. Moreover, the slopes of the iso-price lines will change for given rates of return. A new price line will now be tangent to the $LC$ function and only by chance will the point of tangency be the same as where it was before the change in $k$ occurred. The implication of this is that no single capital budget will be optimal under diverse external market circumstances.

## III. IMPLICATIONS FOR RESEARCH

In the previous section we defined a static equilibrium stock valuation-capital budgeting model. We demonstrated how $r$ and $b$ must vary if the price of a share is to be optimized under the assumption of a given $k$ function and investment-opportunities schedule. We demonstrated the consequence of a shift in either the $LC$ (investment opportunities) schedule, or $k$, as well as the consequences of a corporation's choosing an $r$ or $b$ other than the one dictated by the tangency of the $LC$ schedules and an iso-price line.

If the concept of the psi class is introduced into the $k$ function, the essential features of our equilibrium model are not altered. While the location and slope of the particular iso-price lines will change, the price of the security will still be optimized at the point of tangency between the $LC$ function and the iso-price line.

The model assumed no ranking problems for investment projects: because $r$ is the average return per year on total assets expected by firm and investor and is expected to be a constant, the related problem of finding the marginal profitability of projects having different time streams of returns is suppressed. Risk was not introduced into the $LC$ function because, arguing heuristically, the risk of the investor's discount function ($\psi$ class) is the relevant consideration for firms trying to maximize $P$. Put another way, if firm and investors have the same mean-value forecast of $r$, the risk factor which influences $P$ is that of the investors. Since the model presented in this paper is an equilibrium model, it cannot handle problems in disappointed expectations or consider measured variability as synonomous with risk. In an adjustment model, $\psi$ might best be specified as a function of observed variance around $r$.

The introduction of debt as a variable, however, is more complicated. In this paper it was handled in an arbitrary manner and not treated as a corporate-decision variable. If debt is treated as a variable, another equation, linking debt to the dividend payout, is required. It also may be useful to consider debt in a dynamic context. In an adjustment model there will be an investor $b$-expectation function such as: $b_t^* = b(b_{t-1}, b_{t-2} \ldots)$. A decline in $b^*$ will tend, *ceteris paribus*, to lower $P$. The question then arises: given an investment-opportunities schedule with tangency position at $b > b^*$, should the corporation borrow or reduce dividend payout? Quite possibly the former. Put another way, if investors do not discount increases in leverage too heavily (i.e., if $\phi$ in equation (1.17) is not too large) and the opportunities schedule dictates asset growth, then maximum $P$ suggests both borrowing and paying a $(1 - b^*)$ dividend rate.

## REFERENCES

1. P. L. Cheng and J. P. Shelton, "A Contribution to the Theory of Capital Budgeting—the Multi-Investment Case," *Jour. Finance*, Dec. 1963, *18*, 622–37.
2. D. Durand, "Growth Stocks and the Petersburg Paradox," *Jour. Finance*, Sept. 1957, *12*, 348–63.
3. M. J. Gordon, *The Investment, Financing, and Valuation of the Corporation*, Homewood 1962.
4. W. Gutman, "Book Value-Market Value Patterns," in E. M. Lerner, ed., *Readings in Financial Analysis and Investment Management*, Homewood 1963.
5. P. Hunt, C. M. Williams and G. Donaldson, *Basic Business Finance*, Homewood 1961.
6. R. Lindsay and A. W. Sametz, *Financial Management: An Analytical Approach*, Homewood 1963.
7. J. Lintner, "Dividends, Earnings, Leverage, Stock Prices and the Supply of Capital to Corporations," *Rev. Econ. Stat.*, Aug. 1962, *44*, 243–69.
8. B. G. Malkiel, "Equity Yields and the Structure of Share Prices," *Am. Econ. Rev.*, Dec. 1963, *53*, 1004–32.
9. M. H. Miller, "The Corporation Income Tax and Corporate Financial Policy," in *Stabilization Policies*, Commission on Money and Credit, Englewood Cliffs 1964.
10. —— and F. Modigliani, "Dividend Policy, Growth, and the Valuation of Shares," *Jour. Business*, Oct. 1961, *34*, 411–34.
11. F. Modigliani and M. H. Miller, "The Cost of Capital, Corporation Finance and the Theory of Investment," *Am. Econ. Rev.*, June 1958, *48*, 261–98.

# 13. CAPITAL ASSET PRICES: A THEORY OF MARKET EQUILIBRIUM UNDER CONDITIONS OF RISK*

## WILLIAM F. SHARPE†

Reprinted from *The Journal of Finance*, Vol. *XIX*, No. 3 (September, 1964), pp. 425–42, by permission of the author and the publisher.

## I. INTRODUCTION

One of the problems which has plagued those attempting to predict the behavior of capital markets is the absence of a body of positive microeconomic theory dealing with conditions of risk. Although many useful insights can be obtained from the traditional models of investment under conditions of certainty, the pervasive influence of risk in financial transactions has forced those working in this area to adopt models of price behavior which are little more than assertions. A typical classroom explanation of the determination of capital asset prices, for example, usually begins with a careful and relatively rigorous description of the process through which individual preferences and physical relationships interact to determine an equilibrium pure interest rate. This is generally followed by the assertion that somehow a market risk-premium is also determined, with the prices of assets adjusting accordingly to account for differences in their risk.

A useful representation of the view of the capital market implied in such discussions is illustrated in Figure 1. In equilibrium, capital asset prices have adjusted so that the investor, if he follows rational procedures (primarily diversification), is able to attain any desired point along a *capital market line*.[1] He may obtain a higher expected rate of return on his holdings only by incurring additional risk. In effect, the market presents him with two prices: the *price of time*, or the pure interest rate (shown by the intersection of the line with the horizontal axis) and the *price of risk*, the additional expected return per unit of risk borne (the reciprocal of the slope of the line).

At present there is no theory describing the manner in which the price of

* A great many people provided comments on early versions of this paper which led to major improvements in the exposition. In addition to the referees, who were most helpful, the author wishes to express his appreciation to Dr. Harry Markowitz of the Rand Corporation, Professor Jack Hirshleifer of the University of California at Los Angeles, and to Professors Yoram Barzel, George Brabb, Bruce Johnson, Walter Oi and R. Haney Scott of the University of Washington.

† Associate Professor of Operations Research, University of Washington.

[1] Although some discussions are also consistent with a non-linear (but monotonic) curve.

risk results from the basic influences of investor preferences, the physical attributes of capital assets, etc. Moreover, lacking such a theory, it is difficult to give any real meaning to the relationship between the price of a single asset and its risk. Through diversification, some of the risk inherent in an asset can be avoided so that its total risk is obviously not the relevant influence on its price; unfortunately little has been said concerning the particular risk component which is relevant.

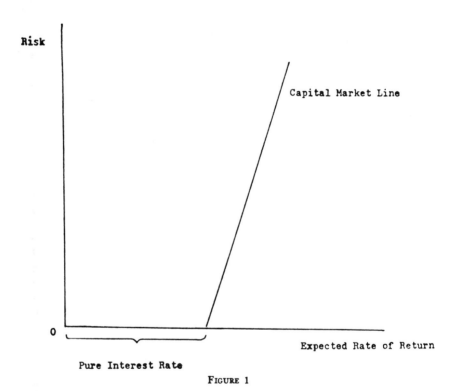

FIGURE 1

In the last ten years a number of economists have developed *normative* models dealing with asset choice under conditions of risk. Markowitz,[2] following Von Neumann and Morgenstern, developed an analysis based on the expected utility maxim and proposed a general solution for the portfolio selection problem. Tobin[3] showed that under certain conditions Markowitz's model implies that the process of investment choice can be broken down into two phases: first, the choice of a unique optimum combination of risky assets;

[2] Harry M. Markowitz, *Portfolio Selection, Efficient Diversification of Investments* (New York: John Wiley and Sons, Inc., 1959). The major elements of the theory first appeared in his article "Portfolio Selection," *The Journal of Finance*, XII (March 1952), 77–91.

[3] James Tobin, "Liquidity Preference as Behavior Towards Risk," *The Review of Economic Studies*, XXV (February 1958), 65–86.

and second, a separate choice concerning the allocation of funds between such a combination and a single riskless asset. Recently, Hicks[4] has used a model similar to that proposed by Tobin to derive corresponding conclusions about individual investor behavior, dealing somewhat more explicitly with the nature of the conditions under which the process of investment choice can be dichotomized. An even more detailed discussion of this process, including a rigorous proof in the context of a choice among lotteries has been presented by Gordon and Gangolli.[5]

Although all the authors cited use virtually the same model of investor behavior,[6] none has yet attempted to extend it to construct a *market* equilibrium theory of asset prices under conditions of risk.[7] We will show that such an extension provides a theory with implications consistent with the assertions of traditional financial theory described above. Moreover, it sheds considerable light on the relationship between the price of an asset and the various components of its overall risk. For these reasons it warrants consideration as a model of the determination of capital asset prices.

Part II provides the model of individual investor behavior under conditions of risk. In Part III the equilibrium conditions for the capital market are considered and the capital market line derived. The implications for the relationship between the prices of individual capital assets and the various components of risk are described in Part IV.

## II. OPTIMAL INVESTMENT POLICY FOR THE INDIVIDUAL

### THE INVESTOR'S PREFERENCE FUNCTION

Assume that an individual views the outcome of any investment in probabilistic terms; that is, he thinks of the possible results in terms of some probability distribution. In assessing the desirability of a particular investment, however, he is willing to act on the basis of only two parameters of this

---

[4] John R. Hicks, "Liquidity," *The Economic Journal*, LXXII (December 1962), 787–802.

[5] M. J. Gordon and Ramesh Gangolli, "Choice Among and Scale of Play on Lottery Type Alternatives," College of Business Administration, University of Rochester, 1962. For another discussion of this relationship see W. F. Sharpe, "A Simplified Model for Portfolio Analysis," *Management Science*, Vol. 9, No. 2 (January 1963), 277–293. A related discussion can be found in F. Modigliani and M. H. Miller, "The Cost of Capital, Corporation Finance, and the Theory of Investment," *The American Economic Review*, XLVIII (June 1958), 261–297.

[6] Recently Hirshleifer has suggested that the mean-variance approach used in the articles cited is best regarded as a special case of a more general formulation due to Arrow. See Hirshleifer's "Investment Decision Under Uncertainty," *Papers and Proceedings of the Seventy-Sixth Annual Meeting of the American Economic Association*, December 1963, or Arrow's "Le Role des Valeurs Boursieres pour la Repartition la Meilleure des Risques," *International Colloquium on Econometrics*, 1952.

[7] After preparing this paper the author learned that Mr. Jack L. Treynor, of Arthur D. Little, Inc., had independently developed a model similar in many respects to the one described here. Unfortunately Mr. Treynor's excellent work on this subject is, at present, unpublished.

distribution—its expected value and standard deviation.[8] This can be represented by a total utility function of the form:

$$U = f(E_W, \sigma_W)$$

where $E_W$ indicates expected future wealth and $\sigma_W$ the predicted standard deviation of the possible divergence of actual future wealth from $E_W$.

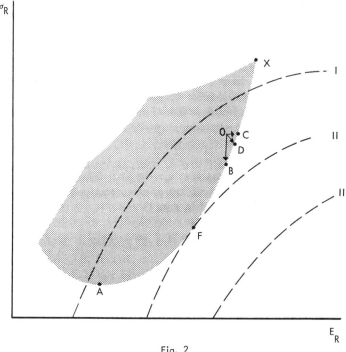

Fig. 2

Investors are assumed to prefer a higher expected future wealth to a lower value, *ceteris paribus* ($dU/dE_W > 0$). Moreover, they exhibit risk-aversion, choosing an investment offering a lower value of $\sigma_W$ to one with a greater level, given the level of $E_W$ ($dU/d\sigma_W < 0$). These assumptions imply that indifference curves relating $E_W$ and $\sigma_W$ will be upward-sloping.[9]

To simplify the analysis, we assume that an investor has decided to commit a given amount ($W_i$) of his present wealth to investment. Letting $W_t$ be his

---

[8] Under certain conditions the mean-variance approach can be shown to lead to unsatisfactory predictions of behavior. Markowitz suggests that a model based on the semi-variance (the average of the squared deviations below the mean) would be preferable; in light of the formidable computational problems, however, he bases his analysis on the variance and standard deviation.

[9] While only these characteristics are required for the analysis, it is generally assumed that the curves have the property of diminishing marginal rates of substitution between $E_W$ and $\sigma_W$, as do those in our diagrams.

terminal wealth and $R$ the rate of return on his investment:

$$R \equiv \frac{W_t - W_i}{W_i},$$

we have

$$W_t = RW_i + W_i.$$

This relationship makes it possible to express the investor's utility in terms of $R$, since terminal wealth is directly related to the rate of return:

$$U = g(E_R, \sigma_R).$$

Figure 2 summarizes the model of investor preferences in a family of indifference curves; successive curves indicate higher levels of utility as one moves down and/or to the right.[10]

THE INVESTMENT OPPORTUNITY CURVE

The model of investor behavior considers the investor as choosing from a set of investment opportunities that one which maximizes his utility. Every investment plan available to him may be represented by a point in the $E_R$, $\sigma_R$ plane. If all such plans involve some risk, the area composed of such points will have an appearance similar to that shown in Figure 2. The investor will choose from among all possible plans the one placing him on the indifference curve representing the highest level of utility (point $F$). The decision can be made in two stages: first, find the set of efficient investment plans and, second, choose one from among this set. A plan is said to be efficient if (and only if) there is no alternative with either (1) the same $E_R$ and a lower $\sigma_R$, (2) the same $\sigma_R$ and a higher $E_R$ or (3) a higher $E_R$ and a lower $\sigma_R$. Thus investment O is inefficient since investments B, C, and D (among others) dominate it. The only plans which would be chosen must lie along the lower right-hand boundary ($AFBDCX$)—*the investment opportunity curve.*

---

[10] Such indifference curves can also be derived by assuming that the investor wishes to maximize expected utility and that his total utility can be represented by a quadratic function of $R$ with decreasing marginal utility. Both Markowitz and Tobin present such a derivation. A similar approach is used by Donald E. Farrar in *The Investment Decision Under Uncertainty* (Prentice-Hall, 1962). Unfortunately Farrar makes an error in his derivation; he appeals to the Von-Neumann-Morgenstern cardinal utility axioms to transform a function of the form:

$$E(U) = a + bE_R - cE_R^2 - c\sigma_R^2$$

into one of the form:

$$E(U) = k_1 E_R - k_2 \sigma_R^2.$$

That such a transformation is not consistent with the axioms can readily be seen in this form, since the first equation implies non-linear indifference curves in the $E_R$, $\sigma_R^2$ plane while the second implies a linear relationship. Obviously no three (different) points can lie on both a line and a non-linear curve (with a monotonic derivative). Thus the two functions must imply different orderings among alternative choices in at least some instance.

To understand the nature of this curve, consider two investment plans—A and B, each including one or more assets. Their predicted expected values and standard deviations of rate of return are shown in Figure 3. If the proportion

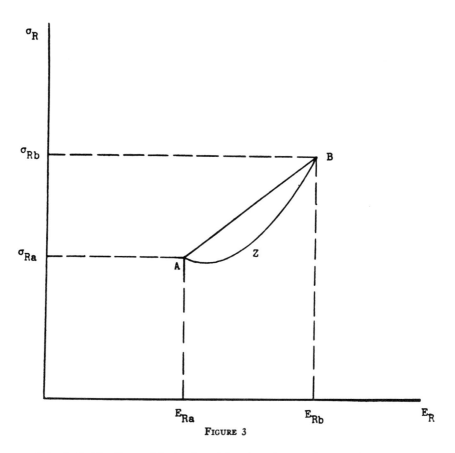

FIGURE 3

$\alpha$ of the individual's wealth is placed in plan A and the remainder $(1-\alpha)$ in B, the expected rate of return of the combination will lie between the expected returns of the two plans:

$$E_{Rc} = \alpha E_{Ra} + (1 - \alpha)E_{Rb}$$

The predicted standard deviation of return of the combination is:

$$\sigma_{Rc} = \sqrt{\alpha^2 \sigma_{Ra}^2 + (1 - \alpha)^2 \sigma_{Rb}^2 + 2r_{ab}\alpha(1 - \alpha)\sigma_{Ra}\sigma_{Rb}}$$

Note that this relationship includes $r_{ab}$, the correlation coefficient between the predicted rates of return of the two investment plans. A value of $+1$ would indicate an investor's belief that there is a precise positive relationship between the outcomes of the two investments. A zero value would indicate a belief that the outcomes of the two investments are completely independent and $-1$ that the investor feels that there is a precise inverse relationship between them. In the usual case $r_{ab}$ will have a value between 0 and $+1$.

Figure 3 shows the possible values of $E_{Rc}$ and $\sigma_{Rc}$ obtainable with different combinations of A and B under two different assumptions about the value of $r_{ab}$. If the two investments are perfectly correlated, the combinations will lie along a straight line between the two points, since in this case both $E_{Rc}$ and $\sigma_{Rc}$ will be linearly related to the proportions invested in the two plans.[11] If they are less than perfectly positively correlated, the standard deviation of any combination must be less than that obtained with perfect correlation (since $r_{ab}$ will be less); thus the combinations must lie along a curve below the line $AB$.[12] $AZB$ shows such a curve for the case of complete independence $(r_{ab} = 0)$; with negative correlation the locus is even more U-shaped.[13]

The manner in which the investment opportunity curve is formed is relatively simple conceptually, although exact solutions are usually quite difficult.[14] One first traces curves indicating $E_R$, $\sigma_R$ values available with simple combinations of individual assets, then considers combinations of combinations of assets. The lower right-hand boundary must be either linear or increasing at an increasing rate $(d^2\sigma_R/dE_R^2 > 0)$. As suggested earlier, the complexity of the relationship between the characteristics of individual assets and the location of the investment opportunity curve makes it difficult to provide a simple rule for assessing the desirability of individual assets, since the effect of an asset on an investor's over-all investment opportunity curve

[11] $E_{Rc} = \alpha E_{Ra} + (1 - \alpha)E_{Rb} = E_{Rb} + (E_{Ra} - E_{Rb})\alpha$

$$\sigma_{Rc} = \sqrt{\alpha^2 \sigma_{Ra}^2 + (1 - \alpha)^2\sigma_{Rb}^2 + 2r_{ab}\alpha(1 - \alpha)\sigma_{Ra}\sigma_{Rb}}$$

but $r_{ab} = 1$, therefore the expression under the square root sign can be factored:

$$\sigma_{Rc} = \sqrt{[\alpha\sigma_{Ra} + (1 - \alpha)\sigma_{Rb}]^2}$$

$$= \alpha\sigma_{Ra} + (1 - \alpha)\sigma_{Rb}$$

$$= \sigma_{Rb} + (\sigma_{Ra} - \sigma_{Rb})\alpha$$

[12] This curvature is, in essence, the rationale for diversification.

[13] When $r_{ab} = 0$, the slope of the curve at point $A$ is

$$-\frac{\sigma_{Ra}}{E_{Rb} - E_{Ra}},$$

at point $B$ it is

$$\frac{\sigma Rb}{E_{Rb} - E_{Ra}}.$$

When $r_{ab} = -1$, the curve degenerates to two straight lines to a point on the horizontal axis.

[14] Markowitz has shown that this is a problem in parametric quadratic programming. An efficient solution technique is described in his article, "The Optimization of a Quadratic Function Subject to Linear Constraints," *Naval Research Logistics Quarterly*, Vol. 3 (March and June, 1956), 111–133. A solution method for a special case is given in the author's "A Simplified Model for Portfolio Analysis," *op. cit.*

depends not only on its expected rate of return $(E_{Ri})$ and risk $(\sigma_{Ri})$, but also on its correlations with the other available opportunities $(r_{i1}, r_{i2}, \ldots, r_{in})$. However, such a rule is implied by the equilibrium conditions for the model, as we will show in part IV.

### THE PURE RATE OF INTEREST

We have not yet dealt with riskless assets. Let $P$ be such an asset; its risk is zero $(\sigma_{Rp} = 0)$ and its expected rate of return, $E_{Rp}$, is equal (by definition) to the pure interest rate. If an investor places $\alpha$ of his wealth in $P$ and the remainder in some risky asset $A$, he would obtain an expected rate of return:

$$E_{Rc} = \alpha E_{Rp} + (1 - \alpha)E_{Ra}$$

The standard deviation of such a combination would be:

$$\sigma_{Rc} = \sqrt{\alpha^2\sigma_{Rp}^2 + (1 - \alpha)^2\sigma_{Ra}^2 + 2r_{pa}\alpha(1 - \alpha)\sigma_{Rp}\sigma_{Ra}}$$

but since $\sigma_{Rp} = 0$, this reduces to:

$$\sigma_{Rc} = (1 - \alpha)\sigma_{Ra}.$$

This implies that all combinations involving any risky asset or combination of assets plus the riskless asset must have values of $E_{Rc}$ and $\sigma_{Rc}$ which lie along a straight line between the points representing the two components. Thus in Figure 4 all combinations of $E_R$ and $\sigma_R$ lying along the line $PA$ are attainable

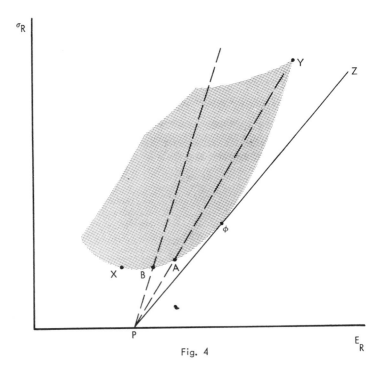

Fig. 4

if some money is loaned at the pure rate and some placed in $A$. Similarly, by lending at the pure rate and investing in $B$, combinations along $PB$ can be attained. Of all such possibilities, however, one will dominate: that investment plan lying at the point of the original investment opportunity curve where a ray from point $P$ is tangent to the curve. In Figure 4 all investments lying along the original curve from $X$ to $\phi$ are dominated by some combination of investment in $\phi$ and lending at the pure interest rate.

Consider next the possibility of borrowing. If the investor can borrow at the pure rate of interest, this is equivalent to disinvesting in $P$. The effect of borrowing to purchase more of any given investment than is possible with the given amount of wealth can be found simply by letting $\alpha$ take on negative values in the equations derived for the case of lending. This will obviously give points lying along the extension of line $PA$ if borrowing is used to purchase more of $A$; points lying along the extension of $PB$ if the funds are used to purchase B, etc.

As in the case of lending, however, one investment plan will dominate all others when borrowing is possible. When the rate at which funds can be borrowed equals the lending rate, this plan will be the same one which is dominant if lending is to take place. Under these conditions, the investment opportunity curve becomes a line ($P\phi Z$ in Figure 4). Moreover, if the original investment opportunity curve is not linear at point $\phi$, the process of investment choice can be dichotomized as follows: first select the (unique) optimum combination of risky assets (point $\phi$), and second borrow or lend to obtain the particular point on $PZ$ at which an indifference curve is tangent to the line.[15]

Before proceeding with the analysis, it may be useful to consider alternative assumptions under which only a combination of assets lying at the point of tangency between the original investment opportunity curve and a ray from $P$ can be efficient. Even if borrowing is impossible, the investor will choose $\phi$ (and lending) if his risk-aversion leads him to a point below $\phi$ on the line $P\phi$. Since a large number of investors choose to place some of their funds in relatively risk-free investments, this is not an unlikely possibility. Alternatively, if borrowing is possible but only up to some limit, the choice of $\phi$ would be made by all those investors willing to undertake considerable risk. These alternative paths lead to the main conclusion, thus making the assumption of borrowing or lending at the pure interest rate less onerous than it might initially appear to be.

---

[15] This proof was first presented by Tobin for the case in which the pure rate of interest is zero (cash). Hicks considers the lending situation under comparable conditions but does not allow borrowing. Both authors present their analysis using maximization subject to constraints expressed as equalities. Hicks' analysis assumes independence and thus insures that the solution will include no negative holdings of risky assets; Tobin's covers the general case, thus his solution would generally include negative holdings of some assets. The discussion in this paper is based on Markowitz' formulation, which includes non-negativity constraints on the holdings of all assets.

## III. EQUILIBRIUM IN THE CAPITAL MARKET

In order to derive conditions for equilibrium in the capital market we invoke two assumptions. First, we assume a common pure rate of interest, with all investors able to borrow or lend funds on equal terms. Second, we assume homogeneity of investor expectations:[16] investors are assumed to agree on the prospects of various investments—the expected values, standard deviations and correlation coefficients described in Part II. Needless to say, these are highly restrictive and undoubtedly unrealistic assumptions. However, since the proper test of a theory is not the realism of its assumptions but the acceptability of its implications, and since these assumptions imply equilibrium conditions which form a major part of classical financial doctrine, it is far from clear that this formulation should be rejected—especially in view of the dearth of alternative models leading to similar results.

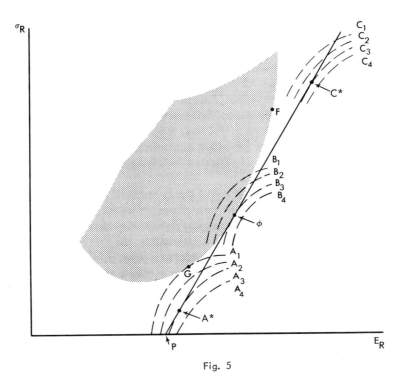

Fig. 5

Under these assumptions, given some set of capital asset prices, each investor will view his alternatives in the same manner. For one set of prices the alternatives might appear as shown in Figure 5. In this situation, an investor with the preferences indicated by indifference curves $A_1$ through $A_4$ would seek to lend some of his funds at the pure interest rate and to invest the remainder in the combination of assets shown by point $\phi$, since this would

[16] A term suggested by one of the referees.

give him the preferred over-all position $A^*$. An investor with the preferences indicated by curves $B_1$ through $B_4$ would seek to invest all his funds in combination $\phi$, while an investor with indifference curves $C_1$ through $C_4$ would invest all his funds plus additional (borrowed) funds in combination $\phi$ in order to reach his preferred position ($C^*$). In any event, all would attempt to purchase only those risky assets which enter combination $\phi$.

The attempts by investors to purchase the assets in combination $\phi$ and their lack of interest in holding assets not in combination $\phi$ would, of course, lead to a revision of prices. The prices of assets in $\phi$ will rise and, since an asset's expected return relates future income to present price, their expected returns will fall. This will reduce the attractiveness of combinations which include such assets; thus point $\phi$ (among others) will move to the left of its initial position.[17] On the other hand, the prices of assets not in $\phi$ will fall, causing an increase in their expected returns and a rightward movement of points representing combinations which include them. Such price changes will lead to a revision of investors' actions; some new combination or combinations will become attractive, leading to different demands and thus to further revisions in prices. As the process continues, the investment opportunity curve will tend to become more linear, with points such as $\phi$ moving to the left and formerly inefficient points (such as $F$ and $G$) moving to the right.

Capital asset prices must, of course, continue to change until a set of prices is attained for which every asset enters at least one combination lying on the capital market line. Figure 6 illustrates such an equilibrium condition.[18] All possibilities in the shaded area can be attained with combinations of risky assets, while points lying along the line $PZ$ can be attained by borrowing or lending at the pure rate plus an investment in some combination of risky assets. Certain possibilities (those lying along $PZ$ from point $A$ to point $B$) can be obtained in either manner. For example, the $E_R$, $\sigma_R$ values shown by point $A$ can be obtained solely by some combination of risky assets; alternatively, the point can be reached by a combination of lending and investing in combination $C$ of risky assets.

It is important to recognize that in the situation shown in Figure 6 many alternative combinations of risky assets are efficient (i.e., lie along line $PZ$), and thus the theory does not imply that all investors will hold the same combination.[19] On the other hand, all such combinations must be perfectly

[17] If investors consider the variability of future dollar returns unrelated to present price, both $E_R$ and $\sigma_R$ will fall; under these conditions the point representing an asset would move along a ray through the origin as its price changes.

[18] The area in Figure 6 representing $E_R$, $\sigma_R$ values attained with only risky assets has been drawn at some distance from the horizontal axis for emphasis. It is likely that a more accurate representation would place it very close to the axis.

[19] This statement contradicts Tobin's conclusion that there will be a unique optimal combination of risky assets. Tobin's proof of a unique optimum can be shown to be incorrect for the case of perfect correlation of efficient risky investment plans if the line connecting their $E_R$, $\sigma_R$ points would pass through point $P$. In the graph on page 83 of this article (*op. cit.*) the constant-risk locus would, in this case, degenerate from a family of ellipses into one of straight lines parallel to the constant-return loci, thus giving multiple optima.

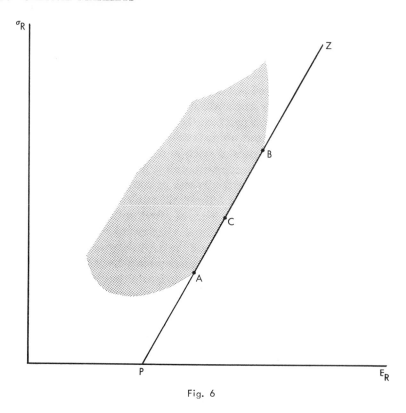

Fig. 6

(positively) correlated, since they lie along a linear border of the $E_R$, $\sigma_R$ region.[20] This provides a key to the relationship between the prices of capital assets and different types of risk.

## IV. THE PRICES OF CAPITAL ASSETS

We have argued that in equilibrium there will be a simple linear relationship between the expected return and standard deviation of return for efficient combinations of risky assets. Thus far nothing has been said about such a relationship for individual assets. Typically the $E_R$, $\sigma_R$ values associated with single assets will lie above the capital market line, reflecting the inefficiency of undiversified holdings. Moreover, such points may be scattered throughout the feasible region, with no consistent relationship between their expected

[20] $E_R$, $\sigma_R$ values given by combinations of any two combinations must lie within the region and cannot plot above a straight line joining the points. In this case they cannot plot below such a straight line. But since only in the case of perfect correlation will they plot along a straight line, the two combinations must be perfectly correlated. As shown in Part IV, this does not necessarily imply that the individual securities they contain are perfectly correlated.

return and total risk ($\sigma_R$). However, there will be a consistent relationship between their expected returns and what might best be called systematic risk, as we will now show.

Figure 7 illustrates the typical relationship between a single capital asset (point $i$) and an efficient combination of assets (point $g$) of which it is a part. The curve $igg'$ indicates all $E_R$, $\sigma_R$ values which can be obtained with feasible combinations of asset $i$ and combination $g$. As before, we denote such a combination in terms of a proportion $\alpha$ of asset $i$ and $(1 - \alpha)$ of combination $g$.

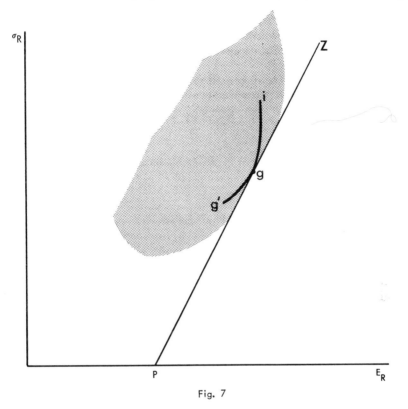

Fig. 7

A value of $\alpha = 1$ would indicate pure investment in asset $i$ while $\alpha = 0$ would imply investment in combination $g$. Note, however, that $\alpha = .5$ implies a total investment of more than half the funds in asset $i$, since half would be invested in $i$ itself and the other half used to purchase combination $g$, which also includes some of asset $i$. This means that a combination in which asset $i$ does not appear at all must be represented by some negative value of $\alpha$. Point $g'$ indicates such a combination.

In Figure 7 the curve $igg'$ has been drawn tangent to the capital market line $(PZ)$ at point $g$. This is no accident. All such curves must be tangent to the capital market line in equilibrium, since (1) they must touch it at the point representing the efficient combination and (2) they are continuous at the point.[21] Under these conditions a lack of tangency would imply that the curve intersects $PZ$. But then some feasible combination of assets would lie to the right of the capital market line, an obvious impossibility since the capital market line represents the efficient boundary of feasible values of $E_R$ and $\sigma_R$.

The requirement that curves such as $igg'$ be tangent to the capital market line can be shown to lead to a relatively simple formula which relates the expected rate of return to various elements of risk for all assets which are included in combination $g$.[22] Its economic meaning can best be seen if the relationship between the return of asset $i$ and that of combination $g$ is viewed in a manner similar to that used in regression analysis.[23] Imagine that we were

[21] Only if $r_{ig} = -1$ will the curve be discontinuous over the range in question.

[22] The standard deviation of a combination of $g$ and $i$ will be:

$$\sigma = \sqrt{\alpha^2 \sigma_{Ri}^2 + (1-\alpha)^2 \sigma_{Rg}^2 + 2r_{ig}\alpha(1-\alpha)\sigma_{Ri}\sigma_{Rg}}$$

at $\alpha = 0$:

$$\frac{d\sigma}{d\alpha} = -\frac{1}{\sigma}[\sigma_{Rg}^2 - r_{ig}\sigma_{Ri}\sigma_{Rg}]$$

but $\sigma = \sigma_{Rg}$ at $\alpha = 0$. Thus:

$$\frac{d\sigma}{d\alpha} = -[\sigma_{Rg} - r_{ig}\sigma_{Ri}]$$

The expected return of a combination will be:

$$E = \alpha E_{Ri} + (1-\alpha)E_{Rg}$$

Thus, at all values of $\alpha$:

$$\frac{dE}{d\alpha} = -[E_{Rg} - E_{Ri}]$$

and, at $\alpha = 0$:

$$\frac{d\sigma}{dE} = \frac{\sigma R_g - r_{ig}\sigma_{Ri}}{E_{Rg} - E_{Ri}}.$$

Let the equation of the capital market line be:

$$\sigma_R = s(E_R - P)$$

where $P$ is the pure interest rate. Since $igg'$ is tangent to the line when $\alpha = 0$, and since $(E_{Rg}, \sigma_{Rg})$ lies on the line:

$$\frac{\sigma_{Rg} - r_{ig}\sigma_{Ri}}{E_{Rg} - E_{Ri}} = \frac{\sigma_{Rg}}{E_{Rg} - P}$$

or:

$$\frac{r_{ig}\sigma_{Ri}}{\sigma_{Rg}} = -\left[\frac{P}{E_{Rg} - P}\right] + \left[\frac{1}{E_{Rg} - P}\right]E_{Ri}.$$

[23] This model has been called the diagonal model since its portfolio analysis solution can be facilitated by re-arranging the data so that the variance-covariance matrix becomes diagonal. The method is described in the author's article, cited earlier.

given a number of (ex post) observations of the return of the two investments. The points might plot as shown in Figure 8. The scatter of the $R_i$ observation around their mean (which will approximate $E_{Ri}$) is, of course, evidence of the total risk of the asset—$\sigma_{Ri}$. But part of the scatter is due to an underlying relationship with the return on combination $g$, shown by $B_{ig}$, the slope of the

Return on Asset 1 (R1)

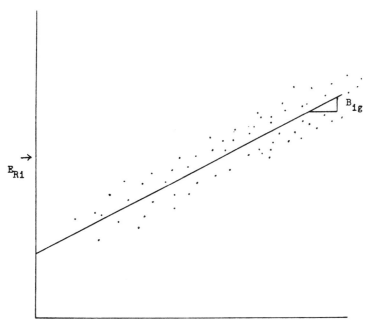

Return on Combination g ($R_g$)

FIGURE 8

regression line. The response of $R_i$ to changes in $R_g$ (and variations in $R_g$ itself) account for much of the variation in $R_i$. It is this component of the asset's total risk which we term the *systematic* risk. The remainder,[24] being uncorrelated with $R_g$, is the unsystematic component. This formulation of the relationship between $R_i$ and $R_g$ can be employed *ex ante* as a predictive model. $B_{ig}$ becomes the *predicted* response of $R_i$ to changes in $R_g$. Then, given $\sigma R_g$ (the predicted risk of $R_g$), the systematic portion of the predicted risk of each asset can be determined.

This interpretation allows us to state the relationship derived from the tangency of curves such as *igg'* with the capital market line in the form shown in Figure 9. All assets entering efficient combination $g$ must have (predicted)

[24] ex post, the standard error.

$B_{ig}$ and $E_{Ri}$ values lying on the line $PQ$.[25] Prices will adjust so that assets which are more responsive to changes in $R_g$ will have higher expected returns than those which are less responsive. This accords with common sense.

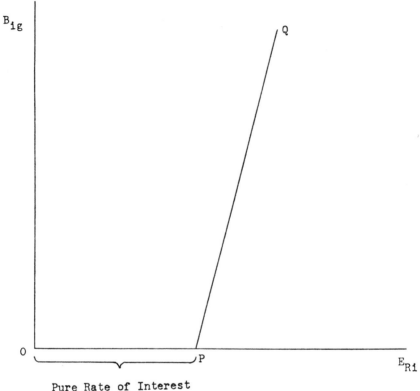

Pure Rate of Interest

FIGURE 9

Obviously the part of an asset's risk which is due to its correlation with the return on a combination cannot be diversified away when the asset is added to the combination. Since $B_{ig}$ indicates the magnitudes of this type of risk it should be directly related to expected return.

25

$$r_{ig} = \sqrt{\frac{B_{ig}^2 \sigma_{Rg}^2}{\sigma_{Ri}^2}} = \frac{B_{ig}\sigma_{Rg}}{\sigma_{Ri}}$$

$$B_{ig} = \frac{r_{ig}\sigma_{Ri}}{\sigma_{Rg}}.$$

The expression on the right is the expression on the left-hand side of the last equation in footnote 22. Thus:

$$B_{ig} = -\left[\frac{P}{E_{Rg} - P}\right] + \left[\frac{1}{E_{Rg} - P}\right]E_{Ri}.$$

The relationship illustrated in Figure 9 provides a partial answer to the question posed earlier concerning the relationship between an asset's risk and its expected return. But thus far we have argued only that the relationship holds for the assets which enter some particular efficient combination ($g$). Had another combination been selected, a different linear relationship would have been derived. Fortunately this limitation is easily overcome. As shown in the footnote,[26] we may arbitrarily select *any* one of the efficient combinations, then measure the predicted responsiveness of *every* asset's rate of return to that of the combination selected; and these coefficients will be related to the expected rates of return of the assets in exactly the manner pictured in Figure 9.

The fact that rates of return from all efficient combinations will be perfectly correlated provides the justification for arbitrarily selecting any one of them. Alternatively we may choose instead any variable perfectly correlated with the

[26] Consider the two assets $i$ and $i*$, the former included in efficient combination $g$ and the latter in combination $g*$. As shown above:

$$B_{ig} = -\left[\frac{P}{E_{Rg} - P}\right] + \left[\frac{1}{E_{Rg} - P}\right] E_{Ri}$$

and:

$$B_{i*g*} = -\left[\frac{P}{E_{Rg*} - P}\right] + \left[\frac{1}{E_{Rg*} - P}\right] E_{Ri*}.$$

Since $R_g$ and $R_{g*}$ are perfectly correlated:

$$r_{i*g*} = r_{i*g}$$

Thus:

$$\frac{B_{i*g*}\sigma_{Rg*}}{\sigma_{Ri*}} = \frac{B_{i*g}\sigma_{Rg}}{\sigma_{Ri*}}$$

and:

$$B_{i*g*} = B_{i*g}\left[\frac{\sigma_{Rg}}{\sigma_{Rg*}}\right].$$

Since both $g$ and $g*$ lie on a line which intercepts the E-axis at $P$:

$$\frac{\sigma_{Rg}}{\sigma_{Rg*}} = \frac{E_{Rg} - P}{E_{Rg*} - P}$$

and:

$$B_{i*g*} = B_{i*g}\left[\frac{E_{Rg} - P}{E_{Rg*} - P}\right].$$

Thus:

$$-\left[\frac{P}{E_{Rg*} - P}\right] + \left[\frac{1}{E_{Rg*} - P}\right] E_{Ri*} = B_{i*g}\left[\frac{E_{Rg} - P}{E_{Rg*} - P}\right]$$

from which we have the desired relationship between $R_{i*}$ and $g$:

$$B_{i*g} = -\left[\frac{P}{E_{Rg} - P}\right] + \left[\frac{1}{E_{Rg} - P}\right] E_{Ri*}.$$

$B_{i*g}$ must therefore plot on the same line as does $B_{ig}$.

rate of return of such combinations. The vertical axis in Figure 9 would then indicate alternative levels of a coefficient measuring the sensitivity of the rate of return of a capital asset to changes in the variable chosen.

This possibility suggests both a plausible explanation for the implication that all efficient combinations will be perfectly correlated and a useful interpretation of the relationship between an individual asset's expected return and its risk. Although the theory itself implies only that rates of return from efficient combinations will be perfectly correlated, we might expect that this would be due to their common dependence on the over-all level of economic activity. If so, diversification enables the investor to escape all but the risk resulting from swings in economic activity—this type of risk remains even in efficient combinations. And, since all other types can be avoided by diversification, only the responsiveness of an asset's rate of return to the level of economic activity is relevant in assessing its risk. Prices will adjust until there is a linear relationship between the magnitude of such responsiveness and expected return. Assets which are unaffected by changes in economic activity will return the pure interest rate; those which move with economic activity will promise appropriately higher expected rates of return.

This discussion provides an answer to the second of the two questions posed in this paper. In Part III it was shown that with respect to equilibrium conditions in the capital market as a whole, the theory leads to results consistent with classical doctrine (i.e., the capital market line). We have now shown that with regard to capital assets considered individually, it also yields implications consistent with traditional concepts: it is common practice for investment counselors to accept a lower expected return from defensive securities (those which respond little to changes in the economy) than they require from aggressive securities (which exhibit significant response). As suggested earlier, the familiarity of the implications need not be considered a drawback. The provision of a logical framework for producing some of the major elements of traditional financial theory should be a useful contribution in its own right.

## 14. THE VALUATION OF RISK ASSETS AND THE SELECTION OF RISKY INVESTMENTS IN STOCK PORTFOLIOS AND CAPITAL BUDGETS*

### JOHN LINTNER

Reprinted by permission of the author and publishers from *The Review of Economics and Statistics*, Vol. *XLVII*, No. 1 (February, 1965), pp. 13–37. (Cambridge, Mass.: Harvard University Press, Copyright, 1965, by the President and Fellows of Harvard College).

## INTRODUCTION AND PREVIEW OF SOME CONCLUSIONS

The effects of risk and uncertainty upon asset prices, upon rational decision rules for individuals and institutions to use in selecting security portfolios, and upon proper selection of projects to include in corporate capital budgets, have increasingly engaged the attention of professional economists and other students of the capital markets and of business finance in recent years. The essential purpose of the present paper is to push back the frontiers of our knowledge of the the logical structure of these related issues, albeit under idealized conditions. The immediately following text describes the contents of the paper and summarizes some of the principal results.

The first two sections of this paper deal with the *problem of selecting* optimal security portfolios by risk-averse investors who have the alternative of investing in risk-free securities with a positive return (or borrowing at the same rate of interest) and who can sell short if they wish. The first gives alternative and hopefully more transparent proofs (under these more general market conditions) for Tobin's important "separation theorem" that

* This paper is another in a series of interrelated theoretical and statistical studies of corporate financial and investment policies being made under grants from the Rockefeller Foundation, and more recently the Ford Foundation, to the Harvard Business School. The generous support for this work is most gratefully acknowledged. The author is also much indebted to his colleagues Professors Bishop, Christenson, Kahr, Raiffa, and (especially) Schlaifer, for extensive discussion and commentary on an earlier draft of this paper; but responsibility for any errors or imperfections remains strictly his own.

[Professor Sharpe's paper, "Capital Asset Prices: A Theory of Market Equilibrium Under Conditions of Risk " (*Journal of Finance*, September 1964) appeared after this paper was in final form and on its way to the printers. My first section, which parallels the first half of his paper (with corresponding conclusions), sets the algebraic framework for sections II, III and VI, (which have no counterpart in his paper) and for section IV on the equilibrium prices of risk assets, concerning which our results differ significantly for reasons which will be explored elsewhere. Sharpe does not take up the capital budgeting problem developed in section V below.]

"... the proportionate composition of the non-cash assets is independent of their aggregate share of the investment balance ..." (and hence of the optimal holding of cash) for risk averters in purely competitive markets when utility functions are quadratic *or* rates of return are multivariate normal.[1] We then note that the same conclusion follows from an earlier theorem of Roy's [19] without dependence on quadratic utilities or normality. The second section shows that *if short sales are permitted*, the best portfolio-mix of risk assets can be determined by the solution of a single simple set of simultaneous equations without recourse to programming methods, and when covariances are zero, a still simpler ratio scheme gives the optimum, whether or not short sales are permitted. When covariances are not all zero and short sales are excluded, a single quadratic programming solution is required, but sufficient.

Following these extensions of Tobin's classic work, we concentrate on the set of risk assets held in risk averters' portfolios. In section III we develop various significant *equilibrium properties within* the risk asset portfolio. In particular, we establish conditions under which stocks will be held long (short) in optimal portfolios even when "risk premiums" are negative (positive). We also develop expressions for different combinations of expected rate of return on a given security, and its standard deviation, variance, and/or covariances which will result in the same relative holding of a stock, *ceteris paribus*. These "indifference functions" provide direct evidence on the moot issue of the appropriate functional relationships between "required rates of return" and relevant risk parameter(s)—and on the related issue of how "risk classes" of securities may best be delineated (if they are to be used).[2] There seems to be a general presumption among economists that relative risks are best measured by the standard deviation (or coefficient of variation) of the rate of return,[3] but in the simplest cases considered—

---

[1] Tobin [21, especially pp. 82–85]. Tobin assumed that funds are to be a allocated only over "monetary assets" (risk-free cash and default-free bonds of uncertain resale price) and allowed no short sales or borrowing. See also footnote 24 below. Other approaches are reviewed in Farrar [3b].

[2] It should be noted that the classic paper by Modigliani and Miller [16] was silent on these issues. Corporations were assumed to be divided into homogeneous classes having the property that all shares of all corporations in any given class differed (at most) by a "scale factor," and hence (a) were perfectly correlated with each other and (b) were perfect substitutes for each other in perfect markets (p. 266). No comment was made on the measure of risk or uncertainty (or other attributes) relevant to the identification of different "equivalent return" classes. Both Propositions I (market value of *firm* independent of capital structure) and II (the linear relation between the expected return on equity shares and the debt-equity ratio for firms within a given class) are derived from the above assumptions (and the further assumption that corporate bonds are riskless securities); they involve no inter-class comparisons, " . . . nor do they involve any assertion as to what is an adequate compensation to investors for assuming a given degree of risk . . . ." (p. 279).

[3] This is, for instance, the presumption of Hirshleifer [8, p. 113], although he was careful not to commit himself to this measure alone in a paper primarily focussed on other issues. For an inductive argument in favor of the standard deviation of the rate of return as the best measure of risk, see Gordon [5, especially pp. 69 and 76]. See also Dorfman in [3, p. 129 ff.] and Baumol [2].

specifically when all covariances are considered to be invariant (or zero)—the indifference functions are shown to be linear between expected rates of return and their *variance*, not standard deviation.[4] (With variances fixed, the indifference function between the $i^{th}$ expected rate of return and its pooled covariance with other stocks is hyperbolic.) There is no simple relation between the expected rate of return required to maintain an investor's relative holding of a stock and its standard deviation. Specifically, when covariances are non-zero and variable, the indifference functions are complex and non-linear *even if* it is assumed that the *correlations* between rates of return on different securities are invariant.

To this point we follow Tobin [21] and Markowitz [14] in assuming that current security prices are given, and that each investor acts on his own (perhaps unique) probability distribution over rates of return given these market prices. In the rest of the paper, we assume that investors' joint probability distributions pertain to dollar returns rather than rates of return,[5] and for simplicity we assume that all investors assign identical sets of means, variances, and covariances to the distribution of these dollar returns. However unrealistic the latter assumption may be, it enables us, in section IV, to derive a set of (stable) equilibrium market prices which at least fully and explicitly reflect the presence of uncertainty *per se* (as distinct from the effects of diverse expectations), and to derive further implications of such uncertainty. In particular, the aggregate market value of any company's equity is equal to the capitalization at the risk-free interest rate of a uniquely defined *certainty-equivalent* of the probability distribution of the aggregate dollar returns to all holders of its stock. For each company, this certainty equivalent is the expected value of these uncertain returns less an adjustment term which is proportional to their aggregate risk. The factor of proportionality is the *same for all companies* in equilibrium, and may be regarded as a *market price of dollar risk*. The relevant risk of each company's stock is measured, moreover, not by the standard deviation of its dollar returns, but by the *sum* of the *variance* of its own aggregate dollar returns *and* their *total covariance* with those of all other stocks.

The next section considers some of the implications of these results for the normative aspects of the capital budgeting decisions of a company whose stock is traded in the market. For simplicity, we impose further assumptions required to make capital budgeting decisions independent of decisions on how the budget is financed.[6] The capital budgeting problem becomes a quadratic programming problem analogous to that introduced earlier for the individual investor. This capital budgeting-portfolio problem is formulated,

---

[4] Except in dominantly " short " portfolios, the constant term will be larger, and the slope lower, the higher the (fixed) level of covariances of the given stocks with other stocks.

[5] The dollar return in the period is the sum of the cash dividend and the increase in market price during the period.

[6] We also assume that common stock portfolios are not " inferior goods," that the value of *all other* common stocks is invariant, and any effect of changes in capital budgets on the *covariances* between the values of different companies' *stocks* is ignored.

its solution is given and some of its more important properties examined. Specifically, the minimum expected return (in dollars of expected present value) required to justify the allocation of funds to a given risky project is shown to be an increasing function of each of the following factors: (*i*) the risk-free rate of return; (*ii*) the "market price of (dollar) risk"; (*iii*) the variance in the project's own present value return; (*iv*) the project's aggregate present value return-covariance with assets already held by the company, and (*v*) its total covariance with other projects concurrently included in the capital budget. All *five* factors are involved explicitly in the corresponding (derived) formula for the minimum acceptable *expected rate* of return on an investment project. In this model, all means and (co)variances of present values must be calculated at the riskless rate $r^*$. We also show that *there can be no "risk-discount" rate* to be used in computing present values to accept or reject individual projects. In particular, the "*cost of capital*" as defined (for uncertainty) anywhere in the literature *is not the appropriate rate* to use in these decisions *even if* all new projects have the same "risk" as existing assets.

The final section of the paper briefly examines the complications introduced by institutional limits on amounts which either individuals or corporations may borrow at given rates, by rising costs of borrowed funds, and certain other "real world" complications. It is emphasized that the results of this paper are not being presented as directly applicable to practical decisions, because many of the factors which matter very significantly in practice have had to be ignored or assumed away. The function of these simplifying assumptions has been to permit a rigorous development of theoretical relationships and theorems which reorient much current theory (especially on capital budgeting) and provide a basis for further work.[7] More detailed conclusions will be found emphasized at numerous points in the text.

## I. PORTFOLIO SELECTION FOR AN INDIVIDUAL INVESTOR: THE SEPARATION THEOREM

### MARKET ASSUMPTIONS

We assume that (1) *each individual* investor can invest any part of his capital in certain *risk-free assets* (e.g., deposits in insured savings accounts[8]) all of which pay interest at a common positive rate, exogenously determined; and that (2) he can invest *any fraction* of his capital *in any* or all of a given finite set of risky securities which are (3) traded in a single *purely competitive market*, free of transactions costs and taxes, at given market prices,[9] which

---

[7] The relation between the results of this paper and the models which were used in [11] and [12] is indicated at the end of section V.

[8] Government bonds of appropriate maturity provide another important example when their "yield" is substituted for the word "interest."

[9] Solely for convenience, we shall usually refer to all these investments as common stocks, although the analysis is of course quite general.

consequently do not depend on his investments or transactions. We also assume that (4) any investor may, if he wishes, borrow funds to invest in risk assets, Except in the final section, we assume that the *interest rate paid* on such loans is the same as he would have received had he invested in risk-free savings accounts, and that there is *no limit* on the amount he can borrow at this rate. Finally (5) he makes all purchases and sales of securities and all deposits and loans at discrete points in time, so that in selecting his portfolio at any "transaction point," each investor will consider only (i) the cash throw-off (typically interest payments and dividends received) within the period to the next transaction point and (ii) changes in the market prices of stocks during the same period. The *return* on any common stock is defined to be the sum of the cash dividends received plus the change in its market price. The return on any portfolio is measured in exactly the same way, including interest received or paid.

ASSUMPTIONS REGARDING INVESTORS

(1) Since we posit the existence of assets yielding *positive risk-free* returns, we assume that each investor has already decided the fraction of his total capital he wishes to hold in cash and non-interest bearing deposits for reasons of liquidity or transactions requirements.[10] Henceforth, we will speak of *an investor's capital* as the stock of funds he has available for profitable investment *after* optimal cash holdings have been deducted. We also assume that (2) each investor will have assigned a *joint probability distribution* incorporating his best judgments regarding the returns on all *individual stocks*, or at least will have specified an expected value and variance to every return and a covariance or correlation to every pair of returns. All expected values of returns are finite, all variances are non-zero and finite, and all correlations of returns are less than one in absolute value (i.e. the covariance matrix is positive-definite). The investor computes the expected value and variance of the total return on any possible *portfolio*, or mix of any specified amounts of any or all of the individual stocks, by forming the appropriately weighted average or sum of these components expected returns, variances and co-variances.

With respect to an investor's *criterion for choices* among different attainable combinations of assets, we assume that (3) if any two mixtures of assets have the *same expected return*, the investor will prefer the one having the *smaller variance* of return, and if any two mixtures of assets have the *same variance* of returns, he will prefer the one having the *greater expected value*. Tobin [21, pp. 75–76] has shown that such preferences are implied by maximization of the expected value of a von Neumann-Morgenstern utility function if *either* (a) the investor's *utility* function is *concave* and *quadratic or* (b) the

---

[10] These latter decisions are independent of the decisions regarding the allocation of remaining funds between risk-free assets with positive return and risky stocks, which are of direct concern in this paper, because the risk-free assets with positive returns clearly dominate with no return once liquidity and transactions requirements are satisfied at the margin.

investor's *utility* function is *concave, and* he has assigned probability distributions such that the *returns* on *all possible portfolios differ at most by a location and scale parameter,* (which will be the case if the joint distribution of all individual stocks is multivariate normal).

### ALTERNATIVE PROOFS OF THE SEPARATION THEOREM

Since the interest rate on riskless savings bank deposits ("loans to the bank") and on borrowed funds are being assumed to be the same, we can treat borrowing as negative lending. Any portfolio can then be described in terms of (i) the *gross* amount invested in stocks, (ii) the fraction of this amount invested in each individual stock, and (iii) the *net* amount invested in loans (a negative value showing that the investor has borrowed rather than lent). But since the *total net* investment (the algebraic sum of stocks plus loans) is a given amount, the problem simply requires finding the jointly optimal values for (1) the ratio of the gross investment in stocks to the total net investment, and (2) the ratio of the gross investment in each individual stock to the total gross investment in stocks. It turns out that although the solution of (1) depends upon that of (2), in our context the latter is independent of the former. Specifically, the *separation theorem* asserts that:

*Given* the assumptions about borrowing, lending, and investor preferences stated earlier in this section, the *optimal proportionate composition of the stock (risk-asset) portfolio* (i.e. the solution to sub-problem 2 above) *is independent of the ratio of the gross investment in stocks to the total net investment.*

Tobin proved this important separation theorem by deriving the detailed solution for the optimal mix of risk assets *conditional* on a given gross investment in this portfolio, and then formally proving the critical invariance property stated in the theorem. Tobin used more restrictive assumptions than we do regarding the available investment opportunities and he permitted no borrowing.[11] Under our somewhat broadened assumptions in these respects, the problem fits neatly into a traditional Fisher framework, with different available combinations of expected values and standard deviations of return on alternative *stock portfolios* taking the place of the original "production opportunity" set and with the alternative investment choices being concurrent rather than between time periods. Within this framework, alternative and

---

[11] Tobin considered the special case where cash with no return was the only riskless asset available. While he formally required that all assets be held in non-negative quantities (thereby ruling out short sales), and that the total value of risk assets held not be greater than the investment balance available without borrowing, these non-negativity and maximum value constraints were not introduced into his formal solution of the optimal investment mix, which in turn was used in proving the invariance property stated in the theorem. Our proof of the theorem is independent of the programming constraints neglected in Tobin's proof. Later in this section we show that when short sales are properly and explicitly introduced into the set of possible portfolios, the resulting equations for the optimum portfolio mix are identical to those derived by Tobin, but that insistence on no short sales results in a somewhat more complex programming problem (when covariances are non-zero), which may, however, be readily handled with computer programs now available.

more transparent proofs of the separation theorem are available which do not involve the actual calculation of the best allocation in stocks over individual stock issues. As did Fisher, we shall present a simple algebraic proof,[12] set out the logic of the argument leading to the theorem, and depict the essential geometry of the problem.[13]

As a preliminary step, we need to establish the relation between the investor's total investment in *any* arbitrary mixture or portfolio of individual stocks, his total net return from all his investments (including riskless assets and any borrowing), and the risk parameters of his investment position. Let the *interest rate* on riskless assets or borrowing be $r^*$, and the *uncertain return* (dividends plus price appreciation) *per dollar invested in the given portfolio of stocks be r*. Let $w$ represent the *ratio* of gross investment in stocks to total *net* investment (stock plus riskless assets minus borrowing). Then the investor's net return per dollar of total net investment will be

(1) $$\tilde{y} = (1 - w)r^* + w\tilde{r} = r^* + w(\tilde{r} - r^*); 0 \leq w < \infty,$$

where a value of $w < 1$ indicates that the investor holds some of his capital in riskless assets and receives interest amounting to $(1 - w)r^*$; while $w > 1$ indicates that the investor borrows to buy stocks on margin and pays interest amounting to the absolute value of $(1 - w)r^*$. From (1) we determine the mean and variance of the net return per dollar of total net investment to be:

(2a) $$\bar{y} = r^* + w(\bar{r} - r^*), \text{ and}$$

(2b) $$\sigma^2_y = w^2\sigma^2_r.$$

Finally, after eliminating $w$ between these two equations, we find that the direct relation between the expected value of the investor's net return per dollar of his total net investment and the risk parameters of his investment position is:

(3a) $$\bar{y} = r^* + \theta\sigma_y, \text{ where}$$

(3b) $$\theta = (\bar{r} - r^*)/\sigma_r.$$

In terms of *any* arbitrarily selected *stock* portfolio, therefore, the investor's *net* expected rate of return on his total net investment is related *linearly* to the *risk* of return on his total net investment as *measured* by the *standard deviation* of his return. Given *any* selected stock portfolio, this linear function corresponds to Fisher's "market opportunity line"; its intercept is the risk-free rate $r^*$ and its slope is given by $\theta$, which is determined by the parameters $\bar{r}$ and $\sigma_r$ of the particular stock portfolio being considered. We also see from (2a) that, by a suitable choice of $w$, the investor can use *any* stock mix (and *its* associated "market opportunity line") to obtain an expected return, $\bar{y}$,

[12] An alternative algebraic proof using utility functions explicitly is presented in the appendix, note I.

[13] Lockwood Rainhard, Jr. has also independently developed and presented a similar proof of the theorem in an unpublished seminar paper.

as high as he likes; but that, because of (2b) and (3b), as he increases his investment $w$ in the (tentatively chosen) mix, the standard deviation $\sigma_y$ (and hence the variance $\sigma^2_y$) of the return on his total investment also becomes proportionately greater.

*Now consider all possible stock portfolios.* Those portfolios having the same $\theta$ value will lie on the same " market opportunity line," but those having different $\theta$ values *will offer different " market opportunity lines"* (between expected return and risk) for the investor to use. The investor's problem is to choose which stock portfolio-mix (or market opportunity line *or* $\theta$ value) to use *and* how intensively to use it (the proper value of $w$). Since *any* expected return $\bar{y}$ can be obtained from *any* stock mix, an investor adhering to our choice criterion will minimize the variance of his over-all return $\sigma^2_y$ associated with *any* expected return he may choose *by confining all his investment in stocks to the mix with the largest $\theta$ value. This portfolio minimizes the variance associated with any $\bar{y}$ (and hence any $w$ value)* the investor may prefer, and *consequently, is independent of $\bar{y}$ and $w$.* This establishes the separation theorem[14] once we note that our assumptions regarding available portfolios[15] insure the existence of a maximum $\theta$.

It is equally apparent that *after* determining the optimal stock portfolio (mix) by maximizing $\theta$, the investor can complete his choice of an over-all investment position by substituting the $\theta$ of this optimal mix in (3) and decide which over-all investment position by substituting of the available ($\bar{y}$, $\sigma_y$) pairs he prefers by referring to his own utility function. Substitution of this best $\bar{y}$ value in (2a) determines a unique best value of the ratio $w$ of gross investment in the optimal stock portfolio to his total net investment, and hence, the optimal amount of investments in riskless savings deposits or the optimal amount of borrowing as well.

This separation theorem thus has four immediate *corollaries* which can be stated:

(*i*) *Given* the assumptions about borrowing and lending stated above, any investor whose choices maximize the expectation of any particular utility function consistent with these conditions will make *identical decisions regarding the proportionate composition of his stock* (risk-asset) *portfolio. This is true regardless of the particular utility function*[16] whose expectation he maximizes.

(*ii*) Under these assumptions, only a *single point* on the Markowitz " Efficient Frontier" *is relevant* to the investor's decision regarding his

---

[14] See also the appendix, note I for a different form of proof.

[15] Specifically, that the amount invested in any stock in any stock mix is infinitely divisible, that all expected returns on individual stocks are finite, that all variances are positive and finite, and that the variance-covariance matrix is positive-definite.

[16] When probability assessments are multivariate normal, the utility function may be polynomial, exponential, etc. Even in the " non-normal" case when utility functions *are* quadratic, they may vary in its parameters. See also the reference to Roy's work in the text below.

investments in risk assets.[17] (The next section shows this point can be obtained directly without calculating the remainder of the efficient set.)

*Given* the same assumptions, (*iii*) the parameters of the investor's particular utility within the relevant set determine *only* the ratio of his total gross investment in stocks to his total *net* investment (including riskless assets and borrowing); and (*iv*) the investor's wealth is also, consequently, relevant to determining the *absolute size* of his investment in individual stocks, but *not* to the *relative distribution* of his gross investment in stocks *among individual issues*.

## THE GEOMETRY OF THE SEPARATION THEOREM AND ITS COROLLARIES

The algebraic derivations given above can be represented graphically as in chart 1. Any given available stock portfolio is characterized by a pair of values $(\sigma, \bar{r})$ which can be represented as a point in a plane with axes $\sigma_y$ and $\bar{y}$.

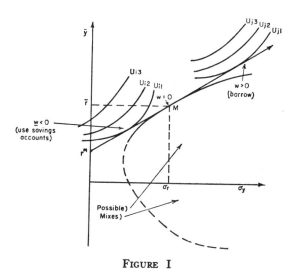

FIGURE I

Our assumptions insure that the points representing all available stock mixes lie in a finite region, all parts of which lie to the right of the vertical axis, and that this region is bounded by a closed curve.[18] The contours of the investor's utility function are concave upward, and any movement in a north and/or west direction denotes contours of greater utility. Equation (3) shows that all the $(\sigma_y, y)$ pairs attainable by combining, borrowing, or lending with *any*

[17] When the above conditions hold (see also final paragraph of this section), the modest narrowing of the relevant range of Markowitz' Efficient Set suggested by Baumol [2] is still larger than needed by a factor strictly proportionate to the number of portfolios he retains in his truncated set! This is true since the relevant set is a single portfolio under these conditions.

[18] See Markowitz [14] as cited in the appendix, note I.

particular stock portfolio lie on a ray from the point $(\theta, r^*)$ through the point corresponding to the stock mix in question. Each possible stock portfolio thus determines a unique "market opportunity line." Given the properties of the utility function, it is obvious that shifts from one possible mix to another which *rotate* the associated market opportunity line *counter clockwise* will *move the investor to preferred positions regardless of the point on the line* he had tentatively chosen. The slope of this market-opportunity line given by (3) is $\theta$, and the limit of the favorable rotation is given by the maximum attainable $\theta$, which identifies the optimal mix $M$.[19] Once this best mix, $M$, has been determined, the investor completes the optimization of his total investment position by selecting the point on the ray through $M$ which is tangent to a utility contour in the standard marner. If his utility contours are as in the $U_i$ set in chart 1, he uses savings accounts and does not borrow. If his utility contours are as in $U_j$ set, he borrows in order to have a gross investment in his best stock mix greater than his net investment balance.

RISK AVERSION, NORMALITY AND THE SEPARATION THEOREM

The above analysis has been based on the assumptions regarding markets and investors stated at the beginning of this section. One crucial premise was investor *risk-aversion* in the form of *preference for expected return and preference against return-variance, ceteris paribus*. We noted that Tobin has shown that *either* concave-*quadratic* utility functions *or* multivariate *normality* (of probability assessments) *and any concave* utility were *sufficient* conditions to validate this premise, but they were *not* shown (or alleged) to be *necessary* conditions. This is probably fortunate because the quadratic utility of income (or wealth!) function, in spite of its popularity in theoretical work, has several undesirably restrictive and implausible properties,[20] and, despite its

---

[19] The analogy with the standard Fisher two-period production-opportunity case in perfect markets with equal borrowing and lending rates is clear. The optimal set of production opportunities available is found by moving along the envelope function of efficient combinations of projects onto ever higher present value lines to the highest attainable. This best set of production opportunities is independent of the investor's particular utility function which determines only whether he then lends or borrows in the market (and by how much in either case) to reach his best over-all position. The only differences between this case and ours lie in the concurrent nature of the comparisons (instead of inter-period), and the rotation of the market opportunity lines around the common pivot of the riskless return (instead of parallel shifts in present value lines). See Fisher [4] and also Hirshleifer [7], figure 1 and section 1a.

[20] In brief, not only does the quadratic function imply negative marginal utilities of income or wealth much "too soon" in empirical work unless the risk-aversion parameter is very small—in which case it cannot account for the degree of risk-aversion empirically found—it also implies that, over a major part of the range of empirical data, common stocks, like potatoes in Ireland, are "inferior" goods. Offering more return at the same risk would so sate investors that they would reduce their risk-investments *because* they were more attractive. (Thereby, as Tobin [21] noted, denying the negatively sloped demand curves for *riskless* assets which are standard doctrine in "liquidity preference theory"—a conclusion which cannot, incidentally, be avoided by "limit arguments" on quadratic utilities such as he used, once borrowing and leverage are admitted.) This function also implausibly implies,

mathematical convenience, multivariate normality is doubtless also suspect, especially perhaps in considering common stocks.

It is, consequently, very relevant to note that by using the Bienaymé-Tschebycheff inequality, Roy [19] has shown that investors operating on his "Safety First" principle (i.e. make risky investments so as to minimize the upper bound of the probability that the realized outcome will fall below a pre-assigned "disaster level") should maximize the ratio of the *excess* expected portfolio return (over the disaster level) to the standard deviation of the return on the portfolio[21]—which is precisely our criterion of max $\theta$ when his disaster level is equated to the risk-free rate $r^*$. This result, of course, does not depend on multivariate normality, and uses a different argument and form of utility function.

The *Separation Theorem*, and its Corollaries (*i*) and (*ii*) above—and all the rest of our following analysis which depends on the maximization of $\theta$—is thus rigorously appropriate in the non-multivariate normal case for Safety-Firsters who minimax the stated upper bound of the chance of doing less well on portfolios including risk assets than they can do on riskless investments, just as it is for concave-expected utility maximizers in the "normal" case. On the basis of the same probability judgments, these Safety-Firsters will use the same proximate criterion function (max $\theta$) and will choose proportionately the same risk asset portfolios as the more orthodox "utility maximizers" we have hitherto considered.

## II. PORTFOLIO SELECTION: THE OPTIMAL STOCK MIX

Before finding the optimal stock mix—the mix which maximizes $\theta$ in (3b) above—it is necessary to express the return on any arbitrary mix in terms of the returns on individual stocks included in the portfolio. Although short sales are excluded by assumption in most of the writings on portfolio optimization, this restrictive assumption is arbitrary for some purposes at least, and we therefore broaden the analysis in this paper to include short sales whenever they are permitted.

COMPUTATION OF RETURNS ON A STOCK MIX, WHEN SHORT SALES ARE PERMITTED

We assume that there are $m$ different stocks in the market, denoted by $i = 1, 2, ..., m$, and treat short sales as negative purchases. We shall use the following basic notation:

---

as Pratt [17] and Arrow [1] have noted, that the insurance premiums which people would be willing to pay to hedge *given* risks *rise* progressively with wealth or income. For a related result, see Hicks [6, p. 802].

[21] Roy also notes that when judgmental distributions *are* multivariate normal, maximization of this criterion *minimizes* the probability of "disaster" (failure to do better in stocks than savings deposits or government bonds held to maturity). It should be noted, however, minimization of the probability of short falls from "disaster" levels in this "normal" case is strictly *equivalent* to expected utility maximization under *all* risk-averters' utility functions. The equivalence is *not* restricted to the utility function of the form (0,1) (zero if "disaster" occurs, one if it doesn't), as claimed by Roy [19, p. 432] and Markowitz [14, p. 293 and following.].

$|h_i|$—The ratio of the gross investment in the $i^{th}$ stock (the market value of the amount bought *or* sold) to the gross investment in all stocks. A positive value of $h_i$ indicates a *purchase*, while a negative value indicates a *short sale*.

$\tilde{r}_i$—The return per dollar invested in a *purchase* of the $i^{th}$ stock (cash dividends plus price appreciation)

$\tilde{r}$—As above, the return per dollar invested in a particular *mix* or *portfolio* of stocks.

Consider now a gross investment in the entire mix, so that the actual investment in the $i^{th}$ stock is equal to $|h_i|$. The returns on purchases and short sales need to be considered separately.

First, we see that if $|h_i|$ is invested in a *purchase* ($h_i > 0$), the return will be simply $h_i \tilde{r}_i$. For reasons which will be clear immediately however, we write this in the form:

$$(4a) \qquad h_i \tilde{r}_i = h(\tilde{r}_i - r^*) + |h_i|\, r^*.$$

Now suppose that $|h_i|$ is invested in a *short sale* ($h_i < 0$), this gross investment being equal to the price received for the stock. (The price received must be deposited in escrow, and in addition, an amount equal to margin requirements on the current price of the stock sold must be remitted or loaned to the actual owner of the securities borrowed to effect the short sale.)[22] In computing the *return* on a short sale, we know that the short seller must pay to the person who lends him the stock any dividends which accrue while the stock is sold short (and hence borrowed), and his capital gain (or loss) is the negative of any price appreciation during this period. In addition, the short seller will receive interest at the riskless rate $r^*$ on the sales price placed in escrow, and he may or may not also receive interest at the same rate on his cash remittance to the lender of the stock. To facilitate the formal analysis, we *assume* that *both interest components* are *always received* by the short seller, and that margin requirements are 100%. In this case, the short seller's *return* per dollar of his gross investment will be $(2r^* - r_i)$, and if he invests

---

[22] In recent years, it has become increasingly common for the short seller to waive interest on his deposit with the lender of the security—in market parlance, for the borrowers of stock to obtain it "flat"—and when the demand for borrowing stock is large relative to the supply available for this purpose, the borrower may pay a cash premium to the lender of the stock. See Sidney M. Robbins, [18, pp. 58–59]. It will be noted that these practices reduce the expected return of short sales without changing the variance. The formal procedures developed below permit the identification of the appropriate stocks for short sale assuming the expected return is $(2r^* - \bar{r}_i)$. If these stocks were to be borrowed "flat" or a premium paid, it would be *simply necessary to iterate the solution after replacing* $(\bar{r}_i - r^*)$ in (4b) and (5) *for these stocks* with the value $(\bar{r}_i)$—and *if*, in addition a premium $p_i$ is paid, the term $(\bar{r}_i + p_i)$ should be substituted (where $p_i \geqq 0$ is the premium (if any) per dollar of sales price of the stock to be paid to lender of the stock). With equal lending and borrowing rates, changes in margin requirements will not affect the calculations. (I am indebted to Prof. Schlaifer for suggesting the use of absolute values in analyzing short sales.)

$|h_i|$ in the short sale ($h_i < 0$), its contribution to his portfolio return will be:

(4b)
$$|h_i|(2r^* - \tilde{r}_i) = h_i(\tilde{r}_i - r^*) + |h_i|r^*.$$

Since the right-hand sides of (4a) and (4b) are identical, the total return per dollar invested in *any* stock mix can be written as:

(5)
$$\tilde{r} = \sum_i [h_i(\tilde{r}_i - r^*) + |h_i|r^*] = r^* + \sum_i h_i(\tilde{r}_i - r^*)$$

because $\sum_i |h_i| = 1$ by the definition of $|h_i|$.

The expectation and variance of the return on any stock mix is consequently

(6a)
$$\bar{r} = r^* + \sum_i h_i(\bar{r}_i - r^*) = r^* + \sum_i h_i \bar{x}_i,$$

(6b)
$$\check{r} = \sum_{ij} h_i h_j \check{r}_{ij} = \sum_{ij} h_i h_j \check{x}_{ij}$$

where $\check{r}_{ij}$ represents the variance $\sigma_{ri j}{}^2$ when $i = j$, and covariances when $i \neq j$. The notation has been further simplified in the right hand expressions by defining:

(7)
$$\tilde{x}_i = \tilde{r}_i - r^*,$$

and making appropriate substitutions in the middle expressions. The quantity $\theta$ defined in (3b) can thus be written:

(8)
$$\theta = \frac{\bar{r} - r^*}{(\check{r})^{1/2}} = \frac{\bar{x}}{(\check{x})^{1/2}} = \frac{\sum_i h_i \bar{x}_i}{(\sum_{ij} h_i h_j \check{x}_{ij})^{1/2}}.$$

Since $h_i$ may be either positive or negative, equation (6a) shows that a portfolio with $\bar{r} < r^*$ and hence with $\theta > 0$ exists if there is one or more stocks with $\bar{r}_i$ not exactly equal to $r^*$. We assume throughout the rest of the paper that such a portfolio exists.

## DETERMINATION OF THE OPTIMAL STOCK PORTFOLIO

As shown in the proof of the Separation Theorem above, the optimal stock portfolio is the one which maximizes $\theta$ as defined in equation (8). We, of course, wish to maximize this value subject to the constraint

(9)
$$\sum_i |h_i| = 1,$$

which follows from the definition of $|h_i|$. But we observe from equation (8) that $\theta$ is a *homogeneous function of order zero* in the $h_i$: the value of $\theta$ is *unchanged by any proportionate* change in all $h_i$. Our problem thus reduces to the simpler one of finding a vector of values yielding the *unconstrained* maximum of $\theta$ in equation (8), after which we may scale these initial solution values to satisfy the constraint.

THE OPTIMUM PORTFOLIO WHEN SHORT SALES ARE PERMITTED

We first examine the partial derivatives of (8) with respect to the $h_i$ and find:

$$(10) \qquad \frac{\partial \theta}{\partial h_i} = (\sigma_x)^{-1} [\bar{x}_i - \lambda(h_i \check{x}_{ii} + \sum_j h_j \check{x}_{ij})],$$

where,

$$(11) \qquad \lambda = \bar{x}/\sigma_x^2 = \sum_i h_i \bar{x}_i / \sum_i \sum_j h_i h_j \check{x}_{ij}.$$

The *necessary and sufficient conditions* on the *relative* values of the $h_i$ for a stationary *and the unique (global) maximum*[23] are obtained by setting the derivatives in (10) equal to zero, which give the set of equations

$$(12) \qquad z_i \check{x}_{ii} + \sum_j z_j \check{x}_{ij} = \bar{x}_i, \quad i = 1, 2, \ldots, m;$$

where we write

$$(13) \qquad z_i = \lambda h_i.$$

It will be noted the set of equations (12)—which are identical to those Tobin derived by a different route[24]—are *linear* in the own-*variances*, pooled *covariances*, and *excess returns* of the respective securities; and since the covariance matrix $\underline{\underline{\check{x}}}$ is positive definite and hence non-singular, this system of equations has a unique solution

$$(14) \qquad z_i^0 = \sum_j \check{x}^{ij} \bar{x}_j$$

where $x^{ij}$ represents the $ij^{th}$ element of $(\check{x})^{-1}$, the inverse of the covariance matrix. Using (13), (7), and (6b), this solution may also be written in terms of the primary variables of the problem in the form

$$(15) \qquad h_i^0 = (\lambda^0)^{-1} \sum_j \check{r}^{ij}(\bar{r}_j - r^*), \text{ all } i.$$

---

[23] It is clear from a comparison of equations (8) and (11), showing that sgn $\theta$ = sgn $\lambda$, that only the vectors of $h_i$ values corresponding to $\lambda > 0$ are relevant to the maximization of $\theta$. Moreover, since $\theta$ as given in (8) and all its first partials shown in (10) are continuous functions of the $h_i$, it follows that when short sales are permitted, any maximum of $\theta$ must be a stationary value, and any stationary value is a maximum (rather than a minimum) when $\lambda > 0$ because $\theta$ is a convex function with a positive-definite quadratic form in its denominator. For the same reason, any maximum of $\theta$ is a unique (global) maximum.

[24] See Tobin, [21], equation (3.22), p. 83. Tobin had, however, formally required no short selling or borrowing, implying that this set of equations is valid under these constraints [so long as there is a single riskless asset (pp. 84–85)]; but the constraints were ignored in his derivation. We have shown that this set of equation *is* valid *when short sales* are properly included in the portfolio *and borrowing* is available in perfect markets in unlimited amounts. The alternative set of equilibrium conditions required when short sales are ruled out is given immediately below. The complications introduced by borrowing restrictions are examined in the final section of the paper.

Moreover, since (13) implies

(16) $$\sum_i |z_i| = \lambda \sum_i |h_i|,$$

$\lambda^0$ may readily be evaluated, after introducing the constraint (9) as

(17) $$\sum_i |z_i^0| = \lambda^0 \sum_i |h_i^0| = \lambda^0.$$

The optimal *relative* investments $z_i^0$ can consequently be scaled to the optimal proportions of the stock portfolio $h_i^0$, by diving each $z_i^0$ by the sum of their absolute values. A comparison of equations (16) and (11) shows further that:

(18) $$\sum_i |z_i^0| = \lambda^0 = \bar{x}^0/\sigma_{x^0}{}^2;$$

i.e., the sum of the absolute values of the $z_i^0$ yields, as a byproduct, the value of the ratio of the expected excess rate of return on the optimal portfolio to the variance of the return on this best portfolio.

It is also of interest to note that if we form the corresponding $\lambda$-ratio of the expected excess return to its variance for each $i^{th}$ stock, we have at the optimum:

(19) $$h_i^0 = (\lambda_i/\lambda^0) - \sum_{j \neq i} h_j^0 \bar{x}_{ij}/\check{x}_{ii} \text{ where}$$

$$\lambda_i = \bar{x}_i/\check{x}_{ii}.$$

The optimal fraction of each security in the best portfolio is equal to the ratio of *its* $\lambda_i$ to that of the entire portfolio, *less* the ratio of its pooled covariance with other securities to its own variance. Consequently, *if* the investor were to act on the assumption that all covariances were zero, he could pick his optimal portfolio mix very simply by determining the $\lambda_i$ ratio of the expected excess return $\bar{x}_i = \bar{r}_i - r^*$ of each stock to its variance $\check{x}_{ii} = \check{r}_{ii}$, and setting each $h_i = \lambda_i/\sum\lambda_i$; for with no covariances,[25] $\sum\lambda_i = \lambda^0 = \bar{x}^0/\sigma_{x_0}{}^2$. With this simplifying assumption, the $\lambda_i$ ratios of each stock suffice to determine the optimal mix by simple arithmetic;[26] in the more general case with non-zero covariances, a single set[27] of linear equations must be solved in the usual way, but no (linear or non-linear) programming is required and no more than one point on the "efficient frontier" need ever be computed, given the assumptions under which we are working.

THE OPTIMUM PORTFOLIO WHEN SHORT SALES ARE NOT PERMITTED

The exclusion of short sales does not complicate the above analysis *if* the investor is willing to act on an assumption of no correlations between the

[25] With no covariances, the set of equations (12) reduces to $\lambda h_i = \bar{x}_i/\check{x}_{ii} = \lambda_i$, and after summing over all $i = 1, 2 \ldots, m$, and using the constraint (9), we have immediately that $|\lambda^0| = \Sigma_i|\lambda_i|$, and $\lambda^0 > 0$ for max $\theta$ (instead of min $\theta$).

[26] Using a more restricted market setting, Hicks [6, p. 801] has also reached an equivalent result when covariances are zero (as he assumed throughout).

[27] See, however, footnote 22, above.

returns on different stocks. In this case, he finds his best portfolio of "long" holding by merely eliminating all securities whose $\lambda_i$-ratio is negative, and investing in the remaining issues in the proportions $h_i = \lambda_i/\Sigma\lambda_i$ in accordance with the preceding paragraph.

But in the more generally realistic cases when covariances are non-zero *and* short sales are not admitted, the solution of a single bilinear or quadratic programming problem is required to determine the optimal portfolio. (All other points on the "efficient frontier," of course, continue to be irrelevant so long as there is a riskless asset and a "perfect" borrowing market.) The optimal portfolio mix is now given by the set of $h_i^0$ which maximize $\theta$ in equation (8) subject to the constraint that all $h_i \geq 0$. As before, the (further) constraint that the sum of the $h_i$ be unity (equation 9) may be ignored in the initial solution for the *relative* values of the $h_i$ [because $\theta$ in (8) is homogeneous of order zero]. To find this optimum, we form the Lagrangian function

$$(20) \qquad \phi(\underline{h}, \underline{u}) = \theta + \sum_i u_i h_i$$

which is to be maximized subject to $h_i \geq 0$ and $u_i \geq 0$. Using (11), we have immediately

$$(21) \qquad \frac{\partial\phi}{\partial h_i} \geq 0 \leftrightarrow \bar{x}_i - \lambda\left(h_i \check{x}_{ii} + \sum_j h_j \check{x}_{ij}\right) + \alpha u_i \geq 0.$$

As in the previous cases, we also must have $\lambda > 0$ for a maximum (rather than a minimum) of $\phi$, and we shall write $z_i = \lambda h_i$ and and $v_i = \alpha u_i$. The necessary and sufficient conditions for the vector of *relative* holdings $z_i^0$ which maximizes $\theta$ in (20) are consequently,[28] using the Kuhn-Tucker theorem [9],

$$(22a) \qquad z_i^0 \check{x}_{ii} + \sum_j z_j^0 \check{x}_{ij} - v_i^0 = \bar{x}_i, \, i = 1, 2, \dots m;$$

[28] Equation (22a–22d) can readily be shown to satisfy the six necessary and two further sufficient conditions of the Kuhn-Tucker theorem. Apart from the constraints $\underline{h} \geq 0$ and $\underline{u} \geq 0$ which are automactically satisfied by the computing algorithm [conditions (22b and 22c)] the four *necessary* conditions are:

(1) $\left[\frac{\partial\phi}{\partial h_i}\right]^0 \leq 0$. This condition is satisfied *as a strict equality* in our solutions by virtue of equation (22a) [See equation (21)]. This strict equality also shows that,

(2) $h_i^0 \left[\frac{\partial\phi}{\partial h_i}\right]^0 = 0$, the first complementary slackness condition is also satisfied.

(3) $\left[\frac{\partial\phi}{\partial u_i}\right]^0 \geq 0$. This condition is satisfied because from equation (20), $\left[\frac{\partial\phi}{\partial u_i}\right]^0 = h_i^0 \geq 0$ by virtue of equation (22b). This same equation shows that the second complementary slackness condition,

(4) $u_i^0 \left[\frac{\partial\phi}{\partial u_i}\right]^0 = 0$, may be written $u_i^0 h_i^0 = 0$ which is also satisfied because of equation (22c) since $\alpha \neq 0$.

The two additional *sufficiency* conditions are of course satisfied because the variance-covariance matrix $\underline{x}$ is positive definite, making $\phi(\underline{h}, \underline{u}^0)$ a concave function on $\underline{h}$, and $\phi(\underline{h}^0, \underline{u})$ a convex function of $\underline{u}$.

where

(22b–d) $$z_i^0 \geq 0, \; v_i^0 \geq 0, \; z_i^0 v_i^0 = 0.$$

This system of equations can be expeditiously solved by the Wilson Simplicial Algorithm [23].

Now let $m'$ denote the number of stocks with strictly positive holdings $z_i^0 > 0$ in (22b), and renumber the entire set of stocks so that the subset satisfying this strict inequality [and, hence also, by (22d) $v_i^0 = 0$] are denoted $1, 2, ..., m'$. *Within this $m'$ subset of stocks found to belong in the optimal portfolio with positive holdings*, we consequently have, using the constraint (19),

(17a) $$\sum_{i=1}^{m'} z_i^0 = \lambda^0 \sum_{i=1}^{m'} h_i^0 = \lambda^0$$

so that the fraction of the optimal portfolio invested in the $i^{\text{th}}$ stock (where $i = 1, 2 \; ..., m'$) is

(23) $$h_i^0 = z_i^0/\lambda^0 = z_i^0 / \sum_{i=1}^{m'} z_i^0.$$

Once again, using (17a) and (11), the sum of the $z_i^0$ within this set of stocks held yields as a by-product the ratio of the expected excess rate of return on the optimal *portfolio* to the variance of the return on this best portfolio:

(18a) $$\sum_{i=1}^{m'} z_i^0 = \lambda^0 = \bar{x}^0/\sigma^2{}_{x^0}.$$

Moreover, since $z_i^0 > 0$ in (22a and 22b) strictly implies $v_i^0 = 0$ by virtue of (22c), equation (22a) *for the subset of positively held stocks $i = 1, 2 ... m'$* is formally identical to equation (12). We can, consequently, use these equations to bring out certain significant properties of the security portfolios which will be held by risk-averse investors trading in perfect markets.[29] *In the rest of this paper, all statements with respect to "other stocks" will refer to other stocks included within the portfolio.*

## III.  RISK PREMIUMS AND OTHER PROPERTIES OF STOCKS HELD LONG OR SHORT IN OPTIMAL PORTFOLIOS

Since the covariances between most pairs of stocks will be positive, it is clear from equation (19) that stocks held long ($h_i^0 > 0$) in a portfolio will generally be those whose expected return is enough greater than the risk-free rate to offset the disutility, so to speak, of the contribution of their variance and pooled covariance to the risk of the entire portfolio. This much is standard doctrine. Positive covariances with other securities held long in the portfolio raise the minimum level of $\bar{x}_i > 0$ which will lead to the inclusion of the $i^{\text{th}}$ stock as a positive holding in the optimal portfolio. But equation

---

[29] More precisely, the properties of portfolios when both the investors and the markets satisfy the conditions stated at the outset of section I. or, alternatively, when investors satisfy Roy's premises as noted previously.

(19) shows that stocks whose expected returns are *less* than the riskless rate (i.e., $\bar{x}_i < 0$ or $\bar{r}_i < r^*$) will *also* be held *long* ($h_i^0 > 0$) *provided* that *either* (*a*) they are *negatively correlated* in sufficient degree with other important stocks *held long* in the portfolio, or (*b*) that they are *positively correlated* in sufficient degree with other important stocks *held short* in the portfolio. The precise condition for $h_i^0 > 0$ when $\bar{x}_i < 0$ is that the weighted sum of the $i^{\text{th}}$ covariances be sufficiently negative to satisfy

(19a)
$$h_i^0 > 0 \leftrightarrow \left| \sum_{j \neq i} h_j^0 \check{x}_{ij} \right| > \left| \bar{x}_i / \lambda^0 \right|,$$

which follows from (19) since $\check{x}_{ii} > 0$.

Since our $\bar{x}_i$ is precisely what is usually called the "risk premium" in the literature, we have just shown that *the "risk premiums" required on risky securities* (i.e. those with $\sigma_i$ and $\sigma_i^2 > 0$) for them *to be held long by optimizing risk-averse investors in perfect markets need not always be positive*, as generally presumed. *They will in fact be negative* under either of the conditions stated in (*a*) and (*b*) above, summarized in (19a). The explanation is, of course, that a long holding of a security which is negatively correlated with other long holdings tends to reduce the variance of the whole portfolio by offsetting some of the variance contributed by the other securities in the portfolio, and this "variance-offsetting" effect may dominate the security's own-variance and even a negative expected excess return $\bar{x}_i < 0$.

Positive correlations with other securities held short in the portfolio have a similar variance-offsetting effect.[30]

Correspondingly, it is apparent from (19) itself that any stock with *positive* excess returns or risk premiums ($\bar{x}_i > 0$) will be held short ($h_i^0 < 0$) in the portfolio *provided that either* (*a*) it is *positively correlated* in sufficient degree with other stocks *held long* in the portfolio, or (*b*) it is *negatively correlated* in sufficient degree with other stocks *held short* in the portfolio. *Positive* (negative) *risk premiums are neither a sufficient nor a necessary condition for a stock to be held long* (short).

INDIFFERENCE CONTOURS

Equation (12) ( and the equivalent set (22a) restricted to stocks actually held in portfolios) also enables us to examine the *indifference contours* between expected excess returns, variances, or standard deviations and covariances of securities which will result in the *same fraction* $h_i^0$ of the investor's portfolio being held in a given security. The general presumption in the literature, as noted in our introduction,[31] is that the market values of

---

[30] Stocks with negative expected excess returns or "risk premiums" ($\bar{x}_i < 0$) will, of course, enter into portfolios only as short sales (provided these are permitted) when the inequality in (19a) is reversed, i.e.
$$h_i^0 < 0 \leftrightarrow \sum_{j \neq i} = h_j^0 \check{x}_{ij} + \bar{x}_i / \lambda^0 < 0.$$ When short sales are not permitted, and (19a) is not satisfied, stocks with $\bar{x}_i < 0$ simply do not appear in the portfolio at all.

[31] See footnote 3 for references and quotations.

risk assets are adjusted in perfect markets to maintain a *linear* relation between expected rates of return (our $\bar{r}_i = \bar{x}_i + r^*$) *and risk* as measured by the *standard deviation* of return $\sigma_i$ on the security in question. This presumption probably arises from the fact that this relation *is* valid for trade offs *between* a riskless security *and* a single risk asset (or a *given mix* of risk assets to be held in fixed proportions). But it can *not* be validly attributed to indifferent trade offs *between* risk assets *within* optimizing risk-asset portfolios. In point of fact, it can easily be shown that there is *a strictly linear indifference contour* between the *expected return* $\bar{r}_i$ (or the expected excess return $\bar{x}_i$) *and the variance* $\sigma_i^2$ (not the standard deviation $\sigma_i$) of the individual security, and this linear function has very straightforward properties. The assumption made in this derivation that the covariances $\sigma_{ij}$ with other securities are invariant is a more reasonable one than is perhaps readily apparent.[32] Subject to the acceptability of this latter assumption, it follows that *risk classes of securities should be scaled in terms of variances* of returns rather than standard deviations (with the level of covariances reflected in the parameters of the linear function). The complexities involved when indifference contours are scaled on covariances or standard deviations are indicated below.

The conclusion that the indifference contour between $\bar{x}_i$ and the variance $\sigma_i^2$ is *linear* in the general case when all covariances $\sigma_{ij}$ are held constant is established in the appendix, note II, by totally differentiating the equilibrium conditions (12) [or the equivalent set (22a) restricted to the $m'$ stocks held in the portfolio]. But *all* pairs of values of $\bar{x}_i$ and $\sigma_i^2$ along the linear indifference contour which holds $h_i^0$ fixed at some given level also rigorously imply that the proportionate mix of *all other* stocks in the portfolio is *also unchanged.* Consequently, we may proceed to derive other properties of this indifference contour by examining a simple "two security" portfolio. (The $i^{\text{th}}$ security is renumbered "1", and "all other" securities are called the second security.) If we then solve the equilibrium conditions[33] (12) in this two-stock case and hold $K = h_1^0/h_2^0$ constant, we have

---

[32] Fixed covariances are directly implied by the assumption that every pair of $i^{\text{th}}$ and $j^{\text{th}}$ stocks are related by a one-common-factor model (e.g. the general state of the economy or the general level of the stock market), so that, letting $\bar{\mu}$ represent the general exogenous factor and $\tilde{\omega}$ the random outcome of endogenous factors under management's control, we have

$$\bar{x}_i = a_i + b_i\bar{\mu} + \tilde{\omega}_i$$

$$\bar{x}_j = a_j + b_j\bar{\mu} + \tilde{\omega}_j$$

with $\bar{\mu}$, $\tilde{\omega}_i$, and $\tilde{\omega}_j$ mutually independent. This model implies

$$\sigma_i^2 = b_i^2\,\sigma_\mu^2 + \sigma_\omega^2, \text{ and } \sigma_{ij} = b_ib_j\sigma_\mu^2,$$

so that if management, say, varies the part under its control, $\tilde{\omega}$ and $\sigma_\omega^2$, the covariance will be unchanged. (This single-common-factor model is essentially the same as what Sharpe [20] calls the "diagonal" model.)

[33] The explicit solution is $z_1^0 = \lambda^0 h_1^0 = (\bar{x}_1\sigma_2^2 - \bar{x}_2\sigma_{12})/(\sigma_1^2\sigma_2^2 - \sigma_{12}^2)$; and $z_2^0 = \lambda^0 h_2^0 = (\bar{x}_2\sigma_1^2 - \bar{x}_1\sigma_{12})/(\sigma_1^2\sigma_1^2 - \sigma_{12}^2)$; where $\lambda^0 = z_1^0 + z_2^0$.

(24)     $K = h_1^0/h_2^0 = \text{constant} = (\bar{x}_1\sigma_2^2 - \bar{x}_2\sigma_{12})/(\bar{x}_2\sigma_1^2 - \bar{x}_1\sigma_{12}$

which leads to the desired explicit expression, using $\bar{r}_1 = \bar{x}_1 + r^*$,

(25)                     $\bar{r}_1 = r^* + W\sigma_{12} + WK\sigma_1^2,$

where

(25a)                    $W = \bar{x}_2/(\sigma_2^2 + K\sigma_{12}).$

Since[34] $WK = \lambda^0 h_1^0$ and $\lambda^0 > 0$, the *slope* of this indifference contour between $\bar{x}_1$ and $\sigma_1^2$ will always be positive when $h_1^0 > 0$ (as would be expected, because when $\sigma_{12}$ is held constant, increased variance requires added return to justify and given positive holding[35]); but when the first stock is held short, its expected (or excess) return and its variance along the contour vary inversely (as they should since "shorts" profit from price declines). Moreover, if we regard $\sigma_{12}$ as an exogenous "shift" parameter, the *constant term* (or intercept) of this indifference contour varies directly[36] with $\sigma_{12}$, and the slope of $\bar{x}_1$ on $\sigma_1^2$ varies inversely[37] with $\sigma_{12}$ in the usual case, when $\bar{x}_2 > 0$.

Now note that (25) and (25a) can be written (25b) $\bar{r}_1 = r^* + \bar{x}_2(\sigma_{12} + K\sigma_1^2)/(\sigma_2^2 + K\sigma_{12})$, which clearly depicts a hyperbolic (rather than linear) indifference contour on $\sigma_{12}$ if $\sigma_1^2$ is regarded as fixed, and a more complex function between $\bar{r}_1$ (or $x_1$) and the standard deviation $\sigma_1$, which may be written (using $\sigma_{12} = \sigma_1\sigma_2\rho$),

(25b′)                $\bar{x}_1 = \dfrac{\bar{x}_2 K\sigma_1^2[1 + \rho(K\sigma_1/\sigma_2)^{-1}]}{\sigma_2^2(1 + \rho K\sigma_1/\sigma_2)}$

The *slope* of the indifference contour between $\bar{x}_1$ and $\sigma_1$ is a still more involved function, which may be written most simply as

(25c)     $\dfrac{\partial \bar{x}_1}{\partial \sigma_1} = \dfrac{\bar{x}_2[2K\sigma_1\sigma_2^2 + (K^2\sigma_1^2\sigma_2 + \sigma_2^3)\rho]}{(\sigma_2^2 + K\sigma_{12})^2}$

$\qquad\qquad = 2K\sigma_1\bar{x}_2 \dfrac{1 + (\rho/2)[(K\sigma_1/\sigma_2) + (\sigma_2/K\sigma_1)]}{\sigma^2(1 + \rho K\sigma_1/\sigma_2)^2}.$

---

[34] Upon substituting (24) in (25) and using the preceding footnote, we have $W = \lambda^0 h_2^0 = z_2^0$, from which it follows that $WK = \lambda^0 h_2^0 h_1^0/h_2^0 = \lambda^0 h_1^0$. As noted earlier, we have $\lambda^0 > 0$ (because the investor maximizes and does not minimize 0). [It may be noted that $W$ is used instead of $z_2^0$ in (25) in order to incorporate the restriction on the indifference contours that $K$ is constant, and thereby to obtain an expression (25a) which does not contain $\bar{x}_1$ and $\sigma_1^2$ (as does $z_2^0$ without the constraint of constant $K$)].

[35] Note that this is true whether the "other security" is held long or short.

[36] Let the constant term in (25) be $C = r^* + W\sigma_{12}$. Then

$\dfrac{\partial C}{\partial \sigma_{12}} = \dfrac{(\sigma_2^2 + K\sigma_{12})\bar{x}_2 - \bar{x}_2\sigma_{12}K}{(\sigma_2^2 + K\sigma_{12})^2} = \dfrac{\bar{x}_2\sigma_2^2}{(\sigma_2^2 + K\sigma_{12})^2}$

which has the same sign as $\bar{x}_2$, independent of the sign of $K$, $\sigma_{12}$, or $\bar{x}_1$.

[37] We have $\partial WK/\partial \sigma_{12} = -K^2\bar{x}_2/(\sigma_2^2 + K\sigma_{12})^2$, which has a sign opposite to that of $\bar{x}_2$.

It is true, in the usual situation with $K > 0$, $\bar{x}_2 > 0$, and $\rho > 0$, that $\bar{x}_1 (=\bar{r}_1 - r^*)$ and $\partial x_1/\partial\sigma_1$ are necessarily positive as common doctrine presumes, *but the complex non-linearity is evident even in this "normal case"* restricted to two stocks—and the *positive risk premium $\bar{x}_1$ and positive slope* on $\sigma_1$, of course, *cannot be generalized.* For instance, in the admittedly less usual but important case with $\bar{x}_2 > 0$ and the intercorrelation $\rho < 0$, *both* $\bar{x}_1$ and $\partial\bar{x}_1/\partial\sigma_1$ are *alternatively negative and positive* over different ranges[38] of $\sigma_1$ for any fixed $h_i^0$ or $K > 0$.

Moreover, *in contrast* to the $\bar{x}_i - \sigma_i^2$ contour examined above, the pairs of values along the $\bar{x}_i - \sigma_i$ contour which hold $h_i^0$ constant do *not* imply an unchanged mix[39] of the other stocks in the optimizing portfolio when $m' > 2$; nor is $\lambda^0$ invariant along an $\bar{x}_i - \sigma_i$ contour, as it is along the $\bar{x}_1 - \sigma_1^2$ contour with covariances constant. For both reasons, the indifference contour between $\bar{x}_1$ and $\sigma_1$ for portfolios of $m' > 2$ stocks is very much more complex than for the two-stock case, whereas the "two-stock" contour (3) between $\bar{x}_1$ and $\sigma_1^2$ is exact for any number of stocks (when "all other" stocks are pooled in fixed proportions, as we have seen they can validly be). We should also observe that there does not seem to be an easy set of economically interesting assumptions which lead to *fixed correlations* as $\sigma_1$ varies (as assumed in deriving $\bar{x}_1 - \sigma_1$ indifference contours) in marked contrast to the quite interesting and plausible "single-factor" model (see footnote 32 above) which directly validates the assumption of fixed covariances used in deriving the $\bar{x}_1 - \sigma_1^2$ indifference contours.

In sum, we conclude that—however natural or plausible it may have seemed to relate risk premiums to standard deviations of return *within* portfolios of risk assets, and to scale risk classes of securities on this same basis—risk premiums can most simply *and* plausibly be related directly to *variances* of returns (with the level of covariances reflected in the parameters of the linear function). Since the principal function of the concept of "risk class" has been to delineate a required level of risk premium, we conclude further that risk classes should also be delineated in the same units (variances) if, indeed, the concept of risk class should be used at all.[40]

---

[38] With $K > 0$, $\bar{x}_2 > 0$, and $\rho < 0$, we have from (25b′)

$$\bar{x}_1 < 0 \text{ if } 0 < K\sigma_1/\sigma_2 < |\rho|, \text{ and}$$

$$\bar{x}_1 > 0 \text{ if } |\rho| < K\sigma_1/\sigma_2 < |\rho^{-1}|.$$

On the other hand, from (25c) we have

$$\partial\bar{x}_1/\partial\sigma_1 < 0 \text{ if } 0 < K\sigma_1/\sigma_2 < |\rho^{-1}| - \sqrt{\rho^{-2} - 1}$$

and

$$\partial\bar{x}_1/\partial\sigma_1 > 0 \text{ if } |\rho^{-1}| - \sqrt{\rho^{-2} - 1} < K\sigma_1/\sigma_2 < |\rho^{-1}|.$$

[39] See appendix, note 11(b).

[40] However, see below, especially the "fifth" through "seventh" points enumerated near the end of Section V.

## IV. MARKET PRICES OF SHARES IMPLIED BY SHAREHOLDER OPTIMIZATION IN PURELY COMPETITIVE MARKETS UNDER IDEALIZED UNCERTAINTY

Our analysis to this point has followed Tobin [21] and Markowitz [14] in assuming that current security prices are *exogenous data*, and that each investor acts on his own (doubtless unique) probability distribution over rates of return, *given* these market prices. I shall continue to make the same assumptions concerning markets and investors introduced in section I. In particular, it is assumed that security markets are purely competitive, transactions costs and taxes are zero, and *all* investors prefer a greater mean rate of return for a given variance and a lesser rate of return variance for any given mean return rate. But in this and the following section I shall *assume* (1) that investors' joint probability distributions pertain to *dollar returns rather than rates* of return—the dollar return in the period being the sum of the cash dividend and the increase of market price during the period. Also, for simplicity, assume that (2) for *any* given set of market prices for all stocks, all investors assign *identical* sets of means, variances, and covariances to the joint distribution of these dollar returns (and hence for *any* set of prices, to the vector of means and the variance-covariances matrix of the rates of return $\tilde{r}_i$ of all stocks), and that all correlations between stocks are $< 1$.

This assumption of identical probability beliefs or judgments by all investors in the market restricts the applicability of the analysis of this and the following section to what I have elsewhere characterized as *idealized uncertainty* [10, pp. 246–247]. But however unrealistic this latter assumption may be, it does enable us to derive a set of (stable) equilibrium market prices— and an important theorem concerning the properties of these prices— which at least fully and explicitly reflect the presence of uncertainty *per se* (as distinct from the effects of diverse judgmental distributions among investors).

Note first that the assumption of identical probability judgments means that (1) *the same stock mix will be optimal for every investor* (although the actual dollar gross investment in this mix—and the ratio, $w$, of gross investment in this mix to his net investment balance—will vary from one investor to the next). It consequently follows that, when the market is in equilibrium, (2) the $h_1^0$ given by equation (15) or (12) can be interpreted as the ratio of the *aggregate market* value of the $i^{th}$ stock to the total aggregate market value of all stocks, and hence, (3) *all $h_i$ will be strictly positive.*

In order to develop further results, define

$V_{0i}$—the aggregate market value of the $i^{th}$ stock at time zero,

$\tilde{R}_i$—the aggregate return on the $i^{th}$ stock (the sum of aggregate cash dividends paid and appreciation in aggregate market value over the transaction period); and $T \equiv \Sigma_i V_{0i}$, the aggregate market value of *all* stock in the market at time zero.

The original economic definitions of the variables in the portfolio optimization problem give

(26a) $$h_i = V_{0i}/T,$$

(26b) $$\tilde{r}_i = \bar{R}_i/V_{0i},$$

(26c) $$\tilde{x}_i = \tilde{r}_i - r^* = (\bar{R}_i - r^*V_{0i})/V_{0i},$$

(26d) $$\check{x}_{ij} = \check{r}_{ij} = \check{R}_{ij}/V_{0i}V_{0j},$$

where $\check{R}_{ij}$ is the covariance of the aggregate dollar returns of the $i^{th}$ and $j^{th}$ stocks (and $\check{R}_{ii}$ is the $i^{th}$ stock's aggregate return variance). The equilibrium conditions (12) may now be written

(12a) $$\frac{\bar{R}_i - r^*V_i^0}{V_{0i}} = \lambda \frac{V_i^0}{T} \frac{\check{R}_{ii}}{(V_{0i})^2} + \lambda \sum_{j \neq i} \frac{V_{0j}}{T} \frac{\check{R}_{ij}}{V_{0i}V_{0j}},$$

which reduces to

(27) $$\bar{R}_i - r^*V_{0i} = (\lambda/T)\left[\check{R}_{ii} + \sum_{j \neq i} \check{R}_{ij}\right]$$

$$= (\lambda/T)\sum_j \check{R}_{ij}.$$

Now $\bar{R}_i - r^*V_{0i}$ represents the *expected* excess of the aggregate dollar return on the $i^{th}$ security over earnings at the riskless rate on its aggregate market value, and $\sum_j \check{R}_{ij}$ represents the aggregate risk (direct dollar return variance and total covariance) entailed in holding the stock. Equation (27) consequently establishes the following:

*Theorem:* Under Idealized Uncertainty, equilibrium in purely competitive markets of risk-averse investors requires that the values of all stocks will have adjusted themselves so that the *ratio* of the expected excess aggregate dollar returns of each stock to the aggregate dollar risk of holding the stock will be *the same for all* stocks (and equal to $\lambda/T$), when the risk of each stock is measured by the variance of its own dollar return and its combined covariance with that of all other stocks.

But we seek an explicit equation[41] for $V_{0i}$, and to this end we note that partial summation of equation (27) over *all other* stocks gives us

(28) $$\sum_{k \neq i}(\bar{R}_k - r^*V_{0k}) = (\lambda/T)\sum_{k \neq i}\sum_j \check{R}_{kj}.$$

After dividing each side of (27) by the corresponding side of (28), and solving for $V_{0i}$, we then find that the aggregate market value of the $i^{th}$ stock is related to the concurrent market values of the *other* $(m - 1)$ stocks by

(29) $$V_{0i} = (\bar{R}_i - W_i)/r^*$$

[41] I do not simply rearrange equation (27) at this point since $(\lambda/T)$ includes $V_{0i}$ as one of its terms (see equation (29d) below).

where

(29a)
$$W_i = \gamma_i \sum_j \check{R}_{ij} = \gamma_i \left( \check{R}_{ii} + \sum_{j \neq i} \check{R}_{ij} \right)$$

and

(29b)
$$\gamma_i = \frac{\sum_{k \neq i} (\bar{R}_k - r^* V_{0k})}{\sum_{k \neq i} \sum_j \check{R}_{kj}}$$

$$= \frac{\sum_{k \neq i} (\bar{R}_k - r^* V_{0k})}{\sum_{k \neq i} \sum_{j \neq i} \check{R}_{kj} + \sum_{j \neq i} \check{R}_{ij}}.$$

Since (29b) *appears* to make the slope coefficient $\gamma_i$ unique to each company, we must note immediately that dividing each side of (27) by its summation over *all* stocks shows that the aggregate market value of the $i^{th}$ stock is *also* related to the concurrent market values of *all* ($m$) stocks[42] by equation (29) when $W_i$ is written as

(29c)
$$W_i = (\lambda/T) \sum_j \check{R}_{ij},$$

and

(29d)
$$\lambda/T = \frac{\sum_i (\bar{R}_i - r^* V_{0i})}{\sum_i \sum_j \check{R}_{ij}}.$$

But from equations (28) and (29b), we see that

(29e)
$$\gamma_i = \gamma_j = \lambda/T,$$

a *common value* for *all companies in the market*. The values of $W_i$ given by (29a) and (29c) are consequently *identical*, and *the subscripts on $\gamma$ should henceforth be ignored*.

In words, equations (29) establish the following further

*Theorem:* Under Idealized Uncertainty, in purely competitive markets of risk-averse investors,

A. the total market value of any stock in equilibrium is equal to the *capitalization* at the *risk-free interest rate $r^*$* of the *certainty equivalent* $(R_i - W_i)$ of its uncertain *aggregate dollar return* $\check{R}_i$;

B. the *difference* $W_i$ between the expected value $\bar{R}_i$ of these returns and their certainty equivalent is *proportional* for *each* company to *its aggregate risk* represented by the *sum* $(\sum_j \check{R}_{ij})$ of the *variance* of these returns and their total covariance with those of all other stocks; and

C. the factor of proportionality $(\gamma = \lambda/T)$ is the *same* for *all* companies in the market.

---

[42] Alternatively, equation (29) and (29c) follow directly from (27) and (29d) may be established by substituting (26a–d) in (11).

Certain corollaries are immediately apparent:

*Corollary I:* Market values of securities are related to standard deviations of dollar returns by way of variances and covariances, *not directly* and *not linearly.*

*Corollary II:* The aggregate risk $(\sum_j R_{ij})$ of the $i^{th}$ stock which is directly relevant to its aggregate market value $V_{0i}$ is simply *its contribution* to the aggregate *variance* of the dollar returns (for *all* holders together) of *all* stocks (which is $\sum_i \sum_j \check{R}_{ij}$).

*Corollary III:* The *ratio* $(\bar{R}_i - W_i)/\bar{R}_i$ of the *certainty-equivalent* of aggregate dollar returns to their expected value is, in general, *different for each* $i^{th}$ company when the market is in equilibrium;[43] but for all companies, this certainty-equivalent to expected-dollar-return ratio is the *same linear function* $\{1 - \gamma[\sum_j \check{R}_{ij}/\bar{R}_j]\}$ of total dollar risk $(\sum_j \check{R}_{ij})$ attributable to the $i^{th}$ stock deflated by its expected dollar return $\bar{R}_i$.

Several further implications also follow immediately. First, note that equation (29) can be written

(29′)
$$V_{0i} = (\bar{R}_i - W_i)/r^*$$
$$= (V_{0i} + \bar{R}_i - W_i)/(1 + r^*)$$
$$= (\bar{H}_i - W_i)/(1 + r^*).$$

Since $\bar{R}_i$ was defined as the sum of the aggregate cash dividend and increase in value in the equity during the period, the *sum* $V_{0i} + \bar{R}_i$ is equal to the expected value of the sum (denoted $\bar{H}_i$) of the cash dividend and end-of-period aggregate market value of the equity, and the elements of the covariance matrix $\check{\underline{H}}$ are identical to those in $\check{\underline{R}}$. *All* equations (29) can consequently be validly rewritten substituting $H$ for $R$ throughout [and $(1 + r^*)$ for $r^*$], *thus explicitly determining all current values* $V_{0i}$ *directly by the joint probability distributions over the end-of-period realizations*[44] $\check{H}_i$. (The value of $W_i$, incidentally, is not affected by these substitutions.) Our assumption that investors hold joint probability distributions over dollar returns $\check{R}_i$ is consequently *equivalent* to an assumption that they hold distributions over end-of-period realizations, and *our analysis applies equally under either assumption.*

Moreover, after the indicated substitutions, equation (29′) *shows that the current aggregate value of any equity is equal to the certainty-equivalent of the sum of its prospective cash receipts (to shareholders) and total market value at the end of the period, discounted at the riskless rate* $r^*$. Similarly, by an extension of the same lines of analysis, the certainty equivalent of the cash dividend

---

[43] From equations (27), (29), (29a), and (29e), this statement is true for all pairs of stocks having different aggregate market values, $V_{0i} \neq V_{0j}$.

[44] Because we are assuming only "idealized" uncertainty, the distribution of these end-of-period realizations will be independent of judgments regarding the dividend receipt and end-of-period market value separately. See Lintner [10] and Modigliani-Miller [16].

and market value at the end of the first period clearly may be regarded as the then-present-values using riskless discount rates of the certainty-equivalents of random receipts still further in the future. *The analysis thus justifies viewing market values as riskless-rate present values of certainty-equivalents of random future receipts*, where certainty-equivalents are related to expected values by way of variances and covariances weighted by adjustment factors $\gamma_{it}$, which may or may not be the same for each future period $t$.

Still another implication of equation (29) is of a more negative character. Those who like (or hope) to find a "risk" discount rate $k_r$ with which to discount expected values under uncertainty will find from (29) that, using a subscript $i$ for the individual firm

$$
(29'') \qquad V_{0i} = \frac{\bar{R}_i}{k_{ri}} = \frac{\bar{R}_i}{r^*(1 - W_i/\check{R}_i)^{-1}}
$$

$$
= \frac{\bar{R}_i}{r^*\left(1 - \gamma \sum_j \check{R}_{ij}/\bar{R}_i\right)^{-1}}
$$

so that

$$
(30) \qquad k_{ri} = r^*\left(1 - \gamma \sum_j \check{R}_{ij}/\bar{R}_i\right)^{-1}
$$

It is apparent that (*i*) the *appropriate "risk" discount rate $k_{ri}$ is unique to each individual company in a competitive equilibrium* (because of the first half of corollary III above); (*ii*) that efforts to derive it complicate rather than simplify the analysis, since (*iii*) it is a *derived* rather than a primary variable; and that (*iv*) it explicitly involves all the elements required for the determination of $V_{0i}$ itself, and, (*v*) does so in a more complex and non-linear fashion.[45] Having established these points, the rest of our analysis returns to the more direct and simpler relation of equation (29).

## V.   CORPORATE CAPITAL BUDGETING UNDER IDEALIZED UNCERTAINTY

Capital budgeting decisions within a corporation affect both the expected value and variances—and hence, the certainty-equivalents—of its prospective aggregate dollar returns to its owners. When the requisite conditions are

---

[45] It may also be noted that even when *covariances* between stocks are constant, the elasticity of $k_{ri}$ with respect to the variance $\check{R}_{ii}$ (and *a fortiori*) to the standard deviation of return is a unique (to the company) multiple of a hyperbolic relation of a variance-expected-return ratio:

$$
(30a) \qquad \frac{\check{R}_{ii}}{k_{ri}} \frac{\partial k_{ri}}{\partial \check{R}_{ii}} = \frac{\gamma \check{R}_{ii}/\bar{R}_i}{1 - \gamma \left(\sum_{j \neq i} \check{R}_{ij}/\bar{R}_i\right) - \gamma \check{R}_{ii}/\bar{R}_i}
$$

satisfied, equation (29) thus provides a normative criterion for these decisions, derived from a competitive equilibrium in the securities market.

In developing these important implications of the results of the last section, I of course maintain the assumptions of idealized uncertainty in purely competitive markets of risk-averse investors with identical probability distributions, and I continue to assume, for simplicity, that there are no transactions costs or taxes. The identity of probability distributions over outcomes now covers corporate management as well as investors, and includes potential corporate investments in the capital budget as well as assets currently held by the company. Every corporate management, *ex ante*, assigns probability zero to default on its debt, and all investors also treat corporate debt as a riskless asset. I thus extend the riskless investment (or borrowing) alternative from individual investors to corporations. Each company can invest any amount of its capital budget in a perfectly safe security (savings deposit or certificate of deposit) at the riskless rate $r^*$, or it may borrow unlimited amounts at the *same* rate in the current or any future period.[46] I also assume that the investment opportunities available to the company in any time period are regarded as independent of the size and composition of the capital budget in any other time period.[47] I also assume there is no limited liability to corporate stock, nor any institutional or legal restriction on the investment purview of any investor, and that the riskless rate $r^*$ is expected by everyone to remain constant over time.

Note that this set of assumptions is sufficient to validate the famous (taxless) Propositions I and II of Modigliani and Miller [15]. In particular, under these severely idealized conditions, for any given size and composition of corporate assets (investments), investors will be indifferent to the *financing* decisions of the company. Subject to these conditions, we can, consequently, derive valid decision rules for capital budgets which do not explicitly depend upon concurrent financing decisions. Moreover, these conditions make the present values of the cash flows *to any* company from its real (and financial) assets and operations equal to the total market value of investors' *claims* to these flows, i.e., to the sum of the aggregate market value of its common (and preferred) stock outstanding and its borrowings (debt).[48] They also make any change in shareholders' claims equal to the change in the present values of flows (before interest deductions) to the company less any change in debt service. The *changes* in the market value of the equity $V_{0i}$ induced

---

[46] The effects of removing the latter assumption are considered briefly in the final section.

[47] This simplifying assumption specifies a (stochastic) comparative static framework which rules out the complications introduced by making investor expectations of future growth in a company's investment opportunities conditional on current investment decisions. I examine the latter complications in other papers [11], and [12].

[48] See Lintner [10]. Note that in [10, especially p. 265, top 1st column] I argued that additional assumptions were needed to validate the "entity theory" under uncertainty—the last sentence of the preceding paragraph, and the stipulation that corporate bonds are riskless meet the requirement. See, however, Modigliani-Miller [16].

by capital budgeting decisions will consequently be precisely equal to

$$(31) \qquad \Delta V_{0i} = \Delta(\bar{R}_i - W_i)/(1 + r^*)$$
$$= \Delta(\bar{H}_i - W_i)/(1 + r^*),$$

where $\Delta \bar{H}_i$ is the net change induced in the *expected* present value at the end of the first period of the cash inflows (net of interest charges) to the $i^{\text{th}}$ company attributable to *its assets*[49] when all present values are computed at the riskless rate $r^*$.

These relationships may be further simplified in a useful way by making three additional assumptions: that (*i*) the *aggregate market value* of *all other* stocks—and (*ii*) the *covariances* $\check{R}_{ij}$ with all other *stocks* are invariant to the capital budgeting decisions of the $i^{\text{th}}$ company; while (*iii*) the (optimal) *portfolio* of risk assets is not an "inferior good" (in the classic Slutsky-Hicks sense) *vis a vis* riskless assets. The reasonableness of (*iii*) is obvious (especially in the context of a universe of risk-averse investors!), and given (*iii*), assumption (*i*) is a convenience which only involves ignoring (generally small) second-order feedback effects (which will not reverse signs); while the plausibility of (*ii*) as a good working first approximation was indicated above (footnote 32).[50]

In this context, we now show that capital budgeting decisions by the $i^{\text{th}}$ firm will raise the aggregate market value of its equity $V_{0i}$—and hence by common agreement be in the interest of its shareholders—so long as the induced change in expected dollar return is greater than the product of the market price $\gamma$ of risk and the induced variance of dollar return, i.e.,

$$(32) \qquad \Delta \bar{R}_i - \gamma \Delta \check{R}_{ii} - \Delta \bar{H}_i - \gamma \Delta \check{H}_{ii} > 0.$$

This assertion (or theorem) can be proved as follows. The total differential of (29) is

$$(29f) \qquad r^* \Delta V_{0i} - \Delta \bar{R}_i + \gamma \Delta \check{R}_{ii} + \left( \sum_j \check{R}_{ij} \right) \Delta \gamma = 0$$

so that under the above assumptions

$$(29g) \qquad \Delta \bar{R}_i \geqq \gamma \Delta \check{R}_{ii} + \left( \sum_j \check{R}_{ij} \right) d\gamma \to \Delta V_{0i} \geqq 0 \to \Delta T \geqq 0.$$

But using (29e) and (29d), we have

$$(29h) \qquad \Delta \gamma = (\Delta \bar{R}_i - \gamma \Delta \check{R}_{ii}) / \sum_i \sum_j \check{R}_{ij}$$

---

[49] By definition, $\Delta H_i$ is the change in the expected sum of dividend payment and market value of the equity at the end of the period. This is made equal to the statement in the text by the assumptions under which we are operating.

[50] It is, however, necessary in general to redefine the variables in terms of *dollar* returns (rather than rates of return), but this seems equally reasonable.

so that

(29i) $$\Delta \bar{R}_i = \gamma \Delta \check{R}_{ii} \to \Delta \gamma = 0 \to \Delta V_{0i} = 0 \to \Delta T = 0,$$

and the first equality in (29i) defines the relevant *indifference function*.[51] Moreover, using (29h) and the fact that $\sum_j \check{R}_{ij} < \sum_i \sum_j \check{R}_{ij}$, we have from (29g):

(29j) $$\Delta \bar{R}_i \geq \gamma \Delta \bar{R}_{ii} \to \Delta \bar{R}_i \geq \gamma \Delta \check{R}_{ii} + \left( \sum_j \check{R}_{ij} \right) \Delta \gamma,$$

and consequently

(29k) $$\Delta \bar{R}_i \geq \gamma \Delta \check{R}_{ii} \to \Delta V_{0i} \geq 0 \to \Delta T \geq 0,$$

from which (32) follows immediately.

In order to explore the implications of (32) further, it will now be convenient to consider in more detail the capital budgeting decisions of a company whose *existing assets* have a present value computed at the rate $r^*$ (and measured at the end of the first period) of $\tilde{H}_o^{(1)}$, a random variable with expected value $\bar{H}_o^{(1)}$ and variance $\check{H}_{oo}$.

The company may be provisionally holding any fraction of $\bar{H}_o$ in savings deposits or CD's yielding $r^*$, and it may use any such funds (or borrow unlimited amounts at the *same* rate) to make new "real" investments. We assume that the company has available a set of new projects $1, 2 \dots j \dots n$ which respectively involve *current* investment outlays of $H_j^{(0)}$, and which have present values of the relevant incremental cash flows (valued at the *end* of the first period) of $\tilde{H}_j^{(1)}$. Since any diversion (or borrowing) of funds to invest in any project involves an opportunity cost of $r^* H_j^{(0)}$, we also have the "excess" dollar end-of-period present value return

(33) $$\tilde{X}_j^{(1)} = \tilde{H}_j^{(1)} - r^* H_{jo}^{(0)}.$$

Finally, we shall denote the $(n + 1)^{\text{th}}$ order covariance matrix (including the existing assets $\tilde{H}_o$) by $\underline{\underline{H}}$ or $\underline{\underline{X}}$ whose corresponding elements $\check{H}_{jk} = \check{X}_{jk}$.

DETERMINATION OF THE OPTIMAL CORPORATE CAPITAL-BUDGET-PORTFOLIO

In this simplified context, it is entirely reasonable to expect that the corporation will seek to maximize the left side of equation[52] (32) as its capital

---

[51] Note that this indifference function can also be derived by substituting equations (26a–d) directly into that found in section III above (equation (6b) in appendix Note II or equation (25) in the text) for the relevant case where covariances are invariant.

[52] Under our assumption that stock portfolios are not inferior goods, sgn $\Delta T =$ sgn $[\Delta \bar{R}_i - \gamma \Delta \check{R}_{ii}]$ so that (although generally small in terms of percentages) the induced change in aggregate values of all stocks will reinforce the induced change in the *relative* value of the $i^{\text{th}}$ stock; the fact that $\Delta \gamma$ also has the same sign introduces a countervailing feedback, but as shown above [note especially (29g)], this latter effect is of second order and cannot reverse the sign of the criterion we use. In view of the overwhelming informational requirements of determining the maximum of a fully inclusive criterion function which allowed formula induced adjustments external to the firm, *and* the fact our criterion is a monotone rising function of this ultimate ideal, the position in the text follows.

budgeting criterion. At first blush, a very complex *integer* quadratic-programming solution would seem to be required, but fortunately we can break the problem down inductively and find a valid formulation which can be solved in essentially the same manner as an individual investor's portfolio decision.

First, we note that if a single project $j$ is added to an existing body of assets $\bar{H}_o^0$, we have

$$(34a) \quad \Delta \bar{R}_i - \gamma \Delta \check{R}_{ii} = \bar{H}_j^{(1)} - r^* H_j^0 - \gamma [H_{jj} + 2\check{H}_{jo}] = X_j^{(1)} - \gamma [\check{X}_{jj} + 2\check{X}_{jo}].$$

Now suppose a project $k$ is also added. The total change from $j$ and $k$ *together* is

$$(34b) \quad (\Delta R_i - \gamma \Delta \check{R}_{ii}) = X_j^{(1)} + X_k^{(1)} - \gamma [\check{X}_{jj} + \check{X}_{kk} + 2\check{X}_{jo} + 2\check{X}_{ko} + 2\check{X}_{jk}],$$

while the *increment* due to adding $k$ *with $j$ already in the budget* is

$$(34c) \quad (\Delta R_i - \gamma \check{R}_{ii}) = \bar{X}_k^{(1)} - \gamma [\check{X}_{kk} + 2\check{X}_{ko} + 2\check{X}_{jk}].$$

Given the goal of maximizing the left side of (32), the $k^{\text{th}}$ project should be added to the budget (already provisionally containing $j$) *if and only if the right side of (34c) is $> 0$*—and if this condition is satisfied, the same test expression written for $j$, given inclusion of $k$, will show whether $j$ should stay in. Equation (34c), appropriately generalized to any number of projects, is thus a *necessary condition* to be satisfied by *each project in an optimal budget*, given the inclusion of all other projects simultaneously satisfying this condition.

The unstructured iterative or search procedure suggested by our two-project development can obviously be short-circuited by programming methods, and the integer aspect of the programming (in this situation) can conveniently be by-passed by assuming that the company may accept all or any fractional part $a_j$, $0 \le a_j \le 1$, of any project (since it turns out that all $a_j$ in the final solution will take on only limiting values). Finally, thanks to this latter fact, the objective of maximizing the left side of (32) is equivalent[53] to maximizing

$$(32') \quad Z = H_o^{(1)} + \sum_j a_j \bar{H}_j^{(1)} - r^* \sum_j a_j H_j^{(0)}$$

$$- \gamma \left[ \sum_j a_j \check{H}_{jj} + 2 \sum_j a_j \check{H}_{jo} + 2 \sum_{j \ne k \ne 0} a_j a_k \check{H}_{jk} \right]$$

$$= \bar{H}_o^{(1)} + \sum_j a_j \bar{X}_j - \gamma \left[ \sum_j a_j \check{X}_{jj} + 2 \sum_j a_j \check{X}_{jo} + 2 \sum_{j \ne k \ne 0} a_j a_k \check{X}_{jk} \right],$$

subject to the constraints that $0 \le a_j \le 1$ for all $a_j$, $j = 1, 2 \dots n$. Not only will all $a_j$ be binary variables in the solution, but the generalized form of the necessary condition (34c) will be given by the solution [see equation (37) below].

[53] For the reason given, the maximum of (32') is the same as it would be if (32') had been written in the more natural way using $a_i^2$ instead of $a_j$ as the coefficient of $\check{H}_{jj}$; the use of $a_j$ is required to make the form of (35') and (37) satisfy the requirement of (34c).

In order to maximize $Z$ in (32′) subject to the constraints on $a_j$, we let $q_j = 1 - a_j$ for convenience, and form the Lagrangian function

$$(35) \qquad \psi(a, \mu, \eta) = Z + \sum_j \mu_j a_j + \sum_j \eta_j q_j$$

which is to be maximized subject to $a_j \geq 0$, $q_i \geq 0$, $\mu_j \geq 0$, and $\eta_j \geq 0$, where $\mu_j$ and $\eta_j$ are the Lagrangian multipliers associated with the respective constraints $a_j \geq 0$ and $q_j \geq 0$. Using (33), we have immediately

$$(35') \qquad \frac{\partial \psi}{\partial a_j} \geq 0 \leftrightarrow \bar{X}_j - \gamma \left[ a_j \breve{X}_{jj} + 2 \sum_j a_j \breve{X}_{jo} + 2 \sum_{k \neq 0} a_k \breve{X}_{jk} \right] + \mu_j - \eta_j \geq 0.$$

Using the Kuhn-Tucker Theorem [9], the necessary and sufficient conditions for the optimal vector of investments $a_j^0$ which maximize $\psi$ in (35) are consequently[54]

$$(36a) \qquad \gamma \left[ a_j^0 X_{jj} + 2a_j^0 X_{jo} + 2 \sum_{k \neq j \neq 0} a_k^0 X_{jk} \right] - \mu_j^0 + \eta_j^0 = \bar{X}_j$$

when

$$(36b, c, d, e) \qquad a_j^0 \geq 0, \quad q_j^0 \geq 0,$$
$$\mu_j^0 \geq 0, \quad \eta_j^0 \geq 0$$

and

$$(36f, g) \qquad \mu_j^0 a_j^0 = 0, \quad \eta_j^0 q_j^0 = 0,$$

where

$$j = 1, 2 \dots n$$

in each set (36a)–(36g).

[54] The proof that the indicated solution satisfies the Kuhn-Tucker conditions with respect to the variables $a_j^0$ and $u_j^0$ is identical to that given above footnote 28 upon the substitution of $\underline{\underline{X}}$ for $\underline{\underline{x}}$, $a_j$ for $h_i$, and $\mu_j$ for $\mu_i$, and need not be repeated. The two additional *necessary* conditions are

$$(3') \qquad \left[ \frac{\partial \psi}{\partial \eta_j} \right]^0 \geq 0,$$

which is satisfied, since from (35) we have $\left[ \dfrac{\partial \psi}{\partial \eta_j} \right]^0 = g_j^0 \geq 0$ by virtue of (36c); and this latter relation shows that the corresponding complementary slackness condition,

$$(4') \qquad \mu_j^0 \left[ \frac{\partial \psi}{\partial \eta_j} \right]^0 = 0,$$

may be written $\mu_j^0 q_j^0 = 0$, and is therefore satisfied because of (36g).

All three sufficiency conditions are also satisfied because the variance-covariance matrix $\underline{\underline{X}}$ is positive definite, making $\psi(a, \underline{u}^0, \underline{n}^0)$ a concave function on $\underline{a}$ and $\psi(a, \underline{u}^0, \underline{n}^0)$ a convex function on both $u$ and $\underline{n}$.

Once again, these equations can be readily solved by the Wilson Simplicial Algorithm [23] on modern computing equipment. It may be observed that this formulation in terms of independent investment projects can readily be generalized to cover mutually exclusive, contingent, and compound projects[55] with no difficulty. It is also apparent that the absence of a financing constraint (due principally to our assumption that new riskless debt is available in unlimited amounts at a fixed rate $r^*$) insures that all projects will either be accepted or rejected *in toto*. All $a_j^0$ will be either 0 or 1, and the troublesome problems associated with fractional projects or recourse to integer (non-linear) programming do not arise.

Consider now the set of *accepted* projects, and denote this subset with asterisks. We then have all $a_{j*}^0 = a_{k*}^0 = 1$; the corresponding $\mu_{j*}^0 = \mu_{k*}^0 = 0$; and for any project $j^*$, the corresponding $\eta_{j*}^0 > 0$ (i.e. *strictly positive*),[56] and the number $\eta_{j*}^0$ is the "dual evaluator" or "shadow price" registering the *net gain* to the company *and* its shareholders of accepting the project. Rewriting the corresponding equation from (36a), we have[57]

$$(37) \qquad \eta_{j*}^0 = \bar{H}_{j*}^{(1)} - r^* H_{j*}^{(0)} - \gamma \left[ \breve{H}_{j*j*} + 2\breve{H}_{j*0} + 2 \sum_{k* \neq j* \neq 0} \breve{H}_{j*k*} \right] > 0.$$

Several important features and implications of these results should be emphasized. First of all, note that we have shown that *even* when uncertainty is admitted in only this highly simplified way, and when any effect of changes in capital budgets on the *covariances* between returns on different companies' *stocks* is ignored, the minimum expected return (in dollars of expected present value $\bar{H}_{j*}^{(1)}$) required to justify the allocation of funds to a given risky project costing a given sum $H_{j*}^0$ is an increasing function of each of the following factors: (*i*) the risk-free rate of return $r^*$; (*ii*) the "market price of dollar risk" $\gamma$; (*iii*) the variance $\breve{H}_{j*j*}$ in the project's own present value return; (*iv*) the project's aggregate present value return-covariance $\breve{H}_{j*0}$ with assets already held by the company, and (*v*) its total covariance $\sum_{k* \neq j* \neq 0} \breve{H}_{j*k*}$ with other projects concurrently included in the capital budget.

Second, it follows from this analysis that, if uncertainty is recognized to be an important fact of life, and risk-aversion is a significant property of relevant utility functions, appropriate *risk-variables* must be introduced *explicitly* into the analytical framework used in analysis, and that these risk-variables will be *essential components* of any optimal decision rules developed. Important insights can be, and have been, derived from "certainty" models, including some *qualitative* notions of the *conditional* effects of changes in

---

[55] See Weingartner [22], 11 and 32–34.

[56] We are of course here ignoring the very exceptional and coincidental case in which $\underline{n}_{j*}^0 = 0$ which implies that $a_{j*}^0$ is indeterminate in the range $0 \leq a_{0j} \leq 1$, the company being *totally indifferent* whether or not all (or any part) of a project is undertaken.

[57] We use $\breve{H}_{j*k*}$ to denote elements of the original covariance matrix $\underline{\underline{H}}$ *after* all rows and columns associated with rejected projects have been removed.

availability of funds due to fund-suppliers' reactions to uncertainty,[58] but such models ignore the decision-maker's problem of optimizing *his* investment decisions in the face of the stochastic character of the outcomes among which *he* must choose.

Third, it is clear that *stochastic considerations are a primary source of interdependencies among projects*, and these must *also enter explicitly* into optimal decision rules. In particular, note that, although own-variances are necessarily positive and subtracted in equation (37), the net gain $n_{j*}^0$ may still be positive and justify acceptance *even if* the expected end-of-period "excess" present-value return $(\check{X}_{j*}^{(1)} = \overline{H}_{j*}^{(1)} - r^* H_{j*}^{(0)})$ is negative[59]—so long as its total present-value-covariances $(\check{H}_{j*0} + \sum_{k* \neq j* \neq 0} \check{H}_{j*k*})$ are also negative and sufficiently large. *Sufficiently risk-reducing investments rationally belong in corporate capital budgets even at the expense of lowering expected present value returns*—an important (and realistic) feature of rational capital budgeting procedure not covered (nor even implied) in traditional analyses.

Fourth, note that, as would by now be expected, for any fixed $r^*$ and $\gamma$, the net gain from a project is a *linear* function of its (present value) *variance* and *covariances* with existing company assets and concurrent projects. Standard deviations are not involved except as a component of (co)variances.

Fifth, the fact that the risk of a project involves all the elements in the bracketed term in (37), including covariances with other concurrent projects, indicates that in practice it will often be extremely difficult, if not impossible, to classify *projects* into respectively homogeneous "risk classes." The practice is convenient (and desirable where it does not introduce significant bias) but our analysis shows it is *not essential*, and the considerations which follow show it to be *a dangerous expedient which is positively misleading as generally employed* in the literature.

Sixth, it must be emphasized that—following the requirements of the market equilibrium conditions (29) from which equations (36), (37), and (38) were derived—*all means and (co)variances of present values have been calculated using the riskless rate $r^*$.* In this connection, recall the non-linear effect on present values of varying the discount rate used in this computation. Also remember the further facts that (*i*) the means and variances of the distributions of present values computed at different discount rates do not vary in proportion to each other when different discount rates are applied to the same set of future stochastic cash flow data, and that (*ii*) the changes induced in the means and variances of the present values of different projects having different patterns and durations of future cash flows will also differ greatly as discount rates are altered. From these considerations alone, it necessarily follows that *there can be no single "risk discount rate"* to use in computing

---

[58] See Weingartner [22] and works there cited. Weingartner would, of course, agree with the conclusion stated here, see pp. 193–194.

[59] Indeed, in extreme cases, a project should be accepted even if the expected end-of-period present value $\overline{H}_{j*}^{(1)}$ is less than cost $H_{j*}^{(0)}$, provided negative correlations with existing assets and other concurrent investments are sufficiently strong and negative.

present values for the purpose of deciding on the acceptance or rejection of *different individual projects* out of a subset of projects *even if all projects in the subset have the same degree of "risk."*[60] The same conclusion follows *a fortiori* among projects with different risks.

Seventh, the preceding considerations, again *a fortiori*, *insure that even if all new projects have the same degree of "risk" as existing assets, the "cost of capital"* (as defined for uncertainty *anywhere* in the literature) *is not the appropriate discount rate to use in accept-reject decisions on individual projects* for capital budgeting.[61] This is true whether the "cost of capital" is to be used as a "hurdle rate" (which the "expected return" must exceed) *or* as a discount rate in obtaining present values of net cash inflows and outflows.

Perhaps at this point the reader should be reminded of the rather heroic set of simplifying assumptions which were made at the beginning of this section. One consequence of the unreality of these assumptions is, clearly, that the results are not being presented as directly applicable to practical decisions at this stage. Too many factors that matter very significantly have been left out (or assumed away). But the very simplicity of the assumptions has enabled us to develop rigorous proofs of the above propositions which do differ substantially from current treatments of "capital budgeting under uncertainty." A little reflection should convince the reader that *all the above conclusions will still hold under more realistic (complex) conditions.*

Since we have shown that selection of individual projects to go in a capital budget under uncertainty by means of "risk-discount" rates (or by the so-called "cost of capital") is fundamentally in error, we should probably note that the decision criteria given by the solutions of equation (36) [and the acceptance condition (37)]—which directly involve the means and variances of present values computed at the riskless rate—do have a valid counterpart in the form of a "required expected rate of return." Specifically, if we let $[\Sigma \breve{H}_{j*}]$ represent the entire bracket in equation (37), and divide through by the original cost of the project $H_{j*}^{(0)}$, we have

$$(38) \qquad \overline{H}_{j*}^{(1)}/H_{j*}^{(0)} = r_{j*} > r^* + \gamma[\sum \breve{H}_{j*}]/H_{j*}^{(0)}.$$

Now the ratio of the expected *end-of-period* present value $\overline{H}_{j*}^{(1)}$ to the initial cost $H_{j*}^{(0)}$—i.e. the left side of (38), which we write $r_{j*}$—is precisely (the

---

[60] Note as a corollary, it also follows that *even if* the world were simple enough that a single "as if" risk-discount rate could in principle be found, the same considerations insure that *there can be no simple function relating the appropriate "risk-discount" rate to the riskless rate r\* and "degree of risk,"* however measured. But especially in this context, it must be emphasized that a single risk-discount rate *would produce non-optimal choices* among projects *even if* (i) all projects could be assigned to meaningful risk-classes, *unless* it were also true that (ii) all projects had the same (actual) time-pattern of net cash flows and the same life (which is a condition having probability measure zero under uncertainty!).

[61] Note particularly that, even though we are operating under assumptions which validate Modigliani and Miller's propositions I and II, and the form of finance is *not* relevant to the choice of projects, we nevertheless cannot accept their use of their $\rho_k$—their cost of capital—as the relevant discount rate.

expected value of) what Lutz called the *net* short term marginal efficiency of the investment [13, p. 159]. We can thus say that the *minimum acceptable expected rate of return* on a project is a (positively sloped) linear function of the ratio of the project's *aggregate incremental* present-value-variance-covariance $(\Sigma \breve{H}_{j*})$ to its cost $H_{j*}^{(0)}$. The slope coefficient is still the "market price of dollar risk," $\gamma$, and the intercept is the risk-free rate $r^*$. (It will be observed that our "accept-reject" rule for individual projects under uncertainty thus reduces to Lutz' rule under certainty—as it should—since with certainty the right-hand ratio term is zero.) To avoid misunderstanding and misuse of this relation, however, several further observations must be emphasized.

*a*) Equation (38)—like equation (37) from which it was derived—states a necessary condition of the (Kuhn-Tucker) optimum with respect to the projects selected. It may validly be *used to choose* the desirable projects out of the larger set of *possible* projects *if the covariances among potential projects* $\breve{H}_{j \neq k \neq 0}$ are all zero.[62] *Otherwise, a programming solution of equation set* (36) *is required*[63] *to find which subset of projects* $H_{j*}$ satisfy either (37) or (38), essentially because the total variance of any project $[\Sigma \breve{H}_j]$ is dependent on which other projects are *concurrently included* in the budget.

*b*) Although the risk-free rate $r^*$ enters equation (38) *explicitly* only as the intercept [or constant in the linear (in)equation form], it must be emphasized again that it *also enters implicitly as the discount rate used in computing the means and variances of all present values which appear* in the (in)equation. *In consequence, (i) any shift* in the value $r^*$ *changes every term* in the function; (*ii*) the changes in $\bar{H}_{j*}^{(1)}$ and $\Sigma \breve{H}_{j*}$ are *non-linear and non-proportional* to each other.[64] Since (*iii*) any shift in the value of $r^*$ changes *every covariance* in equation (36a) *non-proportionately*, (*iv*) the *optimal subset of projects* $j^*$ is *not invariant* to a change in the risk-free rate $r^*$. Therefore (*v*), *in principle, any shift in the value of* $r^*$ *requires a new programming solution of the entire set of equations* (36).

*c*) Even for a predetermined and fixed $r^*$, and even with respect only to *included* projects, the condition expressed in (38) is rigorously *valid only under the full set* of simplifying assumptions stated at the beginning of this section. In addition, the programming solution of equation (36), and its derivative property (38), *simultaneously determines both the optimal composition and the optimal size* of the capital budget *only under this full set* of simplifying assumptions. Indeed, even if the twin assumptions of a fixed riskless rate $r^*$ and of formally unlimited borrowing opportunities at this

---

[62] Note that covariances $\breve{H}_{j0}$ with *existing* assets need not be zero since they are independent of other projects and may be combined with the own-variance $\breve{H}_{jj}$.

[63] In strict theory, an iterative *exhaustive* search over *all possible* combinations *could* obviate the programming procedure, but the number of combinations would be very large in practical problems, and economy dictates programming methods.

[64] This statement is true *even if* the set of projects $j^*$ were invariant to a change in $r^*$ which in general will not be the case, as noted in the following text statement.

rate are retained,[65] *but* other assumptions are (realistically) generalized— specifically to permit expected returns on new investments at any time to depend in part on investments made in prior periods, and to make the "entity value" in part a function of the finance mix used—*then* the (set of) programming solutions merely determines the optimal *mix or composition* of the capital budget *conditional* on each possible aggregate budget size and risk.[66] Given the resulting "investment opportunity function"—which is the three-dimensional Markowitz-type envelope of efficient sets of projects—the optimal capital budget size and risk can be determined directly by market criteria (as developed in [11] and [12])[67] but will depend explicitly on concurrent financing decisions (e.g. retentions and leverage).[68]

## VI.  SOME IMPLICATIONS OF MORE RELAXED ASSUMPTIONS

We have come a fairly long way under a progressively larger set of restrictive assumptions. The purpose of the exercise has not been to provide results *directly* applicable to practical decisions at this stage—too much (other than uncertainty *per se*) that matters greatly in practice has been assumed away— but rather to develop rigorously some of the fundamental implications of uncertainty *as such* for an important class of decisions about which there has been much confusion in the theoretical literature. The more negative conclusions reached—such as, for instance, the serious distortions inherently involved in the prevalent use of a "risk-discount rate" or a "company-risk-class" "cost-of-capital" for project selection in capital budgeting—clearly will hold under more general conditions, as will the primary role under uncertainty of the *risk-free rate* (whether used to calculate *distributions* of present values *or* to form *present values of certainty-equivalents*). But others of our more affirmative results, and especially the particular equations

---

[65] If these assumptions are not retained, the position *and* composition of the investment opportunity function (defined immediately below in the text) are themselves dependent on the relevant discount rate, for the reasons given in the "sixth" point above and the preceding paragraph. (See also Lutz [13, p. 160].) Optimization then requires the solution of a much different and more complex set of (in)equations, simultaneously encompassing finance-mix *and* investment mix.

[66] This stage of the analysis corresponds, in the standard "theory of the firm," to the determination of the optimal mix of factors for each possible scale.

[67] I should note here, however, that on the basis of the above analysis, the correct *marginal expected* rate of return for the investment opportunity function should be the value of $r_j^*$ [see left side equation (38) above] for the marginally included project at each budget size, i.e. the ratio of end-of-period present value computed at the riskless rate $r^*$ to the project cost—rather than the different rate (generally used by other authors) stated in [12, p. 54 top]. Correspondingly, the relevant *average* expected return is the same ratio computed for the budget as a whole. Correspondingly, the relevant *variance* is the variance of this ratio. None of the subsequent analysis or results of [12] are affected by this corrected specification of the inputs to the investment opportunity function.

[68] This latter solution determines the optimal point on the investment opportunity function at which to operate. The optimal *mix* of projects to include in the capital budget is that which corresponds to the optimal point on the investment opportunity function.

developed, are just as clearly inherently conditional on the simplifying assumptions which have been made. While it would be out of place to undertake any exhaustive inventory here, we should nevertheless note the impact of relaxing certain key assumptions upon some of these other conclusions.

The particular formulas in sections II–V depend *inter-alia* on the *Separation Theorem* and each investor's consequent preference for the stock *mix* which maximizes $\theta$. Recall that in proving the Separation Theorem in section I we assumed that the investor could borrow unlimited amounts at the rate $r^*$ equal to the rate on savings deposits. Four alternatives to this assumption may be considered briefly. (1) *Borrowing Limits:* The Theorem (and the subsequent development) holds *provided* that the margin requirements turn out not to be binding; but if the investor's utility function is such that, given the portfolio which maximizes $\theta$, he prefers a $w$ greater than is permitted, *then* the Theorem does not hold and the utility function must be used explicitly to determine the optimal stock mix.[69] (2) *Borrowing rate $r^{**}$ greater than " lending rate " $r^*$:* (a) If the max $\theta$ using $r^*$ implies a $w < 1$, the theorem holds in original form; (b) if the max $\theta$ using $r^*$ implies $w > 1$ *and* (upon recomputation) the max $\theta$ using $r^{**}$ in equations (3b), (7) and (8) implies $w > 1$, the theorem also holds but $r^{**}$ (rather than $r^*$) *must be used* in sections II–V; (c) if max $\theta$ using $r^*$ implies $w > 1$ and max $\theta$ using $r^{**}$ implies $w < 1$, *then* there will be no borrowing *and* the utility function must be used explicitly to determine the optimal stock mix.[70] (3) *Borrowing rate an increasing function of leverage* $(w - 1)$: The theorem still holds under condition (2a) above, but if max $\theta$ using $r^*$ implies $w > 1$ *then the optimal mix and the optimal financing must be determined simultaneously using the utility function* explicitly.[71] (4) The latter conclusion also follows immediately *if the borrowing rate is not independent of the stock mix.*

The *qualitative* conclusions of sections II and III hold even if the Separation Theorem does not, but the formulas would be much more complex. Similarly, the stock market equilibrium in section IV—and the parameters used for capital budgeting decisions in section V—will be altered if different investors in the market are affected differently by the " real world " considerations in the preceding paragraph (because of different utility functions, or probability assessments), or by differential tax rates. Note also that even if all our original assumptions through section IV are accepted for investors, the results in section V would have to be modified to allow for all real world complications in the cost and availability of debt and the tax treatment of debt interest versus other operating income. Finally, although explicitly ruled out in section V, it must be recalled that " limited liability," legal or other institutional restrictions or premiums, or the presence of " market risk " (as distinct from default risk) on corporate debt, *are sufficient both* to make the optimal *project mix* in the capital budget *conditional* on the finance mix (notably

---

[69] See appendix, note III.
[70] See appendix, note IV.
[71] See appendix, note V.

retentions and leverage), *and* the finance mix itself *also* something to be optimized.

Obviously, the need for further work on all these topics is great. The present paper will have succeeded in its essential purpose if it has rigorously pushed back the frontiers of theoretical understanding, and opened the doors to more fruitful theoretical and applied work.

## APPENDIX

### NOTE I—ALTERNATIVE PROOF OF SEPARATION THEOREM AND ITS COROLLARIES

In this note, I present an alternative proof of the *Separation Theorem* and its corollaries using utility functions explicitly. Some readers may prefer this form, since it follows traditional theory more closely.

Let $\bar{y}$ and $\sigma_y$ be the expected value and variance of the rate of return on any asset mixture and $A_0$ be the amount of the investor's total net investment. Given the assumptions regarding the market and the investor, stated in the text, the investor will seek to maximize the expected utility of a function which can be written in general form as

$$(1') \qquad E[U(A_0\bar{y}, A_0\sigma_y)] = \bar{U}(A_0\bar{y}, A_0\sigma_y),$$

subject to his investment opportunities characterized by the risk-free rate $r^*$, at which he can invest in savings deposits or borrow any amount he desires, and by the set of all stock mixes available to him, each of which in turn is represented by a pair of values $(\bar{r}, \sigma_r)$. Our assumptions establish the following properties[72] of the utility function in $(1')$:

$$(1a') \qquad \begin{cases} \partial U/\partial \bar{y} = A_0 \bar{U}_1 > 0; \quad \partial \bar{U}/\partial \sigma_y = A_0 \bar{U}_2 < 0; \\[2mm] \left. \dfrac{d\bar{y}}{d\sigma_y} \right|_U = -\bar{U}_2/\bar{U}_1 > 0; \quad \left. \dfrac{d^2\bar{y}}{d\sigma_y^2} \right|_U > 0. \end{cases}$$

Also, with the assumptions we have made,[73] all available stock mixes will lie *in a finite region* all parts of which are strictly to the right of the vertical axis in the $\sigma_r$, $r$ plane since all available mixes will have positive variance. The boundary of this region will be a closed curve[74] and the region is convex.[75]

---

[72] For formal proof of these properties, see Tobin, [21], pp. 72–77.

[73] Specifically, that the amount invested in any stock in any stock mix is infinitely divisible, that all expected returns on individual stocks are finite, that all variances are positive and finite, and that the variance-covariance matrix is positive-definite.

[74] Markowitz [14] has shown that, in general, this closed curve will be made up of successive hyperbolic segments which are strictly tangent at points of overlap.

[75] Harry Markowitz, [14], chapter VII. The shape of the boundary follows from the fact that the point corresponding to any mix (in positive proportions summing to one) of any two points on the boundary lies to the left of the straight line joining those two points; and all points on and within the boundary belong to the set of available $(\sigma_r, \bar{r})$ pairs because any such point corresponds to an appropriate combination in positive proportions of at least one pair of points on the boundary.

Moreover, since $\bar{U}_1 > 0$ and $\bar{U}_2 < 0$ in (1a'), all mixes within this region are dominated by those whose $(\sigma_r, r)$ values lie on the part of the boundary associated with values of $\bar{r} > 0$, *and* for which changes in $\sigma_r$ and $\bar{r}$ are positively associated. This is Markowitz' Efficient Set or " E-V " Frontier. We may write its equation[76] as

(2') $$\bar{r} = f(\sigma_r), \quad f'(\sigma_r) > 0, \quad f''(\sigma_r) < 0.$$

Substituting (2') in (2) and (3) in the text, we find the first order conditions for the maximization of (1) subject to (2), (3), and (2') to be given by the equalities in

(3a') $$\partial \bar{U}/\partial w = \bar{U}_1(\bar{r} - r^*) + \bar{U}_2\sigma_r \geqq 0.$$

(3b') $$\partial \bar{U}/\partial \sigma_r = \bar{U}_1 w f'(\sigma) + \bar{U}_2 w \geqq 0.$$

which immediately reduce to the two equations [using (3a) from the text]

(4') $$\theta = -\bar{U}_2/\bar{U}_1 = f'(\sigma_r).$$

Second order conditions for a maximum are satisfied because of the concavity of (1') and (2'). The Separation Theorem follows immediately from (4') when we note that the equation of the first and third members $\theta = f'(\sigma)$ *is precisely the condition for the maximization*[77] *of $\theta$*, since

(5a') $$\frac{\partial \theta}{\partial \sigma_r} = \frac{\sigma_r[f'(\sigma_r)] - [\bar{r} - r^*]}{\sigma_r^2} = \frac{f'(\sigma_r) - \theta}{\sigma_r}$$

(5b') $$\frac{\partial^2 \theta}{\partial(\sigma_r)^2} = \frac{\sigma_r f''(\sigma_r) + [f'(\sigma_r) - \theta] - [f'(\sigma_r) - \theta]}{\sigma_r^2}$$

$$= f''(\sigma_r)/\sigma_r < 0 \text{ for all } \sigma_r > 0$$

A necessary condition for the maximization of (1') is consequently the maximization of $\theta$ (as asserted), which is independent of $w$. The value of $(-\bar{U}_2/\bar{U}_1)$, however, directly depends on $w$ (for *any* given value of $\theta$), and a second necessary condition for the maximization of $\bar{U}$ is that $w$ be adjusted to bring this value $(-\bar{U}_2/\bar{U}_1)$ into equality with $\theta$, thereby satisfying the usual tangency condition between utility contours and the market opportunity function (3) in the text. These two necessary conditions are also *sufficient* because of the concavity of (1') and the positive-definite property of the matrix of risk-investment opportunities. Q.E.D.

---

[76] Note that the stated conditions on *the* derivatives in (2') hold even in the exceptional cases of discontinuity. Markowitz [14], p. 153.

[77] This conclusion clearly holds even in the exceptional cases (noted in the preceding footnote) in which the derivatives of $r = f(\sigma_r)$ are not continuous. Equation (3a') will hold as an exact equality because of the continuity of the utility function, giving $\theta = -\bar{U}_2/\bar{U}_1$. By equation (3b'), expected utility $\bar{U}$ increases with $\sigma_r$ for all $f'(\sigma) \geqq -\bar{U}_2/\bar{U}_1 = \theta$, and the max $\sigma_r$ consistent with $f'(\sigma) \geqq \theta$ maximizes $\theta$ by equation (5a').

NOTE II

*a*) Indifference Contours Between $x_i$ and $\sigma_i^2$ When all $\sigma_{ij}$ are Constant

The conclusion that the indifference contour between $\bar{x}_i$ and the variance $\sigma_i^2$ is *linear* in the general case when all covariances $\sigma_{ij}$ are held constant can best be established by totally differentiating the equilibrium conditions (12) in the text [or the equivalent set (22a) restricted to the $m'$ stocks held in the portfolio] which yields the set of equations

$$\lambda^0 \sigma_1^2 \, dh_1^0 + \lambda^0 \sigma_{12} \, dh_2^0 + \cdots + \lambda^0 \sigma_1 \, dh_i^0 +$$

$$\cdots + \lambda^0 \sigma_{1m'} \, dh_{m'}^0 + \frac{\bar{x}_1}{\lambda^0} \, d\lambda^0 = 0$$

$$\vdots$$

(6)
$$\lambda^0 \sigma_{i1}^0 \, dh_1^0 + \lambda^0 \sigma_{i2} \, dh_2^0 + \cdots + \lambda^0 \sigma_i^2 \, dh_i^0 +$$

$$\cdots + \lambda^0 \sigma_{im'} \, dh_{m'}^0 + \frac{\bar{x}_i}{\lambda^0} \, d\lambda^0 = dx_i - \lambda^0 h_i \, d\sigma_i^2$$

$$\vdots$$

$$\lambda^0 \sigma_{m'1} \, dh_1^0 + \lambda^0 \sigma_{m'2} \, dh_2^0 + \cdots + \lambda^0 \sigma_{m'i} \, dh_i^0 +$$

$$\cdots + \lambda^0 \sigma_{m'}^2 \, dh_{m'}^0 + \frac{\bar{x}_{m'}}{\lambda^0} \, d\lambda^0 = 0$$

$$dh_1^0 + dh_2^0 + \cdots + dh_i^0 + \cdots + dh_{m'}^0 = 0$$

Denoting the coefficient matrix on the left by $\underline{\underline{H}}$, and the $i$, $j^{\text{th}}$ element of its inverse by $H^{ij}$, we have by Cramer's rule,

(6a')
$$dh_i^0 = (d\bar{x}_i - \lambda^0 h_i^0 \, d\sigma_i^2)H^{ii}.$$

Since $\underline{\underline{H}}$ is non-singular $h_i^0$ will be constant along an indifference contour if and only if

(6b')
$$d\bar{x}_i = \lambda^0 h_i^0 \, d\sigma_i^2.$$

The indifference contour is strictly linear because the slope coefficient $\lambda^0 h_i^0$ is invariant to the absolute levels of $\bar{x}_i$ and $\sigma_i^2$ when $h_i^0$ is constant, as may be seen by noting that

(6c')
$$d\lambda_0^0 = (d\bar{x}_i - \lambda^0 h_i^0 \, d\sigma_i^2)H^{i\lambda 0}$$

so that

(6d')
$$dh_i^0 = 0 \rightarrow d\lambda_i^0 = 0,$$

when only $\bar{x}_i$ and $\sigma_i^2$ are varied. Moreover, any pair of changes $d\bar{x}_i$ and $d\sigma_i^2$ which hold $dh_i^0 = 0$ by (6a' and b')) imply *no change* in the relative holding $h_j^0$ of *any other* security, since $dh_j^0 = (d\bar{x}_i - \lambda^0 h_i^0 d\sigma_i^2)H^{ij} = 0$ for all $j \neq i$ when $dh_i^0 = 0$. Consequently, *all* pairs of values of $\bar{x}_i$ and $\sigma_i^2$ along the linear indifference contour which holds $h_i^0$ fixed at some given level rigorously imply that the proportionate mix of *all other* stocks in the portfolio is *also unchanged* —as was also to be shown.

*b*) Indifference Contours Between $x_i$ and $\sigma_i$ When $\rho$ Constant

If the equilibrium conditions (12) are differentiated totally to determine the indifference contours between $\bar{x}_i$ and $\sigma_i$, the left-hand side of equations (6′) above will be unaffected, but the right side will be changed as follows: In the $i^{\text{th}}$ equation

$$d\bar{x}_i - \lambda^0\left[2h_i^0\sigma_i - \sum_{j\neq i} h_j^0\sigma_j\rho_{ij}\right] d\sigma_i = d\bar{x}_i - \lambda^0(h_i^0\sigma_i - \bar{x}_i/\sigma_i)\, d\sigma_i$$

replaces $d\bar{x}_i - \lambda^0 h_i^0 d\sigma_i^2$; the last equation is unchanged; and in all other equations $-\lambda^0 h_i^0\sigma_j\rho_{ij}d\sigma_i$ replaces 0. We then have

(7a′)  $$dh_i^0 = \left[d\bar{x}_i - \lambda^0(h_i^0\sigma_i - \bar{x}_i/\sigma_i)\, d\sigma_i\right]H^{ii} - \lambda^0 h_i^0 \sum_{j\neq i} \sigma_j\rho_{ij}\, H^{ij}d\sigma_i;$$

(7b′)  $$dh_j^0 = [d\bar{x}_i - \lambda^0(h_i^0\sigma_i - \bar{x}_i/\sigma_i)\, d\sigma_i]H^{ij} - \lambda^0 h_i^0 \sum_{K\neq i} \sigma_K\rho_{iK}H^{jK}\, d\sigma_i;$$

(7c′)  $$d\lambda^0 = [d\bar{x}_i - \lambda^0(h_i^0\sigma_i - \bar{x}_i/\sigma_i)\, d\sigma_i]H^{i\lambda 0} - \lambda^0 h_i \sum_{K\neq i} \sigma_K\rho_{iK}H^{\lambda 0K}\, d\sigma_i.$$

Clearly, in this case, $dh_i^0 = 0$ does *not* imply $dh_j^0 = 0$, *nor* does it imply $d\lambda^0 = 0$.

NOTE III—BORROWING LIMITS EFFECTIVE

In principle, in this case the investor must compute all the Markowitz efficient boundary segment joining $M$ (which maximizes $\theta$ in figure 1) to the point $N$ corresponding to the greatest attainable $\bar{r}$. Given the fixed margin $w$, he must then project all points on this original (unlevered) efficient set (see equation (2′) above) to determine the new (levered) efficient set of $(\sigma_y, \bar{y})$ pairs

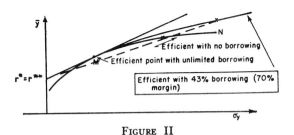

FIGURE II

attainable by using equations (2a, b) in the text; and he will then choose the $(\sigma_y, \bar{y})$ pair from this latter set which maximizes utility. With concave utility functions this optimum $(\sigma_y, \bar{y})$ pair will satisfy the standard optimizing tangency conditions between the (recomputed) efficient set and the utility function. The situation is illustrated in figure 2.

NOTE IV—BORROWING RATE $r^{**}$ IS HIGHER THAN LENDING RATE $r^*$

The conclusions stated in the text are obvious from the graph of this case (which incidentally is *formally* identical to Hirshleifer's treatment of the same case under certainty in [7]). The optimum depends uniquely upon the utility function if it is tangent to the efficient set with no borrowing in the range $MM'$.

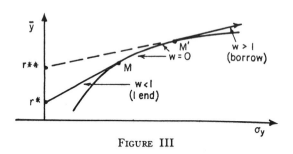

FIGURE III

NOTE V—BORROWING RATE IS DEPENDENT ON LEVERAGE

With $r^{**} = g(w)$, $g'(w) > 0$, and when the optimum $w > 1$ so that borrowing is undertaken, $\theta$ itself from equation (3) in the text becomes a function of $w$, which we will write $\theta(w)$. The optimizing equations, corresponding to (3'a, b) above in note I, then become

(6a')
$$\partial \overline{U}/\partial w = \overline{U}_1[(r - r^{**}) - wg'(w)] + \overline{U}_2 \sigma_r \geq 0$$

(6b')
$$\partial \overline{U}/\partial \sigma_r = \overline{U}_1 wf'(\sigma) + \overline{U}_2 w \geq 0$$

which reduce to the two equations

(7')
$$\theta(w) - wg'(w)/\sigma_r = -\overline{U}_2/\overline{U}_1 = f'(\sigma).$$

The equation of the first and third members $\theta(w) - wg'(w)/\sigma_r = f'(\sigma)$ is *no longer* equal to the *maximization* of $\theta$ itself, *nor* is the solution of this equation *independent* of $w$ which is required for the validity of the Separation Theorem. It follows that the selection of the optimal stock mix (indexed by $\theta$) and of $w$ *simultaneously depend upon the parameter of the utility function* (and, with normal distribution, *also* upon its *form*).   Q.E.D.

BIBLIOGRAPHY

1. Arrow, Kenneth, "Comment on the Portfolio Approach to the Demand for Money and Other Assets," *The Review of Economics and Statistics, Supplement*, XLV (Feb., 1963), 24–27.

2. Baumol, William J., "An Expected Gain-Confidence Limit Criterion for Portfolio Selection," *Management Science*, X (Oct., 1963), 174–82.

3a. Dorfman, Robert, "Basic Economic and Technologic Concepts" in Arthur Maass *et al., Design of Water-Resource Systems* (Cambridge, Harvard University Press, 1962).

3b. Farrar, Donald E., *The Investment Decision Under Uncertainty* (Englewood Cliffs, N.J., Prentice-Hall, 1962).

4. Fisher, Irving, *The Theory of Interest* (New York, 1930).

5. Gordon, Myron J., *The Investment, Financing and Valuation of the Corporation* (Homewood, Illinois: Richard D. Irwin, 1962).

6. Hicks, J. R., "Liquidity," *The Economic Journal*, LXXII (Dec., 1962).

7. Hirshleifer, Jack, "On the Theory of Optimal Investment Decision," *Journal of Political Economy*, LXVI (Aug., 1958).

8. Hirshleifer, Jack, "Risk, the Discount Rate, and Investment Decisions," *American Economic Review*, LI (May, 1961).

9. Kuhn, H. W., and A. W. Tucker, "Nonlinear Programming" in J. Neyman ed., *Proceedings of the Second Berkeley Symposium on Mathematical Statistics and Probability* (Berkeley: University of California Press, 1951), 481–492.

10. Lintner, John, "Dividends, Earnings, Leverage, Stock Prices and the Supply of Capital to Corporations," *Review of Economics and Statistics*, XLIV (August, 1962).

11. Lintner, John, "The Cost of Capital and Optimal Financing of Corporate Growth," *The Journal of Finance*, XVIII (May, 1963).

12. Lintner, John, "Optimal Dividends and Corporate Growth Under Uncertainty," *The Quarterly Journal of Economics*, LXXVIII (Feb., 1964).

13. Lutz, Frederick and Vera, *The Theory of Investment of the Firm* (Princeton, 1951).

14. Markowitz, Harry, *Portfolio Selection* (New York, 1959).

15. Modigliani, Franco and Miller, Merton, "The Cost of Capital, Corporation Finance and the Theory of Investment," *American Economic Review*, XLVIII (June, 1958).

16. Modigliani, Franco and Miller, Merton, "Dividend Policy, Growth and the Valuation of Shares," *Journal of Business*, XXXIV (Oct., 1961).

17. Pratt, John W., "Risk Aversion in the Small and in the Large," *Econometrica*, XXXIII (Jan.–April, 1964), 122–136.

18. Robbins, Sidney M., *Managing Securities* (Boston: Houghton Mifflin Co., 1954).

19. Roy, A. D., "Safety First and the Holding of Assets," *Econometrica*, XX (July, 1952), 431–449.

20. Sharpe, William F., "A Simplified Model for Portfolio Analysis," *Management Science*, IX (Jan., 1963), 277–293.

21. Tobin, James, "Liquidity Preference as Behavior Toward Risk," *Review of Economic Studies*, XXVI (Feb., 1958), 65–86.

22. Weingartner, H. Martin, *Mathematical Programming and the Analysis of Capital Budgeting Problems* (Englewood Cliffs, New Jersey: Prentice-Hall, 1963).

23. Wilson, Robert B., *A Simplicial Algorithm for Concave Programming* (unpublished D.B.A. thesis, Harvard Business School, 1963).

## 15. EQUILIBRIUM IN A CAPITAL ASSET MARKET[1]

JAN MOSSIN[2]*

Reprinted by permission of the author and publisher from *Econometrica*, Vol. 34, No. 4 (October 1966), pp. 768–83.

This paper investigates the properties of a market for risky assets on the basis of a simple model of general equilibrium of exchange, where individual investors seek to maximize preference functions over expected yield and variance of yield on their portfolios. A theory of market risk premiums is outlined, and it is shown that general equilibrium implies the existence of a so-called "market line," relating per dollar expected yield and standard deviation of yield. The concept of price of risk is discussed in terms of the slope of this line.

## 1. INTRODUCTION

In recent years several studies have been made of the problem of selecting optimal portfolios of risky assets ([6, 8], and others). In these models the investor is assumed to possess a preference ordering over all possible port-folios and to maximize the value of this preference ordering subject to a budget restraint, taking the prices and probability distributions of yield for the various available assets as given data.

From the point of view of positive economics, such decision rules can, of course, be postulated as implicitly describing the individual's demand schedules for the different assets at varying prices. It would then be a natural next step to enquire into the characteristics of the whole market for such assets when the individual demands are interacting to determine the prices and the allocation of the existing supply of assets among individuals.

These problems have been discussed, among others, by Allais [1], Arrow [2], Borch [3], Sharpe [7], and also to some extent by Brownlee and Scott [5].

Allais' model represents in certain respects a generalization relative to the model to be discussed here. In particular, Allais does not assume general risk aversion. This generalization requires, on the other hand, certain other assumptions that we shall not need in order to lead to definite results.

Arrow's brief but important paper is also on a very general and even ab-

[1] Revised manuscript received December, 1965.

[2] The author is indebted to Karl Borch, Jacques Drèze, and Sten Thore for their valuable comments and suggestions.

* The Norwegian School of Economics and Business Administration.

stract level. He uses a much more general preference structure than we do here and also allows differences in individual perceptions of probability distributions. He then proves that under certain assumptions there exists a competitive equilibrium which is also Pareto optimal.

Borch has investigated the problem with special reference to a reinsurance market. He suggests, however, that his analysis can be reversed and extended to a more general market for risky assets. The present paper may be seen as an attempt in that direction. The general approach is different in important respects, however, particularly as concerns the price concept used. Borch's price implies in our terms that the price of a security should depend only on the stochastic nature of the yield, not on the number of securities outstanding. This may be accounted for by the particular characteristics of a reinsurance market, where such a price concept seems more reasonable than is the case for a security market. A rational person will not buy securities on their own merits without considering alternative investments. The failure of Borch's model to possess a Pareto optimal solution appears to be due to this price concept.

Generality has its virtues, but it also means that there will be many questions to which definite answers cannot be given. To obtain definite answers, we must be willing to impose certain restrictive assumptions. This is precisely what our paper attempts to do, and it is believed that this makes it possible to come a long way towards providing a theory of the market risk premium and filling the gap between demand functions and equilibrium properties.

Brownlee and Scott specify equilibrium conditions for a security market very similar to those given here, but are otherwise concerned with entirely different problems. The paper by Sharpe gives a verbal-diagrammatical discussion of the determination of asset prices in quasi-dynamic terms. His general description of the character of the market is similar to the one presented here, however, and his main conclusions are certainly consistent with ours. But his lack of precision in the specification of equilibrium conditions leaves parts of his arguments somewhat indefinite. The present paper may be seen as an attempt to clarify and make precise some of these points.

## 2. THE EQUILIBRIUM MODEL

Our general approach is one of determining conditions for *equilibrium of exchange* of the assets. Each individual brings to the market his present holdings of the various assets, and an exchange takes place. We want to know what the prices must be in order to satisfy demand schedules and also fulfill the condition that supply and demand be equal for all assets. To answer this question we must first derive relations describing individual demand. Second, we must incorporate these relations in a system describing general equilibrium. Finally, we want to discuss properties of this equilibrium.

We shall assume that there is a large number $m$ of individuals labeled $i$, $(i = 1, 2, \ldots, m)$. Let us consider the behavior of one individual. He has to select a portfolio of assets, and there are $n$ different assets to choose from, labeled $j$, $(j = 1, 2, \ldots, n)$. The yield on any asset is assumed to be a random variable whose distribution is known to the individual. Moreover, all individuals are assumed to have identical perceptions of these probability distributions.[3] The yield on a whole portfolio is, of course, also a random variable. The portfolio analyses mentioned earlier assume that, in his choice among all the possible portfolios, the individual is satisfied to be guided by its expected yield and its variance only. This assumption will also be made in the present paper.[4]

It is important to make precise the description of a portfolio in these terms. It is obvious (although the point is rarely made explicit) that the holdings of the various assets must be measured in some kind of units. The Markowitz analysis, for example, starts by picturing the investment alternatives open to the individual as a point set in a mean-variance plane, each point representing a specific investment opportunity. The question is: to what do this expected yield and variance of yield refer? For such a diagram to make sense, they must necessarily refer to some unit common to all assets. An example of such a unit would be one dollar's worth of investment in each asset. Such a choice of units would evidently be of little use for our purposes, since we shall consider the prices of assets as variables to be determined in the market. Consequently, we must select some arbitrary "physical" unit of measurement and define expected yield and variance of yield relative to this unit. If, for example, we select one share as our unit for measuring holdings of Standard Oil stock and say that the expected yield is $\mu$ and the variance $\sigma^2$, this means expected yield and variance of yield per share; if instead we had chosen a hundred shares as our unit, the relevant expected yield and variance of yield would have been $100\,\mu$, and $10,000\,\sigma^2$, respectively.

We shall find it convenient to give an interpretation of the concept of "yield" by assuming discrete market dates with intervals of one time unit. The yield to be considered on any asset on a given market date may then be thought of as the value per unit that the asset will have at the next market date (including possible accrued dividends, interest or other emoluments). The terms "yield" and "future value" may then be used more or less interchangeably.

We shall, in general, admit stochastic dependence among yields of different

___

[3] This assumption is not crucial for the analysis, but simplifies it a good deal. It also seems doubtful whether the introduction of subjective probabilities would really be useful for deriving propositions about market behavior. In any case, it may be argued, as Borch [3, p. 439] does: "Whether two rational persons on the basis of the same information can arrive at different evaluations of the probability of a specific event, is a question of semantics. That they may act differently on the same information is well known, but this can usually be explained assuming that the two persons attach different utilities to the event."

[4] Acceptance of the von Neumann—Morgenstern axioms (leading to their theorem on measurable utility), together with this assumption, implies a quadratic utility function for yield (see [4]). But such a specification is not strictly necessary for the analysis to follow, and so, by the principle of Occam's razor, has not been introduced.

assets. But the specification of the stochastic properties poses the problem of identification of "different" assets. It will be necessary to make the convention that two units of assets are of the same kind only if their yields will be identical. The reason for this convention can be clarified by an example. In many lotteries (in particular national lotteries), several tickets wear the same number. When a number is drawn, all tickets with that number receive identical prizes. Suppose all tickets have mean $\mu$ and variance $\sigma^2$ of prizes. Then the expected yield on *two* tickets is clearly $2\mu$, regardless of their numbers. But while the variance on two tickets is $2\sigma^2$ when they have different numbers, it is $4\sigma^2$ when they have identical numbers. If such lottery tickets are part of the available assets, we must therefore identify as many "different" assets as there are different numbers (regardless of the fact that they have identical means and variances). For ordinary assets such as corporate stock, it is of course known that although the yield is random it will be the same on all units of each stock.

We shall denote the expected yield per unit of asset $j$ by $\mu_j$ and the covariance between unit yield of assets $j$ and $k$ by $\sigma_{jk}$. We shall also need the rather trivial assumption that the covariance matrix for the yield of the risky assets is nonsingular.

An individual's portfolio can now be described as an $n$-dimensional vector with elements equal to his holdings of each of the $n$ assets. We shall use $x_j^i$ to denote individual $i$'s holdings of assets $j$ (after the exchange), and so his portfolio may be written $(x_1^i, x_2^i, \ldots, x_n^i)$.

One of the purposes of the analysis is to compare the relations between the prices and yields of different assets. To facilitate such comparisons, it will prove useful to have a *riskless asset* as a yardstick. We shall take the riskless asset to be the $n$th. That it is riskless of course means that $\sigma_{nk} = 0$ for all $k$. But it may also be suggestive to identify this asset with *money*, and with this in mind we shall write specifically $u_n = 1$, i.e., a dollar will (with certainty) be worth a dollar a year from now.

We denote the price per unit of asset $j$ by $p_j$. Now, general equilibrium conditions are capable of determining relative prices only: we can arbitrarily fix one of the prices and express all others in terms of it. We may therefore proceed by fixing the price of the $n$th asset as $q$, i.e., $p_n = q$. This means that we select the $n$th asset as *numéraire*. We shall return to the implications of this seemingly innocent convention below.

With the above assumptions and conventions, the expected yield on individual $i$'s portfolio can be written:

(1)
$$y_1^i = \sum_{j=1}^{n-1} \mu_j x_j^i + x_n^i,$$

and the variance:

(2)
$$y_2^i = \sum_{j=1}^{n-1} \sum_{\alpha=1}^{n-1} \sigma_{j\alpha} x_i^i x_\alpha^j.$$

As mentioned earlier, we postulate for each individual a *preference ordering* (utility function) of the form:

(3) $$U^i = f^i(y_1^i, y_2^i)$$

over all possible portfolios, i.e., we postulate that an individual will behave as if he were attempting to maximize $U^i$. With respect to the form of $U^i$, we shall assume that it is concave, with the first derivative positive and the second negative. This latter assumption of general risk aversion seems to be generally accepted in the literature on portfolio selection. The investor is constrained, however, to the points that satisfy his *budget equation*:

(4) $$\sum_{j=1}^{n-1} p_j(x_j^i - \bar{x}_j^i) + q(x_n^i - \bar{x}_n^i) = 0,$$

where $\bar{x}_j^i$ are the quantities of asset $j$ that he brings to the market; these are given data. The budget equation simply states that his total receipts from the sale of the "old" portfolio should equal total outlays on the "new" portfolio.

Formally, then, we postulate that each individual $i$ behaves as if attempting to maximize (3), subject to (4), (1), and (2). Forming the Lagrangean:

$$V^i = f^i(y_1^i, y_2^i) + \theta^i \left[ \sum_{j=1}^{n-1} p_j(x_j^i - \bar{x}_j^i) + g(x_n^i - \bar{x}_n^i) \right],$$

we can then write the first-order conditions for the maxima for all $i$ as:

$$\frac{\partial V^i}{\partial x_j^i} = f_1^i \mu_j + 2f_2^i \sum_{\alpha=1}^{n-1} \sigma_{j\alpha} x_\alpha^i + \theta^i p_j = 0 \qquad (j = 1, \ldots, n-1),$$

$$\frac{\partial V^i}{\partial x_n^i} = f_1^i + \theta^i q = 0,$$

$$\frac{\partial V^i}{\partial \theta^i} = \sum_{j=1}^{n-1} p_j(x_j^i - \bar{x}_j^i) + q(x_n^i - \bar{x}_n^i) = 0,$$

where $f_1^i$ and $f_2^i$ denote partial derivatives with respect to $y_1^i$ and $y_2^i$, respectively. Eliminating $\theta^i$, this can be written as:

(5) $$-\frac{f_1^i}{f_2^i} = \frac{2 \sum_\alpha \sigma_{j\alpha} x_\alpha^i}{u_j - p_j/q} \qquad (j = 1, \ldots, n-1),$$

(6) $$\sum_{j=1}^{n-1} p_j(x_j^i - \bar{x}_j^i) + q(x_n^i - \bar{x}_n^i) = 0.$$

In (5), the $-f_1^i/f_2^i$ is the marginal rate of substitution $dy_2^i/dy_1^i$ between the variance and mean of yield. Equations (5) and (6) constitute, for each individual, $n$ equations describing his demand for the $n$ assets.

To determine general equilibrium, we must also specify equality between demand and supply for each asset. These market clearing conditions can be written:

(7')
$$\sum_{i=1}^{m} (x_j^i - \bar{x}_j^i) = 0 \qquad (j = 1, \ldots, n).$$

As we would suspect, one of these conditions is superfluous. This can be seen by first summing the budget equations over all individuals:

$$\sum_{i=1}^{m} \sum_{j=1}^{n-1} p_j(x_j^i - \bar{x}_j^i) + q \sum_{i=1}^{m} (x_n^i - \bar{x}_n^i) = 0,$$

or

(8)
$$\sum_{j=1}^{n-1} p_j \sum_{i=1}^{m} (x_j^i - \bar{x}_j^i) + q \sum_{i=1}^{m} (x_n^i - \bar{x}_n^i) = 0.$$

Suppose that (7') were satisfied for all $j$ except $n$. This would mean that the first term on the left of (8) vanishes, so that

$$q \sum_{i=1}^{m} (x_n^i - \bar{x}_n^i) = 0.$$

Hence also the $n$th equation of (7') must hold. We may therefore instead write:

(7)
$$\sum_{i=1}^{m} x_j^i = \bar{x}_j \qquad (j = 1, \ldots, n - 1),$$

where $\bar{x}_j$ denotes the given total supply of asset $j$: $\bar{x}_j = \sum_{i=1}^{m} \bar{x}_j^i$.

This essentially completes the equations describing general equilibrium. The system consists of the $m$ equations (4), the $m(n - 1)$ equations (5) and (6), and the $(n - 1)$ equations (7); altogether $(mn + n - 1)$ equations. The unknowns are the $mn$ quantities $x_j^i$ and the $(n - 1)$ prices $p_j$.

We have counted our equations and our unknowns and found them to be equal in number. But we cannot rest with this; our main task has hardly begun. We shall bypass such problems as the existence and uniqueness of a solution to the system and rather concentrate on investigating properties of the equilibrium values of the variables, assuming that they exist.

We may observe, first of all, that the equilibrium allocation of assets represents a Pareto optimum, i.e., it will be impossible by some reallocation to increase one individual's utility without at the same time reducing the utility of one or more other individuals. This should not need any explicit proof, since it is a well known general property of a competitive equilibrium where preferences are concave. We should also mention the problem of nonnegativity of the solution to which we shall return at a later stage.

## 3. RISK MARGINS

The expected *rate of return* $r_j$ on a unit of a risky asset can be defined by $\mu_j/(1 + r_j) = p_j$, i.e., $r_j = (\mu_j/p_j) - 1$, $(j = 1, \ldots, n - 1)$. Similarly, the rate of return of a unit of the riskless asset $r_n$ is defined by $1/(1 + r_n) = q$, i.e., $r_n = 1/q - 1$. With our earlier interpretation of the riskless asset in mind, $r_n$ may be regarded as the *pure rate of interest*.

The natural definition of the pure rate of interest is the rate of return on a riskless asset. In general, we may think of the rate of return of any asset as separated into two parts: the pure rate of interest representing the "price for waiting," and a remainder, a risk margin, representing the "price of risk." When we set the future yield of the riskless asset at 1 and decided to fix its current price at $q$, we thereby implicitly fixed the pure rate of interest. And to say that the market determines only relative asset prices is seen to be equivalent to saying that the pure rate of interest is not determined in the market for risky assets. Alternatively, we may say that the asset market determines only the risk margins.

The risk margin on asset $j$, $m_j$, is defined by

$$m_j = r_j - r_n = \frac{u_j - p_j/q}{p_j}.$$

To compare the risk margins of two assets $j$ and $k$, we write:

$$\frac{m_j}{m_k} = \frac{\mu_j - p_j/q}{\mu_k - p_k/q}\frac{p_k}{p_j}.$$

We now make use of the equilibrium conditions. From (5) we have:

$$(9) \qquad \frac{\sum\limits_{\alpha} \sigma_{j\alpha} x^i_\alpha}{u_j - p_j/q} = \frac{\sum\limits_{\alpha} \sigma_{k\alpha} x^i_\alpha}{\mu_k - p_k/q} \qquad (j, k = 1, \ldots, n-1).$$

Summing over $i$ and using (7), we then get:

$$(10) \qquad \frac{\sum\limits_{\alpha} \sigma_{j\alpha} \bar{x}_\alpha}{\mu_j - p_j/q} = \frac{\sum\limits_{\alpha} \sigma_{k\alpha} \bar{x}_\alpha}{\mu_k - p_k/q}.$$

These equations define relationships between the prices of the risky assets in terms of given parameters only. We can then write:

$$\frac{m_j}{m_k} = \frac{\bar{x}_j \sum\limits_{\alpha} \sigma_{j\alpha} \bar{x}_\alpha}{\bar{x}_k \sum\limits_{\alpha} \sigma_{k\alpha} \bar{x}_\alpha} \cdot \frac{p_k \bar{x}_k}{p_j \bar{x}_j}.$$

Now, $\bar{x}_j \sum_\alpha \sigma_{j\alpha} \bar{x}_\alpha$ is the variance of yield on the total outstanding stock of asset $j$; $p_j \bar{x}_j$ is similarly the total value, at market prices, of all of asset $j$. Let us denote these magnitudes by $V_j$ and $R_j$, respectively. In equilibrium, therefore, the risk margins satisfy:

$$(11) \qquad \frac{m_j R_j}{V_j} = \frac{m_k R_k}{V_k} \qquad (j, k = 1, \ldots, n-1),$$

i.e., the risk margins are such that *the ratio between the total risk compensation paid for an asset and the variance of the total stock of the asset is the same for all assets.*

## 4. COMPOSITION OF EQUILIBRIUM PORTFOLIOS

We can now derive an important property of an individual's equilibrium portfolio.

When (10) is substituted back in (9), the result is:

$$(12) \qquad \frac{\sum_\alpha \sigma_{j\alpha} x_\alpha^i}{\sum_\alpha \sigma_{j\alpha} \bar{x}_\alpha} = \frac{\sum_\alpha \sigma_{k\alpha} x_\alpha^i}{\sum_\alpha \sigma_{k\alpha} \bar{x}_\alpha}.$$

Now define for each individual $z_j^i = x_j^i / \bar{x}_j$ $(j = 1, \ldots, n - 1)$, i.e., $z_j^i$ is the proportion of the outstanding stock of asset $h$ held by individual $i$. Further, let

$$b_{j\alpha} = \frac{\sigma_{j\alpha} \bar{x}_\alpha}{\sum_\alpha \sigma_{j\alpha} \bar{x}_\alpha},$$

so that $\sum_\alpha j\alpha = 1$. Then (12) can be written

$$(13) \qquad \sum_\alpha b_{j\alpha} z_\alpha^i = \sum_\alpha b_{k\alpha} z_\alpha^i \qquad (j, k = 1, \ldots, n - 1).$$

It is easily proved[5] that these equations imply that the $z_j^i$ are the same for all $j$ (equal to, say, $z^i$), i.e.,

$$(14) \qquad z_j^i = z_k^i = z^i \qquad (j, k = 1, \ldots, n - 1).$$

What this means is that in equilibrium, prices must be such that *each individual will hold the same percentage of the total outstanding stock of all risky assets*. This percentage will of course be different for different individuals, but it means that if an individual holds, say, 2 per cent of all the units outstanding of one risky asset, he also holds 2 per cent of the units outstanding of all the other risky assets. Note that we cannot conclude that he also holds the same percentage of the riskless asset; this proportion will depend upon his attitude towards risk, as expressed by his utility function. But the relation nevertheless permits us to summarize the description of an individual's portfolio by stating (a) his holding of the riskless asset, and (b) the percentage $z^i$ held of the outstanding stock of the risky assets. We also observe that if an individual holds any risky assets at all (i.e., if he is not so averse to risk as to place everything in the riskless asset), then he holds some of *every* asset. (The analysis assumes, of course, that all assets are perfectly divisible.)

Looked at from another angle, (13) states that for any two individuals $r$ and $s$, and any two risky assets $j$ and $k$, we have $x_j^r / x_k^r = x_j^s / x_k^s$, i.e., the ratio between the holdings of two risky assets is the same for all individuals.

With these properties of equilibrium portfolios, we can return to the prob-

---

[5] Let the common value of the $n - 1$ terms $\sum_{\alpha=1}^{n-1} b_{j\alpha} z_\alpha^i$ be $a^i$, and let $c_{j\alpha}$ be the elements of the inverse of the matrix of the $b_{j\alpha}$ (assuming nonsingularity). It is well known that when $\sum_\alpha b_{j\alpha} = 1$, then also $\sum_\alpha c_{j\alpha} = 1$. The solutions for the $z_j^i$ are then: $z_j^i = \sum_\alpha c_{j\alpha} a^i = a^i \sum_\alpha c_{j\alpha} = a^i$, which proves our proposition.

lem of nonnegativity of the solution. With risk aversion it follows from (5) that

$$\sum_\alpha \sigma_{j\alpha} x_\alpha^i \Big/ \Big( \mu_j - \frac{p_j}{q} \Big) > 0.$$

The sum of such positive terms must also be positive, i.e.,

$$\sum_\alpha \sigma_{j\alpha} \bar{x}_\alpha \Big/ \Big( \mu_j - \frac{p_j}{q} \Big) > 0.$$

But then also, $\sum_\alpha \sigma_{j\alpha} x_\alpha^i / \sum_\alpha \sigma_{j\alpha} \bar{x}_\alpha > 0$, so that the $a^i$ of footnote 4 is positive, which then implies $z^i > 0$. Hence, negative asset holdings are ruled out.

Our results are not at all unreasonable. At *any* set of prices, it will be rational for investors to diversify. Suppose that before the exchange takes place investors generally come to the conclusion that the holdings they would prefer to have of some asset are small relative to the supply of that asset. This must mean that the price of this asset has been too high in the past. It is then only natural to expect the exchange to result in a fall in this price, and hence in an increase in desired holdings. What the relations of (14) do is simply to give a precise characterization of the ultimate outcome of the equilibrating effects of the market process.

## 5. THE MARKET LINE

The somewhat diffuse concept of a "price of risk" can be made more precise and meaningful through an analysis of the rate of substitution between expected yield and risk (in equilibrium). Specification of such a rate of substitution would imply the existence of a so-called "market curve." Sharpe illustrates a market curve as a line in a mean-standard deviation plane and characterizes it by saying: "In equilibrium, capital asset prices have adjusted so that the investor, if he follows rational procedures (primarily diversification), is able to attain any desired point along a *capital market line*" (p. 425). He adds that "... some discussions are also consistent with a nonlinear (but monotonic) curve" (p. 425, footnote).

We shall attempt to formulate these ideas in terms of our general equilibrium system.

As we have said earlier, a relation among points in a mean-variance diagram makes sense only when the means and variances refer to some unit common to all assets, for example, a dollar's worth of investment. We therefore had to reject such representations as a starting point for the derivation of general equilibrium conditions. When we study properties of this equilibrium, however, the situation is somewhat different. After equilibrium has been attained, each individual has specific portfolios with specific expected yields and variances of yield. Also, the individual's total wealth, i.e., the value at market prices of his portfolio, has been determined. This wealth, $w^i$, can be expressed as

$$w^i = \sum_{j=1}^{n-1} p_j x_j^i + q x_n^i = \sum_{j=1}^{n-1} p_j \bar{x}_j^i + q \bar{x}_n^i.$$

(The latter equality follows from (6).) We can now meaningfully define, for each individual, the per dollar expected yield of his equilibrium portfolio, $u_1^i$, and the per dollar standard deviation of yield of his equilibrium portfolio, $u_2^i$. These magnitudes are defined in terms of $y_1^i$ and $y_2^i$ by the relations: $u_1^i = y_1^i/w^i$, and $u_2^i = \sqrt{y_2^i}/w^i$. More concretely, we may think of individual $i$'s portfolio as divided into $w^i$ equal "piles," with each asset in equal proportion in all "piles." Each such "pile" has a market value of one dollar; its expected yield is $u_1^i$, and its standard deviation of yield is $u_2^i$. We are interested in the relationship between $u_1^i$ and $u_2^i$.

From (5) we have:

$$\frac{dy_2^i}{dy_1^i} = \frac{2x_j^i \sum_\alpha \sigma_{j\alpha} x_\alpha^i}{(u_j - p_j/q)x_j^i} \qquad (j = 1, \ldots, n-1).$$

But by "corresponding addition,"[6] we also have

$$\frac{dy_2^i}{dy_1^i} = \frac{2 \sum_j \sum_\alpha \sigma_{j\alpha} x_j^i x_\alpha^i}{\sum_j (\mu_j - p_j/q)x_j^i} = \frac{2y_2^i}{(y_1^i - x_n^i) - (w^i - qx_n^i)/q} = \frac{2y_2^i}{y_1^i - w^i q}.$$

We thus have a differential equation in $y_1^i$ and $y_2^i$, the general solution form of which is given by

$$\lambda^i \sqrt{y_2^i} = y_1^i - w^i/q,$$

where $\lambda^i$ is a constant of integration. With this solution, we have

$$\frac{dy_2^i}{dy_1^i} = \frac{2}{\lambda^i} \sqrt{y_2^i},$$

and so $\lambda^i$ can be determined by the condition

$$\frac{2}{\lambda^i} \sqrt{y_2^i} = \frac{2 \sum_a \sigma_{j\alpha} x_\alpha^i}{\mu_j - p_j/q},$$

which gives

$$\lambda^i = \frac{\mu_j - p_j/q}{\sum_\alpha \sigma_{j\alpha} x_\alpha^i} \sqrt{\sum_j \sum_\alpha \rho_{j\alpha} x_j^i x_\alpha^i}.$$

But substituting from (14) $x_j^i = z^i \bar{x}_j$, we end up with

$$\lambda^i = \frac{\mu_j - p_j/q}{\sum_\alpha \sigma_{j\alpha} \bar{x}_\alpha} \sqrt{\sum_j \sum_\alpha \sigma_{j\alpha} \bar{x}_j \bar{x}_\alpha}.$$

[6] If $u = a/b = c/d$, then also $u = (a + c)/(b + d)$.

The important thing to note here is that the righthand side is independent of $i$, so that we conclude that the $\lambda^i$ are the same for all $i$—equal to, say, $\lambda$. This means that all points $(u_1^i, u_2^i)$ lie on a straight line, $u_1 = \lambda u_2 + 1/q$, with

(15)
$$\lambda = \frac{\mu_j - p_j/q}{\sum\limits_\alpha p_{j\alpha}\bar{x}_\alpha} \sqrt{\sum_j \sum_\alpha \sigma_{j\alpha}\bar{x}_j\bar{x}_\alpha}.$$

We note also that according to (10) the factor $(\mu_j - p_j/q)/\sum_\alpha \sigma_{j\alpha}\bar{x}_\alpha$ is the same for all assets, so that the choice of the $j$th asset as "reference point" is perfectly arbitrary.

We shall analyse $\lambda$ in detail in the next section, but it may be worth while to give a general appreciation of the results so far, as they are of some interest in themselves.

We have shown, first of all, that a "market line" in the sense discussed above can be derived from the conditions for general equilibrium (if it exists). Second, the fact that the market line is a straight line means that the rate of substitution between per dollar expected yield and per dollar standard deviation of yield is constant, i.e., for any two individuals $r$ and $s$:

$$\frac{u_1^r - u_1^s}{u_2^r - u_2^s} = \lambda.$$

Third, these results are independent of any individual characteristics, not only with respect to initial holdings, but also with respect to the individuals' utility functions (except, possibly, that they depend upon the first two moments only of the probability distribution for yield). This is not to say that the *value* of $\lambda$ is independent of the utility functions, which is clearly not the case, depending as it does upon the prices which in turn cannot be determined without knowledge of the utility functions. But the demonstration of this general property of equilibrium is nevertheless valuable.

The intercept with the $u_1$-axis, i.e., the point $u_2 = 0$, $u_1 = 1/q$, corresponds to a portfolio consisting entirely of the riskless asset and would be the location for an individual showing an extreme degree of risk aversion. And the further upward along the line an individual is located, the more willing he is to assume risk in order to gain in expected yield.

This concept of the market line as a locus of a finite number of points $(u_1^i, u_2^i)$ describing individual portfolios should be contrasted with the characterization given by Sharpe and cited earlier. At least with the interpretation we have been able to give to the market line, it is not something along which an individual may or may not choose to place himself. It would be misleading to give the impression that if an individual does not behave rationally he is somehow "off" this line. For the market line is not a construct that can be maintained independently of investor behavior, and it has no meaning as a criterion for testing whether an individual behaves rationally or not. Rather, it is a way of summarizing the result of rational behavior, and nothing more. It describes in a concise fashion the market conditions in general equilibrium, and this equilibrium is defined in terms of conditions implied by the attempts of individuals to maximize their utility functions, i.e., to behave rationally (and this is the only meaning that the term "rational behavior" can have in this context). If one or more individuals do not behave rationally, the whole foundation of the analysis is destroyed, and the concept of equilibrium, and hence also of the market line, becomes meaningless. The only statements that (15) does permit are those involving comparisons of different individuals' equilibrium portfolios with respect to their per dollar yield characteristics.

There is one more property of the market equilibrium that should be made explicit, namely, that it is independent of the definition of assets. More precisely: given society's real investments and their stochastic nature, the existence and slope of the market line is (under assumptions to be specified) independent of the distribution of ownership of these investments among companies.

So far, we have not been very precise about the nature of the various risky assets, although company shares were mentioned as examples of assets. Consider now the possibility of a merger of two companies into a new company. How will such a merger affect market equilibrium?

A detailed analysis of this kind of reorganization would evidently require specification of details of the merger agreements. But the most important results can be derived without this knowledge. We shall, as a matter of fact, consider any reorganization of the original $n - 1$ companies into any number $\hat{n}$ of new companies. In the remainder of this section, we shall label the original companies $j$ or $k$—$j, k = 1,\ldots, n - 1$—and retain our earlier notation for the parameters and variables in the original situation. The new companies will be labeled $\alpha$ or $\beta$; $\alpha, \beta = 1,\ldots, \hat{n}$, and the corresponding parameters and variables will be distinguished by hats ($\hat{\mu}_\alpha, \hat{x}^i_\alpha, \hat{w}^i$, etc.). The riskless asset is labeled $n$ in both cases.

We shall make two basic assumptions. The first is that the yield on the securities of a company can be identified with the yield of the real investments that it owns. The second is that the yield on real investments are independent of ownership conditions.

It should be clear that these assumptions imply that we neglect those factors that may account for most real-world mergers, namely, the possibility of reorganization of productive activities so as to improve their yield prospects. Further, it is implicitly taken for granted that the ownership reallocation does not affect investors' perceptions of probability distributions of yield. We are really attempting to compare two entirely different worlds—one with and one without merged companies. There is then no logical reason why there should exist any connections between probability distributions in the two worlds: the $\mu$'s and $\sigma$'s are given data summarizing investors' perceptions when things are organized in a particular way, and would conceivably be different if things were organized differently.

Be that as it may, the immediate results of the assumptions are, first, that the expected yield on total outstanding stock of all companies is the same in both situations, i.e.,

(16)
$$\sum_{j=1}^{n-1} \mu_j \bar{x}_j = \sum_{\alpha=1}^{\hat{n}} \hat{\mu}_\alpha \hat{\bar{x}}_\alpha,$$

and, second, that a similar condition holds for the total variance:

(17)
$$\sum_{j=1}^{n-1}\sum_{k=1}^{n-1} \sigma_{jk}\bar{x}_j\bar{x}_k = \sum_{\alpha=1}^{\hat{n}}\sum_{\beta=1}^{\hat{n}} \hat{\sigma}_{\alpha\beta}\hat{\bar{x}}_\alpha\hat{\bar{x}}_\beta.$$

From (5) we must have, for each $i$ and any $j$ or $\alpha$,

$$\frac{\sum_\beta \hat{\sigma}_{\alpha\beta}\hat{x}_\beta^i}{\hat{\mu}_\alpha - \dfrac{\hat{p}_\alpha}{q}} = \frac{\sum_k \sigma_{jk}x_k^i}{\mu_j - \dfrac{p_j}{q}},$$

so that (by summing over $i$):

(18)
$$\frac{\sum_\beta \hat{\sigma}_{\alpha\beta}\hat{\bar{x}}_\beta}{\hat{\mu}_\alpha - \dfrac{\hat{p}_\alpha}{q}} = \frac{\sum_k \sigma_{jk}\bar{x}_k}{\mu_j - \dfrac{p_j}{q}}.$$

This equation corresponds to (10), and it therefore follows that

$$\frac{\hat{x}_\alpha^i}{\hat{\bar{x}}_\alpha} = \frac{x_j^i}{\bar{x}_j} = z^i,$$

i.e., the proportion held of the outstanding stock of the various risky assets is the same in both situations. Looking now at the expression (15) for $\lambda$, we observe that by (18) the first factor is the same in both situations, and that by (17) this also holds for the second factor. Hence we conclude that the market line remains the same.

By corresponding addition on both sides of (18), we also get

$$\frac{\sum_a\sum_\beta \hat{\sigma}_{\alpha\beta}\,\hat{\bar{x}}_\alpha\hat{\bar{x}}_\beta}{\sum_\alpha \hat{\mu}_\alpha\hat{\bar{x}}_\alpha - \dfrac{1}{q}\sum_\alpha \hat{p}_\alpha\hat{\bar{x}}_\alpha} = \frac{\sum_j\sum_k \sigma_{jk}\bar{x}_j\bar{x}_k}{\sum_j \mu_j\bar{x}_j - \dfrac{1}{q}\sum_j p_j\bar{x}_j}.$$

Therefore,

$$\sum_\alpha \hat{p}_\alpha\hat{\bar{x}}_\alpha = \sum_j p_j\bar{x}_j.$$

Next we can show that each individual will be located at the same point on the market line in both situations, so that his utility remains the same. This is seen by directly observing the means and variances of yield of portfolios in the two cases:

$$\hat{y}_1^i = \sum_\alpha \hat{\mu}_\alpha\hat{x}_\alpha^i + \hat{x}_n^i = z^i\sum_\alpha \hat{\mu}_\alpha\hat{\bar{x}}_\alpha + \hat{x}_n^i = z^i\sum_j \mu_j\bar{x}_j + \hat{x}_n^i$$

$$= \sum_j \mu_j x_j^i + \hat{x}_n^i = y_1^i - x_n^i + \hat{x}_n^i.$$

But since the budget equations must also hold, we have

$$\sum_{\alpha} \hat{p}_{\alpha}\hat{x}^i_{\alpha} + q\hat{x}^i_n = \sum_{j} p_j x^i_j + qx^i_n,$$

$$z^i \sum_{\alpha} p_{\alpha}\hat{x}^i_{\alpha} + q\hat{x}^i_n = z^i \sum_{j} p_j \bar{x}_j + qx^i_n,$$

Therefore, $\hat{x}^i_n = x^i_n$, and so $\hat{y}^i_1 = y^i_1$. Similarly, we find $\hat{y}^i_2 = y^i_2$.

In short, then, everything remains essentially the same as before. Investors will just accept the exchange of securities caused by the reorganization of companies, but will not undertake any further adjustment.

The meaning of these results are, then, that when probability distributions are assumed to apply to the real side of the economy, the organization of productive activities is immaterial from the standpoint of valuation. Accordingly, companies may be formed in the way which is the most efficient for carrying out the productive activities (given such phenomena as economies of scale and the like), and that organization will also prove adequate from a "financial markets" point of view.

## 6. THE PRICE OF RISK

The concept of the "price of risk" can now be explored somewhat more fully in terms of $\lambda$, the slope of the market line. The "price of risk" is not a very fortunate choice of terms: "price of risk reduction" might be more satisfactory, since it is the relief of risk for which we must assume individuals are willing to pay. (We would, to make an analogy, certainly hesitate to use the term "price of garbage" for a city sanitation fee.) The price of risk reduction, however, is not only related to the rate of substitution between expected yield and risk, but must indeed be directly identified with it. That is to say, the only sensible meaning we can impute to the "price of risk reduction" is the amount of expected yield that must be sacrificed in order to reduce risk.

We note that when risk is measured, as we have done above, by the value (in dollars, say) of the standard deviation of yield, then the dimension of the price of risk reduction is that of an interest rate. This observation would lead us to try to establish a relation between $\lambda$ and the risk margins $m_j$, discussed earlier. These risk margins may, of course, also be looked upon as representing prices of risk reduction, each one, however, referring to the risk aspects of that particular asset. We might then suspect that the equilibrating mechanisms of the market are such that all these risk margins are somehow "averaged" out into an overall market price of risk reduction. And it would certainly be reasonable to conjecture that the larger an asset looms in the market, the larger the weight carried by that asset in the total. Such an interpretation of $\lambda$ can indeed be given an exact formulation.

Recalling our earlier definitions of $m_j$, $R_j$, and $V_j$, we can write (15) as:

$$\lambda = \frac{p_j \bar{x}_j m_j}{\bar{x}_j \sum_{\alpha} \sigma_{j\alpha}\bar{x}_{\alpha}} \sqrt{\sum_{j} V_j} = \frac{R_j m_j}{V_j} \sqrt{\sum_{j} V_j}.$$

Since this holds for any $j, j = 1, \ldots, n - 1$, we must also have

(19)
$$\lambda = \frac{\sum_j R_j m_j}{\sum_j V_j} \sqrt{\sum_j V_j} = \frac{\sum_j R_j m_j}{\sqrt{\sum_j V_j}}.$$

This means that $\lambda$ is proportional to an arithmetical average of the $m_j$, the weights for each asset being the outstanding stock of that asset. The factor of proportionality is $\sum_j R_j / \sqrt{\sum_j V_j}$, the mean-standard deviation ratio for the market as a whole.

Another substitution allows us to write $\lambda$ in still another fashion, which also throws some light on its composition. We may write (15) as

$$\lambda = \frac{m_k p_k}{\sum_\alpha \sigma_{k\alpha} \bar{x}_\alpha} \sqrt{\sum_j x_j \sum_\alpha \sigma_{j\alpha} \bar{x}_\alpha}$$

$$= \frac{m_k p_k}{\sum_\alpha \sigma_{k\alpha} \bar{x}_\alpha} \sqrt{\sum_j x_j \frac{(\sum_\alpha \sigma_{j\alpha} \bar{x}_\alpha)^2}{\sum_\alpha \sigma_{j\alpha} \bar{x}_\alpha}}.$$

From (10), however, we get

$$(\sum \sigma_{j\alpha} \bar{x}_\alpha)^2 = (m_j p_j)^2 \left( \frac{\sum_\alpha \sigma_{k\alpha} \bar{x}_\alpha}{m_k p_k} \right)^2.$$

When this is substituted above, the factor $m_k p_k / \sum_\alpha \sigma_{k\alpha} \bar{x}_\alpha$ drops out, and we are left with

$$\lambda = \sqrt{\sum_j \frac{(m_j p_j)^2}{\frac{1}{x_j} \sum_\alpha \sigma_{j\alpha} \bar{x}_\alpha}}.$$

Now define $s_j^2 = \frac{1}{\bar{x}_j} \sum_\alpha \sigma_{j\alpha} \bar{x}_\alpha$; this gives

(20)
$$\lambda = \sqrt{\sum_j \left( \frac{m_j p_j}{s_j} \right)^2}.$$

This expression is not only simple, but affords an interesting interpretation. Since $s_j^2 = V_j / \bar{x}_j^2$, $s_j$ can be interpreted as the standard deviation of yield per unit of asset $j$ (with the given quantities $\bar{x}_j$); i.e., it measures the risk per unit of asset $j$. Hence, $m_j p_j$ is clearly the risk of compensation per unit of asset $j$; $p_j m_j / s_j$ is then the risk compensation per unit of risk on a unit of asset $j$, or, to put it differently, the gain in expected yield per unit's increase in the risk on a unit of asset $j$. The characterization given to $\lambda$ as a description of equilibrium for the market as a whole was completely analogous. Then (20) specifies $\lambda$ as the square root of the sum of squares of the individual components $p_j m_j / s_j$;

this is a natural result of the properties of the standard deviation as a measure of risk.

## REFERENCES

1. Allais, M.: "L'extension des théories de l'équilibre économique général et du rendement social au cas du risque," *Econometrica*, April, 1953.
2. Arrow, K. J.: "The Role of Securities in the Optimal Allocation of Risk-Bearing," *Review of Economic Studies*, 86, 1964.
3. Borch, Karl: "Equilibrium in a Reinsurance Market," *Econometrica*, July, 1962.
4. ———: "A Note on Utility and Attitudes to Risk," *Management Science*, 1963.
5. Brownlee, O. H., and I. O. Scott: "Utility, Liquidity, and Debt Management," *Econometrica*, July, 1963.
6. Markowitz, H.: *Portfolio Selection*, New York, John Wiley and Sons, 1959.
7. Sharpe, W. F.: "Capital Asset Prices: A Theory of Market Equilibrium under Conditions of Risk," *The Journal of Finance*, September, 1964.
8. Tobin, J.: "Liquidity Preference as Behavior Towards Risk," *Review of Economic Studies*, 67, 1959.

# PART IV

## CAPITAL BUDGETING

* * * * * * * * * * * * * * * * * * * *

## 16. THREE PROBLEMS IN RATIONING CAPITAL*

### JAMES H. LORIE† and LEONARD J. SAVAGE‡

Reprinted by permission of the authors and publisher from *Journal of Business*, Vol. XXVIII, No. 4 (October 1955), pp. 56–66.

## I. INTRODUCTION

Corporate executives face three tasks in achieving good financial management. The first is largely administrative and consists in finding an efficient procedure for preparing and reviewing capital budgets, for delegating authority and fixing responsibility for expenditures, and for finding some means for ultimate evaluation of completed investments. The second task is to forecast correctly the cash flows that can be expected to result from specified investment proposals, as well as the liquid resources that will be available for investment. The third task is to ration available capital or liquid resources among competing investment opportunities. This article is concerned with only this last task; it discusses three problems in the rationing of capital, in the sense of liquid resources.

1. Given a firm's cost of capital and a management policy of using this cost to identify acceptable investment proposals, which group of "independent" investment proposals should the firm accept? In other words, how should the firm's cost of capital be used to distinguish between acceptable and unacceptable investments? This is a problem that is typically faced by top management whenever it reviews and approves a capital budget.

* This work was supported in part by the Office of Naval Research and in part by Joel Dean Associates.

† Associate professor of marketing, University of Chicago, and senior consultant, Joel Dean Associates.

‡ Professor of statistics, University of Chicago.

Before presenting the second problem with which this paper deals, the use of the word "independent" in the preceding paragraph should be explained. Investment proposals are termed "independent"—although not completely accurately—when the worth of the individual investment proposal is not profoundly affected by the acceptance of others. For example, a proposal to invest in materials-handling equipment at location A may not profoundly affect the value of a proposal to build a new warehouse in location B. It is clear that the independence is never complete, but the degree of independence is markedly greater than for sets of so-called "mutually exclusive" investment proposals. Acceptance of one proposal in such a set renders all others in the same set clearly unacceptable—or even unthinkable. An example of mutually exclusive proposals would be alternative makes of automotive equipment for the same fleet or alternative warehouse designs for the same site. The choice among mutually exclusive proposals is usually faced later in the process of financial management than is the initial approval of a capital budget. That is, the decision as to which make of automotive equipment to purchase, for example, typically comes later than the decision to purchase some make of equipment.

2. Given a fixed sum of money to be used for capital investment, what group of investment proposals should be undertaken? If a firm pursues a policy of fixing the size of its capital budget in dollars, without explicit cognizance of, or reference to, its cost of capital, how can it best allocate that sum among competing investment proposals? This problem will be considered both for proposals which require net outlays in only one accounting period and for those which require outlays in more than one accounting period. In the latter case, special difficulties arise.

3. How should a firm select the best among mutually exclusive alternatives? That is, when the management of an enterprise, in attempting to make concrete and explicit proposals for expenditures of a type which is included in an approved capital budget, develops more than one plausible way of investing money in conformance with the budget, how can it select the "best" way?

After presenting our solutions to these three problems, we shall discuss the solutions implied by the rate-of-return method of capital budgeting.[1] These solutions are worthy of special attention, since they are based on a different principle from the solutions that we propose and since the rate-of-return method is the most defensible method heretofore proposed in the business literature for maximizing corporate profits and net worth.

## II. THE THREE PROBLEMS

### A. GIVEN THE COST OF CAPITAL, WHAT GROUP OF INVESTMENTS SHOULD BE SELECTED?

---

[1] This method was developed by Joel Dean, who has probably done more than anyone else in applying the formal apparatus of economics to the solution of capital budgeting problems in their business context.

The question of determining the cost of capital is difficult, and we, happily, shall not discuss it. Although there may be disagreement about methods of calculating a firm's cost of capital, there is substantial agreement that the cost of capital is the rate at which a firm should discount future cash flows in order to determine their present value.[2] The first problem is to determine how selection should be made among "independent" investment proposals, given this cost or rate.

Assume that the firm's objective is to maximize the value of its net worth—not necessarily as measured by the accountant but rather as measured by the present value of its expected cash flows. This assumption is commonly made by economists and even business practitioners who have spoken on the subject. It is equivalent to asserting that the corporate management's objective is to maximize the value of the owner's equity or, alternatively, the value of the owner's income from the business. Given this objective and agreement about the significance of the firm's cost of capital, the problem of selecting investment proposals becomes trivial in those situations where there is a well-defined cost of capital; namely, proposals should be selected that have positive present values when discounted at the firm's cost of capital. The things to discount are the net cash flows resulting from the investments, and these cash flows should take taxes into account.

There is nothing unusual or original about this proposed solution. It is identical with that proposed by Lutz and Lutz[3] and is an economic commonplace. Joel Dean in his writings has developed and recommended a method which typically yields the same results for this problem, although the principle of solution is somewhat different, as is discussed later in this article.

The principle of accepting all proposals having positive present value at the firm's cost of capital is obvious, since the failure to do so would clearly mean foregoing an available increment in the present value of the firm's net worth. The principle is discussed here only because it seems a useful introduction to the somewhat more complicated problems that follow. An interesting property of this principle is that adherence to it will result in the present value of the firm's net worth being at a maximum at all points in time.

## B. GIVEN A FIXED SUM FOR CAPITAL INVESTMENT, WHAT GROUP OF INVESTMENT PROPOSALS SHOULD BE UNDERTAKEN?

Some business firms—perhaps most—do not use the firm's cost of capital to distinguish between acceptable and unacceptable investments but, instead, determine the magnitude of their capital budget in some other way that results in

[2] One of the difficulties with the concept of cost of capital is that in complicated circumstances there may be no one rate that plays this role. Still worse, the very concept of present value may be obscure.

[3] Friederich and Vera Lutz, *The Theory of Investment of the Firm* (Princeton: Princeton University Press, 1951). The solution proposed here is identical with the maximization of $V - C$, where $V$ is the present value of future inflows and $C$ is the present value of future outflows. This is discussed in chap. ii of the Lutz book.

fixing an absolute dollar limit on capital expenditures. Perhaps, for example, a corporate management may determine for any one year that the capital budget shall not exceed estimated income after taxes plus depreciation allowances, after specified dividend payments. It is probable that the sum fixed as the limit is not radically different from the sum that would be expended if correct and explicit use were made of the firm's cost of capital, since most business firms presumably do not long persist in policies antithetical to the objective of making money. (The profit-maximizing principle is the one that makes use of the firm's cost of capital, as described previously.) Nevertheless, there are probably some differences in the amount that would be invested by a firm if it made correct use of the firms' cost of capital and the amount that would be invested if it fixed its capital budget by other means, expressing the constraint on expenditures as being a maximum outlay. At the very least, the differences in the ways of thinking suggest the usefulness to some firms of a principle that indicates the "best" group of investments that can be made with a fixed sum of money.

The problem is trivial when there are net outlays in only one accounting period—typically, one year. In such cases, investment proposals should be ranked according to their present value—at the firm's cost of capital—per dollar of outlay required. Once investment proposals have been ranked according to this criterion, it is easy to select the best group by starting with the investment proposal having the highest present value per dollar of outlay and proceeding down the list until the fixed sum is exhausted.[4]

The problem can become more difficult when discontinuities are taken into account. For large firms, the vast majority of investment proposals constitute such a small proportion of their total capital budget that the problems created by discontinuities can be disregarded at only insignificant cost, especially when the imprecision of the estimates of incomes is taken into account. When a project constitutes a large proportion of the capital budget, the problem of discontinuities may become serious, though not necessarily difficult to deal with. This problem can become serious because of the obvious fact that accepting the large proposal because it is "richer" than smaller proposals may preclude the possibility of accepting two or more smaller and less rich proposals which, in combination, have a greater value than the larger proposal. For example, suppose that the total amount available for investment were $1,000 and that only three investment proposals had been made: one requiring a net outlay of $600 and creating an increment in present value of $1,000 and two others, each requiring a net outlay of $500 and each creating an increment in present value of $600. Under these circumstances, the adop-

---

[4] We mention, for completeness, that the outlay or the present value or both for a proposal can be negative. Proposals for which the outlay alone is negative—something for nothing—are always desirable but almost never available. Proposals for which both the outlay and present value are negative can sometimes be acceptable if something sufficiently profitable can be done with ready cash expressed by the negative outlay. The rules which we shall develop can be extended to cover such cases.

tion of the richest alternative, the first, would mean foregoing the other two alternatives, even though in combination they would create an increment in present value of $1,200 as compared with the increment of $1,000 resulting from the adoption of the richest investment alternative. Such discontinuities deserve special attention, but the general principles dealing with them will not be worked out here, primarily because we do not know them.

We shall, however, deal with the more serious difficulties created by the necessity to choose among investment proposals some of which require net cash outlays in more than one accounting period. In such cases a constraint is imposed not only by the fixed sum available for capital investment in the first period but also by the fixed sums available to carry out present commitments in subsequent time periods. Each such investment requires, so to speak, the use of two or more kinds of money—money from the first period and money from each subsequent period in which net outlays are required. We shall discuss only the case of investments requiring net outlays in two periods, for simplicity of exposition and because the principle—although not the mechanics—is the same as for investments requiring net outlays in more than two periods.

1. Let us start with a very simple case. Suppose that all the available opportunities for investment that yield a positive income can be adopted without exceeding the maximum permitted outlay in either time period one or time period two. Clearly, no better solution can be found, because all desirable opportunities have been exhausted. This simple case is mentioned not because of its practical importance, which is admittedly slight, but because it may clarify the more complicated cases that follow.

2. Next, consider a slightly more complicated case. Suppose that the opportunities available require more funds from either time period one or two than are permitted by the imposed constraints. Under these circumstances the problem becomes somewhat more complicated, but it still may not be very complicated. It is still relatively simple if (a) the best use of money available in period one does not exhaust the money available in period two or (b) the best use of money available in period two does not exhaust the money available in period one. In either case the optimum solution—that is, the solution which results in the greatest increment in the net worth of the firm, subject to the two stated constraints—is the one that makes the best possible use of the funds available for investment in one of the two time periods.

This statement is justified by the following reasoning. The imposition of additional restrictions upon the freedom of action of any agency can obviously never increase the value of the best opportunity available to that agency. In the problem at hand, this means that the imposition of an absolute dollar constraint or restriction in time period two can never make it possible to make better use of dollars available in time period one than would have been possible in the absence of that constraint. Thus, if the best possible use is made of the dollars available in time period one, the imposition of a restriction relating to time period two can never mean increased possibilities of

*outlays in more than 1 period* [handwritten marginal note]

profit from the use of funds available in time period one. Therefore, the maximization of the productivity of dollars available in time period one will constitute a maximization of productivity subject to the two constraints as well as to the one constraint. The reasoning is equally valid if we start with the constraint referring to time period two and maximize productivity of money available in that time period and then think of the effect of the additional constraint imposed for time period one.

3. Unfortunately, typical circumstances will probably make the relatively simple solutions unavailable. The solution to the relatively complex problem will—abstracting from discontinuities—require expending the full amount available for investment in each period. To illustrate how the solution is to be reached, consider the average actual net outlay of the two periods as being an outlay in a single "virtual" period and consider the average net outlay that is permitted by the constraints as being the average permitted outlay for the "virtual" period. Plan a budget for this "virtual" period according to the method of the one-period problem with which this section begins. That is, ration the capital available in the "virtual" period among the available investment opportunities so as to maximize the firm's net worth according to the principles stated in the discussion of the one-period problem. If, by accident, this budget happens to require precisely those outlays which are permitted for the first and second periods, it is easy to see that the problem has been solved. No other budget with a higher present value can be devised within the stated constraints for periods one and two.

Typically, the happy accident referred to in the preceding paragraph will not occur. The optimum use of the average amount available for investment in the two periods will typically result in expending too much in one period and not so much as is permitted in the other. Indeed, the happy accident was mentioned only as a step in explaining one method that will work. Though a simple average will almost never work, there is always some weighted average that will, and it can be found by trial and error. We shall describe in some detail a method that is mathematically equivalent to this method of weighted averages. In this method the solution is found by choosing, for suitable positive constants $p_1$ and $p_2$, those, and only those, proposals for which the following quantity is positive: $y - p_1c_1 - p_2c_2$. Here $y$ is the present value of the proposal; $c_1$ and $c_2$ are the present values of the net outlays required in the first and second periods, respectively; and the multipliers $p_1$ and $p_2$ are auxiliary quantities for which there does not seem to be an immediate interpretation but that nonetheless help in solving the problem.[5]

Initially, the values of $p_1$ and $p_2$ will be determined by judgment. Subsequently, they will be altered by trial and error until the amounts to be expended in the first and second periods, according to the rule just enunciated, are precisely the amounts permitted by the constraints. The initial choice of

*subject to constraint*

$P_1 C_1 -$

$P_2 C_2$

---

[5] The multipliers, $p_1$ and $p_2$, are closely related to what are known in mathematics and in economics as "Lagrange multipliers."

values for $p_1$ and $p_2$ is not very important, since a graphical process can usually lead rapidly to the correct values.

Certain special possibilities are worth noting. Proposals of positive present value may have negative cost, that is, release cash, for either period. Some proposals of zero or negative present value may be acceptable because they release cash for one period or both. All such possibilities are automatically covered by the rule as stated and by the rules to be given for later problems.

Finding the correct values for $p_1$ and $p_2$ is sometimes not easy—especially when combined with the problem of selecting among mutually exclusive alternatives—but the task is usually as nothing compared to the interests involved or compared to many everyday engineering problems.[6] The following example may clarify the process.

Nine investments have been proposed. The present value of the net outlays required in the first and second time periods and the present values of the investments are as shown in Table 1. The finance committee has stated that $50 and $20 will be available for capital investment in the first and second periods, respectively. We shall consider these amounts to have present values of $50 and $20, respectively. According to the principle stated above, we must now find appropriate multipliers, $p_1$ and $p_2$.

TABLE 1

| INVESTMENT | OUTLAY— PERIOD 1 ($c_1$) | OUTLAY— PERIOD 2 ($c_2$) | PRESENT VALUE OF INVESTMENT |
|---|---|---|---|
| $a$ | $12 | $ 3 | $14 |
| $b$ | 54 | 7 | 17 |
| $c$ | 6 | 6 | 17 |
| $d$ | 6 | 2 | 15 |
| $e$ | 30 | 35 | 40 |
| $f$ | 6 | 6 | 12 |
| $g$ | 48 | 4 | 14 |
| $h$ | 36 | 3 | 10 |
| $i$ | 18 | 3 | 12 |

Multipliers $p_1$ and $p_2$ were initially set at 1 and 3, respectively. With these values, only for investment $d$ was the expression $(y - p_1c_1 - p_2c_2)$ positive and therefore acceptable. This would have resulted in net outlays of only $6 and $2 in periods one and two, respectively, Clearly, the values initially chosen for $p_1$ and $p_2$ were too great. On the other hand, values of 0.1 and 0.5 for $p_1$ and $p_2$, respectively, are too low, resulting in a positive value of $(y -$

[6] It is true, however, that the numbers in engineering problems are less conjectural; hence the cost of calculation is more likely to be considered worth while.

$p_1c_1 - p_2c_2$) for all investments and required outlays in periods one and two far exceeding the permitted outlays.

Values of 0.33 and 1 for $p_1$ and $p_2$ result in a near-perfect fit. The expression $(y - p_1c_1 - p_2c_2)$ is positive for investments $a$, $c$, $d$, $f$, and $i$. These investments require outlays of $48 and $20 in the first and second periods, as near the permitted outlays of $50 and $20 as discontinuities permit. No other group of investments that is possible within the stated constraints has a greater present value than $70, the present value of this group.[7]

## C. SELECTING THE BEST AMONG MUTUALLY EXCLUSIVE ALTERNATIVES

Before monies are actually expended in fulfilment of an approved capital budget, the firm usually considers mutually exclusive alternative ways of making the generally described capital investment. When the firm is operating without an absolute limit on the dollars to be invested, the solution to the problem of selecting the best alternative is obvious. (Throughout this article, it is assumed that decisions regarding individual investment proposals do not significantly affect the firm's cost of capital.) The best alternative is the one with the greatest present value at the firm's cost of capital.

When the firm is operating subject to the constraint of an absolute dollar limit on capital expenditures, the problem is more difficult. Consider, first, the case in which there are net outlays in only one time period. The solution is found by the following process:

1. From each set of mutually exclusive alternatives, select that alternative for which the following quantity is a maximum: $y - pc$. Here $y$ is the present value of the alternative; $c$ is the net outlay required; and $p$ is a constant of a magnitude chosen initially according to the judgment of the analyst. (Remember that the alternative of making no investment—that is, accepting $y = 0$ and $c = 0$—is always available, so that the maximum in question is never negative.)

2. Compute the total outlays required to adopt all the investment proposals selected according to the principle just specified.

3. If the total outlay required exceeds the total amount available, $p$ should be increased; if the total amount required is less than the amount available for investment, $p$ should be reduced. By trial and error, a value for $p$ can be found that will equate the amount required for investment with that available for investment.

It should be clear that, as the value of $y$ is increased, the importance of the product, $pc$, increases, with a consequent increase in the probability that in each set of mutually exclusive alternatives, an alternative will be selected that requires a smaller net outlay than is required with a smaller value for $p$. Thus increasing $p$ tends to reduce the total amount required to adopt the investment proposals selected according to the principle indicated in (1)

[7] For the three-period problem, the relevant quantity is $(y - p_1c_1 - p_2c_2 - p_3c_3)$ rather than $(y - p_1c_1 - p_2c_2)$.

above. Conversely, reducing $p$ tends to increase the outlay required to adopt the investment proposals selected according to this principle.

When there are net outlays in more than one period, the principle of solution is the same. Instead of maximizing the quantity $(y - pc)$, it is necessary to maximize the quantity $(y - p_1c_1 - p_2c_2)$, where again $c_1$ and $c_2$ are the net outlays in the first and second periods and $p_1$ and $p_2$ are auxiliary multipliers.

Up to this point, we have not discussed the problem of rationing capital among both independent investment proposals and sets of mutually exclusive investment proposals. Superficially, this problem seems different from the one of rationing among mutually exclusive proposals only, but in fact the problems are the same. The identity rests upon the fact that each so-called "independent" proposal is and should be considered a member of the set of proposals consisting of the independent proposal and of the always present proposal to do nothing. When independent proposals are viewed in this way, it can be seen that the case of rationing simultaneously among independent proposals and sets of mutually exclusive proposals is really just a special case of rationing among mutually exclusive proposals according to the principles outlined in the preceding paragraph.

The mechanics of solution are easily worked out. All that is required in order to make the solution the same as the solution for what we have called "mutually exclusive" sets of alternatives is that each so-called "independent" proposal be treated as a member of a mutually exclusive set consisting of itself and of the alternative of doing nothing. Once this is done, it is possible to go into the familiar routine of selecting from each set that proposal for which the express $(y - pc)$, or its appropriate modification to take account of constraints existing in more than one time period, is a maximum. Again, of course, that value of $p$ will have to be found which results in matching as nearly as discontinuities permit the outlays required by the accepted proposals with the outlays permitted by the stated budgetary constraints.

## III. SOME COMPARISONS WITH THE RATE-OF-RETURN METHOD OF CAPITAL RATIONING[8]

Since the rate-of-return method of capital rationing is fully described elsewhere, we shall describe it only briefly.[9] As in the methods described previously, attention is focused exclusively on net cash flows rather than on the data produced by conventional accounting practices. Investment proposals are ranked according to their "rate of return," defined as that rate of discounting which

[8] Joel Dean has pioneered in the development of methods of capital rationing that have an understandable relationship to profit maximization, in contrast to methods still quite widely used in business that rely on such criteria as pay-back, average return on book investment, etc. The method that he advocates is called the "rate-of-return" method.

[9] See Joel Dean, *Capital Budgeting* (New York: Columbia University Press, 1951); "Measuring the Productivity of Capital," *Harvard Business Review*, January–February, 1954.

reduces a stream of cash flows to zero, and selected from this ranking, starting with the highest rate of return.

The rate-of-return solution to the three problems that are the subject of this paper is discussed below.

### A. GIVEN THE COST OF CAPITAL, WHAT GROUP OF INVESTMENTS SHOULD BE SELECTED?

The rate-of-return solution to the problem of selecting a group of independent proposals, given the firm's cost of capital, is to accept all investment proposals having a rate of return greater than the firm's cost of capital. This solution is necessarily identical with the solution proposed previously, except when the present value of some of the proposals is other than a steadily decreasing function of the cost of capital. An intuitive substantiation of this statement is achieved by an understanding of Figure 1. In Figure 1, $I$–$I$ indicates the present value of an investment at different rates of interest; $Oa$ is the firm's cost of capital; $Ob$ is the rate of return on the investment; and $aa'$ is the present value of the investment at the firm's cost of capital. It should be clear from the diagram that any proposal that has a positive ordinate (present value) at the firm's cost of capital will also have a rate of return ($x$-intercept) greater than the cost of capital. (However, it usually takes a little longer to find an intercept than to determine the value of an ordinate at one point.)

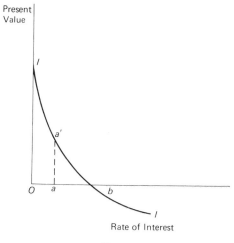

Figure 1

Under what circumstances can the present value of an investment proposal be something other than a steadily decreasing function of the cost of capital? Some investment proposals can intersect the $x$-axis at more than one point. In particular, investment proposals having initial cash outlays, subsequent net cash inflows, and final net cash outlays can intersect the $x$-axis more than once and have, therefore, more than one rate of return. Investments of this nature are rare, but they do occur, especially in the extractive industries. For example, an investment proposal might consist of an investment in an oil pump that gets a fixed quantity of oil out of the ground more rapidly than the pump currently in use. Making this investment would require an initial net outlay (for the new pump), subsequent net incremental cash inflow (larger oil production), and final net incremental cash outlay (the absence of oil production, because of its earlier exhaustion with the use of the higher-capacity new pump).[10] The present value of an investment in such a pump could look like Figure 2. In Figure 2, $I–I$ indicates the present value of the investment; $Oa$ is the firm's cost of capital; $Ob$ and $Oc$ are the two rates of return on the investment; and $aa'$ is the present value of the investment at the firm's cost of capital.

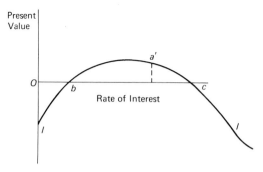

Figure 2

The reasoning behind this apparent paradox of the double rate of return is as follows:

*a*) As the cost of capital of the firm approaches zero, the present value of the investment proposal approaches the algebraic sum of net cash flows and will be negative if this sum is negative.

*b*) As the cost of capital increases, the present value of the final net cash outflow diminishes in importance relative to the earlier flows, and this diminution can cause the present value of the entire proposal to become positive.

*c*) If the cost of capital continues to increase, the significance of all future cash flows tends to diminish, causing the present value of the proposal to approach the initial outlay as a limit.

The rate-of-return criterion for judging the acceptability of investment proposals, as it has been presented in published works, is then ambiguous or anomalous. This is in contrast to the clarity and uniform accuracy of the decisions indicated by the principle proposed earlier, which relates to the

---

[10] These incremental flows are measured with reference to the flows that would have resulted from the use of the smaller pump. Thus the final net outlay is not absolute but rather by comparison with oil (money) that would have been produced had the smaller pump been in use.

present value of an investment at the cost of capital rather than to a comparison between the cost of capital and the rate of return.[11]

### B. GIVEN A FIXED SUM FOR CAPITAL INVESTMENT, WHAT GROUP OF INVESTMENT PROPOSALS SHOULD BE UNDERTAKEN?

The rate-of-return solution to the problem of allocating a fixed sum of money—without reference to cost of capital—among competing proposals is to order the proposals according to their rate of return and to proceed down the ladder thus created until the available funds are exhausted. The group of investment proposals selected by the use of this principle can be different, and probably would usually be different, from the group selected when the criterion is present value rather than rate of return. A difference between the two groups would not exist if the available capital funds were just equal to that amount which would permit investment in all those proposals having a rate of return at least equal to the firm's cost of capital and only those proposals, and if the anomalies mentioned under Section A were not present.

The preceding statements are equivalent to saying that the groups of investments that would be chosen by the use of the two principles or criteria would necessarily be the same only if the fixed sum to be invested happened to be the optimum sum and that investment of any other sum could result in selection of different groups of proposals by use of the two principles. This difference would result from the fact that the different principles can result in a different ranking of proposals within the group that would be accepted if the optimum amount were invested. Table 2 indicates the validity of the statement that the ordering of two investment proposals according to their

TABLE 2

| PERIOD | NET CASH FLOWS | |
| | Investment A ($) | Investment B ($) |
| --- | --- | --- |
| 0– year | − 85 | − 90 |
| 0–1 year | + 17 | + 21 |
| 1–2 years | + 35 | + 33 |
| 2–3 years | + 68 | + 57 |
| 3–4 years | +131 | + 94 |
| 4–5 years | +216 | + 155 |
| 5–6 years | +357 | + 255 |
| 6–7 years | +546 | + 420 |
| 7–8 years | +555 | + 695 |
| 8–9 years | +345 | +1,150 |
| Present value at 20% | +606 | + 853 |
| Rate of return (%) | 66 | 62 |

[11] The rate-of-return rule could be easily modified to remove this ambiguity or anomaly by specifying that the relevant rate of return is the one at which the investment is a decreasing function of the rate of interest.

rate of return can be contrary to their ordering according to their present value per dollar of outlay.

The example of Table 2 illustrates that a proposal with a higher rate of return can have a lower present value and that, therefore, the two rules can conflict. The present-value rule maximizes the present value of the firm's net worth—by definition—and the rate-of-return rule therefore may not.

This discrepancy is undoubtedly of small practical significance. In the first place, firms that ration their capital rationally use the firm's cost of capital as the constraint rather than an absolute dollar sum, and under such rational behavior the two rules yield the same results, with the exception noted previously. (Undoubtedly, no firms long persist in setting absolute dollar constraints that differ significantly in their effects from the cost of capital constraint.) In the second place, the present values of investment proposals, expressed as functions of the cost of capital, are often thoughtful enough not to intersect above the $x$-axis (the rate-of-interest axis), a necessary condition for a conflict between the rate-of-return and present-value principles.

C. SELECTING THE BEST AMONG MUTUALLY EXCLUSIVE ALTERNATIVES

The rate-of-return solution to the problem of selecting the "best" among mutually exclusive investment alternatives, although occasionally tricky in practice, is simply explained as follows:

1. Compute the rate of return for that investment proposal, among the set of mutually exclusive proposals, requiring the least initial net outlay.

2. If the rate of return on the investment requiring the smallest outlay exceeds the firm's cost of capital (or other cutoff rate), tentatively accept that investment. Next compute the rate of return on the incremental outlay needed for the investment requiring the second lowest outlay. If that rate exceeds the firm's cutoff rate, accept the investment requiring the greater outlay in preference to that requiring the lesser. Proceed by such paired comparisons (based on rates of return on incremental outlay) to eliminate all but one investment.

3. If the rate of return on the proposal requiring the least outlay does not exceed the firm's cutoff rate, drop it from further consideration, and compute the rate of return for the proposal requiring the next least outlay. If that rate exceeds the firm's cutoff rate, that investment proposal becomes the bench mark for the first paired comparison. If that rate does not exceed the firm's cutoff rate, drop that proposal from further consideration. The process just described is to be repeated until either a proposal is found with a rate of return exceeding the cost of capital or until all proposals have been eliminated because their rates of return do not exceed the cutoff rate.

The rate-of-return solution to the problem of selecting the best among mutually exclusive investment alternatives is especially subject to the ambiguities and anomalies mentioned under Section A, because the costs and revenues associated with incremental investments required for proposals included in mutually exclusive sets are much more likely to have unusual time shapes and reversals than are the costs and revenues associated with independent investments.

## SUMMARY

We have given solutions to the three problems in budgeting capital so as to maximize the net worth of the firm. The solutions that we have given differ in principle from those implied by the rate of return method of capital rationing. The difference in principle can lead to differences in behavior. Differences in behavior will be rare in coping with problems of the first and third sorts and will be relatively frequent for problems of the second sort. When differences do exist, the rate-of-return solution does not result in maximizing the present value of the firm's net worth.

## 17. RISK, THE DISCOUNT RATE, AND INVESTMENT DECISIONS

### JACK HIRSHLEIFER*

Reprinted from *The American Economic Review*, Vol. *LI*, No. 2 (May, 1961), pp. 112–20, by permission of the author and the publisher.

The problem of risky investment decision has both normative and positive aspects. Looked at normatively, the question is: what is the appropriate technique of analysis—for individuals, firms, or government agencies—to use in evaluating risky investment alternatives? Looking at the problem positively, we ask: why do the mean experienced yields in different risk-classes of securities diverge, even when average yields for the different risk-classes are calculated over many individual securities and over long time-periods to eliminate random effects? If we first examine the positive aspect, the major explanations that have been offered for the yield divergences mentioned above (e.g., the divergences between stock and bond yields, or between earnings on industrial and utility shares) attribute them either to imperfections of capital markets or to market premiums for risk bearing. I will be adopting the latter approach. What I will be presenting is quite a simple market theory of risk, modeled upon Fisher's treatment of time preference and interest (but definitely not modeled upon Fisher's treatment of risk). On the normative side, I attempt to show how the criterion of maximizing present value—now generally accepted, despite some recent heresies, as the guiding principle for evaluation of riskless investment alternatives[1]—must be modified or generalized when risky investments are considered. In brief, I try to indicate the appropriate rate of discount to use, in the present-value formula, to allow for uncertainty of return as well as futurity of return.

* The RAND Corporation and U.C.L.A.

[1] For a discussion of the present-value criterion and a qualified vindication of it against proposed alternative investment criteria, see my paper, "On the Theory of Optimal Investment Decision," *J. P. E.*, Aug., 1958.

## I. THE MEANING OF RISK

First, however, it is absolutely necessary to clarify an elementary point that has been the source of much confusion. There are at least two quite different senses in which investments may be said to be risky. First of all, an investment with a certain nominal or quoted yield (e.g., a corporate bond) is often said to involve a risk of partial or total default. Here risk means only "unfavorable chance." Its measure is the difference between the nominal return and the true mathematical expectation of return. I shall call this difference or bias "expected-value risk," but the concept will not play any important role because I will henceforth ordinarily be speaking of investment yield in the expected-value sense. It is worth remarking, however, that expected-value risk does not occur solely in dealing with investments of fixed nominal yield, like bonds. It has been convincingly demonstrated, for example, that the predicted benefit-cost yields of federal water-resource investment projects are not, on the average, realized. Here also predicted yields are biased estimates of the mathematical expectation of yields.

The concept of risk I will use herein, however, concerns not the expected value but the variability of the probability distribution of outcomes. For concreteness, we may think of the standard deviation, the most common measure of variability, as a quantifier of "variability risk"—or, as we shall say henceforth, simply risk. However, I do not want to commit myself to saying that the standard deviation is *the* measure of risk. It may well be that other moments of the distribution are also involved in determining what we ordinarily call risk-premiums on security yields.[2]

## II. A MARKET THEORY OF THE RISK-PREMIUM

In this section I propose to present only some elements of a theory of the market process by which risk-premiums on investments are determined, in the belief that even a partial theory may serve to bring some order to the subject and settle a few debated points. My basic contention will be that the market risk-premium can be understood as the interaction of individuals' willingness to bear variability risks and of the technical fact of the productivity of risk, given individual endowments of more and less risky income opportunities. I have quite deliberately stated these determinants of the risk-premium to suggest an analogy with the theory of determination of interest—that is, of the time-premium—that we associate primarily with the names of Böhm-Bawerk and Fisher. In what follows I will attempt to develop various aspects of this analogy.

First of all, we can distinguish between widening and deepening of risk in a sense quite parallel to the familiar widening and deepening in time. We widen investments in time when, given the period of the investment, we

[2] Markowitz discusses the question of the appropriate measure of risk in his valuable work, *Portfolio Selection* (Wiley, 1959), pp. 180–201, 287–97. See also James Tobin, "Liquidity Preference as Behavior Towards Risk," *Rev. of Econ. Studies*, Feb., 1958.

increase the aggregate of current sacrifice on behalf of the future; we widen investments in risk when, given the degrees of riskiness of differing securities (for concreteness, we may think in terms of investments with specified standard deviation $\sigma$ of yield per dollar invested), we shift more of our current sacrifice from a relatively low-$\sigma$ to a relatively high-$\sigma$ medium. We deepen investments in time when, holding the aggregate of current sacrifice constant, we shift from quick-yielding to slow-yielding investments; we deepen investments in risk when, given the amount of resources held out of secure media, we shift from lower to higher variability commitments of these resources. As a practical example of the distinction in terms of risk, consider a dry farmer in an arid region where returns are highly uncertain. For a particular set of lands subject to essentially identical conditions, he can widen his risk by cultivating more acres. Or he can deepen his risk by shifting all or part of his operations to lands with still higher variability of outcomes.

In the theory of risk, as in the theory of interest, it is simpler to analyze widening than deepening. This is especially so in the former case, as the standard deviation is a less perfect quantifier for depth of risk than its analogue—the period of production—is for depth in time. However, the main point is that, so long as we stick to the simple widening case, troubles about a perfect measure of depth of risk need not unduly concern us. Once we have made the vital distinction between widening and deepening, I believe it may be possible to grasp intuitively the general consequences of shifts in the depth dimension, even though a theory of the latter will have to wait for another occasion.

Limiting ourselves, then, to the pure widening case, we may start by asking ourselves what we can reasonably assert about the nature of individuals' preferences between, to take the simplest situation, only two investment media —on the assumption that in any case the investor sacrifices current consumption which is certain. One of these media may be taken to be a perfectly secure investment, with a known certain future yield. The other offers a known expected value of yield, subject to a specified type of variability. For concreteness, we may think of the unit of certain yield as, simply, a dollar—and of the unit of risky yield as a lottery ticket representing equal chances of winning $2.00 or nothing. It is necessary, to keep to the simplest possible situation, to assume that the returns from the risky units are perfectly correlated. In other words, if we have 1,000 lottery tickets, we must win either $2,000 or nothing. The correlation assumption prevents the intrusion of the law of large numbers. It is reasonably close to the true situation in our acreage cultivation example, where if the crop fails on any acre it is very likely to fail on all.

With this situation in mind, we can draw indifference curves, between certain yield and uncertain expected yield, that express individuals' risk preferences. Indifference curve $I$ in Figure 1 indicates that the individual in question is indifferent between $500 certain and an expected value of $1,000 representing equal chances of $2,000 or nothing. I feel very easy in asserting convexity of the indifference curves (diminishing marginal rate of substitution between certain income and expected uncertain income). Consider an individual whose initial endowment consists of a risky expected value of $1,000, with no sure income at all. It seems natural to assume that he would be willing initially to sacrifice expected value for certainty at a rate far better than 1 : 1—perhaps as high as 10 : 1. But as his certain wealth or income comes to attain a more balanced relation to his uncertain prospects, the rate of exchange he is prepared to offer for more certainty would become much more moderate.

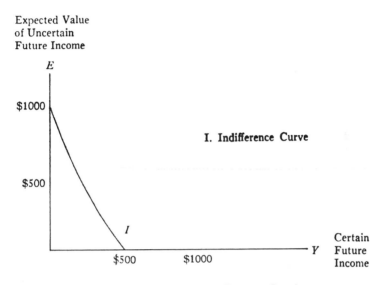

Figure 1. Indifference Curve Between Certain
and Uncertain Income

Indeed, it is conceivable that, given an initial endowment consisting solely of $500 certain, the same individual might be willing to sacrifice more than $1.00 of certain income for an expected value of $1.00. If so, then in this range he would be demonstrating risk-preference rather than risk-aversion. However, for convexity it is not necessary to assert that the individual is ever a risk-preferrer (that is, that the slope of his indifference curve will ever be less than 1 in absolute value)—all that is required is that the rate of exchange he is willing to offer change steadily from one reflecting strong risk-aversion at the upper left to one representing much more moderate risk-aversion or even risk-preference at the lower right.

Having introduced the risk-preference function and the initial endowments, we may now bring in the productive opportunity locus and the market opportunity locus. In a " Robinson Crusoe " situation no market opportunities exist, and the individual must find his optimum in terms of only his preferences, initial endowment, and productive opportunities. The essential point is the concavity of the productive opportunity locus, expressing diminishing marginal (expected) productivity of risk. The idea is that, by shifting his investments from the secure to the risky medium, the individual can first obtain a very favorable rate of exchange, but as he carries the process further it will become less and less favorable. The tangency slope will indicate the equality of the marginal rate of risk-aversion and the marginal productivity of risk-bearing.

Finally, if we bring a market into our two-media world and assume perfect competition, there will be a governing rate of exchange between certain income and expected income, which will be determined in such a way as to equate the sums of individuals' desired holdings in the two media with the actual quantities socially available in terms of original endowments and productive transformations between the two forms. As in the familiar Fisherian solution for time-preference decisions, the insertion of the market exchange line permits attainment of a higher indifference curve than would otherwise be possible. In Figure 2 the " Robinson Crusoe " solution is at $R$,

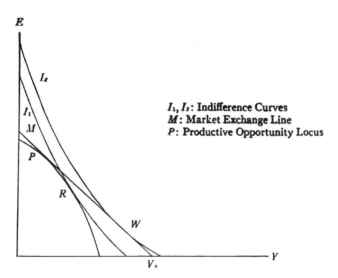

$I_1, I_2$: Indifference Curves
$M$: Market Exchange Line
$P$: Productive Opportunity Locus

FIGURE 2. "Robinson Crusoe" Solution ($R$) and Market Solution ($W$) for Risky Investment

while the market for risk-bearing permits attainment of the point $W$. With the introduction of the market, we may speak of the individual's decision criterion as maximization of certainty-equivalent value ($V_c$ in the diagram), in analogy with the maximization of present value in the theory of time-preference.

I do not feel it necessary to describe how these indifference curves can be made consistent with Friedman-Savage utility-of-wealth functions based upon the von Neumann-Morgenstern postulates. The indifference curves, to use a horrible metaphor, stand on their own feet as descriptive of what seems to me obviously reasonable and typical patterns of behavior. Other analysts have not, so far as I am aware, arrived at the simple results outlined above. I believe the reason is that they unconsciously started with the more difficult deepening case—leading most frequently to the construction of indifference curves between expected value of return and standard deviation of return.[3] Unfortunately, assertions about the shape of these indifference curves carry little immediate conviction, and the situation is not improved by appeal to an underlying Friedman-Savage utility-of-wealth function.

## III. SOME IMPLICATIONS

Without attempting strict proof, I believe a number of irrefutable statements can be derived as implications of the foregoing approach. First and foremost, there will ordinarily be a positive market premium on risk. That is, expected risky yields will be higher than sure yields. This is due to the general tilt of the preference functions illustrated in Figure 1 (expressing reluctance to bear risk) interacting with the fact that risk-bearing is ordinarily productive. That the market does pay positive risk-premiums is a statement so refutable that many people (in particular, Knight) claim it has in fact been refuted. However, I believe that the weight of the evidence indicates that risky media of investment do in fact have higher expected yields than secure media (or, in other words, uncertain expected values are discounted relative to certain values). Over any reasonably long period of measurement, stocks yield more than bonds, and risky bonds more than secure bonds.[4] Of course, this theory does not allow for acceptance of " unfair " gambles. Alternative explanations would have to be sought for the phenomenon of Las Vegas.

A second implication is that individuals will typically diversify. The relationships among the curves are such that interior optima are normal, and corner optima exceptional. A third implication is that—so long as we are dealing with interior rather than corner optima and the assumption of perfect markets applies—on the margin everyone has the same degree of risk-aversion. We should, therefore, exercise care before labelling some individuals " risk-preferrers " and others " risk-avoiders." What is true is that, in the process of attaining marginal equality, some individuals will have shifted away from relatively secure initial endowments and so in a sense sought out risk, while others will have moved in the opposite direction; but this shift will reflect not merely preferences as to risk-bearing but also initial endowments and access to risky productive opportunities.

Translating the third implication above into normative language, we may say that all investors should discount risks at the rate of exchange between certain and risky prospects established by the market for the risk-class within

---

[3] See Tobin, *op. cit.*, pp. 71–82; F. A. and V. Lutz, *The Theory of Investment of the Firm*, pp. 179–92.

[4] That stocks yield more in the long run than bonds is a notorious fact nor requiring demonstration here. The recent study by W. Braddock Hickman, *Corporate Bond Quality and Investor Experience*, supports my contention about bonds—that investors demand an extra premium, over and above the expected loss by default, to hold risky bonds.

which the investment in question falls. This contradicts a traditional view that, in evaluating risky investment opportunities, the investor ought to specify the expected values involved and then discount them by some kind of "caution coefficient" expressing his own preferences toward risk-bearing.[5] The error here has an analogy in the domain of time preference, where theorists have sometimes advised investors to use their personal time-discount rates rather than the market rate in discounting future income prospects. In the latter case, it is not difficult to show that, given a perfect market for exchange of present and future funds, highest levels of satisfaction are attained by maximizing present value calculated at the market rate of discount. Similarly in the case of risk, the optimization rule is to maximize certainty-equivalent value, discounting uncertain expected yields at the market rate of exchange between such yields and certain ones (always assuming that perfect markets exist). In the one case, this implies adjustment of all personal marginal time preferences, by appropriate shifts between present and future funds, to the market time-discount rate; in the other, adjustment of personal risk-preferences, by appropriate shifts between secure and risky media, to the market risk-premium rate.

## IV. CORPORATE FINANCE AND INVESTMENT DECISIONS

The analysis presented above suffices to provide the answer to the simplest problem of corporate finance. If the investment in question involves only widening in time and in risk (i.e., shifting from secure and current funds to future and uncertain ones of a given degree of risk), if it is a new venture so that there are no interactions with returns on past investments, and if only equity financing is involved, the market time-and-risk discount rate should be used in deciding how far to carry the investment. While the list of simplifying conditions sounds formidable, I should comment that the market discount rate in question—the "impure" (inclusive of risk-premium) rate of interest— is at least more of an observable magnitude than the abstract riskless rate of interest. It is assumed that the entrepreneur and the potential investors are both aware of the mathematical expectations of returns at different dates and the appropriate market capitalization rate, $1/\rho$ (where $\rho$ is the "impure" interest rate) for expected yields in that risk-class. The investment in question should, of course, be widened until its marginal expected yield per current certain dollar sacrificed falls to $\rho$.

The listener may possibly have detected by this time a certain resemblance to the line of thought put forward in the recent provocative article by Modigliani and Miller.[6] Modigliani and Miller go beyond the analysis presented here in centering attention upon the market yields of debt-equity combinations and the implications thereof for investment decisions. However, I believe that

---

[5] Irving Fisher, *The Nature of Capital and Income*, p. 277.

[6] Franco Modigliani and Merton H. Miller, "The Cost of Capital, Corporation Finance, and the Theory of Investment," *A. E. R.*, June, 1958, pp. 261–97.

the theoretical analysis of risk-bearing presented here is that implicitly under-lying the Modigliani-Miller paper. The most essential parallel is that Modigliani and Miller select market-value maximization as their criterion (page 264), which in the context is essentially maximization of the certainty-equivalent value described above. The Modigliani-Miller " equivalent-return classes" (pages 266 ff.) seem to be essentially what I have called "risk-classes"; in addition, Modigliani and Miller assume a positive market premium for risk bearing (page 271).

Limitations of time, unfortunately, prevent my presenting a fuller analysis here of what I regard as the major normative conclusion of the Modigliani-Miller analysis: that, setting aside consideration of corporate income tax, even firms with complex debt-equity capital structures should use, in evalu-ating investment alternatives, the discount rate determined by the market in capitalizing pure equity streams of comparable risk (page 288). I believe that this conclusion is basically sound. It is, with some qualifications, quite consistent with the theory of risk bearing presented above, provided one accepts in addition the famous "Proposition I" of Modigliani and Miller: that the "value of the firm," the sum of the market value of its debt and equity, is a constant—determined by capitalizing its expected asset return at the appropriate risky discount rate (page 268). Without getting into tortured debates about what constitutes "arbitrage," I would agree that a divergence between a firm's net asset value and the sum of its debt and equity cannot be expected to persist—unless market imperfections are brought in.

There is one qualification I would like to make here, however, arising out of the theory presented above. Modigliani and Miller describe the discount rate recommended for investment decision as the pure-equity capitalization rate for the asset-earnings of the firm as a whole. Their risk-class concept is a characteristic of the firm rather than of the individual investment. Evidently they are thinking of marginal investments as being equally risky with those previously adopted—what I have called risk-widening rather than risk-deepening. This is justifiable as simplifying the analysis, though the problem remains of evaluating risk-deepening investments. Another problem is created by imperfect correlation of investment returns. While the theoretical analysis above assumed perfect correlation to avoid the operation of the law of large numbers, in the real world the advantages of risk-pooling are very important. In fact, a marginal investment that is individually very risky may substantially reduce the over-all variability risk of the firm's total portfolio of investments. I am inclined to think that the best way of rescuing the analysis is to take note of the fact that, where large numbers of individual investments are involved, the variability of the over-all investment return approaches the value of the average covariance among the individual investments.[7] The risk-classes into which firms are divided, then, would depend very importantly upon the diversity of returns of their portfolios as a whole, and the variability of

[7] See Markowitz, *op. cit.*, p. 111.

individual investments can be correspondingly neglected. The established all-equity discount rate for the firm can then be used without great error in evaluating marginal investments whose individual variability and inter-correlation with other investments are not too divergent from the over-all pattern.

# 18. ON THE THEORY OF OPTIMAL INVESTMENT DECISION[1]

## J. HIRSHLEIFER*

Reprinted from *The Journal of Political Economy*, Vol. *LXVI*, No. 4, (August, 1958), pp. 329–52, by permission of the author and the University of Chicago Press. Copyright, 1958, by the University of Chicago.

This article is an attempt to solve (in the theoretical sense), through the use of isoquant analysis, the problem of optimal investment decisions (in business parlance, the problem of capital budgeting). The initial section reviews the principles laid down in Irving Fisher's justly famous works on interest[2] to see what light they shed on two competing rules of behavior currently proposed by economists to guide business investment decisions—the present-value rule

* University of Chicago

[1] I should like to express indebtedness to many of my colleagues, and especially to James H. Lorie and Martin J. Bailey, for valuable suggestions and criticisms.

[2] Irving Fisher, *The Theory of Interest* (New York: Macmillan Co., 1930), is most widely known. His earlier work, *The Rate of Interest* (New York: Macmillan Co., 1907), contains most of the essential ideas.

and the internal-rate-of-return rule. The next concern of the paper is to show how Fisher's principles must be adapted when the perfect capital market assumed in his analysis does not exist—in particular, when borrowing and lending rates diverge, when capital can be secured only at an increasing marginal borrowing rate, and when capital is "rationed." In connection with this last situation, certain non-Fisherian views (in particular, those of Scitovsky and of the Lutzes) about the correct ultimate goal or criterion for investment decisions are examined. Section III, which presents the solution for multi-period investments, corrects an error by Fisher which has been the source of much difficulty. The main burden of the analysis justifies the contentions of those who reject the internal rate of return as an investment criterion, and the paper attempts to show where the error in that concept (as ordinarily defined) lies and how the internal rate must be redefined if it is to be used as a reliable guide. On the positive side, the analysis provides some support for the use of the present-value rule but shows that even that rule is at best only a partial indicator of optimal investments and, in fact, under some conditions, gives an incorrect result.

More recent works on investment decisions, I shall argue, suffer from the neglect of Fisher's great contributions—the attainment of an optimum through balancing consumption alternatives over time and the clear distinction between production opportunities and exchange opportunities. It is an implication of this analysis, though it cannot be pursued here in detail, that solutions to the problem of investment decision recently proposed by Boulding, Samuelson, Scitovsky, and the Lutzes are at least in part erroneous. Their common error lay in searching for a rule or formula which would indicate optimal investment decisions *independently of consumption decisions.* No such search can succeed, if Fisher's analysis is sound which regards investment as not an end in itself but rather a process for distributing consumption over time.

The present paper deals throughout with a highly simplified situation in which the costs and returns of alternative individual investments are known *with certainty*, the problem being to select the scale and the mix of investments to be undertaken. To begin with, the analysis will be limited to investment decisions relating to two time periods only. We shall see in later sections that the two-period analysis can be translated immediately to the analysis of investments in perpetuities. For more general fluctuating income streams, however, additional difficulties arise whose resolution involves important new questions of principle. The restriction of the solution to perfect-information situations is, of course, unfortunate, since ignorance and uncertainty are of the essence of certain important observable characteristics of investment decision behavior. The analysis of optimal decisions under conditions of certainty can be justified, however, as a first step toward a more complete theory. No further apology will be offered for considering this oversimplified problem beyond the statement that theoretical economists are in such substantial disagreement about it that a successful attempt to bring the solution within the standard body of economic doctrine would represent a real contribution.

## I. TWO-PERIOD ANALYSIS

### A. BORROWING RATE EQUALS LENDING RATE (FISHER'S SOLUTION)

In order to establish the background for the difficult problems to be considered later, let us first review Fisher's solution to the problem of investment decision.[3] Consider the case in which there is a given rate at which the individual (or firm)[4] may borrow that is unaffected by the amount of his borrowings; a given rate at which he can lend that is unaffected by the amount of his loans; and in which these two rates are equal. These are the conditions used by Fisher; they represent a perfect capital market.

In Figure 1 the horizontal axis labeled $K_0$ represents the amount of actual or potential income (the amount consumed or available for consumption) in period 0; the vertical axis $K_1$ represents the amount of income in the same sense in period 1. The individual's decision problem is to choose, within the

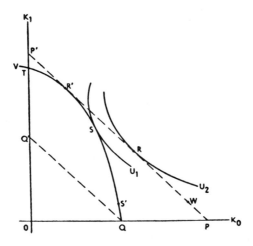

Fɪɢ. 1.—Fisher's solution

opportunities available to him, an optimum point on the graph—that is, an optimum time pattern of consumption. His starting point may conceivably be a point on either axis (initial income falling all in period 0 or all in period 1), such as points $T$ or $P$, or else it may be a point in the positive quadrant (initial income falling partly in period 0 and partly in period 1), such as points $W$ or $S'$. It may even lie in the second or fourth quadrants—where his initial situation involves negative income either in period 0 or in period 1.

---

[3] Fisher's contributions to the theory of capital go beyond his solution of the problem discussed in this paper—optimal investment decision. He also considers the question of the equilibrium of the capital market, which balances the supplies and demand of all the decision-making agencies.

[4] This analysis does not distinguish between individuals and firms. Firms are regarded solely as agencies or instruments of individuals.

The individual is assumed to have a preference function relating income in periods 0 and 1. This preference function would be mapped in quite the ordinary way, and the curves $U_1$ and $U_2$ are ordinary utility-indifference curves from this map.

Finally, there are the investment opportunities open to the individual. Fisher distinguishes between "investment opportunities" and "market opportunities." The former are real productive transfers between income in one time period and in another (what we usually think of as "physical" investment, like planting a seed); the latter are transfers through borrowing or lending (which naturally are on balance offsetting in the loan market). I shall depart from Fisher's language to distinguish somewhat more clearly between "production opportunities" and "market opportunities"; the word "investment" will be used in the more general and inclusive sense to refer to both types of opportunities taken together. Thus we may invest by building a house (a sacrifice of present or future income through a production opportunity) or by lending on the money market (a sacrifice of present for future income through a market or exchange opportunity). We could, equivalently, speak of purchase and sale of capital assets instead of lending or borrowing in describing the market opportunities.

In Figure 1 an investor with a starting point at $Q$ faces a market opportunity illustrated by the dashed line $QQ'$. That is, starting with all his income in time 0, he can lend at some given lending rate, sacrificing present for future income, any amount until his $K_0$ is exhausted—receiving in exchange $K_1$ or income in period 1. Equivalently, we could say that he can buy capital assets—titles to future income $K_1$—with current income $K_0$. Following Fisher, I shall call $QQ'$ a "market line."[5] The line $PP'$, parallel to $QQ'$, is the market line available to an individual whose starting point is $P$ on the $K_0$ axis. By our assumption that the borrowing rate is also constant and equal to the lending rate, the market line $PP'$ is also the market opportunity to an individual whose starting point is $W$, within the positive quadrant.

Finally, the curve $QSTV$ shows the range of productive opportunities available to an individual with starting point $Q$. It is the locus of points attainable to such an individual as he sacrifices more and more of $K_0$ by productive investments yielding $K_1$ in return. This attainability locus Fisher somewhat ambiguously calls the "productive opportunity curve" or "productive transformation curve." Note that in its concavity to the origin the curve reveals a kind of diminishing returns to investment. More specifically, productive investment projects may be considered to be ranked by the expression $(\Delta K_1)/(-\Delta K_0) - 1$, which might be called the "productive rate of return."[6] Here $\Delta K_0$ and $\Delta K_1$ represent the changes in income of periods 0 and 1 associated with the project in question.

---

[5] The slope of the market line is, of course, $-(1 + i)$, where $i$ is the lending-borrowing rate. That is, when one gives up a dollar in period 0, he receives in exchange $1 + i$ dollars in period 1.

[6] For the present it is best to avoid the term "internal rate of return." Fisher uses the expressions "rate of return on sacrifice" or "rate of return over cost."

We may conceive of whole projects being so ranked, in which case we get the average productive rate of return for each such project. Or we may rank infinitesimal increments to projects, in which case we can deal with a marginal productive rate of return. The curve $QSTV$ will be continuous and have a continuous first derivative under certain conditions relating to absence of "lumpiness" of individual projects (or increments to projects), which we need not go into. In any case, $QSTV$ would represent a sequence of projects so arranged as to start with the one yielding the highest productive rate of return at the lower right and ending with the lowest rate of return encountered when the last dollar of period 0 is sacrificed at the upper left.[7] It is possible to attach meaning to the portion of $QSTV$ in the second quadrant, where $K_0$ becomes negative. Such points could not be optimal with indifference curves as portrayed in Figure 1, of course, but they may enter into the determination of an optimum. (This analysis assumes that projects are independent. Where they are not, complications ensue which will be discussed in Sections $E$ and F below.)

As to the solution itself, the investor's objective is to climb onto as high an indifference curve as possible. Moving along the productive opportunity line $QSTV$, he sees that the highest indifference curve it touches is $U_1$ at the point $S$. But this is not the best point attainable, for he can move along $QSTV$ somewhat farther to the point $R'$, which is on the market line $PP'$. He can now move in the reverse direction (borrowing) along $PP'$, and the point $R$ on the indifference curve $U_2$ is seen to be the best attainable.

The investor has, therefore, a solution in two steps. The "productive" solution—the point at which the individual should stop making additional productive investments—is at $R'$. He may then move along his market line to a point better satisfying his time preferences, at $R$. That is to say, he makes the best investment from the productive point of view and then "finances" it in the loan market. A very practical example is building a house and then borrowing on it through a mortgage so as to replenish current consumption income.

[7] An individual starting at $S'$ would also have a "disinvestment opportunity."

[8] The present-value rule is the more or less standard guide supported by a great many theorists. The internal-rate-of-return rule, in the sense used here, has also been frequently proposed (see, e.g., Joel Dean, *Capital Budgeting* [New York: Columbia University Press, 1951], pp. 17–19). Citations on the use of alternative investment criteria may be found in Friedrich and Vera Lutz, *The Theory of Investment of the Firm* (Princeton, N. J.: Princeton University Press, 1951), p. 16. The internal-rate-of-return rule which we will consider in detail (i.e., adopt all projects and increments to projects for which the internal rate of return exceeds the market rate of interest) is *not* the same as that emphasized by the Lutzes (i.e., adopt that pattern of investments maximizing the internal rate of return). The rule considered here compares the incremental or marginal rate of return with a market rate; the other would maximize the average internal rate of return, without regard to the market rate. The latter rule will be shown to be fundamentally erroneous, even in the form the Lutzes accept as their ultimate criterion (maximize the internal rate of return on the investor's owned capital). This point will be discussed in connection with capital rationing in Sec. D, below.

We may now consider, in the light of this solution, the current debate between two competing "rules" for optimal investment behavior.[8] The first of these, the present-value rule, would have the individual or firm adopt all projects whose present value is positive at the market rate of interest. This would have the effect of maximizing the present value of the firm's position in terms of income in periods 0 and 1. Present value, under the present conditions, may be defined as $K_0 + (K_1)/(1 + i)$, income in period 1 being discounted by the factor $1 + i$, where $i$ is the lending-borrowing rate. Since the market lines are defined by the condition that a sacrifice of one dollar in $K_0$ yields $1 + i$ dollars in $K_1$, these market lines are nothing but lines of constant present value. The equation for these lines is $K_0 + (K_1)/(1 + i) = C$, $C$ being a parameter. The present-value rule tells us to invest until the highest such line is attained, which clearly takes place at the point $R'$. So far so good, but note that the rule says nothing about the "financing" (borrowing or lending) also necessary to attain the final optimum at $R$.

The internal-rate-of-return rule, in the form here considered, would have the firm adopt any project whose internal rate is greater than the market rate of interest. The internal rate for a project in the general case is defined as that discounting rate $\rho$ which reduces the stream of net returns associated with the project to a present value of zero (or, equivalently, which makes the discounted value of the associated cost stream equal to the discounted value of the receipts stream). We may write

$$0 = \Delta K_0 + \frac{\Delta K_1}{1 + \rho} + \frac{\Delta K_2}{(1 + \rho)^2} + \cdots + \frac{\Delta K_n}{(1 + \rho)^n}.$$

In the two-period case $\rho$ is identical with the productive rate of return, $(\Delta K_1)/(-\Delta K_0) - 1$. As in the discussion above, if infinitesimal changes are permitted, we may interpret this statement in the marginal sense. The marginal (two-period) internal rate of return is measured by the slope of the productive opportunity curve minus unity. In Figure 1 at each step we would compare the steepness of $QSTV$ with that of the market lines. We would move along $QSTV$ as long as, and just so long as, it is the steeper. Evidently, this rule would have us move along $QSTV$ until it becomes tangent to a market line at $R'$. Again, so far so good, but nothing is said about the borrowing or lending then necessary to attain the optimum.

At least for the two-period case, then, the present-value rule and the internal-rate-of-return rule lead to identical answers[9] which are the same as that reached by our isoquant analysis, so far as *productive* investment decisions are concerned. The rules are both silent, however, about the market exchange between $K_0$ and $K_1$, which remains necessary if an optimum is to be achieved. This second step is obviously part of the solution. Had there been no actual

---

[9] In fact, for the two-period case the rules are identical; it is possible to show that any project (or increment to a project) of positive present value must have an internal rate of return greater than the rate of interest.

opportunity to borrow or lend, the point $S$ would have been the best attainable, and the process of productive investment should not have been carried as far as $R'$. We cannot say that the rules are definitely wrong, however, since with no such market opportunities there would have been no market rate of interest $i$ for calculating present values or for comparison with the marginal internal rate of return. It remains to be seen whether these rules can be restated or generalized to apply to cases where a simple market rate of interest is not available for unlimited borrowing and lending. But it should be observed that, in comparison with isoquant analysis, each of the rules leads to only a partial answer.

### B.  WHEN BORROWING AND LENDING RATES DIFFER

We may now depart from Fisher's analysis, or rather extend it, to a case he did not consider. The borrowing and lending rates are still assumed to be constant, independent of the amounts taken or supplied by the individual or firm under consideration. However, it is now assumed that these rates are not equal, the borrowing rate being higher than the lending rate.[10] In Figure 2 there is the same preference map, of which only the isoquant $U_1$ is shown.

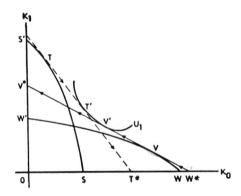

Fig. 2.—Extension of Fisher's solution for differing borrowing and lending rates.

There are now, however, two sets of market lines over the graph; the steeper (*dashed*) lines represent borrowing opportunities (note the direction of the arrows), and the flatter (*solid*) lines represent lending opportunities. The heavy solid lines show two possible sets of productive opportunities, both of which lead to solutions along $U_1$. Starting with amount $OW$ of $K_0$, an investor

[10] If the borrowing rate were lower than the lending rate, it would be possible to accumulate infinite wealth by borrowing and relending, so I shall not consider this possibility. Of course, financial institutions typically borrow at a lower average rate than that at which they lend, but they cannot expand their scale of operations indefinitely without changing this relationship.

with a production opportunity $WVW'$ would move along $WVW'$ to $V$, at which point he would *lend* to get to his time-preference optimum—the tangency with $U_1$ at $V'$. The curve $STS'$ represents a much more productive possibility; starting with only $OS$ of $K_0$, the investor would move along $STS'$ to $T$ and then *borrow* backward along the dashed line to get to $T'$, the tangency point with $U_1$. Note that the total opportunity set (the points attainable through any combination of the market and productive opportunities) is $WVW^*$ for the first opportunity, and $S'TT^*$ for the second.

More detailed analysis, however, shows that we do not yet have the full solution—there is a third possibility. An investor with a productive opportunity locus starting on the $K_0$ axis will never stop moving along this locus in the direction of greater $K_1$ as long as the marginal productive rate of return is still above the borrowing rate—nor will he ever push along the locus beyond the point where the marginal productive rate of return falls below the lending rate. Assuming that some initial investments are available which have a higher productive rate of return than the borrowing rate, the investor should push along the locus until the borrowing rate is reached. If, at this point, it is possible to move up the utility hill by borrowing, productive investment should cease, and the borrowing should take place; the investor is at some point like $T$ in Figure 2. If borrowing decreases utility, however, more productive investment is called for. Suppose investment is then carried on until diminishing returns bring the marginal productive rate of return down to the lending rate. If lending then increases utility, productive investment should halt there, and the lending take place; the investor is at some point like $V$ in Figure 2. But suppose that now it is found that lending also decreases utility! This can only mean that a tangency of the productive opportunity locus and an indifference curve took place when the marginal productive rate of return was somewhere *between* the lending and the borrowing rates. In this case neither lending nor borrowing is called for, the optimum being reached directly in the productive investment decision by equating the marginal productive rate of return with the marginal rate of substitution (in the sense of time preference) along the utility isoquant.

These solutions are illustrated by the division of Figure 3 into three zones. In Zone I the borrowing rate is relevant. Tangency solutions with the market line at the borrowing rate like that at $T$ are carried back by borrowing to tangency with a utility isoquant at a point like $T'$. All such final solutions lie along the curve $OB$, which connects all points on the utility isoquants whose slope equals that of the *borrowing* market line. Correspondingly, Zone III is that zone where the production solution involves tangency with a lending market line (like $V$), which is then carried forward by lending to a final tangency optimum with a utility isoquant along the line $OL$ at a point like $V'$. This line connects all points on the utility isoquants with slope equal to that of the *lending* market line. Finally, Zone II solutions occur when a productive opportunity locus like $QRQ'$ is steeper than the lending rate throughout Zone III but flatter than the borrowing rate throughout Zone I. Therefore, such a locus must be tangent to one of the indifference curves somewhere in Zone II.

By analogy with the discussion in the previous section, we may conclude that the *borrowing* rate will lead to correct answers (to the productive investment decision, neglecting the related financing question) under the present-value rule or the internal-rate-of-return rule—when the situation involves a Zone I solution. Correspondingly, the *lending* rate will be appropriate and lead to correct investment decisions for Zone III solutions. For Zone II solutions, however, neither will be correct. There will, in fact, be some rate between the lending and the borrowing rates which would lead to the correct results.

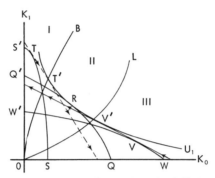

Figure 3. Three Solution Zones for Differing Borrowing and Lending Rates.

Formally speaking, we could describe this correct discount rate as the marginal productive opportunity rate,[11] which will at equilibrium equal the marginal subjective time-preference rate. In such a case neither rule is satisfactory in the sense of providing the productive solution without reference to the utility isoquants; knowledge of the comparative slopes of the utility isoquant and the productive opportunity frontier is all that is necessary, however. Of course, even when the rules in question are considered "satisfactory," they are misleading in implying that productive investment decisions can be correctly made independently of the "financing" decision.

This solution, in retrospect, may perhaps seem obvious. Where the productive opportunity, time-preference, and market (or financing) opportunities stand in such relations to one another as to require borrowing to reach the optimum, the borrowing rate is the correct rate to use in the productive investment decision. The lending rate is irrelevant because the decision on the

---

[11] The marginal productive opportunity rate, or marginal internal rate of return, measures the rate of return on the best alternative project. Assuming continuity, it is defined by the slope of $QRQ'$ at $R$ in Fig. 3. Evidently, a present-value line tangent to $U_1$ and $QRQ'$ at $R$ would, in a formal sense, make the present-value rule correct. And comparing this rate with the marginal internal rate of return as it varies along $QRQ'$ would make the internal-rate-of-return rule also correct in the same formal sense.

margin involves a balancing of the cost of borrowing and the return from further productive investment, both being higher than the lending rate. The lending opportunity is indeed still available, but, the rate of return on lending being lower than the lowest marginal productive rate of return we would wish to consider in the light of the borrowing rate we must pay, lending is not a relevant alternative. Rather the relevant alternative to productive investment is a reduction in borrowing, which in terms of saving interest is more remunerative than lending. Similarly, when the balance of considerations dictates lending part of the firm's current capital funds, borrowing is not the relevant cost incurred in financing productive investment. The relevant alternative to increased productive investment is the amount of lending which must be foregone. While these considerations may be obvious, there is some disagreement in the literature as to whether the lending or the borrowing rate is *the* correct one.[12]

### C. INCREASING MARGINAL COST OF BORROWING

While it is generally considered satisfactory to assume a constant lending rate (the investor does not drive down the loan rate as a consequence of his lendings), for practical reasons it is important to take account of the case in which increased borrowing can only take place at increasing cost. As it happens, however, this complication does not require any essential modification of principle.

Figure 4 shows, as before, a productive opportunity locus $QR'T$ and an indifference curve $U_1$. For simplicity, assume that marginal borrowing costs rise at the same rate whether the investor begins to borrow at the point $R'$, $S'$, or $W'$ or at any other point along $QR'T$ (he cannot, of course, start borrowing at $Q$, having no $K_1$ to offer in exchange for more $K_0$). Under this assumption we can then draw market curves, now concave to the origin, like $R'R$, $S'S$, and $W'W$. The curve $TE$ represents the total opportunity set as the *envelope* of these market curves, that is, $TE$ connects all the points on the market curves representing the maximum $K_0$ attainable for any given $K_1$. By the nature of an envelope curve, $TE$ will be tangent to a market curve at each such point. The optimum is then simply found where $TE$ is tangent to the highest indifference curve attainable—here the curve $U_1$ at $R$. To reach $R$, the investor must exploit his productive opportunity to the point $R'$ and then borrow back along his market curve to $R$.

The preceding discussion applies solely to what was called a Zone I (borrowing) solution in the previous section. Depending upon the nature of

[12] The borrowing rate (the "cost of capital") has been recommended by Dean and by Lorie and Savage (see Joel Dean, *Capital Budgeting* [New York: Columbia University Press, 1951], esp. pp. 43–44; James H. Lorie and Leonard J. Savage, "Three Problems in Rationing Capital," *Journal of Business*, XXVIII [October, 1955], 229–39, esp. p. 229). Roberts and the Lutzes favor the use of the lending rate (see Friedrich and Vera Lutz, *op. cit.*, esp. p. 22; Harry V. Roberts, "Current Problems in the Economics of Capital Budgeting," *Journal of Business*, XXX [January, 1957], 12–16).

the productive opportunity, a Zone II or Zone III solution would also be possible under the assumptions of this section. With regard to the present-value and the internal-rate-of-return rules, the conclusions are unchanged for Zone II and III solutions, however. Only for Zone I solutions is there any modification.

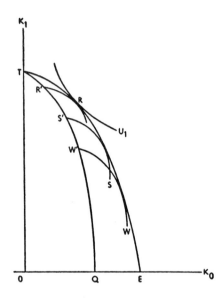

Fig. 4.—Increasing marginal cost of borrowing

The crucial question, as always, for these rules is what rate of discount to use. Intuition tells us that the rate representing *marginal* borrowing cost should be used as the discount rate for Zone I solutions, since productive investment will then be carried just to the point justified by the cost of the associated increment of borrowing.[13] That is, the slope of the envelope for any point on the envelope curve (for example, $R$), is the same as the slope of the productive opportunity curve at the corresponding point ($R'$) connected by the market curve.[14] If this is the case, the discount rate determined by the slope at a tangency with $U_1$ at a point like $R$ will also lead to productive investment being carried to $R'$ by the rules under consideration. Of course, this again is a purely formal statement. Operationally speaking, the rules may not be of much value, since the discount rate to be used is not known in advance independently of the utility (time-preference) function.

[13] I should like to thank Joel Segall for insisting on this point in discussions of the problem. Note that the rate representing marginal borrowing cost is not necessarily the borrowing rate on marginal funds—an increment of borrowing may increase the rate on infra-marginal units.

[14] While this point can be verified geometrically, it follows directly from the analytic properties of an envelope curve.

To simplify notation, in this note I shall denote $K_1$ of Figure 4 as $y$ and $K_0$ as $x$. The

## D. RATIONING OF "CAPITAL"—A CURRENT CONTROVERSY

The previous discussion provides the key for resolving certain current disputes over what constitutes optimal investment decision under a condition of "capital rationing" or "fixed capital budget." This condition is said to exist when the firm, or individual, or perhaps department of government under consideration cannot borrow additional "capital" but is limited instead of making the best use of the "capital" already in its possession or allocated to it.[15] In theoretical literature a closely related idea is expressed by Scitovsky, who, regarding the availability of capital (in the sense of "current capital

---

equation of the productive opportunity locus may be written

$$y_0 = f(x_0).$$ (a)

The family of market curves can be expressed by $y - y_0 = g(x - x_0)$, or

$$F(x,x_0) = f(x_0) + g(x - x_0).$$ (b)

An envelope $y - h(x)$, is defined by the condition that any point on it must be a point of tangency with some member of the family (b). Thus we have

$$h(x) = F(x,x_0)$$ (c)

$$\frac{dh}{dx} = \frac{\partial F(x,x_0)}{\partial x}.$$ (d)

The second condition for an envelope is that the partial derivative of the function (b) with respect to the parameter must equal zero:

$$\frac{\partial F(x,x_0)}{\partial x_0} = 0.$$ (e)

But

$$\frac{\partial F(x,x_0)}{\partial x_0} = \frac{df(x_0)}{dx_0} + (-1)\frac{dg(x-x_0)}{d(x-x_0)}.$$

Hence

$$\frac{df(x_0)}{dx_0} = \frac{dg(x-x_0)}{d(x-x_0)}.$$

Also

$$\frac{\partial F(x,x_0)}{\partial x} = \frac{dg(x-x_0)}{d(x-x_0)}.$$

So, finally,

$$\frac{df(x_0)}{dx_0} = \frac{dg(x-x_0)}{d(x-x_0)} = \frac{\partial F(x,x_0)}{\partial x} = \frac{dh}{dx}.$$

Thus the slope of the productive opportunity locus is the same as the slope of the envelope at points on the two curves connected by being on the same curve.

[15] The expression "capital rationing" was used some time ago by Hart to refer to a non-price limitation on the acquisition of debt or equity financing (see A. G. Hart, "Anticipations, Business Planning, and the Cycle," *Quarterly Journal of Economics*, LI [1937], 273–97). His use of the term does not seem to imply a definitely fixed quantity available and can,

funds ") as the fixed factor limiting the size of the firm, proposes as the investment criterion the maximization of "profit per unit capital invested."[16] Lutz and Lutz, in contrast, assert as their ultimate investment criterion the maximization of the rate of return on the entrepreneur's *owned* capital, which they regard as fixed.[17]

It is of some interest to analyze these concepts in greater detail in terms of our Fisherian model. Scitovsky defines "capital" as current capital funds (our $K_0$) required to bridge the time lapse between factor input and product output.[18] Under this definition, however, "capital" would be fixed to the firm only under rather peculiar conditions; specifically, if there is a discontinuity in the capital funds market such that the marginal borrowing rate suddenly becomes infinite at the firm's level of borrowings.[19] Without discontinuity, an infinitely high marginal borrowing rate could never represent an equilibrium position for the borrower, unless indeed his preference for present income over future income was absolute. And, of course, if the marginal borrowing rate is not infinite, current capital funds could not be said to be fixed. Nevertheless, while this case may be considered peculiar and unlikely to arise in any strict sense, it may be acceptable as a reasonable approximation of certain situations which occur in practice—especially in the short run, perhaps as a result of previous miscalculations. A division of a firm or a department of government may at times be said to face an infinite marginal borrowing rate once a budget constraint is reached—until the next meeting of the board of directors or the Congress provides more funds.

On the other hand, it is difficult to decipher the Lutzes' meaning when they speak of the firm's *owned* capital as fixed. In the Fisherian analysis, "ownership" of current or future assets is a legal form without analytical significance —to buy an asset yielding future income, with current funds, is simply to lend, while selling income is the same as borrowing. In a more fundamental sense, however, we could think of the firm as "owning" the opportunity set or at least the physical productive opportunities available to it, and this perhaps is what the Lutzes have in mind. Thus, Robinson Crusoe's house might

---

in fact, be interpreted simply as indicating a rising marginal cost of capital funds. See also Joel Dean, *Managerial Economics* (Englewood Cliffs, N. J.: Prentice-Hall, Inc., 1951), pp. 586–600. In the sense of a definitely fixed quantity of funds, the term has been used by various authors discussing business or government problems. See J. Margolis, "The Discount Rate and the Benefits-Cost Justification of Federal Irrigation Investment," (Department of Economics, Stanford University, Technical Report No. 23 [Stanford, Calif., 1955]); Lorie and Savage, *op. cit.*, and R. McKean, *Efficiency in Government through Systems Analysis* (New York: John Wiley & Sons, 1958).

[16] T. Scitovsky, *Welfare and Competition* (Chicago: Richard D. Irwin, Inc., 1951), pp. 208–9.

[17] *Op. cit.*, pp. 16–48, esp. pp. 17, 20, 42.

[18] *Op. cit.*, p. 194.

[19] Scitovsky appears to leap from the acceptable argument in the earlier part of his discussion that willingness to lend and to borrow are not *unlimited* to the unacceptable position in his later discussion that current capital funds are *fixed* (*ibid*, pp. 193–200, 208–9).

be considered as his "owned capital"—a resource yielding consumption income in both present and future. The trouble is that the Lutzes seem to be thinking of "owned capital" as the *value* of the productive resources (in the form of capital goods) owned by the firm,[20] but owned physical capital goods cannot be converted to a capital *value* without bringing in a rate of discount for the receipts stream. But since, as we have seen, the relevant rate of discount for a firm's decisions is not (except where a perfect capital market exists) an independent entity but is itself determined by the analysis, the *capital value* cannot in general be considered to be fixed independently of the investment decision.[21]

While space does not permit a full critique of the Lutzes' important work, it is worth mentioning that—from a Fisherian point of view—it starts off on the wrong foot. They search first for an ultimate criterion or formula with which to gauge investment decision rules and settle upon "maximization of the rate of return on the investor's owned capital" on what seem to be purely intuitive grounds. The Fisherian approach, in contrast, integrates investment decision with the general theory of choice—the goal being to maximize utility subject to certain opportunities and constraints. In these terms, certain formulas can be validated as useful proximate rules for some classes of problems, as I am attempting to show here. However, the ultimate Fisherian criterion of choice—the optimal balancing of consumption alternatives over time—cannot be reduced to any of the usual formulas.

Instead of engaging in further discussion of the various senses in which "capital" may be said to be fixed to the firm, it will be more instructive to see how the Fisherian approach solves the problem of "capital rationing." I shall use as an illustration what may be called a "Scitovsky situation," in which the investor has run against a discontinuity making the marginal borrowing rate infinite. I regard this case (which I consider empirically significant only in the short run) as the model situation underlying the "capital rationing" discussion.

An infinite borrowing rate makes the dashed borrowing lines of Figures 2 and 3 essentially vertical. In consequence, the curve *OB* in Figure 3 shifts so far to the left as to make Zone I disappear for all practical purposes. There are then only Zone II and Zone III solutions. An investment-opportunity locus

[20] Lutz and Lutz, *op. cit.*, pp. 3–13.

[21] It is possible, however, that the Lutzes had in mind only the case in which an investor starts off with current funds but no other assets. In this case no discounting problems would arise in defining owned capital, so their ultimate criterion could not be criticized on that score. The objection raised below to the Scitovsky criterion, however—that it fails to consider the *consumption* alternative, which is really the heart of the question of investment decision—would then apply to the Lutzes' rule. In addition, a rule for an investor owning solely current funds is hardly of general enough applicability to be an ultimate criterion. The Lutzes themselves recognize the case of an investor owning no "capital" but using only borrowed funds, and for this case they themselves abandon their ultimate criterion (*ibid.*, p. 42, n. 32). The most general case, of course, is that of an investor with a productive opportunity set capable of yielding him alternative combinations of present and future income.

like $WVW'$ in Figure 3 becomes less steep than the lending slope in Zone III, in which case the investor will carry investment up to the point $V$ where this occurs and then lend until a tangency solution is reached at $V'$, which would be somewhere along the curve $OL$ of Figure 3. If an investment-opportunity locus like $QRQ'$ in Figure 3 is still steeper than the lending rate after it crosses $OL$, investment should be carried until tangency with an indifference curve like $U_1$ is attained somewhere to the left of $OL$, with no lending or borrowing taking place.

In terms of the present-value or internal-rate-of-return rules, under these conditions the decisions should be based on the *lending* rate (as the discounting rate or the standard of comparison) if the solution is a Zone III one. Here lending actually takes place, since movement upward and to the left still remains desirable when the last investment with a rate of return greater than the lending rate is made. If the solution is a Zone II one, the lending rate must not be used. Investments showing positive present value at the lending rate (or, equivalently, with an internal rate of return higher than the lending rate) will be nevertheless undesirable after a tangency point equating the investment-opportunity slope and the time-preference slope is reached. The correct rate, formally speaking, is the marginal opportunity rate.

The solution changes only slightly when we consider an isolated individual like Robinson Crusoe or a self-contained community like a nation under autarchy (or like the world economy as a whole). In this situation neither borrowing nor lending is possible in our sense, only productive opportunities existing. Only Zone II solutions are then possible. This case is the extreme remove from the assumption of perfect capital markets.[22]

As in the case of the Zone II solutions arising without capital rationing, the present-value or internal-rate-of-return rules can be formally modified to apply to the Zone II solutions which are typical under capital rationing. The discount rate to be used for calculating present values or as a standard of comparison against the internal rate of project increments is the rate given by the slope of the Zone II tangency (the marginal productive rate of return); with this rate, the rules give the correct answer. But this rate cannot be discovered until the solution is attained and so is of no assistance in reaching the solution. The exception is the Zone III solution involving lending which can arise in a "Scitovsky situation." Here the lending rate should of course be used. The undetermined discount rate that gives correct results when the rules are used for Zone II solutions can, in some problems, be regarded as a kind of shadow price reflecting the productive rate of return on the best alternative opportunity not being exploited.

The reader may be curious as to why, in the Scitovsky situation, the outcome of the analysis was not Scitovsky's result—that the optimal investment

---

[22] We could, following the principles already laid down, work out without great difficulty the solution for the case in which borrowing is permitted but only up to a certain fixed limit. The effect of such a provision is to provide a kind of "attainability envelope" as in Fig. 4, but of a somewhat different shape.

decision is such as to maximize the (average) internal rate of return on the firm's present capital funds ($K_0$). Thus, in Figure 3, for a firm starting with $OQ$ of $K_0$ and faced with the productive opportunity locus $QRQ'$, the average rate of return ($K_1$ received per unit of $K_0$ sacrificed) is a maximum for an infinitesimal movement along $QRQ'$, since, the farther it moves, the more the marginal and average productive rates of return fall. Such a rule implies staying at $Q$—which is obviously the wrong decision.

How does this square with Scitovsky's intuitively plausible argument that the firm always seeks to maximize its returns on the fixed factor, present capital funds being assumed here to be fixed?[23] The answer is that this argument is applicable only for a factor "fixed" in the sense of no alternative uses. Here present capital funds $K_0$ are assumed to be fixed, but not in the sense Scitovsky must have had in mind. The concept here is that no additional borrowing can take place, but the possibility of *consuming* the present funds as an alternative to investing them is recognized. For Scitovsky, however, the funds *must* be invested. If in fact current income $K_0$ had no uses other than conversion into future income $K_1$ (this amounts to absolute preference for future over current income), Scitovsky's rule would correctly tell us to pick that point on the $K_1$ axis which is the highest.[24] Actually, our time preferences are more balanced; there *is* an alternative use (consumption) for $K_0$. Therefore, even in Scitovsky situations, we will balance $K_0$ and $K_1$ on the margin—and not simply accept the maximum $K_1$ we can get in exchange for all our "fixed" $K_0$.[25] The analyses of Scitovsky, the Lutzes, and many other recent writers frequently lead to incorrect solutions because of their failure to take into account the alternative consumption opportunities which Fisher integrated into his theory of investment decision.

E. NON-INDEPENDENT INVESTMENT OPPORTUNITIES

Up to this point, following Fisher, investment opportunities have been assumed to be independent so that it is possible to rank them in any desired way. In particular, they were ordered in Figure 1 through 4 in terms of decreasing productive rate of return; the resultant concavity produced unique tangency solutions with the utility or market curves. But suppose, now, that there are two mutually exclusive sets of such investment opportunities. Thus we may consider building a factory in the East or the West, but not both—

[23] *Op. cit.*, p. 209.

[24] That is, the point $Q'$ in Fig. 3. This result is of course trivial. Scitovsky may possibly have in mind choice among non-independent sets of investments (discussed in the next section), where each set may have a different intersection with the $K_1$ axis. Here a non-trivial choice could be made with the criterion of maximizing the average rate of return.

[25] Scitovsky may have in mind a situation in which a certain fraction of current funds $K_0$ are set apart from consumption (on some unknown basis) to become the "fixed" current capital funds. In this case the Scitovsky rule would lead to the correct result if it happened that just so much "fixed" capital funds were allocated to get the investor to the point $R'$ on his productive transformation locus of Fig. 3.

contemplating the alternatives, the eastern opportunities may look like the locus $QV'V$, and the western opportunities like $QT'T$ in Figure 5.[26]

Which is better? Actually, the solutions continue to follow directly from Fisher's principles, though too much non-independence makes for troublesome calculations in practice, and in some classes of cases the heretofore inerrant present-value rule fails. In the simplest case, in which there is a constant borrowing-lending rate (a perfect capital market), the curve $QV'V$ is

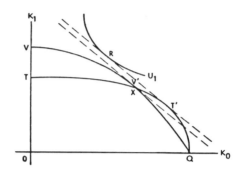

FIGURE 5.   NON-INDEPENDENT INVESTMENT OPPORTUNITIES —TWO ALTERNATIVE PRODUCTIVE INVESTMENT LOCI.

tangent to its highest attainable present-value line at $V'$—while the best point on $QT'T$ is $T'$. It is only necessary to consider these, and the one attaining the higher present-value line ($QT'T$ at $T'$ in this case) will permit the investor to reach the highest possible indifference curve $U_1$ at $R$. In contrast, the internal-rate-of-return rule would locate the points $T'$ and $V'$ but could not discriminate between them. Where borrowing and lending rates differ, as in Figure 2 (now interpreting the productive opportunity loci of that figure as mutually exclusive alternatives), it may be necessary to compare, say, a lending solution at $V$ with a borrowing solution at $T$. To find the *optimum optimorum*, the indifference curves must be known (in Fig. 2 the two solutions attain the same indifference curve). Note that present value is *not* a reliable guide here; in fact, the present value of the solution $V(= W^*)$ at the relevant discount rate for it (the lending rate) far exceeds that of the solution $T(= T^*)$ at its discount rate (the borrowing rate), when the two are actually indifferent. Assuming an increasing borrowing rate creates no new essential difficulty.

Another form of non-independence, illustrated in Figure 6, is also troublesome without modifying principle. Here the projects along the productive investment locus $QQ'$ are not entirely independent, for we are constrained to adopt some low-return ones before certain high-return ones. Again, there is a possibility of several local optima like $V$ and $T$, which can be compared along the same lines as used in the previous illustration.

---

[26] It would, of course, reduce matters to their former simplicity if one of the loci lay completely within the other, in which case it would be obviously inferior and could be dropped from consideration.

F. CONCLUSION FOR TWO-PERIOD ANALYSIS

The solutions for optimal investment decisions vary according to a two-way classification of cases. The first classification refers to the way market opportunities exist for the decision-making agency; the second classification refers to the absence or presence of the complication of non-independent productive opportunities. The simplest, extreme cases for the first classification are: (*a*) a perfect capital market (market opportunities such that lending or borrowing in any amounts can take place at the same, fixed rate) and (*b*) no market

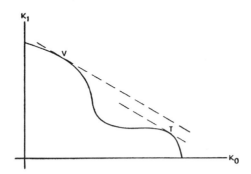

Fɪɢ. 6.—Non-independent investment opportunities—poorer projects prerequisite to better ones.

opportunities whatsoever, as was true for Robinson Crusoe. Where there is a perfect capital market, the total attainable set is a triangle (considering only the first quadrant like *OPP'* in Figure 1, just tangent to the productive opportunity locus. Where there is no capital market at all, the total attainable set is simply the productive opportunity locus itself. It is not difficult to see how the varying forms of imperfection of the capital market fit in between these extremes.

When independence of physical (productive) opportunities holds, the opportunities may be ranked in order of descending productive rate of return. Geometrically, if the convenient (but inessential) assumption of continuity is adopted, independence means that the productive opportunity locus is everywhere concave to the origin, like *QS'TV* in Figure 1. Non-independence may take several forms (see Figs. 5 and 6), but in each case that is not trivial non-independence means that the effective productive opportunity locus is not simply concave. This is obvious in Figure 6. In Figure 5 each of the two alternative loci considered separately is concave, but the effective locus is the scalloped outer edge of the overlapping sets of points attainable by either— that is, the effective productive opportunity locus runs along *QT'T* up to *X* and then crosses over *QV'V*.

With this classification a detailed tabulation of the differing solutions could be presented; the following brief summary of the general principles involved should serve almost as well, however.

1. The internal-rate-of-return rule fails wherever there are multiple tangencies—the normal outcome for non-independent productive opportunities.

2. The present-value rule works whenever the other does and, in addition, correctly discriminates among multiple tangencies whenever a perfect capital market exists (or, by extension, whenever a unique discount rate can be determined for the comparison—for example when all the alternative tangencies occur in Zone I or else all in Zone III).

3. Both rules work only in a formal sense when the solution involves direct tangency between a productive opportunity locus and a utility isoquant, since the discount rate necessary for use of both rules is the marginal opportunity rate—a product of the analysis.

4. The cases when even the present-value rule fails (may actually give wrong answers) all involve the comparison of multiple tangencies arising from non-independent investments when, in addition, a perfect capital market does not exist. One important example is the comparison of a tangency involving borrowing in Zone I with another involving lending in Zone III. Only reference to the utility map can give correct answers for such cases.

5. Even when one or both rules are correct in a not merely formal sense, the answer given is the "productive solution"—only part of the way toward attainment of the utility optimum. Furthermore, this productive decision is optimal only when it can be assumed that the associated financing decision will in fact be made.

## II. A BRIEF NOTE ON PERPETUITIES

A traditional way of handling the multiperiod case in capital theory has been to consider investment decisions as choices between current funds and perpetual future income flows. For many purposes this is a valuable simplifying idea. It cannot be adopted here, however, because the essence of the practical difficulties which have arisen in multiperiod investment decisions is the *reinvestment* problem—the necessity of making productive or market exchanges between incomes in future time periods. In fact, the consideration of the perpetuity case is, in a sense, only a variant of the two-period analysis, in which there is a single present and a single future. In the case of perpetuity analysis, the future is stretched out, but we cannot consider transfer between different periods of the future.

All the two-period results in Section I can easily be modified to apply to the choice between funds and perpetuities. In the figures, instead of income $K_1$ in period 1 one may speak of an annual rate of income $k$. Productive opportunity loci and time-preference curves will retain their familiar shapes. The lines of constant present value (borrow-lend lines) are expressed by the equation $C = K_0 + (k/i)$ instead of $C = K_0 + (K_1)/(1 + i)$. The "internal rate of return" will equal $(k)/(-\Delta K_0)$. The rest of the analysis follows directly, but, rather than trace it out, I shall turn to the consideration of the multiperiod case in a more general way.

## III. MULTIPERIOD ANALYSIS

Considerable doubt prevails on how to generalize the principles of the two-period analysis to the multiperiod case. The problems which have troubled the analysis of the multiperiod case are actually the result of inappropriate generalizations of methods of solution that do lead to correct results in the simplified two-period analysis.

### A. INTERNAL-RATE-OF-RETURN RULE VERSUS PRESENT-VALUE RULE

In the multiperiod analysis there is no formal difficulty in generalizing the indifference curves of Figure 1 to indifference shells in any number of dimensions. Also the lines of constant present value or market lines become hyperplanes with the equation (in the most general form)

$$K_0 + \frac{K_1}{1 + i_1} + \frac{K_2}{(1 + i_1)(1 + i_2)} + \cdots + \frac{K_n}{(1 + i_1)(1 + i_2) \cdots (1 + i_n)} = C,$$

$C$ being a parameter, $i_1$ the discount rate between income in period 0 and 1, $i_2$ the discount rate between periods 1 and 2, and so forth.[27] Where $i_1 = i_2 = \cdots i_n = i$, the expression takes on the simpler and more familiar form

$$K_0 + \frac{K_1}{1 + i} + \frac{K_2}{(1 + i)^2} + \cdots + \frac{K_n}{(1 + i)^n} = C.$$

The major difficulty with the multiperiod case turns upon the third element of the solution—the description of the productive opportunities, which may be denoted by the equation $f(K_0, K_1, \ldots, K_n) = 0$. The purely theoretical specification is not too difficult, however, if the assumption is made that all investment options are independent. The problem of non-independence is not essentially different in the multiperiod case and in the two-period case, and it would enormously complicate the presentation to consider it here. Under this condition, then, and with appropriate continuity assumptions, the productivity opportunity locus may be envisaged as a shell[28] concave to the origin in all directions. With these assumptions, between income in any two periods $K_r$ and $K_s$ (holding $K_t$ for all other periods constant) there will be a two-dimensional productive opportunity locus essentially like that in Figure 1.[29]

[27] I shall not, in this section, consider further the possible divergences between the lending and borrowing rates studies in detail in Sec. I but shall speak simply of "the discount rate" or "the market rate." The principles involved are not essentially changed in the multiperiod case; I shall concentrate attention on certain other difficulties that appear only when more than two periods are considered. We may note that in the most general case the assumption of full information becomes rather unrealistic—e.g., that the pattern of interest rates $i_1$ through $i_n$ is known today.

[28] As in the two-period case, the locus represents not all the production opportunities but only the *boundary* of the region represented by the production opportunities. The boundary consists of those opportunities not dominated by any other; any opportunity represented by an interior point is dominated by at least one boundary point.

[29] The assumption of $n$-dimensional continuity is harder to swallow than two-dimensional continuity as an approximation to the nature of the real world. Nevertheless, the restriction is not essential, though it is an enormous convenience in developing the argument. One possible misinterpretation of the continuity assumption should be mentioned: it does not

Now suppose that lending or borrowing can take place between any two successive periods $r$ and $s$ at the rate $i_s$. The theoretical solution involves finding the multidimensional analogue of the point $R'$ (in Fig. 1)—that is, the point on the highest present-value hyperplane reached by the productive opportunity locus. With simple curvature and continuity assumptions, $R'$ will be a tangency point, thus having the additional property that, between the members of any such pair of time periods, the marginal productive rate of return between $K_r$ and $K_s$ (holding all other $K_t$'s constant) will be equal to the discount rate between these periods. Furthermore, if the condition is met between all pairs of successive periods, it will also be satisfied between any pairs of time periods as well.[30] Again, as in the two-period case, the final solution will involve market lending or borrowing ("financing") to move along the highest present-value hyperplane attained from the intermediate productive solution $R'$ to the true preference optimum at $R$. Note that, as compared with the present value or direct solution, the principle of equating the marginal productive rate of return with the discount rate requires certain continuity assumptions.

---

necessarily mean that the only investment opportunities considered are two-period options between pairs of periods in the present or future. Genuine multiperiod options are allowable—for example, the option described by cash-flows of $-1, +4, +2$, and $+6$ for periods 0, 1, 2, and 3, respectively. The continuity assumption means, rather, that if we choose to move from an option like this one in the direction of having more income in period 1 and less, say, in period 3, we can find other options available like $-1, +4\,e_1, +2, +6 - e_3$, where $e_1$ and $e_3$ represent infinitesimals. In other words, from any point on the locus it is possible to trade continuously between incomes in any pair of periods.

[30] Maximizing the Lagrangian expression $C - \lambda f(K_0, \ldots, K_n)$, we derive the first-order conditions

$$\begin{cases} \dfrac{\partial C}{\partial K_0} = 1 & -\lambda \dfrac{\partial f}{\partial K_0} = 0 \\[2mm] \dfrac{\partial C}{\partial K_1} = \dfrac{1}{1 + i_1} & -\lambda \dfrac{\partial f}{\partial K_1} = 0 \\[2mm] \cdots \cdots \cdots \cdots \cdots \cdots \cdots \\[2mm] \dfrac{\partial C}{\partial K_n} = \dfrac{1}{(1 + i_1)(1 + i_2) \ldots (1 + i_n)} & -\lambda \dfrac{\partial f}{\partial K_n} = 0. \end{cases}$$

Eliminating $\lambda$ between any pair of successive periods:

$$\frac{\partial f / \partial K_r}{\partial f / \partial K_s} = \frac{(1 + i_1)(1 + i_2) \cdots (1 + i_r)(1 + i_s)}{(1 + i_1)(1 + i_2) \cdots (1 + i_r)}$$

$$\left. \frac{\partial K_s}{\partial K_r} \right|_{\substack{K_J \\ (j \neq r,s)}} = 1 + i_s$$

Between non-successive periods:

$$\left. \frac{\partial K_t}{\partial K_r} \right|_{\substack{K_J \\ (j \neq r,t)}} = (1 + i_{r+1})(1 + i_{r+2}) \cdots (1 + i_{t-1})(1 + i_t).$$

Now it is here that Fisher, who evidently understood the true nature of the solution himself, appears to have led others astray. In his *Rate of Interest* he provides a mathematical proof that the optimal investment decision involves setting what is here called the marginal productive rate of return equal to the market rate of interest *between any two periods*.[31] By obvious generalization of the result of the two-period problem, this condition is identical with that of finding the line of highest present value (the two-dimensional projection of the hyperplane of highest present value) between these time periods. Unfortunately, Fisher fails to state the qualification " between any two time-periods " consistently and at various places makes flat statements to the effect that investments will be made wherever the " rate of return on sacrifice " or " rate of return on cost " between any two options exceeds the rate of interest.[32]

Now the rate of return on sacrifice is, for two-period comparisons, equivalent to the productive rate of return. More generally, however, Fisher defines the rate of return on sacrifice in a *multiperiod* sense; that is, as that rate which reduces to a present value of zero the entire sequence of positive and negative periodic differences between the returns of any two investment options.[33] This definition is, for our purposes, equivalent to the so-called " internal rate of return."[34] This latter rate (which will be denoted $\rho$) will, however, be shown to lead to results which are, in general, not correct if the procedure is followed of adopting or rejecting investment options on the basis of a comparison of $\rho$ and the market rate.[35]

B. FAILURE OF THE GENERALIZED " INTERNAL RATE OF RETURN "

Recent thinking emphasizing the internal rate of return seems to be based upon the idea of finding a purely " internal " measure of the time productivity of an investment—that is, the rate of growth of capital funds invested in a

---

[31] *Rate of Interest*, pp. 398–400. Actually, the proof refers only to successive periods, but this is an inessential restriction.

[32] *Ibid.*, p. 155; *Theory of Interest*, pp. 168–69.

[33] *Rate of Interest*, p. 153; *Theory of Interest*, pp. 168–69.

[34] For some purposes it is important to distinguish between the rate which sets the present value of a series of receipts from an investment equal to zero and that rate which does the same for the series of *differences* between the receipts of two alternative investment options (see A. A. Alchian, " The Rate of Interest, Fisher's Rate of Return over Cost, and Keynes' Internal Rate of Return," *American Economic Review*, XLV [December, 1955], 938–43). For present purposes there is no need to make the distinction because individual investment options are regarded as independent increments—so that the receipts of the option in question are in fact a sequence of differences over the alternative of not adopting that option.

[35] As another complication, Fisher's mathematical analysis compares the two-period marginal rates of return on sacrifice with the interest rates of return on sacrifice with the interest rates between those two periods, the latter not being assumed constant throughout. In the multiperiod case Fisher nowhere states how to combine the differing period-to-period interest rates into an over-all market rate for comparison with $\rho$. It is possible that just at this point Fisher was thinking only of a rate of interest which remained constant over time, in which case the question would not arise. The difficulty in the use of the " internal rate " when variations in the market rate over time exist will be discussed below.

project—for comparison with the market rate.[36] But the idea of rate of growth involves a ratio and cannot be uniquely defined unless one can uniquely value initial and terminal positions. Thus the investment option characterized by the annual cash-flow sequence $-1, 0, 0, 8$ clearly involves a growth rate of 100 per cent (compounding annually), because it really reduces to a two-period option with intermediate compounding. Similarly, a savings deposit at 10 per cent compounded annually for $n$ years may seem to be a multiperiod option, but it is properly regarded as a series of two-period options (the "growth" will take place only if at the beginning of each period the decision is taken to reinvest the capital plus interest yielded by the investment of the previous period). A savings-account option without reinvestment would be: $-1, .10, .10, .10, \ldots, 1.10$ (the last element being a terminating payment); with reinvestment, the option becomes $-1, 0, 0, 0, \ldots, (1.10)^n$, $n$ being the number of compounding periods after the initial deposit.

Consider, however, a more general investment option characterized by the sequence $-1, 2, 1$. (In general, all investment options considered here will be normalized in terms of an assumed \$1.00 of initial outlay or initial receipt.) How can a rate of growth for the initial capital outlay be determined? Unlike the savings-account opportunity, no information is provided as to the rate at which the intermediate receipt or "cash throw-off" of \$2.00 can be reinvested. If, of course, we use some external discounting rate (for example, the cost of capital or the rate of an outside lending opportunity), we will be departing from the idea of a purely *internal* growth rate. In fact, the use of an external rate will simply reduce us to a present-value evaluation of the investment option.

In an attempt to resolve this difficulty, one mathematical feature of the two-period marginal productive rate of return was selected for generalization by both Fisher and his successors. This feature is the fact that, when $\rho$ (in the two-period case equal to the marginal productive rate of return $[\Delta K_1]/[-\Delta K_0] - 1$) is used for discounting the values in the receipt-outlay stream, the discounted value becomes zero. This concept lends itself to easy generalization: for any multiperiod stream there will be a similar discounting rate $\rho$ which will make the discounted value equal to zero (or so it was thought). This rate seems to be purely internal, not infected by any market considerations. And, in certain simple cases, it does lead to correct answers in choosing investment projects according to the rule: Adopt the project if $\rho$ is greater than the market rate $r$.

For the investment option $-1, 2, 1$ considered above, $\rho$ is equal to $\sqrt{2}$, or 141.4 per cent. And, in fact, if the borrowing rate or the rate on the best alternative opportunity (whichever is the appropriate comparison) is less than $\sqrt{2}$, the investment is desirable. Figure 7 plots the present value $C$ of the option as a function of the discounting interest rate, $i$, assumed to be constant

---

[36] Sec K. E. Boulding, *Economic Analysis* (rev. ed.; New York: Harper & Bros., 1948), p. 819.

over the two discounting periods. Note that the present value of the option diminishes as $i$ increases throughout the entire relevant range of $i$, from $i = -1$ to $i = \infty$.[37] The internal rate of return $\rho$ is that $i$ for which the present value curve cuts the horizontal axis. Evidently, for any $i < \rho$, present value is positive; for $i > \rho$, it is negative.

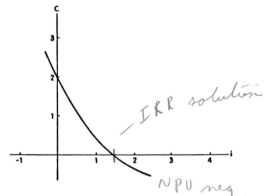

FIG. 7.—Sketch of present value of the option −1, 2, 1.

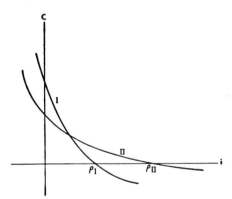

FIG. 8.—Two alternative options

However, the fact that the use of $\rho$ leads to the correct decision in a particular case or a particular class of cases does not mean that it is correct in principle. And, in fact, cases have been adduced where its use leads to incorrect answers. Alchian has shown that, in the comparison of two investment options which are alternatives, the choice of the one with a higher $\rho$ is not in general correct—in fact, the decision cannot be made without knowledge of the appropriate external discounting rate.[38] Figure 8 illustrates two such options,

[37] Economic meaning may be attached to negative interest rates; these are rates of shrinkage of capital. I rule out the possibility of shrinkage rates greater than 100 per cent however.

[38] Alchian, op. cit., p. 939.

I being preferable for low rates of interest and II for high rates. The $i$ at which the crossover takes place is Fisher's rate of return on sacrifice between these two options. But II has the higher internal rate of return (that is, its present value falls to zero at a higher discounting rate) regardless of the actual rate of interest. How can we say that I is preferable at low rates of interest? Because its present value is higher, it permits the investor to move along a higher hyperplane to find the utility optimum attained somewhere on that hyperplane. If II were adopted, the investor would also be enabled to move along such a hyperplane, but a lower one. Put another way, with the specified low rate of interest, the investor adopting I could, if he chose, put himself in the position of adopting II by appropriate borrowings and lendings together with throwing away some of his wealth.[39]

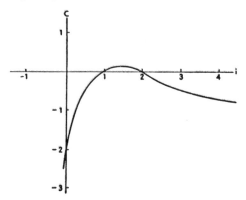

Fig. 9.—Sketch of present value of the investment option $-1, 5, -6$.

Even more fundamentally, Lorie and Savage have shown that $\rho$ may not be unique.[40] Consider, for example, the investment option $-1, 5, -6$. Calculation reveals that this option has a present value of zero at discounting rates of both 100 per cent and 200 per cent. For this investment option present value as a function of the discounting rate is sketched in Figure 9. While

[39] Some people find this so hard to believe that I shall provide a numerical example. For investment I, we may use the annual cash-flow stream $-1, 0, 4$—then the internal rate of return is 1, or 100 per cent. For investment option II, we may use the option illustrated in Figure 7: $-1, 2, 1$. For this investment $p$ is equal to $\sqrt{2}$, or 141.4 per cent. So the internal rate of return is greater for II. However, the present value for option I is greater at an interest rate of 0 per cent, and in fact it remains greater until the cross-over rate, which happens to be at 50 per cent for these two options. Now it is simple to show how, adopting I, we can get to the result II at any interest rate lower than 50 per cent —10 per cent, for example. Borrowing from the final time period for the benefit of the intermediate one, we can convert $-1, 0, 4$ to $-1, 2.73, 1$ (I have subtracted 3 from the final period, crediting the intermediate period with $3/1.1 = 2.73$). We can now get to option II by throwing away the 0.73, leaving us with $-1, 2, 1$. The fact that we can get to option II by throwing away some wealth demonstrates the superiority of I even though $\rho_{II} > \rho_I$, provided that borrowing and lending can take place at an interest rate less than the cross-over discounting rate of 50 per cent.

[40] Op. cit., pp. 236–39.

Lorie and Savage speak only of "dual" internal rates of return, any number of zero values of the present-value function are possible in principle. The option $-1, 6, -11, 6$, illustrated in Figure 10, has zero present value at the discounting rates 0 per cent, and 200 per cent, for example.[41]

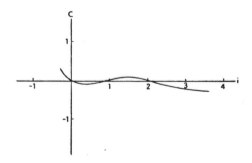

Fig. 10.—Sketch of present value of the investment option $-1, 6, -11, 6$.

In fact, perfectly respectable investment options may have *no* real internal rates (the present value equation has only imaginary roots). The option $-1$, $3, -2\frac{1}{2}$ is an example; a plot would show that its present value is negative throughout the relevant range.[42] It is definitely not the case, however, that all options for which the internal rate cannot be calculated are bad ones. If we merely reverse the signs on the option above to get $1, -3, 2\frac{1}{2}$, we have an option with positive present value at all rates of discount.

These instances of failure of the multiperiod internal-rate-of-return rule (note that in each case the present-value rule continues to indicate the correct

---

[41] The instances discussed above suggest that the alternation of signs in the receipt stream has something to do with the possibility of multiple $\rho$'s. In fact, Descarts' rule of signs tells us that the number of solutions in the allowable range (the number of points where present value equals zero for $i > -1$) is at most equal to the number of reversals of signs in the terms of the receipts sequence. Therefore, a two-period investment option has at most a single $\rho$, a three-period option at most a dual $\rho$, and so forth. There is an interesting footnote in Fisher which suggests that he was not entirely unaware of this difficulty. Where more than a single-sign alternation takes place, he suggests the use of the present-value method rather than attempting to compute "the rate of return on sacrifice" (*Rate of Interest*, p. 155). That any number of zeros of the present value function can occur was pointed out by Paul A. Samuelson in "Some Aspects of the Pure Theory of Capital," *Quarterly Journal of Economics*, LI (1936–37), 469–96 (at p. 475).

[42] Mathematically, the formula for the roots of a three-period option $n_0$, $n_1$, $n_2$ where $n_0 = -1$ is:

$$i = \frac{(n_1 - 2) \pm \sqrt{n_1^2 + 4n_2}}{2}.$$

If $-4n_2$ exceeds $n_1^2$, the roots will be imaginary, and an internal rate of return cannot be calculated. A necessary condition for this result is that the sum of the undiscounted cash flows be negative, but this condition should not rule out consideration of an option (note the option $-1, 5, -6$ in Fig. 9).

answer unambiguously, setting aside the question of the appropriate discounting rate which was discussed in Sec. I) are, of course, merely the symptom of an underlying erroneous conception. It is clear that the idea that $\rho$ represents a growth rate in any simple sense cannot be true; a capital investment of $1.00 cannot grow at a rate both of 100 per cent and of 200 per cent. Even more fundamentally, the idea that $\rho$ is a purely *internal* rate is not true either. Consider the option $-1, 2, 1$ discussed earlier, with a unique $\rho$ equal to $\sqrt{2}$. The intermediate cash throwoff of $2.00 must clearly be reinvested externally of this option. How does the calculation of $\rho$ handle this? This answer is that the mathematical manipulations involved in the calculation of $\rho$ implicitly assume that all intermediate receipts, positive or negative, are treated as if they could be compounded at the rate $\rho$ being solved for.[43] The rate $\rho$ has been characterized rather appropriately as the "solving rate" of interest. But note that this mathematical manipulation, even where it does lead to a unique answer (and, in general, it will not), is unreasonable in its economic implications. There will not normally be other investment opportunities arising for investment of intermediate cash inflows (if required) must be obtained by borrowing at the rate $\rho$. The rate $\rho$, arising from a mathematical manipulation, will only by rare coincidence represent relevant economic alternatives.

The preceding arguments against the use of the usual concept of the "internal rate of return" do not take any account of the possibility of non-constant interest rates over time. Martin J. Bailey has emphasized to me that it is precisely when this occurs (when there exists a known pattern of future variation of $i$) that the internal-rate-of-return rule fails most fundamentally. For in the use of that rule all time periods are treated on a par; the only discounting is via the solving rate defined only in terms of the sequence of cash flows. But with (a known pattern of) varying future $i$, shifts in the relative desirability of income in different periods are brought about. In the usual formulation the internal rate of return concept can take no account of this. In fact, in such a case one might have an investment for which $\rho$ was well defined and unique and still not be able to determine the desirability of the investment opportunity (that is, depending upon the time pattern of future interest rates, present value might be either negative or positive).

The following remarks attempt to summarize the basic principles discussed in this section.

At least in the simplest case, where we do not worry about differences between borrowing and lending rates but assume these to be equal and also constant (constant with respect to the amount borrowed or lent—not constant over time), the multidimensional solution using the present-value rule is a straightforward generalization of the two-period solution. The principle is to

[43] The true significance of the reinvestment assumption was brought out in Ezra Solomon, "The Arithmetic of Capital-budgeting Decisions," *Journal of Business*, XXIX (April, 1956), 124–29, esp. pp. 126–27.

push productive investment to the point where the highest attainable level of present value is reached and then to "finance" this investment by borrowing or lending between time periods to achieve a time-preference optimum.

The main burden of these remarks has been to the effect that the internal-rate-of-return rule, unlike the present-value rule, does not generalize the multi-period case if the usual definition of the internal rate $\rho$ is adopted—that is, as that rate which sets the present value of the discounted income stream equal to zero. I have tried to show the multiperiod generalization which would make the internal-rate-of-return rule still correct: between *every pair* of time periods, the marginal internal rate of return in the sense of the marginal productive rate of return between those two periods, holding income in other periods constant, should be set equal to the market discount rate between those periods. That the usual interpretation of the internal-rate-of-return rule is not in general correct has been illustrated by its failure in particular cases and has been explained by exposing the implicit assumption made in the mathematical manipulation which finds $\rho$—that all intermediate cash flows are reinvested (or borrowed if cash flows are negative) at the rate $\rho$ itself. In addition, $\rho$ does not allow for varying interperiod preference rates (or interest rates) over time. This generalized multiperiod internal rate of return is, therefore, not really internal, nor is the assumption implied about the external opportunities generally correct or even generally reasonable.

## IV. CONCLUDING COMMENTS

The preceding analysis has slighted a great many questions. In addition, lack of time has precluded comparative discussion of the works of other authors, however helpful this might have been.[44]

I have not attempted to generalize the results to the multiperiod case with non-independent investments or with differing or non-constant borrowing and lending rates. On the latter points intuition suggests that whether the borrowing or lending rate in calculating present value is to be used for any time period does not depend upon any characteristics of the investment option under consideration in isolation; it depends rather upon the over-all cash position after adoption of that option as an increment. If, after such adoption, time preference dictates shifting to less income in period $r$ and more in period $t$, any income associated with the option in question falling in period $r$ should

---

[44] I should comment, though, on the important article by Samuelson, *op. cit.* The results here are in part consistent with his, with the following main differences: (1) He limits himself to the analysis of a single investment, whereas I consider the entire investment-consumption pattern over time. (2) He concludes in favor of the present-value rule, discounting at *the* market rate of interest. I have attempted to consider explicitly the problem of what to do when the borrowing and lending rates diverge, or vary as a function of the amount borrowed, and I do not find the present-value rule to be universally valid. Of these differences, the first is really crucial. It is the heart of Fisher's message that investments *cannot* be considered in isolation but only in the context of the other investment and consumption alternatives available. Nevertheless, Samuelson's article suffices to refute a number of fallacies still current in this field of economic theory.

be discounted back to the next earlier period at the lending rate (and that for period $t$ at the borrowing rate). Income in any period $s$ may then have been successively discounted at borrowing rates for a number of periods and lending rates for a number of others before being reduced to a present value.

The main positive conclusion of the paper is that the present-value rule for investment decisions is correct in a wide variety of cases (though not universally) and in a limited sense. The rule tells us to attain the highest possible level of present-value, but the point at which this condition is satisfied (that is, the distribution of incomes in various time periods) is not the final solution. It is, rather, an intermediate " productive " solution which must then be modified by borrowing or lending ("financing") to find the over-all optimum. This becomes particularly clear when we consider the case where lending and borrowing rates differ and thus enter the subcontroversy between those who favor the use of present-value discounting at the cost of capital and those who would discount at the alternative lending rate. Which is correct depends upon the financing necessary to approach the time-preference optimum. Furthermore, if a tangency takes place between the productive opportunity locus and the time-preference utility isoquant at a rate between the lending and the borrowing rates, the " productive " solution requires no financing and the present-value principle is only correct in a formal sense. The present-value rule fails to give correct answers only for certain cases which combine the difficulties of non-independent investments and absence of a perfect capital market. When a perfect capital market exists, the present-value rule is universally correct in the limited sense referred to above. With independent investments but an imperfect capital market, the present-value rule will give answers which are correct but possibly only in a formal sense (the discounting rate used is not an external opportunity but an internal shadow price which comes out of the analysis).

The main negative conclusion is that the internal-rate-of-return rule for the multiperiod case is not generally correct, if the usual definition of the internal rate is adopted as that discount rate which makes the present value of the income stream associated with an investment option equal to zero. The so-called internal rate will only give correct answers in general if restricted to two-period comparisons; I have called this two-period internal rate the productive rate of return. For multiperiod investments the usual internal-rate-of-return rule (compare $\rho$ with the market rate $r$) is not generally correct; however, given certain continuity assumptions, the correct answer will be arrived at by setting the marginal productive rate of return between each *pair* of time periods equal to the discount of market rate between those periods.

More important than the specific detailed conclusions is the demonstration that the Fisherian approach—the analysis of investment decisions as a means of balancing consumption incomes over time, together with the distinction between productive and market investment opportunities—is capable of solving (in the theoretical sense) all the problems posed. This solution is, furthermore, not an excrescence upon the general economic theory of choice but entirely integrated with it, constituting another dimension, so to speak. Since Fisher, economists working in the theory of investment decision have tended to adopt a mechanical approach—some plumping for the use of this formula, some for that. From a Fisherian point of view, we can see that none of the formulas so far propounded is universally valid. Furthermore, even where the present-value rule, for example, is correct, few realize that its validity is conditional upon making certain associated financing decisions as the Fisherian analysis demonstrates. In short, the Fisherian approach permits us to define the range of applicability and the shortcomings of all the proposed formulas—thus standing over against them as the general theoretical solution to the problem of investment decision under conditions of certainty.

# 19. THE DERIVATION OF PROBABILISTIC INFORMATION FOR THE EVALUATION OF RISKY INVESTMENTS

## FREDERICK S. HILLIER*

Reprinted from *Management Science*, Vol. 9, No. 3 (April, 1963), pp. 443–57, by permission of the author and the publisher.

## INTRODUCTION

The amount of risk involved is often one of the important considerations in the evaluation of proposed investments. Thus, a reasonably safe investment with a certain expected rate of return will often be preferred to a much more risky investment with a somewhat higher expected rate of return. This is especially true when the risky investment is so large that the failure to achieve expectations could significantly affect the financial position of the individual or firm. Moreover, despite theoretical arguments against it, research [8] has indicated that many executives maintain this preference even when the personal or corporate resources are more than ample to meet the contingency of adverse events. On the other hand, the prosperity of Las Vegas attests to the fact that some individuals have risk preference rather than risk aversion, i.e., they often select a risky investment with a low or negative expected rate of return because of the possibility of an extremely high return.

Unfortunately, not many expository papers have appeared on practical ways of deriving the type of explicit, well-defined, and comprehensive information that is essential for an accurate appraisal of a risky investment. It is the purpose of this presentation to indicate how, under certain assumptions, such information in the form of the probability distribution of the internal rate of return, present worth, or annual cost of a proposed investment can be derived.

## EXISTING PROCEDURES FOR CONSIDERING RISK

Capital budgeting literature has not yet given much consideration to the analysis of risk; and such procedures as have been suggested for dealing with risk have tended to be either quite simplified or somewhat theoretical. Thus, these procedures have tended either to provide management with only a portion of the information required for a sound decision, or they have assumed the availability of information which is almost impossible to obtain.

* Stanford University, Stanford, California.

The simplified procedures usually amount to reducing the estimates of the possible values of the prospective cash flow during each time period to a single expected value, in either an intuitive or statistical sense, and then analyzing the problem as if each of these expected values were certain to occur.[1] Risk is sometimes included in this analysis by using an interest rate appropriate for the associated degree of risk as the standard for the minimum acceptable internal rate of return or for discounting the cash flow for a particular year. These procedures are the ones generally selected for use currently. However, they suffer the disadvantage of supressing the information regarding the risk of the proposed investment. Thus, while optimistic and pessimistic predictions have both been averaged in to obtain the single measure of the merit of the investment, the executive is not provided with any explicit measure of the risk of the investment. For example, he might be provided with an estimate of the expected rate of return of an investment but not its variance, even though the executive would probably have a distinct preference for an investment with a small variance of the rate of return over another investment with the same expected rate of return and larger variance. As a result, these procedures require the executive to resort to his own intuition for the ultimate consideration of risk.

A useful technique for considering risk which is sometimes used in conjunction with the simplified procedures is sensitivity analysis.[2] This technique involves revising uncertain estimates of prospective cash flows and investigating the sensitivity of the measure of the merit of the investment to such revisions in the estimates. This gives some indication of the effect if one of the original estimates were either too optimistic or too pessimistic. However, sensitivity analysis is quite limited in the amount of information it can provide. For example, it is difficult to draw precise conclusions about the possible effects of combinations of errors in the estimates, even though this is the typical situation of concern. For statistical reasons, it would usually be misleading to consider the case where all the estimates are too optimistic or where all are too pessimistic. In short, sensitivity analysis is useful but its conclusions tend to suffer from a lack of conciseness, precision and comprehensiveness.

A theoretical procedure occasionally suggested would determine the "utility" or degree of merit of each of the possible outcomes of an investment and then determine the expected value of the utility to use as a measure of the merit of the investment.[3] Assuming that valid utilities and associated probabilities are used, this procedure properly weights the merit of both the better and the poorer possible outcomes of an investment so that it accurately and and completely takes risk into account. Thus, expected utility is an ideal measure of the merit of an investment from a theoretical point of view. Unfortunately, utility is a subtle concept, so that the measurement of utility is a difficult task. Therefore, it would be extremely difficult to determine

[1] See, for example, [7], Ch. 13; [2], Ch. 9; [11], pp. 210–213.
[2] See, for example, [7], Ch. 13.
[3] See, for example, [11], pp. 204–216, and [13], Ch. 2.

explicitly, with the needed precision, the utility to management of all the possible outcomes of an investment. From a practical point of view, management usually would have neither the time nor the inclination to participate in such a monumental task in a formal manner. Another procedure which has been suggested by certain economists [10] involves selecting those investments whose expected rate of return exceeds the firm's average cost of capital, including both stocks and bonds, where this cost is a function of the risk associated with the industry and thus (by implication) the investments. However, practical objections can be made regarding the underlying assumptions, including the premise that executives will act solely in the long-run interests of the stockholders, and the difficulty of determining the prospective rate of return of stock. Another interesting approach to this type of problem has recently been reported [12] in the form of a model for investment in the stock market. However, it does not appear that this approach, involving the maximization of expected monetary gains subject to probabilistic constraints on maximum loss during the various periods, can be extended to the general problem of investment under uncertainty.

Finally, mention should be made of the work of Markowitz [9] concerning the analysis of portfolios containing large numbers of securities. Markowitz shows how to determine the portfolio which provides the most suitable combination of expected rate of return and standard deviation of rate of return. While the nature and scope of this problem differs somewhat from the problem dealt with here, there are similarities in the two approaches to the problem of evaluating risky investments. The primary similarities are in the use of the expected value and standard deviation of rate of return and in the treatment of covariances. Furthermore, [9] contains considerable theoretical material which is relevant to the problem posed here. Especially important is the justification given for the use of both the expected value and the standard deviation of rate of return as decision parameters. For example, it is shown that properly using these decision parameters is essentially equivalent to maximizing a quadratic utility function of rate of return.

## COMPARISON OF PROPOSED PROCEDURE WITH EXISTING PROCEDURES

The procedure that will be recommended here is something of a compromise between the simplified procedures and the theoretical procedures described above. While it has some of the same deficiencies, it also enjoys many of the advantages of both types of procedures. It goes beyond the simplified approach to provide additional information, namely, the probability distribution of the selected measure of the merit of the investments. At the same time, this information enables the executive to quickly apply, in an intuitive and implicit sense, the theoretical procedure of evaluating expected utility. Therefore, the techniques that will now be developed are actually tools for more clearly exhibiting the risk involved and should complement, rather than supersede, most current procedures for evaluating investments.

## FORMULATION OF PROBLEM

Consider an investment which will result in cash flows during at least some of the next $n$ years. Let $X_j$ be the random variable which takes on the value of the net cash flow during the $j$-th year, where $j = 0, 1, 2, \ldots, n$. Assume that $X_j$ has a normal distribution with known mean, $\mu_j$, and known standard deviation, $\sigma_j$.

It is recognized that these assumptions regarding $X_j$ will not often be completely justified. In particular, the probability distribution of $X_j$ may not be normal. On the other hand, it would seem that, for many types of prospective cash flows, one's best subjective probability distribution would be nearly a symmetrical distribution resembling the normal distribution. Furthermore, by the Central Limit Theorem, the actual distribution of $X_j$ can sometimes deviate considerably from the normal distribution without significantly affecting the final results. More precisely, looking ahead to Equation 1, if $X_j/(1 + i)^j, j = 0, 1, \ldots, n$, are mutually independent random variables, with finite means and variances, which are either identically distributed or uniformly bounded then (by the Lindeberg Theorem) the Central Limit Theorem will hold and the sum of these random variables will be approximately normal if $n$ is large. If this holds, the probability distribution of the measures of the merit of an investment considered in the following sections will be approximately normal, regardless of whether the $X_j$ random variables are normal or not. Finally, even if the $X_j$ random variables are not normal and the Central Limit Theorem is not applicable, all of the subsequent equations (eq. 1, 2, ..., 13) will still hold. Thus, the mean and variance of the measures of merit will be the same (or nearly the same in the case of internal rate of return) regardless of the normality of $X_j$. The mean and variance (or standard deviation) of these measures, by themselves, provide a substantial basis for evaluating and comparing prospective investments; furthermore, certain weak probability statements can be made by using the Tchebycheff inequality. The only consequence of non-normality is that, without knowledge of the distribution of the measures of merit, precise probability statements cannot be made.

Regarding the other assumptions, present procedures already assume that some measure of the central tendency of each prospective cash flow is known since they require a single forecast of the cash flow. This measure usually corresponds roughly either to $\mu_j$ or to the mode ("most likely value"), which, for the normal distribution, equals $\mu_j$. It should not be much more difficult to estimate $\sigma_j$ than $\mu_j$. Merely keep in mind that about 68% of the probability distribution will lie within $\mu_j \pm \sigma_j$, about 95% within $\mu_j \pm 2\sigma_j$, and about 99.73% within $\mu_j \pm 3\sigma_j$. Thus, estimating $\sigma_j$ is just a more definitive version of that aspect of sensitivity analysis involving the investigation of reasonably likely values of $X_j$.

Some assumption needs to be specified regarding the relationship between the $X_j$ random variables for different values of $j$. The two simplest assumptions are that all the $X_j$ random variables are mutually independent or that they are all completely correlated. Actually, there will be many cases where a compromise between these assumptions is needed since some of the cash flows are reasonably independent whereas others are closely correlated. Therefore, what will be done is to consider the two cases individually and then show how they can be combined.

The desirability of an investment is not always a question that can be answered entirely independently of other investments. The performance of one investment is instead often interrelated with the performance of others. Therefore, for a truly satisfactory investment decision, it would sometimes be desirable to introduce into the analysis some measure or measures of covariance between the investment's merit and that of alternatives or complementary investments. Indeed, Markowitz [9] includes a thorough development of the use of covariance of returns in his analysis. However, this refinement is beyond the scope of this paper. Instead, the problem is confined to describing the desirability of individual prospective investments.

A large number of methods have been advocated for evaluating investments. While it is felt that the approach to be developed here can be applied to most of these methods, only compound interest methods (presently favored by most writers) will be considered. In particular, the three widely advocated discounting procedures—the present worth method, the annual cost method, and the internal rate of return method—as defined by Grant and Ireson [7] will be explored. The objective will be to demonstrate how to obtain a probability distribution for each of these three measures of the merit of an investment.

## PROBABILITY DISTRIBUTION OF PRESENT WORTH

The present worth, $P$, for a proposed productive investment may be defined as:

$$(1) \qquad P = \sum_{j=0}^{n} \left[ \frac{X_j}{(1 + i)^j} \right],$$

where $i$ is the rate of interest which properly reflects the investor's time value of money. The value of $i$ is often described as the minimum attractive rate of return or the cost of capital.

A more general definition of $P$ is sometimes given by specifying possibly distinct values of $i$ for each of the $n$ periods. The following results can be applied with no increased difficulty to the more general case. However, since uniform values of $i$ are almost always used in actual applications, only this simplest case will be considered, so as to concentrate attention on the new features of the proposed procedure.

It should be recognized that, as defined, $P$ is actually a random variable rather than a constant. For purposes of evaluating a proposed investment, the usual procedure is to examine the expected value of $P$,

$$(2) \qquad \mu_P = \sum_{j=0}^{n} \left[ \frac{\mu_j}{(1 + i)^j} \right],$$

although this is often referred to as "the" present worth. Then, if $\mu_P > 0$, the investment would be made since this would increase the expected total wealth of the firm more than investing the same money elsewhere at the marginal rate of return $i$. When comparing mutually exclusive alternatives for the same investment funds, the alternative with the largest value of $\mu_P$ would be preferred, assuming no compensating intangible factors.

Assume initially that $X_0, X_1, \ldots, X_n$ are mutually independent. Therefore, it is well-known that $P$ would have a normal distribution, where the mean is given by Equation 2 and the variance is

(3)
$$\sigma_P^2 = \sum_{j=0}^{n} \frac{\sigma_j^2}{(1+i)^{2j}}.$$

Before illustrating the use of this information, other assumptions leading to different variances will be considered. Assume that $X_0, X_1, \ldots, X_n$ are perfectly correlated. That is, if the value that $X_m$ takes on is $\mu_m + C\sigma_m$, then the value that $X_j$ takes on must be $\mu_j + C\sigma_j$ for $j = 0, 1, \ldots, m, \ldots, n$. Thus, this assumption states, in effect, that if circumstances cause the actual net cash flow during one period to deviate from expectations, then these same circumstances will also affect the net cash flow in all other periods in an exactly comparable manner. For this case, it is clear that $P$ has a normal distribution with a mean as given by Equation 2 and a standard deviation,

(4)
$$\sigma_P = \sum_{j=0}^{n} \left[ \frac{\sigma_j}{(1+i)^j} \right].$$

A more realistic model is one which combines the two assumptions considered above. This model would recognize and make allowance for the fact that, often, some of the cash flows are closely related while the others are reasonably independent. Therefore, the assumption is made that $Y_j$, $Z_j^{(1)}$, $Z_j^{(2)}, \ldots$, and $Z_j^{(m)}$ are the normally distributed random variables such that

(5)
$$X_j = Y_j + Z_j^{(1)} + Z_j^{(2)} + \cdots + Z_j^{(m)},$$

where the new random variables are mutually independent with the exception that $Z_0^{(k)}, Z_1^{(k)}, \ldots, Z_n^{(k)}$ are perfectly correlated for $k = 1, 2, \ldots, m$. In other words, the net cash flow for each period consists of an independent cash flow plus $m$ distinct cash flows which are each perfectly correlated with the corresponding cash flows in the other periods. Therefore, it follows that $P$ has a normal distribution with

(6)
$$\mu_P = \sum_{j=0}^{n} \left[ \frac{\mu_j}{(1+i)^j} \right] = \sum_{j=0}^{n} \frac{E(Y_j) + \sum_{k=1}^{m} E(Z_j^{(k)})}{(1+i)^j},$$

and

(7)
$$\sigma_P^2 = \sum_{j=0}^{n} \left[ \frac{\text{Var}(Y_j)}{(1+i)^{2j}} \right] + \sum_{k=1}^{m} \left( \sum_{j=0}^{n} \left[ \frac{\sqrt{\text{Var}(Z_j^{(k)})}}{(1+i)^j} \right] \right)^2.$$

It is easily seen that the first two cases treated are actually only special cases of this model combining the two assumptions. The first case of complete independence is obtained by setting $m = 0$. The second case of complete correlation is obtained by setting $m = 1$ and $Y_j \equiv 0$. The essential difference between the various special cases is reflected in Equation 7. In particular, given fixed values of $\sigma_j$, $\sigma_P$ is smallest for the case of complete independence and largest for the case of complete correlation.

An even more precise model, from a theoretical point of view, would be one which admitted the possibility of relationship between random variables which falls somewhere between mutual independence and complete correlation. Ideally, one would be given the covariance matrix for $X_0$, $X_1$, ..., $X_n$, so that $\mu_P$ would be given by Eq. 2 and $\sigma_P^2$ would be the weighted sum of the elements of the covariance matrix, where $\sigma_{jk}$ is weighted by $(1 + i)^{-(j+k)}$. Unfortunately, it does not yet appear to be realistic to expect investment analysts to develop reliable estimates for covariances. Therefore, attention will be concentrated on the model summarized by Eq. 5.

Having thus obtained the probability distribution of $P$, this information now provides the executive with some basis for evaluating the risk aspect of the investment decision. For example, suppose that, on the basis of the forecasts regarding prospective cash flow from a proposed investment of $10,000, it is determined that $\mu_P = \$1000$ and $\sigma_P = \$2000$. Ordinarily, the current procedure would be to approve the investment since $\mu_P > 0$. However, with additional information available ($\sigma_P = \$2000$) regarding the considerable risk of the investment, the executive can analyze the situation further. Using widely available tables for the normal distribution, he could note (or be given the information on a drawing of the cumulative distribution function) that the probability that $P < 0$, so that the investment won't pay, is 0.31. Furthermore, the probability is 0.16, 0.023, and 0.0013, respectively, that the investment will lose the present worth equivalent of at least $1000, $3000, and $5000, respectively. Considering the financial status of the firm, the executive can use this and similar information to make his decision. Suppose, instead, that the executive is attempting to choose between this investment and a second investment with $\mu_P = \$500$ and $\sigma_P = \$500$. By conducting a similar analysis for the second investment, the executive can decide whether the greater expected earnings of the first investment justifies the greater risk. A useful technique for making this comparison is to superimpose the drawing of the probability distribution of $P$ for the second investment upon the corresponding drawing for the first investment. This same approach generalizes to the comparison of more than two investments.

## PROBABILITY DISTRIBUTION OF ANNUAL COST

The equivalent uniform annual cost, $A$, for a proposed investment is shown by Grant and Ireson [7] to be

$$(8) \qquad A = -\sum_{j=1}^{n} \left[ \frac{X_j}{(1 + i)^j} \right]\left[ \frac{i(1 + i)^n}{(1 + i)^n - 1} \right] = P\left[ \frac{i(1 + i)^n}{(1 + i)^n - 1} \right].$$

Thus, for given values of $i$ and $n$, $A$ differs from $P$ only by a constant factor. Therefore, the probability distribution of $A$ is found by finding the probability distribution of $P$, as described above, and then multiplying $P$ by this constant factor. The analysis of the risk would also correspond to the analysis when using the present worth method.

## PROBABILITY DISTRIBUTION OF INTERNAL RATE OF RETURN

The internal rate of return, $R$, may be defined as that value of $i$ such that $P = 0$. It is used as a measure of the merit of proposed investments. The highest priority is given to those investments with the highest values of $R$. If adequate funds are available, an established minimum attractive rate of return is often used as a standard for comparison, proposed investments being approved only if their value of $R$ exceeds this standard.

Several writers, including Bernhard [1] and Bierman and Smidt [2], have recently voiced their opinion that the internal rate of return method is inferior to the present worth method. This article is intended to be an introductory exposition of a specific technique for evaluating risk, so the issues raised by these writers will be ignored. Thus, it will be assumed that the circumstances are appropriate for the use of the internal rate of return method, so that, for example, there is a unique value for $R$ with probability essentially one.

The proposed procedure for finding the probability distribution of $R$ is a relatively straight-forward one. It involves finding the probability distribution of $P$ for various values of $i$ in order to find the cumulative distribution function of $R$, and then, if desired, deriving the probability density function of $R$ from its cumulative distribution function. This procedure will now be outlined.

Selecting an arbitrary value of $i$, find the probability distribution of $P$ as described previously. Find the probability that $P < 0$. Then, except under unusual circumstances such as [1] discusses, this is just the probability that $R < i$. This result should be readily apparent since $R = i$ only if $P = 0$ and $R$ normally increases as $P$ increases for a given investment and a fixed value of $i$. Summarizing in equation form,

$$(9) \qquad \text{Prob } \{R < i\} = \text{Prob } \{P < 0 \,|\, i\}.$$

Therefore, to find the cumulative distribution function of $R$, one need merely repeat the calculation of Prob $\{P < 0 \,|\, i\}$ for as many values of $i$ as desired. The calculation of these values provides the basis for a graphical presentation of the cumulative distribution function of $R$. This procedure for deriving the probability distribution of $R$ is illustrated by the example of the following section.

The cumulative distribution function of $R$ can readily be used directly for evaluating an investment. It has a meaningful, yet simple, interpretation which is well-suited for this purpose. However, if desired, the cumulative distribution function can be transformed into the probability density function. Simply recall that the value of the probability density function at a certain $i$ is just the first derivative of the cumulative distribution function at that value of $i$. Alternatively, since the probability distribution of $R$ will usually approximate the normal distribution, the normal curve can be used as an approximate probability density function, where the mean and the standard deviation would be estimated from an examination of the cumulative distribution function.

The assertion that, under the prevailing assumption of the normality of $P$, the probability distribution of $R$ will usually approximate the normal distribution is supported by the following argument. Assume the usual situation that $\mu_o < 0$ and $\mu_j > 0$ for $j = 1, 2, \ldots, n$. Therefore, the first derivative of $\mu_P$ with respect to $i$, $\mu_P'$, is obviously negative (see Equation 6). Assume, as an approximation, that $\mu_P'$ and $\sigma_P$ are constants for all values of $i$. Then, for any numbers, $\Delta$ and $i_o$,

$$\text{Prob}\{P < -\mu_P'\Delta \,|\, i = i_o\} = \text{Prob}\{P < 0 \,|\, i = i_0 + \Delta\},$$

and therefore,

$$\text{Prob}\{R < i_o + \Delta\} = \text{Prob}\{P < -\mu_P'\Delta \,|\, i = i_o\}.$$

Hence, $R$ and $P$ are identically distributed except for the location and scale parameters, mean and standard deviation. Since $P$ is normal, it now follows that the probability distribution of $R$ is the normal distribution. The one shortcoming in this argument is that, in fact, $\mu_P'$ and $\sigma_P$ are not constants. However, the fact that $\mu_P'' > 0$, whereas $\sigma_P' < 0$, means that these two discrepancies tend to cancel each other out.

It would be sometimes desirable, when comparing mutually exclusive investments requiring differing amounts of investment funds, to determine the probability distribution of the internal rate of return on each increment in investment. To illustrate how this would be done, consider two such mutually exclusive investments which can be described by the model involving Equation 5. Let $P(S)$, $P(L)$, and $P(\Delta)$ denote the present worths of the smaller investment, the larger investment, and the incremental investment, respectively. Let $R(\Delta)$ denote the internal rate of return on the incremental investment. Assume that $P(S)$ and $P(L)$ are mutually independent. Therefore, since

$$(10) \qquad P(\Delta) = P(L) - P(S),$$

it is clear that $P(\Delta)$ has a normal distribution with

$$(11) \qquad E\{P(\Delta)\} = E\{P(L)\} - E\{P(S)\},$$

and

$$(12) \qquad \text{Var}\{P(\Delta)\} = \text{Var}\{P(L)\} + \text{Var}\{P(S)\}.$$

Thus, just as before,

$$(13) \qquad \text{Prob}\{R(\Delta) < i\} = \text{Prob}\{P(\Delta) < 0 \,|\, i\},$$

so that the same procedure is now used for finding the probability distribution of $R(\Delta)$ as for $R$.

## EXAMPLE

The XYZ Company is primarily engaged in the manufacture of cameras. They will soon be discontinuing the production of one of their older models, and they are now investigating what should be done with the extra productive capacity that will consequently become available. Two attractive alternatives appear to be available. The first alternative is to expand the production of model A, one of their latest and most popular models. This model was initially marketed last year, and its successful reception plus favorable marketing research indicates that there is and will continue to be a market for this extra production. The second alternative is to initiate the production of model B. Model B would involve a number of revolutionary changes which the re-search department has developed. While no comparable model is now on the market, rumors in the industry indicate that a number of other companies might now have similar models on their drawing boards. Marketing research indicates an exciting but uncertain potential for such a model. Uncertainty regarding the reliability of the proposed new devices, lack of production ex-perience on such a model, and the possibility that the market might be vigor-ously invaded by competing models at any time, all add to the risk involved in this alternative. In short, the decision is between the safe, conservative investment in model A, or the risky but promising investment in model B. It is felt that both of these models will be marketable for the next five years. Due to a lack of investment funds and productive capacity, it has been decided that only one of these alternatives can be selected. It is assumed that the pro-duction of model B would not affect the market for the presently scheduled production of model A.

Detailed studies have been made regarding the after tax cash flow conse-quences of the two alternatives. The analysis of the investment required in model A indicates that considerable new equipment, tooling, and modifica-tion of existing production processes will be needed. It was estimated that the difference in the immediate cash flow because of the investment in model A would be ($- \$400,000$). However, it is recognized that this estimate is only approximate, so that it is appropriate to estimate the standard deviation for this cash flow. Recalling that the probability is 0.6827, 0.9545, and 0.9973, respectively, that the actual cash flow will be within one, two, and three stan-dard deviations, respectively, of the expected cash flow, it was decided that an estimate of \$20,000 was the most appropriate one. In other words, the judgment was that, letting $Y_o$ be the cash flow,

$$\text{Prob}\{-\$400,000 - \sigma \le Y_o \le -\$400,000 + \sigma\} = 0.6827,$$

$$\text{Prob}\{-\$400,000 - 2\sigma \le Y_o \le -\$400,000 + 2\sigma\} = 0.9545,$$

$$\text{Prob}\{-\$400,000 - 3\sigma \le Y_o \le -\$400,000 + 3\sigma\} = 0.9973,$$

most accurately reflects the estimator's subjective probabilities if $\sigma$ is chosen as \$20,000.

Proceeding with a similar analysis, the expected values and standard deviations of the net cash flow for each of the next five years were estimated. Due to the previous experience with model A, these standard deviations were considered to be small. The variation that does exist largely arises from the variation in the production costs, such as maintenance, equipment replacement, and rework costs, and in the state of the economy. Since these conditions tend to vary randomly from year to year, it was decided that the appropriate assumption is that the net cash flows in the various years are mutually independent. One special problem was encountered in determining the standard deviation for the fifth year since this net cash flow combines the regular cash flow for the fifth year plus the effective salvage value of the equipment being used. This standard deviation was obtained by assuming independence, so that the variance of the sum equals the sum of the variances of these cash flows. Thus, even though the standard deviation for the salvage value was estimated at $30,000 and the standard deviation for the rest of the net cash flow at $40,000, the estimated standard deviation of the total net cash flow for the fifth year is $50,000.

Table 1 summarizes the results of the estimating process for model A.

TABLE 1

ESTIMATED NET CASH FLOW DATA IN THOUSANDS OF
DOLLARS FOR MODEL A

| Year | Corresponding Symbol in Eq. 5 | Expected Value | Standard Deviation |
|---|---|---|---|
| 0 | $Y_0$ | −400 | 20 |
| 1 | $Y_1$ | +120 | 10 |
| 2 | $Y_2$ | +120 | 15 |
| 3 | $Y_3$ | +120 | 20 |
| 4 | $Y_4$ | +110 | 30 |
| 5 | $Y_5$ | +200 | 50 |

The procedure for describing the investment in model B was similar. The primary difference was that this investment was considered to generate both a series of correlated cash flows and a series of independent cash flows. Thus, in Equation 5, $m = 1$ instead of $m = 0$ as for the investment in model A. This difference arose because of the uncertainty regarding the reception of model B on the market. Thus, it was felt that if the reception exceeded expectations during the first year or two, it would continue to exceed present expectations thereafter, and vice versa. The resulting conclusion was that the net marketing cash flow, i.e., the net cash flow resulting from the sales income minus the expenses due to the marketing effort and advertising required, for each of the five years should be assumed to be perfectly correlated. On the other hand, it was felt the analysis of the production expenses involved was sufficiently reliable that any deviation from expectations for a given year would be primarily attributable to random fluctuations in production costs, especially in such irregular items as maintenance costs. Therefore, it was concluded that the net production cash flow for each of the five years should be assumed to be mutually independent. The effective equipment salvage value, being essentially independent of the other cash flows, was included in the net production cash flow for the fifth year.

TABLE 2

ESTIMATED NET CASH FLOW DATA IN THOUSANDS OF DOLLARS FOR MODEL B

| Year | Source of Cash Flow | Corresponding Symbol in Eq. 5 | Expected Value | Standard Deviation |
|------|---------------------|-------------------------------|----------------|--------------------|
| 0 | Initial Investment | $Y_0$ | $-600$ | 50 |
| 1 | Production | $Y_1$ | $-250$ | 20 |
| 2 | Production | $Y_2$ | $-200$ | 10 |
| 3 | Production | $Y_3$ | $-200$ | 10 |
| 4 | Production | $Y_4$ | $-200$ | 10 |
| 5 | Production, salvage value | $Y_5$ | $-100$ | $10\sqrt{10}$ |
| 1 | Marketing | $Z_1^{(1)}$ | $+300$ | 50 |
| 2 | Marketing | $Z_2^{(1)}$ | $+600$ | 100 |
| 3 | Marketing | $Z_3^{(1)}$ | $+500$ | 100 |
| 4 | Marketing | $Z_4^{(1)}$ | $+400$ | 100 |
| 5 | Marketing | $Z_5^{(1)}$ | $+300$ | 100 |

Detailed analyses of the various components of total cash flow led, as for model A, to the desired estimates of the expectations and standard deviations of net cash flow for marketing and for production for each of the five years, as well as for the immediate investment required. These results are summarized in Table 2.

The procedure for using these data to derive the probability distribution of present worth will now be illustrated. For this particular company, the appropriate value of $i$ is considered to be $i = 10\%$.

For the investment in Model A, Equations 6 and 7 indicate that, since $m = 0$,

$$\mu_P = \sum_{j=0}^{5} \frac{E(Y_j)}{(1.1)^j} = -400 + \cdots + \frac{200}{(1.1)^5} = +95,$$

$$\sigma_P^2 = \sum_{j=0}^{5} \frac{\text{Var}(Y_j)}{(1.1)^{2j}} = (20)^2 + \cdots + \frac{(50)^2}{(1.1)^{10}} = 2247,$$

so that $\sigma_P = 47.4$. Therefore, the probability distribution of present worth of the investment in model A is a normal distribution with a mean of 95 and a standard deviation of 47.4 (in units of thousands of dollars). Thus, referring to probability tables for the normal distribution to find what proportion of the population is less than the mean minus 95/47.4 standard deviations, it is concluded that

$$\text{Prob}\{P < 0 \,|\, i = 10\%\} = 0.023.$$

Proceeding similarly for the investment in model B, Equations 6 and 7 indicate that, since $m = 1$,

$$\mu_P = \sum_{j=0}^{5} \frac{E(Y_j) + E(Z_j^{(1)})}{(1.1)^j} = -600 + \frac{50}{1.1} + \cdots + \frac{200}{(1.1)^5} = +262,$$

$$\sigma_P^2 = \sum_{j=0}^{5} \frac{\text{Var}(Y_j)}{(1.1)^{2j}} + \left(\sum_{j=0}^{5} \left[\frac{\sqrt{\text{Var}(Z_j^{(1)})}}{(1.1)^j}\right]\right)^2$$

$$= 2500 + \cdots + \frac{1000}{(1.1)^{10}} + \left(\frac{50}{1.1} + \cdots + \frac{100}{(1.1)^5}\right)^2$$

$$= 114{,}700,$$

so that $\sigma_P = 339$. Therefore,

$$\text{Prob }\{P < 0 \,|\, i = 10\%\} = 0.22.$$

This information regarding the probability distribution of present worth permits a precise probabilistic comparison of the two alternative investments. In order to facilitate this comparison, it is sometimes useful to superimpose the two normal curves (or the corresponding cumulative distribution functions) on the same graph.

If the company had desired to use the internal rate of return criterion, the procedure would have been a straight-forward extension of the above procedure for present worth. Thus, given the preceding information regarding present worth, Equation 9 immediately indicates that, for the investment in model A,

$$\text{Prob}\{R < 10\%\} = 0.023,$$

and for the investment in model B

$$\text{Prob}\{R < 10\%\} = 0.22.$$

Using the same procedure for various other values of $i$, the cumulative distribution function of $R$ can be obtained for each of the investments. They are presented subsequently in Figure 1. Comparing these cumulative distribution functions with the cumulative distribution function for the normal distribution, a close similarity is noticed. Thus, a brief examination reveals that, for the investment in model A, the distribution of $R$ is approximately normal with

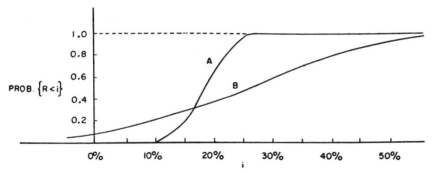

PROB. $\{R < i\}$

FIG. 1. Comparison of the cumulative distribution functions of $R$ for the investments in model A and in model B.

a mean of about 18.5% and a standard deviation of about 4%. For the investment in model B, the distribution of $R$ is approximately normal with a mean of about 25% and a standard deviation of about 20%. This leads to the normal curves given in Figure 2 as the approximate probability density functions of $R$ for the two investments.

Figure 2, or a reasonable facsimile, could also have been obtained directly by determining the slope of the corresponding curves in Figure 1.

If desired, similar information regarding the incremental investment could have been derived from Equations 10, 11, 12, and 13.

The impressive feature of this example is that the decision between the two investments is not an easy one. This is true despite the fact that there is a difference of about $167,000 in the expected present worth and of about 6.5% in the expected rate of return. The great difference in the risk involved compels

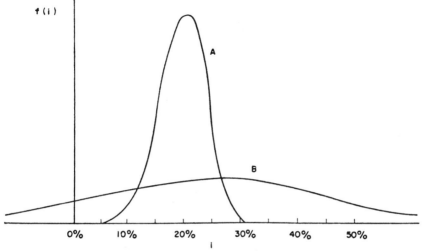

$f(i)$

FIG. 2. Comparison of the approximate probability density functions of $R$ for the investments in Model A and model B.

management to examine carefully the financial position of the firm and evaluate the seriousness of the consequences should the riskier investment fail to achieve expectations. Then, considering the probabilities involved, management would, in effect, implicitly assign utilities to the possible outcomes of the investments and select the investment with the larger expected utility.

## CONCLUSIONS

The risk factor is often an important consideration in the evaluation of a proposed investment. Unfortunately, present procedures for considering risk have not been entirely satisfactory. They have tended either to provide insufficient information or to require the use of essentially unobtainable information. The procedure proposed here appears to largely avoid both of these pitfalls while simultaneously retaining some of the best features of these two types of existing procedures. It requires only that, in addition to an estimate of the expected value of a prospective cash flow, the inexactitude of the estimate be described by an estimate of the standard deviation. On this basis, it then generates an explicit and complete description of the risk involved in terms of the probability distribution of the internal rate of return, present worth, or annual cost. This information then permits management to weigh precisely the possible consequences of the proposed investment and thereby make a sound decision regarding the proposal.

## REFERENCES

1. Bernhard, Richard H., "Discount Methods for Expenditure Evaluation—A Clarification of Their Assumptions," *The Journal of Industrial Engineering*, January–February, 1962, pp. 19–27.
2. Bierman, Harold, Jr., and Smidt, Seymour, *The Capital Budgeting Decision*, The Macmillan Company, New York, 1960.
3. Bowker, Albert H., and Lieberman, Gerald J., *Engineering Statistics*, Prentice-Hall, Englewood Cliffs, New Jersey, 1959.
4. Degarmo, E. Paul, *Engineering Economy*, Third Edition, The Macmillan Company, New York, 1960.
5. English, J. Morley, "New Approaches to Economic Comparison for Engineering Projects," *The Journal of Industrial Engineering*, November–December, 1961, pp. 375–378.
6. Gordon, Myron J., and Shapiro, Eli, "Capital Equipment Analysis: The Required Rate of Profit," *Management Science* (October 1956), pp. 102–110.
7. Grant, Eugene L., and Ireson, W. Grant, *Principles of Engineering Economy*, Fourth Edition, The Ronald Press, New York, 1960.
8. Green, Paul E., "The Derivation of Utility Functions in a Large Industrial Firm," paper given at the First Joint National Meeting of the Operations Research Society of America and the Institute of Management Sciences, 1961.
9. Markowitz, Harry M., *Portfolio Selection*, John Wiley and Sons, New York, 1959.
10. Modigliani, Franco, and Miller, Merton H., "The Cost of Capital, Corporation Finance, and the Theory of Investment," *American Economic Review*, XLVIII, No. 2, June, 1958.

11. Morris, William T., *Engineering Economy*, Richard D. Irwin, Homewood, Illinois, 1960.
12. Naslund, Bertil, and Whinston, Andrew, " A Model of Multi-Period Investment under Uncertainty," *Management Science* (January 1962), pp. 184–200.
13. Schlaifer, Robert, *Probability and Statistics for Business Decisions*, McGraw-Hill, New York, 1959.

## 20.  RISK ANALYSIS IN CAPITAL INVESTMENT

### DAVID B. HERTZ

Reprinted from the *Harvard Business Review*, Vol. 42, No. 1 (January–February, 1964), pp. 95–106, by permission of the publisher.

Of all the decisions that business executives must make, none is more challenging—and none has received more attention—than choosing among alternative capital investment opportunities. What makes this kind of decision so demanding, of course, is not the problem of projecting return on investment under any given set of assumptions. The difficulty is in the assumptions and in their impact. Each assumption involves its own degree—often a high degree—of uncertainty; and, taken together, these combined uncertainties can multiply into a total uncertainty of critical proportions. This is where the element of risk enters, and it is in the evaluation of risk that the executive has been able to get little help from currently available tools and techniques.

There is a way to help the executive sharpen his key capital investment decisions by providing him with a realistic measurement of the risks involved. Armed with this measurement, which evaluates for him the risk at each possible level of return, he is then in a position to measure more knowledgeably alternative courses of action against corporate objectives.

### NEED FOR NEW CONCEPT

The evaluation of a capital investment project starts with the principle that the productivity of capital is measured by the rate of return we expect to receive over some future period. A dollar received next year is worth less to us than a dollar in hand today. Expenditures three years hence are less costly than expenditures of equal magnitude two years from now. For this reason we cannot calculate the rate of return realistically unless we take into account (a) when the sums involved in an investment are spent and (b) when the returns are received.

Comparing alternative investments is thus complicated by the fact that they usually differ not only in size but also in the length of time over which expenditures will have to be made and benefits returned.

It is these facts of investment life that long ago made apparent the short-comings of approaches that simply averaged expenditures and benefits, or lumped them, as in the number-of-years-to-pay-out method. These short-comings stimulated students of decision making to explore more precise methods for determining whether one investment would leave a company better off in the long run than would another course of action.

It is not surprising, then, that much effort has been applied to the development of ways to improve our ability to discriminate among investment alternatives. The focus of all of these investigations has been to sharpen the definition of the value of capital investments to the company. The controversy and furor that once came out in the business press over the most appropriate way of calculating these values has largely been resolved in favor of the discounted cash flow method as a reasonable means of measuring the rate of return that can be expected in the future from an investment made today.

Thus we have methods which, in general, are more or less elaborate mathematical formulas for comparing the outcomes of various investments and the combinations of the variables that will affect the investments.[1] As these techniques have progressed, the mathematics involved has become more and more precise, so that we can now calculate discounted returns to a fraction of a per cent.

But the sophisticated businessman knows that behind these precise calculations are data which are not that precise. At best, the rate-of-return information he is provided with is based on an average of different opinions with varying reliabilities and different ranges of probability. When the expected returns on two investments are close, he is likely to be influenced by "intangibles"—a precarious pursuit at best. Even when the figures for two investments are quite far apart, and the choice seems clear, there lurks in the back of the businessman's mind memories of the Edsel and other ill-fated ventures.

In short, the decision-maker realizes that there is something more he ought to know, something in addition to the expected rate of return. He suspects that what is missing has to do with the nature of the data on which the expected rate of return is calculated, and with the way those data are processed. It has something to do with uncertainty, with possibilities and probabilities extending across a wide range of rewards and risks.

THE ACHILLES HEEL

The fatal weakness of past approaches thus has nothing to do with the mathematics of rate-of-return calculation. We have pushed along this path so far that the precision of our calculation is, if anything, somewhat illusory.

---

[1] See for example, Joel Dean, *Capital Budgeting* (New York, Columbia University Press, 1951); "Return on Capital as a Guide to Managerial Decisions," *National Association of Accounts Research Report*, No. 35, December 1, 1959; and Bruce F. Young, "Overcoming Obstacles to Use of Discounted Cash Flow for Investment Shares," *NAA Bulletin*, March 1963, p. 15.

The fact is that, no matter what mathematics is used, each of the variables entering into the calculation of rate of return is subject to a high level of uncertainty. For example:

The useful life of a new piece of capital equipment is rarely known in advance with any degree of certainty. It may be affected by variations in obsolescence or deterioration, and relatively small changes in use life can lead to large changes in return. Yet an expected value for the life of the equipment—based on a great deal of data from which a single best possible forecast has been developed—is entered into the rate-of-return calculation. The same is done for the other factors that have a significant bearing on the decision at hand.

Let us look at how this works out in a simple case—one in which the odds appear to be all in favor of a particular decision:

The executives of a food company must decide whether to launch a new packaged cereal. They have come to the conclusion that five factors are the determining variables: *advertising and promotion expense, total cereal market, share of market for this product, operating costs, and new capital investment.* On the basis of the "most likely" estimate for each of these variables the picture looks very bright—a healthy 30% return. This future, however, depends on each of the "most likely" estimates coming true in the actual case. If each of these "educated guesses" has, for example, a 60% chance of being correct, there is only an 8% chance that *all five* will be correct (.60 × .60 × .60 × .60 × .60). So the "expected" return is actually dependent on a rather unlikely coincidence. The decision-maker needs to know a great deal more about the *other* values used to make each of the five estimates and about what he stands to gain or lose from various combinations of these values.

This simple example illustrates that the rate of return actually depends on a specific combination of values of a great many different variables. But only the expected levels of ranges (e.g., worst, average, best; or pessimistic, most likely, optimistic) of these variables are used in formal mathematical ways to provide the figures given to management. Thus, predicting a single most likely rate of return gives precise numbers that do not tell the whole story.

The "expected" rate of return represents only a few points on a continuous curve of possible combinations of future happenings. It is a bit like trying to

EXHIBIT I. DESCRIBING UNCERTAINTY — A THROW OF THE DICE

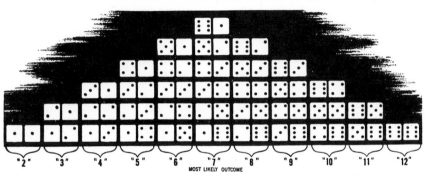

"2"   "3"   "4"   "5"   "6"   "7"   "8"   "9"   "10"   "11"   "12"

MOST LIKELY OUTCOME

predict the outcome in a dice game by saying that the most likely outcome is a "7." The description is incomplete because it does not tell us about all the other things that could happen. In Exhibit I, for instance, we see the odds on throws of only two dice having six sides. Now suppose that each dice has 100 sides and there are eight of them! This is a situation more comparable to business investment, where the company's market share might become any one of 100 different sizes and where there are eight different factors (pricing, promotion, and so on) that can affect the outcome.

Nor is this the only trouble. Our willingness to bet on a roll of the dice depends not only on the odds but also on the stakes. Since the probability of rolling a "7" is 1 in 6, we might be quite willing to risk a few dollars on that outcome at suitable odds. But would we be equally willing to wager $10,000 or $100,000 at those same odds, or even at better odds? In short, risk is influenced both by the odds on various events occurring and by the magnitude of the rewards or penalties which are involved when they do occur. To illustrate again:

Suppose that a company is considering an investment of $1 million. The "best estimate" of the probable return is $200,000 a year. It could well be that this estimate is the average of three possible returns—a 1-in-3 chance of getting no return at all, a 1-in-3 chance of getting $200,000 per year, a 1-in-3 chance of getting $400,000 per year. Suppose that getting no return at all would put the company out of business. Then, by accepting this proposal, management is taking a 1-in-3 chance of going bankrupt.

If only the "best estimate" analysis is used, management might go ahead, however, unaware that it is taking a big chance. If all of the available information were examined, management might prefer an alternative proposal with a smaller, but more certain (i.e., less variable), expectation.

Such considerations have led almost all advocates of the use of modern capital-investment-index calculations to plead for a recognition of the element of uncertainty. Perhaps Ross G. Walker sums up current thinking when he speaks of "the almost impenetrable mists of any forecast."[2]

How can the executive penetrate the mists of uncertainty that surround the choices among alternatives?

### LIMITED IMPROVEMENTS

A number of efforts to cope with uncertainty have been successful up to a point, but all seem to fall short of the mark in one way or another:

1. *More accurate forecasts*—Reducing the error in estimates is a worthy objective. But no matter how many estimates of the future go into a capital investment decision, when all is said and done, the future is still the future. Therefore, however well we forecast, we are still left with the certain knowledge that we cannot eliminate all uncertainty.

[2] "The Judgement Factor in Investment Decisions," *HBR* March–April 1961, p. 99.

2. *Empirical adjustments*—Adjusting the factors influencing the outcome of a decision is subject to serious difficulties. We would like to adjust them so as to cut down the likelihood that we will make a " bad " investment, but how can we do that without at the same time spoiling our chances to make a " good " one? And in any case what is the basis for adjustment? We adjust, not for uncertainty, but for bias.

For example, construction estimates are often exceeded. If a company's history of construction costs is that 90% of its estimates have been exceeded by 15%, then in a capital estimate there is every justification for increasing the value of this factor by 15%. This is a matter of improving the accuracy of the estimate.

But suppose that new-product sales estimates have been exceeded by more than 75% in one-fourth of all historical cases, and have not reached 50% of the estimate in one-sixth of all such cases? Penalties for over-estimating are very tangible, and so management is apt to reduce the sales estimate to "cover" the one case in six—thereby reducing the calculated rate of return. In doing so, it is possibly missing some of its best opportunities.

3. *Revising cutoff rates*—Selecting higher cutoff rates for protecting against uncertainty is attempting much the same thing. Management would like to have a possibility of return in proportion to the risk it takes. Where there is much uncertainty involved in the various estimates of sales, costs, prices, and so on, a high calculated return from the investment provides some incentive for taking the risk. This is, in fact, a perfectly sound position. The trouble is that the decision-maker still needs to know explicitly what risks he is taking—and what the odds are on achieving the expected return.

4. *Three-level estimates*—A start at spelling out risks is sometimes made by taking the high, medium, and low values of the estimated factors and calculating rates of return based on various combinations of the pessimistic, average, and optimistic estimates. These calculations give a picture of the range of possible results, but do not tell the executive whether the pessimistic result is more likely than the optimistic one—or, in fact, whether the average result is much more likely to occur than either of the extremes. So, although this is a step in the right direction, it still does not give a clear enough picture for comparing alternatives.

5. *Selected probabilities*—Various methods have been used to include the probabilities of specific factors in the return calculation. L. C. Grant discusses a program for forecasting discounted cash flow rates of return where the service life is subject to obsolescence and deterioration. He calculates the odds that the investment will terminate at any time after it is made depending on the probability distribution of the service-life factor.

After calculating these factors for each year through maximum service life, he then determines an over-all expected rate of return.[3]

Edward G. Bennion suggests the use of game theory to take into account alternative market growth rates as they would determine rate of return for various alternatives. He uses the estimated probabilities that specific growth rates will occur to develop optimum strategies. Bennion points out:

Forecasting can result in a negative contribution to capital budget decisions unless it goes further than merely providing a single most probable prediction. . . . (With) an estimated probability coefficient for the forecast, plus knowledge of the payoffs for the company's alternative investments and calculation of indifference probabilities . . . the margin of error may be substantially reduced, and the businessman can tell just how far off his forecast may be before it leads him to a wrong decision.[4]

Note that both of these methods yield an expected return, each based on only one uncertain input factor—service life in the first case, market growth in the second. Both are helpful, and both tend to improve the clarity with which the executive can view investment alternatives. But neither sharpens up the range of "risk taken" or "return hoped for" sufficiently to help very much in the complex decisions of capital planning.

## SHARPENING THE PICTURE

Since every one of the many factors that enter into the evaluation of a specific decision is subject to some uncertainty, the executive needs a helpful portrayal of the effects that the uncertainty surrounding each of the significant factors has on the returns he is likely to achieve. Therefore, the method we have developed at McKinsey & Company, Inc., combines the variabilities inherent in all the relevant factors. Our objective is to give a clear picture of the relative risk and the probable odds of coming out ahead or behind in the light of uncertain foreknowledge.

A simulation of the way these factors may combine as the future unfolds is the key to extracting the maximum information from the available forecasts. In fact, the approach is very simple, using a computer to do the necessary arithmetic. (Recently, a computer program to do this was suggested by S. W. Hess and H. A. Quigley for chemical process investments.[5])

To carry out the analysis, a company must follow three steps:

1. Estimate the range of values for each of the factors (e.g., range of selling price, sales growth rate, and so on) and within that range the likelihood of occurrence of each value.

---

[3] "Monitoring Capital Investments," *Financial Executive*, April 1963, p. 19.

[4] "Capital Budgeting and Game Theory," *HBR* November–December 1956, p. 123.

[5] "Analysis of Risk in Investments Using Monte Carlo Techniques," *Chemical Engineering Symposium Series* 42: *Statistics and Numerical Methods in Chemical Engineering* (New York, American Institute of Chemical Engineering, 1963), p. 55.

2. Select at random from the distribution of values for each factor one particular value. Then combine the values for all of the factors and compute the rate of return (or present value) from that combination. For instance, the lowest in the range of prices might be combined with the highest in the range of growth rate and other factors. (The fact that the factors are dependent should be taken into account, as we shall see later.)

3. Do this over and over again to define and evaluate the odds of the occurrence of each possible rate of return. Since there are literally millions of possible combinations of values, we need to test the likelihood that various specific returns on the investment will occur. This is like finding out by recording the results of a great many throws what per cent of "7"s or other combinations we may expect in tossing dice. The result will be a listing of the rates of return we might achieve, ranging from a loss (if the factors go against us) to whatever maximum gain is possible with the estimates that have been made.

For each of these rates the chances that it may occur are determined. (Note that a specific return can usually be achieved through more than one combination of events. The more combinations for a given rate, the higher the chances of achieving it—as with "7"s in tossing dice.) The average expectation is the average of the values of all outcomes weighted by the chances of each occurring.

The variability of outcome values from the average is also determined. This is important since, all other factors being equal, management would presumably prefer lower variability for the same return if given the choice. This concept has already been applied to investment portfolios.[6]

When the expected return and variability of each of a series of investments have been determined, the same techniques may be used to examine the effectiveness of various combinations of them in meeting management objectives.

## PRACTICAL TEST

To see how this new approach works in practice, let us take the experience of a management that has already analyzed a specific investment proposal by conventional techniques. Taking the same investment schedule and the same expected values actually used, we can find what results the new method would produce and compare them with the results obtained when conventional methods were applied. As we shall see, the new picture of risks and returns is different from the old one. Yet the differences are attributable in no way to changes in the basic data—*only to the increased sensitivity of the method to management's uncertainties about the key factors.*

[6] See Harry Markowitz, *Portfolio Selection, Efficient Diversification of Investments* (New York, John Wiley and Sons, 1959); Donald E. Fararr, *The Investment Decision Under Uncertainty* (Englewood Cliffs, New Jersey, Prentice-Hall, Inc., 1962); William F. Sharpe, "A Simplified Model for Portfolio Analysis," *Management Science*, January 1963, p. 277.

INVESTMENT PROPOSAL

In this case a medium-size industrial chemical producer is considering a $10-million extension to its processing plant. The estimated service life of the facility is 10 years; the engineers expect to be able to utilize 250,000 tons of processed material worth $510 per ton at an average processing cost of $435 per ton. Is this investment a good bet? In fact, what is the return that the company may expect? What are the risks? We need to make the best and fullest use we can of all the market research and financial analyses that have been developed, so as to give management a clear picture of this project in an uncertain world.

The key input factors management has decided to use are:

1. Market size.
2. Selling prices.
3. Market growth rate.
4. Share of market (which results in physical sales volume).
5. Investment required.
6. Residual value of investment.
7. Operating costs.
8. Fixed costs.
9. Useful life of facilities.

These factors are typical of those in many company projects that must be analyzed and combined to obtain a measure of the attractiveness of a proposed capital facilities investment.

OBTAINING ESTIMATES

How do we make the recommended type of analysis of this proposal?

Our aim is to develop for each of the nine factors listed a frequency distribution or probability curve. The information we need includes the possible range of values for each factor, the average, and some ideas as to the likelihood that the various possible values will be reached. It has been our experience that for major capital proposals managements usually make a significant investment in time and funds to pinpoint information about each of the relevant factors. An objective analysis of the values to be assigned to each can, with little additional effort, yield a subjective probability distribution.

Specifically, it is necessary to probe and question each of the experts involved—to find out, for example, whether the estimated cost of production really can be said to be exactly a certain value or whether, as is more likely, it should be estimated to lie within a certain range of values. It is that range which is ignored in the analysis management usually makes. The range is relatively easy to determine; if a guess has to be made—as it often does—it is easier to guess with some accuracy a range rather than a specific single value. We have found from past experience at McKinsey & Company, Inc., that a series of meetings with management personnel to discuss such distributions is most helpful in getting at realistic answers to the a priori questions.

(The term "realistic answers" implies all the information management does not have as well as all that it does have.)

The ranges are directly related to the degree of confidence that the estimator has in his estimate. Thus, certain estimates may be known to be quite accurate. They would be represented by probability distributions stating, for instance, that there is only 1 chance in 10 that the actual value will be different from the best estimate by more than 10%. Others may have as much as 100% ranges above and below the best estimate.

Thus, we treat the factor of selling price for the finished product by asking executives who are responsible for the original estimates these questions:

1. Given that $510 is the expected sales price, what is the probability that the price will exceed $550?

2. Is there any chance that the price will exceed $650?

3. How likely is it that the price will drop below $475?

Managements must ask similar questions for each of the other factors, until they can construct a curve for each. Experience shows that this is not as difficult as it might sound. Often information on the degree of variation in factors is readily available. For instance, historical information on variations in the price of a commodity is readily available. Similarly, management can estimate the variability of sales from industry sales records. Even for factors that have no history, such as operating costs for a new product, the person who makes the "average" estimate must have some idea of the degree of confidence he has in his prediction, and therefore he is usually only too glad to express his feelings. Likewise, the less confidence he has in his estimate, the greater will be the range of possible values that the variable will assume.

This last point is likely to trouble businessmen. Does it really make sense to seek estimates of variations? It cannot be emphasized too strongly that the less certainty there is in an "average" estimate, *the more important it is to consider the possible variation in that estimate.*

Further, an estimate of the variation possible in a factor, no matter how judgmental it may be, is always better than a simple "average" estimate, since it includes more information about what is known and what is not known. It is, in fact, this very *lack* of knowledge which may distinguish one investment possibility from another, so that for rational decision making it *must* be taken into account.

This lack of knowledge is in itself important information about the proposed investment. To throw any information away simply because it is highly uncertain is a serious error in analysis which the new approach is designed to correct.

COMPUTER RUNS

The next step in the proposed approach is to determine the returns that will result from random combinations of the factors involved. This requires realistic restrictions, such as not allowing the total market to vary more than some reasonable amount from year to year. Of course, any method of rating the return which is suitable to the company may be used at this point; in the actual case management preferred discounted cash flow for the reasons cited earlier, so that method is followed here.

A computer can be used to carry out the trials for the simulation method in very little time and at very little expense. Thus, for one trial actually made in this case, 3,600 discounted cash flow calculations, each based on a selection of the nine input factors, were run in two minutes at a cost of $15 for computer time. The resulting rate-of-return probabilities were read out immediately and graphed. The process is shown schematically in Exhibit II.

### DATA COMPARISONS

The nine input factors described earlier fall into three categories:

1. *Market analyses.* Included are market size, market growth rate, the firm's share of the market, and selling prices. For a given combination of these factors sales revenue may be determined.

2. *Investment cost analyses.* Being tied to the kinds of service-life and operating-cost characteristics expected, these are subject to various kinds of error and uncertainty; for instance, automation progress makes service life uncertain.

3. *Operating and fixed costs.* These also are subject to uncertainty, but are perhaps the easiest to estimate.

These categories are not independent, and for realistic results our approach allows the various factors to be tied together. Thus, if price determines the total market, we first select from a probability distribution the price for the specific computer run and then use for the total market a probability distribution that is logically related to the price selected.

We are now ready to compare the values obtained under the new approach with the values obtained under the old. This comparison is shown in Exhibit III.

### VALUABLE RESULTS

How do the results under the new and old approaches compare?

In this case, management had been informed, on the basis of the "one best estimate" approach, that the expected return was 25.2% before taxes. When we ran the new set of data through the computer program, however, we got an expected return of only 14.6% before taxes.

This surprising difference not only is due to the fact that under the new approach we use a range of values; it also reflects the fact that we have weighted each value in the range by the chances of its occurrence.

Our new analysis thus may help management to avoid an unwise investment. In fact, the general result of carefully weighing the information and

## EXHIBIT II.  SIMULATION FOR INVESTMENT PLANNING

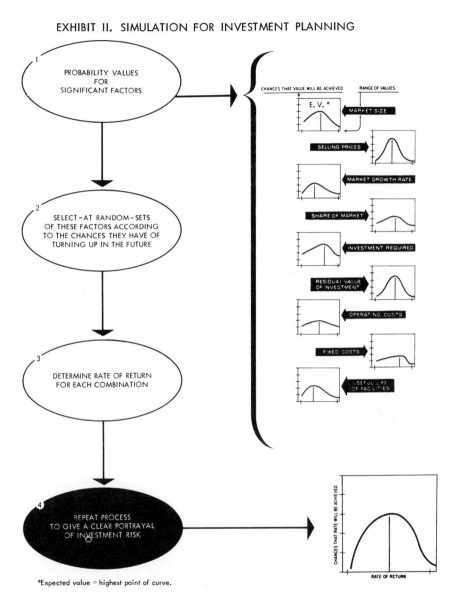

*Expected value = highest point of curve.

Exhibit III
EXHIBIT III
COMPARISON OF EXPECTED VALUES UNDER OLD AND NEW APPROACHES

| | Conventional "best estimate" Approach | New Approach |
|---|---|---|
| MARKET ANALYSES | | |
| 1. *Market size* | | |
| Expected value (in tons) | 250,000 | 250,000 |
| Range | — | 100,000–340,000 |
| 2. *Selling prices* | | |
| Expected value (in dollars/ton) | $510 | $510 |
| Range | — | $385–$575 |
| 3. *Market growth rate* | | |
| Expected value | 3% | 3% |
| Range | — | 0–6% |
| 4. *Eventual share of Market* | | |
| Expected value | 12% | 12% |
| Range | — | 3%–17% |
| INVESTMENT COST ANALYSES | | |
| 5. *Total investment required* | | |
| Expected value (in millions) | $9.5 | $9.5 |
| Range | — | $7.0–$10.5 |
| 6. *Useful life of facilities* | | |
| Expected value (in years) | 10 | 10 |
| Range | — | 5–15 |
| 7. *Residual value (at 10 years)* | | |
| Expected value (in millions) | $4.5 | $4.5 |
| Range | — | $3.5–$5.0 |
| OTHER COSTS | | |
| 8. *Operating costs* | | |
| Expected value (in dollars/ton) | $435 | $435 |
| Range | — | $370–$545 |
| 9. *Fixed Costs* | | |
| Expected value (in thousands) | $300 | $300 |
| Range | — | $250–$375 |

*Note*: Range figures in right-hand column represent approximately 1% to 99% probabilities. That is, there is only a 1 in a 100 chance that the value actually achieved will be respectively greater or less than the range.

lack of information in the manner I have suggested is to indicate the true nature of otherwise seemingly satisfactory investment proposals. If this practice were followed by managements, much regretted over-capacity might be avoided.

The computer program developed to carry out the simulation allows for easy insertion of new variables. In fact, some programs have previously been suggested that take variability into account.[7] But most programs do not allow for dependence relationships between the various input factors. Further, the program used here permits the choice of a value for price from one distribution, which value determines a particular probability distribution (from among several) that will be used to determine the value for sales volume. To show how this important technique works:

Suppose we have a wheel, as in roulette, with the numbers from 0 to 15 representing one price for the product or material, the numbers 16 to 30 representing a second price, the numbers 31 to 45 a third price, and so on. For each of these segments we would have a different range of expected market volumes; e.g., $150,000–$200,000 for the first, $100,000–$150,000 for the second, $75,000–$100,000 for the third, and so forth. Now suppose that we spin the wheel and the ball falls in 37. This would mean that we pick a sales volume in the $75,000–$100,000 range. If the ball goes in 11, we have a different price and we turn to the $150,000–$200,000 range for a price.

Most significant, perhaps, is the fact that the program allows management to ascertain the sensitivity of the results to each or all of the input factors. Simply by running the program with changes in the distribution of an input factor, it is possible to determine the effect of added or changed information (or of the lack of information). It may turn out that fairly large changes in some factors do not significantly affect the outcomes. In this case, as a matter of fact, management was particularly concerned about the difficulty in estimating market growth. Running the program with variations in this factor quickly demonstrated to us that for average annual growths from 3% and 5% there was no significant difference in the expected outcome.

In addition, let us see what the implications are of the detailed knowledge the simulation method gives us. Under the method using single expected values, management arrives only at a hoped-for expectation of 25.2% after taxes (which, as we have seen, is wrong unless there is no variability in the various input factors—a highly unlikely event). On the other hand, with the method we propose, the uncertainties are clearly portrayed:

| Per cent return | Probability of achieving at least the return shown |
|---|---|
| 0% | 96.5% |
| 5 | 80.6 |
| 10 | 75.2 |
| 15 | 53.8 |
| 20 | 43.0 |
| 25 | 12.6 |
| 30 | 0 |

[7] See Frederick S. Hillier, "The Derivation of Probabilistic Information for the Evaluation of Risky Investments," *Management Science*, April 1963, p. 443.

This profile is shown in Exhibit IV. Note the contrast with the profile obtained under the conventional approach. This concept has been used also for evaluation of new product introductions, acquisitions of new businesses, and plant modernization.

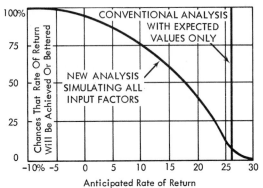

Exhibit IV. Anticipated Rates of Return
Under Old and New Approaches

## COMPARING OPPORTUNITIES

From a decision-making point of view one of the most significant advantages of the new method of determining rate of return is that it allows management to discriminate between measures of (1) expected return based on weighted probabilities of all possible returns, (2) variability of return, and (3) risks.

To visualize this advantage, let us take an example which is based on another actual case but simplified for purposes of explanation. The example involves two investments under consideration, A and B.

When the investments are analyzed, the data tabulated and plotted in Exhibit V are obtained. We see that:

Investment B has a higher expected return than Investment A.

Investment B also has substantially more variability than Investment A. There is a good chance that Investment B will earn a return which is quite different from the expected return of 6.8%, possibly as high as 15% or as low as a loss of 5%. Investment A is not likely to vary greatly from the expected 5% return.

Investment B involves far more risk than does Investment A. There is virtually no chance of incurring a loss on Investment A. However, there is 1 chance in 10 of losing money on Investment B. If such a loss occurs, its expected size is approximately $200,000.

Clearly, the new method of evaluating investments provides management with far more information on which to base a decision.

EXHIBIT V. COMPARISON OF TWO INVESTMENT OPPORTUNITIES

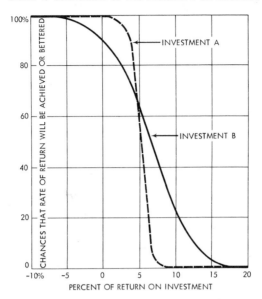

|  | INVESTMENT A | INVESTMENT B |
|---|---|---|
| AMOUNT OF INVESTMENT | $10,000,000 | $10,000,000 |
| LIFE OF INVESTMENT (IN YEARS) | 10 | 10 |
| EXPECTED ANNUAL NET CASH INFLOW | $ 1,300,000 | $ 1,400,000 |
| VARIABILITY OF CASH INFLOW |  |  |
| 1 Chance in 50 of being Greater than | $ 1,700,000 | $ 3,400,000 |
| 1 Chance in 50 of being Less* than | $    00,000 | ($600,000) |
| EXPECTED RETURN ON INVESTMENT | 5.0% | 6.8% |
| VARIABILITY OF RETURN ON INVESTMENT |  |  |
| 1 Chance in 50 of being Greater than | 7.0% | 15.5% |
| 1 Chance in 50 of being Less* than | 3.0% | (4.0%) |
| RISK OF INVESTMENT |  |  |
| Chances of a Loss | Negligible | 1 in 10 |
| Expected Size of Loss |  | $ 200,000 |

*In the case of negative figures (indicated by parentheses) "less than" means "worse than."

## CONCLUSION

The question management faces in selecting capital investments is first and foremost: What information is needed to clarify the key differences among various alternatives? There is agreement as to the basic factors that should be considered—markets, prices, costs, and so on. And the way the future return on the investment should be calculated, if not agreed on, is at least limited to a few methods, any of which can be consistently used in a given company. If the input variables turn out as estimated, any of the methods customarily used to rate investments should provide satisfactory (if not necessarily maximum) returns.

In actual practice, however, the conventional methods do *not* work out satisfactorily. Why? The reason, as we have seen earlier in this article, and as every executive and economist knows, is that the estimates used in making the advance calculations are just that—estimates. More accurate estimates would be helpful, but at best the residual uncertainty can easily make a mockery of corporate hopes. Nevertheless, there is a solution. To collect realistic estimates for the key factors means to find out a great deal about them. Hence the kind of uncertainty that is involved in each estimate can be evaluated ahead of time. Using this knowledge of uncertainty, executives can maximize the value of the information for decision making.

The value of computer programs in developing clear portrayals of the uncertainty and risk surrounding alternative investments has been proved. Such programs can produce valuable information about the sensitivity of the possible outcomes to the variability of input factors and to the likelihood of achieving various possible rates of return. This information can be extremely important as a backup to management judgment. To have calculations of the odds on all possible outcomes lends some assurance to the decision-makers that the available information has been used with maximum efficiency.

This simulation approach has the inherent advantage of simplicity. It requires only an extension of the input estimates (to the best of our ability) in terms of probabilities. No projection should be pinpointed unless we are *certain* of it.

The discipline of thinking through the uncertainties of the problem will in itself help to ensure improvement in making investment choices. For to understand uncertainty and risk is to understand the key business problem— and the key business opportunity. Since the new approach can be applied on a continuing basis to each capital alternative as it comes up for consideration and progresses toward fruition, gradual progress may be expected in improving the estimation of the probabilities of variation.

Lastly, the courage to act boldly in the face of apparent uncertainty can be greatly bolstered by the clarity of portrayal of the risks and possible rewards. To achieve these lasting results requires only a slight effort beyond what most companies already exert in studying capital investments.

## SUMMARY OF NEW APPROACH

After examining present methods of comparing alternative investments, Mr. Hertz reports on his firm's experience in applying a new approach to the problem. Using this approach, management takes the various levels of possible cash flows, return on investment, and other results of a proposed outlay and gets an estimate of the odds for each potential outcome.

Currently, many facilities decisions are based on discounted cash flow calculations. Management is told, for example, that Investment X has an expected internal rate of return of 9.2%, while for Investment Y a 10.3% return can be expected.

By contrast, the new approach would put in front of the executive a schedule which gives him the most likely return from X, but also tells him that X has 1 chance in 20 of being a total loss, 1 in 10 of earning from 4% to 5%, 2 in 10 of paying from 8% to 10%, and 1 chance in 50 of attaining a 30% rate of return. From another schedule he learns what the most likely rate of return is from Y, but also that Y has 1 chance in 10 of resulting in a total loss, 1 in 10 of earning from 3% to 5% return, 2 in 10 of paying between 9% and 11%, and 1 chance in 100 of 30%. Or portrayed graphically:

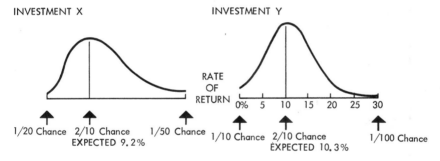

In this instance, the estimates of the rates of return provided by the two approaches would not be substantially different. However, to the decision-maker with the added information, Investment Y no longer looks like the clearly better choice, since with X the chances of substantial gain are higher and the risks of loss lower.

Two things have made this approach appealing to managers who have used it:

1. Certainly in every case it is a more descriptive statement of the two opportunities. And in some cases it might well reverse the decision, in line with particular corporate objectives.

2. This is not a difficult technique to use, since much of the information needed is already available—or readily accessible—and the validity of the principles involved has, for the most part, already been proved in other applications.

The enthusiasm with which managements exposed to this approach have received it suggests that it may have wide application. It has particular relevance, for example, in such knotty problems as investments relating to acquisitions or new products, and in decisions that might involve excess capacity.

## 21. LEVERAGE, DIVERSIFICATION AND CAPITAL MARKET EFFECTS ON A RISK-ADJUSTED CAPITAL BUDGETING FRAMEWORK

### DONALD L. TUTTLE and ROBERT H. LITZENBERGER*

Reprinted from *The Journal of Finance*, Vol. XXIII, No. 3 (June 1968), by permission of the authors and publisher.

Assuming that the primary goal of the firm is the maximization of wealth of its owners, corporate management should choose that group of investments that is expected to have the largest positive effect on the present market value of the firm's outstanding common shares. In its simplest form, traditional capital budgeting theory says the firm should accept independent investment opportunities that promise either internal rates of return larger than the firm's "average cost of capital" or positive net present values with the average cost of capital as the appropriate discount rate.[1] Moreover, under conditions of capital rationing, acceptable opportunities are ranked by size of internal rate of return or net present value per dollar of investment.

Implicit in this simplified approach is the assumption that acceptance of a particular investment opportunity will neither increase nor decrease the risk inherent in the firm's future operating earnings stream. Such an approach is untenable. Economists over the last several decades have concerned themselves with the problem of uncertainty in capital investment decision-making. Keynes [4, p. 145], for example, in 1936 wrote

---

* University of North Carolina. The authors are indebted to Henry Latané whose work in the area of risk and returns laid much of the groundwork for the present paper.

[1] See, for example, Dean [2], Weingartner [21] and Hunt, Williams and Donaldson [3, pp. 456–70]. An "independent" investment opportunity is one whose worth is not profoundly affected by the acceptance of others. That is, proposals are not mutually exclusive nor inclusive. This is the definition used in Lorie and Savage [12, pp. 229–30].

For if a venture is a risky one, the borrower will require a wider margin between his experience of yield and the rate at which he will think it worthwhile to borrow.

The purpose of this paper is to provide an objective basis for screening and ranking opportunities under conditions of uncertainty.[2] Given certain simplifying assumptions, the first section of the paper shows how returns from various investment opportunities can be made risk-equivalent to the firm's cost of equity capital by financing the projects with the proper amount of borrowing or lending. This is accomplished by taking cognizance of a potential linear transformation between return and risk on any investment opportunity by including borrowing or lending as an integral part of the investment decision.[3]

Once the concept of risk-adjusted residual returns to equity has been demonstrated, it is adapted to the standard present value method as a proposed framework for capital budget decision-making. In doing so, the firm's average cost of capital is transformed into the cost of financing a particular project that is relevant to the expected quality—risk and returns—of that project. The cost of financing a given project is the minimum hurdle rate required for the project to positively affect the value of the firm's common equity. This cost of financing is used as the discount rate for the particular project under consideration resulting in a system of multiple discount rates for the firm. The key to calculating this cost of financing is determining the relevant measure of risk associated with the firm's stream of operating earnings. In a concluding section of this part of the paper, it is shown how the personal leverage of individuals who invest in a firm's equity shares can be substituted for corporate leverage in arriving at the cost of financing a project.

The second part of the paper introduces the potential reduction in the risk associated with the firm's stream of operating earnings by the diversification effect of adding a particular project to the firm's present mix of assets.[4] Assuming risk preferences of the market for the firm's common stock are not known, a method for determining the firm's cost of financing a particular project that considers the project's diversification benefits is derived.

In the last part of the paper, the assumption of a market dominated by small investors is removed. Specifically, a market for equity securities that is dominated by large institutional investors is hypothesized. In such a market

---

[2] A number of authors have discussed the need for considering risk as well as returns in capital budgeting. Until recently, however, few writers have offered objective capital budgeting frameworks which actually do consider risk and return. A partial list of this latter group's writings includes Tintner [20, p. 100], Solomon [19], Roberts [16], Lintner [10] and Latané and Tuttle [8].

[3] Several authors have explicitly considered the effect of leverage on the riskiness of investments, whether real (capital budgeting) or financial (portfolio management). Among their published works are Lutz and Lutz [13, pp. 195–99], Latané [6], Sharpe [18], Lintner [11], Latané and Tuttle [9] and Latané [7].

[4] This is a concept explicitly considered in the portfolio management area by Markowitz [14].

the relevant measure of risk used to calculate a project's cost of financing is the risk that cannot be eliminated from institutional portfolios by diversification. Throughout the paper, corporate and personal taxes are omitted from consideration in order to make the analysis as straightforward as possible.

## I. LINEAR TRANSFORMATION OF RISK AND RETURN

At the outset, then, two limiting assumptions will be made. First, we assume a competitive capital market consisting of a large number of small investors, each having an aversion to risk and lacking sufficient funds for diversification. In such a market the implicit rate at which the market capitalizes an expected earnings stream is directly related to the risk inherent in that anticipated earnings stream. If the further assumption is made that the firm's earnings stream approaches normality,[5] the price of the firm's common stock would be a function of its expected rate of return and estimated standard error of its

Figure 1

Market Trade-Off Diagram for Firm A

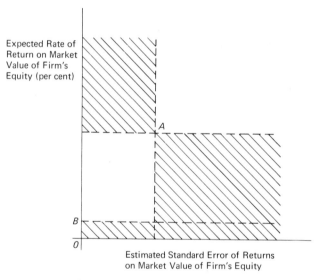

Expected Rate of Return on Market Value of Firm's Equity (per cent)

Estimated Standard Error of Returns on Market Value of Firm's Equity

Point A:  Firm's Current Trade-Off Point

Point B:  Current Level of Effective Interest Rate or
Yield to Maturity on the Firm's Long = Term Debt

[5] There is empirical evidence that investors have a preference for positive skewness and an aversion to negative skewness. See Arditti [1]. If skewness is thought to be a major factor in evaluating the firm's earnings stream and if reasonably accurate ex ante estimates of skewness can be made, it is possible that a measure such as the semi-variance would be a more appropriate single measure of risk.

rate of return.[6] However, the nature of the market trade-off *function* between risk and return is not assumed known. All that is assumed known is the firm's market trade-off *point*, point A in Figure 1 at which the firm is assumed to currently be, akin to Samuelson's point of revealed preference [17, pp. 90–124]. Since investors are assumed to be risk-averse, it can only be assumed the function would *not* be found in the shaded sections of the diagram.

Second, the firm is assumed to face a group of independent investment projects whose anticipated returns are perfectly correlated[7] with the returns expected to be generated by the firm's existing assets. The investment projects faced by this hypothetical firm may be grouped into a three-by-three decision matrix as in Table 1.

TABLE 1

|  | $S_i > S_f$ | $S_i = S_f$ | $S_i < S_f$ |
|---|---|---|---|
| 1 $R_i > R_f$ | ? | accept | accept |
| 2 $R_i = R_f$ | reject | indifferent | accept |
| 3 $R_i < R_f$ | reject | reject | ? |

$R_i$ = the expected internal rate of return offered by the investment project.
$S_i$ = the estimate of the standard error of the expected internal rate of return on the investment project.
$R_f$ = the firm's equity capitalization rate or the expected rate of return on the market value of the firm's outstanding equity without accepting the given investment project.
$S_f$ = the estimate of the standard error of the expected rate of return on the market value of the firm's outstanding common equity.

Under circumstances of perfect correlation of projected returns, an optimal financial policy would call for acceptance of the investment projects grouped in cells 1.2, 1.3, and 2.3, be indifferent to those grouped in cell 2.2, and reject those grouped in cells 2.1, 3.1, and 3.2.

*Risk-Adjusted Internal Rates of Return.*    If the capital budgeting decision is viewed in isolation, an objective method of discriminating between the desirable and the undesirable investment projects in cells 1.1 and 3.3 cannot, in general, be developed without reference to market risk preferences. There

[6] The estimated standard error of returns on a given investment opportunity is defined as the square root of the mean of the square deviations of the realized annual returns from the stream of projected returns on investment of the same subjective quality. For example, an automobile company considering manufacturing a new model could calculate the above statistic using the deviations of the realized annual returns from the stream of projected returns on new models introduced in prior years. Theoretically this information should be available from follow-up reports on capital projects.

[7] Here, as elsewhere in this paper, correlation is measured by the Pearsonian coefficient which represents the proportion of variation in the dependent variable explained by the independent variable.

is, however, one important exception to this general rule. The firm does have the option of neutralizing the risk inherent in a given investment opportunity through long-term borrowing or lending.[8] The return is made "risk-equivalent," thereby eliminating the need for subjectively determining the desirability of one opportunity's return-risk combination against another's.[9]

This is brought about by distinguishing between the risk (estimated standard error) and return on the investment project itself and the comparable residual risk and return to equity from the project. The latter reflects the amount of borrowing or lending which is undertaken; specifically, the latter risk and return are a linear transformation of the former. This is shown below.

Let: $R_0$ = the expected rate of return to equity from the project.

$S_0$ = the estimate of the standard error of the rate of return to equity from the project.

$I$ = the yield to maturity on the firm's long-term debt which is assumed equal to the yield on similar quality debt of the same maturity.

$\alpha$ = the financing ratio for a project; unity plus the project's debt-equity ratio $(1 + D/E)$ where debt is either borrowed or loaned (debt loaned is negative debt). Alternatively it is defined as unity plus the ratio of amounts borrowed to equity investment called for by a project *or* minus the ratio of amounts loaned (invested in debt assets) to equity investment in a project. Or it is the total amount of investment in a project per dollar of equity investment in the project, i.e., $\alpha = (E + D)/E$.

The estimate of the standard error of residual return to equity is

$$S_0 = \alpha S_i \tag{1}$$

When $\alpha$ dollars per dollar of equity are invested in a project (and $\alpha - 1$ dollars are borrowed) the expected return from the project is $\alpha R_i$ and the cost of borrowing is $(\alpha - 1) I$. So the expected residual rate of return to equity when borrowing or lending is permitted is

$$R_0 = R_i + (\alpha - 1) R_i - (\alpha - 1) I \tag{2}$$

which simplifies to

$$R_0 = I + \alpha(R_i - I) \tag{2a}$$

[8] The maturity date of the long-term debt instruments should roughly correspond to the estimated terminal year of the physical investment opportunity.

[9] The authors assume that management wishes to maintain the initial degree of risk inherent in residual earnings to equity. Financial leverage may be altered to maintain this position. The risk that corporate managers wish to maintain in earnings to equity may be a function of their subjective risk preferences or an attempt to maximize the market value of the firm's outstanding common equity. The authors are concerned only with the capitalization of new projects and are not attempting to optimize financial leverage.

The slope of the potential linear transformation between expected return and estimated standard error of return is derived in equations (3) through (5). Now equation (2a) can be restated as

$$R_0 = I + \alpha(R_i - I) \, \alpha \frac{S_i}{S_i} \tag{3}$$

Substituting $S_0$ for $\alpha S_i$ gives

$$R_0 = I + (R_i - I) \frac{S_0}{S_i} \tag{4}$$

Taking the first derivative gives the slope of the potential trade-off between residual return and the risk of equity

$$\frac{dR_0}{dS_0} = \frac{R_i - I}{S_i} \tag{5}$$

Now there is some factor $(\alpha')$ which, when multiplied by the risk of the investment project, $S_i$, will equate $\alpha' S_i$ with the risk of the firm's present mix of assets, $S_f$. In other words, $\alpha'$ is that financing ratio or mix of debt and equity relative to equity[10] that will neutralize the risk effect of the project on the residual return to equity. Thus

$$S_f = \alpha' S_i \tag{6}$$

which becomes

$$\alpha' = \frac{S_f}{S_i} \tag{7}$$

Then the risk effect of a project on residual returns to equity may be neutralized either through long-term lending (or retirement of outstanding debt) of an amount equal to $(1/\alpha') - 1$ of the dollar cost of the investment project if $S_i > S_f$, or the long-term borrowing (or liquidation of long-term debt holdings) of an amount equal to $1 - (1/\alpha')$ of the dollar cost of the project if $S_i < S_f$.[11]

[10] Equity is defined as a source of funds generated internally or obtained externally. Abstracting from personal tax considerations, if perfect capital markets are assumed the cost of these two sources would be identical.

[11] The derivation of these formulations is as follows. Since, by definition, $\alpha' = 1 + $ (Debt/Equity) $= (D + E)/E$, then $1/\alpha' = E/(D + E)$. Therefore

$$\frac{1}{\alpha'} - 1 = \frac{-D}{D + E}$$

which, when multiplied by the cost of the project will give the negative debt (amount to be loaned) associated with the project's financing when $S_i > S_f$ Similarly,

$$1 - \frac{1}{\alpha'} = \frac{D}{D + E}$$

multiplied by the project's cost will give the positive debt (amount borrowed) in the project's financing when $S_i < S_f$.

The risk-adjusted rate of return on an investment project, $R_0$, is shown in equation (8).

$$R'_0 = I + \alpha'(R_i - I) \tag{8}$$

When investment alternatives are independent, our hypothetical firm should accept a given investment project if $R'_0 > R_f$ (i.e., if the risk-adjusted residual return to equity is larger than the firm's equity capitalization rate). This is true because when combined with the proper amount of borrowing or lending, the acceptance of the investment project will have a positive effect on expected earnings to equity holders while being neutral on the estimated standard error of the anticipated earnings stream. Investors being risk-averse will prefer a higher to a lower expected return for a given standard error of returns. The acceptance of the higher return would, therefore, increase the market value of the outstanding common equity of our hypothetical firm.

*Risk-Adjusted Present Values.* The assumptions that the firm has free access to the capital market (no budget constraints) and that the investment projects are independent (not mutually exclusive nor inclusive) were implicit in the previous analysis. Since these conditions are not realistic, some method must be available to *rank* investment projects. As Lorie and Savage [12] have pointed out, the internal rate of return by itself is sometimes not an adequate ranking device when dealing with projects of differing size, differing length and differing time shape of cash flows. A more satisfactory method is ranking by size of present value of a project's expected cash flows. Thus we will adapt the previous analysis to obtain for each project a risk-adjusted cost of financing or discount rate to be used to calculate the project's present value.

As stated earlier, the cost of financing a given project is the minimum hurdle rate required for the acceptance of the project to positively affect the value of the firm's equity. The cost of financing a given project should therefore reflect the amount of borrowing or lending required to neutralize the risk effect on the firm's stream of earnings to equity.

In this context the cost of financing a given investment project, $C_i$, is

$$C_i = \frac{1}{\alpha'} R_f + \left[1 - \frac{1}{\alpha'}\right] I \tag{9}$$

which reduces to

$$C_i = I + \frac{1}{\alpha'}(R_f - I) \tag{10}$$

The acceptance of a given investment project having a positive net present value when discounted by its cost of financing combined with the appropriate financing mix will increase the market value of the firm's previously outstanding shares. In equilibrium the aggregated increase in the market value of the firm's previously outstanding common equity would equal the project's net present value when discounted by its cost of financing. This is true since under our hypothesized market condition the estimated standard error of return to equity and, therefore, the equity capitalization rate, will remain unchanged.

The calculation of risk-adjusted residual returns to equity and costs of financing is illustrated numerically in Table 2 for four hypothetical investment projects. Should there be no budget constraints and if all four projects are independent, projects A and D would be accepted for inclusion in the firm's capital budget.

*Substitution of Personal Leverage.* Professors Modigliani and Miller [15] maintain that investors may substitute personal borrowing and lending for corporate leverage and argue that arbitrage will assure that the market value of the firm's outstanding equity is invariant with respect to leverage.

The Modigliani-Miller theoretical construct, under our hypothesized market conditions, would imply that the firm's cost of equity capital is an increasing linear function of financial leverage. The equity capitalization rate, $R_f$, is according to Modigliani and Miller a linear increasing function of financial leverage as shown below, where $R_e$ is the equity capitalization rate under an all equity capitalization.

$$R_f = R_e + \frac{D}{E}(R_e - I) \tag{11}$$

The estimate of the standard error of return on equity is also a linear increasing function of financial leverage. This is shown below, where $S_e$ is the estimate of the standard error of return on an all equity capitalization.

$$S_f = S_e + \frac{D}{E}S_e \tag{12}$$

The relationship between the equity capitalization rate and the estimate of the standard error of return implicit in the Modigliani-Miller arbitrage argument is the linear relationship

$$R_f = I + \left[1 + \frac{D}{E}\right]\left[\frac{R_e - I}{S_i}S_f\right] \tag{13}$$

The implication of the Modigliani-Miller arbitrage argument is that investors may substitute personal borrowing and lending for corporate leverage in the process of neutralizing the risk effect of the acceptance of a given investment opportunity on earnings to equity. The cost of financing a given investment would similarly be given by equation (10) stated previously

$$C_i = I + \frac{1}{\alpha'}(R_f - I) \tag{10}$$

Thus, the Modigliani-Miller arbitrage theory implies $C_i$ is the cost of financing a given investment project regardless of the amount of borrowing or lending used in its financing. The analysis prior to this section is not, however, contingent on the validity of the Modigliani-Miller thesis, if the firm utilizes corporate borrowing and lending as a tool for risk neutralization.

TABLE 2

CALCULATION OF RISK-ADJUSTED RESIDUAL RATES OF RETURN TO EQUITY AND COSTS OF FINANCING*

| PROJECT | $R_i$ | $R_f$ | $S_i$ | $S_f$ | $\alpha' = \dfrac{S_f}{S_i}$ | $S_0 = \alpha' S_i$ | $I$ | $(R_i - I)$ | $R_0 = I + \alpha'(R - I)$ | DECISION** | $\dfrac{1}{\alpha'}$ | $R_f - I$ | $C_i = I + \dfrac{1}{\alpha_1}(R_f - I)$ |
|---|---|---|---|---|---|---|---|---|---|---|---|---|---|
| A | .40 | .15 | .60 | .30 | .50 | .30 | .05 | .35 | .22 | Accept | 2.00 | .10 | .25 |
| B | .12 | .15 | .25 | .30 | 1.20 | .30 | .05 | .07 | .13 | Reject | .83 | .10 | .13 |
| C | .07 | .15 | .06 | .30 | 5.00 | .30 | .05 | .02 | .15 | Indifferent | .20 | .10 | .07 |
| D | .10 | .15 | .10 | .30 | 3.00 | .30 | .05 | .05 | .20 | Accept | .33 | .10 | .08 |

* Assumes perfect correlation of intrafirm investment yields.
** Assumes investment opportunities are independent.

## II. EFFECT OF DIVERSIFICATION ON COST OF FINANCING

In this section the assumption that the anticipated returns from proposed individual capital projects are perfectly correlated with the expected returns from the firm's present mix of assets is removed. In so doing, the cost of financing a given project must reflect the diversification effect that its acceptance would have on the risk inherent in the returns to equity. This is done by determining the financing ratio, $\alpha'$, that will equate the estimated standard error of returns to equity after acceptance of the project with the same measure calculated before acceptance.

In Appendix A, the estimated standard error of return on the firm's equity *after* accepting and financing project $i$, $S_f'$, is stated in terms of $\alpha$, $S_f$, $P_i$ (the dollar cost of the project), $E$ (the dollar value of the firm's equity at market) and $r_{if}$ (the correlation of the project's anticipated returns with those for the firm). This formulation is then set equal to the estimated standard error before acceptance, $S_f$, and the quadratic equation

$$(P_i S_i^2 + 2Er_{if}S_iS_f)\,\alpha^2 - (2ES_f^2)\,\alpha - (P_iS_f^2) = 0 \tag{14}$$

is derived.

The $\alpha$ that equates $S_f'$ with $S_f$, $\alpha'$, can be found by solving this quadratic equation subject to the constraint that $\alpha' > 0$ since a capital project cannot be sold short.

Under certain circumstances, the formula for $\alpha'$ reduces to much less complex form. Some specific examples will show the value for $\alpha'$ under three sets of circumstances. First, when $r_{if} = 1$ as assumed in the first part of this paper, equation (14) produces a value for $\alpha'$ of

$$\alpha' = \frac{S_f}{S_i} \tag{14a}$$

which was identical to equation (7) derived earlier.

Second, when $r_{if} \to 0$ and $(P_i/E) \to 0$ such that the expected returns from project $i$ are completely uncorrelated with the anticipated returns on the firm's assets and project $i$ is very small relative to the market value of the firm's equity,[12]

$$\alpha' = \infty \tag{14b}$$

This would result in a cost of financing of project $i$ from equation (10) of

$$C_i = I$$

Hence the discount rate for such a project would be the effective interest rate or yield to maturity on the firm's debt issues. This is akin to the certainty-

---

[12] In solving the quadratic formula of equation (14), $a = 0$, $b = -2_f^2$ and $c = 0$ giving

$$a' = [2S_f \pm \sqrt{4S_f^4 - 0}]/0 = \infty$$

equivalent case cited by Knight[13] where the interest rate is the appropriate discount rate.

Last there is the more realistic case where $0 < r_{if} < 1$ and $(P_i/E) \rightarrow 0$. Under these circumstances,[14]

$$\alpha' = \frac{S_f}{r_{if}S_i} \tag{14c}$$

which gives a cost of financing project $i$ of

$$C_i = I + \frac{r_{if}S_i}{S_f}(R_f - I)$$

## III. COST OF FINANCING IN A CAPITAL MARKET DOMINATED BY INSTITUTIONAL INVESTORS

The previous sections of this paper provided a framework for the screening and ranking of investment projects. Throughout this analysis the assumption that the market for equity securities was made up of a large number of risk-averse small investors lacking sufficient funds for diversification was explicit. In view of the ever-increasing role of large institutional investors who utilize information about covariance of security returns, this assumption is unrealistic.

In order to develop a cost of financing in an equity market dominated by large investors, we must determine what these investors consider to be "risk." Now we postulate that investors possessing sufficient capital may reduce the risk inherent in their portfolios of financial assets through diversification. For the large investor whose portfolio of financial assets is well diversified across industries, the risk inherent in a given security, $S_k$, would be a function of the estimate of the standard error of return on equity and the correlation between the security's returns and returns for the securities market, $r_{fm}$. The non-diversifiable risk inherent in an equity security is $r_{fm}S_f$.

In a securities market dominated by large institutional investors the firm's equity capitalization rate would be a function of the interest rate and the non-diversifiable portion of the estimate of its standard error of returns.

$$R_f = f(I, r_{fm}S_f) \tag{15}$$

---

[13] F. H. Knight, [5, pp. 198–99]. In theory, there could be a project $i$ where $r_{if} < 0$ and $(P_i/E) \rightarrow 0$ in which case the cost of financing would be less than $I$ but real world occurrences of negative correlation are likely to be very infrequent.

[14] In this case, $a = 2r_{if}S_iS_f$, $b = -2S_f^2$ and $c = 0$ giving

$$a' = \frac{2S_f^2 \pm \sqrt{4S_f^4 - 0}}{4r_{if}S_iS_f}$$

and since, by definition, $a > 0$, this reduces to

$$a' = \frac{S_f}{r_{if}S_i}$$

In other words, given a certain rate of interest, institutional investors' required rate of return would be dependent only on that part of the risk they cannot avoid through adequately diversifying.

If institutional investors are permitted to borrow and lend freely at a constant rate of interest, then the equilibrium condition for a market dominated by these institutions would call for a linear relationship between the capitalization rate on a firm's equity, $R_f$, and the non-diversifiable portion of estimated standard error of returns, $r_{fm}S_f$.[15] The equilibrium capitalization rate is

$$R_f^* = I + b_f^* (r_{fm}S_f) \qquad (16)$$

where $b_f^*$, the slope of the linear equilibrium relationship, is

$$b_f^* = \frac{dR_f^*}{d(r_{fm}S_f)} = \frac{R_f^* - I}{r_{fm}S_f} \qquad (17)$$

This is shown graphically in Figure 2. In order for equilibrium to occur, $b_f^*$ must be the same for all firms; that is, given a particular level of investor's non-diversifiable risk, $r_{fm}S_f$, $b_f$ times this non-diversifiable risk must (when added to the rate of interest) give the same equity capitalization rate.

Figure 2

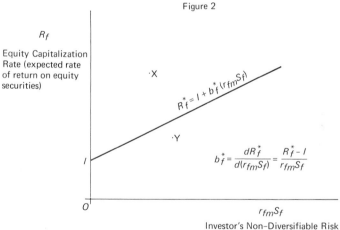

$R_f$

Equity Capitalization Rate (expected rate of return on equity securities)

·X

$R_f^* = I + b_f^* (r_{fm}S_f)$

·Y

$b_f^* = \dfrac{dR_f^*}{d(r_{fm}S_f)} = \dfrac{R_f^* - I}{r_{fm}S_f}$

$O$

$r_{fm}S_f$

Investor's Non-Diversifiable Risk

[15] Institutional lending is equivalent to purchasing debt. It can be shown that ability of institutional lenders to purchase debt would prohibit the market trade-off function from being convex from below ($i'' > 0$). The heroic assumption that institutional investors can borrow unlimited amounts at a constant rate of interest is, of course, not realistic. If institutional borrowing were restricted, and if the market trade-off function were concave downward ($f'' < 0$), increases in a firm's leverage would increase the expected return and risk linearly and the firm's equity price would be bid up to bring expected return into line with market required return for a security in its risk category. A widespread attempt of firms to increase leverage to more optimal levels would increase the aggregate supply of higher risk securities relative to lower risk securities. This would tend to force prices down and equity capitalization rates up for higher risk securities and the opposite for lower risk securities. This process would tend to force linearity upon the market trade-off function.

If a firm's equity capitalization rate, $R_f$, was not in linear equilibrium with the capitalization rates of other firms, opportunities for profitable arbitrage would exist. This arbitrage would take place irrespective of institutional risk preferences. By way of illustration, consider security X offering an expected rate of return (capitalization rate), $R_f$, in excess of the linear equilibrium. Institutional investors would sell a portion of the other securities in their portfolios and purchase security X since combined with borrowing or lending this security has a potentially higher total expected rate of return for a given non-diversifiable standard error than any other security. The price of the security would be bid up until its expected rate of return was brought into linear equilibrium with the non-diversifiable portion of the estimate of its standard error of return. Conversely, consider security Y, having an expected rate of return below the linear equilibrium; investors would sell this security and purchase other equities with the proceeds since the equity securities in equilibrium would have, combined with borrowing or lending, a potentially higher expected total rate of return for a given non-diversifiable standard error. This arbitrage process would continue until the price of the security fell sufficiently to bring its expected rate of return into linear equilibrium. This arbitrage process is illustrated numerically in Table 3 where an equilibrium slope of 0.5 has been arbitrarily selected.

TABLE 3

| SECURITY | PRICE | $R_f$ | $I$ | $r_{fm}S_f$ | $b_f = \dfrac{R_f - I}{r_{fm}S_f}$ | $b_f^*$ | $R_f^*$ | PRICE* |
|---|---|---|---|---|---|---|---|---|
| X | $50.00 | .20 | .05 | .20 | .75 | .5 | .15 | $100.00 |
| Y | $60.00 | .10 | .05 | .15 | .33 | .5 | .125 | $ 30.00 |

Price = price in initial disequilibrium.
$R_f$ = expected rate of return or equity capitalization rate in disequilibrium.
$I$ = interest rate.
$r_{fm}$ = expected correlation of returns from a given security with a market index.
$S_f$ = security's estimated standard error of return.
$b_f$ = relationship of expected return and the non-diversifiable portion of the estimate of the security's expected rate of return in disequilibrium.
$b_f^*$ = equilibrium slope of market tradeoff between non-diversifiable risk and expected return.
$R_f^*$ = equilibrium expected rate of return or equity capitalization rate.
Price* = equilibrium price.

In a market dominated by large institutional investors, corporate management should be concerned with the effect of the acceptance of an investment project on the non-diversifiable portion of the estimated standard error of returns on its equity. If the assumption is made that these large institutional investors are able to borrow and lend at a constant interest rate, the relevant discount rate, in equilibrium, to obtain the present value of an investment project ($C_i$) would be linearly related to the portion of the estimated standard error of returns from the project that cannot be eliminated by diversification across securities.

Again assuming a constant rate of interest the relevant discount rate in equilibrium for an investment project, $C_i^*$, would thus be a function of (1) the linear equilibrium market trade-off between non-diversifiable institutional investors' risk and expected return and (2) institutional investors' non-diversifiable portion of the estimated standard error of returns on the investment project

$$C_i^* = I + b_f^* \, (r_{im} S_i)$$

$$= I + \left[ \frac{R_f^* - I}{r_{fm} S_f} \right] r_{im} S_i \tag{18}$$

Now for any given firm having equity capitalization rate $R_f$, this rate can be transformed linearly into the relevant discount rate for a given investment project, $C_i$ by redefining $1/\alpha'$ in equation

$$C_i = I + \frac{1}{\alpha'} (R_f - I) \tag{10}$$

as the ratio of institutional investors' non-diversifiable risk on the investment project to the institutional investors' non-diversifiable risk on the stream of returns to equity. That is, now

$$\frac{1}{\alpha'} = \frac{r_{im} S_i}{r_{fm} S_f} \tag{19}$$

When the securities market is in equilibrium, $R_f^*$ would equal $R_f$ and therefore $C_i^*$ would be equal to $C_i$. However, when the market is not in equilibrium, $C_i$ is the correct discount rate to be used since it is at this rate that the firm's equity is actually capitalized. $C_i$ represents the firm's opportunity cost of equity funds (whether raised internally or externally) such that in lieu of investing in the project under consideration it could purchase its own shares.

One further point: should institutional investors not be permitted to borrow or lend freely, corporate leverage may be utilized to neutralize institutional investors' non-diversifiable risks on (1) the investment project and (2) the stream of returns to equity. The procedure would be the same as that described in the first and second sections of this paper where the role of large institutions was not assumed significant in the securities markets.

## IV. CONCLUSION

This paper has attempted to develop a rational and objective basis for making capital budgeting decisions under conditions of less than perfect knowledge about the future. Two assumptions were made in order to simplify the initial analysis: (1) a perfectly competitive securities market made up of small, risk-averse investors with non-diversified portfolios and (2) a perfect correlation between returns from the investment project and returns from the firm's mix of assets. Given these it was demonstrated that the internal rate of return on an investment project could be made risk-equivalent to the firm's equity capitalization rate by the proper amount of borrowing or lending. The procedure was based on a linear transformation between return and risk when leverage is introduced. These risk-equivalent rates were then incorporated into the standard present value capital budgeting framework. The possibility of substituting personal for corporate leverage in the process of neutralizing the risk effect of a given investment opportunity was considered next. Since the assumption of perfect correlation of investment project returns and equity returns is not realistic, a new measure of risk on the investment opportunity was derived to reflect the diversification effect of less than perfect correlation between returns.

Finally the assumption of perfectly competitive capital markets made up of small, risk-averse investors with non-diversified portfolios was replaced with the hypothesis that the capital markets are heavily influenced by the actions of large institutional investors. This led to the development of a capital budgeting discount rate which took cognizance of the risk which large institutional investors cannot eliminate from their portfolios of financial assets by diversification across securities.

The procedures described in Sections II and III of the paper which assume different market conditions appear to be substantially different. Actually, the two methods will yield approximately the same results under two widely different situations.

The two methods will yield identical present values when

$$\frac{1}{\alpha'} = \frac{r_{if}S_i}{S_f} = \frac{r_{im}S_i}{r_{fm}S_f} \tag{20}$$

They will be approximately equal on the one hand for a firm whose scope of investment opportunities is in a very narrowly defined industry and whose proposed investment projects are small relative to the size of the firm's existing assets. Here the returns from investment projects under consideration would be expected to follow a cyclical pattern approximating that of earnings for the firm. Therefore the correlation of returns on a given investment project with market returns would be approximately equal to the correlation of the firm's returns with market returns.

On the other hand, for conglomerates having asset mixes that are widely diversified across industry groupings, the coefficient of correlation of the firm's returns with market returns would approximate 1.0; and the correlation of returns from a given investment project with the firm's returns will approximately equal the correlation of returns from that investment project with market returns.

## APPENDIX A

DERIVATION OF A GENERALIZED MODEL FOR THE COST OF FINANCING

While the firm's existing investments cannot be severed and assigned individual market valuations, the aggregate market value of the firm's existing assets is known. The market value of the firm's existing assets financed with equity is the aggregate market value of its outstanding common stock.[16]

The estimated standard error of return on the firm's equity after accepting and financing investment project $i$, $S'_f$, may be derived in a manner similar to the derivation of the variance of a weighted sum of two variables by Markowitz [14, pp. 86–88].

Let: $S_f$ = the estimated standard error of return on the firm's equity *before* accepting and financing project $i$.

$S_0$ = the estimated standard error of return on the equity portion of investment in project $i$.

$w_0$ = the weight for the equity portion of investment in project $i$; the ratio of the dollar amount of equity used in financing project $i$ to the sum of the dollar amount of equity used in financing project $i$ and the market value of the firm's outstanding equity before accepting project $i$.

$w_f$ = $(1 - w_0)$; the weight for the market value of the firm's previously outstanding equity; that ratio of the market value of the firm's equity to the sum of the market value of the firm's equity and the dollar amount of equity investment in project $i$.

$r_{if}$ = the coefficient of correlation of the returns expected to be generated by project $i$ with the anticipated returns on the firm's existing assets.

Then it can be stated that

$$S'_f = \sqrt{w_0^2 S_0^2 + w_f^2 S_f^2 + 2w_0 w_f r_{if} S_0 S_f} \tag{A1}$$

Next we want to restate equation (A1) in terms of $\alpha$.

Let: $E$ = the market value of the firm's outstanding common equity before accepting and financing project $i$.

$P_i$ = the dollar cost of project $i$.

$\dfrac{1}{\alpha} P_i$ = the dollar amount of the investment in project $i$ financed by equity funds.

Since $S_0$ was defined as being equal to $\alpha S_i$ in equation (1), the weights used in equation (A1) may be restated as

$$w_0 = \frac{(1/\alpha)P_i}{E + (1/\alpha)P_i} = \frac{P_i}{\alpha E + P_i} \tag{A2}$$

---

[16] The cost of financing derived here is based on the assumption that the marginal source of equity funds is externally-raised equity. If internal equity funds are available, the market value of the residual returns to equity to be generated by the firm's existing assets is the value of the firm's outstanding equity less a potential liquidation dividend in lieu of the acceptance of new projects.

$$w_f = \frac{E}{E + (1/\alpha)P_i} = \frac{\alpha E}{\alpha E + P_i} \tag{A3}$$

Substituting into equation (A1) yields

$$S'_f = \sqrt{\left[\frac{P_i}{\alpha E + P_i}\right]^2 \alpha^2 S_i^2 + \left[\frac{\alpha E}{\alpha E + P_i}\right]^2 S_f^2 + 2\frac{P_i}{\alpha E + P_i}\frac{\alpha E}{\alpha E + P_i} r_{if}\alpha S_i S_f} \tag{A4}$$

Setting the right side of equation (A4) equal to $S_f$ and solving for $\alpha$ gives the financing ratio that will neutralize the effect of accepting project $i$ on returns to equity. The $\alpha$ that equates $S'_f$ with $S_f$ is $\alpha'$ and the equality reduces to the quadratic equation.

$$(P_i S_i^2 + 2Er_{if}S_i S_f)\alpha^2 - (2ES_f^2)\alpha - (P_i S_f^2) = 0 \tag{A5}$$

## REFERENCES

1. F. Arditti. "Risk and the Required Rate of Return on Equity," *Journal of Finance* XXII (March, 1967), 19–36.
2. J. Dean. "Measuring the Productivity of Capital," *Harvard Business Review* XXXIII (January–February, 1954), 120–130.
3. P. Hunt, C. M. Williams and G. Donaldson. *Basic Business Finance*. Homewood: Richard D. Irwin, Inc., 3rd ed., 1966.
4. J. M. Keynes. *The General Theory of Employment, Interest and Money*. London: Macmillan & Co., 1936.
5. F. H. Knight. *Risk, Uncertainty and Profit*, 1921. Reprints of Economic Classics. New York: Augustus M. Kelly, 1964.
6. H. A. Latané. *Rational Decision Making in Portfolio Management*, Ph.D. Dissertation, University of North Carolina, 1957.
7. ———. "Pure Risk Yields and Long Run Returns," unpublished paper, 1966.
8. ——— and D. L. Tuttle. "Pure Risk Yields and the Cost of Capital," paper presented at the Eastern TIMS meeting, October, 1965.
9. ——— and D. L. Tuttle. "Criteria for Portfolio Building," *Journal of Finance* XXII (September, 1967).
10. J. Lintner. "The Valuation of Risk Assets and the Selection of Risky Investment in Stock Portfolios and Capital Budgets," *Review of Economics and Statistics* (February, 1965), 13–27.
11. ———. "Security Prices, Risk and Maximal Gains from Diversification," *Journal of Finance*, XX (December, 1965), 587–613.
12. J. H. Lorie and L. J. Savage. "Three Problems in Rationing Capital," *Journal of Business*, XXVIII (October, 1955), 229–239.
13. F. and V. Lutz. *The Theory of Investment of the Firm*. Princeton: Princeton University Press, 1951.
14. H. Markowitz. *Portfolio Selection: Efficient Diversification of Investment*. New York: John Wiley & Sons, Inc., 1959.
15. F. Modigliani and M. H. Miller. "The Cost of Capital, Corporation Finance, and the Theory of Investment," *American Economic Review*, XLVIII (June, 1958), 261–297.
16. H. V. Roberts. "Current Problems in the Economics of Capital Budgeting," *Journal of Business* XXX (January, 1957), 12–16.

17. P. A. Samuelson. *Foundations of Economic Analysis*. Cambridge, Mass.: Harvard University Press, 1947.

18. W. F. Sharpe. "A Simplified Model for Portfolio Analysis," *Management Science* IX (January, 1963), 277–293.

19. E. Solomon. "Measuring a Company's Cost of Capital," *Journal of Business* XXVIII (October, 1955), 240–252.

20. G. Tintner. "A Contribution to the Nonstatic Theory of Production," in *Studies in Mathematical Economics and Econometrics*, 1942.

21. H. M. Weingartner. *Mathematical Programming and Analysis of Capital Budgeting Problems*, Englewood Cliffs: Prentice-Hall, Inc., 1963.

## 22. A TIME-STATE-PREFERENCE MODEL OF SECURITY VALUATION**

### STEWART C. MYERS*

Reprinted by permission of the author and the publisher from *Journal of Financial and Quantitative Analysis*, Vol. III, No. 1 (March 1968), pp. 1–33.

## I. INTRODUCTION AND SUMMARY

Determining the market values of streams of future returns is a task common to many sorts of economic analysis. The literature on this subject is extensive at all levels of abstraction. However, most work has not taken uncertainty into account in a meaningful way.

This paper presents a model of security valuation in which uncertainty takes the central role. The model is based on the requirements for equilibrium in a world in which uncertainty is described by a set of possible event-sequences, or states of nature. This "time-state-preference" framework is a

* Assistant Professor of Finance, Sloan School of Management, Massachusetts Institute of Technology.

** This paper is a further development of my doctoral dissertation [20], which was submitted to the Graduate School of Business, Stanford University, in 1967. I am indebted for good advice and apt suggestions to my dissertation committee, Professors Alexander Robichek, Gert von der Linde, and Ezra Solomon. Also, Professor Kenneth Arrow was kind enough to read and comment on the entire dissertation. I wish also to thank Professors Jack Hirshleifer, Avraham Beja, Paul Cootner, and Peter Diamond, as well as this paper's referees, for helpful comments.

My research was supported by a Ford Foundation Doctoral Fellowship and a Ford Foundation Grant to the Sloan School for research in business finance. Neither the Ford Foundation nor the persons cited above are responsible for my opinions or mistakes.

generalized version of that used in articles by Arrow, Debreu, and Hirshleifer, as well as in several more recent studies.[1]

The valuation formulas presented here are, of course, imperfect. They cannot be represented as handy empirical tools. On the theoretical front, moreover, new results and new problems seem always to arrive hand in hand. Although the problems are duly noted, the time-state-preference model will be defended as a plausible approximation and a useful analytical tool.

The paper is organized as follows. The basic time-state-preference model is derived in Section II. This requires careful statement of the assumed market characteristics and the constraints on investors' strategies: although the general characteristics of the formulas obtained are intuitively appealing, their precise form is sensitive to the range of trading opportunities open to investors. The Kuhn-Tucker conditions are used to obtain the necessary conditions for equilibrium. In Section III, the special case discussed by other authors is related to my more general model. Some implications are considered in Section IV.

Finally, I consider the possible effects of "the interdependence of investors' strategies," which arise whenever the value of a security to an investor depends on other investors' beliefs and market strategies. This interdependence leads to price uncertainty, which greatly complicates the necessary conditions for equilibrium. Thus, it is difficult to evaluate its systematic effect, if any, on the structure of security prices. It is possible, however, to make qualitative comments on the nature of the problem and its possible effects.

The main contributions of this paper are as follows:

1. It is a general description of how markets for risky assets would work under a variety of conditions. Although it is more exploratory than definitive, this should not be surprising: work in the area has a relatively short history, and has concentrated mostly on issues that are even broader than those considered here. This paper is one of the first detailed investigations of a particular market under uncertainty.

2. It is widely agreed that the time-state-preference framework as developed by Arrow, Debreu, and Hirshleifer[2] is an important addition to the economist's theoretical tool-kit. This paper shows that the framework is amenable to considerable generalization, and that it allows explicit statement of the effects of certain "imperfections"—e.g., restrictions on short selling or borrowing.

3. The model was originally developed as a contribution to the theory of corporate financial management. Although details are not included here,

---

[1] The framework is due to Arrow [2] and has been extended and expounded by Debreu [5], Ch. VII, and Hirshleifer [9], [10], [11]. See also Radner [24], Drèze [7], Pye [23], Diamond [4], and Beja [3] for examples of related work. Lancaster [14] has used a similar analytical framework in recent discussions of theory of consumer choice.

[2] In the articles already cited.

it has already proved useful in this context.[3] Thus it should be worthwhile to set out the logic of the model in detail as a basis for further work.

## II. THE BASIC TIME-STATE-PREFERENCE MODEL

One way of describing uncertainty about conditions in a future period[4] is to say that one of a set of possible states of nature will occur at that time. Definition of a set of states, in turn, provides a means of describing risk characteristics of securities, since any security can be regarded as a contract to pay an amount which depends on the state which actually occurs.

For instance, we might regard a share of stock as a contract to pay an $x$ dollar dividend if state 1 occurs at $t = 1$, a $y$ dollar dividend if state 2 occurs at $t = 1$, etc. Let the dividend paid be $R(s, t)$ and suppose 100 states of nature are being considered for $t = 1$. Then the set $\{R(s, 1)\} = \{R(1, 1), R(2, 1), \ldots, R(100, 1)\}$ specifies the particular bundle of *contingent payments* which the investor obtains for $t = 1$ by purchasing one share. In this case, $R(1, 1) = x$, $R(2, 1) = y$, and so on.

The following model relates the present value of a security to the present value of the contingent returns the security must pay to its owner. This relationship will be derived from the *necessary* conditions of security market equilibrium. First, however, the assumed characteristics of the market must be carefully specified.

### ASSUMPTIONS

1. *States of Nature.* A state of nature which may occur at time $\tau$ is defined as a particular *sequence of events* during the time span from $t = 1$ to $t = \tau$. Constructing a set of possible states is simply a means of identifying the possible event-sequences relevant to present decisions.

   The concept of an event-sequence is ambiguous, however, if "event" is left undefined, since a possibility that is relevant in one context may not be in another. A benchmark can be established by imagining a set of states defined in such great detail that the knowledge of the state that will occur at any time $t$ would allow specification of every characteristic of the future world from the present to time $t$. Let this set be $S$. The sets of states which would be considered relevant to actual decisions may be regarded as *partitions* of $S$. Thus, if an investor finds it useful to identify a state by "GM's dividend is increased at $t = 1$," the state refers to that subset of $S$ for which this "event" takes place.

   In the model presented here, it is assumed that investors agree on a

---

[3] See Myers [20] [21], Robichek and Myers [25], and Hirshleifer [10], esp. pp. 264–68.

[4] The most common alternative is to specify the mean, variance and possibly other statistical measures of risk and return. See Sharpe [26] and Lintner [16] [17], for formal models using a mean-variance framework, and Hirshleifer [11] for a detailed comparison of the two approaches.

particular partition,[5] which defines a set of states $\{(s, t)\}$. The set is assumed to apply to the time span from $t = 1$ to $t = T$.[6] Conditions at $t = 0$ are known with certainty. The set $\{(s, t)\}$ is sufficiently detailed that, if state $s$ occurs at time $t$, then returns on every security are uniquely specified for period $t$ and all previous periods. Also, the set of states is finite and exhaustive with respect to possible sequences of security returns.[7]

Given these conditions, a security's contingent returns $\{R(s, t)\}$ are not random variables; the return $R(s, t)$ is *certain* to be paid in period $t$ *if* state $s$ occurs. However, it is important to remember that the set $\{(s, t)\}$ does not catalogue all possible future events. Even if it could be known that a particular state $(s, t)$ is to occur, an investor would still face a residual uncertainty about his health, tastes, family status, employment, etc.

2. *The Economy.* We will imagine an economy split into real and financial sectors. For present purposes, "financial sector" and "security markets" are synonymous.

It is clearly meaningless to speak of the equilibrium of security markets except in relation to a particular set of conditions in the real sector. Accordingly, the following items are taken as given:

a. The set of states $\{(s, t)\}$.
b. Investors' assessments of the probabilities that the various states will occur.
c. The (sequences of) security returns contingent on each state $(s, t)$.

Also, it is assumed that investors have given endowments of wealth available for allocation among securities and other uses, which will be referred to collectively as "consumption."

3. *Available Securities.* Taking conditions in the economy's real sector as given necessitates a restriction on the types of securities that may be issued (or retired) in response to security prices at $t = 0$. There is no need to hold supplies of all securities constant; however, it is not consistent to

---

[5] The choice of a particular partition is arbitrary. An even coarser partition than that used here would undoubtedly be more "realistic," since investors would in practice regard computational efforts as a scarce resource. The intuitive meaning of a still finer partition is difficult to pin down, if only because no one person is likely to be *interested* in more than a small subset of the additional event-sequences which could be defined.

The interpretation of time-state-preference models given coarser partitions than $\{(s, t)\}$ is discussed in Section IV.

[6] The horizon $t = T$ is introduced for analytical convenience; it is not a "planning horizon" in the usual sense of the phrase. There is some error because of the lack of explicit analysis of events subsequent to the horizon, but the effect of any such errors on the market's valuation of securities at $t = 0$ may be considered negligible if the horizon is far enough distant in time.

[7] The assumption is that security returns may take specific, discrete values. Continuous variables could just as well be used—e.g., $R_k(s, t)$ could be regarded as a continuous function of $s$ and $t$. Diamond's argument [4] is cast in this form.

admit changes in the supply of securities that are part and parcel of changes in the allocation of resources within the real sector.

To illustrate, suppose that interest rates fall at $t = 0$. In response, a firm issues bonds to finance purchases of additional plant and equipment. Because the additional real assets enable the firm to pay higher returns in some or all future contingencies, a link is created between current interest rates and the bundle of contingent returns which the firm offers to present investors. This is unacceptable if the analysis is to be limited to conditions for equilibrium in the financial sectors.

If, on the other hand, the firm uses the bond issue to retire a portion of its outstanding common stock, conditions in the real sector may be considered unchanged. The substitution of debt for equity in a firm's capital structure is a financing decision, and changes in the firm's real assets or investment strategy are not a necessary consequence.[8]

To generalize, changes in the supply of securities, or the issue of new types of securities, are not ruled out in what follows. It is assumed, however, that such adjustments are not of the sort that imply changed conditions in the real sector. It has already been noted that the concept "equilibrium of security markets" is meaningful only if conditions in the real sector are given.

4. *Market Characteristics.* Markets are assumed to be perfect.

5. *Reinvestment of Contingent Returns.* Investment in securities amounts to the purchase of contingent returns, which may, in general, be either consumed or reinvested when and if they are realized. For this model, however, we will effectively rule out reinvestment by assuming that investors hold their original portfolios unchanged at least until $t = T$. (This assumption is reconsidered in Section V below.) Accordingly, a security's return in $(s, t)$ will be interpreted as the *cash* payment (i.e., dividend, interest, or principal payment) which its owner receives in $(s, t)$. Capital gains or losses will not be considered, except that the price of the security in the most distant future time period under consideration will be treated as if it were a liquidating dividend.[9]

For stocks, this assures that market value is determined solely by the present value of future dividends.

6. *Utility Functions.* Investors choose portfolios which we assume maximize the expected utility of future returns on the portfolio. In addition, the

---

[8] It is true that the contingent returns received by stock- and bond-holders are affected if the firm replaces equity with debt. However, the bundles of contingent returns offered by the firm's securities can still be clearly specified within the set of states $\{(s, t)\}$, provided that (a) there is no change in the total contingent returns paid by the firm on all its outstanding securities and (b) investors are certain about how the firm's total payout is to be divided among stock- and bond-holders in every possible contingency. Although these conditions may not always hold in practice (see Robichek and Myers [25], esp. pp. 15–19), they are a reasonable approximation for present purposes.

[9] However, there is no requirement that all securities offer contingent returns in all time periods from $t = 1$ to $t = T$. Bonds, in particular, will often mature before the horizon period.

total expected utility associated with any portfolio is a linear function of utility functions defined for each state. Specifically, if $\pi(s, t)$ is an investor's judgment of the probability of occurrence of contingency $(s, t)$ and $U(s, t)$ is the utility of returns to be received in $(s, t)$, then the overall utility of a portfolio's contingent returns will be given by

(1) $$\psi = \sum_{s,t} \pi(s, t)U(s, t).$$

The notation $\sum_{s,t}$ denotes summation over all states in the set $\{(s, t)\}$, $t = 1, 2, \ldots, T$.

Further, we assume that each utility function $U(s, t)$ is defined only in terms of returns to be received in $(s, t)$. That is, if an investor holds a portfolio yielding $y$ in $(s, t)$, then the utility of $y$ is independent of the utility of returns in all other contingencies, and vice versa.

This assumption would not be reasonable without our proviso that contingent returns on securities are consumed, rather than reinvested. If, say, the amount $y$ were invested in real assets, the investor's income in subsequent contingencies would be increased. As a consequence, the marginal utility of income in these contingencies would not be the same, in general, as it would be if $y$ were consumed.

In this framework $U'(s, t)$, the marginal utility of income in a given contingency, may be high for either or both of two reasons:[10]

a. Assuming that the investor is risk-averse, $U'(s, t)$ will be relatively high to the extent that the total income to be received in $(s, t)$ is low.
b. The utility of a given amount of money income may differ from state to state, since the utility *functions* $U(s, t)$ are not necessarily the same for each contingency.

One class of reasons why the functions $U(s, t)$ may depend on $(s, t)$ is fairly obvious: differences can arise, for instance, if commodity prices differ from state to state and over time, or if the investor's need for income depends on, say, his age at $(s, t)$.

Another kind of reason follows from the way we have set up the problem. The set $\{(s, t)\}$ assumed for purposes of analysis is exhaustive in the sense that it offers a complete catalogue of possible future returns on *securities*, but it does not catalogue *all* future events exhaustively. The risks inherent in these "uncatalogued" contingencies will not, in general, be independent of the state being considered. An investor will perhaps be less certain of the amount of income he will receive from sources other than securities in wartime, but the occurrence of a war will also affect returns on securities. The functions $U(s, t)$ will reflect such inter-relationships.

Formally, then, the phrase "utility of a contingent return $A$ in $(s, t)$"

---

[10] As noted by Hirshleifer [11], pp. 523–34.

must be taken to mean "the *expected* utility to the investor of the (certain) amount $A$ at time $t$ given that state $s$ occurs." We thus consider only a part of the investor's overall decision problem: the possible incremental effects on his future income of his portfolio choice at $t = 0$.

## THE BASIC MODEL

We begin by considering $N$ different securities which investors can purchase at $t = 0$. These securities may have been issued at $t = 0$, or they may be "left over" from previous periods. The word "share" will be used to refer to a single unit of investment in a given security.

For the $k$th security, the set $\{R_k(s, t)\}$ of contingent returns per share will be written in vector form, and referred to as $R_k$, where

$$R_k = [R_k(0), \ldots, R_k(s, t), \ldots]$$

for $s = 1, 2, \ldots, m(t)$, and for each period $t = 1, 2, \ldots, T$. The "state" $s = 0$ refers to the present—i.e., to $t = 0$—and for each security $R_k(0) = -P_k$, where $P_k$ is the ex-dividend market price per share of the $k$th security at $t = 0$.

We define a dummy security $k = 0$ to be "consumption" at $t = 0$, with

$$R_0 = [1, 0, \ldots, 0].$$

That is, purchasing one share of security zero is interpreted as the consumption of one dollar at $t = 0$. $P_0$, the "price" of consumption, is likewise one dollar.

Consider the portfolio selection problem of a particular investor. Let $h_k$ be the number of shares of the $k$th security which he purchases. His decision problem at $t = 0$ is to choose $[h_0, h_1, \ldots, h_N]$ to maximize expected utility $\psi$, where

(2) $$\psi = \sum_{s,t} \pi(s, t)U(s, t) + U(0),$$

with $U(s, t) = f[\sum_{k=1}^{N} h_k R_k(s, t)]$ and $U(0) = f[h_0]$. The variables $\pi(s, t)$ represent the investor's assessments of the probabilities that the states $(s, t)$ actually will occur. (Note that we have made no assumption ruling out disagreement among investors on the probabilities $\pi(s, t)$.)

In addition, the investor is constrained in that he has only a given amount of wealth, $W$, available for allocation among consumption and investment. The constraint is

(3) $$\phi = \sum_{k=0}^{N} h_k P_k - W = 0.$$

Since consumption and investment in securities are the only available uses for this wealth, Equation (3) is necessarily an equality.

If no short selling or borrowing is permitted, then $h_k \geq 0$ for all $k$. In this case, maximizing Equation (2) subject to the stated constraint is a problem in non-linear programming. The necessary conditions for the maximum may be inferred from the Kuhn-Tucker conditions.[11] If a maximum exists, we know from these conditions that we can assign a positive number $\lambda(\phi)$ to the constraint Equation (3).[12] Maximizing utility implies that

$$(4) \qquad \frac{\delta\psi}{\delta h_k} - \lambda(\phi)\frac{\delta\phi}{\delta h_k} \leq 0,$$

for $k = 0, 1, \ldots, N$. The left hand side of Equation (4) is zero if $h_k > 0$.

Note that $\delta\phi/\delta h_k = P_k$ for $k > 0$, and $\delta\phi/\delta h_0 = 1$. Substituting in Equation (4) for security $k = 0$ (i.e. consumption at $t = 0$), we obtain

$$(5) \qquad \lambda(\phi) = U'(0),$$

where $U'(0)$ is the marginal utility of income used for present consumption.

Using these results, we can rewrite Equation (4) as

$$\delta\psi/\delta h_k - U'(0)P_k \leq 0,$$

or

$$P_k \geq 1/U'(0)[\delta\psi/\delta h_k].$$

Since, for $k \neq 0$, $\delta\psi/\delta h_k = \sum_{s,t} \pi(s, t)U'(s, t)R_k(s, t)$, we have the fundamental result

$$(6) \qquad P_k \geq \sum_{s,t} q(s, t)R_k(s, t),$$

where

$$(7) \qquad q(s, t) = \pi(s, t)\frac{U'(s, t)}{U'(0)}.$$

Equation (6) is the basic valuation formula for the time-state-preference framework. In words, it tells us that when an investor maximizes the expected utility of his portfolio, the price of each security is at least equal to the expectation of the marginal utility associated with a small increment in his holdings of that security, when the utility of money in future contingencies is

---

[11] Kuhn and Tucker [13]. Also, see Dorfman, Samuelson, and Solow [6], Ch. VII, for the exposition which prompted my use of the conditions. Remember that the conditions to be presented are not sufficient for equilibrium. For instance, one necessary condition not mentioned is that the utility functions $U(s, t)$ be convex—i.e., risk-averse. See Arrow [2], p. 95. Also, in the absence of any direct or indirect restraints on the ability of investors to *sell* single contingent payments, we must require that $\pi_i(s, t) > 0$ for all investors (indexed by $i$) and all $(s, t)$. If an investor really believes that the contingency $(s, t)$ is impossible, he will be willing to sell contingent payments in $(s, t)$ in unlimited amounts. This latter point was mentioned to me by Avraham Beja. For a detailed treatment of the existence of equilibrium, see Debreu [5].

[12] Since, from the nature of the problem, the constraint Equation (3) must be satisfied exactly, $\lambda(\phi)$ cannot be zero.

measured in terms of the utility of money used for present consumption. If the investor actually holds that security in his portfolio, then its price is exactly equal to the expectation of the marginal utility associated with the security. The terms $q(s, t)$ thus indicate the present value to this investor of an incremental dollar of portfolio return to be received at time $t$ if state $(s, t)$ occurs.

A necessary condition for equilibrium is that Equation (6) holds for all securities from the point of view of each investor. In effect, it establishes a lower bound on the price of each security, expressed in terms of investors' marginal valuations of contingent returns. For if $P_k$ were less than the right hand side of Equation (6) from the point of view of any investor, then that investor could increase the total expected utility of returns to his portfolio by purchasing security $k$ in at least marginal amounts. Equilibrium cannot exist until all such opportunities are exhausted.

BORROWING

The introduction of investors' borrowing opportunities does not change the necessary conditions for equilibrium given by Equation (6). Borrowing is simply the purchase of a particular type of security. If the $j$th security is a borrowing contract open to an investor, then its contingent cash "returns" can be written in the same format used above:

$$R_j = [R_j(0), \ldots, R_j(s, t), \ldots].$$

The vector $R_j$ is unusual only in that $R_j(0) > Q$ and $R_j(s, t) \leq 0$.

SELLING SHORT

Selling short can be most conveniently analyzed within the present framework by regarding the short sale of security $k$ as the purchase of a dummy security $k^*$ with a vector of contingent returns $R_k^*$ derived from $R_k$. The vector $R_k^*$ will be roughly a mirror image of $R_k$. If there are no margin requirements, then $R_k^* = R_k$, in which case selling security $k$ short is algebraically equivalent to purchasing negative amounts of security $k$, assuming $k^*$ is held to time $t = T$.[13]

It is entirely feasible to incorporate dummy securities such as $k^*$ in the investor's portfolio problem wherever short sales make sense. The necessary conditions for the maximum imply a result comparable to Equation (6) for each dummy security—that is,

---

[13] Given the distant horizon $T$, the short sale becomes a promise to pay security $k$'s dividends from period $t = 1$ to $t = T$ to the lender of the security. The payments include the security's price at $t = T$, which we have interpreted as a liquidating dividend. Thus selling short is the sale of future contingent returns. That we do not actually find short sales undertaken as long-term commitments is apparently due to uncertainty about whether any particular investor could fulfill such a contract. Margin requirements are a reaction to this uncertainty.

(8)
$$P_k^* \geq \sum_{s,t} q(s, t) R_k^*(s, t).$$

This holds with an equality if $h_k^* > 0$.

For the case in which there are no margin requirements, comparison of Equations (6) and (8) leads to an interesting result. As we have observed, for this case $R_k^* = -R_k$, implying that $P_k^* = -P_k$ and that $R_k^*(s, t) = -R_k(s, t)$ for all $(s, t)$. Substituting in Equation (8),

(9)
$$P_k^* \leq \sum_{s,t} q(s, t) R_k(s, t).$$

Equations (6) and (9) taken together require[14]

(10)
$$P_k = \sum_{s,t} q(s, t) R_k(s, t).$$

Note that Equation (10) implies that all investors agree, at the margin, on the equilibrium values of all securities, although not necessarily on the value of any particular contingent return. Because each investor is willing to "take a position" in each security, there can be no such thing as a "clientele effect." That is, investors holding a particular security will *not* value it more highly that other investors do.

On the other hand, Equation (6) *is* in itself consistent with a clientele effect. Any such effect must therefore be ascribed to restricted trading opportunities, not to the existence of uncertainty or differences in investors' expectations.

OTHER CONSTRAINTS

The frictions and imperfections which exist in actual markets, have for the most part, been left out of the above analysis. However, those which impose constraints on investors' portfolio choices can be analyzed with relative ease if portfolio choice is viewed as a problem of non-linear programming.

For example, suppose the investor must invest at least 100 percent of his funds in securities from the set $K$. Now the objective function must be maximized subject to two constraints:

$$\phi_1 = \sum_{k=0}^{N} h_k P_k - W = 0,$$

(11)

$$\phi_2 = bW - \sum_{k \in K} h_k P_k \leq 0.$$

[14] In words, the argument is this. If the investor's total expected utility is reduced by selling a marginal amount of security $k$ short, he will necessarily be better off by purchasing a marginal amount of $k$ long. Conversely, if the investor's total expected utility is reduced by purchasing a marginal amount of security $k$, then it will pay him to sell security $k$ short. Therefore, each investor at equilibrium will be willing to hold at least marginal amounts of each security either long or short in his portfolio. Only if this condition is satisfied will Equations (6) and (9) be consistent.

For securities not included in the set $K$, $\delta\phi_2/\delta h_k = 0$. Here the constraint $\phi_2 = 0$ is irrelevant, and Equation (6) holds. For $k \in K$, however, the Kuhn-Tucker conditions are:

$$(12) \qquad \frac{\delta\psi}{\delta h_k} - \lambda(\phi_1)\frac{\delta\phi_1}{\delta h_k} - \lambda(\phi_2)\frac{\delta\phi_2}{\delta h_k} \leq 0.$$

Computing $\lambda(\phi_1)$ and the partial derivatives, and solving for $P_k$, we have:

$$(13) \qquad P_k = \frac{1}{U'(\phi) - \lambda(\phi_2)} \sum_{s,t} \pi(s, t)U'(s, t)R_k(s, t),$$

assuming that $k$ is actually included in the investor's optimal portfolio. The variable $\lambda(\phi_2)$ is the expected utility lost (at the margin) by investing one dollar in a security $k \in K$ instead of consuming the dollar.[15]

## III. A SPECIAL CASE

We now return to the main thread of the argument. A necessary condition for equilibrium if short sales are permitted, and if there are no margin requirements or other imperfections, is that Equation (10) holds for each investor and each security. For the $i$th investor, then,

$$(10) \qquad P_k = \sum_{s,t} q_i(s, t)R_k(s, t),$$

$k = 1, 2, \ldots, N$. In other words, if there are $N$ securities, equilibrium requires that $N$ equations of this form hold for each investor. The "unknowns" are the variables $q_i(s, t)$, since security prices and contingent returns are taken as given by investors in a perfect market. The set $\{q_i(s, t)\}$ represents the present values of contingent returns to the $i$th investor, given by Equation (7).

In general, there is no requirement that investors agree on the present value of contingent returns. However, consider the special case in which $N \geq M$, where $M$ is the number of future states, and $M$ of the vectors $R_k$ is linearly independent. Here the equations may be solved to yield a unique set of *prices* $\{q_1(1, 1), \ldots, q_i(s, t), \ldots\}$. Moreover, since $P_k$ and $R_k$ are the same for all investors, *the set must be identical for all investors*. Given the structure of security prices at equilibrium, we can thus infer an entirely objective set of prices $\{q(s, t)\}$, where $q(s, t)$ is the price at $t = 0$ of one dollar to be paid contingent on the occurrence of $(s, t)$. We have, therefore:

$$(14) \qquad P_k = \sum_{s,t} q(s, t)R_k(s, t),$$

with $q(s, t) = q_i(s, t)$ for all $i$ and all $(s, t)$.[16]

[15] It is given by $\lambda(\phi_2) = U'(0) - \sum_{s,t} \pi(s, t) U'(s, t) [R_k(s, t)/P_k]$.

[16] This result *may* hold even if short sales are restricted. But this requires that (a) the vectors of returns of available securities—including borrowing and any "dummy securities" used to describe types of trading different from simple purchases—span a cone equivalent to the $M$-dimensional space created by the set $\{(s, t)\}$, and (b) that Equation (16) holds with an equality for all securities and all investors. In this case the number of securities would have to be substantially *more* than the number of states.

In reality, of course, the number of securities is likely to be much less than the number of states. Nevertheless, this simplest possible case is important in several respects.

1. It is customarily argued that, since investors will disagree in their subjective evaluations of the size and risk of streams of future returns, their estimates of the value of these streams will also differ. This may well be true in fact, but Equation (14) establishes that any such disagreement is not a necessary consequence of either (a) the existence of uncertainty or (b) differences in investors' expectations. In fact, Equation (14) implies that all investors would agree on the value of any conceivable bundle of contingent returns, no matter how bizarre, which could be specified in terms of the catalogue of contingencies $\{(s, t)\}$.

2. Equation (14) is closely related to (and, in fact, depends on) the ability of any investor to achieve any desired *pattern* of contingent returns from his portfolio. To be specific, let the vector $X_p$ represent the desired pattern:

$$(15) \qquad X_p = [X_p(1, 1), \ldots, X_p(s, t), \ldots] = \frac{1}{\sum\limits_{s,t} R_p(s, t)} R_p.$$

Here $R_p(s, t)$ is the return of the portfolio in $(s, t)$ and $R_p$ is the vector of these returns. The numbers $X_p(s, t)$ represent the pattern of the contingent returns $R_p(s, t)$. Because $1/\sum\limits_{s,t} R_p(s, t)$ adjusts for the *scale* of the portfolio's returns, $\sum\limits_{s,t} X_p(s, t) = 1$. The pattern of returns for a security can be described similarly:

$$(16) \qquad X_k = [X_k(1, 1), \ldots, X_k(s, t), \ldots] = \frac{1}{\sum\limits_{s,t} R_k(s, t)} R_k.$$

Since, in this special case, there are $M$ securities with linearly independent vectors $X_k$, and there are no margin requirements for short sales, the vectors span the $M$-dimensional space defined by the catalogue of $M$ states. The portfolio vector $X_p$ lies in this same space. It follows that any vector $X_p$ can be obtained by a linear combination of the vectors $X_k$.

To put this another way, we have established that an investor can adjust his portfolio to change a particular contingent return $R_p(s, t)$, while leaving returns in all other contingencies unchanged. In effect, he can buy or sell returns for any contingency. It is as if there were a separate forward market for dollars to be delivered in each future state. Viewed in this light, it is not surprising that a unique set of prices $\{q(s, t)\}$ is a necessary condition for equilibrium.

3. Previous time-state-preference models have, without significant exception, confined their analysis to this special case. In fact, it is usually assumed that trading of contingent returns takes place in explicit markets, rather than implicitly, via portfolio adjustments. Arrow and Hirshliefer, for

instance, have assumed markets for "primitive securities":[17] the primitive security for $(s, t)$ pays one dollar contingent on $(s, t)$, but nothing in any other state. Thus the equilibrium price of such a security would be simply $q(s, t)$.[18]

Without denying the theoretical productivity of this special case,[19] it is important to recognize that the time-state-preference framework can be generalized and adapted to particular market characteristics.

## IV. SOME IMPLICATIONS

This section notes some implications of the time-state-preference model of security valuation. First, the conventional valuation formulas are briefly re-examined. Observations follow on the implications of individual risk aversion for market prices, the interpretation of time-state-preference models if the catalogue of states is not exhaustively defined, and the concept of a risk-equivalent class of securities.

### CONVENTIONAL FORMULAS

Consider the $i$th investor, who holds at least one share of the $k$th stock. Then Equation (12) holds at equilibrium:

$$(10) \qquad P_k = \sum_{s,t} q_i(s, t) R_k(s, t).$$

*Price depends on*
*present value = q*
*expected return = R*

This investor may or may not agree with others on the present value of contingent returns. For simplicity's sake, however, we will drop the subscript $i$ in what follows.

The formulas normally used are:

$$(17) \qquad P_k = \sum_{t=1}^{T} \frac{\bar{R}_k(t)}{(1 + r)^t} = \sum_{t=1}^{T} \frac{C_k(t)}{(1 + i)^t},$$

where $\bar{R}_k(t)$ is the investor's expected return in $t$; $r$ is his required rate of return; $C_k(t)$ is the certainty equivalent of $\bar{R}_k(t)$, and $i$ is the riskless rate of interest. These formulas may be regarded as simplifications of Equation (10). Thus the size of $r$ or $C_k(t)$ depends on (1) the pattern across states of stock $k$'s contingent dividends, (2) the investor's valuations of contingent returns, and (3) his probability assessments. Specifically,[20]

---

[17] See Arrow [2]. Hirshleifer calls these primitive securities "time-state claims." [11], p. 527, and passim.

[18] The set of primitive securities and the $M$ normal securities considered above are simply alternative bases for the vector space defined in terms of $\{(s, t)\}$.

[19] For instance, the special case has generated considerable insight into the problem of determining optimal capital structure for corporations. See Robichek and Myers [25] and Hirshleifer [10], pp. 264–8.

[20] This is purely algebraic juggling. Note that $Z_k(t)D_k(t)$ is equivalent to the vector $[R_k(1, t) \cdots R_k(m(t), t)]$. Also, $Q(t) = [1/\sum_s q(s, t)] [q(1, t) \cdots q(m(t), t)] = (1 + i)^t [q(1, t) \cdots q(m(t), t)]$. That is, $\sum_s q(s, t)$ is the value to the investor of one dollar to be delivered with certainty in period $t$.

(18) $$C_k(t) = Z_k(t)Q'(t)D_k(t),$$

where $D_k(t) = \sum\limits_{s=1}^{m(t)} R_k(s, t)$, a measure of the *scale* of the bundle of contingent returns for period $t$, and $Z_k(t)$ and $Q(t)$ are $1 \times m(t)$ row vectors:

$$Z_k(t) = \frac{1}{D_k(t)}[R_k(1, t) \cdots R_k(m(t), t)]$$

$$Q(t) = \frac{1}{\sum\limits_{s=1}^{m(t)} q(s, t)}[q(1, t) \cdots q(m(t), t)].$$

The variables $\bar{R}_k(t)$ and $C_k(t)$ are related as follows:[21]

(19) $$C_k(t) = \alpha(t)\bar{R}_k(t) = \frac{Z_k(t)Q'(t)}{Z_k(t)\pi'(t)}\bar{R}_k(t).$$

Here $\pi(t)$ is a row vector of the investor's probability assessments $\pi(s, t)$ for period $t$.

There is, of course, no guarantee that investors will agree on the appropriate size for $C_k(t)$, $\bar{R}_k(t)$, $\alpha(t)$ or $r$.

Equation (17) is one among many ways of simplifying the more basic valuation formula, Equation (10). Alternative forms based on continuous compounding and exponential growth are often seen, as are rules of thumb using price-earnings ratios or "multipliers." Given a little algebraic ingenuity, the possible formats are endless.

Consequently, it is pointless to say that any particular simplification is *the* correct way to represent present value.

RISK AVERSION

The next few paragraphs investigate the implications of investors' risk aversion for the structure of security prices. The conclusions are generally consistent with those obtained elsewhere.[22] I repeat them because they serve as a basis for discussing implications of coarse partitions of states, and because of the persistence of the notion that security prices are adequately explained by simply considering the characteristics of individual investors' utility functions.

It is generally accepted that most investors are risk averse. From this, it is

---

[21] This is obtained by multiplying $C_k(t)$ as given by Equation (18) by

$$\frac{\bar{R}_k(t)}{\bar{R}_k(t)} = \frac{\bar{R}_k(t)}{Z_k(t)\pi'(t)D_k(t)} = 1.$$

Confidence in the theoretical appropriateness of certainty equivalents may be somewhat increased by finding that they can be conveniently expressed in a time-state-preference framework. Unfortunately, the required rate $r$ cannot be conveniently expressed—a fact which corroborates Lintner's view that $r$ is not a "primary" variable for theoretical uses. See Lintner [19], pp. 27–8.

[22] See, for instance, Drèze [7], pp. 36–8; Lintner [17], pp. 22–3.

often inferred that "the market" should be risk averse, in the sense that the certainty equivalent of an uncertain return should always be no more than the expectation of the return. In other words, the prediction would be that $\alpha(t) \leq 1$, or that $r \geq i$, where $i$ is the pure rate of interest.

Actually, it is always possible to construct patterns of contingent returns for which $\alpha(t) > 1$ for all $t$,—i.e., such that $r < i$. Note that the numerator and denominator of Equation (18) are weighted averages of relative prices and probabilities, respectively. In general, the relative price for $(s, t)$ may be more or less than $\pi(s, t)$. By changing the weights $Z_k(t)$, therefore, we can always[23] assure that $Z_k(t)Q(t)' > Z_k(t)\pi(t)'$, or that $\alpha(t) > 1$. The economic meaning of this manipulation is that a bundle of contingent returns will be relatively more valuable if it pays higher returns in states in which contingent returns have a high value.

On the other hand, suppose the weights $Z_k(t)$ are chosen randomly, subject to the condition that the elements of $Z_k(t)$ sum to one. The expected result of this experiment is that[24]

$$(20) \qquad E[C_k(t)] = E[Z_k(t)Q'(t)D_k(t)] = \frac{D_k(t)}{m(t)}.$$

That is, period $t$'s bundle of contingent returns is, on the average, exactly as valuable as a *certain* return $D_k(t)/m(t)$. Securities constructed in this manner would tend to be no more or less valuable than riskless securities with the same scale of returns.[25]

These mental experiments indicate that rewards for risk bearing are not explained by uncertainty per se, but by some systematic relationship between the relative sizes of the returns $R_k(s, t)$ and the "prices" $q(s, t)$. In actual markets, the relationship seems to be that returns on most available securities are positively correlated, so that securities tend to pay high returns precisely when most portfolio returns are high and low returns in times of scarcity. The normal risk premium is thus explained, given the inverse relationship between supplies of contingent returns and their present values.

### INTERPRETATION OF THE MODEL GIVEN COARSE PARTITIONS OF STATES

The application of the time-state-preference model within a relatively coarse partition of the set $S$ of possible event-sequences is entirely feasible, given attention to several complicating factors. One of these is that investors will not, in general, adopt identical partitions, so that agreement among

---

[23] If $\pi(t) = Q(t)$, $\alpha(t) = 1$ for any pattern of contingent returns. This is improbable.
[24] That is, the expected value of each of the elements of $Z_k(t)$ is $1/m(t)$; $m(t)$ is the number of states defined for period $t$.
[25] Unfortunately it would not be correct to predict that, on the average, such securities would be priced so that investors would anticipate an *expected* rate of return equal to the riskless rate of interest. Although $E[Z_k(t) Q'(t)] = E[Z_k(t) \pi'(t)]$, it is not true that

$$E[\alpha_t] = E\left[\frac{Z_k(t) Q'(t)}{Z_k(t) \pi'(t)}\right] = 1.$$

investors on the risk characteristics of securities cannot be taken for granted. Nevertheless, postulating agreement will often prove to be appropriate.

Another problem is that our previous definition of contingent returns will no longer serve. Given a partition $\{(\sigma, t)\}$ which is coarser than $\{(s, t)\}$, the returns contingent on $(\sigma, t)$ are the *random* variables $R_k(\sigma, t)$. They cannot be used in the same sense as the variables $R_k(s, t)$—which are *certain* returns, given $(s, t)$—without further explanation.

Adopting the partition $\{(\sigma, t)\}$, the investor's decision problem is to maximize

$$(21) \qquad \psi = \sum_{\sigma,t} \pi(\sigma, t)E[U(\sigma, t)] + U(0),$$

subject to a wealth constraint, where

$$(22) \qquad E[U(\sigma, t)] = E\left[U\left(\sum_{k=1}^{N} h_k \tilde{R}_k(\sigma, t)\right)\right].$$

The value of $E[U(\sigma, t)]$ could be computed readily if the investor had specified the returns $R_k(s, t)$, the probabilities $\pi(s, t)$, given $(\sigma, t)$, and the functions $U(s, t)$; but he does not have this information. A reasonable heuristic tool is to rewrite his decision problem as:

$$(21a) \qquad \psi = \sum_{\sigma,t} \pi(\sigma, t)U^*(\sigma, t) + U(0),$$

$$(22a) \qquad U^*(\sigma, t) = U\left(\sum_{k=1}^{N} h_k C_k(\sigma, t)\right).$$

Here $C_k(\sigma, t)$ is the certainty equivalent of $\tilde{R}_k(\sigma, t)$—that is, if state $(\sigma, t)$ occurs, the investor is indifferent to receiving $\tilde{R}_k(\sigma, t)$ or a certain amount $C_k(\sigma, t)$. The investor is assumed to act as if he is certain to receive a portfolio return of $\sum_{k=1}^{N} h_k C_k(\sigma, t)$ if $(\sigma, t)$ occurs.

The decision problem shown as Equations (21a) and (22a) may be solved by exactly the same procedure used in Section II to derive the basic time-state-preference model. However, this provides an easy way out only if the certainty equivalent can itself be explained without undue complication. Various simple relationships might be assumed if the partition represented by the set $(\sigma, t)$ is not too coarse.[26]

[26] If, for instance, the partition is fine enough to describe all systematic interrelationships among returns, then the returns $\tilde{R}_k(\sigma, t)$ of the $N$ securities are independent random variables. So long as the states $(s, t)$ are not explicitly considered, the securities' returns can be distinguished only by summary measures of the residual uncertainty—e.g., by $\text{Var}[\tilde{R}_k(\sigma, t)]$. Consequently, a relation such as $C_k(\sigma, t) = E[\tilde{R}_k(\sigma, t)] - A \, \text{Var}[\tilde{R}_k(\sigma, t)]$ could be assumed. The result would be a hybrid model, in which a security's price is related to (a) the pattern of its returns across the states $\{(\sigma, t)\}$ and (b) the mean and variability of its contingent returns. It might even be fruitful to set $A = 0$, on the grounds that most of the uncertainty about security returns is resolved by the occurrence of a state $(\sigma, t)$, and that diversification can eliminate most of the residual variance. Note that the covariance of $\tilde{R}_j(\sigma, t)$ and $\tilde{R}_k(\sigma, t)$ would be zero for all $j \neq k$.

One interesting thing is that the special case discussed in Section III is less unlikely when a coarse partition of states is used. The coarser $\{(\sigma, t)\}$, the smaller the number of states, and the more likely it is that the available vectors of security returns will span the vector space associated with $\{(\sigma, t)\}$. It would not be entirely unreasonable, therefore, to attempt to measure the price of one dollar to be delivered (with certainty) at $t = 1$ contingent on, say, an increase in GNP of more than five percent.[27]

## "RISK CLASSES" AS A CONSEQUENCE OF COARSE PARTITIONS

In a time-state-preference framework, the risk characteristics of the $k$th security are determined by its pattern of returns across the possible states of nature. The vector $X_k$, defined by Equation (16), is one way to describe this pattern.

Unfortunately, it is not very helpful to say that securities $j$ and $k$ are in the same risk class if $X_j = X_k$, for this requires the return $R_k(s, t)$ to be the same proportion of $R_j(s, t)$ in every contingency. If this is true, there is little point in calling $j$ and $k$ different securities. The use of such a definition would thus require creating a risk class for every security, and it implies that no two securities can be considered perfect substitutes.

This is not surprising, considering that individuals are assumed to have made the computational investment necessary to evaluate securities within the set of states $\{(s, t)\}$. A smaller computational effort yields a coarser partition, and a corresponding reduction in the investor's ability to distinguish among the risk characteristics of securities. If computation is costly, it is perfectly conceivable that an investor will consider the $j$th and $k$th securities to be perfect substitutes, knowing that $X_j \neq X_k$, but not being able to specify the differences between the two (because of a coarse partition of future states) in any way which would allow a choice between them.[28] Thus the concept of a class of securities with homogeneous risk characteristics—found useful by Modigliani and Miller, for instance[29]—is not unreasonable if computational effort is a scarce resource.

## V. THE INTERDEPENDENCE OF INVESTORS' STRATEGIES

The model of security valuation presented in this paper is not descriptive in any strict sense. On the other hand, the assumptions used are mostly familiar ones; few readers will be surprised to encounter such abstractions as the Perfect Market or the Rational Investor.

---

[27] This would also establish the market price of the certainty equivalent of a random return to be delivered contingent on this event.

[28] However, because of the general benefits of diversification, the investor may hold both securities in his portfolio.

[29] See Modigliani and Miller [18]. These comments are not meant to imply that the concept of a risk class is necessary to the proof of Modigliani and Miller's Proposition I—that the market value of the firm is independent of financial leverage in the absence of taxes on corporate income. The proposition can be readily proved given the detailed partition defined by $\{(s, t)\}$, in which no two securities can be said to belong to the same risk class. See Hirschleifer [10], pp. 264–68, and Robichek and Myers [25].

One novel assumption is that all investors purchase portfolios at $t = 0$ with the certain intention of holding them unchanged at least until period $t = T$. This proviso insures that investors' portfolio choices are *independent*, in the sense that the expected utility of any investor's portfolio depends only on the cash returns of the securities included, and in no way on possible future actions of other investors.

It takes only cursory observation of actual security markets to see that this assumption of a "one-shot" portfolio choice is inaccurate. Investors' strategies are clearly interdependent, for instance, if securities are purchased partly for anticipated capital gains. Here, the return realized by any particular investor depends not only on the state $(s, t)$ occurring, but also on what other investors will think the security is worth.

The interdependence of investors' strategies is a matter of considerable theoretical interest and uncertain practical importance. It is discussed briefly and qualitatively in this section.

### WHY INVESTORS REVISE THEIR PORTFOLIOS

There are two sorts of reasons why an investor may sell securities from his original portfolio.

1. *To provide funds for consumption.* An investor may sell securities if the cash returns on his portfolio do not sustain his "desired" consumption expenditures. Some of these consumption needs, such as retirement income, are fairly predictable, but others are not: security investment serves in part as a cushion or reserve source of funds which may be needed unexpectedly for other uses.

   It is important, however, to look one step behind this proximate cause of the sale of securities. Our previous assumption of a one-shot investment decision is *not necessarily* inconsistent with an investor's providing exactly for a large contingent cash payment, since there may be some portfolio with a pattern of returns across the set of states which is appropriate. If this pattern lies within the cone spanned by the vectors $X_k$ of available securities, then the investor can purchase a portfolio now to meet these contingent needs precisely.

   However, such opportunities do not generally exist for all types of consumption needs, since the actual number of securities is too small to span more than a small portion of the different patterns of portfolio returns which may be desired. Moreover, the problem is only partially solved by postulating the "special case" in which an investor can obtain any conceivable pattern in the vector space defined by the set of states $\{(s, t)\}$. Suppose, for instance, that an investor perceives the possibility of a personal emergency at $t = 1$. He will not be able to provide for the emergency situation by his portfolio choice unless securities exist which give different returns *contingent on the occurrence of the emergency*. Unless this event is related in some way to economic conditions on a broader scale, this will not be the case. One would not expect to find securities offering different returns contingent on the occurrence of an event of purely personal interest.[30] Even in this special case, therefore, an investor's need for a large amount of money income contingent on a personal event cannot always be met without portfolio adjustments when the event occurs.

2. *Portfolio choice is a sequential decision problem.*[31] Whereas the contingent needs just discussed are needs for funds to be consumed, investors may also wish to *reinvest* these funds in other securities. In this case, formal analysis requires explicit treatment of portfolio choice as a *sequential* decision problem. The nature of the problem may be indicated by noting that, in our model, the marginal utility to an investor of money in $(s, t)$ is dependent only on his portfolio choice at $t = 0$, since the returns yielded by the portfolio are determined solely by this choice. In general, however, the return received in $(s, t)$ also depends on (a) the opportunities which develop before time $t$ and (b) the investor's strategy in pursuing these opportunities. In this more general case, the marginal utility of income in $(s, t)$ cannot be deduced solely from consideration of the initial portfolio choice. The result is that this variable cannot be derived and used to evaluate contingent returns in $(s, t)$ without further analysis.

TREATMENT OF THESE PROBLEMS IN THE LITERATURE OF FINANCE

The problems raised by the interdependence of investors' strategies have been recognized, but not emphasized, in the literature. In essence, what has been done is to assume that these problems have no systematic effect on the valuation process.

Suppose we begin by comparing (a) an investor's valuation of an incre-

---

[30] It may be possible for an investor to issue securities which are differentiated in this regard. We see this in practice as insurance. But many risks are not insurable, so that we can count on some emergencies remaining.

The reasons why investors usually cannot issue securities to cover all contingent needs have been discussed by Radner [27] and Arrow [1], pp. 45–56. Transaction costs are an obvious reason. Another is the difficulty of writing a contract in which the duties of the parties depend on which state of nature actually occurs, when the catalogue of states is not exhaustively defined and agreed upon. A third reason is that the very existence of a contract may change the subsequent actions of the parties to it, in turn affecting the probabilities of occurrence of the states on which the contract is contingent. As Arrow [1] notes (p. 55) this problem arises in practice when insurance policies may make the issuing company vulnerable to a "moral hazard."

[31] One of the referees remarked: "The discussion of portfolio choice over time is very weak. The introduction of opportunities developing between $t$ and $T$ means that $(s, t)$ can never be completely specified, which is a good part of what uncertainty is about. Furthermore, information processing is central to what goes on in portfolio management (the sequential problem). In fact, information is of the essence."

The referee is absolutely right. The only defense available is that my model is no weaker in this regard than other formal security valuation models. The tools available are clearly less powerful than we would like; we must do what we can with what we have.

mental share of a security on the assumption that he will hold the share until time $T$ to (b) his valuation of this share, assuming that it is to be sold in some period $t < T$. The bundle of contingent returns he receives in case (b) differs from (a) in the substitution of the security's price at $t$ for the contingent dividends paid by the firm between $t$ and $T$. Since the level and risk characteristics of the security's price at time $t$ are closely associated with those of the security's bundle of contingent returns subsequent to that time, it is a reasonable first approximation to assume that the present value of the price at $t$ and the bundle of subsequent returns is the same. Given this assumption, the value of any security can be expressed solely as a function of its contingent cash returns.

This argument, which has been widely used in the literature,[32] *also justifies any of the results which can be obtained by use of the basic time-state-preference model presented above.*

The difficulty is that the risk characteristics of a security price at some future date $t$ are also dependent on all investors' demands for this security at that time. Therefore, the investor who may sell a security at time $t$ is exposed to uncertainty about other investors' future demands *in addition to* the uncertainty inherent in its bundle of subsequent contingent returns. This *price uncertainty* is precisely why the interdependence of investors' strategies is potentially important to any theory of security valuation. Its actual importance cannot be determined here, but the next subsection considers a situation in which it is likely to be relevant.

### COMMITMENTS TO FUTURE SALE OR PURCHASE OF SECURITIES

Interesting theoretical problems are not always empirically relevant. Could we improve a prediction of the structure of security prices by taking the interdependence of investors' strategies into account? Such an improvement could take place only if (a) securities differ in ways not reflected in their sets of contingent cash returns and (b) these differences are relevant to the investor because of the interdependence of investors' strategies.

The *commitment* to buy or sell a security at a future date (or in a particular state of nature) clearly increases an investor's exposure to price uncertainty; the extent of the increase depends on the extent of the commitment. Therefore, security prices should be affected by the interdependence of investors' strategies where strong commitments are common. It should suffice here to cite two examples.

The many studies of the term structure of interest rates have investigated the effects, if any, of price uncertainty. The liquidity premium found by most such studies is interpreted as an extra payment made by holders of short-term bonds for protection from price uncertainty. It may not be clear, however, how a commitment to buy or sell bonds is involved.

If an investor "needs" a certain amount of funds in ten years, we might

---

[32] For example, see Gordon [8], pp. 131–32, Porterfield [22], p. 19, Lintner [17], p. 27. Lintner uses a slight variant of this assumption in another paper. See [15], p. 69.

refer to $t = 10$ as his "preferred habitat,"[33] since a bond maturing at that time would be ideal for him. Higher anticipated yields on bonds of different maturities may lure him from his habitat, but if he does so, he is exposed to price uncertainty. If the "need" is in fact given, purchasing a five-year bond now commits him to buy another bond at $t = 5$, and bond yields at that time are uncertain. On the other hand, buying a fifteen-year bond effectively commits him to selling, at an uncertain price, at $t = 10$. Thus an investor can be said to commit himself to future sales or purchases when he forsakes his habitat. These commitments are one consideration which may explain the liquidity premiums just noted.[34]

A second type of implied commitment is found in much corporate borrowing, evidenced by the frequent refinancing of corporate issues. Most firms borrow for relatively short periods, compared with the *de facto* maturities of their assets. When this is done, the firm commits itself to refinancing when the borrowed funds are due.[35] If new borrowing is to be undertaken, the firm's shareholders are indirectly exposed to the price uncertainty reflected in uncertainty about the level and term structure of interest rates.

To be sure, the commitment to borrow is not absolute, since the shareholders always have the option of providing additional future financing themselves. This may be done by retention of earnings or by issue of new securities. Unfortunately, the effects of price uncertainty are not avoided in either case. If refinancing by shareholders is anticipated, ownership of the firm's shares implies a commitment to make an additional investment in some future period or contingencies. In general, there is no guarantee that such an investment is consistent with portfolios which would otherwise be optimal at that time.[36] If it is not consistent, we would expect an adverse effect on the present price of the firm's shares. The magnitude of the effect would depend on the firm's debt-equity ratio and the disparity between the maturity structures of its assets and liabilities.

## VII. CONCLUDING NOTE

Hirshleifer has remarked that "one surprising aspect of the time-and-state preference model is that it leads to a theory of decision under uncertainty while entirely excluding the 'vagueness' we usually associate with uncertainty."[37] It should now be clear that such precision is not a necessary characteristic of all time-state-preference models, but only of the special case

[33] The term is Modigliani and Sutch's [19].

[34] They are not sufficient explanations. For instance, see Modigliani and Sutch [19], pp. 183–84.

[35] Robichek and Myers [25] discuss how the necessity to refinance may affect the optimal degree of leverage for highly leveraged firms.

[36] In the "special case" discussed in Section IV above, however, the investor could always offset the effect of the additional investment by short sales and/or sale of other securities in his portfolio. Thus the commitment to invest additional amounts does not constrain his portfolio choice. In less idealized worlds, the commitment may be binding.

[37] Hirshleifer [11], p. 534.

Hirshleifer was concerned with. Given a limited number of securities, restrictions on short sales, the possible effects of the interdependence of investors' strategies, etc., a certain amount of vagueness—i.e. indetermination—seems unavoidable. It should not be surprising that Equation (5), the most basic valuation formula, is an inequality. I do not find this particularly discouraging. Such properties seem to be characteristic of actual problems, not of the models we invent to solve them.

To be sure, it will often be sufficient to assume that prices are determined as if the world were perfectly precise. But we have shown that the usefulness of time-state-preference models does not rest on this assumption.

## REFERENCES

1. Arrow, Kenneth J., *Aspects of the Theory of Risk-Bearing* (Helsinki: Yrjö Jahansson Lectures, 1965).
2. ———, "The Role of Securities in the Optimal Allocation of Risk-Bearing," *Review of Economic Studies*, XXXI (1963–64), pp. 91–96.
3. Beja, Avraham, "A General Framework for the Analysis of Capital Markets and Some Results for Equilibrium," (Unpublished manuscript, Stanford University, 1966).
4. Diamond, Peter A., "The Role of a Stock Market in a General Equilibrium Model with Technological Uncertainty," *American Economic Review*, LVII (September 1967), pp. 759–78.
5. Debreu, Gerard, *The Theory of Value* (New York: John Wiley & Sons, Inc., 1959).
6. Dorfman, Robert, Paul A. Samuelson, and Robert M. Solow, *Linear Programming and Economic Analysis* (New York: McGraw-Hill Book Co., Inc., 1958).
7. Drèze, Jacques H., "Market Allocation Under Uncertainty" (Preliminary draft of paper presented at the First World Congress of the Econometric Society, Rome, September 9–14, 1965).
8. Gordon, Myron J., *The Investment, Financing and Valuation of the Corporation* (Homewood, Ill.: Richard D. Irwin, Inc., 1962).
9. Hirshleifer, J., "Efficient Allocation of Capital in an Uncertain World," *American Economic Review*, LIV (May 1964), pp. 77–85.
10. ———, "Investment Decision Under Uncertainty: Application of the State-Preference Approach," *Quarterly Journal of Economics*, LXXX (May 1966), pp. 252–77.
11. ———, "Investment Decision Under Uncertainty: Choice-Theoretic Approaches," *Quarterly Journal of Economics*, LXXIX (November 1965), pp. 509–36.
12. ———, "On the Theory of Optimal Investment Decision," *Journal of Political Economy*, LXVI (August 1958), pp. 329–52.
13. Kuhn, H. W., and A. W. Tucker, "Nonlinear Programming," in U. Neyman (ed.), *Proceedings of the Second Berkeley Symposium on Mathematical Statistics and Probability* (Berkeley: University of California Press, 1951).
14. Lancaster, Kevin, "Change and Innovation in the Technology of Consumption," *American Economic Review*, LVI (May 1966), pp. 14–23.
15. Lintner, John, "Optimal Dividends and Corporate Growth Under Un-

certainty," *Quarterly Journal of Economics*, LXXVII (February 1964), pp. 49–95.

16. ——, "Security Prices, Risk and Maximal Gains from Diversification," *Journal of Finance*, XX (December 1965), pp. 587–616.

17. ——, "The Valuation of Risk Assets and the Selection of Risky Investments," *Review of Economics and Statistics*, XLVII (February 1967), pp. 13–37.

18. Modigliani, Franco, and M. H. Miller, "The Cost of Capital, Corporation Finance and the Theory of Investment," *American Economic Review*, XLVIII (June 1958), pp. 261–97.

19. ——, and Richard Sutch, "Innovations in Interest Rate Policy," *American Economic Review*, LVI (May 1966), pp. 178–97.

20. Myers, Stewart C., *Effects of Uncertainty on the Valuation of Securities and the Financial Decisions of the Firm* (Unpublished Doctoral Dissertation, Stanford University, 1967).

21. ——, "Procedures for Capital Budgeting Under Uncertainty," Massachusetts Institute of Technology, Sloan School of Management Working Paper 257–67 (mimeo).

22. Porterfield, James T. S., *Investment Decisions and Capital Costs* (Englewood Cliffs, N.J.: Prentice-Hall, Inc., 1965).

23. Pye, Gordon, "Portfolio Selection and Security Prices," *Review of Economics and Statistics*, XLIX (February 1967), pp. 111–15.

24. Radner, Roy, "Competitive Equilibrium Under Uncertainty," Technical Report No. 20, Prepared under Contract Nonr-222(77) for the Office of Naval Research, Center for Research in Management Science (Berkeley, California: University of California, 1967) (mimeo).

25. Robichek, Alexander A., and Stewart C. Myers, "Problems in the Theory of Optimal Capital Structure," *Journal of Financial and Quantitative Analysis*, I (June 1966), pp. 1–35.

26. Sharpe, William F., "Capital Asset Prices: A Theory of Market Equilibrium Under Conditions of Risk," *Journal of Finance*, XIX (September 1964), pp. 425–42.

PART **V**

COST OF CAPITAL

\* \* \* \* \* \* \* \* \* \* \* \* \* \* \* \* \* \* \* \* \* \*

## 23. COST OF DEBT AND EQUITY FUNDS FOR BUSINESS: TRENDS AND PROBLEMS OF MEASUREMENT

### DAVID DURAND*

Reprinted by permission of the author and the publisher from: Durand, D., "Cost of Debt and Equity Funds for Business: Trends and Problems of Measurement," *Conference on Research on Business Finance*, New York: National Bureau of Economic Research, 1952, pp. 215–47.

It does not seem feasible at this time to present a paper that will do justice to the title, "Costs of Debt and Equity Funds for Business: Trends and Problems of Measurement." To me this title implies a critical analysis of available data, and concrete proposals for research. The need for such research is great. We have heard a great deal recently about an alleged shortage of equity capital, and we have actually observed that many corporations finance expansion with cash retained from operations or by borrowing. This may mean, as some have argued, that the usual sources of equity capital have dried up, but it may also mean that corporations find selling stock much less attractive, or perhaps more costly, than other methods of financing. How, therefore, do the costs of stock financing compare with the costs of borrowing, or the costs of retentions? When, if ever, do the costs of financing discourage business expansion? And finally, does the tax structure have any effect on the costs of financing?

I shall deal solely with conceptual problems and, in doing this, ruthlessly brush aside the practical details in hope of clarifying the basic issues. Although we have, I believe, a rather rough notion of what we mean by the cost of raising capital, this notion needs to be sharpened before it is applicable for use in actual measurement. Furthermore, the sharpening process indicates that our conceptual groundwork is inadequate to deal with many

* National Bureau of Economic Research.

questions of investment and capital cost. Hence, the formulation of a working definition of capital cost necessitates reformulating a good deal of basic and generally accepted economic theory. But even if we achieve a satisfactory definition of cost and a sound basic theory, the practical problems of actual measurement are going to be tremendous. However, a good theory should enable us to understand these problems much better, even if it does not diminish them appreciably.

That these problems of measuring capital costs are much the same as the problems that arise in trying to appraise the going concern value of a business enterprise is the general theme of this paper. Almost any method of estimating costs will, I believe, at least imply an evaluation of the common stock of a corporation or the proprietor's interest in an unincorporated business. That is, we can measure the costs of capital about as accurately as we can measure the value of common stock, and any of us who think that stock appraisal is a form of crystal gazing should prepare to include research on the cost of capital in the same category.

Before going on with this argument, I wish to offer a general disclaimer. During the past three months of intermittent work on this paper, I have repeatedly had to revise my opinions, and I expect to have to revise them further in the ensuing three months. I do, of course, expect to stand by two general principles: (1) *Our basic economic theory needs revisions*; (2) *Security appraisal is the key to measuring the cost of capital.* But the details of the argument are, like a timetable, subject to change without notice. This paper is therefore a historical statement of the development of my ideas to date.

Finally, I wish to thank Martin W. Davenport and Wilson F. Payne for contributing a large number of ideas, some of them basic, and for aid in formulating the argument.

## I. BASIC CONSIDERATIONS

A great deal of our economic thinking is derived from a few fundamental notions concerning self-interest. The businessman is supposed to know what is best for him and to act accordingly. From analyzing these self-seeking actions, we hope to derive a theory of economic behavior. This paper is conventional in accepting the principle of self-interest and applying it to the problems of capital cost. If the businessman raises capital to finance a venture, it must be in furtherance of his interests; and any definition of the costs of raising this capital must be consistent with this principle.

This paper is unorthodox, however, in its conception of what actually constitutes a businessman's best interest. Instead of accepting the common dictum that the businessman's interest is to maximize his income, this paper counters with the alternative proposal that the businessman should try to maximize his wealth. This alternative has the advantage of greater flexibility, and for this reason it avoids errors that may result from forcing the principle of maximizing income on situations to which it is strictly inapplicable.

## 1   MAXIMIZING INCOME VS. MAXIMIZING INVESTMENT VALUE

One can attack the principle of maximizing income simply on the grounds that mankind's motives transcend the pecuniary, and that these motives affect his behavior, even in the market place. But leaving these nonpecuniary motives aside, one can also attack the principle of maximizing income on the grounds that it is totally meaningless in any world in which income is expected to change. Suppose, for example, that a businessman has two possible ways to operate his business. Operation A promises him an annual return of $6,500 in perpetuity, and Operation B promises him $10,000 in perpetuity. The principle of maximizing income works well in this example. The businessman will certainly choose Operation B with its higher income (since nonpecuniary motives are ruled out).

But suppose this businessman has another alternative—Operation C—which gets under way slowly and thus promises him $7,000 the first year, $9,000 the second year, and $10,500 thereafter. The principle of maximizing income tells us that Operation C is preferable to Operation A because the income from operation C is certainly larger than that from Operation A. But the principle cannot tell us whether Operation C is also preferable to Operation B. Is the combination of $7,000, $9,000, and $10,500 thereafter greater or less than $10,000 in perpetuity? This difficulty can be readily resolved provided a discount rate or other index of time preference is available, and provided, further, that the principle of maximizing income is appropriately modified.

The table below shows the discounted, or present, value of income under Operations B and C at four arbitrary rates of discount (standard compound interest tables were used). Thus, Operation B is preferable for rates of 10 per cent and above, whereas Operation C is preferable for rates of 9 per cent and below.

| Discount Rate | Discounted Value Operation B | Operation C | Difference (Op. C − Op. B) |
|---|---|---|---|
| 7% | $142,857 | $144,514 | $1,657 |
| 8 | 125,000 | 125,832 | 832 |
| 9 | 111,111 | 111,314 | 203 |
| 10 | 100,000 | 99,711 | −289 |

To effect this simple solution, it was necessary to modify the principle of maximizing income. The statement, "The businessman tries to maximize his income," was changed to read, "The businessman tries to maximize the *discounted value of his future income.*" Of course, some variations in terminology are possible within the revised statement; and, in fact, this paper will henceforth use the term "investment value" to mean the discounted value of an expected income stream.[1]

This revision is more than mere verbiage. The shift from maximization of income to maximization of discounted value has important implications for the measurement of costs and the analysis of investment problems. It emphasizes the basic importance of appraisal and security analysis in molding business decisions. How can the businessman go about maximizing investment value without developing a system of appraisal that is suitable, to him at least?

CHART 1

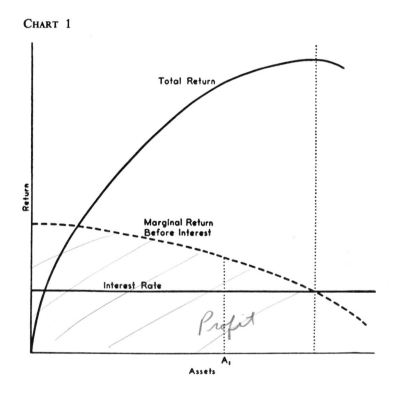

Economic theory has used the principle of maximizing income to demonstrate that business expansion will proceed until the marginal return on capital equals the rate of interest. A brief resumé of the argument is illustrated in Chart 1. Here the marginal return curve represents the rate of return on successive small increments to a businessman's assets. The curve always

[1] Among the possible alternatives are "going-concern value" and "intrinsic value." Some security analysts specifically think of intrinsic value as a sum of discounted future income payments; others are less specific.

slopes downward because the businessman is supposed to make his successive small investments in order of profitability. Since the marginal return represents

TABLE 1

BALANCE SHEET OF THE ABC MANUFACTURING COMPANY

*Assets*

| | | |
|---|---|---|
| Cash | $2,000,000 | |
| Accounts receivable | 5,000,000 | |
| Inventory | 7,000,000 | |
| Total Current | 14,000,000 | |
| Plant and Equipment, less | | |
| depreciation | 16,000,000 | |
| Total | | $30,000,000 |

*Liabilities*

| | | |
|---|---|---|
| Accrued items | $1,000,000 | |
| Accounts payable | 5,000,000 | |
| Total Current | 6,000,000 | |
| Common Stock, 1,000,000 | | |
| shares at $15 per share | 15,000,000 | |
| Surplus | 9,000,000 | |
| | 24,000,000 | |
| Total | | $30,000,000 |

INCOME STATEMENT OF THE ABC MANUFACTURING COMPANY

| | | |
|---|---|---|
| Sales | $30,000,000 | |
| Cost of goods sold | 27,500,000 | |
| Net operating income | | 2,500,000 |
| Dividends paid | | 2,000,000 |
| Transferred to Surplus | | 500,000 |
| Earnings per share | | $2.50 |
| Dividends per share | | $2.00 |
| Net operating income, | | |
| current operations | $2,500,000 | |
| Net operating income, | | |
| proposed operations | 800,000 | |
| | $3,300,000 | |
| Interest | 400,000 | |
| Net income | | $2,900,000 |
| Dividends (old rate) | | 2,000,000 |
| Available for surplus | | $900,000 |

the net return before interest, the distance between this curve and the horizontal line representing the interest rate is the marginal net return after interest. Thus, if the businessman expands his assets to the point $A_1$, his total profit is represented by the area between the marginal return curve, the interest line, the vertical axis, and a vertical line through $A_1$. The maximum possible total profit is attained when assets are expanded to the point where marginal return crosses the interest line.

This demonstration is valid if the returns attributable to the successive investment increments (represented by the curve for marginal return) can be assumed to remain constant and certain over time. But if these returns vary from year to year, and if there is an element of uncertainty as well, the treatment must be reformulated. First, the total profit curve should be supplemented by a curve showing the investment (discounted) value of the expected total profit. Second, some adjustment should be made for the risks that will inevitably be incurred by borrowing. But before modifying Chart 1, a digression on risk in business borrowing is appropriate.

Consider the hypothetical balance sheet and income statement contained in Table 1, and assume that these represent the operations of a closely held, family corporation, so that the stockholders can exert an active and unified influence on the management.[2]

Could such a corporation profitably finance additional plant by issuing $10 million of 4 per cent bonds, provided the expansion were expected to earn $800,000 annually, or 8 per cent? The estimated income statement after the proposed expansion is shown below.

As a practical matter, the current position of this corporation might discourage the investment bankers from handling the issue—even though net operating income would cover interest twice on the new plant alone and over eight times on the entire corporation. Ordinarily, the net current assets are supposed to be sufficient to cover the long-term debt; but the net current assets in this case are only $8 million—a deficiency of $2 million. Of course, an arrangement might be worked out by requiring that the bonds be paid serially, or that dividends should not be paid as long as the net current assets failed to cover the bond issue. Either of these arrangements might curtail dividends for two or three years.

But if the bond issue could be arranged, would the stockholders consider the transaction attractive? The expansion has the advantage of increasing the prospective earnings from $2.50 a share to $2.90. It also has the disadvantage

---

[2] I have a special reason for specifying such a corporation. The stockholders, who are few in number and relatively well acquainted, are apt to take a more active interest in the corporate affairs; and often the stockholders and the management are the same individuals. This gives the family corporation a peculiar degree of unity. In many ways it is like a proprietorship or partnership except for the legal organization in corporate form. In a widely held corporation, however, the stockholders have no such unity, and the management may represent the interests of a small group of stockholders, probably including the managers themselves.

of increasing the risk because the proposed bond issue is so large that dividends might be curtailed for several years—even if the expected earnings were realized; and the entire financial position of the company might be jeopardized if earnings fell off sharply. Somehow the stockholders must balance the greater return against the greater risk, and they can do this by estimating the investment value of their stock. Will the shares be worth more or less following the expansion?

In practice such appraisals are usually difficult and often involve highly complex intangibles. But if the uncomfortable details are left aside, the principle of the appraisal can be very simply illustrated. Suppose, for example, that 12½ per cent, or eight times earnings, is considered a fair capitalization rate as long as the company remains debt free, and that an increase to 15 per cent, or six and two-thirds times earnings, is considered an adequate adjustment to compensate for the risk of carrying $10 million in debt. These assumed rates are completely arbitrary. Although several bases for adjusting capitalization rates to borrowing risks will be discussed in Section II, it is sufficient for the present argument merely to assume that the stockholders consider the rates satisfactory. The necessary stock appraisals can then be made easily, as shown below. These calculations imply that the proposed expansion is inadvisable.

| | |
|---|---:|
| Earnings per share from current operations | $2.50 |
| Multiplier | 8 |
| Investment value per share | $20.00 |
| Projected earnings after expansion | 2.90 |
| Multiplier | 6⅔ |
| Investment value | $19.33 |

Because the stockholders suffer a decline in the investment value of their holdings, the small increase in earnings is not sufficient to compensate for the additional risk.[3]

## 2   REQUIRED RETURN

The preceding example showed that the risks incurred in borrowing may discourage investment, even though the rate of return on the new investment exceeds the interest cost of borrowed money. Specifically, the possibility of earning 8 per cent in this example did not justify borrowing at only half that rate. But a still higher rate of return would have justified the investment. The following calculations show how to ascertain a rate that is just high enough to offset the risk. It is assumed that the risk will be just offset if the prospective

---

[3] Of course, a somewhat smaller increase in the capitalization rate would not depreciate the stock. At 13⅓ per cent, for example, the stock would be worth seven and one-half times $2.90 or $21.75.

per share earnings capitalized at 15 per cent maintain the value of the common stock at $20.00.

| | |
|---|---:|
| Required value of stock per share | $20.00 |
| Capitalization rate | .15 |
| Required earnings, per share | 3.00 |
| Required earnings, 1,000,000 shares | 3,000,000 |
| Earnings previously available | 2,500,000 |
| Additional earnings required | 500,000 |
| Interest charges | 400,000 |
| Required earnings before interest | 900,000 |
| *Rate of required earnings* | *9%* |

The required rate of earnings—9 per cent for this example—is in a sense the cost to this corporation of borrowing the needed money. Of course, it is not an out-of-pocket cost, but a sort of opportunity cost—the minimum rate that the new investment must earn without being actually disadvantageous to the stockholders. But perhaps this is too broad an interpretation of cost, and the reader is, therefore, free to choose for himself. Regardless of his decision, he will find the required rate of earnings an important entity because of the emphasis economists currently place on the determinants of investment. If we can ascertain what new investment has to earn in order to be profitable, we will be much wiser, whether we think this constitutes the cost of capital or something else. For the remainder of this paper the required rate of earnings will be referred to as the *required return* and will be abbreviated, *RR*.

Although the *RR* discussed above refers to bond financing, there is also an *RR* when a corporation sells stock, and sometimes even when it finances expansion with cash retained from operations. If the stockholders in the previous example had been deterred from authorizing the proposed expansion because the expected returns were inadequate to justify the inherent risk incurred by bond financing, they might have considered preferred stock, common stock, and perhaps a judicious combination of common stock and bonds. Would the expected return have been sufficient to justify any of these alternatives? And if not, what rate of return would have been sufficient?

Although this subject will be explored more fully in Section III, a single example may be helpful here. When capital is raised by a common stock issue, the old stockholders will suffer a dilution of earning power and hence a dilution of investment value unless the new investment is capable of earning enough to maintain per share earnings at the old level. The *RR* depends upon the old level of earnings and the price at which the new shares must be sold. If the stockholders of the ABC Company wanted to raise $10 million by selling 500,000 shares on the market at $20.00, the new investment would have to earn $1,250,000 or 12½ per cent to avoid dilution of earnings. Hence 12½ per cent is the *RR*.

### 3   REFORMULATION OF BASIC THEORY

A more realistic presentation of Chart 1 is now in order. Like its predecessor, Chart 2 contains curves representing the marginal return on capital, the interest rate, and the total return. But Chart 2 differs in a number of important

CHART 2

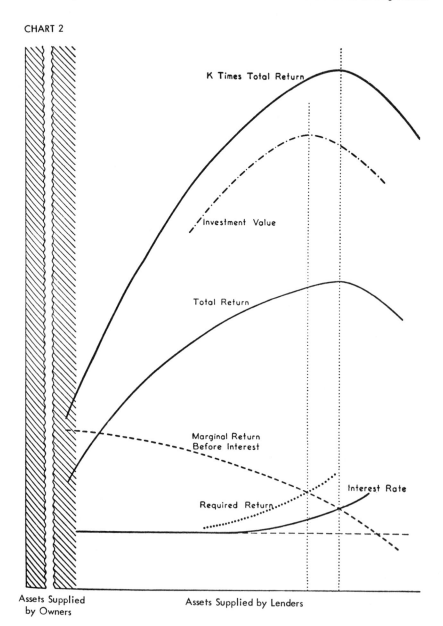

K Times Total Return

Investment Value

Total Return

Marginal Return
Before Interest

Interest Rate

Required Return

Assets Supplied
by Owners

Assets Supplied by Lenders

respects. First, at the left of the chart is a shaded area representing the assets supplied by the owners themselves, which are assumed to remain constant while additional assets are supplied by lenders. Since the owners' assets earn a return, the total return curve is substantially above zero at the point where borrowed assets are zero.

Second, the interest curve is not level, but slopes upward, because a business that borrows heavily will have to pay a higher rate of interest to compensate lenders for bearing additional risk. As drawn, this curve is actually level for a while before turning up, but some readers will undoubtedly prefer a curve that slopes upward at all points, even if only slightly. The interest curve shown in Chart 2 might be called a "marginal interest curve." This implies that the rate for each successive borrowing does not affect the rate on previous borrowings. The marginal interest curve is of such character that the maximum total return occurs when the interest rate equals the marginal return. However, a "total interest curve" is also possible. This implies that all debt must pay the same rate, which increases as the total amount of the debt increases. With the total interest curve, unlike the marginal curve, the maximum total return will occur before the point where the interest rate is equal to the marginal return.[4]

Third, at the very top of the chart is a curve representing the value of the total return when capitalized at a constant rate $K$. This curve—which would represent investment value if borrowing entailed no risk to the owners of the business—naturally reaches its maximum at the same point where total return reaches its maximum. Somewhat below this $K$-times-total-return curve is the assumed actual investment values. When there is no borrowing, investment value is $K$ times total return, and the two curves coincide. But as the volume of the borrowing and the attendant risks increase, total return has to be capitalized at a higher and higher rate; therefore investment value falls farther and farther below $K$ times total return. Naturally, investment value reaches its maximum before total return (or $K$ times total return). This is the point of optimum operation. If a business expands beyond this point, it may attain a higher expected future income, but it will have to incur unjustified risks in the process, which means that the market value of the stock will suffer.

The fourth and final feature of the chart is a curve for the $RR$. As drawn the curve is a marginal curve, that is, it expresses the minimum rate that must be

---

[4] From the viewpoint of practical finance the total interest curve is probably more accurately descriptive than the marginal curve. The best example is the type of business, like some sales finance companies, that raises large amounts of money through short-term bank loans. Although the first loan may carry a lower rate than the second, and this in turn may carry a lower rate than the third, these early loans will eventually have to be renewed, after which they will no longer enjoy their preferential status; hence, in the long run, all debt will carry the same rate. Probably the nearest approach to the marginal curve occurs when a company issues first mortgage bonds at a low rate, later issues second mortgage bonds at a somewhat higher rate, and finally issues debentures at a still higher rate.

earned by successive small investments financed by bonds in order to maintain the investment value of the common stock. By definition, this curve must cross the marginal return curve at the point of optimum operations; to the left of this point, successive investments earn more than the $RR$ and the investment value is therefore enhanced; to the right, successive investments earn less than the $RR$, and the investment value is depreciated. On this particular chart, only a small section of the $RR$ curve is shown. The reason for this is that the shape of the $RR$ curve depends upon the method used for capitalizing earnings. With one method, the $RR$ curve coincides with the interest curve at the point of zero borrowing; but with another method, the $RR$ curve is always above the interest curve. This interesting dilemma will be elaborated in the next section.

For those with a mathematical turn of mind, it may be interesting to note that the $RR$ is expressible in the following equation[5]

$$RR = I + V \frac{dC}{dX}$$

where $(I)$ is the marginal rate of interest, $(V)$ is the investment value, and $\frac{dC}{dX}$ is the rate of change in the capitalization rate (per cent) as the debt burden

---

[5] Let the interest rate $(I)$, the total return $(P)$, the investment value $(V)$, and the capitalization rate $(C)$ all be considered functions of $X$, the amount of money borrowed. Then the equation

$$V = \frac{P}{C}$$

expresses the relation between investment value and total return. After a small increase in $(P)$ resulting from additional borrowing

$$V + \Delta V = \frac{P + \Delta P}{C + \Delta C}$$

To determine the $RR$, it is only the necessary to determine the rate of return that will make $V$ vanish. That is

$$\frac{P + \Delta P}{C + \Delta C} = \frac{P}{C}$$

or

$$\frac{P + (\overline{RR} - I)\Delta X}{C + \Delta C} = \frac{P}{C}$$

Solving for $\overline{RR}$ gives

$$\overline{RR} = I + \frac{P \Delta C}{(C + \Delta C)\Delta X}$$

In the limit this becomes

$$\overline{RR} = I + \frac{P}{C}\left(\frac{dC}{dX}\right)$$

and since $\frac{P}{C}$ is equal to $(V)$, the equation given in the text follows immediately.

increases. This means that the *RR* is equal to the rate of interest as long as the capitalization rate remains constant; but as soon as the capitalization rate begins to increase, the *RR* exceeds the rate of interest. — *risk B*

## II. THE PROBLEM OF SECURITY APPRAISAL

### 1 TWO METHODS OF CAPITALIZING EARNINGS

Any practical application of the principles of the *RR* necessitates a sound, effective, and generally acceptable system of security appraisal. Yet at present no such system exists. Naturally some differences of opinion concerning details may always be expected. But present differences run much deeper than details. On the single question of capitalizing earnings, involved in most

TABLE 2
BALANCE SHEET OF THE PDQ MANUFACTURING COMPANY

*Assets*

| | | |
|---|---|---|
| Cash | $3,000,000 | |
| Accounts receivable | 5,000,000 | |
| Inventory | 7,000,000 | |
| Total Current | 15,000,000 | |
| Plant and equipment, less depreciation | 15,000,000 | |
| Total | | $30,000,000 |

*Liabilities*

| | | |
|---|---|---|
| Accrued items | $1,000,000 | |
| Accounts payable | 4,000,000 | |
| Total Current | 5,000,000 | |
| Bonded debt, 4 per cent debentures | 5,000,000 | |
| Common stock, 1,500,000 shares at $10 per share | 15,000,000 | |
| Earned surplus | 5,000,000 | |
| | 25,000,000 | |
| Total | | $30,000,000 |

INCOME STATEMENT OF THE PDQ MANUFACTURING COMPANY

| | |
|---|---|
| Sales | $30,000,000 |
| Cost of goods sold | 28,000,000 |
| Net operating income | 2,000,000 |
| Interest | 200,000 |

appraisal methods, there appear to be two systems in current use that arise from fundamentally different assumptions, lead to substantially different results in calculating the *RR*, and have radically different implications for financial policy. An analysis of these two systems will therefore prove illuminating and will highlight the need of providing a sound conceptual groundwork for research on investment problems and the costs of capital.

The accompanying sample balance sheet and income statement contain enough data to illustrate the fundamental difference between the two methods of capitalizing earnings. This hypothetical company is financed partly with bonds, partly with common stock; and the problem at hand is to estimate the value of the common stock on the assumption that the bonds, which are well protected, sell in the market at par. Since the purpose of the illustration is to focus attention on the problem of capitalizing earnings, questions of assets and book value will be neglected entirely, and the important matter of the corporate income tax will be deferred for later treatment.

One approach, hereafter called the NOI Method, capitalizes *net operating income* and subtracts the debt as follows:

| | |
|---|---:|
| Net operating income | $2,000,000 |
| Capitalization rate, 10% | × 10 |
| Total value of company | 20,000,000 |
| Total bonded debt | 5,000,000 |
| Total value of common stock | 15,000,000 |
| Value per share, 1,500,000 shares | $10.00 |

The essence of this approach is that the total value of all bonds and stock must always be the same—$20 million in this example—regardless of the proportion of bonds and stock.[6] Had there been no bonds at all, for example, the total value of the common stock would have been $20 million, and had there been $2.5 million in bonds, the value would have been $17.5 million. Hereafter, the total value of all stocks and bonds will be called the "total investment value" of the company.

The alternative approach, hereafter called the NI Method, capitalizes *net income* instead of net operating income. The calculations are as follows:

| | |
|---|---:|
| Net operating income | $2,000,000 |
| Interest | 200,000 |
| Net income | 1,800,000 |
| Capitalization rate, 10% | × 10 |
| Total value of common stock | 18,000,000 |
| Value per share, 1,500,000 shares | $12.00 |

---

[6] If the debt burden should be excessive, proponents of the NOI Method might argue that the total value of all bonds and stock would be depressed below $20 million. This argument could be based on the likelihood of insolvency and subsequent forced dissolution of the company.

Under this method the total investment value does not remain constant, but increases with the proportion of bonds in the capital structure. In the table below, three levels of bond financing are assumed: $5 million, $2.5 million, and no bonds at all. At each level, the value of the stock is obtained, as

| Assumed amount of bonds | None | $ 2,500,000 | $ 5,000,000 |
|---|---|---|---|
| Value of common stock | $20,000,000 | 19,000,000 | 18,000,000 |
| Total investment value | $20,000,000 | $21,500,000 | $23,000,000 |

above, by capitalizing at 10 per cent the residual income after bond interest. The implied relation in this table is that an increase of $2.5 million in bonded debt (total capitalization remaining constant) produces a corresponding increase of $1.5 million in total investment value. However, such a relationship cannot continue indefinitely, as the proponents of the NI Method clearly point out. As the debt burden becomes substantial, the bonds will slip below par, and the stock will cease to be worth ten times earnings.

The difference between the two methods is shown graphically in Chart 3. Here the proportion of bonds in the capital structure is indicated by the share of net operating income (always $2 million in this example) that has to be paid to the bondholders. This method has the advantage of showing bond coverage directly; for when 33⅓ per cent is paid out in interest (indicated by the dotted line), then the interest coverage is three times. The chart itself contains first a horizontal straight line at $20 million representing the total investment value according to the NOI Method. Second, the chart contains an upward sloping straight line representing the total investment value that would result under the NI Method if the bonds were always valued at par and the stock were always capitalized at 10 per cent. Finally, the chart has a curved line showing the total investment value actually implied by the proponents of the NI Method. This curve coincides with the sloping straight line for a considerable distance, but as the proportion of bonds becomes appreciable, the curve falls below the straight line. As drawn here the curve has a definite maximum value, which implies the existence of an optimum  capital structure. Naturally, the shape of the total investment value curve and the position of the maximum, near the three-times-interest-coverage point in this chart, are purely conjectural.

The most obvious difference between the two methods is that the NI Method results in a higher total investment value and a higher value for the common stock except for companies capitalized entirely with stock. For such companies the two methods give identical results provided the same capitalization rate is used.[7] This difference alone marks the NI Method as more liberal than the NOI Method, but the distinction between the optimism of the

[7] Another exception possibly occurs when a business has an excessive debt burden. If the curve for total investment value under the NI Method (Chart 3) were extended, it would meet the level line for the NOI Method at about the point where bond interest is covered 1¾ times, which is considered an excessive debt burden for an industrial corporation.

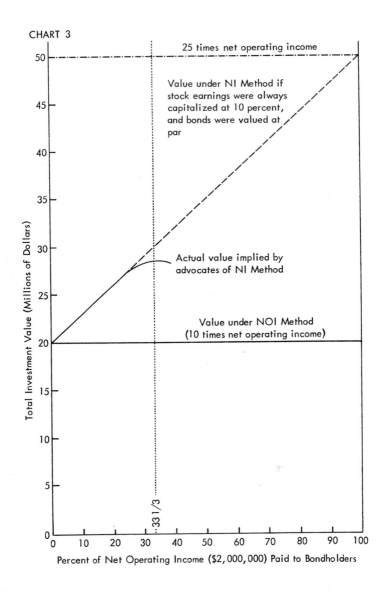

CHART 3

25 times net operating income

50

Value under NI Method if
stock earnings were always
45        capitalized at 10 percent,
and bonds were valued at
par

40

35

Total Investment Value (Millions of Dollars)

30

Actual value implied by
advocates of NI Method

25

Value under NOI Method
(10 times net operating income)

20

15

10

5

33 1/3

0

0   10   20   30   40   50   60   70   80   90   100

Percent of Net Operating Income ($2,000,000) Paid to Bondholders

NI Method and the pessimism of the NOI Method will grow sharper as the discussion progresses. The NI Method, it will appear, takes a very sanguine view of the risks incurred in business borrowing; the NOI Method takes a more sober view.

Proponents of the NOI Method argue that the totality of risk incurred by all security holders of a given company cannot be altered by merely changing the capitalization proportions. Such a change could only alter the proportion of the total risk borne by each class of security holder. Thus if the PDQ

Company had been capitalized entirely with stock—say 2,000,000 shares instead of 1,500,000 as in Table 1—the stockholders would have borne all the risk. With $5 million in bonds in lieu of the additional 500,000 shares, the bondholders would have incurred a portion of this risk. But because the bonds are so well protected, this portion would be small—say in the order of 5 or 10 per cent. Hence the stockholders would still be bearing most of the risk, and with 25 per cent fewer shares the risk per share would be substantially greater.[8]

The advocates of the NI Method take a position that is somewhat less straightforward. Those who adhere strictly to this method contend: first, that conservative increases in bonded debt do not increase the risk borne by the common stockholders; second, that a package of securities containing a conservative proportion of bonds will justifiably command a higher market price than a package of common stock alone. The first contention seems to have little merit; it runs counter to the rigorous analysis offered by the advocates of the NOI Method; and it seems to imply that the security holders of a business can raise themselves by their own bootstraps. Clearly, this contention is a somewhat tempered version of the type of analysis described in Chart 1.[9] The second contention appears to be correct, however, and it certainly merits critical analysis.

Since many investors in the modern world are seriously circumscribed in their actions, there is an opportunity to increase the total investment value of an enterprise by effective bond financing. Economic theorists are fond of

---

[8] This proposition can be stated rigorously in terms of mathematical expectation. In brief, the argument runs along the following lines. The future income of a company has a definite, though perhaps unknown, mathematical expectation. If this income is to be divided up among types of security holder according to some formula, the income of each type will also have a definite mathematical expectation. Finally, the sum of the mathematical expectations for each type will necessarily equal the total for the entire income *no matter how that income is divided up.*

In spite of the logical merits of this proposition, the basic assumption may be objectionable. One of my critics suggests that the totality of risk is increased when a business borrows and that even the NOI Method is optimistic.

[9] The argument illustrated in Chart 1 implies that a business can incur any amount of debt without increasing the proprietors' risk. Recognizing that this is a practical absurdity, the advocates of the NI Method say merely that a business can incur a limited amount of debt without increasing the proprietors' risk.

For example, Benjamin Graham and David L. Dodd, in their book, *Security Analysis* (McGraw-Hill Book Co., second edition, 1940, p. 542), show the effect of indebtedness on earnings by comparing two hypothetical companies. Company A has no bonds at all, and Company B has a conservative bond issue with interest covered more than four times. Because of the leverage imposed by the bond issue, the earnings per common share of Company B fluctuate somewhat more than the earnings per share of Company A. Concerning this, the authors say: "Would it not be fair to assume that the greater sensitivity of Company B to a possible decline in profits is offset by its greater sensitivity to a possible increase?" However, the authors point out that this argument is valid only so long as the indebtedness does not jeopardize the solvency of the company. Should interest be covered only twice (this is an industrial company) the bonds would not be safe and should sell at substantially less than par. The discussion of this point in the third edition of *Security Analysis* (1951, pp. 464 ff.) has been somewhat modified.

saying that in a perfectly fluid world one function of the market is to equalize risks on all investments. If the yield differential between two securities should be greater than the apparent risk differential, arbitragers would rush into the breach and promptly restore the yield differential to its proper value. But in our world, arbitragers may have insufficient funds to do their job because so many investors are deterred from buying stocks or low-grade bonds, either by law, by personal circumstance, by income taxes, or even by pure prejudice. These restricted investors, including all banks and insurance companies, have to bid for high-grade investments almost without regard to yield differentials or the attractiveness of the lower grade investments. And these restricted investors have sufficient funds to maintain yield differentials well above risk differentials. The result is a sort of super premium for safety; and a corporation management can take advantage of this super premium by issuing as many bonds as it can maintain at a high rating grade.

Therefore, a theoretical compromise between the two methods is entirely feasible. One can agree with the advocates of the NOI Method that the totality of risk inherent in the securities of a single company always remains the same, regardless of the capitalization; and one can agree with the advocates of the NI Method that the market will actually and justifiably pay more for the same totality of risk if the company is judicially capitalized with bonds and stock, and no inconsistency whatsoever will be introduced.

To illustrate this type of compromise, suppose it could be determined that well protected bonds like those of the PDQ Company should be valued at 5 per cent if there were no super premium for safety.[10] That is, a 5 per cent differential between bonds at 5 per cent and stock at 10 per cent would just compensate for the risk differential. Suppose further that the demand for bonds by the restricted investors is sufficient to permit floating the 4 per cent bonds of the PDQ Company at par. Hence, 1 per cent is the super premium that the restricted investors must pay for safety. But since the stockholders of the PDQ Company have no need to pay this premium, they are justified in writing down the value of their bonds to a 5 per cent basis. That is, $5 million of 4 per cent bonds would be valued at $4 million in estimating the value of the common stock (because a 4 per cent bond is worth 80 at 5 per cent). The implied calculations are as follows:

| | |
|---|---:|
| Net operating income | $ 2,000,000 |
| Capitalization rate | × 10 |
| | 20,000,000 |
| Stockholders' valuation of bonds (5 per cent basis) | 4,000,000 |
| Value of common stock | 16,000,000 |
| Restricted investors' valuation of bonds (4 per cent basis) | 5,000,000 |
| Total investment value | $21,000,000 |

[10] In making this suggestion, I am not ignoring the practical difficulties of actually estimating this super premium.

If similar calculations are made for other assumed debt loads—say $2 million, $1 million, and no debt at all—the following values for common stock and total investment value will result:

| Face value of bonds[11] | None | $ 1,000,000 | $ 2,000,000 |
|---|---|---|---|
| Value of common stock | $20,000,000 | 19,200,000 | 18,400,000 |
| Total investment value | $20,000,000 | $20,200,000 | $20,400,000 |

This implies that whenever $1 million in stock is funded into bonds, the total investment value will be increased $200,000 thereby. Naturally, this relation will not continue indefinitely, because the restricted investors and the market will not pay a super premium for safety if the volume of bonds is too high for adequate coverage.

CHART 4

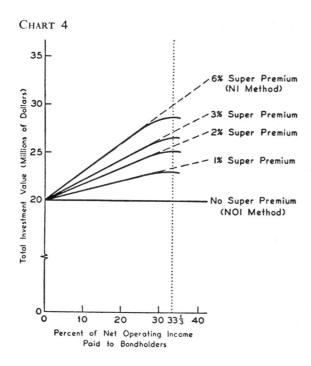

In all of these calculations the amount of the super premium—1 per cent— was arbitrarily assumed, and almost any other amount would have served equally well for illustration. The results, however, would have been different. An increase in the super premium would result in an increase in the value of

[11] Assumed equal to the restricted investors' valuation, also the market valuation.

the stock and the total investment value. This is illustrated graphically in Chart 4, which contains curves showing the relation between total investment value and debt load for five different super premiums. It is interesting to note that a super premium of zero implies the NOI Method, and a super premium of 6 per cent is equivalent to the NI Method.[12] Thus it appears that the two methods may be regarded as optimistic and pessimistic extremes between which a more realistic compromise probably lies. However, the difference between the extremes is so great—as will become evident in subsequent discussion of the *RR*—that the choice of a compromise is subject to great leeway.

Further insight into the differences between the NOI Method, the NI Method, and the described set of compromises can be gained by considering the implied capitalization rate for common stock earnings. The NI Method specifies this rate—10 per cent in the previous example—which remains constant just so long as the debt burden is conservative. The NOI Method and the compromise do not specify a capitalization rate for common stock earnings; nevertheless such a rate is implied, and it can be calculated very easily. For the NOI Method the capitalization rate is given by the simple formula[13]

$$\frac{1 - P}{10 - 25P}$$

where $(P)$ is the proportion of NOI required for bond interest, the figure 10 is the reciprocal of the 10 per cent rate for net operating income, and the figure 25 is the reciprocal of the 4 per cent bond rate. For a compromise appraisal assuming a 1 per cent super premium, this fraction becomes

$$\frac{1 - P}{10 - 20P}$$

where the figure 20 is the reciprocal of the assumed 5 per cent bond rate that would apply if the bonds did not command a super premium. Curves showing

---

[12] The NI Method does not actually imply a 6 per cent super premium. The advocates of the method merely say that conservative borrowing does not increase the stockholders' risk. The idea of the 6 per cent super premium implies that the stockholders' risk is increased but that the high super premium—clearly excessive—completely compensates for this risk.

[13] Let $(N)$ be the net operating income and let $(B)$ be the bond interest. Then $10N$ is the total investment value, $25B$ is the value of the bonds, and $10N - 25B$ is the value of the stock. The capitalization rate is determined by dividing the net income $(N - B)$ by the value of the stock, thus

$$\frac{N - B}{10N - 25B}$$

This fraction can be transformed into the form appearing in the text by letting $P = \dfrac{B}{N}$, which is the proportion of net operating income required for bond interest.

CHART 5

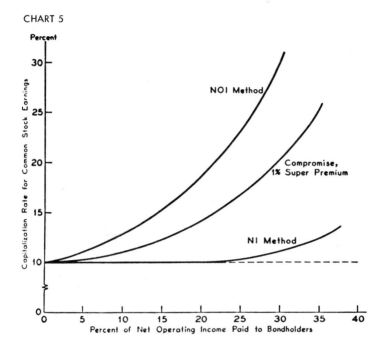

the capitalization rates for three appraisal methods at different levels of bond capitalization appear in Chart 5. The point at which the NI curve starts to turn up and the shape of the curve after this point are, of course, conjectural. The other two curves simply represent the mathematical relationships derived above.

## 2 EFFECT OF APPRAISAL METHOD ON REQUIRED RETURN

If the stockholders (or management) of the PDQ Company should consider raising a moderate amount of new money to finance expansion, they might appropriately ask whether the investment value of their holdings would be enhanced thereby, and they might further ask whether stocks or bonds would offer the more effective medium. If the stockholders should attempt to use the principle of the $RR$ to answer either of these questions, they would discover startling differences in the $RR$ for bond financing depending upon the appraisal method used, but they would discover no such differences in the $RR$ for stock financing.[14] The following table shows the actual results of

[14] I do not wish to imply that all conceivable methods of stock appraisal will result in identical $RR$'s for stock financing. But the NI Method, the NOI Method, and a compromise of the general type described will result in identical $RR$'s.

calculating $RR$'s on the assumption that 4 per cent bonds can be sold at par and that additional common stock can be sold on a 10 per cent basis.[15]

|  | Bonds | Stock |
|---|---|---|
| NI Method | 4% | 10% |
| NOI Method | 10 | 10 |
| Compromise, 1 per cent super premium | 8 | 10 |
| Compromise, 2 per cent super premium | 6⅔ | 10 |

The reader should note that the $RR$'s in the above table depend only on the bond rate (4 per cent), the capitalization rate (10 per cent), and, in the case of the compromise, on the adjusted bond rate (5 and 6 per cent). The capitalization of the company is not relevant so long as the amount of bonds is conservative. But if the debt burden should be excessive, the $RR$ for bond financing will probably rise above the quoted values, and the $RR$ for stock financing will probably fall below the quoted values because additional equity will improve the security behind the bonds and reduce the stockholders' risk.

## 3   EFFECTS OF THE CORPORATE INCOME TAX

To complete the preceding discussion requires at least brief mention of the corporate income tax. Since bond interest is a deductible expense, the corporation can attain definite tax advantages by bond financing. To illustrate,

---

[15] To illustrate the process, $RR$'s for both stock financing and bond financing under the compromise method will be calculated here. Let $s$ be the number of shares of stock, $v$ the investment value per share, $N$ the net operating income, and $B$ the total bond interest. The total investment value is given by the equation

$$sv = 10N - 20B$$

If an additional share of stock is sold at a price equal to $v$, and if the proceeds are invested, net operating income will increase by an amount $\Delta N$. The $RR$ is obtained from solving the equation

$$(s + 1)v = 10(N + \Delta N) - 20B$$

or
$$v = 10\Delta N$$

This means that the additional share must earn 10 per cent on its sale price to justify the expansion.

If, on the other hand, an additional 4 per cent bond were sold, the interest expense would increase by an amount $\Delta B$, and the equation for determining the $RR$ would become

$$sv = 10(N + \Delta N) - 20(B + \Delta B)$$

or
$$0 = 10\Delta N - 20 \Delta B$$

or again
$$\Delta N = 2\Delta B$$

This means that the new investment must earn twice the rate of interest, or 8 per cent.

consider the following abbreviated income statement for an assumed debt-free company.

| | |
|---|---|
| Sales | $30,000,000 |
| Cost of goods sold | 26,666,667 |
| Net operating income (taxable) | 3,333,333 |
| Income tax at 40 per cent[16] | 1,333,333 |
| Net income | $ 2,000,000 |

If the $2 million net is capitalized at 10 per cent, as in the previous example, the result is a total investment value of $20 million, all of which is represented by the common stock. But if a portion of the common stock should be converted into bonds, the income tax would be reduced and the total amount accruing to security holders would be increased; finally, the total investment value would increase—even under the NOI Method of valuation. The following tabulation shows the results that would obtain if the company converted some of its stock into $5 million or 4 per cent bonds.

*Calculation of net income:*

| | |
|---|---|
| Net operating income | $ 3,333,333 |
| Interest | 200,000 |
| Taxable net income | 3,133,333 |
| Income tax at 40 per cent | 1,253,333 |
| Net income | $ 1,880,000 |

*Total investment value by NOI Method:*

| | |
|---|---|
| Net income | $ 1,880,000 |
| Interest | 200,000 |
| Total claims of security holders | 2,080,000 |
| Capitalization factor | 10 |
| Total investment value | $20,800,000 |

*Total investment value by NI Method:*

| | |
|---|---|
| Net income | $ 1,880,000 |
| Capitalization factor | 10 |
| Value of common stock | $18,800,000 |
| Value of bonds | 5,000,000 |
| Total investment value | $23,800,000 |

[16] For the hypothetical examples in this paper, 40 per cent is considered a satisfactory approximation to the 38 per cent corporation rate—particularly since 40 per cent is actually the rate for consolidated returns.

The advantages of bond financing under the income tax are further illustrated by the *RR*'s shown in the table below. In a tax-free world there might be some doubt about the advantages of bond financing; if the NOI Method should be accepted rigidly, the *RR* for bond financing would exactly equal that for stock financing. But with the corporate income tax the *RR* for bond financing is less than that for stock financing, regardless of the method of evaluation. Furthermore, it is noteworthy that the income tax has the effect of increasing the discrepancy between the NI Method and the NOI Method. In the real world, therefore, the choice of a proper method of stock appraisal is even more important than in the theoretical world described previously, where income taxes were assumed nonexistent.

|  | *No Tax*[17] | *40 Per cent Tax*[18] |
| --- | --- | --- |
| Bond financing, NI Method | 4% | 4% |
| Bond financing, NOI Method | 10 | 10 |
| Stock financing, either method | 10 | 16⅔ |

## 4 IMPLICATIONS FOR RESEARCH

The foregoing analysis indicates that significant research in problems involving the cost of capital will be seriously handicapped so long as the

[17] These are the *RR*'s derived on p. 112.

[18] For bond financing, it is obvious that the *RR* will equal the interest rate under the NI Method. As long as the new investment can earn enough to meet the additional interest burden, the earnings for the common stock will not suffer—taxes or no taxes. It is not quite so obvious that the *RR* for stock financing is equal to 16⅔ per cent regardless of appraisal method, but this matter will be amplified further in Section III. Finally, the *RR* for bond financing under the NOI Method will be derived here. When the hypothetical company is capitalized with $5 million of 4 per cent bonds, the total investment value is $20,800,000 as shown, which leaves $15,800,000 for the common stock. If the company sells one more $1,000 bond, the value of the common stock must remain unchanged, and to this end the new investment must earn $140. The following calculations show this.

| | |
| --- | --- |
| Value of Stock | $15,800,000 |
| Value of bonds after expansion | 5,001,000 |
| Total investment value | 20,801,000 |
| Required for interest and stock earnings, | |
| 10 per cent of the above | 2,080,100 |
| Bond interest | 200,040 |
| Required net income after taxes | 1,880,060 |
| Tax | 1,253,373 |
| Required taxable income | 3,133,433 |
| Interest | 200,040 |
| Required net operating income | 3,333,473 |
| Net operating income previously available | 3,333,333 |
| *Additional net operating income required per $1,000* | $140 |

conflict between the NI Method and the NOI Method remains unresolved. Of course, limited research can probably be done now on the cost of common stock financing because the importance of the valuation problem is much less with common stock financing. A discussion of this problem will appear in the next section. But some of the more significant financial problems of the day involve cost comparisons between bond financing and equity financing— including both stock flotations and retentions—and attempts to make such comparisons without first solving the problem of valuation will probably prove futile and misleading. If a research worker wants to suggest that stock financing is much more costly than bond financing, he can do so very easily by accepting the NI Method, which necessarily implies that the cost of bond financing is roughly equal to the long-term interest rate and that the cost of stock financing is roughly equal to the earnings-price ratio for common stocks. But in doing this, he will probably incur bitter, and on the whole justified, criticism from those who favor the NOI Method—and possibly from some of those who favor a compromise.

As an example, Chart 6 traces the yields of industrial stocks and high-grade

**CHART 6**

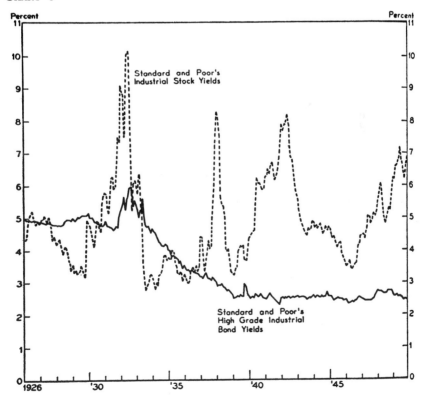

industrial bonds from 1926 through 1949.[19] Charts of this type are sometimes used as evidence that the cost of equity capital in relation to debt capital has been substantially higher in the postwar years than in the late twenties. It is true, of course, that this chart is deficient in a number of details: (1) stock yields, which reflect dividends paid, could be adjusted for earnings; (2) stock yields could also be adjusted for the corporate income tax, and (3) both stock and bond yields could be adjusted for flotation expenses. The net effect of all these adjustments would probably increase the apparent cost of equity in the postwar years. But unfortunately, even when these adjustments are made, the chart is still deficient because the basic methodology is not valid unless the NI Method of valuation is wholeheartedly accepted.

## 5 IMPLICATIONS FOR BUSINESS CYCLE THEORY

According to some writers on business cycle theory the interest rate plays the strategic role of alternately encouraging and discouraging investment. Furthermore, these writers argue, the central monetary authority can exert a substantial stabilizing influence on business by artificially raising the interest rate in prosperous periods and lowering it in depressed periods. Clearly, the force of this argument depends upon a tacit assumption that the cost of raising capital is approximately equal to the interest rate. This, in turn, necessitates another assumption accepting the NI Method, for only with this method is the cost of borrowing equal to the interest rate. Hence, the rejection of the NI Method in favor of the NOI Method, or even one of the compromises previously discussed, would cast grave doubts upon the strategic force of the interest rate in economic life. In particular, if the NOI Method should be rigidly accepted, the interest rate would lose virtually all its significance, and in place of it the stock rate (earnings-price ratio) would emerge as the number one determinant of investment on the cost side.

The preceding analysis may throw new light on a statement by John Maynard Keynes concerning easy money policy. It was Keynes' opinion that easy money would provide little stimulus to business in depressions because the marginal efficiency of capital is apt to be extremely low at such times.[20] Keynes was probably right, but perhaps for the wrong reason. He may have misjudged the importance of cost as a determinant of investment. If businessmen accept the NOI Method of valuation, either explicitly or subconsciously, the RR for new investment will be extremely high during depressions because

[19] The chart was made up from Standard and Poor's stock and bond yields. The actual figures plotted are averages for the middle month of each quarter—that is, February, May, August, and November.

[20] See *The General Theory of Employment, Interest, and Money* (Harcourt, Brace and Company, 1936), p. 316. Here Keynes says: "It is this, indeed, which renders the slump so intractable. Later on, a decline in the rate of interest will be a great aid to recovery and, probably, a necessary condition of it. But for the moment, the collapse in the marginal efficiency of capital may be so complete that no practicable reduction in the rate of interest will be enough."

of low stock prices, and lowering the interest rate will have almost no effect. Possibly, therefore, the high cost of raising capital may discourage new investment during depressions quite as much as the low marginal efficiency of capital. In everyday language, this merely means that businessmen are loath to incur obligations during a depression, and they will not do so, regardless of the interest rate, unless they can expect a return even higher than the one they would expect in a period of prosperity.[21]

## III. A BRIEF ANALYSIS OF EQUITY FINANCING

Viewed as a whole, equity financing includes four general types of transactions: common stock flotations, preferred stock flotations, use of earnings retained from operations, and the conversion of rights or other instruments into common stock. This section, however, will deal only with common stock flotations and the retention of earnings. Furthermore, the treatment is extremely sketchy and serves mainly to amplify and fill in the preceding sections.

### 1  VARIATIONS IN COMMON STOCK FINANCING

The technique of common stock financing varies considerably from flotation to flotation. This is due partly to state laws, partly to market conditions, and partly to matters of taste and judgment. Sometimes a whole stock issue is sold directly to a syndicate, which has the sole responsibility for distributing the issue to the public. At the other extreme, an issue is sometimes sold directly to the stockholders through nonmarketable pre-emptive rights with no provision for public sale. More often, however, a combination method is worked out, which may include the issue of marketable pre-emptive rights and the services of an underwriting syndicate to guarantee sale of the entire issue. Since the technique of the flotation may affect costs and $RR$'s, two examples are worked out here: One describing a straight public sale without rights, the other describing a sale to the stockholders through rights, under the assumption that the stockholders exercise their rights.

### 2  STOCK FLOTATION BY DIRECT SALE TO THE PUBLIC

Table 3 contains a hypothetical balance sheet and income statement. Suppose that the stockholders and management of the XYZ Company see an attractive opportunity to buy additional facilities for $5 million. Suppose further that the management opposes depleting the corporate cash reserves and that the stockholders have no available cash themselves; hence it is necessary to sell securities on the open market, and the management elects to sell common stock. Suppose, finally, that the corporation stock is currently selling on the market at 23 and that a syndicate agrees to sell additional stock at 22 (to allow for a bad market), charging a commission of $2.00 a

---

[21] Using Keynes' language, we might say that businessmen have "a propensity not to borrow" during depressions.

share for the service. The corporation would, therefore, receive $20.00 net for each share sold, and it would have to sell 250,000 new shares to raise the required $5 million. What is the *RR*?

TABLE 3

BALANCE SHEET OF THE XYZ MANUFACTURING COMPANY

*Assets*

| | | |
|---|---|---|
| Cash | $6,000,000 | |
| Accounts receivable | 5,000,000 | |
| Inventory | 4,000,000 | |
| Total Current | 15,000,000 | |
| Plant and Equipment, less depreciation | 15,000,000 | |
| Total | | $30,000,000 |

*Liabilities*

| | | |
|---|---|---|
| Accrued items | $1,000,000 | |
| Accounts payable | 4,000,000 | |
| Total Current | 5,000,000 | |
| Common stock, 1,000,000 shares at $15 per share | 15,000,000 | |
| Surplus | 10,000,000 | |
| | 25,000,000 | |
| Total | | $30,000,000 |

INCOME STATEMENT OF THE XYZ MANUFACTURING COMPANY

| | | |
|---|---|---|
| Sales | $11,000,000 | |
| Cost of goods sold | 6,000,000 | |
| Net operating income | | $5,000,000 |
| Income Tax | | 2,000,000 |
| Net Income | | 3,000,000 |
| Annual dividends | | 1,000,000 |
| Transfer to Surplus | | $2,000,000 |

Probably the simplest solution is to calculate a "market capitalization rate" by dividing the market price of 23 into the per share earnings of $3.00. The result is 13.04 per cent, or 7.66 times earnings. This provides a suitable multiplier if: (1) the market appraisal is considered correct; (2) the market is expected to continue to appraise the stock at the same rate after expansion (except possibly for a short period during the offering, when the stock may fall to about 22); (3) the dividend rate can be ignored; and (4) individual differences among stockholders, say tax status, can be ignored. By means of this capitalization rate, the following calculations show that the new investment must earn $1,250,000 before taxes—or exactly 25 per cent on the additional $5 million—in order to maintain the value of the stock at 23.

ESTIMATED NEW INVESTMENT EARNINGS

| | |
|---|---|
| Required value per share | $23.00 |
| Capitalization rate | .1304 |
| *Required net earnings per share* | *$3.00* |
| Total net earnings, 1,250,000 shares | $3,750,000 |
| Income tax at 40 per cent[22] | 2,500,000 |
| Total required earnings before tax | 6,250,000 |
| Previous earnings before tax | 5,000,000 |
| *Earnings required on new investments* | *$1,250,000* |

The above calculations were made in a somewhat roundabout fashion to illustrate an important point: *For debt-free companies selling stock on the open market, the RR will be the same regardless of what capitalization rate is used.* For example, the stockholders might consider that the market undervalued their stock, and they might prefer to capitalize earnings at 10 per cent, which would make the stock worth $30.00.[23] The above calculations would have to be changed in two respects only: the required price per share ($30.00) and the capitalization rate (10 per cent). These two changes would exactly offset each other, and the required earnings per share would remain $3.00. The subsequent calculations would remain unchanged. All this implies that for debt-free companies selling common stock on the open market, the *RR* is the rate of return required to maintain the original per share earnings—at $3.00 in this example.[24]

This neutral role of the capitalization rate has important practical implications because it considerably simplifies measurement. In actual security appraisal the analyst is ordinarily plagued by two troublesome problems: (1) the estimation of a satisfactory figure for expected earnings, and (2) the

[22] For these simple examples 40 per cent is a satisfactory approximation to the current 38 per cent rate, particularly since 40 per cent is actually the rate for consolidated returns.

[23] It is not only possible but quite likely that the stockholders of a company will value their stock at higher than the market price. If they did not put a higher value on their stock, why would they continue to hold it? The reader is apt to ask at this point: "Well, then, why don't they buy more stock in the market and drive the price up to 30?" The answer is simple. The stockholders are limited by the amount of their resources and the need for diversification.

[24] This principle is not strictly true for indebted companies when the NOI Method is used, or for stock flotations with pre-emptive rights. But it appears to be approximately true. I gather this from investigation of two or three examples, which suggest that very large variations in the capitalization rate have a small effect on the calculated *RR* for stock financing in general. This question might bear further investigation.

choice of a capitalization rate. But if the capitalization rate has no effect on the *RR* for specified types of stock financing, the problem of choosing such a rate can sometimes be sidestepped.

The problem of estimating earnings remains a serious one, however. Actual reported earnings are often not satisfactory because future earnings are more important to stockholders than past earnings. This was brought out dramatically in the early thirties, when many corporations were running deficits and passing dividends; yet their stock was selling substantially above zero on the belief that these corporations had long-run positive earning power. If one should attempt to calculate *RR*'s for the thirties on the basis of the reported deficits, he would obtain perfectly meaningless results. And if he should contemplate estimating the normal, long-run earning power of corporations as it appeared to investors during the thirties—which is the desired figure—he would be facing an almost impossible task.

### 3   A STOCK FLOTATION WITH PRE-EMPTIVE RIGHTS

In the preceding example, the stockholders had inadequate cash reserves, and the new issue had to be sold on the market by a syndicate. In the following example, however, the stockholders are assumed to have sufficient cash to permit buying the issue directly from the company through pre-emptive rights. Suppose that the stockholders are given the right to buy one new share at $21.00 for each four shares held, and that the costs of the flotation are $1.00 a share so that the company again realizes $20.00. This transaction is equivalent to the exchange of $21.00 in cash and four old shares worth $23.00—total $113.00—for five new shares. If the stockholders are not to suffer from the exchange, the five new shares must also be worth $113.00—or $22.60 a share. The necessary calculations for the *RR* are similar to those in the preceding example, except that the required value per share is $22.60 instead of $23.00. The *RR* in this case is $1,141,314 or 22.8 per cent. The slightly lower *RR* in this example is due to two factors: (1) the out-of-pocket flotation expenses were assumed to be lower by this method;[25] (2) the opportunity to buy new stock at slightly less than the market price was exercised by the old stockholders, rather than by outsiders, as in the preceding example.

### 4   FINANCING WITH CASH EARNED AND ACCUMULATED

This example serves mainly to show that business retentions should not be regarded as a costless source of capital. Retentions are costless in one sense only: the management incurs no out-of-pocket expenses as it would in floating securities or arranging a loan. But in almost any other sense retentions involve

---

[25] This is not meant to imply that costs of flotation are typically less for issues floated by means of pre-emptive rights. In fact, a worthwhile project would be to compare actual costs incurred in open market flotations as against pre-emptive rights flotations.

costs like those in other forms of financing. When a management sells stock to the public, it incurs an obligation, through tacit understanding, to invest the proceeds wisely and earn a return for the stockholders. If later the management elects to retain earnings that could be conveniently paid out in dividends, these entail a very clear opportunity cost; for the stockholder loses the opportunity to invest whatever portion of his share of earnings the management chooses to retain. Furthermore, if the management retains earnings and invests them unwisely, the stockholders may incur a very real cost, for the unwise reinvestment of earnings may actually depress the value of the stock.

As presented in Table 3, the XYZ Company earned $3 million, or $3.00 a share, and paid out one-third of this in dividends. What is to be done with the remainder? For the purpose of this discussion, it is assumed that the management has only two choices: (1) to pay an extra dividend of $2.00 a share on one million shares of stock, and (2) to divert this money to purchase $2 million worth of new equipment. Which course is more advantageous to the stockholders, provided it is assumed further that the ample cash balance of the XYZ Company can stand the drain of $2 million without impairing liquidity?

The ensuing discussion rests entirely on the assumption of perfect freedom of choice on the part of the management. Yet in practical affairs managements often do not have such freedom. When a corporation has a low current ratio, its management may have to restrict dividends, even though earned, merely to avoid insolvency. A corporation management may also have to restrict dividends, even though earned, because the terms of a loan agreement or bond indenture stipulate that working capital must be maintained at a specified level. Thus a corporation is sometimes virtually forced to retain earnings. In such instances, it is hardly pertinent to ask which course is more advantageous to the stockholders, and it might be misleading to carry through an estimate of the required return in the manner described below. Clearly this entire question of the costs of retentions is a complicated one, requiring a great deal of thoughtful investigation. The present analysis is merely by way of introduction.

But when there is freedom of choice the management may appropriately consider whether the cash would be worth more converted into plant than it would be as cash in the hands of the stockholders. One factor affecting the decision should be the rate of return earnable on the new investment. If the return is low, the stockholders will be better off to receive the dividends and invest the proceeds in other securities; if the rate is high, they will be better off to have the corporation retain the cash.

Another factor that should affect the decision is the incidence of the personal income tax on stockholders. But taking the personal income tax into account is extremely difficult for two reasons: (1) the great variability in rates between the high income brackets and the low income brackets, and (2) the uncertainty of the eventual tax status of possible capital gains that may arise if the corporation invests its retained cash successfully.[26] Therefore, to obtain an estimate of the *RR* on the new investment requires one arbitrary assumption concerning the income tax bracket to be represented and another concerning the capital gains tax. To make the calculations as simple as possible, it is assumed that the personal income tax on the cash dividend is 50 per cent and that the possibility of an eventual capital gains tax may be ignored.

If the cash dividend is paid, the typical stockholder will have, say, 100 shares of stock worth $23.00 a share[27] and $100.00 in cash after taxes—a total of $2,400 or $24.00 a share. If the cash is retained, the stockholder will have only his shares, which he hopes will be worth at least $24.00. If the shares are to be worth $24.00, the new investment will have to earn $216,667 or 10.8 per cent, as shown below.

| | |
|---|---:|
| Required value per share | $24.00 |
| Capitalization rate | .1304 |
| *Required earnings per share* | *$3.13* |
| Required earnings, 1,000,000 shares | $3,130,000 |
| Income tax at 40 per cent | 2,086,667 |
| Required earnings before tax | 5,216,667 |
| Income previously available | 5,000,000 |
| *Additional income required* | *$216,667* |

The *RR* in this example is ever so much lower than in the previous examples, where *RR*'s of over 20 per cent resulted. The substantial difference is due mainly to the personal income tax, although the avoidance of out-of-pocket flotation costs is also a factor. If there had been no personal income tax, the stockholders would have enjoyed the entire $2.00 dividend—which, with their stock worth $23.00 a share, would have totaled $25.00. Therefore, the new investment would have to earn $433,333 or 21.6 per cent. This is exactly twice as much as the *RR* when the personal income tax is 50 per cent. Although it is doubtful whether corporate officials go through these specific calculations in considering use of retained earnings—when choice is possible—they seem to be generally aware that substantial tax savings are possible through the use of retentions.

[26] For example, if the typical stockholder holds his stock until death, say twenty years hence, how will his estate be taxed at that time?

[27] Some readers may feel that the previously assumed market price of $23.00 a share should reflect the payment of the $2.00 dividend, and that the stock should be worth less than $23.00 after the dividend, say $22.00. This would involve a recalculation of the *RR* to ascertain what rate of return on the new investment would be required to make the stock worth $23.00.

## 5   EQUITY FINANCING IN CONJUNCTION WITH DEBT FINANCING

In all the examples discussed heretofore, *RR*'s were calculated on the supposition that the corporation management had to choose one from among such single possibilities as a bond flotation, a stock flotation, or use of retained earnings. Often, however, financing is a combined process involving both debt and equity in various forms and proportions, and as such it presents an intricate problem in joint costs. What would have been the *RR*, or the cost by any other standard, if the XYZ Company had decided to finance its $5 million plant expansion by (1) using $1 million of its own cash, (2) floating $2 million in bonds, (3) by curtailing dividends until the final $2 million could be retained? Could an *RR* or some other measure of cost be determined for the entire transaction? And could the total cost, however determined, be effectively allocated among the three separate sources of funds? This last question is particularly pertinent to the problem of public utility regulation.

This paper does not propose to discuss joint costs beyond merely mentioning them. The problem clearly exists, and it is probably formidable. With joint costs, as with simple costs for a single form of financing, the solution of the problem certainly hinges upon the valuation of business enterprise.

## IV. CONCLUSION

This paper is limited to a single phase of economic behavior—the financing of assets and the costs incurred therein. By means of a few simple examples I have tried to prove the following proposition: *Given a method of security appraisal, the costs of raising capital can be both defined and measured.* At the same time I have tried to show that there is at present no generally accepted system of appraisal; hence there can be no generally accepted system of measuring costs. It would certainly appear that the first step toward the specific problem of measuring costs is to focus more research on the general problem of appraisal.

"But," the reader is apt to ask at this point, "is there no way to sidestep the appraisal problem and deal with costs directly?" Personally, I think not, though I know of no absolutely conclusive proof. However, any research worker who tries to deal directly with costs is in great danger of falling into one of two rather obvious traps. The first is to define costs in an arbitrary fashion that is amenable to statistical research but irrelevant for economic analysis. An example is the definition of cost currently accepted by many accountants, according to which bond interest is a cost while dividends, even cumulative preferred dividends, are not. If one should accept this definition, he will find a plethora of statistics and a relatively easy problem of measurement, but the "costs" he thus measures will not help him explain the volume of asset expansion or the current preference for debt financing.

The second trap awaiting the unwary research worker is to define costs in a fashion that implies some definite method of appraisal. If, for example, he defines common stock cost as the earnings-price ratio (adjusted for flotation expenses) and bond cost as the interest rate (also adjusted for flotation expenses), he implies the NI Method of valuation; furthermore, he probably implies a belief that borrowing does not entail risk to the borrower. How many of those who support this last definition of cost would also support the view that borrowing entails no extra risk?

Research on the problem of business appraisal does not promise to be easy, by any means. The discussion in this paper has laid chief emphasis on the conflict between the NI Method and the NOI Method of capitalizing earnings. Possibly, this created an impression of oversimplification. Actually, I do not believe that either method, strictly interpreted, is adequate or correct, although I definitely lean in the direction of the NOI Method. But if the NOI Method should be accepted in principle, modifications would almost certainly be required. These might include adjustments for working capital, for book value, and for the super premium for safety, any of which would require careful thought and perhaps considerable statistical analysis.

At the present time, the most fertile field for research on the appraisal problem is probably in the organized security markets. A statistical study of security pricing would probably yield valuable clues for a long-range analysis of capital costs, and it would have the immediate advantage of providing technical information for security analysts and financiers. As conceived here, such a study should be concerned with what might be called "market appraisal," and it would cover such questions as the following: How does an underwriting syndicate arrive at a price to bid for a new security issue? How do investors and traders in the market arrive at prices to bid for traded issues? To what extent do security prices in the market exhibit definite relationships to pertinent factors like earnings prospects and interest coverage? Do the observed relationships imply some specific system of appraisal in use by traders and investors and, if so, is the implied system reasonable? Or, perhaps, is there evidence of many systems? To what extent do traders overlook opportunities for arbitrage between securities?

At the same time a general reformulation of basic economic principles would be highly desirable. What we need is a theory that takes better account of the problem of appraising risks incurred in business expansion. If a project for reformulating basic theory could be incorporated into a statistical analysis of security pricing, two desirable results might be achieved: first, the interpretation of the statistical findings would be less liable to error; second, a truly functional theory of business enterprise would be more likely to emerge.

# 24. THE COST OF CAPITAL, CORPORATION FINANCE, AND THE THEORY OF INVESTMENT

FRANCO MODIGLIANI
and
MERTON H. MILLER*

Reprinted from *The American Economic Review*, Vol. *XLVIII*, No. 3 (June, 1958), pp. 261–97, by permission of the authors and the publisher.

What is the "cost of capital" to a firm in a world in which funds are used to acquire assets whose yields are uncertain; and in which capital can be obtained by many different media, ranging from pure debt instruments, representing money-fixed claims, to pure equity issues, giving holders only the right to a pro-rata share in the uncertain venture? This question has vexed at least three classes of economists: (1) the corporation finance specialist concerned with the techniques of financing firms so as to ensure their survival and growth; (2) the managerial economist concerned with capital budgeting; and (3) the economic theorist concerned with explaining investment behavior at both the micro and macro levels.[1]

In much of his formal analysis, the economic theorist at least has tended to side-step the essence of this cost-of-capital problem by proceeding as though physical assets—like bonds—could be regarded as yielding known, sure streams. Given this assumption, the theorist has concluded that the cost of capital to the owners of a firm is simply the rate of interest on bonds; and has derived the familiar proposition that the firm, acting rationally, will tend to push investment to the point where the marginal yield on physical assets is

* The authors are, respectively, professor and associate professor of economics in the Graduate School of Industrial Administration, Carnegie Institute of Technology. This article is a revised version of a paper delivered at the annual meeting of the Econometric Society, December 1956. The authors express thanks for the comments and suggestions made at that time by the discussants of the paper, Evsey Domar, Robert Eisner and John Lintner, and subsequently by James Duesenberry. They are also greatly indebted to many of their present and former colleagues and students at Carnegie Tech who served so often and with such remarkable patience as a critical forum for the ideas here presented.

[1] The literature bearing on the cost-of-capital problem is far too extensive for listing here. Numerous references to it will be found throughout the paper, though we make no claim to completeness. One phase of the problem which we do not consider explicitly, but which has a considerable literature of its own is the relation between the cost of capital and public utility rates. For a recent summary of the "cost-of-capital theory" of rate regulation and a brief discussion of some of its implications, the reader may refer to H. M. Somers [20].

equal to the market rate of interest.[2] This proposition can be shown to follow from either of two criteria of rational decision-making which are equivalent under certainty, namely (1) the maximization of profits and (2) the maximization of market value.

According to the first criterion, a physical asset is worth acquiring if it will increase the net profit of the owners of the firm. But net profit will increase only if the expected rate of return, or yield, of the asset exceeds the rate of interest. According to the second criterion, an asset is worth acquiring if it increases the value of the owners' equity, *i.e.*, if it adds more to the market value of the firm than the costs of acquisition. But what the asset adds is given by capitalizing the stream it generates at the market rate of interest, and this capitalized value will exceed its cost if and only if the yield of the asset exceeds the rate of interest. Note that, under either formulation, the cost of capital is equal to the rate of interest on bonds, regardless of whether the funds are acquired through debt instruments or through new issues of common stock. Indeed, in a world of sure returns, the distinction between debt and equity funds reduces largely to one of terminology.

It must be acknowledged that some attempt is usually made in this type of analysis to allow for the existence of uncertainty. This attempt typically takes the form of superimposing on the results of the certainty analysis the notion of a "risk discount" to be subtracted from the expected yield (or a "risk premium" to be added to the market rate of interest). Investment decisions are then supposed to be based on a comparison of this "risk adjusted" or "certainty equivalent" yield with the market rate of interest.[3] No satisfactory explanation has yet been provided, however, as to what determines the size of the risk discount and how it varies in response to changes in other variables.

Considered as a convenient approximation, the model of the firm constructed via this certainty—or certainty-equivalent—approach has admittedly been useful in dealing with some of the grosser aspects of the processes of capital accumulation and economic fluctuations. Such a model underlies, for example, the familiar Keynesian aggregate investment function in which aggregate investment is written as a function of the rate of interest—the same riskless rate of interest which appears later in the system in the liquidity-preference equation. Yet few would maintain that this approximation is adequate. At the macroeconomic level there are ample grounds for doubting that the rate of interest has as large and as direct an influence on the rate of investment as this analysis would lead us to believe. At the microeconomic level the certainty model has little descriptive value and provides no real

---

[2] Or, more accurately, to the marginal cost of borrowed funds since it is customary, at least in advanced analysis, to draw the supply curve of borrowed funds to the firm as a rising one. For an advanced treatment of the certainty case, see F. and V. Lutz [13].

[3] The classic examples of the certainty-equivalent approach are found in J. R. Hicks [8] and O. Lange [11].

guidance to the finance specialist or managerial economist whose main problems cannot be treated in a framework which deals so cavalierly with uncertainty and ignores all forms of financing other than debt issues.[4]

Only recently have economists begun to face up seriously to the problem of the cost of capital *cum* risk. In the process they have found their interests and endeavors merging with those of the finance specialist and the managerial economist who have lived with the problem longer and more intimately. In this joint search to establish the principles which govern rational investment and financial policy in a world of uncertainty two main lines of attack can be discerned. These lines represent, in effect, attempts to extrapolate to the world of uncertainty each of the two criteria—profit maximization and market value maximization—which were seen to have equivalent implications in the special case of certainty. With the recognition of uncertainty this equivalence vanishes. In fact, the profit maximization criterion is no longer even well defined. Under uncertainty there corresponds to each decision of the firm not a unique profit outcome, but a plurality of mutually exclusive outcomes which can at best be described by a subjective probability distribution. The profit outcome, in short, has become a random variable and as such its maximization no longer has an operational meaning. Nor can this difficulty generally be disposed of by using the mathematical expectation of profits as the variable to be maximized. For decisions which affect the expected value will also tend to affect the dispersion and other characteristics of the distribution of outcomes. In particular, the use of debt rather than equity funds to finance a given venture may well increase the expected return to the owners, but only at the cost of increased dispersion of the outcomes.

Under these conditions the profit outcomes of alternative investment and financing decisions can be compared and ranked only in terms of a *subjective* "utility function" of the owners which weighs the expected yield against other characteristics of the distribution. Accordingly, the extrapolation of the profit maximization criterion of the certainty model has tended to evolve into utility maximization, sometimes explicitly, more frequently in a qualitative and heuristic form.[5]

The utility approach undoubtedly represents an advance over the certainty or certainty-equivalent approach. It does at least permit us to explore (within limits) some of the implications of different financing arrangements, and it does give some meaning to the "cost" of different types of funds. However, because the cost of capital has become an essentially subjective concept, the utility approach has serious drawbacks for normative as well as analytical

---

[4] Those who have taken a "case-method" course in finance in recent years will recall in this connection the famous Liquigas case of Hunt and Williams [9, pp. 193–96], a case which is often used to introduce the student to the cost-of-capital problem and to poke a bit of fun at the economist's certainty-model.

[5] For an attempt at a rigorous explicit development of this line of attack, see F. Modigliani and M. Zeman [14].

purposes. How, for example, is management to ascertain the risk preferences of its stockholders and to compromise among their tastes? And how can the economist build a meaningful investment function in the face of the fact that any given investment opportunity might or might not be worth exploiting depending on precisely who happen to be the owners of the firm at the moment?

Fortunately, these questions do not have to be answered; for the alternative approach, based on market value maximization, can provide the basis for an operational definition of the cost of capital and a workable theory of investment. Under this approach any investment project and its concomitant financing plan must pass only the following test: Will the project, as financed, raise the market value of the firm's shares? If so, it is worth undertaking; if not, its return is less than the marginal cost of capital to the firm. Note that such a test is entirely independent of the tastes of the current owners, since market prices will reflect not only their preferences but those of all potential owners as well. If any current stockholder disagrees with management and the market over the valuation of the project, he is free to sell out and reinvest elsewhere, but will still benefit from the capital appreciation resulting from management's decision.

The potential advantages of the market-value approach have long been appreciated; yet analytical results have been meager. What appears to be keeping this line of development from achieving its promise is largely the lack of an adequate theory of the effect of financial structure on market valuations, and of how these effects can be inferred from objective market data. It is with the development of such a theory and of its implications for the cost-of-capital problem that we shall be concerned in this paper.

Our procedure will be to develop in Section I the basic theory itself and to give some brief account of its empirical relevance. In Section II, we show how the theory can be used to answer the cost-of-capital question and how it permits us to develop a theory of investment of the firm under conditions of uncertainty. Throughout these sections the approach is essentially a partial-equilibrium one focusing on the firm and "industry." Accordingly, the " prices " of certain income streams will be treated as constant and given from outside the model, just as in the standard Marshallian analysis of the firm and industry the prices of all inputs and of all other products are taken as given. We have chosen to focus at this level rather than on the economy as a whole because it is at the level of the firm and the industry that the interests of the various specialists concerned with the cost-of-capital problem come most closely together. Although the emphasis has thus been placed on partial-equilibrium analysis, the results obtained also provide the essential building blocks for a general equilibrium model which shows how those prices which are here taken as given, are themselves determined. For reasons of space, however, and because the material is of interest in its own right, the presentation of the general equilibrium model which rounds out the analysis must be deferred to a subsequent paper.

# I. THE VALUATION OF SECURITIES, LEVERAGE, AND THE COST OF CAPITAL

## A. THE CAPITALIZATION RATE FOR UNCERTAIN STREAMS

As a starting point, consider an economy in which all physical assets are owned by corporations. For the moment, assume that these corporations can finance their assets by issuing common stock only; the introduction of bond issues, or their equivalent, as a source of corporate funds is postponed until the next part of this section.

The physical assets held by each firm will yield to the owners of the firm— its stockholders—a stream of "profits" over time; but the elements of this series need not be constant and in any event are uncertain. This stream of income, and hence the stream accruing to any share of common stock, will be regarded as extending indefinitely into the future. We assume, however, that the mean value of the stream over time, or average profit per unit of time, is finite and represents a random variable subject to a (subjective) probability distribution. We shall refer to the average value over time of the stream accruing to a given share as the return of that share; and to the mathematical expectation of this average as the expected return of the share.[6] Although individual investors may have different views as to the shape of the probability distribution of the return of any share, we shall assume for simplicity that they are at least in agreement as to the expected return.[7]

This way of characterizing uncertain streams merits brief comment. Notice first that the stream is a stream of profits, not dividends. As will become clear later, as long as management is presumed to be acting in the best interests of the stockholders, retained earnings can be regarded as equivalent to a fully subscribed, pre-emptive issue of common stock. Hence, for present purposes, the division of the stream between cash dividends and retained

---

[6] These propositions can be restated analytically as follows: The assets of the $i$th firm generate a stream:

$$X_i(1),\ X_i(2)\ \cdots\ X_i(T)$$

whose elements are random variables subject to the joint probability distribution:

$$\chi_i[X_i(1),\ X_i(2)\ \cdots\ X_i(t)].$$

The return to the $i$th firm is defined as:

$$X_i = \lim_{T \to \infty} \frac{1}{T} \sum_{t=1}^{T} X_i(t).$$

$X_i$ is itself a random variable with a probability distribution $\phi(X_i)$ whose form is determined uniquely by $\chi_i$. The expected return $\bar{X}_i$ is defined as $\bar{X}_i = E(X_i) = \int x_i X_i \phi_i(X_i) dX_i$. If $N_i$ is the number of shares outstanding, the return of the $i$th share is $x_i = (1/N)X_i$ with probability distribution $\phi_i(x_i)dx_i = \phi_i(Nx_i)d(Nx_i)$ and expected value $x_i = (1/N)\bar{X}_i$.

[7] To deal adequately with refinements such as differences among investors in estimates of expected returns would require extensive discussion of the theory of portfolio selection. Brief references to these and related topics will be made in the succeeding article on the general equilibrium model.

earnings in any period is a mere detail. Notice also that the uncertainty attaches to the mean value over time of the stream of profits and should not be confused with variability over time of the successive elements of the stream. That variability and uncertainty are two totally different concepts should be clear from the fact that the elements of a stream can be variable even though known with certainty. It can be shown, furthermore, that whether the elements of a stream are sure or uncertain, the effect of variability per se on the valuation of the stream is at best a second-order one which can safely be neglected for our purposes (and indeed most others too).[8]

The next assumption plays a strategic role in the rest of the analysis. We shall assume that firms can be divided into "equivalent return" classes such that the return on the shares issued by any firm in any given class is proportional to (and hence perfectly correlated with) the return on the shares issued by any other firm in the same class. This assumption implies that the various shares within the same class differ, at most, by a "scale factor." Accordingly, if we adjust for the difference in scale, by taking the *ratio* of the return to the expected return, the probability distribution of that ratio is identical for all shares in the class. It follows that all relevant properties of a share are uniquely characterized by specifying (1) the class to which it belongs and (2) its expected return.

The significance of this assumption is that it permits us to classify firms into groups within which the shares of different firms are "homogeneous," that is, perfect substitutes for one another. We have, thus, an analogue to the familiar concept of the industry in which it is the commodity produced by the firms that is taken as homogeneous. To complete this analogy with Marshallian price theory, we shall assume in the analysis to follow that the shares concerned are traded in perfect markets under conditions of atomistic competition.[9]

From our definition of homogeneous classes of stock it follows that in equilibrium in a perfect capital market the price per dollar's worth of expected return must be the same for all shares of any given class. Or, equivalently, in any given class the price of every share must be proportional to its expected return. Let us denote this factor of proportionality for any class, say the $k$th

---

[8] The reader may convince himself of this by asking how much he would be willing to rebate to his employer for the privilege of receiving his annual salary in equal monthly installments rather than in irregular amounts over the year. See also J. M. Keynes [10, esp. pp. 53–54].

[9] Just what our classes of stocks contain and how the different classes can be identified by outside observers are empirical questions to which we shall return later. For the present, it is sufficient to observe: (1) Our concept of a class, while not identical to that of the industry is at least closely related to it. Certainly the basic characteristics of the probability distributions of the returns on assets will depend to a significant extent on the product sold and the technology used. (2) What are the appropriate class boundaries will depend on the particular problem being studied. An economist concerned with general tendencies in the market, for example, might well be prepared to work with far wider classes than would be appropriate for an investor planning his portfolio, or a firm planning its financial strategy.

class, by $1/\rho_k$. Then if $p_j$ denotes the price and $\bar{x}_j$ is the expected return per share of the $j$th firm in class $k$, we must have:

$$p_j = \frac{1}{\rho_k} \bar{x}_j;$$
(1)

or, equivalently,

$$\frac{\bar{x}_j}{p_j} = \rho_k, \text{ a constant for all firms } j \text{ in class } k.$$
(2)

The constants $\rho_k$ (one for each of the $k$ classes) can be given several economic interpretations: (a) From (2) we see that each $\rho_k$ is the expected rate of return of any share in class $k$. (b) From (1) $1/\rho_k$ is the price which an investor has to pay for a dollar's worth of expected return in the class $k$. (c) Again from (1), by analogy with the terminology for perpetual bonds, $\rho_k$ can be regarded as the market rate of capitalization for the expected value of the uncertain streams of the kind generated by the $k$th class of firms.[10]

## B. DEBT FINANCING AND ITS EFFECTS ON SECURITY PRICES

Having developed an apparatus for dealing with uncertain streams we can now approach the heart of the cost-of-capital problem by dropping the assumption that firms cannot issue bonds. The introduction of debt-financing changes the market for shares in a very fundamental way. Because firms may have different proportions of debt in their capital structure, shares of different companies, even in the same class, can give rise to different probability distributions of returns. In the language of finance, the shares will be subject to different degrees of financial risk or "leverage" and hence they will no longer be perfect substitutes for one another.

To exhibit the mechanism determining the relative prices of shares under these conditions, we make the following two assumptions about the nature of bonds and the bond market, though they are actually stronger than is necessary and will be relaxed later: (1) All bonds (including any debts issued by households for the purpose of carrying shares) are assumed to yield a constant income per unit of time, and this income is regarded as certain by all traders regardless of the issuer. (2) Bonds, like stocks, are traded in a perfect market, where the term perfect is to be taken in its usual sense as implying that any two commodities which are perfect substitutes for each other must sell, in equilibrium, at the same price. It follows from assumption (1) that all bonds are in fact perfect substitutes up to a scale factor. It follows from assumption (2) that they must all sell at the same price per dollar's worth of return, or what amounts to the same thing must yield the same rate of return. This rate

---

[10] We cannot, on the basis of the assumptions so far, make any statements about the relationship or spread between the various $\rho$'s or capitalization rates. Before we could do so we would have to make further specific assumptions about the way investors believe the probability distributions vary from class to class, as well as assumptions about investors' preferences as between the characteristics of different distributions.

of return will be denoted by $r$ and referred to as the rate of interest or, equivalently, as the capitalization rate for sure streams. We now can derive the following two basic propositions with respect to the valuation of securities in companies with different capital structures:

*Proposition I.* Consider any company $j$ and let $\overline{X}_j$ stand as before for the expected return on the assets owned by the company (that is, its expected profit before deduction of interest). Denote by $D_j$ the market value of the debts of the company; by $S_j$ the market value of its common shares; and by $V_j \equiv S_j + D_j$ the market value of all its securities or, as we shall say, the market value of the firm. Then, our Proposition I asserts that we must have in equilibrium:

(3) $\qquad V_j = (S_j + D_j) = \overline{X}_j/\rho_k$, for any firm $j$ in class $k$.

That is, the *market value of any firm is independent of its capital structure and is given by capitalizing its expected return at the rate $\rho_k$ appropriate to its class.*

This proposition can be stated in an equivalent way in terms of the firm's "average cost of capital," $\overline{X}_j/V_j$, which is the ratio of its expected return to the market value of all its securities. Our proposition then is:

(4) $$\frac{\overline{X}_j}{(S_j + D_j)} = \frac{\overline{X}_j}{V_j} = \rho_k, \text{ for any firm } j, \text{ in class } k.$$

That is, *the average cost of capital to any firm is completely independent of its capital structure and is equal to the capitalization rate of a pure equity stream of its class.*

To establish Proposition I we will show that as long as the relations (3) or (4) do not hold between any pair of firms in a class, arbitrage will take place and restore the stated equalities. We use the term arbitrage advisedly. For if Proposition I did not hold, an investor could buy and sell stocks and bonds in such a way as to exchange one income stream for another stream, identical in all relevant respects but selling at a lower price. The exchange would therefore be advantageous to the investor quite independently of his attitudes toward risk.[11] As investors exploit these arbitrage opportunities, the value of the overpriced shares will fall and that of the underpriced shares will rise, thereby tending to eliminate the discrepancy between the market values of the firms.

By way of proof, consider two firms in the same class and assume for simplicity only, that the expected return, $\overline{X}$, is the same for both firms. Let company 1 be financed entirely with common stock while company 2 has some

[11] In the language of the theory of choice, the exchanges are movements from inefficient points in the interior to efficient points on the boundary of the investor's opportunity set; and not movements between efficient points along the boundary. Hence for this part of the analysis nothing is involved in the way of specific assumptions about investor attitudes or behavior other than that investors behave consistently and prefer more income to less income, *ceteris paribus.*

debt in its capital structure. Suppose first the value of the levered firm, $V_2$, to be larger than that of the unlevered one, $V_1$. Consider an investor holding $s_2$ dollars' worth of the shares of company 2, representing a fraction $\alpha$ of the total outstanding stock, $S_2$. The return from this portfolio, denoted by $Y_2$, will be a fraction $\alpha$ of the income available for the stockholders of company 2, which is equal to the total return $X_2$ less the interest charge, $rD_2$. Since under our assumption of homogeneity, the anticipated total return of company 2, $X_2$, is, under all circumstances, the same as the anticipated total return to company 1, $X_1$, we can hereafter replace $X_2$ and $X_1$ by a common symbol $X$. Hence, the return from the initial portfolio can be written as:

$$(5) \qquad Y_2 = \alpha(X - rD_2).$$

Now suppose the investor sold his $\alpha S_2$ worth of company 2 shares and acquired instead an amount $s_1 = \alpha(S_2 + D_2)$ of the shares of company 1. He could do so by utilizing the amount $\alpha S_2$ realized from the sale of his initial holding and borrowing an additional amount $\alpha D_2$ on his own credit, pledging his new holdings in company 1 as a collateral. He would thus secure for himself a fraction $s_1/S_1 = \alpha(S_2 + D_2)/S_1$ of the shares and earnings of company 1. Making proper allowance for the interest payments on his personal debt $\alpha D_2$, the return from the new portfolio, $Y_1$, is given by:

$$(6) \qquad Y_1 = \frac{\alpha(S_2 + D_2)}{S_1} X - r\alpha D_2 = \alpha \frac{V_2}{V_1} X - r\alpha D_2.$$

Comparing (5) with (6) we see that as long as $V_2 > V_1$ we must have $Y_1 > Y_2$, so that it pays owners of company 2's shares to sell their holdings, thereby depressing $S_2$ and hence $V_2$; and to acquire shares of company 1, thereby raising $S_1$ and thus $V_1$. We conclude therefore that levered companies cannot command a premium over unlevered companies because investors have the opportunity of putting the equivalent leverage into their portfolio directly by borrowing on personal account.

Consider now the other possibility, namely that the market value of the levered company $V_2$ is less than $V_1$. Suppose an investor holds initially an amount $s_1$ of shares of company 1, representing a fraction $\alpha$ of the total outstanding stock, $S_1$. His return from this holding is:

$$Y_1 = \frac{s_1}{S_1} X = \alpha X.$$

Suppose he were to exchange this initial holding for another portfolio, also worth $s_1$, but consisting of $s_2$ dollars of stock of company 2 and of $d$ dollars of bonds, where $s_2$ and $d$ are given by:

$$(7) \qquad s_2 = \frac{S_2}{V_2} s_1, \qquad d = \frac{D_2}{V_2} s_1.$$

In other words the new portfolio is to consist of stock of company 2 and of bonds in the proportions $S_2/V_2$ and $D_2/V_2$, respectively. The return from the stock in the new portfolio will be a fraction $s_2/S_2$ of the total return to stockholders of company 2, which is $(X - rD_2)$, and the return from the bonds will be $rd$. Making use of (7), the total return from the portfolio, $Y_2$, can be expressed as follows:

$$Y_2 = \frac{s_2}{S_2}(X - rD_2) + rd = \frac{s_1}{V_2}(X - rD_2) + r\frac{D_2}{V_2}s_1 = \frac{s_1}{V_2}X = \alpha\frac{s_1}{V_2}X$$

(since $s_1 = \alpha S_1$). Comparing $Y_2$ with $Y_1$ we see that, if $V_2 < S_1 \equiv V_1$, then $Y_2$ will exceed $Y_1$. Hence it pays the holders of company 1's shares to sell these holdings and replace them with a mixed portfolio containing an appropriate fraction of the shares of company 2.

The acquisition of a mixed portfolio of stock of a levered company $j$ and of bonds in the proportion $S_j/V_j$ and $D_j/V_j$ respectively, may be regarded as an operation which "undoes" the leverage, giving access to an appropriate fraction of the unlevered return $X_j$. It is this possibility of undoing leverage which prevents the value of levered firms from being consistently less than those of unlevered firms, or more generally prevents the average cost of capital $\overline{X}_j/V_j$ from being systematically higher for levered than for nonlevered companies in the same class. Since we have already shown that arbitrage will also prevent $V_2$ from being larger than $V_1$, we can conclude that in equilibrium we must have $V_2 = V_1$, as stated in Proposition I.

*Proposition II.*   From Proposition I we can derive the following proposition concerning the rate of return on common stock in companies whose capital structure includes some debt: the expected rate of return or yield, $i$, on the stock of any company $j$ belonging to the $k$th class is a linear function of leverage as follows:

(8) $$i_j = \rho_k + (\rho_k - r)D_j/S_j.$$

That is, *the expected yield of a share of stock is equal to the appropriate capitalization rate $\rho_k$ for a pure equity stream in the class, plus a premium related to financial risk equal to the debt-to-equity ratio times the spread between $\rho_k$ and $r$.* Or equivalently, the market price of any share of stock is given by capitalizing its expected return at the continuously variable rate $i_j$ of (8).[12]

A number of writers have stated close equivalents of our Proposition I although by appealing to intuition rather than by attempting a proof and only to insist immediately that the results were not applicable to the actual

---

[12] To illustrate, suppose $\overline{X} = 1000$, $D = 4000$, $r = 5$ per cent and $\rho_k = 10$ per cent. These values imply that $V = 10,000$ and $S = 6000$ by virtue of Proposition I. The expected yield or rate of return per share is then:

$$i = \frac{1000 - 200}{6000} = .1 + (.1 - .05)\frac{4000}{6000} = 13\tfrac{1}{3} \text{ per cent.}$$

capital markets.[13] Proposition II, however, so far as we have been able to discover is new.[14] To establish it we first note that by definition, the expected rate of return, $i$, is given by:

$$(9) \qquad i_j \equiv \frac{\overline{X}_j - rD_j}{S_j}.$$

From Proposition I, equation (3), we know that:

$$\overline{X}_j = \rho_k(S_j + D_j).$$

Substituting in (9) and simplifying, we obtain equation (8).

C. SOME QUALIFICATIONS AND EXTENSIONS OF THE BASIC PROPOSITIONS

The methods and results developed so far can be extended in a number of useful directions, of which we shall consider here only three: (1) allowing for a corporate profits tax under which interest payments are deductible; (2) recognizing the existence of a multiplicity of bonds and interest rates; and (3) acknowledging the presence of market imperfections which might interfere with the process of arbitrage. The first two will be examined briefly in this section with some further attention given to the tax problem in Section II. Market imperfections will be discussed in Part D of this section in the course of a comparison of our results with those of received doctrines in the field of finance.

*Effects of the present method of taxing corporations.* The deduction of interest in computing taxable corporate profits will prevent the arbitrage process from making the value of all firms in a given class proportional to the expected returns generated by their physical assets. Instead, it can be shown (by the same type of proof used for the original version of Proposition I) that the market values of firms in each class must be proportional in equilibrium to their expected return net of taxes (that is, to the sum of the interest paid and expected net stockholder income). This means we must replace each $\overline{X}_j$ in the original versions of Propositions I and II with a new variable $\overline{X}_j^\tau$ representing the total income net of taxes generated by the firm:

$$(10) \qquad \overline{X}_j^\tau \equiv (\overline{X}_j - rD_j)(1 - \tau) + rD_j \equiv \overline{\pi}_j^\tau + rD_j,$$

[13] See, for example, J. B. Williams [21, esp. pp. 72–73]; David Durand [3]; and W. A. Morton [15]. None of these writers describe in any detail the mechanism which is supposed to keep the average cost of capital constant under changes in capital structure. They seem, however, to be visualizing the equilibrating mechanism in terms of switches by investors between stocks and bonds as the yields of each get out of line with their "riskiness." This is an argument quite different from the pure arbitrage mechanism underlying our proof, and the difference is crucial. Regarding Proposition I as resting on investors' attitudes toward risk leads inevitably to a misunderstanding of many factors influencing relative yields such as, for example, limitations on the portfolio composition of financial institutions. See below, esp. Section I.D.

[14] Morton does make reference to a linear yield function but only "... for the sake of simplicity and because the particular function used makes no essential difference in my conclusions" [15, p. 443, note 2].

where $\bar{\pi}_j^\tau$ represents the expected net income accruing to the common stockholders and $\tau$ stands for the average rate of corporate income tax.[15]

After making these substitutions, the propositions, when adjusted for taxes, continue to have the same form as their originals. That is, Proposition I becomes:

(11) $$\frac{\bar{X}_j^\tau}{V_j} = \rho_k^\tau, \text{ for any firm in class } k,$$

and Proposition II becomes

(12) $$i_j \equiv \frac{\bar{\pi}_j^\tau}{S_j} = \rho_j^\tau + (\rho_k^\tau - r)D_j/S_j$$

where $\rho_k^\tau$ is the capitalization rate for income net of taxes in class $k$.

Although the form of the propositions is unaffected, certain interpretations must be changed. In particular, the after-tax capitalization rate $\rho_k^\tau$ can no longer be identified with the "average cost of capital" which is $\rho_k = \bar{X}_j/V_j$. The difference between $\rho_k^\tau$ and the "true" average cost of capital, as we shall see, is a matter of some relevance in connection with investment planning within the firm (Section II). For the description of market behavior, however, which is our immediate concern here, the distinction is not essential. To simplify presentation, therefore, and to preserve continuity with the terminology in the standard literature we shall continue in this section to refer to $\rho_k^\tau$ as the average cost of capital, though strictly speaking this identification is correct only in the absence of taxes.

*Effects of a plurality of bonds and interest rates.* In existing capital markets we find not one, but a whole family of interest rates varying with maturity, with the technical provisions of the loan and, what is most relevant for present purposes, with the financial condition of the borrower.[16] Economic theory and market experience both suggest that the yields demanded by lenders tend to increase with the debt-equity ratio of the borrowing firm (or individual). If so, and if we can assume as a first approximation that this yield curve, $r = r(D/S)$, whatever its precise form, is the same for all borrowers, then we can readily extend our propositions to the case of a rising supply curve for borrowed funds.[17]

---

[15] For simplicity, we shall ignore throughout the tiny element of progression in our present corporate tax and treat $\tau$ as a constant independent of $(X_j - rD_j)$.

[16] We shall not consider here the extension of the analysis to encompass the time structure of interest rates. Although some of the problems posed by the time structure can be handled within our comparative statics framework, an adequate discussion would require a separate paper.

[17] We can also develop a theory of bond valuation along lines essentially parallel to those followed for the case of shares. We conjecture that the curve of bond yields as a function of leverage will turn out to be a nonlinear one in contrast to the linear function of leverage developed for common shares. However, we would also expect that the rate of increase in the yield on new issues would not be substantial in practice. This relatively slow rise would reflect the fact that interest rate increases by themselves can never be completely satisfactory

Proposition I is actually unaffected in form and interpretation by the fact that the rate of interest may rise with leverage; while the average cost of *borrowed* funds will tend to increase as debt rises, the average cost of funds from *all* sources will still be independent of leverage (apart from the tax effect). This conclusion follows directly from the ability of those who engage in arbitrage to undo the leverage in any financial structure by acquiring an appropriately mixed portfolio of bonds and stocks. Because of this ability, the ratio of earnings (*before* interest charges) to market value—*i.e.*, the average cost of capital from all sources—must be the same for all firms in a given class.[18] In other words, the increased cost of borrowed funds as leverage increases will tend to be offset by a corresponding reduction in the yield of common stock. This seemingly paradoxical result will be examined more closely below in connection with Proposition II.

A significant modification of Proposition I would be required only if the yield curve $r = r(D/S)$ were different for different borrowers, as might happen if creditors had marked preferences for the securities of a particular class of debtors. If, for example, corporations as a class were able to borrow at lower rates than individuals having equivalent personal leverage, then the average cost of capital to corporations might fall slightly, as leverage increased over some range, in reflection of this differential. In evaluating this possibility, however, remember that the relevant interest rate for our arbitrage operators is the rate on brokers' loans and, historically, that rate has not been noticeably higher than representative corporate rates.[19] The

---

to creditors as compensation for their increased risk. Such increases may simply serve to raise $r$ so high relative to $\rho$ that they become self-defeating by giving rise to a situation in which even normal fluctuations in earnings may force the company into bankruptcy. The difficulty of borrowing more, therefore, tends to show up in the usual case not so much in higher rates as in the form of increasingly stringent restrictions imposed on the company's management and finances by the creditors; and ultimately in a complete inability to obtain new borrowed funds, at least from the institutional investors who normally set the standards in the market for bonds.

[18] One normally minor qualification might be noted. Once we relax the assumption that all bonds have certain yields, our arbitrage operator faces the danger of something comparable to " gambler's ruin." That is, there is always the possibility that an otherwise sound concern—one whose long-run expected income is greater than its interest liability—might be forced into liquidation as a result of a run of temporary losses. Since reorganization generally involves costs, and because the operation of the firm may be hampered during the period of reorganization with lasting unfavorable effects on earnings prospects, we might perhaps expect heavily levered companies to sell at a slight discount relative to less heavily indebted companies of the same class.

[19] Under normal conditions, moreover, a substantial part of the arbitrage process could be expected to take the form, not of having the arbitrage operators go into debt on personal account to put the required leverage into their portfolios, but simply of having them reduce the amount of corporate bonds they already hold when they acquire underpriced unlevered stock. Margin requirements are also somewhat less of an obstacle to maintaining any desired degree of leverage in a portfolio than might be thought at first glance. Leverage could be largely restored in the face of higher margin requirements by switching to stocks having more leverage at the corporate level.

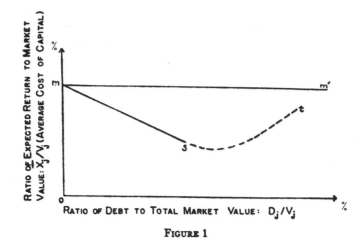

FIGURE 1

operations of holding companies and investment trusts which can borrow on terms comparable to operating companies represent still another force which could be expected to wipe out any marked or prolonged advantages from holding levered stocks.[20]

Although Proposition I remains unaffected as long as the yield curve is the same for all borrowers, the relation between common stock yields and leverage will no longer be the strictly linear one given by the original Proposition II. If $r$ increases with leverage, the yield $i$ will still tend to rise as $D/S$ increases, but at a decreasing rather than a constant rate. Beyond some high level of leverage, depending on the exact form of the interest function, the yield may even start to fall.[21] The relation between $i$ and $D/S$ could conceivably take the form indicated by the curve $MD$ in Figure 2, although in practice the curvature would be much less pronounced. By contrast, with a constant rate of interest, the relation would be linear throughout as shown by line $MM'$, Figure 2.

The downward sloping part of the curve $MD$ perhaps requires some comment since it may be hard to imagine why investors, other than those who like lotteries, would purchase stocks in this range. Remember, however, that the yield curve of Proposition II is a consequence of the more fundamental Proposition I. Should the demand by the risk-lovers prove insufficient to keep

[20] An extreme form of inequality between borrowing and lending rates occurs, of course, in the case of preferred stocks, which can not be directly issued by individuals on personal account. Here again, however, we would expect that the operations of investment corporations plus the ability of arbitrage operators to sell off their holdings of preferred stocks would act to prevent the emergence of any substantial premiums (for this reason) on capital structures containing preferred stocks. Nor are preferred stocks so far removed from bonds as to make it impossible for arbitrage operators to approximate closely the risk and leverage of a corporate preferred stock by incurring a somewhat smaller debt on personal account.

[21] Since new lenders are unlikely to permit this much leverage (cf. note 17), this range of the curve is likely to be occupied by companies whose earnings prospects have fallen substantially since the time when their debts were issued.

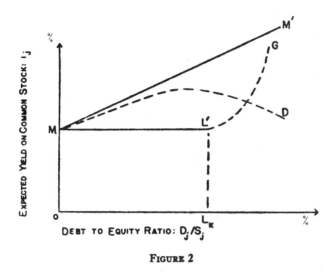

**FIGURE 2**

the market to the peculiar yield-curve $MD$, this demand would be reinforced by the action of arbitrage operators. The latter would find it profitable to own a pro-rata share of the firm as a whole by holding its stock *and* bonds, the lower yield of the shares being thus offset by the higher return on bonds.

D. THE RELATION OF PROPOSITIONS I AND Iı TO CURRENT DOCTRINES

The propositions we have developed with respect to the valuation of firms and shares appear to be substantially at variance with current doctrines in the field of finance. The main differences between our view and the current view are summarized graphically in Figures 1 and 2. Our Proposition I [equation (4)] asserts that the average cost of capital, $\overline{X}^\tau_j/V_j$, is a constant for all firms $j$ in class $k$, independently of their financial structure. This implies that, if we were to take a sample of firms in a given class, and if for each firm we were to plot the ratio of expected return to market value against some measure of leverage or financial structure, the points would tend to fall on a horizontal straight line with intercept $\rho^\tau_k$, like the solid line $mm'$ in Figure 1.[22] From Proposition I we derived Proposition II [equation (8)] which, taking the simplest version with $r$ constant, asserts that, for all firms in a class, the relation between the yield on common stock and financial structure, measured by $D_j/S_j$, will approximate a straight line with slope $(\rho^\tau_k - r)$ and intercept $\rho^\tau_k$. This relationship is shown as the solid line $MM'$ in Figure 2, to which reference has been made earlier.[23]

[22] In Figure 1 the measure of leverage used is $D_j/V_j$ (the ratio of debt to market value) rather than $D_j/S_j$ (the ratio of debt to equity), the concept used in the analytical development. The $D_j/V_j$ measure is introduced at this point because it simplifies comparison and contrast of our view with the traditional position.

[23] The line $MM'$ in Figure 2 has been drawn with a positive slope on the assumption that $\rho^\tau_k > r$, a condition which will normally obtain. Our Proposition II as given in equation (8)

By contrast, the conventional view among finance specialists appears to start from the proposition that, other things equal, the earnings-price ratio (or its reciprocal, the times-earnings multiplier) of a firm's common stock will normally be only slightly affected by "moderate" amounts of debt in the firm's capital structure.[24] Translated into our notation, it asserts that for any firm $j$ in the class $k$,

$$(13) \qquad \frac{\overline{X}_j^{\tau} - rD_j}{S_j} \equiv \frac{\overline{\pi}_j^{\tau}}{S_j} = i_k^*, \text{ a constant for } \frac{D_j}{S_j} \leq L_k$$

or, equivalently,

$$(14) \qquad S_j = \overline{\pi}_j^{\tau}/i_k^*.$$

Here $i_k^*$ represents the capitalization rate or earnings-price ratio on the common stock and $L_k$ denotes some amount of leverage regarded as the maximum "reasonable" amount for firms of the class $k$. This assumed relationship between yield and leverage is the horizontal solid line $ML'$ of Figure 2. Beyond $L'$, the yield will presumably rise sharply as the market discounts "excessive" trading on the equity. This possibility of a rising range for high leverages is indicated by the broken-line segment $L'G$ in the figure.[25]

If the value of shares were really given by (14) then the over-all market value of the firm must be:

$$(16) \qquad V_j \equiv S_j + D_j = \frac{\overline{X}_j^{\tau} - rD_j}{i_k^*} + D_j = \frac{\overline{X}_j^{\tau}}{i_k^*} + \frac{(i_k^* - r)D_j}{i_k^*}$$

That is, for any given level of expected total returns after taxes ($\overline{X}_j^{\tau}$) and assuming, as seems natural, that $i_k^* > r$, the value of the firm must tend to *rise* with debt;[26] whereas our Proposition I asserts that the value of the firm is completely independent of the capital structure. Another way of contrasting our position with the traditional one is in terms of the cost of capital. Solving (16) for $\overline{X}_j^{\tau}/V_j$ yields:

$$(17) \qquad \overline{X}_j^{\tau}/V_j = i_k^* - (i_k^* - r)D_j/V_j.$$

According to this equation, the average cost of capital is not independent of

---

would continue to be valid, of course, even in the unlikely event that $\rho_k^{\tau} < r$, but the slope of $MM'$ would be negative.

[24] See, *e.g.*, Graham and Dodd [6, pp. 464–66]. Without doing violence to this position, we can bring out its implications more sharply by ignoring the qualification and treating the yield as a virtual constant over the relevant range. See in this connection the discussion in Durand [3, esp. pp. 225–37] of what he calls the "net income method" of valuation.

[25] To make it easier to see some of the implications of this hypothesis as well as to prepare the ground for later statistical testing, it will be helpful to assume that the notion of a critical limit on leverage beyond which yields rise rapidly, can be epitomized by a quadratic relation of the form:

$$(15) \qquad \overline{\pi}_j^{\tau}/S_j = i_k^* + \beta(D_j/S_j) + \alpha(D_j/S_j)^2, \qquad \alpha > 0.$$

[26] For a typical discussion of how a promoter can, supposedly, increase the market value of a firm by recourse to debt issues, see W. J. Eiteman [4, esp. pp. 11–13].

capital structure as we have argued, but should tend to *fall* with increasing leverage, at least within the relevant range of moderate debt ratios, as shown by the line *ms* in Figure 1. Or to put it in more familiar terms, debt-financing should be "cheaper" than equity-financing if not carried too far.

When we also allow for the possibility of a rising range of stock yields for large values of leverage, we obtain a U-shaped curve like *mst* in Figure 1.[27] That a yield-curve for stocks of the form *ML'G* in Figure 2 implies a U-shaped cost-of-capital curve has, of course, been recognized by many writers. A natural further step has been to suggest that the capital structure corresponding to the trough of the U is an "optimal capital structure" towards which management ought to strive in the best interests of the stockholders.[28] According to our model, by contrast, no such optimal structure exists—all structures being equivalent from the point of view of the cost of capital.

Although the falling, or at least U-shaped, cost-of-capital function is in one form or another the dominant view in the literature, the ultimate rationale of that view is by no means clear. The crucial element in the position—that the expected earnings-price ratio of the stock is largely unaffected by leverage up to some conventional limit—is rarely even regarded as something which requires explanation. It is usually simply taken for granted or it is merely asserted that this is the way the market behaves.[29] To the extent that the constant earnings-price ratio has a rationale at all we suspect that it reflects in most cases the feeling that moderate amounts of debt in "sound" corporations do not really add very much to the "riskiness" of the stock. Since the extra risk is slight, it seems natural to suppose that firms will not have to pay noticeably higher yields in order to induce investors to hold the stock.[30]

A more sophisticated line of argument has been advanced by David

---

[27] The U-shaped nature of the cost-of-capital curve can be exhibited explicitly if the yield curve for shares as a function of leverage can be approximated by equation (15) of footnote 25. From that equation, multiplying both sides by $S_j$ we obtain: $\bar{\pi}_j^s = \bar{X}_j^s - rD_j = i_k^* S_j + \beta D_j + \alpha D_j^2 / S_j$ or, adding and subtracting $i_k^* D_k$ from the right-hand side and collecting terms,

$$(18) \qquad \bar{X}_j^s = i_k^*(S_j + D_j) + (\beta + r - i_k^*)D_j + \alpha D_j^2 / S_j.$$

Dividing (18) by $V_j$ gives an expression for the cost of capital:

$$(19) \qquad \bar{X}_j^s / V_j = i_k^* - (i_k^* - r - \beta)D_j / V_j + \alpha D_j^2 / S_j V_j = i_k^* - (i_k^* - r - \beta)D_j / V_j + \alpha (D_j / V_j)^2 / (1 - D_j / V_j)$$

which is clearly U-shaped since $\alpha$ is supposed to be positive.

[28] For a typical statement see S. M. Robbins [16, p. 307]. See also Graham and Dodd [6, pp. 468–74].

[29] See *e.g.*, Graham and Dodd [6, p. 466].

[30] A typical statement is the following by Guthmann and Dougall [7, p. 245]: "Theoretically it might be argued that the increased hazard from using bonds and preferred stocks would counterbalance this additional income and so prevent the common stock from being more attractive than when it had a lower return but fewer prior obligations. In practice, the extra earnings from 'trading on the equity' are often regarded by investors as more than sufficient to serve as a 'premium for risk' when the proportions of the several securities are judiciously mixed."

Durand [3, pp. 231–33]. He suggests that because insurance companies and certain other important institutional investors are restricted to debt securities, nonfinancial corporations are able to borrow from them at interest rates which are lower than would be required to compensate creditors in a free market. Thus, while he would presumably agree with our conclusions that stockholders could not gain from leverage in an unconstrained market, he concludes that they can gain under present institutional arrangements. This gain would arise by virtue of the "safety superpremium" which lenders are willing to pay corporations for the privilege of lending.[31]

The defective link in both the traditional and the Durand version of the argument lies in the confusion between investors' subjective risk preferences and their objective market opportunities. Our Propositions I and II, as noted earlier, do not depend for their validity on any assumption about individual risk preferences. Nor do they involve any assertion as to what is an adequate compensation to investors for assuming a given degree of risk. They rely merely on the fact that a given commodity cannot consistently sell at more than one price in the market; or more precisely that the price of a commodity representing a "bundle" of two other commodities cannot be consistently different from the weighted average of the prices of the two components (the weights being equal to the proportion of the two commodities in the bundle).

An analogy may be helpful at this point. The relations between $1/\rho_k$, the price per dollar of an unlevered stream in class $k$; $1/r$, the price per dollar of a sure stream, and $1/i_j$, the price per dollar of a levered stream $j$, in the $k$th class, are essentially the same as those between, respectively, the price of whole milk, the price of butter fat, and the price of milk which has been thinned out by skimming off some of the butter fat. Our Proposition I states that a firm cannot reduce the cost of capital—i.e., increase the market value of the stream it generates—by securing part of its capital through the sale of bonds, even though debt money appears to be cheaper. This assertion is equivalent to the proposition that, under perfect markets, a dairy farmer cannot in general earn more for the milk he produces by skimming some of the butter fat and selling it separately, even though butter fat per unit weight, sells for more than whole milk. The advantage from skimming the milk rather than selling whole milk would be purely illusory; for what would be gained from selling the high-priced butter fat would be lost in selling the low-priced residue of thinned milk. Similarly our Proposition II—that the price per dollar of a levered stream falls as leverage increases—is an exact analogue of

[31] Like Durand, Morton [15] contends "that the actual market deviates from [Proposition I] by giving a changing over-all cost of money at different points of the [leverage] scale" (p. 443, note 2, inserts ours), but the basis for this contention is nowhere clearly stated. Judging by the great emphasis given to the lack of mobility of investment funds between stocks and bonds and to the psychological and institutional pressures toward debt portfolios (see pp. 444–51 and especially his discussion of the optimal capital structure on p. 453) he would seem to be taking a position very similar to that of Durand above.

the statement that the price per gallon of thinned milk falls continuously as more butter fat is skimmed off.[32]

It is clear that this last assertion is true as long as butter fat is worth more per unit weight than whole milk, and it holds even if, for many consumers, taking a little cream out of the milk (adding a little leverage to the stock) does not detract noticeably from the taste (does not add noticeably to the risk). Furthermore the argument remains valid even in the face of institutional limitations of the type envisaged by Durand. For suppose that a large fraction of the population habitually dines in restaurants which are required by law to serve only cream in lieu of milk (entrust their savings to institutional investors who can only buy bonds). To be sure the price of butter fat will then tend to be higher in relation to that of skimmed milk than in the absence of such restrictions (the rate of interest will tend to be lower), and this will benefit people who eat at home and who like skim milk (who manage their own portfolio and are able and willing to take risk). But it will still be the case that a farmer cannot gain by skimming some of the butter fat and selling it separately (firm cannot reduce the cost of capital by recourse to borrowed funds).[33]

Our propositions can be regarded as the extension of the classical theory of markets to the particular case of the capital markets. Those who hold the current view—whether they realize it or not—must assume not merely that there are lags and frictions in the equilibrating process—a feeling we certainly

---

[32] Let $M$ denote the quantity of whole milk, $B/M$ the proportion of butter fat in the whole milk, and let $p_M$, $p_B$ and $p_\alpha$ denote, respectively, the price per unit weight of whole milk, butter fat and thinned milk from which a fraction $\alpha$ of the butter fat has been skimmed off. We then have the fundamental perfect market relation:

(a)
$$p_\alpha(M - \alpha B) + p_B \, \alpha B = p_M M, \qquad 0 \leq \alpha \leq 1,$$

stating that total receipts will be the same amount $p_M M$, independently of the amount $\alpha B$ of butter fat that may have been sold separately. Since $p_M$ corresponds to $1/\rho$, $p_B$ to $1/r$, $p_\alpha$ to $1/i$, $M$ to $\bar{X}$ and $\alpha B$ to $rD$, (a) is equivalent to Proposition I, $S + D = \bar{X}/\rho$. From (a) we derive:

(b)
$$p_\alpha = p_M \frac{M}{M - \alpha B} - p_B \frac{\alpha B}{M - \alpha B}$$

which gives the price of thinned milk as an explicit function of the proportion of butter fat skimmed off; the function decreasing as long as $p_B > p_M$. From (a) also follows:

(c)
$$1/p_\alpha = 1/p_M + (1/p_M - 1/p_B) \frac{p_B \, \alpha B}{p_\alpha(M - \alpha B)}$$

which is the exact analogue of Proposition II, as given by (8).

[33] The reader who likes parables will find that the analogy with interrelated commodity markets can be pushed a good deal farther than we have done in the text. For instance, the effect of changes in the market rate of interest on the over-all cost of capital is the same as the effect of a change in the price of butter on the price of whole milk. Similarly, just as the relation between the prices of skim milk and butter fat influences the kind of cows that will be reared, so the relation between $i$ and $r$ influences the kind of ventures that will be undertaken. If people like butter we shall have Guernseys; if they are willing to pay a high price for safety, this will encourage ventures which promise smaller but less uncertain streams per dollar of physical assets.

share,[34] claiming for our propositions only that they describe the central tendency around which observations will scatter—but also that there are large and *systematic* imperfections in the market which permanently bias the outcome. This is an assumption that economists, at any rate, will instinctively eye with some skepticism.

In any event, whether such prolonged, systematic departures from equilibrium really exist or whether our propositions are better descriptions of long-run market behavior can be settled only by empirical research. Before going on to the theory of investment it may be helpful, therefore, to look at the evidence.

### E.   SOME PRELIMINARY EVIDENCE ON THE BASIC PROPOSITIONS

Unfortunately the evidence which has been assembled so far is amazingly skimpy. Indeed, we have been able to locate only two recent studies—and these of rather limited scope—which were designed to throw light on the issue. Pending the results of more comprehensive tests which we hope will soon be available, we shall review briefly such evidence as is provided by the two studies in question: (1) an analysis of the relation between security yields and financial structure for some 43 large electric utilities by F. B. Allen [1], and (2) a parallel (unpublished) study by Robert Smith [19], for 42 oil companies designed to test whether Allen's rather striking results would be found in an industry with very different characteristics.[35] The Allen study is based on average figures for the years 1947 and 1948, while the Smith study relates to the single year 1953.

*The effect of leverage on the cost of capital.* According to the received view, as shown in equation (17) the average cost of capital, $\overline{X}^{\tau}/V$, should decline linearly with leverage as measured by the ratio $D/V$, at least through most of the relevant range.[36] According to Proposition I, the average cost of capital within a given class $k$ should tend to have the same value $\rho_k^{\tau}$ independently of the degree of leverage. A simple test of the merits of the two alternative hypotheses can thus be carried out by correlating $\overline{X}^{\tau}/V$ with $D/V$. If the traditional view is correct, the correlation should be significantly negative; if our view represents a better approximation to reality, then the correlation should not be significantly different from zero.

---

[34] Several specific examples of the failure of the arbitrage mechanism can be found in Graham and Dodd [6, *e.g.*, pp. 646–48]. The price discrepancy described on pp. 646–47 is particularly curious since it persists even today despite the fact that a whole generation of security analysts has been brought up on this book!

[35] We wish to express our thanks to both writers for making available to us some of their original worksheets. In addition to these recent studies there is a frequently cited (but apparently seldom read) study by the Federal Communications Commission in 1938 [22] which purports to show the existence of an optimal capital structure or range of structures (in the sense defined above) for public utilities in the 1930's. By current standards for statistical investigations, however, this study cannot be regarded as having any real evidential value for the problem at hand.

[36] We shall simplify our notation in this section by dropping the subscript $j$ used to denote a particular firm wherever this will not lead to confusion.

Both studies provide information about the average value of $D$—the market value of bonds and preferred stock—and of $V$—the market value of all securities.[37] From these data we can readily compute the ratio $D/V$ and this ratio (expressed as a percentage) is represented by the symbol $d$ in the regression equations below. The measurement of the variable $\overline{X}^\tau/V$, however, presents serious difficulties. Strictly speaking, the numerator should measure the expected returns net of taxes, but this is a variable on which no direct information is available. As an approximation, we have followed both authors and used (1) the average value of actual net returns in 1947 and 1948 for Allen's utilites; and (2) actual net returns in 1953 for Smith's oil companies. Net return is defined in both cases as the sum of interest, preferred dividends and stockholders' income net of corporate income taxes. Although this approximation to expected returns is undoubtedly very crude, there is no reason to believe that it will systematically bias the test in so far as the sign of the regression coefficient is concerned. The roughness of the approximation, however, will tend to make for a wide scatter. Also contributing to the scatter is the crudeness of the industrial classification, since especially within the sample of oil companies, the assumption that all the firms belong to the same class in our sense, is at best only approximately valid.

Denoting by $x$ our approximation to $\overline{X}^\tau/V$ (expressed, like $d$, as a percentage), the results of the tests are as follows:

Electric Utilities $\quad x = 5.3 + .006d \quad\quad r = .12$
$$(\pm .008)$$

Oil Companies $\quad x = 8.5 + .006d \quad\quad r = .04.$
$$(\pm .024)$$

The data underlying these equations are also shown in scatter diagram form in Figures 3 and 4.

The results of these tests are clearly favorable to our hypothesis. Both correlation coefficients are very close to zero and not statistically significant. Furthermore, the implications of the traditional view fail to be supported even with respect to the sign of the correlation. The data in short provide no

---

[37] Note that for purposes of this test preferred stocks, since they represent an *expected* fixed obligation, are properly classified with bonds even though the tax status of preferred dividends is different from that of interest payments and even though preferred dividends are really fixed only as to their maximum in any year. Some difficulty of classification does arise in the case of convertible preferred stocks (and convertible bonds) selling at a substantial premium, but fortunately very few such issues were involved for the companies included in the two studies. Smith included bank loans and certain other short-term obligations (at book values) in his data on oil company debts and this treatment is perhaps open to some question. However, the amounts involved were relatively small and check computations showed that their elimination would lead to only minor differences in the test results.

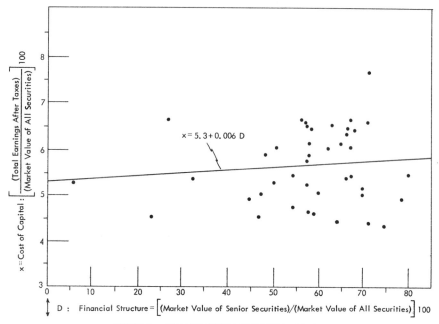

FIGURE 3.   COST OF CAPITAL IN RELATION TO FINANCIAL
STRUCTURE FOR 43 ELECTRIC UTILITIES, 1947–48

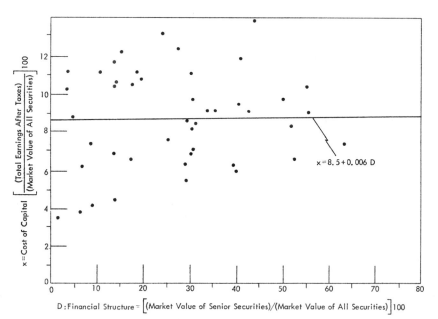

FIGURE 4.   COST OF CAPITAL IN RELATION TO FINANCIAL
STRUCTURE FOR 42 OIL COMPANIES, 1953

evidence of any tendency for the cost of capital to fall as the debt ratio increases.[38]

It should also be apparent from the scatter diagrams that there is no hint of a curvilinear, U-shaped, relation of the kind which is widely believed to hold between the cost of capital and leverage. This graphical impression was confirmed by statistical tests which showed that for both industries the curvature was not significantly different from zero, its sign actually being opposite to that hypothesized.[39]

Note also that according to our model, the constant terms of the regression equations are measures of $\rho_k^\tau$, the capitalization rates for unlevered streams and hence the average cost of capital in the classes in question. The estimates of 8.5 per cent for the oil companies as against 5.3 per cent for electric utilities appear to accord well with a priori expectations, both in absolute value and relative spread.

*The effect of leverage on common stock yields.* According to our Proposition II—see equation (12) and Figure 2—the expected yield on common stock, $\pi^\tau/S$, in any given class, should tend to increase with leverage as measured by the ratio $D/S$. The relation should tend to be linear and with positive slope through most of the relevant range (as in the curve $MM'$ of Figure 2), though it might tend to flatten out if we move far enough to the right (as in the curve $MD'$), to the extent that high leverage tends to drive up the cost of senior capital. According to the conventional view, the yield

---

[38] It may be argued that a test of the kind used is biased against the traditional view. The fact that both sides of the regression equation are divided by the variable $V$ which may be subject to random variation might tend to impart a positive bias to the correlation. As a check on the results presented in the text, we have, therefore, carried out a supplementary test based on equation (16). This equation shows that, if the traditional view is correct, the market value of a company should, for given $\bar{X}^\tau$, increase with debt through most of the relevant range; according to our model the market value should be uncorrelated with $D$, given $\bar{X}^\tau$. Because of wide variations in the size of the firms included in our samples, all variables must be divided by a suitable scale factor in order to avoid spurious results in carrying out a test of equation (16). The factor we have used is the book value of the firm denoted by $A$. The hypothesis tested thus takes the specific form:

$$V/A = a + b(\bar{X}^\tau/A) + c(D/A)$$

and the numerator of the ratio $X^\tau/A$ is again approximated by actual net returns. The partial correlation between $V/A$ and $D/A$ should now be positive according to the traditional view and zero according to our model. Although division by $A$ should, if anything, bias the results in favor of the traditional hypothesis, the partial correlation turns out to be only .03 for the oil companies and $-.28$ for the electric utilities. Neither of these coefficients is significantly different from zero and the larger one even has the wrong sign.

[39] The tests consisted of fitting to the data the equation (19) of footnote 27. As shown there, it follows from the U-shaped hypothesis that the coefficient $\alpha$ of the variable $(D/V)^2/(1 - D/V)$, denoted hereafter by $d^*$, should be significant and positive. The following regression equations and partials were obtained:

Electric Utilities    $x = 5.0 + .017d - .003d^*$; $r_{xd^*.d} = -.15$

Oil Companies    $x = 8.0 + .05d - .03d^*$; $r_{xd^*.d} = -.14$.

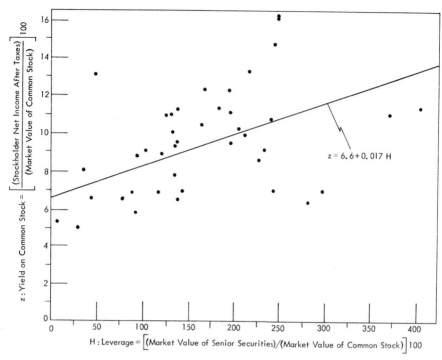

FIGURE 5.　YIELD ON COMMON STOCK IN RELATION TO
LEVERAGE FOR 43 ELECTRIC UTILITIES, 1947−48

curve as a function of leverage should be a horizontal straight line (like $ML'$) through most of the relevant range; far enough to the right, the yield may tend to rise at an increasing rate. Here again, a straight-forward correlation—in this case between $\bar{\pi}^\tau/S$ and $D/S$—can provide a test of the two positions. If our view is correct, the correlation should be significantly positive; if the traditional view is correct, the correlation should be negligible.

Subject to the same qualifications noted above in connection with $\bar{X}^\tau$, we can approximate $\bar{\pi}^\tau$ by actual stockholder net income.[40] Letting $z$ denote in

[40] As indicated earlier, Smith's data were for the single year 1953. Since the use of a single year's profits as a measure of expected profits might be open to objection we collected profit data for 1952 for the same companies and based the computation of $\bar{\pi}^\tau/S$ on the average of the two years. The value of $\bar{\pi}^\tau/S$ was obtained from the formula:

$$\left( \text{net earnings in 1952} \cdot \frac{\text{assets in '53}}{\text{assets in '52}} + \text{net earnings in 1953} \right) \frac{1}{2}$$

$$\div \text{ (average market value of common stock in '53).}$$

The asset adjustment was introduced as rough allowance for the effects of possible growth in the size of the firm. It might be added that the correlation computed with $\bar{\pi}^\tau/S$ based on net profits in 1953 alone was found to be only slightly smaller, namely .50.

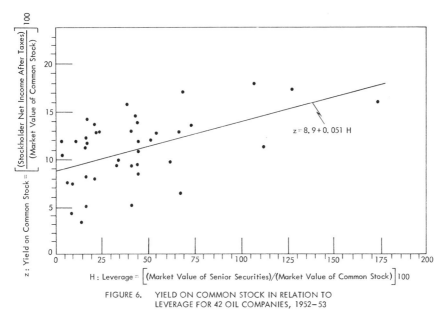

FIGURE 6.   YIELD ON COMMON STOCK IN RELATION TO
LEVERAGE FOR 42 OIL COMPANIES, 1952–53

each case the approximation to $\bar{\pi}^\tau/S$ (expressed as a percentage) and letting $h$ denote the ratio $D/S$ (also in percentage terms) the following results are obtained:

$$\text{Electric Utilities} \quad z = 6.6 + .017h \qquad r = .53$$
$$(+.004)$$

$$\text{Oil Companies} \quad z = 8.9 + .051h \qquad r = .53.$$
$$(\pm.012)$$

These results are shown in scatter diagram form in Figures 5 and 6.

Here again the implications of our analysis seem to be borne out by the data. Both correlation coefficients are positive and highly significant when account is taken of the substantial sample size. Furthermore, the estimates of the coefficients of the equations seem to accord reasonably well with our hypothesis. According to equation (12) the constant term should be the value of $\rho_k^\tau$ for the given class while the slope should be $(\rho_k^\tau - r)$. From the test of Proposition I we have seen that for the oil companies the mean value of $\rho_k^\tau$ could be estimated at around 8.7. Since the average yield of senior capital during the period covered was in the order of $3\frac{1}{2}$ per cent, we should expect a constant term of about 8.7 per cent and a slope of just over 5 per cent. These values closely approximate the regression estimates of 8.9 per cent and 5.1 per cent respectively. For the electric utilities, the yield of senior capital was also on the order of $3\frac{1}{2}$ per cent during the test years, but since the estimate of the mean value of $\rho_k^\tau$ from the test of Proposition I was 5.6 per cent, the slope should be just above 2 per cent. The actual regression estimate for the slope of 1.7 per cent is thus somewhat low, but still within one standard error of its theoretical value. Because of this underestimate of the slope and because of the large mean value of leverage ($\bar{h} = 160$ per cent) the regression estimate of the constant term, 6.6 per cent, is somewhat high, although not significantly different from the value of 5.6 per cent obtained in the test of Proposition I.

When we add a square term to the above equations to test for the presence and direction of curvature we obtain the following estimates:

Electric Utilities   $z = 4.6 + .004h - .007h^2$

Oil Companies   $z = 8.5 + .072h - .016h^2.$

For both cases the curvature is negative. In fact, for the electric utilities, where the observations cover a wider range of leverage ratios, the negative coefficient of the square term is actually significant at the 5 per cent level. Negative curvature, as we have seen, runs directly counter to the traditional hypothesis, whereas it can be readily accounted for by our model in terms of rising cost of borrowed funds.[41]

In summary, the empirical evidence we have reviewed seems to be broadly consistent with our model and largely inconsistent with traditional views. Needless to say much more extensive testing will be required before we can firmly conclude that our theory describes market behavior. Caution is indicated especially with regard to our test of Proposition II, partly because of possible statistical pitfalls[42] and partly because not all the factors that might have a systematic effect on stock yields have been considered. In particular, no attempt was made to test the possible influence of the dividend pay-out ratio whose role has tended to receive a great deal of attention in current research and thinking. There are two reasons for this omission. First, our main objective has been to assess the prima facie tenability of *our* model, and in this model, based as it is on rational behavior by investors, dividends per se play no role. Second, in a world in which the policy of dividend stabilization is widespread, there is no simple way of disentangling the true effect of dividend payments on stock prices from their apparent effect, the latter reflecting only the role of dividends as a proxy measure of long-term

[41] That the yield of senior capital tended to rise for utilities as leverage increased is clearly shown in several of the scatter diagrams presented in the published version of Allen's study. This significant negative curvature between stock yields and leverage for utilities may be partly responsible for the fact, previously noted, that the constant in the linear regression is somewhat higher and the slope somewhat lower than implied by equation (12). Note also in connection with the estimate of $\rho_k^\tau$ that the introduction of the quadratic term reduces the constant considerably, pushing it in fact below the a priori expectation of 5.6, though the difference is again not statistically significant.

[42] In our test, *e.g.*, the two variables $z$ and $h$ are both ratios with $S$ appearing in the denominator, which may tend to impart a positive bias to the correlation (*cf.* note 38). Attempts were made to develop alternative tests, but although various possibilities were explored, we have so far been unable to find satisfactory alternatives.

earning anticipations.[43] The difficulties just mentioned are further compounded by possible interrelations between dividend policy and leverage.[44]

## II. IMPLICATIONS OF THE ANALYSIS FOR THE THEORY OF INVESTMENT

### A.  CAPITAL STRUCTURE AND INVESTMENT POLICY

On the basis of our propositions with respect to cost of capital and financial structure (and for the moment neglecting taxes), we can derive the following simple rule for optimal investment policy by the firm:

*Proposition III.* If a firm in class $k$ is acting in the best interest of the stockholders at the time of the decision, it will exploit an investment opportunity if and only if the rate of return on the investment, say $\rho^*$, is as large as or larger than $\rho_k$. That is, *the cut-off point for investment in the firm will in all cases be $\rho_k$ and will be completely unaffected by the type of security used to finance the investment.* Equivalently, we may say that regardless of the financing used, the marginal cost of capital to a firm is equal to the average cost of capital, which is in turn equal to the capitalization rate for an unlevered stream in the class to which the firm belongs.[45]

To establish this result we will consider the three major financing alternatives open to the firm—bonds, retained earnings, and common stock issues—and show that in each case an investment is worth undertaking if, and only if, $\rho^* \geqq \rho_k$.[46]

Consider first the case of an investment financed by the sale of bonds. We know from Proposition I that the market value of the firm before the investment was undertaken was:[47]

$$(20) \qquad V_0 = \overline{X}_0/\rho_k$$

[43] We suggest that failure to appreciate this difficulty is responsible for many fallacious, or at least unwarranted, conclusions about the role of dividends.

[44] In the sample of electric utilities, there is a substantial negative correlation between yields and pay-out ratios, but also between pay-out ratios and leverage, suggesting that either the association of yields and leverage or of yields and pay-out ratios may be (at least partly) spurious. These difficulties however do not arise in the case of the oil industry sample. A preliminary analysis indicates that there is here no significant relation between leverage and pay-out ratios and also no significant correlation (either gross or partial) between yields and pay-out ratios.

[45] The analysis developed in this paper is essentially a comparative-statics, not a dynamic analysis. This note of caution applies with special force to Proposition III. Such problems as those posed by expected changes in $r$ and in $\rho_k$ over time will not be treated here. Although they are in principle amenable to analysis within the general framework we have laid out, such an undertaking is sufficiently complex to deserve separate treatment. *Cf.* note 17.

[46] The extension of the proof to other types of financing, such as the sale of preferred stock or the issuance of stock rights is straightforward.

[47] Since no confusion is likely to arise, we have again, for simplicity, eliminated the subscripts identifying the firm in the equations to follow. Except for $\rho_k$, the subscripts now refer to time periods.

and that the value of the common stock was:

$$(21) \qquad\qquad S_0 = V_0 - D_0 .$$

If now the firm borrows $I$ dollars to finance an investment yielding $\rho^*$, its market value will become:

$$(22) \qquad\qquad V_1 = \frac{\overline{X}_0 + \rho^* I}{\rho_k} = V_0 + \frac{\rho^* I}{\rho_k}$$

and the value of its common stock will be:

$$(23) \qquad S_1 = V_1 - (D_0 + I) = V_0 + \frac{\rho^* I}{\rho_k} - D_0 - I$$

or using equation (21),

$$(24) \qquad\qquad S_1 = S_0 + \frac{\rho^* I}{\rho_k} - I.$$

Hence $S_1 \gtreqless S_0$ as $\rho^* \gtreqless \rho_k$.[48]

To illustrate, suppose the capitalization rate for uncertain streams in the $k$th class is 10 per cent and the rate of interest is 4 per cent. Then if a given company had an expected income of 1,000 and if it were financed entirely by common stock we know from Proposition I that the market value of its stock would be 10,000. Assume now that the managers of the firm discover an investment opportunity which will require an outlay of 100 and which is expected to yield 8 per cent. At first sight this might appear to be a profitable opportunity since the expected return is double the interest cost. If, however, the management borrows the necessary 100 at 4 per cent, the total expected income of the company rises to 1,008 and the market value of the firm to 10,080. But the firm now will have 100 of bonds in its capital structure so that, paradoxically, the market value of the stock must actually be reduced from 10,000 to 9,980 as a consequence of this apparently profitable investment. Or, to put it another way, the gains from being able to tap cheap, borrowed funds are more than offset for the stockholders by the market's discounting of the stock for the added leverage assumed.

Consider next the case of retained earnings. Suppose that in the course of its operations the firm acquired $I$ dollars of cash (without impairing the earning power of its assets). If the cash is distributed as a dividend to the

---

[48] In the case of bond-financing the rate of interest on bonds does not enter explicitly into the decision (assuming the firm borrows at the market rate of interest). This is true, more-over, given the conditions outlined in Section I.C, even though interest rates may be an increasing function of debt outstanding. To the extent that the firm borrowed at a rate other than the market rate the two $I$'s in equation (24) would no longer be identical and an additional gain or loss, as the case might be, would accrue to the shareholders. It might also be noted in passing that permitting the two $I$'s in (24) to take on different values provides a simple method for introducing underwriting expenses into the analysis.

stockholders their wealth $W_0$, after the distribution, will be:

$$(25) \qquad W_0 = S_0 + I = \frac{\overline{X}_0}{\rho_k} - D_0 + I$$

where $\overline{X}_0$ represents the expected return from the assets exclusive of the amount $I$ in question. If however the funds are retained by the company and used to finance new assets whose expected rate of return is $\rho^*$, then the stockholders' wealth would become:

$$(26) \qquad W_1 = S_1 = \frac{\overline{X}_0 + \rho^* I}{\rho_k} - D_0 = S_0 + \frac{\rho^* I}{\rho_k}$$

Clearly $W_1 \gtreqless W_0$ as $\rho^* \gtreqless \rho_k$ so that an investment financed by retained earnings raises the net worth of the owners if and only if $\rho^* > \rho_k$.[49]

Consider finally, the case of common-stock financing. Let $P_0$ denote the current market price per share of stock and assume, for simplicity, that this price reflects currently expected earnings only, that is, it does not reflect any future increase in earnings as a result of the investment under consideration.[50] Then if $N$ is the original number of shares, the price per share is:

$$(27) \qquad P_0 = S_0 / N$$

and the number of new shares, $M$, needed to finance an investment of $I$ dollars is given by:

$$(28) \qquad M = \frac{I}{P_0}.$$

As a result of the investment the market value of the stock becomes:

$$S_1 = \frac{\overline{X}_0 + \rho^* I}{\rho_k} - D_0 = S_0 + \frac{\rho^* I}{\rho_k} = NP_0 + \frac{\rho^* I}{\rho_k}$$

and the price per share:

$$(29) \qquad P_1 = \frac{S_1}{N + M} = \frac{1}{N + M} \left[ NP_0 + \frac{\rho^* I}{\rho_k} \right]$$

[49] The conclusion that $\rho_k$ is the cut-off point for investments financed from internal funds applies not only to undistributed net profits, but to depreciation allowances (and even to the funds represented by the current sale value of any asset or collection of assets). Since the owners can earn $\rho_k$ by investing funds elsewhere in the class, partial or total liquidating distributions should be made whenever the firm cannot achieve a marginal internal rate of return equal to $\rho_k$.

[50] If we assumed that the market price of the stock did reflect the expected higher future earnings (as would be the case if our original set of assumptions above were strictly followed) the analysis would differ slightly in detail, but not in essentials. The cut-off point for new investment would still be $\rho_k$, but where $\rho^* > \rho_k$ the gain to the original owners would be larger than if the stock price were based on the pre-investment expectations only.

Since by equation (28), $I = MP_0$, we can add $MP_0$ and subtract $I$ from the quantity in brackets, obtaining:

$$P_1 = \frac{1}{N + M}\left[(N + M)P_0 + \frac{\rho^* - \rho_k}{\rho_k}I\right]$$

(30)

$$= P_0 + \frac{1}{N + M}\frac{\rho^* - \rho_k}{\rho_k}I > P_0 \text{ if, and only if, } \rho^* > \rho_k.$$

Thus an investment financed by common stock is advantageous to the current stockholders if and only if its yield exceeds the capitalization rate $\rho_k$.

Once again a numerical example may help to illustrate the result and make it clear why the relevant cut-off rate is $\rho_k$ and not the current yield on common stock, $i$. Suppose that $\rho_k$ is 10 per cent, $r$ is 4 per cent, that the original expected income of our company is 1,000 and that management has the opportunity of investing 100 having an expected yield of 12 per cent. If the original capital structure is 50 per cent debt and 50 per cent equity, and 1,000 shares of stock are initially outstanding, then, by Proposition I, the market value of the common stock must be 5,000 or 5 per share. Furthermore, since the interest bill is $.04 \times 5,000 = 200$, the yield on common stock is $800/5,000 = 16$ per cent. It may then appear that financing the additional investment of 100 by issuing 20 shares to outsiders at 5 per share would dilute the equity of the original owners since the 100 promises to yield 12 per cent whereas the common stock is currently yielding 16 per cent. Actually, however, the income of the company would rise to 1,012; the value of the firm to 10,120; and the value of the common stock to 5,120. Since there are now 1,020 shares, each would be worth 5.02 and the wealth of the original stockholders would thus have been increased. What has happened is that the dilution in expected earnings per share (from .80 to .796) has been more than offset, in its effect upon the market price of the shares, by the decrease in leverage.

Our conclusion is, once again, at variance with conventional views,[51] so much so as to be easily misinterpreted. Read hastily, Proposition III seems to imply that the capital structure of a firm is a matter of indifference; and that, consequently, one of the core problems of corporate finance—the problem of the optimal capital structure for a firm—is no problem at all. It may be helpful, therefore, to clear up such possible misunderstandings.

### B.   PROPOSITION III AND FINANCIAL PLANNING BY FIRMS

Misinterpretation of the scope of Proposition III can be avoided by remembering that this Proposition tells us only that the type of instrument used to finance an investment is irrelevant to the question of whether or not

---

[51] In the matter of investment policy under uncertainty there is no single position which represents "accepted" doctrine. For a sample of current formulations, all very different from ours, see Joel Dean [2, esp. Ch. 3], M. Gordon and E. Shapiro [5], and Harry Roberts [17].

the investment is worth while. This does not mean that the owners (or the managers) have no grounds whatever for preferring one financing plan to another; or that there are no other policy or technical issues in finance at the level of the firm.

That grounds for preferring one type of financial structure to another will still exist within the framework of our model can readily be seen for the case of common-stock financing. In general, except for something like a widely publicized oil-strike, we would expect the market to place very heavy weight on current and recent past earnings in forming expectations as to future returns. Hence, if the owners of a firm discovered a major investment opportunity which they felt would yield much more than $\rho_k$, they might well prefer not to finance it via common stock at the then ruling price, because this price may fail to capitalize the new venture. A better course would be a pre-emptive issue of stock (and in this connection it should be remembered that stockholders are free to borrow and buy). Another possibility would be to finance the project initially with debt. Once the project had reflected itself in increased actual earnings, the debt could be retired either with an equity issue at much better prices or through retained earnings. Still another possibility along the same lines might be to combine the two steps by means of a convertible debenture or preferred stock, perhaps with a progressively declining conversion rate. Even such a double-stage financing plan may possibly be regarded as yielding too large a share to outsiders since the new stockholders are, in effect, being given an interest in any similar opportunities the firm may discover in the future. If there is a reasonable prospect that even larger opportunities may arise in the near future and if there is some danger that borrowing now would preclude more borrowing later, the owners might find their interests best protected by splitting off the current opportunity into a separate subsidiary with independent financing. Clearly the problems involved in making the crucial estimates and in planning the optimal financial strategy are by no means trivial, even though they should have no bearing on the basic decision to invest (as long as $\rho^* \geqq \rho_k$).[52]

Another reason why the alternatives in financial plans may not be a matter of indifference arises from the fact that managers are concerned with more than simply furthering the interest of the owners. Such other objectives of the management—which need not be necessarily in conflict with those of the owners—are much more likely to be served by some types of financing arrangements than others. In many forms of borrowing agreements, for example, creditors are able to stipulate terms which the current management may regard as infringing on its prerogatives or restricting its freedom to

[52] Nor can we rule out the possibility that the existing owners, if unable to use a financing plan which protects their interest, may actually prefer to pass up an otherwise profitable venture rather than give outsiders an "excessive" share of the business. It is presumably in situations of this kind that we could justifiably speak of a shortage of "equity capital," though this kind of market imperfection is likely to be of significance only for small or new firms.

maneuver. The creditors might even be able to insist on having a direct voice in the formation of policy.[53] To the extent, therefore, that financial policies have these implications for the management of the firm, something like the utility approach described in the introductory section becomes relevant to financial (as opposed to investment) decision-making. It is, however, the utility functions of the managers per se and not of the owners that are now involved.[54]

In summary, many of the specific considerations which bulk so large in traditional discussions of corporate finance can readily be superimposed on our simple framework without forcing any drastic (and certainly no systematic) alteration of the conclusion which is our principal concern, namely that for investment decisions, the marginal cost of capital is $\rho_k$.

### C.   THE EFFECT OF THE CORPORATE INCOME TAX ON INVESTMENT DECISIONS

In Section I it was shown that when an unintegrated corporate income tax is introduced, the original version of our Proposition I,

$$\overline{X}/V = \rho_k = \text{a constant}$$

must be rewritten as:

(11)
$$\frac{(\overline{X} - rD)(1 - \tau) + rD}{V} = \frac{\overline{X}^\tau}{V} = \rho_k^\tau = \text{a constant.}$$

Throughout Section I we found it convenient to refer to $\overline{X}^\tau/V$ as the cost of capital. The appropriate measure of the cost of capital relevant to investment decisions, however, is the ratio of the expected return *before* taxes to the market value, *i.e.*, $\overline{X}/V$. From (11) above we find:

(31)
$$\frac{\overline{X}}{V} = \frac{\rho_k^\tau - \tau_r(D/V)}{1 - \tau} = \frac{\rho_k^\tau}{1 - \tau}\left[1 - \frac{\tau r D}{\rho_k^\tau V}\right],$$

which shows that the cost of capital now depends on the debt ratio, decreasing, as $D/V$ rises, at the constant rate $\tau r/(1 - \tau)$.[55] Thus, with a corporate income

---

[53] Similar considerations are involved in the matter of dividend policy. Even though the stockholders may be indifferent as to payout policy as long as investment policy is optimal, the management need not be so.  Retained earnings involve far fewer threats to control than any of the alternative sources of funds and, of course, involve no underwriting expense or risk. But against these advantages management must balance the fact that sharp changes in dividend rates, which heavy reliance on retained earnings might imply, may give the impression that a firm's finances are being poorly managed, with consequent threats to the control and professional standing of the management.

[54] In principle, at least, this introduction of management's risk preferences with respect to financing methods would do much to reconcile the apparent conflict between Proposition III and such empirical findings as those of Modigliani and Zeman [14] on the close relation between interest rates and the ratio of new debt to new equity issues; or of John Lintner [12] on the considerable stability in target and actual dividend-payout ratios.

[55] Equation (31) is amenable, in principle, to statistical tests similar to those described in Section I.E. However we have not made any systematic attempt to carry out such tests so far, because neither the Allen nor the Smith study provides the required information. Actually,

tax under which interest is a deductible expense, gains can accrue to stock-holders from having debt in the capital structure, even when capital markets are perfect. The gains however are small, as can be seen from (31), and as will be shown more explicitly below.

From (31) we can develop the tax-adjusted counterpart of Proposition III by interpreting the term $D/V$ in that equation as the proportion of debt used in any additional financing of $V$ dollars. For example, in the case where the financing is entirely by new common stock, $D = 0$ and the required rate of return $\rho_k^S$ on a venture so financed becomes:

$$(32) \qquad \rho_k^S = \frac{\rho_k^\tau}{1 - \tau}.$$

For the other extreme of pure debt financing $D = V$ and the required rate of return, $\rho_k^D$, becomes:

$$(33) \qquad \rho_k^D = \frac{\rho_k^\tau}{1 - \tau}\left[1 - \tau\frac{r}{\rho_k^\tau}\right] = \rho_k^S\left[1 - \tau\frac{r}{\rho_k^\tau}\right] = \rho_k^S - \frac{r}{1 - \tau}r.^{56}$$

For investments financed out of retained earnings, the problem of defining the required rate of return is more difficult since it involves a comparison of the tax consequences to the individual stockholder of receiving a dividend versus having a capital gain. Depending on the time of realization, a capital gain produced by retained earnings may be taxed either at ordinary income tax rates, 50 per cent of these rates, 25 per cent, or zero, if held till death. The rate on any dividends received in the event of a distribution will also be a variable depending on the amount of other income received by the stock-holder, and with the added complications introduced by the current dividend-credit provisions. If we assume that the managers proceed on the basis of reasonable estimates as to the average values of the relevant tax rates for the owners, then the required return for retained earnings $\rho_k^R$ can be shown to be:

$$(34) \qquad \rho_k^R = \rho_k^\tau \frac{1}{1 - \tau}\frac{1 - \tau_d}{1 - \tau_g} = \frac{1 - \tau_d}{1 - \tau_g}\rho_k^S$$

---

Smith's data included a very crude estimate of tax liability, and, using this estimate, we did in fact obtain a negative relation between $\bar{X}/V$ and $D/V$. However, the correlation $(-.28)$ turned out to be significant only at about the 10 per cent level. While this result is not con-clusive, it should be remembered that, according to our theory, the slope of the regression equation should be in any event quite small. In fact, with a value of $\tau$ in the order of .5, and values of $\rho_k^\tau$ and $r$ in the order of 8.5 and 3.5 per cent respectively (cf. Section I.E) an increase in $D/V$ from 0 to 60 per cent (which is, approximately, the range of variation of this variable in the sample) should tend to reduce the average cost of capital only from about 17 to about 15 per cent.

[56] This conclusion does not extend to preferred stocks even though they have been classed with debt issues previously. Since preferred dividends except for a portion of those of public utilities are not in general deductible from the corporate tax, the cut-off point for new financ-ing via preferred stock is exactly the same as that for common stock.

where $\tau_d$ is the assumed rate of personal income tax on dividends and $\tau_g$ is the assumed rate of tax on capital gains.

A numerical illustration may perhaps be helpful in clarifying the relationship between these required rates of return. If we take the following round numbers as representative order-of-magnitude values under present conditions: an after-tax capitalization rate $\rho_k^\tau$ of 10 per cent, a rate of interest on bonds of 4 per cent, a corporate tax rate of 50 per cent, a marginal personal income tax rate on dividends of 40 per cent (corresponding to an income of about \$25,000 on a joint return), and a capital gains rate of 20 per cent (one-half the marginal rate on dividends), then the required rates of return would be: (1) 20 per cent for investments financed entirely by issuance of new common shares; (2) 16 per cent for investments financed entirely by new debt; and (3) 15 per cent for investments financed wholly from internal funds.

These results would seem to have considerable significance for current discussions of the effect of the corporate income tax on financial policy and on investment. Although we cannot explore the implications of the results in any detail here, we should at least like to call attention to the remarkably small difference between the "cost" of equity funds and debt funds. With the numerical values assumed, equity money turned out to be only 25 per cent more expensive than debt money, rather than something on the order of 5 times as expensive as is commonly supposed to be the case.[57] The reason for the wide difference is that the traditional view starts from the position that debt funds are several times cheaper than equity funds even in the absence of taxes, with taxes serving simply to magnify the cost ratio in proportion to the corporate rate. By contrast, in our model in which the repercussions of debt financing on the value of shares are taken into account, the *only* difference in cost is that due to the tax effect, and its magnitude is simply the tax on the "grossed up" interest payment. Not only is this magnitude likely to be small but our analysis yields the further paradoxical implication that the stockholders' gain from, and hence incentive to use, debt financing is actually smaller the lower the rate of interest. In the extreme case where the firm could borrow for practically nothing, the advantage of debt financing would also be practically nothing.

---

[57] See *e.g.*, D. T. Smith [18]. It should also be pointed out that our tax system acts in other ways to reduce the gains from debt financing. Heavy reliance on debt in the capital structure, for example, commits a company to paying out a substantial proportion of its income in the form of interest payments taxable to the owners under the personal income tax. A debt-free company, by contrast, can reinvest in the business all of its (smaller) net income and to this extent subject the owners only to the low capital gains rate (or possibly no tax at all by virtue of the loophole at death). Thus, we should expect a high degree of leverage to be of value to the owners, even in the case of closely held corporations, primarily in cases where their firm was not expected to have much need for additional funds to expand assets and earnings in the future. To the extent that opportunities for growth were available, as they presumably would be for most successful corporations, the interest of the stockholders would tend to be better served by a structure which permitted maximum use of retained earnings.

## III. CONCLUSION

With the development of Proposition III the main objectives we outlined in our introductory discussion have been reached. We have in our Propositions I and II at least the foundations of a theory of the valuation of firms and shares in a world of uncertainty. We have shown, moreover, how this theory can lead to an operational definition of the cost of capital and how that concept can be used in turn as a basis for rational investment decision-making within the firm. Needless to say, however, much remains to be done before the cost of capital can be put away on the shelf among the solved problems. Our approach has been that of static, partial equilibrium analysis. It has assumed among other things a state of atomistic competition in the capital markets and an ease of access of those markets which only a relatively small (though important) group of firms even come close to possessing. These and other drastic simplifications have been necessary in order to come to grips with the problem at all. Having served their purpose they can now be relaxed in the direction of greater realism and relevance, a task in which we hope others interested in this area will wish to share.

## REFERENCES

1. F. B. Allen, "Does Going into Debt Lower the 'Cost of Capital'?," *Analysts Jour.*, Aug. 1954, *10*, 57–61.
2. J. Dean, *Capital Budgeting*. New York 1951.
3. D. Durand, "Costs of Debt and Equity Funds for Business: Trends and Problems of Measurement" in Nat. Bur. Econ. Research, *Conference on Research in Business Finance*. New York 1952, pp. 215–47.
4. W. J. Eiteman, "Financial Aspects of Promotion," in *Essays on Business Finance* by M. W. Waterman and W. J. Eiteman. Ann Arbor, Mich. 1952, pp. 1–17.
5. M. J. Gordon and E. Shapiro, "Capital Equipment Analysis: The Required Rate of Profit," *Manag. Sci.*, Oct. 1956, *3*, 102–10.
6. B. Graham and L. Dodd, *Security Analysis*, 3rd ed. New York 1951.
7. G. Guthmann and H. E. Dougall, *Corporate Financial Policy*, 3rd ed. New York 1955.
8. J. R. Hicks, *Value and Capital*, 2nd ed. Oxford 1946.
9. P. Hunt and M. Williams, *Case Problems in Finance*, rev. ed. Homewood, Ill. 1954.
10. J. M. Keynes, *The General Theory of Employment, Interest and Money*. New York 1936.
11. O. Lange, *Price Flexibility and Employment*. Bloomington, Ind. 1944.
12. J. Lintner, "Distribution of Incomes of Corporations among Dividends, Retained Earnings and Taxes," *Am. Econ. Rev.*, May 1956, *46*, 97–113.
13. F. Lutz and V. Lutz, *The Theory of Investment of the Firm*. Princeton 1951.
14. F. Modigliani and M. Zeman, "The Effect of the Availability of Funds, and the Terms Thereof, on Business Investment" in Nat. Bur. Econ. Research, *Conference on Research in Business Finance*. New York 1952, pp. 263–309.
15. W. A. Morton, "The Structure of the Capital Market and the Price of Money," *Am. Econ. Rev.*, May 1954, *44*, 440–54.
16. S. M. Robbins, *Managing Securities*. Boston 1954.

17. H. V. Roberts, "Current Problems in the Economics of Capital Budgeting," *Jour. Bus.*, 1957, *30* (1), 12–16.
18. D. T. Smith, *Effects of Taxation on Corporate Financial Policy*. Boston 1952.
19. R. Smith, "Cost of Capital in the Oil Industry," (hectograph). Pittsburg: Carnegie Inst. Tech. 1955.
20. H. M. Somers, "'Cost of Money' as the Determinant of Public Utility Rates," *Buffalo Law Rev.*, Spring 1955, **4**, 1–28.
21. J. B. Williams, *The Theory of Investment Value*. Cambridge, Mass. 1938.
22. U.S. Federal Communications Commission, *The Problem of the "Rate of Return" in Public Utility Regulation*. Washington 1938.

## 25. THE COST OF CAPITAL, CORPORATION FINANCE, AND THE THEORY OF INVESTMENT: COMMENT

### DAVID DURAND*

Reprinted from *The American Economic Review*, Vol. *XLIX*, No. 4, (September, 1959), pp. 639–55, by permission of the author and the publisher.

In a recent contribution on security valuation and the cost of capital Franco Modigliani and M. H. Miller [11] (hereafter MM) have enunciated three propositions that contradict widely accepted beliefs and some earlier conclusions of mine [2]. This paper will not attempt to deny these propositions in their own properly limited theoretical context. Instead, it will analyze MM's underlying assumptions, which are subtle and restrictive; and it will indicate some of the difficulties of using these assumptions to support [11, p. 264] "an operational definition of the cost of capital and a workable theory of investment."

Of MM's propositions the first is basic. Proposition I states that, in a perfect market, the total value of all outstanding securities of a firm is independent of its capital structure. More specifically, if firm $j$ has outstanding stock and debt instruments values at $S_j$ and $D_j$ and if its expected average earnings are $\overline{X}_j$ before interest, then the total value of its securities [11, p. 268, equation (3)] is

$$V_j \equiv (S_j + D_j) = \overline{X}_j/\rho_k,$$

where $\rho_k$ is a constant capitalization factor for all firms in "equivalent return" class $k$. In such a class, which [11, p. 266] "plays a strategic role in the rest of the analysis," future net income per share of all firms, though

---

* The author is professor of industrial management, Massachusetts Institute of Technology.

subject to unknown variations, are certain to be perfectly correlated, each with every other.[1]

There are at least four devices that will aid in building a foundation under Proposition I. One is to assume that arbitrage is possible between securities in an equivalent return class. Another is to assume that a "firm" falls into none of the standard categories—proprietorship, partnership, or corporation —but is a sort of hybrid, having marketable securities like a corporation, proration of income like a partnership, and allocation of financial responsibility like neither. A third is to exclude risk. And a fourth is to assume a long-run equilibrium in which stocks sell at book value. But all of these devices are unrealistic, and MM have accepted none of them wholeheartedly. Thus, while they speak of arbitrage, MM describe a process that is not arbitrage at all, but a switch. Or again, they include all firms in one category— calling them corporations, but failing to endow them with distinctively corporate characteristics. They admit risk to the extent of minor uncertainties, but not major hazards. And finally, although they do not discuss the relation between stock prices and book value, some but not all of their treatment of dividend policy seems to assume that stocks sell at book value. This paper will expose the difficulties of justifying Proposition I for real corporations in a world where arbitrage is usually impossible, where substitutes for arbitrage are restrained and risky, and where stocks rarely sell at book value.

## I. PROPOSITION I AND ARBITRAGE: AN ILLUSTRATIVE EXAMPLE

True arbitrage, when possible, is a powerful equalizer; but it is not ordinarily possible in corporate securities. To clarify the issue, this section presents an artificial example of an equivalent return class of corporations in which the possibility of arbitrage will practically guarantee Proposition I; subsequent sections will show how this example fails to account for the real problems of corporation finance.

Petrolease is a fictitious corporation whose business consists in leasing oil properties; it earns $10 per share on the average, all of which it pays out in dividends. Leverfund is a fictitious open-end investment trust, whose assets consist solely of Petrolease shares. It operates under the following conditions, some of which are unusual: (1) for every share of Petrolease that it holds, it must have outstanding one share of its own stock and one $100 bond paying interest at 5 per cent; (2) it incurs no expenses and pays out all earnings; (3) as an open-end fund, it will issue on demand one share and one bond while simultaneously acquiring, by purchase or exchange, a Petrolease

---

[1] MM offer a specific definition for an equivalent return class of debt-free firms [11, p. 266]: namely, "that the return on the shares issued by any firm in any given class is proportional to (and hence perfectly correlated with) the return on the shares of any other firm in the same class." Although MM are not equally specific for indebted firms, the obvious extension is that their returns are perfectly correlated ($Y = A + BX$) but not proportional ($Y = BX$).

share, or it will redeem on demand one share and one bond while divesting itself of a Petrolease share; (4) since it makes no loading charge, the buyer (or seller) of a bond and share pays (or receives) the same combined price that Leverfund pays (or receives) for a share of Petrolease; (5) in the open market, securities of both corporations trade without commissions. As a result of conditions (1) and (2), the income per share of Leverfund averages $5 and is exactly equal to the income per share of Petrolease minus $5. Thus, the incomes per share of Leverfund and Petrolease are prefectly correlated and the two corporations must belong to the same equivalent return class.

The peculiarities of Leverfund and Petrolease guarantee that an approximation to Proposition I will hold between them; together a bond and share of the one must sell for about the same price as a share of the other. Any discrepancy will provide traders with opportunities for profit, the exploitation of which will tend to reduce, and perhaps eventually eliminate, the discrepancy.

The most spectacular opportunity is through arbitrage. If a bond and share of Leverfund are selling in the open market for more than a share of Petrolease, a short-term trader can realize a quick profit by buying, say, 100 shares of Petrolease and simultaneously selling short 100 bonds and shares of Leverfund. Then, at his leisure, he exchanges his long Petrolease shares for Leverfund securities and delivers the latter against his short commitment. A single aggressive arbitrager can thus exert terrific equalizing pressure, for he can continue his operations just as long as any discrepancy remains—even to the extent of buying up and exchanging all outstanding shares of Petrolease.

But note, the effectiveness of this arbitrage depends upon equivalence in exchange between a share of Petrolease and a bond and share of Leverfund, not upon equivalence of income.[2] If, for example, personal income from bond interest were taxed at a lower rate than dividends, astute investors would prefer a bond and share of Leverfund to a share of Petrolease and would regard a price discrepancy as normal. But the arbitragers could still profit by buying Petrolease and selling Leverfund.

MM repeatedly speak of one security as a "perfect substitute" for another merely on the grounds that it represents an equal amount of income. Now, in fact, a share of Petrolease is not a perfect substitute for a bond and share of Leverfund; for one thing, a Petrolease stockholder has no vote for Leverfund directors. But owing to the possibility of exchange, a share of Petrolease is a good enough substitute for a bond and share of Leverfund, and vice versa, to

[2] Arbitrage between Petrolease and Leverfund belongs to the category of "kind" arbitrage. According to Weinstein [14, p. 2], a transaction of this type is defined as "the simultaneous purchase and sale of equivalent articles or securities in the same or different markets." Here the meaning of equivalence is rather special, implying that the articles or securities are essentially different but, "through the terms of their issuance or through special circumstance, may become equal to each other." Later [14, p. 66], Weinstein specifies: "By equivalent securities is meant a convertible bond or stock, a right or option warrant, or a stock of one company which may be exchanged for the stock of the same or another company."

permit the arbitrage operations that assure the validity of Proposition I between the two corporations. The importance of these details becomes apparent if Leverfund is simply transformed into a closed-end trust—bearing, say, the name Closecorp. Then, even though a share of Petrolease still stands behind a bond and share of Closecorp—maintaining income equivalence as with Leverfund—exchange is no longer possible. Neither is arbitrage, and the realization of Proposition I must depend upon other equalizing operations.

One substitute for arbitrage, to be mentioned in passing, is what might be called a hedge position,[3] to provide income without investment. If Closecorp sells at a 5 per cent premium, an operator might sell short 100 bonds and shares, investing the proceeds in 105 shares of Petrolease; then, since the income from 100 shares of Petrolease would suffice exactly to cover interest and dividend requirements on his short position, he would derive as net income the dividends from 5 shares of Petrolease. But this sort of transaction may be hard to arrange, owing to the many restrictions on short selling; and it exposes the operator to numerous risks—including the risk of being caught in a corner (cf. Macaulay [10, pp. vii–viii, 19–20]). Although corners are less frequent than formerly, the recent episode of E. L. Bruce on the American Stock Exchange indicates that some danger is still present.

Another substitute for arbitrage is the switching of investment accounts from comparatively unattractive issues into others that seem to offer a higher return for the same risk. MM commit a common error in confusing switching with arbitrage, but the distinction is important. Arbitrage can be effective if only a few professional traders are alert and aggressive. Switching, however, to be equally effective, may require the active cooperation of a large body of investors.

As an example of switching, suppose that Closecorp stock is selling in the market at 68, Closecorp bonds at 100, and Petrolease stock at 160. According to MM a leverage-loving investor who holds 300 shares of Closecorp stock outright should sell it and buy Petrolease on margin. A switch arranged according to the table below will achieve an increase of $200 in net income

*Before Switching*
300 Closed Corp. at $ 68   value $20,400   yielding $1,500

*After Switching*

| | | | | |
|---|---|---|---|---|
| 340 Petrolease | at 160 | 54,000 | yielding | 3,400 |
| Margin loan at 5% interest[4] | | 34,000 | costing | 1,700 |
| Net investment | | $20,400 | | $1,700 |

---

[3] Perhaps the use of the term "hedge" is a little loose in this context (cf. Weinstein [14, p. 76]).

[4] MM [11, p. 268] assume that the investor pays the same rate on his "bonds" (i.e., margin loan) that Leverfund pays on its bonds.

with no loss of stability; for, by arranging to pay in interest exactly $5 of his dividend receipts from each share of Petrolease, which is what Closecorp pays, the investor assures himself that his net income will exhibit exactly the same percentage fluctuations as Closecorp dividends. From such considerations MM [11, p. 270] "conclude therefore that levered companies cannot command a premium over unlevered companies because investors have the opportunity of putting the equivalent leverage into their portfolio [sic] directly by borrowing on personal account." But this is only a limited opportunity for most investors, who are deterred from aggressive margin buying by the legal and institutional restrictions placed upon it (see Section II) or by its intrinsic risks (see Section III).

Because of these deterrents, Proposition I can be no more than an inequality for Petrolease and Closecorp. In simplest terms, Closecorp securities enjoy a wider market than does Petrolease stock. Almost any investor who would buy a share of Petrolease should find a satisfactory—though not perfect—substitute in a bond and share of Closecorp, and he should willingly switch if the substitute fell to a discount.[5] Thus, as long as investors are fairly alert, Closecorp cannot sell much below Petrolease. But the reverse does not hold. Closecorp stock has a special appeal to risk-takers, and its bonds have a special appeal both to the safety-minded and to those barred from buying stock. For Closecorp to command a premium, it suffices that this specialized demand for its bonds and for its shares should exceed the available supply of these securities. After all, the essential difference between Closecorp and Leverfund is the limitation on the amount of securities that the former can issue in the short run. When Leverfund securities command a premium, the arbitragers can immediately increase the supply by buying up and exchanging Petrolease shares; they cannot do this for Closecorp.

In the long run, of course, Closecorp can expand, issuing more bonds and high-leverage shares to meet the specialized demand for these instruments; and in taking this step it will reap the benefits of low cost capital—that is until it issues enough securities to satisfy the demand. Here, then, is another substitute for arbitrage, which MM have neglected—the financial operations of corporations.

Here, also, is a paradox. If those of us who doubt the existence of equilibria advise corporate managers to remain alert and to exploit every opportunity to reduce their cost of capital by adjusting capital structure, we shall help to establish MM's equilibrium; whereas MM, by offering assurance that these opportunities do not arise, are sabotaging their own goal. Perhaps a realistic resolution to the paradox would be to recognize that any particular functional relation between total security value and capital structure is unlikely to remain stable over the long run—especially if it affords corporations an obvious opportunity to minimize capital cost by adopting one particular structure.

---

[5] There will be a few exceptions—institutions like the College Retirement Equities Fund, which are required to invest only in common stock.

Once the relation is widely recognized, everyone will attempt to exploit it; and a new relation, though not necessarily equilibrium, will result.

In practice this means that those who seek to reduce capital cost by adjusting capital structure must ascertain conditions in the current market, and act rapidly to exploit them. For instance, the stock market decline in September 1946 inaugurated a period of several years in which bonds yields were low and stock yields were high. For the first quarter of 1950, when [2] was in preparation, Standard and Poor's reported yields of 2.6 per cent for high-grade utility bonds as against dividend yields of 5.35 and earnings yields of 8.1 per cent for utility stocks. Those levels offered corporations a golden opportunity to finance with bonds. Nine years later, in the first quarter of 1959, bond yields were up to 4.3 per cent, while dividend yields and earnings yields were down to 3.9 and 5.4 per cent. The ratio of bond yields to stock yields had more than doubled. Thus, utility companies that availed themselves of the opportunity to sell bonds on comparatively favorable terms in 1950 and stock on comparatively favorable terms in 1959 must have acquired their capital at appreciably lower cost than those selling stock in 1950 and bonds in 1959.

## II. MARKET IMPERFECTIONS: RESTRICTIONS ON MARGIN BUYING

MM visualize a highly competitive market, almost but not quite free of restrictions. Specifically, they write [11, pp. 280–81]:

Those who hold the current view—whether they realize it or not—must assume not merely that there are lags and frictions in the equilibrating process—a feeling we certainly share, claiming for our propositions only that they describe the central tendency around which observations will scatter—but also that there are large and *systematic* imperfections in the market which permanently bias the outcome.

Between the "current view" and their own, MM have left much middle ground. Whenever the market deviates from equilibrium, it provides someone with an opportunity for profit. But whom? MM's development of Proposition I, whether they realize it or not, accords investors exclusive rights to profit by giving them full responsibility to correct deviations from equilibrium. But why discriminate against the corporations? One likely reason, not mentioned by MM, is that market imperfections prevent corporations from issuing or redeeming securities as fast as investors can switch accounts. But even so market deviations may resist investors' corrective actions long enough for corporations to partake of the profits, unless the investors' speed is coupled with adequate volume; and a host of institutional restrictions limit the volume of switching operations that investors can arrange on short notice—especially switching from high-leverage stocks held outright into low-leverage stocks on margin, which is MM's prescribed corrective when high-leverage stocks command a premium.

Margin requirements under Regulation T can place a very substantial legal limitation on the volume of corrective margin switching that investors can generate. In the previously mentioned switch from 300 Closecorp outright at 68 into 340 Petrolease on margin at 160, the investor's equity was but 36 per cent of the total holding, which would be legally insufficient under the 90 per cent limitation in effect when this comment was prepared, or even under the 50 per cent limitation when MM published [11]. Of course, an investor with a large portfolio could legalize the transaction by hypothecating some of his other securities against his loan—but only at the expense of reducing his ability to take advantage of similar switching opportunities between other pairs of stocks.

Moreover, even the small amount of margin buying permitted some investors under Regulation T is withheld from many of our largest investors, the institutions. Mutual funds, fire and casualty companies, closed end trusts, life insurance companies, and most personal trust funds are prevented from buying stocks on margin—either by direct prohibitions in their charters or by the rather general acceptance of the prudent man rule. Together these institutional investors command a tremendous volume of investable or invested funds, most of which are simply not available for the purchase of low-leverage shares on margin, even when they fall to a discount.

MM suggest [11, pp. 278–81] that the restrictions under which institutional investors operate are, in effect, only a vehicle through which individual investors express their subjective risk preferences; cautious individuals commit their funds to conservative financial intermediaries. But this is only half the story. Nowadays, investment trusts are set up to pursue a variety of goals. An investor who wishes to plunge can entrust his savings to a high-leverage trust. The trust achieves its leverage not by buying on margin, but by selling bonds; and although the two operations are equivalent in many respects, there is an important difference. A bond issue requires time to arrange! So, if the market remains out of equilibrium long enough to provide investment trusts with extraordinary opportunities to profit by selling bonds, nonfinancial corporations can enjoy the same opportunities.

To sum up, those of us who take a middle-of-the-road view believe neither in a permanent equilibrium nor in a permanent and consistent departure from equilibrium. We suspect that switching operations by investors—hampered as they are by margin restrictions, brokers' commissions, tax considerations, and other institutional limitations—are insufficient in volume to maintain the market anywhere near equilibrium; and we regard the financing operations of nonfinancial corporations as an integral part of any equilibrating process that may be in operation. Even though corporations cannot act with the speed of a floor trader or of an aggressive investor, they can deal in large sums when they do act. Indeed, in June 1958, when MM's paper [11] appeared, margin requirements were at a 3-year low; yet the volume of loans by all commercial banks for purchasing or carrying securities ($5.6 billion reported by the Federal Reserve Board) was slightly less than the funded debt of just one corporate system ($5.7 billion for American Telephone and Telegraph).

## III. THE RISKS OF MARGIN BUYING

MM would argue [11, p. 269] that the investor who switches from an outright position in Closecorp to a margined position in Petrolease incurs no additional risk, because he merely exchanges "one income stream for another stream, identical in all relevant respects but selling at a lower price." But this argument does not apply to corporate stockholders in a world of high risk, though it might apply either to stockholders in a world of low risk or to limited partners in a world of high risk. If Petrolease earnings were absolutely certain to remain above $5 per share, fluctuating only slightly about the $10 average, the income stream from Petrolease on margin would certainly equal the stream from Closecorp outright, and neither the margin lender nor the Closecorp bondholder would run any risk of default. Possibly MM had such safety in mind when they wrote [11, p. 268]: "All bonds (including any debts assumed by households for the purpose of carrying shares) are assumed to yield a constant income per unit of time, and this income is regarded as certain by all traders regardless of the issuer." But this is a strange statement for anyone who addresses himself to the question [11, p. 261]: "What is the 'cost of capital' to a firm in a world in which funds are used to acquire assets whose yields are uncertain, ...?"

In a world where yields are really uncertain, Petrolease income may fall below $5 per share. Indeed, it may cease entirely if the oil wells run dry. If Closecorp were specially chartered as a limited partnership or joint venture with pro-rata allocation of responsibility, the outright holder of Closecorp stock would owe, in the event of financial disaster, as much to Closecorp bondholders as the margined holder of Petrolease would owe to his bank or broker. But as a corporate stockholder, the leverage-loving investor with 300 shares of Closecorp at 68 enjoys most of the benefits of a levered position in Petrolease without all of the attendant risks; for he has limited his liability to the amount of his investment, $20,400. If, however, he follows MM's advice and switches into 340 shares of Petrolease on margin at 160—regulations permitting—he incurs a liability of $34,000 for his margin loan, and his maximum loss increases to $54,400. In practice, of course, he runs little risk of losing the entire $54,400; his bank or broker, in self defense, will sell him out before Petrolease becomes worthless. But this protection against maximum loss greatly increases the risk of lesser loss. In the days when promiscuous margin buying was permitted, a temporary price decline in a generally rising market often resulted in the liquidation of over-extended accounts.

## IV. THE PROBLEM OF RETENTION AND GROWTH

In the switching example, income equivalence between Closecorp and Petrolease depended on the assumption of 100 per cent dividend payout. This would be completely realistic for partnerships, since the law considers that a partner receives his pro-rata share of the firm's income, whether paid out or not; and it is almost realistic for such corporations as regulated investment trusts. But it will not do for corporations at large. MM do not actually assume 100 per cent payout; instead they say [11, p. 266]:

> As will become clear later, as long as management is presumed to be acting in the best interests of the stockholders, retained earnings can be regarded as equivalent to a fully subscribed, pre-emptive issue of common stock. Hence, for present purposes, the division of the stream between cash dividends and retained earnings in any period is a mere detail.

But what do "present purposes" include? A little thought will show that they do not include the delineation of an equivalent return class, which is the cornerstone of MM's argument. Suppose, for example, that two equity-financed corporations earn regularly a definite rate $\rho^*$ on assets of $A$, and that they retain no earnings. Then the assets of each will remain constant at $A$, and the earnings at $A\rho^*$ per year. Earnings per share will be proportional, and the two corporations must belong to the same class. But as soon as one corporation starts to retain earnings and to reinvest them profitably its assets and earnings will begin to increase; and this will suffice to transfer it into a new class, since its earnings per share will now be imperfectly correlated with those of the other corporation.

MM's proposal to regard retentions as a fully subscribed, pre-emptive stock issue will not avoid this difficulty unless stocks sell at book value. Before the corporation of the preceding paragraph started to expand, it earned $A\rho^*$—or $A\rho^*/N$ per share on $N$ shares having book value $B_0 = A/N$. With a capitalization rate of $\rho_k$, the stock had a price of $P_0 = A\rho^*/\rho_k N$ and a ratio to book value of $P_0/B_0 = \rho^*/\rho_k$. Now, in the first year of its expansion, the corporation retains and reinvests $I = A\rho^*X$ to yield the same rate $\rho^*$; and this enables it to earn $A\rho^*(1 + \rho^*X)$. MM wish to regard $I$, the amount retained, as the proceeds of a stock sale, but they neglect to set the price $P_f$ at which this hypothetical transaction is to take place—a detail, perhaps, but an important one! Except when $\rho^* = \rho_k$ and $P_0 = B_0$, no single price $P_f$ will meet both of two requirements: first, to maintain earnings per share unchanged and thus keep the corporation in the same class; and second, to provide a genuine equation between the amount retained and the hypothetical stock issue.

A price of $P_f = B_0$, for example, will meet only the first requirement. At this price the corporation must issue new shares numbering:

$$\text{(1)} \qquad \frac{I}{B_0} = \frac{A\rho^*X}{A/N} = \rho^*NX,$$

and these together with $N$ old shares will show the same earnings,

$$\text{(2)} \qquad \frac{A\rho^*(1 + \rho^*X)}{N(1 + \rho^*X)} = A\rho^*/N,$$

as before expansion. But the price $P_f = B_0$ will not meet the second condition because the hypothetical subscriber to this stock issue is, in effect, forced to acquire shares at $B_0$ when the market price is $P_0$; and he must either enjoy a profit $P_0 - B_0$ or suffer a loss $B_0 - P_0$.

Finding a price $P_f$ to meet the second requirement, by equating a dollar's worth of retentions to a dollar's worth of issued stock, is difficult. Such a price will depend, when $\rho^* \neq \rho_k$ and $P_0 \neq B_0$, on the entire future growth of the corporation; and to obtain a solution, one must stipulate an arbitrary growth pattern. From the standpoint of algebra, one of the more tractable patterns is uniform growth in perpetuity, resulting from the retention and reinvestment each year of a fraction $X$ of earnings to yield precisely $\rho^*$. Then the required price is given by:

$$(3) \qquad P_f = \frac{A\rho^*(1 - N)}{(\rho_k - \rho^*X)N},$$

which is a standard actuarial formula for the present value of an income stream starting at $A\rho^*(1 - X)/N$, growing at a rate $\rho^*X$, and discounted at $\rho_k$ (cf. Todhunter [13, pp. 48–49]). Clearly $P_f$ is independent of retentions only when $\rho^* = \rho_k$; then $P_f = A/N \equiv B_0$. But when $\rho^* > \rho_k$, (3) gives $P_f > B_0$, with $P_f$ approaching infinity as $\rho^*X$ approaches $\rho_k$. Thus in addition to resting on highly artificial assumptions, (3) sometimes leads to absurdities (cf. Durand [5]). Williams [15, pp. 89–94, 129–34] suggests other growth formulae, which are also artificial but avoid the absurdities.

Whether the corporation fails or succeeds in finding, for its hypothetical stock issue, the exact price $P_f$ that meets the second requirement, any choice of $P_f \neq B_0$ will affect its earnings per share and transfer it into a new class.[6] Hence, if MM wish to include in their equivalent return classes companies expanding at various rates, or if they wish to reduce the division of corporate income between dividends and retained earnings to a mere detail, then they must assume some sort of long-run equilibrium in which $\rho^* = \rho_k$ and $P_0 = B_0$. Indeed, they have explicitly [11, pp. 288–91] assumed $\rho^* \geq \rho_k$, on the grounds that investments yielding $\rho^* < \rho_k$ are detrimental to the stockholders. They could equally well have ruled out $\rho^* > \rho_k$ on grounds of competition; if an area of investment opportunity yields $\rho^* > \rho_k$, it will attract additional capital until the discrepancy disappears. Such an argument should be no great hurdle for those who believe that the presence of "large and *systematic* imperfections in the market which permanently bias the outcome … is an assumption that economists, at any rate, will instinctively eye with some skepticism" [11, p. 281].

---

[6] Possibly this argument contains a subtlety that requires explanation. A corporation can, of course, start in a given equivalent return class, go through a period of expansion, and return to the same class at the close of its expansion—even if it earns $\rho^* > \rho_k$ on its investments. But this is not the point. It is the prospect of expansion, not the act itself, that causes the difficulty. Oddly enough, MM recognize [11, p. 290, fn. 50] that a proposed expansion may, because of its potential effect on earnings per share, influence stock prices; but they seem to have overlooked the havoc that this kind of anticipation plays with their concept of an equivalent return class.

Although an outright assumption that $\rho^* = \rho_k$ and $P_0 = B_0$ would have done much to shore up MM's theoretical argument, it would have done nothing to establish this argument as realistic or operational. In the operating world stocks do not sell at book value—not even approximately. A list recently released by the New York Stock Exchange [16] shows great variation in popular stocks—ranging from New York Central, at about one-tenth book value to International Business Machines at about seven times. This is one kind of evidence of market imperfection that is easy to obtain.

In an expanding economy where stock prices deviate from book value, the interaction between the growth rate and the ratio of price to book value is an important dynamic factor bearing on security values and the cost of capital. Writing on the utility industry, where the problem is well recognized, Tatham [12, p. 36] points out that utility stocks in recent years have generally commanded a premium over book value, thus assuring investors of a " potential increase in value and earnings during a period of expansion," which "provides one of the basic attractions of utility common stocks for investment purposes." By this "potential increase" Tatham refers specifically to growth in earnings per share resulting from successive issues of stock above book value; but he could have extended his argument to include expansion financed by borrowing or by retained earnings.[7] All this means that although retentions can often be regarded as a fully subscribed, pre-emptive stock issue, the division of earnings between dividends and retentions is anything but a mere detail when stocks do not sell at book value.

TABLE 1

REGRESSION ANALYSIS OF THE STOCKS OF 25 LARGE BANKS OUTSIDE
NEW YORK CITY, EARLY 1953

| Regression Equations | Residual Sum of Squares |
|---|---|
| $\log_{10}P = .07 + .97 \log_{10}B$ | .151298 |
| $\log_{10}P = .54 + .49 \log_{10}B + .54 \log_{10}E$ | .094283 |
| $\log_{10}P = .96 + .22 \log_{10}B + .91 \log_{10}E + .70 \log_{10}D/E$ | .036081 |

That investors do not in fact regard dividend policy as a mere detail is now attested by considerable empirical evidence (cf. Durand [3] [4], Gordon [6], Graham and Dodd [8, Ch. 34], Johnson, Shapiro, and O'Meara [9]). Table 1 summarizes a regression analysis of price $P$ on book value $B$, earnings

[7] In addition to Tatham, Durand [4, Ch. 4] and Gordon and Shapiro [7] describe the mechanism by which this "potential increase " is realized and discuss its implications for the analysis of cost of capital. MM [11, pp. 288–91] describe the mechanism very clearly, but neglect the implications.

$E$, and dividends $D$, for a group of 25 bank stocks—one of six groups analyzed recently.[8] The special arrangement in the table is designed to show the successive reductions in the residual sum of squares due first to earnings, $E$, and then to the ratio of dividends to earnings, $D/E$. In particular, the reduction due to $D/E$ (i.e., .094283 − .036081 = .058202) is far too great to attribute to chance (since the $F$-ratio .058202 × 21/.036081 = 33.87 far exceeds even the .001 point for 1 and 21 degrees of freedom) and indicates that the payout ratio exerts a significant influence on price—even after the combined influence of book value and earnings have been taken into account. Table 2 summarizes regression analyses of four groups of public utility stocks.[9] Here the ratio of price to book value, $P/B$, is related to earnings over book value, $E/B$, and dividends over earnings, $D/E$. The reduction in the sum of squares is highly significant in the first two groups, but not at all significant in the last two. The combined experience of all groups taken together is significant.

TABLE 2

REGRESSION ANALYSIS OF FOUR GROUPS OF PUBLIC
UTILITY STOCKS (20 STOCKS PER GROUP), EARLY 1955

| Group | Regression Equations | Residual Sum of Squares |
|-------|---------------------|--------------------------|
| I. Northeast | $\log_{10}P/B = 1.18 + .96 \log_{10}E/B$ | .031033 |
| | $\log_{10}P/B = 1.32 + 1.04 \log_{10}E/B = .60 \log_{10}D/E$ | .017997 |
| | $F = 17 \times .013036/.017997 = 12.314$ | .013036 |
| II. Midwest | $\log_{10}P/B = .90 + .70 \log_{10}E/B$ | .019481 |
| | $\log_{10}P/B = 1.16 + .90 \log_{10}E/B + .46 \log_{10}D/E$ | .011770 |
| | $F = 17 \times .007711/.011770 = 11.137$ | .007711 |
| III. West | $\log_{10}P/B = .97 + .77 \log_{10}E/B$ | .042596 |
| | $\log_{10}P/B = 1.11 + .87 \log_{10}E/B + .28 \log_{10}D/E$ | .040625 |
| | $F = 17 \times .001971/.040625 = .825$ | .001971 |
| IV. South | $\log_{10}P/B = 1.13 + .90 \log_{10}E/B$ | .049213 |
| | $\log_{10}P/B = 1.27 + 1.00 \log_{10}E/B + .30 \log_{10}D/E$ | .041994 |
| | $F = 17 \times .007219/.041994 = 2.922$ | .007219 |

[8] For further analysis, see Durand [4]. The original data for this example appear in [4, p. 29, Table 5].

[9] These analyses come from a larger study on public utility stock prices and the cost of capital, financed by a grant from the Sloan Research Fund of the School of Industrial Management, Massachusetts Institute of Technology. The main results have yet to be published. The computations were performed on the I.B.M. 704 computer at the M.I.T. Computation Center.

MM are inclined to scoff at evidence like the above, arguing that [11, pp. 287–88] "in a world in which the policy of dividend stabilization is widespread, there is no simple way of disentangling the true effect of dividend payments on stock prices from their apparent effect, the latter reflecting only the role of dividends as a proxy measure of long-term earning anticipations." Are not MM trying to extinguish the fire by pouring on more fuel? In addition to the true effect, they introduce an apparent effect, which may also influence stock prices and the cost of capital—presumably by creating or correcting wrong impressions. In the earlier and less responsible days of Wall Street, an unscrupulous insider, like General Daniel E. Sickles of the Erie (cf. Dewing [1, p. 744, fn. 6]) might often attempt to mislead the public by manipulating dividends and issuing false earning statements. And even today, when blatant manipulation is far less common, psychological influences remain. If a conscientious corporation manager believes that the public is underestimating the earning power of his company and that a dividend change might improve the public's estimate, should he not make the change? There are many ways, some devious, in which dividend policy can influence stock prices and the cost of capital; and the available evidence indicates conclusively that at least some of them are effective.

Even if the available evidence does not suffice to disentangle all these influences, it offers some interesting hints. The bank stocks covered by Table 1 had an average price about 5 per cent above book value—with a range from 22 per cent below for The National Shawmut to 83 per cent above for the Bank of America. The utility stocks covered by Table 2 all sold above book value—with a range from 11 per cent for Consolidated Edison and Pennsylvania Water and Power to 222 per cent for Scranton Electric. With stocks selling above book value, a dollar retained is worth more than a dollar paid out—as implied earlier in this section—and investors seeking long-term appreciation should prefer stocks paying low dividends. If these investors dominate the market, negative regression coefficients for $D/E$ are the natural result. The positive coefficients in Tables 1 and 2 imply dominance by another type of investor—possibly one who looks at dividend data instead of analyzing the earnings account, but more probably one with a genuine need for regular dividend income (cf. Durand [4, p. 47]). After all, there is a difference between capital gains and income—and especially between unrealized capital gains and realized income. In effect, our evidence on dividend policy is just good enough to be frustrating; it leaves us no doubt whatsoever that dividend policy exerts an influence on stock prices and the cost of capital, while failing to explain precisely how the influence is exerted.

## V. PROBLEMS OF EMPIRICAL ANALYSIS

The empiricist who would investigate the cost of capital to corporations will encounter a host of obstacles, and among the first will be the gathering of reliable and pertinent data. He will find price quotations sometimes hard to acquire and often erratic or nominal—particularly quotations for corporate bonds, most of which are rather inactively traded nowadays, and some of which, the so-called private placements, are not traded at all. He will find dividend rates, although easy enough to ascertain for regular payers like American Telephone and Telegraph, very troublesome when irregular payments, stock dividends, and extras are the rule. And he will find earnings even harder than dividends to ascertain precisely, for they are subject to the vagaries of accounting practice as well as the vicissitudes of business conditions.

Another obstacle, which is crucial for MM's approach, is the difficulty of assembling a sample of corporations capable of supporting a comparative, or cross-section, type of analysis. The empirical analyst will be unable to assemble any sample meeting the rigid requirements of MM's equivalent class; but this in itself is hardly disastrous, since samples showing no variation in dividend policy and growth rate will not yield much information. The real difficulty is to find samples that are reasonably homogeneous in most respects, and yet show enough variation in growth rate, capital structure, and the like to bring out the influence of these factors. One can often find two or three, and sometimes more, corporations with characteristics sufficiently uniform to bear comparative analysis—an approach long known and used by security analysts. But if an analyst restricts his samples in order to keep them homogeneous, he must perforce keep them small; and if he attempts to expand them to the point where they are numerically satisfactory, he must pay a price in lost homogeneity. This problem arose recently in a study of 117 bank stocks (Durand [3] and [4]). A sample of 117 would be large enough to support a respectable cross-section analysis—if it were homogeneous. But a division of this sample into six subsamples, coupled with some tests for heterogeneity, revealed striking differences. Within the subsamples, moreover, there was further evidence of heterogeneity; in fact, a surprisingly large number of banks exhibited characteristics that rendered them virtually unique [4, pp. 19–20 and 60–62].

Taken all together these obstacles of sparse quotations, uncertain dividends, ambiguous earnings, and heterogeneous stock groups rather narrowly limit the ability of the empirical analyst to detect, let alone measure, the various factors affecting cost of capital. Indeed, only the strongest factors are likely to be discernible through the haze of unwanted perturbations; the subtler ones easily remain unnoticed. To date, in fact, dividend payout is one of the few factors that have proved strong enough to be repeatedly discernible; yet its specific influence is neither clear-cut nor easy to interpret. The available evidence appears inadequate to answer most of the interesting questions. Does the typical positive correlation between price and payout imply that investors are using dividend data to forecast company prospects or merely expressing an honest preference for cash income? To what extent is the price-payout relation obfuscated by growth-conscious investors, who prefer retentions to income? Can one measure reliably the price-payout relation for individual companies? And how does the conscientious manager set dividend policy to accommodate a medley of present and potential stockholders in greatly varied personal circumstances and tax brakets?

The influence, if any, of leverage on cost of capital has so far escaped detection in cross sections—both in the oils and utilities mentioned by MM, and in the bank stocks. But in view of the difficulties of empirical analysis, this is merely evidence of lack of evidence. On MM's scatter diagram [11, p. 283, Figure 3], relating cost of capital to financial structure for 43 utilities in 1947–48, the ratio of "total earnings after taxes" to "market value of all securities" (i.e., cost by MM's definition) ranges roughly from $4\frac{1}{4}$ to $7\frac{1}{2}$ per cent, with well over a third of the observations falling outside the range from 5 to $6\frac{1}{2}$ per cent. In the face of so much scatter, could anyone be assured of detecting a consistent variation of, say, $\frac{1}{4}$ per cent? And a variation in capital cost of this magnitude would not be financially insignificant to a corporation manager or a public utilities commission. On assets of $1,000,000,000 savings of $\frac{1}{4}$ per cent would amount to the tidy sum of 2,500,000 per year. I submit that MM's apparently negative cross-section evidence is essentially inconclusive—especially when history provides positive evidence of periods like 1948–50, which were unusually favorable to bond financing, and others like 1958–59, which were unusually favorable to stock financing. The real significance of the lack of evidence in these cross-sections is to warn us that many important questions in corporation finance, the cost of capital, and the theory of investment are not easily answered with available data.

## VI. CONCLUSION

MM have cut out for themselves the extremely difficult, if not impossible, task of being pure and practical at the same time. Starting with a perfect market in a perfect world, they have taken a few steps in the direction of realism; but they have not made significant progress, considering their avowed purpose of achieving an "operational definition of the cost of capital." Their treatment of risk affords, perhaps, the clearest example. In allowing corporate earnings to fluctuate somewhat—presumably about a fairly definite central value—MM have postulated a world that is not 100 per cent riskless; but it is a remarkably safe world—being free from the risk of bond default, margin calls, foreclosures, or major disasters of any sort. In a world so safe, the effect of risk on the cost of capital, corporation finance, or the theory of investment is not apparent.

Or again, MM's treatment of the equilibrating mechanism in an imperfect market is unrealistic and also inconsistent. MM have endowed investors with unrestricted freedom to switch accounts whenever the market deviates from equilibrium; but for undisclosed reasons they do not extend equal freedom to corporations. If MM wish to assume a perfectly free market, they should realize that corporations unhampered by the practical costs and delays of issuing or redeeming securities can immediately exploit any departure from equilibrium, and it is then arguable that investors can never profit by switching accounts because corporate financing activities will maintain an equilibrium in which profitable switching is impossible. To be realistic, we must recognize that switching operations by investors, financing operations by corporations, and even arbitrage operations where possible, are all subject to restrictions—though not the same ones—and that each of these operations will exert some leveling effect on the market in spite of restrictions. A conscientious equilibrium theorist should advise, nay urge, all interested operators—investors or corporations—to exploit their available opportunities as vigorously as possible. MM, however, advise corporations that there is no opportunity to reduce cost of capital by judicious adjustment of capital structure; and thus they promote complacency, a form of market imperfection.

Finally, and most important, MM have underestimated the difficulty of setting up an equivalent return class, which is the cornerstone of their theory. To the practically minded, it is unthinkable to postulate the existence of two or more separate and independent corporations with income streams that can fluctuate at random and yet be perfectly correlated from now until doomsday; and the artificial example of Petrolease and Closecorp, which are not completely independent, provides no exception. But the difficulty goes much deeper. The concept of an equivalent return class, derived from notions of static equilibrium, is not adaptable to a highly dynamic economy in which stocks do not sell at book value.

Indeed, MM's approach to the cost of capital, as a ratio of current earnings to market price, is essentially static. Dynamically speaking, the cost of capital should measure the inducement—in terms of current earnings *plus long-term growth potential*—required to attract new investment fast enough to meet the needs of an expanding economy. This is the approach for a public utility commission desirous of assuring service in a growing community, for a bank supervisor worried lest the deterioration of bank capital ratios may jeopardize the ability of banks to finance expansion, and certainly for anyone concerned with the ability of this nation to maintain its position of economic leadership.

It is not easy to formulate an operational definition of the cost of capital for a dynamic economy where markets are imperfect, where price-to-book-value ratios vary from one-tenth to seven, and where investors and their advisory services discriminate between income and appreciation. Indeed, it may turn out to be impossible. But we shall make more progress in the long run by frankly recognizing the obstacles to achievement than by accepting false goals attainable by ignoring these obstacles.

## REFERENCES

1. A. S. Dewing, *The Financial Policy of Corporations*, 5th ed. New York 1953, Vol. 1.
2. D. Durand, "Costs of Debt and Equity Funds for Business: Trends and Problems of Measurement " in Nat. Bur. Econ. Research, *Conference on Research in Business Finance*, New York 1952, pp. 215–47.

3. ——, "Bank Stocks and the Analysis of Covariance," *Econometrica*, Jan. 1955, *23*, 30–45.

4. ——, *Bank Stock Prices and the Bank Capital Problem*, Occasional Paper 54, Nat. Bur. Econ. Research, New York 1957.

5. ——, "Growth Stocks and the Petersburg Paradox," *Jour. Finance*, Sept. 1957, *12*, 348–63.

6. M. J. Gordon, "Dividends, Earnings, and Stock Prices," *Rev. Econ. Stat.*, May 1959, *41*, 99–105.

7. M. J. Gordon and E. Shapiro, "Capital Equipment Analysis: The Required Rate of Profit," *Manag. Sci.*, Oct. 1956, *3*, 102–10.

8. B. J. Graham and D. L. Dodd in collaboration with C. Tatham, Jr., *Security Analysis*, 3rd ed. New York 1951.

9. L. R. Johnson, E. Shapiro, and J. O'Meara, Jr., "Valuation of Closely Held Stock for Federal Tax Purposes: Approach to an Objective Method," *Univ. Penn. Law Rev.*, Nov. 1951, *100*, 166–95.

10. F. R. Maculay in collaboration with D. Durand, *Short Selling on the New York Stock Exchange* (Twentieth Century Fund, Mimeo.). New York 1951.

11. F. Modigliani and M. H. Miller, "The Cost of Capital, Corporation Finance and the Theory of Investment," *Am. Econ. Rev.*, June 1958, *48*, 261–97.

12. C. Tatham, Jr., "Book Value and Market Prices of Electric Utility Common Stocks," *Analysts Jour.*, Nov. 1953, *9*, 33–36.

13. R. Todhunter, *The Institute of Actuaries' Text-Book on Compound Interest and Annuities Certain*, 4th ed., revised by R. C. Simmonds and T. P. Thompson. Cambridge, England 1937.

14. M. H. Weinstein, *Arbitrage in Securities*. New York and London 1931.

15. J. B. Williams, *The Theory of Investment Value*. Cambridge, Mass. 1938.

16. New York Stock Exchange, "Book Value and Market Value," *The Exchange*, June 1958, *19*, 9–11.

# 26. THE COST OF CAPITAL, CORPORATION FINANCE, AND THE THEORY OF INVESTMENT: REPLY

FRANCO MODIGLIANI
and
MERTON H. MILLER*

Reprinted from *The American Economic Review*, Vol. *XLIX*, No. 4 (September, 1959), pp. 655–69, by permission of the authors and the publisher.

In this reply to the two preceding comments, we shall concentrate on certain issues raised by David Durand. To J. R. Rose we can only apologize for having led him astray by our failure to adjust explicitly the definition of a "class" [3, p. 266, par. 2] when we introduced debt financing (Sec. I.B). We should have said more clearly, in the very beginning perhaps, that what determines membership in a class is the stream generated by the assets held by the firm, not the stream accruing to the *shares*. The two streams, of course, happen to be completely equivalent in our first special case of no borrowing, but only in that case. We hope the above emendation plus a study of Durand's numerical parable of Petrolease, Leverfund and Closecorp will clear up the misunderstanding.

We do not propose to go over Durand's comment point by point partly for reasons of space, and partly because on many issues we have little to add to (or retract from) what we originally wrote. There are, however, four issues where Durand's comments (plus correspondence we have had with many others) have led us to believe that some further elaboration of our model and our approach to the empirical problems might serve a useful purpose.

Before proceeding to this task, however, we should like to remind readers of the considerable areas of agreement between Durand and us which are easy to overlook in critical exchanges of this kind. Despite his sternly critical tone, he agrees (1) that our conclusions, which "contradict widely accepted beliefs" can be regarded as valid at least "in their own properly limited theoretical context" (see p. 640); and (2) that for all the attention that leverage has received in the literature of finance "the influence, if any, of leverage on the cost of capital has so far escaped detection" (p. 652). Not only is there agreement on these basic matters, but Durand's paper represents the kind of thoughtful and thought-provoking response we hoped we would get

* The authors are respectively, Professor and Associate Professor of Economics in the Graduate School of Industrial Administration, Carnegie Institute of Technology. They wish to thank their colleague Gert von der Linde for a number of helpful suggestions.

to the invitation in the closing paragraph of our paper. He has probed carefully to find inadequacies in our treatment of perfect markets, and he has endeavored to explore the implications of certain market imperfections for the usefulness of our approach. We feel, however, that he has not been conspicuously successful on either front, largely because he has focused on the apparent limitations of the perfect market model instead of trying to surmount these limitations by extending our basic approach.

## I. THE ABILITY OF INVESTORS AND SPECULATORS TO ENFORCE PROPOSITION I

Section I of Durand's note is largely devoted to denying that the behavior of investors and speculators can be counted on to enforce Proposition I. Some of the issues raised in his discussion are largely semantic, notably whether certain transactions can or cannot properly be called arbitrage. In our paper, we chose to include under the general heading of arbitrage, the operation of simultaneously selling a commodity and replacing it with a perfect substitute because it has, in common with dictionary arbitrage, two essential features: (1) simultaneous purchase and sale of (2) perfect substitutes. We regret that our stretching of the language has annoyed Durand, who would prefer to confine this word to cases where the commodities bought and resold were identical, rather than merely perfect substitutes. Unfortunately, Durand's stretching of the word "switch" annoys us just as much because it obscures the distinction between our transaction in perfect substitutes—let us call it a "roll-over" for the sake of harmony—and ordinary switches by investors between different securities in response either to changes in tastes or to shifts of the budget line. As we tried to warn readers in our paper [3, especially n. 13] the failure to appreciate this distinction has been responsible for much of the confusion which has surrounded the analysis of capital markets.

Reservations might also be entered about his use of the word "hedge" to describe the operation, closely akin to arbitrage à la Durand-Weinstein, whereby any investor—and not the holders of the overpriced shares only—can exploit a price discrepancy by simultaneously going short on the overpriced shares and long on the undervalued ones. There is little point, however, in pursuing these terminological issues. For, whatever the nomenclature, Durand does not seem to disagree that in perfect markets[1] enough mechanisms are available to investors and speculators to prevent value discrepancies in a class from being more than ephemeral. And, on our part, we entirely agree with him that real world markets are never perfect and hence that conclusions based on the assumption of perfect markets *need not* have empirical validity.

---

[1] The term perfect market is to be taken in its usual sense of implying perfect information and absence of transaction costs. In addition to these standard attributes, we also require for a perfect capital market that the rate of interest (or, more generally, the rate of interest function) be the same for all borrowers and lenders. See [3, p. 268].

In particular, we have always been fully aware of the fact that, because of various "imperfections" and institutional limitations, "home-made" leverage obtained, for example, from margin buying was not identical with corporate leverage.[2] Such home-made leverage may well be inferior in some respects, though there are other respects in which it would seem to have positive advantages over corporate leverage.[3] But, in contrast to Durand, we saw little value in enumerating imperfections or trying to weight the relative merits of the two kinds of leverage. No amount of a priori speculation, we felt, could ever settle the issue of how close the substitutability is between home-made and corporate leverage, to say nothing of how close it would have to be to prevent any significant discrepancies in values from emerging. As is true elsewhere in positive economics, the most effective method of testing alternative assumptions is to test their consequences. If home-made leverage were as poor a substitute for corporate leverage as Durand and traditional doctrines (by implication) suggest, then levered companies would command a substantial premium in the market at least over some not insignificant range of capital structures. "Noise" in the data, of course, may well obscure this premium in particular samples; but if the cost advantages of (permanent) corporate borrowing were as large as traditional discussions suggest, they could and would be detected.[4] All we can say is that so far they haven't been detected; and consequently, implausible as it may seem to finance specialists, the assumption that home-made leverage of one kind or another is serving as a substitute for corporate leverage cannot yet be rejected in discussions of the cost-of-capital problem.

[2] That the concept of home-made leverage as a substitute for corporate leverage is at least not unknown to a large number of investors would seem to be indicated by the reference to it in a popular investment manual [1]. We might remind potential arbitrageurs also that margin buying is not the only way to participate in the equilibrating process. See [3, p. 262, n. 19].

[3] While an individual who pledges securities as collateral runs the risk of losing more than his original equity in the securities, the fact that his general credit stands behind the loan is one reason why interest costs on such loans are as low as they are. By the same token, the existence of limited liability forces lenders to corporations to expect somewhat higher rates and to impose more numerous and severe restrictions on corporate financial (and even operating policies) than would otherwise be the case. Not only are such restrictions unlikely to enhance the earnings prospects of levered corporations, but precisely because they cannot protect the bond-holders against temporary adversity by drafts on the wealth of the stockholders, levered corporations expose their stockholders to the risk of "gambler's ruin." See [3, p. 274, n. 18]. Similar kinds of offsetting advantages and disadvantages arise, for example, from the circumstance that the borrowing in one case may be short-term and in the other, long-term.

[4] It is important to stress that the essentially zero correlation we found between leverage and cost of capital cannot be attributed solely to noise in the data. If noise alone had been responsible, we would not have been likely to get the results we did for our tests of Proposition II (see pp. 285–286) or for the supplementary tests described in note 55. In connection with the interpretation of the empirical findings, it also strikes us to be a matter of little consequence whether the premium on levered capital structures has not been detected because it is not there or only, as Durand suggests, because it is too small to be noticed.

## II. THE ROLE OF FINANCIAL OPERATIONS BY CORPORATIONS

To the above conclusion Durand raises the objection that Proposition I may hold not through the behavior of investors, but as a result of financial operations by corporations. That is, if some financial structures were to command a premium over others, this, he argues, would afford "corporate managers an opportunity to reduce their cost of capital by adjusting capital structures"; and in exploiting such opportunities, they would tend to cause the discrepancies in valuation to disappear. Hence the fact that Proposition I holds need not mean that the cost of capital is independent of financial arrangements; on the contrary, it may tend to hold because the very opposite is true.

The first point to note in connection with this line of reasoning is that it offers no support whatever for the traditional U-shaped cost-of-capital curve, the main target of our paper. For these temporary premiums, arising because the process of adjustment to equilibrium takes time in less than perfect markets, are of an entirely different sort from the permanent premiums on mixed over pure equity structures which are presumed to arise, in the traditional view, from the fact that debt money is always "cheaper" than equity money. In fact, these temporary premiums imply no lasting shape for the market cost-of-capital function, let alone the orthodox U with its unique "optimum." Depending upon where along our equilibrium horizontal line the adjustments happen to be lagging at the moment, we may have a U, an inverted U or any other shape, regular or irregular, namable or unnamable.

The next point that must be stressed is that Durand has failed to indicate explicitly what can be gained by whom and how, through adjustment of capital structures to exploit temporary bumps; or how this adjustment affects our conclusions concerning the cost of capital. As a matter of fact, he has even failed to explain what *he* means by the cost of capital—although, if taken literally, he would seem to be concerned with the cost of capital to management, whatever that might be. Nor has he provided any concrete illustrations to help us understand just what he has in mind. The only illustration given refers not to the exploitation of "bumps" prevailing at a given point of time, but to the exploitation of changes *over time* in bond and stock yields—a quite separate issue which we shall consider later. This failure to be specific is not altogether surprising. Systematic analysis would have disclosed that temporary deviations from the relation between market value and leverage implied by Proposition I, do not significantly affect our conclusions concerning the cost of capital (as defined by us), or otherwise provide management with significant opportunities to benefit stockholders through adjustment of capital structures.[5]

---

[5] While we doubt that even extremely "alert" managements, for reasons to be discussed, can reap important gains for their stockholders by exploiting the bumps, we have no doubts whatever that nonalert managements can produce losses for their stockholders. On this

By way of illustration, suppose that in a given class, total earnings were generally capitalized at 15 per cent and the market rate of interest were 5 per cent. For some reason, however, companies with leverage ratios of around 20 per cent suddenly became so popular with investors that their stocks sold at a premium. Instead of yielding the 17 per cent indicated by our equation (8), these stocks are bid up to the point where they yield only 15 per cent. This, in turn, implies that the ratio of expected return to total market value, $\overline{X}/V$, for such companies is only 13.3 per cent as compared with the 15 per cent prevailing for all other members of the class. Durand would presumably argue that companies with leverage ratios above 20 per cent could raise the total market value of their securities by selling stock and retiring bonds; and vice versa for companies with leverage below 20 per cent. Such operations would increase the supply of stock in the popular leverage range. This, in turn, would tend to satisfy the "specialized demand" and contribute to the disappearance of the premium.

But how and to what extent would this benefit the stockholders of the adjusting corporations? The effect of these manipulations would be to raise the price of their shares for as long as the premium happened to last. Such a temporary price rise, however, could offer a real advantage only to those stockholders who, like our arbitrageurs, were wise enough to dispose of the stock before the premium disappeared. The faithful stockholders would reap no gain at all (and might even be inconvenienced). It is not obvious, therefore, that a management which passed up this kind of opportunity would be derelict or complacent, especially when we take into account the cost and time lags of such capital structure adjustments and their possible conflict with the other policy considerations we mentioned [3, pp. 292–93, Sec. IIB]. And since there are no clear or strong incentives for undertaking these adjustments, little, if anything, would seem to be lost in not considering adjustments on the supply side a significant part of the equilibrating mechanism underlying Proposition I.

We may next inquire: what in our example would be the cost of capital as we have defined it, that is the minimum rate of return required for an investment to be advantageous to the stockholders? The answer to this question may appear, at first sight, to depend on the initial capital structure and on the form of financing to be adopted. The cost of capital would seem to be 13.3 per cent for companies which already have the optimum structure and propose to finance new investment with the currently popular 20 per cent debt-80 per cent equity mixture. For companies with no debt currently, a cut-off rate as low as 5 per cent might seem justified (in the sense that it would raise the market value of the shares) if the firm could, by the debt-financing

_____

point, we actually took some pains in our Section II to warn managers that our statement that capital structure was a matter of indifference did not mean that they should become so complacent as, say, to float stock when the price of their shares was temporarily depressed, or to borrow at interest rates above the minimum obtainable in the market

of such projects, get into the popular leverage range.[6] These appearances, however, are deceptive. For, in so far as debt-free companies are concerned, unless the yield of the investment is sufficiently greater than 15 per cent, it would be possible to increase the market value per share even more by using the debt issue to buy the company's own stock. More to the point, if the bonds are used to finance new investments, then unless the yield of the projects is at least 15 per cent, the value of the stock will actually fall, once the temporary premium disappears, to less than it would have been if the investments had not been undertaken at all. Under these conditions, would Durand really be prepared to conclude that the appropriate cut-off rate for debt-free firms was anything but the same 15 per cent which would prevail everywhere in the class after the random bumps had disappeared?

For firms already in the premium zone, and thus able to finance new investment partly with " overpriced " stock the situation is more complicated. Here it can be shown that any investment yielding less than 15 per cent, but at least 13.3 per cent, might actually be slightly advantageous to the old stockholders (provided they were shrewd enough not to acquire the new issue) even after the temporary premium had disappeared. Their gain, how- ever, is made *entirely* at the expense of new stockholders to whom the management sold the temporarily overpriced shares.[7] Whether or not it is incumbent on management to engage in this sort of "exploitation" is, fortunately, an issue we need not face here since so far no one has been able to point to value discrepancies for an alert management to exploit.[8]

---

[6] If the investment yielded 5 per cent $+ \varepsilon$ ($\varepsilon$ being any positive number), and were financed by bonds at 5 per cent interest, then the expected return to the stockholders would increase precisely by $\varepsilon$. Since the new structure would be in the premium range where the capitaliza- tion rate for common stock is 15 per cent, i.e., the same as the rate prevailing for the original unlevered stock, the undertaking of the investment would increase the market value of the stock by $(\varepsilon/.15)$.

[7] If the new stock issue is acquired by the old owners in proportion to their ownership, the operation will turn out to be damaging to them, the moment the bump disappears unless the investment yields at least 15 per cent. More generally, if the sale of overpriced stock is regarded as undesirable from an ethical and goodwill point of view, recourse must be had to bond or other temporary financing, just as in the reverse case of a temporary undervaluation of the stock discussed in our paper [3, p. 292]; but this course can be justified only if the investment yields no less than 15 per cent. Thus even for companies already in the premium range, there are good reasons for regarding 15 per cent as the appropriate cut-off rate or cost of capital.

[8] Durand's remarks sometimes suggest that he is concerned with another type of market imperfection, the premium attaching not to particular financial structures, but to the securi- ties of individual companies. In this case, the securities of at least some firms would have no " perfect " substitutes. Such firms would be confronted with a partly isolated and protected market entirely analogous to those underlying the theory of monopoly and of monopolistic competition; in fact, the notion of a class would then play the same role, and be subject to the same limitations as the notion of a group in the original Chamberlinian construction. Even for this type of imperfection it is not clear that the interests of the stockholders would be served by exploiting an existing premium through further issues as Durand seems to suggest (p. 643), since such a policy would reduce the market price of the shares.

There remains finally, to consider the issues raised by Durand's only concrete illustration. These issues are of an entirely different nature from the ones just discussed. They have nothing to do with the market imperfections which are supposedly Durand's main concern nor with the U-shaped cost-of-capital curve which was ours. They involve rather, the dynamic aspects of the investment and financing problem which, as repeatedly stated, we did not pretend to cover in our original paper.[9]

In the limited space available here, the most we can do is to point out that the basic conclusion of our static analysis with regard to the cost of capital will remain essentially valid even when we take into account changes over time in the capitalization rates—in so far as these changes are anticipated by the market and hence reflected in the current capitalization rates. That is to say, in general, an investment will be worth undertaking from the point of view of the current owners, if and only if its yield, $\rho^*$, is no smaller than the *current* capitalization rate for the class $\rho_k$.[10] Furthermore, this is so regardless of financial arrangements, in the sense that the criterion will lead to the highest (equilibrium) current market value for the shares no matter how the investment is financed.

Of course, future changes in interest rates and the over-all cost of capital are not always correctly anticipated by the market. Hence even though all capital structures are equally good in terms of *current* market valuations, when unanticipated changes do occur some capital structures will turn out *ex post* to have been preferable. Preferable not in the sense of enabling the *company* to secure its capital at a lower cost—for this is an essentially meaningless concept—but rather in the specific sense of being more advantageous to stockholders who bought in before the change occurred. To illustrate, a 10 per cent fall over time in the market capitalization rate $\rho_k$ in a given class —interest rates and income expectations constant—will increase the total market value, $V$, by 10 per cent; and since the market value of debt is constant, it will increase the market value of the stock, $S$, of levered companies by even more than 10 per cent to an extent increasing with leverage.[11]

But it is one thing to say that if management can successfully guess an unexpected fall (rise) in $\rho_k$ it can reap gains for the stockholders by adopting a levered (unlevered) capital structure, and quite another to suggest that, because of this possibility, management should be encouraged, as it were, to speculate on these changes with the stockholders' money. For such speculation can

---

[9] See e.g., [3, p. 273, n. 16]. We did, however, touch briefly on a certain class of essentially dynamic problems [3, p. 292] with a view not to solving them, but rather to showing how the analysis could be extended to handle them.

[10] The main qualification needed as a result of dynamic considerations is that when the capitalization rate is expected to fall, the static criterion is necessary but not sufficient. There are certain circumstances in which it may be preferable to postpone an investment, if such a postponement is feasible, thereby rejecting the investment now even though it currently meets the static test.

[11] It can be similarly verified that a rise in interest rates—$\rho_k$ constant—will increase $S$ for companies with long-term debt issued before the rise.

also reap losses when the guess is wrong. We cannot help feeling that Durand's stress on the desirability of speculative adjustments is at least partly the wisdom of hindsight. It is easy in 1959 to call attention to the gains that management might have reaped for the stockholders by having a large proportion of debt in 1950 when interest rates were only 2.6 per cent and average stock yields 8.1 per cent, knowing that stock yields fell thereafter to 5.4 per cent and bond yields rose to 4.3 per cent. Apparently, however, it was not so easy in 1950 to see that bond yields were about to rise and stock yields about to fall (or else these changes would have taken place then and there).[12] There is abundant evidence showing how hard it is for anyone to outguess the market consistently and it is obviously impossible for a majority to do so. Consequently, we, at least, are not yet convinced that corporation managers, in choosing their capital structures and planning their investment programs, should give major consideration to the possible windfall gains (or losses) they may earn for the stockholders if the current market consensus about the level of future yields should turn out to be wrong.[13]

## III. DIVIDENDS, GROWTH OPPORTUNITIES AND THE THEORY OF SHARE PRICES

Durand is quite correct in pointing out that we nowhere provided an explicit description of how our model would explain relative share prices in the face of differential opportunities for growth by firms. Our omission, plus his own efforts at filling our gap, have apparently convinced him that our model cannot accomplish this task.

The fact is that the analysis can be extended in fairly straightforward fashion to accommodate growth without requiring any essential modification in the conclusions already established with the simpler model. To have developed this generalization in adequate detail, however, was impossible within the space limitations imposed on the original paper. Nor did it seem wise, in view of the controversial nature of the leverage issue, to open up a

[12] Nor does it follow, as Durand suggests, that managements choosing to issue stock rather than bonds in 1959 have advantaged their stockholders, for that will depend on the *future* course of bond yields and capitalization rates. Actually, to be certain that levered shares fared better than the others between even 1950 and 1959, we should look at the behavior of $\rho_k$, not of the average current yields of shares. From just the information provided by Durand, one cannot rule out the possibility that $\rho_k$ in fact rose in this period, the lower average yield of shares reflecting merely the rise in interest rates. If so, there might have been no net advantage to the stockholders of levered companies since the rise in $\rho_k$ might have offset the favorable effect of rising bond yields!

[13] Note that corporate managers (at least in nonfinancial corporations) who failed to engage in this type of speculation because they felt that it was not properly their function or because it was a task at which they had no comparative advantage, would not be depriving their stockholders of a potential source of gain by their failure to speculate. For, unlike the case of the " bumps," where the gains, if any, could only be reaped by financial adjustments at the corporate level, the shareholder always has the option of speculating on future market movements by arranging his own leverage position.

dividend policy dispute at the same time. Although, again for space reasons, many facets of the problem must be deferred to a forthcoming paper, we shall try to sketch out here at least enough of the theory to make it plain that no inconsistencies or peculiar assumptions about book-values are involved in the generalization.

Consider first the concept of a risk-equivalent "class," the analogue in our analysis to the "industry" of ordinary price theory. In the more general model, two companies will be said to be in the same class at a specific point in time, $t$, if the elements of the streams generated by the physical assets each holds *at time t* are perfectly correlated and proportional. Membership in the class at each point in time is thus to be determined only by reference to the assets held at that point. Hence, there is no contradiction in the fact that firms in the same class are adding to their assets and income at very different rates over time.[14]

Having attached a meaning to the notion of risk-equivalence of differently growing streams we can consider the relative valuation of shares of "equal risk" but different growth potentials.[15] In order to handle, one at a time, the issues raised by Durand, we shall take for granted, until the end of this section, that investors behave rationally and that capital markets are perfect. These assumptions imply, among other things, that investors are concerned only with the total income they receive from a security and are indifferent as to whether this income takes the form of dividends or of capital gains. When such is the case, the market value of any firm will depend only on the earning power of the assets currently held and on the size and relative profitability of the investment opportunities that the firm is expected to undertake in the future.[16] More specifically, let:

[14] Note also that our definition of a class [3, p. 266] reduces to the broader definition above, in the special case in which (a) all firms in the class can acquire future income at the same terms (equivalent growth potentials) and (b) all the managements act in the best interests of the stockholders and hence pursue equivalent investment policies.

[15] In the matter of our treatment of the risk (or more properly the uncertainty) surrounding equity streams, we should like to take strong exception to Durand's observations at several points but especially in his concluding comments on page 653 that our model assumes "a remarkably safe world" and that that is why the "effect of risk on the cost of capital . . . is not apparent." We cannot see how anyone reading our discussion [pp. 265–66] could infer that we are only "Allowing corporate earnings to fluctuate somewhat—presumably about a fairly definite central value" or that we have somehow ruled out "major disaster of any sort." We did, of course, assume in our first model that *bonds* were completely riskless and perhaps this is the basis of his objections. We felt, and still feel, however, that this is an entirely satisfactory first approximation because, if for no other reason, the quantitative restrictions typically imposed by lenders to reduce their risk have in practice been remarkably successful.

Durand's impatience with our notion of a risk-equivalent class even at the level of theory (p. 653) is also puzzling. We hope that those who have tried to face up to the logical difficulties involved in applying the ordinary present-value apparatus (which is certainty analysis) to uncertain streams will recognize some merit in our risk-equivalent class as a method of dealing with some of these well-known difficulties.

[16] See, in this connection, footnote 21 below.

$\overline{X}_j(t)$ = the expected return (in the sense of our note [3, p. 265, n. 6]) of the assets held by firm $j$ at time $t$;

$k_j(t)$ = the expected volume of purchases of new assets by firm $j$ in period $t$, expressed for convenience as a percentage of the expected return on the assets held at $t$;

$\rho_j^*(t)$ = the expected rate of return on the assets acquired at $t$;

$\rho_k$ = the capitalization rate in class $k$ for the uncertain, but "non-growing" stream $\overline{X}_j(0)$ (i.e., one for which $k_j(t) = 0$ for all $t$). Alternatively, $\rho_k$ may be thought of as the yield investors would earn on the securities of a company in the class with no differential earning opportunities (i.e., one for which $\rho_j^*(t) = \rho_k$ for all $t$ regardless of $k_j(t)$).

It can then be readily shown (although the formal proof must be postponed to a forthcoming paper) that the market value of the firm will be given by:

(1) $\quad V_j(0) \equiv S_j(0) + D_j(0)$

$$= \overline{X}_j(0)\left[\sum_{t=0}^{t=\infty}\left(1 + k_j(t)\frac{\overline{X}_j(t)}{\overline{X}_j(0)}\cdot\frac{\rho^*(t) - \rho_k}{\rho_k}\right)(1 + \rho_k)^{-t}\right].$$

It follows further from the first three definitions given above that

$$\frac{\overline{X}_j(t)}{\overline{X}_j(0)}$$

can itself be expressed entirely in terms of the quantities $k_j(\tau)$ and $\rho^*(\tau)$, $\tau = 0, 1, \ldots, t - 1$ by means of the recursive relation:

(2) $\qquad \overline{X}_j(t) = \overline{X}_j(t - 1)[1 + k_j(t - 1)\rho_j^*(t - 1)] \quad t = 1, 2, \ldots, \infty.$

Hence, the value of the infinite summation in the right-hand side of (1) is, in the final analysis, a function of all the $k_j(t)$, $\rho_j^*(t)$ and $\rho_k$ and can be conveniently denoted by $1/\psi_j(k_j(t); \rho_j^*(t); \rho_k)$. We can then rewrite (1) as:

(1') $\qquad V_j(0) = \overline{X}_j(0)/\psi_j(k_j(t); \rho_j^*(t); \rho_k)$

where the function $\psi_j$ is defined by (1) and (2).

Equations (1) and (1') should make clear what is involved in extending our original analysis to encompass growth. Instead of the single capitalization rate for current expected earnings in the class,

$$\frac{\overline{X}_j(0)}{V_j(0)} = \rho_k \text{ for all } i$$

—this rate being also the same as the cost of capital in the class—we now get a multiplicity of composite capitalization rates

$$\frac{\overline{X}_j(0)}{V_j(0)} = \psi_j.^{17}$$

But, and this is the important point, all these composite capitalization rates for current earnings are reducible to the single cost of capital in the class $\rho_k$, and the parameters $\rho_j^*(t)$ and $k_j(t)$ which characterize the opportunities expected to be available and to be exploited by the firm for investing funds at a rate of return higher than the cost of capital, $\rho_k$.[18]

Equations (1) and (1') may also be helpful in making clearer the precise meaning of our assertion [3, p. 266] that, in perfect markets, dividend policy is a "mere detail." This statement has been misunderstood by some readers because they make the tacit, but unwarranted, assumption that the ability of the firm to exploit profitable opportunities is limited by—or at any rate intimately connected with—its dividend policy. This assumption is unwarranted because dividend retention is but one of the many sources through which expansion can be financed. Furthermore, in the absence of market imperfections such as flotation costs, and institutional factors such as tax laws, this source has no advantage or disadvantage over other sources from the point of view of the cost of funds. Hence, the possibility of exploiting opportunities is independent of dividend policy. Once a decision has been made as to which opportunities are to be exploited, the only role of dividend

[17] The function $\psi_j$ can, of course, be specialized by making some definite assumptions about the nature of the $\rho^*{}_j(t)$ and the $k_j(t)$. If, for example, one assumes $\rho^*{}_j(t) = \rho^* = a$ constant, $k_j(t) = k = $ a constant for all $t$, and if one neglects leverage then (1) reduces to:

(2)      $$S_j(0) = \overline{X}_j(0)\frac{1-k}{\rho_k - k\rho^*}$$      ($\rho_k > k\rho^*$ or $\rho^*$, whichever is smaller),

the valuation formula given by Durand. In using this simple specialization one need not be unduly concerned about Durand's "growth stock paradox" (see his reference [5]). The case in which $k\rho^* \geq \rho_k$ is not a *substantive* paradox at all, but an artifact attributable solely to the partial equilibrium nature of his analysis. In a general equilibrium framework (which we shall present in still another forthcoming paper), $\rho_k$, the capitalization rate, is not an independently given constant as in (1) [or the special case (2)], but a *variable*. Its actual value will be whatever is necessary to clear the market, given among other things, the growth opportunities available. If it were really true that for some corporation $k\rho^*$ was expected to remain indefinitely at say, 50 per cent per annum ($k$ being less than one), the $\rho_k$ for all stocks of "equal risk" would have to be at least 50 per cent. From what one knows about stock yields and growth potentials, this hardly seems an event worth worrying about; but it is in no way paradoxical.

[18] The use of the words "rate of return *higher than* $\rho_k$" in the above sentence is correct as long as we can expect all firms to follow an optimal investment policy, for then no firm will ever exploit opportunities yielding less than $\rho_k$. If so, the market price will reflect only the availability of high-yield opportunities and the capitalization rate $X_j(0)/V_j(0)$ will never be larger than $\rho_k$. If, however, we want to take into account the empirically relevant possibility of firms being expected to exploit "unprofitable" opportunities, then the words "higher than $\rho_k$" in the above sentence should be replaced by "different from $\rho_k$." For firms expected to adopt unprofitable investments, the market capitalization may, of course, be higher than $\rho_k$. On this point, see also footnote 19 below.

policy is to determine what proportion of each year's investment $k_j(t)\overline{X}_j(t)$ is to be financed from retained earnings—the equivalent of a fully subscribed preemptive issue—and what proportion from outside sources.[19] Similarly, from the point of view of the stockholder, the only significance of dividend policy is to determine how much of the earnings of the firm will accrue to him in the form of cash, and how much in the form of capital gains (or losses). We need hardly add that this explication of the "irrelevance" of dividend policy is in no way dependent, as Durand repeatedly suggests, on any special assumption about the ratio of price to book value.[20]

## IV. THE EFFECT OF DIVIDENDS ON STOCK PRICES: THE EMPIRICAL FINDINGS AND THEIR INTERPRETATION

We hope that the discussion in the previous section has been sufficiently explicit, even though the formal proofs have been omitted, so that it no longer requires any great act of faith to accept our original conclusion, *viz.*, that in a world of perfect markets and rational behavior, a firm's dividend policy, other things equal, will have no effect either on the value of the firm or its cost of capital. We can then take the next step and enquire whether this conclusion is a valid or useful approximation in real-world capital markets.[21]

[19] Admittedly, this is not what most people have in mind when they bristle at our assertion that dividend policy is a mere detail under perfect capital markets. Their thoughts usually leap immediately to cases of the Montgomery Ward type, in which supposedly everyone but the management felt that a cessation of the hoarding policy and a more generous dividend would have raised the price of the shares. To reason this way, however, is to forget the vital *ceteris paribus*, namely *given the investment policy*. In our terminology, what was at fault was not the dividend policy as such, but the decision to invest in cash (i.e., $\rho^*$ was too low). We doubt, in other words, that the stockholders would have been better served had management decided to finance *the same volume of hoards* not out of retained earnings, but out of new stock issues.

[20] The relation between the market value of a firm and its book value—the latter being defined not in the accounting sense, but in the economic sense of the reproduction cost of a firm's assets—will depend on many things. Some (such as drastic revaluations of a firm's prospects) do not lend themselves readily to further analysis; others (such as the relation of internal yields [the $\rho^*(t)$] to external yields [the $\rho_k$] can be more systematically explored by means of various specializations of equation (1). If, for example, one assumes that $\rho^*_j(t) = \rho_k$ for all $j$ and all $t$ then, with certain minor supplementary assumptions, one can obtain Durand's case of price equal to book-value throughout the class. This case, however (which stands in roughly the same relation to our general formulation as the "no-rent" case stands to the general theory of supply functions) is merely one of a large number of interesting possibilities.

[21] The issue under discussion—whether and to what extent market valuation is affected by current dividend policy—which is a very real issue, should not be confused with a different and entirely empty issue. This is the question whether what is capitalized is the stream of earnings and earning opportunities ratable to a share or a stream of revenues accruing to the holder of the share and consisting of cash dividends plus capital gains. This is an empty issue for it can be readily shown that both of these views, when properly stated and understood, lead to identical implications; in particular, they both imply that, given the investment policy of the firm, market valuation in perfect markets is independent of current dividend payments or long-run payout policy.

On this issue, Durand cites a number of recent empirical studies and presents some results from his own researches which, he claims, leave "no doubt whatsoever that dividend policy exerts an influence on stock prices and the cost of capital." We have to enter a strong dissent; for, as we warned in our paper [3, p. 287 and 288, n. 43] having precisely the studies he mentions in mind, the existing empirical tests are hopelessly inadequate for determining the effect, if any, of payout policy on stock prices or on the cost of capital.

What is the nature of this supposedly irrefutable evidence? It consists, by and large, of cross-section studies in which price is correlated in various ways with dividends and with *current income*. In general, dividends turn out to have high gross and net correlations with price. From this, it is concluded that our valuation formula (1), which involves earnings but not dividends, cannot be an adequate representation of reality. Note, however, that the earnings variable in our equation is not *current* earnings, $X$, but $\overline{X}_o$, the *expected value* of the (uncertain) earnings of the assets currently held. This difference may seem a small one at first glance, but it actually holds the main clue to the puzzle.

For if there is one thing we can assert with confidence about the firms in any sample, it is that the earnings they report for any short period like a year are affected by a great many random disturbances and temporary distortions. (See, in this connection, Durand's comment p. 651.) To the extent that these temporary disturbances are recognized as such, they will, of course, be discounted by investors and will not be reflected in market prices. Current income, in other words, is at best only an approximate and often very imperfect measure of $\overline{X}_o$, the "noise-free" earnings potential upon which rational investors would base their valuations. Furthermore, and this is what causes most of the trouble, there are many other variables which, like $X$, are correlated with (i.e., contain information about) the unobservable but crucial $\overline{X}_o$. In particular, whenever corporations follow a policy of stabilizing dividends—and the excellent studies of Lintner (see, e.g., [2]) leave no doubt that the majority of the publicly held corporations usually do—dividends will contain considerable information about $\overline{X}_o$, possibly even more than $X$. Hence, when one runs regression of price against dividends, either alone or in combination with $X$, significant positive coefficients would result even in a world in which we knew for certain that $\overline{X}_o$ alone was being capitalized and that dividend policy had no independent effect whatever on price.

The following example may clarify the nature of the difficulty. Suppose to take the simplest case, that we have two (unlevered) corporations with $\overline{X}_{01} = \overline{X}_{02} = \$5$ per share and with identical long-run payout policies of 40 per cent. Let us suppose that the market price of each is determined exclusively by "noise-free" earnings. If then, the capitalization rate is .1, both shares sell at \$50. Imagine now that firm 1 suffers a run of bad luck during the current year—or merely that its accountant decides to write off some assets—so that current income falls momentarily to \$3. Since management recognizes the situation as temporary, it does not take the drastic step of cutting its dividend which remains \$2. Firm 2, on the other hand, has had some temporary good fortune which pushes its income up to say \$8. Again, since the extra income is in the nature of a windfall, management does not raise the dividend above \$2, since that would not be maintainable given its 40 per cent payout target. Suppose now, given this situation and the data we have generated, we conduct one of the popular tests and see whether dividend policy affects stock prices. If we compare, say, price-earnings ratios with current dividend-payout ratios, we find:

$$\frac{P_1}{X_1} = \frac{50}{X_{01} + 2} = \frac{50}{3} = 16.667 \qquad \frac{D_1}{X_1} = \frac{2}{3} = .667$$

$$\frac{P_2}{X_2} = \frac{50}{X_{02} + 3} = \frac{50}{8} = 6.25 \qquad \frac{D_2}{X_2} = \frac{2}{8} = .25$$

One would certainly be tempted, from such striking results, to draw the conclusion, which we know to be false in this case, that the payout ratio (dividend policy) does have a marked effect on stock prices.[22] We get these striking results, of course, only because dividends here contain information about $\overline{X}_o$.

It is, of course, one thing to say that the informational content of dividends *could* fully account for the empirical correlations of Durand and others, and quite another to say that it *does*. At the moment, the evidence is insufficient to settle this question, as Durand himself eventually concedes (p. 651). We have some new, and we hope much sharper, tests under development, and we hope others will join us in our attempt to disentangle the two effects. But the task is by no means a simple one and definitive results may be a long time in coming.

But even if more conclusive tests were to provide adequate evidence that the apparent effect of dividends is entirely attributable to the information they convey about long-run earnings prospects, would we not, in any event, be forced to abandon our position that dividend policy has no effect on the cost of capital? That such is not the case can perhaps best be seen by considering another variable frequently used in statistical tests, to wit, the book value per share. Like dividends, this variable shows up well in correlations with $P$ (often even when both $D$ and $X$ are included in the relation). But, unlike $D$, there seems to be little question that the effect of $B$ is wholly informational. Or, to put it in a slightly different way, few specialists these days would argue for book value, as they do for dividends, that because of the demonstrated high correlations with price, a firm could count on raising the price of its

---

[22] For the benefit of sophisticates who know all about the dangers of spurious ratio correlation, we hasten to point out that it is not the use of ratios per se that makes dividends appear to influence price. As we shall show in more detail in our forthcoming paper, in any sample containing substantial numbers of dividend stabilizers, dividends will, in general, appear significant in relation to $X$ regardless of the form of the test.

shares permanently, simply by writing up its book value, if nothing else changed in the situation. The word *permanently* is the important one in this context. For, in view of the customary informational content of book value, we cannot exclude the possibility that its manipulation will temporarily succeed in misleading the market.

What has been said for book value can be repeated for dividends. Because changes in dividend are usually an indication that other things have changed, they may temporarily affect the market even when other things have, in fact, not changed. Indeed, we are quite ready to believe that as many investors were gulled by Daniel Sickles' watered dividends as by Daniel Drew's watered stocks! All we argue is that changes in dividends will have such an effect only in so far as they are not perceived as manipulations and that the effect will be temporary unless the message is confirmed by deeds.

In summary, pending adequate evidence, we are not willing to accept the proposition that dividend manipulations can be exploited to lower permanently the cost of capital. For this proposition would imply either that investors are incurably irrational or that corporate managers really can fool all of the people all of the time.

## V. CONCLUDING REMARKS

We are grateful to Durand for giving us this opportunity to clarify certain points in our paper and to show our approach is actually a good deal more general than he and others seem to have realized. We have been the first to stress that our paper was intended to be no more than the beginning of the attack on the cost of capital and related problems; and we have indicated areas both fundamental and applied in which the implications of our model remain to be totally or partially explored. We are as aware as Durand of the obstacles in the path. But we hope to have shown that Durand's nihilism is premature; that the framework developed in our paper has already permitted some progress; and that it represents at least a promising point of departure for a further systematic attack on the many remaining problems.

## REFERENCES

1. L. Barnes, *Your Investments*. American Research Council, Larchmont, N.Y. 1959.
2. J. Lintner, "Distribution of Incomes of Corporations among Dividends, Retained Earnings and Taxes," *Am. Econ. Rev.*, May 1956, **46,** 97–113.
3. F. Modigliani and M. H. Miller, "The Cost of Capital Corporation Finance and the Theory of Investment," *Am. Econ. Rev.*, June 1958, **48,** 261–97.

# 27. CORPORATE INCOME TAXES AND THE COST OF CAPITAL: A CORRECTION

FRANCO MODIGLIANI
and
MERTON H. MILLER*

Reprinted from *The American Economic Review*, Vol. *LIII*, No. 3, (June, 1963), pp. 433–43, by permission of the authors and the publisher.

The purpose of this communication is to correct an error in our paper "The Cost of Capital, Corporation Finance and the Theory of Investment" (this *Review*, June 1958). In our discussion of the effects of the present method of taxing corporations on the valuation of firms, we said (p. 272):

The deduction of interest in computing taxable corporate profits will prevent the arbitrage process from making the value of all firms in a given class proportional to the expected returns generated by their physical assets. Instead, it can be shown (by the same type of proof used for the original version of Proposition I) that the *market values of firms in each class must be proportional in equilibrium to their expected returns net of taxes* (that is, to the sum of the interest paid and expected net stockholder income). (Italics added.)

The statement in italics, unfortunately, is wrong. For even though one firm may have an *expected* return after taxes (our $\bar{X}^\tau$) twice that of another firm in the same risk-equivalent class, it will not be the case that the *actual* return after taxes (our $X^\tau$) of the first firm will always be twice that of the second, if the two firms have different degrees of leverage.[1] And since the distribution of returns after taxes of the two firms will not be proportional, there can be no "arbitrage" process which forces their values to be proportional to their expected after-tax returns.[2] In fact, it can be shown—and this time it really will be shown—that "arbitrage" will make values within any class a function

---

* The authors are, respectively, Professor of Industrial Management, School of Industrial Management, Massachusetts Institute of Technology, and Professor of Finance, Graduate School of Business, University of Chicago.

[1] With some exceptions, which will be noted when they occur, we shall preserve here both the notation and the terminology of the original paper. A working knowledge of both on the part of the reader will be presumed.

[2] Barring, of course, the trivial case of universal linear utility functions. Note that in deference to Professor Durand (see his Comment on our paper and our reply, this *Review*, Sept. 1959, *49*, 639–69) we here and throughout use quotation marks when referring to arbitrage.

not only of expected after-tax returns, but of the tax rate and the degree of leverage. This means, among other things, that the tax advantages of debt financing are somewhat greater than we originally suggested and, to this extent, the quantitative difference between the valuations implied by our position and by the traditional view is narrowed. It still remains true, however, that under our analysis the tax advantages of debt are the *only* permanent advantages so that the gulf between the two views in matter of interpretation and policy is as wide as ever.

## I. TAXES, LEVERAGE, AND THE PROBABILITY DISTRIBUTION OF AFTER-TAX RETURNS

To see how the distribution of after-tax earnings is affected by leverage, let us again denote by the random variable $X$ the (long-run average) earnings before interest and taxes generated by the currently owned assets of a given firm in some stated risk class, $k$.[3] From our definition of a risk class it follows that $X$ can be expressed in the form $\overline{X}Z$, where $\overline{X}$ is the expected value of $X$, and the random variable $Z = X/\overline{X}$, having the same value for all firms in class $k$, is a drawing from a distribution, say $f_k(Z)$. Hence the random variable $X^\tau$, measuring the after-tax return, can be expressed as:

$-$ *EBiT*

$$(1) \quad X^\tau = (1-\tau)(X - R) + R = (1 - \tau)X + \tau R = (1 - \tau)\,\overline{X}Z + \tau R$$

where $\tau$ is the marginal corporate income tax rate (assumed equal to the average), and $R$ is the interest bill. Since $E(X^\tau) \equiv \overline{X}^\tau = (1 - \tau)\overline{X} + \tau R$ we can substitute $\overline{X}^\tau - \tau R$ for $(1 - \tau)\overline{X}$ in (1) to obtain:

$$(2) \qquad X^\tau = (\overline{X}^\tau - \tau R)Z + \tau R = \overline{X}^\tau\left(1 - \frac{\tau R}{\overline{X}^\tau}\right)Z + \tau R.$$

Thus, if the tax rate is other than zero, the shape of the distribution of $X^\tau$ will depend not only on the " scale " of the stream $\overline{X}^\tau$ and on the distribution of $Z$, but also on the tax rate and the degree of leverage (one measure of which is $R/\overline{X}^\tau$). For example, if $\mathrm{Var}\,(Z) = \sigma^2$, we have:

$$\mathrm{Var}(X^\tau) = \sigma^2(\overline{X}^\tau)^2\left(1 - \tau\,\frac{R}{\overline{X}^\tau}\right)^2$$

[3] Thus our $X$ corresponds essentially to the familiar EBIT concept of the finance literature. The use of EBIT and related "income" concepts as the basis of valuation is strictly valid only when the underlying real assets are assumed to have perpetual lives. In such a case, of course, EBIT and "cash flow" are one and the same. This was, in effect, the interpretation of $X$ we used in the original paper and we shall retain it here both to preserve continuity and for the considerable simplification it permits in the exposition. We should point out, however, that the perpetuity interpretation is much less restrictive than might appear at first glance. Before-tax cash flow and EBIT can also safely be equated even where assets have finite lives as soon as these assets attain a steady state age distribution in which annual replacements equal annual depreciation. The subject of finite lives of assets will be further discussed in connection with the problem of the cut-off rate for investment decisions.

implying that for given $\overline{X}^\tau$ the variance of after-tax returns is smaller, the higher $\tau$ and the degree of leverage.[4]

## II. THE VALUATION OF AFTER-TAX RETURNS

Note from equation (1) that, from the investor's point of view, the long-run average stream of after-tax returns appears as a sum of two components: (1) an uncertain stream $(1 - \tau)\overline{X}Z$; and (2) a sure stream $\tau R$.[5] This suggests that the equilibrium market value of the combined stream can be found by capitalizing each component separately. More precisely, let $\rho^\tau$ be the rate at which the market capitalizes the expected returns net of tax of an unlevered company of size $\overline{X}$ in class $k$, i.e.,

$$\rho^\tau = \frac{(1 - \tau)\overline{X}}{V_U} \quad \text{or} \quad V_U = \frac{(1 - \tau)\overline{X}}{\rho^\tau};^6 \qquad V = \frac{E}{K}$$

and let $r$ be the rate at which the market capitalizes the sure streams generated by debts. For simplicity, assume this rate of interest is a constant independent of the size of the debt so that

$$r = \frac{R}{D} \quad \text{or} \quad D = \frac{R}{r}.^7$$

Then we would expect the value of a levered firm of size $\overline{X}$, with a permanent level of debt $D_L$ in its capital structure, to be given by:

---

[4] It may seem paradoxical at first to say that leverage *reduces* the variability of outcomes, but remember we are here discussing the variability of total returns, interest plus net profits. The variability of stockholder net profits will, of course, be greater in the presence than in the absence of leverage, though relatively less so than in an otherwise comparable world of no taxes. The reasons for this will become clearer after the discussion in the next section.

[5] The statement that $\tau R$—the tax saving per period on the payments—is a sure stream is subject to two qualifications. First, it must be the case that firms can always obtain the tax benefit of their interest deductions either by offsetting them directly against other taxable income in the year incurred; or, in the event no such income is available in any given year, by carrying them backward or forward against past or future taxable earnings; or, in the extreme case, by merger of the firm with (or its sale to) another firm that can utilize the deduction. Second, it must be assumed that the tax rate will remain the same. To the extent that neither of these conditions holds exactly then some uncertainty attaches even to the tax savings, though, of course, it is of a different kind and order from that attaching to the stream generated by the assets. For simplicity, however, we shall here ignore these possible elements of delay or of uncertainty in the tax saving; but it should be kept in mind that this neglect means that the subsequent valuation formulas overstate, if anything, the value of the tax saving for any given permanent level of debt.

[6] Note that here, as in our original paper, we neglect dividend policy and "growth" in the sense of opportunities to invest at a rate of return greater than the market rate of return. These subjects are treated extensively in our paper, "Dividend Policy, Growth and the Valuation of Shares," *Jour. Bus.*, Univ. Chicago, Oct. 1961, 411–33.

[7] Here and throughout, the corresponding formulas when the rate of interest rises with leverage can be obtained merely by substituting $r(L)$ for $r$, where $L$ is some suitable measure of leverage.

(3)
$$V_L = \frac{(1-\tau)\overline{X}}{\rho^\tau} + \frac{\tau R}{r} = V_U + \tau D_L.^8$$

In our original paper we asserted instead that, within a risk class, market value would be proportional to expected after-tax return $\overline{X}^\tau$ (cf. our original equation [11]), which would imply:

(4)
$$V_L = \frac{\overline{X}^\tau}{\rho^\tau} = \frac{(1-\tau)\overline{X}}{\rho^\tau} + \frac{\tau R}{\rho^\tau} = V_U + \frac{r}{\rho^\tau}\tau D_L.$$

We will now show that if (3) does not hold, investors can secure a more efficient portfolio by switching from relatively overvalued to relatively undervalued firms. Suppose first that unlevered firms are overvalued or that

$$V_L - \tau D_L < V_U.$$

An investor holding $m$ dollars of stock in the unlevered company has a right to the fraction $m/V_U$ of the eventual outcome, i.e., has the uncertain income

$$Y_U = \left(\frac{m}{V_U}\right)(1-\tau)\overline{X}Z.$$

Consider now an alternative portfolio obtained by investing $m$ dollars as follows: (1) the portion,

$$m\left(\frac{S_L}{S_L + (1-\tau)D_L}\right),$$

is invested in the stock of the levered firm, $S_L$; and (2) the remaining portion,

$$m\left(\frac{(1-\tau)D_L}{S_L + (1-\tau)D_L}\right),$$

is invested in its bonds. The stock component entitles the holder to a fraction,

$$\frac{m}{S_L + (1-\tau)D_L},$$

of the net profits of the levered company or

$$\left(\frac{m}{S_L + (1-\tau)D_L}\right)[(1-\tau)(\overline{X}Z - R_L)].$$

The holding of bonds yields

$$\left(\frac{m}{S_L + (1-\tau)D_L}\right)[(1-\tau)R_L].$$

[8] The assumption that the debt is permanent is not necessary for the analysis. It is employed here both to maintain continuity with the original model and because it gives an upper bound on the value of the tax saving. See in this connection footnote 5 and footnote 9.

Hence the total outcome is

$$Y_L = \left(\frac{m}{(S_L + (1 - \tau)D_L)}\right)[(1 - \tau)\bar{X}Z]$$

and this will dominate the uncertain income $Y_U$ if (and only if)

$$S_L + (1 - \tau)D_L \equiv S_L + D_L - \tau D_L \equiv V_L - \tau D_L < V_U.$$

Thus, in equilibrium, $V_U$ cannot exceed $V_L - \tau D_L$, for if it did investors would have an incentive to sell shares in the unlevered company and purchase the shares (and bonds) of the levered company.

Suppose now that $V_L - \tau D_L > V_U$. An investment of $m$ dollars in the stock of the levered firm entitles the holder to the outcome

$$Y_L = (m/S_L)[(1 - \tau)(\bar{X}Z - R_L)]$$
$$= (m/S_L)(1 - \tau)\bar{X}Z - (m/S_L)(1 - \tau)R_L.$$

Consider the following alternative portfolio: (1) borrow an amount $(m/S_L)$ $(1 - \tau)D_L$ for which the interest cost will be $(m/S_L)(1 - \tau)R_L$ (assuming, of course, that individuals and corporations can borrow at the same rate, $r$); and (2) invest $m$ plus the amount borrowed, i.e.,

$$m + \frac{m(1 - \tau)D_L}{S_L} = m\frac{S_L + (1 - \tau)D_L}{S_L} = (m/S_L)[V_L - \tau D_L]$$

in the stock of the unlevered firm. The outcome so secured will be

$$(m/S_L)\left(\frac{V_L - \tau D_L}{V_U}\right)(1 - \tau)\bar{X}Z.$$

Subtracting the interest charges on the borrowed funds leaves an income of

$$Y_U = (m/S_L)\left(\frac{V_L - \tau D_L}{V_U}\right)(1 - \tau)\bar{X}Z - (m/S_L)(1 - \tau)R_L$$

which will dominate $Y_L$ if (and only if) $V_L - \tau D_L > V_U$. Thus, in equilibrium, both $V_L - \tau D_L > V_U$ and $V_L - \tau D_L < V_U$ are ruled out and (3) must hold.

## III. SOME IMPLICATIONS OF FORMULA (3)

To see what is involved in replacing (4) with (3) as the rule of valuation, note first that both expressions make the value of the firm a function of leverage and the tax rate. The difference between them is a matter of the size and source of the tax advantages of debt financing. Under our original formulation, values within a class were strictly proportional to expected earnings after taxes. Hence the tax advantage of debt was due solely to the fact that the deductibility of interest payments implied a higher level of after-tax income for any given level of before-tax earnings (i.e., higher by the amount $\tau R$ since $\bar{X}^\tau = (1 - \tau)\bar{X} + \tau R$). Under the corrected rule (3), however, there is an additional gain due to the fact that the extra after-tax earnings, $\tau R$, represent a sure income in contrast to the uncertain outcome $(1-\tau)\overline{X}$. Hence $\tau R$ is capitalized at the more favorable certainty rate, $1/r$, rather than at the rate for uncertain streams, $1/\rho^{\tau}$.[9]

Since the difference between (3) and (4) is solely a matter of the rate at which the tax savings on interest payments are capitalized, the required changes in all formulas and expressions derived from (4) are reasonably straightforward. Consider, first, the before-tax earnings yield, i.e., the ratio of expected earnings before interest and taxes to the value of the firm.[10] Dividing both sides of (3) by $V$ and by $(1-\tau)$ and simplifying we obtain:

$$(31.c) \qquad \frac{\overline{X}}{V} = \frac{\rho^{\tau}}{1-\tau}\left[1 - \tau\frac{D}{V}\right]$$

which replaces our original equation (31) (p. 294). The new relation differs from the old in that the coefficient of $D/V$ in the original (31) was smaller by a factor of $r/\rho^{\tau}$.

Consider next the after-tax earnings yield, i.e., the ratio of interest payments plus profits after taxes to total market value.[11] This concept was discussed extensively in our paper because it helps to bring out more clearly the differences between our position and the traditional view, and because it facilitates the construction of empirical tests of the two hypotheses about the valuation process. To see what the new equation (3) implies for this yield we need merely substitute $\overline{X}^{\tau} - \tau R$ for $(1-\tau)\overline{X}$ in (3) obtaining:

$$(5) \qquad V = \frac{\overline{X}^{\tau} - \tau R}{\rho^{\tau}} + \tau D = \frac{\overline{X}^{\tau}}{\rho^{\tau}} + \tau\frac{\rho^{\tau} - r}{\rho^{\tau}}D,$$

from which it follows that the after-tax earnings yield must be:

$$(11.c) \qquad \frac{\overline{X}^{\tau}}{V} = \rho^{\tau} - \tau(\rho^{\tau} - r)D/V.$$

This replaces our original equation (11) (p. 272) in which we had simply

[9] Remember, however, that in one sense formula (3) gives only an upper bound on the value of the firm since $\tau R/r = \tau D$ is an exact measure of the value of the tax saving only where both the tax rate and the level of debt are assumed to be fixed forever (and where the firm is certain to be able to use its interest deduction to reduce taxable income either directly or via transfer of the loss to another firm). Alternative versions of (3) can readily be developed for cases in which the debt is not assumed to be permanent, but rather to be outstanding only for some specified finite length of time. For reasons of space, we shall not pursue this line of inquiry here beyond observing that the shorter the debt period considered, the closer does the valuation formula approach our original (4). Hence, the latter is perhaps still of some interest if only as a lower bound.

[10] Following usage common in the field of finance we referred to this yield as the "average cost of capital." We feel now, however, that the term "before-tax earnings yield" would be preferable both because it is more immediately descriptive and because it releases the term "cost of capital" for use in discussions of optimal investment policy (in accord with standard usage in the capital budgeting literature).

[11] We referred to this yield as the "after-tax cost of capital." Cf. the previous footnote.

$\overline{X}^\tau/V = \rho^\tau$. Thus, in contrast to our earlier result, the corrected version (11.c) implies that even the after-tax yield is affected by leverage. The predicted rate of decrease of $\overline{X}^\tau/V$ with $D/V$, however, is still considerably smaller than under the naive traditional view, which, as we showed, implied essentially $\overline{X}^\tau/V = \rho^\tau - (\rho^\tau - r)D/V$. See our equation (17) and the discussion immediately preceding it (p. 277).[12] And, of course, (11.c) implies that the effect of leverage on $\overline{X}^\tau/V$ is *solely* a matter of the deductibility of interest payments whereas, under the traditional view, going into debt would lower the cost of capital regardless of the method of taxing corporate earnings.

Finally, we have the matter of the after-tax yield on *equity* capital, i.e., the ratio of net profits after taxes to the value of the shares.[13] By subtracting $D$ from both sides of (5) and breaking $\overline{X}^\tau$ into its two components—expected net profits after taxes, $\overline{\pi}^\tau$, and interest payments, $R = rD$—we obtain after simplifying:

$$(6) \qquad S = V - D = \frac{\overline{\pi}^\tau}{\rho^\tau} - (1 - \tau)\left(\frac{\rho^\tau - r}{\rho^\tau}\right)D.$$

From (6) it follows that the after-tax yield on equity capital must be:

$$(12.c) \qquad \frac{\overline{\pi}^\tau}{S} = \rho^\tau + (1 - \tau)[\rho^\tau - r]D/S$$

which replaces our original (12), $\overline{\pi}^\tau/S = \rho^\tau + (\rho^\tau - r)D/S$ (p. 272). The new (12.c) implies an increase in the after-tax yield on equity capital as leverage increases which is smaller than that of our original (12) by a factor of $(1 - \tau)$. But again, the linear increasing relation of the corrected (12.c) is still fundamentally different from the naive traditional view which asserts the cost of equity capital to be completely independent of leverage (at least as long as leverage remains within "conventional" industry limits).

## IV. TAXES AND THE COST OF CAPITAL

From these corrected valuation formulas we can readily derive corrected measures of the cost of capital in the capital budgeting sense of the minimum prospective yield an investment project must offer to be just worth undertaking from the standpoint of the present stockholders. If we interpret earnings stream as perpetuities, as we did in the original paper, then we actually have two equally good ways of defining this minimum yield: either by the required increase in before-tax earnings, $d\overline{X}$, or by the required increase in earnings net of taxes, $d\overline{X}(1 - \tau)$.[14] To conserve space, however, as well as to

---

[12] The $i_k{}^*$ of (17) is the same as $\rho^\tau$ in the present context, each measuring the ratio of net profits to the value of the shares (and hence of the whole firm) in an unlevered company of the class.

[13] We referred to this yield as the "after-tax cost of equity capital." Cf. footnote 9.

[14] Note that we use the term "earnings net of taxes" rather than "earnings after taxes." We feel that to avoid confusion the latter term should be reserved to describe what will actually appear in the firm's accounting statements, namely the net cash flow including the

maintain continuity with the original paper, we shall concentrate here on the before-tax case with only brief footnote references to the net-of-tax concept.

Analytically, the derivation of the cost of capital in the above sense amounts to finding the minimum value of $d\bar{X}/dI$ for which $dV = dI$, where $I$ denotes the level of new investment.[15] By differentiating (3) we see that:

$$(7) \qquad \frac{dV}{dI} = \frac{1 - \tau}{\rho_\tau} \frac{d\bar{X}}{dI} + \tau \frac{dD}{dI} \geq 1 \quad \text{if} \quad \frac{d\bar{X}}{dI} \geq \frac{1 - \tau \dfrac{dD}{dI}}{1 - \tau} \rho^\tau.$$

Hence the before-tax required rate of return cannot be defined without reference to financial policy. In particular, for an investment considered as being financed entirely by new equity capital $dD/dI = 0$ and the required rate of return or marginal cost of equity financing (neglecting flotation costs) would be:

$$\rho^S = \frac{\rho^\tau}{1 - \tau}.$$

This result is the same as that in the original paper (see equation [32], (p. 294) and is applicable to any other sources of financing where the remuneration to the suppliers of capital is not deductible for tax purposes. It applies, therefore, to preferred stock (except for certain partially deductible issues of public utilities) and would apply also to retained earnings were it not for the favorable tax treatment of capital gains under the personal income tax.

For investments considered as being financed entirely by new debt capital $dI = dD$ and we find from (7) that:

$$(33.\text{c}) \qquad\qquad \rho^D = \rho^\tau$$

which replaces our original equation (33) in which we had:

$$(33) \qquad\qquad \rho^D = \rho^S - \frac{\tau}{1 - \tau} r.$$

Thus for borrowed funds (or any other tax-deductible source of capital) the marginal cost or before-tax required rate of return is simply the market rate of capitalization for net of tax unlevered streams and is thus independent of both the tax rate and the interest rate. This required rate is lower than that implied

---

tax savings on the interest (our $\bar{X}^\tau$). Since financing sources cannot in general be allocated to particular investments (see below), the after-tax or accounting concept is not useful for capital budgeting purposes, although it can be extremely useful for valuation equations as we saw in the previous section.

[15] Remember that when we speak of the minimum required yield on an investment we are referring in principle only to investments which increase the *scale* of the firm. That is, the new assets must be in the same "class" as the old. See in this connection, J. Hirshleifer, "Risk, the Discount Rate and Investment Decisions," *Am. Econ. Rev.*, May 1961, 51, 112–20 (especially pp. 119–20). See also footnote 16.

by our original (33), but still considerably higher than that implied by the traditional view (see pp. 276–77 of our paper) under which the before-tax cost of borrowed funds is simply the interest rate, $r$.

Having derived the above expressions for the marginal costs of debt and equity financing it may be well to warn readers at this point that these expressions represent at best only the hypothetical extremes insofar as costs are concerned and that neither is directly usable as a cut-off criterion for investment planning. In particular, care must be taken to avoid falling into the famous " Liquigas " fallacy of concluding that if a firm intends to float a bond issue in some given year then its cut-off rate should be set that year at $\rho^D$; while, if the next issue is to be an equity one, the cut-off is $\rho^S$. The point is, of course, that no investment can meaningfully be regarded as 100 per cent equity financed if the firm makes any use of debt capital—and most firms do, not only for the tax savings, but for many other reasons having nothing to do with "cost" in the present static sense (cf. our original paper pp. 292–93). And no investment can meaningfully be regarded as 100 per cent debt financed when lenders impose strict limitations on the maximum amount a firm can borrow relative to its equity (and when most firms actually plan on normally borrowing less than this external maximum so as to leave themselves with an emergency reserve of unused borrowing power). Since the firm's long-run capital structure will thus contain both debt and equity capital, investment planning must recognize that, over the long pull, *all* of the firm's assets are really financed by a mixture of debt and equity capital even though only one kind of capital may be raised in any particular year. More precisely, if $L^*$ denotes the firm's long-run " target " debt ratio (around which its actual debt ratio will fluctuate as it "alternately" floats debt issues and retires them with internal or external equity) then the firm can assume, to a first approximation at least, that for any particular investment $dD/dI = L^*$. Hence, the relevant marginal cost of capital for investment planning, which we shall here denote by $\rho^*$, is:

$$\rho^* = \frac{1 - \tau_L{}^*}{1 - \tau} \rho^\tau = \rho^S - \frac{\tau}{1 - \tau} \rho^D L^* = \rho^S(1 - L^*) + \rho^D L^*.$$

That is, the appropriate cost of capital for (repetitive) investment decisions over time is, to a first approximation, a weighted average of the costs of debt and equity financing, the weights being the proportions of each in the "target" capital structure.[16]

[16] From the formulas in the text one can readily derive corresponding expressions for the required net-of-tax yield, or net-of-tax cost of capital for any given financing policy. Specifically, let $\bar{\rho}(L)$ denote the required net-of-tax yield for investment financed with a proportion of debt $L = dD/dI$. (More generally $L$ denotes the proportion financed with tax deductible sources of capital.) Then from (7) we find:

(8)                    $$\bar{\rho}(L) = (1 - \tau)\frac{d\bar{X}}{dI} = (1 - L\tau)\rho^\tau$$

and the various costs can be found by substituting the appropriate value for $L$. In particular,

## V. SOME CONCLUDING OBSERVATIONS

Such, then, are the major corrections that must be made to the various formulas and valuation expressions in our earlier paper. In general, we can say that the force of these corrections has been to increase somewhat the estimate of the tax advantages of debt financing under our model and consequently to reduce somewhat the quantitative difference between the estimates of the effects of leverage under our model and under the naive traditional view. It may be useful to remind readers once again that the existence of a tax advantage for debt financing—even the larger advantage of the corrected version—does not necessarily mean that corporations should at all times seek to use the maximum possible amount of debt in their capital structures. For one thing, other forms of financing, notably retained earnings, may in some circumstances be cheaper still when the tax status of investors under the personal income tax is taken into account. More important, there are, as we pointed out, limitations imposed by lenders (see pp. 292–93), as well as many other dimensions (and kinds of costs) in real-world problems of financial strategy which are not fully comprehended within the framework of static equilibrium models, either our own or those of the traditional variety. These additional considerations, which are typically grouped under the rubric of " the need for preserving flexibility," will normally imply the maintenance by the corporation of a substantial reserve of untapped borrowing power. The tax advantage of debt may well tend to lower the optimal size of that reserve, but it is hard to believe that advantages of the size contemplated under our model could justify any substantial reduction, let alone their complete elimination. Nor do the data indicate that there has in fact been a substantial increase in the use of debt (except relative to preferred stock) by the corporate sector during the recent high tax years.[17]

---

if we substitute in this formula the " target " leverage ratio, $L^*$, we obtain:

$$\bar{\rho}^* \equiv \bar{\rho}(L^*) = (1 - \tau L^*)\rho^\tau$$

and $\bar{\rho}^*$ measures the average net-of-tax cost of capital in the sense described above.

Although the before-tax and the net-of-tax approaches to the cost of capital provide equally good criteria for investment decisions when assets are assumed to generate perpetual (i.e., nondepreciating) streams, such is not the case when assets are assumed to have finite lives (even when it is also assumed that the firm's assets are in a steady state age distribution so that our $X$ or EBIT is approximately the same as the net cash flow before taxes). See footnote 3 above. In the latter event, the correct method for determining the desirability of an investment would be, in principle, to discount the net-of-tax stream at the net-of-tax cost of capital. Only under this net-of-tax approach would it be possible to take into account the deductibility of depreciation (and also to choose the most advantageous depreciation policy for tax purposes). Note that we say that the net-of-tax approach is correct " in principle " because, strictly speaking, nothing in our analysis (or anyone else's for that matter) has yet established that it is indeed legitimate to " discount " an uncertain stream. One can hope that subsequent research will show the analogy to discounting under the certainty case is a valid one; but, at the moment, this is still only a hope.

[17] See, e.g., Merton H. Miller, "The Corporate Income Tax and Corporate Financial Policies," in *Staff Reports to the Commission on Money and Credit* (forthcoming).

As to the differences between our modified model and the traditional one, we feel that they are still large in quantitative terms and still very much worth trying to detect. It is not only a matter of the two views having different implications for corporate financial policy (or even for national tax policy). But since the two positions rest on fundamentally different views about investor behavior and the functioning of the capital markets, the results of tests between them may have an important bearing on issues ranging far beyond the immediate one of the effects of leverage on the cost of capital.

# 28. A TEST OF COST OF CAPITAL PROPOSITIONS†

## J. FRED WESTON*

Reprinted from *The Southern Economic Journal*, Vol. *XXX*, No. 2 (October, 1963), pp. 105–12, by permission of the author and the publisher.

Modigliani and Miller have thrown traditional concepts of cost of capital into turmoil.[1] In view of the broad implications of their propositions, this study has sought to test their propositions and underlying assumptions by further empirical analysis. While this study represents only one additional set of measurements, the findings are reported because the results differ significantly from those of Modigliani and Miller. A comparison of the empirical results illuminates the theory. In addition, measurement problems important for other empirical studies are brought to the fore.

## MODIGLIANI AND MILLER PROPOSITIONS AND TRADITIONAL THEORY

The Modigliani and Miller propositions, as well as their summary of the traditional propositions, may be set forth briefly. The Modigliani-Miller

* University of California at Los Angeles.

† I am grateful to the Bureau of Business and Economic Research, UCLA for research assistance. Louis Blumberg, Phoebe Cottingham and Roger Weiland helped gather the data upon which the analysis is based. Professor Raymond Jessen helped on a number of aspects of the statistical work. Mr. William Anderson of the Western Data Processing Center UCLA assisted in the use of the BIMED 06 Program for running the regressions. I also benefited from discussions with my colleagues in the Finance Area at the Graduate School of Business, UCLA. Suggestions by the editors of this *Journal* stimulated improvements in the manuscript.

[1] Franco Modigliani and Merton H. Miller, "The Cost of Capital, Corporation Finance, and the Theory of Investments," *The American Economic Review*, June 1958, pp. 261–96. Also see their "Reply," *The American Economic Review*, September, 1959, pp. 655–69.

theory is identical with Durand's NOI approach.[2] Durand compared two theories of the valuation of the earnings of a corporation, describing one as the capitalization of net operating earnings (NOI approach) and the other as capitalization of net income (NI approach).

In the NOI approach the value of a corporation is determined by capitalizing the corporation's net operating income. The value of the company's stocks and bonds must conform to this total. In the NI approach, the cost of debt is deducted from net operating income to give net income. The appropriate capitalization rate is applied to net income available to common stock to determine the value of the company's common stock. The market value of the common stock is then added to the market value of the company's bonds to determine the total value of the company.

Durand's Net Operating Income approach and Modigliani and Miller's Proposition I are logically equivalent. Both state that the net operating income of a business firm, divided by the appropriate capitalization rate, gives the value of the enterprise to which the value of the bonds and stocks of the firm must conform. Thus, Proposition I of Modigliani and Miller can be expressed as follows: the value of a business corporation is equal to its net operating income divided by the capitalization rate appropriate for application to the leverage-free earnings of a firm in a specified risk class.[3] This NOI approach can be expressed in the symbols of Modigliani and Miller.[4]

$$V_j = (S_j + D_j) - \overline{X}_j/\rho_\kappa \equiv (NOI)_j/\rho_\kappa \qquad \text{Proposition I}$$

$V_j$ = the market value of all the firm's securities or the market value of the firm

$S_j$ = the market value of the firm's common shares

$D_j$ = the market value of the debts of the company

$\overline{X}_j$ = the expected return on the assets owned by the company, which equals its net operating income—NOI

$\rho_\kappa$ = the capitalization rate appropriate to the risk class of the firm[5]

Proposition II is another way of stating Proposition I. Modigliani and Miller's elaborate rationalization of Proposition II is unnecessary. If Proposition I is accepted, Proposition II follows directly.

$$(1) \qquad i_j = \frac{\overline{X}_j - rD_j}{S_j}$$

Definitional identity: This is equation (9) in Modigliani and Miller, *op. cit.*, p. 271.

[2] David Durand, "Costs of Debt and Equity Funds for Business: Trends and Problems of Measurement," *Conference on Research in Business Finance* (New York: National Bureau of Economic Research, Inc., 1952), p. 227.

[3] Modigliani and Miller, *op. cit.*, p. 268.

[4] *Ibid.*

[5] The analysis at this point will not take taxes into account in order to simplify the exposition. In the empirical analysis presented later, the formulations employed will be on an after-corporate-income-tax basis.

Where: $i$ = expected yield on common stock
$r$ = expected cost of debt

(2) $$\bar{X}_j = \rho_\kappa V_j = \rho_\kappa (D_j + S_j)$$  Proposition I

(3) $$i_j = \frac{\rho_\kappa S_j + \rho_\kappa D_j - rD_j}{S_j}$$

Substitute from (2) into (1).

(4) $$i_j = \rho_\kappa + (\rho_\kappa - r)\frac{D_j}{S_j}$$  Proposition II

The two propositions of Modigliani and Miller are of great significance. Proposition I states that regardless of the degree of leverage employed by a company, its cost of capital will be the same. The cost of capital function of a firm will be unaffected by leverage.

The second proposition shows the implications of the NOI approach. Proposition II states that the earnings/price ratio on the common stock of a company in a given risk class is a linear function of leverage, the slope being the difference between the company's cost of capital and the cost of debt. It is a precise formulation for determining the earnings-price ratio of a company's stock as a function of its overall cost of capital, its cost of debt, and the degree of leverage employed.

It will be useful at this point to compare the Net Operating Income or the Modigliani and Miller theory with what Modigliani and Miller describe as the traditional approach. Modigliani and Miller point out that in contrast to their Proposition II, "the conventional view among finance specialists is to start from the proposition that other things equal, the earnings-price ratio (or its reciprocal the times-earnings multiplier) of a firm's common stock will normally be only slightly affected by 'moderate' amounts of debt in the firm's capital structure."[6] They point out that the crucial element in the theory—that the expected earnings-price ratio of the stock is largely unaffected by leverage up to some conventional limit—"is rarely even regarded as something which requires explanation."[7]

While the traditional approach clearly disagrees with the NOI approach, it is not the NI approach in pure form. It is a modified NI theory in the following sense. It suggests that if a large corporation employs moderate amounts of leverage, the interest on debt and the capitalization factor applied to the earnings available for common stock do not rise to the same degree that risk premiums accompanying the leverage employed by individuals would increase. Thus increasing the proportion of debt employed to finance a firm would increase the expected market value of the firm up to some critical proportion of leverage. Beyond that point, capitalization factors rise sufficiently to offset

---

[6] *Ibid.*, p. 276. They also cite illustrations of this position in the literature.
[7] *Ibid.*, p. 278.

the added earnings available to common stock, resulting in a decline in the market value of the firm. Hence the firm's overall cost of capital would fall, then rise.

Space does not permit an exegesis of the "traditional finance theory" by a historical survey of the literature. The support for the traditional view rests upon the nature of the corporation and investor behavior. The corporate institution is a device which shifts a portion of financial risk from owners to creditors. Since the risk to owners is limited to the amount which they have committed to the corporate enterprise the owners reduce their probable loss. While their losses are limited to the amount actually invested in the enterprise, their gains are not so restricted. Personal leverage does not have the same limited-risk characteristic.

A related support for the assumptions of the traditional theorems is based on investment standards. Moderate increases in leverage are not regarded as increasing risk so long as the minimum standards for debt ratios or earnings coverage of fixed charges are met.[8]

The corporate institution and investment standards make corporate leverage advantageous over personal leverage. Since personal leverage is not a perfect substitute for corporate leverage, the arbitrage operations described by Modigliani and Miller are not possible. The present discussion does not question their underlying assumptions; it merely indicates the rationale of competing assumptions. The realism of assumptions cannot be tested directly. In a policy area such as business finance, the ultimate test of the underlying assumptions is the ability of the derived propositions to predict. We can evaluate the rival assumptions about the behavior of investors by further empirical studies described in the following section.

## EMPIRICAL TESTS OF THE INFLUENCE OF LEVERAGE ON THE COST OF CAPITAL

The essentials of two alternative models for the cost of capital have been set forth. The choice between the two models must ultimately depend upon their conformity with the real world. The predictive implications of the alternative theories will be tested as a basis for selecting between the two models.

As in economic theory generally, to test a model directly often involves serious inadequacies. A very critical part of the Modigliani and Miller formulation is the concept of a risk class. Their identification of a risk class with an industry suffers from all the problems of the non-homogeneity of "an industry." The defects are aggravated in the risk class concept because the dependent variables which they seek to explain are particularly sensitive to differences in characteristics between firms conventionally grouped in a given "industry" by government or financial agencies.

[8] Benjamin Graham. David L. Dodd, and Sidney Cottle, *Security Analysis* (New York: McGraw-Hill Book Co., 1962), pp. 248–9; Harry Sauvain, *Investment Management* (Englewood Cliffs, N.J.: Prentice Hall, 1959), pp. 220–1; Douglas A. Hayes, *Investments: Analysis and Management* (New York: Macmillan Company, 1961), pp. 175–88.

The differences between firms in the oil industry, in particular, are great. For example, in a group of 42 oil companies used by Modigliani and Miller would be found the following diversity: fully-integrated oil companies, oil companies strong in refining, oil companies strong in distribution; some regional in their operations, some with heavy investments in troubled international regions; some with stable, assured or rising income from petrochemicals or uranium or other minerals. Furthermore, lease obligations, which are common in the oil industry, are not reflected in Modigliani and Miller's data on debt. It is obviously not plausible to regard a group of companies with such wide ranging diversity in significant characteristics as a homogeneous risk class.

As a consequence, in my study the empirical tests are confined to the electrical utility industry. The utility industry is not free of the problem, but utilities are probably less heterogeneous than oils. The initial results are set forth in Table I. (The symbols of Modigliani and Miller are generally followed.) The Modigliani-Miller findings for 1947–48 are compared with mine for 1959. Our findings for the earnings-price ratio are almost identical in form. The intercept is somewhat lower, and the slope is somewhat smaller, which is consistent with the change in equity markets between the two periods of

TABLE I
COST OF CAPITAL CALCULATIONS, ELECTRIC UTILITIES, 1959 )

| Year | M & M 1947–1948 | Weston 1959 |
|---|---|---|
| A. Earnings to price ratio | $z = 6.6 + .017h$ <br> $(\pm.004)$ <br> $r = .53$ | $z = 4.91 + .014h$ <br> $(\pm.004)$ <br> $r = .43$ |
| B. Cost of capital (investor viewpoint) | $x = 5.3 + .006d$ <br> $(\pm.008)$ <br> $r = .12$ <br> $n = 43$ | $x = 4.27 + .027d$ <br> $(\pm.007)$ <br> $r = .46$ <br> $n = 55$ |
| C. Cost of capital (financial manager viewpoint) | | $x = 5.07 - .010d$ <br> $(\pm.007)$ <br> $r = -.193$ |
| D. Cost of capital (risk measure of leverage) | | $x = 5.25 - .017d*$ <br> $(\pm.008)$ <br> $r = -.283$ |

Where:

$z$  = yield on common stock

$h$  = market value of senior securities divided by market value of common stock

$x$  = cost of capital equals total earnings after taxes divided by market value of all securities

$d$  = market value of senior securities divided by market value of all securities

$d*$ = market value of debt divided by market value of all securities

time. The correlation coefficient is somewhat smaller, but almost of equal significance in view of the fact that my sample size is approximately 30 per cent larger.

The significant contrast occurs, however, when the cost of capital function is calculated. Three measures of the cost of capital are set forth. Equation B takes the investor viewpoint (as did Modigliani and Miller) in which the cost of debt is taken at its full value into the weighted cost of capital calculations. The second method, under part C of the Table, takes the financial manager's viewpoint in which the cost of debt is on an after tax basis.[9] A third concept of cost of capital takes the financial manager's viewpoint, but removes preferred stock from the numerator of the leverage measure. Only fixed charges on debt carry risks of insolvency. Dividends on preferred stock do not constitute a fixed charge in this sense. It is logical therefore to measure leverage from the risk standpoint as the ratio of debt to the total market value of the company.[10]

When the investor viewpoint is taken, the cost of capital function has a positive slope. The regression coefficient is significant as well as is the correlation coefficient. This result differs fundamentally from Modigliani and Miller's findings. When the financial manager's viewpoint is taken, the cost of capital function has a negative slope, but is no longer significant. When the risk-measure of leverage is used, the negative slope of the cost of capital function becomes significant at the five per cent level.

What is the explanation for the difference between my results and those of Modigliani and Miller for equation B of Table I and why does the slope of the regression equation become negative in equation C? The answer to the second part of the question provides the key to the answer to the first part. The explanation will be aided by an examination of the quantitative relations. For my study the cost of debt and the cost of equity functions are approximately:

(1) $$r = 5 + .01d$$

(2) $$z = 4 + .06d$$

The Modigliani-Miller procedures suggest that the weighted cost of capital is:

(3) $$x = krd + i(1 - d)$$

The symbols all have the same meaning as in Table I. The new symbol, $k$, is 1 for the investor (M & M) viewpoint and .5 for the financial manager

[9] The rationale for the distinction and the circumstances under which the investor viewpoint versus the financial manager viewpoint would be taken are set forth cogently in John F. Childs, *Long-Term Financing* (Englewood Cliffs, N.J.: Prentice-Hall, 1961), Ch. X, "Profit Goals—Cost of Capital," especially pages 340–44.

[10] Of course, preferred stock (typically non-participating) enables a firm to trade on the equity. For an analysis of the effectiveness of trading on the equity, preferred stock would be included in senior obligations. In the present situation where we are investigating risk aspects of leverage, it is more appropriate to exclude preferred stock from senior obligations.

view-point. For the $r$ and $i$ functions given above, the cost of capital function may be determined.

(4) $\qquad$ For $k = 1, x = -.05d^2 + 1.06d + 4$

(5) $\qquad$ For $k = .5, x' = -.055d^2 - 1.44d + 4$

The value of $d$ (a measure of leverage) in equations (4) and (5) ranges from .1 to under 1.0. In this range, $x$ is positive throughout corresponding to equation B for the 1959 data, in Table I. Conversely, it is clear that $x'$ would be negative throughout the range of $d$, consistent with equation C of Table I. This analysis provides a formal explanation for the switchover from a positive slope in my results for the cost of capital function measured from an investor viewpoint and a negative slope for the cost of capital measured from the financial manager's viewpoint. This is also the key to explanation of the difference between my results and those of Modigliani-Miller in section B of Table I. The full explanation is most readily seen after the influence of growth is analyzed in the following section.

## INFLUENCE OF GROWTH ON THE COST OF CAPITAL

To this point my analysis has attempted to follow as closely as possible the original paper of Modigliani and Miller, including their empirical tests. Since the size of firms and the growth rate of their earnings are additional possible influences on the cost of capital, my study was broadened to include these additional variables. The investor viewpoint was used in these studies to permit direct comparison with the Modigliani-Miller data.

Table II shows that the growth in earnings per share has a significant influence on the cost of equity financing. However, the partial regression coefficient for the influence of leverage on equity yields is no longer significant. The influence of growth on the total cost of capital is also highly significant. But the sign of the leverage term is now negative, consistent with the declining segment of the cost of capital function predicted by traditional theory. Thus, when the influences on the cost of capital are partitioned through multiple regression analysis, the results are consistent with traditional theory. In view of the strong influence of growth on the cost of capital function, the relation between the cost of capital and leverage will depend on how growth is correlated with leverage. The regression equations in sections C and D of Table II show that leverage is a negative function of growth.

Thus the apparent positive correlation between leverage and equity yields observed by Modigliani and Miller actually represents the negative correlation between current equity yields and growth. The partial regression relationships show that when the influence of growth is removed, leverage is not significantly correlated with current earnings-price ratios for the range of leverage employed.

The partial regression analysis of the weighted cost of capital yields similar results. When the influence of growth is isolated, leverage is found to be

TABLE II

MULTIPLE REGRESSION ANALYSIS OF COST OF
CAPITAL, ELECTRIC UTILITIES, 1959

A.  $z = 6.75 - .0029h^* + 0.0A - .1352E$
    $\quad\quad\quad (\pm.0159) + (\pm.0002) \quad (\pm.0454)$
    $\quad\quad\quad\quad \beta = .0253 \quad\quad\quad\quad \beta = .4110$
    $R = .4032$

B.  $x = 5.91 - .0265d^* + 0.0A - .0822E$
    $\quad\quad\quad (\pm.0079) \quad (\pm.0001) \quad (\pm.0024)$
    $\quad\quad\quad\quad \beta = .4333 \quad\quad\quad\quad \beta = .4702$
    $R = .5268$

C.  $d = 51.66 - 1.78E \quad\quad r = -0.58$
    $\quad\quad\quad (\pm.34)$

D.  $d^* = 39.59 - 1.16E \quad\quad r = -0.48$
    $\quad\quad\quad (\pm.29)$

Where

$z$ = yield on common stock

$x$ = cost of capital equals total earnings after taxes divided by market value of all securities

$d$ = market value of senior securities divided by the market value of all securities

$h^* = d^*$ = market value of debt divided by the market value of all securities

$A$ = total assets as book value

$E$ = compound growth rate in earnings per share per annum, 1949–1959

$\beta$ = beta coefficient which normalizes the regression coefficient to measure its relative influence in the dependent variables

$R$ = multiple correlation coefficient.

negatively correlated with the cost of capital. Traditional theory suggests that firms have an aversion to debt and are likely to be operating in the range of a declining cost of capital.[11] The apparent lack of influence of leverage on the *overall cost of capital* observed by Modigliani-Miller is due to the negative correlation of leverage with earnings growth. When the net effects are measured, the cost of capital is found to be significantly negatively correlated with both leverage and growth. The reason why Modigliani-Miller found no correlation between the cost of capital and leverage in that leverage is correlated with other influences which change the gross relationship between cost of capital and leverage.[12]

The data showing the influence of growth on equity yields and the cost of capital function help explain the positive slope obtained for the cost of capital function for 1959 in Table I. The empirical data utilized by Modigliani and

[11] N. H. Jacoby and J. F. Weston, "Financial Policies for Regularizing Business Investment," *Regularization of Business Investment* (Princeton, N.J.: Princeton University Press, 1954), pp. 386–387.

[12] The beta coefficient for earnings growth in the regression for the yield on equity funds is much larger than the beta coefficient for leverage. In the regression for cost of capital, the two beta coefficients are approximately equal.

Miller were for the late 1940's when equity prices were depressed and earnings/price ratios were high. Interest yields were low and inflexible, reflecting the support of the Government bond market by the Federal Reserve System. In contrast, my study for the year 1959 was a period of buoyant equity prices, large premiums for prospective growth, and low current earnings to current price ratios. The current cost of equity money relative to the cost of debt money was low. As shown in equations (1) and (2) of the preceding section, the intercept of the cost of debt function was higher than the intercept for the cost of equity function. In the Modigliani-Miller data, however, $r$ is estimated at 3.5 and the intercept of the cost of equity function (shown in section A of Table I) is 6.6.

The strands may now be brought together. My data show that leverage is negatively correlated with growth. Growth also lowers the (current) cost of equity money. Hence we both found that the cost of equity money was a positive function of leverage. In Modigliani-Miller's data, we observe a rising cost of equity function and a constant and lower cost of debt function. As leverage is increased, the cost of capital is pushed up by the rising cost of equity function, but is pulled down because the lower cost of debt is weighted more heavily. Modigliani and Miller's data for the late 1940's indicate that the pull of the opposing forces was about balanced so that the cost of capital function appeared not to have a significant slope.

In my data for 1959, the current cost of equity money is relatively low because current prices reflected the future growth of earnings. The cost of debt was somewhat higher. Hence in equation B of Table I where the cost of debt is taken into the measurements at its full level, the cost of capital function would rise with leverage. The rising cost of equity is offset only slightly because the cost of debt is relatively high. When the cost of debt is reduced by one-half, the greater weighting of debt cost as leverage increases, pulls down the cost of capital as shown in equation C of Table I.[13]

## MEASUREMENT OF THE COST OF EQUITY FUNDS WITH GROWTH

In the studies utilized by Modigliani and Miller, the ratio of current earnings to the current market price of common stock is used as a measure of the cost of equity financing. This is invalid. As their own subsequent writing has demonstrated, the cost of equity financing must add to current yields a corrective for a growth factor in order to obtain a relevant measure of the cost of

---

[13] It has been observed that strong firms employ low debt ratios, but by customary financial standards could employ much higher debt ratios. Professor John P. Shelton has suggested a rationale for this. If strong firms have low equity costs, the relative gain from employing debt is small or negative. Hence it is not irrational for such firms to employ low debt ratios. This observation, as well as the discussion above, depends on a relatively low cost of equity function. But this in turn implies use of the current earnings-price ratio, rather than relating expected future earnings to the current price, to measure the cost of equity money.

equity financing.[14] For example, in my study the average dividend yield on common stock for the year 1959 was 3.96 per cent. The average compound rate of growth in either dividends or earnings per share over the eleven-year period, 1949–1959, was approximately 6 per cent. The estimate of the electrical utility industry cost of equity money for 1959 is 9.96 per cent, employing the Modigliani and Miller formula.[15] The current earnings-price ratio understates the cost of capital of a company with growing earnings.[16]

Thus the use of current earnings to current price would not be accurate for a measure of the cost of capital function. However, in the Modigliani-Miller studies and the present study which replicates their procedures, we are concerned not with the absolute level of the cost of capital, but how it varies with leverage and other factors. Hence the slopes of the functions and their relative levels may be little affected by using the ratio of current earnings to current price, although the absolute levels of the functions will be affected.

## INDIRECT TESTS OF THE INFLUENCE OF LEVERAGE ON THE COST OF CAPITAL

In view of the measurement disputes, some broad proxy tests may be applied. We can formulate the following hypothesis. In an industry in which earnings instability is relatively small, decision-makers in different firms would be expected to view prospective risks in a similar fashion. As a consequence, traditional theory would predict a clustering of leverage ratios in a relatively narrow range for an industry or risk class in which the instability of earnings was characteristically small.

On the other hand, if we observe a wide range of variations in earnings among firms in the same industry group, we would expect decision-makers to view risks differently in view of the greater instability of earnings in the industry. The spread of leverage ratios employed would be expected to be much larger. But the Miller and Modigliani theory would predict that leverage ratios would vary randomly in both types of industries since leverage does not affect a firm's cost of capital.

A test of the influence of leverage on cost of capital is provided by the two studies used by Modigliani and Miller as well as my own. In the electrical utilities industry, which is an approximation to the first type of industry described (in which the instability of earnings is small), there is a clustering of

[14] Merton H. Miller and Franco Modigliani, "Dividend Policy, Growth, and the Valuation of Shares," *Journal of Business*, October, 1961, pp. 411–32.

[15] *Ibid.*, pp. 421–22.

[16] Some recent studies provide additional discussion of these problems. See Haskel Benishay, "Variability in Earnings-Price Ratios of Corporate Equities," *The American Economic Review*, March, 1961, pp. 80–94; and "Reply," *The American Economic Review*, March, 1962, pp. 209–16; Myron J. Gordon, *The Investment, Financing, and Valuation of the Corporation* (Homewood, Ill.: Richard D. Irwin, 1962); Myron J. Gordon, "Variability in Earnings-Price Ratios: Comment," *The American Economic Review*, March, 1962, pp. 203–8; John Lintner, "Dividends, Earnings, Leverage, Stock Prices and the Supply of Capital to Corporations," *Review of Economics and Statistics*, August, 1962, pp. 243–69.

leverage ratios within a very narrow range. The oil industry illustrates the second class of industry. It is an industry characterized by great variation among firms in earnings stability and great instability of earnings for individual firms. A wide range of leverage is employed by firms in this industry as predicted by traditional business finance theory.

Thus, the multiple regression analysis of the influence of leverage and growth on the cost of capital, as well as the broad proxy tests provided by observed differences in leverage policies followed, strongly indicate that leverage does have an influence on a firm's cost of capital. There is, thus, strong theoretical and empirical evidence that the traditional theory of business finance remains a better predictor of the real world than the Modigliani and Miller propositions.

## CONCLUSIONS

This paper has shown that the Modigliani and Miller propositions are Durand's NOI approach to valuation presented in a new garb. Proposition I states that the value of a firm is obtained by capitalizing its net operating income; the sum of bond and stock values must conform to this figure. This theorem is based upon the assumption that personal leverage and corporate leverage are completely substitutable. Proposition II is an identity which is a definition of the earnings/price ratio. When Proposition I (the value of debt plus stock must total the value of the firm) is substituted in the identity, the earnings/price ratio can be expressed as a linear equation. The intercept of the equation is the firm's cost of capital; its slope is the difference between the firm's cost of capital and the cost of debt, with leverage as the independent variable.

The considerable disagreement on the NOI approach continues to surround its new appearance in the form of the Modigliani and Miller propositions. While Modigliani and Miller found two empirical studies apparently consistent with their propositions, their proof is deficient in important respects. A serious weakness of their empirical studies is the failure to investigate the nature of the relationship between leverage and other factors influencing a firm's cost of capital. The present study shows that leverage is a negative linear function of earnings growth. Thus the lack of correlation between the cost of capital and leverage is due to the counterbalancing influence of earnings growth on leverage. The partial correlation measures show that both leverage and earnings growth were significantly correlated with the cost of capital.

The apparent overwhelming empirical support of the generality of the Modigliani and Miller propositions rests upon measuring the gross influences of leverage and growth and attributing all the influence to leverage. When the influence of growth is isolated, the net influence of leverage on the cost of capital is found to be consistent with traditional business finance theory, rather than with the Modigliani and Miller propositions.

## 29. THE COST OF CAPITAL, CORPORATION FINANCE, AND THE THEORY OF INVESTMENT: COMMENT

DAWSON E. BREWER

and

JACOB B. MICHAELSEN*

Reprinted from *The American Economic Review*, Vol. *LV*, No. 3 (June, 1965), pp. 516–24, by permission of the authors and the publisher.

In the June 1958 issue of this *Review*, Franco Modigliani and Merton H. Miller (hereafter MM) presented a model of corporate leverage which challenged the traditional view that an optimum capital structure exists. They demonstrated quite convincingly that, within the context of the model's assumptions, arbitrage operations will make the market value of the firm independent of its capital structure. While considerable attention has been given to the validity or " realism " of these assumptions,[1] little has been given to the feasibility of the tests MM proposed to distinguish between these two views of the effects of leverage. These tests are based on what MM believed to be the implication of each view for the following two relationships: (1) that between the expected yield on a firm's shares and its debt-equity ratio; and (2) that between the weighted average of the expected yields on a firm's shares and bonds and its debt-equity ratio. The purpose of this communication is to show that these implications differ in important respects from what MM supposed them to be, and that even when the appropriate corrections are made, serious doubt remains as to whether either view can be contradicted by the data.

## I. IMPLICATIONS OF THE ALTERNATIVE VIEWS IN THE ABSENCE OF CORPORATE INCOME TAXES

MM based their entire analysis on Proposition I, which asserts that "*the average cost of capital to any firm is completely independent of its capital structure and is equal to the capitalization rate of a pure equity stream of its class*" [3, pp. 268–69; their italics]. Proposition I may be written as follows:[2]

---

* The authors are, respectively, acting assistant professor and assistant professor of business administration at the University of California, Berkeley. They acknowledge the helpful comments of Professors Modigliani and Miller. The views expressed are those of the authors alone.

[1] See, for example, D. Durand [1] and J. Lintner [2].

[2] With some exceptions, which will be noted when they occur, we shall preserve the notation used by MM. For convenience, subscripts denoting individual firms have been omitted.

$$(1) \qquad\qquad \rho_k = i\frac{S}{V} + r\frac{D}{V},$$

where $i$ and $r$ are, respectively, the expected yields on the firm's shares and bonds, $S$ is the value of its shares, $D$ is the value of its bonds and $V = (S + D)$.[3] We may solve for the relationship between the expected yields on the firm's securities and its debt-equity ratio by rearranging (1) as follows:

$$(2) \qquad\qquad i = \rho_k + (\rho_k - r)D/S, \text{ and}$$

$$(3) \qquad\qquad r = \rho_k - (i - \rho_k)S/D.$$

The stock-yield function (2) is identical to their Proposition II [3, p. 271], which they similarly derived from Proposition I. However, MM failed to recognize that Proposition I also implies the bond-yield function (3). As a result, they posited a form for (2) which is inconsistent with their assumption about investors' attitudes toward risk. To determine the permissible forms which (2) can take, it will be necessary to first make clear the constraints which attitudes toward risk place upon both (2) and (3).

While the validity of Proposition I does not depend on the attitudes of investors toward risk as MM correctly argued, these attitudes nevertheless play an important role in their analysis. Thus, by making $\rho_k$ greater than the expected yield on riskless bonds, they implicitly assumed risk aversion. From this it follows that, since shares become progressively more risky as leverage increases, the expected yield on shares must be an increasing function of the debt-equity ratio. MM neglected this corollary when they attempted to include a rising supply curve of borrowed funds in their analysis. To accommodate risky bonds, they assumed "as a first approximation that this yield curve, $r = r(D/S)$, whatever its precise form, is the same for all borrowers" [3, p. 273]. MM then supposed the marginal cost of borrowed funds could rise so rapidly as to cause the yield on shares to fall. This possibility is represented by the downward-sloping segment of the $MD$ curve in their Figure 2 [3, p. 275] which is inconsistent with the assumed risk aversion.

Since these yield curves are interdependent, they need not be considered separately. Focusing on the properties of the share-yield curve, $i = i(D/S)$, risk aversion requires $i' > 0$. The implications of this constraint can be seen by differentiating (2) with respect to $D/S$, which yields:

---

[3] This expression follows directly from their equation [4] [3, p. 268]:

$$\frac{\bar{X}}{(S + D)} = \frac{\bar{X}}{V} = \rho_k,$$

where $\bar{X}$ is the expected return on the firm's assets. Let $(\bar{X} - \bar{R})$ be the expected return on the firm's shares and $\bar{R}$ the expected return on its bonds so that $\bar{X} = (\bar{X} - \bar{R}) + \bar{R}$. Letting $iS = (\bar{X} - \bar{R})$ and $rD = \bar{R}$, we have

$$\frac{(\bar{X} - \bar{R})}{V} + \frac{\bar{R}}{V} = \rho_k,$$

which is equivalent to (1) above. See note 5 for a more detailed discussion of these expected returns.

(4) $$i' = (\rho_k - r) - r'(D/S)$$

From (3) we know that $r = \rho_k$ when the firm is completely financed by debt, at which point the bonds are exactly equivalent to unlevered shares.[4] Because the distribution of returns to assets, $\phi(X)$, has some dispersion, bonds must become risky prior to this point so that $r'$ must exceed zero beyond some finite level of leverage.[5] As a consequence the bond-yield curve is subject to certain general constraints independent of the exact form of $\phi(X)$.

Inspection of (4) reveals that $i' = 0$ when $\rho_k - r = r'D/S$. Unless $r'$ approaches zero as $\rho_k - r$ approaches zero, the share-yield curve will pass through a maximum as does MM's $MD$ curve. To avoid this, $r$ must approach $\rho_k$ asymptotically as $D/S$ approaches infinity which entails $r'' < 0$ over this same range. (In the limit, both $r'$ and $r''$ tend to be zero). Differentiating (4) with respect to $D/S$ yields

(5) $$i'' = -2r' - r''D/S,$$

which is equal to zero when both $r'$ and $r''$ are zero and when $2r' = -r''D/S$. If riskless bonds can be issued, $i$ will be a linear function of $D/S$ over this range. As debt becomes risky, we may suppose $r'$ and $r''$ to both be positive so that $i''$ becomes negative. Since $r'' < 0$ for the upper range of $D/S$, $i''$ may well become positive as complete debt financing is approached. Share- and bond-yield curves with these characteristics are depicted in Figure 1.

---

[4] The promised yield on these bonds could be infinite since the coupon must reflect the most favorable return on assets. However, the expected value of the coupon will be less than the promised value so that the expected yield on bonds will never exceed $\rho_k$.

[5] In their footnote 6 [3, p. 265] the return on the assets $X$ is defined as a random variable subject to the probability distribution $\phi(\bar{X})$ which differs among firms by almost a scale factor. The expected return is

$$\bar{X} = E(X) = \int_a^b X\phi(X)dX,$$

where $a$ and $b$ represent, respectively, the lower and upper limits of $\phi(X)$ and $\int_a^b \phi(X)dX = 1.0$. The expected return on bonds is

$$\bar{R} = \int_a^R X\phi(X)dX + R\int_R^b \phi(X)dX,$$

where $R$ is the promised coupon.

The expected return on shares is

$$\bar{\pi} = \int_R^b (X - R)\phi(X)dX$$

$$= \int_R^b X\phi(X)dX - R\int_R^b \phi(X)dX.$$

Substituting from the expression for $\bar{R}$ yields

$$\bar{\pi} = \int_a^b X\phi(X)dX - \bar{R}$$

$$= \bar{X} - \bar{R}.$$

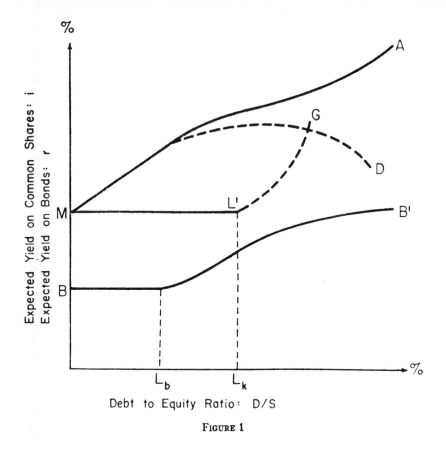

FIGURE 1

The axes in Figure 1 are the same as those in MM's Figure 2 [3, p. 275], facilitating the comparison of their curves with ours. $MA$ is the share-yield curve and $BB'$ the bond-yield curve implied by our analysis. $MD$ is the share-yield curve MM believed might result from a rising bond-yield curve. (Consistent with the ambiguity in their discussion of the bond-yield curve, they did not include one in their Figure 2.) $ML'G$ represents MM's interpretation of the traditional view that up to some "reasonable" amount of leverage, $L_k$, share yields remain constant but rise sharply beyond it.[6]

The shapes of our share- and bond-yield curves are to some extent arbitrary, since they depend on the exact forms of the density function $\phi(X)$ and the utility functions describing investors' attitudes toward $\phi(X)$, neither of which can be specified a priori. Even so, this particular pair of curves serves to illustrate, as could any one of a large number of others, the constraints imposed by risk aversion. The magnitude of $L_b$, the debt-equity ratio beyond

[6] See [3, p. 277].

which bonds become risky, could range from zero to some large finite value, its magnitude here depending on the particular form of $\phi(X)$ we assumed.

To distinguish between the traditional view and the MM model, the relationship between the yield on shares and the debt-equity ratio must be observed over a range where negative curvature could be detected if it exists. Clearly, a finding of positive curvature could contradict neither hypothesis.[7] However, this difficulty can be avoided by observing instead the relationship between the weighted average cost of capital and leverage. In the absence of taxes, the MM model implies a linear horizontal relationship whereas the traditional view implies a U-shaped one.[8] Observable behavior will reflect the impact of the corporate income tax so that its effect on the weighted average cost of capital must be taken into account. Let us turn, then, to MM's analysis of the effect of taxes.

## II. IMPLICATIONS OF THE ALTERNATIVE VIEWS IN THE PRESENCE OF THE CORPORATE INCOME TAX

The special treatment accorded interest payments under the corporate income tax is likely to render regression analyses of the kind proposed by MM ineffective as a means of distinguishing between these alternative views for two reasons. First, as MM recognized in their recent correction [4] of their earlier discussion of the effects of the tax, the forms of the relationship between the weighted average cost of capital and debt-equity ratios are similar for both views under the tax. Second, and perhaps more important, the tax provides an incentive for rational managers to use debt. As we shall show, maximizing behavior is likely to lead to similar debt-equity ratios for all firms in the same risk class; consequently, the relationship between debt-equity ratios and the average cost of capital (and between the debt-equity ratio and the expected yield on shares as well) may be extremely difficult to estimate from the behavior of firms in a given risk class.

To illustrate these points, let us consider MM's equation (3) [4, p. 436], the counterpart to Proposition I corrected for the impact of taxes. It asserts that "the value of a levered firm of size $\overline{X}$, with a permanent level of debt $D_L$ in its capital structure" is as follows:

$$V_L = \frac{(1 - \tau)\overline{X}}{\rho^\tau} + \frac{\tau R}{\dot{r}} = V_u + \tau \dot{D}_L,$$

where $\tau$ is the tax rate, $\rho^\tau$ is the cost of capital for an unlevered firm under the tax (or equivalently, for a levered firm under the tax if interest payments did not receive special treatment), and $\dot{r}$ is the riskless rate of interest. We have altered their notation, denoting the present value of the tax saving as $\tau \dot{D}_L$, to

---

[7] If $L_k$ can be determined a priori so that firms with $D/S > L_k$ can be excluded from the analysis, a finding of a positive slope for the share-yield curve would contradict the traditional view.

[8] See Figure 1 [3, p. 275] for a graph of these alternatives.

emphasize the fact that the tax saving is a function of the promised rather than the expected coupon.

The value of tax saving depends on the promised coupon, $R$, because the full amount of the promise is deductible from earnings in determining tax liabilities and can always be realized, if necessary, in the market for tax losses.[9] Because $\tau R$ is thus certain, it must be discounted by the riskless rate of interest.[10] The promised and expected coupons are identical when bonds are riskless, so that no distinction between them need be made in this special case. However, this distinction becomes important when bonds are risky. The value of risky bonds is $D_L = \bar{R}^\tau/r^\tau$, the expected returns on the bonds including the possible returns from the sale of tax losses discounted by the expected yield.[11] Since $\bar{R}^\tau < R$ and $\dot{r} < r^\tau$, $(\bar{R}^\tau/r^\tau) = (\tau D_L < \tau R/\dot{r})$.

The implications of this can be seen by rewriting their equation (3) as

(6)
$$V_L = V_u + \frac{\tau R}{\dot{r}} = V_u + \frac{\tau r^* D_L}{\dot{r}}$$

where $r^* = R/D_L$, the promised yield. $R$ can be quite large since the highest possible return before interest and taxes, which determines the minimum coupon for complete debt financing, can be quite large. Neglect of the difference between promised and riskless yields understates the value of the levered firm by

$$\tau D_L \frac{(r^* - \dot{r})}{\dot{r}}$$

Equation (6) poses a problem which we shall mention only in passing; namely, if $V_L$ varies directly with $\tau R/\dot{r}$, it appears that all firms would be completely financed by debt. However, this would destroy the market for tax

[9] See footnote 5 [4, p. 435].

[10] This can be seen as follows: the expected return on a firm's bonds under the tax is

$$\bar{R}^\tau = \bar{R} + \tau \int_a^R (R - X)\phi(X)dX,$$

where $\bar{R}$ is as defined in note 5, and the second term is the increment due to the market for tax losses. The expected return on shares is simply

$$\bar{\pi}^\tau = (1 - \tau) \int_R^b (X - R)\phi(X)dX.$$

The expected return on bonds and shares, $\bar{R}^\tau + \bar{\pi}^\tau$, is

$$\bar{X}^\tau = (1 - \tau) \int_a^b X\phi(X)dX + \tau R \int_a^b \phi(X)dX$$

$$= (1 - \tau)\bar{X} + \tau R(1.0).$$

Thus, if a market for tax losses exists, $\tau R$ is certain.

[11] Because the tax saving provides additional protection for the holder of risky bonds, the expected yield on them under the tax is lower than that given by the rising portion of $BB'$ in Figure 1.

losses, since firms would no longer have tax liabilities, with the result that $\tau R$ would no longer be certain. Rather than considering here the implications of this, we shall assume that institutional constraints, such as those imposed by the Internal Revenue Service, suffice to prevent complete debt financing and so insure the existence of a market for tax losses.[12]

It follows from (6) that the weighted average after-tax cost of capital is

$$(7) \qquad \dot{\rho}^\tau = \frac{\bar{X}\tau}{V_L} = \rho^\tau - \tau \frac{r^*}{\dot{r}}(\rho^\tau - \dot{r})\frac{D_L}{V_L}.$$

This differs from MM's expression for $\rho^\tau$ (in their notation $\bar{X}/V_L$) as given in their equation (11.c) [4, p. 439] in two ways. First, the fact that the tax saving depends on the promised yield is made explicit by the factor $r^*/\dot{r}$: by omitting this factor MM implicitly assumed it to be unity, which is correct only for riskless bonds. And second, the fact that the tax saving is certain is made explicit by the identification of bond yield in the tax adjustment term as the riskless yield, $\dot{r}$. Since this tax adjustment term increases with leverage, $\rho^\tau$ is clearly a declining function of leverage. The rate of decline is greater over range of leverage for which bonds are risky than MM's equation (11.c) suggests.

To see how (7) differs from the weighted average cost of capital under the tax implied by the traditional view, consider MM's interpretation of this relationship as given by their equation (17), [3, p. 277], which we write as

$$(8) \qquad \dot{\rho}^\tau = i^\tau - (i^\tau - r^\tau)D/V$$

to make it clear that the expected yield on bonds is the relevant one in this function.[13] Differentiating (8) with respect to $D/V$ reveals that

$$(9) \qquad \dot{\rho}^{\tau'} = i^{\tau'} - (i^{\tau'} - r^\tau) - (i^{\tau'} - r^{\tau'})D/V.$$

For leverage less than or equal to $L_k$, (9) reduces to

$$(10) \qquad \dot{\rho}^{\tau'} = -(\rho^\tau - r^\tau) + r^{\tau'}D/V$$

because $i^\tau$ is then equal to $\rho^\tau$, a constant. As long as bonds are riskless, $\dot{\rho}^{\tau'} = -(\rho^\tau - \dot{r})$, which is more steeply inclined than $-\tau(\rho^\tau - \dot{r})$, the slope of (7). But when the bonds become risky, and for leverage beyond $L_k$, the slope

---

[12] There is nothing in the MM model which precludes complete debt financing by all firms. Indeed, they state that strategic considerations "not fully comprehended within the framework of static equilibrium models, either our own or those of the traditional variety [4, p. 442]," prevent such behavior.

[13] In [4, p. 439] MM restate their equation (17) [3, p. 277] as $\bar{X}^\tau/V = \rho^\tau - (\rho^\tau - r)D/V$ to facilitate its comparison with their equation (11.c). As our equations (7) and (8) make clear, this comparison is valid only when promised, expected, and riskless yields are identical; when bonds are risky, divergences between these yields make the two expressions more nearly alike for at least some range of leverage. Moreover, this version of the traditional view obscures the fact that $i^\tau$ increases for leverage beyond $L_k$. The substitution of $\rho^\tau$ for $i^\tau$ is appropriate only when $i^\tau$ is constant.

(8) becomes less steep—and hence more closely approximates that of (7) over some range of debt-equity ratios.

Because the traditional hypothesis does not place constraints on the share- and bond-yield curves like those imposed by the MM hypothesis, it is not possible to specify the exact shape of the weighted average cost of capital curve on a priori grounds. As a result, even though the slopes of (7) and (8) diverge over the range of leverage for which (8) turns up—presumably (8) is U-shaped under the tax as well as in its absence—it is not possible to deter- mine the range of debt-equity ratios over which the slopes are similar. To distinguish between (7) and (8), then, requires observation of firms over nearly the entire range of possible leverage so that, if the traditional hypothesis were correct, the upward-sloping portion of the U-shaped curve could be observed. As we shall show, it is unlikely that firms with debt-equity ratios in the relevant range can be found.

Recourse to estimation of the share-yield curve is unlikely to circumvent this difficulty since the basic shape of MM's share-yield curve is unaltered by the tax. The following expression for the weighted average cost of capital under he tax, paralleling (1), will help to illustrate this:

$$(11) \qquad \dot{\rho}^\tau = i^\tau \frac{S}{V_L} + r^\tau \frac{D}{V_L}.$$

From (7) and (11) it follows that

$$(12) \qquad i^\tau = \frac{\bar{\pi}^\tau}{S} = \rho^\tau + (\rho^\tau - r^\tau)D/S - \tau \frac{r^*}{\dot{r}}(\rho^\tau - \dot{r})D/S,$$

which differs from MM's expression for $\bar{\pi}^\tau/S$ as given in equation (12.c) [4, p. 439] in the same way that our equation (7) differs from their equation (11.c); namely, by the presence of $r^*/\dot{r}$ and $\dot{r}$ in the tax-adjustment term. The share- yield curve described by (12) is similar in shape to the $MA$ curve in Figure 1 but is displaced to the right.[14] Although (12) differs from the traditional view represented by $ML'G$ in Figure 1, a finding of positive curvature is consistent with both hypotheses. As in the absence of taxes, only a finding of negative curvature can serve to distinguish between them.[15]

Turning now to the second and more intractable difficulty noted above, it would appear that firms in a given risk class would have utilized debt up to the limits of the institutional constraints facing them or up to the optimum amount, if such exists, to maximize $V_L$. Under both hypotheses, then, firms in a given class will tend to have the same debt-equity ratios. Consequently, a scatter diagram of either expected yields on shares or weighted averages of expected yields on bonds and shares plotted against debt-equity ratios should

[14] We abstract here from the possible implications of the tax for the yield on the shares of an unlevered form; $\rho^\tau$ need not be equal to $\rho_k$.

[15] See note 7.

form a tight cluster (ideally a point).[16] The interpretation to be given the slope of a line fitted to such a scatter, such as the regression coefficients reported by MM [3, p. 281–87] for the oil and utility industries, is far from clear. Apart from measurement error, wide dispersion probably indicates the inclusion in the sample of firms from different risk classes. It may, therefore, be necessary to expand both hypotheses to include the effects of variation of institutional constraints and of optimal debt-equity ratios among risk classes to determine which of them describes the effects of leverage on market value in the real world. In the absence of such an undertaking it appears likely that tests quite different from those discussed here will be necessary to distinguish between the two hypotheses.

## REFERENCES

1. David Durand, "The Cost of Capital in an Imperfect Market: A Reply to Modigliani and Miller," *Am. Econ. Rev.*, Sept. 1959, **49**, 639–55.
2. John Lintner, "Dividends, Earnings, Leverage, Stock Prices and the Supply of Capital to Corporations," *Rev. Econ. Stat.*, Aug. 1962, **44**, 243–69.
3. Franco Modigliani and Merton H. Miller, "The Cost of Capital, Corporation Finance and the Theory of Investments," *Am. Econ. Rev.*, June 1985, **48**, 261–97.
4. —— and ——, "Taxes and the Cost of Capital: A Correction," *Am. Econ. Rev.*, June 1963, **53**, 433–43.

[16] We abstract from the unsettled questions of how expected yields are to be measured or whether they exist in the sense used by MM. In much of the traditional literature expected and promised yields on bonds are not carefully distinguished. This might be the source of some of the current controversy, since the weighted average of expected yields on shares and promised yields on bonds will be a U-shaped curve under both hypotheses.

## 30. THE COST OF CAPITAL, CORPORATION FINANCE, AND THE THEORY OF INVESTMENT: REPLY

FRANCO MODIGLIANI
and
MERTON H. MILLER*

Reprinted from *The American Economic Review*, Vol. *LV*, No. 3, (June, 1965), pp. 524–27, by permission of the authors and the publisher.

Although we can appreciate the ingenuity with which Messrs. Brewer and Michaelsen have developed parts of their argument, we fear that they have underestimated the limitations of their theoretical analysis and overestimated the significance of even their valid results for empirical applications.

Taking up the various points in their paper in order, consider first their treatment of the much-mooted falling zone in the expected yield curve for shares. We referred to such a zone only very casually in our original paper and only because the possibility of its existence was a somewhat surprising implication of our Proposition I (namely, that with perfect capital markets, no taxes, and identical borrowing functions for firms and individuals, the value of any firm must be independent of its financial structure). We did not push the matter further at that time partly because we considered the point to be of no practical consequence and partly because there seemed to be no more that could validly be said about such a zone within the confines of our basic assumptions. Nothing in the Brewer-Michaelsen paper leads us to believe we were wrong in these judgments. To reason, as they do, that a $\rho_k$ larger than the riskless rate of interest implies "risk aversion," which in turn implies $\rho_k$ greater than $r$ everywhere, and hence a monotonically increasing yield curve is merely to play with words. No precise definition of "risk aversion" in this context is provided, let alone a proof that risk aversion (everywhere?) is implied by $\rho_k$ greater than riskless $r$. Nor is this very surprising. The concept of risk aversion may perhaps have some heuristic value for rationalizing the gross behavior of the yield curves in commonsense terms; but we doubt that the term can ever be defined with sufficient precision and generality to derive conclusions of the kind Brewer and Michaelsen assert.[1]

---

* The writers are, respectively, professor of economics and industrial management at Massachusetts Institute of Technology and professor of finance and economics at the University of Chicago.

[1] The difficulties that arise with respect to defining risk aversion are merely one symptom of what is the real obstacle to specifying the relations between $\rho_k$ and $r$, namely that these

Brewer and Michaelsen are on sounder ground in their derivation of the shape of the share-yield curve, *given* a bond-yield curve (or vice versa). That, as they show, is a straightforward matter of curve tracing, and we have no particular quarrel with it. We must admit, however, to being puzzled as to why they think their discussion of the curvature properties has any significant bearing on problems of empirical testing. As they themselves acknowledge, there would always be other and more direct implications by which to distinguish the two models (in particular, by reference to the behavior of total market value in response to differences in capital structure). Even in terms of the yield curves, there would be no very serious difficulties, in principle, in distinguishing between their curves $MA$ and $ML'G$ (particularly since the slope and curvature of $MA$ can be directly predicted, as they show, from $ML'G$ and an estimate of $\rho_k$). Whether, in practice, the two curves could be distinguished by simple regressions of yield on leverage, is, of course, another matter. But the uncertainties surrounding the usefulness of this particular type of test have nothing much to do with the sorts of questions raised by Brewer and Michaelsen.

Turning next to the issue of the proper measure of the value of the tax saving on debt, we fear that their proposed new expressions are based on a misunderstanding (for which we must take some of the blame) of what we meant by the "certainty" of the tax deduction for interest payments. What we perhaps should have said more clearly is that our formulas would be valid when the tax deduction was exactly as certain or uncertain as the interest payment itself (or, equivalently, that the government's liability to the creditors is essentially the same as that of an ordinary stockholder).[2] Operationally, this means that the amount of the interest deduction for tax purposes is conditional on the

---

relations can be adequately treated only in the framework of a general equilibrium model of valuation under uncertainty. Hopefully, recent advances in this direction by Arrow (in " Le Rôle des Valeurs Boursières pour la Répartition la Meilleure des Risques," *International Colloquium on Econometrics*, 1952) and developed by Hirshleifer ("Investment Decision Under Uncertainty," forthcoming), may open up some new lines of attack.

[2] In fact, under this "stockholder" interpretation for the government's share, it is possible to derive our tax formulas directly from the no-tax case. If we let the superscripts $G$, $P$, and $T$ stand, respectively, for the government's "ownership" interest, the private sector's ownership interest, and the combined holdings of both groups; and if we assume that the government " owns " the fraction of the total common stock, then from Proposition I, we will have for an unlevered firm $V_U^T = S_U^P + S_U^G = \bar{X}/\rho_k$. The value of the purely private interest in that firm will then be

$$V_U^P = S_U^P = (1 - \tau)V_U^T = \bar{X}(1 - \tau)/\rho_k.$$

For a levered firm we will have

$$V_L^T = S_L^P + S_L^G + D_L^P = \bar{X}/\rho_k,$$

so that the private interest is

$$V_L^P = S_L^P + D_L^P = D_L^P + (1 - \tau)[\bar{X}/\rho_k - D_L^P] = V_U^P + \tau D_L^P$$

exactly as in our equation (3).

amount of the interest actually paid to the bondholders either by the issuing corporation, or, in the event of the sale of the issuing firm, by the corporation acquiring the issuing firm and its accumulated tax losses. If so, the present value of the tax saving on interest should be computed by discounting the "expected value of the tax saving—the tax saving itself being in principle a random variable—at the very same rate the market applies to the stream of expected interest payments in arriving at the market value of the debt. And this, in turn, will lead to precisely our $\tau D_L$ as the required present value. In practice, of course, the government's liability is not exactly the same as that of the stockholders. The complexity of our tax laws is such that cases can arise in which the government's liability to the creditors may be somewhat greater or may well be smaller. On the whole, however, we feel that our assumption represents a good first approximation; and certainly a far better one than that implied by Brewer and Michaelsen's equations (6), (7), and (12). These formulas, since they assume that the tax saving is certain in the literal sense, whether or not the interest is paid, amount to saying that the government assumes an absolutely unlimited liability to the bondholders and in perpetuity to boot!

Even if their formulas were acceptable descriptions of valuation under existing tax laws, we would find it hard to take seriously their claim to have disclosed new and "intractable" difficulties for empirical testing. For one thing, such discrepancies as would exist between their valuations and ours would be substantial only at levels of leverage far higher than any we normally observe. Nor would their higher estimate of the tax subsidy change the picture materially in the matter of choice of capital structure. We have noted many times that if one looks only at the tax subsidy to debt in our model (or at the "gains" from leverage under the simple traditional model), then one might expect every firm in the class to have the same debt ratio and that it would be as large as the tax laws or creditor restrictions permit. Similarly, under the more sophisticated traditional model, all firms would presumably always be at the unique "optimum" debt ratio for the class. In the real world, however, such tight clustering does not seem to occur; and the differences in capital structure in most industries we have looked at are larger than can be convincingly accounted for by measurement errors or mixing of risk classes. We have always acknowledged that we have no completely specified model to account for these observed differences, though we think we can see some of the important elements out of which such a more general theory will someday be built.

In the meantime, however, empirical research need not grind to a halt. Differences in capital structure, for whatever reasons, do exist and they can be exploited to shed much light on the controversy over the effects of financial policy on market valuation. This is not to say, of course, that the empirical problems are easy or straightforward; on the contrary, they present a most severe challenge to the econometrician. Until this challenge has been accepted by finance specialists, may we propose a moratorium on all further speculations about what might or might not be true about valuation?

# 31. A COMMENT ON THE MODIGLIANI-MILLER COST OF CAPITAL THESIS

## A. JAMES HEINS and CASE M. SPRENKLE*

Reprinted from *The American Economic Review*, Vol. *LIX*, No. 4, Part I (September, 1969), pp. 590–92, by permission of the authors and the publisher.

William L. Baldwin and Thomas J. Velk [1] point out a basic flaw in the famous Modigliani-Miller cost of capital thesis [2]. The purpose of this article is to show that the flaw, while clearly present, can be repaired and that the M-M conclusions are not affected.

The M-M thesis basically asserts that two firms cannot have different market values simply by reason of different financial structures. Using the M-M formulation, consider two firms for which the expected return is the same, $\bar{X}$. Both firms are of the same risk class; that is, the random variable $X$ representing the distribution of possible earnings before interest on any debt is the same for both. Company 1 is financed entirely by stock $S_1$, and Company 2 by stock $S_2$ and debt $D_2$. Thus:

(1) $\qquad V_1 = S_1 \qquad$ the market value of Company 1

(2) $\qquad V_2 = S_2 + D_2 \qquad$ the market value of Company 2

The object is to show that $V_1$ must equal $V_2$ under the condition that the total earnings variable, $X$, is the same for both firms. M-M do this by the following counter examples.

Suppose the value of the levered firm is greater than that of the unlevered firm, i.e., $V_1 < V_2$. Consider an investor who owns $\alpha S_2$ of the stock in Company 2. His return can be written as:

(3) $\qquad\qquad Y_2 = \alpha(X - rD_2)$

where $r$ is the rate of interest the firm pays on its debt.

Now suppose the investor sells his stock in Company 2, $\alpha S_2$, and buys an amount of stock in Company 1 equal to $\alpha(S_2 + D_2)$, financing the purchase with the proceeds, $\alpha S_2$, and by borrowing the remainder, $\alpha D_2$, at the interest rate $r$ by pledging his holdings as collateral. His new return would be:

* University of Illinois, Urbana.

$$Y_1 = \frac{\alpha(S_2 + D_2)}{S_1} X - r\alpha D_2$$

(4)

$$= \alpha \frac{V_2}{V_1} X - r\alpha D_2$$

Now, since $Y_1$ is greater than $Y_2$ if $V_2 > V_1$, M-M allege that arbitrage will drive $V_2$ and $V_1$ together and equilibrate $Y_1$ and $Y_2$.

Baldwin and Velk correctly point out that, while $Y_1$ is indeed greater than $Y_2$, $\sigma_{Y1}$ is also greater than $\sigma_{Y2}$. That is, the variance of returns on the holding of $\alpha(S_2 + D_2)$ dollars of stock 1 is greater than the variance on the holding of $\alpha S_2$ dollars of stock 2 if $V_2$ is greater than $V_1$. This follows from the proposition that multiplying a random variable, in this case $X$, by a number larger than one, in this case $V_2/V_1$, will increase its variance. Thus, using M-M's own necessary relationship that increasing the variance around some expected return will decrease the value of that return, one cannot assert that investors will arbitrage by bidding up the price of $Y_1$, i.e., the value of firm 1, to equilibrate $V_1$ and $V_2$.[1]

While at first blush this would seem to weaken the M-M argument significantly, it turns out that the M-M arbitrage case can be made simply by having the investor buy $\alpha S_1$ of the stock in Company 1 rather than $\alpha(S_2 + D_2)$. In other words, M-M have used the wrong example to show the arbitrage possibilities.

To show this, assume again that $V_2 > V_1$, but this time have our hypothetical investor sell $\alpha S_2$ and buy stock in Company 1 equal to $\alpha S_1$, borrowing the difference, $\alpha S_1 - \alpha S_2$, at interest rate $r$. In this case his return can be stated as:

(5)
$$Y_1^* = \alpha X - r\alpha(S_1 - S_2)$$

Now, from (1) and (2):

(6)
$$V_1 - V_2 = S_1 - S_2 - D_2$$
$$S_1 - S_2 = V_1 - V_2 + D_2$$

Substitute (6) into (5):

(5a)
$$Y_1^* = \alpha X - r\alpha(V_1 - V_2 + D_2)$$
$$= \alpha X - r\alpha D_2 - r\alpha(V_1 - V_2)$$

And recall:

---

[1] An unknown reviewer has reminded us that this criticism is valid only if there are positive probabilities that $X$ turns out to be negative. If the probability that $X$ is less than zero is equal to zero $P(X < 0) = 0$, then although the variance will be greater each possible return to the investor following the M-M arbitrage process will be greater than or equal to the corresponding return from continuing to hold stock in Company 1, and thus the M-M arbitrage process would in fact take place. That is, if $P(X < 0) = 0$ then $Y^1$ from equation (4) will be greater than or equal to $Y^2$ from equation (3) for any outcome $X$. Presumably, however, there is more interest in the existence of an arbitrage process that holds no matter what the expected returns may be.

$$(3) \qquad Y_2 = \alpha(X - rD_2) = \alpha X - r\alpha D_2$$

The variance of $Y_1^*$ is the same as the variance of $Y_2$ since adding or sub-tracting a number from a random variable does not change its variance. But, if $V_1 < V_2$, then $Y_1^* > Y_2$. That is, if $V_2$ is greater than $V_1$, it is possible to construct a portfolio, in this case $\alpha S_1$, that has a greater return than holdings of stock in Company 2, but *has the same variance*. Note also that $Y_1^* = Y_2$ if, and only if, $V_1 = V_2$.

The crucial difference in the arbitrage cases is that under the M-M scheme the investor borrows $\alpha D_2$ dollars whereas in our case the investor borrows only $\alpha(S_1 - S_2) = \alpha(V_1 - V_2 + D_2) < \alpha D_2$ if $V_2 > V_1$. Total ownership in stock 1 for M-M will be $\alpha(S_2 + D_2) = \alpha V_2$ whereas in our case it will be $\alpha S_2 + \alpha(V_1 - V_2 + D_2) = \alpha V_1$, and of course, $\alpha V_1 < \alpha V_2$ if $V_2 > V_1$.

For the opposite case $V_2 < V_1$; that is, the levered firm has a lower market value, M-M make a similar error in constructing their counter example. In this case, M-M's investor holds $\alpha S_1$ of stock in Company 1 yielding a return:

$$(7) \qquad Y_1 = \alpha X$$

M-M have the investor sell his $\alpha S_1$ holdings and buy stock in Company 2 in the amount of $\alpha S_1(S_2/V_2)$ and lend the remainder, $\alpha S_1(D_2/V_2)$, at interest rate $r$. His return on this portfolio is:

$$(8) \qquad \begin{aligned} Y_2 &= \alpha \frac{V_1}{V_2}(X - rD_2) + r\alpha D_2 \frac{V_1}{V_2} \\ &= \alpha \frac{V_1}{V_2} X \end{aligned}$$

M-M then conclude that, since $V_1 > V_2$, $Y_2 > Y_1$, and arbitrage will take place. But, as in the previous example $\sigma_{Y2} > \sigma_{Y1}$, and, assuming risk aversion, one cannot conclude that $Y_2$ will be preferred to $Y_1$; that is, arbitrage will not necessarily take place.

This result is obtained as before, because M-M have their investor follow the wrong strategy. Suppose that the investor sells his $\alpha S_1$ holding and buys $\alpha S_2$ dollars of stock in Company 2 and lends the remainder, $\alpha(S_1 - S_2)$ at interest rate $r$. His return on this portfolio will be:

$$(9) \qquad Y_2^* = \alpha(X - rD_2) + r\alpha(S_1 - S_2)$$

And recalling (6):

$$(9a) \qquad Y_2^* = \alpha X + r\alpha(V_1 - V_2)$$

Here $Y_2^* > Y_1$ if $V_1 > V_2$, but $\sigma_{Y1}^* = \sigma_{Y1}$. Thus, under this strategy we can conclude that arbitrage will take place, and thus that $V_2$ must be driven up to equal $V_1$.

M-M's mistake involves having their investor buy too much stock in Company 2 ($\alpha S_1(S_2/V_2)$) and lend too little ($\alpha S_1(D_2/V_2)$). Our investor buys only $\alpha S_2$ in stock (smaller than $\alpha S_1(S_2/V_2)$ if $V_1 > V_2$) and lends $\alpha(S_1 - S_2)$ (larger than $\alpha S_1(D_2/V_2)$ if $V_1 > V_2$).

The upshot of all this is that M-M are correct in saying that arbitrage will drive the market values of the two firms together; but the nature of the arbitrage process is different from that laid out in their original article.[2]

## REFERENCES

1. W. L. Baldwin and T. J. Velk, "Uncertainty of the Income Stream in the Modigliani-Miller Model," *Quart. Rev. Econ. Bus.* (forthcoming).
2. F. Modigliani and M. H. Miller, "The Cost of Capital, Corporation Finance, and the Theory of Investment," *Amer. Econ. Rev.*, June 1958, *48*, 261–97.

[2] This statement assumes away the many other comments about the viability of the M-M process that have been made in the literature.

## 32. REPLY TO HEINS AND SPRENKLE

### FRANCO MODIGLIANI and MERTON H. MILLER*

Reprinted from *The American Economic Review*, Vol. *LIX*, No. 4, Part I (September, 1969), pp. 592–95, by permission of the authors and the publisher.

In the preceding paper, A. James Heins and Case N. Sprenkle [2] offer a new proof of our proposition that the value of a firm is independent of its capital structure. They developed this proof initially to meet certain objections raised by W. L. Baldwin and T. J. Velk in [1] to our original proof in [5]; and on this score H and S seem to us to have been entirely successful. Unfortunately, however, they have chosen to deal with the B and V arguments in a way that seems likely to lead to further confusions, both about the real limitations of our proof and the real advantages of the new proposed alternative.

The trouble stems mainly from their insistence (following the unhappy example set by Baldwin and Velk) on restating our proof in terms of the variances of returns to the arbitraging shareholder. Why anyone would want to introduce the variance of returns into the proof is particularly hard for us to understand since the essential motivation underlying our original arbitrage proof, after all, was precisely to avoid having to establish tradeoffs between the moments of the probability distribution of returns. Instead, we were able to show that unless the equilibrium conditions were met, one distribution of

* The authors are members of the faculty of Massachusetts Institute of Technology and University of Chicago, respectively.

returns would completely *dominate* the other. That is, it would yield higher returns for every admissible value of the random variable $X$.[1]

The last qualification is important, for as we shall explain below, negative values of $X$ make little economic sense in this context and hence can be excluded from the domain of admissible values. Given this exclusion, it should be quite clear from equations (4) and (5) of H and S that $V_2 > V_1$ would indeed imply $Y_1 \geq Y_2$ for all admissible values of $X$. Hence, $Y_1$ would be preferred to $Y_2$ by any investor for whom more wealth was better than less; and would be so preferred *despite the fact that the variance of $Y_1$ happens to be larger than that of $Y_2$*. It is only when negative values for $X$ are admitted that the proof would fail since, for such values of $X$, $Y_1$ would be smaller than $Y_2$ and hence $Y_1$ would no longer strictly dominate $Y_2$.[2]

But while the nonnegativity restriction on $X$ means that our original proof remains entirely valid, H and S have certainly done a useful service in providing a proof that can dispense with that particular restriction. What their preoccupation with variances seems to have kept them from realizing, however, is that their proof is by no means the only one with that virtue. Among these alternative proofs there is one in particular that we would like to present here because it is so much easier to understand and, in a sense that will presently become clear, is more general than either our original proof or the H and S extension of it. This proof consists of showing that if the levered and unlevered firms did not have the same market value, then it would be possible for holders of the shares of the overvalued firm to form a portfolio based on the shares in the undervalued firm in such a way as to produce the *identical* (random) outcome for a smaller net investment. Since the investor would clearly be better off to take the cheaper of the two alternatives, an incentive would exist to sell the overpriced shares and buy the other as long as the disequilibrium persisted.

More formally, using the mnemonic notation $V_U \equiv S_U$ for the value of the unlevered firm $V_L \equiv S_L + D_L$ for that of the levered firm and $X$ as before for the (identical) stream generated by each firm; consider first the case of an investor holding the fraction $\alpha$ of the shares in the unlevered corporation. That holding entitles him to a return of $\alpha X$ for a total investment on his part of $\alpha S_U \equiv \alpha V_U$. But an identical return of $\alpha X$ can also be obtained for a total investment of $\alpha V_L$ as follows:

---

[1] It is true that we ourselves on occasion have used variances of returns in discussing our propositions (see, for example, our [7, especially Section I], but only as a way of making the common sense of the final result easier for some to see and not as an essential part of the argument.

[2] As indeed H and S eventually recognize in their note 1. That the validity of our original proof requires the restriction $X \geq 0$ has, of course, been pointed out by a number of people over the years, most insistently perhaps, by William Sher. See, for example, [8].

| Transaction | Investment Required | Return Produced |
|---|---|---|
| 1. Buy the fraction $\alpha$ of the shares in the levered firm. | $\alpha S_L \equiv \alpha(V_L - D_L)$ | $\alpha(X - rD_L)$ |
| 2. Buy the fraction $\alpha$ of the bonds of the levered firm. | $\alpha D_L$ | $\alpha r D_L$ |
| Totals | $\alpha V_L$ | $\alpha X$ |

Hence, if $V_U > V_L$ our investor would not want to hold his shares in the unlevered firm since he could obtain exactly the same return by the transactions indicated in the table for a net investment smaller by $\alpha(V_U - V_L)$.

Similarly, in the other direction. The holder of the fraction $\alpha$ of the levered firm obtains a return of $\alpha(X - rD_L)$ at a cost of $\alpha S_L \equiv \alpha(V_L - D_L)$. But, by matching the components of this return separately an identical return can be obtained from the unlevered shares at a cost of $\alpha(V_U - D_L)$:

| Transaction | Investment Required | Return Produced |
|---|---|---|
| 1. Buy the fraction $\alpha$ of the shares of the un-levered firm. | $\alpha S_U \equiv \alpha V_U$ | $\alpha X$ |
| 2. Borrow $\alpha D_L$ on personal account. | $-\alpha D_L$ | $-\alpha r D_L$ |
| Totals | $\alpha(V_U - D_L)$ | $\alpha(X - rD_L)$ |

Hence, if $V_L > V_U$ our holder of the levered shares could obtain exactly the same return for an outlay smaller by $\alpha(V_L - V_U)$ so that shares in the levered firm would not be held. Thus, as with our original proof, we are able to rule out both inequalities and, hence, may validly conclude that only $V_L = V_U$ is compatible with equilibrium in the capital markets.

This new proof based on cost minimization is more general than the original M and M or the H and S proof in that it requires no assumption as to how the saving achieved by switching portfolios is to be invested (or, indeed, as to whether it be invested at all). By contrast, our earlier proof implicitly added the unnecessary restriction that the saving be entirely reinvested in the under-valued shares, while the H and S version adds the equally unnecessary restriction that the saving be reinvested in the undervalued shares in such a way as to maintain the initial variance of returns. In addition to its greater generality in this respect, the new proof is also considerably more transparent. The gain on this count is particularly striking when we turn from the no-tax case to the much messier one in which a corporate income tax is admitted (as in our [7])—a case in which under the original proof it required something of the instincts of a Swiss currency speculator to be able to see how to construct a dominating holding. Consider now, however, the case of an investor owning the fraction $\alpha$ of the shares of the levered firm. His outlay of $\alpha S_L$ for these shares would entitle him to a return of $\alpha(X - rD_L)(1 - \tau) = \alpha X(1 - \tau) - \alpha(1 - \tau)rD_L$ where $X$ is equal to the return before corporate taxes and $\tau$ is the corporate tax rate. But by using the unlevered shares and personal borrowing to match each of the components of the returns separately, the investor could obtain an identical return as follows:

| Transaction | Investment Required | Return Produced |
|---|---|---|
| 1. Buy the fraction $\alpha$ of the shares of the unlevered firm. | $\alpha S_U \equiv \alpha V_U$ | $\alpha X(1 - \tau)$ |
| 2. Borrow $\alpha(1 - r)D_L$ on personal account. | $-\alpha(1 - \tau)D_L$ | $-\alpha(1 - \tau)rD_L$ |
| Totals | $\alpha(V_U - (1 - \tau)D_L)$ | $\alpha(X - rD_L)(1 - \tau)$ |

Hence, if $S_L > V_U - (1 - \tau)D_L$ or equivalently if $S_L + D_L \equiv V_L > V_U + \tau D_L$ the investor would not want to hold his shares in the levered firm since he could buy exactly the same return at a saving of $\alpha(V_L - (V_U + \tau D_L))$. The proof in the other direction is equally straightforward and by now should not need to be spelled out in detail.

Having shown how and why alternative proofs can be provided that do not require the exclusion of negative values for $X$, we may turn now to explain our earlier assertion that such values can, in any event, safely be ruled out on economic grounds. This explanation is offered here, we hasten to add, not as a justification of our earlier approach, but in the hopes of clarifying some of the real limitations on arbitrage proofs whether of the original or newer varieties.

To understand the basis of our assertion, it is important to remember that our $X$ does not stand for the earnings generated by a firm during a given period—an amount that can certainly be negative. It represents, rather, the return that actually accrues to those who own the firm's securities. Precisely how that return is to be defined will depend on the further purposes of the analysis. Where, for example, the concern is to derive the proposition within the framework of standard portfolio theory, then $X$ would be defined as the one period return, that is, as the sum of any cash payments received during the period plus the terminal value of the firm's assets. In our original paper, our concern was rather to derive the proposition in a way that would relate more directly to standard discussions of the cost of capital and capital budgeting and would do so despite the fact that no generally valid method for discounting uncertain streams was (or is yet) available. For this purpose, it proved convenient to define $X$ as the average return per period that would accrue to someone who held the shares in perpetuity; and then, by analogy with the perpetuity formula in the certainty case, to define the value of the firm as the capitalized value of the mathematical expectation of that average return. Under either interpretation of $X$, however, it should be clear that $X$ is intended to represent a gross return. Hence, it would have to be positive (or at worst zero) for both the bondholders and the shareholders, at least as long as the latter are assumed not to be subject to assessments or other devices that remove the normal limitations on their liability to the corporations' creditors.

Although the existence of limited liability at the corporate level thus permits us to banish the case of $X < 0$, a similar difficulty in establishing the necessary dominance will emerge if limited liability is not assumed to extend also to individuals on their personal leverage operations. For, in that event, the exact matching of returns on levered and unlevered shares would be prevented by the possibility of occurrence of $0 < X < rD_L$, the limited liability of the corporation then leading to a return of zero for holders of levered shares, but to a negative return for those borrowing against the unlevered shares and now faced with an additional call to pay off their creditors. Thus, given corporate limited liability, a completely rigorous arbitrage proof, whether of the old or new variety, requires either the further restriction that $X > rD_L$, or, the assumption that, by one means or another, individuals as well as corporations are able effectively to limit their liability.[3]

To say this is not to suggest, of course, that the same restrictions are equally necessary for the validity of the fundamental conclusion itself. Alternative approaches can and have been developed which show that the independence proposition may hold in equilibrium even where the restrictions above are relaxed or eliminated (see especially Stiglitz [9] and Hirshleifer [3] (4]). Nor should such results be particularly surprising. Even without invoking the usual sorts of "positivist" considerations (as, e.g., in our [6], especially Section I), we know that a substantial cushion of "slack" must be present in the arbitrage proofs, which are so conservative, after all, as actually to require a complete dominance of one distribution over another before they will admit the slightest equilibrating movement in prices. Such extreme conservatism, however, is not without its compensations. It does permit the essential point to be made with a much less formidable apparatus than required for the alternative, general equilibrium proofs. Hence, the simple arbitrage proofs, despite their seemingly restricted range, can still play a useful role in discussions of the capital structure problem—a role that may

---

[3] Although not stated in quite these terms, these limitations seem to us at least to have been clearly implied first by our assumption that all interest payments were riskless (which would have to mean $X \geq rD$ if corporations had limited liability) and later, when we relaxed the riskless borrowing assumption, by our assumption that the interest rate *function*, whatever form it might take, be the same for individuals as for corporations. A very thorough discussion of the whole problem is given by Stiglitz in [9]. Stiglitz shows, among other things, incidentally, that many of the other restrictive assumptions in the proof can be dropped or relaxed (most notably the presumed existence of homogeneous risk classes) if limited liability is assumed for individuals.

hopefully be enhanced by the newer and even simpler versions here presented.

REFERENCES

1. W. L. Baldwin, and T. J. Velk, "Uncertainty of the Income Stream in the Modigliani-Miller Model," *Quart. Rev. Econ. Bus.*, forthcoming.
2. A. J. Heins and C. M. Sprenkle, "A Comment on The Modigliani-Miller Cost of Capital Thesis," *Amer. Econ. Rev.*, current issue.
3. J. Hirshleifer, "Investment Decision Under Uncertainty: Choice Theoretic Approaches," *Quart. J. Econ.*, Nov. 1965, *79*, 509–36.
4. ———, "Investment Decision Under Uncertainty: Applications of the State Preference Approach," *Quart. J. Econ.*, May 1966, *80*, 611–17.
5. F. Modigliani and M. H. Miller, "The Cost of Capital, Corporation Finance and the Theory of Investment," *Amer. Econ. Rev.*, June 1958, *48*, 261–97.
6. ———, "Reply to Rose and Durand," *Amer. Econ. Rev.*, Sept. 1959, *49*, 655–59.
7. ———, "Corporate Income Taxes and the Cost of Capital: A Correction," *Amer. Rev.*, June 1963, *53*, 433–43.
8. W. Sher, "The Cost of Capital and Corporation Finance Involving Risk." A paper presented at the Winter Meetings of the Econometric Society, Evanston, Dec. 1968. Multilithed, Duquesne Univ., Pittsburgh.
9. J. E. Stiglitz, "A Re-examination of the Modigliani-Miller Theorem." Cowles Foundation Discussion Paper, No. 242. Yale Univ., Dec. 1967.

## 33. A RE-EXAMINATION OF THE MODIGLIANI-MILLER THEOREM

### JOSEPH E. STIGLITZ*

Reprinted from *The American Economic Review*, Vol. *LIX*, No. 5 (December, 1969) pp. 784–93, by permission of the author and the publisher.

In their classic paper of 1958, Franco Modigliani and Merton H. Miller demonstrated that the cost of capital for a firm was independent of the debt-equity ratio [13]. Although much of the subsequent discussion has focused on the realism of particular assumptions [3] [7], there have been few attempts to

* Associate professor, Cowles Foundation, Yale University. This is a revised version of Cowles Foundation Discussion Paper No. 242, presented at the December 1967 meetings of the Econometric Society. The research described in this paper was carried out under grants from the National Science Foundation and from the Ford Foundation. I am deeply indebted to D. Cass, A. Klevorick, M. Miller, and W. Nordhaus for extensive discussions on these problems and detailed comments on a previous draft.

delineate exactly the class of assumptions under which the M-M theorem obtains.[1] In particular, five limitations of the M-M proof may be noted:

1. It depended on the existence of risk classes.
2. The use of risk classes seemed to imply objective rather than subjective probability distributions over the possible outcomes.
3. It was based on partial equilibrium rather than general equilibrium analysis.
4. It was not clear whether the theorem held only for competitive markets.
5. Except under special circumstances, it was not clear how the possibility of firm bankruptcy affected the validity of the theorem.

In Section 1, we show in the context of a general equilibrium state preference model that the M-M theorem holds under much more general conditions than those assumed in their original study. The validity of the theorem does not depend on the existence of risk classes, on the competitiveness of the capital market, or on the agreement of individuals about the probability distribution of outcomes.[2]

The two assumptions which do appear to be important for our proof are (a) individuals can borrow at the same market rate of interest as firms and (b) there is no bankruptcy.[3] But it is these assumptions which appear to be the center of much of the criticism of the M-M analysis. In Section II, we show that the M-M results may still be valid even if there are limitations on individual borrowing, and in Section III, we show that the possibility of bankruptcy raises more serious problems, although the M-M theorem can still be shown to hold under somewhat more stringent conditions.

## I. THE BASIC THEOREM

Consider a firm whose gross returns, $X$ (before paying bondholders but after paying all non-capital factors of production) are uncertain. We can consider $X$ as a function of the state of the world $\theta$. One dollar invested in a perfectly safe bond yields a gross return of $r^*$, so that $r^* - 1$ is the market rate of interest. If there is any chance of bankruptcy, the nominal rate $\hat{r}$ which the firm must pay on its bonds will depend on the number issued. If principal payments plus interest exceed gross profits, $X$, the firm goes bank-

---

[1] Exceptions are the work of Hirschleifer [9] [10] and Robichek and Meyers [19], who used the Arrow–Debreu model (which assumes at least as many securities as states of the world) and the doctoral dissertation of G. Pye [18]. More recently Sher [21] has concerned himself with some of the difficulties raised by bankruptcy. For other general equilibrium portfolio (stock-market) models, see Sharpe [20], Lintner [11], Mossin [17], and Diamond [6].

[2] Except that they must agree that there is zero probability of bankruptcy. See discussion in text.

[3] It should be clear that these assumptions are not completely independent. Presumably, one of the most important reasons individuals cannot borrow at the same rate as firms is that there is a higher probability of default.

rupt, and the gross profits are divided among the bondholders.[4] Thus the gross return on a dollar invested in the bonds of the firm depends on state $\theta$.

$$(1) \qquad \bar{r}(\theta) = \begin{cases} \hat{r} & \text{if } \hat{r} B \leq X(\theta) \\ \dfrac{X(\theta)}{B} & \text{if } \hat{r} B \geq X(\theta). \end{cases}$$

Earnings per dollar invested in equity in state $\theta$ are given by

$$(2) \qquad e(\theta) = \begin{cases} [X(\theta) - \hat{r}B]/E & \text{if } \hat{r}B \leq X(\theta) \\ 0 & \text{if } \hat{r}B \geq X(\theta) \end{cases}$$

where $E$ is the value of the firm's equity. The value of the firm is

$$(3) \qquad V = E + B.$$

Individuals will be assumed to evaluate alternative portfolios in terms of their income patterns across the states of nature.

We now prove the following proposition.

Assume there is no bankruptcy and individuals can borrow and lend at the market rate of interest. If there exists a general equilibrium with each firm having a particular debt-equity ratio and a particular value, then there exists another general equilibrium solution for the economy with any firm having any other debt-equity ratio but with the value of all firms and the market rate of interest unchanged.

*Proof.* Let $w^j$ be the $j$th individual's wealth, $E_i^j$, the value of his shares of the $i$th firm, $B^j$ the number of bonds he owns.[5] Assume the $i$th firm, whose value is $V_i$, issues $B_i$ bonds. The $j$th individual's budget constraint may be written

$$(4) \qquad w_j = \sum_i E_i^j + B^j.$$

If we let $\alpha_i^j = E_i^j/E_i$, the share of the $i$th firm's equity owned by the $j$th individual, (4) becomes

$$(5) \qquad w^j = \sum_i \alpha_i^j E_i + B^j.$$

Then his income in state $\theta$ may be written

---

[4] Throughout the discussion we limit ourselves to a two-period model. In a two-period model, a firm either makes its interest payments or goes bankrupt. In a multi-period model, the firm can, in addition, defer the interest or principal payments. If there is a positive probability of such deferral, the market will force the firm to pay a higher nominal rate of interest. If there are large transaction costs involved in bankruptcy or deferral, the M-M theorem would not hold. Throughout the discussion we shall assume that there are no flotation costs and no taxes.

[5] By convention, one bond costs one dollar.

$$(6) \qquad Y^j(\theta) = \sum_{i=1}^{n} (X_i - r^*B_i)\alpha_i^j + r^*\left(w^j - \sum_{i=1}^{n} \alpha_i^j(V_i - B_i)\right)$$

$$= \sum_{i=1}^{n} X_i\alpha_i^j + r^*\left(w^j - \sum_{i=1}^{n} \alpha_i^j V_i\right).$$

If, as $B_i$ changes, $V_i$ remains unchanged, the individual's opportunity set does not change, and the set of $\alpha_i^j$ which maximizes the individual's utility is unchanged. If

$$\sum_j \alpha_i^j = 1$$

before, i.e., demand for shares equalled supply of shares, it still does. The total net demand for bonds is

$$\sum_i \left(w^j - \sum_i \alpha_i^j(V_i - B_i)\right) + \sum_i B_i = \sum_j w^j - \sum_i V_i.$$

If the market was in equilibrium initially,

$$\sum_j w^j - \sum_i V_i = 0,$$

i.e., excess demand equalled zero. If as the debt-equity ratio changes, all $V_i$ remain unchanged, excess demand remains at zero.

An alternative way of seeing this is the following. We may rewrite (6) as

$$(6') \qquad Y^j(\theta) = \sum_i e_i(\theta) E_i^j + r^*\left(w^j - \sum_{i=1}^{n} E_i^j\right).$$

Assume now that the first firm, say, issues no bonds. If we let carets denote the values of the various variables in this situation, the opportunity set is given by

$$(6'') \qquad \hat{Y}^j(\theta) = \sum_i \hat{e}_i(\theta)\hat{E}_i^j + \hat{r}^*\left(w^j - \sum_i \hat{E}_i^j\right).$$

Assume $r^* = \hat{r}^*$, $E_i = \hat{E}_i$, $i \geq 2$. Then from (2), $e_i(\theta) = \hat{e}_i(\theta)$, $i \geq 2$. If $\hat{E}_1 = E_1 + B_1$, then the opportunity sets described by (6') and (6'') are identical. To see this, assume that for each dollar of equity he owned in the first firm in the initial situation, the individual borrows $B_1/E_1$ in addition to $B^j$

$$\text{so } \hat{B}^j = B^j + E_1^j \frac{B_1}{E_1}.$$

With the proceeds of the loan he increases his holdings of equities in the first firm, so

$$(7) \qquad \hat{E}_1^j = E_1^j + E_1^j \frac{B_1}{E_1} = E_1^j \left(\frac{V_1}{E_1}\right).$$

His income in state $\theta$ is then given by

$$\hat{Y}^j(\theta) = \frac{X_1 E_1^j}{E_1} + \sum_{i=2}^{n} e_i(\theta)E_i^j + r^*\left(w^j - \sum_{i=2}^{n} E_i^j - \frac{E_1^j V_1}{E_1}\right)$$

(8)

$$= \left(\frac{X_1 - r^*B_1}{E_1}\right) E_1^j + \sum_{i=2}^{n} e_i(\theta)E_i^j + r^*\left(w^j - \sum_{i=1}^{n} E_i^j\right)$$

which is identical to (6').

Since his opportunity set has not been changed as a result of the change in the debt-equity ratio of the firm, if he was maximizing his utility in the initial situation, the optimal allocation in the new situation is identical to that in the initial situation with the one modification given above.

We now need to show that the markets for the firm's equities and the market for bonds will clear. Summing (7) over all individuals, we obtain

$$\sum_{j} \hat{E}_1^j = \frac{V_1}{E_1} \sum_{j} E_1^j.$$

Thus the demand for equities has increased by a factor $V_1/E_1$. But since $\hat{E}_1/E_1 = V_1/E_1$, the supply has increased by exactly the same proportion, so if demand equalled supply before it also does now. Similarly, the increase in the demand for bonds by individuals equals $(B_1/E_1) \sum E_1^j = B_1$. But this exactly equals the decrease in the demand for bonds by the first firm.

It should be emphasized that in this proof, $X(\theta)$ is subjectively determined; moreover no assumptions about the size of firms, the source of the uncertainty, and the existence of risk classes have been made. The only restriction on the individual's behavior is that he evaluates alternative portfolios in terms of the income stream they generate. The two crucial assumptions were (a) all individuals agree that for all firms $X_i(\theta) > r^*B$ for all $\theta$ (see Section III); and (b) individuals can borrow and lend at the market rate of interest. This assumption is considerably weaker than the assumpton of a competitive capital market, since no assumption about the number of firms has been made: the market rate of interest need not be invariant to the supply of bonds by any single firm.

## II. LIMITATIONS ON INDIVIDUAL BORROWING

One of the main objections raised to the M-M analysis is that individuals cannot borrow at the same rate of interest as firms. First, it should be noted (see [13]) that the analysis does not require that individuals actually borrow from the market, but only that they change their holdings of bonds. A problem can arise then only if an individual has *no* bonds in his portfolio.

Although the requirement that all individuals hold bonds does place restrictions on the possible debt-equity ratios of different firms, there still need not be an optimal debt-equity ratio for any single firm. Assume we have some general equilibrium situation where $B^i \geq 0$ for all $j$. Then so long as $B_i$ satisfy the inequalities.

(9)
$$\sum_i \alpha_i^j B_i \geq w^j - \sum_i \alpha_i^j V_i \quad \text{for all } j$$

all individuals will be lenders. If there were two firms, the constraints (9) would imply that $(B_1, B_2)$ lie in the shaded area shown in Figure 1. For any pair of $(B_1, B_2)$ in the region, there will exist a general equilibrium in which the values of both firms are identical to that in the original situation.

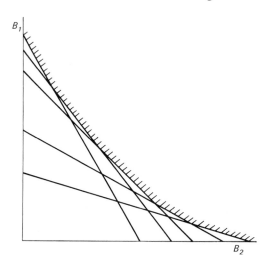

Figure 1

So far, none of our results have depended on the existence of risk classes.[6] The following two results depend on more than one firm having the same pattern of returns across the states of nature.

We shall first show that if there are two (or more) firms with the same pattern of returns and individuals can sell short, then, the two firms must have the same value, independent of the debt-equity ratio.

We follow M-M in assuming for simplicity that one of the two firms has no outstanding debt, so $V_1 = E_1$. The second firm issues $B_2$ bonds, so $V_2 = B_2 + E_2$.

Consider first an individual who owns $\alpha_1$ of the shares of the first firm, yielding an income pattern $\alpha_1 X_1(\theta)$. If instead he purchases $\alpha_1$ of the shares of the second firm, at a cost of $\alpha_1 E_2$, and buys $\alpha_1 B_2$ bonds, his income in state $\theta$ is $\alpha_1(X_2(\theta) - r^*B_2) + \alpha_1 r^*B_2 = \alpha_1 X_2(\theta)$ which is identical to his income in state $\theta$ in the previous situation. But the cost of purchasing $\alpha_1$ of the shares of the first company is $\alpha_1 V_1$ which is *greater* than $\alpha_1(E_2 + B_2) = \alpha_1 V_2$ if $V_1 > V_2$. Accordingly, if $V_1$ were greater than $V_2$, all holders of shares in the first company would sell their shares and purchase shares in the second firm, driving the value of the second firm up and that of the first down. Now consider an individual who wishes to lend money. If he sells short $\alpha_2$ of the shares

---

[6] Two firms, $i$ and $j$ are in the same risk class if $X_i(\theta) = \lambda X_j(\theta)$ for all $\theta$. In the remainder of the discussion we shall assume for convenience, that $\lambda = 1$.

of the second firm and buys $\alpha_2$ of the shares of the first firm, he receives a perfectly safe return of[7] $-\alpha_2(X_2 - r^*B_2) + \alpha_2 X_1 = \alpha_2 r^* B_2$ at a net cost of $-\alpha_2(V_2 - B_2) + \alpha_2 V_1$ so the return per dollar is

$$r^* \frac{B_2}{V_1 - (V_2 - B_2)} = r^* \frac{1}{1 + \dfrac{V_1 - V_2}{B_2}}$$

If $V_1 < V_2$, the individual can obtain a perfectly safe return in excess of $r^*$. It follows immediately that equilibrium in the capital market requires $V_1 = V_2$.[8]

Similar arguments can be used to show the following.

If there are three or more firms in the same risk class, and the firms with the highest and lowest debt-equity ratios have the same value, then the value of all other firms must be the same.

This is true whether individuals can borrow or can sell securities short. This result rules out the possibility of a U-shaped curve relating the value of the firm to the debt-equity ratio.[9]

## III. BANKRUPTCY

Bankruptcy presents a problem for the usual proofs of the M-M theorem on two accounts: first, it means that the nominal rate of interest which the firm must pay on its bonds will increase as the number of bonds increases. (M-M have treated the case where it increases at exactly the same rate for all firms and individuals.) Second, if a firm goes bankrupt, it is no longer possible for an individual to replicate the exact patterns of returns, except if he can buy on margin, using the security as collateral; and if he defaults, he only forfeits the security and none of his other assets. To see this, consider the two alternative policies considered in Section I; in the one case, the firm issues no bonds (hence no chance of default) and in the other it issues $\hat{B}$ bonds. We

[7] As usual, we assume no transactions costs and that there is no cash requirement or short sales. (See fn. 9.)

[8] This proof has the advantage that no restrictions on the sign of $X(\theta)$ need be made. Although the case of $X(\theta) < 0$ is not very interesting from an economic point of view, some authors (e.g. [21]) have drawn attention to the difficulties which arise in the original M-M proof when $X(\theta) < 0$.

[9] Taxes and bankruptcy may alter this conclusion. Recently, Baumol and Malkeil [2] have argued that if there are costs of transactions, the levered company may have a higher value than the unlevered company. They argue that if, in order to undertake the arbitrage operations required by the M-M analysis, the individual had to borrow, the total value of transactions would be greater than if the company provided the desired leverage. If there are sizeable transactions costs, in order for the net income from the two firms to be the same, the levered company must have a higher value than the unlevered firm. Transactions costs cannot be adequately analyzed in terms of the two-period model that they (and we) use, but even in the context of a two-period model, it is not clear that their point is correct. If the individual has bonds in his portfolio, or if there are two companies, one with high leverage and one with low leverage, the individual can simply change his portfolio composition.

have shown how the individual by buying stock on margin in the latter case can exactly replicate the returns in the former situation in those states where the firm does not go bankrupt if the value of the firm is the same in the two situations. But if the firm goes bankrupt in some state, $\theta'$, in the one case his return is zero, while in the other his return per dollar invested is

$$\frac{X(\theta')}{V} \left( 1 + \frac{\hat{B}}{\hat{E}} \right) - \hat{r} \frac{\hat{B}}{\hat{E}} < 0.$$

If, however, he can forfeit the security then his return will again be zero.

Of course, if the firm has a positive probability of going bankrupt, it will have to pay a higher nominal rate of interest. But if the individual is to use the security as collateral, he, too, will have to pay a higher nominal rate of interest. And indeed, it is clear that the two will be exactly the same, since the pattern of returns on the bonds in bankruptcy will be the same. Thus, we have shown that

if a firm has a positive probability of going bankrupt, and an individual can borrow using those securities as collateral (so that if his return from the securities is less than his borrowings, he can forfeit the securities) the value of the firm is invariant to the debt-equity ratio.

It should be noted that the validity of this proposition does not require 100 percent margins. The required margin is only $\hat{B}/V$.

Individuals may, of course, not be able to make the limited liability arrangements or to obtain the level of margin required by the above analysis. Then, a firm by pursuing alternative debt-equity policies may be able to offer patterns of returns which the individual cannot obtain in any other manner (i.e., by purchasing shares in one or more other firms), and the value of the firm may consequently vary as the firm changes its debt-equity ratio. In the following subsections, we consider some special situations, in which M-M results may still be valid, even though there is a finite probability of bankruptcy.

RISK CLASSES

If there are a large number of firms in the same risk class, then potentially they can all supply the same pattern of returns. If all firms maximize their value, then in market equilibrium all firms will have the same value.[10] Firms may have different debt-equity ratios and the same value for a number of reasons. For instance, assume that some individuals, for some reason or other, prefer a low debt equity-ratio, and some prefer a high debt-equity ratio. Then, some firms may have a high debt-equity ratio, some a low one. If one firm observes another firm in the same risk class with a different debt-equity ratio but a higher value, it will change its debt-equity ratio. Thus the observation that all firms in a given risk class have the same value but possibly different debt-equity ratios can be taken as evidence that firms are value

[10] Recall that we have assumed for expositional convenience that $X_j(\theta) = X_i(\theta)$ for all firms in the risk class.

maximizers and are in market equilibrium. It is not necessarily evidence that the arbitrage activities described by Modigliani and Miller have occurred, or that the value of the firm would be the same at some debt-equity ratio other than those actually observed.

Assume the market is in equilibrium, with $V = \rho EX$ for all members of the risk class. The securities sold by a firm are completely described by the risk class and the debt-equity ratio. A new, small firm is created, belonging to the same risk class, with mean return $\tilde{X}$. If it chooses a debt-equity ratio used by other firms in the same risk class, the price of its shares must be the same as those of the other firms (since they are identical) so its value will be $\tilde{X}\rho$. But, if it chooses some other debt-equity ratio, its value may be lower (if, for instance, there is a positive probability of bankruptcy).[11]

MEAN-VARIANCE ANALYSIS AND THE SEPARATION THEOREM

In this subsection we consider the special case where all individuals evaluate alternative income patterns in terms of their mean and variance. For simplicity, let us assume that only the first firm issues enough bonds to go bankrupt. If all individuals agree on the probability distribution of returns for each firm, it can be shown that the

...total market value of any stock in equilibrium is equal to the *capitalization* at the *risk-free interest rate* $r^*$, of the *certainty equivalent*... of its uncertain *aggregate dollar return*; ... the difference... between the expected value of these returns and their certainty equivalent is *proportional* for each company to *its aggregate risk* represented by the *sum* of the *variance* of these returns and their total covariance with those of all other stocks, and the factor of proportionality is the *same* for *all* companies in the market. [11, pp. 26–27].

This implies that

$$(10) \quad E_i + B_i = \left\{ \bar{X} - k \sum_{j=1}^{n} \mathscr{E}(X_i - \bar{X}_i)(X_j - \bar{X}_j) \right\} \Big/ r^* \qquad i = 2, \ldots, n$$

$$(11) \qquad E_1 = \left\{ \bar{Z} - k \sum_{j=1}^{n} \mathscr{E}(Z - \bar{Z})(X^j - \bar{X}j) \right\} \Big/ r^*$$

$$(12) \qquad B_1 = \left\{ \bar{r}B_1 - k \sum_{j=1}^{n} \mathscr{E}(\tilde{r} - \bar{r}) B_1(X_j - X_j) \right\} \Big/ r^*$$

where $\mathscr{E}$ is the expectations operator,

$$Z = \max(X_1 - \hat{r}B_1, 0), \qquad \mathscr{E}Z = \bar{Z},$$
$$\mathscr{E}X_j = \bar{X}_j, \qquad \mathscr{E}\tilde{r} = \bar{r},$$

and

$$k = r^* \left( \sum_i (X_i - \bar{X}_i) \Big/ \sum_i \sum_j \mathscr{E}(X_i - \bar{X}_i)(X_j - \bar{X}_j) \right).$$

[11] This also may occur with taxes if interest payments are tax deductible and if capital gains are treated preferentially. See [8].

Then adding $B_1$ and $E_1$, ((11) and (12)), we obtain

$$V_1 = E_1 + B_1 = \left\{ \bar{X}_1 - k \sum_{j=1}^{n} \mathcal{E}(X_1 - \bar{X}_1)(X_j - \bar{X}_j) \right\} \Big/ r^*$$

independent of the debt-equity ratio.

The intuitive reason for this should be clear: it is well-known that if all individuals agree on the probability distribution of the risky assets, if there exists a safe asset, and if individuals evaluate income patterns in terms of mean and variance, the ratio in which different risky assets are purchased will be the same for all individuals, i.e. all the relevant market opportunities can be provided by the safe asset and a single mutual fund which (in market equilibrium) will contain all the risky assets, including the risky bonds. More generally, whenever the ratio in which different risky assets are purchased is the same for all individuals, then the M-M theorem will be true even with bankruptcy. For a complete discussion of the conditions under which the separation theorem obtains, see Cass and Stiglitz [4].

If, however, (a) all individuals do not agree on the probability distribution of $X_i(\theta)$ or, (b) the conditions under which the separation theorem is valid do not obtain, then the value of the firm will in general depend on the debt-equity ratio.[12]

### ARROW-DEBREU SECURITIES

Arrow [1] and Debreu [5] have formulated a model of general equilibrium under uncertainty in which individuals can buy and sell promises to pay if a given state of the world occurs. See also Hirshleifer [10]. A stock market security and a bond can be viewed as a bundle of these Arrow-Debreu

---

[12] For then, issuing a risky bond (a high debt-equity ratio) changes the relevant market opportunities available to the individual. For the M-M result to be valid, the debt-equity ratio can have no real effects on the economy. But it is easy to show that the assumptions (a) marginal utility of income in each state of nature is independent of the debt-equity ratio, and (b) the value of the firm is independent of the debt-equity ratio are in general inconsistent with the first order conditions for expected utility maximization being satisfied by all individuals (if bankruptcy may occur). To see this, observe that if an individual chooses his portfolio to maximize $\mathcal{E}U(Y(\theta))$, where $U'' < 0$, then a necessary and sufficient condition for the optimal allocation (assuming short sales are allowed) may be written $\mathcal{E}U'e_i = \mathcal{E}U'r^*$, or from (2), $[\mathcal{E}U'(X_j - \hat{r}_jB_j]/\mathcal{E}U'r^* = E_j$
where $\mathcal{S}$ is defined as the set of states of nature for which $X_j(\theta) \geq \hat{r}_jB_j$. Assume $U'(Y(\theta))$ is invariant for all $\theta$ and for all individuals to the $j$th firm's debt-equity ratio. Then,

$$dE_j/dB_j = -\frac{\hat{r}_j}{r^*}\left(1 + \frac{d \ln \hat{r}_j}{d \ln B_j}\right)(\mathcal{E}U'/\mathcal{E}U');$$

and if the value of the firm is to be unchanged, $dE_j/dB_j = -1$. But unless all individuals have identical utility functions _and_ indentical assessments of the probability of bankruptcy ($\mathcal{E}U'/\mathcal{E}U'$) will differ for different individuals, so $dE_j/dB_j = -1$ only if marginal utilities in some states of nature change for some individuals.

It should be observed that when the actions of a firm can change the opportunity set, there is no reason that firms necessarily, will maximize market value.

securities. If there is a sufficient number of different firms, equal to or greater than the number of states of nature, then the market opportunities available to the individual (by purchasing or selling short different amounts of the market securities) are identical to those of a corresponding Arrow-Debreu market. If a promise to pay one dollar in state $\theta$ has a price $p^*(\theta)$,[13] then the value of the firm's equity is

$$E = \sum_{\mathcal{S}} (X(\theta) - \hat{r}B)p^*(\theta).$$

If

$$\hat{r} = \left[ 1 - \sum_{\mathcal{S}'} \frac{X(\theta)}{B} p^*(\theta) \right] \Big/ \sum_{\mathcal{S}} p^*(\theta)$$

where $\mathcal{S} \equiv \{\theta \,|\, X(\theta) \geq \hat{r}B\}$, i.e. the states of nature in which the firm does not go bankrupt, and $\mathcal{S}' \equiv \{\theta \,|\, X(\theta) < \hat{r}B\}$, then

$$E = \sum_{\theta} X(\theta)p^*(\theta) - B$$

i.e.

$$V = E + B = \sum_{\theta} X(\theta)p^*(\theta)$$

independent of the debt-equity ratio.

Three observations are in order: First, individuals do not need to agree on the probability of different states of nature occurring, i.e. they may disagree on the probability distribution of the returns to any firm.[14] Second, if there are fewer firms than states of nature, whether there are as many securities as states of nature is a function of the debt-equity ratio. If there are four states of nature and two firms, and if neither firm issues enough securities to go bankrupt, then there will only be three securities, but if one of the firms goes bankrupt, there will be four. Although the latter situation will be Pareto optimal (the marginal rate of substitution between consumption in any two states identical for all individuals), the value of the firm which goes bankrupt may be larger or smaller in the former situation than in the latter.[15]

Third, if we take literally the Arrow–Debreu definition of a state of nature, there undoubtedly will be more states of nature than firms. Yet, in some sense, most of these states are not very different from one another. For example,

---

[13] If there are no Arrow–Debreu securities on the market, $p^*(\theta)$ is the net cost to the individual of increasing his income in state $\theta$ by one dollar, i.e. by buying and selling short different securities. If there are more securities than states of nature, market equilibrium requires that the set of market prices generated by considering any subset of market securities which span the states of nature be independent of the particular subset chosen. For a more thorough discussion of these problems, see [4].

[14] They must, however, not assign zero probabilities to different states of nature occurring.

[15] In this situation we cannot assume that firms will necessarily maximize market value. (See fn. 12.)

much of the variation in the return on stocks can be explained by the business cycle. If in any given business cycle state, the variance of the return were very small, and there were a small number of identifiable business cycle states, then the economy might look very much as if it were described by an Arrow–Debreu securities market.[16]

BANKRUPTCY AND PERFECT CAPITAL MARKETS

The usual criterion for a perfectly competitive market is that the price of a commodity or factor an individual (or firm) buys or sells be independent of the amount bought or sold and be the same for all individuals in the economy. On this basis, it has been argued that the capital market is imperfectly competitive: (a) as a firm issues more bonds the rate of interest it pays may go up; (b) individuals may have to pay a higher interest rate than firms, and some firms higher than others; (c) lending rates may differ from borrowing rates. In this section, we have, however, considered perfectly competitive capital markets (with bankruptcy) in which all three of these would be true.[17] See also [22]. Thus the possibility of bankruptcy makes somewhat questionable the interpretation of much of this evidence of an imperfect capital market. The crucial fallacy lies in the implicit assumption that one firm's bond is identical to another firm's bond, and that bonds a firm issues when it has a low debt-equity ratio and those which it issues when it has a high debt-equity ratio are the same. But they are not. They give different patterns of returns. If there is any chance of default, a bond gives a variable return (i.e., is a risky asset). Just as there is no reason to expect butter and cheese, even though they are related commodities, to have the same price, so there is no reason to expect the nominal rate of interest where there is a low debt-equity ratio to be the same as when there is a high debt-equity ratio. Even the discrepancy between borrowing and lending rates does not imply imperfect capital markets, for when a person lends to the bank and the account is insured by FDIC, he can assume there is a zero probability of bankruptcy, but when the bank lends back to the same individual, it cannot make the same assumption.

## REFERENCES

1. K. J. Arrow, "The Role of Securities in the Optimal Allocation of Risk Bearing," *Rev. Econ. Stud.*, Apr. 1964, *31*, 91–96.
2. W. Baumol and B. Malkiel, "The Firm's Optimal Debt-Equity Combination and the Cost of Capital," *Quart. J. Econ.*, Nov. 1967, *18*, 547–78.
3. D. E. Brewer and J. B. Michaelson, "The Cost of Capital, Corporation Finance, and the Theory of Investment: Comment," *Amer. Econ. Rev.*, June 1965, *55*, 516–23.
4. D. Cass and J. E. Stiglitz, "The Structure of Preferences and Returns and

---

[16] The point is that under these conditions the individual, by diversification of his portfolio, can essentially eliminate the variations in returns within a given business cycle state.

[17] Transactions cost may also partly explain (b) and (c).

Separability in Portfolio Allocation: A Contribution to the Pure Theory of Mutual Funds," *Cowles Foundation Discussion Paper*, May 1969.

5. G. Debreu, *The Theory of Value*, New York 1959.
6. P. Diamond, "The Role of a Stock Market in a General Equilibrium Model with Technological Uncertainty," *Amer. Econ. Rev.*, Sept. 1967, *57*, 759–76.
7. D. Durand, "Cost of Capital, Corporation Finance, and the Theory of Investment: Comment," *Amer. Econ. Rev.*, Sept. 1959, *49*, 639–55.
8. D. E. Farrar and L. L. Selwyn, "Taxes, Corporate Financial Policy, and Return to Investors," *Nat. Tax J.* Dec. 1967, *20*, 444–54.
9. J. Hirshleifer, "Investment Decision under Uncertainty: Choice Theoretic Approaches," *Quart. J. Econ.*, Nov. 1965, *79*, 509–36.
10. ———, "Investment Decision under Uncertainty: Applications of the State-Preference Approach," *Quart. J. Econ.*, May 1966, *80*, 237–77.
11. J. Lintner, "The Valuation of Risk Assets and the Selection of Risky Investments in Stock Portfolios and Capital Budgets," *Rev. Econ. Statist.*, Feb. 1965, *47*, 13–37.
12. H. Markowitz, *Portfolio Selection*, New York 1959.
13. F. Modigliani and M. H. Miller, "The Cost of Capital, Corporation Finance, and the Theory of Investment," *Amer. Econ. Rev.*, June 1958, *48*, 261–97.
14. ———, "Reply to Rose and Durand," *Amer. Econ. Rev.*, Sept. 1959, *49*, 665–69.
15. ———, "Corporate Income Taxes and the Cost of Capital: A Correction," *Amer. Econ. Rev.*, June 1963, *53*, 433–43.
16. ———, "Reply to D. E. Brewer and J. B. Michaelson," *Amer. Econ. Rev.*, June 1965, *55*, 524–27.
17. J. Mossin, "Equilibrium in a Capital Asset Market," *Econometrica*, Oct. 1966, *34*, 768–83.
18. G. Pye, "Investment Rules for Corporations," doctoral dissertation, M. I. T. 1963.
19. A. A. Robichek and S. C. Myers, "Problems in the Theory of Optimal Capital Structure," *J. Finance Quant. Anal.*, June 1966, *1*, 1–35.
20. W. F. Sharpe, "Capital Asset Prices: A Theory of Market Equilibrium under Conditions of Risk," *J. Finance*, Sept. 1964, *19*, 425–42.
21. W. Sher, "The Cost of Capital and Corporation Finance Involving Risk." A paper presented at the winter meetings of the Econometric Society, Evanston, Illinois, Dec. 1968.
22. G. Stigler, "Imperfections in the Capital Market," *J. Polit. Econ.*, June 1967, *75*, 287–93.

## 34. LEVERAGE AND THE COST OF CAPITAL

EZRA SOLOMON*

Reprinted from *The Journal of Finance*, Vol. *XVIII*, No. 2 (May, 1963), pp. 273–79, by permission of the author and the publisher.

The proper use of debt financing is one of the major decision areas of corporate financial management. My paper confines itself to just one facet of the many considerations which jointly determine the optimal use of debt—namely, the effect that a change in financial leverage has, or can be assumed to have, on a company's cost of capital. In particular, it addresses itself to the thesis put forward by Modigliani and Miller that, apart from a tax effect, a company's cost of capital is independent of the degree of leverage in its financial structure.[1]

### I

To isolate the effect of leverage alone from the many other factors that may be involved in using debt wisely, it is useful to conduct the analysis in terms of the following simplified model:

Let $X$ be a company which holds or acquires only one kind of asset. Each dollar invested in these assets generates a flow of operating earnings, before taxes, which provides a rate of return of $k$ per annum of a given quality with respect to the certainty or uncertainty with which it can be expected to occur. We will assume that this company may use any mixture of only two kinds of financing—pure, externally derived: equity, on the one hand, and pure debt, on the other. Third, we assume that the structure of market capitalization rates is given and that this *structure* does not change over time.

The following notation will be used:

| | |
|---|---|
| Total market value of company's securities | $V$ |
| Market value of bonds | $B$ |
| Market value of stock | $S$ |
| Leverage | $L = B/S$ |
| Operating earnings (before taxes or interest) | $O$ |
| Debt charges | $F$ |
| Residual earnings on equity (before taxes) | $E = O - F$ |

* Professor of finance and director, International Center for the Advancement of Management Education, Stanford University.

[1] Franco Modigliani and Merton H. Miller, "The Cost of Capital, Corporation Finance and the Theory of Investment," *American Economic Review*, June, 1958.

| | |
|---|---|
| Rate of return on investment | $k$ |
| Pretax over-all capitalization rate (cost of capital) | $k_o = Q/V$ |
| Pretax equity capitalization rate (cost of equity capital) | $k_e = E/S$ |
| Pretax debt capitalization rate (cost of debt capital) | $k_i = F/B$ |
| Pretax marginal cost of borrowing | $m = \Delta F/\Delta B$ |

For the all-equity case we have $k_e = k_o = k$. When debt is used, we have $k_e > k_o$. Specifically, regardless of the valuation theory one embraces, the relationship $k_e = k_o + (k_o - k_i)B/S$ and $k_o = k_e S + k_i B$ must hold.[2] The heart of the leverage question can now be stated as follows: What happens to $V$ and $k_o$ as we increase the degree of leverage (other things remaining unchanged) from $L = O$ to $L \to \infty$ ?

For the purpose of analysis there are two ways in which leverage can be altered in the model. We can assume that Company X *substitutes* debt for equity in its capital structure, i.e., it issues debt and uses the proceeds to redeem outstanding stock. This model has the virtue that it keeps the asset structure constant as leverage changes and therefore permits a direct comparison of $V$ at one level of leverage with $V$ at other levels. But it does not allow for the easy identification of the marginal cost of debt as this is generally measured. As we shall see, this variable is an important key to the entire leverage question.

An alternative model for analyzing changes in leverage is to permit Company X to expand, i.e., to issue more and more debt, using the proceeds to acquire additional assets. This permits an easy identification of the marginal cost of each increment of debt. However, in order not to contaminate the leverage effect, it is necessary to assume that each new asset acquired generates operating earnings, before tax, of a same size and quality as those produced by existing assets.

On the whole, the latter model is more convenient for present purposes, and we shall use it. Modigliani and Miller have generally used the former model in their illustrations, but it is relatively easy to restate their conclusions and arguments in terms of the latter.

Introducing positive amounts of debt into the model introduces the problem of corporate income and the complication that interest payments are deductible in computing taxes. However, everybody agrees that the tax-effect factor does tend to lower the over-all cost of capital of a more highly levered

---

[2] These two relationships are derived as follows:

(a) Since $k_e = E/S = O - F/S$ and $O = k_o V = k_o(B + S)$ and $F = k_i B$, we have

$$k_e = \frac{k_o(B + S) - k_i B}{S},$$

$$= k_o + (k_o - k_i)B/S.$$

(b) Since $k_o = O/V = (E + F)/(B + S)$ and $E = k_e S$ and $F = k_i B$, we have

$$k_o = \frac{k_e S + k_i B}{B + S}.$$

company relative to a less levered company, and we can conveniently ignore the tax effect in addressing ourselves to the more controversial issues.

## II

Ignoring the tax effect, the Modigliani-Miller position is that Company X's over-all cost of capital $k_o$ is constant for all levels of leverage from $L = O$ to $L \to \infty$. If $k_o^*$ is used to represent the over-all cost of capital for a more levered company and $k_o$ to represent the over-all cost of capital for a less levered company in the same risk class, their basic thesis is that, except for the tax effect, $k_o^* = k_o$ for any and all levels of leverage.

It is useful to divide their basic thesis into two component statements. Still ignoring the tax effect, these are (1) an increase in borrowing (and hence in leverage), no matter how moderate or "judicious," can never lower a company's cost of capital; (2) an increase in borrowing (and hence in leverage), no matter how immoderate or "excessive," can never raise a company's cost of capital.

Almost all the analytical controversy generated thus far by the Modigliani-Miller thesis seems to have centered on the first of these two component statements and on the proof put forward on its behalf by its proponents. The proof offered by Modigliani-Miller is that a process akin to arbitrage, in which individual investors engage in "home-made" leverage as a substitute for corporate leverage will keep $k_o^*$, the capitalization rate for the more levered situation, equal to $k_o$, the capitalization rate for the less levered situation.

The traditional position is that, even if the tax effect of leverage is ignored, moderate leverage can lower $k_o^*$ relative to $k_o$.[3] The traditionalists' counter-argument to Modigliani and Miller's arbitrage model is that home-made leverage is not a perfect substitute for corporate leverage and that the equilibrating mechanism posited in the arbitrage model may not fully erase the tendency for $k_o^*$ to fall below $k_o$.

While this aspect of the controversy is an interesting one, it is not of great practical consequence for the issue at hand. Whether, in a tax-free world, the traditional view that $k_o$ does fall is correct or whether the Modigliani-Miller argument that $k_0$ does not fall is correct, in a world of taxable corporate incomes in which interest payments are tax-deductible, everybody agrees that, up to a certain "judicious" limit of debt, $k_o$ declines as leverage is increased.

The really crucial part of the Modigliani-Miller thesis is their second statement, namely, that $k_o$ will not rise, no matter how far the use of leverage is carried. This conclusion might hold if we assume that the rate of interest paid on debt does not rise as leverage is increased. At least it is possible, given this assumption, to invoke the "arbitrage" argument in order to show that it *should* hold if investors behave rationally.

But in practice $k_i$, the average rate of interest paid on debt, must rise as

---

[3] For an explicit statement of the traditional position, see Harry G. Guthmann and Herbert E. Dougall, *Corporate Financial Policy* (3rd ed.; Englewood Cliffs: Prentice-Hall, 1955), p. 245.

leverage is increased. For extreme leverage positions, i.e., as the company approaches an all-debt situation, it is clear that $k_i$ will be at least equal to $k_o$. Given the general attitude of bondholders and bond-rating agencies, it is highly likely that $k_i$ will be *above* $k_o$ for positions of extreme leverage.

Now as $k_i$, the average cost of debt, rises, the marginal cost of borrowing, $m = \Delta F/\Delta B$, must be above $k_i$. Therefore, there is some point of leverage at which Company X finds that $m$, the marginal cost of more debt, is higher than its average cost of capital, $k_o$. Again taking into account the general attitudes of those who supply debt funds, this point is likely to be reached quite rapidly if leverage is increased beyond levels acceptable to the debt markets.

For all practical purposes, the point at which a company finds that $m \geq k_o$ represents the maximum use of leverage, for it can be argued that no rational company will finance with more pure debt if it can do so more cheaply by using a mixture of debt and equity similar to that outstanding in its existing structure. If this fact is accepted, then the argument between Modigliani and Miller and the traditional position vanishes. Both would agree that leverage is clearly excessive if carried beyond the point at which the rising marginal cost-of-debt curve intersects the over-all cost of capital at that point.

## III

Assuming that the straightforward logic of this argument is accepted, what we are left with is something very similar to the U-shaped $k_o$ curve envisaged by traditional theory. This is outlined in Figure 1. In the early or moderate

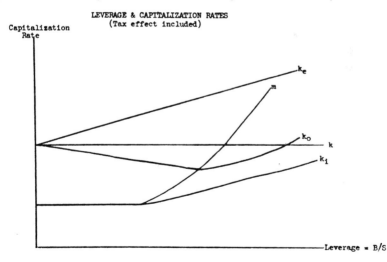

FIG. 1.—Traditional version

phases of leverage, $k_o$ declines, possibly because of market imperfections but at the very least because of the tax-effect factor. As leverage reaches and then exceeds the limits acceptable to the debt markets, $m$ rises rapidly, and the tax advantage of even more leverage is offset by the rising cost of each further increment of debt. When $m$ rises above $k_o$, any further increase in leverage will bring about a rise in $k_o$. We thus have a clearly determinate point or range of optimal leverage.

Unfortunately, Modigliani and Miller have not been willing to accept this conclusion. Instead, they argue that $k_o$ remains constant even when leverage is increased beyond the point at which $m > k_o$. According to them, what brings about this startling and wholly illogical result is that $k_e$, the cost of equity capital, *falls* as leverage is increased through the use of increments of debt which cost more than $k_o$. The behavior of the capitalization rates, as they view it, is outlined in Figure 2.

This device of having $k_e$ fall as leverage is increased leads squarely into a second dilemma. We now have to assume that rational investors in the equity markets capitalize a more uncertain stream of residual earnings at a *lower* $k_e$ than they capitalize a less uncertain stream.

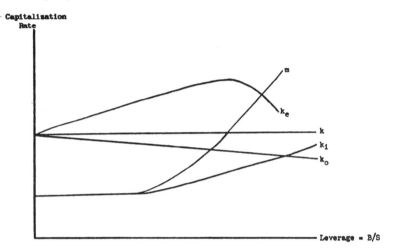

FIG. 2.—Modigliani and Miller version

It is difficult to reconcile this assumption with Modigliani and Miller's own assumptions about rational investor behavior and reasonably perfect markets. The only explanation they offer in support of a $k_e$ curve that *falls* as leverage is increased is as follows: "Should demand by risk-lovers prove insufficient to keep the market to this peculiar yield-curve, this demand would be reinforced by the action of arbitrage operators."[4]

The introduction of subjective risk preference as a major determinant of equity prices just for this phase of the leverage argument is hardly admissible unless one is also prepared to accept it for other phases of leverage.

As a last line of defense in support of a constant $k_o$, even under these circumstances, Modigliani and Miller simply assert that arbitrage will see to it that $k_e^*$, the equity-capitalization rate for the overly levered stream of net earnings, is kept sufficiently *below* $k_e$, the rate for the less-levered stream,

[4] *Op. cit.*, p. 276.

so as to maintain an equality between $k_o^*$ and $k_o$. If we examine the relationships between the various capitalization rates for situations in which $m > k_o$, we find that this assertion is not justified. Indeed, the opposite is true. Rational investor behavior, including the equilibrating process envisaged in their arbitrage model, will push $k_e^*$ *above* $k_e$ and $k_o^*$ above $k_o$.

## IV

There is, therefore, no legitimate basis for assuming that $k_e$ will *fall* as leverage is increased and hence no basis for assuming that $k_o$ can remain constant as leverage is increased through the use of debt issues which involve a marginal cost higher than $k_o$. Given this conclusion, it must follow that the cost of capital $k_o$ rises with increased leverage whenever $m > k_o$.

In short, the thesis that a company's cost of capital is independent of its financial structure is not valid. As far as the leverage effect *alone* is concerned (and ignoring all the other considerations that might influence the choice between debt and equity), there does exist a clearly definable optimum position —namely, the point at which the marginal cost of more debt is equal to, or greater than, a company's average cost of capital.

# 35. THE COST OF CAPITAL AND OPTIMAL FINANCING OF CORPORATE GROWTH

## JOHN LINTNER*

Reprinted from *The Journal of Finance*, Vol. *XVIII*, No. 2 (May, 1963), pp. 292–310, by permission of the author and the publisher.

The interest of professional economists in the theory of corporate finance and capital budgeting has increased markedly within the last decade.[1] Nevertheless, the literature is still marked by confusion and even contradiction: the decision rules which have been proposed for determining the optimal capital budget in a corporation and its optimal capital structure and reliance on different sources of financing are mutually inconsistent in the sense that they

* Professor of Business Administration, Graduate School of Business Administration, Harvard University.

[1] This paper is one part of a series of interrelated theoretical and statistical studies of corporate and financial policies being made at the Harvard Business School under a grant of the Rockefeller Foundation for work in the general area of profits in the functioning of the economy. The Foundation's generous support for this work is most gratefully acknowledged. Major parts of this paper are based upon the longer manuscripts [a18], [b8], [b9], and [b10]. (The coverage of [a19], as previously announced, was cut back to [b8].)

would lead to (often substantially) different decisions under given sets of circumstances.

None of the marked differences in decision rules advanced in the literature reviewed here can be attributed to different assumed *goals*, since all the authors to be cited have, explicitly, offered their respective criteria as the means to accomplish the same ultimate objective—the greatest satisfaction of common stockholders' preferences. Moreover, since increased current share valuations *ceteris paribus* obviously increase shareholders' current wealth, which in turn clearly implies greater utility, this criterion of optimizing shareholders' utility has in practice been identified with the maximization of the current market value of the common stock. Further, all authors assumed maximizing behavior to be universal and financial markets to be purely competitive. *These premises and specifications are accepted without question and maintained throughout the present paper.*

## I. INTRODUCTION

*Disagreements on optimal size of capital budgets and cost of capital.*—The seriousness of the conflicts in the literature on the theory of corporate finance and capital budgeting is clearly indicated in the markedly different conclusions offered by eminent economists regarding the determination of the optimal size of capital budgets.

The Lutzes, in their classic study a decade ago [a20],[2] concluded that investment within the firm should be increased up to the point where this course no longer added more to the collective stockholders' "net profits prospects" than further outside investment. Cash flows from borrowing and debt service are to be deducted from those of the internal investment plan, the resulting stream of net cash flows is to be discounted at the yield of the preferred maturity of outside riskless investment (government bonds), and internal investments are to be increased only so long as the certainty equivalents of the resulting present values exceed the cost of the investment.

Roberts [a28] concurs in the use of the outside lending rate and the netting of cash flows from borrowings and repayments, but argues that the discount rate should be the external yield available on outside investments having (subjectively) similar risk, and he equates this with the *current earnings yield* of the company's own stock.[3] His decision rule is: Investments are to be made so long as the present value of prospective incremental receipts exceeds that of incremental cash outflows, when both flows are discounted at a rate equal to the current earnings yield on the stock. The relevant investment fund flows are the same for the Lutzes and Roberts in any given case; but Roberts' discount rate is much greater, and it has not been shown that this difference offsets the Lutzes' utility adjustment of present values to certainty equivalents.

---

[2] Especially chaps. xiii–xvii.

[3] Spencer and Siegelman [b13] have recently advocated the same rule with the proviso that the earnings yield should be measured as it would be "when the firm has what the market considers to be a well-balanced capital structure."

Dean [a4] and, more recently, Modigliani-Miller [a23; a25], Kuh [a16], Benishay [b3], and Weston [a34; b15] have also capitalized corporate earnings to determine market values and have all argued that the current earnings yield on common stock is the proper discount rate when no debt is outstanding, but otherwise they urge the use of a *current-market-value weighted average cost of debt and equity capital* as the proper discount rate. This is often a substantially *lower* figure than the current earnings yield on the equity when debt is outstanding;[4] and these authors do not net debt charges from investment fund flows. For given investment projects, the relevant fund flows for these authors are larger than for Lutz and Roberts; their further use of a lower discount rate when debt is outstanding clearly implies acceptance of projects (and thereby extensions of the size of the capital budget) which would not be made under Roberts' rule (and presumably under the Lutzes).

Similarly, Solomon [a30], like Roberts, advises netting cash flows due to borrowing from those of individual investment projects, but he substitutes the ratio of "estimated future average earnings per share" to current market price as his recommended discount rate. In growing companies this is an even *higher* figure than the current earnings yield on equity. For Solomon and Roberts, the relevant investment fund flows from given projects are the same (i.e., both deduct interest costs when debt is used in financing the project), but Solomon's rule will reject projects that Roberts' rule would accept in growth situations because of the latter's lower discount rate.

A still different rule has been advanced by Walter [a33] who advocated discounting investment opportunities at the rate at which current and future dividends are capitalized; this rate being defined as "the underlying yield on safe securities (government bonds?) and the required risk premiums."[5] Similarly, Bodenhorn [a2] has also urged the use of the market discount rate for comparable risk, and Modigliani and Miller in a new paper [a25] have also fixed upon the market discount rate as the proper cost of capital.[6] In some contexts (see below, *passim*), growth opportunities will make current earnings yields less than current market discount rates, and these authors' rule would lead to rejection of projects which Roberts' rule would accept, and they would correspondingly reduce the size of capital budgets and the rate of growth below the levels his rule would justify. In other contexts, the

---

[4] This is true even when the market-value weights urged by Modigliani and Miller are used; further differences are produced by Dean's advocacy of book-value weights; but, for reasons already clear in the literature, this latter position is invalid.

[5] Since Walter ignores borrowing, strict comparison of his rule with that of other authors can be made only in situations where there is no borrowing; but the conflict in the decisions implied on given sets of data is clear in this class of cases. If different decisions will be made in non-leverage cases, the rules necessarily have different implications in general.

[6] They have thus abandoned the identification of the market discount rate with current earnings yield *in the absence of debt* which provided the decision rule in their earlier paper [a23]. In the presence of growth opportunities, they agree with Solomon that the relevant cost-of-capital is greater than current earnings yield, but their figure is lower (and very much lower in strong growth situations) than his ratio of *future average* earnings to current prices and will thus accept many projects he would reject.

opposite would occur. The rule advanced by Shapiro and Gordon [a14], based upon the sum of the current dividend yield and the expected growth rate, would in general lead to still different decisions, and, as our final illustration, we note that Gordon in later writings [a11-13; b4] has advanced a still different requirement.

So far we have emphasized differences in rules for accepting investments and setting the optimal size of the capital budget. We should also note that the various authors differ on whether—and how—their respective preferred "cost-of-capital" figure varies as a function of the existing capital structure (primarily the mix of debt and equity capital) and also as a function of the form of the new financing to be used for the capital budget—the proportion of retained earnings, additional debt, and/or new issues of equity capital.

Modigliani and Miller [a23 and a25] take the limiting position that (apart from the relatively small discrimination in favor of debt financing under the corporate income tax) the cost of capital is *independent* of both the existing capital structure and the mix of new financing, a position apparently also shared by Dean. Others—notably Solomon, Kuh, Weston, Gordon, Duesenberry [a6], Schwartz [b11], and myself [a17, 18 and b7]—argue that the cost of capital is a function of the financing mix, although, once again, there are substantial differences in the exact form of the dependence. Indeed, the rules for decisions regarding *how* the investments should be financed differ as seriously as those for determining the size of the capital budget itself—i.e., those determining the *amount* of finance (whatever the type) to be used.

Since all these authors have defined their optima in terms of maximization of the current market value of existing equity issues, all these differences in the decision rules come down fundamentally either to differences in assumptions regarding the character of the corporations investment opportunities themselves (to which we revert below) or to differences in the models the various authors have used to explain (*a*) the determination of stock-market prices when there is no debt outstanding and (*b*) the effects of leverage on those prices. Indeed, in the latter two respects, the more significant differences can be traced to the respective author's choice of one of two basic assumptions within each of the two categories just noted: specifically, to whether or not (1) [as alleged in "pure earnings" theories], *ceteris paribus*, the valuation of unlevered equities is determined by (expectational) current earnings *independent* of dividends and (2) [as held in "entity value" theories] the market valuation of the corporate entity is independent of its capitalization, apart from corporate tax differentials due to the deductibility of debt interest.

*Further context of present paper.*—In the usual "theory of the firm," there are two separate (or at least separable) parts to the analysis: (*a*) given production functions and supply conditions in factor markets, how can the firm minimize the cost of producing each possible quantity of output? and (*b*) given the results of such isoquant-cum-budget-line analysis and specified product market conditions, what *quantity* of output produced and sold will maximize profit? The necessary and sufficient conditions for the validity of the "pure earnings and company investment" and "entity value" theories can best be analyzed under an assumption that time vectors of investment budgets and corporate earnings are fixed throughout all time independent of dividends and the finance mix.

These issues were examined in detail in a previous paper [b7]. That analysis corresponded in our financial context to the "theory of the production of a given output" ("output" here being vectors of capital budgets and their associated earnings). Corresponding to the second major problem in the standard theory of the firm, there is the further major issue for the theory of corporate financing and capital budgeting: "given the minimum 'cost' (i.e., optimal finance mix) for each possible size of capital budget, what is the optimal size of the capital budget under any given functional relationship between size-of-budget and corporate earnings?" This latter issue is the primary focus of the present paper.

Some of the central results of the previous paper, however, obviously provide an essential basis for the present one: specifically, that both the "pure earnings" theory (investors indifferent to particular dividend vectors) and the "entity value" theory (the sum of market values of equity and debt invariant to debt) are invalid even with the time vectors of earnings and investments fixed forevermore if the market context involves (1) costs of issuing securities, or (2) any personal tax differentials, or (3) any lack of prescience and identity in investors' subjective probability distributions, or (4) any combination of them;[7] that the model making stock prices depend essentially upon the (present values of the) time vectors of cash dividend flows to investors remains valid even under these fully generalized neoclassical conditions, while the alternatives are valid if and only if stated in forms identically reducible to this dividend theory; and that the significance of time vectors of earnings (and of company investments) lies in its implications for the prospective stream of dividends, rather than vice versa.

In the present paper, I consequently rely essentially on "present values of dividends models"[8] and, removing the constraint of fixed investment budgets, examine optimal decision rules for the finance mix and size of the capital budget of a corporation and its optimal (expected average) rate of growth over time. Since all these matters depend on the proper determination of the relevant "cost of capital," this issue also provides a common concern throughout the paper.

In keeping with space limitations and the interests of this group, this paper will focus on the important, but necessarily limited, objective of setting forth the essential logic of some of the more fundamental conclusions I have reached on these issues. To this end, I will outline the basic structure of some of the more useful analytical models I have been developing, present some rigorous proofs, and motivate others. A full set of rigorous mathematical derivations

[7] Also, of course, any corporate tax differentials between interest and other income will invalidate the "entity value" theory.

[8] See n. 15 below.

and proofs and a more complete and general analysis of these and related issues will be found elsewhere. Among other simplifications, I shall assume throughout this paper that all tax rates are zero; that the (riskless) discount rates $k\tau = k$ are constant over time; and that the variance of profit rates with no growth and no debt $\sigma_{p_0}^2$ is given and constant over time.

Finally, two definitions are needed at the outset which, for convenience, are stated in general form to cover uncertainty—certainty being the limiting case for each when all variances approach zero. Specifically, *the marginal cost of (a given type of) capital* for the corporation is the *minimum* (expectation of) *rate of return required on a marginal investment* for the shareholders to be better off (value of existing equity greater) *with* the incremental-investment-cum-this-incremental-financing *than without either* the increment to the capital budget *or* this financing. Similarly, *corporate earnings* or *profits* (after taxes and interest) for any period are defined to be equal to the maximum cash dividend which (expectationally) *could* be paid in that period consistent with (pro-forma) no outside financing *and* with the *expectation* that a similarly large dividend *could* then be paid in future periods subject to the same constraint (this pro-forma constraint tying the earnings back to earnings on present assets.)[9]

## II. UNLEVERED FIRMS UNDER CERTAINTY

Certain issues can most conveniently be handled under the simplifying assumption of certainty. First of all, it can readily be shown that, *even in the absence of issue costs, taxes, or uncertainty*, the *relevant marginal cost of capital for the corporation is not equal to the discount rate k* unless (*a*) the " investment opportunity " or " profit " function relating the average rate of internal return,[10] $p_t$, per dollar of new investment is *strictly independent* of the amounts of investments made in earlier or subsequent periods, *or* (*b*) the profit function at every point in time exhibits strictly constant returns to scale *and* these returns $p_t = k$. The absence of costs, taxes, and uncertainty, together with a profit function $p_t = \psi_t(F_t^* \ldots)$ in which $\psi_t$ is strictly independent of the dollar size of the company's aggregate investments (capital budget) $F_\tau^*$ for all $\tau \neq t$, are *sufficient conditions* to make the discount rate $k$ the appropriate cost of capital because under the fully idealized neoclassical conditions all marginal rates of substitution for all companies and investors are equal to the discount rate $k$ in equilibrium, as demonstrated by Fisher thirty years ago [*a*10].

---

[9] See n. 17, p. 250, in [*b*7].

[10] In this paper, I shall consistently use decision rules in the form of marginal internal rate of return $\geq$ marginal cost of capital. Under the assumptions made concerning the efficient set of the (portfolio) of investment opportunities facing the firm (and the simplifying assumption of constant discount rates over time), these rules are strictly equivalent to the alternative statement of rules in the form of present values exceeding costs. Cross-sectional non-independence of investment opportunities are subsumed in the efficient opportunity set; perfect capital markets are assumed throughout; and major lumpiness in discrete investment projects causes no trouble when our assumptions regarding the regularity and smoothness of the envelope of the efficient set are satisfied. Cf. [*b*5 and *b*2].

Under these very restrictive conditions, all investments are perfect substitutes at the margin, and, in keeping with standard classical theory, the company should include all increments of investment in each period which have a marginal rate of return $\rho$ on their dollar cost $\geq$ the discount rate $k$. Allowance for issue costs and taxes, however, requires important modifications even under certainty (cf. [b7, a23, a30, and a33], although, with no taxes, the minimum acceptable return $\rho_0 = k$ *so long as* all investments whose $\rho \geq k$ do not exhaust current earnings.[11]

But models based on the profit function $\psi_t$ *restricted* by an independence assumption regarding $F_\tau^*$, $\tau \neq t$, are at best inadequate to handle—and in general[12] are inherently biased with respect to—the essential elements and issues of growth and change over time which constitute the primary focus of this paper. For this restriction on $\psi_t$ implies that the (average *and* marginal) profitability of *any given dollar-sized* capital budget for, say, IBM, du Pont, Avon, or General Motors in 1962 is independent of the capital investments they have made in the last one, three, five, ten, or even twenty years—which is obviously not true. In particular, this restriction on $\psi_t$ ignores the hard fact that—especially in the major oligopolistic industries which account for such large fractions of plant and equipment expenditures and of total equity values, but also quite generally—the position of a firm in its industry and the profitability of further new investments depend heavily upon whether it has led or lagged in the introduction of new products, new capacity, new cost-reducing technologies, research and development, long-range advertising, and other promotion of product-market position, and so on in the recent and more remote past.[13] All this is true not only in the short run but, cumulatively, in the longer run as well.

To encompass the essence of the problems involved in decisions for continuing growth and to incorporate basic determinants of the profit opportunities available to potentially growing firms at given points in time, the function $\psi_t$ must explicitly depend on investments in other periods (or, as their surrogate, recent realized—or "normalized"—levels of earnings). The central implications of such dependence are brought out most simply in the

[11] The reason is that such costs simply insure that new investments in this range, if made, will be financed by retained earnings. See [b7].

[12] In this respect, they will be acceptable as a first approximation only for firms selling in markets within which no seller has or creates any significant (product) market power which affects the profitability of future investments, where investments include outlays for product promotion as recognized in Dean [a4].

[13] See Lintner [a17], Duesenberry [a6], and Meyer-Kuh [a22]. The importance of including outlays for advertising, research and development, and other promotion of product-market position in the capital budget, when the outlays are intended to affect receipts in subsequent periods, has been emphasized by Dean.

It should be emphasized that we assume throughout this paper that *financial* markets are strictly and universally *purely competitive* (except for the fact that any given company is the sole issuer of its own securities), but this does not require us to ignore well-known facts of life in the *product*-market place—which do affect in a fundamental way the properties of the firm's profit-opportunity function.

profit function originally advanced by Preinreich [a27] and Williams [a35] a quarter of a century ago and more recently also adopted by Gordon-Shapiro and Gordon in which the function $\psi_t$ is invariant over time when written in the form

$$p_t = \psi_t^*(F^*/Y^*, \ldots) = \psi_t^*(f, \ldots) = p(f, \ldots) = p \text{ constant over time,} \quad (1)$$

where $Y^*$ is the corporation's aggregate earnings in the current period, and $f = F^*/Y^*$. Since $p$ will not in general be invariant with respect to $f$, we also have $p'(f) \leq 0$ but constant over time as a function of $f$, and there will be a marginal rate of return, defined as

$$\rho = \frac{\delta f p(f)}{\delta f} = p(f) + f p'(f), \quad (1a)$$

which will also be constant over time for given $f$, with the further property that $\delta\rho/\delta f \leq 0.$[14]

Since *the criterion* ordering the desirability of alternative outcomes is the market price of the common equity, the profit function (1) must be incorporated into a model of stock price which specifies price as a function of both the profit opportunities of the company and the amounts and types of financing used to finance its internal investments or capital budget. As a first step, note that using continuous compounding for convenience, so that $Y_t^*$ is the instantaneous rate of earnings flow, the rate of growth $g^*$ of $Y_t^*$ is

$$g^* = g_{Y_t}^* = d \log Y_t^*/dt = f p(f). \quad (2)$$

With aggregate dividends determined by $D_t^* = x Y_t^*$, where $x$ is the dividend payout ratio, which is a decision variable also assumed to be constant over time, it is clear that the growth rates of dividends and earnings will be equal and that the aggregate dividend distribution at any time $t$ will be

$$D_t^* = x Y_t^* = x Y_0^* e^{g^* t}.$$

Stock prices at any given time, however, reflect the values of the streams properly attributable to the *then outstanding* shares of stock. Let $N_t$ be the number of shares at time $t$, and we have $D_t = D_t^*/N_t$ and $Y_t = Y_t^*/N_t$. It follows that if new shares are issued at the relative rate $n = g_{Nt} = d \log N_t/dt$ and we let $g$ without asterisk represent the rate of growth of dividends and earnings on shares outstanding at time $t$, we have

$$g = d \log D_t/dt = d \log Y_t/dt = d \log D_t^*/dt - d \log N_t/dt = g^* - n \quad (3)$$

so that

$$D_t = x Y_t = x Y_0 e^{(g^* - n)t} = x Y_0 e^{gt} = D_0 e^{gt}. \quad (4)$$

[14] These latter stipulations incorporate the economist's usual (and seemingly very realistic) assumption that marginal rates of return on investment budgets are not infinitely elastic *as of any given point of time* throughout most of their relevant range; that they become so only with respect to outside investments in the market after all internal investments having higher marginal returns have been exhausted. Cf. Duesenberry [a6].

Since the sum of current cash returns (here dividend yields $= D_t/P_t = y_d$) plus rates of growth in own price for all assets must equal the current market rate of discount in equilibrium in perfect markets, the basic *equilibrium price condition* is $y_d + d \log P_t/dt = k_t$. The solution of this differential equation for market price, recognizing (4) and letting $x$ be constant for simplicity, is

$$P_t = \frac{D_t}{k - g} = \frac{D_0 e^{gt}}{k - g} = \frac{D_0 e^{(g^* - n)t}}{k - (g^* - n)} = \int_t^\infty D_{t e}^{-(\tau - t)(k - g)} \, d\tau, \quad k > g, \quad (5)$$

which, by derivation, will satisfy the criterion cross-sectionally over different stocks and securities *and* will do so continuously over time.[15] For the *current* price of the stock, $P_0$, equation (5) reduces to

$$P_0 = \frac{D_0}{k - g} = \frac{x Y_0}{k - g} = \frac{x Y_0}{k - (g^* - n)}, \quad k > g. \quad (5a)$$

Since, in the absence of issue costs, taxes, and uncertainty, all forms of financing are perfect substitutes at the margin, the marginal costs of each are the same. The minimum acceptable marginal rate of return to justify any additional internal investment under these conditions, however financed, can most easily be found for retained earnings. With $n = 0$ and $g^* = g$, and letting the retention ratio $r = 1 - x$,

$$\frac{\delta P_0}{\delta r} = P_0 \left[ -\frac{1}{x} + \frac{\delta g/\delta r}{k - g} \right] \geq 0 \quad \text{as} \quad \frac{\delta g}{\delta r} = \rho \geq \frac{k - g}{x} = Y_0/P_0 = y_e, \quad (6)$$

where $y_e$ is the current earnings yield on the stock. The marginal internal rate of return $\rho = \delta g/\delta r$ in this case because $\delta f/\delta r = 1$ and[16] $\rho = \delta f p(f)/\delta f = \delta g/\delta r$.

Under fully idealized neoclassical conditions with opportunities for constant growth forever, the optimizing decision rule is to accept all investments having $\rho \geq y_e$, the current earnings yield.[17] But $y_e$ is equal to the discount rate $k$ only in the special case where profit opportunities are infinitely elastic

---

[15] In [b8] we give the more general form of this model in which dividend payouts (earnings) growth rates, rates of issuing new securities, and discount rates are all unique functions, each varying in any way over time, and show that the resulting model also has the properties just stated in the text. A *corollary* of critical importance is that any alternative model of stock prices (such as various models based on earnings) will satisfy this criterion of legitimacy in classical theory *if and only if* it is *identically reducible* to the dividend model. (For further elaboration see Lintner [b7].) We consequently do not need to use any such alternatives to dividend models in this paper.

[16] Alternatively, by definition

$$p(f) = \frac{1}{f} \int_0^f \rho(f) \, df \quad \text{or} \quad g = \int_0^f \rho(f) \, df,$$

and the text relation follows by direct differentiation.

[17] This is precisely the rule advanced by Modigliani-Miller in [a23], which was derived from a "corporate earnings" model and under essentially static assumptions; but, as noted in Lintner [b7], for use in dynamic situations their original definition of "current earnings" must be altered to the more traditional concept in which *current* rates of earnings flows (rather than the undiscounted time-average they proposed) are used directly in the numera-

throughout—i.e., strictly constant returns regardless of the size of the investment budget in each period—and at a level equal to $k$.[18] This establishes the second half of the proposition made at the beginning of this section. The extremely unrealistic character of these conditions indicates that the common assertion that optimal investment budgets can be set by equating the corporation's $\rho$ to $k$ is generally in error, even under otherwise idealized conditions, when steady growth is assumed.[19]

Indeed, if the company is operating in the region of diminishing returns so that $\rho < p$—and this is surely the usual case—then $\rho_0 < k$ so long as the company is paying any dividends:[20] the minimum marginal returns *to the company* which will lead investors under the conditions being assumed to prefer added company investment is necessarily (and often very significantly) *less* than the discount rate $k$, which *inter alia* reflects returns available on alternative investments.[21] The explanation is that from equation (5) $\delta P/\delta r > 0$ as $x\rho + g \geq k$. The marginal return for the *investor* from added investment within the company is equal to the sum of the dividend payout applied to the marginal internal return within the company *plus* the growth rate on the retention itself, and if this *sum* is greater than the discount rate, he will prefer the retention.[22]

It must be also emphasized that the marginal cost of capital (m.c.c.) is the *current* earnings yield $y_e = Y_0/P_0$, *not* the ratio of future or "average future" earnings to current price, as frequently proposed [e.g., in a30, a23, and a26]. Moreover, the earnings yield *declines* with increasing size of capital budget *up*

---

tor of the relevant *current* earnings yield. It is a nice paradox that our model basing values on dividend flows in the steady-growth case under certainty leads to an optimizing rule based on straight *current* earnings yield—which had been advocated by most earnings theorists all along on the basis of a price model which is *not* generally valid in dynamic contexts! (see Lintner [b7, p. 249]); that the "market rate" used to discount dividends in these models is seldom the correct cutoff rate; and that the equation of earnings yields to market "discount" rates often presumed holds up in growth situations only on very restrictive additional conditions on profit opportunities.

[18] Since $y_e = (k - g)/x = [k - (1 - x)p]/x$, we have $xy_e + (1 - x)p = k$, so that $y_e \gtreqless k$ as $p \gtreqless k$, since $0 \leq x \leq 1$. But $p < k$ can, of course, be ruled out in any well-managed corporation, and we are left with $y_e \leq k$ as $p \geq k$.

[19] This error is Gordon and Shapiro's conclusion to this effect [a14] has been noted by Bodenhorn [a2]. The still more recent paper of Modigliani and Miller [a25], however, continues to use the discount rate $k$ as the cost of capital in the "steady growth" case.

[20] From eq. (6) we have $x\rho_0 = k - (1 - x)p$ or $k = p - (p - \rho_0)x$. If $x > 0$ and $\rho_0 < p$, then $p > k$, and the conclusion follows from the second preceding footnote, since $\rho_0 = y_e$.

[21] This is, of course, contrary to the case treated above, where profit opportunities were independent of investment rates in other periods. The reason for the perhaps surprising conclusion that $\rho_0' < k$ clearly lies in the different assumptions on investment opportunities.

[22] It will be noted that *this result does not depend upon any tax differentials* between ordinary income and capital gains rates such as have been so much emphasized in the literature. The broader significance of the result is to emphasize the importance of the distinction between marginal return requirements *to the company* and marginal returns to investors; for even though $\rho_0 < k$, the investor's return given above *does* meet the opportunity costs of returns on alternative investments reflected in $k$.

to the optimum scale of investment, since with $y_e = (k - g)/x$, $\delta y_e/\delta r = (y_e - \rho)/x < = > 0$ as $\rho > = $ or $< y_e$: the *act of making appropriate company investments reduces* $y_e$ [= m.c.c. under present assumptions] and does *not* raise it as alleged elsewhere (e.g., [a30]); *only improper investment raises* $y_e$.

Before turning to uncertainty, I should also show that the internal returns required to justify expansion financed externally in the face of underpricing and new issue costs are substantially greater than so far recognized. The basic valuation model is still equation (5), but with new stock issues the aggregate size of the capital budget now is $F_t^* = Y_t^* - D_t^* + S_t^*$, where $S_t^*$, is the *net dollar proceeds* to the company from any newly issued shares. Dividing through by $Y_t^*$, we now have $f = r + s$ for use in equations (1) and (1a). Differentiating equation (5) partially with respect to $s$ gives

$$\frac{\delta P_0}{\delta s} = - \frac{P_0 \left[ \dfrac{dn}{ds} - \dfrac{\delta g^*}{\delta s} \right]}{k - g^* + n} \gtreqless 0 \quad \text{as} \quad \frac{\delta g^*}{\delta s} = \frac{\delta g^*}{\delta f} = \rho \gtreqless \frac{dn}{ds}. \tag{7}$$

To relate $s$ to $n$, the relative rate of issuing new shares, first note that, in the absence of issue costs, net proceeds to the company are equal to the price to the buyers and also that, under classical certainty, the aggregate market demand for the company's equity shares is infinitely elastic at the initial (pre-new issue) price earnings ratio, $y_e$.[23] Under *these* conditions,[24] $s = n/y_e$ and $dn/ds = y_e$, so that required returns for "costless" new equity financing are the same as those found above for retained earnings.[25]

But in real life there are both fixed and variable costs of issuing new equity securities and, in addition, some "sweetening" in the form of pricing under the current market is usually required to sell new securities.[26] Such overt

---

[23] This is true under these conditions because aggregate market value (in the absence of debt) is independent of number of shares, so that *both* price per share and earnings per share are rectangular hyperbolas in terms of number of shares, and the ratio is constant at $y_e$. This formulation has also been used by Kuh in [a16].

[24] Where $P_t^*$ is the aggregate market value of the stock in the absence of new issues, and $N_t$ the total number of shares outstanding at time $t$, the price per share $P_t$ in the absence of new issue costs is determined by $N_t P_t = P_t^*$, where $P_t^*$ is a constant independent of $\Delta N_t = dN_t/dt$ the number of new shares issued in the given time interval. Also $N_t = N_{t0} + \Delta N_t$, where $N_{t0}$ is the number of shares in the absence of new issues; $S_t^*$, the aggregate net proceeds of the new share issues, will then be

$$S_t^* = \int_{N_{t0}}^{N_{t0} + \Delta N_t} \frac{P_t^*}{N} dN = P_t^* \int_0^n dn = P_t^* n.$$

Consequently, $s_t = S_t^*/Y_t^* = P_t^* n/Y_t^* = n/y_e$.

[25] The equivalence of required returns when retentions or new stock issues are used *under these conditions* to finance expansion—and hence the indifference of shareholders between more dividends cum more new issues vs. more retentions cum smaller new issues (and so a larger percentage of ownership represented by given initial share holdings)—can also be confirmed by showing that the total differential of $P_0$ in equation (12a) with $f$ (and consequently $g^*$) fixed is equal to zero.

[26] Strictly speaking, "underpricing" would never be required in classical markets under certainty, but I have shown in [b7] that (a) it is unavoidable under uncertainty whenever

costs and underpricing can be summarized by making the (average) *net proceeds per share* on the new issue be $p_{t0}(a - bn) - c$,[27] so that[28] $s = [n/y_{e0}](a - bn) - c$, $0 < a \leq 1$, $0 < b < 1$, $n \geq 0$, $c > 0$. With these costs recognized $dn/ds = y_{e0}/(a - 2bn)$, and $\delta P_0/\delta s >$ or $= 0$ only so long as $\rho >$ or $= y_{e0}/(a - 2bn)$, where $t_{e0} = Y_t/P_{t0}$ as defined above. The proper cutoff on new stock issues (even in "growth" situations) is the ratio of the *current* (not future) earnings to the *marginal* net proceeds per share $P_0(a - 2bn)$ of the new stock—and not simply $P_0a$ as commonly proposed (e.g., in [a30]). Moreover, since the return required to justify expansion financed by stock issues in the presence of any unavoidable "underpricing" and of any overt issue costs is greater than that required to finance expansion by retained earnings, there is a vertical shift in the "supply or cost of capital function." Investors will consequently always prefer, in the context of the present model, that investment budgets be financed with retained earnings instead of new stock issues as long as retained earnings are available—i.e., so long as $x > 0$ and $r < 1$. Companies optimizing for shareholders, however, *should* expand capital budgets further by issuing new shares after retentions are exhausted, so long as the stated marginal condition can be satisfied. Finally, it is apparent that the absence of current dividends does not nullify the applicability of our present model based explicitly on dividend flows: the value of *currently* outstanding stock is still simply the present value of the dividends which will be paid in the future on the presently outstanding shares.[29]

## III. FIRMS UNDER UNCERTAINTY

I now turn to some important general conclusions required by the fact of uncertainty. The first is that, as I pointed out two years ago,[30] while decision rules for determining the optimal size and project composition of capital

---

diverse probability distributions over outcomes is admitted and (*b*) its impact is essentially the same (though different perhaps in degree) as fixed and variable costs under certainty. To save space in the present exposition the two have been treated together at this point.

[27] The subscript zero refers to values that would have obtained if *n* were zero; $(1 - a)$ represents the minimum fractional underpricing required to sell *any* new stock, while *b* covers both the variable cash costs of issuing new securities *and* the *further* underpricing which is dependent on the size of the new issue—the units of both *a* and *b* being fractions of $P_{t0}$ as defined; *c* denotes the *fixed* overt cash cost per share of new issues.

[28] With new issue costs recognized, using symbols defined just above, *aggregate* net proceeds to the company are $S_t^* = P_{t0}^* n(a - bn) - c$; the equation given follows after dividing by $Y_t^*$ when $y_{e0} = Y_t^*/P_{t0}^*$. It should be noted that uncertainties concerning the *b* or *c* will further increase the marginal cost of new outside equity relative to that of retained earnings.

[29] Both the latter two points can be nicely illustrated by considering the simple case of a company whose investment opportunities over a period of *m* years will be so rich that no dividends should be paid during this time, after which its special investment opportunities will be gone and it will pay all subsequent (constant) earnings in dividends. The present value of the stock will be $P_0 = e^{-km}Y_m/k$ and $Y_m = Y_0 e^{(g^* - n)m}$. Maximizing $P_0$ involves maximizing $Y_m$, which leads immediately to the optimizing rule given above.

[30] [a18]; the final page of Hirshleifer's paper [b6] at the same meetings makes the same point. See also my [b8] and [b9].

budgets are generally identical under neoclassical certainty, *they are essentially different under uncertainty: the problem of optimizing the composition of a capital budget of any given size is formally identical with problems of selecting optimal security portfolios.*[31] In the rest of this paper, I shall focus on the optimal determination of the size of the capital budget and the mix of internal funds and debt to be used in its financing, simply assuming that a Markowitz-type "efficient set" analysis has already been made which yields a three-dimensional (per time period) "profit possibility function" relating amount of investment (size of budget), expected average profit rates, and variance of return.

In keeping with our emphasis here on (expectationally) steady growth, however, I assume specifically that $\psi_t(f, \hat{p}, \hat{\sigma}_p^2) = 0$ is invariant over time with $f = F_t^*/Y_t^*$ constant at some level to be determined, and that $\delta\hat{p}/\delta f \leq 0$, which is constant over time for any $f$ and $\sigma_p^2$ as is the marginal expected rate of return $\rho_\Lambda = \delta f\hat{p}/\delta f$. Also, to simplify the development and concentrate on the budget-portfolio returns required in the presence of given company-investment risks, I will assume that the profit-rate-variance $\sigma_p^*$ of the budget is fixed or prespecified, that it is invariant over time, and that *it* is also invariant to the size of the budget. Since $\sigma_p^2 > 0$ (even when $f = 0$, so that $\hat{g} = 0$), however, and since $g = fp(f)$, in general the variance of the growth rate $\sigma_p^2 = (1 + a_1 f^2)\sigma_p^2$, which does depend on size of budget although invariant over time for given $f$. Cumulated growth over a period $t$ in length, $\bar{g}t$ is then a random variable with $\sigma_{(\bar{g}t)}^2 = t\sigma_g^2$.

In what follows, I examine certain important properties of the *comparative stochastic dynamics* of capital budgeting, corporate financing, and growth, seeking the marginal cost of capital (as previously defined), and the decision rules for the optimal determination of $f$ (and its components, relative rates of retentions $r$ and borrowing $\theta$) on the assumption (management's and investor's expectation) that the values of $f$, $r$, and $\theta$ decided upon will be held constant over time.

With the current price of the stock now a random variable, our *criterion* becomes maximization of the expected value of this current market price, and, to save space, I shall here simply assume[32] that this expected value is

---

[31] As a result, individual investments (projects) may be eminently desirable components of optimizing project-portfolio-budgets because of low variances and/or covariances with other components (and existing assets) in spite of relatively low expected returns. Also, a project having a large variance in its own quasi-rents but low or negative covariances with other existing and future investments will often make a much smaller contribution to company-wide variance (risk) than other projects with low own-variances and substantial intercorrelations with other company investments in terms of cash flows. Indeed, many investment proposals are accepted in capital budgets in order to reduce risks and not to raise returns—something incongruous in conventional theoretical contexts of capital budgeting, but surely to be expected in the present framework. It should be clear that throughout I take $p$ and $\sigma_p^2$ to refer to profit *before* interest.

[32] Some of the deductive justification is given in Hirshleifer [b6] and Smith [b11]. See also my [b8]. For those who prefer to use the alternative criterion of the certainty-equivalent of the probability distribution of the present values of the uncertain streams, I will simply

equal to the *present* value (computed essentially at the risk-free discount rate[33]) of the *certainty equivalents* of the uncertain income (dividend) receipts in the stream. I also assume that, at the time of the company decision (i.e., on pre-existing data and expectations), all investors hold the portfolios they most prefer. Any change in the retention ratio (dividend payout), leverage, or expected growth rate of the $i$-th company which increases the present value of its stock will increase its shareholders' wealth and be in their interest.

Our problem essentially involves the terms of trade between expected receipts and varying risks on a given security—"deepening" in Hirshleifer's terminology [b6] rather than (or along with) the much simpler "widening" case he examined. It is clear, however, that the functional relation between certainty-equivalents, expected returns, and risks must fall between two limiting cases.

On the one hand, in the limit, under the extreme simplifying assumption that all trades are between single risk assets (or portfolios of fixed proportions) and *riskless* securities, we know that all investors' marginal rates of substitution are equal in equilibrium to market-determined exchange lines which are linear in expected return and $\sigma$ as a measure of risk. But continuing to assume purely competitive markets (as I do throughout), the exchange lines governing expected prices for given expected returns (or expected returns required for given prices) *within the set of risk assets* and when "money illusion" is absent, involve both $\sigma$ and $\sigma^2$. The second limiting case is provided by the observation that market equilibrium with interior solutions requires that the marginal rate of substitution on the latter function not exceed that on investors' utility functions—and in the absence of good viable markets for trading in the relevant disjoint future uncertain receipts, the latter must in themselves provide the certainty equivalents. (See my [b8] and [b9].)

Consider now the second limiting case, letting investors' utility functions, following Tinbergen [b14],[34] be hyperbolic of the form $U(\tilde{D}_t) = 1 -$

---

observe that, under a very general set of assumptions otherwise, all the general conclusions drawn below also hold under this alternative criterion where it is viable.

[33] To a reasonably good approximation, these present values can be computed at the risk-free discount rate $k_0$ for the average or representative company. Provisional present values of all securities computed with discount rates $k_i = k_0$ may, however, lead to switching and other adjustments, which results in changes in (expected) market prices. When all portfolios are in full adjustment on the basis of a given set of underlying expectations, parameter values, supplies of securities, etc., the expected price of any $i$-th security can be equated to the present value of its certainty equivalents computed at a discount rate $k_i = k_0 + k_{ci}$, where $k_{ci}$ (either $+$ or $-$) reflects the impact of changes in share price $P_i$ due to switches, covariances, etc. In the text I drop subscripts and implicitly assume $k_{ci}$ to be invariant, but, in general, $k_{ci}$ will vary with $\sigma$ and compound to results stated below.

[34] Quadratic utility functions, however, are patently inappropriate in the context of our concern with long-run growth, even if variances are minimal or zero. A point is soon reached beyond which further increases in dividend (and growth) would *reduce* the utility of the receipt. The hyperbolic form adopted here is free of this disability and has other important advantages [cf. b8].

$(C_0/D_t)^{a_1}$, $a > 0$. Then [35] $E[U(\breve{D}_t)] = 1 - (C_0/\breve{D}_t)^{a_1} = 1 - (C_0/\breve{D}_t)^{a_1} = 1 - (C_0/D_0)^{a_1}e^{-a_1 t(\hat{g} - a_1\sigma_g^2/2)}$ so that the certainty equivalent is $\breve{D}_t = D_0 e^{t(\hat{g} - a_1\sigma_g^2/2)}$, from which the stock price is

$$P_0 = \int_0^\infty D_0 e^{-t[k - \hat{g} + a_1\sigma_g^2/2]}\,dt = \frac{D_0}{k - \hat{g} + a_1\sigma_g^2/2}, \quad k + a_1\sigma_g^2/2 > \hat{g}. \quad (8)$$

The impact of uncertainty can be clearly seen in the marginal cost of funds for internally financed expansion, which is

$$\frac{\delta P_0}{\delta r} = P_0\left[ -\frac{1}{x} + \frac{\rho_\Lambda - a_1(\delta\sigma_g^2/\delta r)/2}{k - \hat{g} + a_1\sigma_g^2/2} \right] > 0 \text{ as } \rho_\Lambda > y_e + a_1 a_1 f\sigma_p^2 = \text{m.c.c.} \quad (9)$$

*Uncertainty, of course, raises the earnings yield,* but the more subtle and far-reaching result is that, *in addition, the marginal cost of capital* (here retained earnings) *is greater than the earnings yield by amounts which vary directly with size of the capital budget f* and the size of the coefficient $a_1$ in $\sigma_p^2 = (1 + agf^2)\sigma_p^2$. (Note also that this result was reached even though the marginal profit variance $\sigma_p^2$ on the capital budget itself was assumed constant. If $\sigma_p^2$ also varies with $f$, the result is compounded.) Moreover, I have shown elsewhere [b8] that these results are quite general. In particular, if viable markets for all future time periods exist which establish exchange lines along which $\hat{g} - a_2\sigma_g - a_3\sigma_g^2$ are equally valued (the first limiting case above is covered by setting $a_3 = 0$), these same conclusions hold, with the excess of m.c.c. over $y_e$ varying directly with the market exchange coefficients $\alpha_2$ and $\alpha_3$ instead of directly with $\alpha_1$, the coefficient of risk aversion on the utility function itself. Finally (as also shown in [b8]), m.c.c. $y_e$ necessarily, and by amounts that increase essentially exponentially with the size of budget, if when viewed as of $t_0$, the variance $\sigma_{p_t}^2$ of the profitability of new investments to be made at different times in the future is a monotone increasing function of their futurity. With this very plausible and persuasive feature incorporated in the models, the conclusions stated above hold *even if* [36] $a_1 = 0$.

These results lead directly to other fundamental conclusions. Even though leverage per se has not yet been considered explicitly, it necessarily follows from the preceding analysis that *the conventional weighted-average-cost-of-capital rule is inherently erroneous and down-biased.* Even if a weighted average of equity and debt costs were the proper criterion, the average of earnings yield and interest cost would be *too low* because the relevant marginal cost of retained earnings is *greater* than the earnings yield (and the relevant marginal cost of outside equity still larger). If, for instance, both retained earnings and debt are to be used in financing, standard production theory insures that (*a*) the optimal *mix* will involve the *equalization of the two* (interdependent) *marginal costs* and (*b*) the relevant marginal cost of (optimal-mix) finance

---

[35] Cf. Aitchison and Brown [b1, p. 8].

[36] The reason is essentially that increased retentions and growth shift relatively more of the income stream into the further future and thereby increase the relevant weighted average uncertainty of the stream.

for any sized budget will be *equal to the* (equalized) *marginal costs of each type of finance used.*

Even with quoted interest rates well below equity yields, there is, of course, no problem in having marginal costs of debt equal to marginal equity costs: not only are marginal interest costs with much use of debt substantially above stated or coupon rates, but—just as non-zero profit-rate variances make the *relevant* marginal costs of equity greater than earnings yields—it is reasonable to expect that the *relevant marginal costs of debt will similarly be greater than even the marginal overt interest costs.* And so they are.[37] Although borrowing per se does not affect $\sigma_p^2$, the variance of the profit rate before interest, by introducing fixed interest charges it necessarily increases $\sigma_{p_a}^2$, the profit rate variance after interest, and consequently $\sigma_g^2$, which is the variance more directly relevant to the shareholder.[38] Moreover, it does so at every point in time and cumulatively over time—and as interest costs increase with increased borrowing, it does so in necessarily non-linear fashion even on the standard deviation and a fortiori so on the variance. Such (non-linearly) increasing shareholder risks with increasing corporate borrowing raise the relevant marginal costs of debt (minimum expected marginal returns on investments) *above* its marginal overt interest cost (which is its true marginal cost under certainty)—and by margins which progressively increase with the relative amount of the debt financing—for precisely the same economic reason that any increase in risks in the shareholders' income stream due to added retentions raises *their* true marginal cost above the earnings yield (which would have been their proper marginal cost under certainty).

## IV. CONCLUSION

In conclusion, it should be emphasized that *so long as* the marginal expected return on the capital budget is > *this* m.c.c. of debt (making full allowance for its risk impact), *debt-financing-cum-investment raises* the (expected value of) the *current stock price*—and consequently *lowers current earnings yields*, contrary to the common impression. *Only unjustified debt-financed-expansion raises current earnings yields.* Of course, $\rho_\Lambda$ < m.c.c. (debt) *until r* (or *s*) is substantially positive; but in these models, *after r* and *s* have been optimized under the constraint of no (permanent)[39] borrowing $\rho_\Lambda$ will often be > m.c.c. (debt) and permanent borrowing is desirable (because it raises share values)

[37] This analysis is free of the straitjacket of the "entity value" theory for reasons given in detail in [b7].

[38] If $a_1 > 0$, as is surely the usual case, borrowing increases this variance in compound and non-linear fashion [since $(1 + a_1 f^2)\sigma_{p_a}^2$ is a product]. With borrowing in the picture, $f = r + \theta$, where $\theta$ is the new borrowing and all variables as before as ratios to current earnings.

[39] In view of the emphasis on comparative dynamics, $\theta$ is defined as a fraction of earnings, and, with positive growth, total debt grows continuously over time as in the Domar models. Our $\theta$ does not include temporary borrowing to even out stochastic variations in income flows.

up to a well-defined optimum,[40] again contrary to theoretical models now current; alternatively, so long as the equity financing exceeds a certain pace, there is an optimal finance-mix involving both equity and debt for each relative size of budget $f$, and along this finance-mix "expansion path," budget size $f$ should be increased until the condition $\rho_\Lambda \geq$ m.c.c. is no longer satisfied.[41]

## BIBLIOGRAPHY

*a*1–*a*35. These references refer to the correspondingly numbered items in the bibliography to item *b*7 below.

*b*1. Aitchison, J., and Brown, J. A. C. *The Lognormal Distribution* (Cambridge: Cambridge University Press, 1957).

*b*2. Bailey, Martin J. "Formal Criteria for Investment Decisions," *Journal of Political Economy*, Vol. LXVII (October, 1959).

*b*3. Benishay, Haskell. "Variability in Earnings-Price Ratios," *American Economic Review*, Vol. LI (March, 1961).

*b*4. Gordon, Myron J. *The Investment, Financing and Valuation of the Corporation* (Homewood, Ill.: R. D. Irwin, 1962).

*b*5. Hirshleifer, Jack. "On the Theory of Optimal Investment Decision," *Journal of Political Economy*, Vol. LXVI (August, 1958).

*b*6. ——. "Risk, the Discount Rate, and Investment Decisions," *American Economic Review*, Vol. LI (May, 1961).

*b*7. Lintner, John. "Dividends, Earnings, Leverage, Stock Prices and the Supply of Capital to Corporations," *Review of Economics and Statistics*, Vol. XLIV (August, 1962).

*b*8. ——. "Optimal Dividends and Corporate Growth under Uncertainty," *Quarterly Journal of Economics*, forthcoming (November, 1963).

*b*9. ——. "The Valuation of Risk Assets and the Selection of Risky Investments," *Review of Economics and Statistics*, forthcoming (November, 1963).

*b*10. ——. "Optimal Risk Bearing, Retentions and Leverage in Corporate Growth," forthcoming.

*b*11. Schwartz, Eli. "Theory of the Capital Structure of the Firm," *Journal of Finance*, Vol. XIV (March, 1959).

*b*12. Smith, Vernon L. "Comment on Risk, the Discount Rate and Investment Decisions," *American Economic Review*, Vol. LI (May, 1961).

*b*13. Spencer, Milton H., and Siegelman, Louis. *Managerial Economics* (Homewood, Ill.: R. D. Irwin, 1959).

*b*14. Tinbergen, Jan. "The Optimum Rate of Saving," *Economic Journal*, Vol. LXVI (December, 1956).

*b*15. Weston, J. Fred. *Managerial Finance* (New York: Holt, Rinehart & Winston, 1962).

---

[40] After borrowing is optimized subject to $r$ (or $s$) fixed at *its* optimum assuming no debt, further retentions will often *become* justified (due to interaction effects between costs of equity and debt capital) and so on interatively to the global optimum.

[41] Depending on parameter values, it is entirely possible (and probably frequent in practice) that $\rho_\Lambda <$ m.c.c. (debt) for all values of $r$ (and $s$), in which case the optimum borrowing $\theta = 0$ throughout.

## 36. PORTFOLIO ANALYSIS, MARKET EQUILIBRIUM AND CORPORATION FINANCE

ROBERT S. HAMADA*

Reprinted from *The Journal of Finance*, Vol. *XXIV*, No. 1 (March, 1969), pp. 13–31, by permission of the author and the publisher.

## I. INTRODUCTION

At least three conceptual frameworks have been developed to study the effects of uncertainty on financial and economic decision-making in recent times. Of these, the homogeneous risk-class concept constructed to eliminate the need for a general equilibrium model by Modigliani and Miller [20, 21, 22], henceforth abbreviated to MM, is most familiar to those interested in corporation finance. On the other hand, the most common basis for making personal or institutional investment decisions is the portfolio model first developed by Markowitz [16, 17]. Little has been developed rigorously to cross the finance fields using either of these two uncertainty frameworks.[1]

More recently, a third uncertainty model has been revived by Hirshleifer [8, 9, 10] and labeled the time-state preference approach.[2] This last model is undoubtedly the most general approach to uncertainty and was used by Hirshleifer [10] to prove the famous MM no-tax Proposition I. Unfortunately, thus far, this generality has its cost. Using a time-state preference formulation, it is difficult to test its propositions empirically (since markets do not exist for each state) or to derive practical decision rules for capital budgeting within the firm.

The purpose of this paper is to derive the three MM Propositions using the standard deviation-mean portfolio model in a market equilibrium context. This approach to some of the major issues of corporation finance enables us

* Graduate School of Business, University of Chicago. The generous support of the Ford Foundation and the research committee of the Graduate School of Business is gratefully acknowledged. I am indebted to Eugene Fama, Merton Miller, and Myron Scholes for their helpful comments in the preparation of this paper.

[1] The notable exception is the article by Lintner [13] which considered corporate capital budgeting questions in the context of a market equilibrium portfolio model. Lintner's treatment of this problem will be discussed in Section V.

[2] Hirshleifer restated the Arrow-Debreu [1, 4] objects of choice in the classical Irving Fisher [7] framework, where the objects of choice are consumption or income bundles at explicit times and states-of-the-world.

to derive these propositions in a somewhat more direct way than with the use of the risk-class assumption and the arbitrage proof of the MM paper. Instead, a model is substituted relating the maximization of stockholder expected utility to the selection of portfolios of assets to, finally, the financing and investment decisions within the corporation. A link will be provided between two branches of the field of finance that have so far been evolving more or less separately.

In Section II, the assumptions are enumerated and the equilibrium capital asset pricing model is presented. MM's Propositions I and II, the effects of the financing decision on equity prices, are proved in Section III for the no corporate income tax case. Section IV is devoted to the corporate tax effect on this financing decision. A derivation and discussion of the cost of capital for investment decisions within the firm (MM's Proposition III) in the no-tax case are the topics of Section V. And in Section VI, the cost of capital considering corporate taxes is derived.

## II. ASSUMPTIONS AND THE EQUILIBRIUM RISK-RETURN RELATIONSHIP

### A. ASSUMPTIONS

The assumptions are divided into two sets. The following are required for the portfolio-capital asset pricing model.[3]

1. There are perfect capital markets. This implies that information is available to all at no cost, there are no taxes and no transaction costs, and all assets are infinitely divisible. Also, all investors can borrow or lend at the same rate of interest and have the same portfolio opportunities.
2. Investors are risk-averters and maximize their expected utility of wealth at the end of their planning horizon or the one-period rate of return over the horizon.[4] In addition, it is assumed that portfolios can be assessed solely by their expected rate of return and standard deviation of this rate of return. Of two portfolios with the same standard deviation, the criterion of choice would lead to the selection of that portfolio with the greater mean; and of two portfolios with the same expected rate of return, the investor would select the one with the smaller risk as measured by the

[3] The first two sections of Fama's paper [6] is recommended as the clearest exposition of this model for the homogeneous expectations case. The extension to the case of differing judgments by investors can be found in Bierwag and Grove [2] and Lintner [14, pp. 600–601]. We shall not use the heterogeneous expectations framework here since it will not add to the primary purpose of this paper and may only serve to take the focus away from our major concern.

[4] The rate of return is defined as the change in wealth divided by the investor's initial wealth, where the change in wealth includes dividends and capital gains. Note that this is a one-period model, in common with Lintner's [13, 14] and in many respects with MM's [20, 21, 22].

standard deviation. This implies that either the investor's utility function is quadratic or that portfolio rates of return are multivariate normal.[5]

3. The planning horizon is the same for all investors and their portfolio decisions made at the same time.

4. All investors have identical estimates of expected rates of return and the standard deviations of these rates.[6]

In addition to these four assumptions, we shall require the following for the subsequent sections:

5. Expected bankruptcy or default risk associated with debt-financing, as well as the risk of interest rate and purchasing power fluctuation, are assumed to be negligible relative to variability risk on equity. Thus, the corporation is assumed to be able to borrow or lend at the same risk-free rate as the individual investor.

6. Dividend policy is assumed to have no effect on the market value of a firm's equity or cost of capital. Having made our initial assumption of perfect capital markets, it was shown by MM in [19] that this need not be an additional assumption as long as there is rational investor behavior and the financing and investment policies of the corporation can be considered independent. If assumption (5) is valid, this second requirement should be met.

7. Though future investment opportunities available to the firm at rates of return greater than the cost of capital undoubtedly are reflected in the current market price, we shall ignore them here. They can be considered a capitalized quantity independent of the issues raised by MM's three propositions as long as the firm has a long-run financing policy (if the financing mix affects the cost of capital) and if the marginal rate of return of a new investment (to be compared to the subsequently derived cost of capital) includes all, direct and indirect, contributions to cash flow provided by this investment.[7]

---

[5] See Tobin [27, pages 82–85] for a justification; the need for the restrictive normal probability distribution assumption is not strictly required, as Fama [5] has generalized much of the results of the Sharpe-Lintner model for other members of the stable class of distributions where the standard deviation does not exist. It can be further noted, as Lintner [13, pages 18–19] does, that Roy [24] has shown that investors who minimize the probability of disaster (who use the "safety-first" principle) will have roughly the same investment criterion for risky assets.

[6] See footnote 3.

[7] This latter requirement is the issue raised by Miller in [18] on Lintner's growth papers [11, 12]. Lintner assumed that the indirect effects, such as shifting the firm's investment productivity schedule to a more profitable level in all future time periods, are the same for all projects and therefore do not have to be included in the marginal rate of return of the project under consideration. Instead, we are requiring that all effects and opportunities introduced by the acceptance of this project be taken into account explicitly in the marginal rate of return. For one practical method of doing this, see Magee [15].

## B. ASSET PRICES AND MARKET EQUILIBRIUM

Represent the rate of return of a portfolio or risky asset by the random variable $R$. From assumption (2), the expected rate of return, $E(R)$, and the standard deviation, $\sigma(R)$, of portfolios are the objects of choice; this leads to the formation, by each individual investor, of an efficient set of risky portfolios according to the principles provided by Markowitz [16, 17]. Introducing a riskless asset with a rate of return $R_F$ leads to a new efficient set combining a single risky portfolio, $M$ (which was on the previous efficient set), with various proportions of the risk-free asset (this includes borrowing as well as lending).

Because maximum expected utility for a risk-averter requires a tangency of his expected utility curve with this efficient set, and because all investors have the same expectations, risky portfolio $M$ would be combined by all investors in some proportion with the riskless asset. And market equilibrium requires all outstanding, risky assets to be held in the proportion of their market value to the total market value of all assets. This is the composition of portfolio $M$, henceforth called the market portfolio.

From this construct, the following Sharpe-Lintner-Mossin [25, 13, 14, 23] equilibrium relationship can be derived for any individual risky asset $i$ in the market:[8]

$$E(R_i) = R_F + \frac{[E(R_M) - R_F]}{\sigma^2(R_M)} \operatorname{cov}(R_i, R_M) \tag{1}$$

Note that $\dfrac{E(R_M) - R_F}{\sigma^2(R_M)}$ is the same for all assets and can be viewed as a measure of market risk aversion, or the price of a dollar of risk. Substituting a constant $\lambda$ for this expression in (1), we have:

$$E(R_i) = R_F + \lambda \operatorname{cov}(R_i, R_M) \tag{1a}$$

Equation (1a) supplies us with a formal market relationship between any asset's required rate of return and its individual risk, as measured by $\operatorname{cov}(R_i, R_M)$.

## III. THE FINANCING DECISION ASSUMING NO CORPORATE TAXES

### A. EFFECT OF LEVERAGE ON STOCKHOLDERS' EQUITY

This section will deal with MM's Proposition I—the effects on equity value and perceived risk as a firm alters its capital structure. The quality of equity will no longer be the same and is directly dependent on the corporation's debt-equity ratio. For this purpose, we have constructed the following: assume equilibrium exists and there is a corporation, $A$, with no debt in its capital

---

[8] See [6] for the derivation of equation (1).

structure. Defining $S_A$ as the present equilibrium market value of the equity of this debt-free firm, $E(S_{AT})$ as the expected market value for this same firm one period later, $E(\text{div})$ as the expected dividends paid over this period, and $E(X_A)$ as expected earnings net of depreciation but prior to the deduction of interest and tax payments, assumptions (6) and (7) allow us to write the following relationship for the dollar return:

$$E(X_A) = E(\text{div}) + E(S_{AT}) - S_A. \tag{2}$$

Employing the definition of the expected rate of return, we have:

$$E(R_A) \equiv \frac{E(\text{div}) + E(S_{AT}) - S_A}{S_A} = \frac{E(X_A)}{S_A} \tag{3}$$

giving us a relation for the rate of return required by corporation $A$'s shareholders.

Now assume that corporation $A$ decides to alter its capital structure without changing any of its other policies. This implies its assets, both present and future, remain the same as before. All it decides to do is to simultaneously issue some debt (at the riskless rate, $R_F$) and purchase as much of its equity as it can with the proceeds. Let us denote the equity of this same real firm, after the issuance of debt, as $B$.[9] The rate of return required by the remaining stockholders is given by adjusting (2), and thus (3):

$$E(R_B) = \frac{E(X_A) - R_F D_B}{S_B} \tag{4}$$

Two points concerning (4) should be emphasized. First, the earnings from assets is $E(X_A)$, since this is the same "real" firm as $A$. And secondly, the interest payments, $R_F D_B$, as noted in assumption (5), is not a random variable.

Next, from (1a), the equilibrium required rate of return-risk relationship is substituted into (3) and (4) to yield:[10]

$$R_F + \lambda \operatorname{cov}(R_A, R_M) = \frac{E(X_A)}{S_A} \tag{3a}$$

$$R_F + \lambda \operatorname{cov}(R_B, R_M) = \frac{E(X_A) - R_F D_B}{S_B} \tag{4a}$$

[9] This construction can be readily extended to the cases where a firm already has debt and is considering either increasing or decreasing the proportion of debt in its capital structure. Also, if we rigidly honor the one-period planning horizon restriction, then the situation should be more precisely worded: equilibrium at $t = 0$ with equity $A$ included and market price for risk $\lambda$. Firm $A$ adds debt at $t = 0 + \varepsilon$ and general equilibrium restored immediately with market risk aversion remaining the same. This comparative statics framework will be used throughout this paper.

[10] $\lambda$ is not strictly equal in (3a) and (4a) since one equity, $B$, has been substituted for another, $A$. Because $\lambda$ includes the effects of *all* capital assets, the substitution of $B$ for $A$ should have a negligible effect on the value of the market price of risk.

Intuitively, equity $B$ should be riskier than $A$ since its dollar return is a residual after fixed interest commitments are paid. Thus, $\text{cov}(R_B, R_M)$ should be greater than $\text{cov}(R_A, R_M)$. In addition, the expected return to the two equities are different so that it is not immediately clear what the relationship between $S_A$ and $S_B$ should be in equilibrium. To pursue this point, rearrange (3a) and (4a) to isolate $E(X_A)$ and equate the two relations:

$$S_A[R_F + \lambda \, \text{cov}(R_A, R_M)] = S_B\left[\lambda \, \text{cov}(R_B, R_M) + R_F\left(1 + \frac{D_B}{S_B}\right)\right] \quad (5)$$

The next step is to note the definition of the covariance:

$$\text{cov}(R_A, R_M) = E\left\{\left[\frac{X_A}{S_A} - E\left(\frac{X_A}{S_A}\right)\right][R_M - E(R_M)]\right\}$$

$$= \frac{1}{S_A} \, \text{cov}(X_A, R_M). \quad (6)$$

Similarly:[11]

$$\text{cov}(R_B, R_M) = \frac{1}{S_B} \, \text{cov}(X_A, R_M). \quad (7)$$

Substituting (6) and (7) into (5), we find:

$$S_A\left[\frac{\lambda}{S_A} \, \text{cov}(X_A, R_M) + R_F\right] = S_B\left[\frac{\lambda}{S_B} \, \text{cov}(X_A, R_M) + R_F\left(1 + \frac{D_B}{S_B}\right)\right]$$

which reduces to:

$$S_A = S_B + D_B \quad (8)$$

---

[11] If the "feel" for the covariance of asset earnings with $R_M$ is difficult, we can use the definition:

$$R_M = \sum_{k=1}^{T} \frac{S_k}{S_T} R_k = \frac{1}{S_T} \sum_{k=1}^{T} X_k$$

where $S_T$ is the market value of all capital assets and $T$ the total number of risky assets, $k$, outstanding. Then:

$$\text{cov}(X_A, R_M) = \frac{1}{S_T} \sum_{k=1}^{T} \text{cov}(X_A, X_k). \quad (6a)$$

Substituting (6a) into (6) and (7), respectively, yields:

$$\text{cov}(R_A, R_M) = \frac{1}{S_A S_T} \sum_{k=1}^{T} \text{cov}(X_A, X_k) \quad (6b)$$

$$\text{cov}(R_B, R_M) = \frac{1}{S_B S_T} \sum_{k=1}^{T} \text{cov}(X_A, X_k) \quad (7a)$$

Thus we have an expression for the covariance between dollar returns. Whether we use (6) or (6b) and (7) or (7a) makes no difference since the covariance terms cancel out in the following step. The important point is the weights, $1/S_A$ and $1/S_B$, multiplying the covariances.

To complete our proof of MM's Proposition I, the relationship between $V$, the total market value of the firm, and earnings is required. Since by definition,

$$V = S_B + D_B$$

then from (8) and (3):

$$V = S_A = \frac{E(X_A)}{E(R_A)} \tag{9}$$

The total value of the firm depends only on the expected earnings from its assets, the uncertainty of this earning (expressed by $\text{cov}(R_A, R_M)$), and the market factors $\lambda$ and $R_F$. The financing mix is irrelevant, given our assumptions.

Having established the entity theory of value without the use of the homogeneous risk-class assumption, we are now in a position to discuss a switching mechanism to replace the MM arbitrage operation. Substituting (4) for $E(R_i)$ and (7a) for $\text{cov}(R_i, R_M)$ in (1a), and noting that the number of shares, $n_B$, times the price per share, $P_B$, is equal to $S_B$, we obtain for $\lambda$:

$$\lambda = \frac{[E(X_A) - R_F D_B - n_B R_F P_B]}{\dfrac{1}{S_T} \displaystyle\sum_{k=1}^{T} \text{cov}(X_A, X_k)}. \tag{10}$$

Equation (10) is meant to emphasize the point that the ratio of the expected return (over and above the risk-free return) to the risk of any equity must be a constant and equal to $\lambda$, the market price per unit of risk, in equilibrium. Thus if $P_B$ should, for any reason, rise above its equilibrium price, then the right-hand side of (10) would fall below $\lambda$. Investors would have an incentive to sell security $B$ and buy any other outstanding asset from which they could obtain $\lambda$. This switching would drive down the price of $B$ and restore the equality (10) requires in equilibrium.

Alternatively, if $P_B$ should fall below its equilibrium price, the right-hand side of (10) would rise above $\lambda$. Since the excess rate of return for risk is now greater than what is obtainable on all other assets, investors would bid for $B$, driving up $P_B$. Thus, this switching operation is implicitly being substituted for the MM arbitrage operation in the proof presented here.[12]

### B. LEVERAGE AND THE EXPECTED RATE OF RETURN

Having derived (8), to find the effect of leverage on the expected rate of return (MM's Proposition II) is merely a matter of arithmetic manipulation. Recalling that equity $B$ is the same physical firm as $A$ except that debt is in its capital structure, the following equilibrium conditions can be noted by substituting (6) and (7) into (1a):

---

[12] If, during the switching process prior to the restoration of equilibrium, an investor finds himself not at his maximum utility point, he would also rearrange the proportion of his riskless asset and his portfolio $M$.

$$E(R_A) = R_F + \frac{\lambda}{S_A} \text{cov}(X_A, R_M) \qquad (11)$$

$$E(R_B) = R_F + \frac{\lambda}{S_B} \text{cov}(X_A, R_M). \qquad (11a)$$

Subtracting (11) from (11a), and using our result (8), we have:

$$E(R_B) - E(R_A) = \lambda \, \text{cov}(X_A, R_M)\left[\frac{D_B}{S_B S_A}\right]. \qquad (12)$$

From (11):

$$\lambda \, \text{cov}(X_A, R_M) = S_A[E(R_A) - R_F]. \qquad (11b)$$

And substituting (11b) in (12), we obtain MM's Proposition II:

$$E(R_B) = E(R_A) + [E(R_A) - R_F]\left(\frac{D_B}{S_B}\right). \qquad (13)$$

That is, the capitalization rate for a firm's equity, or the rate of return required by investors, increases linearly with the firm's debt-equity ratio.

## IV. THE FINANCING DECISION WITH CORPORATE TAXES

Maintaining the framework of Sections II and III, the corporate tax case follows without difficulty. The rate of return, $R$, must be defined on an after corporate income tax basis so that individual investors will now select their portfolios with respect to after-tax expected rates of return and the standard deviation of these after-tax rates of return. Otherwise, the equilibrium risk-rate of return relationship presented in Section II will not be altered.[13]

Consideration of the firm's financing decision requires only the modification of equations (2), (3a), and (4a) to take into account the corporate tax:

$$E[X_A(1 - \tau)] = E(\text{div}) + E(S_{AT}) - S_A \qquad (2a)$$

$$E(R_A) = \frac{E[X_A(1 - \tau)]}{S_A} = R_F + \lambda \, \text{cov}(R_A, R_M) \qquad (3b)$$

$$E(R_B) = \frac{E[(X_A - R_F D_B)(1 - \tau)]}{S_B} = R_F + \lambda \, \text{cov}(R_B, R_M) \qquad (4b)$$

where $\tau$ is the corporate tax rate and equities $A$ and $B$ refer to the same real firm—$A$ with no debt and $B$ with some debt in the capital structure.[14]

Rearranging (3b) and (4b) to isolate the tax-adjusted expected asset earnings, $(1 - \tau)E(X_A)$, and equating the two relations, we obtain:

$$S_A[R_F + \lambda \, \text{cov}(R_A, R_M)] = S_B\left\{\lambda \, \text{cov}(R_B, R_M) + R_F\left[1 + \frac{D_B}{S_B}(1 - \tau)\right]\right\}. \qquad (14)$$

[13] Problems of Pareto optimality will not be considered here.
[14] See footnote 10.

As in the no-tax case, investigation of the two covariance terms is required next, which yields:

$$\text{cov}(R_A, R_M) = \frac{(1 - \tau)}{S_A} \text{cov}(X_A, R_M) \tag{15}$$

and[15]

$$\text{cov}(R_B, R_M) = \frac{(1 - \tau)}{S_B} \text{cov}(X_A, R_M). \tag{16}$$

Substitution of (15) and (16) into (14) gives us:

$$S_A = S_B + (1 - \tau)D_B. \tag{17}$$

Since the total market value of a firm can be expressed as:

$$V = S_B + D_B$$

we have from (17):

$$V = S_A + \tau D. \tag{18}$$

Therefore, without debt, the total value of the firm is simply $S_A$. As the corporation increases its leverage, the aggregate equity value for the remaining shareholders increases by $\tau D$, the government subsidy given to debt financing through tax-deductible interest payments. The entity value of the firm no longer holds.

Since the first half of (3b) gives us a relationship for $S_A$, we can express (18) as:

$$V = \frac{(1 - \tau)E(X_A)}{E(R_A)} + \tau D. \tag{19}$$

Again, MM's result is reproduced in a market equilibrium setting.[16]

## V. INVESTMENT ANALYSIS AND THE COST OF CAPITAL ASSUMING NO CORPORATE TAXES

It was stated in assumption (2) that investors maximize their expected utility of terminal wealth. Corporation managers can increase their shareholders' utility by investing in new projects within the firm such that their stock price would rise as a result of this decision. If the stock, in addition, should change its risk characteristic, $\text{cov}(R_i, R_M)$, the stockholder can always sell his equity in the firm, realize the gain, and be better off than before. Because his wealth is now larger than originally anticipated, he is able to reach a higher utility position. Thus, to be consistent with the portfolio-asset

---

[15] See footnote 11.

[16] The effect of leverage on the expected equity rate of return (MM's Proposition II) for the corporate tax case can be derived in a manner analogous to that used in Section III B.

pricing model, the criterion for capital budgeting decisions must ensure that the change in equity value, as a result of the project selection, will at least be larger than any new equity required to finance this project.

Defining $dI$ as the purchase cost of the incremental investment and $dE \cdot F \cdot$ as the new equity (either new stock issues or retained earnings) required to finance this investment, the capital budgeting criterion can be written as:

$$\frac{dS}{dI} \geq \frac{dE \cdot F \cdot}{dI} \tag{20}$$

for the project, $dI$, to be acceptable.[17]

A. DERIVATION OF THE COST OF CAPITAL

Having derived the following valuation relationship in Section III A,

$$V = \frac{E(X_A)}{E(R_A)} = \frac{E(X_A)}{R_F + \lambda \operatorname{cov}(R_A, R_M)}$$

it can be shown that:[18]

$$V = \frac{E(X_A)}{R_F} - \frac{[E(X_T) - R_F S_T] \sum_k \operatorname{cov}(X_A, X_k)}{R_F \sigma^2(X_T)} \tag{21}$$

where $X_T$ is the sum of dollar earnings from all risky capital assets combined. Furthermore, (21) is equivalent to:[19]

---

[17] It can be shown that this criterion is the same as the one proposed by MM, i.e. $dV/dI \geq 1$, since

$$\frac{dV}{dI} = \frac{dS}{dI} + \frac{dD}{dI} \text{ and } \frac{dE \cdot F \cdot}{dI} + \frac{dD}{dI} = 1.$$

[18] By definition,

$$\lambda = \frac{E(R_M) - R_F}{\sigma^2(R_M)}$$

and substituting

$$R_M = \sum_{k=1}^{T} \left(\frac{S_k}{S_T}\right)\left(\frac{X_k}{S_k}\right) = \frac{X_T}{S_T}, \quad \lambda = \frac{S_T[E(X_T) - R_F S_T]}{\sigma^2(X_T)}.$$

And from footnote 11,

$$\operatorname{cov}(R_A, R_M) = \frac{1}{S_A S_T} \sum_{k=1}^{T} \operatorname{cov}(X_A, X_k),$$

so that substitution and rearrangement yields (21).

In this section, the effects of the firm's investment on all of the variables will be explicitly noted—this will even include the market variables $\lambda$, $S_T$, and $X_T$. If we were to remain strictly within our initial framework, any new investment must only be a combination of what is already available in the market. Ignoring the effects on the market variables will be discussed at the end of this section.

[19] This is the same as Lintner's [13, page 26] equation (29). The subtraction of $(\lambda/S_T) \sum_k \operatorname{cov}(X_A, X_k)$ from expected earnings adjusts for risk.

$$V = \frac{E(X_A)}{R_F} - \frac{\frac{\lambda}{S_T} \sum_k \text{cov}(X_A, X_k)}{R_F}. \tag{21a}$$

Since the market value of firm $A$'s equity is part of the market value of all capital assets combined, $S_T$, (21a) is still not a completely reduced form. Defining:

$$S_T' = \sum_{k=A}^{T} S_k = \text{market value of all equity except } A,$$

then $S_T = S_T' + S_A$.

Substituting this in (21) yields:

$$S = \frac{E(X_A)\sigma^2(X_T) - [E(X_T) - R_F(S_T' - D)] \sum_k \text{cov}(X_A, X_k)}{R_F[\sigma^2(X_T) - \sum_k \text{cov}(X_A, X_k)]} - D. \tag{21b}$$

Applying the capital budgeting criterion (20) to (21b), solving for the dollar return on the marginal investment, and noting that $\dfrac{dD}{dI} + \dfrac{dE \cdot F \cdot}{dI} = 1$, we obtain:[20]

$$\frac{dE(X_A)}{dI} \geq R_F + \frac{\lambda}{S_T} \left[ \frac{d \sum_k \text{cov}(X_A, X_k)}{dI} - Z \frac{d\sigma^2(X_T)}{dI} \right]$$

$$+ Z\left[ \frac{dE(X_T)}{dI} - R_F\left(1 + \frac{dS_T'}{dI} - \frac{dD}{dI}\right)\right] \tag{22}$$

where $Z$ is defined as

$$\frac{\sum_k \text{cov}(X_A, X_k)}{\sigma^2(X_T)} = \frac{V}{S_T}\left[ \frac{E(R_A) - R_F}{E(R_M) - R_F}\right].$$

The next step is to consider the effect of this incremental investment on the expected value and variance of $X_T$,[21] and solve for the dollar return on the investment, $\dfrac{dE(X_A)}{dI}$, commonly called the marginal internal rate of return, on the left-hand side of the inequality. The assumption that investors maximize their expected utility leads to the criterion that the firm should make

---

[20] The term, $dD/dI$, in (22) does not mean that the form of financing will affect the cost of capital. It appears only because a completely general equilibrium framework is not considered here—we neglected the condition that ex ante borrowing must equal ex ante lending in the bond market so that debt floated by firm $A$ would affect $R_F$ and other parameters. This is truly a third-order effect which can be neglected. It will also be seen later that the $dD/dI$ term is unimportant.

capital budgeting decisions that ensure $\dfrac{dS}{dI} \geq \dfrac{dE \cdot F \cdot}{dI}$, which in turn leads to the criterion that the expected marginal internal rate of return of a project must be larger than some quantity. This quantity, the cut-off rate for the marginal investment, or the cost of capital, is:

$$\text{cost of capital} = \frac{R_F}{1-Z} +$$

$$\frac{\lambda}{S_T}\left\{\frac{d\sum_k \text{cov}(X_A, X_k)}{dI} - \left(\frac{Z}{1-Z}\right)\left[\frac{d\sigma^2(X_T')}{dI} + \frac{d\,\text{cov}(X_T', X_A)}{dI}\right]\right\}$$

$$+ \left(\frac{Z}{1-Z}\right)\left[\frac{dE(X_T')}{dI} - R_F\left(\frac{1+dS_T'}{dI} - \frac{dD}{dI}\right)\right] \quad (23)$$

At this point, some approximations will be made.[22] Notice that in the denominator of the definition of $Z$ is $S_T$, the aggregate market value of all capital assets combined (which includes stocks, real estate, insurance, etc.), a very large sum. Thus the last half of the second term of (23) can be assumed to be negligible since it is mutiplied by, among other things, $\dfrac{1}{S_T^2}$. In addition, the change due to an incremental investment in Firm $A$ of the expected earnings and the market value of all assets other than $A$, $\dfrac{dE(X_T')}{dI}$ and $\dfrac{dS_T'}{dI}$, will be assumed to be zero when multiplied by $\dfrac{Z}{1-Z}$, itself a very small fraction. Finally, since $\dfrac{dD}{dI}$ is bounded by one and zero, the term $\left(\dfrac{Z}{1-Z}\right)R_F\dfrac{dD}{dI}$ will be neglected. Therefore, we are left with the approximated cost of capital expression:

---

[21] These are:

$$\frac{dE(X_T)}{dI} = \frac{dE(X_T')}{dI} + \frac{dE(X_A)}{dI}$$

and

$$\frac{d\sigma^2(X_T)}{dI} = \frac{d\sigma^2(X_T')}{dI} + \frac{d\sigma^2(X_A)}{dI} + 2\frac{d\,\text{cov}(X_T', X_A)}{dI}$$

$$= \frac{d\sum_k \text{cov}(X_A, X_k)}{dI} + \frac{d\sigma^2(X_T')}{dI} + \frac{d\,\text{cov}(X_T', X_A)}{dI}$$

where $X_T' = \sum\limits_{k \neq A} X_k = $ dollar earnings from all capital assets except equity $A$.

[22] The reason for presenting the full cost of capital equation instead of assuming away these feedback effects from the beginning is to allow the reader to judge for himself the validity of these approximations (a procedure not followed by Lintner [13] and which will be discussed shortly).

$$\text{cost of capital} = R_F + \frac{\lambda}{S_T} \left[ \frac{d \sum_k \text{cov}(X_A, X_k)}{dI} \right]. \tag{24}$$

## B. INTERPRETATION OF THE COST OF CAPITAL

Comparing (24) to the valuation equation (21a), suggests an interpretation of our derived cost of capital. If the investment is riskless, i.e., does not increase the adjustment term,

$$\frac{\lambda}{S_T} \sum_k \text{cov}(X_A, X_k),$$

applied by the market (in equation 21a) to account for the risk of the firm's total earnings, then the expected marginal internal rate of return of this investment must only surpass the risk-free rate of interest. By not increasing this adjustment term in (21a),

$$\frac{\lambda}{S_T} \left[ \frac{d \sum_k \text{cov}(X_A, X_k)}{dI} \right]$$

must be zero for the investment. Therefore, the second half of the cost of capital equation takes into account the effect of the specific investment on this market risk-adjustment, which is then subtracted from the new expected earnings prior to being capitalized at the riskless rate to yield the new total market value of the firm. The cost of capital is thus composed of the riskless rate plus a premium for the risk of the particular project.

We can arrive at this same intepretation by noticing that:

$$\frac{\lambda}{S_T} = \frac{V_A[E(R_A) - R_F]}{\sum_k \text{cov}(X_A, X_k)} \tag{25}$$

so that the risk premium in the cost of capital expression (24) is:

$$[E(R_A) - R_F] \left[ \frac{\dfrac{d \sum_k \text{cov}(X_A, X_k)}{dI}}{\dfrac{\sum_k \text{cov}(X_A, X_k)}{V_A}} \right] \tag{25a}$$

where $[E(R_A) - R_F]$ can be viewed as the risk premium prior to the acceptance of the project in question. Thus to obtain a project's appropriate risk premium, this existing premium is multiplied by the fractional change in the firm's risk per dollar of invested capital caused by the investment.[23]

[23] This discussion of the cost of capital, equation (24), gives us an interpretation of our previous approximations. All terms that were approximated to be zero were indeed second-order effects due to changes in $\lambda$ caused by the investment and the inclusion of firm $A$'s equity in $S_T$.

Having explained the meaning of our cost of capital, we can compare it to the one proposed by MM. They suggest using the capitalization rate for a debt-free firm; that is:

$$E(R_A) = R_F + \lambda \operatorname{cov}(R_A, R_M).$$

The use of $E(R_A)$ as the cost of capital is appropriate for any investment that preserves their valuation relationship

$$V_A = \frac{E(X_A)}{E(R_A)} = \frac{E(X_A)}{R_F + \left(\dfrac{\lambda}{S_T}\right)\left(\dfrac{1}{V_A}\right) \sum\limits_{k} \operatorname{cov}(X_A, X_k)} \tag{26}$$

after the investment is accepted. Assuming that $R_F$, $\lambda$, and $S_T$ are not affected by capital budgeting decisions in firm $A$, the type of investment that will maintain the above relation is restricted to one with the following characteristic:[24]

$$\frac{d \sum\limits_{k} \operatorname{cov}(X_A, X_k)}{dI} = \frac{\sum\limits_{k} \operatorname{cov}(X_A, X_k)}{V}. \tag{27}$$

The right-hand side of (27) is a measure of the existing risk per dollar invested. Therefore, we can conclude that MM's cost of capital is applicable for all new investments that have the same effect on risk per dollar invested (the left-hand side of (27)) as existing assets. Because of their use of the equivalent risk-class concept to derive the cost of capital, this conclusion is not surprising. $E(R_A)$ can be used as the cost of capital only for pure scale or non-diversifying investments that do not change the firm's risk class.

Now with a market equilibrium framework developed, we are able to obtain the cost of capital for all investments, scale-changing or otherwise. To show that our cost of capital expression will be the same as MM's result for a non-diversifying project, substitute (27) in (24) to obtain:

[24] The property of an investment that will preserve the linear homogeneity of (26) so that $E(R_A)$ is the correct cost of capital, can be found by differentiating the right-hand side of (26) with respect to $dI$

$$\frac{dI}{dV} = \frac{\left[R_F + \dfrac{\lambda}{S_T V} \sum\limits_{k} \operatorname{cov}(X_A, X_k)\right] \dfrac{dE(X_A)}{dI} - E(X_A) \dfrac{\lambda}{S_T} \left\{d\left[\dfrac{1}{V} \sum\limits_{k} \operatorname{cov}(X_A, X_k)\right]/dI\right\}}{\left[R_F + \dfrac{\lambda}{S_T V} \sum\limits_{k} \operatorname{cov}(X_A, X_k)\right]^2}$$

Only if

$$\frac{d\left[\dfrac{1}{V} \sum\limits_{k} \operatorname{cov}(X_A, X_k)\right]}{dI} = \frac{V \dfrac{d \sum\limits_{k} \operatorname{cov}(X_A, X_k)}{dI} - \left[\sum\limits_{k} \operatorname{cov}(X_A, X_k)\right] \dfrac{dV}{dI}}{V^2} = 0$$

will MM's cost of capital be appropriate. Setting the numerator in the last expression equal to zero and noting that the cost of the investment, $dI$, must be financed by debt and/or equity so that $dI = dS + dD = dV$, condition (27) in the text is obtained.

$$\text{cost of capital} = R_F + \frac{\lambda}{S_T V} \sum_k \text{cov}(X_A, X_k)$$

$$= R_F + \lambda \, \text{cov}(R_A, R_M).$$

Lintner [13], in contrast to MM, required his investments to meet a much more stringent condition. He assumed that the change in the covariance of firm $A$'s earnings with the earnings of all other firms caused by the marginal investment is zero; that is,[25]

$$\frac{d \sum\limits_{k \neq A} \text{cov}(X_A, X_k)}{dI} = 0$$

Then his cost of capital, in our context, becomes:

$$\text{cost of capital (Lintner)} = R_F + \frac{\lambda}{S_T} \frac{d\sigma^2(X_A)}{dI}.$$

To indicate the implication of this assumption, rearrange our (25) to obtain:

$$\sum_k \text{cov}(X_A, X_k) = S_T \frac{V_A[E(R_A) - R_F]}{\lambda} \tag{25a}$$

which shows how large the sum of covariances must be, considering the magnitude of $S_T$. To suggest that the risk in all future projects is only the effect on the firm's variance is to consider only a very small part of the total riskiness of the investment. If we substitute $\sigma^2(X_A)$ for $\sum\limits_k \text{cov}(X_A, X_k)$ in (25a), the equality would hardly remain. As a result, Lintner's cost of capital is much smaller than that which would have been used for the firm had it started from scratch today. For the average investment made by the average firm, it would seem that MM's cost of capital is much more accurate than Lintner's suggested approach (even disregarding MM's proviso that it be applied only to scale-changing investments). Lintner's [13] attack on MM's work appears unjustified.[26]

[25] Lintner [13, page 23] justifies this assumption by referring to Sharpe's [26] diagonal model, whereby all assets are dependent on a common underlying market factor, $D$. Then:

$$R_k = \alpha_k + \beta_k R_D + \varepsilon_k \qquad k = 1, 2 \ldots, T; \qquad k \neq A$$
$$R_A = \alpha_A + \beta_A R_D + \varepsilon_A$$

and $\text{cov}(\varepsilon_A, \varepsilon_k) = \text{cov}(\varepsilon_A, R_D) = \text{cov}(\varepsilon_k, R_D) = 0$ are specified. Lintner then makes the critical assumption that the random disturbance term, $\varepsilon_A$, is all that can be (or is) affected by capital budgeting decisions in firm $A$. Then of course, $\text{cov}(R_A, R_k) = \beta_A \beta_k \sigma^2(R_D)$ and is independent of changes in $E(\varepsilon_A)$ and $\sigma(\varepsilon_A)$. But why cannot new investments affect $\beta_A$, as did previous investments? Otherwise, how did $\beta_A$ get there initially? Lintner, alone, should not be criticized on this point. Many others have suggested using the Markowitz portfolio approach on the real assets of the firm and therefore ignoring all market effects on risk—for the latest example, see Cohen and Elton [3].

[26] Having assumed the major part of the risk effect of a new investment to be zero, Lintner goes on to emphasize such minor points as the covariance of an investment's earnings with concurrent projects' earnings. And just for this, he suggests using a pro-

## VI. THE EFFECT OF CORPORATE TAXES ON THE COST OF CAPITAL

A. DERIVATION OF THE COST OF CAPITAL

Consideration of corporate income taxes does not require us to alter the procedure followed in Section V. The valuation formula for this case can be expressed as:[27]

$$S = \frac{(1 - \tau)E(X_A)}{R_F} + \tau D - \frac{\frac{\lambda}{S_T} \sum_k \text{cov}(_\tau X_A, _\tau X_k)}{R_F} - D \qquad (28)$$

where after-tax asset earnings, $(1 - \tau)X$, is denoted by the left-hand subscript $\tau$ on $X$.

Applying the capital budgeting criterion, $\dfrac{dS}{dI} \geq \dfrac{dE \cdot F \cdot}{dI}$ to (28), rearranging, and noting that $\dfrac{dD}{dI} + \dfrac{dE \cdot F \cdot}{dI} = 1$, we obtain:

$$(1 - \tau)\frac{dE(X_A)}{dI} \geq R_F\left(1 - \tau\frac{dD}{dI}\right) + \frac{\lambda}{S_T}\left[\frac{d \sum_k \text{cov}(_\tau X_A, _\tau X_k)}{dI}\right]. \qquad (29)$$

The left-hand side of (29) is the after-tax expected marginal internal rate of return of an investment and it must be at least equal to the right-hand side, otherwise stockholders' wealth will not be maximized. Therefore, the after-tax cost of capital is:

$$\text{cost of capital} = R_F\left(1 - \tau\frac{dD}{dI}\right) + \frac{\lambda}{S_T}\left[\frac{d \sum_k \text{cov}(_\tau X_A, _\tau X_k)}{dI}\right]. \qquad (30)$$

---

gramming approach! Lintner also seems to have forgotten that his (and our and MM's) model is strictly valid for only one horizon period (our assumption 2) when criticizing MM and when discussing the effects of changes in $R_F$. Theoretically, as soon as a new investment is made by the firm, it must be financed and a new equity created. This changes the set of capital assets available to the investor and a new equilibrium (and parameters) must be determined. This is truly a major disadvantage and whether or not it invalidates the model for practical purposes awaits empirical results.

[27] Starting with equation (19), we have:

$$S = \frac{(1 - \tau)E(X_A)}{E(R_A)} + \tau D - D = \frac{(1 - \tau)E(X_A)}{R_F + \lambda \, \text{cov}(R_A, R_M)} + \tau D - D$$

where the subscript $A$ represents the firm if it did not have any debt and the $R$'s are on an after-tax basis. Since

$$\text{cov}(R_A, R_M) = \frac{1}{S_A S_T} \sum_k \text{cov}(_\tau X_A, _\tau X_k)$$

and

$$S_A = V - \tau D = S - \tau D + D,$$

equation (28) is obtained. Also, the comments made in Section V, part A, are recognized, so that we shall henceforth ignore the effects of $dI$ on the market variables $\lambda$, $S_T$, and $X_T$.

We can interpret this result by comparing it to (28). First, consider a risk-less project; then $\dfrac{d \sum\limits_{k} \text{cov}(_\tau X_A, _\tau X_k)}{dI} = 0$. Its after-tax marginal internal rate of return must be greater than only the risk-free rate less the tax subsidy given to debt financing in order for the present shareholders' equity to increase. The tax subsidy is the product of the dollar interest cost, $R_F \dfrac{dD}{dI}$, and the tax rate, $\tau$. Thus, the cost of capital for a riskless project is $R_F - \tau R_F \dfrac{dD}{dI}$, the answer provided by (30).

Next, consider a project that has some risk. It will, in addition to the costs discussed for the riskless project, affect the risk adjustment term in (28). The last term in our cost of capital relation clearly considers the investment's impact on this term.

This result can be compared again to the MM cost of capital. They applied the capital budgeting criterion, $\dfrac{dV}{dI} \geq 1$, to our equation (19), to obtain:[28]

$$\text{cost of capital (MM)} = [E(R_A)]\left(1 - \tau \frac{dD}{dI}\right)$$

$$= R_F\left(1 - \tau \frac{dD}{dI}\right) + \frac{\lambda\left(1 - \tau \dfrac{dD}{dI}\right)}{S_T S_A} \sum_k \text{cov}(_\tau X_A, _\tau X_k) \tag{31}$$

An investment which will preserve the linear homogeneity of (19) so that (31) will be its cost of capital must satisfy the following condition:[29]

$$\frac{d \sum\limits_{k} \text{cov}(_\tau X_A, _\tau X_k)}{dS_A} = \frac{\sum\limits_{k} \text{cov}(_\tau X_A, _\tau X_k)}{S_A} \tag{32}$$

As in the no-tax case, a project with this property is one that merely changes the scale of the firm. Assuming that equity was the sole source of previous capital, the right-hand side of (32) defines the risk per dollar already invested in the corporation. New investments must have this same ratio of MM's cost of capital to be applicable. In (32), proportional changes in risk are expressed on a pure equity basis; otherwise the consequence of the debt tax subsidy on effective capital required to finance the project would not be taken into consideration.

To show that MM's result is a special case of the cost of capital derived here, the relationship between the purchase cost of the investment, $dI$, and the effective capital required, $dS_A$, allows us to express (32) as:[30]

---

[28] See reference [20] or [22].

[29] The same procedure described in footnote 24 is used to obtain equation (32).

[30] Since $dI$ must be financed with debt and/or equity, then $dI = dS + dD \equiv dV$. And

$$\frac{d \sum_k \text{cov}(_{\tau}X_A, _{\tau}X_k)}{dI} = \frac{\left(1 - \tau \frac{dD}{dI}\right) \sum_k \text{cov}(_{\tau}X_A, _{\tau}X_k)}{S_A} \tag{32a}$$

so that MM's cost of capital is obtained when (32a) is substituted in (30).

B. SUGGESTIONS FOR ESTIMATING THE COST OF CAPITAL

Nothing will be added to MM's recommendation concerning the financing of specific projects. The long-run target debt ratio, $L^*$, for the firm's capital structure should be recognized as the financing mix for all of the firm's investments regardless of how any individual project is financed. Then, $\frac{dD}{dI} = L^*$, and (30) can be expressed as:

$$\text{cost of capital} = R_F(1 - \tau L^*) + \frac{\lambda}{S_T} \left[ \frac{d \sum_k \text{cov}(_{\tau}X_A, _{\tau}X_k)}{dI} \right] \tag{30a}$$

For small or nondiversifying investments, it is proposed that management assume that each effective invested dollar of the new project, $dS_A$, affects the covariance of the corporation's earnings with all other earnings as the average effective dollar of the corporation's existing assets, $S_A$, affects this covariance. Then MM's cost of capital can be used.

Major investments, in contrast to those discussed above, require a direct solution of (30a). For the risk premium, we can note the following equivalent forms:

$$\frac{\lambda}{S_T} \left[ \frac{d \sum_k \text{cov}(_{\tau}X_A, _{\tau}X_k)}{dI} \right]$$

$$= \frac{\lambda}{S_T} \frac{d \, \text{cov}(_{\tau}X_A, _{\tau}X_T)}{dI}$$

$$= \frac{\lambda}{S_T} [\text{cov}(_{\tau}X_{A0} + _{\tau}X_{A1}, _{\tau}X_T + _{\tau}X_{A1}) - \text{cov}(X_{\tau A0}, _{\tau}X_T)]$$

$$= \lambda \, \text{cov}(_{\tau}X_{A1}, R_M) + \frac{\lambda}{S_T} [\text{cov}(_{\tau}X_{A0}, _{\tau}X_{A1}) + \sigma^2(_{\tau}X_{A1})] \tag{30b}$$

where $_{\tau}X_{A0}$, $_{\tau}X_{A1}$, and $_{\tau}X_T$ are defined as tax-adjusted earnings from firm $A$'s

---

from (18), we have $dS_A = dV - \tau dD$, so that

$$dS_A = dI - \tau dD = dI\left(1 - \tau \frac{dD}{dI}\right).$$

Substituting this last expression in (32) results in (32a).

existing assets, from the new investment under consideration, and from all capital assets in the market, respectively.[31]

Use of the Sharpe [26] diagonal model is possible in estimating the project's major risk component, $\lambda \operatorname{cov}(_\tau X_{A1}, R_M)$, if the rate of return of a value-weighted index, such as the S & P Index, can be assumed to be a "good" proxy for $R_M$ and the systematic risk in $_\tau X_{A1}$ can be explained by a simple linear relationship with $R_M$.[32] Then:

$$_\tau X_{A1} = a + bR_M + \varepsilon \tag{33}$$

where $a$ and $b$ are parameters and $E(\varepsilon) = \operatorname{cov}(R_M, \varepsilon) = 0$. Applying (33) to the definition of the covariance, we have:

$$
\begin{aligned}
\lambda \operatorname{cov}(_\tau X_{A1}, R_M) &= \lambda E\{[bR_M + \varepsilon - bE(R_M)][R_M - E(R_M)]\} \\
&= \lambda b \sigma^2(R_M) \\
&= b[E(R_M) - R_F]
\end{aligned}
$$

so that $b$ and $E(R_M)$ are all that must be estimated.

## VII. CONCLUSION

Two major issues of corporation finance, the financing and investment decisions of the firm, have been analyzed in this paper in the framework of the Sharpe-Lintner-Mossin market equilibrium capital asset pricing model, itself an extension of the Markowitz-Tobin portfolio model. The effects of the financing decision on aggregate equity values were the topics of Sections III and IV. The famous MM Propositions I and II were found to hold when put to the market equilibrium model, both in the no tax case (Section III) and when corporate taxes were taken into account (Section IV). Thus the assumption of homogeneous risk-classes, constructed expressly to eliminate a full-blown market equilibrium model, and the arbitrage proof are no longer necessary. In place of arbitrage, a switching operation was discussed.

Sections V and VI were devoted to developing and interpreting the cost of capital, the minimum required rate of return individual projects within the firm must surpass in order that their shareholders not suffer a decrease in

---

[31] For completeness, we should consider the covariance of the tax-adjusted earnings of project 1 with all the other projects, $n$, included in the year's capital budget. Then to (30b) must be added

$$\frac{\lambda}{S_T} [2 \sum_n \operatorname{cov}(_\tau X_{A1}, {_\tau X_n})].$$

However, this term, as well as $\operatorname{cov}(_\tau X_{A0}, {_\tau X_{A1}})$ and $\sigma^2(_\tau X_{A1})$, contributes very little to the cost of capital risk premium because it is multiplied by $\dfrac{\lambda}{S_T}$. In view of this small effect and that a programming approach is required (since this covariance is not known until the entire capital budget is determined simultaneously), we shall disregard it.

[32] We are not assuming that all of the $k$ capital assets are related to $R_M$ by (33). Therefore, the comments made by Fama [6] on the Sharpe-Linter conflict do not apply to the less restrictive model employed here.

expected utility. MM's recommended cost of capital was found to be a special case (for nondiversifying investments) of the one developed here, albeit a most important special case. Then comparing Lintner's cost of capital to MM's, the latter version was thought to be more accurate in the majority of cases faced by the firm. Finally, cursory suggestions to estimate the cost of capital were made.

It might be of interest to note that MM's discussions suggest an equilibrium portfolio model was implicitly being employed. For instance, they associated a rise in expected equity yields, when leverage increased, to an increased premium induced by the need to bear greater variability risk. And when discussing their arbitrage operation, we can quote [21, footnote 11]:

In the language of the theory of choice, the exchanges are movements from inefficient points in the interior to efficient points on the boundary of the investor's opportunity set; and not movements between efficient points along the boundary . . . .

That their propositions are shown to hold in the portfolio model under market equilibrium conditions a decade later (and slightly earlier for Proposition I in the time-state preference framework) should be regarded as a tribute to their partial equilibrium concept of the homogeneous risk-class.

But a word of caution is necessary in conclusion. We opened the analytical part of this paper with an enumeration of the assumptions. The results presented here are conditional on these assumptions not grossly violating reality.

## REFERENCES

1. K. J. Arrow. "The Role of Securities in the Optimal Allocation of Risk-Bearing," *Review of Economic Studies*, April, 1964.
2. G. Bierwag and M. Grove. "On Capital Asset Prices: Comment," *Journal of Finance* (March, 1965), pp. 89–93.
3. K. Cohen and E. Elton. "Inter-temporal Portfolio Analysis Based on Simulation of Joint Returns," *Management Science* (Sept., 1967), pp. 5–18.
4. G. Debreu. *Theory of Value*. New York: John Wiley and Sons, 1959. Chap. 7.
5. E. Fama. "Risk, Return and General Equilibrium in a Stable Paretian Market." Unpublished manuscript, June, 1967.
6. ———. "Risk, Return and General Equilibrium: Some Clarifying Comments." *Journal of Finance* (March, 1968), pp. 29–40.
7. I. Fisher. *The Theory of Interest*. New York: Macmillan, 1930. Reprinted, Augustus M. Kelley, 1961.
8. J. Hirshleifer. "Efficient Allocation of Capital in an Uncertain World," *American Economic Review* (May, 1964), pp. 77–85.
9. ———. "Investment Decision Under Uncertainty: Choice-Theoretic Approaches," *The Quarterly Journal of Economics* (November, 1965), pp. 509–36.
10. ———. "Investment Decision Under Uncertainty: Applications of the State-Preference Approach," *The Quarterly Journal of Economics* (May, 1966), pp. 252–77.

11. J. Lintner. "The Cost of Capital and Optimal Financing of Corporate Growth," *Journal of Finance* (May, 1963), pp. 292–310.

12. ———. "Optimal Dividends and Corporate Growth Under Uncertainty," *Quarterly Journal of Economics* (February, 1964), pp. 49–95.

13. ———. "The Valuation of Risk Assets and The Selection of Risky Investments in Stock Portfolios and Capital Budgets," *Review of Economics and Statistics* (February, 1965), pp. 13–37.

14. ———. "Security Prices, Risk, and Maximal Gains from Diversification," *Journal of Finance* (December, 1965), pp. 587–615.

15. J. Magee. "Decision Trees for Decision Making," *Harvard Business Review* (July–August, 1964), pp. 126–38.

16. H. Markowitz. "Portfolio Selection," *Journal of Finance* (March 1952), pp. 77–91.

17. ———. *Portfolio Selection: Efficient Diversification of Investments.* New York: John Wiley and Sons, Inc., 1959.

18. M. Miller. "Discussion," *Journal of Finance* (May, 1963), pp. 313–16.

19. M. Miller and F. Modigliani. "Dividend Policy, Growth, and the Valuation of Shares," *Journal of Business* (October, 1961), pp. 411–33.

20. ———. "Some Estimates of the Cost of Capital to the Electric Utility Industry, 1954–57," *American Economic Review* (June, 1966), pp. 333–91.

21. Modigliani and Miller. "The Cost of Capital, Corporation Finance and the Theory of Investment," *American Economic Review* (June, 1958), pp. 261–97.

22. ———. "Corporate Income Taxes and the Cost of Capital: A Correction," *American Economic Review* (June, 1963), pp. 433–43.

23. J. Mossin. "Equilibrium in a Capital Asset Market," *Econometrica* (October, 1966), pp. 768–83.

24. A. Roy. "Safety First and the Holding of Assets," *Econometrica* (July, 1952), pp. 431–49.

25. W. Sharpe. "Capital Asset Prices: A Theory of Market Equilibrium under Conditions of Risk," *Journal of Finance* (September, 1964), pp. 425–42.

26. ———. "A Simplified Model for Portfolio Analysis," *Management Science* (January, 1963), pp. 277–93.

27. J. Tobin. "Liquidity Preference as Bahavior Towards Risk," *Review of Economic Studies* (February, 1958), pp. 65–86.

PART **VI**

DIVIDEND POLICY

\* \* \* \* \* \* \* \* \* \* \* \* \* \* \* \* \* \* \* \*

# 37. DIVIDEND POLICY: ITS INFLUENCE ON THE VALUE OF THE ENTERPRISE

JAMES E. WALTER*

Reprinted from *The Journal of Finance*, Vol. *XVIII*, No. 2 (May, 1963), pp. 280–91, by permission of the author and the publisher.

The question before the house is whether dividends are in some sense of the word weighted differently from retained earnings at the margin in the minds of marginal investors. As evidenced by the current literature on the subject, the answer is by no means self-evident.

Although the problem that confronts us can be approached in a variety of ways, our preference is to commence with net cash flows from operations and to consider the effect of additions to, and subtractions from, these flows upon stock values.[1] Not only does this starting point by-pass certain measurement problems, but it also directs attention to the relevant variables in a manner that other approaches may not.

Net cash flows from operations are available for (1) the payment of interest and principal on debt or the equivalent and (2) capital expenditures and dividend payments. Operating cash flows can, of course, be supplemented in any period by debt or equity financing. Debt financing creates obligations to pay out cash in future periods and thereby reduces cash flows available for capital expenditures and dividends in those periods. Equity financing, in turn, diminishes the *pro rata* share of total cash flows available for dividends and reinvestment.

---

* University of Pennsylvania.

[1] As a point of departure, *net cash flows from operations* lie somewhere between (1) net cash flow and (2) net operating income. See, for example, Bodenhorn (1). For an illustrative breakdown and an explanation of the manner in which net operating cash flows are derived from balance sheets and income statement, refer to chapter 11 of Walter (12).

The stockholder shares in the operating cash flows of each period to the degree that cash dividends are declared and paid and in future cash flows insofar as they are reflected in the market price of the stock.[2] In like fashion, the purchaser of a share of stock acquires (1) a finite stream of anticipated cash dividends and (2) an anticipated market price at the end of his holding period. The market price of the stock at any time can be said to be determined by the expectations of marginal investors (as these anticipations pertain to the dividend stream and to the terminal market price) and by their system of weighting the possible outcomes per period and through time.

To focus directly upon the potential influence of variations in dividend policy in this scheme of things, it is useful, first, to draw an analogy to the stream-splitting approach to the cost of capital. Consideration is then afforded (1) the conditions under which adjustments in dividend payout exert no effect upon stock price and (2) the consequences of modifying these conditions to take account of the economic power of large corporations and other aspects of observed behavior. The final item treated in this article is that of statistical testing.

The assumptions that prevail throughout the analysis are commonplace. One is that the satisfaction which investors derive from owning stock is wholly (or almost wholly) monetary in character. A second is that investors do the best that they can; they operate, however, in a competitive capital market and are unable to stack the results.

Corporate management—we may add—is also keenly aware of the potential impact of its actions upon stock price (if only because of stock options). Management may nonetheless be confronted with such *mixed* motivations as self-preservation and avoidance of anti-trust action. The consequence is that maximization of stock price need not be the sole objective.[3]

So far as uncertainty is concerned, it is supposed that—unless otherwise stated—people think whatever they think about the future. Whether this assumption is appropriate remains to be seen.

No attempt is made in this treatment of dividend policy to run the gamut from perfect foresight to generalized uncertainty. Papers by Miller and Modigliani (10) and Lintner (7)—among others—have already proceeded along these lines. Rather, the intention is to show where dividends fit into the underlying analytical scheme, to spotlight certain assumptions that underlie recent statements pertaining to the neutrality of dividend policy, and to propose extensions in the theory designed to recognize deficiencies in the perfectly competitive model.

---

[2] It almost goes without saying that an existing shareholder periodically compares the objective market price with his subjective version of anticipated dividend streams and terminal prices to determine whether to hold or liquidate. In this respect, his behavior resembles that of a prospective buyer.

[3] For justification, we have only to refer to the statistics on concentration of economic power.

## ANALOGY TO COST OF CAPITAL

Before the thrust shifted to dividends, the basic issue in the cost of capital discussion was one of dividing the stream of operating cash flows (or some reconcilable variant thereof) between debt and equity in such a manner as to maximize the market value of the enterprise. Modigliani and Miller (8), it may be remembered, dramatized the stream-splitting aspect by drawing an analogy to the price effect of separating the whole milk into cream and skim milk. Their contention that, even in the face of institutional limitations, the farmer cannot gain by splitting the milk stream was subsequently subjected to empirical testing by Durand (3) and shown to be invalid.

When dividends enter the picture, the issue becomes one of dividing the stream of operating cash flows among debt, dividends, and reinvestment in such a way as to achieve the same result. The principal difference in the character of the analysis is that it may no longer be feasible to assume that the size and shape of the stream of operating cash flows is independent of the manner in which it is subdivided.[4]

Much the same as contractual interest payments and other financial outlays, the continuation of cash dividends at their prevailing (or regular) rate can be—and commonly is—assigned a priority by management.[5] In such instances, the burden of oscillations in operating cash flows is placed upon lower-priority outlays, namely, capital and related expenditures, unless management is both willing and able to compensate by adjusting the level of external financing.[6] Even if management is willing to seek funds outside the firm, moreover, the uncertainties inherent in the terms under which external financing can be obtained in the future reduce the likelihood of such action in the event of operating cash deficiencies in any period. The upshot is that current cash dividends may well be capitalized somewhat differently from anticipated future cash flows (net of current dividends, to avoid double-counting).

It may be observed that the relative instability of expenditures designed to augment future cash flows shows up even in the aggregate. The change from year to year for new plant and equipment averaged 19 per cent for all manufacturing corporations in the post-war period (to 1961), as compared with 9 per cent for cash dividends. The maximum declines from one year to the

---

[4] Although the milk-separating analogy implies that the dimensions of the stream are unaffected by its division between debt and equity, even this need not be a fundamental difference in character. As evidenced by Donaldson (2), decisions by management to borrow or not to borrow sometimes affect growth, that is, the level of future cash flows.

[5] Cf., for example, Lintner (6), in which observed corporate behavior involves gradual adjustments of dividends to earnings and "greater reluctance to reduce than to raise dividends. . . . "

[6] The term "capital and related expenditures" refers to all outlays that affect operating cash flows over several periods. Either by reason of previous commitments or because of their importance to the continued operation of the business, certain elements of these expenditures may have priorities that equal or exceed those connected with the payment of cash dividends.

next were 40 per cent for new plant and equipment and but 2 per cent for dividends.

Again, as in the case of debt versus equity, investor reactions to dividend policy changes can nullify in whole or in part their price effect. Whenever the stockholder is dissatisfied with the dividend payout, the balance between present and future income can be redressed by buying or selling shares of stock and perhaps by other means as well (for instance, by "lending" or "borrowing" on the same *risk* terms that cash dividends are paid). If dividends are deemed insufficient, the desired proportion of current income can be obtained by periodically selling part of the shares owned. If current income is too high, cash dividends can be used to acquire additional shares of stock.

The one thing that shareholders cannot do through their purchase and sale transactions is to negate the consequences of investment decisions by management. If—as may well be the case—investment decisions tend to be linked with dividend policy, their neglect in the analysis of dividend effects seems inappropriate.

## CONDITIONS FOR DIVIDEND EFFECT

The conditions under which changes in dividend payout have minimal influence upon stock values can now be stated. For the most part, they follow from the logics of stream-splitting.

1. *Condition No. 1: The level of future cash flows from operations (that is, the growth rate) is independent of the dividend-payout policy.*—In essence, this condition implies that the impact of a change in dividend payout upon operating cash flows will be *exactly* offset (or negated) by a corresponding and opposite change in supplemental (or external) financing.

For those who believe that the cost of capital is unaffected by the capital structure, either debt or equity financing is a legitimate means of neutralizing dividend policy changes. For those who believe otherwise, an increase in dividends can be offset only by the sale of equity shares. In the latter instance, then, the capital structure must also be taken as independent of the dividend-payout policy.

If attention is confined to offsetting transactions in equity shares for the sake of simplicity and generality, the following result obtains: An increase in dividend payout will leave operating cash flows unchanged in the aggregate, but the share of future cash flows accruing to existing stockholders will decline, since additional stock has to be sold to finance the planned capital outlays. The existing shareholder can, of course, reconstitute his former *pro rata* position by purchasing shares in the market with his incremental dividends.

Implicit in these remarks is the presumption that the market completely capitalizes anticipated growth in operating cash flows. New shares are thus acquired at a price that returns new investors *only* the going market rate for the relevant class of risks. The present value of extraordinary returns from investment by the corporation goes to existing stockholders (or whoever was around at the time when the prospect of these returns was first recognized by ͵the market), rather than to new shareholders.

To the degree that the anticipated level of operating cash flows, that is, the growth rate, is connected with the dividend payout for one reason or another the market value of the firm may be conditioned by variations in dividend payout. The policy changes must, of course, be unexpected, and their price effect hinges at least partly upon the relation between the *internal* and *market* rates of return. If the former exceeds the latter, the present value of a dollar employed by the firm (other things being equal) will be greater than a dollar of dividends distributed and invested elsewhere. This issue was considered in my 1956 paper (11).

Condition No. 1 can readily be extended to take account of tax differentials. The amended version is that operating cash flows *net* of taxes paid thereon by shareholders are unaffected by the dividend payout. As things stand, this criterion simply does not hold; neither—it might be added—does the corresponding condition hold in the case of debt versus equity.[7]

2. *Condition No. 2: The weights employed are independent of the dividend-payout policy.*—In other words, the discount factors or weights, that is, the ratios of indifference values between one period and the next, are invariant with respect to changes in dividend payout.

Gordon (4) argues that the weights employed must also be constant between periods and that such is unlikely to be the case under uncertainty. That is to say, looking forward from period zero, the ratios of the indifference values between periods 0 and 1, 1 and 2, and so on have to be all the same.

In order to evaluate this possible addition to Condition No. 2, it is pertinent to recall Condition No. 1. If the level of total operating cash flows is unaffected by the policy revision, a change in current cash dividends will alter the stockholder's stake in future cash flows. The gain or loss in current dividends will just equal the gain or loss in the present value of future cash flows (or dividends, if you wish), provided that the system of weights remains unchanged. Gordon's point is thus unacceptable because the firm has to go into the market for funds to replace those paid out in dividends and, in so doing, has to pay the market rate.

Returning to the question of the independence of the weights used from the dividend-payout policy, a change in dividend payout undoubtedly disturbs the investors in that stock to some extent unless the modification was anticipated previously. Insofar as costs of one kind or another, indivisibilities, and other factors prevent the shareholders thus activated from completely reconstituting their *old* position and thereby give rise to a new and different equili-

---

[7] The price effect of tax differentials may well be less than might be supposed. For example, the marginal tax rates implied in a comparison or recent yields on tax-exempts of high quality with those on United States government securities are on the order of 15–25 per cent.

brium point, the weights employed will adjust in some measure. The role played by friction in the system is, however, well known, and there is little need to dwell upon this aspect.

More significant, perhaps, is the fact that the substitution of future cash flows for present dividends superimposes an element of market risk upon the basic uncertainty of the operating cash-flow stream. As contrasted with cash dividends in which the stockholder receives a dollar for each dollar declared, there is no telling what price the shareholder will realize in the market at any given time for his stake in future cash flows.

It is, of course, true that the corporation would confront the same market risk if it—rather than the shareholder—were forced to enter the capital market. It is also true that realized prices may average out over a period of time. The fact remains that the firm may well be better able to adjust for—as well as to assume—this class of risk.

Whether further conditions ought to be introduced is a moot point. A recent article by John Lintner (7), for example, concludes that "generalized uncertainty" is itself sufficient to insure that shareholders "will *not* be indifferent to whether cash dividends are increased (or reduced) by substituting new equity issues for retained earnings to finance given capital budgets."

As a generalization, this conclusion is suspect, for it appears to be inconsistent with a logical extension of Lintner's earlier analysis under idealized uncertainty. It is difficult to see why two or two million investors cannot be indifferent at a given price for a variety of reasons. If so, generalized uncertainty can—but perhaps need not—produce the same *surface* result as idealized uncertainty.[8]

In any event, Condition No. 2 is sufficiently broad to embrace the foregoing aspect of the uncertainty issue. To the degree that Lintner's proposition is valid, generalized uncertainty produces an effect that resembles that associated with the presence of costs and frictions in the system.

## IMPERFECT COMPETITION, REGULATED ENTERPRISE, AND NON-ECONOMIC CONSIDERATIONS

That the conditions for no dividend effect fail to hold in certain important respects has already been established here and elsewhere. At this stage, there is little point in discussing further the consequences of differences in tax treatment, new-issue and other costs associated with external financing, and uncertainty itself (although the *on balance* effect will be considered toward the end of the paper). It is nonetheless relevant—in view of their neglect in the literature—to extend the examination of dividend effects beyond the oft-used competitive model that presupposes rational behavior in the traditional economic sense and to consider the influence of such things as management leeway, economic slack, and intramarginal pricing policies. The following remarks represent a preliminary effort in this direction.

[8] To add to the confusion, moreover, see n. 35 in Lintner (7).

In the bulk of corporations with which it is possible to deal statistically, management has considerable leeway in decision making. Their histories of earnings and dividends—not to mention their economic power—are such that their survival in the foreseeable future seemingly does not hinge upon single modes of behavior. The presence of generalized uncertainty implies, moreover, that there is often no best *visible* course of action.

The frequently observed association between dividend-payout policy, capital structure, and rate of growth is a useful case in point; the survival of the corporation ordinarily does not depend, in the short run at least, upon any specific rate of growth. The prime considerations affecting growth, apart from profit opportunities, are (1) willingness of corporations to go into the public market place for additional funds and (2) their attitude toward dividends (including their willingness to return unneeded funds to the investors).

For firms that are reluctant to get involved in external financing (and there appear to be many), then, the burden of expansion rests upon residual internal sources, that is, operating cash flows *less* cash dividends and debt servicing *net* of additions to debt. Decisions to increase or decrease dividends thus condition the value of the enterprise as long as the returns on new investments differ from the market rate.

The sword cuts both ways. Wherever the available investment opportunities are unable to earn their keep, the specter of liquidating dividends or repurchase of shares or debt retirement arises. If there is no debt outstanding and if the repurchase of shares is not contemplated, the burden of liquidation falls upon dividend payout.

The fact that many of the corporations that normally constitute the statistical samples used in testing dividend hypotheses are characterized by negatively sloping demand curves is also worth noting. Suppose, for instance, that such firms do not charge what the traffic will bear in the sense of equating discounted marginal revenues with discounted marginal costs. Instead, let us assume that they employ some sort of a full-cost pricing policy.

Insofar as these companies assign priorities to the payment of dividends and regard them as a cost (that is, as an obligation of the firm that should be met if possible), the dividend-payout policy will affect stock prices. Decisions to alter the dividend payout under the full-costing approach will, sooner or later, be reflected in product prices (although the impact may be barely visible to the naked eye). If the new prices more nearly approach optimum prices from a profit-maximization standpoint, the effect is to increase stock values. If the reverse obtains, values diminish.

The foregoing consideration may be especially significant in the case of regulated companies whose prices are set by edict rather than by competitive forces. The dividends that regulatory bodies explicitly or implicitly permit to be incorporated in the elements that determine product or service prices will be reflected in stock values.

Closely connected with, but extending beyond, the matter of product or service pricing is the question of operating slack. Our experience has been that most profitable firms are able in some measure to curtail their non-operating and operating outlays without interfering with future cash flows. To the extent that a change in dividend-payout policy conditions the amount of slack in the system, the value of the firm is modified by such changes.

The impact of a revision in dividend policy need not show up immediately; it may await a softness in operating cash flows. As mentioned previously, Lintner (6) and others cite evidence that some fraction of cash dividends is commonly placed well up on the priority scale. The upshot is that managements' reactions to unanticipated reductions in operating cash flows may lead not only to the adjustment of lower-priority outlays but also to the elimination of slack from the system before dividend-payout policies (once established) are altered.

In summary, it is not our purpose to overemphasize the importance of the foregoing extension of the competitive model. The point is simply that hypothesis building in this area has barely begun to scratch the surface. With this in mind, let us turn to the important matter of statistical testing.

## STATISTICAL TESTING

The woods are currently replete with statistical analyses designed to demonstrate the significance (or non-significance) of the diverse factors that may influence stock prices. While it is not our aim to add further to the mounting pile, it is meaningful to mention certain problems of a statistical nature, referred to in the recent literature, that have a bearing on the testing of most hypotheses and, in particular, on the testing of an imperfectly competitive model. Specifically, the comments that follow focus upon the notion of a random variable and collinearity.

In their 1958 article (8), Modigliani and Miller alluded to the peril of relying upon "a single year's profits as a measure of expected profits." Later (9), they argued—as have others—that investors may accept current dividends as an indirect measure of profit expectations.

The difficulties inherent in the use of a random variable to reveal expectations are well known. The realized value of a random variable in any period is ordinarily but one of several values that might have obtained; it may bear little relation—in any visible sense of the word—to the underlying expectation. With this in mind, recent studies have tended to employ averages of one kind or another for the earnings variable. Kolin (5), using an exponential weighting system, has found earnings thus measured to be superior to current dividends in explaining the relative valuation of stocks.

Notwithstanding the fact that current dividends test out more significantly than current earnings, it is important to remember that they, too, are random variables. There is on the surface (apart from the relative stability) little more to recommend current dividends as a measure of expected dividends than there is to presuppose that current earnings adequately reflect anticipated earnings.

Looking to Lintner's earlier work (6), in which dividends were said to adjust gradually to a target payout ratio, an interesting and relevant reversal of the information-content proposition comes to mind. It is entirely possible (as well as quite reasonable) for some weighted average of earnings to be a good surrogate for dividend expectations. In other words, the improved results obtained by Kolin (5) may well be entirely consistent with the *dividend* hypothesis.

In a subsequent piece (10), Miller and Modigliani remarked upon the omission of relevant variables. Pointing a critical finger at certain studies (one of mine and two of Durand were cited!), they stipulated that "no general prediction is made (or can be made) by the theory [i.e., theirs] about what will happen to the dividend coefficient if the crucial growth term is omitted."[9] Except by oblique footnote reference to Gordon's work, however, they neglected to add that specification of the individual coefficient may be difficult even if a growth term is included.

The issue in question is *collinearity*. In his analysis of a linear function that includes both dividends and earnings, Gordon (4) pointed to the instability present in the coefficients whenever a strong correlation existed between two explanatory variables. His finding was: "They [i.e., the coefficients] vary over a very wide range and they cannot be used to make reliable estimates on the variation in share price with each variable." Kolin (5), in turn, referred to the danger of a "severe loss of accuracy due to near singularity of the correlation matrix of independent variables that would occur if the two highly collinear variables were present in the same regression." His concern was with the stochastic properties that might be introduced by computer programs that treat "all digits of the words that are input to the inversion program as error free digits."

It follows that the correlation between dividend payout and growth (that is, the level of future cash flows), which seems likely to exist in many instances, contributes to the difficulty of interpreting results obtained from regression analyses. At the extreme, as Miller and Modigliani (10) affirmed, there may be "no way to distinguish between the effects of dividend policy and investment policy."

Other pitfalls to statistical testing readily come to mind. Perhaps the most significant (in the context of this paper) is the character of the sample used in relation to the hypothesis being tested. More specifically, it seems incongruous to utilize samples drawn from the universe of either regulated monopolies or very large corporations to test competitive behavior.

## CONCLUSIONS

The implication of the foregoing treatment is that the choice of dividend policies almost always affects the value of the enterprise. The general conditions for neutrality are simply not satisfied in the world as we know it. The

---

[9] Actually, my study should not be castigated on this score, for it incorporated variables that measure both growth and internal rate of return.

dimensions of the cash-flow stream (both before and after account is taken of taxes imposed on recipients of dividends and capital gains) are conditioned by dividend-payout policy; efforts by investors to negate the effects of policy changes are frequently of limited avail; and so on.

In the real world (again, as we know it), it is insufficient to contemplate the effects of dividends under perfectly (or even purely) competitive circumstances. The fact that a great many firms exercise some control over their own destinies deserves to be recognized. Once the possibility of imperfections is admitted, the potential association between dividends and the level of future cash flows, among other things, becomes clear.

Standard objections to dividend neutrality, that is, differences in tax treatment and costs of external financing, ordinarily favor the retention of earnings. Interdependence between dividend-payout policy and capital outlays, on the other hand, can work either way; it all depends on the profitability of the enterprise.

Statistical analyses designed to support the "pure earnings" hypothesis—or any other hypothesis, for that matter—remain ambiguous. For one thing, uncertainties exist as to precisely what is being measured. For another, the closer the linkage between dividend policy and dimensions of the total stream, the less meaningful are the coefficients attached to each independent variable.

Be that as it may, we are not opposed to statistical analyses. What we do say, however, is that judgment must ultimately rest on the power of the theory generated.


# REFERENCES

1. Bodenhorn, D. "On the Problem of Capital Budgeting," *Journal of Finance*, XIV (December, 1959), 473–92.
2. Donaldson, G. *Corporate Debt Capacity* (Boston: Harvard Business School, 1961).
3. Durand, D. "The Cost of Capital in an Imperfect Market: A Reply to Modigliani and Miller," *American Economic Review*, Vol. XLIX (June, 1959).
4. Gordon, M. *The Investment, Financing and Valuation of the Corporation* (Homewood, Ill.: R. D. Irwin, 1962).
5. Kolin, M. "The Relative Price of Corporate Equity with Particular Reference to Investor Valuation of Retained Earnings and Dividends" (unpublished manuscript).
6. Lintner, J. "Distribution of Incomes of Corporations among Dividends, Retained Earnings and Taxes," *American Economic Review*, XLVI (May, 1956), 97–113.
7. ———. "Dividends, Earnings, Leverage, Stock Prices and the Supply of Capital to Corporations," *Review of Economics and Statistics*, XLIV (August, 1962), 243–70.
8. Modigliani, F., and Miller, M. "The Cost of Capital, Corporation Finance and the Theory of Investment," *American Economic Review*, XLVIII (June, 1958), 261–97.

9. ———. "The Cost of Capital, Corporation Finance and the Theory of Investment: Reply," *ibid.*, XLIV (September, 1959), 655–69.

10. ———. "Dividend Policy, Growth, and the Valuation of Shares," *Journal of Business*, XXXIV (October, 1961), 411–33.

11. Walter, J. "Dividend Policies and Common Stock Prices," *Journal of Finance*, XI (March, 1956), 29–41.

12. ———. *The Investment Process* (Boston: Harvard Business School, 1962), Chap. xi.

## 38. OPTIMAL INVESTMENT AND FINANCING POLICY

### M. J. GORDON*

Reprinted from *The Journal of Finance*, Vol. *XVIII*, No. 2 (May, 1963), pp. 264–72, by permission of the author and the publisher.

In two papers[1] and in a recent book[2] I have presented theory and evidence which lead to the conclusion that a corporation's share price (or its cost of capital) is not independent of the dividend rate. As you may know, MM (Modigliani and Miller) have the opposite view, and they argued their position at some length in a recent paper.[3] Moreover, the tone of their paper made it clear that they saw no reasonable basis on which their conclusion could be questioned. Since they were so sure of their conclusion, it would seem advisable for me to review carefully my thinking on the subject, and this meeting appears to be a good time and place to do so.

## I.

Let us begin by examining MM's fundamental proof that the price of a share is independent of its dividend. They defined the value of a share at $t = 0$ as the present value of (1) the dividend it will pay at the end of the first period, $D_1$, plus (2) the ex-dividend price of the share at the end of the period, $P_1$:

$$P_0 = \frac{1}{1 + k} [D_1 + P_1].$$   (1)

* Professor of business economics, University of Rochester.

[1] "Dividends, Earnings and Stock Prices," *Review of Economics and Statistics*, May, 1959, pp. 99–105; "The Savings, Investment and Valuation of the Corporation," *ibid.*, February, 1962, pp. 37–51.

[2] *The Investment Financing and Valuation of the Corporation* (Homewood, Ill.: R. D. Irwin, 1962).

[3] "Dividend Policy, Growth, and the Valuation of Shares," *Journal of Business*, October, 1961, pp. 411–33.

They then asked what would happen if the corporation, say raised its dividend but kept its investment for the period constant by selling the additional number of shares needed to offset the funds lost by the dividend increase. They demonstrated that the ex-dividend price of the stock at the end of the period would go down by exactly the same amount as the increase in the dividend. Since the sum $D_1 + P_1$ remains the same, $P_0$ is unchanged by the change in the dividend.

I will not review their proof of the theorem in detail because I find nothing wrong with it under the assumption they made that the future is certain. However, after proving the theorem a number of times under different conditions, they withdrew the assumption of certainty and made the dramatic announcement, "our first step, alas, must be to jettison the fundamental valuation equation."[4] Under uncertainty, they continued, it is not "at all clear what meaning can be attached to the discount factor...."[5] The implication which they made explicit in discussing my work is that under uncertainty we cannot represent investors as using discount rates to arrive at the present value of an expectation of future receipts.

It would seem that all is lost. But no! On the very next page we are told that their "fundamental conclusion need not be modified merely because of the presence of uncertainty about the future course of profits, investment, or dividends...."[6] By virtue of the postulates of "imputed rationality" and "symmetric market rationality," it remains true that "dividend policy is irrelevant for the determination of market prices."[7]

Their paper continued with a discussion of market imperfections, in which they note that the most important one, the capital gains tax, should create a preference for low payout rates. They concede that it may nevertheless be true that high payout rates sell at a premium, but they found "... only one way to account for it, namely as a result of systematic irrationality on the part of the investing public." They concluded with the hope that "... investors, however naive they may be when they enter the market, do sometimes learn from experience; and perhaps, occasionally even from reading articles such as this."[8]

It would seem that under uncertainty they might have been less sure of their conclusion for two reasons. First, under uncertainty an investor need not be indifferent as to the distribution of the one-period gain on a share between the dividend and price appreciation. Since price appreciation is highly uncertain, an investor may prefer the expectation of a $5 dividend and a $50 price to a zero dividend and a $55 price without being irrational. Second, the expectation of a stock issue at $t = 1$ may have a depressing influence on the price at $t = 0$. What MM did was both change the dividend and change the number of new shares issued. Can we be so sure that the price of a share will not change when these two events take place?

[4] Miller and Modigliani, *op. cit.*, p. 426.
[5] *Ibid.*, p. 427.    [6] *Ibid.*, p. 428.    [7] *Ibid.*, p. 429.    [8] *Ibid.*, p. 432.

## II.

Let us turn now to the proof of the MM position on the dividend rate that I presented in my *RES* paper and book. The reasons for presenting this proof will be evident shortly. Consider a corporation that earned $Y_0$ in the period ending at $t = 0$ and paid it all out in dividends. Further, assume that the corporation is expected to continue paying all earnings in dividends and to engage in no outside financing. Under these assumptions the company is expected to earn and pay $Y_0$ in every future period. If the rate of return on investment that investors require on the share is $k$, we may represent the valuation of the share as follows:

$$P_0 = \frac{Y_0}{(1 + k)^1} + \frac{Y_0}{(1 + k)^2} + \frac{Y_0}{(1 + k)^3} + \cdots + \frac{Y_0}{(1 + k)^t} + \cdots. \tag{2}$$

We may also say that $k$ is the discount rate that equates the dividend expectation of $Y_0$ in perpetuity with the price $P_0$.

Next, let the corporation announce at $t = 0$ that it will retain and invest $Y_1 = Y_0$ during $t = 1$ and that it expects to earn a rate of return of $k = Y_0/P_0$ on the investment. In each subsequent period it will pay all earnings out in dividends. Share price is now given by the expression

$$P_0 = \frac{0}{(1 + k)^1} + \frac{Y_0 + kY_0}{(1 + k)^2} + \frac{Y_0 + kY_0}{(1 + k)^3} + \cdots + \frac{Y_0 + kY_0}{(1 + k)^t}. \tag{3}$$

Notice that the numerator of the first term on the right side is zero. It is the dividend and not the earnings in the period, since the investor is correctly represented as using the dividend expectation in arriving at $P_0$. If he were represented as looking at the earnings expectation, then as Bodenhorn[9] noted, he would be double-counting the first period's earnings.

It is evident that, as a result of the corporation's decision, the investor gives up $Y_0$ at the end of $t = 1$ and receives, in its place, $kY_0$ in perpetuity. The distribution of dividends over time has been changed. It is also evident that $kY_0$ in perpetuity discounted at $k$ is exactly equal to $Y_0$. Hence $P_0$ is unchanged, and the change in the distribution over time of the dividends had no influence of share price. In general, the corporation can be expected to retain and invest any fraction of the income in any period without share price being changed as a consequence, so long as $r$, the return on investment, is equal to $k$. If $r > k$ for any investment, $P_0$ will be increased, but the reason is the profitability of investment and not the change in the time distribution of dividends.

Assume now that when the corporation makes the announcement which changes the dividend expectation from the one given by equation (2) to the one given by equation (3), investors raise the discount rate from $k$ to $k'$. For the

[9] Diran Bodenhorn, "On the Problem of Capital Budgeting," *Journal of Finance*, December, 1959, pp. 473–92.

moment let us not wonder why the discount rate is raised from $k$ to $k'$, i.e., why the rate of return investors require on the share is raised as a consequence of the above change in the dividend expectation. If this takes place, equation (3) becomes

$$P'_0 = \frac{0}{(1 + k')^1} + \frac{Y_0 + kY_0}{(1 + k')^2} + \frac{Y_0 + kY_0}{(1 + k')^3} + \cdots + \frac{Y_0 + kY_0}{(1 + k')^t} + \cdots. \quad (3a)$$

It is clear that with $k' > k$, $P'_0 < P_0$.

Let us review what happened. The dividend policy changed: the near dividend was reduced, and the distant dividends were raised. This caused a rise in the discount rate, and the result was a fall in the price of the share. I, therefore, say that the change in dividend policy changed the share's price.

In response to this argument, MM stated that I fell into "the typical confounding of dividend policy with investment policy."[10] I don't understand their reasoning. It is well known that when the rate of return on investment is set equal to the discount rate, changing the level of investment has no influence on share price. By this means, I neutralized the profitability of investment. It seems to me perfectly clear that I did not confound investment and dividend policy; I changed the discount rate. Share price changed with the dividend rate in the above example because the discount rate was changed. The issue, therefore, is whether the behavior of investors under uncertainty is correctly represented by a model in which the discount rate that equates a dividend expectation with its price is a function of the dividend rate.

I cannot categorically state that $k$ is a function of the rate of growth in the dividend, i.e., the dividend rate, but I can present some theoretical considerations and empirical evidence in support of the theorem. It seems plausible that (1) investors have an aversion to risk or uncertainty, and (2), given the riskiness of a corporation, the uncertainty of a dividend it is expected to pay increases with the time in the future of the dividend. It follows from these two propositions that an investor may be represented as discounting the dividend expected in period $t$ at a rate of $k_t$, with $k_t$ not independent of $t$. Furthermore, if aversion to risk is large enough and/or risk increases rapidly enough with time, $k_t$ increases with $t$.

It is therefore possible, though not certain, that investor behavior is correctly approximated by the statement that, in arriving at the value of a dividend expectation, they discount it at the rates $k_t$, $t = 1, 2 \ldots$, with $k_t > k_{t-1}$. In this event the single discount rate we use in stock value models is an increasing function of the rate of growth in the dividend. In short, dividend policy influences share price. To illustrate the conclusion, let us rewrite equation (2):

$$P_0 = \frac{Y_0}{(1 + k_1)^1} + \frac{Y_0}{(1 + k_2)^2} + \frac{Y_0}{(1 + k_3)^3} + \cdots \frac{Y_0}{(1 + k_t)^t} + \cdots. \quad (4)$$

We now look on the $k$ of equation (2) as an average of the $k_t$ of equation (4)

---

[10] Miller and Modigliani, *op. cit.*, p. 425.

such that if the entire dividend expectation is discounted at this single rate, it results in the same share price. The discount rate $k$ is an average of the $k_t$ with $Y_0$, the weight assigned to each item.

Once again let the corporation retain $Y_1 = Y_0$ and invest it to earn $k Y_0$ per period in perpetuity. Using the sequence of discount rates $k_t$, the same as that appearing in equation (4), the valuation of the new dividend expectation becomes

$$P_0' = \frac{0}{(1 + k_1)^1} + \frac{Y_0 + kY_0}{(1 + k_2)^2} + \frac{Y_0 + kY_0}{(1 + k_3)^3} + \cdots + \frac{Y_0 + kY_0}{(1 + k_t)^t} + \cdots. \quad (5)$$

The shareholder gives up $Y_0$ and gets $k Y_0$ in perpetuity, but the latter is now discounted at the rates $k_t, t = 2 \rightarrow \infty$, and it can be shown that $k Y_0$ so discounted is less than $Y_0$. Hence $P_0' < P_0$, and dividend policy influences share price. It also can be shown that $k'$, the new average of the same $k_t$, is greater than $k$. In general, reducing the near dividends and raising the distant dividends (lowering the dividend rate) changes the weights of the $k_t$ and raises their average.

## III.

To summarize the theoretical part of my argument, I started with two assumptions: (1) aversion to risk and (2) increase in the uncertainty of a receipt with its time in the future. From these assumptions I proceeded by deductive argument to the proposition that the single discount rate an investor is represented as using to value a share's dividend expectation is an increasing function of the rate of growth in the dividend. The consequence of the theorem is that dividend policy per se influences the value of a share. The assumptions have enough intuitive merit, I believe, that the theorem may in fact be true.

Before proceeding to the empirical evidence, I would like to comment briefly on two other criticisms MM directed at my argument. First, they differentiated between my " purely subjective discount rate and the objective market-given yields" and stated: "To attempt to derive valuation formulas from these purely subjective discount factors involves, of course, an error...."[11] My assumptions and empirical results may be questioned, but where is the error? Does the theorem fail to follow from the assumptions? Why, as they suggest, is it logically impossible for an investor to arrive at the value of a share by estimating its future dividends and discounting the series at a rate appropriate to its uncertainty?

The following MM criticism of my argument I find even more confusing. They stated: " Indeed if they [investors] valued shares according to the Gordon approach and thus paid a premium for higher payout ratios, then holders of the low payout shares would actually realize consistently higher returns on their investment over any stated interval of time."[12] Under this reasoning two shares cannot sell at different yields regardless of how much they differ in risk because the holders of the higher-yield share would "actually realize

---

[11] *Ibid.*, p. 424.
[12] *Ibid.*, p. 425.

consistently higher returns over any stated interval of time." Do MM deny that investors have an aversion to risk?

To test the theorem empirically, I proceeded as follows. The valuation of a share may be represented by the expression

$$P_0 = \int_0^\infty D_t e^{-kt} \, dt, \tag{6}$$

where $D_t$ is the dividend expected in period $t$ and $k$ is an operator on the $D_t$ that reduces them to their present value to the investor. Equation (6) is a perfectly general statement that is not open to question. However, to use the equation in empirical work, we must specify how investors arrive at $D_t$ from observable variables. For this, I assumed that investors expect a corporation will: (1) retain the fraction $b$ of its income in each future period; (2) earn a rate of return, $r$, on the common equity investment in each future period; (3) maintain the existing debt-equity ratio; and (4) undertake no new outside equity financing. Under the above assumptions the current dividend is $D_0 = (1 - b)Y_0$, and its rate of growth is $br$. Further, the entire dividend expectation is represented by these two variables, and equation (6) is equal to:

$$P_0 = \frac{(1 - b)Y_0}{k - br}. \tag{7}$$

The above four assumptions may be criticized as being too great a simplification of reality. I have admitted their limitations, and I welcome improvement, but I know of no other empirical model that contains as rich and accurate a statement of the dividend expectation provided by a share. Most empirical work, including the published work of MM, represents the investor as expecting that the corporation will pay all earnings in dividends and engage in no outside financing. They, therefore, also ignore the influence of the profitability of investment on share price. This model incorporates a prediction of the corporation's investment and rate of return on the investment in each future period. The expected investment in period $t$ is the fraction $b$ of the period's income plus the leverage on the retention that maintains the corporation's existing debt-equity ratio. Further, the influence of this retention and borrowing on the dividend expectation is incorporated in the model.

The interesting thing about the model as it stands is that it is consistent with the MM position and should provoke no objection. To see this, let us make their assumption that $k$ is independent of $b$ and, to neutralize the profitability of investment, let $r = k$. In this model, dividend policy is represented by $b$ the retention rate, so that, if we take the derivative of $P_0$ with respect to $b$, we establish the relation between share price and the dividend rate. We find that $\partial P / \partial b = 0$. The value of a share is independent of the dividend rate—exactly what MM argue.

One can use this model in empirical work under the assumption that $k$ is independent of $br$. I did and obtained poor results. Since I found good theoretical grounds for believing that $k$ is an increasing function of $br$, it would seem reasonable to explore the hypothesis, and that is what I did. If $k$ is an increasing function of $br$, we can write equation (7) as

$$P_0 = A_0[(1 - b)Y_0][1 + br]^{\alpha_2}. \tag{8}$$

In this expression, $A_0$ represents the influence of all variables other than the current dividend, $(1 - b)Y_0$, and its rate of growth, $br$. When $b = 0$, $P_0$ is the multiple $A_0$ of $Y_0$. As $br$ increases, the dividend, $(1 - b)Y_0$, falls and $br$ rises, the former lowering price and the latter raising price. Whether $P_0$ rises or falls with $b$ depends on $r$, the profitability of investment, and on $\alpha_2$. The expression $\alpha_2$ may be looked on as how much investors are willing to pay for growth. Its value depends on how fast the $k_t$ rise with $t$, that is, on how fast uncertainty increases with time and on the degree of investor aversion to risk.

It should be noted that equation (8) is not merely a stock value model. Given the investor's valuation of a share, $A_0$ and $\alpha_2$, and, given the profitability of investment, $r$, the model may be used t‸ find the retention rate (equal to the investment rate under our assumptions) that maximizes the value of a share. Extensions of the model developed elsewhere[13] allow its use to find the investment and the financing, retention, debt, and new equity that maximize share price.

The empirical results I obtained with the above model have been published in detail,[14] and all I will say here is that they are very good. Although the results compare favorably with earlier work, they are not good enough to settle the question. MM[15] and Benishay[16] have pointed out that my independent variables are not free of error, and the consequence is that the parameter estimates have a downward basis. Kolin[17] has reported that his empirical work revealed no relation between dividend policy and share price. As things stand, I would say that the influence of dividend policy on share price is a question that requires further study. The axiomatic basis of the MM position is certainly not so powerful as to force the acceptance of their conclusions.

## IV.

I should like to close with a brief comment on the two major camps that are emerging with respect to the theory of corporation finance. In both camps optimal policy is taken as the policy that maximizes the value of the corporation. Although corporations may not make investment and financing decisions with only this objective in mind, managements are certainly not indifferent to the prices at which their corporations' securities sell. Hence the policy question posed has practical significance.

[13] M. J. Gordon, *The Investment, Financing and Valuation of the Corporation* (Homewood, Ill.: R. D. Irwin, 1962).

[14] *Ibid.*

[15] Franco Modigliani and Merton Miller, "The Cost of Capital Corporation Finance, and Theory of Investment: Reply," *American Economic Review*, September, 1959, pp. 655–69.

[16] Haskel Benishay, "Variability in Earnings-Price Ratios: Reply," *American Economic Review*, March, 1962, pp. 209–16.

[17] Marshal Kolin, *The Relative Price of Corporate Equity* (Boston: Harvard Business School).

In one camp, where we find MM, it is argued that a corporation's cost of capital is a constant—i.e., independent of the method and level of financing. Optimal policy is the investment that equates the marginal return on investment with this cost of capital. The inescapable conclusion is that financing policy is not a problem. The opposite position is that a corporation's cost of capital varies with the method and level of financing. My judgment is that the theoretical and empirical evidence we have favors this position.

However, regardless of which view prevails, the battle should be lively and productive. For a long time the position that cost of capital is a constant was held almost exclusively by economists, who were sophisticated in methods of theoretical and econometric analysis but knew little of finance. By contrast, the position that the cost of capital is a variable was held by finance men, who were familiar with their subject but not with advanced methods of theoretical and empirical research. People in each group talked only to those who agreed with them, and in consequence not much was said. The situation has changed, it will change further, and the promise is that the lively debate and active research in progress will advance our knowledge on the subject.

## 39. DIVIDEND POLICY, GROWTH, AND THE VALUATION OF SHARES*

MERTON H. MILLER†

and

FRANCO MODIGLIANI‡

Reprinted from *The Journal of Business of the University of Chicago*, Vol. *XXXIV*, No. 4, (October, 1961), pp. 411–33, by permission of the authors and the University of Chicago Press, Copyright, 1961, by the University of Chicago.

The effect of a firm's dividend policy on the current price of its shares is a matter of considerable importance, not only to the corporate officials who must set the policy, but to investors planning portfolios and to economists seeking to understand and appraise the functioning of the capital markets. Do companies with generous distribution policies consistently sell at a premium over those with niggardly payouts? Is the reverse ever true? If so, under what conditions? Is there an optimum payout ratio or range of ratios that maximizes the current worth of the shares?

Although these questions of fact have been the subject of many empirical studies in recent years no consensus has yet been achieved. One reason appears to be the absence in the literature of a complete and reasonably rigorous statement of those parts of the economic theory of valuation bearing directly on the matter of dividend policy. Lacking such a statement, investigators have not yet been able to frame their tests with sufficient precision to distinguish adequately between the various contending hypotheses. Nor have they been able to give a convincing explanation of what their test results do imply about the underlying process of valuation.

In the hope that it may help to overcome these obstacles to effective empirical testing, this paper will attempt to fill the existing gap in the theoretical literature on valuation. We shall begin, in Section I, by examining the effects of differences in dividend policy on the current price of shares in an ideal economy characterized by perfect capital markets, rational behavior, and perfect certainty. Still within this convenient analytical framework we shall go on in Sections II and III to consider certain closely related issues that

* The authors wish to express their thanks to all who read and commented on earlier versions of this paper and especially to Charles C. Holt, now of the University of Wisconsin, whose suggestions led to considerable simplification of a number of the proofs.

† Professor of finance and economics, University of Chicago.

‡ Professor of economics, Northwestern University.

appear to have been responsible for considerable misunderstanding of the role of dividend policy. In particular, Section II will focus on the longstanding debate about what investors "really" capitalize when they buy shares; and Section III on the much mooted relations between price, the rate of growth of profits, and the rate of growth of dividends per share. Once these fundamentals have been established, we shall proceed in Section IV to drop the assumption of certainty and to see the extent to which the earlier conclusions about dividend policy must be modified. Finally, in Section V, we shall briefly examine the implications for the dividend policy problem of certain kinds of market imperfections.

## I. EFFECT OF DIVIDEND POLICY WITH PERFECT MARKETS, RATIONAL BEHAVIOR, AND PERFECT CERTAINTY

*The meaning of the basic assumptions.* Although the terms "perfect markets," "rational behavior," and "perfect certainty" are widely used throughout economic theory, it may be helpful to start by spelling out the precise meaning of these assumptions in the present context.

1. In "perfect capital markets," no buyer or seller (or issuer) of securities is large enough for his transactions to have an appreciable impact on the then ruling price. All traders have equal and costless access to information about the ruling price and about all other relevant characteristics of shares (to be detailed specifically later). No brokerage fees, transfer taxes, or other transaction costs are incurred when securities are bought, sold, or issued, and there are no tax differentials either between distributed and undistributed profits or between dividends and capital gains.

2. "Rational behavior" means that investors always prefer more wealth to less and are indifferent as to whether a given increment to their wealth takes the form of cash payments or an increase in the market value of their holdings of shares.

3. "Perfect certainty" implies complete assurance on the part of every investor as to the future investment program and the future profits of every corporation. Because of this assurance, there is, among other things, no need to distinguish between stocks and bonds as sources of funds at this stage of the analysis. We can, therefore, proceed as if there were only a single type of financial instrument which, for convenience, we shall refer to as shares of stock.

*The fundamental principle of valuation.* Under these assumptions the valuation of all shares would be governed by the following fundamental principle: the price of each share must be such that the rate of return (dividends plus capital gains per dollar invested) on every share will be the same throughout the market over any given interval of time. That is, if we let

$d_j(t)$ = dividends per share paid by firm $j$ during period $t$

$p_j(t)$ = the price (ex any dividend in $t-1$) of a share in firm $j$ at the start of period $t$, we must have

$$\frac{d_j(t) + p_j(t + 1) - p_j(t)}{p_j(t)} = \rho(t) \text{ independent of } j; \tag{1}$$

or equivalently,

$$p_j(t) = \frac{1}{1 + \rho(t)} [d_j(t) + p_j(t + 1)] \tag{2}$$

for each $j$ and for all $t$. Otherwise, holders of low-return (high-priced) shares could increase their terminal wealth by selling these shares and investing the proceeds in shares offering a higher rate of return. This process would tend to drive down the prices of the low-return shares and drive up the prices of high-return shares until the differential in rates of return had been eliminated.

*The effect of dividend policy.* The implications of this principle for our problem of dividend policy can be seen somewhat more easily if equation (2) is restated in terms of the value of the enterprise as a whole rather than in terms of the value of an individual share. Dropping the firm subscript $j$ since this will lead to no ambiguity in the present context and letting

$n(t)$ = the number of shares of record at the start of $t$

$m(t + 1)$ = the number of new shares (if any) sold during $t$ at the ex dividend closing price $p(t + 1)$, so that

$n(t + 1) = n(t) + m(t + 1)$

$V(t) = n(t) p(t)$ = the total value of the enterprise and

$D(t) = n(t) d(t)$ = the total dividends paid during $t$ to holders of record at the start of $t$,

we can rewrite (2)

$$V(t) = \frac{1}{1 + \rho(t)} [D(t) + n(t)p(t + 1)]$$

$$= \frac{1}{1 + \rho(t)} [D(t) + V(t + 1) - m(t + 1)p(t + 1)]. \tag{3}$$

The advantage of relating the fundamental rule in this form is that it brings into sharper focus the three possible routes by which current dividends might affect the current market value of the firm $V(t)$, or equivalently the price of its individual shares, $p(t)$. Current dividends will clearly affect $V(t)$ via the first term in the brackets, $D(t)$. In principle, current dividends might also affect $V(t)$ indirectly via the second term, $V(t + 1)$, the new ex dividend market value. Since $V(t + 1)$ must depend only on future and not on past events, such could be the case, however, only if both (a) $V(t + 1)$ were a function of future dividend policy and (b) the current distribution $D(t)$ served to convey some otherwise unavailable information as to what that future dividend policy would be. The first possibility being the relevant one from the standpoint of assessing the effects of dividend policy, it will clarify matters to assume, provisionally, that the future dividend policy of the firm is known and given for $t + 1$ and all subsequent periods and is independent of the actual dividend decision in $t$. Then $V(t + 1)$ will also be independent of the current dividend decision, though it may very well be affected by $D(t + 1)$ and all subsequent distributions. Finally, current dividends can influence $V(t)$ through the third term, $-m(t + 1) p(t + 1)$, the value of new shares sold to outsiders during the period. For the higher the dividend payout in any period the more the new capital that must be raised from external sources to maintain any desired level of investment.

The fact that the dividend decision effects price not in one but in these two conflicting ways—directly via $D(t)$ and inversely via $-m(t) p(t + 1)$—is, of course, precisely why one speaks of there being a dividend policy *problem*. If the firm raises its dividend in $t$, given its investment decision, will the increase in the cash payments to the current holders be more or less than enough to offset their lower share of the terminal value? Which is the better strategy for the firm in financing the investment: to reduce dividends and rely on retained earnings or to raise dividends but float more new shares?

In our ideal world at least these and related questions can be simply and immediately answered: the two dividend effects must always exactly cancel out so that the payout policy to be followed in $t$ will have *no* effect on the price at $t$.

We need only express $m(t + 1) \cdot p(t + 1)$ in terms of $D(t)$ to show that such must indeed be the case. Specifically, if $I(t)$ is the given level of the firm's investment or increase in its holding of physical assets in $t$ and if $X(t)$ is the firm's total net profit for the period, we know that the amount of outside capital required will be

$$m(t + 1)p(t + 1) = I(t) - [X(t) - D(t)]. \tag{4}$$

Substituting expression (4) into (3), the $D(t)$ cancel and we obtain for the value of the firm as of the start of $t$

$$V(t) \equiv n(t)p(t) = \frac{1}{1 + \rho(t)} [X(t) - I(t) + V(t + 1)]. \tag{5}$$

Since $D(t)$ does not appear directly among the arguments and since $X(t)$, $I(t)$, $V(t + 1)$ and $\rho(t)$ are all independent of $D(t)$ (either by their nature or by assumption) it follows that the current value of the firm must be independent of the current dividend decision.

Having established that $V(t)$ is unaffected by the current dividend decision it is easy to go on to show that $V(t)$ must also be unaffected by any future dividend decision as well. Such future decisions can influence $V(t)$ only via their effect on $V(t + 1)$. But we can repeat the reasoning above and show that $V(t + 1)$—and hence $V(t)$—is unaffected by dividend policy in $t + 1$; that $V(t + 2)$—and hence $V(t + 1)$ and $V(t)$—is unaffected by dividend policy in $t + 2$; and so on for as far into the future as we care to look. Thus, we may conclude that given a firm's investment policy, the dividend payout policy it chooses to follow will affect neither the current price of its shares nor the total return to its shareholders.

Like many other propositions in economics, the irrelevance of dividend policy, given investment policy, is "obvious, one you think of it." It is, after all, merely one more instance of the general principle that there are no "financial illusions" in a rational and perfect economic environment. Values there are determined solely by "real" considerations—in this case the earning power of the firm's assets and its investment policy—and not by how the fruits of the earning power are "packaged" for distribution.

Obvious as the proposition may be, however, one finds few references to it in the extensive literature on the problem.[1] It is true that the literature abounds with statements that in some "theoretical" sense, dividend policy ought not to count; but either that sense is not clearly specified or, more frequently and especially among economists, it is (wrongly) identified with a situation in which the firm's internal rate of return is the same as the external or market rate of return.[2]

A major source of these and related misunderstandings of the role of the dividend policy has been the fruitless concern and controversy over what investors "really" capitalize when they buy shares. We say fruitless because as we shall now proceed to show, it is actually possible to derive from the basic principle of valuation (1) not merely one, but several valuation formulas each starting from one of the "classical" views of what is being capitalized by investors. Though differing somewhat in outward appearance, the various formula can be shown to be equivalent in all essential respects including, of course, their implication that dividend policy is irrelevant. While the controversy itself thus turns out to be an empty one, the different expressions do have some intrinsic interest since, by highlighting different combinations of variables they provide additional insights into the process of valuation and they open alternative lines of attack on some of the problems of empirical testing.

## II. WHAT DOES THE MARKET "REALLY" CAPITALIZE?

In the literature on valuation one can find at least the following four more or less distinct approaches to the valuation of shares: (1) the discounted cash flow approach; (2) the current earnings plus future investment opportunities approach; (3) the stream of dividends approach; and (4) the stream of earnings approach. To demonstrate that these approaches are, in fact, equivalent it will be helpful to begin by first going back to equation (5) and developing from it a valuation formula to serve as a point of reference and comparison. Specifically, if we assume, for simplicity, that the market rate of yield $\rho(t) = \rho$

---

[1] Apart from the references to it in our earlier papers, especially [16], the closest approximation seems to be that in Bodenhorn [1, p. 492], but even his treatment of the role of dividend policy is not completely explicit. (The numbers in brackets refer to references listed below, pp. 365–366).

[2] See below p. 354.

for all $t$,[3] then, setting $t = 0$, we can rewrite (5) as

$$V(0) = \frac{1}{1 + \rho}[X(0) - I(0)] + \frac{1}{1 + \rho} V(1). \tag{6}$$

Since (5) holds for all $t$, setting $t = 1$ permits us to express $V(1)$ in terms of $V(2)$ which in turn can be expressed in terms of $V(3)$ and so on up to any arbitrary terminal period $T$. Carrying out these substitutions, we obtain

$$V(0) \sum_{t=0}^{T-1} \frac{1}{(1 + \rho)^{t+1}} [X(t) - I(t)] + \frac{1}{(1 + \rho)^T} V(T). \tag{7}$$

In general, the remainder term $(1 + \rho)^{-T} V(T)$ can be expected to approach zero as $T$ approaches infinity[4] so that (7) can be expressed as

$$V(0) = \lim_{T \to \infty} \sum_{t=0}^{T-1} \frac{1}{(1 + \rho)^{t+1}} [X(t) - I(t)], \tag{8}$$

which we shall further abbreviate to

$$V(0) = \sum_{t=0}^{\infty} \frac{1}{(1 + \rho)^{t+1}} [X(t) - I(t)]. \tag{9}$$

4) *The discounted cash flow approach.* Consider now the so called discounted cash flow approach familiar in discussions of capital budgeting. There, in valuing any specific machine we discount at the market rate of interest the stream of cash receipts generated by the machine; plus any scrap or terminal value of the machine; and minus the stream of cash outlays for direct labor, materials, repairs, and capital additions. The same approach, of course, can also be applied to the firm as a whole which may be thought of in this context as simply a large, composite machine.[5] This approach amounts to defining the value of the firm as

$$V(0) = \sum_{t=0}^{T-1} \frac{1}{(1 + \rho)^{t+1}} [\mathscr{R}(t) - \mathscr{O}(t)] + \frac{1}{(1 + \rho)^T} V(T), \tag{10}$$

[3] More general formulas in which $\rho(t)$ is allowed to vary with time can always be derived from those presented here merely by substituting the cumbersome product.

$$\prod_{\tau=0}^{t} [1 + \rho(\tau)] \text{ for } (1 + \rho)^{t+1}.$$

[4] The assumption that the remainder vanishes is introduced for the sake of simplicity of exposition only and is in no way essential to the argument. What is essential, of course, is that $V(0)$, i.e., the sum of the two terms in (7), be finite, but this can always be safely assumed in economic analysis. See below, n. 14.

[5] This is, in fact, the approach to valuation normally taken in economic theory when discussing the value of the *assets* of an enterprise, but much more rarely applied, unfortunately, to the value of the liability side. One of the few to apply the approach to the shares as well as the assets is Bodenhorn in [1], who uses it to derive a formula closely similar to (9) above.

where $\mathscr{R}(t)$ represents the stream of cash receipts and $\mathcal{O}(t)$ of cash outlays, or, abbreviating, as above to

$$V(0) = \sum_{t=0}^{\infty} \frac{1}{(1 + \rho)^{t+1}} [\mathscr{R}(t) - \mathcal{O}(t)]. \tag{11}$$

But we also know, by definition, that $[X(t) - I(t)] = [\mathscr{R}(t) - \mathcal{O}(t)]$ since, $X(t)$ differs from $\mathscr{R}(t)$ and $I(t)$ differs from $\mathcal{O}(t)$ merely by the "cost of goods sold" (and also by the depreciation expense if we wish to interpret $X(t)$ and $I(t)$ as net rather than gross profits and investment). Hence (11) is formally equivalent to (9), and the discounted cash flow approach is thus seen to be an implication of the valuation principle for perfect markets given by equation (1).

*The investment opportunities approach.* Consider next the approach to valuation which would seem most natural from the standpoint of an investor proposing to buy out and operate some already-going concern. In estimating how much it would be worthwhile to pay for the privilege of operating the firm, the amount of dividends to be paid is clearly not relevant, since the new owner can, within wide limits, make the future dividend stream whatever he pleases. For him the worth of the enterprise, as such, will depend only on: (a) the "normal" rate of return he can earn by investing his capital in securities (i.e., the market rate of return); (b) the earning power of the physical assets currently held by the firm; and (c) the opportunities, if any, that the firm offers for making additional investments in real assets that will yield more than the "normal" (market) rate of return. The latter opportunities, frequently termed the "good will" of the business, may arise, in practice, from any of a number of circumstances (ranging all the way from special locational advantages to patents or other monopolistic advantages).

To see how these opportunities affect the value of the business assume that in some future period $t$ the firm invests $I(t)$ dollars. Suppose, further, for simplicity that starting in the period immediately following the investment of the funds, the projects produce net profits at a constant rate of $\rho^*(t)$ per cent of $I(t)$ in each period thereafter.[6] Then the present worth as of $t$ of the (perpetual) stream of profits generated will be $I(t)\rho^*(t)/\rho$, and the "good will" of the projects (i.e., the difference between worth and cost) will be

$$I(t)\frac{\rho^*(t)}{\rho} - I(t) = I(t)\left[\frac{\rho^*(t) - \rho}{\rho}\right].$$

The present worth as of now of this future "good will" is

$$I(t)\left[\frac{\rho^*(t) - \rho}{\rho}\right](1 + \rho)^{-(t+1)},$$

---

[6] The assumption that $I(t)$ yields a uniform perpetuity is not restrictive in the present certainty context since it is always possible by means of simple, present-value calculations to find an equivalent uniform perpetuity for any project, whatever the time shape of its actual returns. Note also that $\rho^*(t)$ is the *average* rate of return. If the managers of the firm are behaving rationally, they will, of course, use $\rho$ as their cut-off criterion (cf. below p. 347). In this event we would have $\rho^*(t) \geq \rho$. The formulas remain valid, however, even where $\rho^*(t) < \rho$.

and the present value of all such future opportunities is simply the sum

$$\sum_{t=0}^{\infty} I(t) \frac{\rho^*(t) - \rho}{\rho} (1 + \rho)^{-(t+1)}.$$

Adding in the present value of the (uniform perpetual) earnings, $X(O)$, on the assets currently held, we get as an expression for the value of the firm

$$V(0) = \frac{X(0)}{\rho} + \sum_{t=0}^{\infty} I(t) \frac{\rho^*(t) - \rho}{\rho} (1 + \rho)^{-(t+1)}. \tag{12}$$

To show that the same formula can be derived from (9) note first that our definition of $\rho^*(t)$ implies the following relation between the $X(t)$:

$$X(1) = X(0) + \rho^*(0)I(0),$$
$$\dots\dots\dots\dots\dots\dots\dots\dots\dots\dots\dots\dots$$
$$X(t) = X(t - 1) + \rho^*(t - 1)I(t - 1)$$

and by successive substitution

$$X(t) = X(0) + \sum_{\tau=0}^{t-1} \rho^*(\tau)I(\tau),$$

$$t = 1, 2 \cdots \infty.$$

Substituting the last expression for $X(t)$ in (9) yields

$$V(0) = [X(0) - I(0)](1 + \rho)^{-1}$$

$$+ \sum_{t=1}^{\infty} \left[ X(0) + \sum_{\tau=0}^{t-1} \rho^*(\tau)I(\tau) - I(t) \right] (1 + \rho)^{-(t+1)}$$

$$= X(0) \sum_{t=1}^{\infty} (1 + \rho)^{-t} - I(0)(1 + \rho)^{-1}$$

$$+ \sum_{t=1}^{\infty} \left[ \sum_{\tau=0}^{t-1} \rho^*(\tau)I(\tau) - I(t) \right] (1 + \rho)^{-(t+1)}$$

$$= X(0) \sum_{t=1}^{\infty} (1 + \rho)^{-t} + \sum_{t=1}^{\infty} \left[ \sum_{\tau=0}^{t-1} \rho^*(\tau)I(\tau) - I(t - 1) \right]$$

$$\times (1 + \rho) \left| (1 + \rho)^{-(t+1)}. \right.$$

The first expression is, of course, simply a geometric progression summing to $X(0)/\rho$, which is the first term of (12). To simplify the second expression note that it can be rewritten as

$$\sum_{t=0}^{\infty} I(t) \left[ \rho^*(t) \sum_{\tau=t+2}^{\infty} (1 + \rho)^{-\tau} - (1 + \rho)^{-(t+1)} \right].$$

Evaluating the summation within the brackets gives

$$\sum_{t=0}^{\infty} I(t) \left[ \rho^*(t) \frac{(1 + \rho)^{-(t+1)}}{\rho} - (1 + \rho)^{-(t+1)} \right]$$

$$= \sum_{t=0}^{\infty} I(t) \left[ \frac{\rho^*(t) - \rho}{\rho} \right] (1 + \rho)^{-(t+1)},$$

which is precisely the second term of (12).

Formula (12) has a number of revealing features and deserves to be more widely used in discussions of valuation.[7] For one thing, it throws considerable light on the meaning of those much abused terms "growth" and "growth stocks." As can readily be seen from (12), a corporation does not become a "growth stock" with a high price-earning ratio merely because its assets and earnings are growing over time. To enter the glamor category, it is also necessary that $\rho^*(t) > \rho$. For if $\rho^*(t) = \rho$, then however large the growth in assets may be, the second term in (12) will be zero and the firm's price-earnings ratio would not rise above a humdrum $1/\rho$. The essence of "growth" in short, is not expansion, but the existence of opportunities to invest significant quantities of funds at higher than "normal" rates of return.

Notice also that if $\rho^*(t) < \rho$, investment in real assets by the firm will actually reduce the current price of the shares. This should help to make clear among other things, why the "cost of capital" to the firm is the same regardless of how the investments are financed or how fast the firm is growing. The function of the cost of capital in capital budgeting is to provide the "cut-off rate" in the sense of the minimum yield that investment projects must promise to be worth undertaking from the point of view of the current owners. Clearly, no proposed project would be in the interest of the current owners if its yield were expected to be less than $\rho$ since investing in such projects would reduce the value of their shares. In the other direction, every project yielding more than $\rho$ is just as clearly worth undertaking since it will necessarily enhance the value of the enterprise. Hence, the cost of capital or cut-off criterion for investment decisions is simply $\rho$.[8]

Finally, formula (12) serves to emphasize an important deficiency in many recent statistical studies of the effects of dividend policy (such as Walter [19] or Durand [4, 5]). These studies typically involve fitting regression equations in which price is expressed as some function of current earnings and dividends.

---

[7] A valuation formula analogous to (12) though derived and interpreted in a slightly different way is found in Bodenhorn [1]. Variants of (12) for certain special cases are discussed in Walter [20].

[8] The same conclusion could also have been reached, of course, by "costing" each particular source of capital funds. That is, since $\rho$ is the going market rate of return on equity any new shares floated to finance investment must be priced to yield $\rho$; and withholding funds from the stockholders to finance investment would deprive the holders of the chance to earn $\rho$ on these funds by investing their dividends in other shares. The advantage of thinking in terms of the cost of capital as the cut-off criterion is that it minimizes the danger of confusing "costs" with mere "outlays."

A finding that the dividend coefficient is significant—as is usually the case—is then interpreted as a rejection of the hypothesis that dividend policy does not affect valuation.

Even without raising questions of bias in the coefficients,[9] it should be apparent that such a conclusion is unwarranted since formula (12) and the analysis underlying it imply only that dividends will not count given current earnings *and growth potential*. No general prediction is made (or can be made) by the theory about what will happen to the dividend coefficient if the crucial growth term is omitted.[10]

*The stream of dividends approach.* From the earnings and earnings opportunities approach we turn next to the dividend approach, which has, for some reason, been by far the most popular one in the literature of valuation. This approach too, properly formulated, is an entirely valid one though, of course, not the only valid approach as its more enthusiastic proponents frequently suggest.[11] It does, however, have the disadvantage in contrast with previous approaches of obscuring the role of dividend policy. In particular, uncritical use of the dividend approach has often led to the unwarranted inference that, since the investor is buying dividends and since dividend policy affects the amount of dividends, then dividend policy must also affect the current price.

Properly formulated, the dividend approach defines the current worth of a share as the discounted value of the stream of dividends to be paid on the share in perpetuity. That is

$$p(t) = \sum_{\tau=0}^{\infty} \frac{d(t + \tau)}{(1 + \rho)^{\tau+1}}. \tag{13}$$

To see the equivalence between this approach and previous ones, let us first restate (13) in terms of total market value as

$$V(t) = \sum_{\tau=0}^{\infty} \frac{D_t(t + \tau)}{(1 + \rho)^{\tau+1}}, \tag{14}$$

[9] The serious bias problem in tests using current reported earnings as a measure of $X(0)$ was discussed briefly by us in [16].

[10] In suggesting that recent statistical studies have not controlled adequately for growth we do not mean to exempt Gordon in [8] or [9]. It is true that his tests contain an explicit "growth" variable, but it is essentially nothing more than the ratio of retained earnings to book value. This ratio would not in general provide an acceptable approximation to the "growth" variable of (12) in any sample in which firms resorted to external financing. Furthermore, even if by some chance a sample was found in which all firms relied entirely on retained earnings, his tests then could not settle the question of dividend policy. For if all firms financed investment internally (or used external financing only in strict proportion to internal financing as Gordon assumes in [8]) then there would be no way to distinguish between the effects of dividend policy and investment policy (see below p. 354).

[11] See, e.g., the classic statement of the position in J. B. Williams [21]. The equivalence of the dividend approach to many of the other standard approaches is noted to our knowledge only in our [16] and, by implication, in Bodenhorn [1].

where $D_t(t + \tau)$ denotes that portion of the total dividends $D(t + \tau)$ paid during period $t + \tau$, that accrues to the shares of record as of the start of period $t$ (indicated by the subscript). That equation (14) is equivalent to (9) and hence also to (12) is immediately apparent for the special case in which no outside financing is undertaken after period $t$, for in that case

$$D_t(t + \tau) = D(t + \tau) = X(t + \tau) - I(t + \tau).$$

To allow for outside financing, note that we can rewrite (14) as

$$V(t) = \frac{1}{1 + \rho} \left[ D_t(t) + \sum_{\tau=1}^{\infty} \frac{D_t(t + \tau)}{(1 + \rho)^{\tau}} \right]$$

$$= \frac{1}{1 + \rho} \left[ D(t) + \sum_{\tau=0}^{\infty} \frac{D_t(t + \tau + 1)}{(1 + \rho)^{\tau+1}} \right]. \tag{15}$$

The summation term in the last expression can be written as the difference between the stream of dividends accruing to all the shares of record as of $t + 1$ and that portion of the stream that will accrue to the shares newly issued in $t$, that is,

$$\sum_{\tau=0}^{\infty} \frac{D_t(t + \tau + 1)}{(1 + \rho)^{\tau+1}} = \left( 1 - \frac{m(t + 1)}{n(t + 1)} \right) \sum_{\tau=0}^{\infty} \frac{D_{t+1}(t + \tau + 1)}{(1 + \rho)^{\tau+1}} \tag{16}$$

But from (14) we know that the second summation in (16) is precisely $V(t + 1)$ so that (15) can be reduced to

$$V(t) = \frac{1}{1 + \rho} \left[ D(t) + \left( 1 - \frac{m(t + 1)p(t + 1)}{n(t + 1)p(t + 1)} \right) V(t + 1) \right]$$

$$= \frac{1}{1 + \rho} [D(t) + V(t + 1) - m(t + 1)p(t + 1)], \tag{17}$$

which is (3) and which has already been shown to imply both (9) and (12).[12]

There are, of course, other ways in which the equivalence of the dividend approach to the other approaches might have been established, but the method presented has the advantage perhaps of providing some further insight into the reason for the irrelevance of dividend policy. An increase in current dividends, given the firm's investment policy, must necessarily reduce the

---

[12] The statement that equations (9), (12), and (14) are equivalent must be qualified to allow for certain pathological extreme cases, fortunately of no real economic significance. An obvious example of such a case is the legendary company that is expected *never* to pay a dividend. If this were literally true then the value of the firm by (14) would be zero; by (9) it would be zero (or possibly negative since zero dividends rule out $X(t) > I(t)$ but not $X(t) < I(t)$); while by (12) the value might still be positive. What is involved here, of course, is nothing more than a discontinuity at zero since the value under (14) and (9) would be positive and the equivalence of both with (12) would hold if that value were also positive as long as there was some period $T$, however far in the future, beyond which the firm would pay out $\varepsilon > 0$ per cent of its earnings, however small the value of $\varepsilon$.

terminal value of existing shares because part of the future dividend stream that would otherwise have accrued to the existing shares must be diverted to attract the outside capital from which, in effect, the higher current dividends are paid. Under our basic assumptions, however, $\rho$ must be the same for all investors, new as well as old. Consequently the market value of the dividends diverted to the outsiders, which is both the value of their contribution and the reduction in terminal value of the existing shares, must always be precisely the same as the increase in current dividends.

*The stream of earnings approach.* Contrary to widely held views, it is also possible to develop a meaningful and consistent approach to valuation running in terms of the stream of earnings generated by the corporation rather than of the dividend distributions actually made to the shareholders. Unfortunately, it is also extremely easy to mistate or misinterpret the earnings approach as would be the case if the value of the firm were to be defined as simply the discounted sum of future total earnings.[13] The trouble with such a definition is not, as is often suggested, that it overlooks the fact that the corporation is a separate entity and that these profits cannot freely be withdrawn by the shareholders; but rather that it neglects the fact that additional capital must be acquired at some cost to maintain the future earnings stream at its specified level. The capital to be raised in any future period is, of course, $I(t)$ and its opportunity cost, no matter how financed, is $\rho$ per cent per period thereafter. Hence, the current value of the firm under the earnings approach must be stated as

$$V(0) = \sum_{t=0}^{\infty} \frac{1}{(1 + \rho)^{t+1}} \left[ X(t) - \sum_{\tau=0}^{t} \rho I(\tau) \right].$$

(18)

That this version of the earnings approach is indeed consistent with our bsaic assumptions and equivalent to the previous approaches can be seen by regrouping terms and rewriting equation (18) as

$$V(0) = \sum_{t=0}^{\infty} \frac{1}{(1 + \rho)^{t+1}} X(t) - \sum_{t=0}^{\infty} \left( \sum_{\tau=t}^{\infty} \frac{\rho I(t)}{(1 + \rho)^{\tau+1}} \right)$$

$$= \sum_{t=0}^{\infty} \frac{1}{(1 + \rho)^{t+1}} X(t) - \sum_{t=0}^{\infty} \frac{1}{(1 + \rho)^{t+1}}$$

$$\times \left( \sum_{\tau=0}^{\infty} \frac{\rho I(t)}{(1 + \rho)^{\tau+1}} \right).$$

(19)

[13] In fairness, we should point out that there is no one, to our knowledge, who has seriously advanced this view. It is a view whose main function seems to be to serve as a "straw man" to be demolished by those supporting the dividend view. See, e.g., Gordon [9, esp. pp. 102–3]. Other writers take as the supposed earnings counter-view to the dividend approach not a relation running in terms of the *stream* of earnings but simply the proposition that price is proportional to current earnings, i.e., $V(0) = X(0)/\rho$. The probable origins of this widespread misconception about the earnings approach are discussed further below (p. 354).

Since the last inclosed summation reduces simply to $I(t)$, the expression (19) in turn reduces to simply

$$V(0) = \sum_{t=0}^{\infty} \frac{1}{(1+\rho)^{t+1}} [X(t) - I(t)], \tag{20}$$

which is precisely our earlier equation (9).

Note that the version of the earnings approach presented here does not depend for its validity upon any special assumptions about the time shape of the stream of total profits or the stream of dividends per share. Clearly, however, the time paths of the two streams are closely related to each other (via financial policy) and to the stream of returns derived by holders of the shares. Since these relations are of some interest in their own right and since misunderstandings about them have contributed to the confusion over the role of dividend policy, it may be worthwhile to examine them briefly before moving on to relax the basic assumptions.

## III. EARNINGS, DIVIDENDS, AND GROWTH RATES

*The convenient case of constant growth rates.* The relation between the stream of earnings of the firm and the stream of dividends and of returns to the stockholders can be brought out most clearly by specializing (12) to the case in which investment opportunities are such as to generate a constant rate of growth of profits in perpetuity. Admittedly, this case has little empirical significance, but it is convenient for illustrative purposes and has received much attention in the literature.

Specifically, suppose that in each period $t$ the firm has the opportunity to invest in real assets a sum $I(t)$ that is $k$ per cent as large as its total earnings for the period; and that this investment produces a perpetual yield of $\rho^*$ beginning with the next period. Then, by definition

$$X(t) = X(t-1) + \rho^* I(t-1) = X(t-1)[1 + k\rho^*]$$
$$= X(0)[1 + k\rho^*]^t \tag{21}$$

and $k\rho^*$ is the (constant) rate of growth of total earnings. Substituting from (21) into (12) for $I(t)$ we obtain

$$V(0) = \frac{X(0)}{\rho} + \sum_{t=0}^{\infty} \left(\frac{\rho^* - \rho}{\rho}\right) kX(0)[1 + k\rho^*]^t (1+\rho)^{-(t+1)}$$
$$= \frac{X(0)}{\rho}\left[1 + \frac{k(\rho^* - \rho)}{1 - \rho} \sum_{t=0}^{\infty} \left(\frac{1 + k\rho^*}{1 + \rho}\right)^t\right]. \tag{22}$$

Evaluating the infinite sum and simplifying, we finally obtain[14]

$$V(0) = \frac{X(0)}{\rho}\left[1 + \frac{k(\rho^* - \rho)}{\rho - k\rho^*}\right] = \frac{X(0)(1 - k)}{\rho - k\rho^*}, \tag{23}$$

[14] One advantage of the specialization (23) is that it makes it easy to see what is really involved in the assumption here and throughout the paper that the $V(0)$ given by any of our summation formulas is necessarily finite (cf. above, n.4). In terms of (23) the condition is

which expresses the value of the firm as a function of its current earnings, the rate of growth of earnings, the internal rate of return, and the market rate of return.[15] Note that (23) holds not just for period 0, but for every $t$. Hence if $X(t)$ is growing at the rate $k\rho^*$, it follows that the value of the enterprise, $V(t)$, also grows at that rate.

*The growth of dividends and the growth of total profits.* Given that total earnings (and the total value of the firm) are growing at the rate $k\rho^*$ what is the rate of growth of dividends per share and of the price per share? Clearly, the answer will vary depending on whether or not the firm is paying out a high percentage of its earnings and thus relying heavily on outside financing. We can show the nature of this dependence explicitly by making use of the

---

clearly $k\rho^* < \rho$, i.e., that the rate of growth of the firm be less than market rate of discount. Although the case of (perpetual) growth rates greater than the discount factor is the much-discussed "growth stock paradox" (e.g. [67]), it has no real economic significance as we pointed out in [16, esp. n.17, p. 664]. This will be apparent when one recalls that the discount rate $\rho$, though treated as a constant in partial equilibrium (relative price) analysis of the kind presented here, is actually a variable from the standpoint of the system as a whole. That is, if the assumption of finite value for all shares did not hold, because for some shares $k\rho^*$ was (perpetually) greater than $\rho$, then $\rho$ would necessarily rise until an over-all equilibrium in the capital markets had been restored.

[15] An interesting and more realistic variant of (22), which also has a number of convenient features from the standpoint of developing empirical tests, can be obtained by assuming that the special investment opportunities are available not in perpetuity but only over some finite interval of $T$ periods. To exhibit the value of the firm for this case, we need only replace the infinite summation in (22) with a summation running from $t = 0$ to $t = T - 1$. Evaluating the resulting expression, we obtain

$$V(0) = \frac{X(0)}{\rho} \left\{ 1 + \frac{k(\rho^* - \rho)}{\rho - k\rho^*} \left[ 1 - \left( \frac{1 + k\rho^*}{1 + \rho} \right)^T \right] \right\} \tag{22a}$$

Note that (22a) holds even if $k\rho^* > \rho$, so that the so-called growth paradox disappears altogether. If, as we should generally expect, $(1 + k\rho^*)/(1 + \rho)$ is close to one, and if $T$ is not too large, the right hand side of (22a) admits of a very convenient approximation. In this case in fact we can write

$$\left[ \frac{1 + k\rho^*}{1 + \rho} \right]^T \cong 1 + T(k\rho^* - \rho)$$

the approximation holding, if, as we should expect, $(1 + k\rho^*)$ and $(1 + \rho)$ are both close to unity. Substituting this approximation into (22a) and simplifying, finally yields

$$V(0) \cong \frac{X(0)}{\rho} \left[ 1 + \frac{k(\rho^* - \rho)}{\rho - k\rho^*} T(\rho - k\rho^*) \right]$$

$$= \left[ \frac{X(0)}{\rho} + kX(0) \left( \frac{\rho^* - \rho}{\rho} \right) T \right]. \tag{22b}$$

The common sense of (22b) is easy to see. The current value of a firm is given by the value of the earning power of the currently held assets plus the market value of the special earning opportunity multiplied by the number of years for which it is expected to last.

fact that whatever the rate of growth of dividends per share the present value of the firm by the dividend approach must be the same as by the earnings approach. Thus let

$g$ = the rate of growth of dividends per share, or, what amounts to the same thing, the rate of growth of dividends accruing to the shares of the current holders (i.e., $D_o(t) = D_o(0)[1 + g]^t$);

$k_r$ = the fraction of total profits retained in each period (so that $D(t) = X(0)[1 - k_r]$);

$k_e = k - k_r$ = the amount of external capital raised per period, expressed as a fraction of profits in the period.

Then the present value of the stream of dividends to the original owners will be

$$D_0(0) \sum_{t=0}^{\infty} \frac{(1+g)^t}{(1+\rho)^{t+1}} = \frac{D(0)}{\rho - g} = \frac{X(0)[1 - k_r]}{\rho - g}. \tag{24}$$

By virtue of the dividend approach we know that (24) must be equal to $V(0)$. If therefore, we equate it to the right hand side of (23), we obtain

$$\frac{X(0)[1 - k_r]}{\rho - g} = \frac{X(0)[1 - (k_r + k_e)]}{\rho - k\rho^*}$$

from which it follows that the rate of growth of dividends per share and the rate of growth of the price of a share must be[16]

$$g = k\rho^* \frac{1 - k_r}{1 - k} - k_e\rho \frac{1}{1 - k}. \tag{25}$$

Notice that in the extreme case in which all financing is internal ($k_e = 0$ and $k = k_r$), the second term drops out and the first becomes simply $k\rho^*$. Hence the growth rate of dividends in that special case is exactly the same as that of total profits and total value and is proportional to the rate of retention $k_r$. In all other cases, $g$ is necessarily less than $k\rho^*$ and may even be negative, despite a positive $k\rho^*$, if $\rho^* < \rho$ and if the firm pays out a large fraction of its income in dividends. In the other direction, we see from (25) that even if a firm is a "growth" corporation ($\rho^* > \rho$) then the stream of dividends and price per share must grow over time even though $k_r = 0$, that is, even though it pays out *all* its earnings in dividends.

---

[16] That $g$ is the rate of price increase per share as well as the rate of growth of dividends per share follows from the fact that by (13) and the definition of $g$

$$p(t) = \sum_{\tau=0}^{\infty} \frac{d(t+\tau)}{(1+\rho)^{\tau+1}} = \sum_{\tau=0}^{\infty} \frac{d(0)[1+g]^{t+\tau}}{(1+\rho)^{\tau+1}}$$

$$= (1+g)^t \sum_{\tau=0}^{\infty} \frac{d(\tau)}{(1+\rho)^{\tau+1}} = p(0)[1+g]^t.$$

The relation between the growth rate of the firm and the growth rate of dividends under various dividend policies is illustrated graphically in Figure 1 in which for maximum clarity the natural logarithm of profits and dividends have been plotted against time.[17]

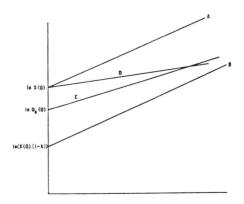

FIG. 1.— Growth of dividends per share in relation to growth in total earnings:
A. Total earnings: $\ln X(t) = \ln X(0) + k\rho^* t$;
B. Total earnings minus capital invested: $\ln [X(t) - I(t)] = \ln X(0) [1 - k] + k\rho^* t$;
   Dividends per share (all financing internal): $\ln D_0(t) = \ln D(0) + gt = \ln X(0) [1 - k] + k\rho^* t$;
C. Dividends per share (some financing external): $\ln D_0(t) = \ln D(0) + gt$;
D. Dividends per share (all financing external): $\ln D_0(t) = \ln X(0) + [(k/1 - k) (\rho^* - \rho)]t$.

Line A shows the total earnings of the firm growing through time at the constant rate $k\rho^*$, the slope of A. Line B shows the growth of (1) the stream of total earnings minus capital outlays and (2) the stream of dividends to the original owners (or dividends per share) in the special case in which all financing is internal. The slope of B is, of course, the same as that of A and the (constant) difference between the curves is simply $\ln(1 - k)$, the ratio of dividends to profits. Line C shows the growth of dividends per share when the firm uses both internal and external financing. As compared with the pure retention case, the line starts higher but grows more slowly at the rate $g$ given by (25). The higher the payout policy, the higher the starting position and the slower the growth up to the other limiting case of complete external financing, Line D, which starts at $\ln X(0)$ and grows at a rate of $(k/1 - k) \cdot (\rho^* - \rho)$.

*The special case of exclusively internal financing.* As noted above the growth rate of dividends per share is not the same as the growth rate of the firm except in the special case in which all financing is internal. This is merely one of a number of peculiarites of this special case on which, unfortunately, many writers have based their entire analysis. The reason for the preoccupation with this special case if far from clear to us. Certainly no one would

[17] That is, we replace each discrete compounding expression such as $X(t) = X(0) \times [1 + k\rho^*]^t$ with its counterpart under continuous discounting $X(t) = X(0)e^{k\rho^* t}$ which, of course, yields the convenient linear relation in $X(t) = \ln X(0) + k\rho^* t$.

suggest that it is the only empirically relevant case. Even if the case were in fact the most common, the theorist would still be under an obligation to consider alternative assumptions. We suspect that in the last analysis, the popularity of the internal financing model will be found to reflect little more than its ease of manipulation combined with the failure to push the analysis far enough to disclose how special and how treacherous a case it really is.

In particular, concentration on this special case appears to be largely responsible for the widely held view that, even under perfect capital markets, there is an optimum dividend policy for the firm that depends on the internal rate of return. Such a conclusion is almost inevitable if one works exclusively with the assumption, explicit or implicit, that funds for investment come *only* from retained earnings. For in that case *dividend policy* is indistinguishable from *investment policy*; and there is an optimal investment policy which does in general depend on the rate of return.

Notice also from (23) that if $\rho^* = \rho$ and $k = k_r$, the term $[1 - k_r]$ can be canceled from both the numerator and the denominator. The value of the firm becomes simply $X(0)/\rho$, the capitalized value of current earnings. Lacking a standard model for valuation more general than the retained earnings case it has been all too easy for many to conclude that this dropping out of the payout ratio $[1 - k_r]$ when $\rho^* = \rho$ must be what is meant by the irrelevance of dividend policy and that $V(0) = X(0)/\rho$ must constitute the "earnings" approach.

Still another example of the pitfalls in basing arguments on this special case is provided by the recent and extensive work on valuation by M. Gordon.[18] Gordon argues, in essense, that because of increasing uncertainty the discount rate $\hat{\rho}(t)$ applied by an investor to a future dividend payment will rise with $t$, where $t$ denotes not a specific date but rather the distance from the period in which the investor performs the discounting.[19] Hence, when we use a single uniform discount rate $\rho$ as in (22) or (23), this rate should be thought of as really an average of the "true" rates $\hat{\rho}(t)$ each weighted by the size of the expected dividend payment at time $t$. If the dividend stream is growing exponentially then such a weighted average $\rho$ would, of course, be higher the greater the rate of growth of dividends $g$ since the greater will then be the portion of the dividend stream arising in the distant as opposed to the near future. But if all financing is assumed to be internal, then $g = k_r\rho^*$ so that given $\rho^*$, the weighted average discount factor $\rho$ will be an increasing function

[18] See esp. [8]. Gordon's views represent the most explicit and sophisticated formulation of what might be called the "bird-in-the-hand" fallacy. For other, less elaborate, statements of essentially the same position see, among others, Graham and Dodd [11, p. 433] and Clendenin and Van Cleave [3].

[19] We use the notation $\hat{\rho}(t)$ to avoid any confusion between Gordon's purely subjective discount rate and the objective, market-given yields $\rho(t)$ in Sec. I above. To attempt to derive valuation formulas under uncertainty from these purely subjective discount factors involves, of course, an error essentially analogous to that of attempting to develop the certainty formulas from "marginal rates of time preference" rather than objective market opportunities.

of the rate of retention $k_r$ which would run counter to our conclusion that dividend policy has no effect on the current value of the firm or its cost of capital.

For all its ingenuity, however, and its seeming foundation in uncertainty, the argument clearly suffers fundamentally from the typical confounding of dividend policy with investment policy that so frequently accompanies use of the internal financing model. Had Gordon not confined his attention to this special case (or its equivalent variants), he would have seen that while a change in dividend policy will necessarily affect the size of the expected dividend payment on the share in any future period, it need not, in the general case, affect either the size of the *total* return that the investor expects during that period or the degree of uncertainty attaching to that total return. As should be abundantly clear by now, a change in dividend policy, given investment policy, implies a change only in the distribution of the total return in any period as between dividends and capital gains. If investors behave rationally, such a change cannot affect market valuations. Indeed, if they valued shares according to the Gordon approach and thus paid a premium for higher payout ratios, then holders of the low payout shares would actually realize consistently higher returns on their investment over any stated interval of time.[20]

*Corporate earnings and investor returns.* Knowing the relation of $g$ to $k\rho^*$ we can answer a question of considerable interest to economic theorists, namely: What is the precise relation between the earnings of the corporation in any period $X(t)$ and the total return to the owners of the stock during that period?[21] If we let $G_t(t)$ be the capital gains to the owners during $t$, we know

[20] This is not to deny that growth stocks (in our sense) may well be "riskier" than nongrowth stocks. But to the extent that this is true, it will be due to the possibly greater uncertainty attaching to the size and duration of future growth opportunities and hence to the size of the future stream of total returns quite apart from any questions of dividend policy.

[21] Note also that the above analysis enables us to deal very easily with the familiar issue of whether a firm's cost of equity capital is measured by its earnings/price ratio or by its dividend/price ratio. Clearly, the answer is that it is measured by neither, except under very special circumstances. For from (23) we have for the earnings/price ratio

$$\frac{X(0)}{V(0)} = \frac{\rho - k\rho^*}{1 - k},$$

which is equal to the cost of capital, $\rho$, only if the firm has no growth potential (i.e., $\rho^* = \rho$). And from (24) we have for the dividend/price ratio

$$\frac{D(0)}{V(0)} = \rho - g,$$

which is equal to $\rho$ only when $g = 0$; i.e., from (25), either when $k = 0$; or, if $k > 0$, when $\rho^* < \rho$ and the amount of external financing is precisely

$$k_e \frac{\rho^*}{\rho} k[1 - k_r],$$

so that the gain from the retention of earnings exactly offsets the loss that would otherwise be occasioned by the unprofitable investment.

that

$$D_t(t) + G_t(t) = X(t)(1 - k_r) + gV(t) \tag{26}$$

since the rate of growth of price is the same as that of dividends per share. Using (25) and (26) to substitute for $g$ and $V(t)$ and simplifying, we find that

$$D_t(t) + G_t(t) = X(t)\left[\frac{\rho(1 - k)}{\rho - k\rho^*}\right]. \tag{27}$$

The relation between the investors' return and the corporation's profits is thus seen to depend entirely on the relation between $\rho^*$ and $\rho$. If $\rho^* = \rho$ (i.e., the firm has no special "growth" opportunities), then the expression in brackets becomes 1 and the investors returns are precisely the same as the corporate profits. If $\rho^* < \rho$, however, the investors' return will be less than the corporate earnings; and, in the case of growth corporations the investors' return will actually be greater than the flow of corporate profits over the interval.[22]

*Some implications for constructing empirical tests.* Finally the fact that we have two different (though not independent) measures of growth in $k\rho^*$ and $g$ and two corresponding families of valuation formulas means, among other things, that we can proceed by either of two routes in empirical studies of valuation. We can follow the standard practice of the security analyst and think in terms of price per share, dividends per share, and the rate of growth of dividends per share; or we can think in terms of the total value of the enterprise, total earnings, and the rate of growth of total earnings. Our own

---

[22] The above relation between earnings per share and dividends plus capital gains also means that there will be a systematic relation between retained earnings and capital gains. The "marginal" relation is easy to see and is always precisely one for one regardless of growth or financial policy. That is, taking a dollar away from dividends and adding it to retained earnings (all other things equal) means an increase in capital gains of one dollar (or a reduction in capital loss of one dollar). The "average" relation is somewhat more complex. From (26) and (27) we can see that

$$G_t(t) = k_r X(t) + k X(t)\frac{\rho^* - \rho}{\rho - k\rho^*}.$$

Hence, if $\rho^* = \rho$ the total capital gain received will be exactly the same as the total retained earnings per share. For growth corporations, however, the capital gain will always be greater than the retained earnings (and there will be a capital gain of

$$k X(t)\left[\frac{\rho^* - \rho}{\rho - k\rho^*}\right]$$

even when all earnings are paid out). For non-growth corporations the relation between gain and retentions is reversed. Note also that the absolute difference between the total capital gain and the total retained earnings is a constant (given, $\rho$, $k$ and $\rho^*$) unaffected by dividend policy. Hence the *ratio* of capital gain to retained earnings will vary directly with the payout ratio for growth corporations (and vice versa for non-growth corporations). This means, among other things, that it is dangerous to attempt to draw inferences about the relative growth potential or relative managerial efficiency of corporations solely on the basis of the ratio of capital gains to retained earnings (cf. Harkavy [12, esp. pp. 289–94]).

preference happens to be for the second approach primarily because certain additional variables of interest—such as dividend policy, leverage, and size of firm—can be incorporated more easily and meaningfully into test equations in which the growth term is the growth of total earnings. But this can wait. For present purposes, the thing to be stressed is simply that two approaches, properly carried through, are in no sense *opposing* views of the valuation process; but rather equivalent views, with the choice between them largely a matter of taste and convenience.

## IV. THE EFFECTS OF DIVIDEND POLICY UNDER UNCERTAINTY

*Uncertainty and the general theory of valuations.* In turning now from the ideal world of certainty to one of uncertainty our first step, alas, must be to jettison the fundamental valuation principle as given, say, in our equation (3)

$$V(t) \frac{1}{1 + \rho(t)} [D(t) + n(t)p(t + 1)]$$

and from which the irrelevance proposition as well as all the subsequent valuation formulas in Sections II and III were derived. For the terms in the bracket can no longer be regarded as given numbers, but must be recognized as " random variables " from the point of view of the investor as of the start of period $t$. Nor is it at all clear what meaning can be attached to the discount factor $1/[1 + \rho(t)]$ since what is being discounted is not a given return, but at best only a probability distribution of possible returns. We can, of course, delude ourselves into thinking that we are preserving equation (3) by the simple and popular expedient of drawing a bar over each term and referring to it thereafter as the mathematical expectation of the random variable. But except for the trivial case of universal linear utility functions we know that $V(t)$ would also be affected, and materially so, by the higher order moments of the distribution of returns. Hence there is no reason to believe that the discount factor for expected values, $1/[1 + \rho(t)]$, would in fact be the same for any two firms chosen arbitrarily, not to mention that the expected values themselves may well be different for different investors.

All this is not to say, of course, that there are insuperable difficulties in the way of developing a testable theory of rational market valuation under uncertainty.[23] On the contrary, our investigations of the problem to date have convinced us that it is indeed possible to construct such a theory—though the construction, as can well be imagined, is a fairly complex and space-consuming task. Fortunately, however, this task need not be undertaken in this paper

---

[23] Nor does it mean that all the previous certainty analysis has no relevance whatever in the presence of uncertainty. There are many issues, such as those discussed in Sec. I and II, that really relate only to what has been called the pure " futurity " component in valuation. Here, the valuation formulas can still be extremely useful in maintaining the internal consistency of the reasoning and in suggesting (or criticizing) empirical tests of certain classes of hypotheses about valuation, even though the formulas themselves cannot be used to grind out precise numerical values for specific real-world shares.

which is concerned primarily with the effects of dividend policy on market valuation. For even without a full-fledged theory of what *does* determine market value under uncertainty we can show that dividend policy at least is *not* one of the determinants. To establish this particular generalization of the previous certainty results we need only invoke a corresponding generalization of the original postulate of rational behavior to allow for the fact that, under uncertainty, choices depend on expectations as well as tastes.

*"Imputed rationality" and "symmetric market rationality."* This generalization can be formulated in two steps as follows. First, we shall say that an individual trader "imputes rationality to the market" or satisfies the postulate of "imputed rationality" if, in forming expectations, he assumes that every other trader in the market is (a) rational in the previous sense of preferring more wealth to less regardless of the form an increment in wealth may take, and (b) imputes rationality to all other traders. Second, we shall say that a market as a whole satisfies the postulate of "symmetric market rationality" if every trader both behaves rationally and imputes rationality to the market.[24]

Notice that this postulate of symmetric market rationality differs from the usual postulate of rational behavior in several important respects. In the first place, the new postulate covers not only the choice behavior of individuals but also their expectations of the choice behavior of others. Second, the postulate is a statement about the market as a whole and not just about individual behavior. Finally, though by no means least, symmetric market rationality cannot be deduced from individual rational behavior in the usual sense since that sense does not imply imputing rationality to others. It may, in fact, imply a choice behavior inconsistent with imputed rationality unless the individual actually believes the market to be symmetrically rational. For if an ordinarily rational investor had good reason to believe that other investors would not behave rationally, then it might well be rational for him to adopt a strategy he would otherwise have rejected as irrational. Our postulate thus rules out, among other things, the possibility of speculative "bubbles" wherein an individually rational investor buys a security he knows to be overpriced (i.e., too expensive in relation to its expected *long-run* return to be attractive as a permanent addition to his portfolio) in the expectation that he can resell it at a still more inflated price before the bubble bursts.[25]

[24] We offer the term "symmetric market rationality" with considerable diffidence and only after having been assured by game theorists that there is no accepted term for this concept in the literature of that subject even though the postulate itself (or close parallels to it) does appear frequently. In the literature of economics a closely related, but not exact, counterpart is Muth's "hypothesis of rational expectations" [18]. Among the more euphonic, though we feel somewhat less revealing, alternatives that have been suggested to us are "putative rationality" (by T. J. Koopmans), "bi-rationality" (by G. L. Thompson), "empathetic rationality" (by Andrea Modigliani), and "pan-rationality" (by A. Ando).

[25] We recognize, of course, that such speculative bubbles have actually arisen in the past (and will probably continue to do so in the future), so that our postulate can certainly not be taken to be of universal applicability. We feel, however, that it is also not of universal inapplicability since from our observation, speculative bubbles, though well publicized when they occur, do not seem to us to be a dominant, or even a fundamental, feature of actual

*The irrelevance of dividend policy despite uncertainty.* In Section I we were able to show that, given a firm's investment policy, its dividend policy was irrelevant to its current market valuation. We shall now show that this fundamental conclusion need not be modified merely because of the presence of uncertainty about the future course of profits, investment, or dividends (assuming again, as we have throughout, that investment policy can be regarded as separable from dividend policy). To see that uncertainty about these elements changes nothing essential, consider a case in which current investors believe that the future streams of total earnings and total investment whatever actual values they may assume at different points in time will be identical for two firms, 1 and 2.[26] Suppose further, provisionally, that the same is believed to be true of future total dividend payments from period one on so that the only way in which the two firms differ is possibly with respect to the prospective dividend in the current period, period 0. In terms of previous notation we are thus assuming that

$$\tilde{X}_1(t) = \tilde{X}_2(t) \qquad t = 0 \cdots \infty$$

$$\tilde{I}_1(t) = \tilde{I}_2(t) \qquad t = 0 \cdots \infty$$

$$\tilde{D}_1(t) = \tilde{D}_2(t) \qquad t = 1 \cdots \infty$$

the subscripts indicating the firms and the tildes being added to the variables to indicate that these are to be regarded from the standpoint of current period, not as known numbers but as numbers that will be drawn in the future from the appropriate probability distributions. We may now ask: "What will be the return, $\tilde{R}_1(0)$ to the current shareholders in firm 1 during the current period?" Clearly, it will be

$$\tilde{R}_1(0) = \tilde{D}_1(0) + \tilde{V}_1(1) - \tilde{m}_1(1)\tilde{p}_1(1). \tag{28}$$

But the relation between $\tilde{D}_1(0)$ and $\tilde{m}_1(1)\,\tilde{p}_1(1)$ is necessarily still given by equation (4) which is merely an accounting identity so that we can write

$$\tilde{m}_1(1)\tilde{p}_1(1) = \tilde{I}_1(0) - [\tilde{X}_1(0) - \tilde{D}_1(0)], \tag{29}$$

and, on substituting in (28), we obtain

$$\tilde{R}_1(0) = \tilde{X}_1(0) - \tilde{I}_1(0) + \tilde{V}_1(1) \tag{30}$$

---

market behavior under uncertainty. That is, we would be prepared to argue that, as a rule and on the average, markets do not behave in ways which do not obviously contradict the postulate so that the postulate may still be useful at least as a first approximation, for the analysis of long-run tendencies in organized capital markets. Needless to say, whether our confidence in the postulate is justified is something that will have to be determined by empirical tests of its implications (such as, of course, the irrelevance of dividend policy).

[26] The assumption of two identical firms is introduced for convenience of exposition only, since it usually is easier to see the implications of rationality when there is an explicit arbitrage mechanism, in this case, switches between the shares of the two firms. The assumption, however, is not necessary and we can, if we like, think of the two firms as really corresponding to two states of the same firm for an investor performing a series of "mental experiments" on the subject of dividend policy.

for firm 1. By an exactly parallel process we can obtain an equivalent expression for $\tilde{R}_2(0)$.

Let us now compare $\tilde{R}_1(0)$ with $\tilde{R}_2(0)$. Note first that, by assumption, $\tilde{X}_1(0) = \tilde{X}_2(0)$ and $\tilde{I}_1(0) = \tilde{I}_2(0)$. Furthermore, with symmetric market rationality, the terminal values $\tilde{V}_i(1)$ can depend only on prospective future earnings, investment and dividends from period 1 on and these too, by assumption, are identical for the two companies. Thus symmetric rationality implies that every investor must expect $\tilde{V}_1(1) = \tilde{V}_2(1)$ and hence finally $\tilde{R}_1(0) = \tilde{R}_2(0)$. But if the return to the investors is the same in the two cases, rationality requires that the two firms command the same current value so that $V_1(0)$ must equal $V_2(0)$ regardless of any difference in dividend payments during period 0. Suppose now that we allow dividends to differ not just in period 0 but in period 1 as well, but still retain the assumption of equal $\tilde{X}_i(t)$ and $\tilde{I}_i(t)$ in all periods and of equal $\tilde{D}_i(t)$ in period 2 and beyond. Clearly, the only way differences in dividends in period 1 can effect $\tilde{R}_i(0)$ and hence $V_i(0)$ is via $\tilde{V}_i(1)$. But, by the assumption of symmetric market rationality, current investors know that as of the start of period 1 the then investors will value the two firms rationally and we have already shown that differences in the current dividend do not affect current value. Thus we must have $\tilde{V}_1(1) = \tilde{V}_2(1)$—and hence $V_1(0) = V_2(0)$—regardless of any possible difference in dividend payments during period 1. By an obvious extension of the reasoning to $\tilde{V}_i(2)$, $\tilde{V}_i(3)$, and so on, it must follow that the current valuation is unaffected by differences in dividend payments in any future period and thus that dividend policy is irrelevant for the determination of market prices, given investment policy.[27]

*Dividend policy and leverage.* A study of the above line of proof will show it to be essentially analogous to the proof for the certainty world, in which as we know, firms can have, in effect, only two alternative sources of investment funds: retained earnings or stock issues. In an uncertain world, however, there is the additional financing possibility of debt issues. The question naturally arises, therefore, as to whether the conclusion about irrelevance remains valid even in the presence of debt financing, particularly since there may very well be interactions between debt policy and dividend policy. The answer is that it does, and while a complete demonstration would perhaps be too tedious and repetitious at this point, we can at least readily sketch out the main outlines of how the proof proceeds. We begin, as above, by establishing the conditions from period 1 on that lead to a situation in which $\tilde{V}_1(1)$ must be brought into equality with $\tilde{V}_2(1)$ where the $V$, following the approach in our

---

[27] We might note that the assumption of symmetric market rationality is sufficient to derive this conclusion but not strictly necessary if we are willing to weaken the irrelevance proposition to one running in terms of long-run, average tendencies in the market. Individual rationality alone could conceivably bring about the latter, for over the long pull rational investors could enforce this result by buying and holding "undervalued" securities because this would insure them higher long-run returns when eventually the prices became the same. They might, however, have a long, long wait.

earlier paper [17], is now to be interpreted as the total market value of the firm, debt plus equity, not merely equity alone. The return to the original investors taken as a whole—and remember that any individual always has the option of buying a proportional share of both the equity and the debt—must correspondingly be broadened to allow for the interest on the debt. There will also be a corresponding broadening of the accounting identity (4) to allow, on the one hand, for the interest return and, on the other, for any debt funds used to finance the investment in whole or in part. The net result is that both the dividend component and the interest component of total earnings will cancel out making the relevant (total) return, as before, $[\tilde{X}_i(0) - \tilde{I}_i(0) + \tilde{V}_i(1)]$ which is clearly independent of the current dividend. It follows, then, that the value of the firm must also therefore be independent of dividend policy given investment policy.[28]

*The informational content of dividends.* To conclude our discussion of dividend policy under uncertainty, we might take note briefly of a common confusion about the meaning of the irrelevance propossition occasioned by the fact that in the real world a change in the dividend rate is often followed by a change in the market price (sometimes spectacularly so). Such a phenomenon would not be incompatible with irrelevance to the extent that it was merely a reflection of what might be called the "informational content" of dividends, an attribute of particular dividend payments hitherto exluded by assumption from the discussion and proofs. That is, where a firm has adopted a policy of dividend stabilization with a long-established and generally appreciated "target payout ratio," investors are likely to (and have good reason to) interpret a change in the dividend rate as a change in management's views of future profit prospects for the firm.[29] The dividend change, in other words, provides the occasion for the price change though not its cause, the price still being solely a reflection of future earnings and growth opportunities. In any particular instance, of course, the investors might well be mistaken in placing this interpretation on the dividend change, since the management might really only be changing its payout target or possibly even attempting to "manipulate" the price. But this would involve no particular conflict with the irrelevance proposition, unless, of course, the price changes in such cases were not reversed when the unfolding of events had made clear the true nature of the situation.[30]

---

[28] This same conclusion must also hold for the current market value of all the shares (and hence for the current price per share), which is equal to the total market value minus the given initially outstanding debt. Needless to say, however, the price per share and the value of the equity at *future* points in time will not be independent of dividend and debt policies in the interim.

[29] For evidence on the prevalance of dividend stabilization and target ratios see Lintner [15].

[30] For a further discussion of the subject of the informational content of dividends, including its implications for empirical tests of the irrelevance proposition, see Modigliani and Miller [16, pp. 666–68].

## V.  DIVIDEND POLICY AND MARKET IMPERFECTIONS

To complete the analysis of dividend policy, the logical next step would presumably be to abandon the assumption of perfect capital markets. This is, however, a good deal easier to say than to do principally because there is no unique set of circumstances that constitutes "imperfection." We can describe not one but a multitude of possible departures from strict perfection, singly and in combinations. Clearly, to attempt to pursue the implications of each of these would only serve to add inordinately to an already overlong discussion. We shall instead, therefore, limit ourselves in this concluding section to a few brief and general observations about imperfect markets that we hope may prove helpful to those taking up the task of extending the theory of valuation in this direction.

First, it is important to keep in mind that from the standpoint of dividend policy, what counts is not imperfection per se but only imperfection that might lead an investor to have a systematic preference as between a dollar of current dividends and a dollar of current capital gains. Where no such systematic preference is produced, we can subsume the imperfection in the (random) error term always carried along when applying propositions derived from ideal models to real-world events.

Second even where we do find imperfections that bias individual preferences—such as the existence of brokerage fees which tend to make young "accumulators" prefer low-payout shares and retired persons lean toward "income stocks"—such imperfections are at best only necessary but not sufficient conditions for certain payout policies to command a permanent premium in the market. If, for example, the frequency distribution of corporate payout ratios happened to correspond exactly with the distribution of investor preferences for payout ratios, then the existence of these preferences would clearly lead ultimately to a situation whose implications were different in no fundamental respect from the perfect market case. Each corporation would tend to attract to itself a "clientele" consisting of those preferring its particular payout ratio, but one clientele would be entirely as good as another in terms of the valuation it would imply for the firm. Nor, or course, is it necessary for the distributions to match exactly for this result to occur. Even if there were a "shortage" of some particular payout ratio, investors would still normally have the option of achieving their particular saving objectives without paying a premium for the stocks in short supply simply by buying appropriately weighted combinations of the more plentiful payout ratios. In fact, given the great range of corporate payout ratios known to be available, this process would fail to eliminate permanent premiums and discounts only if the distribution of investor preferences were heavily concentrated at either of the extreme ends of the payout scale.[31]

---

[31] The above discussion should explain why, among other reasons, it would not be possible to draw any valid inference about the relative preponderance of "accumulators" as opposed to "income" buyers or the strength of their preferences merely from the weight attaching to dividends in a simple cross-sectional regression between value and payouts (as is attempted in Clendenin [2, p. 50] or Durand [5, p. 651]).

Of all the many market imperfections that might be detailed, the only one that would seem to be even remotely capable of producing such a concentration is the substantial advantage accorded to capital gains as compared with dividends under the personal income tax. Strong as this tax push toward capital gains may be for high-income individuals, however, it should be remembered that a substantial (and growing) fraction of total shares outstanding is currently held by investors for whom there is either no tax differential (charitable and educational institutions, foundations, pension trusts, and low-income retired individuals) or where the tax advantage is, if anything, in favor of dividends (casualty insurance companies and taxable corporations generally). Hence, again, the " clientele effect " will be at work. Furthermore, except for taxable individuals in the very top brackets, the required difference in before-tax yields to produce equal after-tax yields is not particularly striking, at least for moderate variations in the composition of returns.[32] All this is not to say, of course, that differences in yields (market values) caused by differences in payout policies should be ignored by managements or investors merely because they may be relatively small. But it may help to keep investigators from being too surprised if it turns out to be hard to measure or even to detect any premium for low-payout shares on the basis of standard statistical techniques.

Finally, we may note that since the tax differential in favor of capital gains is undoubtedly the major *systematic* imperfection in the market, one clearly cannot invoke "imperfections" to account for the difference between our irrelevance proposition and the standard view as to the role of dividend policy found in the literature of finance. For the standard view is not that low-payout companies command a premium; but that, in general, they will sell at a discount![33] If such indeed were the case—and we, at least, are not prepared to concede that this has been established—then the analysis presented in this paper suggests there would be only one way to account for it; namely, as the result of systematic irrationality on the part of the investing public.[34]

To say that an observed positive premium on high payouts was due to

[32] For example, if a taxpayer is subject to a marginal rate of 40 per cent on dividends and half that or 20 per cent on long-term capital gains, then a before-tax yield of 6 per cent consisting of 40 per cent dividends and 60 per cent capital gains produces an after-tax yield of 4.32 per cent. To net the same after-tax yield on a stock with 60 per cent of the return in dividends and only 40 per cent in capital gains would require a before-tax yield of 6.37 per cent. The difference would be somewhat smaller if we allowed for the present dividend credit, though it should also be kept in mind that the tax on capital gains may be avoided entirely under present arrangements if the gains are not realized during the holder's lifetime.

[33] See, among many, many others, Gordon [8, 9], Graham and Dodd [11, esp. chaps. xxxiv and xxxvi], Durand [4, 5], Hunt, Williams, and Donaldson [13, pp. 647–49], Fisher [7], Gordon and Shapiro [10], Harkavy [12], Clendenin [2], Johnson, Shapiro, and O'Meara [14], and Walter [19].

[34] Or, less plausibly, that there is a systematic tendency for external funds to be used more productively than internal funds.

irrationality would not, of course, make the phenomenon any less real. But it would at least suggest the need for a certain measure of caution by long-range policy-makers. For investors, however naive they may be when they enter the market, do sometimes learn from experience; and perhaps, occasionally, even from reading articles such as this.

## REFERENCES

1. Bodenhorn, Diran. "On the Problem of Capital Budgeting," *Journal of Finance*, XIV (December, 1959), 473–92.
2. Clendenin, John. "What Do Stockholders Like?" *California Management Review*, I (Fall, 1958), 47–55.
3. Clendenin, John, and Van Cleave, M. "Growth and Common Stock Values," *Journal of Finance*, IX (September, 1954), 365–76.
4. Durand, David. *Bank Stock Prices and the Bank Capital Problem.* ("Occasional Paper," No. 54) New York: National Bureau of Economic Research, 1957.
5. ——. "The Cost of Capital and the Theory of Investment: Comment," *American Economic Review*, XLIX (September, 1959), 639–54.
6. ——. "Growth Stocks and the Petersburg Paradox," *Journal of Finance*, XII (September, 1957), 348–63.
7. Fisher, G. R. "Some Factors Influencing Share Prices," *Economic Journal*, LXXI, No. 281 (March, 1961), 121–41.
8. Gordon, Myron. "Corporate Saving, Investment and Share Prices," *Review of Economics and Statistics* (forthcoming).
9. ——. "Dividends, Earnings and Stock Prices," *ibid.*, XLI, No. 2, Part I (May, 1959), 99–105.
10. Gordon, Myron, and Shapiro, Eli. "Capital Equipment Analysis: The Required Rate of Profit," *Management Science*, III, 1956, 102–10.
11. Graham, Benjamin, and Dodd, David. *Security Analysis.* 3rd ed. New York: McGraw-Hill Book Company, 1951.
12. Harkavy, Oscar, "The Relation between Retained Earnings and Common Stock Prices for Large Listed Corporations," *Journal of Finance*, VIII (September, 1953), 283–97).
13. Hunt, Pearson, Williams, Charles, and Donaldson, Gordon. *Basic Business Finance.* Homewood, Ill.: Richard D. Irwin, 1958.
14. Johnson, L. R., Shapiro, Eli, and O'Meara, J. "Valuation of Closely Held Stock for Federal Tax Purposes: Approach to an Objective Method," *University of Pennsylvania Law Review*, C, 166–95.
15. Lintner, John. "Distribution of Incomes of Corporations among Dividends, Retained Earnings and Taxes," *American Economic Review*, XLVI (May, 1956), 97–113.
16. Modigliani, Franco, and Miller, Merton. "The Cost of Capital, Corporation Finance and the Theory of Investment: Reply," *American Economic Review*, XLIX (September, 1959), 655–69.
17. ——. "The Cost of Capital, Corporation Finance and the Theory of Investment," *ibid.*, XLVIII (1958), 261–97.
18. Muth, John F. "Rational Expectations and the Theory of Price Movements," *Econometrica* (forthcoming).

19. Walter, James E. "A Discriminant Function for Earnings-Price Ratios of Large Industrial Corporations," *Review of Economics and Statistics*, XLI (February, 1959), 44–52.
20. ——. "Dividend Policies and Common Stock Prices," *Journal of Finance*, XI (March, 1956), 29–41.
21. Williams, John B. *The Theory of Investment Value*. Cambridge, Mass.: Harvard University Press, 1938.

# 40. DIVIDEND POLICY: AN EMPIRICAL ANALYSIS*

EUGENE F. FAMA and HARVEY BABIAK†

Reprinted from *The Journal of the American Statistical Association*, Vol. 63 (December, 1968), pp. 1132–61, by permission of the authors and the publisher.

Starting with the "partial adjustment model" suggested by Lintner [10, 11], this paper examines the dividend policies of individual firms. The Lintner model, in which the change in dividends from year $t - 1$ to year $t$ is regressed on a constant, the level of dividends for $t - 1$, and the level of profits for $t$, explains dividend changes for individual firms fairly well relative to other models tested. But a model in which the constant term is suppressed and the level of earnings for $t - 1$ is added, provides the best predictions of dividends on a year of data not used in fitting the regressions.

Though the dividend policy of individual firms is certainly a subject of economic interest, perhaps much of the novelty of the paper is methodological: specifically, the way in which a validation sample, simulations, and prediction tests are used to investigate results obtained from a pilot sample. To avoid spurious results that could follow from the extensive data-dredging involved in finding "good-fitting" dividend models, only half of the available firms are used in the original search, the remaining firms serving as a check on the findings. In addition, since the models tested are autoregressive, their statistical properties cannot always be evaluated analytically. This problem is surmounted to some extent by using simulations to study the results and conclusions obtained from the data for individual firms. The novelty in this use of simulations is that they are directed towards checking specific empirical results rather than establishing the properties

* We have benefitted from the comments of P. Brown, Z. Griliches, H. Thornber, A. Zellner, and especially H. Roberts and R. Roll. The study was financed with funds granted to the Graduate School of Business, University of Chicago, by the Ford Foundation and by a grant from the National Science Foundation.
† University of Chicago.

of some general model. Finally, the conclusions drawn from the regression analysis and from the simulations are again checked by using the various models to predict dividend changes for a new year of data. The coherence in the results obtained with these various tests justifies strong conclusions with respect to the "best" dividend models and their properties.

## 1. INTRODUCTION

This paper studies the determinants of dividend payments by individual firms. The starting point is the work of Lintner [10, 11], recently extended by Brittain [2, 3]. Lintner's model is an application of the partial adjustment model (cf. [16]). For any year $t$ the target dividends ($D_u^*$) for firm $i$ are related to profits ($E_{it}$) according to

$$D_{it}^* = r_i E_{it}, \tag{1}$$

where $r_i$ is the firm's target ratio of dividends to profits. In any given year the firm will only partially adjust to the target dividend level, so that the change in dividend payments from year $t - 1$ to year $t$ is assumed to be

$$\Delta D_{it} = D_{it} - D_{i, t-1} = a_i + c_i(D_{it}^* - D_{i, t-1}) + u_{it}, \tag{2}$$

where $c_i$ is the "speed-of-adjustment coefficient" and $u_{it}$ is an error term. Substitution of (1) into (2) yields[1]

$$\Delta D_{it} = a_i + c_i r_i E_{it} - c_i D_{i, t-1} + u_{it}, \tag{3}$$

or

$$\Delta D_{it} = \alpha_i + \beta_{1i} D_{i, t-1} + \beta_{2i} E_{it} + u_{it}, \tag{4}$$

where $\alpha_i = a_i, \beta_{1i} = - c_i$, and $\beta_{2i} = c_i r_i$.

Although Lintner and Brittain develop (4) to explain dividend decisions of individual firms, most of their empirical work involves aggregate data. In this study the model will be applied to data for individual firms. The problem will be approached as follows:

(a) Most of the behavioral models consistent with (4) imply that the current dividend is a function of current and past earnings. Section 2 provides a rough test of this postulated distributed lag effect.

(b) Sections 3 and 4 are concerned more directly with testing (4) as a description of dividend changes. Issues that arise in estimating the coefficients of (4) will be considered, and alternative models will be examined.

(c) In Section 5 Monte Carlo experiments will be used to study statistical properties of the various dividend models that cannot be examined analytically.

---

[1] Lintner was led to the partial adjustment model (2) as a result of interviews with the managements of 28 firms. But the partial adjustment model is not the only behavioral justification of (4). For a discussion see [2, pp. 27–31].

(d) Finally, in Section 6 a new year of data will be used to compare the predictions of the "best" regression models with those of various "naive" forecasting procedures.

## 2. DIVIDENDS AND DISTRIBUTED LAGS: A PRELIMINARY TEST

Most dividend models implicitly assume that the current dividend payments of the firm are a distributed lag function of current and past profits. Before examining models that assume specific lag structures, it is appropriate to test whether the data lend any support to the notion of a lagged response. Table 1 provides distributions by sign $\Delta D_{it}$, conditional on the signs of the per share profits changes $\Delta E_{it}$ (Panel A), $\Delta E_{it}$ and $\Delta E_{i,t-1}$ (Panel B), and $\Delta E_{it}$, $\Delta E_{i,t-1}$ and $\Delta E_{i,t-2}$ (Panel C). The table is taken from pooled annual data on 392 major industrial firms for the 19 years 1946–64.[2]

Table 1 seems to provide evidence for a distributed lag relationship between profits and dividend changes. In Panel A when $\Delta E_{it} > 0$, in 65.8 per cent of the cases $\Delta D_{it} > 0$. In Panel B when both $\Delta E_{it}$ and $\Delta E_{i,t-1}$ are positive, the proportion of positive dividend changes is 74.8, while when $\Delta E_{it}$ is positive but $\Delta E_{i,t-1}$ is negative, there are only 54.1 per cent dividend increases. Finally, in Panel C, in 80.7 per cent of the cases where there were three consecutive increases in annual profits, the current dividend per share was also increased; on the other hand, two successive profits increases preceded by a decrease resulted in an increased current dividend in 66.9 per cent of the cases. Similar statements apply to dividend and profit decreases. Further support for some sort of distributed lag dividend model is the evidence in Table 1 that the effects of a given change in profits on the dividend stream decline over time. For example, if two out of three of the profits changes ($\Delta E_{it}$, $\Delta E_{i,t-1}$, $\Delta E_{i,t-2}$) are negative, the proportion of negative $\Delta D_{it}$ for the sequence $(-\,-\,+)$ is higher than for the sequence $(-\,+\,-)$ which in turn is higher than for the sequence $(+\,-\,-)$.

Finally, a parenthetical comment. Table 1 provides some evidence that earnings changes, or at least their signs, are nearly independent. The last columns of Panels B and C shows the expected percentages of different profits sequences under the assumption that successive changes in profits are independent, with the estimated probabilities of positive and negative changes given by the observed relative frequencies $P(+) = .593$ and $P(-) = .407$. The observed percentages of each sequence of earnings changes are shown in the second to last column of the table. The differences between the actual and expected percentages are small.

In the adaptive expectations model, an alternative behavioral model often

---

[2] The basic data file consists of annual financial statement information on 900 major industrial firms for the period 1946–64, as reported on the Compustat tapes of the Standard Statistics Corporation. Our sample includes only the 392 firms for which 19 years of complete data on all variables needed in the various tests are available. The profits variable in Table 1 is net income per share (income after depreciation and taxes divided by an adjusted measure of number of shares outstanding). The reported number of shares outstanding is adjusted to eliminate the effect of stock dividends and splits.

TABLE 1

DISTRIBUTION BY SIGN OF $\Delta D_t$, CONDITIONAL ON $\Delta E_t$, $\Delta E_{t-1}$, AND $\Delta E_{t-2}$

| | | | $\Delta D_t$ | | | | | | | | |
|---|---|---|---|---|---|---|---|---|---|---|---|
| | | | − | | 0 | | + | | | | |
| $\Delta E_t$ | $\Delta E_{t-1}$ | $\Delta E_{t-2}$ | # | % of Row Total | # | % of Row Total | # | % of Row Total | Total | % of Column Total | Expected % |
| **Panel A** | | | | | | | | | | | |
| + | | | 752 | 20.3 | 517 | 13.9 | 2,437 | 65.8 | 3,706 | 59.3 | |
| − | | | 1,002 | 39.5 | 455 | 17.9 | 1,083 | 42.6 | 2,540 | 40.7 | |
| | | Totals | 1,754 | 28.1 | 972 | 15.5 | 3,520 | 56.4 | 6,246 | 100.0 | |
| **Panel B** | | | | | | | | | | | |
| + | + | | 288 | 13.8 | 238 | 11.4 | 1,562 | 74.8 | 2,088 | 33.4 | 35.2 |
| + | − | | 464 | 28.7 | 279 | 17.2 | 875 | 54.1 | 1,618 | 25.9 | 24.1 |
| − | + | | 515 | 33.4 | 261 | 16.9 | 766 | 49.7 | 1,542 | 24.7 | 24.1 |
| − | − | | 487 | 48.8 | 194 | 19.4 | 317 | 31.8 | 998 | 16.0 | 16.6 |
| | | Totals | 1,754 | 28.1 | 972 | 15.5 | 3,520 | 56.4 | 6,246 | 100.0 | 100.0 |
| **Panel C** | | | | | | | | | | | |
| + | + | + | 131 | 10.9 | 101 | 8.4 | 967 | 80.7 | 1,199 | 19.2 | 20.9 |
| + | + | − | 157 | 17.7 | 137 | 15.4 | 595 | 66.9 | 889 | 14.2 | 14.3 |
| + | − | + | 234 | 25.0 | 159 | 17.0 | 542 | 58.0 | 935 | 15.0 | 14.3 |
| + | − | + | 262 | 31.5 | 123 | 14.8 | 447 | 53.7 | 832 | 13.3 | 14.3 |
| − | + | − | 230 | 33.7 | 120 | 17.6 | 333 | 48.7 | 683 | 10.9 | 9.8 |
| − | + | + | 253 | 35.6 | 138 | 19.4 | 319 | 44.9 | 710 | 11.4 | 9.8 |
| − | − | + | 323 | 48.4 | 111 | 16.6 | 233 | 34.9 | 667 | 10.7 | 9.8 |
| − | − | − | 164 | 49.5 | 83 | 25.1 | 84 | 25.4 | 331 | 5.3 | 6.7 |
| | | Totals | 1,754 | 28.1 | 972 | 15.5 | 3,520 | 56.4 | 6,246* | 100.0 | 100.0 |

* Note that the total number of observations should be $16 \times 392 = 6,272$. The missing 26 observations are the cases where $\Delta E = 0$. Since there were so few of them, we simply excluded these cases from the tabulation.

used to derive (4), it is assumed that dividends are linearly related to long-run expected profits.

$$D_{it} = r_i E_{it}^* + u_{it},$$

and the change at $t$ in long-run expected profits is related to profits observed at $t$ by

$$E_{it}^* - E_{i,t-1}^* = \lambda_i(E_{it} - E_{i,t-1}^*).$$

But if successive earnings changes are independent, the optimal value of $\lambda_i$ is 1, and

$$D_{it} - D_{i,t-1} = a_i + r_i E_{it} - D_{i,t-1} + u_{it}.$$

Thus the coefficient of the lagged dividend term is $-1$. In fact, the estimated average value of this coefficient (Table 2 Panel A) is $-.37$, which suggests that adaptive expectations is an inappropriate specification.

## 3. INITIAL TESTS OF THE LINTNER MODEL

In this section we begin to examine (4) as a description of the dividend be-havior of firms. We shall be concerned with (a) the fact that (4) contains a lagged dependent variable as an explanatory variable, (b) determination of the appropriate measure of profits; and finally (c) whether the intercept in (4) is 0 or close to it.

### A. DESIGN OF TESTS

The available data were used to test many different models. In such data-dredging there is the danger that a particular model works well (in terms of multiple $R^2$) only because it happens by chance to conform to the random elements in the sample at hand. Two steps were taken in this study to guard against this result. First, the data for half of the available firms were used in "screening" for the best models; data for the remaining firms were used to "validate" the initial results. Second, when the "best" models had been chosen, their predictive value was examined (see Section 6) by applying them to a new year of data.

The procedure used in allocating firms to one-half of the sample or the other was as follows. First, we attempted to determine in advance all the variables that would be required in the models to be examined. Then those companies with nineteen years of data on all variables were selected, ordered alphabetically within each industry, and allocated alternately into one-half of the sample or the other. Originally 412 firms were identified as having full information. Predictably, after testing a few models, additional models were suggested; as a result, the two subsamples eventually dwindled to 201 and 191 firms.

The first four panels of Table 2 summarize the cross-sectional distributions of parameter estimates obtained when least squares was used to estimate the

# TABLE 2

## CROSS-SECTIONAL DISTRIBUTIONS OF REGRESSION COEFFICIENTS FOR THE MODELS OF (5)*

| | (1) $P$ | (2) $R^2$ | (3) $\hat{\alpha}$ | (4) $t(\hat{\alpha})$ | (5) $\hat{\beta}_1$ | (6) $t(\hat{\beta}_1)$ | (7) $\hat{\beta}_2$ | (8) $t(\hat{\beta}_2)$ | (9) $\hat{\beta}_3$ | (10) $t(\hat{\beta}_3)$ | (11) $\hat{\rho}_1$ | (12) $\hat{\rho}_2$ | (13) $\hat{\rho}_3$ |
|---|---|---|---|---|---|---|---|---|---|---|---|---|---|
| **Panel A** | | | | | | | | | | | | | |
| $E_t$ = Net Income | | | | | | | | | | | | | |
| $\bar{P}$ | | .432 | .062 | .26 | −.366 | −3.10 | .168 | 3.39 | | | −.093 | −.094 | −.057 |
| $\hat{\sigma}(P)$ | | .236 | .390 | 2.04 | .386 | 2.41 | .112 | 2.05 | | | .227 | .239 | .255 |
| .10 | | .094 | −.158 | −1.39 | −.664 | −5.31 | .048 | 1.00 | | | −.382 | −.405 | −.403 |
| .25 | | .270 | −.054 | − .68 | −.490 | −3.91 | .091 | 1.89 | | | −.243 | −.255 | −.231 |
| .50 | | .439 | .010 | .13 | −.303 | −2.74 | .155 | 3.17 | | | −.094 | −.083 | −.047 |
| .75 | | .615 | .094 | .99 | −.201 | −1.92 | .225 | 4.49 | | | .061 | .053 | .125 |
| .90 | | .725 | .307 | 1.79 | −.127 | −1.18 | .294 | 5.70 | | | .195 | .228 | .245 |
| **Panel B** | | | | | | | | | | | | | |
| $E_t$ = Net Income + Depreciation | | | | | | | | | | | | | |
| $\bar{P}$ | | .409 | .038 | .22 | −.428 | −3.19 | .136 | 3.14 | | | −.027 | −.077 | −.057 |
| $\hat{\sigma}(P)$ | | .226 | .480 | 2.28 | .421 | 2.47 | .111 | 1.99 | | | .235 | .231 | .238 |
| .10 | | .094 | −.279 | −1.95 | −.710 | −5.28 | .033 | .98 | | | −.341 | −.372 | −.350 |
| .25 | | .245 | −.106 | − .97 | −.540 | −3.88 | .075 | 1.90 | | | −.184 | −.232 | −.220 |
| .50 | | .406 | .003 | .03 | −.382 | −2.94 | .122 | 2.95 | | | −.025 | −.081 | −.061 |
| .75 | | .561 | .117 | 1.22 | −.254 | −1.94 | .187 | 4.13 | | | .137 | .070 | .104 |
| .90 | | .700 | .355 | 2.22 | −.174 | −1.33 | .256 | 5.36 | | | .271 | .224 | .245 |
| **Panel C** | | | | | | | | | | | | | |
| $E_t$ = Net Income | | | | | | | | | | | | | |
| $\bar{P}$ | | .466 | .109 | .45 | −.452 | −2.99 | .160 | 3.04 | .061 | .46 | −.111 | −.128 | −.092 |
| $\hat{\sigma}(P)$ | | .226 | .494 | 2.06 | .376 | 2.29 | .120 | 2.11 | .294 | 1.52 | .213 | .235 | .247 |
| .10 | | .150 | −.214 | −.144 | −.789 | −5.25 | .032 | .68 | −.177 | −1.29 | −.379 | −.437 | −.405 |
| .25 | | .309 | −.060 | − .69 | −.597 | −3.72 | .084 | 1.65 | −.043 | − .45 | −.263 | −.287 | −.267 |
| .50 | | .471 | .028 | .34 | −.402 | −2.67 | .147 | 2.68 | .040 | .40 | −.155 | −.120 | −.104 |
| .75 | | .632 | .180 | 1.30 | −.266 | −1.72 | .220 | 4.14 | .144 | 1.36 | .003 | .024 | .086 |
| .90 | | .749 | .501 | 2.20 | −.158 | −1.06 | .294 | 5.47 | .315 | 2.26 | .183 | .180 | .221 |

**Panel D**
$E_t$ = Net Income

| | | | | | | | | |
|---|---|---|---|---|---|---|---|---|
| $\bar{P}$ | .377 | −.317 | −3.38 | .165 | 4.03 | −.067 | −.059 | −.022 |
| $\hat{\sigma}(P)$ | .241 | .351 | 1.91 | .099 | 2.07 | .234 | .240 | .251 |
| .10 | .027 | −.537 | −5.69 | .056 | 1.80 | −.356 | −.386 | −.352 |
| .25 | .206 | −.415 | −4.32 | .096 | 2.82 | −.230 | −.220 | −.202 |
| .50 | .383 | −.280 | −3.13 | .146 | 3.72 | −.058 | −.049 | −.011 |
| .75 | .542 | −.182 | −2.23 | .211 | 4.89 | .101 | .092 | .158 |
| .90 | .672 | −.110 | −1.24 | .278 | 6.36 | .218 | .228 | .293 |

**Panel E**
"Screening" Subsample
$E_t$ = Net Income

| | | | | | | | | |
|---|---|---|---|---|---|---|---|---|
| $\bar{P}$ | .392 | −.342 | −3.47 | .165 | 4.16 | −.075 | −.090 | −.041 |
| $\hat{\sigma}(P)$ | .244 | .463 | 1.90 | .099 | 2.13 | .222 | .249 | .263 |
| .10 | .029 | −.554 | −5.67 | .054 | 1.99 | −.350 | −.415 | −.397 |
| .25 | .214 | −.442 | −4.36 | .097 | 2.86 | −.238 | −.257 | −.227 |
| .50 | .414 | −.285 | −3.14 | .148 | 3.87 | −.071 | −.092 | −.052 |
| .75 | .580 | −.183 | −2.38 | .215 | 5.09 | .077 | .082 | .153 |
| .90 | .681 | −.113 | −1.43 | .288 | 6.36 | .212 | .225 | .295 |

**Panel F**
"Validation" Subsample
$E_t$ = Net Income

| | | | | | | | | |
|---|---|---|---|---|---|---|---|---|
| $\bar{P}$ | .360 | −.290 | −3.29 | .164 | 3.91 | −.059 | −.025 | −.002 |
| $\hat{\sigma}(P)$ | .236 | .162 | 1.90 | .098 | 1.99 | .246 | .226 | .236 |
| .10 | .025 | −.506 | −5.69 | .059 | 1.73 | −.383 | −.345 | −.399 |
| .25 | .205 | −.397 | −4.18 | .096 | 2.63 | −.226 | −.166 | −.182 |
| .50 | .361 | −.275 | −3.04 | .146 | 3.62 | −.042 | −.024 | .023 |
| .75 | .536 | −.182 | −2.13 | .209 | 4.74 | .116 | .129 | .169 |
| .90 | .672 | −.095 | −1.04 | .273 | 6.36 | .241 | .250 | .272 |

\* The regression equation is

$$\Delta D_t = \hat{\alpha} + \hat{\beta}_1 D_{t-1} + \hat{\beta}_2 E_t + \hat{\beta}_3 A_t + \hat{u}_t.$$

To simplify the notation, the firm subscript $i$ that appears in (5) is omitted.

coefficients of different versions of

$$\Delta D_{it} = \alpha_i + \beta_{1i} D_{i, t-1} + \beta_{2i} E_{it} + \beta_{3i} A_{it} + u_{it}, \quad t = 1947 - 1964 \quad (5)$$

for each of the 392 firms in the total sample. $D_{it}$ is dividends per share paid by firm $i$ during year $t$, $E_{it}$ is profits per share, $A_{it}$ is depreciation per share, and $u_{it}$ is a random disturbance term. In Panels A, C, and D the profits variable $E_{it}$ is net income, whereas in Panel B it is cash flow (net income plus depreciation). In Panels A, B, and D the depreciation variable $A_{it}$ is suppressed, and in Panel D the constant term $\alpha_i$ is also suppressed.

The cross-sectional distributions of the estimated regression coefficients of (5) are in columns (3), (5), (7) and (9) of Table 2, while the distributions of their "$t$" values (ratios of coefficients to estimated standard errors) are in columns (4), (6), (8) and (10). Column (1) shows the distribution of the co-efficient of determination ($R^2$), while columns (11)–(13) present the auto-correlation coefficients ($\hat{\rho}_1, \hat{\rho}_2, \hat{\rho}_3$) of the estimated regression residuals for one, two, and three year lags. For each parameter or its corresponding "$t$" value, Table 2 presents seven summary statistics: the mean and standard deviation ($\bar{P}$ and $\hat{\sigma}(P)$), and five fractiles (the .10, .25, .50, .75, and .90). (Note that a single line of the table does not correspond to the regression for a given company. For example, the .5 fractile line does not summarize the results for the "median company" but rather shows the medians of each of the parameter distributions.)

The tests of (5) will be discussed in terms of the entire sample of 392 firms. But, as noted above, the research procedure was first to study the results obtained for the 201 firms in the "screening" subsample and then to check these on the 191 firms in the "validation" subsample. For the models of Panels A-D of Table 2, the results for the two subsamples were almost identical. A sample comparison is provided by Panels E and F, which summarize the model of Panel D for the two separate subsamples.

## B. SOME STATISTICAL ISSUES

Equation (5) contains a lagged value of the dependent variable as an explanatory variable.[3] In finite samples this leads to bias of unknown magnitude in the ordinary least squares regression coefficients. If there is also serial dependence in the error term $u_t$, the regression coefficients will not even be consistent. For the moment we shall not be concerned with the bias in the estimated coefficients. In Section 5, after obtaining evidence about the "best" form of dividend model, simulations will be used to study the properties of the sampling distributions of the coefficients.

But the existence of bias or inconsistency or both is not in itself sufficient reason for rejecting ordinary least squares. From a sampling theory viewpoint, biased coefficients do not necessarily lead to biased predictions of the dependent variable, and estimating techniques (such as instrumental variables) de-

---

[3] If the lagged dividend term on the left of (5) is transferred to the right, the coefficients of $E_t$ and $A_t$ will be the same as in (5), and the coefficient of $D_{t-1}$ will be $1 + \beta$.

signed to produce consistency often lead to regression coefficients with larger small sample dispersion than the inconsistent least squares estimates (cf. [12]). From a Bayesian or decision theory viewpoint, in choosing point estimators, the only consideration is expected loss; bias and inconsistency are never of direct concern.

## C. THE EARNINGS VARIABLE

We turn now to a comparison of the results for the different models summarized in Tabel 2. First, for all models both lagged dividends and some measure of current profits are important variables in explaining dividend changes. For example, in Panel A, which is the Lintner model (4), more than 75 per cent of the estimated coefficients of $D_{t-1}$ (expected to be negative) have "$t$" values less than $-1.92$ and 75 per cent of the estimated coefficients of $E_t$ (expected to be positive) have "$t$" values greater than 1.89.[4]

Brittain [2, 3] argues that in the war and postwar periods the changes in the tax laws with respect to depreciation (five-year equipment writeoffs, allowances for accelerated depreciation, etc.) invalidate reported depreciation figures as either estimates or proxies for the economic costs associated with capital usage. He contends that after 1941, instead of net income, firms were more likely either to use cash flow (net income plus depreciation) as the measure of their ability to pay dividends, or to use net income and depreciation separately, presumably paying out a smaller proportion of the latter since part of the measured depreciation figure is true amortization of capital.[5]

Unlike his aggregate data for all manufacturing corporations and for individual industries, Brittain's data for individual firms lend little support to his profits hypothesis. The results in Table 2 confirm this negative conclusion. All five fractiles of the distribution of adjusted $R^2$ in the net income model of Panel A are at least as large as the corresponding fractiles for the cash flow model of Panel B.[6] But the differences between the values of $R^2$ are small. Similarly, all five fractiles of the distribution of adjusted $R^2$ in Panel C, in which net income and depreciation are included as separate variables, are greater than the corresponding fractiles for the net income model of Panel A,

[4] Given the lagged variable issue, and the possibility of serial correlation in the disturbances, the "$t$" values provide only rough indications of the "importance" of the variables.

[5] Brittain's primary goal in [2] is to relate changes over time in target payout ratios to public policy factors. In addition to his results with respect to depreciation tax laws, he finds that in the entire 1920–60 period changes in target payout ratios can in part be accounted for by changes in personal income tax rates, and especially changes in the tax treatment of dividends and capital gains. Since most of the changes in the personal income tax laws were enacted prior to 1946, we can avoid this issue here.

[6] Let $\bar{R}^2$ be the ratio of the "explained" sum of squares from the regression to the total sum of squares. Then $R^2$, adjusted for degrees of freedom, is

$$R^2 = 1 - (1 - \bar{R}^2)\frac{T - \delta}{T - K - \delta},$$

where $T$ is the sample size (always 18 in our case), $K$ is the number of explanatory variables, and $\delta$ is 1 if the model includes a constant and 0 otherwise. (Cf. [6, p. 217].)

but again the differences are small. Panel C shows quite clearly why the cash flow model of Panel B performs relatively poorly. The cash flow model constrains the coefficients of net income and depreciation to be equal. The distributions of $\hat{\beta}_2$ and $\hat{\beta}_3$, the estimated coefficients of net income and depreciation, in Panel C indicate that there is no correspondence between the values of the two coefficients. Whereas the net income variable enters strongly into the model, the "$t$" values for the coefficients of the depreciation variable are generally of trivial magnitude.

In the remainder of the paper we follow Lintner and use net income as the measure of profits. As a check, when various models are used in Section 6 to predict a new year of dividend data, depreciation will be included as an explanatory variable in some of the models.

### D. THE CONSTANT TERM IN THE LINTNER MODEL

Lintner [11, p. 107] argues that a constant term (expected to be positive) should be included in (5) "to reflect the greater reluctance to reduce than to raise dividends which was commonly observed as well as the influence of the specific desire for a gradual growth in dividend payments found in about a third of the companies visited." In Panel A of Table 2 the mean and median values of $t(\hat{\alpha})$ for the different firms are indeed positive, though close to 0. Under the assumption that the $t(\hat{\alpha})$ are independent drawings from a $t$ distribution with mean 0 and $18 - 3 = 15$ degrees of freedom, 80 per cent of the observed values would be expected to fall between $t(\hat{\alpha}) = \pm 1.34$ and 50 per cent between $t(\hat{\alpha}) = \pm .69$. The actual distribution in column (4) of Panel A deviates only slightly (in the positive direction) from this.[7] But when the constant is suppressed in Panel D, the distribution of adjusted $R^2$ shifts downward. For example, the median value of $R^2$ falls from .439 to .383. Since this evidence is somewhat conflicting, we defer further consideration of the role of the constant until Sections 5 and 6, where simulations and predictive tests will be used to judge the importance of the constant term in dividend models.

## 4. TESTS OF THE LAG STRUCTURE

Griliches [7] suggests that in cases where (4) may seem appropriate on the basis of behavioral considerations, the underlying lag structure which (4) implies can be tested against a wide range of alternatives simply by comparing the results obtained when (4) is applied to the data with those obtained from estimating equations involving additional lagged values of one or both of the earnings and dividend variables. Panels A-D of Table 3 summarize the cross-sectional distributions of estimates obtained when the model

$$\Delta D_{it} = \alpha_i + \beta_{1i} D_{i,t-1} + \beta_{2i} D_{i,t-2} + \beta_{3i} E_{it} + \beta_{4i} E_{i,t-1} + u_{it} \qquad (6)$$

was applied to each of the 392 firms in the sample.

---

[7] The values of $\alpha$ depend on the levels of the dividend and profits variables for each firm. The standardization implicit in the "$t$" ratio makes the estimates roughly comparable from firm to firm.

A plausible dividend model can be derived by combining the partial adjustment and adaptive expectations models. Dividend changes follow the partial adjustment model

$$\Delta D_i = a + c(D_t^* - D_{t-1}) + u_i,$$

but now target dividends are proportional to long-run expected earnings,

$$D_t^* = rE_{t,}^*,$$

and long-run expected earnings are given by,

$$E_t^* - E_{t-1}^* = b(E_t - E_{t-1}^*).$$

Waud [19] shows that if $b \neq 1$ the estimating equations for this model will contain a constant, $E_t$, $D_{t-1}$ and $D_{t-2}$, i.e., the model of Panel A Table 3. Comparison of Panel A Table 3 with Panel A Table 2 indicates that adding the lagged dividend $D_{t-2}$ does not improve upon the explanation of annual dividend changes provided by the Lintner model. The mean and median values of adjusted $R^2$ for the two models are almost identical. The fact that this model performs no better than the simple partial adjustment model of (1)–(4) suggests that the optimal value of the smoothing constant $b$ is in general close to 1. This is consistent with the tentative hypothesis, advanced in Section 2, that year-to-year changes in net income are nearly independent. This negative conclusion with respect to the role of $D_{t-2}$ is also supported by comparison of Panels B and C of Table 3. Again adding $D_{t-2}$ to the equation leads to no noticeable improvement in $R^2$.

For the lagged profits variable $E_{t-2}$ the results are slightly more positive. Comparing Panel A Table 2 with Panel B Table 3, we see that addition of the lagged profits term raises the mean $R^2$ by .037, about a nine per cent improvement. The low "$t$" values for $\hat{\beta}_4$, which seem to indicate that lagged profits do not have "significant" explanatory power, may be due to multicollinearity between $E_t$ and $E_{t-1}$. This is supported by the fact that the "$t$" values for the coefficient of $E_t$ also drop substantially when $E_{t-1}$ is added to the model.[8]

One model that is consistent with the partial adjustment hypothesis and that can be used to explain the presence of a lagged profits term in the dividend model assumes that the process generating the annual profits of firm $i$ can be represented as

$$E_{it} = (1 + \lambda_i)E_{i,t-1} + v_{it}, \tag{7}$$

where $v_{it}$ is a serially independent error term. Target dividends are still

$$D_{it}^* = r_i E_{it}, \tag{8}$$

but now it is assumed that there is full adjustment of dividends to the expected

---

[8] Note that successive levels of profits may be highly correlated, even though (as suggested in Section 2) changes in profits are nearly independent.

TABLE 3

CROSS-SECTIONAL DISTRIBUTIONS OF REGRESSION COEFFICIENTS FOR THE MODELS OF (6)*

| | (1) $P$ | (2) $R^2$ | (3) $\hat{\alpha}$ | (4) $t(\hat{\alpha})$ | (5) $\hat{\beta}_1$ | (6) $t(\hat{\beta}_1)$ | (7) $\hat{\beta}_2$ | (8) $t(\hat{\beta}_2)$ | (9) $\hat{\beta}_3$ | (10) $t(\hat{\beta}_3)$ | (11) $\hat{\beta}_4$ | (12) $t(\hat{\beta}_4)$ | (13) $\hat{\rho}_1$ | (14) $\hat{\rho}_2$ | (15) $\hat{\rho}_3$ |
|---|---|---|---|---|---|---|---|---|---|---|---|---|---|---|---|
| **Panel A** | | | | | | | | | | | | | | | |
| $\bar{P}$ | | .432 | .061 | .14 | −.381 | −1.79 | .003 | .06 | .166 | 3.11 | | | −.100 | −.139 | −.045 |
| $\hat{\sigma}(P)$ | | .241 | .431 | 1.44 | .447 | 1.69 | .340 | 1.20 | .122 | 2.08 | | | .192 | .222 | .242 |
| .10 | | .122 | −.170 | −1.34 | −.741 | −3.77 | −.278 | −1.40 | .040 | .84 | | | −.362 | −.425 | −.358 |
| .25 | | .259 | −.062 | −.62 | −.559 | −2.66 | −.144 | −.76 | .085 | 1.72 | | | −.233 | −.283 | −.215 |
| .50 | | .440 | .009 | .09 | −.351 | −1.61 | .022 | .13 | .156 | 2.94 | | | −.096 | −.133 | −.035 |
| .75 | | .607 | .104 | .86 | −.156 | −.67 | .172 | .87 | .232 | 4.10 | | | .032 | .000 | .122 |
| .90 | | .735 | .327 | 1.76 | −.028 | −.14 | .320 | 1.62 | 3.04 | 5.51 | | | .146 | .131 | .255 |
| **Panel B** | | | | | | | | | | | | | | | |
| $\bar{P}$ | | .469 | .056 | .16 | −.402 | −2.70 | | | .150 | 2.74 | .043 | .65 | −.077 | −.078 | −.075 |
| $\hat{\sigma}(P)$ | | .238 | .383 | 1.77 | .344 | 1.85 | | | .128 | 2.06 | .121 | 1.55 | .216 | .238 | .243 |
| .10 | | .138 | −.170 | −1.56 | −.759 | −4.33 | | | .025 | .50 | −.078 | −1.06 | −.348 | −.397 | −.392 |
| .25 | | .317 | −.066 | −.79 | −.530 | −3.40 | | | .072 | 1.29 | −.020 | −.28 | −.217 | −.238 | −.237 |
| .50 | | .487 | .006 | .08 | −.333 | −2.58 | | | .138 | 2.42 | .035 | .53 | −.086 | −.067 | −.085 |
| .75 | | .643 | .093 | .94 | −.208 | −1.79 | | | .206 | 3.89 | .096 | 1.44 | .079 | .080 | .093 |
| .90 | | .772 | .294 | 1.70 | −.137 | −1.15 | | | .287 | 5.21 | .172 | 2.44 | .204 | .212 | .248 |
| **Panel C** | | | | | | | | | | | | | | | |
| $\bar{P}$ | | .467 | .036 | −.01 | −.473 | −1.77 | .055 | .29 | .142 | 2.46 | .061 | .78 | −.047 | −.151 | −.071 |
| $\hat{\sigma}(P)$ | | .250 | .422 | 1.42 | .423 | 1.30 | .320 | 1.14 | .139 | 2.09 | .130 | 1.49 | .153 | .225 | .234 |
| .10 | | .124 | −.254 | −1.80 | −.849 | −3.35 | −.236 | −1.11 | .011 | .14 | −.066 | −1.04 | −.224 | −.443 | −.370 |
| .25 | | .294 | −.089 | −.90 | −.671 | −2.53 | −.100 | −.45 | .060 | 1.09 | −.009 | −.11 | −.131 | −.309 | −.221 |
| .50 | | .493 | −.004 | −.04 | −.437 | −1.69 | .069 | .30 | .129 | 2.18 | .045 | .67 | −.041 | −.144 | −.063 |
| .75 | | .645 | .092 | .77 | −.260 | −.92 | .231 | 1.09 | .204 | 3.54 | .121 | 1.44 | .036 | −.011 | .087 |
| .90 | | .781 | .345 | 1.70 | −.074 | −.31 | .362 | 1.63 | .293 | 4.86 | .205 | 2.53 | .136 | .152 | .228 |

**Panel D**

| | | | | | | | | | | |
|---|---|---|---|---|---|---|---|---|---|---|
| $\bar{P}$ | .416 | −.399 | −2.76 | .149 | 3.07 | .028 | .46 | −.047 | −.039 | −.033 |
| $\hat{\sigma}(P)$ | .244 | .300 | 1.43 | .116 | 2.31 | .129 | 1.64 | .222 | .240 | .243 |
| .10 | .081 | −.610 | −4.53 | .033 | .77 | −.105 | −1.39 | −.350 | −.371 | −.345 |
| .25 | .254 | −.443 | −3.57 | .072 | 1.48 | −.031 | — .48 | −.204 | −.192 | −.221 |
| .50 | .433 | −.299 | −2.70 | .139 | 2.71 | .025 | .41 | −.042 | −.041 | −.026 |
| .75 | .592 | −.179 | −1.91 | .209 | 4.15 | .083 | 1.30 | .099 | .114 | .141 |
| .90 | .739 | −.102 | −1.08 | .284 | 5.80 | .147 | 2.32 | .243 | .260 | .289 |

**Panel E — "Screening" Subsample**

| | | | | | | | | | | |
|---|---|---|---|---|---|---|---|---|---|---|
| $\bar{P}$ | .433 | −.374 | −2.96 | .145 | 3.04 | .040 | .63 | −.045 | −.060 | −.052 |
| $\hat{\sigma}(P)$ | .252 | .371 | 1.56 | .115 | 2.28 | .138 | 1.63 | .216 | .245 | .244 |
| .10 | .071 | −.658 | −4.86 | .035 | .80 | −.080 | −1.16 | −.353 | −.399 | −.352 |
| .25 | .261 | −.484 | −3.87 | .071 | 1.48 | −.016 | — .28 | −.190 | −.210 | −.237 |
| .50 | .467 | −.321 | −2.78 | .136 | 2.63 | .030 | .47 | −.035 | −.057 | −.055 |
| .75 | .622 | −.191 | −1.91 | .204 | 4.30 | .098 | 1.43 | .098 | .106 | .100 |
| .90 | .739 | −.119 | −1.35 | .274 | 5.56 | .161 | 2.71 | .241 | .249 | .273 |

**Panel F — "Validation" Subsample**

| | | | | | | | | | | |
|---|---|---|---|---|---|---|---|---|---|---|
| $\bar{P}$ | .398 | −.302 | −2.56 | .154 | 8.09 | .016 | .27 | −.050 | −.017 | −.012 |
| $\hat{\sigma}(P)$ | .235 | .192 | 1.37 | .118 | 2.33 | .117 | 1.62 | .229 | .231 | .241 |
| .10 | .105 | −.567 | −4.10 | .029 | .72 | −.112 | −1.73 | −.343 | −.335 | −.336 |
| .25 | .254 | −.411 | −3.24 | .074 | 1.49 | −.047 | — .72 | −.226 | −.156 | −.172 |
| .50 | .396 | −.289 | −2.54 | .142 | 2.76 | .016 | .32 | −.044 | −.002 | .004 |
| .75 | .549 | −.163 | −1.90 | .219 | 4.09 | .069 | 1.22 | .108 | .127 | .171 |
| .90 | .741 | −.089 | .80 | .312 | 6.42 | .136 | 2.00 | .253 | .278 | .298 |

* The regression equation is

$$\Delta D_t = \hat{a} + \hat{\beta}_1 D_{t-1} + \hat{\beta}_2 D_{t-2} + \hat{\beta}_3 E_t + \hat{\beta}_4 E_{t-1} + \hat{u}_t.$$

earnings change $\lambda_i E_{i,t-1}$ and partial adjustment to the remainder:

$$\Delta D_{it} = a_i + c_i[r_i(E_{it} - \lambda_i E_{i,t-1}) - D_{i,t-1}] + r_i\lambda_i E_{i,t-1} + u_{it}, \quad (9)$$

$$\Delta D_{it} = a_i - c_i D_{i,t-1} + c_i r_i E_{it} + r_i\lambda_i(1 - c_i)E_{i,t-1} + u_{it}. \quad (10)$$

This interpretation of the lagged earnings model will be examined more fully in the next two sections.

The tests of the lag structure have been discussed in terms of the sample of 392 firms. In fact the research procedure was first to study the results obtained for the 201 firms in the "screening" subsample and then to check these on the 191 firms in the "validation" subsample. For the models of Panels A-D of Table 3, the results for the two subsamples were again almost identical. A sample comparison is provided by Panels E and F of Table 3, which summarize the model of Panel D for the two separate subsamples.

In the course of this study many other dividend models were tried, but without much success. For example, past, current, and future capital expenditure variables (levels and changes) were introduced separately and in combination into (5) and (6). In no case did the capital expenditure variables produce an improvement of as much as .02 in the average value of adjusted $R^2$. We have also tried models in which the current dividend change is considered a function of current and past *changes* in earnings and dividends; by the $R^2$ criterion, none of these performed as well as the Lintner model (4).

## 5. SIMULATIONS

In this section Monte Carlo experiments will be used to study some statistical issues mentioned earlier. The simulations will be concerned with (a) the effects on the sampling distributions of the estimated regression coefficients of the fact that models (5) and (6) contain lagged values of the dependent variable as explanatory variables; (b) the effects of fitting dividend models with constant terms when the constant is inappropriate; (c) the effects of misspecification of distributed lag structures; (d) measuring the serial dependence in the disturbances of these lagged variable models; and (e) determining efficient procedures for estimating various parameters of economic interest in the models.

Throughout these simulations we shall be concerned with the sampling distributions of estimated regression parameters, given the underlying population values of these parameters. Thus our analysis is in the context of the "sampling theory" approach to statistics. By contrast, in the Bayesian and "likelihood theory" approaches, interest would center around the distributions of the population values of the parameters, given the observed sample values. It is interesting to note that lagged variable models provide one case where the "sampling theory" and Bayesian (or likelihood theory) approaches lead to different views of estimation problems, even when the Bayesian uses diffuse prior distributions. (Cf. [1] [18] [22].)

TABLE 4

CROSS-SECTIONAL DISTRIBUTIONS OF REGRESSION COEFFICIENTS FOR
SIMULATIONS OF (13) WITH NO EARNINGS TREND*

| | (1)<br>PARAMETER | (2)<br>$R^2$ | (3)<br>$\hat{\alpha}$ | (4)<br>$t(\hat{\alpha})$ | (5)<br>$\hat{\beta}_1$ | (6)<br>$t(\hat{\beta}_1)$ | (7)<br>$\hat{\beta}_2$ | (8)<br>$t(\hat{\beta}_2)$ |
|---|---|---|---|---|---|---|---|---|
| Panel A | $\bar{P}$ | .436 | | | −.493 | −3.91 | .160 | 4.29 |
| $\theta = 2.0$ | $\hat{\sigma}(P)$ | .160 | | | .145 | 1.25 | .041 | 1.38 |
| | .10 | .199 | | | −.704 | −5.44 | .113 | 2.63 |
| | .25 | .328 | | | −.598 | −4.67 | .129 | 3.27 |
| | .50 | .448 | | | −.471 | −3.83 | .155 | 4.22 |
| | .75 | .547 | | | −.392 | −3.04 | .188 | 5.21 |
| | .90 | .624 | | | −.317 | −2.41 | .218 | 5.86 |
| Panel B | $\bar{P}$ | .466 | | | −.501 | −4.40 | .160 | 4.89 |
| $\theta = 1.7$ | $\hat{\sigma}(P)$ | .208 | | | .147 | 2.38 | .050 | 2.99 |
| | .10 | .177 | | | −.699 | −6.57 | .113 | 2.15 |
| | .25 | .313 | | | −.584 | −5.18 | .134 | 3.20 |
| | .50 | .482 | | | −.479 | −4.06 | .155 | 4.46 |
| | .75 | .618 | | | −.408 | −2.95 | .188 | 5.84 |
| | .90 | .740 | | | −.345 | −2.33 | .228 | 7.55 |
| Panel C | $\bar{P}$ | .476 | .034 | .16 | −.533 | −3.92 | .161 | 3.79 |
| $\theta = 2.0$ | $\hat{\sigma}(P)$ | .147 | .187 | 1.21 | .157 | 1.19 | .055 | 1.49 |
| | .10 | .288 | −.155 | −1.25 | −.727 | −5.33 | .104 | 2.23 |
| | .25 | .381 | −.076 | −.67 | −.625 | −4.53 | .128 | 2.83 |
| | .50 | .486 | .014 | .12 | −.512 | −3.82 | .159 | 3.82 |
| | .75 | .585 | .123 | 1.00 | −.423 | −3.16 | .195 | 4.64 |
| | .90 | .647 | .258 | 1.70 | −.359 | −2.50 | .225 | 5.50 |
| Panel D | $\bar{P}$ | .507 | .048 | .14 | −.539 | −4.35 | .157 | 4.27 |
| $\theta = 1.7$ | $\hat{\sigma}(P)$ | .192 | .314 | 1.21 | .157 | 2.09 | .082 | 2.81 |
| | .10 | .265 | −.183 | −1.23 | −.737 | −6.52 | .103 | 1.73 |
| | .25 | .356 | −.096 | −.71 | −.637 | −5.02 | .129 | 2.67 |
| | .50 | .521 | .008 | .06 | −.516 | −4.05 | .156 | 3.91 |
| | .75 | .648 | .149 | .87 | −.434 | −3.14 | .195 | 5.33 |
| | .90 | .755 | .293 | 1.81 | −.352 | −2.46 | .230 | 6.92 |

* The regression equation is

$$\Delta D_t = \hat{\alpha} + \hat{\beta}_1 D_{t-1} + \hat{\beta}_2 E_t + \hat{u}_t.$$

The data are generated by the model of (11) and (12) with $\lambda = 0$ in (12). Thus the population values of the coefficients are $\alpha = 0$, $\beta_1 = -.45$ and $\beta_2 = .15$.

A. DESIGN OF THE TESTS

We stress that the goal of the simulations is limited: to obtain insights into the empirical results for the firm data presented in the previous sections. Thus the simulation process will be designed to capture as many features as possible

TABLE 5

CROSS-SECTIONAL DISTRIBUTIONS OF REGRESSION COEFFICIENTS FOR
SIMULATIONS OF (13) WITH EARNINGS TREND*

| | (1) PARAMETER | (2) $R_2$ | (3) $\hat{\alpha}$ | (4) $t(\hat{\alpha})$ | (5) $\hat{\beta}_1$ | (6) $t(\hat{\beta}_1)$ | (7) $\hat{\beta}_2$ | (8) $t(\hat{\beta}_2)$ |
|---|---|---|---|---|---|---|---|---|
| Panel A | $\bar{P}$ | .464 | | | −.513 | −3.85 | .165 | 4.58 |
| $\theta = 2.0$ | $\hat{\sigma}(P)$ | .165 | | | .146 | 1.24 | .040 | 1.40 |
| | .10 | .246 | | | −.698 | −5.55 | .122 | 2.87 |
| | .25 | .360 | | | −.604 | −4.67 | .138 | 3.65 |
| | .50 | .461 | | | −.496 | −3.70 | .160 | 4.29 |
| | .75 | .580 | | | −.427 | −3.03 | .187 | 5.44 |
| | .90 | .673 | | | −.352 | −2.57 | .213 | 6.56 |
| Panel B | $\bar{P}$ | .468 | | | −.513 | −4.15 | .168 | 5.00 |
| $\theta = 1.7$ | $\hat{\sigma}(P)$ | .206 | | | .139 | 2.15 | .046 | 3.37 |
| | .10 | .217 | | | −.708 | −6.48 | .121 | 2.75 |
| | .25 | .287 | | | −.601 | −5.02 | .139 | 3.28 |
| | .50 | .444 | | | −.502 | −3.64 | .160 | 4.26 |
| | .75 | .610 | | | −.415 | −2.83 | .187 | 5.83 |
| | .90 | .751 | | | −.363 | −2.43 | .218 | 7.62 |
| Panel C | $\bar{P}$ | .502 | −.004 | −.05 | −.561 | −3.87 | .176 | 4.20 |
| $\theta = 2.0$ | $\hat{\sigma}(P)$ | .160 | .158 | 1.23 | .164 | 1.26 | .051 | 1.41 |
| | .10 | .287 | −.200 | −1.58 | −.744 | −5.51 | .112 | 2.59 |
| | .25 | .399 | −.112 | −.98 | −.675 | −4.70 | .145 | 3.21 |
| | .50 | .508 | −.006 | −.04 | −.534 | −3.69 | .172 | 3.96 |
| | .75 | .620 | .098 | .81 | −.454 | −3.00 | .207 | 5.06 |
| | .90 | .701 | .162 | 1.36 | −.365 | −2.53 | .238 | 6.12 |
| Panel D | $\bar{P}$ | .508 | .002 | −.06 | −.560 | −.413 | .182 | 4.59 |
| $\theta = 1.7$ | $\hat{\sigma}(P)$ | .194 | .345 | 1.20 | .159 | 1.89 | .073 | 3.22 |
| | .10 | .266 | −.260 | −1.58 | −.779 | −6.44 | .122 | 2.33 |
| | .25 | .354 | −.030 | −.99 | −.666 | −4.82 | .143 | 3.03 |
| | .50 | .502 | −.011 | −.05 | −.540 | −3.77 | .169 | 3.94 |
| | .75 | .654 | .110 | .74 | −.444 | −2.89 | .205 | 5.34 |
| | .90 | .763 | .250 | 1.47 | −.376 | −2.50 | .236 | 7.06 |

* The model is

$$\Delta D_t = \hat{\alpha} + \hat{\beta}_1 D_{t-1} + \hat{\beta}_2 E_t + \hat{u}_t.$$

The data are generated by (11) and (12) with $\lambda = .1$ in (12). Thus the population values of the coefficients are $\alpha = 0$, $\beta_1 = -.45$ and $\beta_2 = .15$.

of the firm data. For example, the sample size and coefficient values will correspond closely to the firm data, and distributions of disturbance terms will be chosen to produce cross-sectional distributions of $R^2$ close to those observed in the firm data.

The data for the initial simulations are generated by the model

$$\Delta D_t = -.45 D_{t-1} + .15 E_t + u_t, \tag{11}$$

$$E_t = (1 + \lambda) E_{t-1} + e_t. \tag{12}$$

Expression (11) can be interpreted as the Lintner "partial adjustment" model of (3) and (4) with intercept $\alpha = 0$, "speed of adjustment coefficient" $c = -\beta_1 = .45$, and target payout ratio $r = -\beta_2/\beta_1 = .33$. In (12) two values of $\lambda$ will be used in the tests: $\lambda = 0$, and $\lambda = .1$.

To generate simulated "data" samples for (11) and (12) it is necessary to choose starting values, $E_0$ and $D_0$, and to specify the process generating the disturbance terms $u_t$ and $e_t$. Initially successive values of $u_t$ and $e_t$ will be independent, identically distributed random variables with mean 0. In half of the simulations $u_t$ and $e_t$ are normal with $SIQ(u)$, the semi-interquartile range of the distribution of $u$, equal to 1.0 and $SIQ(e) = .21$. In the other half $u$ and $e$ are generated from symmetric stable distributions with characteristic exponent $\theta = 1.7$, again with $SIQ(u) = 1.0$ and $SIQ(e) = .21$. The stable and normal samples are related in the sense that a single random sample of "cumulative probabilities" (random numbers uniformly distributed over the interval 0-1) was generated, and then inverse functions for the normal and stable $\theta = 1.7$ distributions were used to get the two samples of $u$. The same procedure was used for $e$. Generating the disturbance terms in this way should enable us to isolate the effects of distributional assumptions.[9]

Under each distributional assumption 201 samples of 20 observations on $u_t$ and $e_t$ have been generated. For each eample $E_0 = 1.0$ and $D_0 = .33$ and then (11) and (12) are used to generate $D_1$ through $D_{20}$ and $E_1$ through $E_{20}$, first for $\lambda = 0$ and then for $\lambda = .1$. Thus there are four sets of data (201 samples per set and 20 observations per sample), each set corresponding to a pair of assumptions concerning the distributions of the disturbance terms and the trend in earnings. Least squares is then used to estimate the coefficients of

$$\Delta D_t = \alpha + \beta_1 D_{t-1} + \beta_2 E_t + u_i \qquad t = 1, 2, \ldots, 20, \tag{13}$$

for each sample of 20 observations. The cross-sectional distributions of the estimates are presented in Tables 4 and 5. To check that the results do not de-

---

[9] The normal distribution is itself symmetric stable or Paretian with characteristic exponent $\theta = 2.0$. The normal is the only stable distribution for which second and higher order moments exist. For $\theta < 2$, moments of order less than $\theta$ exist, while those of order equal to and greater than $\theta$ do not. Heuristically, nonnormal symmetric stable distributions have higher densities around their medians and in their extreme tails than the normal—properties which seem to describe empirical distributions for many economic variables. (Cf. [4], [14], and [17].) Since variances of nonnormal stable distributions do not exist, least squares estimating procedures would seem inappropriate. Though they are certainly inefficient, some justification for their use has been provided by Wise [21]. Further justification will be provided by the results of our simulations.

It would have been desirable to study the distributions of the residuals $u_{it}$ for the dividend models fit to the firm data. But with samples of 18, the results would not be meaningful.

pend critically on the choice of starting values, the models in Table 4 were replicated using randomly selected values of $E_0$ and $D_0$. The results were almost identical.

## B. LAGGED VARIABLE BIAS

Given that the model is otherwise correctly specified, how does the presence of a lagged value of the dependent variable as an explanatory variable affect the distributions of the estimated regression coefficients of (13)? The question can be answered by reference to Panel A Table 4. The sampling distribution of $\hat{\beta}_1$, with a mean value of $-.493$, and a median of $-.471$, is centered to the left of the true value $\beta_1 = -.45$. On the other hand, the sampling distribution of $\hat{\beta}_2$ is centered to the right of the true value $\beta_2 = .15$, with a mean of $.160$ and a median of $.155$.

Panel B Table 4 presents results for the same model as Panel A but for the case where all random variables are generated by stable $\theta = 1.7$ rather than normal distributions. This change has little effect on the sampling distributions of the regression coefficients. The mean values of the coefficients are close to those for the normal model in Panel A, and the fractiles of the cross-sectional distributions are similar. On the other hand, the cross-sectional distributions of the "$t$" values for the coefficients are much more disperse in the stable $\theta = 1.7$ case. For example, for the normal model of Panel A Table 4 the interquartile range of the distribution of $t(\hat{\beta}_1)$ is 1.63, whereas for the stable model of Panel B it is 2.23. Thus when the disturbances are generated by a stable distribution with $\theta = 1.7$, the distributions of the ordinary least squares regression coefficients are well-behaved (in the sense of being close to those obtained when the disturbances are normal), but inferences based on the normal regression model will be misleading. The problem arises from the fact that the estimates of the standard errors of the regression coefficients computed under the normality assumption are downward biased estimates of dispersion when the disturbances are stable with characteristic exponent $\theta < 2$.[10]

---

[10] Consider the model

$$y_t = \beta x_t + u_t \qquad t = 1, 2, \ldots, n,$$

where the $x_t$ are fixed numbers and the $u_t$ are independent drawings from a symmetric stable distribution with $\theta \leq 2$. If $\sigma$ is the semi-interquartile range of the distribution of $u$, the least squares estimate of $\beta$ will have a symmetric stable distribution with the same characteristic exponent $\theta$ as $u$ and with semi-interquartile range

$$\sigma(\hat{\beta}) = \sigma \frac{\sum_{t=1}^{n} |x_t|^\theta}{\left( \sum_{t=1}^{n} x_t^2 \right)^\theta} \qquad \text{(Wise [21]).} \quad (14)$$

If in general $\sum x_t^2 > |x_t|$, then $\sigma(\hat{\beta})$ is a decreasing function of $\theta$ for $\theta > 1$. Thus if we apply standard normal regression theory (i.e., assume $\theta = 2$) when in fact $\theta < 2$, estimates of the dispersion in the distribution of $\beta$ will be downward biased. (Moreover, the bias will *increase* with the sample size $n$.) In the simulations the values of $x_t$ are not fixed: outliers from the distribution of $x_t$ will tend to occur more frequently in the stable $\theta = 1.7$ model than in the normal model, accentuating the effects discussed above.

The simulations summarized in Table 4 are for $\lambda = 0$ in (12), i.e., no earnings trend. But during 1946–64 a majority of firms had positive earnings trends. The results for $\lambda = .1$, summarized in Panels A and B of Table 5, indicate that any such trend effects are minor; the cross-sectional distributions of coefficient estimates and their "$t$" values in Table 5 are close to those for the corresponding models in Panels A and B of Table 4.

## C. THE CONSTANT TERM

The simulations summarized in Tables 4 and 5 also provide evidence on the effects of estimating the dividend model with a constant term when the population value of the constant is 0. Some of the pertinent results are presented in Table 6, along with corresponding results for the Compustat firm data from Panels A and D of Table 2. In several respects the simulations reproduce fairly well the results for the firm data. As in the firm data, including the constant in the estimating equation in the simulations leads to an increase in the values of adjusted $R^2$. In the firm data the average value of $\hat{\beta}_1$, the coefficient of $D_{t-1}$, goes from $-.317$ to $-.366$ when the constant is added to the model. In the simulations, including the constant seems to increase the downward bias of $\hat{\beta}_1$; the average value goes from $-.513$ to $-.561$. Finally, there is also some similarity between the distributions of $t(\hat{\alpha})$ for the firm and the simulated data.

The success of the simulations in reproducing results observed in the firm data suggests that for most firms the constant in the dividend model is close to zero. But, as in all simulations, there is the danger that the success of the simulations in capturing features of the empirical data may result from factors other than the constant term that were overlooked in the analysis. Fortunately, independent evidence on the role of the constant term will be obtained in the prediction tests of Section 6.

## D. TESTING THE LAG STRUCTURE

We saw in Section 4 that in the data for individual firms, including a lagged earnings variable in the dividend model increases adjusted $R^2$, though the increases are small. Simulations can be used to examine the effects of the lagged earnings variable both when the true dividend generating process involves this variable and when it does not. In the latter case we simply examine the effects of including a lagged earnings variable in the estimating equation when in fact the data are generated by (11), which does not involve the lagged earnings variable. The relevant results appear in Table 7. The underlying data samples are the same as those in Tables 4 and 5. For a dividend generating process involving the lagged earnings variable we return to (10), setting $\lambda = .1$, $\alpha = 0$, $c = .45$, and $r = .33$. Thus the process is

$$\Delta D_t = \beta_1 D_{t-1} + \beta_2 E_t + \beta_3 E_{t-1} + u_t \tag{15}$$

$$= -.45 D_{t-1} + .15 E_t + .018 E_{t-1} + u_t \tag{16}$$

TABLE 6

COMPARISONS OF CROSS-SECTIONAL DISTRIBUTIONS OF REGRESSION PARAMETERS FOR FIRM DATA AND SIMULATIONS, AND FOR MODELS WHICH INCLUDE AND EXCLUDE THE CONSTANT TERM*

| (1) | $R^2$ FIRM DATA | | $R^2$ SIMULATIONS | | $t(\hat\alpha)$ FIRM DATA | $t(\hat\alpha)$ SIMULATIONS | $\hat\beta_1$ FIRM DATA | | $\hat\beta_1$ SIMULATIONS | | $\hat\beta_2$ FIRM DATA | | $\hat\beta_2$ SIMULATIONS | |
|---|---|---|---|---|---|---|---|---|---|---|---|---|---|---|
| | (2) | (3) | (4) | (5) | (6) | (7) | (8) | (9) | (10) | (11) | (12) | (13) | (14) | (15) |
| Parameter | With Constant | Without Constant | With Constant | Without Constant | With Constant | With Constant | With Constant | Without Constant | With Constant | Without Constant | With Constant | Without Constant | With Constant | Without Constant |
| Model | | | | | | | | | | | | | | |
| $\bar P$ | .432 | .377 | .502 | .464 | .26 | −.05 | −.366 | −.317 | −.561 | −.513 | .168 | .165 | .176 | .165 |
| $\hat\sigma(P)$ | .236 | .241 | .160 | .165 | 2.04 | 1.23 | .386 | .351 | .164 | .146 | .112 | .099 | .051 | .040 |
| .10 | .094 | .027 | .287 | .246 | −1.39 | −1.58 | −.664 | −.537 | −.774 | −.698 | .048 | .056 | .112 | .122 |
| .25 | .270 | .206 | .399 | .360 | −.68 | −.98 | −.490 | −.415 | −.675 | −.604 | .091 | .096 | .145 | .138 |
| .50 | .439 | .383 | .508 | .461 | .13 | −.04 | −.303 | −.280 | −.534 | −.496 | .155 | .146 | .172 | .160 |
| .75 | .615 | .542 | .620 | .580 | .99 | .81 | −.201 | −.182 | −.454 | −.427 | .225 | .211 | .207 | .187 |
| .90 | .725 | .672 | .701 | .673 | 1.79 | 1.36 | −.127 | −.110 | −.365 | −.352 | .294 | .278 | .238 | .213 |

* The regression model is

$$\Delta D_t = \hat\alpha + \hat\beta_1 D_{t-1} + \hat\beta_2 E_t + \hat u_t.$$

In the simulations the population values of the coefficients are $\alpha = 0$, $\beta_1 = -.45$, $\beta_2 = .15$; the values of $E_t$ are generated by $E_t = 1.1 E_{t-1} + v_t$. The results for the firm data are from panels A and D of Table 2 while the simulation results are from the normal models of Panels A and C of Table 5.

TABLE 7

CROSS-SECTIONAL DISTRIBUTION OF REGRESSION COEFFICIENTS FOR
SIMULATIONS OF (15) WHERE TRUE VALUE OF $\beta_3 = 0$*

| | (1)<br>PARAMETER | (2)<br>$R^2$ | (3)<br>$\hat{\beta}_1$ | (4)<br>$t(\hat{\beta}_1)$ | (5)<br>$\hat{\beta}_2$ | (6)<br>$t(\hat{\beta}_2)$ | (7)<br>$\hat{\beta}_3$ | (8)<br>$t(\hat{\beta}_3)$ |
|---|---|---|---|---|---|---|---|---|
| Panel A | $\bar{P}$ | .433 | − .543 | − 2.95 | .144 | 2.85 | .033 | .49 |
| $\theta = 2.0$ | $\hat{\sigma}(P)$ | .186 | .203 | 1.16 | .057 | 1.35 | .079 | 1.13 |
| No | .10 | .190 | − .827 | − 4.35 | .074 | 1.29 | − .065 | − .92 |
| Earnings | .25 | .318 | − .674 | − 3.52 | .106 | 1.96 | − .012 | − .19 |
| Trend | .50 | .464 | − .516 | − 2.75 | .143 | 2.80 | .034 | .45 |
| | .75 | .557 | − .383 | − 2.23 | .181 | 3.64 | .080 | 1.12 |
| | .90 | .649 | − .310 | − 1.69 | .219 | 4.68 | .124 | 1.78 |
| Panel B | $\bar{P}$ | .467 | − .551 | − 3.17 | .145 | 3.37 | .032 | .46 |
| $\theta = 1.7$ | $\hat{\sigma}(P)$ | .230 | .201 | 1.51 | .072 | 2.58 | .091 | 1.18 |
| No | .10 | .159 | − .841 | − 4.86 | .059 | .80 | − .066 | − .99 |
| Earnings | .25 | .300 | − .672 | − 3.75 | .111 | 1.89 | − .019 | − .26 |
| Trend | .50 | .500 | − .536 | − 2.84 | .143 | 2.92 | .033 | .41 |
| | .75 | .629 | − .415 | − 2.27 | .177 | 4.61 | .083 | 1.04 |
| | .90 | .751 | − .312 | − 1.79 | .218 | 6.02 | .143 | 1.71 |
| Panel C | $\bar{P}$ | .450 | − .532 | − 2.88 | .149 | 3.01 | .026 | .37 |
| $\theta = 2.0$ | $\hat{\sigma}(P)$ | .184 | .199 | 1.00 | .058 | 1.37 | .079 | 1.09 |
| With | .10 | .213 | − .815 | − 4.11 | .080 | 1.38 | − .078 | − .97 |
| Earnings | .25 | .337 | − .656 | − 3.45 | .111 | 2.09 | − .033 | − .42 |
| Trend | .50 | .473 | − .519 | − 2.77 | .148 | 2.96 | .033 | .44 |
| | .75 | .582 | − .376 | − 2.16 | .183 | 3.82 | .080 | 1.06 |
| | .90 | .661 | − .296 | − 1.66 | .220 | 4.83 | .114 | 1.67 |
| Panel D | $\bar{P}$ | .474 | − .535 | − 3.09 | .150 | 3.55 | .024 | .31 |
| $\theta = 1.7$ | $\hat{\sigma}(P)$ | .224 | .201 | 1.36 | .073 | 2.60 | .093 | 1.15 |
| With | .10 | .167 | − .796 | − 4.61 | .072 | 1.06 | − .079 | − 1.13 |
| Earnings | .25 | .347 | − .637 | − 3.67 | .121 | 1.95 | − .031 | − .41 |
| Trend | .50 | .493 | − .521 | − 2.82 | .151 | 3.13 | .024 | .34 |
| | .75 | .636 | − .385 | − 2.30 | .181 | 4.78 | .067 | .96 |
| | .90 | .753 | − .305 | − 1.74 | .227 | 6.08 | .143 | 1.63 |

* The regression model is $\Delta D_t = \hat{\beta}_1 D_{t-1} + \hat{\beta}_2 E_t + \hat{\beta}_3 E_{t-1} + \hat{u}_t$. In the data generating process the values of the coefficients are $\beta_1 = -.45, \beta_2 = .15, \beta_3 = 0$.

where $\beta_1 = -c = -.45$, $\beta_2 = cr = .15$, $\beta_3 = r\lambda(1 - c) = .018$. The same samples of disturbances used in the previous simulations were used to obtain observations on (16). The regressions for this model are summarized in Table 8. In both Tables 7 and 8 the model fit to the data is (15).

When the data for individual firms are used to estimate the coefficients of (15), the average value of $R^2$ is .416 (Panel D Table 3) versus .377 when the

TABLE 8

CROSS-SECTIONAL DISTRIBUTION OF REGRESSION COEFFICIENTS FOR
SIMULATIONS OF (15) WHERE TRUE VALUE OF $\beta_3$ = .018*

| | | (1) | (2) | (3) | (4) | (5) | (6) | (7) | (8) |
|---|---|---|---|---|---|---|---|---|---|
| | | P | $R^2$ | $\hat{\beta}_1$ | $t(\hat{\beta}_1)$ | $\hat{\beta}_2$ | $t(\hat{\beta}_2)$ | $\hat{\beta}_3$ | $t(\hat{\beta}_3)$ |
| Panel A | $\bar{P}$ | .458 | −.456 | −3.74 | .169 | 4.63 | | |
| $\theta = 2.0$ | $\hat{\sigma}(P)$ | .180 | .134 | 1.20 | .039 | 1.35 | | |
| | .10 | .217 | −.642 | −5.32 | .125 | 2.83 | | |
| | .25 | .350 | −.540 | −4.56 | .139 | 3.62 | | |
| | .50 | .479 | −.442 | −3.62 | .164 | 4.62 | | |
| | .75 | .601 | −.366 | −2.85 | .193 | 5.54 | | |
| | .90 | .664 | −.282 | −2.24 | .223 | 6.32 | | |
| Panel B | $\bar{P}$ | .486 | −.465 | −4.23 | .170 | 5.22 | | |
| $\theta = 1.7$ | $\hat{\sigma}(P)$ | .219 | .133 | 2.14 | .043 | 2.87 | | |
| | .10 | .200 | −.658 | −6.40 | .126 | 2.58 | | |
| | .25 | .334 | −.540 | −4.99 | .142 | 3.38 | | |
| | .50 | .504 | −.449 | −3.82 | .164 | 4.77 | | |
| | .75 | .625 | −.378 | −2.88 | .193 | 6.17 | | |
| | .90 | .754 | −.310 | −2.28 | .228 | 7.87 | | |
| Panel C | $\bar{P}$ | .466 | −.519 | −3.04 | .149 | 3.03 | .043 | .59 |
| $\theta = 2.0$ | $\hat{\sigma}(P)$ | .188 | .190 | 1.06 | .057 | 1.37 | .081 | 1.11 |
| | .10 | .218 | −.783 | −4.38 | .083 | 1.43 | −.055 | − .81 |
| | .25 | .342 | −.642 | −3.61 | .113 | 2.07 | −.016 | − .22 |
| | .50 | .505 | −.499 | −2.92 | .149 | 2.93 | .045 | .62 |
| | .75 | .606 | −.371 | −2.34 | .183 | 3.85 | .098 | 1.34 |
| | .90 | .677 | −.288 | −1.79 | .215 | 4.95 | .132 | 1.86 |
| Panel D | $\bar{P}$ | .493 | −.522 | −3.32 | .150 | 3.55 | .041 | .58 |
| $\theta = 1.7$ | $\hat{\sigma}(P)$ | .226 | .184 | 1.58 | .073 | 2.60 | .092 | 1.18 |
| | .10 | .190 | −.763 | −4.87 | .075 | 1.02 | −.063 | − .84 |
| | .25 | .356 | −.623 | −3.97 | .122 | 1.98 | −.014 | − .19 |
| | .50 | .517 | −.504 | −2.93 | .152 | 3.12 | .043 | .52 |
| | .75 | .657 | −.383 | −2.43 | .183 | 4.79 | .091 | 1.16 |
| | .90 | .772 | −.306 | −1.82 | .225 | 6.13 | .155 | 1.92 |

* The regression model is $\Delta D_t = \hat{\beta}_1 D_{t-1} + \hat{\beta}_2 E_t + \hat{\beta}_3 E_{t-1} + \hat{u}_t$. In the data generating process the values of the coefficients are $\beta_1 = -.45$, $\beta_2 = .15$, and $\beta_3 = .018$.

lagged earnings variable $E_{t-1}$ is excluded (Panel D Table 2). In the simulations a systematic increase in $R^2$ is only observed in Table 8, where the dividend generating process involves the lagged earnings variable directly. In Table 7, where the dividend generating process does not involve $E_{t-1}$, no such systematic increase in $R^2$ is observed when this variable is included in the estimating equation. In Panels B and D of Table 7 the average values of $R^2$ (.467 and

.474) are slightly higher than the values in Panel B Table 4 (.466) and Panel B Table 5 (.468) for the corresponding models in which $E_{t-1}$ is excluded. But in Panels A and C of Table 7 the average values of $R^2$ (.433 and .450) are slightly lower than the values (.436 and .464) for the corresponding models of Panel A Table 4 and Panel A Table 5. On the other hand, when the dividend generating process in the simulations involves $E_{t-1}$ directly, including this variable in the estimating equation increases the values of adjusted $R^2$, though only very slightly. From Panel A Table 8 to Panel C the average $R^2$ increases from .458 to .466, while from Panel B to Panel D the increase is from .486 to .493. Thus the simulations support the evidence in the firm data that the lagged earnings variable has explanatory value.

### E. TESTING FOR SERIAL DEPENDENCE IN THE ESTIMATED REGRESSION RESIDUALS

Griliches [7] has shown that common measures of dependence like the auto-correlation coefficient often do not provide a powerful test of independence for the residuals from lagged variable regression models. In such models the estimated autocorrelation coefficient is substantially biased towards 0. In Monte Carlo experiments on the model

$$y_t = \alpha + \beta_1 y_{t-1} + \beta_2 x_t + u_t, \qquad x_t \text{ exogenous}$$
$$u_t = .5u_{t-1} + \varepsilon_t, \qquad \varepsilon_t \text{ normal and serially uncorrelated,}$$

Malinvaud [12] documents the bias of the autocorrelation coefficient estimated from the $\hat{u}_t$. Though the population value of the coefficient is .5, the sample values are widely dispersed about a mean of .3. Nevertheless, Malinvaud's results indicate that, though the power of the test of independence provided by the autocorrelation coefficient is weakened when the regression model contains lagged endogenous variables, the test still provides fairly reliable information concerning the direction (positive or negative) of any serial dependence in the residuals and will produce values systematically different from 0 when the serial dependence is strong.

In this section we shall try to obtain evidence on the degree of serial dependence in the residuals of our dividend models by comparing the cross-sectional distribution of residual autocorrelation coefficients obtained for the Lintner model (4) from the Compustat firm data with the distributions obtained from a simulated model of the same form but with various levels of serial dependence in the disturbances. The process generating the simulation data is again (11) but with the additional specification

$$u_t = \rho u_{t-1} + v_t. \tag{17}$$

Three values of $\rho$ are used: 0, $-.2$, and .2. The 201 normal samples of 20 observations each obtained earlier for $u_t$ in (11) are used here for $v_t$. The equation fit to the data is (4) but with the constant suppressed. The cross-sectional distributions of $\hat{\rho}$, the first order autocorrelation of the estimated regression residuals, are presented in Table 9. The results for the Compustat firm data in column (1) are from Panel D Table 2.

TABLE 9

CROSS-SECTIONAL DISTRIBUTIONS OF FIRST ORDER AUTOCORRELATION
COEFFICIENTS FOR COMPUSTAT FIRMS AND FOR SIMULATIONS*

|  |  | SIMULATIONS† | | |
|  | COMPUSTAT FIRMS | $\rho = 0$ | $\rho = -.2$ | $\rho = .2$ |
|  | (1) | (2) | (3) | (4) |
| $\bar{\hat{\rho}}$ | $-.067$ | $-.057$ | $-.174$ | .061 |
| $\sigma(\hat{\rho})$ | .234 | .189 | .179 | .197 |
| .10 | $-.356$ | $-.297$ | $-.388$ | $-.197$ |
| .25 | $-.230$ | $-.188$ | $-.313$ | $-.080$ |
| .50 | $-.058$ | $-.066$ | $-.183$ | .064 |
| .75 | .101 | .076 | $-.060$ | .208 |
| .90 | .218 | .181 | .063 | .289 |

\* The regression model is

$$\Delta D_t = \hat{\beta}_1 D_{t-1} + \hat{\beta}_2 E_t + \hat{u}_t.$$

Data for the simulations are generated by

$$\Delta D_t = -.45 D_{t-1} + .15 E_t + u_t \qquad u_t = \rho u_{t-1} + v_t$$

$$E_t = E_{t-1} + e_t; \quad e_t \text{ and } v_t \text{ serially independent and normal.}$$

† In the *absence* of the lagged variable problem, the estimated autocorrelation of the residuals would have bias of order approximately $-1/N$ (Cf. [8] or [20]), which in samples of size 20 is about $-.05$. If the mean values of $\hat{\rho}$ for $\rho = -.2$, $(-.174)$, and for $\rho = .2$, $(.061)$, are corrected for bias, they will be close in absolute value. If the mean of $\hat{\rho}$ for $\rho = 0$ were likewise corrected, it would be close to 0.

It seems safe to conclude that positive autocorrelation of order $\rho = .2$ or greater is not a general phenomenon for the Compustat firms. In the simulations, the mean and fractiles of the distribution of $\hat{\rho}$ obtained when $\rho = .2$ are much larger than for the firm data in column (1). In fact the cross-sectional distribution of $\hat{\rho}$ for the firms seems to be somewhere between those for $\rho = 0$ and $\rho = -.2$ in the simulations, and indeed somewhat closer to that for $\rho = 0$ in the simulations than for $\rho = -.2$.

Comparisons of cross-sectional distributions of $\hat{\rho}$ have been carried out for stable $\theta = 1.7$ models as well as for normal models. They have also been carried out for lagged variable dividend equations of the form of (6). The results support completely the conclusions drawn here.

On balance the comparisons of $\hat{\rho}$ for the simulations and the firm data seem to support the following conclusions concerning the magnitude of the auto-correlations in the disturbances for the dividend models fit to the firm data. When autocorrelations for firms are nonzero, they will generally be negative and somewhere between 0 and $-.2$. More important, strong positive *or* negative serial dependence in the disturbances of the dividend models fit to the firm data is certainly not a general phenomenon.

# TABLE 10

## CROSS-SECTIONAL DISTRIBUTIONS OF SPEED-OF-ADJUSTMENT COEFFICIENTS ($\hat{c}$), TARGET PAYOUT RATIOS ($\hat{r}$), AND THE RATE OF GROWTH OF EARNINGS ($\hat{\lambda}$)*

| Model of | SPEED OF ADJUSTMENT COEFFICIENTS ($\hat{c}$) | | | | | | | TARGET PAYOUT RATIOS ($\hat{r}$) | | | | | | RATE OF GROWTH $\hat{\lambda}$ | |
| --- | --- | --- | --- | --- | --- | --- | --- | --- | --- | --- | --- | --- | --- | --- | --- |
| | (1) Panel A Table 4 | (2) Panel C Table 4 | (3) Panel A Table 5 | (4) Panel A Table 7 | (5) Panel A Table 8 | (6) Panel C Table 8 | (7) | (8) Panel A Table 4 | (9) Panel C Table 4 | (10) Panel A Table 7 | (11) Panel A Table 8 | (12) Panel C Table 8 | (13) | (14) Panel C Table 8 | (15) Panel D Table 8 |
| $\bar{P}$ | .493 | .533 | .513 | .543 | .456 | .519 | .543 | .337 | .316 | .308 | .384 | .329 | .324 | .044 | −5.593 |
| $\hat{\sigma}(P)$ | .145 | .157 | .146 | .203 | .134 | .190 | .152 | .083 | .112 | .214 | .089 | .183 | .062 | 18.119 | 58.650 |
| .10 | .317 | .359 | .352 | .310 | .282 | .288 | .360 | .255 | .197 | .136 | .324 | .159 | .257 | −.193 | −.294 |
| .25 | .392 | .423 | .427 | .383 | .366 | .371 | .433 | .299 | .267 | .196 | .350 | .208 | .298 | −.080 | −.093 |
| .50 | .471 | .512 | .496 | .516 | .442 | .499 | .526 | .334 | .322 | .261 | .369 | .284 | .326 | .269 | .165 |
| .75 | .598 | .625 | .604 | .674 | .540 | .642 | .626 | .364 | .373 | .377 | .397 | .423 | .350 | 1.106 | .824 |
| .90 | .704 | .727 | .698 | .827 | .642 | .783 | .765 | .419 | .427 | .521 | .444 | .567 | .386 | 2.480 | 2.840 |
| $\hat{\sigma}^2(P)$ | .0210 | .0246 | .0213 | .0412 | .0180 | .0361 | .0231 | .0069 | .0125 | .0458 | .0079 | .0335 | .0038 | 328.2981 | 3439.8225 |
| $(\bar{P} - P)^2$ | .0018 | .0069 | .0040 | .0086 | .0000 | .0048 | .0086 | .0000 | .0002 | .0005 | .0029 | .0000 | .0000 | .0031 | 32.4102 |
| M.S.E. | .0228 | .0315 | .0253 | .0498 | .0180 | .0409 | .0317 | .0069 | .0127 | .0463 | .0108 | .0335 | .0038 | 328.3012 | 3472.2327 |

* For all columns except (5), (6), (11), (12), (14) and (15) the dividend generating process is

$$(11) \quad \Delta D_t = -.45 D_{t-1} + .15 E_t + u_t; \qquad (12) \quad E_t = (1 + \lambda)E_{t-1} + e_t; \qquad (17) \quad u_t = \rho u_{t-1} + v_t.$$

For columns (5), (6), (11), (12), (14) and (15) the process is (12) and (17) plus (18) $\Delta D_t = -.45 D_{t-1} + .15 E_{t-1} + u_t.$

In the models of columns (3), (5), (6), (11), (12), (14) and (15), $\lambda = .1$ in (12), while for all others $\lambda = 0$. The first order coefficient $\rho = 0$ in (17) for all columns except (7) and (13) and for these $\rho = -.2$.

The regression equation fit to the data is $\Delta D_t = \hat{a} + \hat{\beta}_1 D_{t-1} + \hat{\beta}_2 E_t + \hat{u}_t$ for columns (1), (2), (3), (5), (7), (8), (9), (11), (13) with $\hat{a}$ constrained to be 0 for all columns except (2) and (9). For the models of columns (4), (6), (10), (12), (14) and (15) the regression equation is

$$\Delta D_t = \hat{\beta}_1 D_{t-1} + \hat{\beta}_2 E_t + \hat{\beta}_3 E_{t-1} + \hat{u}_t.$$

F. SPEED OF ADJUSTMENT COEFFICIENTS, TARGET PAYOUT RATIOS, AND THE RATE OF GROWTH OF EARNINGS

Simulations can provide valuable evidence on properties of the estimates of three parameters of economic interest in the various dividend models: the speed-of-adjustment coefficient $c$, the target payout ratio $r$, and the rate of growth of earnings $\lambda$. Table 10 summarizes the cross-sectional distributions of $\hat{c}$, $\hat{r}$, and $\hat{\lambda}$ for different simulation models and provides the mean square error (M.S.E.) for each of the distributions. The table allows us to examine the distributions of these parameters both in cases where the regression equation fit to the data is of the same form as the model generating the data and in cases where the regression model is misspecified in some way. Except for column (15), Table 10 concentrates entirely on normal models. The results for the corresponding stable $\theta = 1.7$ models are again almost identical. Table 11 presents distributions of the three parameters obtained from the Compustat firm data.

TABLE 11

Cross-Sectional Distributions of the Speed-of-Adjustment Coefficient ($\hat{c}$), the Target Payout Ratio ($\hat{r}$) and the Rate of Growth of Earnings ($\hat{\lambda}$) for the 392 Compustat Firms*

| MODEL | $\Delta D_t = \hat{\alpha} + \hat{\beta}_1 D_{t-1}$ $+ \hat{\beta}_2 E_t + \hat{u}_t$ | | $\Delta D_t = \hat{\beta}_1 D_{t-1} +$ $\hat{\beta}_2 E_t + \hat{u}_t$ | | $\Delta D_t = \hat{\beta}_1 D_{t-1} + \hat{\beta}_2 E_t +$ $\hat{\beta}_3 E_{t-1} + \hat{u}_t$ | | |
|---|---|---|---|---|---|---|---|
| (1) | (2) | (3) | (4) | (5) | (6) | (7) | (8) |
| P | $\hat{c}$ | $\hat{r}$ | $\hat{c}$ | $\hat{r}$ | $\hat{c}$ | $\hat{r}$ | $\hat{\lambda}$ |
| $\bar{P}$ | .366 | .816 | .317 | .604 | .339 | .404 | .147 |
| $\hat{\sigma}(P)$ | .386 | 5.044 | .351 | .445 | .300 | 2.941 | 10.522 |
| .10 | .127 | .157 | .110 | .369 | .102 | .081 | $-.163$ |
| .25 | .201 | .337 | .182 | .476 | .179 | .248 | $-.056$ |
| .50 | .303 | .509 | .280 | .574 | .299 | .440 | .059 |
| .75 | .490 | .683 | .415 | .660 | .443 | .719 | .402 |
| .90 | .664 | .974 | .537 | .774 | .610 | 1.159 | 1.558 |

* $\hat{c} = -\hat{\beta}_1$, $\hat{r} = -\hat{\beta}_2/\hat{\beta}_1$, and $\hat{\lambda} = -(\hat{\beta}_1\hat{\beta}_3)/[\hat{\beta}_2(1 + \hat{\beta}_1)]$. The fact that $\hat{r}$ and $\hat{\lambda}$ involve products and ratios of the regression coefficients (which are themselves random variables) seems to destroy the value of the mean and standard deviation as measures of location and dispersion for the distribution of $\hat{r}$ and $\hat{\lambda}$.

The simulation data used to obtain the distributions of the speed-of-adjustment coefficient $\hat{c}$ and the target payout ratio $\hat{r}$ in columns (1) and (8) of Table 10 were generated by the two variable model (11) and (12) with serially independent disturbances and no earnings trend. The regression equation fit to the data is also the two variable Lintner model with the constant suppressed, so that the data-generating process and the regression equation have the same form. The M.S.E. for the distribution of $\hat{c}$ is .0228 with .0210 due to the variance of the estimates and .0018 due to bias. The M.S.E. for the distribution of $\hat{r}$ is .0069 but all of it is due to variance since the bias is essentially 0. The absence of bias in the estimates of $r$ is interesting. Malinvaud [13] shows that the estimates of $\beta_1$ and $\beta_2$ in (15) are negatively correlated. But it is nevertheless surprising that this apparently causes the ratio of the coefficients to provide an unbiased estimate of the target payout ratio, in spite of the fact that both of the coefficients are themselves biased.

In the model of columns (2) and (9) of Table 10 the data generating process (and in fact the data themselves) are the same as in column (1), but the regression equation is the two variable Lintner model with the constant. Including the constant when this is inappropriate causes the dispersion in the distributions of $\hat{c}$ and $\hat{r}$ to increase. The bias of $\hat{c}$ is also increased and bias is now apparently also present in the estimates of $r$. The net effect is an increase in the M.S.E. of both coefficients. Similar results, at least with respect to the dispersion of $\hat{c}$ and $\hat{r}$ are also observed in the firm data of Table 11; suppressing the constant leads to substantial reductions in dispersion.

Next we consider the effects of autocorrelation in the disturbances on the distributions of $\hat{c}$ and $\hat{r}$. In the model of columns (7) and (13) of Table 10 the dividend generating process is the same as that used in obtaining columns (1) and (8) except that the disturbances follow a first order process with $\rho = -.2$. The regression equation fit to the data is the two variable model with the constant suppressed, the same as in columns (1) and (8). Autocorrelation in the disturbances has about the same effect on the speed of adjustment coefficient $\hat{c}$ as including the constant in the estimating equations when this is inappropriate; the distributions of $\hat{c}$ in columns (2) and (7) are very similar in terms of bias and dispersion, both of which are slightly higher than for the correctly specified regression equation of column (1). For the target payout ratio $\hat{r}$, however, things are much different. Autocorrelation in the disturbances in the form of a first order process with $\rho = -.2$ apparently *improves* the estimates of $r$. In column (13) Table 10 the mean value $\hat{r} = .324$ is close to the true value $r = .333$, and the dispersion in the distribution of $\hat{r}$ is lower than for any other model. The M.S.E. of $\hat{r}$ is .0038 versus .0069 in column (8) for the same model without serial correlation.

Table 10 also shows the effects of misspecification of the lag structure on the distributions of the estimates of $\hat{c}$ and $\hat{r}$. Consider first the case where the dividend data are generated by the two-variable model (11) with no trend in earnings or autocorrelated disturbances, but a three-variable regression equation, including the "unnecessary" lagged earnings variable $E_{t-1}$, is fit to the data. The resulting distributions of $\hat{c}$ and $\hat{r}$ are in columns (4) and (10) of Table 10. The M.S.E.'s of both $\hat{c}$ and $\hat{r}$ are substantially higher than those of any other model. Thus, including the lagged earnings variable in the regression model when this is inappropriate leads to problems in estimating the coefficients $c$ and $r$.

Suppose now the dividend generating process includes the lagged earnings variable $E_{t-1}$ directly and this variable is also included in the estimating equation. The distributions of $\hat{c}$ and $\hat{r}$ obtained in this case are in columns (6) and (12) of Table 10. Though the estimating equation includes exactly the same variables as the equation generating data, the M.S.E.'s of the distributions of $\hat{c}$ and $\hat{r}$ are high relative to those of other models, and this is primarily a result of the high degree of dispersion in these distributions. The high dispersion relative to two-variable models can be traced directly to increased multicollinearity between the variables in the estimating equation when $E_{t-1}$ is included. For example, for the model without the lagged earnings variable summarized in Panel A Table 4, the average values of $t(\hat{\beta}_1)$ and $t(\hat{\beta}_2)$ are $-3.91$ and 4.29 respectively. For the corresponding model with the lagged earnings variable, summarized in Panel A Table 7, the average values of $t(\hat{\beta}_1)$ and $t(\hat{\beta}_2)$ are $-2.95$ and 2.85 respectively.

In fact, at least in these simulations, better estimates (in terms of M.S.E.) of $c$ and $r$ are obtained by omitting $E_{t-1}$ from the estimating equation, even though the dividend generating process involves this variable. In column (5) Table 10 the distribution of $\hat{c}$ has smaller bias, variance, and M.S.E. than the distribution for the "correct" three-variable estimating equation in column (6). The corresponding distribution of $\hat{r}$ for the two-variable estimating equation in column (11) shows estimates with higher bias than those obtained with the three-variable equation in column (12), but the low variance obtained with the two-variable model more than offsets the increased bias: the M.S.E. of the distribution of $\hat{r}$ for the two-variable model is less than one-third that of the three-variable model. These results suggest that perhaps in the firm data the two-variable dividend model, involving $D_{t-1}$ and $E_t$, should sometimes be used to estimate the parameters $c$ and $r$ even though one may suspect that the generating process also involves the lagged earnings variable $E_{t-1}$. This anomalous conclusion, however, results from the high degree of muticollinearity between successive values of $E$ that was incorporated into the simulations. In a study concerned with precise estimation of $c$ and $r$ for the firm data, one would want to check the degree of multicollinearity. Certainly an optimal procedure would be contingent on the observed levels of dependence.

Finally, columns (14) and (15) of Table 10 present the cross-sectional distributions of the rate of growth of earnings $\hat{\lambda}$ obtained when the dividend data are generated according to the three-variable model (16) and the three-variable equation (15) is fit to the data. The estimated values of $\hat{\lambda}$ are given by $\hat{\lambda} = -\hat{\beta}_1 \hat{\beta}_3 / \hat{\beta}_2 (1 + \hat{\beta}_1)$, and the true value is $\lambda = .1$. In the model of column (14) the disturbances in (16) are normal, while in the model of column (15) they are stable $\theta = 1.7$. We conclude immediately that the regression model does not provide meaningful estimates of $\hat{\lambda}$. Apparently the complicated function of random variables (the $\hat{\beta}$'s) used to estimate $\lambda$ produces a sampling distribution which provides very little information about the rate of growth parameter. This conclusion is also supported by the distribution of $\hat{\lambda}$ obtained for the Compustat firm data in column (8) Table 11.

## 6. PREDICTIONS OF 1965 DIVIDENDS

In this section we examine the results obtained when various dividend models are used to predict the changes in dividends per share paid by individual firms during 1965. Let $\hat{D}_{i,65}$ be the predicted and $D_{i,65}$ the actual dividend for firm $i$ for 1965. The raw prediction error is then

$$\hat{u}_{i,65} = (\hat{D}_{i,65} - \hat{D}_{i,64}) - (D_{i,65} - D_{i,64})$$
$$= \hat{D}_{i,65} - D_{i,65}.$$

The dispersion of the distribution of $\hat{u}$ for any given dividend model will vary from firm to firm. To construct meaningful cross-sectional distributions of prediction errors, it is necessary to "standardize" the units used in measuring the errors. We therefore define the standardized prediction error

$$\varepsilon_i = \frac{\hat{u}_{i,65}}{M_i}.$$

In half the tests $M_i = \hat{\sigma}(\Delta D_i)$, the standard deviation of the dividend changes of firm $i$ over the period 1946–64, while in the other half $M_i = IQ(\Delta D_i)$, the interquartile range of the annual dividend changes.

The five "naive" models ($N1$–$N5$) and nine regression models ($R1$–$R9$) used to make dividend predictions for 1965 are presented in Table 12. The coefficient estimates for $R1$–$R3$ are from the regressions used in constructing Panels A, C, and D of Table 2. The coefficients for $R5$ and $R6$ are from the regressions used in constructing Panels B and D of Table 3. For each firm $R7$ is that model of the models $R1$–$R6$ which had the highest multiple $R^2$ in the regression analyses. Thus, the actual model used for $R7$ differs from firm to firm. Similarly, for each firm $R8$ is the "best" of $R1$, $R2$, and $R5$, the regression models which include a constant, while $R9$ is the "best" of $R3$, $R4$, and $R6$, the models in which the constant is suppressed. For each of the models Table 13 provides the number of firms ($N$) for which a forecast of 1965 dividends was made, the average absolute value of the standardized prediction errors ($\sum_{i=1}^{N}|\varepsilon_i|/N$), the mean square prediction error ($\sum_{i=1}^{N}\varepsilon_i^2/N$), the average ($\bar{\varepsilon}$), squared average ($\bar{\varepsilon}^2$), standard deviation $\hat{\sigma}(\varepsilon)$, variance $\hat{\sigma}^2(\varepsilon)$, interquartile range $IQ(\varepsilon)$, and interdecile range $ID(\varepsilon)$ of the errors, along with five fractiles of the cross-sectional distribution of $\varepsilon$.

How do these prediction tests compare to the earlier results concerning the "best" dividend models? Table 13 includes results for four criteria (average absolute error, mean square error, and the interquartile and interdecile ranges) for judging the predictive power of the various dividend models. For each criterion two versions of the standardized prediction error are used, making a total of eight summary comparisons of the models. If for the moment we exclude the summary models $R7$–$R9$, in five of these comparisons the regression model $R6$ produces the minimum value of the test criterion, and $R6$ ranks no lower than fourth in the remaining three comparisons. In the regressions on the firm data the best model, in terms of average $R^2$, was $R5$, the model with

TABLE 12
DESCRIPTIONS OF DIVIDEND PREDICTION MODELS

NAIVE MODELS

| MODEL | DESCRIPTION | PREDICTED 1965 DIVIDEND CHANGE $(\hat{D}_{i,65} - D_{i,64})$ EQUALS | EXCEPTIONS |
|---|---|---|---|
| $N1$ | No change | $0$ | — |
| $N2$ | Same dollar change | $D_{i,64} - D_{i,63}$ | If $\hat{D}_{i,65} < 0$, let $\hat{D}_{i,65} = 0$ |
| $N3$ | Average dollar change | $\dfrac{D_{i,64} - D_{i,46}}{18}$ | If $\hat{D}_{i,65} < 0$, let $\hat{D}_{i,65} = 0$ |
| $N4$ | Average rate of growth | $D_{i,64}(e^r - 1)$; $r = \dfrac{\log D_{i,64} - \log D_{i,46}}{18}$ | If $D_{i,46} = 0$, the first positive dividend is used in the numerator and the denominator is correspondingly reduced |
| $N5$ | Same percentage change | $D_{i,64}\left(\dfrac{D_{i,64}}{D_{i,63}} - 1\right)$ | If $D_{i,63} = 0$ and $D_{i,64} > 0$, no prediction is made. If $D_{i,63} = 0$ and $D_{i,64} = 0$, let $\hat{D}_{i,65} = 0$ |

REGRESSION MODELS

| MODEL | PREDICTED 1965 DIVIDEND CHANGE $(\hat{D}_{i,65} - D_{i,64})$ EQUALS |
|---|---|
| $R1$ | $\hat{\alpha}_i + \hat{\beta}_{1i}D_{i,64} + \hat{\beta}_{2i}E_{i,65}$ |
| $R2$ | $\hat{\alpha}_i + \hat{\beta}_{1i}D_{i,64} + \hat{\beta}_{2i}E_{i,65} + \hat{\beta}_{3i}A_{i,65}$ |
| $R3$ | $\hat{\beta}_{1i}D_{i,64} + \hat{\beta}_{2i}E_{i,65}$ |
| $R4$ | $\hat{\beta}_{1i}D_{i,64} + \hat{\beta}_{2i}E_{i,65} + \hat{\beta}_{3i}A_{i,65}$ |
| $R5$ | $\hat{\alpha}_i + \hat{\beta}_{1i}D_{i,64} + \hat{\beta}_{2i}E_{i,65} + \hat{\beta}_{3i}E_{i,64}$ |
| $R6$ | $\hat{\beta}_{1i}D_{i,64} + \hat{\beta}_{2i}E_{i,65} + \hat{\beta}_{3i}E_{i,64}$ |
| $R7$ | Best of $R1$–$R6$ for each individual firm |
| $R8$ | Best of $R1$, $R2$ or $R5$ (i.e., with constants) |
| $R9$ | Best of $R3$, $R4$ or $R6$ (i.e., without constants) |

the constant and lagged earnings variable. In the predictions $R6$, the same lagged earnings model *but with the constant suppressed,* is best.

This negative result with respect to the importance of the constant term is supported by the forecasting tests for the other regression models. $R3$ (the Lintner model with the constant suppressed) outperforms $R1$ (the same model with the constant) in six out of eight of the summary comparisons of distributions of prediction errors. The constant-suppressed model $R4$ outperforms $R2$ in every comparison. These results confirm the earlier conclusions drawn from the simulations (which were concerned with models $R1$, $R3$, $R5$, and $R6$). In the simulations, including the constant term in the regression models led to a slight increase in $R^2$, though the data generating process did not involve the constant.

The evidence uniformly suggests that, for a majority of firms, models with the constant suppressed provide better predictions of dividend changes than models in which the value of the constant is left completely free. But from a Bayesian viewpoint, our treatment of the constant throughout the paper has considered only the extreme cases of diffuse and dogmatic prior beliefs. If we had chosen the Bayesian route, we would have been forced to admit that our *a priori* feelings concerning the constant would have been summarized by a distribution closely but not completely concentrated about zero. Imposing such a prior distribution on the data would guarantee that the posterior distribution of the constant was also closely concentrated about zero. Since it would rule out wild values of the estimated constant, this approach could lead to even better predictions of dividend changes than simply suppressing the constant.

The prediction tests also confirm the earlier conclusions with respect to the relevant measure of earnings to be used in dividend models. Following the suggestions of Brittain [2, 3], $R2$ and $R4$ contain both net income and depreciation as explanatory variables; following Lintner [11], $R1$ and $R3$ contain only net income. For six to eight of the summary measures of prediction error, model $R1$ is better than $R2$, and $R3$ outperforms $R4$ in seven of eight comparisons. Thus, for most firms the depreciation variable adds little to the prediction of dividends.

Can predictions of dividend changes be improved by using the model that has the highest $R^2$ for each firm? The results for models $R3–R9$ in Table 13 indicate that the answer is negative. $R9$ produces the minimum prediction error in column (10) Panel B, but in the remaining seven tests models $R7–R9$ are dominated by one of the other models (usually $R6$).

In most of the tests the naive model $N2$ (same dollar change) performs well relative to the various regression models. When testing many naive models, however, one is likely to find by chance alone at least one that performs well. The reason for the good performance of $N2$ is easy to find. For the Compustat firms the average change in net income from 1964–65 was very close to the change from 1963–64. $N2$ would not perform so well in years when this was not the case.

Finally, the four summary measures (average absolute error, mean square error, and the interquartile and interdecile ranges) of the distributions of prediction errors are certainly not of equal value. The primary concern here is determining which of the various dividend models works best for a large majority of firms; it is unreasonable to expect that any given model will be appropriate for all firms. If a model works well for most firms but is completely inappropriate for a few firms, this is the best we can expect. We certainly do not want to give heaviest weight to the prediction errors of the

TABLE 13

CROSS-SECTIONAL DISTRIBUTIONS OF 1965 PREDICTION ERRORS FOR NAIVE MODELS ($N$) AND VARIOUS "GOOD FITTING" REGRESSION MODELS ($R$)

| (1) | (2) | (3) | (4) | (5) | (6) | (7) | (8) | (9) | (10) | (11) | (12) | (13) | (14) | (15) |
|---|---|---|---|---|---|---|---|---|---|---|---|---|---|---|
| | | | | | | | | | | FRACTILES | | | | |
| MODEL | $N$ | $\bar{\varepsilon}$ | $\dfrac{\sum|\varepsilon_i|}{N}$ | $\dfrac{\sum \varepsilon_i^2}{N}$ | $\hat{\sigma}^2(\varepsilon)$ | $\bar{\varepsilon}^2$ | $\hat{\sigma}(\varepsilon)$ | $IQ(\varepsilon)$ | $ID(\varepsilon)$ | .10 | .25 | .50 | .75 | .90 |
| Panel A | | | | | | | | | | | | | | |
| Prediction | | | | | | | | | | | | | | |
| error for firm | | | | | | | | | | | | | | |
| $i$ is divided by | | | | | | | | | | | | | | |
| $\hat{\sigma}(\Delta D_i)$ | | | | | | | | | | | | | | |
| N1 | 369 | −1.05 | 1.24 | 3.29 | 2.19 | 1.10 | 1.48 | 1.64 | 3.07 | −3.04 | −1.66 | −.77 | −.01 | .03 |
| N2 | 369 | −.29 | .94 | 2.20* | 2.12 | .08 | 1.45 | 1.17* | 2.92 | −1.87 | −.89 | −.07 | .28 | 1.05 |
| N3 | 369 | −.68 | 1.07 | 2.44 | 1.98* | .46 | 1.41* | 1.40 | 3.04 | −2.52 | −1.24 | −.47 | .15 | .52 |
| N4 | 369 | −.26 | 1.06 | 2.29 | 2.22 | .07 | 1.49 | 1.49 | 3.21 | −2.00 | −1.01 | −.18 | .47 | 1.21 |
| N5 | 366 | −.08 | 1.06 | 3.01 | 3.00 | .01 | 1.73 | 1.31 | 3.32 | −1.75 | −.85 | −.02 | .46 | 1.57 |
| R1 | 369 | −.10 | .93 | 3.64 | 3.63 | .01 | 1.90 | 1.21 | 2.62 | −1.38 | −.60 | .03 | .61 | 1.24 |
| R2 | 369 | −.10 | 1.02 | 3.56 | 3.55 | .01 | 1.88 | 1.35 | 2.83 | −1.50 | −.67 | .07 | .68 | 1.33 |
| R3 | 369 | −.06 | .90 | 3.32 | 3.32 | .00 | 1.82 | 1.25 | 2.54 | −1.34 | −.57 | .08 | .67 | 1.20 |
| R4 | 369 | −.01* | .96 | 3.04 | 3.04 | .00 | 1.74 | 1.27 | 2.70 | −1.47 | −.54 | .19 | .73 | 1.23 |
| R5 | 369 | −.04* | .92 | 2.80 | 2.80 | .00 | 1.67 | 1.21 | 2.59 | −1.34 | −.55 | .05 | .66 | 1.25 |
| R6 | 369 | −.02 | .88* | 2.36 | 2.36 | .00 | 1.54 | 1.24 | 2.50* | −1.31 | −.56 | .10 | .68 | 1.19 |
| R7 | 369 | −.05 | .99 | 3.48 | 3.48 | .00 | 1.87 | 1.23 | 2.72 | −1.38 | −.57 | .10 | .66 | 1.34 |
| R8 | 369 | −.06 | .99 | 3.48 | 3.48 | .00 | 1.87 | 1.27 | 2.72 | −1.38 | −.59 | .10 | .68 | 1.34 |
| R9 | 369 | .01* | .93 | 2.94 | 2.94 | .00 | 1.72 | 1.25 | 2.64 | −1.36 | −.52 | .11 | .73 | 1.28 |

Panel B — Prediction error for firm $i$ is divided by $IQ(\Delta D_i)$

| | $N$ | | | | | | | | | | | | | |
|---|---|---|---|---|---|---|---|---|---|---|---|---|---|---|
| N1 | 361 | −1.06 | 1.28 | 4.77 | 3.65 | 1.12 | 1.91 | 1.54 | 2.79 | −2.76 | −1.57 | −.72 | −.02 | .03 |
| N2 | 361 | −.31 | 1.00 | 3.72 | 3.62 | .10 | 1.90 | 1.16 | 2.64 | −1.80 | −.87 | −.07 | .29 | .84 |
| N3 | 361 | −.72 | 1.13 | 3.87 | 3.36 | .51 | 1.83 | 1.37 | 2.81 | −2.32 | −1.20 | −.46 | .17 | .49 |
| N4 | 361 | −.36 | 1.10 | 3.45 | 3.32 | .13 | 1.82 | 1.47 | 3.18 | −2.04 | −.97 | −.19 | .51 | 1.14 |
| N5 | 359 | .05 | 1.28 | 12.88 | 12.88 | .00 | 3.59 | 1.25 | 2.96 | −1.61 | −.81 | −.03 | .45 | 1.35 |
| R1 | 361 | .07 | 1.00 | 3.14 | 3.13 | .01 | 1.77 | 1.09* | 2.81 | −1.36 | −.51 | .06 | .58 | 1.45 |
| R2 | 361 | .04* | 1.06 | 3.23 | 3.23 | .00 | 1.80 | 1.32 | 2.67 | −1.31 | −.63 | .10 | .69 | 1.36 |
| R3 | 361 | .14 | .96 | 2.82 | 2.80 | .02 | 1.67 | 1.14 | 2.55 | −1.18 | −.52 | .10 | .61 | 1.37 |
| R4 | 361 | .19 | 1.03 | 3.17 | 3.13 | .04 | 1.77 | 1.15 | 2.51 | −1.21 | −.47 | .18 | .69 | 1.30 |
| R5 | 361 | .10 | .99 | 2.75 | 2.74 | .01 | 1.66 | 1.14 | 2.65 | −1.17 | −.51 | .06 | .63 | 1.48 |
| R6 | 361 | .14 | .93* | 2.32* | 2.30* | .02 | 1.52* | 1.15 | 2.49 | −1.08 | −.49 | .11 | .66 | 1.41 |
| R7 | 361 | .08 | 1.03 | 2.85 | 2.84 | .01 | 1.69 | 1.27 | 2.70 | −1.24 | −.58 | .13 | .69 | 1.46 |
| R8 | 361 | .07 | 1.03 | 2.83 | 2.82 | .01 | 1.68 | 1.30 | 2.70 | −1.24 | −.58 | .13 | .72 | 1.46 |
| R9 | 361 | .17 | .95 | 2.36 | 2.33 | .03 | 1.53 | 1.14 | 2.47* | −1.11 | −.44 | .12 | .69 | 1.35 |

* Minimum value for column and panel.

† In the annual data for 1946–64 the total number of firms was 392. During 1956, 23 of these firms "disappeared" from the Compustat tapes. No predictions were made for these firms. In addition, for 8 of the remaining firms $IQ(\Delta D_i) = 0$; that is, each of these firms changed dividends per share less than 9 times during the period 1946–64.

few firms for which the model examined is completely inappropriate. But since these firms are likely to have the largest prediction errors, the mean square error criterion gives them heaviest weight. For our purposes the inter-quartile and interdecile ranges provide a more representative picture of the cross-sectional distributions of prediction errors produced by each model, but these also have their shortcomings. Any interfractile range criterion puts heavy weight on just two points of the distribution. The average absolute error criterion provides a much more even weighting of individual prediction errors than either mean square error or interfractile ranges.

The rankings of the models (excluding the summary models $R7$–$R9$) by size of average absolute error are as follows.

| RANK | 1 | 2 | 3 | 4 | 5 | 6 | 7 | 8 | 9 | 10 | 11 |
|---|---|---|---|---|---|---|---|---|---|---|---|
| $M_i = \hat{\sigma}(\Delta D_i)$ | R6 | R3 | R5 | R1 | N2 | R4 | R2 | N4 | N5 | N3 | N1 |
| $M_i = IQ(\Delta D_i)$ | R6 | R3 | R5 | R1 | N2 | R4 | R2 | N4 | N3 | N5 | N1 |

It is clear that for this criterion the rankings of the various models do not depend much on whether the prediction errors are measured in units of standard deviation of dividend changes or in units of the interquartile ranges.

## 7. CONCLUSIONS

The regressions on the firm data, the simulations, and the prediction tests provide consistent evidence on dividend models for individual firms. The two variable Lintner model (4), including a constant term, $D_{t-1}$, and $E_t$, performs well relative to other models; in general, however, deleting the constant and adding the lagged profits variable $E_{t-1}$ leads to a slight improvement in the predictive power of the model. In applying dividend models to the data of most firms, net income seems to provide a better measure of profits than either cash flow or net income and depreciation included as separate variables in the model. Finally, in the models tested here, serial dependence in the disturbances does not seem to be a serious problem.

## REFERENCES

1. Barnard, G. A., Jenkins, G. M., and Winsten, C. B., "Likelihood Inference and Time Series," *Journal of the Royal Statistical Society*, Series A (General), Vol. 125 (1962), 321–72.
2. Brittain, John A., *Corporate Dividend Policy* (Washington: The Brookings Institution, 1966).
3. Brittain, John A., "The Tax Structure and Corporate Dividend Policy," *American Economic Review* (May, 1964), 272–87.
4. Fama, Eugene F., "The Behavior of Stock Market Prices," *Journal of Business* (January, 1965), 34–105.
5. Fama, Eugene F., and Roll, Richard, "Some Properties of Symmetric Stable Distributions," *Journal of the American Statistical Association* (September, 1968).

6. Goldberger, Arthur S., *Econometric Theory* (New York: John Wiley and Sons, 1964).
7. Griliches, Zvi, "Distributed Lags: A Survey," *Econometrica* (January, 1967), 16–49.
8. Kendall, M. G., "Note on Bias in the Estimation of Autocorrelation," *Biometrika* (1954), 403–04.
9. Koyck, L. M., *Distributed Lags and Investment Analysis* (Amsterdam: North Holland Publishing Co., 1954).
10. Lintner, John, "The Determinants of Corporate Saving," in *Savings in the Modern Economy*, edited by W. W. Heller (Minneapolis: University of Minnesota Press, 1963), 230–55.
11. Lintner, John, "Distribution of Incomes among Dividends, Retained Earnings and Taxes," *American Economic Review* (May, 1956), 97–113.
12. Malinvaud, Edmond, "Estimation et Prévision dans les Modèles Économiques Autoregressifs," *Revue de l'Institut International de Statistique* Vol. 29, No. 2 (1961), 1–32.
13. Malinvaud, Edmond, *Statistical Methods of Econometrics* (Amsterdam: North Holland Publishing Co., 1966), Chs. 13–15.
14. Mandelbrot, Benoit, "The Variation of Certain Speculative Prices," *Journal of Business* (October, 1963), 394–419.
15. Miller, Merton H., and Modigliani, Franco, "Dividend Policy, Growth and the Valuation of Shares," *Journal of Business* (October, 1961), 411–33.
16. Nerlove, Marc, *Distributed Lags and Demand Analysis* (Washington: U.S.D.A. Agriculture Handbook No. 141, 1958).
17. Roll, Richard, "The Efficient Market Model Applied to U.S. Treasury Bill Rates," unpublished Ph.D. thesis, Graduate School of Business, University of Chicago, March, 1968.
18. Thornber, Hodson, "Finite Sample Monte Carlo Studies: An Autoregressive Illustration," *Journal of the American Statistical Association* (September, 1967), 801–18.
19. Waud, Roger N., "Small Sample Bias Due to Misspecification in the 'Partial Adjustment' and 'Adaptive Expectations' Models," *Journal of the American Statistical Association* (December, 1966), 1130–52.
20. White, John S., "Asymptotic Expansions for the Mean and Variance of the Serial Correlation Coefficient," *Biometrika* (1961), 85–94.
21. Wise, John, "Linear Estimators for Linear Regression Systems Having Infinite Residual Variances," unpublished paper presented to the Berkeley-Stanford Mathematical Economics Seminar (October, 1963).
22. Zellner, Arnold, and Tiao, George C., "Bayesian Analysis of the Regression Model with Autocorrelated Errors," *Journal of the American Statistical Association* (September, 1964), 763–78.